ARTS AND CULTURE

AN INTRODUCTION TO THE HUMANITIES

VOLUME 2

ARTS AND CULTURE

AN INTRODUCTION TO THE HUMANITIES

Third Edition

Janetta Rebold Benton
Pace University, New York

Robert DiYanni
New York University

Upper Saddle River, New Jersey 07458

Library of Congress Cataloging-in-Publication Data

Benton, Janetta Rebold
    Arts and culture : an introduction to the humanities / Janetta Rebold Benton, Robert DiYanni.—3rd ed.
        p. cm.
    Includes index.
    ISBN 978–0–13–157860–9   (v. 1)—ISBN 978–0–13–232171–6   (v. 2)—ISBN 978–0–13–228391–5   (v. 3)
    1. Arts—History.   I. DiYanni, Robert.   II. Title.
    NX440.B46 2008
    700.9—dc22

                                                                                    2006039000

Editor-in-Chief: *Sarah Touborg*
Acquisitions Editor: *Amber Mackey*
Editorial Assistant: *Carla Worner*
Marketing Director: *Brandy Dawson*
Executive Marketing Manager: *Marissa Feliberty*
VP, Director of Production and Manufacturing:
    Barbara Kittle
Marketing Assistant: *Irene Fraga*
Senior Managing Editor: *Lisa Iarkowski*
Production Liaison: *Joe Scordato*
Production Editor: *Bruce Hobart*
Production Assistant: *Marlene Gassler*
Manufacturing Manager: *Nick Sklitsis*
Manufacturing Buyer: *Sherry Lewis*
Creative Design Director: *Leslie Osher*
Art Director: *Anne Nieglos*
Interior and Cover Designer: *Jill Lehan*

Cover Art: *Cameraphoto Arte, Venice/Art Resource, NY*
Director, Image Resource Center: *Melinda Patelli*
Manager, Rights and Permissions: *Zina Arabia*
Manager, Visual Research: *Beth Brenzel*
Manager, Cover Visual Research & Permissions:
    Karen Sanatar
Image Permission Coordinator: *Debbie Latronica*
Photo Researcher: *Francelle Carapetyan, Image
    Research Editorial Services*
Copy Editor: *Tally Morgan*
Composition: *Pine Tree Composition, Inc.*
Printer/Binder: *R. R. Donnelley Sons, Inc.*
Cover Printer: *Phoenix Color Corp.*
Text: *This book was set in 10/12 Janson.*
*Credits and acknowledgments borrowed from other
    sources and reproduced, with permission, in this
    textbook appear on pages 489-491).*

For our children:
Alexander, Ethan, Meredith, and Leland;
Karen and Michael.

Pearson Prentice Hall™ is a trademark of Pearson Education, Inc.
Pearson™ is a registered trademark of Pearson plc
Prentice Hall™ is a registered trademark of Pearson Education, Inc.

Pearson Education Ltd
Pearson Education Singapore, Pte. Ltd
Pearson Education, Canada, Ltd
Pearson Education—Japan

Pearson Education Australia PTY, Limited
Pearson Education North Asia Ltd
Pearson Education de Mexico, S.A. de C.V.
Pearson Education Malaysia, Pte. Ltd

10 9 8 7 6 5 4 3 2 1
ISBN 0-13-232171-8
978-0-13-232171-6

CHAPTER 22

Modern Africa and Latin America 385

CHAPTER 23

Mid-Twentieth Century and Later 419

CHAPTER 21

Early Twentieth Century   337

CHAPTER 24

Diversity in Contemporary Life   453

As in our first two editions of *Arts and Culture*, we provide in this Third Edition an introduction to the world's major civilizations—to their artistic achievements, their history, and their cultures. Through an integrated approach to the humanities, *Arts and Culture* offers an opportunity to view works of art, read literature, and listen to music in historical and cultural contexts.

Works of art from different cultures reveal common human experiences of birth and death, love and loss, pleasure and pain, hope and frustration, elation and despair. Study of the humanities—literature, philosophy, history, religion, and the arts—reveals what others value and believe, inviting each of us to consider our personal, social, and cultural values in relation to those of others.

In studying the humanities, we focus our attention on works of art that reflect and embody the central values and beliefs of particular cultures and specific historical moments. In our approach we consider the following questions:

1. *What kind of artwork is it? To what artistic category does it belong?* These questions lead us to consider a work's type.

2. *Why was the artwork made? What was its function, purpose, or use? Who was responsible for producing it? Who paid for or commissioned it?* These questions lead us to consider the context of a work.

3. *What does the work express or convey? What does it reveal about its creator? What does it reveal about its historical and social context?* These questions lead us to considerations of a work's meaning.

4. *How was the artwork made or constructed?* This question leads us to consider materials and techniques.

5. *What are the parts or elements of a work of art? How are these parts related to create a unified artwork?* These questions lead us to considerations of formal analysis, understanding the ways the artwork satisfies aesthetically.

6. *What social, cultural, and moral values does the work express, reflect, or embody?* This question leads us to consider the social, cultural, and moral values of an artwork.

In *Arts and Culture*, we highlight the individual artistic qualities of numerous works, always in view of the cultural worlds in which they were created. We discuss each work's significance in conjunction with the social attitudes and cultural values it embodies, without losing sight of its individual expression and artistic achievement.

Two important questions underlie our choice of works in *Arts and Culture:* (1) What makes a work a masterpiece of its type? (2) What qualities of a work of art enable it to be appreciated over time? These questions imply that certain qualities appeal to something fundamental and universal in all of us, no matter where or when we may live. These are the aesthetic principles and predilections that link all of us together.

MAKING CONNECTIONS

We believe that a study of the humanities involves more than an examination of the artistic monuments of civilizations past and present. In our view, it also involves a consideration of how forms of human achievement in many times and places echo and reinforce, as well as alter and modify each other. An important aspect of humanities study involves seeing connections among the arts and ideas of a given culture and discovering relationships between the arts and ideas of different cultures. We have highlighted three forms of connections that are especially important:

1. *Interdisciplinary connections* among artworks of an individual culture
2. *Cross currents* among artworks of different cultures
3. Transhistorical links between past and present, *then and now*
4. The *cultural impact* or influence of one culture on later cultures

These forms of connection invite our readers to locate relationships among various humanities disciplines and to identify links between the achievements of diverse cultures. Discovering such connections can be intellectually stimulating and emotionally stirring since the forms of human experience reflected in the works of art of many cultures resonate with common human concerns. These artworks address social questions about who we are, philosophical questions about why we exist at all, and religious questions concerning what awaits us after death. These and other perennial questions and the varying perspectives taken on them have been central to many cultures, and find expression in their arts. To highlight these questions, we have included the following features throughout the text.

INTERDISCIPLINARY CONNECTIONS

For example, one type of interdisciplinary connection appears in the ways the music and architecture of Renaissance Florence were influenced by mathematical proportion and ancient notions of "harmony." Mathematics played a crucial role in all the arts of the Renaissance. Architects were guided in the design of their buildings by mathematical ratios and proportions; composers likewise wrote music that reflected mathematical ratios in both its melody and harmony.

CULTURAL **CROSS CURRENTS**

These reflect the ways artistic ideals, literary movements, and historical events influence the arts of other cultures. For example, Turkish military music found its way into the symphonies and piano compositions of Viennese composers, such as Mozart and Beethoven. Japanese woodblock prints influenced the art of the Impressionist painter Claude Monet and the Post-Impressionist painter Vincent van Gogh. And the dynamic cybernetic sculpture of contemporary artist Wen-Ying Tsai weds Western technology with ancient Chinese aesthetic principles.

THEN & NOW

Also considered are connections between the past and present. *Then & Now* offers discussions of a wide range of subjects that form various types of historical bridges.

CULTURAL IMPACT

This feature appears at the end of the end of each chapter. It explains the influence of one culture or civilization on later ones, showing how the essential, broad themes explored in the chapter continue to impact today's world.

GLOBAL COVERAGE

Arts and Culture includes a wide-ranging overview of the world's civilizations. In addition to Western culture, we examine the civilizations of Africa, China, India, Japan, Latin America, and Mesoamerica. We emphasize the contributions of women, from the eleventh-century writings of the Japanese Murasaki Shikibu, the twelfth-century music of the German Hildegard of Bingen, and the fourteenth century writings of the Italian Christine de Pizan, to the Renaissance painting of the Italian Properzia de'Rossi, or the Baroque still lives by the Flemish Clara Peeters, to the Rococo art of the French painter Marie-Louise-Elisabeth Vigée-Le Brun and the numerous women writers, painters, sculptors, architects, and photographers of the nineteenth and twentieth centuries from many parts of our world. In the final chapter of *Arts and Culture* we bring together a broad spectrum of styles, voices, and perspectives, which, although focusing on contemporary multicultural America, reflects trends and influences from around the globe. We highlight a number of current issues in the arts including how technology has globalized the arts. The numerous and varied contributions of artists and writers include works by Native American painters such as Lisa Fifield and Jaune Quick-to-See

Smith, Latina/Latino writers such as Sandra Cisneros and Oscar Hijuelos, and Australian Aborigine artists.

Throughout the book, we have tried to present the arts and cultures of the world to suggest their richness, variety, and humanity. As a reader of *Arts and Culture* you can find in these pages the background necessary to understand not only the artistic achievements of many civilizations but also the representation of human experience in all its complexity. In a time of rapid social change when the world's cultures are becoming increasingly globalized, it has become necessary to understand the values of human beings around the world. The common humanity we share has been recorded, inscribed, and celebrated in arts and achievements of all cultures.

LEARNING TOOLS FOR STUDENTS

Arts and Culture offers a number of learning tools for students. A helpful starter kit appears at the beginning of the book, giving readers a brief introduction to the study of the visual arts, literature, music, history, and philosophy. Each chapter begins with a full-page timeline and Chapter Overview to introduce the chapter's content. Maps and tables appear within each chapter to further illustrate and organize important information. Each chapter ends with a list of key terms as well as suggested websites for further study. A glossary appears at the end of the book; terms in the glossary are highlighted in boldface in the text.

BOOK FORMAT

For flexibility in teaching, *Arts and Culture* is available in three volumes: Volume I contains chapters 1-13, Volume II contains chapters 13-24, and the Combined Volume contains chapters 1-24. Chapter 13 on The Renaissance and Mannerism in Italy appears in both Volumes I and II, so instructors have the flexibility to cover the Renaissance while using either volume. Additionally, reading selections appear at the end of each chapter in Volumes I and II, but not in the Combined Volume; instructors preferring a single volume text without readings may select the Combined Volume.

NEW IN THE THIRD EDITION

In this Third Edition of *Arts and Culture*, we have preserved the book's key features but have made important adjustments and necessary corrections of fact and perspective throughout. We have also expanded and contracted various discussions to create a better balance among the arts and humanities and to improve the historical contexts. In doing so, we have added many new photographs to accompany new discussions, in addition to replacing numerous photographs from the previous edition with images that better reflect the original artwork.

EXPANDED COVERAGE OF HUMANITIES FROM AROUND THE GLOBE

We have responded to requests to expand coverage of humanities from around the globe. Chapter 7 on Indian Civilization has been revised and expanded with new material. Former chapter 9 on Early Chinese and Japanese Civilizations has been expanded into two new chapters, Chapter 8 on Early Chinese Civilization and Chapter 9 on Early Japanese Civilization, each with extensive new material. Chapter 10 has been augmented with new material on early African civilization, along with coverage of the early Americas. In the second half of the book, we have revised our coverage of China and Japan, expanding the material in chapter 19 on Chinese Civilization and in chapter 20 on Japanese Civilization. Chapter 22 on Modern Africa and Latin America has also been revised and expanded with new material.

INCREASED FOCUS ON WOMEN ARTISTS

Twenty-four women painters, sculptors, and photographers, from the sixteenth to the twentieth century, active in various parts of the globe, have been added. The Third Edition of *Arts and Culture* places greater emphasis on the accomplishments of women than is found in any other book on global humanities.

CRITICAL THINKING

In addition to retaining the popular boxed features from the first two editions, we have added a new feature in each chapter. This Critical Thinking boxed feature invites students to do just that—think critically about an aspect of culture relevant to each chapter.

NEW TOPICS FOR CONNECTIONS, CROSS CURRENTS, AND THEN & NOW BOXES

We have updated several of the boxed features. New topics have been provided for all of the special boxed features: Then & Now, Connections, and Cross Currents.

NEW READINGS

Many of the reading selections at the end of each chapter in Volumes I and II are new. Some longer works have been scaled back to make space for a greater variety of selections.

NEW ORGANIZATION OF INFORMATION

Highlights of our new content include a new organization of the chapters, combining Prehistoric, Mesopotamian, and Egyptian Civilizations, a separate chapter for Early Chinese and for Early Japanese Civilizations, and major restructuring of the chapters on the twentieth century.

FACULTY AND STUDENT RESOURCES TO ACCOMPANY *ARTS AND CULTURE*

Music for the Humanities CD—This music CD is included with each new copy of the text. Musical selections represent important works from a broad variety of time periods and styles.

Humanities Notes—This tool is designed to help students organize their course notes. For each chapter of the book, it includes key illustrations and short extracts from the text with a space next to each where students may take notes. *Humanities Notes* can be packaged at a substantial discount with the book upon request.

OneKey—OneKey is Prentice Hall's exclusive course management system that delivers all student and instructor resources in one place. Powered by Blackboard and WebCT, OneKey offers an abundance of online study and research tools for students and a variety of teaching and presentation resources for instructors, including an easy-to-use gradebook and access to an image library. For more information, go to www.prenhall.com/onekey

Companion WebsiteTM—With the *Arts and Culture* Companion Website, students have access to this extensive online study resource, which includes quizzes, web links, chapter objectives, and more. Please visit the Companion Website at www.prenhall.com/benton.

Instructor's Manual with Tests—An invaluable professional resource and reference for new and experienced instructors, providing chapter summaries, further topics for discussion, activities, and hundreds of sample test questions, these resources are carefully organized to make preparation, classroom instruction, and student testing smoother and more effective. ISBN: 978-0-13-228392-2.

TestGen—This computerized test management program allows instructors to select items from the test bank and design their own exams. ISBN: 978-0-13-228393-9.

Fine Art Slides and Videos—For qualified adopters, slides and videos are available. Contact your local Prentice Hall representative for more information.

The Prentice Hall *Atlas of the Humanities*—Prentice Hall collaborates with Dorling Kindersley, the world's most innovative producer of maps and atlases. This atlas features mulit-dimensional maps that include global, thematic, regional, and chronological perspectives showing political, economic, and cultural changes over time. It is available at a significant discount when packaged with the text. ISBN: 978-0-13-238628-9.

ACKNOWLEDGMENTS

Arts and Culture represents the cooperative efforts of many people. The book originated with a suggestion fifteen years ago by Tony English, then of Macmillan Publishing. Work on the project began with Tony and his Macmillan colleagues and continued with Prentice Hall when Simon & Schuster acquired Macmillan in 1993. At Prentice Hall we had the good fortune to work with Bud Therien, Publisher, who oversaw the book's development in every respect, and Clare Payton, Development Editor, who helped shape the first edition.

Also deserving of particular mention for their work on the first edition are Sylvia Moore for her contribution to the introductory materials, Jenny Moss for her work on the timelines and glossary, and Ailsa Heritage and Andrea Fairbrass for their imaginative work on the maps.

We owe thanks to Henry Sayre, without whom we could not have completed the first edition of *Arts and Culture* on schedule. Professor Sayre helped us shape the drafts of our chapters, melding our styles and recommending organizational changes that have resulted, we believe, in an integrated and compelling overview of the humanities.

For the Third Edition, we owe a special debt of gratitude to Amber Mackey, Acquisitions Editor, who ably shepherded *Arts and Culture*, through the revision process. Our thanks also go to Sarah Touborg, Editor-in-Chief; Melissa Feliberty, Executive Marketing Manager; Leslie Osher, Creative Director; Bruce Hobart, Production Editor; and Carla Worner, Editorial Assistant.

We would like to thank the following reviewers, who offered us wise counsel: Jane Anderson Jones, Manatee Community College; Richard Mahon, Riverside Community College; Brian A. Pavlac, King's College; Danney Ursery, St. Edward's University; Richard A. Voeltz, Cameron University; and Katherine Wyly, Hillsborough Community College.

We want to thank Margaret Manos for her excellent work on early versions of the manuscript, and for her wise and extremely helpful advice in making decisions on what to cut and what to add for the previous edition. In addition, we would like to extend our appreciation to A. Daniel Frankforter of Pennsylvania State University, for his many helpful corrections and suggestions on the history portions; to Jane Pyle of Miami Dade College for expanding our music coverage; to Stephen Addiss of the University of Richmond for his work revising and expanding our Asian chapters; to Jonathan T. Reynolds of Northern Kentucky University for his expansion of the African chapters; and, finally, to Bill Christy of Ohio University for his work on the timelines, key terms, and web links.

We also wish to thank our reviewers for this third edition. Their comments and suggestions helped us in many ways. Thanks to: Lynn Spencer, Brevard Community College; Richard A. Voeltz, Cameron University; Scott H. Boyd, College of DuPage; Richard Mahon, Riverside Community College; and Jane Anderson Jones, Manatee Community College.

We would also like to thank each other for offering mutual support, encouragement, advice, and help throughout a long and sometimes arduous process of writing, revising, and editing. Our families, too, deserve our thanks, for without their patience and understanding we could not have completed our work with equanimity and good humor. In particular, the encouragement and loving support of our spouses, Elliot Benton and Mary DiYanni, enabled us to do our work on *Arts and Culture* with a minimum of anxiety and a maximum of pleasure.

Arts and Culture is an introduction to the humanities, from the earliest times to the present day. The goal of the book is to familiarize readers with a fundamental body of art, history, and ideas as a basis for understanding Western and non-Western cultures. In demonstrating the interrelationships between the creators of art and the historical and social forces at work in various cultures, the text fosters an understanding of the creative process and the uses of the arts.

THE HUMANITIES AND THE ARTS

The humanities are those areas of thought and creation whose subject is human experience. They include history, philosophy, religion, and the arts. Broadly speaking, the arts are objects or experiences created by human beings. The role of the human creator, therefore, is central to any study of the arts since, ultimately, the arts and humanities are a record of human experience and concerns. The arts convey information—a lyric poem or a water-color can describe or portray a summer's day, for example—yet this is not their primary function. More importantly, the arts give form to what is imagined, express human beliefs and emotions, create beauty, move, persuade, and entertain their audiences.

The arts include visual art and architecture, drama, music, and literature, and photography and film. Seeing the arts within their historical and social context is necessary for understanding their development. For example, the figure of the biblical giant-killer, David, was popular during the Renaissance in the Italian city-state of Florence. Michelangelo's *David* was commissioned by the Florentine city officials (see fig. 13.27). Florence had recently fought off an attempt at annexation by the much larger city-state of Milan. Thus, the biblical David slaying the giant, Goliath, became a symbol of Florentine cleverness and courage in defense of independence. It is a theme particular to its time and place, yet one that has been used throughout history to express the success of the "little" person against powerful exploiters.

RECORDS OF CULTURE

We study what survives, which is not necessarily all that once existed. Not all arts survive the passage of time. Art can be divided into the durable and the ephemeral, or short-lived. Surviving objects tend to be large (the Pyramids) or hidden (the contents of tombs). Until human beings created the means of capturing moving images and sounds, the ephemeral arts such as music and dance could be described but not reexperienced. Therefore, some of the oldest arts—music and dance of the ancient world, for example—are lost. With the development of writing, humans began the long process of liberating themselves from the tyranny of time. They began to communicate across space and time, leaving a record of their lives. In our own century, we have seen our recording abilities explode from sound recording and silent movies at the turn of the century into the digitized world of the CD-ROM and the Internet today. The result has been an unprecedented expansion in the humanities.

THE ROLE OF THE ARTIST

The functions of the artist and the artwork have varied widely during the past five thousand years. In our time, the artist is seen as an independent worker, dedicated to the expression of a unique subjective experience. Often the artist's role is that of the outsider, a critical or rebellious figure. He or she is a specialist who has usually undergone advanced training in a university department of art or theater, or a school with a particular focus, such as a music conservatory. In our societies, works of art are presented in specialized settings: theaters, concert halls, performance spaces, galleries, and museums. There is usually a sharp division between the artist and her or his audience of nonartists. We also associate works of art with money: art auctions in which paintings sell for millions of dollars, ticket sales to the ballet, or fundraising for the local symphony.

In other societies and in parts of our own society, now and in the past, the arts are closer to the lives of ordinary people. For the majority of their history, artists have expressed the dominant beliefs of a culture, rather than rebelling against them. In place of our emphasis on the development of a personal or original style, artists were trained to conform to the conventions of their art form. Nor have artists always been specialists; in some societies and periods, all members of a society participated in art. The modern Western economic mode, which treats art as a commodity for sale, is not universal. In societies such as that of the Navajo, the concept of selling or creating a salable version of a sand painting would be completely incomprehensible. Selling Navajo sand paintings created as part of a ritual would profane a sacred experience.

Artists' identities are rarely known before the Renaissance, with the exception of the period of Classical Greece, when artists were highly regarded for their individual talents and styles. Among artists who were known, there were fewer women than men. In the twentieth century, many female artists in all the disciplines have been recognized.

Their absence in prior centuries does not indicate lack of talent, but reflects lack of opportunity. The necessary social, educational, and economic conditions to create art rarely existed for women in the past.

Artists of color have also been recognized in the West only recently. The reasons for this absence range from the simple—there were few Asians in America and Europe prior to the middle of the nineteenth century—to the complexities surrounding the African diaspora. The art of indigenous peoples, while far older than that of the West, did not share the same expressive methods or aims as Western art. Until recently, such art was ignored or dismissed in Western society by the dominant cultural gatekeepers.

CONTEXTS AND AESTHETICS

Our understanding of the arts depends in part on our knowledge of the historical and social context surrounding a work. For instance, for whom was a particular work intended—a private or a public audience? What was or is its setting—public, private, accessible, or hidden? How is the work related to the economic workings of its time: for example, was it commissioned by a ruler, a religious organization, a group of guildspeople, a corporation? Was it created by nuns or monks, by peasants, or by specially-trained craftspersons? Each of these considerations expands our understanding of a given work, even when we cannot know all the answers.

The branch of philosophy devoted to thinking about the arts is called "aesthetics." Aesthetic knowledge is both intuitive and intellectual; that is, we can grasp a work of art on an emotional level while at the same time analyzing it. There is no single, unquestionable body of aesthetic knowledge, although philosophers have tried to create universal systems. Each culture has its own aesthetic preferences. In addition, different disciplines and different styles within a culture reflect different aesthetic values.

FORM AND CONTENT

When discussing works of art, it is useful to distinguish between the form of the artwork and its content. The form of a work of art is its structural or organizing principle—the shape of its content. A work's content is what it is about—its subject matter. At its most basic, formal analysis provides a description of the apparent properties of an artwork. Artists use these properties to engineer our perception and response. In music, for example, a formal analysis would discuss the melody, the harmony, and the structure. In visual art, comparable elements would be line, color, and composition. The goal of formal analysis is to understand how an artwork's form expresses its content.

Contextual approaches to the arts seek to situate artworks within the circumstances of their creation. Histori-

ans of the arts conduct research aimed at recreating the context of a given work. Armed with this information, the historian interprets the work in light of that context. Knowing, for example, that *Guernica* (see fig. 21.20), Pablo Picasso's anti-war painting, depicts an aerial bombing of a small village of unarmed civilians in the Spanish Civil War, drives its brutal images of pain and death home to viewers. Picasso chose black, white, and grey for this painting because he learned of the attack through the black and white photojournalism of the newspapers. Knowing the reason for this choice, which may otherwise have seemed arbitrary to modern viewers of the work, adds to the meaning of the image. Picasso's choice of black and white also intensifies the horrors he depicts.

CRITICAL THINKING

Among the most important purposes of any study of the arts and humanities is to develop habits of mind, including critical thinking. By critical thinking, we do not mean "being critical" of something in the ordinary sense. Rather, we mean developing a capacity to analyze and synthesize, compare and contrast, understand causes and effects, understand, appreciate, and evaluate the cultural productions—the architecture, sculpture, painting, photography, film, literature, music, philosophy, and other arts of all civilizations, whether ancient or modern, and whether similar to or radically different from our own.

Critical Thinking in this sense involves asking questions, making observations and connections, drawing inferences and provisional interpretive conclusions about the meaning of artworks and considering their importance to the civilizations in which they were created. It also involves considering basic issues, such as: what does it mean to live in a society as an individual human being? To what extent does living in one kind of society, in a particular civilization at a particular historical moment, affect one's thoughts, perceptions, attitudes, and feelings? How does the world view of ancient Africans, Babylonians, Chinese, Egyptians, Greeks, Romans, Sumerians, and others compare and contrast with one another and with those of people living in different cultures around the world today?

Each chapter of *Arts and Culture* contains much information and analysis that invites such considerations. And, although the book does not contain study questions or review assignments (those can be found in supplements to *Arts and Culture*), it does contain, in each chapter, a highlighted brief discussion labeled "Critical Thinking." You are invited to think about the issues raised in each of those discussions, as for example, why cows are considered sacred in India, a Hindu civilization, along with the effects of treating cows as sacred animals, as well as considering what "sacred cows," in a metaphorical sense, exist in your own culture.

An additional thought about such critical thinking questions is that when we study civilizations of the past, we are not just studying cultural artifacts and learning about historical events. Additionally, we are learning about people, human beings, who, like us, experience joy and sorrow, frustration and elation, pleasure and pain. And, finally, here we will use the word "critical" in still another sense, for the study of the humanities disciplines through history is critical to understanding ourselves in today's world. We put before you for critical consideration the notion that studying the humanities not only adds to your stock of knowledge, while enriching your own life and imaginatively extending its possibilities but also deepens your appreciation of other peoples and their values.

STARTER KIT

THE HUMANITIES

This Starter Kit provides you with a brief reference guide to key terms and concepts for studying the humanities. The following section will give you a basis for analyzing, understanding, and describing art forms.

COMMONALITIES

We refer to the different branches of humanities—art and architecture, music, literature, philosophy, history—as **disciplines.** The various humanistic disciplines have many key terms in common. However, each discipline has defining characteristics, a distinct vocabulary, and its own conventions, so that the same word may mean different things in different disciplines.

Every work of art has two core components: form and content. **Form** refers to the arrangement, pattern, or structure of a work, how a work is presented to our senses. **Content** is what a work is about its meaning or substance. The form might be a Tang Dynasty painting; the content might be the beauty of nature in a particular place. To comprehend how the form expresses the content is one of the keys to understanding a work of art, music or literature.

The term **artist** is used for the producer of artworks in any discipline. All artworks have a **composition,** the arrangement of its constituent parts. **Technique** refers to the process or method that produced the art. The **medium** is the physical material that makes up the work, such as oil paint on canvas.

STYLE

We use the term **style** to mean several different things. Most simply, style refers to the manner in which something is done. Many elements form a style. Artists working at the same time and place are often trained in the same style. When mentioned in a text, historical styles are usually capitalized, as in *Classical Greek* art, referring to the arts of that particular time and place, which shared distinct characteristics. If used with lowercase letters, such as *classical* style, the term refers to works which, although not from Classical Greece, are similar in character to Classical Greek art, or to Roman art, which was largely derived from Greek forms.

Conventions are accepted practices, such as the use of a frontal eye in a profile face, found in the art of the ancient Egyptians, or the use of the sonnet form by Shakespeare and his contemporaries.

FUNCTIONS AND GENRES

In the most general terms, the functions of the arts can be divided into religious and secular art. **Religious** or liturgical art, music, or drama is used as part of the ritual of a given religion. Art that is not religious art is termed **secular** art. Secular art is primarily used to provide pleasure and entertainment, but among other functions has been its use in the service of political or propaganda ends.

Each discipline has subsets, called **genres.** In music, for example, we have the symphony, a large, complex work for orchestra, in contrast to a quartet, written for only four instruments. In literature we might contrast the novel, with its extended narrative and complexities of character, with the compression of a short story. From the seventeenth to the nineteenth centuries, certain subjects were assigned higher or lower rank by the academies that controlled the arts in most European countries. Portrait painting, for example, was considered lower than history painting. That practice has been abandoned; today the genres are usually accorded equal respect and valued for their distinctive qualities.

THE VISUAL ARTS

The visual arts are first experienced by sight, yet they often evoke other senses such as touch or smell. Because human beings are such visual creatures, our world is saturated with visual art, in advertising, on objects from CD covers to billboards, on TV and the Internet. The visual arts occur in many varieties of two-dimensional and three-dimensional forms, from painting, printmaking, and photography, to sculpture and architecture.

As is the case with other arts, the origins of the visual arts are now lost. However, their development represents a milestone in human civilization. Drawing, the representation of three-dimensional forms (real or imagined) on a two-dimensional surface, is an inherent human ability, and failure to draw by a certain stage in a child's growth is a sign of serious trouble. The creation and manipulation of images was and is a first step toward mastery of the physical world itself.

The visual arts use different methods. **Representation** is an ancient function of visual art, in which a likeness of an object or life form is produced. Artists use different methods to represent a subject (what is actually depicted, such as a portrait of a person, a still life, a landscape, a historical event, etc.). If the work is realistic, the subject is accurately depicted and readily recognizable. If the work is abstracted, the subject, although not photographically

Visual Arts

Line: A mark on a surface. Lines may be continuous or broken. They are used to create patterns and textures, to imply three dimensions, and to direct visual movement.

Shape: An area with identifiable boundaries. Shapes may be **organic,** based on natural forms and thus rounded or irregular, or they may be **geometric,** based on measured forms.

Mass: The solid parts of a three-dimensional object. An area of space devoid of mass is called **negative space;** while **positive space** is an area occupied by mass.

Form: The shape and structure of something. In discussion of art, form refers to visual aspects such as line, shape, color, texture, and composition.

Color: The sensation produced by various wavelengths of light. Also called **hue.** Red, blue, and yellow are the **primary colors,** which cannot be made from mixing other colors. **Secondary colors** (orange, green, and purple) are hues produced by mixing two primary colors.

Value: The lightness or darkness of an area of color, or as measured between black and white. The lighter, the higher in value it is; the **darker,** the lower in value.

Texture: The appearance or feel of a surface, basically smooth or rough. Texture may be actual, as the surface of a polished steel sculpture, or implied, as in a painting of human flesh or the fur of an animal.

Composition: The arrangement of the formal components of a work, most frequently used to describe the organization of elements in a drawing or painting.

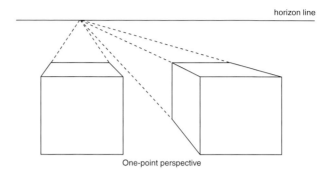

horizon line

One-point perspective

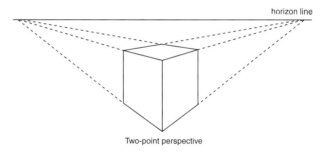

horizon line

Two-point perspective

Perspective: A system of portraying three-dimensional space on a two-dimensional surface. In **one-point** linear perspective, lines recede toward a single **vanishing point** on the horizon line. In **two-point** perspective there are two vanishing points. **Atmospheric** or **aerial** perspective uses properties of light and air, in which objects become less distinct and cooler in color as they recede into distance.

recorded, is nevertheless identifiable. If the work is nonobjective there is no longer a recognizable subject.

Realistic paintings, drawings, and prints often create an illusion of pictorial space (an illusion of three dimensions on a two-dimensional surface) by using perspective. There are two types: 1) atmospheric perspective, and 2) linear perspective, both defined in the box above. These are characteristic of Western art, whereas Eastern art tends to Emphasize the picture plane. Landscapes, as Zho Jan's *Seeking the Tao in the Autumn Mountains* (Figure 8.8), does not employ Western methods of creating illusions of space. Inscriptions, as in Shitao's *Searching for the Past* (Figure 19.5), by stressing the picture plane, further compress the sense of space. Abstract and nonobjective art, arising in the twen-

tieth century, are more concerned with the elements on the picture plane (the surface of the paper or canvas) rather than in creating an illusion of depth.

FORMAL ANALYSIS

To analyze a work of visual art formally, its visual elements are considered without reference to the content, whereas moving to more sophisticated levels involves the content as well. At its simplest, the content is what is represented, the subject matter, whether a person, an orange, or a flag. However, the image may not stop with the representation; there may be a symbolic element. It is useful to distinguish between signs and symbols. **Signs** convey visual information

FIGURE 0.1 Edvard Munch, *The Scream*, 1893, tempera and casein on cardboard, 36 × 29″ (91.3 × 73.7 cm), Nasjonal-galleriet, Oslo. © 2003 The Munch Museum/The Munch-Ellingson Group/Artists Rights Society (ARS), New York/ADAGP, Paris. J. Lathion/© Nasjionalgalleriet 02.

strokes. The composition is dynamic; the artist has used exaggerated diagonals to suggest a dramatic perspective for the bridge. The figure at the front is the focal point. The craft is secondary to the expressive purpose of the work.

It should be obvious that in *The Scream* more is going on than the preceding analysis indicates. Three people are on a bridge at sunset. Two are walking away; one stands transfixed with his hands over his ears. The expression on his face functions as a sign to convey shock or horror. To understand the significance of his expression, we turn to the historical context and the artist's life. Munch, a Norwegian artist who worked in the late-nineteenth and early-twentieth centuries, was one of the artists who rejected conventions and created personal symbolic systems, based largely on his experience. *The Scream* is usually interpreted as representing a screaming person. This is not correct. As we know from the artist's diary, the work refers to the "scream of nature." The image captured is a powerful evocation of a sensitive man overwhelmed by nature's power, which his companions cannot sense. The swirling lines suggest the impact of screaming nature on this person. The blood-red sky resonates as a symbol of savage nature oblivious to the puny humans below.

COMPONENTS OF THE VISUAL ARTS

The basic elements used to construct a work of visual art are line, shape, mass, form, color, value, texture, and composition. While many drawings are executed in black mediums, such as pencil and charcoal, on a white ground, color is a vital ingredient of art, especially important in conveying information as well as emotion to the viewer. Color affects us both physically and psychologically and has significance to us both in our personal lives and in our cultural traditions.

There can be no color without light. In the seventeenth century, Sir Isaac Newton observed that when sunlight passed through a glass prism it was broken up, or **refracted,** into rainbow colors. Our perception of color depends upon reflected light rays of various wavelengths. Theorists have arranged colors on a **color wheel** (fig 0.2) that is well-known to students of painting and even young schoolchildren. On it are the **primary colors**—red, yellow, and blue—and **secondary colors**—orange, green, and purple. Some wheels show **tertiary colors** such as yellow-green and red-purple. The primary colors cannot be created by mixing other colors, but secondary and tertiary colors are made, respectively, by mixing two primaries, or primaries and secondaries, together. **Complementary** colors are those opposite each other on the wheel, so that red is opposite from green, orange from blue, and yellow from purple. Many artists have studied and worked with the **optical effects** of color, especially the French Impressionist Claude Monet and the Post-Impressionist Georges Seurat.

economically by means of images or words. **Symbols** are images that have resonance, or additional meaning. Works of visual art may use both signs and symbols. Artists use symbolic systems, part of the visual language of their time. Like all languages, these must be learned. Sometimes artists create their own symbols.

Iconography is the language of symbols. The **iconography** of a work of art is often religious in nature. For example, different representations of Jesus derive from incidents in his life. To understand the deeper levels of the work, it is necessary to understand the iconography. The use of personal iconography by an artist is a relatively recent development of the past few centuries.

The following analysis of *The Scream* by Edvard Munch (fig. 0.1) will serve as an example of this process. Viewed formally, the major visual elements used by Munch in this painting are line and color. There are two kinds of lines: the geometric lines that form the sharply receding bridge contrast with the swirling organic lines of the main figure and the landscape, sea, and sky. There is little or no modelling or shading. The colors contrast bright red and yellow with rich blue, offset by neutral tones. *The Scream* is a painting executed on cardboard with rapid, loose brush-

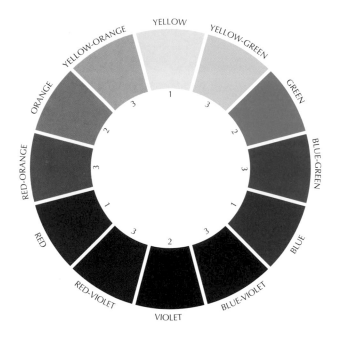

FIGURE 0.2 Color wheel.

SCULPTURE

A sculpture is a three-dimensional form made by carving, modeling, or assembling. Unlike paintings, drawings, and prints, which have two dimensions (height and width), sculptures have three dimensions (height, width, and depth).

Subtractive Sculpture. Using materials that have natural solid mass, such as stone, wood, or ivory, the sculptor shapes the work of art by removing material, cutting it away, usually with a hammer and chisel. The finished work must fit within the dimensions of, for example, the block of marble. Obviously, the work must be planned carefully in advance, for if a major error is made in carving, such as breaking off an extremity of a figure, correction is virtually impossible.

Physical strength may be required to carve in stone, as the *Seated Buddha* (Figure 7.6) of schist. However, greater control is required to carve in wood, as the Yoruba mask from the Republic of Benin (Figure 22.1), due to the varying resistance offered by the wood, depending upon whether the sculptor cuts with or against the grain.

Marble is the traditional medium for sculpture. Marble, limestone, and sandstone are all essentially calcium carbonate, the difference being the size and density of the crystalline structure of the stone. Limestone and sandstone are grainier, softer, and more easily worked than marble. They have a mat surface, whereas marble can be polished to a shine.

Additive Sculpture. Using materials that have no natural mass, shape, or dimensions, such as plaster, clay, or wax,

the sculptor gradually builds up the desired form by modeling it. The scale of the sculpture is not limited, as it would be by the size of a block of stone or piece of wood. Because the material is soft, an **armature** (a rigid structure, usually of metal) may be needed for support. The artist can continually revise the form while working, and can easily make changes. For this reason, wax and clay are often used to make small studies for sculpture to be carved on a larger scale in stone.

Alternatively, a work modeled in clay or wax, which are rather impermanent materials, may be cast in metal—traditionally, bronze is used. A small **statuette** can be cast solid, as the tiny bronze horse shown in Figure 2.15, but a large piece, as the huge statue of Marcus Aurelius shown in Figure 4.19, must be hollow. This is not only because of the expense and weight, but because, were it solid, the bronze, which must be heated to make it molten for the casting process, would crack as it gradually cooled.

The material selected by the sculptor affects the form of the finished work, or, conversely, the sculptor selects the material according to the form he or she wishes to create. For example, bronze is very strong—a figure made of bronze could be posed as if balancing on one toe, whereas the same figure, if carved of stone, would be likely to break.

Assembled Sculpture. A modern type of sculpture is the **mobile,** invented by the American **Alexander Calder.** As the name suggests, the sculpture, which is usually suspended from the ceiling, actually moves with every breeze. As Figure 23.11 shows, the colored shapes are linked together, and a delicate balance carefully achieved. Calder also created **stabiles,** which used the same brightly colored metal shapes, but rest on the ground and do not move.

Another modern form of sculpture is the **assemblage** made of **found objects,** sometimes called **ready-mades.** As the term "assemblage" suggests, the mixed-media sculpture is created by assembling or compiling various bits, pieces, and objects, as was done by **Robert Rauschenberg** in Figure 23.13.

ARCHITECTURE

Architecture is a branch of the visual arts that combines practical function and artistic expression; it is art to inhabit. The function served by a building usually determines its form. In addition to the purely useful purpose of providing shelter, architecture answers prevailing social needs. The use of architects to design and erect public and religious structures has given rise to many innovative forms throughout history. Architecture reflects the society in which it is built. Structural systems depend upon the available building materials, technological advancements, the intended function of the building, and aesthetics of the culture. The relationship between a building and its **site,** or location, is integral to architecture. The Greek Parthenon (fig. 0.3), for example, crowns a hill overlooking Athens. The elevated location indicates its importance, and the pathway one must ascend to reach the Parthenon is part of the experience. A striking example of the adaptation of architecture to the natural environment is seen in homes of the Anasazi culture at Mesa Verde, Colorado, built into the cliff (Fig. 10.14).

LITERATURE

SPEECH, WRITING, AND LITERATURE

Literature differs from the visual arts since it is not built from physical elements, such as paint and stone; nor is it composed of sound as is music, but from words, the basic elements of language. Paint and sound have no intrinsic meaning; words do. Speech depends on meaningful units of sound—words, which are the building blocks of communication in language. Literature presupposes language, with its multitudes of meaning (content), its **grammar** (rules for construction), and its **syntax**, the arrangement of words.

Language, essentially communicative, has many functions. We use language to make emotional contact with others: for example, a parent using baby talk to a child too young to understand the meaning of words. Through language we convey information to each other, as in the classroom, where a dialogue between teacher and student is part of the educational process. All literature is language, but not all language is literature. Distinguishing between literature and other forms of language is sometimes difficult, but refinement in language and careful structure or form typically characterize literature.

FIGURE 0.3 Ictinus and Callicrates, Parthenon, Acropolis, Athens, 448–432 B.C.E.

Literature, in the broadest sense, is widely apparent in everyday life. Popular songs, magazine essays, greeting card verse, hymns and prayers are all forms of literature. One meaning of the word *literature,* in fact, is what is written. Generally, however, the term "literature" is reserved for those works that exhibit "the best that has been thought and said," works that represent a culture's highest literary achievements.

LITERACY AND LITERATURE

The Development of Literature. Literature predates literacy. Ancient literature was **oral**—spoken—rather than written. To make it easier to remember and recite, much of this was in the form of song or poetry. The invention of writing enabled people to communicate across space and time. It was with this invention that recorded history was born. The earliest writings of the ancient world are businesslike records of laws, prayers, and commerce—informative but not expressive. When mechanical methods of printing were developed, literacy spread. Today, universal literacy is a goal in all civilized countries.

The Functions of Literature. Literature serves a variety of social functions. One of its most ancient functions is as **religious literature,** the prayers and mythology of a given culture. The myths of the Greeks and Romans have exerted a powerful influence on Western culture; their origins lie deep in the history of Egypt and Mesopotamia. **Epic literature,** such as the African Epic of Son Jara, or the sagas from Norway and Iceland, were passed down by oral tradition. Literature distinct from liturgical or epic forms was invented by the ancient Greeks, and, broadly speaking included history, philosophy, drama, and poetry. Novels and short stories as we know them today were a much later development. The novel in its modern form was named for tales popular in Italy in the late-thirteenth century, though the novel is generally identified with prose narratives that developed in the eighteenth century in Europe.

Since literature is a communicative act, it is important to consider the audience and setting. Silent reading is a recent development, alien to the oral roots of literature. Most literature through the ages was meant to be recited, sung, or read aloud in groups ranging from general public gatherings to the intimate setting of the private home. Authors today may give readings from their work in libraries, bookstores, and educational institutions.

FORMS OF LITERATURE

Literature can be divided into fiction and nonfiction, poetry and prose.

Poetry is distinguished by its concentrated and precise language, "the best words in the best order," as one poet defined it. **Diction** is the poet's selection of words, and

Architecture

Architect: One who designs and supervises the construction of buildings. Ideally, the architect is part builder with a sound knowledge of engineering principles, materials, structural systems, and other such practical necessities, as well as part artist who works with form, space, scale, light, and other aesthetic properties.

Scale: The relative size of one thing compared to another. The relationship of a building to another element, often the height of a human being.

Site: The location of an object or building. Care must be taken to choose a solid, attractive, and appropriate building site.

Structural System: The engineering principles used to create a structure. Two basic kinds of structural system are the **shell** system, where one or more building materials such as stone or brick provide both support and covering, and the **skeleton and skin** system, as in modern skyscrapers with steel skeletons and glass skin.

Column: A supporting pillar consisting of a base, a cylindrical shaft, and a decorative capital at the top. Three Classical orders, established in ancient Greece, are the **Doric, Ionic,** or **Corinthian,** identified by the capital.

Post and Lintel: A basic structural system dating from ancient times that uses paired vertical elements (posts) to support a horizontal element (lintel).

Arch, Dome, and Vault: An arch consists of a series of wedged-shaped stones, called **voussoirs,** locked in place by a **keystone** at the top center. In principle, an arch rotated 180 degrees creates a **dome.** A series of arches forms a **barrel** or **tunnel vault.** When two such vaults are constructed so that they intersect at right angles, a **cross** or **groin vault** is created. Roman and Romanesque masons used semi-circular arches, whereas Gothic masons built with pointed arches to create vaults that were reinforced with **ribs,** permitting large openings in the walls. The true arch, dome, and vault are dynamic systems—the lateral thrust that they exert must be buttressed externally to prevent collapse.

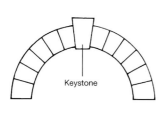

Romanesque

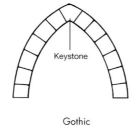

Gothic

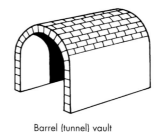

Barrel (tunnel) vault

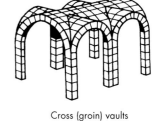

Cross (groin) vaults

syntax the ordering of those words in sentences. Other poetic elements include images—details that evoke sense perception—along with metaphor and other forms of comparison. With its roots in song, poetry of many eras and places exhibits rhyme and other types of sound play as well as rhythm and meter, the measured pattern of accent in poetic lines. Drama, plays intended for performance, are sometimes written in verse, rhymed or unrhymed, as, for example, in **blank verse.**

Language that is not poetry is **prose.** Not all prose is literature; some, such as journalism or technical writing, is purely descriptive or informative, as some visual art is purely representational. Literature can be fiction or nonfiction, or a combination of both. Fiction is a work of the imagination. Fictional forms can be long and complex, as in a novel or play, or short and concise, as in a novella or short story. Nonfiction, which deals with actual events or persons, includes expressions of opinion, such as political essays. Functions of nonfiction include explanation, persuasion, commentary, exposition, or any blend of these. Sometimes philosophic essays and works of history are included in the category of literature.

Fiction and drama, and much nonfiction as well, create their effects through elements such as the plot, or story line, characters, description of the setting, dialogue between the characters, and exposition, or explanation. The latter is presented in the voice of a narrator, who may represent the author using the third-person perspective, or may instead be a character expressing a first-person point of view.

Literature

Fiction: Literature that is imaginative, rather than descriptive of actual events. Typical fictional forms are the short story and the novel, which has greater length and complexity.

Nonfiction: An account of actual events and people. Forms of nonfiction include essays, biography and autobiography, and journalistic writing, as for newspapers and magazines.

Narrative: The telling of a story; a structured account of events.

Narrator: The storyteller from whose **point of view** the story is told. The point of view can be **first-person** or **third-person,** and may shift within the work. The narrator can be **omniscient,** knowing everything, or limited to what she or he can know personally or be told by others.

Plot: The plan or story line. To plot a story is to conceive and arrange the action of the characters and the sequence of events. Plots typically involve **rising action,** events that complicate the plot and move it forward to a **climax,** the moment of greatest intensity. This is followed by the **denouement,** the resolution of the plot.

Characters: The people in a literary work. The leading character is known as the **protagonist,** a word stemming from ancient Greek drama in which the protagonist was opposed by an **antagonist.**

Dialogue: Conversation between two or more characters. Drama is mainly rendered through dialogue; it is used in fiction to a lesser extent.

Setting: Where the events take place; includes location, time, and situation. In theatrical productions, a **set** is the scenery, sometimes very elaborate, constructed for a stage performance. In films the set is the sound stage or the enclosure where a scene is filmed.

Exposition: Explanatory material, which, especially in drama, often lays out the current situation as it arises from the past.

In common with visual art and music, literature has **themes,** or overarching ideas that are expressed by all the elements working together. The structure of a work of literature is analogous to the composition of a symphony or a painting. Writers use symbolism, much as visual artists do. A successful work of literature will likely establish a mood, hold the reader's interest through a variety of incidents or ideas with evident focus, yet possess an overall sense of unity.

Autobiography, as a separate literary and historical endeavor, began with the *Confessions* of St. Augustine (354–430 C.E.), in which he told the story of his life and the progress of his religious convictions. Autobiography is history written from a subjective point of view. The memoir, so popular in recent years, is descended from this first, spiritual autobiography.

Biography is a branch of both literature and history. The author's role is complicated because a biographer must check the facts of the subject's life, usually by interviewing both the subject and many other people. Deciding the major theme of a person's life, the relationship between that person and his or her time, and considering what is true as well as what is germane are the biographer's responsibility. Different biographers may offer quite different interpretations of a subject's life.

History is a powerful force that shapes the humanities as a whole. The writing of history varies across cultures, and as cultures change, history itself is continuously under revision. The leaders of some societies would never allow the publication of versions of history that vary from their orthodox beliefs, no matter what the facts might be. Because history is an interpretative discipline, several versions of events may coexist, with scholars arguing and defending the merits of each. This is particularly true in our multicultural and pluralist era.

MUSIC

We are surrounded by sounds at all times. The art that derives from our sense of hearing is music, order given to sounds by human intent. A temporal art, one that exists in time, music is the least material of the arts, its basic elements being sound and silence. Silence in music is analogous to a painter's, sculptor's, or architect's use of negative space: unoccupied but important, so that the intervals between the notes are necessary parts of a musical piece. Music permeates our daily lives—in the movies, on radio and television, in elevators and stores. The success of the Sony Walkman and the recently developed MP3 players reflects our human desire to surround ourselves with music.

Until the development of sound recording, music was one of the **ephemeral** arts, like dance and live theater, which exist only for the duration of their performances. Until the late Middle Ages, music in the West was not written down, or **notated.** It was taught by ear, passed on from one generation to the next.

SOCIAL AND RITUAL ROLES

Music has many different functions. It has been and remains a major element in religious ritual. It is also used frequently in collective labor; the regular rhythm that characterizes work songs keeps the pace steady and makes the work more fun. For example, aerobics classes and workout tapes depend on music to motivate exercisers and help them keep the pace. On the other hand, parents use lullabies to lull their babies to sleep.

Since the late Middle Ages, Western music has developed many conventional types. These genres vary with the audience, the instruments, and the musical structures. **Liturgical** music was designed for churches, used sacred texts, and took advantage of church acoustics. The soaring vaults of Gothic cathedrals were perfect for the music of the Middle Ages. Music known as **chant** or **plainsong** is simply the human voice singing a religious text without instrumental accompaniment. When the voice is unaccompanied, it is known as **a cappella.** When the sound is made by specialized devices, called **instruments,** the music is termed **instrumental.**

Secular, that is nonreligious, music brought about other forms. **Chamber music,** instrumental music that was originally played in palaces for royalty and nobility, calls for more intimate spaces, a small ensemble of players, and small audiences. **Orchestral music** is the most public and complex form, involving a full orchestra and a concert hall, where the acoustics, or quality of sound, is very important. **Popular music,** often shortened to **pop,** appeals to a wide audience. It includes rock, folk, country, rap, and other types of music. **Jazz** is an improvisational form that arose in the United States from blues and ragtime. **Musical theater,** as the name implies, is a combination of drama and music. Its songs often enter the pop repertoire as **show tunes. Opera,** a narrative in which both dialogue and exposition is sung, combines music with literature and drama.

INSTRUMENTS

Musical instruments, which vary widely across cultures, can nevertheless be grouped in families. Probably most ancient are the **percussion** instruments, which make noise as they are struck. Drums, blocks, cymbals, and tambourines are percussion instruments. **Stringed** instruments, deriving from the hunting bow, have strings stretched between two points; sounds are produced when they are plucked, strummed, bowed, or struck. **Woodwinds** are hollow instruments that were originally made of wood, such as the flute, recorder, and panpipes. **Reed** instruments, such as the oboe, are woodwinds that use a mouthpiece created from a compressed reed. **Brasses** are metal horns like the tuba, trumpet, and cornet. In addition to their musical function, brasses were long used by the military to communicate over distances in battle or in camp. Using a prearranged trumpet call, the commander could sound "retreat" or "charge."

MUSICAL QUALITIES AND STRUCTURE

Musical structure ranges from a simple tune or rhythm to the intricacy of a symphony or an opera. The tone, or sound of a specific quality, is the basis of all music, using varieties of high or low pitches and timbres with varying intensity and tempos. Music appeals to our emotions through tempo, musical color or timbre, and harmonic structure. We associate different emotions with different timbres. The harp, for example, evokes gentleness or calm, whereas brasses evoke more stirring emotions.

Musical structure can be simple, such as Ravel's *Bolero*, which uses the repetition of a single melody with increased tempo and volume to build to a climax. Increases in tempo generate excitement, literally increasing the listener's heart rate and breathing speed. These qualities were used to good advantage in Blake Edwards's film *10*. Composers of movie music manipulate our emotions expertly, heightening the appeal of the action.

The comparatively uncomplicated pop songs we sing are based on melodies, a succession of notes, with accompanying words. We are also familiar with the 32-bar structure of most pop and rock music, in which **verses** alternate with repeated **choruses.** To appreciate and enjoy more complex music, some understanding of structure is important. The simple song "Row, Row, Row Your Boat," familiar to many of us from childhood, is a **round** or **canon;** the same melody is sung by each voice, but voices enter one after the other, creating overlapping notes, or **chords.** More elaborate forms stemming from such simple structures are found in **classical** music, beginning with European music of the eighteenth and nineteenth centuries.

Harmonic structure is a complex topic. Western music is written in **keys,** a system of notes based on one central note, such as the key of C Major. The different keys have their own emotional connotations. A **minor key** is often associated with sadness; a **major key** seems happier or more forceful. Notes that seem to fit together are consonant, while clashing notes are dissonant. Generally, consonance seems peaceful or happy to most people, while dissonance may be unsettling.

Music

Acoustics: The qualities of sound, often used to describe the relationship between sound and architecture, as in a concert hall.

Vibrations: Trembling or oscillating motions that produce sound. When singers or stringed instruments produce a wavering sound, causing a fluctuation in pitch, it is termed **vibrato.**

Pitch: The sound produced by vibrations. The speed of vibrations controls the pitch: slow vibrations produce low pitches; fast vibrations produce high pitches.

Tempo: The speed at which music is played or sung. This is shown on sheet music, usually in Italian terms, by **tempo marks** that indicate the desired speed. A device called a **metronome** can indicate tempo with precision.

Timbre: The characteristic sound or tonal quality of an instrument or voice. Also termed **color,** it can refer to the combination produced by more than one instrument's timbres, as **orchestral color.**

Tone: A sound of specific pitch and quality, the basic building material of music. Its properties are pitch, timbre, duration, and intensity.

Note: The written symbol for a tone, shown as **whole notes, half notes,** etc. These indicate the time a note is held, with a corresponding **rest** sign. **Notation** is the use of a set of symbols to record music in written form.

Melody: The succession of notes or pitches played or sung. Music with a single melodic line is called **monophony,** while music with more than one melodic line is **polyphony.**

Texture: In music, this refers to the number of diffent melodic lines; the greater the number, the thicker the texture.

Harmony: The combination of notes sung or played at one time, or **chords;** applies to homophonic music. **Consonance** refers to the sound of notes that are agreeable together; **dissonance** to the sound of notes that are discordant.

NON-WESTERN MUSIC

Music of the non-Western world shares with Western music a tradition of early oral transmission and an affiliation with the values and beliefs of its originating culture. Like Western music, too, music of non-Western traditions has undergone change and reflects the influence of musical traditions with which it has had contact over the centuries.

Nonetheless, there are distinctive differences among the world's many and varied musical traditions, and a number of differences between Western and non-Western musical forms, textures, and harmonic, melodic, and rhythmic systems. Pentatonic scales, for example (the 5-note scales illustrated by the black piano keys), are of non-Western origin. Micro-tones, pitches that exist between the half-tone steps of traditional Western musical scales, are another non-Western influence. So too are the intricate rhythmic patterns of Indian music, as performed by tabla players as they accompany master musicians performing on the sitar, an instrument that produces sounds, pitches, and harmonies beyond the scope of those common to Western music.

The best way to learn about and listen to music from other times, places, and traditions, is to understand it within its cultural context and to approach differences with an open mind and an attentive ear. Whether you are listening to Japanese shakuhachi music, which has a ceremonial quality, or to Indonesian gamelan music, with its uniquely orchestral combination of xylophone, bronze bowls, gongs, flutes, percussive and plucked instruments, or to African Mbira music, with its repetitive melodies and strong dance connections, the route to understanding and enjoyment is to be willing to entertain new sounds, new combinations of instruments, and new musical experiences.

HISTORY, RELIGION, AND PHILOSOPHY

History, the recording and explanation of events, and philosophy, the search for truth, have both influenced the arts. These subjects have themselves evolved as humanistic disciplines. **Aesthetics,** the branch of philosophy concerned with the functions, practice, and appreciation of the arts, along with their role in society, is an important part of this book and of cultural studies in general.

HISTORY

Unlike expressive literature, or fiction, history is an inquiry into and report upon real events and people. Until the Greek historian Herodotus, traveling in the Mediterranean lands of the sixth century B.C.E., turned his questioning and skeptical eye on the received beliefs and tales of peoples he met, history was inseparable from religious faith and folk memory. Herodotus began as a kind of cultural anthropologist, and he deliberately distinguished his historical writing from the epic tradition by writing prose. Historians have since developed methods of inquiry, questioning the likelihood of stories and delving into the motives of their informants. They learned to consider nonhistorical accounts and records as checks on the official versions of events. They began to consider the psychological motives of the people they chronicled. The artistry of their presentation became a part of the discipline.

RELIGION AND PHILOSOPHY

Religion has played a crucial role in the development of the arts, which provide images, sounds, and words for use in worship, prayers, and religious stories. **Theology,** study of the nature of the divine, prescribes religious practices, moral beliefs, and rules for social behavior. The dominant religion in a culture often controls the art, either directly by training artists and commissioning art, or indirectly. The medieval Catholic belief in the efficacy of **relics** to heal or give aid, for example, led to the practice of pilgrimage, and from that to the creation of churches and cathedrals. As religious orders acquired holy relics, they housed them in shrines within the churches. Problems arose when the many pilgrims who came to be healed and blessed disrupted services. Romanesque architects then developed the **ambulatory,** or walkway, that allowed pilgrims to see the relics without interrupting worshipers at a service, thereby altering religious architecture. Different religions hold different aesthetic beliefs. Nudity was acceptable in the temple statues of Classical Greece and Hindu India. Islam prohibits any figurative images in places of worship, and some Native Americans believe a permanent house of worship is itself inappropriate.

In many cultures, philosophy and religion are intertwined. Confucianism, Taoism, Hinduism, and Buddhism are all based on intricate philosophical systems that become allied with various social and religious beliefs and practices. Like religion, philosophy is concerned with the basic truths and principles of the universe. Both are also concerned with human perception and understanding of these truths, and with the development of moral and ethical principles for living.

ARTS AND CULTURE

An Introduction to the Humanities

Chapter 13

History

1494	First French invasion of Italy
ca. 1495	Savonarola takes control of Florence
1494–1512	Medici exiled from Florence
1516–23	Leo X controls Florence
1519	Charles V becomes Holy Roman Emperor
1523–27	Clement VII controls Florence
1527	Sack of Rome
1553–63	Council of Trent

Arts and Architecture

ca. 1425–30s	Donatello, *David*
1427–28	Masaccio, *Trinity*
1425–52	Ghiberti, *Gates of Paradise*
1430	Dufay Alma Redemptoris Mater
1436	Brunelleschi finishes dome for Florence Cathedral; Dufay, "Il Duomo"
1453–55	Donatello, *Mary Magdalene*
1438–45	Fra Angelico, *Annunciation*
1445–ca. 1452	Michelozzo, Palazzo Medici-Riccardi
ca. 1484–86	Botticelli, *Birth of Venus*
ca. 1499	Michelangelo, *Pietà*
1502	Josquin des Près, "Ave Maria . . . virgo serena"
ca. 1503	Leonardo da Vinci, *Mona Lisa*
1508–12	Michelangelo, ceiling of Sistine Chapel
1510–11	Raphael, *School of Athens*
ca. 1520	Properzia de Rossi, *Joseph and Potiphar's Wife*
1524–59	Laurentian Library
1534–40	Parmigianino, *Madonna with the Long Neck*
1543–54	Cellini, *Perseus*
ca. 1559	Sofonisba Anguissola, *Portrait of the Artist's Sister Minerva*
1565	Palestrina, *Pope Marcellus Mass*

Literature and Philosophy

1327–72	Petrarch, *Canzonieri*
1429	Bruni finishes *History of Florence*
1435–50	Alberti, *De pictura/De re aedificatoria*
ca. 1455	Gutenberg and the printing press
1462	Platonic Academy of Philosophy
ca. 1484–86	Ficino, *Theologia Platonica*
1486	Pico, *Oration on the Dignity of Man*
1524–59	Castiglione, *Book of the Courtier*
1534–40	Machiavelli, *The Prince*
1550	Vasari, *Lives*
1553–63	Cellini, *Autobiography*

The Renaissance
and Mannerism in Italy

Leonardo da Vinci, *The Last Supper*, refectory, Santa Maria delle Grazie, Milan, 1495–98, tempera and oil on plaster, 15′2″ × 28′10″ (4.60 × 8.80 m). Scala/Art Resource, NY.

MAP 13.1   The division of Italy into city-states at the end of the fifteenth century.

CHAPTER OVERVIEW

THE EARLY RENAISSANCE
Rebirth of interest in antiquity, the individual, and nature

THE HIGH RENAISSANCE
The maturation of the arts

MANNERISM
Moving away from the classical ideal

THE EARRLY RENAISSANCE

The transition from the Middle Ages to the Renaissance was gradual. The intense religiosity of the Middle Ages persisted into the Renaissance, though it came to coexist with a more worldly philosophy and a more secular outlook. A number of important broad changes developed during the Renaissance, such as the development of nation states, the advent of commercial capitalism, the emergence of the middle class, and the rise of rationalist thought. European exploration of the Americas was abetted by scientific and technological developments, especially in navigation. And the invention of movable type, which allowed for printing, expanded the world of learning.

Of particular importance in Europe, originally in Italy, was a reinvigoration of classical learning based on the literary and philosophical writings of the Greeks and Romans. This development, called "classical humanism," was a defining Renaissance intellectual preoccupation. The influence of Greco-Roman antiquity on Renaissance Europe was pervasive, and included an impact on social, political, and diplomatic life, as well as upon education and the arts. Of great importance is the part played by Arab scholars in preserving ancient Greek scholarship, which enabled European scholars like Petrarch and Boccaccio to benefit from their labors.

In Italy, changes were developing across the social, political, and economic spectrums. Italy underwent significant urbanization, increased political stability, and economic expansion, along with increasing contact with other societies. Venice, for example, was a crossroads for East–West commercial exchanges, and also for exchange of customs and ideas.

The French word **Renaissance,** meaning "rebirth," was first employed in the nineteenth century to describe the period from the early fifteenth century to the middle of the next. The Italians of the time believed this period marked a radical break from the past and a reinvention of the civilization and ideals of classical Greece and Rome.

The Renaissance was characterized by—in addition to this interest in classical art, literature, law, and ideals—an interest in the individual person, now emerging from the anonimity of the Middle Ages, as well as a new fascination with nature and the physical world. A number of Italian city-states had grown powerful in Italy—the kingdom of Naples in the south, the church states around Rome, and in the north, the duchy of Milan and the republics of Venice and Florence. Located on the main road connecting Rome with the north, Florence had become the center of trade, and European banking had been established with credit operations available to support and spur on an increase in trade (fig. 13.1).

Florence itself was ruled by its guilds, or *arti.* The seven major guilds, which were controlled by bankers, lawyers, and exporters, originally ran the civic government, but by the middle of the fourteenth century all the guilds, even the lesser guilds of middle-ranking tradesmen, had achieved some measure of political voice, and the city prided itself on its "representative" government and its status as a republic. Still, the long-standing division between those who favored the Holy Roman Emperor and those who favored the popes continued unabated. Such civil strife, sometimes marked by street battles, had one inevitable result. By the fifteenth century, what Florence needed most was a leader with enough political skill, power, and wealth to stop the feuding.

FIGURE 13.1 A map of Florence in 1490.

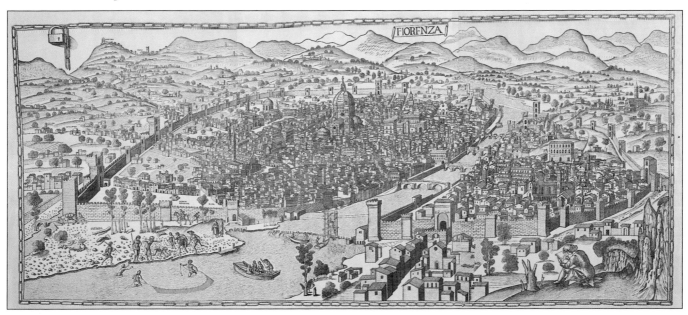

THE MEDICIS' FLORENCE

A single family, the Medici, led Florence to its unrivaled position as the cultural center of Renaissance Europe in the fifteenth century. The family had begun to accumulate its fortune by lending money to other Florentines out of income derived from its two wool workshops. GIOVANNI DI BICCI DE' MEDICI [geo-VAHN-nee dee BEE-chee deh MED-uh-chee] (1360–1429) multiplied this fortune by setting up branch banks in major Italian cities and creating close financial allegiances with the papacy in Rome, allegiances that tended to switch the balance of power, making secular concerns more important than religious ones to the Vatican.

Cosimo de' Medici. COSIMO [CAH-zee-moh] (1389–1464), the son of Giovanni Di Bicci, led the family to a position of unquestioned preeminence, not only in Florence but, as branches of the Medici banks opened elsewhere, throughout Europe. Although never the official leader of the city, Cosimo ruled from behind the scenes. By 1458, Pope Pius II said of Cosimo that "He is King in everything but name."

Cosimo's power was based on calculated acts of discretion and benevolence. Cosimo built the first public library since ancient times and stocked it with ancient manuscripts and books, chiefly Greek and Roman, with a special eye toward the works of Plato and Aristotle. At some point, Cosimo employed virtually every major Italian artist, architect, writer, philosopher, or scholar of the day.

In many ways, Cosimo's largesse simply solidified what was already fact—Florence had been a cultural center since the middle of the fourteenth century (see Chapter 12). The growing wealth of the city itself, together with the peace brought by Cosimo's leadership, created an atmosphere in which the arts could prosper, and this in turn contributed to the increasing sophistication of its citizenry.

Lorenzo the Magnificent. The city's dream of achieving the status of the Golden Age of Athens was fully realized by LORENZO [LOR-enn-zoh] (1449–1492), Cosimo's grandson, who assumed his place as head of the

FIGURE 13.2 Giorgio Vasari, *Posthumous Portrait of Lorenzo the Magnificent,* oil on canvas, Galleria degli Uffizi, Florence. SCALA/Art Resource, NY. The impressive presence of Lorenzo, as well as his broken nose, are recorded in this painting by Vasari, author of the *Lives of the Most Eminent Sculptors, Painters, and Architects.*

Medici family at the age of twenty in 1469, inaugurating twenty-three years of influence. Lorenzo's father, PIERO [pea-AIR-oh] (1416–1469), cursed with ill health, had ruled for only five years after Cosimo before his own death, but he had raised Lorenzo in Cosimo's image, and Lorenzo quickly established himself as a force to be reckoned with. "Lorenzo the Magnificent" he was called (fig. 13.2), and he lived with a sense of grandeur. He was one of the leading

Table 13-1		POPES DURING THE RENAISSANCE AND MANNERIST PERIODS			
The Catholic popes of the fifteenth and sixteenth centuries and the dates they reigned:					
Boniface IX	1389–1404	Innocent VIII	1484–1492	Paul IV	1555–1559
Innocent VII	1404–1406	Alexander VI	1492–1503	Pius IV	1559–1565
Gregory XII	1406–1415	Pius III	1503	St. Pius V	1566–1572
Martin V	1417–1431	Julius II	1503–1513	Gregory XIII	1572–1585
Eugene IV	1431–1447	Leo X	1513–1521	Sixtus V	1585–1590
Nicholas V	1447–1455	Adrian VI	1522–1523	Urban VII	1590
Callistus III	1455–1458	Clement VII	1523–1534	Gregory XIV	1590–1591
Pius II	1458–1464	Paul III	1534–1549	Innocent IX	1591
Paul II	1464–1471	Julius III	1550–1555	Clement VIII	1592–1605
Sixtus IV	1471–1484	Marcellus II	1555		

Cross Currents

MONTEZUMA'S TENOCHTITLAN

While Florence stood as the center of the Early Renaissance world, in the other hemisphere stood a city of equal grandeur, one that the Europeans did not know existed until Hernán Cortés invaded Mexico in 1519. It was called Tenochtitlan, and it was the capital of Montezuma's Aztec empire.

The Aztecs, who founded the city, believed they had been ordered by their god Huitzilopochtli to wander until they saw an eagle perched upon a prickly pear, or *tenochtli*. They finally encountered such a vision in 1325 on an island in the marshes of Lake Texcoco in the Valley of Mexico. There they built their city, connecting it to the mainland by four causeways. By the end of the fifteenth century, it was a metropolis inhabited by 150,000 to 200,000 people and ruled by a priest and emperor, Montezuma.

The *Codex Mendoza* (fig. 13.3) is the fullest account that we have of early sixteenth-century Aztec life. It consists of seventy-two annotated pictorial pages together with sixty-three more pages of re-lated Spanish commentary. It was compiled under the supervision of Spanish friars and at the request of the Spanish crown in about 1541 to aid in their colonial expansion.

As depicted by Aztec scribes, the city is represented by the eagle on the cactus, the shield and arrows symbolizing war, and the waterways dividing the city into equal quadrants. At the heart of the city was the Great Pyramid, imaged by the scribes in the temple at the top. Here, the Aztecs worshiped both Huitzilopochtli, god of the sun and of warfare, and Tlaloc, god of rain and fertility, and here they engaged in ritual human sacrifice to both gods by cutting out the still-beating hearts of their victims, then decapitating them.

As the cultural center of the Aztec civilization, Tenochtitlan was magnificent, grander in fact than anything in Europe at the time. In the words of one of Cortés's soldiers: "When we saw . . . that straight and level causeway going towards Tenochtitlan, we were amazed. . . . Some of our soldiers even asked whether the things that we saw were not a dream."

FIGURE 13.3 *The Founding of Tenochtitlan,* page from the *Codex Mendoza,* Aztec, sixteenth century, ink and color on paper, $81\frac{7}{10} \times 12\frac{3}{8}''$ (21.5 × 31.5 cm), The Bodleian Library, Oxford. The skull rack just to the right of center is one of the very few images in the Codex that openly acknowledges the practice of human sacrifice in Aztec life.

---

poets of his day, as well as an accomplished musician, playing the lute and composing dances. He surrounded himself with scholars, built palaces and parks, sponsored festivals and pageants, all the while dipping deeply into the city's coffers, which he controlled, as well as his own. He commissioned little in the way of painting, preferring instead to spend money on gemstones and ancient vases, which he believed to be better investments. Many of the precious stones in his collection, for example, were valued at over a thousand florins (the coin of the day), whereas a painting by Botticelli might be bought for as little as a hundred florins. Spend Lorenzo did, and by the time of his death in 1492, the Medici bank was in financial trouble and Florence itself was verging on bankruptcy.

Although the Medici ruled Florence with minor interruptions until 1737, they never again held the same power and authority as Cosimo and Lorenzo. Outside Florence, the most important patron of the Renaissance in Rome would be Lorenzo's son, Pope Leo X. In generations to come, several female Medici descendants would marry the most powerful figures in Europe—Catherine de' Medici (1519–89) was queen to Henry II of France, and Marie de' Medici (1573–1642) was queen consort to Henry IV of France.

THE HUMANIST SPIRIT

Cosimo, Piero, and Lorenzo de' Medici were all **humanists**—they believed in the worth and dignity of the individual. Celebrating human reason, spirit, and physical beauty, the humanists echoed the Greek philosopher Protagoras in seeing human beings as the measure of all things. Seeking to discover what was best about humanity, they turned to the culture of classical antiquity. In the literature, history, rhetoric, and philosophy of ancient Greece and Rome, they discovered what the Latin scholar and poet PETRARCH [PEH-trark] (1304–72) a century before had called a "golden wisdom." Cosimo and Lorenzo worked to make Florence the humanist capital of the world, a place where the golden wisdom of the ancients might flourish.

Petrarch is often called the father of humanism, and in many ways he determined its high moral tone. He believed that learning was the key to living a virtuous life, and that life should be an eternal quest for truth. Every individual leading a virtuous life in the pursuit of knowledge and truth would provide a basis for improving humanity's lot. He encouraged an appreciation of beauty, in nature and in human endeavor, which he thought to be a manifestation of the divine. For Petrarch, reading the ancients was like having conversations with them, and he took to writing letters to the ancients as if they were personal friends, even family. He called the poet Virgil his brother and Cicero his father. In the writings of the ancients, Petrarch sensed their uniquely human (noble and ignoble) qualities.

In the middle of the fourteenth century, Petrarch's friend, the writer Boccaccio, was one of the first men to study Greek since the classical age itself. During the next fifty years, humanist scholars combed monastery libraries for long-ignored ancient Greek texts and translated them into Latin and Italian. By 1400, the works of Homer, Aeschylus, Sophocles, Euripides, Aristophanes, Herodotus, Thucydides, and all of Plato's dialogues were available. In addition, after the fall of Constantinople to the Muslim forces of the Ottoman Turks in 1453, ending the already weakening Byzantine Empire, Greek scholars flooded into Italy. Greek learning spread with the rapid rise of printing in Italy following Johann Gutenberg's invention of printing with movable type in 1455. Between 1456 and 1500, more books were published than had been copied by manuscript scribes in the previous thousand years. Many of these were in vernacular (or native) Italian, which contributed to the growing literacy of the middle class. By the sixteenth century, many educated persons owned the complete works of Plato.

THE PLATONIC ACADEMY OF PHILOSOPHY

The center of humanist study was the Platonic Academy of Philosophy in Florence, founded by Cosimo de' Medici in 1462 and supported with special enthusiasm by Lorenzo the Magnificent. The academy sponsored **Neoplatonism,** or a "new Platonism," which sought to revive Platonic ideals in contemporary culture, especially as espoused by the Roman philosopher PLOTINUS [Ploh-TINE-us] (205–270 C.E.). The Platonic Academy was an important example of the shift of interest from Aristotle during the Middle Ages to Plato during the Renaissance.

Marsilio Ficino. At the head of the academy was MARSILIO FICINO [fi-CHEE-noh] (1433–99), who translated both Plato and Plotinus into Latin and wrote the *Theologia Platonica* (1482). Ficino's Neoplatonism was a conscious rereading of Plato (see Chapter 3), particularly his dualistic vision of the psyche (roughly equivalent to the soul or spirit) trapped in the body, but Ficino thought we could glimpse the higher world of forms or ideas through study and learning, and so he looked to Plotinus. Plotinus argued that the material and spiritual worlds could be united through ecstatic, or mystical, vision. Following Plotinus, Ficino conceived of beauty in the things of this world as God's means of making himself manifest to humankind. The contemplation and study of beauty in nature—and in all things—was a form of worship, a manifestation of divine or spiritual love, and Plato's ideas about love were central to Ficino's philosophy. Like erotic love, spiritual love is inspired by physical beauty, but spiritual love moves beyond the physical to an intellectual plane and, eventually, to such an elevated spiritual level that it results in the soul's union with God. Thus, in Neoplatonic terms, Lorenzo's fondness for gems was a type of spiritual love, as was Petrarch's love for Laura, celebrated in his sonnets, and so was the painter Botticelli's love of the human form (both discussed later in this chapter). If in real things one could discover the divine, realism became, in Neoplatonic terms, a form of idealism. In fact, Ficino saw "Platonic love," the love of beauty, as a kind of spiritual bond on which the strongest kind of community could be constructed. In this way, Neoplatonism even had political implications. The Neoplatonists even had political implications. The Neoplatonists envisioned Florence as a city whose citizenry was spiritually bound together in a common love of the beautiful.

Pico della Mirandola. Another great Neoplatonic philosopher at the academy was PICO DELLA MIRANDOLA [PEA-coh DELL-ah mee-RAN-doh-lah] (1463–94), whose religious devotion, intense scholarship, and boundless optimism attracted many followers. His *Oration on the Dignity of Man* (1486) encapsulates one of the central impulses of the Renaissance: humankind serving as a link between the lower orders of nature, including animals, and the higher spiritual orders, of which angels are a part. For Pico, human beings possess free will; they can make of themselves what they wish. Though linked with the lower order of matter, they are capable of rising to the higher realm of spirit and ultimately being united with God. Each person's destiny is thus a matter of individual choice.

In the *Oration*, Pico presents God speaking to Adam, telling him that "in conformity with thy free judgment in whose hands I have placed thee, thou art confined by no bonds, and constrained by no limits." God also tells Adam directly that he is "the molder and maker" of himself, who "canst grow downward into the lower natures which are brutes" or "upward from the mind's reason into the higher natures which are divine." This central tenet of humanist philosophy is often misunderstood to mean that an emphasis on the individual results in or implies a rejection of God. Although Pico, and humanists in general, place the responsibility for human action squarely on humans and not on the Almighty, Pico also believed the human mind—with its ability to reason and imagine—could conceive of and move toward the divine. It follows that individual genius, which was allowed to flower in Renaissance Italy as never before in Western culture, is the worldly manifestation of divine truth.

ARCHITECTURE

Renaissance architecture reflects a renewed interest in ancient Roman models for mathematically derived proportions as well as logic of construction.

Filippo Brunelleschi.   The greatest architect of the Early Renaissance was FILIPPO BRUNELLESCHI [brewnuh-LESS-key] (1377–1446), whose triumph is the dome of Florence Cathedral (fig. 13.4). Measuring $138\frac{1}{2}$ feet wide and 367 feet high, it was the largest dome since the Pantheon built in 125 C.E. (see Chapter 4). Although influenced by antique architecture, the octagonal dome of Florence Cathedral does not look like the hemispherical dome of the ancient Roman Pantheon. Using the basic structural principles perfected in the pointed arches of Gothic cathedrals, Brunelleschi produced a dome with less outward thrust than a hemispherical one. Because his predecessor, Arnolfo di Cambio, had designed the base of the dome to be extraordinarily wide, Brunelleschi flanked his octagonal dome with three half domes to buttress it.

Brunelleschi used stone at the bottom of the dome; for the upper portion, he used brick. The heavier material at the bottom produced a self-buttressing system, an idea seen in the Pantheon. Brunelleschi's innovation was to build a double dome with an inner and an outer shell—a

FIGURE 13.4   Filippo Brunelleschi, Florence Cathedral, dome, 1420–36; lantern completed 1471. Brunelleschi managed to erect this enormous double-shell pointed dome without the use of temporary scaffolding. It is the major landmark of Florence.

dome within a dome that was much lighter than the solid concrete dome of the Pantheon. The octagonal dome is reinforced by eight major ribs, visible on the exterior, plus three minor ribs between every two major ribs (fig. 13.5). Finally, Michelozzo added an open structure to crown the roof, a **lantern.** The metal lantern's weight stabilized the whole, its downward pressure keeping the ribs from spreading apart at the top.

Leon Battista Alberti. The other great architect of the day, LEON BATTISTA ALBERTI [al-BEAR-tee] (1404–72), was celebrated both as an architect and as an author. He was the first to detail the principles of linear perspective in his treatise *De pictura (On Painting)*, written in 1434–35. His ten books on architecture, *De re aedificatoria*, completed about 1450, were inspired by the late-first-century B.C.E. Roman writer Vitruvius, who had himself written an encyclopedic ten-volume survey of classical architecture.

Alberti worked to create beauty in architecture that derived from harmony among all parts, using mathematics to determine the proportions of his buildings. A prime example is the church of Sant' Andrea in Mantua (fig. 13.6), designed in 1470 and completed after his death. Hampered by an older building on the site, Alberti had to adapt his ideal design for the church to the preexisting surroundings. His solution exemplifies Renaissance theory. For the facade he combined the triangular pediment of a classical temple with the arches characteristic of ancient Roman triumphal arches—one large central arch flanked by two smaller arches. The facade balances horizontals and verticals, with the height of the facade equaling the

FIGURE 13.6 Leon Battista Alberti, Sant' Andrea, Mantua, facade, designed 1470. An ideal demonstration of the Early Renaissance devotion to the antique, the design of this facade combines the form of an ancient temple with that of an ancient triumphal arch.

FIGURE 13.5 Line drawing of Brunelleschi's dome for Florence Cathedral, indicating the double-shell construction.

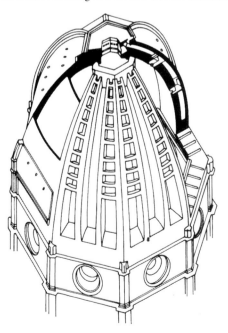

width. Four colossal Corinthian pilasters paired with small pilasters visually unite the stories of the facade. Large and small pilasters of the same dimensions appear in the nave, linking the exterior and interior in a harmonious whole.

Michelozzo di Bartolommeo. In fifteenth-century Florence, wealthy families customarily hired architects to build fortresslike palaces, emblematic of their power. The Palazzo Medici-Riccardi (fig. 13.7), designed by MICHELOZZO DI BARTOLOMMEO [MEE-kel-LOTZ-oh] (1396–1472), was begun in 1445 and probably completed by 1452. Although built for Cosimo de' Medici, the Riccardi family acquired the palazzo in the seventeenth century. Located on a corner of the Via Larga, the widest street in Florence, it is an imposing residence, dignified yet grand, that heralded its resident—the city's most powerful person—literally and metaphorically at the center of the city's cultural and political life.

Michelozzo created an austere three-story stone building. The stonework, beginning with a ground level of rusticated stone (the same rough-hewn masonry used in fortifications), becomes increasingly smoother from bottom story to top. Michelozzo further differentiated the

FIGURE 13.7 Michelozzo di Bartolommeo, Palazzo Medici-Riccardi, Florence, exterior, begun 1445, probably completed by 1452; ground-floor windows by Michelangelo, ca. 1517. Typical of Early Renaissance palazzi, the facades of this massive city residence, built for Cosimo de' Medici the Elder, are neatly divided into three stories with evenly spaced windows.

levels visually by successively diminishing the height of each, although they all remain over twenty feet high. Typical of the Renaissance, the division of the stories is neat and clear, and the divisions are formed by classical moldings.

The Renaissance interest in orderliness is seen also in the even spacing of the windows. The form of window used—two arched openings within an overriding arch— was already popular in the Middle Ages. At the top of the palazzo, a heavy projecting cornice fulfills both aesthetic and architectural roles. The cornice serves visually to frame and conclude the architectural composition; it also sent the rainwater wide of the wall. The Medici coat of arms with its seven balls appears on the corners of the second story. What are now its ground-level windows were originally arches that opened onto the street creating a *loggia*, or covered gallery. (The arches were filled and the windows added in the sixteenth century by Michelangelo.)

The first story provided offices and storage rooms for the Medici business; the family's living quarters were on the second level.

The rooms of the Palazzo Medici-Riccardi are arranged around a central colonnaded courtyard, a typical Florentine system in which the palace is turned in on itself, ostensibly for protection but also for privacy and quiet. Whereas the plain exterior reflected the original owner's public posture as a careful, even conservative man, the inside, especially the second floor, or *piano nobile* (the grand and "noble" family rooms of the palace), displayed ostentatious grandeur.

SCULPTURE

Renaissance culture promoted the notion of individual genius by encouraging competitions among artists for prestigious public and religious commissions. In 1401, the Florentine humanist historian Leonardo Bruni sponsored a competition to determine who would make the doors of Florence Cathedral's octagonal **baptistery,** the small structure seen in the left foreground in fig 12.13, separate from the main church, where baptisms are performed. Seven sculptors were asked to submit depictions of the sacrifice of Isaac.

Lorenzo Ghiberti. The winner of the competition was the young sculptor LORENZO GHIBERTI [ghee-BAIR-tee] (1378–1455), and his reaction typifies the heightened sense of self-worth that Renaissance artists felt about their artistic abilities and accomplishments: "To me was conceded the palm of victory by all the experts. . . . To me the honor was conceded universally and with no exception. To all it seemed that I had at that time surpassed the others."

So well were these doors received that as soon as they were completed Ghiberti was commissioned to make a second set for the east side of the baptistery. These, depicting ten stories from the Old Testament, were completed in 1452. Impressed by their beauty, Michelangelo called them the "gates of paradise," and the name stuck. *The Gates of Paradise* face the cathedral facade, occupying the most prominent position on the baptistery.

The panels are fewer in number and larger in size; scenes are set in simple square formats, and this time the whole square is gilded rather than just the raised areas. Each panel includes several scenes. The first, *The Creation* (fig. 13.8), portrays five scenes from Genesis. At the top, God creates the heavens and earth. At the bottom left, Adam is created from the earth. The central scene depicts Eve being created from Adam's rib. To the left and behind, Adam and Eve are tempted by Satan in the guise of a serpent. And to the right, Adam and Eve are expelled from the Garden of Eden. This is simultaneous presentation of events that took place sequentially, a technique called continuous narration.

FIGURE 13.8   Lorenzo Ghiberti, *The Creation of Adam and Eve*, relief panel from the *Gates of Paradise*, east doors, Baptistery, Florence, 1425–52, gilt bronze, $31\frac{1}{4} \times 31\frac{1}{4}''$ (79.4 × 79.4 cm), now in the Museo dell'Opera del Duomo, Florence. Because of their beauty, Michelangelo referred to these doors as the "Gates of Paradise."

FIGURE 13.9   Donatello, *Feast of Herod*, relief panel from baptismal font, Baptistery, Siena, ca. 1423–27, gilt bronze, $23\frac{1}{2}'' \times 23\frac{1}{2}''$ (59.7 × 59.7 cm). Donatello's harsh drama contrasts with Ghiberti's fluid charm.

Donatello.   Ghiberti's interest in correct perspective, proper proportions, and the accurate representation of nature was shared by DONATELLO [don-ah-TELL-oh] (1386–1466). His *Feast of Herod* (fig. 13.9), a gilded bronze relief made ca. 1423–27 for the font in the baptistery of Siena Cathedral, is a triumph in the creation of perspectival space. Although perspective had been employed by the ancient Romans in their murals, the principles of Renaissance **linear perspective** are believed to have been developed by Filippo Brunelleschi, whom Ghiberti had defeated in the original competition for the Florentine baptistery doors. These principles were later codified by the architect Leon Battista Alberti in his *De pictura (On Painting)*. In the simplest terms, perspective allows the picture plane (or surface of the picture) to function as a window through which a scene is presented to the viewer.

The effectiveness of linear perspective in organizing a composition and in creating the illusion of pictorial space cannot be overstated. The actual physical space of Donatello's *Feast of Herod* is shallow, but perspective creates the illusion of a deep space, with two courtyards behind the foreground action. In each courtyard the people are progressively smaller. The floor pattern, drawn in linear perspective, enhances the illusion of recession. Donatello's emphasis on the mathematical discipline of his design and his rigorous application of the laws of perspective are balanced by the dramatic and emotional content of the scene.

Indeed, the *Feast of Herod* possesses a dramatic force never before seen in Italian sculpture. The composition is split down the middle so there are two competing centers of attention, an unusual device. John the Baptist's head is brought on a platter to Herod on the left, and Salome dances seductively on the right. This split adds to the emotional impact and tension of the composition.

Donatello depicted a very different subject, one popular in the Early Renaissance, the shepherd boy David (fig. 13.10) who slew the giant, Goliath, with a stone from his slingshot. In Donatello's *David* (ca. 1425–30s), the stone is still in David's sling, although Goliath's head lies beneath David's foot. By depicting David both before and after the conflict, Donatello provides a condensed version of the story. With the first large-scale nude created since Roman antiquity, Donatello portrays his hero as an adolescent male wearing only a hat and boots. According to the Bible, David casts off only his armor as too cumbersome for battle. To depict David in the nude is to link him to heroic nudes of antiquity. In addition, David adopts the antique *contrapposto* posture, in which the weight of the body rests on one leg, elevating the hip and the opposite shoulder, putting the spine into an S curve.

Between 1453 and 1455, Donatello carved his polychromed wooden figure of *Mary Magdalene* (fig. 13.11), which stands over six feet high. After a sermon by Pope Gregory the Great in 594, in which he made a suggestive comparison to Mary Magdalene's sinfulness, she came to be identified as a prostitute. She remained among the followers of Jesus, is said to have annointed him with oil after his crucifixion, to have attended to his burial, and discov-

FIGURE 13.10   Donatello, *David*, ca. 1425–30, bronze, height 5′2¼″ (1.58 m), Museo Nazionale del Bargello, Florence. Scala/Art Resource, NY. The Early Renaissance interest in antiquity and the accurate portrayal of the nude are evidenced in Donatello's work.

FIGURE 13.11   Donatello, *Mary Magdalene*, 1453–55, wood, painted and gilded, height 6′2″ (1.88 m), Museo dell'Opera del Duomo, Florence. Scala/Art Resource, NY. Not only beauty, but also its absence can be used to create emotionally moving art, as in this portrayal of the repentant sinner.

ered his resurrection. Donatello depicts her after years of living in the desert, rejecting the life of the body in anticipation of the immortal life of the soul after a spiritual resurrection. Her body now gaunt, her arms and legs withered, she prays. Donatello's figure is intentionally unnerving, even repulsive. It is the striking absence of beauty that makes her both powerful and memorable.

PAINTING

Masaccio.   Of all the Early Renaissance painters, it was MASACCIO [mah-SAH-chee-oh] (1401–29), in his short life, who carried the naturalistic impulse in painting furthest. In the 1436 Italian edition of *On Painting*, Alberti named Masaccio, along with Brunelleschi, Donatello, and Ghiberti, as a leading artist of the day.

Masaccio's extraordinary inventiveness is evident in the frescoes painted on the walls of the Brancacci Chapel in Santa Maria del Carmine, Florence, completed in 1428. In one, *The Tribute Money* (fig. 13.12), Masaccio depicts the scene from the Bible in which Jesus orders his disciples to "render unto Caesar that which is Caesar's, and unto God the things that are God's." In the center, Jesus, in response to the arrival of a Roman tax collector, tells his disciple Peter to look for money in the mouth of a fish. On the left, having removed his cloak, Peter takes the money from the fish. On the right, he gives the money to the tax collector. It is an example of continuous narration.

Masaccio's figures are harmoniously arranged, the main figure group placed to the left of center, balancing the

FIGURE 13.12   Masaccio, *The Tribute Money,* Brancacci Chapel, Santa Maria del Carmine, Florence, finished 1428, fresco, 8′1″ × 19′7″ (2.3 × 6.0 m). A narrative based on Matthew 17:24–27 is related in a three-part perfectly balanced composition, seemingly illuminated by light coming from the chapel windows. Perspective converges to a point behind Jesus' head, thereby directing the viewer's eyes to Jesus.

visually heavier group on the far right. The entire space is carefully composed by the one-point perspective of the architecture, the vanishing point behind Jesus's head. The depth of the whole scene is further enhanced by means of **atmospheric (aerial) perspective,** duplicating in point the optical phenomenon of the atmosphere's ability to modify the clarity and color of objects at a distance.

The figures seem to stand in a three-dimensional space. The tax collector, wearing the short tunic, has turned his back to us, and stands in a *contrapposto* pose, balanced, relaxed, and natural. When Vasari later wrote that "Masaccio made his figures stand upon their feet," he was praising the naturalism of such poses. The tax collector also echoes our own relationship to the space; real viewers and painted figures alike look at Jesus. All the faces are individualized, not idealized, and reflect Masaccio's models, real people of the peasant class of Florence. Masaccio's use of strong contrast between light and shadow creates an illusion of three-dimensional, almost sculptural, figures moving in space. They are lit from the right in imitation of physical reality, since the windows in the Brancacci Chapel are to the right of the fresco.

Masaccio's fresco of the *Trinity with the Virgin, St. John the Evangelist, and Donors* (fig. 13.13), in Santa Maria Novella in Florence, of ca. 1427–28, summarizes several characteristics of the Renaissance. The Renaissance interest in lifelike portraiture can be seen in the life-size de-

pictions of two members of the Lenzi family who commissioned the work. Unlike the anonymous marginal figures of donors seen in medieval paintings, these donors have a real presence in the scene. So successful was Masaccio in his use of linear perspective that the chapel appears to recede into the wall; the vanishing point is just below the bottom of the cross, five feet from the floor, approximately eye level for the adult viewer. Situated deeper in the space and therefore drawn smaller than the Lenzis, Mary and John the Evangelist plead with Jesus on behalf of humankind. The only figure to defy natural logic is God, for his feet are on the back wall, yet he holds the cross in the foreground. The Renaissance interest in the antique is seen in the coffered barrel vault, Ionic and Corinthian capitals, and the moldings—all based upon ancient Roman models.

Piero della Francesca.   PIERO DELLA FRANCESCA [pea-AIR-oh del-uh-fran-CHES-kah] (ca. 1406/12–1492) was also deeply interested in portraiture, a reflection of the Renaissance concern for the individual. His double depiction of Battista Sforza and Federico da Montefeltro (figs. 13.14 and 13.15) shows wife and husband holding their heads motionless, high above the landscape behind them. They are noble, elevated, grand. The profile presentation was especially popular in the Early Renaissance, revealing the sitter's most distinctive features.

FIGURE 13.14   Piero della Francesca, *Battista Sforza*, 1472–73, oil on panel, $18\frac{1}{2}'' \times 13''$ (47 × 33 cm), Galleria degli Uffizi, Florence. SCALA/Art Resource, NY. The profile portrait was favored in the Early Renaissance; later the three-quarter view became popular.

Piero began the portraits in 1472, the year the countess died, suggesting her portrait was made from her death mask. She is shown in the fashion of the times, with her plucked and shaved forehead, her elaborate hairstyle, and sparkling jewels. The count was ruler of Urbino, which had begun to compete with Florence as an intellectual center. He was a gentleman, scholar, bibliophile, and warrior, whose court included humanists, philosophers, poets, and artists. A left profile view was chosen because the count had lost his right eye and the bridge of his nose to a sword in a tournament. It is nonetheless with unsparing realism that Piero presents him "warts and all." We can assume the countess and count looked exactly like this, and that Piero faithfully recorded all the crannies and crevices of their facial terrain.

Fra Angelico.   FRA ANGELICO [FRAH an-JELL-ee-coh] (ca. 1400–55), nicknamed "Angelic Brother" by his brother Dominican monks, was the most popular painter in Florence in the first half of the fifteenth century. His

FIGURE 13.13   Masaccio, *Trinity with the Virgin, St. John the Evangelist, and Donors*, Santa Maria Novella, Florence, probably 1427 or 1428, fresco, 21′ × 10′5″ (6.5 × 3.2 m). The architectural setting demonstrates the Early Renaissance interest in the antique and in spatial illusion; the naturalistic portrayal of the life-size donors indicates the new concern for the individual.

FIGURE 13.15   Piero della Francesca, *Federico da Montefeltro*, 1472–73, oil on panel, $18\frac{1}{2} \times 13''$ (47 × 33 cm), Galleria degli Uffizi, Florence. Scala/Art Resource, NY. In this pair of portraits, wife and husband are recorded with unsparing realism. An accident in combat accounts for the count's curious profile.

Annunciation (fig. 13.16), painted between 1438 and 1445 in the monastery of San Marco in Florence, was part of a vast project in which Fra Angelico painted on the walls in one of the cloisters, the chapter house, upstairs in the corridors, and especially in the monks' dormitory cells with the help of assistants. It would be difficult to create gentler, more graceful gestures than those of Mary and Gabriel in this scene. Their crossed arms are a sign of respect as well as a reference to Jesus's cross and prefiguration of his crucifixion. In the garden to the left are accurate depictions of real plants, but Fra Angelico, in medieval fashion, has spaced them evenly across the ground so each maintains its separate identity. The architecture of the space is rendered with typical Early Renaissance respect for the laws of perspective, but Fra Angelico has placed his figures in the architectural setting without regard to proper relative scale. The scene is accurately set within the architecture of San Marco, newly finished by the architect Michelozzo; thus the Annunciation is shown to take place in a specific and contemporary building. The immediacy and conviction of the event were enhanced for the monks who saw the angel Gabriel addressing Mary in their own monastery.

Sandro Botticelli.   SANDRO BOTTICELLI [bott-tee-CHEL-lee] (1445–1510) received his artistic training as an assistant to Fra Filippo Lippi, a painter who had worked with Fra Angelico.

His *Primavera* (fig. 13.17), painted about 1482, is a complex allegory of spring taken from the Latin writers Horace and Lucretius. It embodies the growing interest in classical literature and pagan mythology of the Neoplatonists of the Florentine Academy. Botticelli was himself a member of this Neoplatonist circle, which also included Lorenzo de' Medici. *Primavera* was commissioned by Lorenzo di Pierfrancesco de' Medici, a cousin of Lorenzo's, for a chamber next to his bedroom.

Botticelli was unconcerned with the representation of deep space; his orange grove behind functions more like a stage backdrop than an actual landscape. However, Botticelli is, above all, a master of line, and the emphasis of his work is on surface pattern. Neither solid nor three dimensional, his figures are clearly outlined, and they seem to flow along the rhythmic lines of a dance or procession. The painting moves from right to left, as if blown on the breath of Zephyrus, god of the west wind, shown with his cheeks puffed out on the far right. Next is Chloris, the spring nymph, with a leafy vine coming from her mouth. Beside her is Flora, the goddess of flowers, strewing their path with petals. In the middle stands Venus, goddess of love, shown pregnant as a symbol of her fruitfulness in spring. With her, the movement of the scene almost comes to a halt, but she gestures toward the three Graces as Cupid, above her, shoots an arrow in their direction. The three Graces themselves, daughters of Zeus and the personifications of beauty and charm, twirl and whirl us around, but they too seem to spin to the left where finally Mercury, messenger of the gods, holds up his caduceus, or staff, as if to halt the entire procession.

Botticelli's *Birth of Venus* (fig. 13.18), of ca. 1484–86, was also painted for Lorenzo di Pierfrancesco de' Medici, and also depicts a subject from antique pagan mythology, made acceptable to the Christian church by equating Venus with Jesus's mother Mary on the grounds that both were sources of love. According to Neoplatonic interpretation, the birth of Venus is equivalent to the birth of the human soul, as yet uncorrupted by the matter of the world. In Neoplatonic terms, the soul is free to choose for itself whether to follow a path toward sin and degradation or to attempt to regain, through the use of reason, a spiritual perfection manifested in the beauty of creation and felt in the love of God. To love beauty is to love not the material world of sensual things, but rather the world's abstract and spiritual essence.

In 1494, a Dominican friar, Girolamo Savonarola, who had lived in the same monastery of San Marco in Florence that Fra Angelico had painted, took control of the city.

FIGURE 13.16   Fra Angelico, *Annunciation*, monastery of San Marco, Florence, 1438–45, fresco, 7′6″ × 10′5″ (2.29 × 3.18 m). Fra Angelico cleverly painted the Annunciation as if it were taking place within the actual architecture of the monastery of San Marco.

Savonarola proclaimed that Florence had condemned itself to perdition, saying that its painters—artists such as Botticelli—"make the Virgin look like a harlot." A bonfire was built in the Piazza della Signoria, the main square of the city, and on it signs of vanity—clothing, wigs, false beards, make-up, and mirrors as well as books, board games, and paintings were burned.

EARLY RENAISSANCE MUSIC

March 15, 1436, was a day of dedication for the completed Florence Cathedral, now crowned by Brunelleschi's extraordinary dome. A procession wound its way through the city's streets and entered the cathedral, led by Pope Eugene IV and seven cardinals, thirty-six bishops, and untold numbers of church officials, civic leaders, artists, scholars, and musicians. The papal choir included one of the greatest figures in Renaissance music, the composer Guillaume Dufay. The choir performed a motet called informally "Il Duomo" composed by Dufay especially for the occasion. As one eyewitness recalled, "The whole space of the temple was filled with such choruses of harmony, and such a concert of diverse instruments, that it seemed (not without reason) as though the symphonies and songs of the angels and of divine paradise had been sent forth from Heaven to whisper in our ears an unbelievable celestial sweetness."

Guillaume Dufay.   More than any other composer, GUILLAUME DUFAY [dew-FAY] (1400–74) shaped the musical language of the Early Renaissance. Born in northern France, Dufay served first as a music teacher for the French court of Burgundy, then as a court composer in Italy, working at various times in Bologna, Florence, and Rome. A musical celebrity, he was often solicited to compose music for solemn occasions, such as the dedication of "Il Duomo."

The English had developed pleasing harmonies using a three-note interval (rather than the four-, five-, or eight-note intervals of the Middle Ages), but it was Dufay who used this triadic harmony in polyphonic and imitative style. Dufay was a composer of the increasingly popular "parody mass," where a popular song of the day was inserted into a liturgical mass. Congregations loved the familiar secular tune used in their daily worship. However, com-

FIGURE 13.17   Sandro Botticelli, *Primavera*, ca. 1482 (?), tempera on panel, 6'8" × 10'4" (2.03 × 3.15 m), Galleria degli Uffizi, Florence. Neoplatonic theory is given visual form in this allegory, perhaps a depiction of the Floralia, an ancient Roman celebration of spring. It was made for a cousin of Lorenzo de' Medici, ruler of Florence.

posers of parody masses were careful to hide the pop tune in a slow-moving tenor line to escape criticism from the clergy.

Dufay wrote music in all the popular genres of his time: masses for liturgies, Latin motets, or compositions for multiple voices; music for ceremonies; and French and Italian *chansons*, or songs, for the pleasure of his patrons and friends. In each genre, Dufay's melodies and rhythms were more easily identifiable than those of earlier composers.

Motets.   Dufay wrote many **motets:** one-movement compositions that set a sacred text to polyphonic choral music, usually with no instrumental accompaniment. Dufay's motet *Alma Redemptoris Mater*, composed in about 1430, fuses medieval *polyphony*—that is, the simultaneous singing of several voices each independent of the others—with a newer Early Renaissance form. The result was a multimelodic, rather than merely a multivoiced, musical style, with more lyrical, less chantlike melodies and a more sensuous sound. Earlier composers typically put the *plainchant* melody, or main melody, in the lowest voice, but Dufay puts the main melody in the highest or uppermost voice, where it can be better heard. He also avoids the

rhythmic distortion of medieval composition. The three voices of Dufay's *Alma Redemptoris Mater*—bass, tenor, and soprano—maintain rhythmic independence (also a late medieval characteristic) until the third and last section of the motet. Then Dufay blocks them together in chords to emphasize the text's closing words, which ask Mary to be merciful to sinners; the chords, arranged in graceful harmonies, soothe the listener's ears more than those of the traditional medieval motet. In this last part Dufay adds an additional voice by giving the sopranos two different parts to sing. In doing so, he moves toward the four-part texture of soprano, alto, tenor, and bass that was to become the norm for later Renaissance vocal music.

Word Painting.   Dufay's emphasis on lyrics is an early example of **word painting,** in which the meaning of words is underscored and emphasized through the music that accompanies them. One sixteenth-century musical theorist offered composers this suggestion: "When one of the words expresses weeping, pain, heartbreak, sighs, tears, and other similar things, let the harmony be full of sadness." A composer might also employ a descending melodic line (going from high to low), or a bass line, to

FIGURE 13.18   Sandro Botticelli, *Birth of Venus*, ca. 1484–86, tempera on canvas, 6′7″ × 9′2″
(2.01 × 2.79 m), Galleria degli Uffizi, Florence. SCALA/Art Resource, NY. Botticelli painted
this important revival of the nude based upon antique prototypes.

express anguish; conversely, an ascending line (going from
low to high), utilizing soprano voices, might express joy
and hope. This increasing sense of the drama of language,
comparable to the Renaissance artists' attention to the
drama of the stories they chose to depict—Donatello's
Mary Magdalene (see fig. 13.11), for example—led Renaissance composers to use music to enrich the feelings
their music expressed, and to support the meaning of a
song's text, whether sacred or secular. Though little music
had survived from ancient Greece, humanist philosophers
like Ficino understood that Aristotle had considered music
the highest form of art and the rhythms of Greek music
imitated the rhythms of Greek poetry, for which it served
as a setting. Thus word painting as the intimate relation of
sound and sense has classical roots.

As in the Middle Ages, musicians like Dufay were employed by the churches, towns, and courts. However, unlike music in the Middle Ages, which served mostly
religious ends, music in the Renaissance became increasingly secularized. Musicians still depended on such patronage, but commissions came from wealthy burghers
and aristocrats such as the Medici family, as well as from

the church, which remained the staunchest of musical patrons. The nobility commissioned secular works to accompany formal occasions such as coronations, weddings,
processions, and even political events. However, before
long secular music also found its way into sacred settings.
Dufay, for instance, introduced the popular French folksong "*L'Homme armé*" ("The Man in Armor") into a mass,
and other composers soon followed suit, creating an entire
musical genre known as *chanson masses*, or "song masses."

Musical accomplishment was one of the marks of an
educated person in the Renaissance, and most people
among the nobility both played an instrument and sang.
Moreover, many uneducated people were accomplished
musicians; in fact, the music of the uneducated masses—
their songs and dances—was most influenced by the secular music of the age. Music was an integral part of an
evening's entertainment. Although it was common for professionals to provide this entertainment, increasingly individuals at a party might entertain the group. Dance, too,
became the focus of social gatherings, and much of the instrumental music of the day was composed to accompany
dances. By the Early Renaissance, instruments had evolved

Connections

MATHEMATICAL PROPORTIONS: BRUNELLESCHI AND DUFAY

Mathematics played an important part in all the arts of the Renaissance. Architects designed buildings guided by mathematical ratios and proportions. Painters employed the mathematical proportions governed by linear perspective. Composers wrote music that reflected mathematical ratios between the notes of a melody and in the intervals between notes sounded together in harmony. Poets structured their poems according to mathematical proportions.

One especially striking set of relationships exists between the proportions of the dome built by Filippo Brunelleschi for Florence Cathedral and "Il Duomo," the motet for four voices that Guillaume Dufay wrote for its dedication in 1436. Its formal title is *Nuper Rosarum Flores (Flowers of Roses)*, the word *flores* referring to Florence itself. The mathematical ratios in Dufay's motet are evident in its rhythm rather than its melody. The slower-moving lower voices of the two tenors proceed in strict rhythmic progressions that reflect the ratio of 6:4:2:3. The initial ratio of 6:4 is reducible to 3:2; thus it is a mirror reverse ratio of 3:2:2:3, which appears in the number of beats in each of the work's four sections: 6, 4, 4, and 6. In addition, Dufay's motet contains a total of 168 measures, proportionally divided into four harmonious parts of 56, 56, 28, and 28 measures each. The last two parts contain exactly half the number of measures of the first two, creating a mathematically harmonious and intellectually pleasing structure.

Brunelleschi's dome's proportions exhibit mathematical ratios that are 6:4:2:3, just as in Dufay's motet. This is the ratio of the internal dimensions to the external ones. And motet and dome both have a doubling. Dufay's motet employs a doubling of the tenor voices, which sing the lower melody five notes apart. Brunelleschi's dome is a double shell, having an internal and an external structure.

The structure of a Petrarchan sonnet also employs a harmonious mathematical ratio for its basic structure. The Petrarchan sonnet is composed of fourteen lines, which typically break into two parts: an octave of eight lines and a sestet of six that yield a ratio of 8:6, which reduces to 4:3. Moreover, both the octave and the sestet usually split evenly into two equal parts: 4 + 4 and 3 + 3, yielding a further neatly symmetrical balanced pair of proportions in both octave and sestet of 1:1.

In these and numerous other instances of Renaissance architecture and music, as well as perspectivist painting, sculptural proportions, and poetry, mathematics lies at the heart of the harmonious nature of the works. This concern with geometric symmetry and mathematical proportions illustrates one more way in which the arts of the Renaissance were a legacy of the golden age of Greece.

---

to look much as they do today. The lute was used both as a solo instrument and to accompany singers. Bowed instruments came in all sizes; wind instruments with brass mouthpieces and single and double reeds were used in festivals and in church. Instruments were classified as either loud (*haut*) or soft (*bas*), which also designated the activity for which the instrument was intended. Before this time, instruments had always performed vocal parts. During the Renaissance, music was written specifically for particular instruments without regard for the capability of the human voice.

Movable type contributed to the growth and popularity of music during the Renaissance. The first collection of music printed in movable type, *One Hundred Songs*, was published in 1501 in Venice by Ottaviano de' Petrucci. Half a century later, printed music was widely available to scholars and amateurs alike. With the greater availability of printed scores, Renaissance composers became more familiar with each other's works and began to influence one another. Amateurs were able to buy and study the same music, and soon songs and dances in particular achieved the kind of widespread popularity that today might put a song into the "Top Ten."

LITERATURE

Petrarch. The first great figure of Italian Renaissance letters, and the first important representative of Italian Renaissance humanism, was Petrarch, a scholar and prolific writer, whose work simultaneously reflects the philosophy of Greek antiquity and the new ideas of the Renaissance. Born Francesco Petrarca in Arezzo and taken, at the age of eight, to Avignon, where the papal courts had moved in 1309, Petrarch studied law in Bologna and Montpellier, then returned in 1326 to Avignon. Petrarch once said of himself, "I am a pilgrim everywhere," for he also traveled widely in France and Italy, hunting down classical manuscripts.

Unlike his Florentine predecessor, Dante Alighieri, whose *Divine Comedy* (see Chapter 12) summed up the sensibility of late medieval culture, Petrarch positioned himself at the beginning of a new literary and artistic era, one that placed greater emphasis on human achievement. Without rejecting the importance of spirituality and religious faith, Petrarch celebrated human accomplishment as the crowning glory of God's creation but praised human beings for their achievements as well.

Petrarch's work is poised between two powerful, intertwined impulses: the religious and moral impulse of the early medieval thinkers, such as St. Augustine, and the humanist dedication to the disciplined study of ancient writers, coupled with a desire for artistic excellence.

Petrarch was especially affected by the elegance and beauty of early Latin literature. However, he disliked the Latin of the Middle Ages, seeing in it a barbarous falling off from the heights of eloquence exemplified by ancient Roman writers such as Virgil, Horace, Ovid, Seneca, and Cicero. Petrarch strove to revive classical literature rather than absorb its elements into contemporary Italian civilization. He considered classical culture a model to be emulated and an ideal against which to measure the achievements of other civilizations. For Petrarch, ancient culture was not merely a source of scientific information, philosophical knowledge, or rhetorical rules; it was also a spiritual and intellectual resource for enriching the human experience. Petrarch would help first Italy, and then Europe, recollect its noble classical past. And although Petrarch did not invent humanism, he breathed life into it and was its tireless advocate.

Soon after his return to Avignon in 1326, Petrarch fell in love with a woman whose identity is unknown, but whom he called Laura in his *Canzoniere (Songbook).* This collection of 366 poems—**sonnets, ballads, sestinas,** madrigals, and **canzoni** (songs)—was written and reworked over more than forty years. Many of the poems are about love, and they are notable for their stylistic elegance and formal perfection. The poems about Laura are the most famous and the most beautiful.

The Petrarchan Sonnet. Thematically, Petrarch's sonnets introduced what was to become a predominant subject of Renaissance lyric poetry: the expression of a speaker's love for a woman and his experience of the joy and pain of love's complex and shifting emotions. Laura's beauty and behavior cause the poet/speaker to sway between hope and despair, pleasure and pain, joy and anguish. Throughout the sequence of poems, Laura remains unattainable. Like so many figures in Renaissance painting, she is at once a real person and an ideal form, a contradiction expressed in the ambivalent feelings the poet/speaker has about her. Petrarch's popularity spawned a profusion of imitators, who borrowed from his situations, psychological descriptions, figurative language, and particularly his sonnet form. Petrarch's sonnets also inspired poets throughout Europe to write their own sonnet sequences. The most famous examples in English are Philip Sidney's *Astrophel and Stella* (1591), Edmund Spenser's *Amoretti* (1595), and William Shakespeare's 154 sonnets. Petrarch's sonnet structure established itself as one of the two dominant sonnet patterns used by poets.

The Petrarchan (sometimes called the Italian) sonnet is organized in two parts: an octave of eight lines and a sestet of six. The octave typically identifies a problem or situation, and the sestet proposes a solution; or the octave introduces a scene, and the sestet comments on or complicates it. The rhyme scheme of the Petrarchan sonnet reinforces its logical structure, with different rhymes occurring in octave and sestet. The octave rhymes *abba abba* (or *abab abab*), and the sestet rhymes *cde cde* (or *cde ced; cde dce;* or *cd, cd, cd*).

The following sonnet was the most popular poem in the European Renaissance; it depicts the lover's ambivalence in a series of paradoxes.

> I find no peace and all my war is done,
> I fear and hope, I burn and freeze like ice;
> I fly above the wind yet can I not arise,
> And nought I have and all the world I sesan.
> That loseth nor locketh holdeth me in prison   *5*
> And holdeth me not, yet can I escape nowise;
> Nor letteth me live nor die at my devise,
> And yet of death it giveth me occasion.
> Without eyes, I see, and without tongue I plain,
> I desire to perish, and yet I ask health,   *10*
> I love an other, and thus I hate my self,
> I feed me in sorrow and laugh in all my pain,
> Likewise displeaseth me both death and life,
> And my delight is cause of this strife.

THE HIGH RENAISSANCE

In the High Renaissance, focus shifted from Florence to Rome due to the wealth and power of the popes. Lavish artistic patronage was provided especially by Pope Julius II (1503–13), patron of Bramante, Raphael, and Michelangelo, and Pope Leo X (1513–21), who also patronized Michelangelo (and excommunicated Martin Luther). Rome had now become a city in which the two major national traditions of Italy converged—Classicism and Christianity.

The High Renaissance begins around 1485 or 1490 in Italy. Only one generation long, the High Renaissance was a short yet extremely important period that was to prove enormously influential on future art. Although there is no precise conclusion to the High Renaissance, the period may be said to come to a close at the death of Raphael in 1520, because this artist's paintings are widely held to epitomize the Renaissance style. Alternatively, the Renaissance may be said to have ended when Rome was sacked and burned by troops serving the Holy Roman Emperor Charles V (in Germany) in 1527. Many artists fled the city, thereby further spreading the ideas of Italy over western Europe.

The High Renaissance continued Early Renaissance interests in humanism, classicism, and individualism, artists and authors perfecting some of the ideas of their Early Renaissance predecessors and developing ideas of their own.

PAINTING

Leonardo da Vinci.   Born in Vinci, about twenty miles west of Florence, LEONARDO DA VINCI [lay-o-NAR-doh dah VIN-chee] (1452–1519) was the illegitimate son of a peasant named Caterina and Ser Piero, a Florentine lawyer, or notary. Leonardo later joined his father in Florence, and in 1469 he entered the workshop of Andrea del Verrocchio, whose other apprentices included Sandro Botticelli. Giorgio Vasari wrote of Leonardo's "beauty as a person," describing him as "divinely endowed" and "so pleasing in conversation that he won all hearts." But he was, Vasari noted, unstable in temperament, often abandoning projects, constantly searching and restless.

Leonardo was sent to Milan by Lorenzo the Magnificent in 1481 or 1482 as an ambassador, charged with presenting an ornate lyre to the duke, Ludovico Sforza, as a gesture of peace. Leonardo chose to remain in Milan. In Florence, Leonardo had been known as a painter and sculptor, but he was, he told the duke, primarily a designer of military and naval weaponry and only secondarily an architect, painter, drainage engineer, and sculptor. He was, in short, the epitome of what we have come to call the "Renaissance" or "universal man," a person not merely capable but talented in an extraordinarily wide range of endeavors.

Leonardo was fascinated by all aspects of nature, as is amply evidenced in his *Madonna of the Rocks* (fig. 13.19), begun in 1483, soon after his arrival in Milan. This is the first time Mary has been depicted in a grotto. The geology—cliffs, mountains, and a grotto filled with stalactites and stalagmites—comes out of his lifelong fascination with the effects of wind and water on the environment. Hurricanes and deluges, eddies and currents of moving water, particularly intrigued him. The *Madonna of the Rocks* demonstrates Leonardo's preoccupation with the interrelated effects of perspective, light, color, and optics. Naturalistic lighting and atmospheric perspective are taken to new heights.

Leonardo developed a technique for modeling forms called **chiaroscuro.** In Italian, *chiaro* means "clear" or "light," and *oscuro* means "obscure" or "dark." Chiaroscuro describes Leonardo's technique of working in areas of light and dark in space. Leonardo also developed a painting technique called **sfumato** (in Italian, "smoky"), which is the intentional suppression of the outline of a figure in a hazy, almost smoky atmosphere. Leonardo's figures do not so much emerge from the darkness of the grotto as they are immersed in it, surrounded by it, even protected by it, as if the grotto were the womb of the earth itself and Mary the site's resident mother goddess. In the *Madonna of the Rocks,* the child Jesus blesses his cousin John, the infant John the Baptist, who represents the congregation of Christians, literally protected by Mary's cloak but figuratively taken under her wing. The figures form a triangular or pyramid grouping, a favorite Renaissance compositional device.

FIGURE 13.19   Leonardo da Vinci, *Madonna of the Rocks,* ca. 1483, oil on panel, $6'6\frac{1}{2}''$ × 4' (2.0 × 1.2 m), Musée du Louvre, Paris. SCALA/Art Resource, NY. Leonardo, both artist and scientist, created a grotto setting with stalactites, stalagmites, and identifiable foliage, an unusual environment for these religious figures.

Leonardo's greatest achievement in Milan was *The Last Supper* (fig. 13.20), painted between 1495 and 1499. The orderly composition of *The Last Supper* clarifies the painting's meaning. The largest of the three windows on the back wall is directly behind Jesus, thereby emphasizing him. The curved pediment, which arches above his head, serves as a halo. He is perfectly centered in the mural, and all perspective lines converge toward a vanishing point directly behind his head, leading the viewer's eyes to him. The twelve apostles are arranged six on each side, divided into four equal groups of three figures. The result is a composition that is symmetrically balanced on either side around the central figure of Jesus, whose arms are extended diagonally so that he forms an equilateral triangle in the center. The arrangement of the five segments is somewhat theatrical—action building from the wings, leading to the central calm figure of Jesus.

FIGURE 13.20   Leonardo da Vinci, *The Last Supper*; refectory, Santa Maria delle Grazie, Milan, 1495–98, tempera and oil on plaster, 15′ 2″ × 28′10″ (4.60 × 8.80 m). Scala/Art Resource, NY. The mural's poor condition is due to the experimental media in which Leonardo painted. Nevertheless, his ability to merge form and content, using perspective to create simultaneously an illusion of a cubic space and focus the viewer's attention on Jesus, can still be appreciated.

Leonardo chose the most psychologically powerful moment in the story: Jesus has just announced that one of his apostles will betray him, and they respond with dismay. Judas, his betrayer, sits with John and Peter directly to the left of Jesus, his face lost in shadow as he leans away, clutching a money bag in his right hand. We know from preparatory sketches that Leonardo wanted to depict a different emotion on each of the apostles' faces. The most difficult thing to paint, Leonardo said, was "the intention of Man's soul." It could only be shown by pose, facial expression, and surrounding events and figures. Painting Judas and Jesus, apparently, gave Leonardo the most difficulty. Vasari tells the story:

> The prior [of Santa Maria delle Grazie] was in a great hurry to see the picture done. He could not understand why Leonardo would sometimes remain before his work half a day together, absorbed in thought. . . . [Leonardo] made it clear that men of genius are sometimes producing most when they seem least to labor, for their minds are then occupied in the shaping of those conceptions to which they afterward give form. He told the duke [Sforza, under whose protection the monastery was] that two heads were yet to be done: that of the Savior, the likeness of which he could not hope to find on earth and . . . the other, of Judas. . . . As a last resort he could always use the head of that troublesome and impertinent prior.

Leonardo solved his problem with Judas by grouping him with Peter and John. "I say," Leonardo explained in his *Notebooks*, "that in narratives it is necessary to mix closely together direct contraries, because they provide a great contrast with each other, and so much more if they are adjacent, that is to say the ugly to the beautiful."

Sometime in 1503, after Leonardo had been forced to return to Florence, he painted the *Mona Lisa* (fig. 13.21), a portrait of Lisa di Antonio Maria Gherardini, the twenty-four-year-old wife of a Florentine official, Francesco del Gioconda—hence the painting is sometimes called *La Gioconda*. Mona Lisa appears relaxed and natural. Leonardo presents his sitter in a half-length, three-quarter view, the hands showing. With this pose, set against a landscape background, Leonardo established a type. In accordance with the fashion of the time, her high forehead indicates Mona Lisa's nobility—the effect achieved by her shaved hairline and absence of eyebrows. The sitter's lofty mind is indicated by the stormy weather shown in the background. The fame of this painting rests on the sitter's facial expression. Leonardo was concerned with not only the exterior, but also with the interior, with the psychological subtleties of individual personality.

THE REINVENTION OF ROME

In the middle of the fifteenth century, Pope Nicholas V had close ties to the Florentine humanists, especially to Leon Battista Alberti, who made a massive survey of classical architecture, *De re aedificatoria*. With Alberti as his

FIGURE 13.21　Leonardo da Vinci, *Mona Lisa*, ca. 1503, oil on panel, $2'6\frac{1}{4}'' \times 1'9''$ (76.8 × 53.3 cm), © Musée du Louvre, Paris/Reunion des Musées National/Art Resource, NY. Probably the most famous painting in the world, Mona Lisa's mysterious smile continues to intrigue viewers today.

FIGURE 13.22　Melozzo da Forlì, *Sixtus IV Appoints Platina Head of the Vatican Library*, 1480–81, fresco, $13'1'' \times 10'4''$ (3.99 × 3.15 m), Pinacoteca Vaticana, Rome. Platina kneels before Pope Sixtus IV while the Pope's nephews stand behind. In the middle is Cardinal Giuliano della Rovere, later Pope Julius II.

chief consultant, Nicholas V began to rebuild Rome's ancient churches and initiated plans to remake the Vatican as a new sacred city. Nicholas V also began to assemble a massive classical library, paying humanist scholars to translate ancient Greek texts into Latin and Italian.

The New Vatican.　The Vatican library became one of the chief preoccupations of Pope Sixtus IV (reigned 1471–84). With Platina as its head, the library became a true "Vatican," or "public," library, with rules for usage, a permanent location, and an effective, permanent administration. Platina's appointment is celebrated in a fresco painted by Melozzo da Forlì for the library (fig. 13.22). The Latin couplets below the scene, written by Platina himself, outline Sixtus's campaign to restore the city of Rome, rebuilding churches, streets, walls, bridges, and aqueducts, but praise Sixtus IV most of all for the creation of the library. By 1508, the Vatican Library was said to be the "image" of Plato's Academy. Athens had been reborn in Rome.

Archaeological discoveries led to Rome's reinvention as the classical center of learning and art. Sixtus established a museum in 1474 to house the recently uncovered Etruscan bronze statue of the she-wolf that had nourished Romulus and Remus, the mythical twin founders of the city (see Chapter 4). Other discoveries followed: *Spinario*, a Hellenistic bronze of a youth pulling a thorn from his foot; *Hercules*, the life-size bronze discovered in the ruined temple of Hercules in the Forum Boarium; and two antique marble river gods that came from the ruins of the Constantinian baths.

To execute Pope Nicholas's plans for a new Vatican palace, Sixtus IV commissioned the Sistine Chapel, which he named after himself, and inaugurated plans for its decoration. Perugino and Botticelli, among others, painted frescoes for the chapel's walls, which were completed in 1482. Sixtus's nephew, Pope Julius II (reigned 1503–13), continued Sixtus's plans. Classical sculpture was placed in the Vatican's sloping gardens: the *Apollo Belvedere*, which had been discovered during excavations, and the *Laocoön* (see Chapter 3), found buried in the ruins of some Roman baths. Composers were hired to write new hymns. Josquin des Près served in the sixteen- to twenty-four-member *Sistina Cappella*, or Sistine Choir, from 1476 to 1484. Soon the rough rhythms of medieval poetry were supplanted by the softer, finer meter of the Horatian odes. To add to the pomp of the liturgical processions, Julius established a large chorus to perform exclusively in St. Peter's, the *Cappella Giulia*, or Julian Choir, which remains active to this day. And, most important, Julius invited Raphael and Michelangelo to work in Rome.

PAINTING AND SCULPTURE

Raphael. When RAPHAEL [RAFF-ay-el], born Raffaello Santi of Urbino (1483–1520), was invited to Rome in 1508, he was not yet twenty-five years old, but his renown as a painter was well established. He had grown up surrounded by culture and beauty. He studied painting under his father, Giovanni Santi, a painter for the dukes of Urbino. In Perugia he studied with Perugino.

One of Raphael's first major works is directly indebted to Perugino's *Jesus Delivering the Keys*. It is the *Marriage of the Virgin* (fig. 13.23), signed and dated 1504, the year he came to Florence. As in Perugino's work, the composition is divided into a foreground with large figures, a middle ground of open space with smaller figures, and a background with a temple and tiny figures. In the foreground, Mary and Joseph wed. The story says that Joseph, although older than the many other suitors, was selected because, among all the symbolic rods presented to Mary, his alone flowered. Beside him a disgruntled suitor snaps his own rod in half over his knee. The absence of facial expression is a stylistic habit derived from Perugino, which Raphael would soon discard under the influence of Leonardo and Michelangelo. Everything in Raphael's painting is measured and rendered in careful perspective, as is emphasized by the pattern of rectangles that cross the square. In fact, so powerful is the perspective grid that the viewer's eyes are led away from the marriage in the foreground to the temple behind, creating a competing focal point, in contrast to Leonardo da Vinci's use of perspective to focus the viewer's attention on the most important person in a scene (fig. 13.20).

Raphael became famous for his paintings of the Madonna and Child. His *Madonna of the Meadows* (fig. 13.24), painted in 1505, is typical of his style: pale, sweet, and serious. She is maternal and meditative, thinking ahead to Jesus's passion, prefigured by the cross offered by the infant St. John, who in turn is identified by the camel-hair garment he would wear as an adult. In most Early Renaissance depictions of this subject, the Madonna is elevated on a throne. Raphael's Madonna has descended to our earthly level; she even sits upon the ground—in this pose she is referred to as the "Madonna of Humility." The

FIGURE 13.23 Raphael, *Marriage of the Virgin*, 1504, oil on panel, 5′7″ × 3′10½″ (1.70 × 1.18 m), Giancarlo Costa/Brera Gallery, Milan. Raphael's carefully composed scene includes figures in the foreground, middleground, and background. The lines of perspective lead to a central plan building (the type favored by Bramante); the marriage is shown taking place in the foreground, dividing the composition.

differences between the sacred and the secular are minimized—even the figures' halos have become thin gold bands.

A master of composition, with ease and grace, Raphael contrasts the curved and rounded shapes of his substantial figures with their triangular and pyramidal positions in space. The triangular format recalls that of Leonardo's *Madonna of the Rocks* (fig. 13.19), but the difference between the dark grotto setting of Leonardo's painting and Raphael's pastoral countryside is instructive. Raphael's composition is simpler, possessing far less contrast between light and dark. His figures are more tightly grouped. Leonardo's children have serious facial expressions, lending them the emotional complexity of adults; Raphael's are far more playful.

Beginning in 1508, Julius II commissioned Raphael to paint frescoes in several rooms in the Vatican Palace, including the Stanza della Segnatura, the room where papal

FIGURE 13.24   Raphael, *Madonna of the Meadows*, 1505, oil on panel, $44\frac{1}{2}'' \times 34\frac{1}{4}''$ (113 × 87 cm), Kunsthistorisches Museum, Vienna. Erich Lessing/Art Resource, NY. Often considered the epitome of High Renaissance painters, Raphael was celebrated for his ability to arrange several figures into compact units. Mary, Jesus, and John the Baptist form a pyramid, a favorite Renaissance compositional device.

documents were signed. The *School of Athens* (fig. 13.25) embodies the Renaissance humanist's quest for classical learning and truth. In the center of this bilaterally symmetrical composition are the ancient Greek philosophers, Plato and Aristotle. The figure of the older Plato, which might be a portrait of Leonardo da Vinci, holds Plato's *Timaeus* and points upward, indicating the realm of his ideal Forms. The younger Aristotle holds his *Ethics* and points toward earth, indicating the philosopher's emphasis on material reality. The scene includes representations of Diogenes or Socrates, sprawling on the steps in front of the philosophers; Pythagoras, calculating on a slate at the lower left; Ptolemy, holding a globe at the right; and Euclid in front of him, inscribing a slate with a compass. Michelangelo is shown as the philosopher Heraclitus in the foreground leaning on a block of marble while sketching. Raphael painted his own portrait, the second figure from the right, looking at us. Pope Julius had made Raphael "prefect of antiquities," in charge of the papal ex-

cavation and preservation of antiques. Perhaps because of this, the setting is based on the ancient Roman baths and has the classical statues of Apollo (god of sunlight, rationality, and poetry) and Minerva (goddess of wisdom).

Michelangelo.   MICHELANGELO BUONARROTI [my-kuhl-AN-gel-oh] (1475–1564), born near Florence, lived as a child in the Palazzo Medici there, which served not only as Lorenzo the Magnificent's home but also as an art school, and there he studied sculpture under Giovanni Bertoldo, once a student of Donatello. In Lorenzo's palace, bursting with Neoplatonic and humanist ideas, Michelangelo was nurtured on the virtues of antique classical sculpture. As a boy, in Florence, he studied fresco painting under Domenico del Ghirlandaio and routinely copied the frescoes by Giotto in Santa Croce and those by Masaccio in Santa Maria del Carmine. He was, like so many Renaissance artists, skilled in many areas—painting, architecture, poetry—but in his own mind he was a sculptor.

Michelangelo believed the figure is imprisoned within the block of marble in the same way the soul is trapped within the body. In fact, to release the figure from the marble was a matter of subtraction, as the sculptor chiseled away the shell of stone that hid the figure within. Michelangelo's approach to sculpture was, in short, profoundly Neoplatonic; sculpture, from his point of view, both revealed and liberated the human ideal, as the first stanza of the following poem by him suggests:

> Even the best of artists can conceive no idea
> That a single block of marble will not contain
> In its excess, and such a goal is achieved
> Only by the hand that obeys the intellect.
>   The evil which I flee and the good I promise myself   5
> Hides in you, my fair, proud, and divine lady;
> And working against my very life,
> My skill is contrary to my purpose.
> My ill cannot be blamed upon your beauty,
>   Your harshness, bad fortune, or your disdain,   10
> Nor upon my destiny or my fate,
> If in your heart you bear both death and mercy
> At the same time, and if my lowly talent
> Ardently burning, can draw forth only death.

Unlike Leonardo, who believed beauty was found in nature, Michelangelo believed beauty was found in the imagination. One of his earliest sculptures is a *Pietà* (fig. 13.26), meaning "pity." The term refers to depictions of Mary mourning over the dead Jesus in her lap. Commissioned by a French cardinal, Michelangelo bragged his *Pietà* would be "the most beautiful work in marble that exists today in Rome." In order to heighten the viewer's feelings of pity and sorrow, Michelangelo made the figure of Jesus disproportionately small in comparison to the monumental figure of Mary. Despite the fact that Jesus died as a grown man of thirty-three, Mary is portrayed as a very young woman; the poignant implication is that Mary thinks back to when Jesus was an infant in her lap.

FIGURE 13.25 Raphael, *School of Athens*, 1510–11, fresco, 19 × 27′ (5.79 × 8.24 m), Stanza della Segnatura, Vatican Museums, Rome. Raphael painted several rooms in the Vatican for Pope Julius II, a great patron of the arts. Statues of Apollo and Minerva flank Plato and Aristotle, shown surrounded by scientists and philosophers of antiquity, some of whom have been given the facial features of Raphael's contemporaries.

Michelangelo carved the enormous *David* (fig. 13.27) between 1501 and 1504. The statue, which is over 13 feet tall, was intended to stand 40 feet above the ground on a buttress on Florence Cathedral. However, when it was finished, the city officials designated it a "masterpiece," too good to be placed so high on the cathedral; instead it was placed in front of the Palazzo Vecchio in the Piazza della Signoria. There, in the square where political meetings took place, it would symbolize not only freedom of speech, but the Republic of Florence itself, free from foreigners, papal domination, and Medici rule. (The Medici had been exiled in 1494.)

The *David*'s pose is taken from antiquity, with the weight on one leg in the *contrapposto* position. The sculptor's virtuosity is most evidenced in David's tightly muscled form, his tendons and veins recorded. A sense of enormous pent-up energy emerges, of latent power about to

explode, and the question seems to be less *if* he will move than *when*. The absence of attire recalls the heroic nudes of antiquity and avoids linking the *David* to a specific time period; instead *David* has universal meaning. He represents the battle between good and evil, as well as every person who must face their foe.

Michelangelo was called to Rome in 1505 to create the monumental tomb of Pope Julius II. The project was halted by Julius II himself soon after Michelangelo's arrival when the pope decided that finishing the painting of the Sistine Chapel, a project initiated by his predecessor Sixtus IV, should take priority. Michelangelo is reputed to have said, "Painting is for women, sculpture for men." Reluctantly, he began to paint. The ceiling, which covers more than 5,800 square feet, is nearly seventy feet high. Michelangelo would have to work long hours on scaffolding, paint dripping on him. The center of the ceiling features the story of

FIGURE 13.26 Michelangelo, *Pietà*, 1498/99–1500, marble, height 5′8½″ (1.70 m), St. Peter's, Vatican, Rome. Araldo de Luca, Roma/Vatican Museums, Rome, Italy/Fabbrica di San Pietro. "Pietà" refers to the depiction of Mary mourning over Jesus, lying across her lap. Although the subject was developed in Gothic Germany, the most famous *Pietà* is surely Michelangelo's version.

Creation—nine scenes from Genesis. Four further scenes from the Old Testament appear in the corners. Old Testament prophets and ancient pagan sibyls (female prophets) are included, along with Jesus's ancestors, and assorted medallions, *putti* (cherubs), and male nudes. There are over three hundred figures in all, many of which have no known meaning. Michelangelo claimed that Julius II let him paint what he pleased, but the complexity of the program suggests he had advisers. Neoplatonist numerology, symbolism, and philosophy inform many of the subjects and pagan stories and motifs are also evident. Old Testament stories are used to prefigure those in the New Testament.

In the scene of the *Creation of Adam* (fig. 13.28), God, noble and powerful, flies in swiftly, bringing Eve with him under his arm. Compare this scene with Ghiberti's depiction in the *Gates of Paradise* (see fig. 13.8). Michelangelo's dynamic God contrasts with a listless Adam, whose figure Michelangelo derived from an ancient Roman coin. Momentarily, God will give Adam his soul and bring him fully to life, for their fingers are about to touch. Note the masculine musculature of the figures; even the female figures on the Sistine ceiling are based on male models. Michelangelo's figures are heroic and powerful, yet they have a grace and beauty.

FIGURE 13.27 Michelangelo, *David*, 1501–04, marble, height 13′5″ (4.09 m), Galleria dell'Accademia, Florence. A magnificent marble man, akin to the heroic nudes of antiquity and undated by costume, David becomes a universal symbol of the individual facing unseen conflict.

FIGURE 13.28   Michelangelo, *Creation of Adam*, detail of Sistine Chapel ceiling, 1511–12, fresco, 9′2″ × 18′ 8″ (2.79 × 5.69 m), Vatican, Rome. Adam's enormous latent power will be released in the next instant when swift-moving God, with Eve already under his arm, brings him to life.

In both the tenseness of its mood and its distortion of human anatomy, Michelangelo's fresco of *The Last Judgment* (fig. 13.29) reflects the Mannerist style. Although his plan for St. Peter's, built in 1546, embodies the ideals of the High Renaissance, much of Michelangelo's late work leaves those ideals far behind. A new spirit entered his art in *The Last Judgment*, commissioned for the altar wall of the Sistine Chapel in 1534 by a dying Pope Clement VII. Painted between 1536 and 1541, it lacks the optimism and sense of beauty that define Michelangelo's work on the ceiling. His figures, no longer beautifully proportioned, now look twisted and grotesque, with heads too small for their giant, inflated bodies. The space is filled with bodies that are larger at the top of the picture than the bottom; no illusion of realistic depth is even intended here.

However, this style befits Michelangelo's subject. The dead are dragged from their graves and pulled upward to be judged by Jesus. Mary, at his side, cringes at the vision. At his feet, to his right, is St. Bartholomew. Legend states that Bartholomew was martyred by being skinned alive, and he holds his skin in his hand. But the face is a self-portrait of Michelangelo, and such grimness extends to the whole painting. The hands of Bartholomew's flayed skin seem to reach downward, to the chasm of hell that opens at the bottom of the painting, where a monstrous Charon (the ferryman of the dead) guides his boat across the River Styx, driving the damned before him into perpetual torment.

Properzia de' Rossi.   PROPERZIA DE' ROSSI [Pro-PEHR-tzee-ah deh RAW-see] (ca. 1490–1530), from Bologna, is known for her work in miniature, carving entire scenes on the pit of an apricot or a peach! Yet she also sculpted on a huge scale, for de' Rossi won a competition to create sculpture for the facade of the church of San Petronio in Bologna, from which the scene of *Joseph and Potiphar's Wife* (fig. 13.30) is believed to come. The semiclad wife of the Egyptian officer Potiphar has failed to seduce Joseph; she reaches quickly to grab for his cloak as he flees her bed. The sense of animation achieved is notable, the draperies and hair of Joseph and of Potiphar's wife shown to respond to the speed of their movements. Properzia de' Rossi died at the age of 39—one can only wonder what she would have achieved had her productive years been extended.

Figure 13.29 Michelangelo, *The Last Judgment*, Sistine Chapel, 1536–41, fresco, 48 × 44′ (14.63 × 13.41 m), Vatican Museums, Rome. Michelangelo's optimism and the idealized beauty of the ceiling of this chapel are now replaced with a pessimistic view and anatomical anomalies.

Critical Thinking

THE QUESTION OF ART RESTORATION

Among questions debated strongly in recent years is the extent to which works of art that have deteriorated over the centuries should be restored, or even cleaned. Cleaning refers to removing grime and soot, or layers of varnish from works. Restoration involves repairing elements that have become damaged and replacing missing elements. One major example that occasioned strenuous debate was the cleaning of the Sistine Chapel frescoes painted by Michelangelo, and which had, over the centuries, become darkened with dirt. Another example is the restoration of Leonardo da Vinci's *Last Supper*, which took twenty years, and involved not only cleaning, but also filling in some missing sections of the image with new paint.

Among the arguments against cleaning Michelangelo's work was that the cleaning agents might also remove some of the original pigment, and could damage the painting irretrievably by removing the darkened colors that over many generations people had become accustomed to seeing and revealing a brighter set of hues that some considered garish. Against adding newly painted sections to Leonardo's work were those who said the great painting would effectively no longer be Leonardo's. Countering these arguments were those who claimed that cleaning the Sistine frescoes would restore them to how Michelangelo originally painted them. Similarly, those who favored restoring Leonardo's *Last Supper* believe that the painting has now been restored to its former glory.

Which point of view do you find more convincing, and why? What other issues do you think should be evaluated when a major art masterpiece is being considered for cleaning and/or restoration? What do you think should be done with Leonardo's *Mona Lisa*, which is the most famous prime candidate for cleaning today?

FIGURE 13.30   Properzia de' Rossi, *Joseph and Potiphar's Wife*, ca. 1520, marble bas-relief, $19'\frac{1}{4}''\times 18'\frac{1}{8}''$ (49 × 46 cm), Museo di San Petronio, Bologna. Powerful full figures, so admired during the High Renaissance, move rapidly through space in this compact composition, the garments revealing the bodies beneath as well as enhancing the action.

ARCHITECTURE

Donato Bramante. DONATO BRAMANTE's [bra-MAHN-tay] (1444–1514) reputation was based largely on a building called the Tempietto, or "little temple" (fig. 13.31) constructed from 1502 on the site where St. Peter was believed to have been crucified. Commissioned by Ferdinand and Isabella of Spain (patrons of the explorer Christopher Columbus), the Tempietto is an adaptation of a classical temple of the Doric order (see Chapter 2), including a complete entablature.

The building itself is set on a stepped base and surrounded by a **peristyle,** or continuous row of columns. The first story is topped by a balustrade, or carved railing, inside of which is a **drum,** or circular wall, on which Bramante set a classically hemispheric dome. The plan, with its deeply recessed spaces, creates a dramatic play of light and dark, despite the relatively small scale of the building itself.

THE NEW ST. PETER'S BASILICA

In 1506, Pope Julius II decided to tear down the old St. Peter's Basilica, which had stood at the Vatican since the time of Constantine in the early fourth century, and re-

FIGURE 13.31 Donato Bramante, Tempietto, San Pietro in Montorio, Rome, 1502–after 1511. Small in size but of great importance, the Tempietto demonstrates the reuse of ancient pagan architecture for Renaissance Christian purposes.

(a)

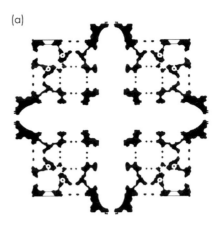

(b)

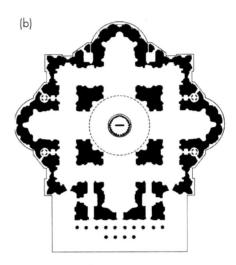

(c)

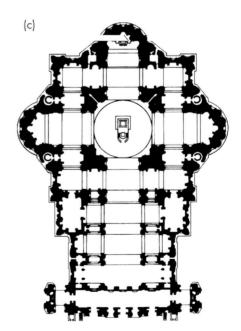

FIGURE 13.32 Floor plans for St. Peter's, Rome, by (a) Bramante, (b) Michelangelo, and (c) Carlo Maderno. Although Bramante and Michelangelo intended Greek-cross plans, the long nave of the Latin-cross plan was added by Maderno to accommodate the crowds of people.

place it with a new church more befitting the dignity and prestige of the papacy. To this end he appointed Donato Bramante as architect.

Bramante's plan for St. Peter's Basilica (fig. 13.32) is, essentially, a grander version of the Tempietto, over 450 feet in diameter instead of 15. Instead of basing his plan on the traditional longitudinal Latin cross (three short arms and one long one), Bramante chose to utilize a Greek cross (four arms of equal length) with a central dome. The plan is symmetrical and harmonious, symbolizing the perfection of God, topped by an enormous dome modeled after the Pantheon's.

Michelangelo's St. Peter's.   With the deaths of Julius II in 1513 and of Bramante in 1514, work ceased temporarily. After several other architects, including Raphael, attempted to revise Bramante's plan, Michelangelo was appointed architect in 1546. He described Bramante's original design as "clear and straightforward." He wrote, "Indeed, every architect who has departed from Bramante's plan . . . has departed from the right way." Nevertheless, Michelangelo modified the original (fig. 13.32). Instead of an interior of interlocking Greek crosses, Michelangelo simplified the scheme, in part, due to structural necessity. The four main piers had to be massively enlarged to support the dome, causing Michelangelo to simplify the remaining interior space. Michelangelo also intended a double-columned portico across the front.

Michelangelo did not live to see the completion of his plan. The dome was finished in 1590 (fig. 13.33), with a somewhat higher and more pointed profile than Michelangelo had intended, in part because of engineering requirements, the vertical shape minimizing the lateral thrust exerted by the dome. In 1606, Pope Paul V appointed the architect Carlo Maderno to restore the church to a Latin-cross plan (fig. 13.32).

FIGURE 13.33   View of St. Peter's, Rome. St. Peter's underwent so many changes that only a hint of the simplicity of Bramante's and Michelangelo's original Greek cross plans remains.

VENICE

Throughout the fifteenth century and into the sixteenth, Venice was one of the most powerful city-states in all of Europe, exercising control over the entire Adriatic and much of the eastern Mediterranean. It was celebrated in Vittore Carpaccio's *Lion of St. Mark* (fig. 13.34), painted in 1516 for a government office in the city's Ducal Palace.

FIGURE 13.34   Vittore Carpaccio, *Lion of St. Mark*, 1516, oil on canvas, $4'6\frac{3}{4}'' \times 12'1''$ (1.40 × 3.70 m), Ducal Palace, Venice. The winged lion was a symbol of the Evangelist Mark and of Venice. This painting documents the early sixteenth-century appearance of the city, with its campanile, Ducal Palace, and the domes of St. Mark's Cathedral.

The lion is the symbol of the city's patron saint, Mark the Evangelist, whom God was said to have visited on the Evangelist's arrival at the Venice lagoon, thereby designating Venice as the saint's final resting place. Greeting St. Mark, God's angel is said to have announced, "Peace unto you, Mark, my evangelist," the Latin words inscribed on the tablet held in the lion's paws. The lion stands with its front paws on land and its hind paws in the water, signifying Venice's dominion over land and sea. Behind the lion, to the left, is the Ducal Palace, the seat of government and law and the source of the city's order and harmony. The Byzantine domes of St. Mark's Cathedral rise behind it, the basis of the city's moral fabric, and the giant campanile (bell tower) that dominates St. Mark's Square stands on the far left housing the five bells of St. Mark's, one of which chimed to announce the beginning and end of each working day. Behind the lion to the right is a fleet of Venetian merchant ships, the source of the city's wealth and prosperity.

Venetian Oil Painting.   Surrounded by water and built over a lagoon, humidity made fresco painting, so popular elsewhere in Europe, virtually impossible in Venice. From 1475, after **oil painting** (pigments mixed with linseed oil) was developed in The Netherlands, fresco painting in Venice gradually ceased. The use of oil on canvas led in turn to a new kind of painting. Applying colors in glazes—that is, in layers of transparent color—created by mixing a little pigment with a lot of linseed oil, painters were able to create a light that seemed to emanate from the depths of the painting itself. Furthermore, the texture of the canvas itself was exploited. Stroked over a woven surface, the brush deposits more paint on the top of the weave and less in the crevices. This textured surface in turn "catches" actual light, lending an almost shimmering vibrancy.

Titian.   Tiziano Vecelli of Venice, known as TITIAN [TISH-un] (ca. 1488/90-1576) favored paintings with complex iconography—in fact, Titian classified his paintings as poetry. Characteristic of the Renaissance interest in antiquity, the subject of Titian's festive *Bacchanal* (fig. 13.35), painted ca. 1518, derives from Classical mythology; Bacchus is the ancient Roman god of wine. Titian popularized the type of strawberry blond female seen here, portrayed with his characteristically sensuous handling of

FIGURE 13.35   Titian, *Bacchanal*, ca. 1518, oil on canvas, 5'8$\frac{7}{8}$" × 6'4" (1.75 × 1.93 m), Museo del Prado Madrid. Botticelli's slender Early Renaissance figure type (figs. 13.17–18) matured in the work of High Renaissance painters such as Titian to a full-bodied ideal of beauty.

flesh. The richness of Titian's paintings is due in part to his use of an underpainting of red bolus (an earth pigment) in many of his works, rather than the usual green-black underpainting. He also used **impasto**—thick paint made by mixing the pigment with beeswax. Titian is associated with the so-called "golden glow" of Venetian painting, achieved, in part, by adding a bit of yellow pigment to the final protective glaze applied to the painting.

MUSIC

The reinvention of Rome required the reinvention of music—a new St. Peter's needed a new mass to fill its vast space with sound.

Josquin des Près. The most important composer of the new Rome took on the job: JOSQUIN DES PRÈS [JOZ-skanh de-PRAY] (1440–1521), from Flanders. It was Josquin who led the Sistine Choir as Michelangelo painted the ceiling and Raphael worked in the papal suites. Like Dufay, Josquin spent many years in Italy, serving the Sforza family in Milan, the Estes at their court in Ferrara, and finally several Roman popes, including Sixtus IV (for whom he directed the Sistine Choir), Julius II, and Leo X. So highly regarded was Josquin that the French king Louis XII and the Austrian queen Margaret both bid for his services. His contemporaries extolled him as "the Father of Musicians" and "the best of composers." An enchanted Martin Luther remarked that Josquin was "the master of the notes; they must do as he wills."

Josquin composed approximately two hundred works—motets, **masses,** and **chansons** (songs). His many motets and chansons attest to his interest in exploring new trends in setting words to music. His motet "Ave Maria . . . virgo serena" ("Hail, Mary . . . Serene Virgin") (1502) exemplifies his style. The opening employs imitative counterpoint with the melody for the words "Ave Maria" first heard in the soprano, then repeated in succession by the alto, the tenor, and the bass while the original parts continue, as in a round. On the words *gratia plena* ("full of grace") Josquin introduces a new, second melody, again in the soprano, which is again passed from one voice to the next. Josquin overlaps the voices in both melodies, allowing the altos to enter, for example, before the sopranos have sung the complete melody. This overlapping of voices enriches the music's texture, giving it body and providing it with a continuous and fluid motion. Josquin also allows two voices, and sometimes three or four, to sing the same melody simultaneously—a duet between the two lower voice parts (tenor and bass), for instance, will imitate a duet between alto and soprano. The motet concludes serenely with emphatic slow chords on the words *O mater Dei, memento mei* ("O mother of God, remember me"). Just before this ending, Josquin introduces a significant silence that sounds at first like an ending. He uses this silence to focus the listener's attention on the true ending, which comes immediately after. The dignified serenity and graceful restraint of Josquin's "Ave Maria . . . virgo serena" can be compared with the quiet beauty and restrained elegance of Raphael's madonnas.

Palestrina. The music of the Italian GIOVANNI PIERLUIGI DA PALESTRINA [pal-uh-STREE-nah] (1525–94) came to dominate the church throughout most of the sixteenth century. As the church came under attack from the north for its excessive spending and ornate lavishness, it responded by simplifying the mass and the music designed to accompany it. Although it considered banning polyphony altogether, thinking it too elaborate to be easily understood by laypeople, in the end the church endorsed the controlled and precise style of Palestrina.

Palestrina held a number of important church positions. He was organist and choirmaster of the large chorus that performed exclusively in St. Peter's, the *Cappella Giulia* (Julian Choir), and he was music director for the Vatican. His music evokes the Gregorian roots of traditional church music and relies directly on the emotional appeal of the listener's potential union with God. He wrote nearly a thousand compositions, including over a hundred masses. Among the most beautiful of all Palestrina's works is his *Pope Marcellus Mass,* written in honor of the pope and set for an **a cappella**—or unaccompanied—choir in six voice parts: soprano, alto, two tenors, and two basses. It contains music for the Kyrie, Gloria, Credo, Sanctus, Benedictus, and Agnus Dei, as did the Gregorian Mass before it, and Palestrina utilizes the traditional Gregorian melodies connected with each of these parts of the mass. Still, it is clearly Renaissance in its style, utilizing an orderly and clear imitative polyphony that allows the listener to follow each of the voices in the mass as they weave together with precision.

LITERATURE

Baldassare Castiglione. BALDASSARE CASTIGLIONE [KAS-till-YOH-nay] (1478–1529) was a courtier to the Italian ducal courts, first at the court of Francesco Gonzaga, the ruler of Mantua in the early sixteenth century, and then at the court of Urbino, established by Federico da Montefeltro, the father of Guidobaldo da Montefeltro, in whose service Castiglione prospered. Later unrest caused him to return to service in Duke Francesco's court. After serving as ambassador to Rome, Castiglione was appointed by Pope Clement VII as papal ambassador to Spain, where he lived out the remaining years of his life.

While at Urbino, Castiglione wrote the *Book of the Courtier,* which memorializes, celebrates, and idealizes life at court, especially Urbino. It is cast in the form of a series of dialogues spread out over four evenings at the court of Urbino. The central topic is the manners, education, and behavior of the ideal courtier, whose virtues Castiglione extols. The courtier must be a man of courage with experience in war; he must be learned in the classics and in classical languages; he must be able to serve his prince with generosity. Castiglione's ideal courtier had to be physically and emotionally strong, able to perform feats requiring agility, skill, courage, and daring. His physical prowess was measured by his grace as a dancer and elegance as a singer and musician. He was also expected to be an engaging and witty conversationalist, a good companion, an elegant writer, even a bit of a poet. In short, Castiglione's courtier was the ideal Renaissance gentleman—of sound mind, body, and character, and learned in the ideas of Renaissance humanism.

Castiglione's blending of the soldier and the scholar, his merging of the ideals of medieval chivalry with those of Renaissance humanism, made his *Book of the Courtier* popular both in its own time and afterward. Castiglione himself was no exception and embodied the ideals his book celebrated. Raphael's portrait of Castiglione (fig. 13.36) displays many of the qualities Castiglione extols, from the

FIGURE 13.36 Raphael, *Baldassare Castiglione*, ca. 1515, oil on panel, transferred to canvas, $32\frac{1}{4}''\times26\frac{1}{2}''$ (81.9 × 67.3 cm), Musée du Louvre, Paris. J.G. Berizzi/Reunion des Musées National, France/Art Resource, NY. Castiglione wrote about the qualities of the ideal courtier; it is not surprising that Raphael, a refined gentleman, was a personal friend of his. Perhaps some of the calm restraint recommended by Castiglione is seen in Raphael's portrait with its restricted range of color.

nobility of the graceful head to the intelligence of the shining eyes, complemented by the elegant refinement of the attire.

Niccolò Machiavelli.   A contemporary of Castiglione, NICCOLO MACHIAVELLI [mak-ee-ah-VEL-ee] (1469–1527), also wrote a guidebook on behavior—*The Prince*, a manual for princes and rulers.

Like Castiglione, Machiavelli was well educated in the Renaissance humanist tradition. Like Castiglione's courtier, Machiavelli's prince is a model of an ideal. The difference between the two writers' "ideals," however, is dramatic: Castiglione supported the tenets of Renaissance humanism, but Machiavelli challenged them by introducing a radically different set of standards, standards that inform, among other things, Mannerist art.

Young Machiavelli was employed as a clerk and secretary to the Florentine magistrates responsible for war and internal affairs. From 1498 to 1512, he also served as an ambassador to, among others, the Holy Roman Emperor Maximilian, the king of France, and Pope Julius II. During his lifetime, the Italian city-states were almost continually at war either with one another or with other countries, such as France and Spain. Machiavelli himself suffered from the changing fortunes of the ruling families: When the Medici came to power in Florence, for instance, he was accused of conspiracy, tortured, and imprisoned. Later, when the Medici government collapsed, he was accused of being a Medici sympathizer.

The Prince was written in 1513 and published in 1532 after Machiavelli's death. It quickly acquired fame or, as some would have it, notoriety. Based on a series of premises about human nature—none favorable—*The Prince* asserts that people are basically selfish, deceitful, greedy, and gullible. Accordingly, Machiavelli advises princes to rule in ways that play on these fundamental human characteristics. A prince can be—indeed, should be—hypocritical, cruel, and deceitful when necessary. He should keep faith with no one but himself and employ ruthlessness and cunning to maintain his power over the people. As Machiavelli writes, "it is far better to be feared than loved," although he notes, "the prince must nonetheless make himself feared in such a way that, if he is not loved, he will at least avoid being hated."

The view of human beings that forms the foundation of Machiavelli's arguments in *The Prince* reflects political expediency, based on Machiavelli's observation of Florentine politics and the politics of other city-states and countries he visited as a Florentine ambassador. Having witnessed the instability of power in Italy, particularly the surrender of parts of Italy to France and Spain, Machiavelli wrote that a ruler must be strong enough to keep himself in power, for only with the strength of absolute power could he rule effectively.

Machiavelli's *The Prince* was the most widely read book of its time, after the Bible. The questions it raises about the relationship between politics and morality, the starkly realistic depiction of power it presents, and the authority, immediacy, and directness with which it is written, ensured its success. Whatever we may think of its vision of human nature or of the advice it offers rulers, it is hard to deny the power of its language, the strength of its convictions, and force of its arguments.

MANNERISM

Mannerism was defined as a style in 1914 by Walter Friedländer; the term **Mannerism** derived from the Italian *manièra* (manner of style, suggesting affectation). The style is also referred to as the Manièra as well as the anti-Classical style, although the artists today labeled as Mannerists considered themselves classical. Mannerism originally referred only to painting, and meant that one painted "in the manner of . . ." Later, it came to have a negative connotation, one associated with affectation, academicism, and decadence: Mannerism became a derogatory term connoting artificiality and artistic decline on the grounds that artists did not assimilate the style of a master, but only affected it. Today, Mannerism is no longer considered a decline, for it is felt the distorted elements that characterize the style give spiritual feeling and convey emotion. The Mannerist period dates from approximately 1520 to 1600, the style seen especially in Italy, centering in Rome and Florence, although it was also fashionable in France and elsewhere.

Mannerism coincides with a period of political and religious unrest. The sack of Rome in 1527 by the troops of Charles V, six months of murder and destruction, undermined the confidence of the Renaissance humanists. Religious feelings were strong in the time of the Reformation and Counter-Reformation. In an age of anxiety, an era of crisis, the clarity and confidence of the High Renaissance was lost, replaced by ambiguity and despair. The emotional impact of Mannerist art is likely to be tense and disturbing.

Never intended to have broad public appeal, Mannerism was a court style oriented to the tastes of the upper class. It was formulated to appeal to the sophisticated, elegant, aristocratic sensibilities of the sixteenth century. Thus, although the style was in vogue for a long period of time, its audience was restricted and it was not to have significant impact on future artistic trends. Mannerism, therefore, is not considered as important in the history of culture as the preceding Renaissance style or the succeeding Baroque style.

PAINTING

Mannerism was a departure from Renaissance ideals. Whereas Renaissance painting was characterized by clear presentations of subject matter, balanced compositions, normal body proportions, scientific spatial constructions, and preference for primary colors, Mannerist painting, in contrast, was characterized by intentionally obscure subject matter, unbalanced compositions, bodies with distorted proportions and contorted poses, confusing spatial constructions, and a preference for secondary and acidic colors. Facial expressions may be strained or inappropriate for the subject. Aesthetic forms became of greater concern than content.

Parmigianino. Among the most characteristic examples of the Mannerist departure from the Renaissance norm is the *Madonna with the Long Neck* (fig. 13.37), painted 1534–40 by PARMIGIANINO [par-mee-jah-NEE-noh]

FIGURE 13.37 Parmigianino, *Madonna with the Long Neck*, 1534–40, oil on panel, 7′1″ × 4′4″ (2.16 × 1.32 m), Galleria degli Uffizi, Florence. Scala/Art Resource, NY. Comparison with Raphael's High Renaissance *Madonna of the Meadows* (see fig. 13.24) makes obvious the Mannerist preference for distorted figures and spatial ambiguity.

(1503–40) of Parma. The figures are perfect, but, in contrast to the classical canon of proportions admired in the Renaissance, they have become unreal, other worldly, elongated and ethereal, artificial and affected, graceful and refined beyond nature's capabilities. Mary is especially large, with an almost balloonlike inflation through the hips and thighs. Only a complete absence of bones and joints would explain the curving contours of Mary's right hand.

The composition is unbalanced and spatially ambiguous. The figures are crowded on the left side, yet the open area on the right side is almost empty. The column in the background is a symbol of the torture of Jesus, because he was bound to a column and flagellated. The tiny prophet emphasizes the odd and unclear spatial arrangement—the viewer looks up to the foreground figures but down to the prophet.

Bronzino.   Another representative of the Mannerist or anti-Classical style is Bronzino (1503–72), court painter to Cosimo de' Medici. Mannerism was noted to be the style of the courts and was not intended to appeal to the general public. Bronzino's painting of the *Allegory of Venus* (figure 13.38), ca. 1546, demonstrates the intentional ambiguity of Mannerist iconography. The two main figures are Venus and Cupid, their relationship shown to be uncomfortably erotic. On the right, Folly throws roses. In the upper right, Father Time uncovers the follies of love—or perhaps he tries to hide them! The figure in the right background, with the body of a snake and the left and right hands reversed, is Deceit—the masks suggest falseness. The figures in the left background are probably Hatred and Inconstancy. Typically Mannerist is the complexity and obscurity of the **allegory,** which has been interpreted in various ways by historians.

Like the subject, the composition is also unclear. Characteristic of Mannerism is the absence of a single center of focus—the figures seem to compete with each other for the viewer's attention. The figures completely fill the composition, choking the space. Still and tense, their poses are elegant but affected, agitated, and exaggerated—and certainly difficult for a person to actually assume. Relative scale of the figures is inconsistent. Their uneasy expressions cause them to appear disturbed, and they are intended to disturb the viewer in this style that is distorted psychologically and physically. The colors are acid and metallic, the style of painting linear and hard with harsh lighting. Figures weave in and out in a paper-thin space, crowded, limited, and confined, set against a heavy and impenetrable background. Spatial contradictions abound—a floor plan of this space and its inhabitants cannot be drawn, for neither linear nor aerial perspective is used.

Tintoretto.   The leader of the Mannerists in Venice was Tintoretto (1518–94), whose real name was Jacopo Robusti, painter of the *Last Supper* (fig. 13.39) of 1592–94. The coveted Renaissance iconographic clarity, seen in Leonardo da Vinci's depiction of this subject (fig. 13.20),

FIGURE 13.38   Agnolo Bronzino, *Allegory with Venus and Cupid,* ca. 1546, oil on panel, 4′9½″ × 3′9¼″ (1.46 × 1.16 m), National Gallery, London. Typically Mannerist are the intentionally complex iconography (including an oddly erotic encounter between Venus and Cupid) and the pictorial space choked with figures.

is gone. In fact, the viewer may need some time to find Jesus in this scene, for the perspective leads the viewer's eyes away from Jesus and out of the composition, many figures compete with Jesus for the viewer's attention, and Jesus is pushed back into the space. He is singled out only by his central position and aureole of light. The lighting is unnatural, radiating from Jesus and the hanging lamp, from which the smoke turns into floating transparent angels. Judas is singled out from the apostles as the only figure on the opposite side of the table. The table is not parallel to the picture plane, as in Renaissance portrayals of the Last Supper, but placed on a strong diagonal into depth—the rapid recession is characteristic of Tintoretto. This Mannerist portrayal of the Last Supper is set in a tavern, an unusually commonplace location for a religious event.

Yet there is no possibility of mistaking this for a genre scene. Religious drama and emotion derive from Tintoretto's striking composition and lighting. Far from a calm, stable, static depiction, Tintoretto's verve changed Leonardo da Vinci's format for the Last Supper and broke Leonardo's hold on this subject. But Tintoretto's presen-

FIGURE 13.39   Tintoretto, *The Last Supper*, 1592–94, oil on canvas, 12′ × 18′8″ (3.66 × 5.69 m), San Giorgio Maggiore, Venice. SCALA/Art Resouce, NY. In striking contrast to the compositional clarity of Leonardo da Vinci's High Renaissance depiction (see fig. 13.20), the viewer may have some difficulty in locating Jesus in Tintoretto's Mannerist version of this subject, for the perspective leads away from, rather than toward, Jesus.

tation has been criticized for losing sight of the spirituality of the subject, with too much stress placed on the incidental activity in the foreground. Instead, Tintoretto's greatest concern was the aesthetic problem and the potential of light, movement, and drama.

El Greco.   One of the most interesting artists whose work displays Mannerist qualities is known as EL GRECO [el GRECK-oh] (1541–1614), or "the Greek." Domenikos Theotokopoulos was born on the island of Crete. He studied in Venice from about 1566, where he was deeply influenced by Titian, and then for seven years in Rome. In 1577, he emigrated to Spain, going first to Madrid and then to Toledo.

The most important of his major commissions is *The Burial of Count Orgaz* (fig. 13.40) of 1586. Legend held that at the count's burial in 1323, Saints Augustine and Stephen appeared and lowered him into his grave even as his soul was seen ascending to heaven. In the painting, the

burial and the ascension occur in two separate realms, neither of which fits spatially with the other, and both of which are packed with figures. On the lower portion, El Greco has painted the local contemporary aristocracy—people he knew—in attendance at the funeral, not the aristocracy of the count's day. In fact, El Greco's eight-year-old son stands at the lower left next to St. Stephen, and above him, looking out at the viewer from the back row, is quite possibly El Greco himself.

The top half of the scene is as spatially ambiguous as any example of Mannerist painting. A crowd of saints enters from a deep space at the top right. A chorus of angels playing instruments occupies a sort of middle space on the left. In the foreground, St. John and the Virgin Mary greet the angel who arrives with the soul of the count, shown about the size of a baby, as if to emphasize its innocence. John and Mary plead the count's case with Jesus, who is peculiarly small and seated far enough in the distance almost to occupy the vanishing point to the heavens. The most no-

FIGURE 13.40 El Greco, *The Burial of Count Orgaz*, 1586, oil on canvas, 16′ × 11′10″ (4.88 × 3.61 m), Church of San Tomé, Toledo. Although El Greco's distorted figures were once attributed to astigmatism, they are now recognized as part of the Mannerist preference for elongated bodily proportions.

table aspect of El Greco's style is exemplified by Jesus' right arm, which stretches far forward into the space above Mary's head. The elongated hands and arms are the most "mannered" feature of El Greco's art, and yet it is difficult to label his work "Mannerist." His aim is to move his audience by conveying a sense of the spiritual, almost mystical power of deeply religious faith and conviction. In this, his painting anticipates that of the Baroque age, and captures something of the power of the great Spanish mystics of his own day, Teresa of Avila and Ignatius Loyola, both of whom would be made saints in Rome in 1622.

Sofonisba Anguissola. Castiglione's *Book of the Courtier* advocated that aristocrats, be they male or female, be educated in social arts, and that women, specifically, should learn to paint, not as a career, but as part of training for aristocratic life. SOFONISBA ANGUISSOLA [So-fo-NEES-bah Ahn-gwee-SO-lah] (1528/35– 1625), from Cremona, and her five younger sisters studied painting and all became painters; only the youngest sibling, a boy, did not. In 1560, Anguissola became a painter at the court of Philip II in Madrid, indicating her international fame. The high regard in which she was held is made clear by the generous dowry the Spanish monarchy provided for her first marriage in 1570.

Sofonisba Anguissola frequently painted self-portraits, which were much in demand due to her fame, as well as portraits of her family, such as fig. 13.41 of one of her sisters, Minerva. Her sitters appear relaxed, almost alive; Giorgio Vasari noted that she created "breathing likenesses." Minerva wears a large gold medallion of the ancient Minerva, goddess of wisdom and the arts.

Lavinia Fontana. LAVINIA FONTANA [La-VEEN-nee-eh Fohn-THAN-nah] (1552–1614) grew up in Bologna, where she was instructed by her father, the artist Prospero Fontana. She is believed to be the first woman in western Europe to establish herself as a professional artist equal to her male contemporaries in fame. Her *Portrait of a Noblewoman* (fig. 13.42) is representative of her work; although women artists were likely to specialize in portraiture, Fontana's repertoire included religious and mythological subjects as well. Her husband and fellow

FIGURE 13.41 Sofonisba Anguissola, *Portrait of the Artist's Sister Minerva*, ca. 1564, oil on canvas, 33½ × 26″, Milwaukee Art Museum. Gift of the family of Mrs. Fred Vogel, Jr. As was customary for women artists of this era, Anguissola specialized in portraits. Such realistic records are one of the manifestations of the interest accorded the individual that began during the Renaissance.

FIGURE 13.42 Lavinia Fontana, *Portrait of a Noblewoman*, ca. 1580, oil on canvas, $45\frac{1}{4}$″ × $35\frac{1}{4}$″ (114.9 × 89.5 cm), National Museum of Women in the Arts, Washington, DC. Gift of Wallace and Wilhelmina Holladay. This portrait of an unknown Bolognese lady is believed to be a marriage portrait because red was the customary color of a wedding gown in Bologna; she is shown wearing one of the garments, and some of the gems, in her trousseau. The dog is a standard symbol of marital fidelity.

FIGURE 13.43 Benvenuto Cellini, *Saltcellar of Francis I*, 1539–43, gold with enamel, $10\frac{1}{4}$″ × $13\frac{1}{8}$″ (26 × 33.3 cm), Kunsthistorisches Museum, Vienna, Austria. An example of extreme elegance and opulence, this table ornament contained salt and pepper.

painter Gian Paolo Zappi worked as her assistant. She was the mother of eleven children, although was survived by only three of them. In 1604 she moved to Rome to work as a portrait painter for Pope Paul V. The appeal of Fontana's style lies in the meticulously painted details of the costume, her superb technical skill in depicting various textures, and the absence of a distracting background, thereby placing all attention on the subject.

SCULPTURE

By the mid-sixteenth century, Mannerism was the dominant style in France, largely as a result of the influence of Italian artists who moved there after the sack of Rome in 1527. Benvenuto Cellini's sculpture and writings reflected the full flowering of the style.

FIGURE 13.44 Benvenuto Cellini, *Perseus*, 1545–54, bronze, height 18′ (5.4 m), Loggia dei Lanzi, Florence. Even the depiction of the decapitation of the ancient mythological gorgon Medusa, blood gushing, attains elegance in the Mannerist style.

Then & Now

THE VENICE GHETTO

One of the most horrifying events in twentieth-century history is the Holocaust, the anti-Semitism movement in Hitler's Germany that led to the murder of more than six million Jews. One of the reasons Hitler could so easily control the Jewish population in Europe was that he created ghettos for the vast majority of Jews in the major European capitals. The earliest known segregation of Jews into their own distinct neighborhoods occurred in Spain and Portugal in the fourteenth century, but a large ghetto was established in Frankfurt in 1460. Ghettos in Venice appeared early in the sixteenth century.

A Jewish presence in Venice dates to the early fourteenth century, and by 1381 the city had authorized Jews to live in the city, practice usury—the lending of money with interest—and sell secondhand clothes and objects, which led to the profession of pawnbroking. In 1397, all Jews were expelled, ostensibly because of irregularities that had been discovered in the monetary practices of Jewish bankers and merchants. They were permitted to visit the city for no more than fifteen consecutive days and forced to wear an emblem identifying their religion. But this order became more and more laxly enforced, and the Venetian Jewish community flourished until 1496, when they were once again banished, and this time only permitted to stay in Venice for two weeks a year.

In 1508, Julius II formed an alliance with the rest of Italy and Europe against Venice, and when his army approached the city in the spring of 1509, the large Jewish community that lived on the mainland at the lagoon's edge fled to Venice proper. Many Jewish leaders offered much-needed financial support, and the city found itself in a quandary about where they should be allowed to live. The issue was hotly debated for seven years. Franciscan sermons routinely warned that God would punish the city if Jews were admitted. Finally, on March 29, 1516, a substantial majority of the Senate approved a proposal to move the Jews en masse to an islet linked to the rest of the city by two points of access that could be closed at night. In this way, Venice could make use of the skills—and money—of the Jewish community and still segregate them.

The island to which they were banished was the site of a new foundry. The Venetian word for the smelting process is *gettare*, and the new foundry built on the island was named *getto nuovo*. Soon the island itself was called Ghetto Nuovo, and the word "ghetto" entered the language, and came to be used throughout Europe to describe the areas in cities where Jewish communities were to be found.

Benvenuto Cellini. BENVENUTO CELLINI [che-LEE-nee] (1500–71) was a Florentine who worked in France for King Francis I (reigned 1515–47). Cellini made an extraordinary gold and enamel *Saltcellar of Francis I* (fig. 13.43), between 1539 and 1543. It is functional, yet elegant and fantastic. Salt is represented by the male figure Neptune, because salt comes from the sea (the salt is actually in a little boat), and pepper is represented by the female figure Earth, because pepper comes from the earth (the pepper is actually in a little triumphal arch). On the base are complex allegorical figures of the four seasons and four parts of the day, meant to evoke both festive seasonal celebrations and the daily meal schedule. Cellini wrote that figures should be elongated; these with small heads and boneless limbs are graceful and charming.

The Autobiography of Benvenuto Cellini. Among the most widely read of Renaissance works, Cellini's *Autobiography* is notable for the way in which it portrays the Italian Mannerist sculptor and goldsmith. His response to his patron, the duke of Florence, Cosimo de' Medici, who had just commissioned a new sculpture, *Perseus* (fig. 13.44), shows his Mannerist extravagance. When the duke questioned Cellini's ability to complete a sculpture in bronze, the artist responded with supreme confidence. In Cellini's account of the incident, the artist is portrayed as heroic, brave, violent, passionate, promiscuous, and entirely committed to his art.

Like the elongated figures in Parmigianino's paintings, Cellini's exaggerated portrayal of himself and others, in his *Autobiography*, typifies the Mannerist tendency. Unlike Parmigianino's delicacy and grace, however, Cellini is all drama and vigor. Cellini's *Autobiography*, in the end, is akin to his *Saltcellar of Francis I*. His sculpture extends the Mannerist style to its limits—the decorous Classical ideal of his Renaissance predecessors is gone.

ARCHITECTURE

Mannerist architects responded to the revival of the antique in unorthodox ways. The vestibule of the Laurentian Library in Florence (fig. 13.45) was built as the Medici family library above the monastery of the church of San Lorenzo. Begun by Michelangelo in 1524, the staircase was designed between 1558 and 1559, and the room was completed by GIORGIO VASARI [va-SAH-ree] (1511–74) and AMMANATI [ah-mahn-AH-tee] (1511–92). One of the most peculiar rooms ever built, the foyer has among its oddities that it is two stories high and thus higher than it is long or wide. The niches (wall recesses) are smaller at the bottom than at the top, and the same inversion of the norm is true of the pilasters that flank the niches. The columns are set into the wall, not in front of it, reversing the usual column and wall relationship. Scroll brackets, usually supporting elements, are rendered nonfunctional by their placement. The impression is one of walls pushing in, crushing the visitor. Finally, the staircase has three separate flights at the bottom but only one into the doorway at the top—a guaranteed traffic problem. This intriguing and uncomfortable room, in which everything is contrary to the classical rules of architecture, may be regarded as an ingenious Mannerist interpretation of the antique vocabulary.

The architect ANDREA PALLADIO (1508–80), from Vicenza in northern Italy, created a building in the Mannerist style that was to be highly influential—the Villa Rotunda (fig. 13.46), ca. 1567–70, one of many villas he built in and around Vicenza. The Villa Rotunda demonstrates the extreme to which Palladio carried his passion for symmetry and ancient architecture, since all four sides are identical, each mimicking an ancient temple facade with a triangular pediment supported on columns. The central dome recalls that of the ancient Roman Pantheon (Chapter 4, fig. 4.13). Certainly the result is harmonious, dignified, majestic, with an impressive grandeur. Yet the idea of a home as inviting and welcoming has been transformed into something intimidating: The visitor is humbled by the ascent of many steps required to gain entry, and, although the spacious main floor was used for entertaining, the bedrooms upstairs have low ceilings.

Palladio was not only an architect but also an author: His *Four Books on Architecture*, published in 1570, became the handbook of architects. An admirer of classical architecture, as the Villa Rotunda demonstrates, the ancient architect's logic is replaced by impracticality in the Mannerist's reinterpretation.

FIGURE 13.45 Michelangelo, Vasari, and Ammanati, vestibule of Laurentian Library, begun 1524, staircase completed 1559, monastery of San Lorenzo, Florence. The antique architectural vocabulary has been used to create a space in which the visitor is unlikely to feel comfortable. The stairs, which seem to flow downward, fill most of the floor space and, because three flights lead to a single doorway at the top, a traffic jam is likely.

Cultural Impact

The Renaissance changed the way human beings thought of themselves. People were no longer content to see themselves simply as a part of a larger social or religious group. With the Italian Renaissance emerged the notion of the individual self, an idea that would be celebrated two centuries later in the age of Romanticism.

One legacy of the Italian Renaissance was a restless intellectual energy. The independent thought and critical scrutiny encouraged during the Renaissance would result in the scientific revolution of the seventeenth century, as thinkers like Copernicus and Galileo built on the advances of that earlier time.

The power of individual artistic genius is most evident perhaps, among Italy's painters and sculptors. Who better than Raphael, Leonardo, and Michelangelo epitomize the genius of the Renaissance and its cultural influence? The very concept of the "Renaissance man," a multitalented individual who operates at the peak of perfection in many areas, is synonymous with these splendid artists, whose achievements have never been surpassed.

Outside the arts proper, the political ideas of Macchiavelli have been profoundly influential. Machiavelli's realistic approach to governing established principles by which rulers not only of his own day, but also of future eras, would rule. More quiet but no less influential were the social ideals of Renaissance court etiquette, especially those set down by Castiglione. His ideals of behavior established a standard for educated people of his own and future centuries to emulate.

FIGURE 13.46   Andrea Palladio, Villa Rotunda, Vicenza, ca. 1567–70. This home takes the idea of symmetry and repetition beyond the limits of practicality, for all four sides look exactly the same. Palladio's passion for his antique prototype—the Roman Pantheon (see Chapter 4)—led him to create this Mannerist example.

KEY TERMS

Renaissance
humanist
Neoplatonism
lantern
baptistery
linear perspective
atmospheric (aerial)

motet
word painting
sonnet
ballad
sestina
canzoni

chiaroscuro
sfumato
peristyle
drum
oil painting
impasto

mass
chanson
a cappella
Mannerism
allegory

WWW. WEBSITES FOR FURTHER STUDY

http://www.nga.gov/collection/gallery/gg4/gg4-main2.html
(A virtual tour of the early Renaissance in Florence, with many excellent images from the period.)

http://www.artchive.com/artchive/D/donatello.html
(This is the Artchive, a website with virtually every major artist in every style from every era in art history. It is an excellent resource.)

http://www.michelangelo.com/buon/bio-index2.html
(This site is a comprehensive resource for the life and career of Michelangelo.)

http://www.GreatBuildings.com/buildings/St Peters of Rome.html
(The Great Buildings site is an excellent tool for architecture of all eras.)

READINGS

PICO DELLA MIRANDOLA
ORATION ON THE DIGNITY OF MAN

Pico della Mirandola's Oration on the Dignity of Man *is a preface to a disputation he prepared to debate the Roman Church on theological and phisophical questions. His oration focuses on the centrality and importance of the individual human being, including the potential for perfectibility. A kind of humanist manifesto, Pico's oration celebrates human potentiality and demonstrates his skill at argumentation.*

Most esteemed Fathers,[1] I have read in the ancient writings of the Arabians that Abdala the Saracen[2]" on being asked what, on this stage, so to say, of the world, seemed to him most evocative of wonder, replied that there was nothing to be seen more marvelous than man. And that celebrated exclamation of Hermes Trismegistus,[3] "What a great miracle
is man, Asclepius"[4] confirms this opinion.
And still, as I reflected upon the basis assigned for these estimations, I was not fully persuaded by the diverse reasons advanced by a variety of persons for the preeminence of human nature; for example: that man is the intermediary between creatures, that he is the familiar of the gods above him as he is lord of the beings beneath him; that, by the acuteness of his senses, the inquiry of his reason and the light of his intelligence, he is the interpreter
of nature, set midway beween the timeless unchanging and the flux of time; the living union (as the Persians say), the very marriage hymn of the world, and, by David's testimony[5]
but little lower than the angels. These reasons are all, without question, of great weight; nevertheless, they do not touch the principal reasons, those, that is to say, which justify man's unique right to such unbounded admiration.
Why, I asked, should we not admire the angels themselves and the beatific choirs more?
At long last, however, I feel that I have come to some understanding of why man is the most fortunate of living things and, consequently, deserving of all admiration; of what may be the condition in the hierarchy of beings assigned to him, which draws upon him the envy, not of the brutes alone, but of the astral beings and of the very intelligences which dwell beyond the confines of the world. A thing surpassing belief and smiting the soul with

wonder. Still, how could it be otherwise? For it is on this ground that man is, with complete justice, considered and called a great miracle and a being worthy of all admiration.
Hear then, oh Fathers, precisely what this condition of man is; and in the name of your humanity, grant me your benign audition as I pursue this theme.
God the Father, the Mightiest Architect, had already raised, according to the precepts of His hidden wisdom, this world we see, the cosmic dwelling of divinity, a temple most august. He had already adorned the supercelestial region with Intelligences, infused the heavenly globes with the life of immortal souls and set the fermenting dungheap of
the inferior world teeming with every form of animal life. But when this work was done, the Divine Artificer still longed for some creature which might comprehend the meaning of so vast an achievement, which might be moved with love at its beauty and smitten with awe at its grandeur. When, consequently, all else had been completed, ... in the very last place, He bethought Himself
of bringing forth man. Truth was, however, that there remained no archetype according to which He might fashion a new offspring, nor in His treasure-houses the wherewithal to endow a new son with a fitting inheritance, nor any place, among the seats of the universe, where this new creature might dispose himself to contemplate the world. All space was already filled; all things had been distributed in the highest, the middle and the lowest orders. Still, it was not in the nature of the power of the Father to fail in this last creative élan; nor was it in the nature of that supreme Wisdom to hesitate through lack of counsel in so crucial a matter; nor, finally, in the nature of His beneficent love to compel the creature destined to praise the divine generosity in all other things to find it wanting in himself.
At last, the Supreme Maker decreed that this creature, to whom He could give nothing wholly his own, should have a
share in the particular endowment of every other creature. Taking man, therefore, this creature of indeterminate image, *70*
He set him in the middle of the world and thus spoke to him:
"We have given you, Oh Adam, no visage proper to yourself,
nor any endowment properly your own, in order that whatever
place, whatever form, whatever gifts you may, with premeditation, select, these same you may have and possess through your own judgment and decision. The nature of all other creatures is defined and restricted within laws which We have laid down; you, by contrast, impeded by no such restrictions, may, by your own free will, to whose custody We
have assigned you, trace for yourself the lineaments of your *80*
own nature. I have placed you at the very center of the world,
so that from that vantage point you may with greater ease glance round about you on all that the world contains. We

---

[1]The assembly of clergymen to whom the oration was to be addressed.
[2]The Arabic philosopher and translator Abd-Allah Ibn al Muqaffa (718–775).
[3]The Greek name (Hermes Thrice-Great) for the Greek god Thoth, the presumed author of a body of occult philosophy that mingled Neoplatonism, alchemy, and mystical interpretations of the Scriptures.
[4]The Greek god of healing and medicine.
[5]In Psalms 8.6.

have made you a creature neither of heaven nor of earth,
neither mortal nor immortal, in order that you may, as the
free and proud shaper of your own being, fashion
    yourself in
the form you may prefer. It will be in your power to
    descend
to the lower, brutish forms of life; [or] you will be
    able, through
your own decision, to rise again to the superior orders
    whose
life is divine."   *90*
Oh unsurpassed generosity of God the Father, Oh
    wondrous
and unsurpassable felicity of man, to whom it is granted
to have what he chooses, to be what he wills to be! The
    brutes,
from the moment of their birth, bring with them, as
    Lucilius[6]
says, "from their mother's womb" all that they will ever
posses. The highest spiritual beings were, from the very
moment of creation, or soon thereafter, fixed in the
    mode of
being which would be theirs through measureless
    eternities.
But upon man, at the moment of his creation, God
    bestowed
seeds pregnant with all possibilities, the germs of every
form of life. Whichever of these a man shall cultivate, the
same will mature and bear fruit in him. If vegetative, he
will become a plant; if sensual, he will become brutish; if
    rational,
he will reveal himself a heavenly being; if intellectual, he
will be an angel and the son of God. And if,
    dissatisfied with
the lot of all creatures, he should recollect himself into the
center of his own unity, he will there, become one
    spirit with
God, in the solitary darkness of the Father, Who is set
    above
all things, himself transcend all creatures.
Who then will not look with awe upon this our
    chameleon,   *110*
or who, at least, will look with greater admiration on any
other being? This creature, man, whom Asclepius the
Athenian, by reason of this very mutability, this nature
capable of transforming itself, quite rightly said was
symbolized in the mysteries by the figure of Proteus.
    This is
the source of those metamorphoses, or
    transformations, so
celebrated among the Hebrews and among the
    Pythagoreans;[7] . . .
. . . while the Pythagoreans transform men guilty of
crimes into brutes or even, if we are to believe Empedo-
cles,[8] into plants; and Mohamet,[9] imitating them, was

known frequently to say that the man who deserts the
divine law becomes a brute. And he was right; for it is
    not the bark that
makes the tree, but its insensitive and unresponsive nature; nor the hide which makes the beast of burden, but
its brute and sensual soul; nor the orbicular form which
makes the heavens, but their harmonious order. Finally,
    it is not freedom
from a body, but its spiritual intelligence, which makes
the angel. If you see a man dedicated to his stomach,
crawling on the ground, you see a plant and not a man;
or if you see a man bedazzled by the empty forms of the
    imagination, as
by the wiles of Calypso,[10] and through their alluring so-
licitations made a slave to his own senses, you see a brute
and not a man. If, however, you see a philosopher, judging and distinguishing all things according to the rule of
reason, him shall you hold in veneration, for he is a creature of heaven and not of earth; if, finally, a pure con-
templator, unmindful of the body, wholly
    withdrawn into
the inner chambers of the mind, here indeed is neither a
creature of earth nor a heavenly creature, but some
higher divinity, clothed with human flesh:

PETRARCH

SONNET 159

*The following poem is just one of the many in which Petrarch cel-
ebrated his beloved Laura. Consider how the poet refers to Neoplatonic and humanist ideas. Petrarch was master of the extended
metaphor; here it comprises the entire sonnet.*

From what part of the Heavens, from what Idea
did Nature take the model to derive
that lovely face of charm by which she chose
to show down here her power up above?

What fountain nymph, what woodland goddess ever   *5*
let such fine hair of gold flow in the breeze?
How did a heart collect so many virtues
the sum of which is guilty of my death?

Who seeks for divine beauty seeks in vain,
if he has not yet looked upon those eyes   *10*
and seen how tenderly she makes them move;

he does not know how love can heal and kill,
who does not know the sweetness of her sighs,
the sweetness of her speech, how sweet her smile.

FRANCOIS VILLON

*Francois Villon (1431–ca. 1474), was a poet and a vagabond and,
some claim, a thief. He is as well known for his life as for his poems.
The following ballads with their repeating refrains memorably evoke
certain realities about life and death.*

---

[6]A Roman writer of satires (180–102 B.C.E.).
[7]Followers of the Greek philosopher and mathematician Pythagoras (fl.
530 B.C.E.).
[8]A Greek philosopher and poet (495–435 B.C.E.).
[9]The prophet Muhammad (570–632).

---

[10]In Greek mythology, a sea nymph who lured Odysseus to remain with
her for seven years.

THE BALLAD OF DEAD LADIES[1]

Tell me now in what hidden way is
Lady Flora the lovely Roman?
Where's Hipparchia, and where is Thais,
Neither of them the fairer woman?
Where is *Echo*, beheld of no man,
Only heard on river and mere,—
She whose beauty was more than human? . . .
But where are the snows of yester-year?

Where's Héloise, the learned nun,
For whose sake Abeillard, I ween,
Lost manhood and put priesthood on?
(From Love he won such dule and teen!)
And where, I pray you, is the Queen
Who willed that Buridan should steer
Sewed in a sack's mouth down the Seine? . . .
But where arc the snows of yester-year?

White Queen Blanche, like a queen of lilies,
With a voice like any mermaiden,—
Bertha Broadfoot, Beatrice, Alice,
And Ermengarde the lady of Maine,—
And that good Joan whom Englishmen
At Rouen doomed and burned her there,—
Mother of God, where are they then? . . .
But where are the snows of yester-year?

Nay, never ask this week, fair lord,
Where they are gone, nor yet this year,
Save with this much for an overword,—
But where are the snows of yester-year?

BALLADE OF FORGIVENESS[1]

Brothers and sisters, Celestine,
Carthusian, or Carmelite,
Street-loafers, fops whose buckles shine,
Lackeys, and courtesans whose tight
Apparel gratifies the sight,
And little ladies'-men who trot
In tawny boots of dreadful height:
I beg forgiveness of the lot.

Young whores who flash their teats in sign
Of what they hawk for men's delight,
Ape-handlers, thieves and, soused with wine,
Wild bullies looking for a fight,
And Jacks and Jills whose hearts are light,
Whistling and joking, talking rot,
Street-urchins dodging left and right:
I beg forgiveness of the lot.

Excepting for those bloody swine
Who gave me, many a morn and night,
The hardest crusts on which to dine;
Henceforth I'll fear them not a mite.
I'd belch and fart in their despite,
Were I not sitting on my cot.

Well, to be peaceful and polite,
I beg forgiveness of the lot.

May hammers, huge and heavy, smite
Their ribs, and likewise cannon-shot.
May cudgels pulverize them quite.
I beg forgiveness of the lot.

VITTORIA DA COLONNA

I LIVE ON THIS DEPRAVED AND LONELY CLIFF

Vittoria da Colonna (1490–1547), one of the most celebrated women of the Italian Renaissance, was a member of the nobility and a friend to prominent artists and writers. She is generally recognized as the inspiration for a number of Michelangelo's poems. In all her own poems, exclusively written in sonnet form, Vittoria da Colonna describes her relationship with and love for her husband. The following poem contains Neoplatonic light imagery, popular in Renaissance lyric poetry.

I live on this depraved and lonely cliff
like a sad bird abhorring a green tree
or plashing water; I move forcefully
away from those I love, and I am stiff
even before myself, so that my thoughts   5
may rise and fly to him: sun I adore
and worship. Though their wings could hurry more,
they race only to him; the forest rots
until the instant when they reach that place.
Then deep in ecstasy, though brief, they feel   10
a joy beyond all earthly joy. I reel,
and yet if they could recreate his face
as my mind, craving and consuming, would,
then here perhaps I'd own the perfect good.

BALDASSARE CASTIGLIONE

from the *Book of the Courtier*

The Book of the Courtier *was not published until 1528, but it is one of the most representative books of the Italian High Renaissance. It is also one of the most highly regarded. The English scholar Roger Ascham (1515–68) claimed that, when diligently read, Castiglione's book was more instructive than a three-year sojourn in Italy. Among other things, it offered practical advice to the Renaissance gentleman on how to get ahead. However, it was in some respects a bit naive, as Machiavelli's* The Prince *would show.*

"Then, as for the physical appearance of the courtier, I would say that all that is necessary is that he should be neither too small nor too big, since either of these two conditions causes a certain contemptuous wonder and men built in this way are stared at as if they were monsters. However, if one is forced to choose between the two evils, then it is better to be on the small side than unduly large; for men who are so huge are often found to be rather thick-headed, and moreover, they are also unsuited for sport and recreation, which I think most important for the courtier. So I wish our courtier to be well built, with finely proportioned members, and I would have him demonstrate strength and lightness and suppleness and be good at all the physical exercises befitting a warrior. Here, I believe, his first duty is to know how to handle expertly every

---

[1]Translated by Dante Gabriel Rossetti.
[1]Translated by Richard Wilbur.

kind of weapon, either on foot or mounted, to understand all their finer points, and to be especially well informed about all those weapons commonly used among gentlemen. For apart from their use in war, when perhaps the finer points may be neglected, often differences arise between one gentleman and another and lead to duels, and very often the weapons used are those that come immediately to hand. So, for safety's sake, it is important to know about them. And I am not one of those who assert that all skill is forgotten in a fight; because anyone who loses his skill at such a time shows that he has allowed his fear to rob him of his courage and his wits.

"I also believe that it is of the highest importance to know how to wrestle, since this often accompanies combat on foot. Next, both for his own sake and for his friends, the courtier should understand about seeking restitution and the conduct of disputes, and he should be skilled in seizing the advantage, and in all this he must show both courage and prudence. Nor should he be too anxious for these engagements, save when his honour demands it; for, as well as the considerable danger that an uncertain outcome brings with it, whoever rushes into these things precipitately and without urgent cause deserves to be gravely censured, even if he is successful. However, when a man has committed himself so far that he cannot withdraw without reproach then both in the preliminaries and in the duel itself he should be very deliberate. He should always show readiness and courage; and he should not behave like those who are always quibbling and arguing over points of honour, and when they have the choice of weapons, select those which can neither cut nor prick, arm themselves as if they had to face a cannonade, and, thinking it enough if they are not defeated, retreat all the time and keep on the defensive, giving proof of utter cowardice, and in this way making themselves the sport of children, like those two men from Ancona who fought at Perugia a little while ago, and made everyone who saw them burst out laughing."

"And who were they?" asked Gaspare Pallavicino.

"Two cousins," answered Cesare.

"And in their fighting, more like two dear brothers," said the Count. Then he continued:

"Weapons are also often used in various sports during peace-time, and gentlemen often perform in public spectacles before the people and before ladies and great lords. So I wish our courtier to be an accomplished and versatile horseman and, as well as having a knowledge of horses and all the matters to do with riding, he should put every effort and diligence into surpassing the rest just a little in everything, so that he may always be recognized as superior. And as we read of Alcibiades, that he surpassed all those peoples among whom he lived, and each time in regard to what they claimed to be best at, so this courtier of ours should outstrip all others, and in regard to the things they know well. Thus it is the peculiar excellence of the Italians to ride well with the rein, to handle spirited horses very skilfully, and to tilt and joust; so in all this the courtier should compare with the best of them. In tourneys, in holding his ground, in forcing his way forward, he should compare with the best of the French; in volleying, in running bulls, in casting spears and darts, he should be outstanding among the Spaniards. But, above all, he should accompany his every act with a certain grace and fine judgement if he wishes to earn that universal regard which everyone covets." . . .

"If I remember rightly, my dear Count, it seems to me that you have repeated several times this evening that the courtier has to imbue with grace his movements, his gestures, his way of doing things and in short, his every action. And it appears to me that you require this in everything as the seasoning without which all other attributes and good qualities would be almost worthless. Now I admit that everyone should easily be persuaded of this, seeing that, by the very meaning of the word, it can be said that a man who behaves with grace finds it with others. You have said that this is very often a natural, God-given gift, and that even if it is not quite perfect it can be greatly enhanced by application and effort. It seems to me that those who are born as fortunate and as rich in such treasures as some we know have little need of any further instruction, since the gracious favour they have received from heaven raises them, almost despite themselves, higher than they might have desired, and makes everyone both like and admire them. I do not argue about this, since it is not in our power to acquire it of ourselves. But regarding those who receive from Nature only so much as to make it possible for them to acquire grace through enterprise, application and effort, I should like to know by what art, teaching and method they can gain this grace, both in sport and recreation which you believe are so important, and in everything else they say or do. Now since by praising this quality so highly you have, I believe, aroused in all of us a strong desire to obtain it, because of the task given you by signora Emilia, you are also obliged to satisfy us by teaching the way to do so." . . .

"Therefore anyone who wants to be a good pupil must not only do things well but must also make a constant effort to imitate and, if possible, exactly reproduce his master. And when he feels he has made some progress it is very profitable for him to observe different kinds of courtiers and, ruled by the good judgement that must always be his guide, take various qualities now from one man and now from another. Just as in the summer fields the bees wing their way among the plants from one flower to the next, so the courtier must acquire this grace from those who appear to possess it and take from each one the quality that seems most commendable. And he should certainly not act like a friend of ours, whom you all know, who thought that he greatly resembled King Ferdinand the Younger of Aragon, but had not tried to imitate him except in the way he raised his head and twisted a corner of his mouth, a habit which the King had acquired through illness. There are many like this, who think they are marvellous if they can simply resemble a great man in some one thing; and often they seize on the only defect he has. However, having already thought a great deal about how this grace is acquired, and leaving aside those who are endowed with it by their stars, I have discovered a universal rule which seems to apply more than any other in all human actions or words: namely, to steer away from affectation at all costs, as if it were a rough and dangerous reef, and (to use perhaps a novel word for it) to practise in all things a certain nonchalance which conceals all artistry and makes whatever one says or does seem uncontrived and effortless. I am sure that grace springs especially from this, since everyone knows how difficult it is to accomplish some unusual feat perfectly, and so facility in such things excites the greatest wonder; whereas, in contrast, to labour at what one is doing and, as we say, to make bones over it, shows an extreme lack of grace and causes everything, whatever its worth, to be discounted. So we can truthfully say that true art is what does not seem to be art; and the most important thing is to conceal it, because if it is revealed this discredits a man completely and ruins his reputation. I remember once having read of certain outstanding orators of the ancient world who, among the other things they did, tried hard to make everyone believe that they were ignorant of letters; and, dissembling their knowledge, they made their speeches appear to have been composed very simply and according to the promptings of Nature and truth rather than effort and artifice. For if the people had known of their skills, they would have been frightened of being deceived. So you see that to reveal intense application and skill robs everything of grace. Who is there among you who doesn't laugh when our Pierpaolo dances in that way of his, with those little jumps and with his legs stretched on tiptoe, keeping his head motionless as if he were made of wood, and all so laboured that he seems to be counting every step? Who is so blind that he doesn't see in this the clumsiness of affectation? And in contrast we see in many of the men and women who are with us now, that graceful and nonchalant spontaneity (as it is often called) because of which they seem to be paying little, if any, attention to the way they speak or laugh or hold themselves, so that those who are watching them imagine that they couldn't and wouldn't ever know how to make a mistake."

Then, without waiting, Bernardo Bibbiena said:

"Well, it seems that our Roberto has now found someone who will praise his style of dancing, which you all despise. For if the excellence we are discussing consists in being nonchalant, and displaying indifference, and thinking of anything except what one is actually doing, then when it comes to dancing Roberto is without equal, because to demonstrate that he isn't thinking what he is doing he lets his clothes fall from his back and his slippers from his feet, and he dances away without bothering to pick them up."

The Count went on: "Since you wish me to continue with the discussion, I shall now say something about our faults. Do you not realize that what you are calling nonchalance in Roberto is in fact affectation, since he evidently goes to great pains to show that he is not thinking about what he is doing? He is really taking too much thought, and by passing the bounds of moderation his nonchalance is affected and inappropriate, and it has exactly the opposite effect of what is intended, namely the concealment of art. So although nonchalance is praiseworthy as such, when it leads to someone letting the clothes fall off his back it degenerates as easily into affectation as does a meticulous regard for one's personal appearance (also praiseworthy as such), when it means holding one's head rigid for fear of spoiling one's coiffure, or carrying a mirror in the fold of one's cap and a comb in one's sleeve, and walking through the streets always followed by a page with a brush and sponge. For this kind of self-regard and nonchalance goes too much to extremes, which is always a fault and the opposite of the pure and agreeable simplicity which appeals to everyone. Notice how ungraceful a rider is when he forces himself to sit bolt upright in the saddle, as is said, in the Venetian way, in comparison with another who sits on his horse as free and relaxed as if he were on the ground. How much more agreeable and admired is a warrior when he is modest, saying little and boasting hardly ever, than one who is forever singing his own praises

and threatening all and sundry with his swearing and bragging! And this is simply the affectation of wanting to appear a bold fellow. The same applies whatever one's profession; indeed, it holds good for every single thing we do or say."

At this, the Magnifico Giuliano remarked: "It certainly holds true in music, in which it is very wrong to have two perfect consonances one after the other; for our sense of hearing abhors this, whereas it often likes a second or a seventh, which in itself is a harsh and unbearable discord. This is because to continue in perfect consonances produces satiety and offers a harmony which is too affected; but this disappears when imperfect consonances are introduced to establish the contrast which keeps the listener in a state of expectancy, waiting for and enjoying the perfect consonances more eagerly and delighting in the discord of the second or seventh, as in a display of nonchalance."

"So you see," answered the Count, "that affectation is as dangerous in music as in other things. Moreover, it is said to have been proverbial among certain great painters of the ancient world that excessive diligence is harmful; and Protogenes is said to have been censured by Apelles for not knowing when to take his hands from the board."

Then Cesare added: "It seems to me that our Fra Serafino shares this same fault of not being able to take his hands from the board, at least not before all the food has been taken away as well."[1]

The Count laughed and continued: "What Apelles meant was that when painting Protogenes did not know when he had done enough; in other words, he was blaming him for finishing his work too thoroughly. So this quality which is the opposite of affectation and which we are now calling nonchalance, apart from being the real source of grace, brings with it another advantage; for whatever action it accompanies, no matter how trivial it is, it not only reveals the skill of the person doing it but also very often causes it to be considered far greater than it really is. This is because it makes the onlookers believe that a man who performs well with so much facility must possess even greater skill than he does, and that if he took great pains and effort he would perform even better. To give other examples, consider a man using weapons, and about to throw a dart or handle a sword or some other weapon. If, without thinking about it, he casually takes up a position at the ready, so naturally that it seems as if his whole body assumes the right posture without any strain, then even if he does nothing more he demonstrates that he is in complete command of what he is doing. Similarly in dancing, a single step, a single unforced and graceful movement of the body, at once demonstrates the skill of the dancer. When a musician is singing and utters a single word ending in a group of notes with a sweet cadence, and with such ease that it seems effortless, that touch alone proves that he is capable of far more than he is doing. Then again, in painting, a single line which is not laboured, a single brush stroke made with ease, in such a way that it seems that the hand is completing the line by itself without any effort or guidance, clearly reveals the excellence of the artist, about whose competence everyone will then make his own judgement. The same happens in al-

---

[1]The pun, untranslatable into English, relies on the use of the same word *tavola* for both table and board or panel.

most every other thing. Our courtier, therefore, will be judged to be perfect and will show grace in everything, and especially in his speech, if he shuns affectation. However, affectation is a vice of which only too many people are guilty, and sometimes our Lombards more than others, who, if they have been away from home for a year, on their return immediately start speaking Roman or Spanish or French, and God knows what. And all this springs from the over-anxiety to show how much they know; so that they put care and effort into acquiring a detestable vice. Certainly it would require a great deal of effort on my part if in these discussions of ours I wished to use those old Tuscan words which the Tuscans of today have discarded; and what's more I'm sure you would all laugh at me."

At this, Federico remarked: "It is true that in talking among ourselves as we are doing now it would perhaps be wrong to use those old Tuscan words; because, as you say, they would prove tedious both for the speaker and his listeners, and many of us would have difficulty in understanding them. But for myself I believe that it would be wrong not to make use of them in writing, because they impart considerable grace and authority to what is written, and they produce a style which is more dignified and sonorous than can be achieved with modern words."

To this, the Count replied: "I can hardly think how grace and authority may be conferred by words which should be eschewed not only (as you yourself admit) in the kind of conversation we are enjoying at the moment but also in any conceivable circumstance. For if any man of good judgement had to make a speech on a serious subject before the very senate of Florence, which is the capital of Tuscany, or had to discuss important business in private with a highranking Florentine, or even amusing things with a close friend, or romantic affairs with ladies or gentlemen, or had to join in the jesting and joking at feasts, games or anywhere else, whatever the time, place or subject, I am certain that he would go out of his way to avoid using those old Tuscan words. And if he did use them, as well as making a fool of himself he would give no little annoyance to anyone listening. So it seems to me very curious to accept as good in writing those very words which are shunned as wrong in all kinds of conversation, and to insist that what is never appropriate in speech should be highly appropriate when it comes to writing. For it is my belief that writing is nothing other than a kind of speech which remains in being after it has been uttered, the representation, as it were, or rather the very life of our words. And so in speech, which ceases to exist as soon as it is uttered, some things are perhaps tolerable which are not so in writing; because writing preserves the words and submits them to the judgement of the reader, who has the time to give them his considered attention. Therefore it is right that greater pains should be taken to make what is written more polished and correct; not, however, that the written words should be different from those which are spoken, but they should be chosen from the most beautiful of those employed in speech. If we were to allow in writing what is not allowed in speech, in my opinion there would be one very unfortunate result: namely, more liberties could be taken in an area demanding the strictest discipline, and all the endeavour that goes into writing would be harmful instead of beneficial. So surely the rule is that what is proper in writing is also proper in speaking; and the finest

speech resembles the finest writing. Moreover, I believe that it is more important to make one's meaning clear in writing than in speaking; because unlike someone listening, the reader is not always present when the author is writing. However, I would praise any man who, as well as shunning the use of many old Tuscan words, also makes certain, whether he is writing or speaking, that he employs words in current usage in Tuscany or elsewhere in Italy which possess a certain grace when they are pronounced. It seems to me that anyone who follows some other practice runs the risk of that affectation which attracts so much censure and about which we were talking a moment ago."

Then Federico said: "I cannot deny, Count, that writing is a kind of speech. I would say, however, that if the spoken word is at all obscure what is said will fail to penetrate the mind of the listener and, since it will not be understood, will be useless. And this is not the case with writing, for if the words used by the writer carry with them a certain, I will not say difficulty but veiled subtlety, and so are not as familiar as those commonly used in speech, they give what is written greater authority and cause the reader to be more attentive and aware, and so reflect more deeply and enjoy the skill and message of the author; and by judiciously exerting himself a little he experiences the pleasure that is to be had from accomplishing difficult tasks. If the reader is so ignorant that he cannot overcome these difficulties, that is not the fault of the writer and his language should not, on this account, be judged to lack beauty. Therefore in writing I believe that it is right to use Tuscan words, and only those employed by the ancient Tuscans, because that is a convincing proof, tested by time, that they are sound and effective in conveying what they mean. Furthermore, they possess the grace and dignity which great age imparts not only to words but also to buildings, statues, pictures and to everything that is able to endure. And often simply by such splendour and dignity they beautify one's diction, through whose force and eloquence everything, no matter how mean, can be so embellished that it deserves the highest praise. But this matter of contemporary usage, on which you put so much stress, seems to me highly dangerous and very often wrong. If some solecism or other is adopted by many ignorant people, this, in my opinion, hardly means that it should be accepted as a rule and followed by others. What is more, current practice varies a great deal, and there's not a city in Italy where the mode of speech is not different from everywhere else. However, since you have not felt obliged to declare which of them is the best, a man might just as well take up Bergamasque as Florentine and, according to you, this would be perfectly correct. It seems to me, therefore, that if one wants to avoid all misgivings and be absolutely certain, one has to decide to imitate someone who by common consent is accepted as sound, and to employ him continuously as a guide and protection against hostile critics. And this model (I mean in the vernacular) should be none other, I think, than Petrarch or Boccaccio; and whoever strays from these two has to grope his way, like a man walking through the darkness without a light, and will frequently take the wrong path. But nowadays we are so headstrong that we are contemptuous of doing what the best men did in the ancient world, namely, of practising imitation. But unless we do I believe it is impossible to write well. It seems to me that there is convincing proof of this in Virgil who, although his inspired judgement and genius were such that he made it impossible for anyone afterwards to hope to imitate him successfully, yet himself wished to imitate Homer."

NICCOLO MACHIAVELLI

from *The Prince*

Fundamentally, Machiavelli's The Prince *is a book about power, especially how power is seized and administered. The political arena is a jungle in which the strongest prevail, a relentlessly competitive world in which maintaining moral standards and ethical behavior is merely naive. For the prince who wants to retain his power, the end justifies the means. To gain and hold power, Machiavelli notes, the prince requires the cunning of the fox and the strength of the lion. The heart of Machiavelli's advice appears in the chapters extolling the "virtues" of a prince; an excerpt follows.*

XV. THE THINGS FOR WHICH MEN, AND ESPECIALLY PRINCES, ARE PRAISED OR BLAMED

It now remains for us to see how a prince must govern his conduct towards his subjects or his friends. I know that this has often been written about before, and so I hope it will not be thought presumptuous for me to do so, as, especially in discussing this subject, I draw up an original set of rules. But since my intention is to say something that will prove of practical use to the inquirer, I have thought it proper to represent things as they are in real truth, rather than as they are imagined. Many have dreamed up republics and principalities which have never in truth been known to exist; the gulf between how one should live and how one does live is so wide that a man who neglects what is actually done for what should be done learns the way to self-destruction rather than self-preservation. The fact is that a man who wants to act virtuously in every way necessarily comes to grief among so many who are not virtuous. Therefore if a prince wants to maintain his rule he must learn how not to be virtuous, and to make use of this or not according to need.

So leaving aside imaginary things, and referring only to those which truly exist, I say that whenever men are discussed (and especially princes, who are more exposed to view), they are noted for various qualities which earn them either praise or condemnation. Some, for example, are held to be generous, and others miserly (I use the Tuscan word rather than the word avaricious: we call a man who is mean with what he possesses, miserly, and a man who wants to plunder others, avaricious).[1] Some are held to be benefactors, others are called grasping; some cruel, some compassionate; one man faithless, another faithful; one man effeminate and cowardly, another fierce and courageous; one man courteous, another proud; one man lascivious, another pure; one guileless, another crafty; one stubborn, another flexible; one grave, another frivolous; one religious, another sceptical; and so forth. I know everyone will agree that it would be most laudable if a prince possessed all the qualities deemed to be good among those I have enumerated. But, because of conditions in the world, princes cannot have those qualities, or observe them completely. So a prince has of necessity to be so prudent that

he knows how to escape the evil reputation attached to those vices which could lose him his state, and how to avoid those vices which are not so dangerous, if he possibly can; but, if he cannot, he need not worry so much about the latter. And then, he must not flinch from being blamed for vices which are necessary for safeguarding the state. This is because, taking everything into account, he will find that some of the things that appear to be virtues will, if he practises them, ruin him, and some of the things that appear to be vices will bring him security and prosperity.

XVI. GENEROSITY AND PARSIMONY

So, starting with the first of the qualities I enumerated above, I say it would be splendid if one had a reputation for generosity; nonetheless if you do in fact earn a reputation for generosity you will come to grief. This is because if your generosity is good and sincere it may pass unnoticed and it will not save you from being reproached for its opposite. If you want to acquire a reputation for generosity, therefore, you have to be ostentatiously lavish; and a prince acting in that fashion will soon squander all his resources, only to be forced in the end, if he wants to maintain his reputation, to lay excessive burdens on the people, to impose extortionate taxes, and to do everything else he can to raise money. This will start to make his subjects hate him, and, since he will have impoverished himself, he will be generally despised. As a result, because of this generosity of his, having injured many and rewarded few, he will be vulnerable to the first minor setback, and the first real danger he encounters will bring him to grief. When he realizes this and tries to retrace his path he will immediately be reputed a miser.

So as a prince cannot practise the virtue of generosity in such a way that he is noted for it, except to his cost, he should if he is prudent not mind being called a miser. In time he will be recognized as being essentially a generous man, seeing that because of his parsimony his existing revenues are enough for him, he can defend himself against an aggressor, and he can embark on enterprises without burdening the people. So he proves himself generous to all those from whom he takes nothing, and they are innumerable, and miserly towards all those to whom he gives nothing, and they are few. In our own times great things have been accomplished only by those who have been held miserly, and the others have met disaster. Pope Julius II made use of a reputation for generosity to win the papacy but subsequently he made no effort to maintain this reputation, because he wanted to be able to finance his wars. The present king of France has been able to wage so many wars without taxing his subjects excessively only because his long-standing parsimony enabled him to meet the additional expenses involved. Were the present king of Spain renowned for his generosity he would not have started and successfully concluded so many enterprises.

So a prince must think little of it, if he incurs the name of miser, so as not to rob his subjects, to be able to defend himself, not to become poor and despicable, not to be forced to grow rapacious. Miserliness is one of those vices which sustain his rule. Someone may object: Caesar came to power by virtue of his generosity, and many others, because they practised and were known for their generosity, have risen to the

---

[1]The two words Machiavelli uses are *misero* and *avaro*.

as it seemed, must have frightened away your mortal fever! The fever feared that it might catch it too, as we did!" All my poor household relieved in like measure from anxiety and overwhelming labour, went at once to buy earthen vessels in order to replace the pewter I had cast away. Then we dined together joyfully; nay, I cannot remember a day in my whole life when I dined with greater gladness or a better appetite.

After I had let my statue cool for two whole days, I began to uncover it by slow degrees. The first thing I found was that the head of Medusa had come out most admirably, thanks to the air-vents; for, as I had told the Duke, it is the nature of fire to ascend. Upon advancing farther, I discovered that the other head, that, namely, of Perseus, had succeeded no less admirably; and this astonished me far more, because it is at a considerably lower level than that of the Medusa. Now the mouths of the mould were placed above the head of Perseus and behind his shoulders; and I found that all the bronze my furnace contained had been exhausted in the head of this figure. It was a miracle to observe that not one fragment remained in the orifice of the channel, and that nothing was wanting to the statue. In my great astonishment I seemed to see in this the hand of God arranging and controlling all.

I went on uncovering the statue with success, and ascertained that everything had come out in perfect order, until I reached the foot of the right leg on which the statue rests. There the heel itself was formed, and going farther, I found the foot apparently complete. This gave me great joy on the one side, but was half unwelcome to me on the other, merely because I had told the Duke that it could not come out. However, when I reached the end, it appeared that the toes and a little piece above them were unfinished, so that about half the foot was wanting. Although I knew that this would add a trifle to my labour, I was very well pleased because I could now prove to the Duke how well I understood my business. It is true that far more of the foot than I expected had been perfectly formed; the reason of this was that from causes I have recently described, the bronze was hotter than our rules of art prescribe; also that I had been obliged to supplement the alloy with my pewter cups and platters, which no one else, I think, had ever done before.

Having now ascertained how successfully my work had been accomplished, I lost no time in hurrying to Pisa, where I found the Duke. He gave me a most gracious reception, as did also the Duchess; and although the major-domo had informed them of the whole proceedings, their Excellencies deemed my performance far more stupendous and astonishing when they heard the tale from my own mouth. When I arrived at the foot of Perseus, and said it had not come out perfect just as I previously warned his Excellency, I saw an expression of wonder pass over his face, while he related to the Duchess how I had predicted this beforehand. Observing the princes to be so well disposed towards me, I begged leave from the Duke to go to Rome. He granted it in most obliging terms, and bade me return as soon as possible to complete his Perseus; giving me letters of recommendation meanwhile to his ambassador, Averardo Serristori.

CHAPTER 14

HISTORY

1520	Pope Leo X excommunicates Luther
1521	Diet of Worms condemns Luther
1529–35	Reformation Parliament in England
1534	Henry VIII declared head of Church of England
1535	Shrine to St. Thomas à Becket in Canterbury Cathedral destroyed; Henry VIII orders monasteries destroyed
1542	Frisius invents triangulation
1550	Images and altars ordered removed from English churches
1553–58	Mary restores Catholicism in England
1555	Peace of Augsburg ends German religious wars
1559	Elizabeth reestablished as head of Church of England
1566	Van Eyck's *Ghent Altarpiece* hidden by church supporters
1598	Edict of Nantes ends French religious wars
1609	Galileo adapts telescope to astronomy

ARTS AND ARCHITECTURE

ca. 1426	Campin, *Mérode Altarpiece*
1425–32	Van Eyck, *Ghent Altarpiece*
1500	Dürer, *Self-Portrait*
1505–10	Bosch, *Garden of Earthly Delights*
1519 f.	Da Cortona (?), *Château of Chambord*
1529–35	Luther, lyrics to "A Mighty Fortress Is Our God"
1540	Holbein the Younger, *Henry VIII*
1551	Van Hemessen, *Portrait of a Lady*
1566–67	Bruegel the Elder, *Peasant Wedding*
1595	Morley, madrigal composer, "Now Is the Month of Maying"
1591–96	Smythson, Hardwick Hall
1598	Weelkes, madrigal composer, "As Vesta Was Descending"

LITERATURE AND PHILOSOPHY

1509	Erasmus, *The Praise of Folly*
1517	Sir Thomas More, *Utopia*
1519	Luther, "Ninety-Five Theses"
1520	Erasmus, *Familiar Conversations*
1536	Calvin, *Institutes of the Christian Religion*
1542	Jesuit order founded
1543	Vesalius, *Seven Books on the Structure of the Human Body*
1549	Copernicus, *On the Revolutions of Celestial Bodies*
1550	Cranmer's *Book of Common Prayer* required in all English churches
1559	First Index of Prohibited Books
1593	Montaigne, *Essays*
1595	Marlowe, *Dr. Faustus*
1603	Gilbert, *Concerning the Magnet*
1609	Shakespeare, *Hamlet*
1620	Kepler, *On the Motion of Mars*
1628	Bacon, *Novum Organum*
1628	Harvey, *On the Circulation of Blood*

The Renaissance
in Northern Europe

Albrecht Dürer, *Self-Portrait*, 1500, oil on panel, $26\frac{1}{4} \times 19\frac{1}{4}''$ (66.3 × 49 cm),
Alte Pinakothek, Munich.

Empire of Charles V ca. 1551

NORWAY

SWEDEN

NORTH
SEA

DENMARK

BALTIC SEA

ATLANTIC

OCEAN

ENGLAND   NETHERLANDS

London

Bruges

Ghent

Rhine R.

HOLY
ROMAN
EMPIRE

POLAND-LITHUANIA

Elbe R.

Oder R.

Vistula R.

Prague   MORAVIA

Paris   Seine R.

Loire R.

Nuremburg

Augsburg

Danube R.

Vienna

FRANCE

BURGUNDY

AUSTRIA

STYRIA

HUNGARY

Rhône R.

Po R.

VENETIAN REPUBLIC

ADRIATIC SEA

OTTOMAN EMPIRE

Danube R.

SPAIN

NAVARRE

CASTILE

Madrid

ARAGON

Barcelona

Tagus R.

CORSICA

PAPAL
STATES

Rome

Naples

KINGDOM
OF
SARDINIA

KINGDOM
OF
NAPLES

MEDITERRANEAN

KINGDOM
OF
SICILY

AFRICA

SEA

CRETE

0   250   500 Miles

0   250   500 Kilometers

MAP 14.1   The empire of Charles V, ca. 1551.

CHAPTER OVERVIEW

THE EARLY RENAISSANCE IN NORTHERN EUROPE
The Low Countries establish high standards in the visual arts

THE HIGH RENAISSANCE IN NORTHERN EUROPE
The age of discovery, political and religious conflict, Shakespeare, and the portrait

THE EARLY RENAISSANCE IN NORTHERN EUROPE

THE "REBIRTH" OF CLASSICAL VALUES EMERGED in northern Europe and in England more slowly than in Italy. Inevitably, trade and commerce brought Italian ideas northward, where they influenced the artistic traditions. As trade grew, it brought prosperity to an ever more influential merchant class, who soon became the most important patrons of their day.

THE COLUMBIAN EXCHANGE

With the voyages of the Italian navigator Christopher Columbus and the Portuguese navigator Vasco de Gama, European penetration of the Americas became well established, following previous voyages of Portuguese mariners, especially those of Henry the Navigator in the early fifteenth century. Successive Portuguese voyages resulted in their colonizing the Madeira and Azores islands in the Atlantic, as well as the Cape Verde islands off the west coast of Africa. By the mid-fifteenth century, Portuguese traders had expanded their trade in guns and textiles for African gold to include trade in slaves. Although Africa had long engaged in its own slave trade, the Portuguese vastly increased its volume and varied the destinations of slaves to offshore African islands, Atlantic islands, North and South America, and the Caribbean region.

The voyages of Christopher Columbus, underwritten by the Spanish King and Queen, Ferdinand and Isabella, did not reach the "Indies" in Asia by sailing west, as Columbus had calculated. Nor did Columbus bring back the silks and spices he had envisioned when he set sail on these voyages. These voyages, however, did open the way for other European mariners from England, France, Holland, and Spain to follow in his wake and to explore and exploit opportunities for trade and for colonizing the Americas and the Caribbean. In the centuries following Columbus's and de Gama's voyages, the conquest, settlement, and exploitation of native peoples of the Americas and Africa by Europeans was firmly established.

The natural resources of the new world were brought to Europe, such that to a large degree, the wealth of the Americas fueled the amassing of fortunes in art by European courts. Moreover, new world products, such as cocoa, cotton, and tobacco, became staples of European consumers. One of the great ironies of the period from the fourteenth through sixteenth centuries is that an age grounded in humanistic ideals and anchored in religious morality could result in the exploitation of African slaves and the destruction of native Indian civilizations in Mexico and Peru.

GHENT AND BRUGES

In the Low Countries, the areas known today as Belgium and The Netherlands, there was a number of substantial cities by the dawn of the fifteenth century. Cities such as Ghent were commercial centers, surrounded by agricultural lands and located, for trading purposes, along the rivers and coast. In 1340, Ghent was a flourishing textile center producing tapestries, lace, and other fine textiles, which it exported to the world from its substantial port on the River Scheldt. But by 1400, it had lost its place as the region's commercial center, supplanted by the nearby port of Bruges, which had become the financial capital of all northern Europe. There were many reasons for Bruges's rise, among them Ghent's devastating population loss to the Black Plague. Perhaps the most important reason was that Bruges, not Ghent, became the favorite city of the dukes of Burgundy, especially Philip the Good (1396–1467). Philip dreamed of creating a court culture that might compete with that of the French, and early in the fifteenth century he moved his court from Dijon to Bruges. Meanwhile, the Medicis founded an important branch of their bank in Bruges and fresh news of the Florentine cultural scene was always at hand.

Philip's grandfather, Philip the Bold, and his brother, Jean, duke of Berry, were great patrons of art in northern Europe, just as the Medici were in southern Europe. (Jean commissioned the Limbourg brothers' illuminated book of hours, completed in 1416; see Chapter 12.) Their court was obsessed with chivalry and encouraged chivalrous entertainments—jousts, tournaments, pageants, and processions. They dressed in gold-threaded cloth, ermine, and jewels; they commissioned the finest tapestries; and they surrounded themselves with poets, musicians, scholars, and painters. Unfortunately, by the late fifteenth century, the harbor at Bruges was filled with silt, and the city, dwindling in size, lost importance as a financial capital. Virtually untouched and forgotten for four hundred years, it remains today as one of the best examples of an Early Renaissance city in Europe, its streets and buildings still very much as they were.

FLEMISH OIL PAINTING

Oil paint had been used for centuries to paint stone and metal, but it was not used on wood panels until the early fifteenth century. In the past, painters had used egg tempera. In **egg tempera** (pigments mixed with egg yolk), an artist must work quickly because the mixture dries rapidly. Subtle modeling is difficult to achieve in egg tempera, since the paint does not blend readily and is fairly opaque. Oil paint (pigments mixed with linseed oil) stays wet a long time, so color can be blended and reworked right on the painting surface. Depicting subtle texture—soft skin, fluffy hair, velvet, wood, metal, or plaster—is possible in oil paint.

Robert Campin. One of the first important examples of the oil painting technique is the *Mérode Altarpiece* (fig. 14.1), attributed to the Master of Flémalle, ROBERT CAMPIN [cam-PEN] (ca. 1375–1444), a member of both the Tournai painters' guild and the city council.

FIGURE 14.1 Robert Campin (Master of Flémalle), *Mérode Altarpiece*, ca. 1426, egg tempera and oil on panel, center $25\frac{3}{16} \times 24\frac{7}{8}''$ (64.1 × 63.2 cm), each wing $25\frac{3}{8} \times 10\frac{7}{8}''$ (64.5 × 27.6 cm), The Cloisters Collection, 1956 (56. 70), Metropolitan Museum of Art, New York. Illusions of texture and atmosphere are made possible by painting in oil rather than egg tempera, the medium favored during the Middle Ages. Equally innovative is the depiction of the Annunciation in a middle-class fifteenth-century Flemish home.

The altarpiece still echoes medieval conventions: For instance, the large size of Mary and Gabriel indicates their importance, not realistic relative scale. Yet it also introduces a new matter-of-fact attention to the details of reality, facilitated by the use of oil paint. Painting around 1426, Campin employed a mixed technique in the altarpiece, using egg tempera for the underpainting, then proceeding immediately to paint over it in oil.

The altarpiece is a **triptych**—a three-paneled painting. The triptych wings are hinged and can be closed to protect the painting inside, and when they are opened out at an angle, the altarpiece can stand up unaided. This is the earliest known depiction of the Annunciation as taking place not in a church or holy realm but in a home. Here the traditional religious subject has been combined with an accurate observation of daily life.

The central panel depicts the Annunciation. In the left panel, a prosperous merchant, the patron, Ingelbrecht of Mechlin, and his wife look in through an open doorway, witnessing the miraculous event. This clever device establishes an ingenious spatial relationship uniting the two panels.

The artist documents each object in tiny detail. Every part of the painting catches and holds the viewer's eyes. This interest in detail is suffused with religious symbolism. For example, the lion finials on the bench are symbols of

watchfulness as well as of Jesus and his resurrection; the dog finials are symbols of fidelity and domesticity. The candle refers to the light brought into the world by Jesus. The lily, a symbol of purity, is the flower of Jesus's mother Mary (Madonna lily). Perhaps the most interesting symbolic detail is the tiny figure coming in the window on rays of light, heading for Mary's abdomen. This miniature man, carrying a tiny cross, is a prefiguration of Jesus—in the next instant the Incarnation will take place. Every object, even an ordinary household item, could carry **iconographic** (or symbolic) implications. An unusual example of symbolism is seen on the right panel, where Mary's husband Joseph makes mousetraps in his carpentry shop, a fifteenth-century Flemish carpenter's shop complete with tools. Presumably this iconography derives from St. Augustine's description of the Lord's cross as a mousetrap for the devil, and his death as the bait by which the devil would be caught.

Jan van Eyck. In the 1420s, the painter JAN VAN EYCK [van IKE] (ca. 1390–1441) served Philip the Good, not only as a painter but also as a diplomat to Spain and Portugal. In Portugal, he painted portraits of Philip's future bride, Princess Isabella, so that Philip, back in Flanders, might see what she looked like. He became renowned not only at the Burgundian court but among notables visiting from abroad, especially the Italians. By the middle

of the next century, Giorgio Vasari was referring to him in his *Lives* as the "inventor of oil painting."

Like Robert Campin, van Eyck recorded the world in minute detail. Jan van Eyck completed his *Ghent Altarpiece*, in 1432, just a few years after the *Mérode Altarpiece*. The *Ghent Altarpiece* is a much more ambitious work in which he was probably aided by his brother Hubert. Located in St. Bavon Cathedral in Ghent, this enormous **polyptych**—a painting consisting of multiple panels—has twenty-six panels. When shut, it depicts the Annunciation (fig. 14.2) across four panels cleverly painted to form one room. Even the frame enters the pictorial illusion, casting shadows into the room. In the center of the lower tier are John the Baptist and John the Evangelist, the former identified by his camel hair garment and the lamb he is holding, the latter by a chalice with snakes. These figures are painted to appear to be sculptures set in architectural niches. Van Eyck has painted light falling from the right as

it might in nature, heightening a sense of verisimilitude. St. Bavon was dedicated to John the Baptist, the patron saint of the city of Ghent.

A deed dated May 13, 1535, establishes Joos Vijd, on the left, and his wife Elizabeth Borluut, on the right, as founders of the chapel where the altarpiece stood. An inscription on the outer frame reads: "Hubert van Eyck, the most famous painter ever known, started this work of art at the request of Joos Vijd; his brother Jan, who was the second in art, finished the monumental commission. With this verse the donor consigns the work to your charge on May 6, 1432." Little is known about Hubert van Eyck. Still, mention of the artists on the work itself indicates a shift from the anonymity of the medieval guild system toward the recognition of individual artists.

When opened, the altarpiece focuses on the salvation and redemption of humankind (fig. 14.3). The glowing colors of the interior contrast with the somber colors of the exterior panels. The central panel on the lower level depicts the *Adoration of the Lamb:* The Mystic Lamb is sacrificed, its blood spurting into the chalice, which symbolizes Jesus's sacrifice. In the foreground is the Fountain of Life, symbolizing the mass from which grace unceasingly flows. The crowds of people paying homage to the Lamb include Old Testament prophets and patriarchs, classical poets and philosophers, New Testament apostles, and people of all classes, times, and places. Various body types and facial expressions individualize the figures with their blemishes and deformities included. Realism is heightened by the use of atmospheric perspective (see Chapter 13). The colors and the edges of objects in the background are not as intense or as sharp as those in the foreground; distant hills merge with the sky. This differs from the *Mérode Altarpiece* in which the artist gave each object equal focus, whether in the foreground or background.

Unlike the lower panels, the upper panels do not form a unified composition. In the center is either God or Jesus, adorned in a scarlet mantle and gemstones that appear to catch the light. This figure seems to incorporate all aspects of the Trinity within himself—the Father, Son, and Holy Ghost. The outermost figures are Adam and Eve, the earliest large-scale nudes in northern European panel painting. Highly naturalistic, they were obviously painted from models. Eve's protruding abdomen is the fashionable figure of the day rather than an indication of pregnancy. Adam is shown with his mouth slightly open, as if speaking. Drawn as if seen from below, the bottom of Adam's foot is visible as he steps on the frame, because the viewer must look up at these figures.

Van Eyck's particular genius is further demonstrated in his commissioned portrait of *Giovanni Arnolfini and His Wife Giovanna Cenami*, often called *The Arnolfini Wedding* (fig. 14.4). On the back wall, above the mirror, are the words "*Johannes de Eyck fuit hic. 1434*" ("Jan van Eyck was here. 1434"). We see reflections in the mirror: the backs of

FIGURE 14.2   Jan and Hubert van Eyck, *Ghent Altarpiece* (closed), ca. 1425–32, oil on panel, $11'5\frac{1}{4}'' \times 7'6\frac{3}{4}''$ (3.4 × 2.3 m), St. Bavon, Ghent. Although Gabriel and Mary are too large to stand up, the space is ingeniously depicted as if continuous through all four panels behind the frame—which itself appears to cast shadows into the room.

FIGURE 14.3 Jan and Hubert van Eyck, *Ghent Altarpiece* (open), ca. 1425–32, oil on panel, 11′5$\frac{3}{4}$″ × 15′1$\frac{1}{2}$″ (3.4 × 4.6 m), St. Bavon, Ghent. Because of the lower center scene in which the multitudes are shown venerating the Lamb of God (Agnus Dei), this monumental polyptych is sometimes referred to as the *Mystic Lamb*.

Arnolfini and Cenami and, beyond them, two other figures, standing in the same place as the viewer. The man in the red turban is perhaps the artist himself, suggesting he was, in fact, present as witness.

Giovanni Arnolfini was an Italian merchant working in Bruges as an agent for the Medicis. The painting expresses the prosperity of the merchant class in fifteenth-century Bruges with their lavish textiles and dazzling finery. His wife's protruding abdomen again does not suggest pregnancy but a fashionable physique, probably achieved by a small padded sack over the abdomen and emphasized by the cut of the garment and posture of its wearer.

Although it has long been assumed the couple are shown in a bridal chamber, exchanging marriage vows, recent arguments suggest instead we are witness here not to a marriage but to an engagement, and the room is not a bedroom but the main room of Arnolfini's house. The moment is not unlike that described by Shakespeare in *Henry V,* when the English king proposes to Katherine, the French princess: "Give me your answer; i' faith, do; and so clap hands and a bargain: how say you lady?" Such a touching of the hands was the common sign of a mutual agreement to wed. As for the room itself, it has been pointed out

that canopy beds were "furniture of estate," commonly displayed in the principal room of the house as a sign of the owner's prestige.

The painting is replete with objects that hold iconographic significance, in **disguised symbolism.** Thus St. Margaret, patron saint of childbirth, adorns the bedpost. The couple's shoes are off to signify they stand on holy ground. Ten scenes in the mirror frame represent the passion of Jesus, and the single candle in the chandelier represents the all-seeing God. The dog, as noted, is a symbol of fidelity and domesticity. God's presence on earth was believed to be found in ordinary everyday objects.

Hieronymus Bosch. Very different from Jan van Eyck's efforts to portray the real world are those of HIERONYMUS BOSCH [BOSH] (1450 or 1453–1516). He takes his name from s-Hertogenbosch [s-HER-toe-gen-bos] in southern Holland (now called Den Bosch) where he grew up and worked. Off the main roads, isolated from progressive ideas, this was a middle class, commercial town situated within an area of religious, political, social, and economic unrest. In Bosch's world, people believed in witches, astrology was taught at the universities, and vi-

FIGURE 14.4 Jan van Eyck, *Giovanni Arnolfini and His Wife Giovanna Cenami*, signed and dated 1434, oil on panel, $32\frac{1}{4} \times 23\frac{1}{2}''$ (83.8 × 57.2 cm), National Gallery, London. The growing interest in portraiture is evidenced here. Cenami's protruding abdomen was a fashion of the times, achieved by padding and posture (note Eve's comparable contour in the *Ghent Altarpiece*) rather than an impetus for the exchanging of wedding vows.

sions were accepted as fact. Although a member of a Catholic fraternity until his death in 1516, Bosch was openly critical of certain religious practices.

Bosch's work displays an extraordinary imagination and a highly personal style, his painting teeming with bizarre and menacing creatures, part human, part animal. Painting **alla prima** [AH-la PREE-ma]—without any preliminary drawing—his draftsmanship looks fragile and delicate. Where other Flemish painters stressed solid dimensionality, Bosch chose dreamy transparency. While his contemporaries painted illusions of nature, Bosch painted a phantasmagorical world. Bosch was less interested in the painterly problems of light and shadow, and more concerned with the moralistic import of his subjects.

Bosch's *Hay Wain* (fig. 14.5), a triptych painted ca. 1495–1500, illustrates the Flemish proverb, "The world is a hay wagon and each seeks to grab what he can." The hay wagon is a symbol of worldly goods and pleasures, and the painting is a satire on the evils of greed. Characteristically, Bosch fills this painting with a multitude of vignettes. In the center panel all classes of people fight each other for the hay. Some are crushed under the wheels. A quack physician fills his purse. Nuns, supervised by a gluttonous monk, stuff hay into a bag. On top of the hay a man plays a lute

while the dancing demon on the right plays his nose like a flute, and a couple kiss in the bushes. Only the angel on the left notices Jesus above. The left panel is a scene of Original Sin. Rebel angels are thrown out of heaven and the sky is full of monsters. On the right panel is hell—to which the wagon, pulled by devils, is rolling.

Bosch's most famous painting, the *Garden of Earthly Delights* (fig. 14.6), probably painted between 1505 and 1510, is, like the *Hay Wain*, a sermon on earthly folly and its punishment in hell. Again, creation is shown on the left panel and hell on the right. But here the pleasures of the flesh, portrayed on the central panel, are the focus of punishment.

The central panel is populated by innumerable tiny humans, bizarre animals, and fantastic plants. The huge fruits are perishables, such as cherries, strawberries, and blackberries—rotting fruit is a recurrent image. The implication is that pleasure, too, is short lived. In this realm, people cavort amorously. Gluttonous lovers sit inside a berry, luring people in. Other lovers are surrounded by a transparent capsule, unaware that their conduct is seen by all.

The left panel portrays the creation of Eve, her presentation to Adam, the Tree of Knowledge, and the begin-

FIGURE 14.5   Hieronymus Bosch, *Hay Wain*, ca. 1495–1500 (?), oil on panel, center $4'7\frac{1}{8}'' \times 3'3\frac{3}{8}''$ (1.40 × 1.00 m), each wing $4'9\frac{1}{8}'' \times 2'2''$ (147 × 66 cm), Museo del Prado, Madrid. Another version of this painting is in the Escorial, near Madrid—scholars debate which is the original. People of all types try to grab the hay, which, according to a proverb, represents material possessions.

FIGURE 14.6 Hieronymus Bosch, *Garden of Earthly Delights*, ca. 1505–10, oil on panel, center 7′2″ × 6′4″ (2.20 × 1.95 m), each wing 7′2½″ × 3′2″(2.20 × 0.97 m), Derechos reservados © Museo Nacional del Prado, Madrid. Bosch's predilection for the bizarre, his juxtapositions of seemingly unrelated objects, and their irregular scale foreshadow Salvador Dalí and twentieth-century Surrealism (see Chapter 21).

ning of sin with the Fall. The right panel is a vision of hell. At the top, cities burn. A pair of ears is separated by a knife, but held together by an arrow. There is a convent, roofed by a horse's skull and populated by demons. A knight is devoured by dogs. Musical instruments serve as instruments of torture. At this time lust was called the "music of the flesh," and the bagpipe referred specifically to the male sexual organ. A bird-creature consumes and excretes the damned. A miser vomits gold coins into a sewer. Every type of sin receives its punishment in hell. Is the face looking out at us below the bagpipe a self-portrait? If so, Bosch has placed himself in hell!

Although much of Bosch's meaning escapes us, some aspects are clear. When he portrayed a mother superior pig giving a dying man an embrace, Bosch was cryptically criticizing the Church practice of extracting wills that benefited monasteries. Members of the clergy during Bosch's time were often corrupt, living in licentious luxury even as they preached austerity and abstinence to others.

The German artist Albrecht Dürer later said of Bosch's paintings that nothing like them was ever "seen before nor thought of by any other man." Bosch's vision of the Church soon became part of a general call for reform, as other artists, writers, and intellectuals began to attack the Church.

THE HIGH RENAISSANCE IN NORTHERN EUROPE

THE HABSBURG PATRONAGE

Bosch became the favorite northern painter of Philip II of Spain, the richest and greatest collector of art in the last half of the sixteenth century. Not only did Philip own the *Garden of Earthly Delights*, but he owned over thirty other paintings attributed to Bosch. The painter's work evidently struck a chord with the elegant, highly educated, and refined prince.

Philip II was the nephew of Charles V, emperor of the Holy Roman Empire, and of Mary of Hungary, the emperor's sister. The HABSBURG [HAPS-burg] Charles V controlled Spain, the Low Countries, the German empire, Hungary, Spanish America, and parts of Italy. Although not a strong supporter of the arts, Charles discovered the paintings of Titian in 1532 and became, together with Mary, the artist's chief patron. Mary of Hungary also served as governor of the Netherlands from 1531 to 1556, and in that time developed a passion for fifteenth-century Flemish painting, acquiring, among others, van Eyck's portrait of *Giovanni Arnolfini and His Wife Giovanna Cenami* (see fig. 14.4).

Then & Now

ICONOCLASM AND THE ATTACK ON THE ARTS

The iconoclastic practices of sixteenth-century European Protestants were focused on the destruction of "idolatrous" images of God. From the Protestant point of view, such images diminished God by making him appear like humankind. This logic quickly extended to all images within churches, which could distract the worshiper from the true contemplation of salvation. It was not a question of artistic merit; the statues were viewed solely for their sacrilegious content.

Since 1985, artists in the United States have also been attacked for creating art considered obscene or blasphemous, specifically those works that, to some people, challenge the very idea of Christianity and the values they associate with a Christian lifestyle. Recent attacks have had a political flavor because the art and artists in question—Robert Mapplethorpe and Andreas Serrano, for ex-

ample—were funded in part by the National Endowment for the Arts. The attackers argue that the government, supported by taxpayers' money, should not fund work that offends or upsets those who pay for it.

Senator Alphonse D'Amato, a Republican from New York, tore a photograph of one of Serrano's works into pieces on the floor of the U.S. Senate on May 18, 1989. "This so-called piece of art is a deplorable, despicable display of vulgarity," he exclaimed. On July 26, 1989, Senator Jesse Helms, a Republican from North Carolina, introduced an amendment to legislation funding the National Endowment that would prohibit the use of appropriated funds to, among other things, "promote, disseminate, or produce . . . obscene or indecent materials, including but not limited to depictions of sadomasochism, homoeroticism, the exploitation of children, or individuals engaged in sex acts; or . . . material which denigrates the objects or

beliefs of the adherents of a particular religion or non-religion."

Supporters of artists' rights of self-expression found the last word of that statement particularly alarming, because, if the amendment were to be passed, the government could prohibit funding of any material that denigrated *anyone's* belief about *anything*. It seemed to many like government-supported censorship.

The amendment failed, and thus began a legislative battle that continues to this day. Should the government take on the role of artistic patron? If not, who will? Many of the country's great dance companies, symphony orchestras, theater companies, artists, and writers depend on government funds to complete their projects.

Thus the link between Renaissance iconoclasm and today's debates over funding of the arts is clear. How our current society settles the debate remains in question.

Financed by gold and silver from the Americas, Philip added to the great collections of his uncle and aunt. Like Charles V and Mary before him, he favored Titian, granting him an annual stipend and allowing him to paint whatever he chose. When Titian died in 1576, Philip had amassed dozens of his paintings. From Flanders, Philip collected works by Campin and Bosch. By the time Philip was done, he had brought more than 1,500 paintings to Spain.

ERASMUS AND NORTHERN HUMANISM

Like Bosch, the northern humanist scholar DESIDERIUS ERASMUS [ee-RAZ-mus] (1466–1536), born in Rotterdam, The Netherlands, saw the religious world of late-fifteenth- and early-sixteenth-century Europe through a critical lens, but he was no iconoclast. In *A Pilgrimage for Religion's Sake*, he marveled at the shrine to Thomas à Beckett in Canterbury Cathedral: "Ye Gods! What a show was there of silken vestments, what a power of golden candlesticks. . . . Treasures beyond all calculation [were] displayed. The most worthless thing there was gold, every

part glowed, sparkled and flashed with rare and large gems, some of which were bigger than a goose egg."

Erasmus blended the study of classical civilization with Christian faith. Combining critical intelligence with spiritual conviction, Erasmus brought together the thought of Plato with that of St. Paul, and the philosophy of Aristotle with that of St. Augustine. Educated by the Brethren of the Common Life, an order of laymen who modeled their lives on that of Jesus Christ, he joined an Augustinian monastery in 1487 and was ordained a priest in 1492. Erasmus traveled widely, studying and teaching in most of the cultural centers of Europe, including England. At Oxford, he became friends with Sir Thomas More; at Cambridge, he was Professor of Divinity and of Greek.

Erasmus wrote his *Familiar Conversations* (1519) to attack abuses within the Catholic Church. Erasmus's readers found the satire scathingly accurate. His *Conversations* was so antagonistic to the clergy that Charles V, the Holy Roman Emperor, issued an edict that any teacher using the work in the classroom would be liable to immediate execution. Forty editions of the book were published in Erasmus's lifetime, and John Milton, more than a hundred years later, remarked that everyone was still reading it at

Cambridge. His most famous work, however, is *The Praise of Folly*, a satire of hypocrisy and pretension in his time.

Erasmus did not set himself up as a counterauthority to the Catholic Church. His goal was to purify the church from within by ridiculing its abuses and thereby stimulating internal reform.

THOMAS MORE

Sir Thomas More (1478–1535), to whom Erasmus dedicated his *Praise of Folly*, was, like Erasmus, a scholar and a Christian humanist. More rose to power during the reign of King Henry VIII, the English king who broke away from the Roman Catholic Church to establish the Church of England. A man of conscience, More lost his life for refusing to support Henry in his split with the Roman Church, and especially in his effort to annul his marriage. Henry had More executed for treason.

More is also known for his *Utopia*, which depicts an ideal state in which economic and social equality prevail and in which citizens are free to pursue religion and learning as they wish. In More's utopian society, citizens worked, studied, and took recreation in a balanced life guided by moral values and ethical principles, although not dominated by any particular religion.

MARTIN LUTHER AND THE REFORMATION

If one individual could be said to dominate the history of sixteenth-century Europe, that person would be MARTIN LUTHER [LOO-ther] (1483–1546) the key figure in the Protestant **Reformation.** Like Erasmus, Luther (fig. 14.7) was an Augustinian monk and a humanist scholar, and, again like Erasmus, he was no iconoclast, although he was well aware that his teachings sparked iconoclastic frenzy. He was an avid lover of the arts, especially music. He wrote hymns for his new Protestant church services. Many are still sung, especially "A Mighty Fortress Is Our God." Two centuries later, Johann Sebastian Bach used Luther's chorales, embellishing them in his cantatas.

Luther was a professor of philosophy and biblical studies at Wittenberg [VIT-en-burg] University. At Wittenberg Latin was the language of instruction, and the method of teaching was a detailed study of the classics with particular attention to Aristotle's logic. The learning process depended on **disputations,** or debates. Faculty and students attended weekly disputations, which were judged on success according to the rules of logic.

The faculty of Wittenberg University came largely from an Augustinian monastery in the city, where Luther was a monk. Luther specialized in the language and grammar of the Bible. After 1516, he studied in particular the Greek New Testament in the edition of Erasmus. The task of making his own translation into German led him to rethink the question of salvation. Salvation, he now believed,

FIGURE 14.7   Lucas Cranach, *Portrait of Martin Luther*, ca. 1526, oil on panel, 15 × 9″ (38.1 × 22.9 cm), Uffizi Gallery, Florence. SCALA/Art Resource, NY. Cranach was a staunch supporter of Luther, whose criticism of church practices, such as indulgences, began the Protestant Reformation.

was not delivered through achievement but through faith. According to Luther, the gospel repudiates "the wicked idea of the entire kingdom of the pope . . . [with its idea that] a Christian man must be uncertain about the grace of God toward him. If this opinion stands, then Christ is completely useless. . . . Therefore the papacy is a veritable torture chamber of consciousness and the very kingdom of the devil."

Such language would obviously offend Rome, but the incident that drew Luther to the attention of Pope Leo X was the publication, on October 31, 1517, of his "Ninety-Five Theses." The clergy had long accepted payment for indulgences, which supposedly remitted penalties to be suffered in the afterlife (including release from purgatory) and paved the purchaser's way to heaven. Luther was particularly incensed by the conduct of the Dominican monk

TETZEL [TET-sel]. "As soon as the coin into the box rings," Tetzel would remind his audience, "a soul from purgatory to heaven springs." Frederick the Wise had banned Tetzel from Wittenberg, but the city's populace simply went out to meet him in the countryside. When the people informed Luther, who also served as their pastor, that they no longer needed to confess or attend mass because they had purchased lifetime indulgences from the Dominican monk, Luther was outraged, and the "Ninety-Five Theses" soon followed.

Luther's ideas were given greater impact by the advent of printing—Luther considered the printing press a gift from God. In 1500, there were over two hundred printing presses in Europe; soon there were seven in Wittenberg alone, pumping out the writings of the so-called heretic Martin Luther as fast as they could. Over 750,000 copies of Luther's German translation of the Bible were in circulation by the time of his death in 1546.

Luther concluded that every nonessential religious practice needed to be stripped away. For Luther, nonessentials included scholastic philosophy and church ritual, along with its hierarchy, sacraments, organizational structure, and even its prayers and services. Believers could be "justified by faith alone."

Luther crystallized reformist ideas that were simmering in other countries besides Germany, most importantly Switzerland and England. Aside from the sale of indulgences, at issue were three fundamental concerns: (1) the opulence and worldliness of the Roman Church; (2) the idea that faith, not good works, led to a person's salvation;

MAP 14.2 The Reformation in Europe, ca. 1560.

and (3) the tension between religious tradition as embodied in the papacy and Scripture, including both Old and New Testaments, as the supreme authority in matters of faith and morals. Luther and other Protestant reformers sought to simplify the elaborate rituals of the Roman Church by returning to spiritual essentials. In addition, Protestant reformers, especially Luther, believed that in order to achieve salvation one had to believe in God, and that God's mercy alone, not an individual's good acts, determined one's spiritual salvation. Moreover, central to the reformers' ideas was an emphasis on the importance of the individual conscience—one's unmediated, personal relationship with God, rather than a relationship mediated by priests, doctrines, and religious tradition.

Luther was also community minded. No one, he believed, should have to beg in Wittenberg. Every city should take care of its poor. Disappointed by the unwillingness of the populace of Wittenberg to contribute to the community chest (established by him in late 1520 to provide social welfare), Luther scolded his congregation for being "unthankful beasts," and, declaring his unwillingness to be "the shepherd of such pigs," actually quit preaching until the situation was remedied. He argued, "Christ and all saints are one spiritual body, just as the inhabitants of a city are one community and a body, each citizen being a member of the other and of the entire city." Thus Luther laid religious grounds for social democracy and equality, ideas that would, in the next century, lead to social revolution throughout Europe and the Americas.

JOHN CALVIN AND THE *INSTITUTES* OF THE *CHRISTIAN RELIGION*

While Luther was reforming in Germany, another more radical Protestant leader was active in Geneva in Switzerland, JOHN CALVIN [KAL-vin] (1509–64), a French humanist who underwent a religious conversion of great intensity. Calvin's reformist views were not well received in France, and he fled to Switzerland, where he published his *Institutes of the Christian Religion* in Basel and later set up a theocratic state—that is, a state ruled by a religious figure or group—in Geneva.

Calvin's reforms, like Luther's, involved stripping away what he considered external and distracting to true Christian piety. He rejected images of saints and limited the use of music to psalms. Many other activities were prohibited in Calvin's Geneva, including feasting and dancing; wearing rouge, jewelry, and lace, and dressing immodestly; swearing, gambling, and playing cards; reading immoral books and engaging in sexual activity outside of marriage. People caught breaking the rules were warned the first time, fined the second, and severely punished after that. Some were banished, others executed.

Like Luther, Calvin recognized the Bible as the supreme source of knowledge and the only recourse for religious living. His *Institutes* drew out the principles embedded in biblical teaching. They include the following:

1. Human beings are born in total depravity as a result of Adam's fall, whereby they inherit original sin.
2. The will of God is absolute and all-powerful.
3. Faith is superior to good works, since humans lack the capacity to choose to do works that are truly good in God's eyes.
4. Salvation comes through God's freely given grace rather than through any acts of the people.
5. God divinely predestines some to eternal salvation—the Elect—and others to eternal perdition—the Damned; and since no one knows with absolute certainty whether he or she is one of the Elect, all must live as if they were, obeying God's commands.

Calvin identified the Elect by their unambiguous profession of faith, their upright life, and their pious participation in the sacraments, whose number, like Luther, Calvin reduced.

From Geneva Calvinism spread into France, the Netherlands, England, Scotland, and North America, impacting the social, political, and intellectual life of all these countries. The Calvinist attitude can be traced in the rise of the Puritans, in Milton's *Paradise Lost* and the works of seventeenth-century American Puritan writers Edward Taylor and Cotton Mather, and in nineteenth-century works such as Nathaniel Hawthorne's *The Scarlet Letter* and Herman Melville's *Moby-Dick*.

ICONOCLASM

Iconoclasm [eye-KON-o-KLAZ-em] is the systematic destruction of religious icons because of their religious connotations. As anti-Catholic reform movements spread throughout northern Europe in the sixteenth century, an iconoclastic fever spread with them. The widespread destruction of religious images resulted from popular resentment against a church grown worldly and corrupt. The Old Testament prohibition against images that led to idolatry was cited as the justification for this destruction. The art that had flourished under the patronage of Julius II and Leo X became the very symbol of the papacy's corruption. In Zurich, the religious leader ULRICH ZWINGLI [ZWING-glee] even prohibited the use of music in worship. John Calvin wrote, "Therefore it remains that only those things are to be sculpted or painted which the eyes are capable of seeing: let not God's majesty, which is far above the perception of the eyes, be debased through unseemly representations." Such sentiments led church supporters to dismantle the *Ghent Altarpiece* in 1566 and safeguard it in the tower of St. Bavon.

The most virulent iconoclasm occurred in England, beginning when King Henry VIII (fig. 14.8) ordered the destruction of the monasteries in 1535. Henry's motives were as much political as they were religious. When he

Cross Currents

DÜRER DESCRIBES MEXICAN TREASURES

When Hernán Cortés landed in Mexico in 1519, he did so as the representative of King Charles V of Spain, the Hapsburg ruler who actually lived in Vienna. Cortés sent Charles a series of letters recounting his conquests there, and with them a collection of treasures. When these treasures arrived in Brussels, Albrecht Dürer was among the many who came to see them.

Among the collection was the famous Dresden Codex, a folding-screen manuscript made of bark paper dating to as early as the thirteenth century. It recounts agricultural rituals, establishes the Mayan calendar, and, in its drawings of costumes and gods, is by far the most detailed description of Mayan life we have today. Only its having been sent back to Europe saved it from the total destruction of all "pagan" and "idolatrous" manuscripts ordered by Diego de Landa, Charles V's first appointee as bishop of Yucatán.

But Dürer was most impressed by the extraordinary gold- and metalwork sent from the "New World": "I saw the things brought to the King from the New Golden Land," Dürer wrote, "a sun en-tirely of gold, a whole fathom wide; likewise, a moon, made entirely of silver, and just as big; also, a variety of other curiosities from weapons, to armor, and missiles. . . . These things were all so precious that they were valued at a hundred thousand gilders. But I have never seen in all my days anything that caused my heart to rejoice so as these things have. For I saw among them amazing art objects, and I marveled over the subtle ingenuity of the men in distant lands who made them." This Aztec goldwork was, however, soon melted down by Charles for currency, the fate of almost all such metalwork sent to Europe from Mexico.

FIGURE 14.8   Hans Holbein the Younger, *Henry VIII*, ca. 1540, oil on panel, $2'9\frac{1}{2}'' \times 2'5\frac{1}{2}''$ (82.6 × 75 cm), Galleria Nazionale d'Arte Antica, Rome. Scala/Art Resource, NY. The English monarch is shown in wedding dress—an attire he donned six times. As Holbein records, at the age of forty-nine he was already, as he was described in his later years, a "man-mountain."

wanted to divorce Catherine of Aragon and marry Anne Boleyn, from whom he hoped for a male heir, as a Catholic he could not do so. Frustrated after six years of negotiations with Pope Clement VII in Rome, Henry eliminated papal authority in England. Thus the Church of England was born—the Anglican Church—and it granted his divorce. (An heir was born, although Henry was disappointed, since the child was a girl—the future Queen Elizabeth I.)

Henry first attacked the monasteries, the ruins of many of which still stand: Glastonbury, the mythological burial place of King Arthur, and Tintern Abbey, which later inspired a poem by William Wordsworth. When Shakespeare wrote of "these bare ruin'd choirs where late the sweet birds sang," he was referring to such ruins. Thomas Cromwell, Henry's minister, ordered the destruction of the objects of idolatry, particularly "feigned images . . . abused with pilgrimages or offerings." Soon the shrine to St. Thomas à Beckett in Canterbury Cathedral was torn down and his sainthood recanted.

THE AGE OF DISCOVERY

Ever since Marco Polo had returned from China in the thirteenth century, the European view of the globe had undergone continual revision. In the two centuries after 1450, European explorations mapped the details of the world. Fueled by both missionary and economic zeal, European exploration also spawned an encounter with peoples and cultures hitherto unknown.

Renaissance Explorers. In 1488, the Portuguese explorer BARTOLOMEU DIAS [DEE-es] was blown far south off the West African coast by an enormous storm. Heading northeast afterwards, he had rounded what came to be called the Cape of Good Hope, thus suggesting that Africa was surrounded by water. In 1497, the Portuguese explorer VASCO DA GAMA [VAS-koe de GAM-uh] followed Dias's route and reached India ten months and fourteen days after setting out from Lisbon. Meanwhile, Christopher Columbus had made landfall in the Bahamas in 1492, and in 1500 the Portuguese PEDRO CABRAL [ka-BRAHL] pushed west from the bulge of Africa and landed in what is now Brazil. Magellan sailed around the tip of South America, across the Pacific to the Philippines, across the Indian Ocean and around Africa, thus circumnavigating the globe. On September 8, 1522, the eighteen survivors of Ferdinand Magellan's crew arrived back in Cadiz, Spain, three years after setting out.

The age of discovery was an age of doubt. Thus not only geography underwent revision in the sixteenth century. Likewise, the Reformation placed in doubt the authority of institutional orthodoxy. In asserting that authority resided in the individual, Luther echoed a humanist trend. Luther's emphasis on individual conscience, on private judgment, and the individual act of faith was part of the cultural transformation that led to the secularization of society and the rise of scientific investigation.

Nicolas Copernicus. In the spirit of geographical "discovery" the Polish astronomer NICOLAS COPERNICUS [koh-PUR-ni-kus] (1473–1543) published *On the Revolutions of Celestial Bodies* in the year of his death. Building on the work of the ancient Greek geographer and astronomer Ptolemy, whose writings had been rediscovered and translated in 1410, Copernicus argued that earth and the other planets orbit the sun, rather than the sun and planets revolving around earth. But theologians refused to believe the earth was not at the center of the universe, and Copernicus's book was placed on the Index of Prohibited Books in 1616. Even so, Copernicus's work could not be suppressed.

The New Scientists. In England, Francis Bacon (1562–1626) advocated a "scientific method" in which actual observations needed to be made in planned experiments. Hypotheses could be tested and proved; there was no room in science for blind "faith."

In the same year that Copernicus published *On the Revolutions of Celestial Bodies*, ANDREAS VESALIUS [vi-SAY-lee-es] (1514–64) published his *Seven Books on the Structure of the Human Body*, which illustrated the anatomy of the human body based on actual observations. In England, Sir William Harvey discovered capillaries in the human circulation system, solving the mystery of how blood returned to the heart from the arteries. The English mathematician JOHN NAPIER [NAY-pee-er] discovered the logarithm, freeing mathematicians from arduous calculation. In 1542, GEMMA FRISIUS [FREE-zi-yus] discovered new principles for increasing accuracy in surveying and mapmaking, using the technique of triangulation.

PAINTING AND PRINTMAKING

Albrecht Dürer. If any artist in the north can be said to embody the ideals of the Renaissance and the spirit of discovery that defines it, it is ALBRECHT DÜRER [DYOU-ruhr] (1471–1528), painter, printer, draftsman, theoretician, writer, humanist, and publisher. His output was enormous, consisting of more than a hundred paintings and over a thousand drawings and prints.

Dürer was born in Nuremberg; his mother was a German, his father a Hungarian goldsmith. Like his Italian counterpart Leonardo da Vinci, Dürer was fascinated with nature and studied it intensely. Throughout his career, Dürer made various studies of animals, birds, and plants, all sketched or painted from life.

Dürer produced a number of self-portraits. In that of 1500 (fig. 14.9), he admires himself in a most self congratulatory way. "Art," he wrote, "derives from God; it is God who has created all art; it is not easy to paint artistically. Therefore, those without aptitude should not attempt it, for it is an inspiration from above." Dürer believed he was endowed with a God-given gift, a humanistic and individualistic view that he shared with Michelangelo and other Renaissance artists.

Despite his genius at painting, Dürer's fame derives from his prints. In **woodcuts** and **engravings,** through the precision and detail of his work as well as the richness and variety of his effects, Dürer was able to achieve monumentality on the scale of a sheet of paper. Among the many series of prints that Dürer produced is the *Apocalypse,* published in 1498, consisting of fifteen woodcuts with the

Table 14-1	RELIGIOUS REFORMERS IN WESTERN EUROPE	
Reformer	Country	Significance
Desiderius Erasmus (1466–1533)	The Netherlands	*The Praise of Folly*
Martin Luther (1483–1546)	Germany	The 95 Theses
Ulrich Zwingli (1484–1531)	Switzerland (Zurich)	Iconoclasm
John Calvin (1509–64)	Switzerland (Geneva)	Predestination
King Henry VIII (1491–1547)	England	Destruction of monasteries

FIGURE 14.9   Albrecht Dürer, *Self-Portrait*, 1500, oil on panel, $26\frac{1}{4} \times 19\frac{1}{4}''$ (66.3 × 49 cm), Alte Pinakothek, Munich. Dürer, carrying the Renaissance interest in the self further than most, completed several self-portraits throughout his life. Here, hardly subtle, Dürer depicts himself in Christlike mode.

FIGURE 14.10   Albrecht Dürer, *Four Horsemen of the Apocalypse*, 1497–98, woodcut, $15\frac{1}{2} \times 11\frac{1}{8}''$ (39.4 × 28.3 cm), gift of Junius S. Morgan, 1919. Metropolitan Museum of Art, New York. Dürer's genius elevated graphic art (printmaking) to a fine art. When making a woodcut, the artist draws a reverse image on a block of wood, then cuts away the wood from the drawing. The remaining raised areas of the wooden block are inked, the paper is pressed onto the block, and an image of the raised area is made.

text printed on the reverse. Reissued several times, this series did much to spread his fame. From the *Apocalypse* series comes the gruesome *Four Horsemen of the Apocalypse* (fig. 14.10). Death, War, Pestilence, and Famine are riding rampant over the burghers, artisans, merchants, and other citizens of Nuremberg. In a woodcut, the negative, or white, areas of the final print are cut into the block while the black areas are uncut, and remain raised in relief. Ink is rolled over the surface, paper is placed on the inked surface, and the image transferred to the paper by applying pressure to the back of the paper.

Adam and Eve (fig. 14.11) is an engraving, signed and dated on the plaque on the tree branch, "Albrecht Dürer of Nuremberg made this in 1504." An engraving is printed from a design inscribed in the surface of a metal plate. Using a sharp **burin,** or steel gouging tool, the design is cut into the surface of a metal plate. Ink is rubbed into these recesses and the surface of the plate is wiped clean. Damp paper is then placed on the inked plate. The pressure of a printing press is required to force the paper into the recesses to pick up the ink. For both engravings and wood-

cuts, the image that is printed is a mirror reversal of the original.

After visiting Italy, Dürer became increasingly interested in the human figure, and his depictions of Adam and Eve essentially an excuse to study the male and female nude. Dürer used mathematical proportions and drew from Italian works and interpretations of antiquity. His Adam resembles the Hellenistic Greek *Apollo Belvedere*, which had been recently discovered, and his Eve recalls the classical *Venus de Milo*.

Dürer included symbols of the four humors, a notion derived from classical philosophy, in the background of *Adam and Eve:* The cat is choleric (angry); the rabbit sanguine (confident); the elk melancholic (depressed); and the ox phlegmatic (impassive).

In 1515, Dürer was made court painter to Emperor Maximilian I. Now among the rich and famous, Dürer had a shop of people working for him. In later years he worked

FIGURE 14.11   Albrecht Dürer, *Adam and Eve*, 1504, engraving, $9\frac{1}{8} \times 7\frac{5}{8}''$ (25.1 × 19.4 cm), Philadelphia Museum of Art, Philadelphia. In an engraving, the recessed areas are printed. The artist cuts the lines into a metal plate, the recessed lines take the ink, paper is applied to the inked plate, and the ink is transferred to the paper by the pressure of a printing press.

FIGURE 14.12   Hans Holbein the Younger, *Erasmus of Rotterdam*, ca. 1523, oil on panel, $16\frac{1}{2} \times 12\frac{1}{2}''$ (42 × 31.4 cm), Musée du Louvre, Paris. Reunion des Musées Nationaux/Art Resource, NY. Holbein's portrait of the Dutch humanist Erasmus, shown as he records his ideas, conveys his intellectual authority.

more and more on theories of measurement and proportion. Like Leonardo da Vinci, Dürer relied on Vitruvius's scheme of human proportions, and in 1525 he published *The Teaching of Measurements with Rule and Compass (Manual of Measurements)* and later *Four Books on Human Proportions.* Concerned with practical application, Dürer designed devices to aid the artist in doing perspective drawings. In all, his interests in antiquity, the natural world, anatomy, and perspective were analogous to those of his Italian contemporaries.

Although Dürer did paint and print religious subjects, most were executed early in his career. In 1519, Dürer became a follower of Martin Luther. As the Reformation gained momentum, painters in the north turned more and more to secular subjects.

Hans Holbein the Younger. The art of HANS HOLBEIN THE YOUNGER [HOLE-bine] (1497/98–1543) reflects this increasing secularity. Holbein's fame grew from his portraiture, and he painted many important people. Born in Augsburg into a family of artists, he worked in the shop of his father, Hans Holbein the Elder, and he studied in Basel, Switzerland, where in 1519 he set up

shop. Around 1523, Holbein painted *Erasmus of Rotterdam* (fig. 14.12), a portrait of the famous Dutch humanist who had settled in Basel in 1521. Holbein revered Erasmus, became his close friend, and portrayed him several times.

Erasmus provided Holbein with letters of introduction to the English court, where he was to become famous. In 1536, Holbein became court painter to Henry VIII, producing portraits of the king and his family (see fig. 14.8). As Henry's court painter, Holbein painted portraits of his prospective brides. Holbein's working method was to begin with a chalk sketch, the face drawn in careful detail, the body and costume loosely indicated. Later, the portrait was painted in his studio. The sitter could send to Holbein's studio any garment she or he wished to be shown wearing; no one was expected to pose while waiting for Holbein to craft every puff and pleat. These portraits display exquisite line and sensitive modeling. Holbein varied the format of his portraits, but he always made the sitter look dignified.

Caterina van Hemessen. Caterina Van Hemessen (1527/8 – ca. 1566), one of the most important women painters of the Renaissance in northern Europe, also

FIGURE 14.13   Caterina van Hemessen, *Portrait of a Lady*, 1551, oil on oak, 9 × 7″ (23 × 18 cm), National Gallery, London. Tiny in size, this portrait is an example of the sixteenth-century vogue for miniature portraits. Van Hemessen's sitters, seemingly avoiding eye contact with the viewer, maintain their quiet composure.

specialized in portraiture, as many women artists did. Her father was the Flemish Mannerist painter Jan Sanders van Hemessen of Antwerp. The example seen in fig. 14.13 is typical of her work in its small-scale depiction of a single figure standing against a dark monochromatic background. This reserved simplicity accorded with the taste of the time and brought her great success, for she was patronized by Queen Mary of Hungary, then ruling the Low Countries for her brother, Charles I of Spain. In 1556, when Mary returned to Spain, her invitation to van Hemessen and her husband to join her there was accepted. When Mary died, she left van Hemessen and her husband ample funds to allow them to return to Antwerp and live comfortably.

Pieter Bruegel the Elder.   In contrast to Holbein's and van Hemessen's work at court, PIETER BRUEGEL THE ELDER [BROY-gul] (ca. 1525–1569) portrayed the peasantry and the countryside. Little is known about his life. When he was born remains uncertain; where, perhaps in Flanders. He visited Rome to study humanism, classicism,

and the new trends, but the trip seems to have had little impact on his art. In 1563, he married his teacher's daughter and moved from Antwerp to Brussels, where he was to remain. His two sons became painters.

Bruegel earned considerable income by imitating the paintings of Hieronymus Bosch, which were extremely popular by the middle of the sixteenth century. But his best paintings depict the daily life of ordinary people, known as **genre painting.** Typical of his paintings is the *Harvesters* (fig. 14.14) of 1565. Bruegel was commissioned to paint a series of scenes of the months of the year with, presumably, one painting representing every two months; the *Harvesters* represents August and September. Bruegel gave the landscape prominence; nature no longer served merely as a setting for a portrait or religious event. The Limbourg brothers (see Chapter 12) had completed a series on the months of the year in their book of hours in 1416; what is new in Bruegel's paintings is the way in which the landscape is shown. The figures, rather than being placed in front of a landscape background, are now integrated into the setting. The colors convey the feeling of a warm summer afternoon—rich yellows and tans in the foreground, cool greens in the background.

Bruegel's *Peasant Wedding* (fig. 14.15), of ca. 1566–67, records the commotion of a rustic wedding. The smiling bride sits before a dark hanging cloth, hands clasped. Two men carrying bowls of rice pudding on wooden planks create the foreground. The bagpiper looks at this dessert, which, because rice was not a local product, was considered a delicacy. The composition of the *Peasant Wedding* is carefully constructed to appear informal and draw the viewer into the event. The foreground is brought close to the viewer by the figures in the lower left, including a child licking his fingers. The arrangement in space is diagonal; the diagonal line of the planks on which the dessert is served continues to recede down the table all the way to the back of the hall. Bruegel uses areas of flat color and simplified forms to create a decorative, patterned quality. His strong, stocky figures convey the robustness and earthy liveliness of this celebration.

ARCHITECTURE

As the merchant class rose in importance, secular patronage of the arts grew, along with interest in personal luxury and the display of wealth as a means of expressing power and prestige. Castles were obvious examples of the owner's importance. The most splendid of these were the **châteaux** (castles) of France. A concentration of Renaissance castles is found in the Loire [LWAR] valley, which was an especially agreeable area because of its fine climate and abundant game.

Château of Chambord.   Perhaps the most extraordinary of the French Renaissance châteaux is that of Chambord

FIGURE 14.14 Pieter Bruegel the Elder, *Harvesters*, 1565, oil on panel, $3'10\frac{1}{2}'' \times 5'3\frac{1}{4}''$ (1.18 × 1.61 m), Rogers Fund, 1919. Metropolitan Museum of Art, New York. A genuine interest in landscape as a subject, rather than as mere background, first appears in Bruegel's series of paintings depicting the months and their corresponding labors.

[sham-BORE] (fig. 14.16), begun in 1519 for the king, Francis I. The original architect is believed to have been an Italian, DOMENICO DA CORTONA [dah kor-TOE-nuh] (d. 1549). The largest of all Renaissance châteaux, Chambord has 440 rooms, 365 chimneys (one for every day of the year), fourteen big staircases, and seventy smaller staircases. The plan of Chambord is that of a medieval castle with a central keep, four corner towers, a surrounding wall, and, originally, a moat. Yet Chambord was built not for defense but for display.

The château at Chambord has two extraordinary features, one outside, the other inside. Outside, on the flat roof, is a tiny town with winding streets, squares, and turrets. To walk on the roof is to wander in an intricate fairyland in the sky. Inside, the main attraction is the central double-spiral staircase. Built within a circle 30 feet in diameter and 80 feet to the roof, the two spiral staircases intertwine, but do not meet—two people on opposite

staircases can see each other across the central well, but they cannot touch.

Hardwick Hall. England's castles with massive fortifications and small windows gradually gave way to airy homes with huge glass windows. These were built for the newly enfranchised nobility created by Henry VIII, when he granted church lands to his supporters. Hardwick Hall (fig. 14.17), built 1591–96 and probably the work of the leading English architect ROBERT SMYTHSON [SMITH-son] (ca. 1535–1614), is one example. It was built for the able and determined Elizabeth of Shrewsbury, also known as Bess of Hardwick, who amassed a fortune from her four marriages and as a businesswoman in her own right.

The plan of Hardwick Hall is symmetrical and compact, built with a central great hall and square corner towers. The layout is innovatively arranged to separate rooms for public functions from those for private activities. The

FIGURE 14.15   Pieter Bruegel the Elder, *Peasant Wedding*, ca. 1566–67, oil on panel, $3'8\frac{1}{8}'' \times 5'4'$ (1.10 × 1.60 m), Kunsthistorisches Museum, Vienna. Unlike his contemporaries, Bruegel was concerned not so much with the individual as with the type and, in particular, with the peasant class.

FIGURE 14.16   Domenico da Cortona (?), Château of Chambord, Loire Valley, begun in 1519, north facade. It is possible to ascend the monumental double-spiral staircase to the roof—where a little town has been constructed atop this extraordinary French castle.

FIGURE 14.17 Robert Smythson (?), Hardwick Hall, Derbyshire, 1591–96, facade. The importance of large windows as a sign of wealth is made clear by the comment, "Hardwick Hall, more glass than wall," to describe this English castle.

floors are divided according to function and the more ceremonial the use of a room, the higher it is located in the house. Thus the great hall and the areas used by servants are on the ground floor; the private family apartments on the next floor; and the state rooms at the top of the house. Hardwick Hall includes an invention of the English Renaissance, a **long gallery**—an unusually long room in which to take exercise during bad weather.

Hardwick Hall's massiveness and symmetry are characteristic of Elizabethan architecture. Hardwick Hall was noted in particular for the great size of its windows, made memorable by the line coined at the time, "Hardwick Hall, more glass than wall." Note, too, that the size of the windows increases as the floors ascend, corresponding to the luxury and prestige of the functions of the rooms within.

SECULAR MUSIC

During the Renaissance, **secular music** (music not associated with religious meanings or ceremonies) became increasingly popular. Giorgione and Titian's *Fête champêtre* (see fig. 13.36) documents this popularity in its depiction of people playing instruments. Unlike sacred vocal music, which typically set Latin or Greek texts to music, secular vocal music was composed for lyrics in the vernacular, the spoken language. Although secular vocal compositions were written in Italian, French, Spanish, German, Dutch, and English, there were two main schools of madrigal writing—English in the north and Italian in the south.

The **madrigal** is a vocal composition for a small group of singers, usually with no accompaniment. Like sacred motets (religious texts set to a polyphonic composition), madrigals were composed in polyphonic style, with multiple voice parts. (For an explanation of polyphony, see Chapter 13.) Unlike motets, however, which were performed by a small choir singing the same text in polyphony, madrigals were performed by a few singers, each of whom sang a different vocal part. The madrigal particularly appealed to an educated audience and was a popular court entertainment.

Typically settings of short lyric poems, madrigals were often about love and frivolity. The madrigalist's challenge was to set the poem to music perfectly. Madrigalists often tried to outdo each other, and their language and musical settings were often witty. They were especially inventive in setting words associated with weeping, sighing, trembling, and dying.

Thomas Weelkes. A composer best known for his madrigals, THOMAS WEELKES [WILKS] (1575–1623) was the organist at Chichester Cathedral. His madrigal "As Vesta Was Descending" was included in an early-seventeenth-century collection of madrigals, *The Triumph of Oriana*, to honor Queen Elizabeth I (fig. 14.18). Written for six voices—two sopranos, alto, two tenors, and bass—Weelkes's madrigal was a setting of the following poem:

> As Vesta was from Latmos hill descending,
> She spied a maiden Queen the same ascending,
> Attended only by all the shepherds swain,
> To whom Diana's darlings came running down amain:
> First two by two, then three by three together,
> Leaving their goddess all alone, hasted thither,
> And mingling with the shepherds of her train,
> With mirthful tunes her presence entertain.
> Then sang the shepherds and nymphs of Diana,
> Long live fair Oriana.

Weelkes takes advantage of the poem's opportunities for word painting. On the words "descending" and "ascending," for example, he uses descending and ascending musical lines, respectively. He also expresses the description of the attendants running "two by two, then three by three together, / Leaving their goddess all alone," by having first

FIGURE 14.18   Levina Bening Teerling, *Elizabeth I as a Princess*, ca. 1559, oil on oak panel, $42\frac{3}{4}'' \times 32\frac{1}{4}''$ (108.5 × 81.8 cm), The Royal Collection © 2004 Her Majesty Queen Elizabeth II, Windsor Castle, Windsor. Royal Collection Enterprises Ltd. The books are indicative of Elizabeth's love of learning and support of the arts.

two singers then three, and finally all six join in before dropping back to a solo singer. Weelkes also uses fast notes for the words "running down amain," and he writes lively and upbeat music for the line "With mirthful tunes her presence entertain." Finally, for the word "long" in the last line, Weelkes provides singers with their longest held note. (For a further explanation of word painting, see Chapter 13.)

Thomas Morley.   Another well-known composer of madrigals was Thomas Morley (1557–1603). Morley favored **homophonic texture,** in which a single melody, not several, is employed with harmonic support. He also uses the same music for each stanza of the poem below, with the nonsense syllables *fa-la* sung as a refrain. The playfulness of the music complements the playfulness of the words, which, as with much Elizabethan poetry, reveal a true love of the language.

Morley's madrigal, "Now Is the Month of Maying," scored for five voices, describes the flirting and courtship games common in the countryside. Morley's melody has the rhythm and tunefulness of a folk dance. It is structured in two parts, each of which is repeated and each of which concludes with the *fa-la* refrain. Here is the text:

> Now is the month of maying,
> When merry lads are playing, fa la,
> Each with his bonny lass
> Upon the greeny grass. Fa la.
> The spring, clad all in gladness,
> Doth laugh at winter's sadness, fa la,
> And to the bagpipe's sound
> The nymphs tread out their ground. Fa la.
> Fie then! why sit we musing,
> Youth's sweet delight refusing? Fa la,
> Say, dainty nymphs, and speak,
> Shall we play barley break? Fa la.

The lyrics to both Weelkes's and Morley's madrigals depict delicate nymphs and good-natured shepherds, lighthearted diversions that appealed to the privileged classes.

LITERATURE

Michel de Montaigne.   The fame of MICHEL DE MONTAIGNE [mahn-TAYN] (1533–92) rests on his *Essays*, which exemplify Renaissance individualism grounded in a humanism derived from Greco Roman antiquity. Montaigne's *Essays*, however, are distinguished less by depth of knowledge of the past than by a profound knowledge of the self.

Montaigne was born in Bordeaux, southern France. Montaigne studied law, spent time at court, and became a member of the Bordeaux parliament, serving as an arbitrator between the warring Protestant and Catholic royal factions. At thirty-eight, Montaigne retired to his castle, where he had a library, and devoted himself to reflection and writing. (At forty-eight, he came out of retirement to serve two terms as mayor of Bordeaux in 1581–85.)

Montaigne's early essays (in French, *essais*) contain numerous quotations from antiquity. In his second book of essays, however, he relied less on the authority of the past and more on expressing views in his own voice. In his third and last book of essays, Montaigne used quotations sparingly, presenting an original self-portrait.

Montaigne said that he wrote about himself because he knew himself better than he knew anything else. In "Of Experience," he wrote that "no man ever treated of a subject that he knew and understood better than I do this . . . and in this I am the most learned man alive." Montaigne notes, however, that he exists in a state of flux. "I must adapt my history to the moment," he wrote, for "I may presently change, not only by chance, but also by intention." And thus his essays are "a record of diverse and changeable events, of undecided, and . . . contradictory ideas."

Montaigne asks questions in his essays, without providing answers. "Perhaps" and "I think" are among his most frequently used expressions, and *"Que sais-je?"* ("What do I know?") is his most recurring question. The very name for the genre he created, *essai*, means trial or attempt, suggesting a process rather than a product, openness rather than conclusiveness, a journey and not a destination. As much as his essays reveal him, they also reveal readers to themselves. Montaigne's search for questions rather than answers, coupled with his affirmation of the individual, makes his work a landmark of Renaissance humanism. The modern novelist Virginia Woolf put it this way: "This talking of oneself, following one's own vagaries, giving the whole map, weight, colour, and circumference of the soul in its confusion, its variety, its imperfection—this art belonged to one man only: to Montaigne."

William Shakespeare.

WILLIAM SHAKESPEARE [SHAYK-speer] (1564–1616) is the greatest writer in the English language, a reputation that rests on thirty-seven plays and 154 sonnets exploring complex states of mind and feeling in exuberant language rich with metaphor. His command is particularly evident in his **soliloquies**, meditative reflections spoken aloud. From *Hamlet* (fig. 14.19) alone, we glean the following sayings:

> In my mind's eye;
> I must be cruel only to be kind;
> Brevity is the soul of wit;
> To be or not to be, that is the question;
> Neither a borrower nor a lender be;
> Something's rotten in the state of Denmark;
> What a piece of work is a man.

Shakespeare was born in Stratford-upon-Avon in April 1564. He attended the local school, but did not go on to Oxford or Cambridge. Instead, in 1582, at the age of eighteen, he married Anne Hathaway, who bore him three children in as many years. At that time Shakespeare began writing and acting in plays. Although many tributes have been paid to Shakespeare, one stands above the rest: his

FIGURE 14.19   Title page, *Hamlet* (1603), The Huntington Library, California. This is the title page of the first quarto edition of the play that was printed.

contemporary Ben Jonson's judgment that "he is not for an age, but for all time."

Shakespeare's sonnets have drama as well as melodic lyricism. Their range is wide, including melancholy, despair, hope, shame, guilt, fear, jealousy, and exhilaration. Written during the 1590s, they were not published until 1609—(though two were printed in a 1599 collection, *The Passionate Pilgrim*, without Shakespeare's authorization). Like John Donne's poems, Shakespeare's sonnets circulated in manuscript before publication and were much admired.

Shakespeare's soliloquies further reveal the human spirit. In a soliloquy, Macbeth uses obsessive, bitter language to lament his ruined scheme. The following from Act V, Scene i occurs when Macbeth discovers that though he is now king, his wife is dead:

Connections

SHAKESPEARE AND MUSIC

Shakespeare employs music in his plays for various purposes. He uses music to suggest a change in locale and time, indicating that the action of a play has shifted scene. Music signals the entrance or exit of an important character; trumpet flourishes announce the arrival or departure of royalty. Trumpets also sound a battle charge.

Music and Character Revelation

Perhaps the most important function of music in Shakespeare's plays is to reveal character. Shakespeare's characters disclose their states of mind through the songs they sing. In *Hamlet*, the young Ophelia reveals her unstable mental state through singing about love, loss, and death. In *Othello*, Desdemona, Othello's wife, conveys an ominous foreboding about her imminent death in the "Willow Song."

Musical Imagery

Shakespeare's plays are also rife with musical images. Some of these are simple passing references, such as those in *Romeo and Juliet*. When Romeo and Juliet part, Juliet cries out in disappointment, "the lark sings so out of tune, / Straining harsh discords and unpleasing sharps." Often, however, Shakespeare developed elaborate patterns of musical imagery. A striking example occurs when Hamlet speaks to his boyhood friends Rosencrantz and Guildenstern, who are about to betray him. In complaining about their deceit, Hamlet likens himself to a recorder, or flute, playing in the background, and also to a plucked and fretted instrument:

> HAMLET   Why, look you now, how unworthy a thing you make of me! You would play upon me, you would seem to know my stops, you would pluck out the heart of my mystery, you would sound me from my lowest note to the top of my compass; and there is much music, excellent voice, in this little organ, yet cannot you make it speak. 'Sblood, do you think I am easier to be played on than a pipe? Call me what instrument you will, though you can fret me, you cannot play upon me.
>
> *Act III, Scene ii, ll. 349–57*

In this elaborated metaphor, everything Hamlet says proves to be literally true.

Composers and Instruments

Instruments used for Shakespearean music include brass, woodwind, strings, and percussion (fig. 14.20). Trumpets were the most frequently used brass instrument; wooden flutes and recorders of various sizes were the most common woodwind instruments. Stringed instruments included the violin, harp, lyre, and lute, among others. Percussion was almost always supplied by a tabor or drum, which often was accompanied by a fife, the smallest of the flutes.

Shakespeare did not compose the music that accompanied his plays. In Shakespeare's lifetime, his contemporaries, such as Thomas Morley, set his words to music, including "O Mistress Mine" from *Twelfth Night*, which Morley may have written at Shakespeare's request. Other music used to accompany songs included traditional arrangements that antedated the plays, as with the "Willow Song," sung by Desdemona in *Othello*, and the gravedigger's song "In Youth When I Did Love" from *Hamlet*.

FIGURE 14.20   Anonymous, *Le Concert champêtre: la musique* (*The Country Concert*), Italian School, sixteenth century. Musée de l'Hotel l'Allemant, Bourges. Giraudon/Art Resource, New York. Here is a depiction of a typical chamber music ensemble, consisting of a harpsichord, lute, recorder, and bass viol.

Critical Thinking

WHO WROTE "SHAKESPEARE'S PLAYS"?

Among issues in literary studies that have reappeared over the centuries is that of whether William Shakespeare is the actual author of plays such as *Hamlet*, *Julius Caesar*, and *Romeo and Juliet*. Those arguing against Shakespeare's authorship claim that he was not sufficiently well educated to have written such masterpieces, with their wide range of knowledge and their brilliant language. These critics of Shakespearean authorship offer alternative authors, including, among others, Sir Francis Bacon and Edward De Vere, the Seventh Earl of Oxford, and the Renaissance playwright Christopher Marlowe, all of whom were extremely well educated and themselves very good writers.

Defenders of Shakespeare claim that the preponderance of evidence is in favor of his authorship of the plays. These defenders offer as evidence that Shakespeare's name is on the first printed editions and that he was an actor and part owner of an acting company that needed new material, which he wrote as a normal part of his theatrical work. They refer to contemporary paintings of Shakespeare and to his extensive knowledge of Italy, classics, and the law, which runs throughout his plays.

How would you go about deciding whether Shakespeare wrote the plays attributed to him? What questions would you have in pursuing your investigation of the matter? What kinds of evidence would you look for? What types of sources would you consult, and what kinds of credentials for the writers of those sources would you find credible?

Tomorrow, and tomorrow, and tomorrow
Creeps in this petty pace from day to day,   *20*
To the last syllable of recorded time;
And all our yesterdays have lighted fools
The way to dusty death. Out, Out, brief candle!
Life's but a walking shadow, a poor player
That struts and frets his hour upon the stage   *25*
And then is heard no more. It is a tale
Told by an idiot, full of sound and fury
Signifying nothing.

Written in **blank verse**—verse in unrhymed **iambic pentameter** (each line has ten syllables with alternating stresses)—the soliloquy portrays Macbeth's despair over the apparent meaninglessness of life.

Shakespeare's plays capture the imagination. The political astuteness in *Julius Caesar* and *Antony and Cleopatra* is complemented by the playful comedy in *As You Like It* and *Much Ado About Nothing*, and the tempered romance of Shakespeare's final plays, of which *The Tempest* is the glorious example.

The drama of the Elizabethan Age (1558–1603) shares features with Greek drama. The Elizabethan dramatists wrote domestic tragedies, tragedies of character, and revenge tragedies, of which *Hamlet* is the great example. The Elizabethan dramatists also wrote comedies of manners and comedies of humors, which extended the range of earlier romantic and satiric comedies. In both Greek and Elizabethan theater, props were few, scenery was simple, and the dialogue alone indicated changes of locale and time.

An Elizabethan playhouse such as the Globe (fig. 14.21), where Shakespeare's plays were staged, had a much smaller seating capacity than the large Greek amphitheaters, which could seat thousands. The Globe could accommodate about 2,300 people, including roughly eight hundred groundlings who, exposed to the weather, stood around the stage. The stage itself projected from an inside wall into their midst. More prosperous spectators sat in one of the three stories that encircled the stage. The reduced size of the Elizabethan theater and the projection of its stage made for a greater intimacy between actors and audience. Although actors still had to project their voices and exaggerate their gestures, they could be heard and seen without the aid of the megaphonic masks and elevated shoes of the ancient Greek theater. Elizabethan actors could modulate their voices to vary pitch, stress, and intonation in ways unsuited to the Greek stage. They could also make wider and more subtle use of facial expression and gesture.

In addition to greater intimacy, the Elizabethan stage also offered more versatility than its Greek counterpart. Although the Greek *skene* building could be used for scenes occurring above the ground, such as a god descending from above by means of a crane (**deus ex machina**), the Greek stage was really a single-level acting area. Not so the Elizabethan stage, which contained a second-level balcony, utilized in *Othello* and in *Romeo and Juliet*, for instance. Shakespeare's stage also had doors at the back for entrances and exits, a curtained alcove useful for scenes of intrigue, and a stage-floor trapdoor, used for the ghost's entrance in *Hamlet*.

These and other of Shakespeare's plays were given varied readings. *Julius Caesar* and other Roman plays, such as *Coriolanus*, were given classical settings to highlight Renaissance interest in the classical world. *Romeo and Juliet*, in contrast, was set in the Italian Renaissance, and *Hamlet* was set in the north, in Denmark.

Cultural Impact

The Reformation of the Roman Church, which emerged from the Renaissance emphasis on individualism, had profound effects on western European society. With the decline of the authority of the Catholic Church, Europeans began to follow alternative religious beliefs and practices. Soon after Luther, Calvin, Zwingli, and Henry VIII had splintered the Catholic Church, their own churches fragmented and factionalized. In the ensuing centuries, numerous religious denominations were established, and hundreds of Protestant churches emerged.

A more general consequence of the Protestant Reformation was an emphasis on wealth. Personal wealth commanded respect as a mark of social status and a sign of divine favor. The virtues of discipline and effort necessary to achieving worldly success were Protestant values and fed directly into the emergence of capitalism.

The invention of movable type led to mass printing of reformist theological tracts. Gutenberg's press changed the way information was packaged, processed, and disseminated. Among the world's major revolutions, mechanized printing had an effect that lasted to the end of the millennium; only now in the twenty-first century, is the new age of electronic technology vying to displace print as the prime medium of communication.

The power of the individual genius creating works of enduring influence also finds expression in the north, more powerfully perhaps, in the work of its writers than in that of its painters, sculptors, and architects, who led the Renaissance in Italy. Who better than Montaigne and Shakespeare to epitomize the heights of achievement during the Elizabethan age, as they invented genres such as the personal essay and perfected those of the sonnet and the revenge tragedy? Moreover, Shakespeare set the standard for poetic excellence and dramatic accomplishment, his 37 plays having been translated into many of the world's languages and continue to be studied and dramatized today.

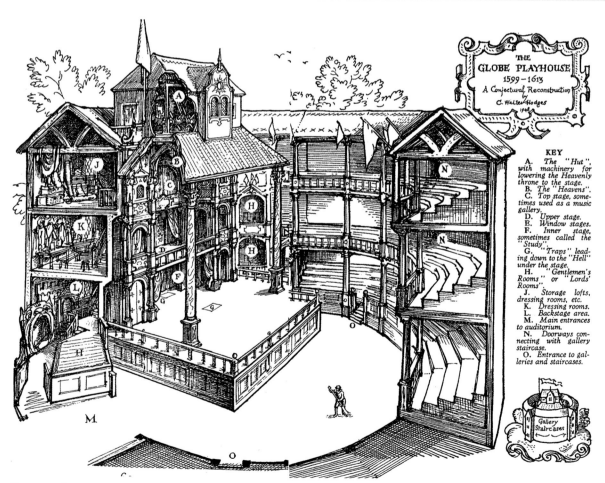

KEY

A. The "Hut", with machinery for lowering the Heavenly throne to the stage.
B. The "Heavens".
C. Top stage, sometimes used as a music gallery.
D. Upper stage.
E. Window stages.
F. Inner stage, sometimes called the "Study".
G. "Traps" leading down to the "Hell" under the stage.
H. "Gentlemen's Rooms" or "Lords' Rooms".
J. Storage lofts, dressing rooms, etc.
K. Dressing rooms.
L. Backstage area.
M. Main entrances to auditorium.
N. Doorways connecting with gallery staircase.
O. Entrance to galleries and staircases.

FIGURE 14.21   Shakespeare's Globe Playhouse, London, 1599–1613. C. Walter Hodges, *Shakespeare and the Players*, London, 1948. This imaginative reconstruction by C. Walter Hodges depicts the open-air theater where *Hamlet* and other plays by Shakespeare were first performed.

KEY TERMS

egg tempera
triptych
polyptych
disguised symbolism
alla prima
Reformation

disputation
iconoclasm
woodcut
engraving
burin
genre painting

châteaux
long gallery
secular music
madrigal
homophonic texture
soliloquy

blank verse
iambic pentameter
deus ex machina

WWW. WEBSITES FOR FURTHER STUDY

http://www.metmuseum.org/works_of_art/collection.asp
(Campin's The Annunciation Triptych exhibits the stylistic tendencies of the early Netherlands style.)

http://artchive.com/artchive/V/van_eyck.html
(This is the Artchive, a Website with virtually every major artist in every style from every era in art history. It is an excellent resource.)

http://mexplaza.udg.mx/wm/paint/auth/bosch/delight/
(The Webmuseum of Paris displays and discusses Bosch's most famous and unconventional picture, The Garden of Earthly Delights.)

http://www.iep.utm.edu/h/humanism.htm#Erasmus
(The Internet Encyclopedia of Philosophy is an excellent source for all the major philosophers.)

http://www.txdirect.net/users/rrichard/science.htm
(This is the Internet Chronology of Scientific Developments, listing all the important scientists from the sixteenth through the twentieth century.)

READINGS

DESIDERIUS ERASMUS

from *The Praise of Folly*

Erasmus's The Praise of Folly *(1509) is the most important satirical work of the Renaissance. Erasmus casts a wide net, catching all manner of vanities, arrogance, selfishness, pomposity, and other human failings. He criticizes clerics, scholars, teachers, theologians, and scientists. In the following passage, Erasmus, speaking in the voice of Folly, zeroes in on the clerics, then moves on to princes and courtiers, using sharply piercing wit.*

Next to them in bliss come those who are popularly called "men of religion" and "monks." Both names are completely false since most of them avoid religion as much as they can, and wherever you go you can't help running into these men who've "withdrawn" from the world. I simply can't imagine what would be more wretched than their condition, unless I helped them out in all sorts of ways. For everyone loathes them so much that simply for one of them to show his face is considered bad luck; yet they flatter themselves gloriously. First, they think it a main point of piety to be ignorant of good letters, preferably not to be able to read at all. Then when like donkeys in church they bray out their psalms (memorized indeed, but not understood) they can imagine they are ravishing the ears of the saints with infinite delight. A good many of them make an excellent living out of their beggars' rags, bellowing for bread from door to door, and shoving into inns, carriages, and boats to the great prejudice of other beggars. And thus these delightful fellows represent themselves to us as apostles—by virtue of their filth, stupidity, grossness, and impudence, forsooth!

What can be funnier than their habit of doing everything by the book, as if following mathematical rules that it would be a sin to break? So many knots are required in the shoelace, a cloak can have only so many colors and must be of a certain material, the girdle must also be of a certain material and so many straws wide, the cowl can be cut only one way and capable of holding only so many pecks, the hair must be trimmed to the length of so many fingers, sleep is permitted for only so many hours. This rigid equality, imposed on people so very different in body and mind, is most unequal in its effects, as who can help seeing? And yet by these tricks they succeed in feeling superior not only to ordinary laymen but to one another—so that these men dedicated to apostolic charity will make frightful scenes over a habit worn with the wrong girdle or a bit too dark in color. Some you can find so severely religious that they use only rough Cilician cloth for their outer robe, though the undergarment is of fine Milesian wool; a variation of this trick is to wear linen on the outside, wool inside. Still others reject mere contact with money as if it were a most contagious poison, though they are less scrupulous about wine-bibbing or intimate relations with women.

Finally, they all try as hard as possible not to agree with each other in their way of life; they are far less interested in resembling Christ than in differing among themselves. Thus they take special delight in their various names, some calling themselves "Cordeliers" but then subdividing their order into "Coletans," "Friars Minor," "Minims," and "Bullists." Again we have the "Benedictines" and the "Bernardines," the "Brigetines" and the "Augustinians," the "Williamites" and the "Jacobites"—as if it was their last concern to be known as Christians.

The greater number of them insist so vehemently on their own ceremonies and petty traditions that they think a single heaven will hardly be adequate reward for such outstanding merit—never imagining that Christ, despising all these observances, will judge by his own standard, which is that of charity. One monk will point to his paunch, distended by eating every conceivable variety of fish; another will pour forth psalms by the bushel. Another will number up his myriads of fasts, and account for his bursting belly by the fact that he eats only one meal at midday. Another points to his huge pile of ceremonies performed, so many they couldn't be laden on seven naval transports. Another brags that for sixty years he has never touched money except with fingers protected by two pairs of gloves. Still another wears a cowl so dirty and slimy that no sailor would let it touch his body. Another boasts that for more than half a century he has led the life of a sponge, always fixed to the same spot; his neighbor claims credit for a voice hoarsened by constant singing; another for a lethargy contracted during years of solitude; and still another for a tongue atrophied during years of silence. But Christ, interrupting their boasts (which otherwise would never end), will ask, "Where did this new race of Jews come from? I recognize no law but my own, and about it I hear nothing whatever. Long ago, speaking openly and using no intricate parables, I promised that my father's kingdom would be granted, not to cowls, prayers, or fasts, but to works of faith and charity. Nor do I recognize those who make too much of their own merits and want to seem more sanctified than me; let them go live in the heavens of Abraxa or, if they want, get a new heaven built for them outside mine by the men whose foolish traditions they have preferred before my commandments." When they hear these words, and see sailors and coachmen preferred before them, with what expressions do you suppose they will stare at each other? But meanwhile they cherish their own comfortable illusions, not without help from me.

Even though they have no political power, nobody dares to scorn the monks, least of all the mendicants, because they hold the keys of everyone's secret life under the seal of the confessional, as they call it. Revealing such secrets they consider very wrong, unless when they're drunk, and want to please the company with spicy stories; then they sketch the outlines of the tale, but allusively, leaving out all the names. But if anyone stirs up these hornets, then they defend themselves in public sermons, alluding indirectly and subtly to their enemy, so that only a complete dummy will fail to get the point. And there'll be no end to their yapping till you stop their mouths with a bone.

Tell me, now, what comic actor or street-corner charlatan would you rather watch in action than these fellows making their sermons? Though they can't avoid ridiculous blunders, they try to imitate everything the old rhetoricians have handed down on the art of discourse. Good lord, how they gesticulate, how they change pitch, how they crow and strut and fling themselves wildly about, putting on special expressions from time to time, and getting everything mixed up in their outcries. And this art of oratory they hand down as a secret tradition from brother to brother: gradually, they limp painfully through the first part, break out in a wild clamor even though they're in the dullest part of their subject, and then fall silent so abruptly you'd think they were out of breath. Finally, they've learned from the rhetoricians that it's a good idea to indulge a little humor now and then, so they try to mix a few jokes in with their talk; "Lord help us all," how gracefully they do it, and how *à propos*—you'd say it was a clear case of "an ass with a lyre." From time to time, they give a little satirical nip, too, but they take care to tickle rather than wound. And in fact they never flatter more than when they pretend to be "speaking most sharply." In short, the whole performance is such that you'd swear the preachers must have studied with street-corner charlatans, who are better performers, indeed, but follow the same procedures so closely that it's obvious one group must have learned its rhetorical tricks from the other.

And yet these preachers find that, thanks to my assistance, their audiences imagine that they're hearing a modern Demosthenes or a Cicero. Shopkeepers and women are the hearers they like best, and they try hardest to please them, because the former if stroked the right way may be coaxed into untying their moneybags, and the ladies, among many other reasons for liking the clergy, know they can always find there an understanding ear in which to pour out their grievances against their husbands.

You see now, I guess, how much men of the cloth owe to me, since with their petty little ceremonies, their trifling formulas, and loud mouths, they can wield a practical tyranny over the laity, and pass themselves off as actual Saint Pauls or Saint Anthonys. But I'm happy to be rid of these shoddy play-actors, who are as good at taking my gifts without showing gratitude as they are at putting up a show of piety for the public. For now I'd like to say something about princes and courtiers who, like the free and liberal-minded men they are, seek my favors quite openly and unabashedly. These noblemen, if they have just half an ounce of good heart, must surely lead the most wretched lives in the world, and the most to be avoided. For what man would ever dream of trying to seize royal power by perjury or parricide if he reflected what a heavy burden falls on the shoulders of anyone who assumes the part of a true prince? If he wants to guide the ship of state, he must think continually of the public welfare, not his own; indeed, he can consider nothing but the public good. He must not depart by a finger's breadth from the laws he has designed and promulgated; he must see to the integrity of all his officers and magistrates. His own life is exposed to public scrutiny; thus, if his manners are virtuous, he can be a star to steer by, and of the utmost benefit in all human affairs—or if, on the contrary, he is like a deadly comet, he can bring total destruction in his wake. Other men's vices are not so obvious, nor are they so far-reaching in their effects. A prince stands on such an eminence that if something turns him ever so slightly from the path of honesty, a moral pestilence spreads through thousands of his subjects. Then because a ruler's position brings with it many things to distract him from virtue, such as pleasure, leisure, flattery, and luxury, he must be vigilant and keen to avoid disgracing his office. Finally, passing over all the plots, jealousies, and other perils that threaten, he is subject to the judgment of that one true King who will exact retribution for his least failing, and the more strictly, the greater has been his authority. If a prince would reflect on these and similar matters—and he would if he were wise—I doubt if he would enjoy either his evening dinner or a good night's sleep.

But now, thanks to my bounty, princes dismiss all these problems and send them to Jericho; they look out for their own sweet selves and won't even admit anyone to their presence who can't keep the conversation light, and far away from disagreeable subjects. They suppose they're performing all the duties of a prince if they ride regularly to hounds, keep a stable full of fine horses, sell government offices for their own profit, and think every day of a new way to squeeze money out of the citizens and funnel it into the royal treasury. But these tricks are always performed under cover of precedent, so that even if the proceedings are iniquitous, they can at least make a pretence of equity; and they're always accompanied by a few words of flattery, to keep on the good side of public opinion.

Picture to yourself a man, like quite a few existing nowadays, who is ignorant of the law, almost an open enemy of the public good, concerned only with his own private advantage, a hater of liberty, learning, and truth, thinking of nothing less than the welfare of his country, but judging everything by his own pleasures, his own profit. Now hang a golden chain on his neck to symbolize the linkage of all the virtues, and set on his head a crown studded with gems to remind him that he should excel everyone else in heroic qualities. Put a scepter in his hand to symbolize justice and a heart free from corruption, and give him a purple robe to show his outstanding devotion to the welfare of his country. If a prince were to compare these symbols with his actual behavior, I think he might be ashamed of his trappings, and fear lest some satiric commentator might turn all his fine apparel into a ridiculous joke.

Courtiers are another story. Though generally they're the most meeching, slavish, stupid, abject creatures conceivable, they fancy themselves the most distinguished of men. In one respect, they take the prize for modesty, because they content themselves with the gold, gems, purple robes, and other insignia of virtue while relinquishing to others all concern for the virtues themselves. One thing makes them perfectly happy if they can address the king as "Sire," if they can speak three words of greeting to him, and then fill out the rest of their speech with formulas like "Serene Majesty," "Your Lordship," and "Your Imperial Highness." The rest of their talent is just barefaced flattery. And these are the proper skills of a noble courtier. But if you look more closely at their way of life, you'll find they are nothing but Phaeacians, or Penelope's suitors—you know the rest of the poem, which Echo can give you better than I. They sleep till noon, when some miserable, mercenary little priest comes to their bedside and runs through mass for them almost before they're awake. Next to breakfast, which is hardly finished before it's lunchtime. Then on to dicing, draughts, betting, comedians, fools, drabs, games, and dirty stories, with a goodie to nibble on every so often between these activities. Dinner time now, followed by drinks, more than one, you can be sure. And in this way, without a moment's boredom, hours, days, months, years, and ages glide away. I myself get thoroughly sick of them, and take off, when I see them "putting on the dog," their ladies preening themselves on their long trains as if that made them superior beings, the men elbowing one another out of the way so they can be seen standing next to the prince, or when they string heavy gold chains around their necks, as if trying to show off their muscles at the same time as their money.

For a long time now, this courtly manner of life has been eagerly imitated by the loftiest Popes, Cardinals, and Bishops, some of whom have even surpassed their originals. But does anyone think what the priest's linen vestment means by its snow-white color, that it is the sign of a spotless life? Or what is the meaning of that two-horned mitre, with each point rising to a tight knot, if not to indicate absolute knowledge of the Old and New Testaments? Or why his hands are covered with gloves, if not to keep them clean of all contact with human affairs, and free to administer the sacraments? Why does he carry a crozier, if not to take vigilant care of the flock entrusted to him? Why the cross carried before him if not to signify victory over all human appetites? If any one of the clergy were to reflect on these and many other similar matters, I ask you, wouldn't he live a pretty sorry and wretched life? But now they're perfectly content, as long as they've stuffed themselves. As for watching over the flock, they either let Christ take care of that chore or put it off on curates and the "Brethren," as they call them. They never even think of the meaning of their title "Bishop," which means "overseer," and implies work, caring, taking pains. Yet when it comes to raking in the revenues, they're sharp-sighted enough; no "careless oversight" there.

Likewise the Cardinals, if they reflected that they are successors to the Apostles, and that the same things are required of them as of their predecessors, might consider that they are not masters but administrators of spiritual gifts, for which an exact accounting will have to be rendered. They might even philosophize for a moment over their vestments, and ask themselves a few questions. For example: what is the meaning of this white outer garment, if not supreme, spotless innocence of life? Why the purple beneath, if not to show an ardent love of God? And again, that capacious cloak spreading out to envelop not only the Most Reverend Father but his mule as well—and sufficient to cover even a camel—does it not signify universal charity, extending to every person everywhere, in the form of teaching, exhorting, correcting, admonishing, pacifying quarrels, resisting wicked princes, and freely expending for the benefit of the Christian community not only his money but his blood? And why do they need money at all if they stand in the place of the Apostles, who were all poor men? If they thought over these matters, as I say, they wouldn't be so ambitious for the post, might even resign it—or at least live lives as strenuous and devoted as those of the original Apostles.

And the Popes themselves, vicars of Christ, if they tried to imitate his life—his poverty, his toil, his teaching, his suffering on the cross, his contempt of life—if they ever thought of the name "Pope," which means Father, or their title "Your Holiness," what soul on earth would be more downcast? Who would purchase that position at the expense of all his belongings, or would defend it, once bought, with sword, poison, and violence of every sort? Think how many comforts would be lost to them if they ever admitted a gleam of reason! Reason, did I say? Rather, just a grain of the salt Christ spoke of. Off they would go, all those riches, honors, powers, triumphs, appointments, dispensations, special levies and indulgences; away with the troops of horses, mules, flunkies, and all the pleasures that go with them! (You'll note what a marketplace, what a harvest, what an ocean of pleasures I've crammed into a few words.) Instead of which, wisdom would

bring wakeful nights, long fasts, tears, prayers, sermons, hours of study, sighs, and a thousand other griefs of that sort. And let's not forget the other circumstances, all those scribes, copyists, notaries, advocates, prosecutors, and secretaries, all those mule-drivers, stable hands, money-changers, pimps, and—I almost added something gentler, but I'm afraid it would grate on certain ears. In short, this whole gang of people which battens on the Holy See—sorry, I meant to say, "which distinguishes it"—would be reduced to want. What a crime! abominable and inhuman; and to make it worse, the highest princes of the church and true lights of the world would be reduced to taking up scrip and staff.

But as things stand now, whatever work may be called for in the church is passed along to Peter and Paul, who have ample free time; if there's any splendor or pleasure being given out, that our church leaders are willing to take on. And so it happens that, thanks to my efforts, no class of men live more comfortably or with less trouble. They think they've amply fulfilled Christ's commandments if they play the part of bishop with mystical and almost theatrical pomp, with formulas of Your Beatitude, Your Reverence, and Your Holiness, salted with some blessings and anathemas. Performing miracles is, for them, old-fashioned and obsolete, not at all in tune with modern times; teaching the people is hard work, prayer is boring, tears are weak and womanish, poverty is degrading, and meekness is disgraceful, quite unworthy of one who barely admits even the greatest kings to kiss his feet. Death is a most unattractive prospect, and the idea of dying on a cross is quite out of the question.

All that's left to them in the way of weapons are those good words and fair speeches described by Paul (and of those things they are sufficiently generous)—along with interdicts, suspensions, warnings many times repeated, anathemas, fearful images, and that horrifying thunderbolt with which, by a mere nod of the head, they dispatch the souls of mortal men to the depths of Tartarus. It's a weapon that the most holy fathers in God and vicars of Christ on earth launch at no one more fiercely than at those who, instigated by the Devil, try to whittle away the patrimony of Peter to a mere morsel. This patrimony, though the Evangelist says, "We have left all and followed you," is understood to include farmlands, taxes, tithes, and judicial privileges. Ablaze with Christian zeal, they fight with fire and sword to defend these belongings, at no small expense of Christian blood—and all the time they declare that this is the apostolic way to defend the church, the bride of Christ, by putting to flight her enemies, as they call them. As if, indeed, there were any enemies of the church more pernicious than impious popes, who by their silence allow Christ to be forgotten, lock him up behind their money-making laws, contaminate his teachings with their interpretations, and murder him with their atrocious manner of life.

MARTIN LUTHER

Ninety-Five Theses; or, Disputation on the Power and Efficacy of Indulgences

The following are the ninety-five theses Martin Luther nailed to the door of Castle Church at Wittenberg in 1517. They were essentially an invitation to debate and quickly became a rallying point for criticism of church practices. The indulgences Luther was attacking were pardons from sin given out by church officials in exchange for monetary donations.

The central concern of the ninety-five theses is with penance, which for Luther was a permanent inner attitude. He believed that indulgences misled the faithful into believing they could be absolved of their sins simply through their outward purchase. Luther, however, held that sincere repentance was necessary for the forgiveness of sin and the remission of punishment. Luther begins his ninety-five theses with references to these more general issues of sin and repentance. The first mention of "indulgence" comes in the twenty-first thesis.

Out of love and zeal for truth and the desire to bring it to light, the following theses will be publicly discussed at Wittenberg under the chairmanship of the reverend father Martin Lutther,[1] Master of Arts and Sacred Theology and regularly appointed Lecturer on these subjects at that place. He requests that those who cannot be present to debate orally with us will do so by letter.[2]

In the Name of Our Lord Jesus Christ. Amen.

1. When our Lord and Master Jesus Christ said, "Repent" [Matt. 4:17],[3] he willed the entire life of believers to be one of repentance.

2. This word cannot be understood as referring to the sacrament of penance, that is, confession and satisfaction, as administered by the clergy.

3. Yet it does not mean solely inner repentance; such inner repentance is worthless unless it produces various outward mortifications of the flesh.

4. The penalty of sin[4] remains as long as the hatred of self, that is, true inner repentance, until our entrance into the kingdom of heaven.

5. The pope neither desires nor is able to remit any penalties except those imposed by his own authority or that of the canons.[5]

6. The pope cannot remit any guilt, except by declaring and showing that it has been remitted by God; or, to be sure, by remitting guilt in cases reserved to his judgment. If his right to grant remission in these cases were disregarded, the guilt would certainly remain unforgiven.

7. God remits guilt to no one unless at the same time he humbles him in all things and makes him submissive to his vicar, the priest.

8. The penitential canons are imposed only on the living, and, according to the canons themselves, nothing should be imposed on the dying.

9. Therefore the Holy Spirit through the pope is kind to us insofar as the pope in his decrees always makes exception of the article of death and of necessity.[6]

10. Those priests act ignorantly and wickedly who, in the case of the dying, reserve canonical penalties for purgatory.

11. Those tares of changing the canonical penalty to the penalty of purgatory were evidently sown while the bishops slept [Matt. 13:25].

12. In former times canonical penalties were imposed, not after, but before absolution, as tests of true contrition.

13. The dying are freed by death from all penalties, are already dead as far as the canon laws are concerned, and have a right to be released from them.

14. Imperfect piety or love on the part of the dying person necessarily brings with it great fear; and the smaller the love, the greater the fear.

15. This fear or horror is sufficient in itself, to say nothing of other things, to constitute the penalty of purgatory, since it is very near the horror of despair.

16. Hell, purgatory, and heaven seem to differ the same as despair, fear, and assurance of salvation.

17. It seems as though for the souls in purgatory fear should necessarily decrease and love increase.

18. Furthermore, it does not seem proved, either by reason or Scripture, that souls in purgatory are outside the state of merit, that is, unable to grow in love.

19. Nor does it seem proved that souls in purgatory, at least not all of them, are certain and assured of their own salvation, even if we ourselves may be entirely certain of it.

20. Therefore the pope, when he uses the words "plenary remission of all penalties," does not actually mean "all penalties," but only those imposed by himself.

21. Thus those indulgence preachers are in error who say that a man is absolved from every penalty and saved by papal indulgences.

22. As a matter of fact, the pope remits to souls in purgatory no penalty which, according to canon law, they should have paid in this life.

23. If remission of all penalties whatsoever could be granted to anyone at all, certainly it would be granted only to the most perfect, that is, to very few.

24. For this reason most people are necessarily deceived by that indiscriminate and high-sounding promise of release from penalty.

25. That power which the pope has in general over purgatory corresponds to the power which any bishop or curate has in a particular way in his own diocese or parish.

26. The pope does very well when he grants remission to souls in purgatory, not by the power of the keys, which he does not have,[7] but by way of intercession for them.

27. They preach only human doctrines who say that as soon as the money clinks into the money chest, the soul flies out of purgatory.

---

[1]Luther spelled his name Lutther in this preamble.

[2]There was actually no debate, for no one responded to the invitation. The contents of the ninety-five theses were soon widely disseminated by word of mouth and by the printers, and in effect a vigorous debate took place that lasted for a number of years.

[3]The Latin form, *poenitentiam agite,* and the German, *tut Busse,* may be rendered in two ways, "repent," and "do penance."

[4]Catholic theology distinguishes between the "guilt" and the "penalty" of sin.

[5]The canons, or decrees of the church, have the force of law. Those referred to here and in Theses 8 and 85 are the so-called penitential canons.

---

[6]Commenting on this thesis in the *Explanations of the Ninety-Five Theses,* Luther distinguishes between temporal and eternal necessity "Necessity knows no law." "Death is the necessity of necessities."

[7]This is not a denial of the power of the keys that is, the power to forgive and to retain sin, but merely an assertion that the power of the keys does not extend to purgatory.

28. It is certain that when money clinks in the money chest, greed and avarice can be increased; but when the church intercedes, the result is in the hands of God alone.

29. Who knows whether all souls in purgatory wish to be redeemed, since we have exceptions in St. Severinus and St. Paschal,[8] as related in a legend.

30. No one is sure of the integrity of his own contrition, much less of having received plenary remission.

31. The man who actually buys indulgences is as rare as he who is really penitent; indeed, he is exceedingly rare.

32. Those who believe that they can be certain of their salvation because they have indulgence letters will be eternally damned, together with their teachers.

33. Men must especially be on their guard against those who say that the pope's pardons are that inestimable gift of God by which man is reconciled to him.

34. For the graces of indulgences are concerned only with the penalties of sacramental satisfaction[9] established by man.

35. They who teach that contrition is not necessary on the part of those who intend to buy souls out of purgatory or to buy confessional privileges[10] preach unchristian doctrine.

36. Any truly repentant Christian has a right to full remission of penalty and guilt,[11] even without indulgence letters.

37. Any true Christian, whether living or dead, participates in all the blessings of Christ and the church; and this is granted him by God, even without indulgence letters.

38. Nevertheless, papal remission and blessing are by no means to be disregarded, for they are, as I have said [Thesis 6], the proclamation of the divine remission.

39. It is very difficult, even for the most learned theologians, at one and the same time to commend to the people the bounty of indulgences and the need of true contrition.

40. A Christian who is truly contrite seeks and loves to pay penalties for his sins; the bounty of indulgences, however, relaxes penalties and causes men to hate them—at least it furnishes occasion for hating them.

41. Papal indulgences must be preached with caution, lest people erroneously think that they are preferable to other good works of love.

42. Christians are to be taught that the pope does not intend that the buying of indulgences should in any way be compared with works of mercy.

43. Christians are to be taught that he who gives to the poor or lends to the needy does a better deed than he who buys indulgences.

44. Because love grows by works of love, man thereby becomes better. Man does not, however, become better by means of indulgences but is merely freed from penalties.

45. Christians are to be taught that he who sees a needy man and passes him by, yet gives his money for indulgences, does not buy papal indulgences but God's wrath.

46. Christians are to be taught that, unless they have more than they need, they must reserve enough for their family needs and by no means squander it on indulgences.

47. Christians are to be taught that the buying of indulgences is a matter of free choice, not commanded.

48. Christians are to be taught that the pope, in granting indulgences, needs and thus desires their devout prayer more than their money.

49. Christians are to be taught that papal indulgences are useful only if they do not put their trust in them, but very harmful if they lose their fear of God because of them.

50. Christians are to be taught that if the pope knew the exactions of the indulgence preachers, he would rather that the basilica of St. Peter were burned to ashes than built up with the skin, flesh, and bones of his sheep.

51. Christians are to be taught that the pope would and should wish to give of his own money, even though he had to sell the basilica of St. Peter, to many of those from whom certain hawkers of indulgences cajole money.

52. It is vain to trust in salvation by indulgence letters, even though the indulgence commissary, or even the pope, were to offer his soul as security.

53. They are enemies of Christ and the pope who forbid altogether the preaching of the Word of God in some churches in order that indulgences may be preached in others.

54. Injury is done the Word of God when, in the same sermon, an equal or larger amount of time is devoted to indulgences than to the Word.

55. It is certainly the pope's sentiment that if indulgences, which are a very insignificant thing, are celebrated with one bell, one procession, and one ceremony, then the gospel, which is the very greatest thing, should be preached with a hundred bells, a hundred processions, a hundred ceremonies.

56. The treasures of the church,[12] out of which the pope distributes indulgences, are not sufficiently discussed or known among the people of Christ.

57. That indulgences are not temporal treasures is certainly clear, for many [indulgence] preachers do not distribute them freely but only gather them.

58. Nor are they the merits of Christ and the saints, for, even without the pope, the latter always work grace for the inner man, and the cross, death, and hell for the outer man.

59. St. Laurence said that the poor of the church were the treasures of the church, but he spoke according to the usage of the word in his own time.

---

[8]Luther refers to this legend again in the *Explanations of the Ninety-Five Theses.* The legend is to the effect that these saints, Pope Severinus (638–640) and Pope Paschal I (817–824), preferred to remain longer in purgatory that they might have greater glory in heaven.

[9]Satisfaction is that act of the penitent, in connection with the sacrament of penance, by means of which he pays the temporal penalty for his sins. If at death he is in arrears in paying his temporal penalty for venial sins, he pays the penalty in purgatory. Indulgences are concerned with this satisfaction of the sacrament of penance—they permit a partial or complete (plenary) remission of temporal punishment. According to Roman Catholic theology, the buyer of an indulgence still has to confess his sins, be absolved from them, and be truly penitent.

[10]These are privileges entitling the holder of indulgence letters to choose his own confessor and relieving him, the holder, of certain satisfactions.

[11]To justify the placing of absolution before satisfaction, contrary to the practice of the early church, theologians distinguished between the guilt and the penalty of sin.

---

[12]The treasury of merits is a reserve fund of good works accumulated by Christ and the saints upon which the pope could draw when he remitted satisfaction in indulgences.

60. Without want of consideration we say that the keys of the church[13] given by the merits of Christ are that treasure;

61. For it is clear that the pope's power is of itself sufficient for the remission of penalities and cases reserved by himself.

62. The true treasure of the church is the most holy gospel of the glory and grace of God.

63. But this treasure is naturally most odious for it makes the first to be last [Matt. 20:16].

64. On the other hand the treasure of indulgences is naturally most acceptable for it makes the last to be first.

65. Therefore the treasures of the gospel are nets with which one formerly fished for men of wealth.

66. The treasures of indulgences are nets with which one now fishes for the wealth of men.

67. The indulgences which the demagogues acclaim as the greatest graces are actually understood to be such only insofar as they promote gain.

68. They are nevertheless in truth the most insignificant graces when compared with the grace of God and the piety of the cross.

69. Bishops and curates are bound to admit the commissaries of papal indulgences with all reverence.

70. But they are much more bound to strain their eyes and ears lest these men preach their own dreams instead of what the pope has commissioned.

71. Let him who speaks against the truth concerning papal indulgences be anathema and accursed;

72. But let him who guards against the lust and license of the indulgence preachers be blessed;

73. Just as the pope justly thunders against those who by any means whatsoever contrive harm to the sale of indulgences.

74. But much more does he intend to thunder against those who use indulgences as a pretext to contrive harm to holy love and truth.

75. To consider papal indulgences so great that they could absolve a man even if he had done the impossible and had violated the mother of God is madness.

76. We say on the contrary that papal indulgences cannot remove the very least of venial sins as far as guilt is concerned.

77. To say that even St. Peter, if he were now pope, could not grant greater graces is blasphemy against St. Peter and the pope.

78. We say on the contrary that even the present pope, or any pope whatsoever, has greater graces at his disposal, that is, the gospel, spiritual powers, gifts of healing, etc., as it is written in I Cor. 12[:28].

79. To say that the cross emblazoned with the papal coat of arms, and set up by the indulgence preachers, is equal in worth to the cross of Christ is blasphemy.

80. The bishops, curates, and theologians who permit such talk to be spread among the people will have to answer for this.

81. This unbridled preaching of indulgences makes it difficult even for learned men to rescue the reverence which is due the pope from slander or from the shrewd questions of the laity,

82. Such as: "Why does not the pope empty purgatory for the sake of holy love and the dire need of the souls that are there if he redeems an infinite number of souls for the sake of miserable money with which to build a church? The former reasons would be most just; the latter is most trivial."

83. Again, "Why are funeral and anniversary masses for the dead continued and why does he not return or permit the withdrawal of the endowments founded for them, since it is wrong to pray for the redeemed?"

84. Again, "What is this new piety of God and the pope that for a consideration of money they permit a man who is impious and their enemy to buy out of purgatory the pious soul of a friend of God and do not rather, because of the need of that pious and beloved soul, free it for pure love's sake?"

85. Again, "Why are the penitential canons, long since abrogated and dead in actual fact and through disuse, now satisfied by the granting of indulgences as though they were still alive and in force?"

86. Again, "Why does not the pope, whose wealth is today greater than the wealth of the richest Crassus,[14] build this one basilica of St. Peter with his own money rather than with the money of poor believers?"

87. Again, "What does the pope remit or grant to those who by perfect contrition already have a right to full remission and blessings?"[15]

88. Again, "What greater blessing could come to the church than if the pope were to bestow these remissions and blessings on every believer a hundred times a day, as he now does but once?"[16]

89. "Since the pope seeks the salvation of souls rather than money by his indulgences, why does he suspend the indulgences and pardons previously granted when they have equal efficacy?"[17]

90. To repress these very sharp arguments of the laity by force alone, and not to resolve them by giving reasons, is to expose the church and the pope to the ridicule of their enemies and to make Christians unhappy.

91. If, therefore, indulgences were preached according to the spirit and intention of the pope, all these doubts would be readily resolved. Indeed, they would not exist.

92. Away then with all those prophets who say to the people of Christ, "Peace, peace," and there is no peace! [Jer. 6:14].

93. Blessed be all those prophets who say to the people of Christ, "Cross, cross," and there is no cross!

94. Christians should be exhorted to be diligent in following Christ, their head, through penalties, death, and hell;

---

[13]The office of the keys: the preaching of the gospel, the celebrating of the sacraments, the remitting of sins to the penitent, and the excommunicating of impenitent sinners.

[14]Marcus Licinius Crassus (115–53 B.C.E.), also called Dives ("the Rich"), was noted for his wealth and luxury by the classical Romans. Crassus means "the Fat."

[15]See Theses 36 and 37.

[16]The indulgence letter entitled its possessor to receive absolution once during his lifetime and once at the approach of death.

[17]During the time when the jubilee indulgences were preached, other indulgences were suspended.

95. And thus be confident of entering into heaven through many tribulations rather than through the false security of peace [Acts 14:22].

LOUISE LABE

Sonnet 18 "Kiss Me Again, Rekiss Me, Kiss Me More"

French poet LOUISE LABÉ [LAH-bay] (1525–66), a renowned equestrian and archer, is reputed to have fought on horseback in battles with the Spanish and to have participated in jousting tournaments. In her poetry, however, she concentrated on love. The following sonnet echoes a love poem by the ancient Roman poet Catullus, who asks his Lesbia to kiss him numerous times. The poem, with its witty and imaginative playfulness, is quite suggestively erotic.

Kiss me again, rekiss me, kiss me more,
give me your most consuming, tasty one,
give me your sensual kiss, a savory one,
I'll give you back four burning at the core.
Are you up in arms? Well, I'll give you ten   *5*
erotic kisses for your appetite
and we will mingle kisses and excite
our bodies with an easy joy again.
Then we will live a double life, and each
of us will be alone and yet will blend   *10*
our love. Love, please allow a little madness:
I'm always hurt and live with temperate speech,
veiling these days in which I find no gladness
if I can't leave myself and find my friend.

QUEEN ELIZABETH I

Speech to the English Troops at Tilbury

The reign of Queen Elizabeth I of England (1558–1603) represents one of the most glorious periods of English history and includes the early career of Shakespeare. Elizabeth was an accomplished woman of letters and used public occasions to demonstrate her knowledge of Greek and Latin, which she learned as part of her humanistic education.

Queen Elizabeth also translated many important literary works from their original language, including the Bible (the Psalms), and works from Plutarch, Seneca, and Petrarch. In addition, she wrote poetry and prose. The following speech was given to her troops as they were poised to do battle with the Spanish. In it, she exhibits great mastery of the classical tenets of rhetoric as well as an ability to rally her men to defend England.

My loving people,

We have been persuaded by some that are careful of our safety, to take heed how we commit our selves to armed multitudes, for fear of treachery; but I assure you I do not desire to live to distrust my faithful and loving people. Let tyrants fear, I have always so behaved myself that, under God, I have placed my chiefest strength and safeguard in the loyal hearts and good-will of my subjects; and therefore I am come amongst you, as you see, at this time, not for my recreation and disport, but being resolved, in the midst and heat of the battle, to live or die amongst you all; to lay down for my God, and for my kingdom, and my people, my honour and my blood, even in the dust. I know I have the body but of a weak and feeble woman; but I have the heart and stomach of a king, and of a king of England too, and think foul scorn that Parma or Spain, or any prince of Europe, should dare to invade the borders of my realm; to which rather than any dishonour shall grow by me, I myself will take up arms, I myself will be your general, judge, and rewarder of every one of your virtues in the field. I know already, for your forwardness you have deserved rewards and crowns; and We do assure you in the word of a prince, they shall be duly paid you. In the mean time, my lieutenant general shall be in my stead, than whom never prince commanded a more noble or worthy subject; not doubting but by your obedience to my general, by your concord in the camp, and your valour in the field, we shall shortly have a famous victory over those enemies of my God, of my kingdom, and of my people.

MICHEL DE MONTAIGNE

Of Cannibals

In his essay "Of Cannibals," Montaigne defends, surprisingly, cannibal culture—"that other world" in which men capture, kill, cook, and eat their enemies. This world, considered by Montaigne's contemporaries to be wholly uncivilized, Montaigne finds "civilized" in comparison to sixteenth-century Europe. He proves his point by comparing cannibalism to the Renaissance methods of punishment—being drawn and quartered—or literally pulled apart alive—for instance. To Montaigne, "there is more barbarity in eating a man alive than in eating him dead; and in tearing by tortures and the rack a body still full of feeling, in roasting him bit by bit . . . than in roasting and eating him after he is dead."

One of Montaigne's main concerns is the "human disease" of war, and he contrasts the methods and motivations of war in the two cultures. Throughout his essay, Montaigne characterizes the cannibals as honest, courageous, and intelligent while presenting the Europeans as cowardly and cruel. As he notes, "the worth and value of a man is in his heart and his will." In its use of difference to shed light on the moral and cultural attitudes of his countrymen, "Of Cannibals" can be compared with Jonathan Swift's Gulliver's Travels *(Chapter 16). Like Swift, Montaigne utilizes humor, irony, and surprise to prod his readers to examine their cultural values.*

When King Pyrrhus passed over into Italy, after he had reconnoitered the formation of the army that the Romans were sending to meet him, he said: "I do not know what barbarians these are" (for so the Greeks called all foreign nations), "but the formation of this army that I see is not at all barbarous." The Greeks said as much of the army that Flamininus brought into their country, and so did Philip, seeing from a knoll the order and distribution of the Roman camp, in his kingdom, under Publius Sulpicius Galba. Thus we should beware of clinging to vulgar opinions, and judge things by reason's way, not by popular say.

I had with me for a long time a man who had lived for ten or twelve years in that other world which has been discovered in our century, in the place where Villegaignon landed, and which he called Antarctic France.[1] This discovery of a

---

[1] In Brazil, in 1557.

boundless country seems worthy of consideration. I don't know if I can guarantee that some other such discovery will not be made in the future, so many personages greater than ourselves having been mistaken about this one. I am afraid we have eyes bigger than our stomachs, and more curiosity than capacity. We embrace everything, but we clasp only wind.

Plato brings in Solon, telling how he had learned from the priests of the city of Saïs in Egypt that in days of old, before the Flood, there was a great island named Atlantis, right at the mouth of the Strait of Gibraltar, which contained more land than Africa and Asia put together, and that the kings of that country, who not only possessed that island but had stretched out so far on the mainland that they held the breadth of Africa as far as Egypt, and the length of Europe as far as Tuscany, undertook to step over into Asia and subjugate all the nations that border on the Mediterranean, as far as the Black Sea; and for this purpose crossed the Spains, Gaul, Italy, as far as Greece, where the Athenians checked them; but that some time after, both the Athenians and themselves and their island were swallowed up by the Flood.

It is quite likely that that extreme devastation of waters made amazing changes in the habitations of the earth, as people maintain that the sea cut off Sicily from Italy—

'Tis said an earthquake once asunder tore
These lands with dreadful havoc, which before
Formed but one land, one coast.

VIRGIL

—Cyprus from Syria, the island of Euboea from the mainland of Boeotia; and elsewhere joined lands that were divided, filling the channels between them with sand and mud:

A sterile marsh, long fit for rowing, now
Feeds neighbor towns, and feels the heavy prow.

HORACE

But there is no great likelihood that that island was the new world which we have just discovered; for it almost touched Spain, and it would be an incredible result of a flood to have forced it away as far as it is, more than twelve hundred leagues; besides, the travels of the moderns have already almost revealed that it is not an island, but a mainland connected with the East Indies on one side, and elsewhere with the lands under the two poles; or, if it is separated from them, it is by so narrow a strait and interval that it does not deserve to be called an island on that account.

It seems that there are movements, some natural, others feverish, in these great bodies, just as in our own. When I consider the inroads that my river, the Dordogne, is making in my lifetime into the right bank in its descent, and that in twenty years it has gained so much ground and stolen away the foundations of several buildings, I clearly see that this is an extraordinary disturbance; for if it had always gone at this rate, or was to do so in the future, the face of the world would be turned topsy-turvy. But rivers are subject to changes: now they overflow in one direction, now in another, now they keep to their course. I am not speaking of the sudden inundations whose causes are manifest. In Médoc, along the seashore, my brother, the sieur d'Arsac, can see an estate of his buried under the sands that the sea spews forth; the tops of some buildings are still visible; his farms and domains have changed into very thin pasturage. The inhabitants say that for some time the sea has been pushing toward them so hard that they have lost four leagues of land. These sands are its harbingers; and we see great dunes of moving sand that march half a league ahead of it and keep conquering land.

The other testimony of antiquity with which some would connect this discovery is in Aristotle, at least if that little book *Of Unheard-of Wonders* is by him. He there relates that certain Carthaginians, after setting out upon the Atlantic Ocean from the Strait of Gibraltar and sailing a long time, at last discovered a great fertile island, all clothed in woods and watered by great deep rivers, far remote from any mainland; and that they, and others since, attracted by the goodness and fertility of the soil, went there with their wives and children, and began to settle there. The lords of Carthage, seeing that their country was gradually becoming depopulated, expressly forbade anyone to go there any more, on pain of death, and drove out these new inhabitants, fearing, it is said, that in course of time they might come to multiply so greatly as to supplant their former masters and ruin their state. This story of Aristotle does not fit our new lands any better than the other.

This man I had was a simple, crude fellow[2]—a character fit to bear true witness; for clever people observe more things and more curiously, but they interpret them; and to lend weight and conviction to their interpretation, they cannot help altering history a little. They never show you things as they are, but bend and disguise them according to the way they have seen them; and to give credence to their judgment and attract you to it, they are prone to add something to their matter, to stretch it out and amplify it. We need a man either very honest, or so simple that he has not the stuff to build up false inventions and give them plausibility; and wedded to no theory. Such was my man; and besides this, he at various times brought sailors and merchants, whom he had known on that trip, to see me. So I content myself with his information, without inquiring what the cosmographers say about it.

We ought to have topographers who would give us an exact account of the places where they have been. But because they have over us the advantage of having seen Palestine, they want to enjoy the privilege of telling us news about all the rest of the world. I would like everyone to write what he knows, and as much as he knows, not only in this, but in all other subjects; for a man may have some special knowledge and experience of the nature of a river or a fountain, who in other matters knows only what everybody knows. However, to circulate this little scrap of knowledge, he will undertake to write the whole of physics. From this vice spring many great abuses.

Now, to return to my subject, I think there is nothing barbarous and savage in that nation, from what I have been told, except that each man calls barbarism whatever is not his own practice; for indeed it seems we have no other test of truth and reason than the example and pattern of the opinions and customs of the country we live in. *There* is always the perfect religion, the perfect government, the perfect and accomplished manners in all things. Those people are wild, just as we call wild the fruits that Nature has produced by herself and in her normal course; whereas really it is those that we have changed

---

[2]The traveler Montaigne spoke of him at the beginning of the chapter.

artificially and led astray from the common order, that we should rather call wild. The former retain alive and vigorous their genuine, their most useful and natural, virtues and properties, which we have debased in the latter in adapting them to gratify our corrupted taste. And yet for all that, the savor and delicacy of some uncultivated fruits of those countries is quite as excellent, even to our taste, as that of our own. It is not reasonable that art should win the place of honor over our great and powerful mother Nature. We have so overloaded the beauty and richness of her works by our inventions that we have quite smothered her. Yet wherever her purity shines forth, she wonderfully puts to shame our vain and frivolous attempts:

> *Ivy comes readier without our care;*
> *In lonely caves the arbutus grows more fair;*
> *No art with artless bird song can compare.*
>
> PROPERTIUS

All our efforts cannot even succeed in reproducing the nest of the tiniest little bird, its contexture, its beauty and convenience; or even the web of the puny spider. All things, says Plato, are produced by nature, by fortune, or by art; the greatest and most beautiful by one or the other of the first two, the least and most imperfect by the last.

These nations, then, seem to me barbarous in this sense, that they have been fashioned very little by the human mind, and are still very close to their original naturalness. The laws of nature still rule them, very little corrupted by ours; and they are in such a state of purity that I am sometimes vexed that they were unknown earlier, in the days when there were men able to judge them better than we. I am sorry that Lycurgus and Plato did not know of them; for it seems to me that what we actually see in these nations surpasses not only all the pictures in which poets have idealized the golden age and all their inventions in imagining a happy state of man, but also the conceptions and the very desire of philosophy. They could not imagine a naturalness so pure and simple as we see by experience; nor could they believe that our society could be maintained with so little artifice and human solder. This is a nation, I should say to Plato, in which there is no sort of traffic, no knowledge of letters, no science of numbers, no name for a magistrate or for political superiority, no custom of servitude, no riches or poverty, no contracts, no successions, no partitions, no occupations but leisure ones, no care for any but common kinship, no clothes, no agriculture, no metal, no use of wine or wheat. The very words that signify lying, treachery, dissimulation, avarice, envy, belittling, pardon—unheard of. How far from this perfection would he find the republic that he imagined: *Men fresh sprung from the gods* [Seneca].

> *These manners nature first ordained.*
>
> VIRGIL

For the rest, they live in a country with a very pleasant and temperate climate, so that according to my witnesses it is rare to see a sick man there; and they have assured me that they never saw one palsied, bleary-eyed, toothless, or bent with age. They are settled along the sea and shut in on the land side by great high mountains, with a stretch about a hundred leagues wide in between. They have a great abundance of fish and flesh which bear no resemblance to ours, and they eat them with no other artifice than cooking. The first man who rode a horse there, though he had had dealings with them on several other trips, so horrified them in this posture that they shot him dead with arrows before they could recognize him.

Their buildings are very long, with a capacity of two or three hundred souls; they are covered with the bark of great trees, the strips reaching to the ground at one end and supporting and leaning on one another at the top, in the manner of some of our barns, whose covering hangs down to the ground and acts as a side. They have wood so hard that they cut with it and make of it their swords and grills to cook their food. Their beds are of a cotton weave, hung from the roof like those in our ships, each man having his own; for the wives sleep apart from their husbands.

They get up with the sun, and eat immediately upon rising, to last them through the day; for they take no other meal than that one. Like some other Eastern peoples of whom Suidas tells us, who drank apart from meals, they do not drink then; but they drink several times a day, and to capacity. Their drink is made of some root, and is of the color of our claret wines. They drink it only lukewarm. This beverage keeps only two or three days; it has a slightly sharp taste, is not at all heady, is good for the stomach, and has a laxative effect upon those who are not used to it; it is a very pleasant drink for anyone who is accustomed to it. In place of bread they use a certain white substance like preserved coriander. I have tried it; it tastes sweet and a little flat.

The whole day is spent in dancing. The younger men go to hunt animals with bows. Some of the women busy themselves meanwhile with warming their drink, which is their chief duty. Some one of the old men, in the morning before they begin to eat, preaches to the whole barnful in common, walking from one end to the other, and repeating one single sentence several times until he has completed the circuit (for the buildings are fully a hundred paces long). He recommends to them only two things: valor against the enemy and love for their wives. And they never fail to point out this obligation, as their refrain, that it is their wives who keep their drink warm and seasoned.

There may be seen in several places, including my own house, specimens of their beds, of their ropes, of their wooden swords and the bracelets with which they cover their wrists in combats, and of the big canes, open at one end, by whose sound they keep time in their dances. They are close shaven all over, and shave themselves much more cleanly than we, with nothing but a wooden or stone razor. They believe that souls are immortal, and that those who have deserved well of the gods are lodged in that part of heaven where the sun rises, and the damned in the west.

They have some sort of priests and prophets, but they rarely appear before the people, having their home in the mountains. On their arrival there is a great feast and solemn assembly of several villages—each barn, as I have described it, makes up a village, and they are about one French league from each other. The prophet speaks to them in public, exhorting them to virtue and their duty; but their whole ethical science contains only these two articles: resoluteness in war and affection for their wives. He prophesies to them things to come and the results they are to expect from their undertakings, and urges them to war or holds them back from it; but this is on the condition that when he fails to prophesy correctly, and if things turn out otherwise than he has predicted, he is cut into a thousand pieces if they catch him, and condemned as a false prophet. For this reason, the prophet who has once been mistaken is never seen again.

Divination is a gift of God; that is why its abuse should be punished as imposture. Among the Scythians, when the soothsayers failed to hit the mark, they were laid, chained hand and foot, on carts full of heather and drawn by oxen, on which they were burned. Those who handle matters subject to the control of human capacity are excusable if they do the best they can. But these others, who come and trick us with assurances of an extraordinary faculty that is beyond our ken, should they not be punished for not making good their promise, and for the temerity of their imposture?

They have their wars with the nations beyond the mountains, further inland, to which they go quite naked, with no other arms than bows or wooden swords ending in a sharp point, in the manner of the tongues of our boar spears. It is astonishing what firmness they show in their combats, which never end but in slaughter and bloodshed; for as to routs and terror, they know nothing of either.

Each man brings back as his trophy the head of the enemy he has killed, and sets it up at the entrance to his dwelling. After they have treated their prisoners well for a long time with all the hospitality they can think of, each man who has a prisoner calls a great assembly of his acquaintances. He ties a rope to one of the prisoner's arms, by the end of which he holds him, a few steps away, for fear of being hurt, and gives his dearest friend the other arm to hold in the same way; and these two, in the presence of the whole assembly, kill him with their swords. This done, they roast him and eat him in common and send some pieces to their absent friends. This is not, as people think, for nourishment, as of old the Scythians used to do, it is to betoken an extreme revenge. And the proof of this came when they saw the Portuguese, who had joined forces with their adversaries, inflict a different kind of death on them when they took them prisoner, which was to bury them up to the waist, shoot the rest of their body full of arrows, and afterward hang them. They thought that these people from the other world, being men who had sown the knowledge of many vices among their neighbors and were much greater masters than themselves in every sort of wickedness, did not adopt this sort of vengeance without some reason, and that it must be more painful than their own; so they began to give up their old method and to follow this one.

I am not sorry that we notice the barbarous horror of such acts, but I am heartily sorry that, judging their faults rightly, we should be so blind to our own. I think there is more barbarity in eating a man alive than in eating him dead; and in tearing by tortures and the rack a body still full of feeling, in roasting a man bit by bit, in having him bitten and mangled by dogs and swine (as we have not only read but seen within fresh memory, not among ancient enemies, but among neighbors and fellow citizens, and what is worse, on the pretext of piety and religion), than in roasting and eating him after he is dead.

Indeed, Chrysippus and Zeno, heads of the Stoic sect, thought there was nothing wrong in using our carcasses for any purpose in case of need, and getting nourishment from them; just as our ancestors, when besieged by Caesar in tile

city of Alésia, resolved to relieve their famine by eating old men, women, and other people useless for fighting.

The Gascons once, 'tis said, their life renewed
By eating of such food.

JUVENAL

And physicians do not fear to use human flesh in all sorts of ways for our health, applying it either inwardly or outwardly. But there never was any opinion so disordered as to excuse treachery, disloyalty, tyranny, and cruelty, which are our ordinary vices.

So we may well call these people barbarians, in respect to the rules of reason, but not in respect to ourselves, who surpass them in every kind of barbarity.

Their warfare is wholly noble and generous, and as excusable and beautiful as human disease can be; its only basis among them is their rivalry in valor. They are not fighting for the conquest of new lands, for they still enjoy that natural abundance that provides them, without toil and trouble with all necessary things in such profusion that they have no wish to enlarge their boundaries. They are still in that happy state of desiring only as much as their natural needs demand; anything beyond that is superfluous to them.

They generally call those of the same age, brothers; those who are younger, children; and the old men are fathers to all the others. These leave to their heirs in common the full possession of their property, without division or any other title at all than just the one that Nature gives to her creatures in bringing them into the world.

If their neighbors cross the mountains to attack them and win a victory, the gain of the victory is glory, and the advantage of having proved the master in valor and virtue; for apart from this they have no use for the goods of the vanquished, and they return to their own country, where they lack neither anything necessary nor that great thing, the knowledge of how to enjoy their condition happily and be content with it. These men of ours do the same in their turn. They demand of their prisoners no other ransom than that they confess and acknowledge their defeat. But there is not one in a whole century who does not choose to die rather than to relax a single bit, by word or look, from the grandeur of an invincible courage; not one who would not rather be killed and eaten than so much as ask not to be. They treat them very freely, so that life may be all the dearer to them, and usually entertain them with threats of their coming death, of the torments they will have to suffer, the preparations that are being made for that purpose, the cutting up of their limbs, and the feast that will be made at their expense. All this is done for the sole purpose of extorting from their lips some weak or base word, or making them want to flee, so as to gain the advantage of having terrified them and broken down their firmness. For indeed, if you take it the right way, it is in this point alone that true victory lies:

It is no victory
Unless the vanquished foe admits your mastery.

CLAUDIAN

The Hungarians, very bellicose fighters, did not in olden times pursue their advantage beyond putting the enemy at their mercy. For having wrung a confession from him to this effect, they let him go unharmed and unransomed, except, at most, for exacting his promise never again to take up arms against them.

We win enough advantages over our enemies that are borrowed advantages, not really our own. It is the quality of a porter, not of valor, to have sturdier arms and legs; agility is a dead and corporeal quality; it is a stroke of luck to make our enemy stumble, or dazzle his eyes by the sunlight; it is a trick of art and technique, which may be found in a worthless coward, to be an able fencer. The worth and value of a man is in his heart and his will; there lies his real honor. Valor is the strength, not of legs and arms, but of heart and soul; it consists not in the worth of our horse or our weapons, but in our own. He who falls obstinate in his courage, *if he has fallen, he fights on his knees* [Seneca]. He who relaxes none of his assurance, no matter how great the danger of imminent death; who, giving up his soul, still looks firmly and scornfully at his enemy—he is beaten not by us, but by fortune; he is killed, not conquered.

The most valiant are sometimes the most unfortunate. Thus there are triumphant defeats that rival victories. Nor did those four sister victories, the fairest that the sun ever set eyes on—Salamis, Plataea, Mycale, and Sicily—ever dare match all their combined glory against the glory of the annihilation of King Leonidas and his men at the pass of Thermopylae.

Who ever hastened with more glorious and ambitious desire to win a battle than Captain Ischolas to lose one? Who ever secured his safety more ingeniously and painstakingly than he did his destruction? He was charged to defend a certain pass in the Peloponnesus against the Arcadians. Finding himself wholly incapable of doing this, in view of the nature of the place and the inequality of the forces, he made up his mind that all who confronted the enemy would necessarily have to remain on the field. On the other hand, deeming it unworthy both of his own virtue and magnanimity and of the Lacedaemonian name to fail in his charge, he took a middle course between these two extremes, in this way. The youngest and fittest of his band he preserved for the defense and service of their country, and sent them home; and with those whose loss was less important, he determined to hold this pass, and by their death to make the enemy buy their entry as dearly as he could. And so it turned out. For he was presently surrounded on all sides by the Arcadians, and after slaughtering a large number of them, he and his men were all put to the sword. Is there a trophy dedicated to victors that would not be more due to these vanquished? The role of true victory is in fighting, not in coming off safely; and the honor of valor consists in combating, not in beating.

To return to our story. These prisoners are so far from giving in, in spite of all that is done to them, that on the contrary, during the two or three months that they are kept, they wear a gay expression; they urge their captors to hurry and put them to the test; they defy them, insult them, reproach them with their cowardice and the number of battles they have lost to the prisoners' own people.

I have a song composed by a prisoner which contains this challenge, that they should all come boldly and gather to dine off him, for they will be eating at the same time their own fathers and grandfathers, who have served to feed and nourish his body. "These muscles," he says, "this flesh and these veins are your own, poor fools that you are. You do not recognize that the substance of your ancestors' limbs is still contained in them. Savor them well; you will find in them the taste of your own flesh." An idea that certainly does not smack of barbarity. Those that paint these people dying, and who show the execution, portray the prisoner spitting in the face of his slayers and scowling at them. Indeed, to the last gasp they never stop braving and defying their enemies by word and look. Truly here are real savages by our standards; for either they must be thoroughly so, or we must be; there is an amazing distance between their character and ours.

The men there have several wives, and the higher their reputation for valor the more wives they have. It is a remarkably beautiful thing about their marriages that the same jealousy our wives have to keep us from the affection and kindness of other women, theirs have to win this for them. Being more concerned for their husbands' honor than for anything else, they strive and scheme to have as many companions as they can, since that is a sign of their husbands' valor.

Our wives will cry "Miracle!" but it is no miracle. It is a properly matrimonial virtue, but one of the highest order. In the Bible, Leah, Rachel, Sarah, and Jacob's wives gave their beautiful handmaids to their husbands; and Livia seconded the appetites of Augustus, to her own disadvantage; and Stratonice, the wife of King Deiotarus, not only lent her husband for his use a very beautiful young chambermaid in her service, but carefully brought up her children, and backed them up to succeed to their father's estates.

And lest it be thought that all this is done through a simple and servile bondage to usage and through the pressure of the authority of their ancient customs, without reasoning or judgment, and because their minds are so stupid that they cannot take any other course, I must cite some examples of their capacity. Besides the warlike song I have just quoted, I have another, a love song, which begins in this vein: "Adder, stay; stay, adder, that from the pattern of your coloring my sister may draw the fashion and the workmanship of a rich girdle that I may give to my love; so may your beauty and your pattern be forever preferred to all other serpents." This first couplet is the refrain of the song. Now I am familiar enough with poetry to be a judge of this: not only is there nothing barbarous in this fancy, but it is altogether Anacreontic. Their language, moreover, is a soft language, with an agreeable sound, somewhat like Greek in its endings.

Three of these men, ignorant of the price they will pay some day, in loss of repose and happiness, for gaining knowledge of the corruptions of this side of the ocean; ignorant also of the fact that of this intercourse will come their ruin (which I suppose is already well advanced: poor wretches, to let themselves be tricked by the desire for new things, and to have left the serenity of their own sky to come and see ours!)—three of these men were at Rouen, at the time the late King Charles IX was there. The king talked to them for a long time; they were shown our ways, our splendor, the aspect of a fine city. After that, someone asked their opinion, and wanted to know what they had found most amazing. They mentioned three things, of which I have forgotten the third, and I am very sorry for it; but I still remember two of them. They said that in the first place they thought it very strange that so many grown men, bearded, strong, and armed, who were around the king (it is likely that they were talking about the Swiss of his guard) should submit to obey a child, and that one of them was not chosen to command instead. Second (they have a way in their language of speaking of men as halves of one another), they had noticed that there were among us men full and gorged with all sorts of good things, and that their other halves were beggars at their doors, emaciated with hunger and poverty; and they thought it strange that these needy halves could endure such an injustice, and did not take the others by the throat, or set fire to their houses.

I had a very long talk with one of them; but I had an interpreter who followed my meaning so badly, and who was so hindered by his stupidity in taking in my ideas, that I could get hardly any satisfaction from the man. When I asked him what profit he gained from his superior position among his people (for he was a captain, and our sailors called him king), he told me that it was to march foremost in war. How many men followed him? He pointed to a piece of ground, to signify as many as such a space could hold; it might have been four or five thousand men. Did all his authority expire with the war? He said that this much remained, that when he visited the villages dependent on him, they made paths for him through the underbrush by which he might pass quite comfortably.

All this is not too bad—but what's the use? They don't wear breeches.

WILLIAM SHAKESPEARE

William Shakespeare (1564–1616), the most famous English writers and one of the world's greatest poets and dramatists, is also perhaps its most popular. Shakespeare's fame and popularity rest on his plays primarily, though his 154 sonnets remain perennially in fashion. Samples of the sonnets are followed by famous soliloquies from a few of the plays.

Shall I Compare Thee to a Summer's Day?

Shall I compare thee to a summer's day?
Thou art more lovely and more temperate.
Rough winds do shake the darling buds of May,
And summer's lease hath all too short a date.
Sometime too hot the eye of heaven shines,   5
And often is his gold complexion dimmed;
And every fair from fair sometime declines,
By chance, or nature's changing course, untrimmed;[1]
But thy eternal summer shall not fade,
Nor lose possession of that fair thou ow'st,°   *ownest*   10
Nor shall Death brag thou wand'rest in his shade,
When in eternal lines to time thou grow'st.
    So long as men can breathe or eyes can see.
    So long lives this, and this gives life to thee.
                                                        [#18, 1609]

---

[1]**untrimmed**   stripped or divested of beauty.

When, in Disgrace With Fortune and Men's Eyes

When, in disgrace with Fortune and men's eyes,
I all alone beweep my outcast state,
And trouble deaf heaven with my bootless° cries,   *fruitless*
And look upon myself and curse my fate,
Wishing me like to one more rich in hope,   5
Featured like him, like him with friends possessed,
Desiring this man's art, and that man's scope,
With what I most enjoy contented least;
Yet in these thoughts myself almost despising,
Haply I think on thee, and then my state,   10
Like to the lark at break of day arising
From sullen earth, sings hymns at heaven's gate;
    For thy sweet love rememb'red such wealth brings,
    That then I scorn to change my state with kings.
                                                        [#29, 1609]

Not Marble, Nor the Gilded Monuments

Not marble, nor the gilded monuments
Of princes, shall outlive this pow'rful rhyme,
But you shall shine more bright in these contents
Than unswept stone, besmeared with sluttish° time.   *dirty*   5
When wasteful war shall statues overturn,
And broils root out the work of masonry,
Nor Mars his sword nor war's quick fire shall burn
The living record of your memory.
'Gainst death and all oblivious enmity
Shall you pace forth; your praise shall still find room   10
Even in the eyes of all posterity
That wear this world out to the ending doom.°
                                                    judgment day
    So, till the judgment that yourself arise,
    You live in this, and dwell in lovers' eyes.
                                                        [#15, 1609]

Let Us Not To the Marriage of True Minds

Let me not to the marriage of true minds
Admit impediments; love is not love
Which alters when it alteration finds,
Or bends with the remover to remove.
Oh no, it is an ever-fixed mark
That looks on tempests and is never shaken;
It is the star to every wandering bark
Whose worth's unknown, though his height be taken.
Love's not time's fool, though rosy lips and cheeks
Within his bending sickle's compass come;
Love alters not with his brief hours and weeks,
But bears it out even to the edge of doom.
    If this be error and upon me proved,
    I never writ, nor no man ever loved.

That Time of Year Thou May'st in Me Behold

That time of year thou may'st in me behold
When yellow leaves, or none, or few, do hang
Upon those boughs which shake against the cold,
Bare ruined choirs where late the sweet birds sang.
In me thou see'st the twilight of such day   5

As after sunset fadeth in the west,
Which by-and-by black night doth take away,
Death's second self that seals up all in rest.
In me thou see'st the glowing of such fire
That on the ashes of his youth doth lie,   *10*
As the deathbed whereon it must expire,
Consumed with that which it was nourished by.
 This thou perceiv'st, which makes thy love more strong,
 To love that well which thou must leave ere long.

All the World's A Stage

from *As You Like It,* II, vii, 139–166

JAQUES.   All the world's a stage,
And all the men and women merely players;
They have their exits and their entrances,
And one man in his time plays many parts,
His acts being seven ages. At first, the infant,   *5*
Mewling° and puking° in the nurse's arms.
          crying/vomiting
Then the whining schoolboy, with his satchel
And shining morning face, creeping like snail
Unwillingly to school. And then the lover,
Sighing like furnace, with a woeful ballad   *10*
Made to his mistress' eyebrow. Then a soldier,
Full of strange oaths and bearded like the pard,°
          leopard
Jealous° in honor, sudden° and quick in quarrel,
          zealous/rash
Seeking the bubble reputation
Even in the cannon's mouth. And then the justice,   *15*
In fair round belly with good capon lined,[2]
With eyes severe and beard of formal cut,
Full of wise saws° and modern instances;°
         maxims/examples
And so he plays his part. The sixth age shifts
Into the lean and slippered pantaloon,[3]   *20*
With spectacles on nose and pouch on side;
His youthful hose, well saved, a world too wide
For his shrunk shank, and his big manly voice,
Turning again toward childish treble, pipes
And whistles in his° sound. Last scene of all,   *its 25*
That ends this strange eventful history,
Is second childishness and mere oblivion,
Sans teeth, sans eyes, sans taste, sans everything.[4]

Now Is the Winter of Our Discontent

from *Richard III* I, i, 1–41

RICHARD. Now is the winter of our discontent
Made glorious summer by this sun of York;
And all the clouds that loured upon our house
In the deep bosom of the ocean buried.
Now are our brows bound with victorious wreaths,   *5*
Our bruisèd arms hung up for monuments,°
         memorials

Our stern alarums° changed to merry meetings,
         alarms
Our dreadful marches to delightful measures.°
         dances
Grim-visaged War hath smoothed his wrinkled
 front,°   *forehead*
And now, instead of mounting barbèd steeds   *10*
To fright the souls of fearful adversaries,
He capers nimbly in a lady's chamber
To the lascivious pleasing of a lute.
But I, that am not shaped for sportive tricks
Nor made to court an amorous looking glass;   *15*
I, that am rudely stamped, and want° love's majesty
         lack
To strut before a wanton ambling nymph;
I, that am curtailed of this fair proportion,
Cheated of feature° by dissembling Nature,
        bodily form
Deformed, unfinished, sent before my time   *20*
Into this breathing world scarce half made up,
And that so lamely and unfashionable
That dogs bark at me as I halt by them;
Why, I, in this weak piping time of peace,[5]
Have no delight to pass away the time,   *25*
Unless to spy my shadow in the sun
And descant on mine own deformity.[6]
And therefore, since I cannot prove a lover
To entertain these fair well-spoken days,
I am determinèd to prove a villain   *30*
And hate the idle pleasures of these days.
Plots have I laid, inductions° dangerous,   *plans*
By drunken prophecies, libels, and dreams,
To set my brother Clarence and the King
In deadly hate the one against the other;   *35*
And if King Edward be as true and just
As I am subtle, false, and treacherous,
This day should Clarence closely be mewed up°
         imprisoned
About a prophecy which says that *G*
Of Edward's heirs the murderer shall be.   *40*
Dive, thoughts, down to my soul.

Friends, Romans, Countrymen

from *Julius Caesar.* III. a, 75–109

ANTONY. Friends, Romans, countrymen, lend me your ears;
I come to bury Caesar, not to praise him.
The evil that men do lives after them,
The good is oft interred with their bones;
So let it be with Caesar. The noble Brutus   *5*
Hath told you Caesar was ambitious.
If it were so, it was a grievous fault,
And grievously hath Caesar answered it.[7]
Here, under leave of Brutus and the rest
(For Brutus is an honorable man,   *10*

---

[2]**capon lined** a capon is a bribe offered to a judge.
[3]**pantaloon** figure in the Italian *commedia dell'arte;* a ridiculous old man.
[4]**Sans** French for "without."

[5]**piping . . . peace** The pipe, or wooden flute, was associated with peacetime.
[6]**descant** a musical term meaning "to compose variations on a theme."
[7]**answered** paid the penalty

So are they all, all honorable men),
Come I to speak in Caesar's funeral.
He was my friend, faithful and just to me;
But Brutus says he was ambitious,
And Brutus is an honorable man.   *15*
He hath brought many captives home to Rome,
Whose ransoms did the general coffers° till;   *treasury*
Did this in Caesar seem ambitious?
When that the poor have cried, Caesar hath wept;
Ambition should be made of sterner stuff.   *20*
Yet Brutus says he was ambitious;
And Brutus is an honorable man.
You all did see that on the Lupercal
I thrice presented him a kingly crown,
Which he did thrice refuse. Was this ambition?   *25*
Yet Brutus says he was ambitious;
And sure he is an honorable man.
I speak not to disprove what Brutus spoke,
But here I am to speak what I do know.
You all did love him once, not without cause;   *30*
What cause withholds you then to mourn for him?
O judgment, thou art fled to brutish beasts,
And men have lost their reason! Bear with me;
My heart is in the coffin there with Caesar,
And I must pause till it come back to me.   *35*

To Be, or Not To Be

from *Hamlet*, III, i, 56–90

HAMLET.   To be, or not to be: that is the question:
Whether 'tis nobler in the mind to suffer
The slings and arrows of outrageous fortune,
Or to take arms against a sea of troubles,
And by opposing end them. To die, to sleep—   *5*
No more—and by a sleep to say we end
The heartache, and the thousand natural shocks
That flesh is heir to! 'Tis a consummation
Devoutly to be wished. To die, to sleep—
To sleep—perchance to dream: ay, there's the rub,°
                                                    obstacle   10
For in that sleep of death what dreams may come
When we have shuffled off this mortal coil,
Must give us pause. There's the respect°   *consideration*
That makes calamity of so long life:
For who would bear the whips and scorns of time,   *15*
Th' oppressor's wrong, the proud man's contumely,
The pangs of despised love, the law's delay,
The insolence of office, and the spurns
That patient merit of th' unworthy takes,
When he himself might his quietus° make
                                                    settlement 20
With a bare bodkin°? Who would fardels° bear,
                                                    dagger/burdens
To grunt and sweat under a weary life,
But that the dread of something after death,
The undiscovered country, from whose bourn°
                                                    region
No traveler returns, puzzles the will,   *25*
And makes us rather bear those ills we have,
Than fly to others that we know not of?
Thus conscience does make cowards of us all,

And thus the native hue of resolution
Is sicklied o'er with the pale cast of thought,   *30*
And enterprises of great pitch and moment,
With this regard° their currents turn awry,
                                                    consideration
And lose the name of action.—Soft you now,
The fair Ophelia!—Nymph, in thy orisons°   *prayers*
Be all my sins remembered.   *35*

O Reason Not the Need!

from *King Lear.* II, iv, 263–285

LEAR.   O reason not the need! Our basest beggars
Are in the poorest thing superfluous.
Allow not nature more than nature needs,
Man's life is cheap as beast's. Thou art a lady:
If only to go warm were gorgeous,   *5*
Why, nature needs not what thou gorgeous wear'st,
Which scarcely keeps thee warm. But, for true need—
You heavens, give me that patience, patience I need.
You see me here, you gods, a poor old man,
As full of grief as age, wretched in both.   *10*
If it be you that stirs these daughters' hearts
Against their father, fool° me not so much
                                                    humiliate
To bear it tamely; touch me with noble anger,
And let not women's weapons, water drops,
Stain my man's cheeks. No, you unnatural hags!   *15*
I will have such revenges on you both
That all the world shall—I will do such things—
What they are, yet I know not; but they shall be
The terrors of the earth. You think I'll weep.
No, I'll not weep.   *20*

Storm and tempest.

I have full cause of weeping, but this heart
Shall break into a hundred thousand flaws°
                                                    fragments
Or ere° I'll weep. O Fool, I shall go mad!   *before*

Our Revels Now Are Ended

From *The Tempest*, IV, i, 148–163

ARIEL.   Our revels now are ended. These our actors,
As I foretold you, were all spirits and
Are melted into air, into thin air;
And, like the baseless fabric of this vision,
The cloud-capped towers, the gorgeous palaces,   *5*
The solemn temples, the great globe itself,
Yea, all which it inherit,° shall dissolve.   *occupy it*
And, like this insubstantial pageant faded,
Leave not a rack° behind. We are such stuff
                                                    wisp of cloud
As dreams are made on, and our little life   *10*
Is rounded with a sleep. Sir, I am vexed.
Bear with my weakness; my old brain is troubled.
Be not disturbed with my infirmity.
If you be pleased, retire into my cell
And there repose. A turn or two I'll walk   *15*
To still my beating mind.

CHAPTER 15

The Baroque Age

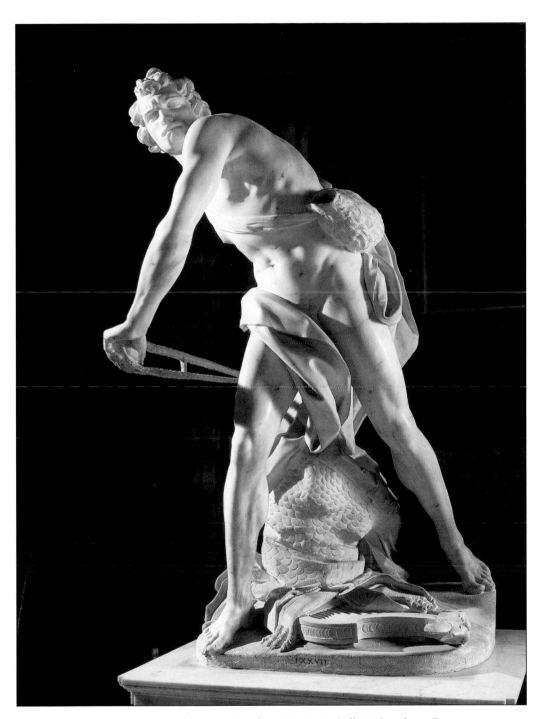

Gianlorenzo Bernini, *David*, marble, 1623, height 5'7"(1.7 m), Galleria Borghese, Rome.

MAP 15.1 Europe in the early 1700s.

CHAPTER OVERVIEW

THE BAROQUE IN ITALY
Drama and illusion dominate the arts

THE BAROQUE OUTSIDE ITALY
Diversity rules the arts and sciences

THE BAROQUE IN ITALY

THE TERM **BAROQUE,** FROM THE PORTUGUESE word *barrocco*, meaning a large, irregularly shaped pearl, was initially used as a pejorative, or negative, term. Gradually it came to describe the complex, multifaceted, international phenomenon of the Baroque. Baroque artists intended to involve their audiences emotionally. Formally,

the style is characterized by drama and theatricality seen in a heightened realism and illusions of motion. Classical elements are used without classical restraint. Emotionalism is enhanced by striking contrasts of light and shadow.

At least as important in defining the Baroque style is understanding the patronage that supported it. Church-sponsored art in Rome thrived during the Counter-Reformation. Although secular patrons were important in the development of Baroque art (particularly Philip IV in Spain and Marie de' Medici and Louis XIV in France), the Church in Rome assumed the role of the center of the Baroque art world.

As pope succeeded pope, each brought with him an entourage of family and friends who expected and received lucrative positions in the government and who vied with each other to give expression to their newfound wealth and position. The popes commissioned palaces and chapels—along with paintings and sculptures to decorate them. Artists flocked to Rome to take advantage of the situation.

THE COUNTER-REFORMATION IN ROME

In response to Martin Luther's "Ninety-Five Theses" and the Protestant Reformation that followed, the Catholic Church sought to remake Rome as the cultural center of the Western world. Thus once again Roman popes became great patrons of art and architecture. The strategy to defend Rome's prestige and dominion was continued for over a hundred years, culminating in the twenty-one-year pontificate of Urban VIII (1623–44).

The theological justification for this patronage came at the Council of Trent, which convened in three sessions from 1545 to 1563 to address the crisis of the Reformation. The council decided to counter the Protestant threat "by means of the stories of the mysteries of our Redemption portrayed by paintings or other representations, [whereby] the people [shall] be instructed and confirmed in the habit of remembering, and continually revolving in mind the articles of faith." The council further suggested that religious art be directed toward clarity (to increase understanding), realism (to make it more meaningful in everyday fashion), and emotion (to arouse piety and religious fervor). Taken together, these goals epitomized the Catholic **Counter-Reformation.**

According to the council's recommendations, art ought to be easily understood. Music had to be accessible and lyrics intelligible. Literature should celebrate religious values and ideals. These recommendations were intended to counter the Mannerist style. Mannerist painting tended to be refined, stylized, virtuosic, decorative, and complex in color, structure, and allegorical content. Baroque art was to make direct statements on religious subjects familiar to the common people. Still, from the Mannerists, Baroque artists inherited a reliance on emotionally charged and dramatic action. The Council of Trent began a renewal of faith, stirring religious fervor through church art and architecture, and through liturgies, rituals, and dogmas.

Two new religious orders emerged from the Council of Trent, the Oratorians and the Jesuits. Both were of central importance to the religious mission.

The Oratorians. Founded by St. Philip Neri, the Oratorians were groups of Catholics, laymen and clergy, who met informally for spiritual conversation, study, and prayer. They met not in churches but in prayer halls called **oratories.** They were not a religious order: They took no vows, and members could leave at any time. Music played an essential role in their religious devotions, especially vocal music. The composer who was most important for them was Palestrina (see Chapter 13), whose *Laude,* or songs of praise, were easy to sing. Later, musical performances became increasingly dramatic. Eventually, they resembled unstaged miniature music dramas and were the forerunners of the oratorios written by George Frederick Handel.

The Jesuits. In 1534, the Jesuit order of Catholic priests was established by St. Ignatius Loyola, and there was nothing informal about the Jesuits' organization or goals. The order was to follow a militaristic discipline. Members followed strict vows of poverty, chastity, and obedience while pursuing a rigorous education in preparation for their missionary role. Jesuit priests played an important part in the religious life of the age, serving as confessors and spiritual advisers to prominent artists such as Bernini and to political leaders, including Queen Christina of Sweden.

The most influential aspect of Jesuit spirituality derives from the writings of the order's founder, St. Ignatius. His *Spiritual Exercises,* published in 1548, guide believers through a sequence of spiritual practices to intensify their relationship with God. The *Exercises* involve each of the senses so the individual might obtain more than just intellectual understanding. For example, when contemplating sin and hell, the soul is exhorted to consider in order: the sights of hell (flames); the sounds of hell (groans of the damned and shrieks of devils); the smells of hell (the fetid stench of corrupting bodies); the tastes of hell (the suffering of hunger and thirst); and the tactile experience of hell (the intense heat, which scorches the body and boils the blood). Such exercises involved the emotions in religious experience, the hallmark of Baroque sensibility.

Complementing the work of the Oratorians and the Jesuits were the writings of sixteenth- and seventeenth-century Spanish mystics such as St. John of the Cross, who wrote *The Dark Night of the Soul,* and St. Teresa of Avila, who wrote an autobiography. Both blended the contemplative life with a commitment to a life of action. Teresa of Avila was canonized by Pope Gregory XV in 1622, along with Philip Neri and Ignatius of Loyola.

THIRTY YEARS' WAR

During the thirty-year period from 1618 to 1648, a series of wars raged throughout central Europe. On one side was a coalition consisting of the Austrian Hapsburg Holy Roman Emperors, Ferdinand I and II, with their Spanish cousin King Philip IV. Opposing them were Denmark, France, Holland, and Sweden. In addition, various German principalities fought on both sides. There was also a religious dimension to the war, with Lutherans, Catholics, and Calvinists fighting one another at various times.

The war occurred when the Peace of Augsburg (1555), which had ended violence between Lutherans and Catholics in Germany, became frayed. Tensions were exacerbated by rising political tensions throughout Europe, as Denmark, France, Spain, and Sweden all had designs, for different reasons, on German lands. Fought primarily on German lands, the war resulted in the deaths of about one-third of the German population.

The consequences of the war were significant. Spain declined both politically and militarily, with Portugal declaring its independence from Spain in 1640. With Germany fractured into many competing territories, France grew in power. Other effects included an end to the age of mercenaries, or hired soldiers. The Peace of Westphalia (1648), which concluded the Thirty Years' War, ended the era of the Holy Roman Empire and religious unity, inaugurating a new era in which sovereign nation states controlled politics and diplomacy in Europe.

ARCHITECTURE AND SCULPTURE IN ROME

St. Peter's Basilica. The Church's most visible effort to arouse the faithful was the continued work on the new St. Peter's Basilica, work initiated by Pope Julius II in 1502 (see Chapter 13). In 1607, Pope Paul V commissioned CARLO MADERNO [mah-DEHR-no] (1556–1629) as Vatican architect to convert Michelangelo's Greek-cross plan into a Latin cross plan complete with a new facade. There was a practical reason for this: The long nave of the Latin cross plan provided space for more people to attend services. The interior space Maderno created was the largest of any church in Europe, meant to evoke the vastness of God himself.

Maderno's facade (fig. 15.1) followed Michelangelo's conception of using the colossal order to unite the stories and of topping the entrance with a triangular pediment. In fact, Maderno's composition is even more theatrical than Michelangelo intended. Pope Paul V conceived of the church facade as a backdrop to his own public appearances

FIGURE 15.1 Carlo Maderno, facade of St. Peter's, Rome, 1607–15, height 147′(44.81 m), width 374′(114 m). The facade is treated like a theatrical performance that builds from the wings: Starting from the corners, the pilasters double, then become columns, which then also double, and, finally, the center section seems to push out to meet the visitor.

and required a balcony from which he could bless the people below. An architectural crescendo rises from the sides of the facade toward the central portal, generating a dramatic, which is to say Baroque, effect.

Gianlorenzo Bernini. The theatricality of Maderno's facade was only a beginning. When Maderno died in 1629, Pope Urban VIII replaced him with GIANLORENZO BERNINI [ber-NEE-nee] (1598–1680), who had collaborated with Maderno for five years. Although Bernini considered himself a classicist, he fused his classicism with extraordinary drama and emotion. His sculpture and architecture are the essence of Baroque art.

In 1657, Bernini, now working for another pope, designed and supervised the building of a **colonnade,** or row of columns, in front of St. Peter's. Beginning in two straight covered walkways, or **porticoes,** the Doric columns extend down a slight incline from the church facade, then swerve into two enormous curved porticoes, surrounding and embracing the open space of the piazza, like "the motherly arms of the church," as Bernini himself put it (fig. 15.2). Forgoing the square and circular forms of the Renaissance, Bernini's colonnade uses the more dynamic ellipse and trapezoid. In the center of the oval plaza stands an **obelisk,** or four-sided shaft topped by a pyramid. From there, lines on the pavement radiate out to the colonnade. Finally, surmounting each inner column is a different statue, creating an irregular silhouette along the top of the colonnade.

Bernini's sculpture of *David* (fig. 15.3), carved in 1623 and characteristic of his style, deserves comparison to Michelangelo's High Renaissance *David* (see Chapter 13). In its depiction of drama, Bernini's work is close to Hellenistic sculpture as embodied in the *Laocoön* (Chapter 3), which Bernini had studied. Michelangelo's *David*, by contrast, seems restrained. Bernini captures the split second before David flings the stone that kills Goliath, implying a second figure to "complete" the action. *David's* pose and facial expression charge the space surrounding the sculpture with tension, so effectively that people viewing the statue avoid standing between *David* and his implied target.

Bernini's *Ecstasy of St. Teresa* (fig. 15.4) is the most impressive sculpture created to celebrate the life of a Counter-Reformation saint. Bernini designed it for the Cornaro Chapel of Santa Maria della Vittoria in Rome and positioned it in an oval niche above the altar, framed by green marble pilasters. Created between 1645 and 1652, the multimedia sculpture depicts the moment in St. Teresa's autobiography when she says an angel pierced her heart with a flaming golden arrow, causing her to swoon in pleasure and agony. "The pain was so great that I screamed aloud," she wrote, "but at the same time I felt such infinite sweetness that I wished the pain to last forever. . . . It was the sweetest caressing of the soul by God."

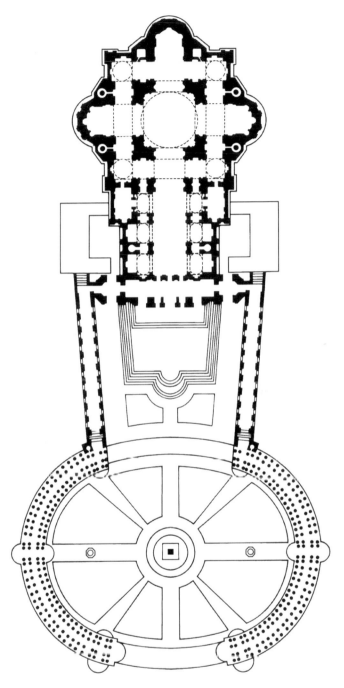

FIGURE 15.2 St. Peter's Rome, plan. Maderno's Latin cross plan of St. Peter's is preceded by Bernini's colonnades that create a dynamic architectural environment of eliptical and trapezoidal shapes.

Abandoning Renaissance restraint, Bernini captures the sensuality of her ecstasy.

Francesco Borromini. FRANCESCO BORROMINI [Bor-ro-MEE-nee] (1599–1667) joined his uncle, Carlo Maderno, in Rome in 1619 and was soon working for Bernini in St. Peter's. But Borromini quickly became Bernini's chief rival, and unlike the worldly Bernini,

FIGURE 15.3 Gianlorenzo Bernini, *David,* marble, 1623, height 5′ 7″ (1.7 m), Galleria Borghese, Rome. Unlike Michelangelo's static *David,* Bernini's is caught at the split second when the direction of the action is about to reverse—much like the ancient Greek *Discus Thrower.* Bernini effectively indicates the position of the giant Goliath, something that is sensed by viewers, who quickly move out of the implied line of fire.

Borromini was a secretive and unstable man whose life ended in suicide.

Borromini is best known for San Carlo alle Quattro Fontane (fig. 15.5), or St. Charles of the Four Fountains, named for the fountains at the junction where it is located in Rome. The interior of the church was designed between 1638 and 1641, and the facade between 1665 and 1667. On a tiny and irregular plot, Borromini built a tiny and irregular church: San Carlo could fit easily within Saint Peter's. Deviating from the classical tradition, the columns are of no known order—instead, Borromini designed a new order of his own. Rather than building with the traditional flat surfaces of ancient architecture, Borromini made the stone facade seem elastic, curving in and out, the

stone appearing to undulate in a serpentine concave-convex motion. So three dimensional is this facade that it almost becomes sculpture, rippling with light and shade in Rome's sunlight.

Borromini designed San Carlo alle Quattro Fontane with a double facade, a clever solution to a practical problem. The church faces so small an intersection that it is not possible to stand back far enough to view the facade in its entirety. Borromini's double facade divides the surface into two smaller compositions, yet the entablature of the lower story forms the balcony of the upper story, typical of the Baroque concern for unity of design.

Borromini's extravagant style was popular. The head of the religious order for whom San Carlo alle Quattro Fontane was built wrote with great pride, "Nothing similar can be found anywhere else in the world. This is attested by the foreigners who . . . try to procure copies of

FIGURE 15.4 Gianlorenzo Bernini, *Ecstasy of St. Teresa,* overview of Cornaro Chapel, 1645–52, height of figure group 11′ 6″ (3.51 m), Santa Maria della Vittoria, Rome. This dramatic depiction of Teresa's written description is literally theatrical, for the chapel is arranged like a theater, complete with box seats occupied by marble figures of members of the Cornaro family.

FIGURE 15.5 Francesco Borromini, San Carlo alle Quattro Fontane, Rome 1638–67, width of facade 34′(10.36 m). Because this church is located at an intersection of narrow streets, the viewer cannot easily see the entire facade. Borromini therefore created two separate compositions, undulating and sculptural, linked by the entablature of the lower story that forms a balcony for the upper story.

the plan. We have been asked for them by Germans, Flemings, Frenchmen, Italians, Spaniards, and even Indians."

PAINTING IN ITALY

As with sculptors and architects, the demand for painters during the Counter-Reformation was enormous. Although some were hired to work permanently for a given patron, by far the majority worked in studios in Rome, displaying their works in progress and seeking commissions. Competition for the best artists was fierce, and as a result their social standings (and fees) rose ever higher.

Caravaggio. One of the most important art patrons was Cardinal Scipione Borghese, nephew of Pope Paul. Bor-

ghese's villa contained a vast quantity of paintings and frescoes and was set in a large park full of niches and statuary. One of Borghese's favorite painters was CARAVAGGIO [ka-ra-VAH-joh] (1573–1610), whose real name was Michelangelo Merisi but who took his name from his birthplace, the village of Caravaggio near Milan. Caravaggio was a bohemian artist with a terrible temper who led a short and turbulent life (with a long police record bordering on the criminal). Despite his lifestyle, Caravaggio was a great religious painter whose work established the major direction of painting in the Baroque age.

Caravaggio painted the *Calling of St. Matthew* (fig. 15.6) in about 1599–1602 for the private chapel of the Contarelli family in the Church of San Luigi dei Francesi in Rome. A large painting, it depicts the climactic moment of Matthew's calling. As told in the Bible, Matthew 9:9. Jesus points to the tax collector Matthew, who gestures with disbelief, as if to say, "Who? Me?"

This biblical tale, shown in the everyday environment of a Roman tavern, is enacted by people who could have been Caravaggio's contemporaries (who were probably the models for the work). Although Matthew and his associates are richly attired, the two figures on the right are in rags. Jesus's halo is barely visible. Yet a religious atmosphere is created by Caravaggio's dramatic use of light, known as **tenebrism**—a "dark manner," in which light and dark contrast strongly, the highlights picking out only what the artist wants the viewer to see. The light comes from above, like a spotlight centering on an actor on stage, but no obvious light source is shown.

Caravaggio also painted the *Entombment* (fig. 15.7), executed in 1603 for a chapel in Santa Maria in Vallicella, Rome, the church of St. Philip Neri's Congregation of the Oratory. The light reveals only a hint of the setting; clarity is achieved by Caravaggio's highlighting of select figures and features. The platform on which his figures stand is at the viewers' eye level and seems to extend into the viewers' space, increasing the impact of the scene by drawing them toward it, and making them feel virtual participants in the event. Indeed, the implication is that the viewer is in the tomb itself, ready to receive Jesus's body. The figures are placed so close to the picture plane that the elbow of the man who grasps Jesus's legs seems to project into the viewer's space.

The *Entombment* makes the words of the sermon visible, explicit, almost tangible. Caravaggio portrays Jesus's associates as people much like himself. He did not raise his subjects to the level of the heroic, as had customarily been done. This aspect of Caravaggio's art was not well received by his contemporaries who felt he had gone too far in reducing the distinction between heaven and earth.

Artemisia Gentileschi. The emotional and dramatic side of the Baroque is demonstrated also by ARTEMISIA GENTILESCHI [jen-tee-LESS-kee] (1593–ca. 1653). Born in Rome, her style seems to have been influenced by

FIGURE 15.6   Caravaggio, *Calling of St. Matthew*, ca. 1599–1602, oil on canvas, 11′ 1″ × 11′5″(3.38 × 3.48 m). Contarelli Chapel, San Luigi dei Francesi, Rome. Although Matthew is seated in a tavern when he receives Jesus's call, Caravaggio uses tenebristic lighting to reveal the religious nature of this event.

that of her father, Orazio Gentileschi, a painter in Caravaggio's style. She was herself known as one of several "Caravaggisti," or "night painters," whose work was identifiable by the use of tenebrism.

Gentileschi's paintings often depicted the popular biblical subjects of Bathsheba and David and of Judith and Holofernes. Her *Judith Slaying Holofernes* (fig. 15.8), painted ca. 1620, conveys intrigue and violence. The beautiful Jewish widow Judith saved her people from Nebuchadnezzar's Assyrian army by enticing their leader, Holofernes, into a tent where he drank himself to sleep. She then cut off his head with his own sword. The unnerving drama is enhanced by the dark tenebristic lighting that spotlights the actors as if on stage. The large figures fill the picture and seem to crowd forward as if about to burst through the picture plane.

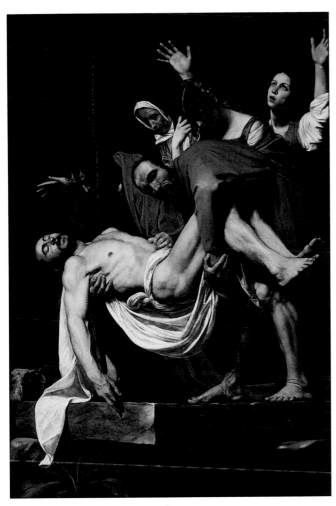

FIGURE 15.7 Caravaggio, *Entombment*, 1603, oil on canvas, 9′ 10$\frac{1}{8}$″ × 6′ 7$\frac{15}{16}$″(3.00 × 2.03 m), Musei Vaticani, Pinacoteca, Rome. Scala/Art Resource, NY. The painting's impact is enhanced by bringing the figures close to the picture plane. By locating the stone slab at eye level, Caravaggio suggests the viewer is actually in the tomb, ready to receive Jesus's body.

FIGURE 15.8 Artemisia Gentileschi, *Judith Slaying Holofernes*, ca. 1620, oil on canvas, 6′6$\frac{1}{3}$″ × 5′4″(1.99 × 1.63 m). Galleria degli Uffizi, Florence. Scala/Art Resource, NY. Drama and horror are magnified by the proximity of the figures and by the powerful spotlight focusing attention on the beheading, leaving all else in shadow.

Gentileschi's paintings have been linked to a sexual assault at the age of fifteen by one of her teachers. Later she was tortured in court with a thumbscrew (a device designed to compress the thumb to the point of smashing it) to verify the validity of her accusation.

Elisabetta Sirani. During her brief life of only twenty-seven years, the extremely prolific painter ELISABETTA SIRANI [Elis-ah-BEHT-tah see-RAH-nee] (1638–65) of Bologna was in charge of the family shop and supported her parents and three siblings through the sale of her art. Known for the speed with which she produced finished paintings, she achieved international fame and her paintings were sought by the most important patrons. Her early death followed immediately after severe abdominal pains. When an autopsy discovered perforated ulcers, the maid accused of poisoning her was acquitted.

Her painting of the *Virgin and Child* (fig. 15.9), dated to 1663, shows the sentimentality that charmed her patrons. Mary's gesture could be no gentler without losing hold of her twisting infant, whose animation contrasts to Mary's slow movement. The exchange of gazes endears, as Mary leans forward so that Jesus may crown her with a flower garland. Sirani signed her work in the embroidered band on the pillow on which Jesus sits.

Giovanna Garzoni. In contrast to the Baroque emotional drama and obscuring shadows is the work of GIOVANNA GARZONI [Gee-oh-VAHN-nah Gar-ZONE-ee] (1600–70), for although she painted various subjects, she is remembered for her depictions of still life, a subject already popular in Northern Europe from the late sixteenth century onward. In the *Plate of White Peas* (fig. 15.10) the composition is simple and the subject is ordinary, down to the degree of decay beginning to appear on the leaves and pods. The appeal of Garzoni's paintings is based largely upon her impressive technical skill and ability to simulate in paint what the eye sees, down to the tiniest and most meticulously rendered detail.

FIGURE 15.10 Giovanna Garzoni, *Plate of White Peas*, undated, tempera on parchment, $9\frac{3}{4}'' \times 13\frac{1}{2}''$ (25 × 33 cm). Palazzo Pitti, Florence. Technically, working in a water-based medium on animal skin and painting the tiniest details, this recalls medieval manuscript illuminations. But the extreme degree of fidelity to the visible world and direct study from a model in Garzoni's work contrasts with the medieval preference for distortion and avoidance of firsthand study of nature.

FIGURE 15.9 Elisabetta Sirani, *Virgin and Child*, 1663, oil on canvas, $34'' \times 27\frac{1}{2}''$ (86.4 × 69.9 cm), National Museum of Women in the Arts, Washington, DC. Gift of Wallace and Wilhelmina Holladay. Conservatin funds generously provided by the Southern California State Committee of the National Museum of Women in the Arts. The Baroque interest in emotion, in this case sweet, sentimental, and touching, is seen in Sirani's painting. Also characteristic of the Baroque are the lush full-bodied figures and the facility with which they are painted.

Like some successful male artists of her day, Garzoni did not marry and instead traveled from one city to the next. Thus, she accommodated her patrons in Venice, Florence, Naples, and Rome, arriving there by 1654 and remaining in this city thereafter.

Fra Andrea Pozzo. The epitome of the illusionistic Baroque ceiling fresco was achieved by FRA ANDREA POZZO [POT-zoh] (1642–1709), in his depiction of the *Triumph of St. Ignatius of Loyola* (fig. 15.11), of 1691–94, on the nave ceiling of Sant'Ignazio, Rome. The effect is astonishing; the solid vault of the ceiling has been painted away. It is an extreme example of what the Italians called *quadratura*, used to trick the eye into believing that the architecture of the church, its columns and arches, extends past the actual ceiling. The perspective is calculated to be seen from a specific point marked on the floor. When standing there, it is difficult to determine where the real architecture ends and the painted architecture begins. The center of the ceiling appears to be open sky from which saints and angels descend. Some sit on painted architecture or clouds; others fly through space in a dazzling display of Baroque artistic dexterity.

MUSIC IN ITALY

Claudio Monteverdi and Early Opera. It is hardly surprising, given the dramatic theatricality of Baroque painting, that the Baroque era produced the musical form known as **opera**, the Italian word for "a work." *Opera drammatica in musica*, "a dramatic work in music," has been abbreviated to "opera." Combining vocal music, instrumental music, and theater, an opera is a staged drama sung to the accompaniment of an orchestra. Opera developed among a group of humanists in Florence, who were interested in reviving the arts of ancient Greece. The creation of accompanied melodies with dramatic presentation was thought to be similar to the original Greek performances that had occurred between acts of plays. The emotional content of the voice, accompanied by instruments and combined with drama, was one of the most powerful forms to develop during the Baroque era. Opera epitomized the spirit of the Baroque in its flamboyant and theatrical style.

The first operas were written and performed before 1600, but the first notable work in the genre, *Orfeo* (*Orpheus*) by CLAUDIO MONTEVERDI [mon-teh-VAIR-dee] (1567–1643), was composed for his patron, the duke of Mantua, in 1607. It retells the Greek myth of Orpheus, the poet and musician who goes down to Hades, the underworld, to bring back his dead wife, Eurydice.

FIGURE 15.11   Fra Andrea Pozzo, *Triumph of St. Ignatius of Loyola*, 1691–94, ceiling fresco, Sant Ignazio, Rome. If the viewer stands directly below the center of this quintessentially Baroque illusionistic ceiling painting, it is not possible to see where the actual architecture ends and the painted architecture begins.

The opera includes **recitative,** a form of musically heightened speech midway between spoken dialogue and melodic aria. Orpheus's recitative is a monologue in the "agitated style," which expresses musically the feelings described by the text. For example, the melody descends on the words *più profondi abissi* ("deepest abysses") and ascends to accompany the words *a riverder le stelle* ("to see again the stars").

Singing the women's parts in opera throughout the Baroque were "castrati," men who had been castrated before puberty to maintain their "boy soprano" vocal qualities. The high register of the boy, coupled with the strength and power of an adult voice, was popular with audiences during the seventeenth and eighteenth centuries. The demand for vocal virtuosity in lead singers in opera and later in solo performances meant castrati often had much wealth and prestige.

The orchestra accompanying Baroque operas consisted of groups of small ensembles and was used to affect the "feelings" produced by the libretto, or text. Pastoral scenes might be accompanied by recorders or scenes of heaven by a harp. This process paved the way for program music in the centuries to follow.

Antonio Vivaldi and the Concerto Grosso.   Invented by ARCANGELO CORELLI [ko-REL-lee] (1653–1713), the **concerto grosso** is an instrumental musical form consisting of three parts, or movements, for soloists and orchestra pitted against one another in dramatic contrast. Typically, the first movement of a Baroque concerto is energetic and spirited, the second is slow but with increasing tension, and the third and final movement more vigorous than the first, releasing the tensions built up earlier.

One of the most prolific Baroque composers of the concerto was ANTONIO VIVALDI [vee-VAHL-dee] (1678–1741), who wrote 450 concertos, forty operas, and numerous vocal and chamber works. Born in Venice in 1678, Vivaldi, an ordained priest, spent most of his life as music master at a Venetian school for orphaned girls. Many of his works were composed for student recitals.

Vivaldi's most popular work is *The Four Seasons,* a set of four concertos for solo violin and orchestra. Each of Vivaldi's four concertos—Winter, Spring, Summer, and Fall—is accompanied by a sonnet describing the appropriate season. In the original edition, the words were printed above musical passages that depicted the words in sound. The Spring Concerto, for instance, includes descriptions of chirping birds returning to the meadows, and has accompanying sections called "bird calls" in which one violin "calls" and another answers it.

The first eight lines of the sonnet are distributed throughout the first movement of the Spring Concerto, an Allegro in E major. The movement opens with a phrase played twice in succession, once loud and once softly as an echo. This is followed by a **ritornello** passage that will return repeatedly throughout the movement. The ritor-nello section is played by the entire instrumental group in alternation with sections for the solo violin. The ritornello form pervades not only Vivaldi's music but the Baroque concerto generally. Different textures in solo and ensemble sections are supplemented by abrupt contrasts in dynamics from loud to soft (terraced dynamics) and by contrasting imitations of bird-song and storm.

But interesting as such musical scene painting may be, the primary interest of Vivaldi's music is its use of themes, textures, and tone colors in structured repetitions and contrasts that identify him as a master of the concerto style. Inventive within a formal structure, Vivaldi's music was soon admired throughout Europe, and closely studied by Johann Sebastian Bach, the great composer of the age. The play between control and freedom appealed to an age at once attracted to the classicism of a Bernini colonnade and the fantasy of a Borromini facade.

THE BAROQUE OUTSIDE ITALY

Baroque art, especially painting, originated in Italy. Many of the Baroque artists whom we identify with other countries either lived, worked, or studied in Rome, including the French painter Nicolas Poussin, the Spanish painter Diego Velázquez, and the Flemish painter Peter Paul Rubens. If they did not go to Rome, they were usually influenced by Roman Baroque painting, particularly Caravaggio, who enjoyed a considerable reputation outside Italy. Nonetheless, the Baroque thrived outside Italy: in the low countries, Flanders and Holland, where a flourishing mercantile class became deeply interested in the arts; in Spain, where Philip IV amassed a collection; in England, where Charles I did the same; in France, where Marie de' Medici, regent for the young King Louis XIV, exerted influence over the French court; and in Germany, where Baroque music was particularly well received.

PAINTING IN HOLLAND

During the reign of Philip II of Spain, the northern provinces of The Netherlands rebelled against his repression of Protestants and formed a new Dutch republic; the southern provinces remained Catholic and loyal to Spain, thus creating the separate countries of Holland and Flanders.

A distinct brand of Baroque painting emerged in Holland, which in the seventeenth century was a country of merchants and tradespeople who found themselves, freed of Spanish rule, the sudden beneficiaries of having Amsterdam, the maritime center and commercial capital of Europe, as their capital city.

In Holland not just religious and political leaders but also merchants and tradespeople collected art. The English traveler Peter Mundy in 1640 claimed that "none go beyond" the Dutch "in the affection of the people to pictures. . . . All in general strive to adorn their houses, especially the outer or street room, with costly pieces. Butchers and bakers not much inferior in their shops, which are fairly set forth, yea many times blacksmiths, cobblers, etc., will have some picture or other by their forge and their stall."

Frans Hals. FRANS HALS [hals] (ca. 1580–1666) was born in Antwerp and worked in Haarlem as a portraitist. An extrovert, the painter's jovial personality comes across in a number of his paintings. Hals's sitters usually appear to be in a good mood, more at home in a tavern than in a church. Differing from the stiff formality of earlier portraiture, the *Jolly Toper* (fig. 15.12) of ca. 1628–30 is balancing a wine glass and gesturing broadly, perhaps caught in conversation. Hals broke with the fashion of the time, which was to paint with careful contours, delicate modeling, and attention to detail. Instead, his paint ranged from thick impasto to thin fluid glazes and he left the separate brushstrokes clearly visible. This spontaneity of technique matched the liveliness of his subject.

Judith Leyster. The most important follower of Frans Hals was JUDITH LEYSTER [LIE-ster] (1609–60), a

FIGURE 15.13 Judith Leyster, *Boy Playing a Flute*, 1630–35, oil on canvas, $28\frac{1}{2} \times 24\frac{1}{8}$"(72.4 × 61.3 cm), Nationalmuseum, Stockholm. Leyster's ability to convey a sense of life, of animation, is comparable to Hals's. The seemingly casual quality of both subject and painting technique is actually achieved with great care.

FIGURE 15.12 Frans Hals, *Jolly Toper*, ca. 1628–30, oil on canvas, $31\frac{7}{8} \times 26\frac{1}{4}$"(81.0 × 66.7 cm), Rijksmuseum, Amsterdam. Breaking from the stiffness of earlier portraits, this man appears to have been caught in mid-sentence—perhaps offering that glass of wine. Hals's dashing brushstrokes accord with and enhance the quality of spontaneity.

Dutch painter whose name came from her family's brewery in Haarlem, the Leysterre (Pole Star). So close are their painting styles that several works long thought to be by Hals have been found to be by Leyster. Like Hals, Leyster depicted animated scenes from daily life, as in the *Boy Playing a Flute* (fig. 15.13), painted 1630–35. Like Caravaggio, Leyster used limited colors and tenebristic lighting. And, as in Caravaggio's paintings, the figure occupies a shallow space, close to the picture plane. The boy's glance to the left would endanger the balance of this composition, were it not for the musical instruments hanging on the wall to the right. As with Hals, the seemingly casual brushwork and composition skillfully create an impression of relaxed ease.

Rembrandt van Rijn. In Amsterdam, the most important painter was REMBRANDT VAN RIJN [REM-brant] (1606–69), who took Caravaggio's Baroque lighting to new heights. Born in Leyden, the son of a miller, Rembrandt abandoned his studies of classical literature at the University of Leyden to study painting. In 1634, he married Saskia van Ulenborch, who came from a wealthy family. Between 1634 and 1642, now extremely successful, Rembrandt had many commissions and owned a large house and art collection in Amsterdam. Saskia was his great joy and often his model, but her early death in 1642 marked a turning point in Rembrandt's life—it was in this year that he painted *The Night Watch*.

The Night Watch (fig. 15.14) was one of Rembrandt's most important public commissions, paid for by the Amsterdam civic guard. All the men portrayed in this huge informal group portrait had contributed equally to the cost (their names appear on the shield hanging on the far wall). Its original title was *Captain Frans Banning Cocq Mustering His Company*, but it was dubbed *The Night Watch* in the eighteenth century because it had darkened with age. In actuality, the painting shows Cocq's company in the morning, welcoming Marie de' Medici, Queen of France, at Amsterdam's city gate.

The composition moves along diagonals. Originally, Captain Cocq and his lieutenant were not in the center but walking toward it (the painting has been cut on the left and bottom). Originally their next steps would have placed them in the center; because the viewer intuitively expects the focal point to be in the center, Rembrandt cleverly implies their movement.

The most remarkable aspect of the painting is the light, which creates atmosphere, unifies the composition, links the figures, highlights expressive features, and subordi-

FIGURE 15.14 Rembrandt van Rijn, *Captain Frans Banning Cocq Mustering His Company* (*The Night Watch*), 1642, oil on canvas, 11′11″ × 14′4″ (3.63 × 4.37 m), Rijksmuseum, Amsterdam. This enormous group portrait is often interpreted as marking the turning point in Rembrandt's life. His wife Saskia died in 1642, his popularity as an artist declined, and his financial problems began. The event depicted took place in the morning, but, because of gradual darkening, the painting has come to be known as *The Night Watch*.

FIGURE 15.15 Rembrandt van Rijn, *Christ Preaching*, ca. 1652, etching, $6\frac{1}{8} \times 8\frac{1}{8}''$ (15.6 × 20.6 cm). Metropolitan Museum of Art, New York, bequest of Mrs. H. O. Havermeyer, 1929. The H. O. Havermeyer Collection (29. 107. 18). The strong contrasts of light and dark seen in Rembrandt's paintings have their equivalent in his prints.

FIGURE 15.16 Rembrandt van Rijn, *Portrait of the Artist as an Old Man*, 1669, oil on canvas, $23\frac{1}{4} \times 20''$ (59.0 × 51.0 cm), Royal Picture Gallery Mauritshuis, The Hague. Rembrandt painted himself throughout his life, not in a laudatory manner like Albrecht Dürer, but as a means of self-analysis and personal reflection more akin to the later self-portraits of Vincent van Gogh.

nates unimportant details. The figures of Captain Cocq and his lieutenant received the greatest emphasis; the others felt cheated, but the picture was considered good enough to hang in the company's clubhouse.

Rembrandt also worked as a printer, a medium devoted to the play of light and dark. His etching of *Christ Preaching* (fig. 15.15), of ca. 1652, is set in Amsterdam's Jewish ghetto. Rembrandt felt sympathy for the Jewish people as victims of persecution. Using cross-hatching to model the masses and shadows, Rembrandt's subtle effects range from the faintest lines of gray to the richest areas of black. In **etching,** as in engraving, the design comes from incisions made in the surface. When an etching is made, first, a metal plate is coated with a waxy film. Next, the design is scraped or scratched through the wax to expose the plate, a process far less arduous than engraving the plate itself. The plate is then placed in a mild acid bath that eats into the exposed areas of metal. Finally, the waxy layer is removed from the plate, ink is wiped into the grooves, and the plate is printed on paper under pressure exerted by a printing press.

Rembrandt recorded his own life in many self-portraits—sixty in oil alone. His last *Self-Portrait* (fig. 15.16) was painted in 1669, the year of his death. The textured handling of paint is masterful, the colors luminous and glowing, but the contours are looser, the brushstrokes broader, the surface not as smooth as in his earlier paintings. Rembrandt is weary and disillusioned. Yet he remains dignified; in none of his self-portraits does he appear bit-

ter, resentful, or self-pitying. Introspective and honest, he presented himself as he was.

Pieter de Hooch. Everyday life, in its humblest details, is documented in the paintings of the Dutch artist PIETER DE HOOCH [hoogk] (1629–after 1684). In *The Bedroom* (fig. 15.17) of about 1663, a woman chats with a girl as she changes linens. Notable is de Hooch's carefully observed lighting; the woman is bathed by light from the window, while the dark interior contrasts with the warm sunlight on the cityscape visible through the door.

Jan Vermeer. Born in Delft, JAN VERMEER [vur-MEER] (1632–75) painted only for local patrons. He specialized in domestic scenes that document everyday life. Like Rembrandt Vermeer was fascinated by light, but of a very different kind. Where Rembrandt's light is theatrical, Vermeer's is scientific. Vermeer's use of light reveals every textural nuance.

In *Young Woman with a Water Pitcher* (fig. 15.18) of ca. 1664–65, characteristic of Vermeer, a single female figure is depicted performing an ordinary action, indoors, at a table with objects on it, light coming from a window on the left, the figure silhouetted against a pale-colored wall. Ver-

meer's clear and luminous light pervades the space, unlike Rembrandt's light, which falls in shafts. Neither the subtle gradations across the back wall nor the reflections of the table rug in the metal basin are overlooked. The viewer can almost feel the starched linen headdress, its two sides subtly differentiated by the fall of light, the polished metal pitcher, and the basin. The woman is posed within a composition of rectangles drawn in perspective. Vermeer's intimate scene of a woman absorbed in household tasks conveys a mood of serenity and peace.

Rachel Ruysch. This interest in careful observation and detailed recording done with an almost scientific attention to detail is seen in the work of the Dutch artist RACHEL RUYSCH (1664–1750), whose fame derives from the many still lifes of flowers she executed during a long and productive life. In 1679 she began an apprenticeship with a flower painter. Her *Roses, Convolvulus, Poppies, and Other Flowers in an Urn on a Stone Ledge* (fig. 15.19), an early work from the 1680s, shows her to have been an especially adept student. This scientifically accurate record of a variety of flowering plants includes both familiar and exotic species. Some are still buds, others are

FIGURE 15.17 Pieter de Hooch, *The Bedroom*, ca. 1663, oil on canvas, 20 × 24″ (50.8 × 61.0 cm), National Gallery of Art, Washington, D.C. Widener Collection. © Board of Trustees, The intimate details of everyday life are the center of interest of de Hooch's Baroque Dutch painting.

FIGURE 15.18 Jan Vermeer, *Young Woman with a Water Pitcher,* ca. 1664–65, oil on canvas, 18 × 16″ (45.7 × 40.6 cm), Metropolitan Museum of Art, New York, gift of Henry G. Marquand, 1889. Great importance is given by Vermeer to light—not for Baroque bravura, but to scientifically observe and record every detail, and to note every subtle gradation and reflection.

FIGURE 15.19 Rachel Ruysch. *Roses, Convolvulus, Poppies, and Other Flowers in an Urn on a Stone Ledge,* ca. 1745, oil on canvas, $42\frac{1}{2}$ × 33″(108 × 84 cm), National Museum of Women in the Arts, Washington, DC. Gift of Wallace and Wilhelmina Holladay. A much-appreciated painter of flower still lifes, a subject favored by the Dutch, Ruysch's popularity was based on her perfect assymetric flower arrangements, the most colorful flowers emerging from the characteristically dark gloom. Taking a scientific approach to Nature, she included a variety of types of plants and recorded the tiniest details of each.

in full bloom, and still others are now decaying. Ruysch's interest in variety includes the decorative shapes, colors, and textures. She had learned the importance of careful observation of Nature from her father, the scientist Frederik Ruysch; later she returned the favor by teaching her father to paint.

Ruysch joined the painters' guild in The Hague in 1701. Commissions for her large flower still lifes came from various parts of the globe. In 1708, she accepted an invitation to be court painter to Johann Wilhelm, the Elector Palatine of Bavaria, in Düsseldorf.

PAINTING IN FLANDERS

Peter Paul Rubens. Although born in Germany, PETER PAUL RUBENS [REW-bens] (1577–1640) established himself as an artist in Antwerp, the capital of Catholic Flanders. Between 1600 and 1608, at the very height of Caravaggio's career, he was in Italy, where he studied the Baroque masters, the antique, and the High Renaissance. He copied the "old masters" and enjoyed a good reputation in Italy, painting in a style that combined influences from the north and the south.

Intelligent, talented, sociable, energetic, and equipped with a good business sense, Rubens became extremely successful. He set up shop in Antwerp, and by 1611, with two hundred painters and students working in his studio, was the most financially successful artist of the age. He built a large home containing his studio and an art collection including works by Raphael, Titian, Tintoretto, van Eyck, and Bruegel. He received commissions from the Church, the city of Antwerp, and private individuals, but it was the royal courts of Europe that garnered him the most fame and fortune. He was court painter to the Duke of Mantua, and to the Spanish regents of The Netherlands, Albert and Isabella. Commissions came also from Charles I of England and Philip IV of Spain, both of whom presented him with a knighthood. In 1621, Marie de' Medici of France gave him the commission that would establish his international reputation.

After the death of her husband, Henry IV, Marie de' Medici served as regent for her young son, Louis XIII.

Connections

VERMEER AND THE ORIGINS OF PHOTOGRAPHY

It appears that Vermeer used a device known as the **camera obscura** to execute his paintings. First used in the Renaissance for verifying perspective, the camera obscura was used by Dutch painters as a tool for observation comparable to the microscope and the telescope. At its simplest, the device is an enclosed box with a tiny hole in one side through which shines a beam of external light, projecting the scene outside as an inverted image on the opposite, interior wall of the box. Thus the *camera obscura* is like the modern-day camera, but it lacks light-sensitive paper or film on which to record the image. In Vermeer's time, it could be the size of a room in which the artist could stand fully upright and trace the image, Or, as is probable in the case of Vermeer, the pinhole was lensed in such a way that he could focus the image on a translucent intermediary screen that he could closely copy.

Not only did the camera obscura transform a three-dimensional view to a two-dimensional image; it revealed intriguing details about the play of light. Often in Vermeer's paintings the light seems to force the image out of focus. Photographers call such spots in a photograph "discs of confusion." Although fleeting to the naked eye, Vermeer could study this optical effect through the lens of his camera obscura and capture it on canvas.

While it would be another 150 years until photographic chemistry was perfected, the physics upon which photography is based was already at work in Vermeer's images.

She asked Rubens to create a cycle of twenty-one large oil paintings portraying her life. His aim was to glorify the queen. A master of narrative, Rubens's solution was to dramatize even the ordinary. In the scene of *Marie de' Medici, Queen of France, Landing in Marseilles* (fig. 15.20), the queen is merely disembarking in the southern French city of Marseilles, yet Fame flies above, blowing a trumpet, and Neptune, god of the sea, accompanied by mermaids, rises from the waves to welcome her.

The drama of the composition is characteristic of the Baroque style, as is the love of movement in an open space. Everything becomes active to the point of agitation, even when not required by the subject. Rubens painted in terms of rich, luminous, glowing color and light rather than in terms of line. Every stroke, every form, is united by the sweeping movements of Rubens's design and the sheer exuberance of his lush forms, which appeal more to the eye than to the mind.

Aided by his early experience as a court page as well as his fluency in five languages (Greek, Italian, French, Spanish, and Flemish), Rubens served as an adviser and emissary for the Flemish court. When he visited the court of Philip IV in Spain from September 1628 until late April 1629, he stayed in the royal palace in Madrid and was visited almost daily by the young king.

After his first wife died in 1626, Rubens married Hélène Fourment, a distant relative, and began a second family. He was fifty years old, his bride sixteen, and they had four children in five years. *The Garden of Love* (fig. 15.21), ca. 1638, expresses the pleasures of life, with a robust grandeur approaching animal exuberance. Certainly Rubens's main interest in this work is in the voluptuous female figure. Only with difficulty could this scene be made any more sumptuous—or sensuous.

FIGURE 15.20　Peter Paul Rubens, *Marie de' Medici, Queen of France, Landing in Marseilles*, 1622–25, oil on canvas, 5'1" × 3'11⅔"(1.55 × 1.21 m), Musée du Louvre, Paris, Reunion des Musées Nationaux. Jean Lewandowski/Art Resource, NY. With the diagonal movements typical of the Baroque, brilliant color, sensuous textures, and dashing brushwork, Rubens raised his depiction of an unglamorous queen at an ordinary event to the level of high drama.

FIGURE 15.21 Peter Paul Rubens, *The Garden of Love*, ca. 1638, oil on canvas, 6′6″ × 9′3½″(1.98 × 2.83 m), Museo Nacional del Prado, Madrid. Rubens is known for his rich, lush style—applied to the setting and, especially, to the figures. The term *Rubenesque* has been coined to describe voluptuous fleshy females.

Anthony van Dyck. Rubens's assistant from 1618 to 1620, Anthony van Dyck (1599–1641), became painter to the court of Charles I in England and perhaps the greatest portrait painter of the age. His *Portrait of Charles I at the Hunt* (fig. 15.22), of 1635, captures the king's self-assurance. Van Dyck contrasts the king with the anxious groom and the pawing, nervous horse behind him, underscoring Charles's command of all situations.

Clara Peeters. Another aspect of Flemish painting is represented by Clara Peeters (1594–after 1657) from Antwerp, who signed her first painting at the age of fourteen. A still life painter, her specialty was the depiction of breakfasts or elaborate banquet tables. Of the latter type is her *Table with a Tart and a White Pitcher* (fig. 15.23) of 1611, painted when she was only seventeen years old. This complex table setting records a complete gourmet meal. Her technical ability in depicting different textures and surfaces reached a peak in the skillful handling of reflections, as here on the polished metal plate or glass goblet, which sometimes included miniature self-portraits.

Beneath the surface beauty of such still life paintings lies deeper symbolic meaning, often alluding to the brevity of life. In moralizing *vanitas* pictures, obvious symbols are a snuffed-out candle, hour glass, or skull, while more subtle are flowers that are dying or eaten by insects and fruits that are decaying or peeled, as seen here. The meaning of such symbols was well known to Peeters's intended audience.

PAINTING IN ENGLAND

Mary Beale. The interest in portraiture in seventeenth-century Europe also appears in the work of Mary Beale (1632–97), who specialized in portraiture, a genre particularly appreciated by the British. The artist Sir Peter Lely invited Beale to copy paintings in his extensive personal art collection in London. After Lely's death, Beale satisfied the

FIGURE 15.22   Anthony van Dyck, *Portrait of Charles I at the Hunt*, 1635, oil on canvas, approx. 9 × 7′ (2.74 × 2.13 m), Musée du Louvre, Paris. Reunion des Musées Nationaux. Art Resource, NY. Working in Rubens's rich, painterly style with loose brushwork and a range of textural effects, van Dyck captures the haughtiness of the posturing king.

demand for copies of his paintings: So adept was she at this, and so similar were their styles, that it is possible some portraits by Beale have been incorrectly attributed to Lely. After marrying Charles Beale, she began a professional apprenticeship and by 1670 was working independently as an artist. An example of her skill at this time in portraiture is seen in the likeness she created of *John Wilkins DD* (fig. 15.24) of ca. 1670. Painted in subdued colors, the Bishop of Chester is shown seated, the depiction straight forward, as he looks directly at the viewer.

Beale's husband aided her by preparing her canvases and colors, and even becoming an art dealer. Notebooks survive in which he kept track of her work and the large number of commissions she completed each year. One of her two sons became a portraitist.

PAINTING IN SPAIN

Diego Velázquez.   Philip IV had become king of Spain in 1621 at the age of sixteen, and from the outset he relied heavily on the advice of Gaspar de Guzmán, the count of Olivares. Olivares wanted Philip's court to be recognized as the most prominent in Europe; he appointed DIEGO VELAZQUEZ [ve-LAHS-kez] (1599–1660) to the position of royal painter. Velázquez was highly honored by the king, who ultimately knighted and conferred on him the Order of Santiago, usually reserved for noblemen. Velázquez painted many portraits of the royal family, and he seems to have made his sitters no prettier or more handsome than they actually were. Velázquez lived most of his life in Madrid, although shortly after Rubens's visit and at Rubens's sugges-

FIGURE 15.23   Clara Peeters, *Table with a Tart and a White Pitcher*, 1622, 75 × 73 cm. Museo del Prado, Madrid, Spain. Erich Lessing/Art Resource, NY. Such still life paintings appeal to our senses—of visual beauty and, as encouraged by the level of realism, also to our senses of taste and of smell. A luxurious way of life is implied, perhaps the viewer's for the taking: Objects extend over the edge of the table, suggesting that we might reach across the picture plane and help ourselves to these delicious foods.

tion, Philip granted Velázquez permission to visit Italy in order to study art in 1629. There he absorbed the lessons of the Italian Baroque and brought them back to Spain. Throughout his career, his style became progressively richer, the color lusher, the figures more animated.

Velázquez's most celebrated painting is the *Maids of Honor*, or *Las Meninas* (fig. 15.25), painted in 1656. Originally called *Family of Philip IV*, the painting raises the question: Is this a formal portrait? Or is it a genre scene? In fact, it is both. A glass of water has just been brought to Princess Margarita, the five-year-old daughter of Philip IV and his second wife, Queen Mariana. Margarita's maids, friends, a nun, a dwarf, a dog, and others gather round. Yet this scene from everyday life is portrayed on a huge scale. Velázquez includes himself painting a large canvas in the foreground.

On the back wall of the room are the reflections of the queen and king, apparently in a mirror. They stand where the viewer stands in relation to the pictorial space. Is the viewer looking at a portrait of the Infanta Margarita, or are the king and queen having their portraits painted by Velázquez and their child has come to watch? Velázquez unites the world of the sitter and the world of the viewer. Velázquez implies yet a third space to be reached by ascending the stairs on the back wall.

When Velázquez's masterpiece took its place in Philip IV's collection, it joined over 1500 paintings in the king's collection at the Buen Retiro, the new residence that Olivares and Philip built on the outskirts of Madrid in the early 1630s. Together with Philip II's massive collection, Spain, by 1650, owned much of the Western world's great art.

PAINTING IN FRANCE

Nicolas Poussin. NICOLAS POUSSIN [poo-SAN] (1594–1665) represents the classicizing and restrained tendency within the usually dramatic Baroque.

Favoring academic history painting, his *Rape of the Sabine Women* (fig. 15.26), of ca. 1636–37, shows Romulus,

FIGURE 15.24   Mary Beale, *John Wilkins DD*, ca. 1670, oil on canvas, 49 × 39½"(124.5 × 100.5 cm). Bodleian Library, Oxford. The British interest in portraiture is evidenced here. The abundant and richly textured textiles of the costume, furniture, and curtain add to the sought-after impression of elevated social standing.

on the left, raising his cloak to signal his men to abduct the Sabine women to be their wives. The figures make wild gestures and expressions, yet the action is frozen and the effect unmoving. This style is intended to appeal more to the mind than to the eye; appreciation of the painting depends largely upon knowing the story depicted. Poussin said the goal of painting was to represent noble subjects to morally improve the viewer. His approach to painting was disciplined, organized, and theoretical. Poussin worked in terms of line rather than color—in this he was the opposite of Rubens.

Louise Moillon.   Among all seventeenth-century French painters of still life, LOUISE MOILLON [Loo-EEZ Mwa-YON] (1610–96) of Paris is regarded as the finest. Both her father, Nicolas Moillon, who died when she was nine, and her stepfather, François Garnier, were painters and art dealers. A child prodigy, she was selling paintings by the time she was ten. Although the Royal Academy of Painting and Sculpture, discussed below, regarded still life as of less merit than religious or historical subjects or portraiture, the artists elected to membership during the seventeenth century included still life painters. In fig. 15.27,

FIGURE 15.25   Diego Velázquez, *Maids of Honor (Las Meninas)*, 1656, oil on canvas, 10′ 5″ × 9′ (3.17 × 2.74 m), Museo del Prado, Madrid. Velázquez depicts himself in this group portrait in the process of painting just such a large canvas. Much as in Jan van Eyck's Arnolfini wedding portrait (fig. 14.4), the presence of people (here the king and queen) in the viewer's space is indicated by their reflection in the mirror on the back wall.

FIGURE 15.26 Nicolas Poussin, *Rape of the Sabine Women*, ca. 1636–37, oil on canvas, 5′7⅞″ × 6′10⅝″(1.55 × 2.10 m). Metropolitan Museum of Art, New York. In spite of the dramatic subject and technical perfection of drawing, Poussin's academic style renders his characters as frozen actors on a stage, unlikely to elicit an emotional response in the viewer.

Still Life with Cherries, Strawberries, and Gooseberries, painted when she was only twenty and already an artist of note, Moillon created a simple composition, perfectly balanced, the blank background focusing all attention on the objects. The textures, sizes, and shapes of the fruits as well as of their containers form intentional contrasts.

The French Academy. Beginning with the reign of KING LOUIS XIV [LOO-ee] (1638–1715), who came to the throne as a child in 1643 and ruled outright from 1661 until 1715, Paris became increasingly the center of the Western art world, even if many of its most important painters, such as Poussin, preferred to live and work in Rome. Louis XIV's reign was the longest in European history, and assisted by his chief adviser, Jean-Baptiste Colbert, he soon established control over art and architecture. He did this through the Royal Academy of Painting and Sculpture, established in Paris in 1648 and known more simply as the French Academy. Its purpose was to

define absolute standards by which to judge the art of the period.

Favored above all other painters was Poussin, but the Academy's insistence on Poussin's supremacy alienated many younger members of the Academy inclined not toward Poussin's cool classicism, but toward Rubens's dashing bravura. By the end of the seventeenth century, the Academy had split into two opposing groups—those who favored line and those who favored color. The former, adherents to the style of Poussin and referred to as **poussinistes,** argued that line was superior because it appealed to the mind, whereas color appealed only to the senses. The latter, preferring the style of Rubens, were called **rubénistes** and maintained that color was truer to nature; line appealed only to an educated mind, but color appealed to all. Both sides agreed on this point. Thus, to ask whether line or color is superior is to question whether the educated person or the lay person is the ultimate audience for art, a debate that continues to this day.

FIGURE 15.27 Louise Moillon, *Still Life with Cherries, Strawberries, and Gooseberries*, 1630, oil on panel, $12\frac{5}{8} \times 19\frac{1}{8}''$ (32 × 48.5 cm). Norton Simon Foundation, Pasadena, CA. Moillon's speciality was fruit still lifes. This display of her extraordinary technical skill includes the drops of water on the table which are given a prominent location in the center foreground, ensuring that they do not go unnoticed by the viewer. More realistic records of the visible world would have to wait until the invention of photography.

ARCHITECTURE

The Louvre. As head of the French Academy, Colbert invited Bernini to Paris in 1664 to present plans for the facade for the new east wing of the royal palace of the Louvre [LOOV]. But Bernini's approach was deemed too radical, and furthermore, French architects did not think the design of a French palace should fall to an Italian. Therefore, to conceive a new plan, Colbert appointed a French council: architect LOUIS LE VAU [luh VO] (1612–70), painter CHARLES LE BRUN [luh BRUN] (1619–90), a previous director of the French Academy, and architect CLAUDE PERRAULT [peh-ROH] (1613–88), who later published a French edition of the ancient architect Vitruvius. A strict, linear classicism was the result (fig. 15.28). The center of the facade looks like a Roman temple with Corinthian columns; wings of paired columns ex-tend on each side, and the building ends in forms reminiscent of a Roman triumphal arch. The king was so pleased that he insisted the new facade be duplicated on the palace's other faces.

The Palace of Versailles. Louis XIV then turned his attention to the building of a new royal palace at Versailles [vair-SIGH], eleven miles southwest of Paris. It was begun in 1669 by Le Vau, who managed to design the garden facade but died within the year. JULES HARDOUIN-MANSART [man-SAR] (1646–1708) took over and enlarged the palace to the extraordinary length of 1,903 feet.

The visitor arriving at Versailles from Paris is greeted by the principal facade, designed to focus on the three windows of Louis XIV's bedroom in the center. The entire palace and gardens are arranged symmetrically on this axis.

Critical Thinking

ART FORGERIES

Among the problems confronting art dealers and purchasers today is that of forgery—works of art which have been created to look like important paintings, sculptures, or artifacts from the past, usually from ancient times, but are copies meant to deceive. Forgery exists because artworks are valuable, and forgers aim to cash in on that fact.

Among recent forgeries is that of an ancient Greek sculpture of a kouros, or young male nude standing figure, pur-chased by the J. Paul Getty Museum in California. Although the work appeared to be from the sixth-century B.C.E. historians were divided as to its authenticity. After listening to arguments on both sides, the museum purchased the statue, in large part because geological analysis indicated that its marble had come from an ancient quarry site and because it had appropriate papers to designate its provenance—its history of former ownership.

In a recent book, *Blink*, Malcolm Gladwell explains how the forged sculp-ture was created, why some people were fooled by it, and how some experts knew, seemingly instinctively, that the Getty kouros was a fake, even though many details suggested its authenticity.

What do you think is necessary for an expert to detect a forgery? What kinds of tests might be done as part of the investigation into a work's authenticity? To what extent do you think tests, such as those done on the dating of a work's materials, are enough to decide such issues? To what extent is an art historian's experience of value in deciding such matters?

FIGURE 15.28   Louis Le Vau, Charles Le Brun, Claude Perrault, east facade, Palais du Louvre, Paris, 1667–70. All vestiges of Baroque sensuality have been banished here in favor of a strict revival of elements found in ancient Roman architecture.

Versailles was the seat of the government of France and once housed ten thousand people. Even the humblest attic room at Versailles was preferred to living on one's own estate, because only through contact with the king was there the possibility of obtaining royal favor. The most spectacular of the many splendid rooms of the palace of Versailles is the Hall of Mirrors (fig. 15.29), designed about 1680, the work of Hardouin-Mansart, Le Brun, and Antoine Coysevox. Tunnel-like in its dimensions (240 feet long, but only 34 feet wide, and 43 feet high), the Hall of Mirrors overlooks the gardens through seventeen arched windows reflected in seventeen arched mirrors. Furnished with silver furniture and orange trees, and hung white brocade curtains, lit by innumerable flickering candles, mirrored to reflect marble, gilding, stucco, wood, and paint, it is one of the ultimate examples of French Baroque elegance.

St. Paul's Cathedral. Although England had lagged behind the continent artistically, Sir Christopher Wren (1632–1723) quickly brought it to the fore. In addition to being an architect, Wren was professor of astronomy at Oxford University and was also knowledgeable in anatomy, physics, mathematics, sailing, street paving, and embroidery. He even invented a device for copying documents by having a second pen attached to the first and writing double.

During the Great Fire of 1666, much of London was destroyed, including the original Gothic church of St. Paul's. Wren joined the royal commission for rebuilding the city, and although his master plan for its reconstruction was rejected, he did design many local churches. His masterpiece was the new St. Paul's cathedral (fig. 15.30), built 1675–1710.

St. Paul's cathedral may be regarded as a Baroque reinterpretation of the ancient Roman Pantheon (see Chapter 4). Wren designed a dome like that of the Pantheon, but raised it high on double drums and topped it with a lantern, and he modeled his triangular pediment on the

FIGURE 15.29 Jules Hardouin-Mansart and Charles Le Brun, Hall of Mirrors, Palace of Versailles, ca. 1680. Typically Baroque is the combination of a variety of materials to enhance the opulence of the overall impact. Imagine the effect with the flickering light of hundreds of candles reflected in the arched mirrors.

FIGURE 15.30   Sir Christopher Wren, facade, St. Paul's Cathedral, London, 1675–1710, length 514′ (156.67 m), width 250′ (76.20 m), height of dome 366′ (111.56 m). The facade of St. Paul's in London deserves comparison with that of St. Peter's in Rome (fig. 15.1). Although the basic dome, pediment, and columns derive from antiquity, the Baroque influence is evident in the paired columns and double facade.

Pantheon's but supported it on two stories of columns, which, characteristic of the Baroque, are grouped in pairs. The lower story of columns is as wide as the nave and aisles, the upper as wide as the nave. Particularly Baroque are the broken silhouettes of the towers at each corner.

It is possible that Wren intended St. Paul's to be the St. Peter's of the north. Like the dome of St. Peter's in Rome, the dome of St. Paul's is as wide as the nave and aisles. Although smaller than St. Peter's, St. Paul's is considered artistically superior for its stylistic consistency; St. Paul's is also the only major cathedral in Western Europe to be completed by the person who designed it. St. Peter's lacks small-scale features with which to interpret its vastness;

St. Paul's includes such details on both the exterior and interior.

BAROQUE MUSIC OUTSIDE ITALY

Handel and the Oratorio.   Late in the Baroque age, Italian opera such as Monteverdi's began to go out of style, particularly in the north where Protestants thought the form frivolous. One of the most successful composers of Italian opera of the day was GEORGE FREDERICK HANDEL [HAN-del] (1685–1759), a German composer who emigrated to England in the early 1700s. Handel was renowned as an organist and a prodigious composer in many musical genres, including keyboard works, orchestral suites, and concertoes for various instruments. Lauded and commissioned by the Hanoverian kings, he profoundly influenced English music for a century after his death.

By the mid-1720s Handel had composed nearly forty operas, but recognizing the growing English distaste for the form, he turned to composing **oratorios.** An oratorio is a sacred opera sung without costume and without acting because it was forbidden to present biblical characters in a public theater. Handel relied on a heightened musical drama to make up for the lack of theater. Written in English, Handel's oratorios employ the many musical forms of opera, such as **arias** (solo songs), recitatives, duets, ensemble singing, and choruses, and all were set to orchestral accompaniment.

Handel's most famous oratorio is his *Messiah*, a composition of enormous scope that rivals the most ambitious projects of Baroque art and architecture—Bernini's colonnade for the Vatican square, Rubens's cycle of paintings celebrating the life of Marie de' Medici and Milton's epic *Paradise Lost*. *Messiah* includes approximately fifty individual pieces, lasting, collectively, about three hours. Its three parts are based on the biblical texts of Isaiah, the Psalms, the Gospels, Revelations, and the Pauline Epistles. The first part concerns the prophecy of the birth of Christ; the second focuses on his suffering, especially the crucifixion; the third encompasses his resurrection and the redemption of the world.

The tone of *Messiah* is jubilant and celebratory. One particularly inspirational section is the second part of the oratorio, concluding with the famous "Hallelujah Chorus," which is based on Revelations 11:15. The text is as follows:

a. Hallelujah! Hallelujah!
b. For the Lord God omnipotent reigneth
c. The Kingdom of this world is become the Kingdom of Our Lord and of His Christ.
d. And He shall reign for ever and ever
   King of Kings and Lord of Lords
   And He shall reign for ever and ever
   Hallelujah! Hallelujah!

The opening of this exultant chorus is noteworthy for its repeated and emphatic Hallelujahs (a), followed by a sudden contrasting quieter section (b). An even softer section begins with (c) "The Kingdom of this world," which is quickly followed by the majestic fugue of (d) "And he shall reign for ever and ever." As the chorus moves exuberantly toward its dramatic conclusion, Handel splits the voices. The top voice is split into two voices, soprano and alto, and they rise higher and higher on the phrase "King of Kings and Lord of Lords." The bottom voice is also divided into two voices, tenor and bass, which sing "for ever and ever, Hallelujah!" The four voices are bolstered by the jubilance of beating drums and trumpeting brass. The entire effect is one of Baroque drama, a play between the "light" of the soprano voices and brass contrasted with the "darkness" of the drums and bass line, capturing the essence of the crucifixion's simultaneous sorrow and joy.

Composed in an astonishing twenty-three days, *Messiah* was first performed not in London but in Dublin, in 1742, for the relief of prisoners and wards of the state. It was not until 1750 that the London public fully responded to the work. Upon completing *Messiah* Handel's eyes are said to have filled with tears, and he is reputed to have said, "I did think I did see all Heaven before me, and the Great God Himself!"

Johann Sebastian Bach.   The other great Baroque composer is JOHANN SEBASTIAN BACH [BAHK] (1685–1750), the grand master of the Baroque style and musical art forms of his age, and as thorough and thoughtful a musician as ever lived. Bach's output includes music for voices and instruments in every major form of the era except opera. His works for keyboard include hundreds of pieces that are used today as teaching pieces. He played and composed solo works for a number of instruments, including violin and harpsichord (fig. 15.31), and was master of the organ, on which he could improvise at will the most complicated fugues.

A **fugue** is composed of three or four independent parts of which one part, or voice, states a theme, which is then imitated in succession by each of the other voices. As the

FIGURE 15.31   Jerome de Zentis, harpsichord, 1658. Maker: Girolamo Zenti. Robet Harding/Metropolitan Museum of Art, New York. A keyboard instrument that was often intricately decorated, the Baroque harpsichord had strings that were plucked by mechanical plectra inside the body of the instrument.

Cross Currents

THE BAROQUE IN MEXICO

When the Spanish explorers led by Hernán Cortés came to America in 1519, they spread Catholicism with zeal. With the support of Jesuits, missionaries, and the political and financial backing of European governments, seventeenth-century South America boasted a strong European cultural connection, including no fewer than five universities, the largest and most important of which was in Mexico City.

Mexican-born writers and artists worked hand in hand with their European-born counterparts to create a native architecture and literature that spoke to the European cultural heritage. Great Baroque structures were built, the leading example of which is the Chapel of the Rosary in the Church of Santo Domingo in Puebla (fig. 15.32), completed about 1690. Like much Mexican art, it melds local traditions and Catholic icons. Here local artisans crafted images in polychrome stucco that, although they represent Christian figures, possess the faces and dresses of native Mexicans. Meandering vines weave across the ceilings, and gold leaf covers the altar. So

elaborate is the whole that the style is called the "exuberant Baroque."

Among the most noteworthy and influential of Mexican Baroque writers was SOR JUANA INÉS DE LA CRUZ [soar HWA-nah] (1648–95), who was born near Mexico City. Hailed as the "Phoenix of Mexico" and "America's Tenth Muse" during her lifetime, Sor Juana is considered one of the finest Spanish American writers of her time. Although a nun, she also became the confidante of prominent leaders and intellectuals throughout Spanish America.

Her poetry speaks to women across cultures and centuries in a language that is by turns playful and ironically critical of men's failures, as shown in the first and last stanzas from her aptly titled poem, "She Demonstrates the Inconsistency of Men's Wishes in Blaming Women for What They Themselves Have Caused":

> Silly, you men—so very adept
> at wrongly faulting womankind,
> not seeing you're alone to blame
> for faults you plant in woman's mind. . .
> I well know what powerful arms 5
> you wield in pressing for evil:
> your arrogance is allied
> with the world, the flesh, and the devil.

FIGURE 15.32 Chapel of the Rosary, Church of Santo Domingo, Puebla, Mexico, ca. 1690. Free of any preconceptions that would limit their decorative impulses, the artists who fashioned this interior were able to press the Baroque sensibility to its very limits.

second voice takes over the theme from the first, the first continues playing in **counterpoint,** music that differs from the main theme. The third voice takes over from the second, the second continues on in counterpoint, and so on. The driving rhythm of Bach's fugues create drama and tension, as the musical voices seem to chase one another, only to be resolved when they come together peacefully at the end.

Bach developed to perfection the art of such *polyphonic* music, or music for multiple voices. As a young church organist, Bach demonstrated a talent for improvising on hymn tunes, so much so that complaints were lodged against him "for having made many curious variations in the chorale and mingled many strange tones in it." He was at work on his *Art of the Fugue,* an encyclopedic compendium of fugues for study and performance, when he died.

Bach's professional career began with a position as organist at a church in Arnstadt. Then he served for nine years as court organist and chamber musician at the court

of the duke of Weimar, composing many works for the organ. Next Bach served as director of music for the prince of Cöthen, where he composed a set of six concertos dedicated to the Margrave of Brandenburg, subsequently known as *The Brandenburg Concertos.* Bach's longest musical post was as music director of the Church of St. Thomas in Leipzig, where for twenty-seven years he served as organist, choirmaster, composer, and music director. At Leipzig, Bach produced his religious vocal music, including the *B Minor Mass,* the *St. John* and *St. Matthew Passions,* and numerous church cantatas, of which he wrote nearly three hundred, more than two hundred of which survive. A **cantata** is a work for a single singer or group of singers accompanied by instruments.

Among these is the famous *Cantata No. 80: Ein feste Burg ist unser Gott (A Mighty Fortress Is Our God),* composed in 1715, revised in 1724, and based on the hymn, or chorale, by Martin Luther. Like many of Bach's sacred, or church, cantatas, this one was written for Lutheran services. The cantatas were performed by eight to twelve singers and an orchestral ensemble of eighteen to twenty-four musicians (although Bach often complained he had to make do with wretched musicians and underprepared vocalists). Luther's original chorale, which is in itself a centerpiece of Protestant hymnology, appears in eloquent and simple majesty in a four-part harmonization as the final movement of Bach's cantata.

Bach's music gained worldwide popularity when a composer of the Romantic era, Felix Mendelssohn (1809–47), arranged for a performance of Bach's *Passion According to St. Matthew* some eighty years after Bach's death. Since that time, Bach has been considered the consummate composer of Baroque music. His musical style has been adapted to a variety of genres. Jazz performers study Bach's improvisational style and his theoretical techniques. Groups such as the Swingle Singers and the Thomas Gabriel Trio have adapted Bach's works in a fusion of jazz and Baroque styles. His polyphonic compositions are well suited to computer-generated music such as the series of Wendy Carlos's *Switched On Bach.* The parodies of Peter Schickele, who uses the pseudonym PDQ Bach, entertain us with comedic renditions of Bach's music.

THE SCIENCE OF OBSERVATION

The precision of Bach's fugues and Vermeer's paintings echo the scientific spirit of the Baroque age. Francis Bacon's development of the principles of the scientific method (see Chapter 14), with its emphasis on the careful observation of physical phenomena, resounded throughout the Baroque age in a vast array of scientific discoveries and inventions. Precise observation required new tools for seeing, and these new observations in turn created new knowledge.

Anton van Leeuwenhoek. In Holland, for instance, a lens maker named ANTON VAN LEEUWENHOEK [LAY-ven-huck] (1632–1723) transformed the magnifying glasses used by lace makers and embroiderers into powerful microscopes capable of seeing small organisms. He investigated everything under his microscope (including all of his bodily fluids). Leeuwenhoek quickly realized that the world was teeming with microorganisms he called "little animals." He was the first person to see protozoa and bacteria and the first to describe the red blood cell. Leeuwenhoek was also fascinated with the mechanisms of sight, particularly with the fact that the eye is itself a lens. He dissected insect and animal eyes, and actually looked through them himself. He describes looking at the tower of the New Church through the eye of a dragonfly: "A great many Towers were presented, also upside down, and they appeared no bigger than does the point of a small pin to our Eye."

Johannes Kepler. JOHANNES KEPLER [KEP-ler] (1571–1630) had been equally interested in the eye, and in

1604 he was the first to describe it as an optical instrument with a lens used for focusing (fig. 15.33). "Vision," he wrote, "is brought about by a picture of the thing seen being formed on the concave surface of the retina."

"I leave to natural philosophers to discuss the way in which this picture is put together by the spiritual principles of vision residing in the retina and the nerves," he wrote, "and whether it is made to appear before the soul or tribunal of the faculty of vision by a spirit within the cerebral cavities, or the faculty of vision, like a magistrate sent by the soul, goes out from the council

FIGURE 15.33 Illustration of the theory of the retinal image, from René Descartes, *La Dioptrique* (Leiden, 1637), Bancroft Library, Berkeley, California. No image better illustrates the importance of scientific observation to the Baroque sensibility. Even the eye itself is defined here as a scientific instrument.

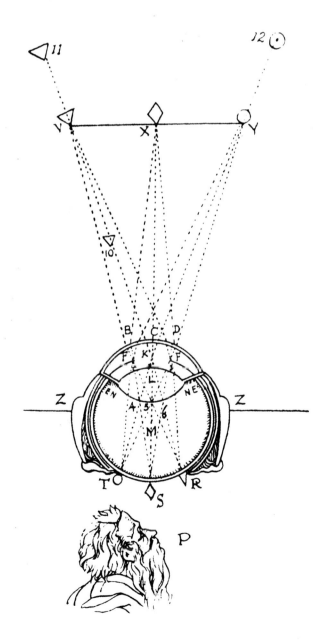

chamber of the brain to meet this image in the optic nerves and retina, as it were descending to a lower court." Kepler is interested in the *fact* of vision, not its metaphysical meaning.

Galileo Galilei. Kepler's friend GALILEO GALILEI [ga-li-LAY-o] (1564–1642) was the first to develop the telescope and use it to observe the heavens. Through it he saw and described craters on the moon, the phases of Venus, and sunspots, and he theorized, in one of the important advances of physics, that light takes time to get from one place to another—that, either as a particle or wave, it travels at a uniform speed that is measurable. Galileo's astronomical findings confirmed Copernicus's theory that the earth circled the sun, a position the Church still did not accept. In 1615, Galileo was forced to defend his ideas before Pope Paul V in Rome, but his efforts failed, and he was prohibited from either publishing or teaching his findings. When Pope Urban VIII, an old friend, was elected pope, Galileo appealed to the papacy again, but again he was condemned, this time much more severely. He was made to admit the error of his ways in public and sentenced to prison for the rest of his life. Friends intervened, and in the end he was merely banished to a comfortable villa outside Florence.

PHILOSOPHY

René Descartes. Kepler's effort to distinguish the science of observation from the contemplation of the subjective or spiritual matters of the mind was well known to RENÉ DESCARTES [day-CART] (1595–1650). Descartes actually published the illustrated model of the retinal image (fig. 15.33) in his own work. But Descartes was interested in what Kepler was not. He was, in fact, the very "natural philosopher" to whom Kepler left the problem of what happened to the image once it registered itself on the retina. Descartes did for modern philosophy what Bacon had done for science, and so he is often called the "Father of Modern Philosophy."

Descartes used doubt as a point of departure and philosophical debate. He began with a series of systematic questions that led him to doubt the existence of everything. At that point, he asked himself if there was anything at all he could know with certainty. His answer was that the only thing he could conceive of "clearly" and "distinctly" (his two essential criteria) was that he existed as a doubting entity. Descartes formulated this fundamental concept in Latin: *Cogito, ergo sum*, which means "I think, therefore I am." According to Descartes, this *cogito* provided the foundation, principle, and model for all subsequent knowledge,

MAP 15.2   World exploration, 1271–1611.

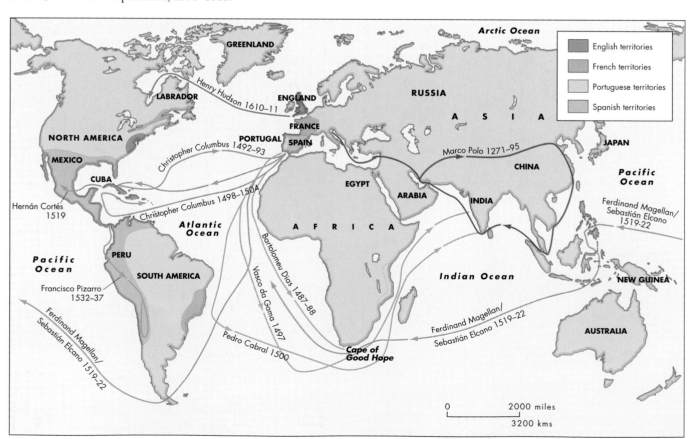

which he held to the same standards of evidence and rationality.

Turning his attention from himself to the world, Descartes allowed that the only thing he could *know* for certain about the material world is that it too exists. He believed there was an absolute division between mind and matter. Matter could be studied mathematically and scientifically, its behavior predicted by the new science of physics. How the mind knows something is altogether different. When we observe an object in the distance—the sun, for instance—it appears to be small, but we know through scientific observation that it is much larger than it appears. Knowledge, Descartes recognized, cannot rest on perception alone. This had been demonstrated by Copernicus's theory of the universe: We may perceive ourselves to be standing still, but we are on a planet spinning quickly through space.

This recognition led Descartes to ask how we can know that which we cannot perceive. Most important, how can we know that God exists, if we cannot perceive him? Descartes decided, finally, that if we are too imperfect to trust even our own perceptions, and yet we are still able to *imagine* a perfect God, then God must exist. If he did not, then he would be unimaginable. In other words, what is "clearly" and "distinctly" perceived by the mind—*Cogito, ergo sum*—must be true. Descartes's answer was somewhat paradoxical and would lead to much philosophical debate in the centuries to come.

Thomas Hobbes.   During the Baroque age, the question of how to govern increasingly occupied philosophical thinkers. In England, the situation reached a crisis point when Charles I challenged Parliament's identity as the king's partner in rule. Civil war erupted, and in 1649, a Commonwealth was established, led by the Puritan Oliver Cromwell as, essentially, a military dictatorship. The monarchy was restored in 1660 after the republic failed, but the relationship between parliament and monarch remained murky. Finally, in 1688, James II was expelled in the bloodless "Glorious Revolution," and Mary and William of Orange, James's daughter and son-in-law, ascended the throne. They immediately accepted the rights of all citizens under the law, recognizing in particular Parliament's right to exercise authority over financial matters, and England became a limited monarchy.

In this atmosphere, the debate about who should govern and how was addressed by two political philosophers with very different points of view. Mirroring Descartes's emphasis on the primacy of perception was the philosopher Thomas Hobbes (1588–1679). Educated as a classicist, Hobbes was particularly impressed by the geometry of Euclid, and he came to believe the reasoning on which geometry is based could be extended to social and political life. After visiting with Galileo in Italy, Hobbes became even more convinced this was true. The power of Galileo's science of observation and its ability to describe the movement of the solar system could be extended to the observation of human beings in their relations to one another.

Hobbes's philosophy, published in 1651 in a book entitled *Leviathan* (fig. 15.34), would be read by many as an apology for, or defense of, monarchical rule. Hobbes believed that humans are driven by two primal forces, the fear of death and the desire for power. If government does nothing to check these impulses, humankind simply self-destructs. But Hobbes also believed that humans recognize their essential depravity and therefore choose to be governed. They enter into what he called the **social contract,** by which the people choose to give up sovereignty over themselves and bestow it on a ruler. They agree to carry out all the ruler's commands, and in return the ruler agrees to keep the peace.

FIGURE 15.34   Frontispiece of *Leviathan*, 1651, Bancroft Library, Berkeley, California. An image of the social contract, the body of the king is made up of hundreds of his subjects. He rules over a world at peace, its cities well fortified and its countryside well groomed.

Then & Now

THE TELESCOPE

Galileo's telescope (fig. 15.35) changed the way people thought of their solar system. It demonstrated conclusively that the earth and other planets orbited around the sun. The modern-day Hubble Space Telescope is rapidly enhancing our understanding of the solar system's place in the universe. Deployed into Earth's orbit on April 24, 1990, from the space shuttle *Discovery*, the 12.5-ton satellite is able to look directly at the cosmos unhindered by Earth's atmosphere. It has revealed galaxy forms as far as twelve billion light-years away, which may be the furthest reaches of our universe.

Galileo was able to see other galaxies, which he called *nebulae* (clouds). Hubble's photographs suggest that these *nebulae* are really clumps of gas that generate new stars. Enormous jets of gas erupt out of these gas clumps at speeds up to 300 miles per second and are shot trillions of miles out into space. This is

the stuff, scientists believe, of which solar systems are made. Hubble has shown these whirling jets all at once form a star and shoot out jets of matter that will form something like our own solar system. The implication is that some stars, even in our own galaxy, may possess solar systems similar to our own, and hence the possibility of life.

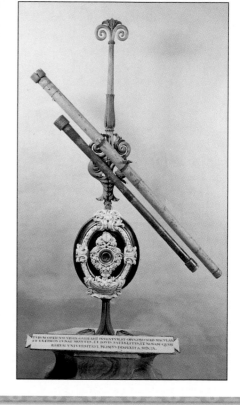

FIGURE 15.35   Galileo Galilei, Telescope, 1609, Museum of Science, Florence. With a telescope such as this, Galileo was able to contradict the Ptolemaic view of the universe.

John Locke.   JOHN LOCKE [lock] (1632–1704), repudiating Hobbes, believed people are perfectly capable of governing themselves. Locke's *Essay on Human Understanding*, published in 1690, argues that the human mind is at birth a *tabula rasa*, or "blank slate." Then two great "fountains of knowledge," our environment as opposed to our heredity, and our reason as opposed to our faith, fill this blank slate with learning as the person develops. Locke argued, furthermore, in his *Second Treatise on Government*, also published in 1690, that humans are "by nature free, equal, and independent." They accept the rule of government, he argues, because they find it convenient to do so, not because they are innately inclined to submit to au-

thority. Such ideas set the stage for the political revolutions of the eighteenth century.

LITERATURE

Unlike Renaissance writers, who were often content to catalog the beauties of the beloved, Baroque writers explore the mysteries of love, both erotic and divine. Baroque writers, overall, also spend considerably more time exploring their relationship to God, often in passionate and dramatic terms. Religious and secular Baroque writing, poetry in particular, often dramatizes emotional and personal encounters between speaker and listener (whether God or lover).

Table 15–1 SEVENTEENTH-CENTURY SCIENTISTS AND PHILOSOPHERS	
Scientists	Anton van Leeuwenhoek (1632–1723): The microscope
	Johannes Kepler (1571–1639): The science of vision
	Galileo Galilei (1564–1642): The telescope
Philosophers	Thomas Hobbes (1588–1679): *The Leviathan* social contract
	René Descartes (1595–1650): *Cogito, ergo sum* (I think, therefore I am)
	John Locke (1632–1704): *Essay on Human Understanding;* tabula rasa (blank slate)

Molière and the Baroque Stage. During the Baroque era, stage plans differed from those of Shakespeare and classical Greece. Seventeenth-century plays took place indoors on a stage, with a **proscenium arch,** an arch that stands in front of the scene and divides the stage from the auditorium. A supporting curtain separates the audience from the actors. The plays were enacted on a box stage, which represented a room with a missing fourth wall, allowing the audience to look in on the action. This is still the most popular stage in use.

Unelaborate painted scenery served as a backdrop for the action. Candles and lanterns illuminated actors and audience. Costume tended toward the ornate, as in Elizabethan drama. On both Elizabethan and Baroque stages, actors were costumed in the contemporary dress appropriate to the social status of the characters they portrayed. An innovation in seventeenth-century drama was that female actresses assumed women's roles for the first time, enabling more extensive, more frequent, and more realistic love scenes. As in the earlier eras of drama, however, language still did much of the work.

The conventions of the French theater of the time were inspired by the classical drama of Greece and Rome. Like its ancient antecedents, the seventeenth-century French theater observed what are known as the three **unities:** the unity of time, the unity of place, and the unity of action. A play's action had to be confined to a twenty-four-hour period. The place should be a single setting. The action must be unified in a single plot. Plays that violated these unities were thought crude and inelegant by their audience, which consisted largely of courtiers and aristocrats. The three great practitioners of the French Baroque theater all observed the unities—its two great tragedians, PIERRE CORNEILLE [kor-NAY] (1606–1684) and JEAN RACINE [ra-SEEN] (1639–1699), and its great comic genius Jean-Baptiste Poquelin, known by his stage name MOLIÈRE [mol-YAIR] (1622–1673).

Corneille's themes are patriotism and honor. Racine's plays concentrate on the moral dilemmas of the Greek tragedies. But of the three, Molière's satiric comedy is the most accessible, resorting, as it often does, to slapstick, pratfalls, and the sorts of comic predicaments modern audiences still enjoy. Among his masterpieces is *Tartuffe,* which satirizes fraud and religious hypocrisy. The play also pokes fun at the gullibility of those who allow themselves to be taken in by greedy, self-serving sanctimony.

When *Tartuffe* was first staged in 1664, it antagonized some who considered it an attack on religion. Even though Molière retitled it *The Impostor* to indicate Tartuffe's fraudulence, the play was censored and banned. To defend himself and his play against such charges, Molière wrote three prefaces and later changed his original ending. The publicity enhanced the play's popularity, and the work was returned to the stage under the protection of the king. Its unending popularity, however, is due neither to royal protection nor to notoriety, but rather to the ingenuity of its plot, the vitality of its characterization, and the brilliance of its language.

John Donne. JOHN DONNE [dun] (1572–1631) is considered among the finest poets of his, or indeed of any, age. He wrote prose as well as verse, and his poetry includes amorous lyrics, philosophical poems, devotional sonnets and hymns, elegies, epistles, and satires.

Born into a Roman Catholic family in anti-Catholic England, Donne attended Oxford and Cambridge Universities, though he neither took an academic degree nor practiced law. He later converted to Anglicanism and was appointed private secretary to Sir Thomas Egerton, a high court official. When Donne secretly married his employer's niece, Anne More, he was dismissed and prohibited from obtaining court appointment, first by Egerton and later by King James I, who wanted Donne to become an Anglican preacher. This Donne eventually did, being ordained to the ministry in 1615 and made dean of St. Paul's Cathedral in London in 1621, where he served until his death ten years later.

Donne's "A Valediction: Forbidding Mourning," a philosophical love poem, is noted for its extended analogy or conceit comparing lovers to the two feet of a geometrician's compasses.

As virtuous men pass mildly away,
    And whisper to their souls to go,
While some of their sad friends do say,
    The breath goes now, and some say, no:
So let us melt, and make no noise,   5
    No tear-floods, nor sigh-tempests move;
'Twere profanation of our joys
    To tell the laity our love.
Moving of th' earth brings harms and fears,
    Men reckon what it did and meant,   10
But trepidation of the spheres,
    Though greater far, is innocent.
Dull sublunary lovers' love
    (Whose soul is sense) cannot admit
Absence, because it doth remove   15
    Those things which elemented it.
But we by a love so much refined,
    That ourselves know not what it is,
Inter-assured of the mind,
    Care less, eyes, lips, and hands to miss.   20
Our two souls therefore, which are one,
    Though I must go, endure not yet
A breach, but an expansion,
    Like gold to airy thinness beat.
If they be two, they are two so   25
    As stiff twin compasses are two;
Thy soul the fixed foot, makes no show
    To move, but doth, if th' other do.
And though it in the center sit,
    Yet when the other far doth roam,   30
It leans, and hearkens after it,
    And grows erect, as that comes home.
Such wilt thou be to me, who must
    Like th' other foot, obliquely run:

Thy firmness makes my circle just,   *35*
  And makes me end, where I begun.

Contemporary sources note that Donne addressed this poem to his wife as he was preparing in 1611 for a continental journey. He had premonitions of disaster, which turned out to be well founded because his wife gave birth to a stillborn child while he was abroad. In the first two stanzas the speaker urges his wife not to make a public spectacle of their grief on parting. The poet/speaker compares their leave-taking with the death of virtuous men, who depart life quietly and peacefully. He urges her to emulate their behavior, arguing that theatrical displays of unhappiness profane their deeply private relationship.

Throughout the next four stanzas the speaker contrasts the couple's higher, more spiritual love with the love of the sensual. Their love, intellectual and spiritual, transcends the senses. In these stanzas, Donne introduces the first of his two important conceits: that the lovers' souls are not really separated but are almost infinitely expanded to fill the intervening space between them, as gold expands when beaten into paper-thin sheets. The comparison with gold suggests the value of love and its prominent position in their lives. This use of concrete reality to illuminate a spiritual condition typifies Donne's amalgamation of disparate realms of experience.

The last part of Donne's "A Valediction: Forbidding Mourning," however, extends his conceit over three stanzas. The compass is a symbol of constancy and change, since it both moves and remains stationary. The compass also inscribes a circle, symbol of perfection. These ideas of constancy and perfection are worked through in detail as the speaker/poet explains how one foot of the compass moves only in relation to the other, returning "home" when the two feet of the compass are brought together.

Anne Bradstreet.   Among Donne's near contemporaries is Anne Bradstreet (1612–72), the first major poet in American literature. Born Anne Dudley to a Puritan family in Northampton, England, she sailed with her parents and her new husband, Simon Bradstreet, to Massachusetts in 1630. As secretary to the Massachusetts Bay Company, Simon often traveled on company business, leaving Anne alone. On several occasions she wrote poems about their separation. "A Letter to Her Husband, Absent upon Public Employment" is an example.

Though best known today for her domestic lyrics, in her own day Bradstreet was known for a cycle of historical poems based on the four ages of humanity. Donne's philosophical poems, and Bradstreet's domestic ones, can be compared with the art of Vermeer, whose paintings, although few in number, embody near perfection of form and idea. The following poem to her husband is an example.

TO MY DEAR AND LOVING HUSBAND

If ever two were one, then surely we.
If ever man were lov'd by wife, then thee.
If ever wife was happy in a man,
Compare with me, ye women, if you can.
I prize thy love more than whole Mines of gold
Or all the riches that the East doth hold.
My love is such that Rivers cannot quench,
Nor ought but love from thee give recompence.
Thy love is such I can no way repay.
The heavens reward thee manifold, I pray.
Then while we live, in love let's so persever
That when we live no more, we may live ever.

John Milton.   John Milton (1608–74) represents a facet of Baroque sensibility that John Donne lacked. Unlike Donne, whose poems are mostly brief lyrics, Milton had a monumental conception of poetry attuned to the epic. Like the architect Bernini, the painter Rubens, and the composers Bach and Handel, Milton worked on a grand scale.

No poet more than Milton embodies a grand ideal of the poetic vocation. He believed a poet had to prepare the mind and soul through study and prayer before attempting to produce great art.

One kind of preparation was his study of the classical writers of ancient Greece and Rome—Homer, Virgil, Ovid, and Theocritus. Another was his study of the complete Bible, which he is said to have memorized. Following these studies Milton wrote poetry at once serious in outlook and grand in manner, befitting one who wanted to "leave something so written to aftertimes as they should not willingly let it die."

Combining the ideals of classical humanism and biblical morality more thoroughly and more profoundly than any other writer in English, Milton presents a summation of High Renaissance art and Christian humanism. From the Greeks and Romans Milton derived a sense of civic responsibility. Milton valued statesmen, who by virtue of their nobility, intellectuality, and vision might ensure the survival of humane values. In later life, Milton found his ideal in the Puritan leader Oliver Cromwell, for whom he wrote a series of prose works.

Milton's life can be divided into three parts. First, he prepared for his vocation. This period culminated in the publication of "Lycidas," his elegy on the death of a drowned friend, followed by a two-year tour of Europe. Second, from about 1640 to 1660 was a twenty-year span of political involvement, during which he wrote prose rather than poetry. In the service of the Puritan cause, Milton produced pamphlets and tracts on various theological and ecclesiastical issues, such as Christian doctrine and divorce. When the English monarchy was restored to the Stuart line, Milton was imprisoned and his property confiscated. Set free a short time later, he lived out the third part of his life in relative isolation working on his great epic poems. Milton lived the last two decades of his life in blindness caused, in part, by his exhausting work on behalf of the Puritans.

Milton spent the last fifteen years of his life writing and publishing his most ambitious works: *Paradise Lost* (1667), *Paradise Regained* (1671), and *Samson Agonistes* (1671). In these poems, especially in *Paradise Lost*, Milton attempted, in his words, "to justify the ways of God to man." This idea of justification reflected Milton's blend of Puritan theology and classical humanism. Milton reinterpreted the events of Genesis—humankind's fall from grace, and its banishment from the Garden of Eden. Milton emphasized the central belief of Christianity: the incarnation of God-as-man in Jesus Christ, who came to atone for the sin of humanity's first parents. Christ's sacrifice thus gained for human beings the chance for eternal life—providing they live in accordance with biblical teachings.

We should note, however, that although Milton's major life work was his epic, *Paradise Lost*, he also wrote a few exquisite sonnets. The two reprinted here, one on his blindness, the other on his deceased wife, are perhaps his finest efforts in the genre.

WHEN I CONSIDER HOW MY LIGHT IS SPENT

When I consider how my light is spent
    Ere half my days in this dark world and wide,
    And that one talent which is death to hide
    Lodg'd with me useless, though my soul more bent
To serve therewith my Maker, and present
    My true account, lest he returning chide,
    "Doth God exact day-labour, light denied?"
    I fondly ask. But Patience, to prevent
That murmur, soon replies: "God doth not need
    Either man's work or his own gifts: who best
    Bear his mild yoke, they serve him best. His state
Is kingly; thousands at his bidding speed
    And post o'er land and ocean without rest:
    They also serve who only stand and wait."

ON HIS DECEASED WIFE

METHOUGHT I saw my late espoused saint
    Brought to me like Alcestis from the grave,
    Whom Jove's great son to her glad husband gave,
Rescued form death by force, though pale and faint.
Mine, as whom wash'd from spot of child-bed taint
    Purification in the old Law did save,
    And such, as yet once more I trust to have
Full sight of her in Heaven without restraint,
Came vested all in white, pure as her mind:

Her face was veil'd yet to my fancied sight
Love, sweetness, goodness, in her person shin'd
So clear, as in no face with more delight.
    But O, as to embrace me she inclin'd,
    I wak'd; she fled; and day brought back my night.

Miguel de Cervantes. During the sixteenth century in Spain, a narrative form known as the **picaresque** began to develop. The picaresque novel details the life of a *pícaro*, a rogue or knave who wanders from adventure to adventure, and marks the birth of the novel as a literary art form. Like Chaucer's *Canterbury Tales*, the picaresque novel probably developed out of the pilgrimage tradition, in particular the pilgrimage across northern Spain to Santiago de Compostela, the burial place of St. James, which in the eleventh and twelfth centuries had been the object of European pilgrimages. Whereas the *Canterbury Tales* is a compendium of stories about different pilgrims, the picaresque novel focuses on a single hero.

One characteristic feature of the picaresque novel is its pseudo-autobiographical nature. Narrated always by the hero, the point of view is clearly his, prejudiced and partial. He is an observer of society, and, perhaps as a result, he is expert at recognizing fraud and deception.

The greatest of all picaresque novels is *Don Quixote*, by MIGUEL DE CERVANTES [ser-VAHN-tez] (1548–1616). It is in fact more than a picaresque novel, satirizing the form even as it goes beyond it in complexity and ambition. Composed between 1603 and 1615, *Don Quixote* was translated in the seventeenth century into English, French, Italian, and German. The central character, Don Quixote, the hero, wants, most of all, to become a "knight errant," the kind of hero he has read about in books, who saves ladies from evil and defeats dragons in combat. In fact, he is at once noble and a buffoon. What he sees and what is the truth are two entirely different things. His horse is "all skin and bones," but in his eyes, it is a noble "steed." His companion is a peasant boy, re-dubbed his "squire," Sancho Panza. His lady, the lovely Dulcinea, is actually one Aldonza Lorenzo, who "never knew or was aware of" his love for her. And the giants he fights are not giants at all, but windmills. The novel represents, for the first time in Western literature, the conflict between reality and the imagination, and although Don Quixote's imagination brings him to the edge of total madness, it ennobles him as well.

Cultural Impact

The Baroque era celebrated individual genius while endorsing new forms of social cooperation and artistic patronage. Begun in Italy, the Baroque style spread throughout Europe. In Italy the Counter-Reformation fueled an emotional embrace of the spiritual world, seen especially in the sculpture and architecture of Bernini.

The Baroque style influenced the creation of public buildings and monuments, as well as domestic architecture. The monuments of southern Baroque architecture were funded not by private donors but by public commission of court or church. Piazzas and fountains abounded in Italy, with forms alluding to religious history and Greco-Roman mythology.

The Roman Church and Counter-Reformation spirituality retained influence on the music of the southern Baroque. However, Baroque music became as much a secular as a religious art. Opera, invented in Italy during the early Baroque, initially took its subjects from myth, history, and legend. This trend continued in later centuries, as the influence of opera became more prominent.

The impact of the Baroque in northern Europe was quieter and less flamboyant, with the north revealing a more subdued but no less sustained shift of cultural expression. In England and in Holland, for example, artistic patronage shifted from court and church to wealthy patrons, who commissioned works honoring themselves and their world. This celebration of social ideals and middle-class prosperity are hallmarks of the northern Baroque. Portraits by Rembrandt of prominent individuals and of members of civic organizations exemplify this desire for recognition and honor.

Northern Baroque painters such as Rembrandt and Rubens amassed huge fortunes. Rembrandt was to lose his and died nearly destitute. Rubens, however, oversaw a large studio and inaugurated a major industry—the production of masterpieces with the aid of teams of assistants.

The situation was otherwise for literature, which was only occasionally commissioned and almost exclusively composed by an individual. John Donne's poems circulated in manuscript only to be published after his death. While employing Renaissance poetic conventions and playfully undermining them, Donne and his followers seasoned poetry with wit and ingenuity. Donne's influence appears in such later poets as Emily Dickinson in the nineteenth century and T. S. Eliot in the twentieth.

Unlike their counterparts in the south, composers of the northern Baroque were not exclusively in the employ of the Roman Church. Thus, although J. S. Bach and G. F. Handel both wrote reams of music for religious occasions, both composed much music for court and private entertainment as well. Their music, and the music of Baroque masters in the south such as Antonio Vivaldi, was designed to challenge the virtuosity of the performer, an emphasis that would be taken much further later, especially during the Romantic era.

Perhaps the greatest legacy of the northern Baroque was the emergence of objectivity with the inductive method of Baconian science and the rational analytical method of Cartesian philosophical thought. Casting everything into doubt until proof could be established, Bacon and Descartes changed science and philosophy forever.

Finally, the expansion of colonial empires spread European values and ideals around the globe, particularly to the shores on the Americas, where they took root and sprouted during the eras of the Enlightenment and Romanticism.

KEY TERMS

Baroque
Counter-Reformation
oratories
portico
obelisk
tenebrism

opera
recitative
concerto grosso
ritornello
etching
camera obscura

poussinistes/rubénistes
oratorio
aria
fugue
counterpoint
cantata

social contract
proscenium arch
unities
picaresque

www. WEBSITES FOR FURTHER STUDY

http://galileo.rice.edu/gal/urban.html
(A site on the Maffeo Barberini, also known as Pope Urban VIII, one of the most powerful and influential popes.)

http://www.fordham.edu/halsall/source/loyola-spirex.html
(An excerpt from The Spiritual Exercises of Ignatius Loyola, founder of the Jesuit order.)

http://www.artchive.com/artchive/C/caravaggio/calling of st matthew.jpg.html
(This is the Artchive, a website with virtually every major artist in every style from every era in art history. It is an excellent resource.)

http://w3.rz-berlin.mpg.de/cmp/monteverdi.html
(A good site on Monteverdi and the beginning of opera.)

http://www.ucmp.berkeley.edu/history/leeuwenhoek.html
(The biography of Antony Leeuwenhoek, discoverer of bacteria and inventor of the microscope.)

READINGS

IGNATIUS OF LOYOLA

from *The Spiritual Exercises*

Ignatius of Loyola's Spiritual Exercises *provided both clerical and lay Church members with a guidebook for spiritual development. As leaders of the Counter-Reformation, the Jesuits advocated strict obedience to the tenets of Roman Catholicism, both for themselves and for lay people. In the following meditation, Ignatius prescribes activities and forms of contemplation that will conjure up vivid images and evoke strong emotional and spiritual responses in the participant.*

THE FIFTH EXERCISE

The Fifth Exercise is a meditation on Hell. It contains, after a preparatory prayer and two preludes, five points and a colloquy.

Let the preparatory prayer be the usual one.

The first prelude is a composition of place, which is here to see with the eyes of the imagination the length, breadth, and depth of Hell.

The second prelude is to ask for that which I desire. It will be here to ask for an interior perception of the pains which the lost suffer, in order that if I through my faults forget the love of the Eternal Lord, at least the fear of punishment may help me not to fall into sin.

The first point will be to see with the eyes of the imagination these great fires, and the souls as it were in bodies of fire.

The second will be to hear with the ears of the imagination the wailings, the howlings, the cries, the blasphemies against Christ our Lord and against all the saints.

The third will be to smell the smoke, the sulphur, the filth, and the putrid matter.

The fourth will be to taste with the taste of the imagination bitter things, such as tears, sadness, and the worm of conscience.

The fifth will be to feel with the touch of the imagination how the fires touch and burn the souls.

Making a colloquy to Christ our Lord, bring to memory the souls which are in Hell, some because they did not believe His coming, others because believing they did not act according to His commandments; making of them three classes: the first, those who lived before His coming; the second, those who were alive during His lifetime; and the third, those who lived after His life in this world: and then give thanks that He has not, by putting an end to my life, permitted me to fall under any of these classes. In like manner consider how up till now He has always had towards me such pity and mercy; and then finish with a *Pater noster.*

RENÉ DESCARTES

from *The Meditations*

In the following passage from his Meditations, *Descartes explores the nature of his own mind, focusing particularly on what he knows with certainty. His "Second Meditation" shows Descartes discover-* ing what he is—"*A thing that thinks.*" The Meditations *in their entirety reveal a human mind reasoning in various manifestations—doubting, affirming, denying, willing, refusing, understanding, and imagining.*

SECOND MEDITATION

OF THE NATURE OF THE HUMAN MIND, AND THAT IT IS EASIER TO KNOW THAN THE BODY

Yesterday's Meditation has filled my mind with so many doubts that henceforth it is no longer in my power to forget them, and yet I do not see how I shall be able to solve them; and just as if I had suddenly fallen into very deep water, I am so taken aback that I can neither find foothold at the bottom, nor swim to keep myself at the top. I shall make an effort, nevertheless, and follow again the same road I went over yesterday, by putting away from me all in which I shall be able to imagine the least doubt, just as if I knew it to be absolutely false, and I shall continue to follow this path, until I have met with something that is certain; or at least, if I can do nothing else, until I have learned for certain that nothing in the world is certain. Archimedes, to draw the terrestrial globe from its place, and transport it elsewhere, asked no more than one firm and immovable point: in the same way, I shall have the right to conceive high hopes, if I am happy enough to find but one certain and indubitable thing.

I assume, therefore, that everything that I see is false; I persuade myself that of all the things which my memory, stored with dreams, represents to me, none have ever existed; I suppose that I have no sense; I believe that body, shape, extension, motion, and place are only fictions of my mind. What, then, shall be esteemed true? Nothing, perhaps, but that nothing in the world is certain.

But how do I know that there is not some other thing, different from these that I have just pronounced uncertain, of which there cannot be the slightest doubt? Is there not a God, or some other power which puts these thoughts into my mind? Not necessarily; for it may be that I am capable of producing them myself. I, at least, then, am I not something? But I have already denied that I had any senses or any body; nevertheless I hesitate, for what follows? Am I so dependent on the body and on the senses that I cannot exist without them? But I persuaded myself that there was nothing in the whole world, no sky, no earth, no spirits, no bodies; did I not therefore also persuade myself that I did not exist? Far from it; beyond doubt I existed if I persuaded myself, or even if I only thought something. But there is an unknown deceiver, very powerful and very cunning, who employs all his energy in continually deceiving me; therefore there is no doubt that I exist, if he deceives me; let him deceive me as much as he will, he will never be able to make me to be nothing, so long as I shall think I am something. So having pondered that well, and examined everything carefully, it must after all be concluded and held as unquestionable that this proposition—*I am, I exist*—is necessarily true, every time that I pronounce it, or conceive it in my mind.

But I do not yet know quite clearly what I am, I, who am certain that I am: so that henceforth I must take careful heed not to imprudently mistake some other thing for myself, so as not to err in this knowledge, which I maintain to be more certain and evident than all which I have had formerly.

This is why I shall now consider entirely anew what I believed myself to be before I entered upon these last thoughts, and from my old opinions I shall lop off all which can be in the slightest degree opposed to the reasons I have already alleged, so that there may remain just that which is perfectly certain and indubitable, and that alone. What, then, have I believed myself to be hitherto? Without doubt, I thought I was a man; but what is a man? Shall I say that it is a rational animal? No indeed, for I should afterwards have to find out what an animal is, and what rational is, and thus from one single question I should be launched, without knowing it, into an infinity of others more difficult and complex, and I would not misuse the little time and leisure remaining to me, by employing it in unravelling difficulties of the kind. But I will here dwell rather on the consideration of the thoughts which heretofore took rise of themselves in my mind, and with which my nature alone inspired me, when I applied myself to the contemplation of my being. I considered myself first as having a face, hands, arms, and all the mechanism of flesh and bones, such as it appears in a corpse, which I designated "body." Moreover, I reflected that I nourished myself, that I walked, felt, and thought, and I connected all these actions with the soul; but I did not stop to think what this soul was; or rather, if I did so, I imagined it something extremely rare and subtle, as a wind, a flame, or a very volatile air insinuated and diffused throughout my more material parts. As to what the body was, in nowise did I doubt of its nature, but I thought I knew it very distinctly; and if I had wished to explain it according to the notions I then had of it, I would have described it in this way. By the body I understand all which can be limited by some fixture, which can be contained in some place, and occupy a space in such a manner that all other bodies are excluded therefrom; which is sensible either to touch, or sight, or hearing, or taste, or smell; which can be moved in many ways, not indeed by itself, but by something extraneous which comes into contact with it, and from which it receives the impression; for I do not believe at all that the power of moving of oneself, or of feeling, or of thinking, belongs to the nature of the body; on the contrary, I was astonished, rather, to see that in some bodies faculties of the kind were to be met with.

But I, what am I, now that I assume that there is a certain genius who is extremely powerful, and, if I dare say so, malicious and crafty, who uses all his power and industry to deceive me? Can I be sure that I have the least of all those things that I have just said belonged to the nature of the body? I pause to consider that attentively; I revolve all these things in my mind, and I find none of them which I can say are in me. There is no need for me to stay to enumerate them. Let us pass, therefore, to the attributes of the soul, and see if there are any which may be in me. The first attributes are [the faculties of] feeding myself and of walking; but if it is true that I have no body, it is also true that I can neither walk nor feed. Another is sensibility, but neither can we feel without the body besides, I have at times thought I felt many things during sleep, which on waking I have discovered that I had not really felt. Another is thought, and here I find that thought is an attribute which belongs to me; it alone cannot be separated from me. *I am, I exist*—that is certain, but for how long? As long as I think; for, perhaps, if I entirely ceased to think, I should at the same time entirely cease

to be. I now admit nothing, which is not of necessity true; therefore, strictly speaking, I am *only a thing which thinks*, that is to say, a mind, an understanding, or a reason, terms whose signification was formerly unknown to me. Now I am a real thing, and truly existent, but what thing? I have said it,—a thing which thinks. What more? I will exert my imagination, to see if I am not something more yet. I am not this collection of members which is called the human body; I am not a volatile and penetrating air diffused through these members; I am not a wind, a breath, a vapour, or any of the things which I can feign and imagine myself, since I have assumed all that to be nothing, and since without changing this assumption I find that I do not cease to be certain that I am something.

But perhaps it is true that these very things which I suppose not to exist, because they are unknown to me, are not in reality different from myself, whom I know? I cannot say; I do not now dispute it; I cannot give my opinion except on things which are known to me: I know that I exist, and I am seeking what I am—I, whom I know to be. Now it is very certain that the knowledge of my being, thus taken exactly, does not depend on the things whose existence is not yet known to me; consequently, it does not depend on any of those that I can feign by my imagination. And even these terms "feign" and "imagination" warn me of my error. For I should feign indeed if I imagined myself to be something, since to imagine is nothing else than to contemplate the figure or image of a material thing: now I already know for certain that I am, and that at the same time it may be that all these images, and generally all the things which are connected with the bodily nature, are only dreams or chimeras. Following which, I see clearly, that I have as little reason in saying, I will excite my imagination in order to know more exactly what I am, as if I said, I am now awake, and perceive something real and veritable, but because I do not yet perceive it plainly enough, I will send myself to sleep expressly in order that my dreams may represent it to me with even more truth and evidence. And therefore I know clearly that nothing which I can comprehend by means of the imagination belongs to this knowledge that I have concerning myself, and that there is need to call off and deflect the mind from this mode of conception, in order that it may more exactly know its nature.

But what, then, am I? *A thing which thinks.* What is a thing which thinks? It is a thing which doubts, understands, conceives, affirms, denies, wills, wills not, which also imagines, and feels.

MIGUEL CERVANTES

from *Don Quixote*

Cervantes's Don Quixote *is often considered to be the first modern western novel. Its central characters, Don Quixote, the idealistic Knight of the Sorrowful Countenance, and his down-to-earth companion, Sancho Panza, are well-known literary characters. The following passage introduces Don Quixote de La Mancha and his companion, and it describes one of the book's most famous scenes— the episode of the windmills. In these brief chapter episodes, Cervantes reveals much about each of his contrasting characters and just as much about their relationship.*

PART ONE OF THE INGENIOUS GENTLEMAN DON QUIXOTE OF LA MANCHA

Chapter I

WHICH DESCRIBES THE CONDITION AND PROFESSION OF THE FAMOUS GENTLEMAN DON QUIXOTE OF LA MANCHA

Somewhere in La Mancha, in a place whose name I do not care to remember, a gentleman lived not long ago, one of those who has a lance and ancient shield on a shelf and keeps a skinny nag and a greyhound for racing. An occasional stew, beef more often than lamb, hash most nights, eggs and abstinence on Saturdays, lentils on Fridays, sometimes squab as a treat on Sundays—these consumed three-fourths of his income.[1] The rest went for a light woolen tunic and velvet breeches and hose of the same material for feast days, while weekdays were honored with dun-colored coarse cloth. He had a housekeeper past forty, a niece not yet twenty, and a man-of-all-work who did everything from saddling the horse to pruning the trees. Our gentleman was approximately fifty years old; his complexion was weathered, his flesh scrawny, his face gaunt, and he was a very early riser and a great lover of the hunt. Some claim that his family name was Quixada, or Quexada, for there is a certain amount of disagreement among the authors who write of this matter, although reliable conjecture seems to indicate that his name was Quexana. But this does not matter very much to our story; in its telling there is absolutely no deviation from the truth.

And so, let it be said that this aforementioned gentleman spent his times of leisure—which meant most of the year—reading books of chivalry with so much devotion and enthusiasm that he forgot almost completely about the hunt and even about the administration of his estate; and in his rash curiosity and folly he went so far as to sell acres of arable land in order to buy books of chivalry to read, and he brought as many of them as he could into his house; and he thought none was as fine as those composed by the worthy Feliciano de Silva,[2] because the clarity of his prose and complexity of his language seemed to him more valuable than pearls, in particular when he read the declarations and missives of love, where he would often find written: *The reason for the unreason to which my reason turns so weakens my reason that with reason I complain of thy beauty.* And also when he read: . . . *the heavens on high divinely heighten thy divinity with the stars and make thee deserving of the deserts thy greatness deserves.*

With these words and phrases the poor gentleman lost his mind, and he spent sleepless nights trying to understand them and extract their meaning, which Aristotle himself, if he came back to life for only that purpose, would not have been able to decipher or understand. Our gentleman was not very happy with the wounds that Don Belianis gave and received, because he imagined that no matter how great the physicians and surgeons who cured him, he would still have his face and

entire body covered with scars and marks. But, even so, he praised the author for having concluded his book with the promise of unending adventure, and he often felt the desire to take up his pen and give it the conclusion promised there; and no doubt he would have done so, and even published it, if other greater and more persistent thoughts had not prevented him from doing so. He often had discussions with the village priest—who was a learned man, a graduate of Sigüenza[3]—regarding who had been the greater knight, Palmerín of England or Amadís of Gaul; but Master Nicolás, the village barber, said that none was the equal of the Knight of Phoebus, and if any could be compared to him, it was Don Galaor, the brother of Amadís of Gaul, because he was moderate in everything: a knight who was not affected, not as weepy as his brother, and incomparable in questions of courage.

In short, our gentleman became so caught up in reading that he spent his nights reading from dusk till dawn and his days reading from sunrise to sunset, and so with too little sleep and too much reading his brains dried up, causing him to lose his mind. His fantasy filled with everything he had read in his books, enchantments as well as combats, battles, challenges, wounds, courtings, loves, torments, and other impossible foolishness, and he became so convinced in his imagination of the truth of all the countless grandiloquent and false inventions he read that for him no history in the world was truer. He would say that El Cid Ruy Díaz[4] had been a very good knight but could not compare to Amadís, the Knight of the Blazing Sword, who with a single backstroke cut two ferocious and colossal giants in half. He was fonder of Bernardo del Carpios[5] because at Roncesvalles[6] he had killed the enchanted Roland by availing himself of the tactic of Hercules when he crushed Antaeus, the son of Earth, in his arms. He spoke highly of the giant Morgante because, although he belonged to the race of giants, all of them haughty and lacking in courtesy, he alone was amiable and well-behaved. But, more than any of the others, he admired Reinaldos de Montalbán,[7] above all when he saw him emerge from his castle and rob anyone he met, and when he crossed the sea and stole the idol of Mohammed made all of gold, as recounted in his history. He would have traded his housekeeper, and even his niece, for the chance to strike a blow at the traitor Guenelon.[8]

The truth is that when his mind was completely gone, he had the strangest thought any lunatic in the world ever had, which was that it seemed reasonable and necessary to him, both for the sake of his honor and as a service to the nation, to become a knight errant and travel the world with his armor and his horse to seek adventures and engage in everything he had read that knights errant engaged in, righting all manner

---

[1]Cervantes describes typical aspects of the ordinary life of the rural gentry. The indications of reduced circumstances include the foods eaten by Don Quixote: beef, for example, was less expensive than lamb.

[2]The author of several novels of chivalry; the phrases cited by Cervantes are typical of the language in these books that drove Don Quixote mad.

[3]The allusion is ironic: Sigüenza was a minor university, and its graduates had the reputation of being not very well educated.

[4]A historical figure (eleventh century) who has passed into legend and literature.

[5]A legendary hero, the subject of ballads as well as poems and plays.

[6]The site in the Pyrenees, called Roncesvaux in French, where Charlemagne's army fought the Saracens in 778.

[7]A hero of the French chansons de geste; in some Spanish versions, he takes part in the battle of Roncesvalles.

[8]The traitor responsible for the defeat of Charlemagne's army at Roncesvalles.

of wrongs and, by seizing the opportunity and placing himself in danger and ending those wrongs, winning eternal renown and everlasting fame. The poor man imagined himself already wearing the crown, won by the valor of his arm, of the empire of Trebizond at the very least; and so it was that with these exceedingly agreeable thoughts, and carried away by the extraordinary pleasure he took in them, he hastened to put into effect what he so fervently desired. And the first thing he did was to attempt to clean some armor that had belonged to his great-grandfathers and, stained with rust and covered with mildew, had spent many long years stored and forgotten in a corner. He did the best he could to clean and repair it, but he saw that it had a great defect, which was that instead of a full sallet helmet with an attached neckguard, there was only a simple headpiece; but he compensated for this with his industry, and out of pasteboard he fashioned a kind of half-helmet that, when attached to the headpiece, took on the appearance of a full sallet. It is true that in order to test if it was strong and could withstand a blow, he took out his sword and struck it twice, and with the first blow he undid in a moment what it had taken him a week to create; he could not help being disappointed at the ease with which he had hacked it to pieces, and to protect against that danger, he made another one, placing strips of iron on the inside so that he was satisfied with its strength; and not wanting to put it to the test again, he designated and accepted it as an extremely fine sallet.

Then he went to look at his nag, and though its hooves had more cracks than his master's pate and it showed more flaws than Gonnella's horse, that *tantum pelus et ossa fuit*,[9] it seemed to him that Alexander's Bucephalus and El Cid's Babieca were not its equal. He spent four days thinking about the name he would give it; for—as he told himself—it was not seemly that the horse of so famous a knight, and a steed so intrinsically excellent, should not have a worthy name; he was looking for the precise name that would declare what the horse had been before its master became a knight errant and what it was now; for he was determined that if the master was changing his condition, the horse too would change its name to one that would win the fame and recognition its new position and profession deserved; and so, after many names that he shaped and discarded, subtracted from and added to, unmade and remade in his memory and imagination, he finally decided to call the horse Rocinante,[10] a name, in his opinion, that was noble, sonorous, and reflective of what it had been when it was a nag, before it was what it was now, which was the foremost nag in all the world.

Having given a name, and one so much to his liking, to his horse, he wanted to give one to himself, and he spent another eight days pondering this, and at last he called himself *Don Quixote*,[11] which is why, as has been noted, the authors of this absolutely true history determined that he undoubtedly must have been named Quixada and not Quexada, as others have claimed. In any event, recalling that the valiant Amadís

had not been content with simply calling himself Amadís but had added the name of his kingdom and realm in order to bring it fame, and was known as Amadís of Gaul, he too, like a good knight, wanted to add the name of his birthplace to his own, and he called himself *Don Quixote of La Mancha*,[12] thereby, to his mind, clearly stating his lineage and country and honoring it by making it part of his title.

Having cleaned his armor and made a full helmet out of a simple headpiece, and having given a name to his horse and decided on one for himself, he realized that the only thing left for him to do was to find a lady to love; for the knight errant without a lady-love was a tree without leaves or fruit, a body without a soul. He said to himself:

"If I, because of my evil sins, or my good fortune, meet with a giant somewhere, as ordinarily befalls knights errant, and I unseat him with a single blow, or cut his body in half, or, in short, conquer and defeat him, would it not be good to have someone to whom I could send him so that he might enter and fall to his knees before my sweet lady, and say in the humble voice of surrender: 'I, lady, am the giant Caraculiambro, lord of the island Malindrania, defeated in single combat by the never sufficiently praised knight Don Quixote of La Mancha, who commanded me to appear before your ladyship, so that your highness might dispose of me as you chose'?"

Oh, how pleased our good knight was when he had made this speech, and even more pleased when he discovered the one he could call his lady! It is believed that in a nearby village there was a very attractive peasant girl with whom he had once been in love, although she, apparently, never knew or noticed. Her name was Aldonza Lorenzo;[13] and he thought it a good idea to call her the lady of his thoughts, and, searching for a name that would not differ significantly from his and would suggest and imply that of a princess and great lady, he decided to call her *Dulcinea of Toboso*,[14] because she came from Toboso, a name, to his mind, that was musical and beautiful and filled with significance, as were all the others he had given to himself and everything pertaining to him.

Chapter VIII

REGARDING THE GOOD FORTUNE OF THE VALOROUS DON QUIXOTE IN THE FEARFUL AND NEVER IMAGINED ADVENTURE OF THE WINDMILLS, ALONG WITH OTHER EVENTS WORTHY OF JOYFUL REMEMBRANCE

As they were talking, they saw thirty or forty of the windmills found in that countryside, and as soon as Don Quixote caught sight of them, he said to his squire:

"Good fortune is guiding our affairs better than we could have desired, for there you see, friend Sancho Panza, thirty or more enormous giants with whom I intend to do battle and

---

[9]Pietro Gonnella, the jester at the court of Ferrara, had a horse famous for being skinny. The Latin translates as "was nothing but skin and bones."

[10]Rocín means "nag"; *ante* means "before," both temporally and spatially.

[11]*Quixote* means the section of armor that covers the thigh.

[12]La Mancha was not one of the noble medieval kingdoms associated with knighthood.

[13]Aldonza, considered to be a common, rustic name, had comic connotations.

[14]Her name is based on the word *dulce* ("sweet").

whose lives I intend to take, and with the spoils we shall begin to grow rich, for this is righteous warfare, and it is a great service to God to remove so evil a breed from the face of the earth."

"What giants?" said Sancho Panza.

"Those you see over there," replied his master, "with the long arms; sometimes they are almost two leagues long."

"Look, your grace," Sancho responded, "those things that appear over there aren't giants but windmills, and what looks like their arms are the sails that are turned by the wind and make the grindstone move."

"It seems clear to me," replied Don Quixote, "that thou art not well-versed in the matter of adventures: these are giants; and if thou art afraid, move aside and start to pray whilst I enter with them in fierce and unequal combat."

And having said this, he spurred his horse, Rocinante, paying no attention to the shouts of his squire, Sancho, who warned him that, beyond any doubt, those things he was about to attack were windmills and not giants. But he was so convinced they were giants that he did not hear the shouts of his squire, Sancho, and could not see, though he was very close, what they really were; instead, he charged and called out:

"Flee not, cowards and base creatures, for it is a single knight who attacks you."

Just then a gust of wind began to blow, and the great sails began to move, and, seeing this, Don Quixote said:

"Even if you move more arms than the giant Briareus,[1] you will answer to me."

And saying this, and commending himself with all his heart to his lady Dulcinea, asking that she come to his aid at this critical moment, and well-protected by his shield, with his lance in its socket, he charged at Rocinante's full gallop and attacked the first mill he came to; and as he thrust his lance into the sail, the wind moved it with so much force that it broke the lance into pieces and picked up the horse and the knight, who then dropped to the ground and were very badly battered. Sancho Panza hurried to help as fast as his donkey could carry him, and when he reached them he discovered that Don Quixote could not move because he had taken so hard a fall with Rocinante.

"God save me!" said Sancho. "Didn't I tell your grace to watch what you were doing, that these were nothing but windmills, and only somebody whose head was full of them wouldn't know that?"

"Be quiet, Sancho my friend," replied Don Quixote. "Matters of war, more than any others, are subject to continual change; moreover, I think, and therefore it is true, that the same Frestón the Wise who stole my room and my books has turned these giants into windmills in order to deprive me of the glory of defeating them: such is the enmity he feels for me; but in the end, his evil arts will not prevail against the power of my virtuous sword."

"God's will be done," replied Sancho Panza.

He helped him to stand, and Don Quixote remounted Rocinante, whose back was almost broken. And, talking about their recent adventure, they continued on the road to Puerto Lapice,[2] because there, said Don Quixote, he could not fail to find many diverse adventures since it was a very heavily trafficked place; but he rode heavyhearted because he did not have his lance; and expressing this to his squire, he said:

"I remember reading that a Spanish knight named Diego Pérez de Vargas, whose sword broke in battle, tore a heavy bough or branch from an oak tree and with it did such great deeds that day, and thrashed so many Moors, that he was called Machuca, the Bruiser, and from that day forward he and his descendants were named Vargas y Machuca.[3] I have told you this because from the first oak that presents itself to me I intend to tear off another branch as good as the one I have in mind, and with it I shall do such great deeds that you will consider yourself fortunate for deserving to see them and for being a witness to things that can hardly be believed."

"It's in God's hands," said Sancho. "I believe everything your grace says, but sit a little straighter, it looks like you're tilting, it must be from the battering you took when you fell."

"That is true," replied Don Quixote, "and if I do not complain about the pain, it is because it is not the custom of knights errant to complain about any wound, even if their innards are spilling out because of it."

"If that's true, I have nothing to say," Sancho responded, "but God knows I'd be happy if your grace complained when something hurt you. As for me, I can say that I'll complain about the smallest pain I have, unless what you said about not complaining also applies to the squires of knights errant."

Don Quixote could not help laughing at his squire's simplemindedness; and so he declared that he could certainly complain however and whenever he wanted, with or without cause, for as yet he had not read anything to the contrary in the order of chivalry. Sancho said that it was time to eat. His master replied that he felt no need of food at the moment, but that Sancho could eat whenever he wished. With this permission, Sancho made himself as comfortable as he could on his donkey, and after taking out of the saddlebags what he had put into them, he rode behind his master at a leisurely pace, eating and, from time to time, tilting back the wineskin with so much gusto that the most self-indulgent tavern-keeper in Málaga might have envied him. And as he rode along in that manner, taking frequent drinks, he did not think about any promises his master had made to him, and he did not consider it work but sheer pleasure to go around seeking adventures, no matter how dangerous they might be.

In short, they spent the night under some trees, and from one of them Don Quixote tore off a dry branch to use as a lance and placed on it the iron head he had taken from the one that had broken. Don Quixote did not sleep at all that night but thought of his lady Dulcinea, in order to conform to what he had read in his books of knights spending many sleepless nights in groves and meadows, turning all their thoughts to memories of their ladies. Sancho Panza did not do the same; since his stomach was full, and not with chicory water, he slept the entire night, and if his master had not called him, the rays of the sun shining in his face and the song of numerous birds joyfully greeting the arrival of the new day would have

---

[1]A monstrous giant in Greek mythology who had fifty heads and a hundred arms.

[2]An entrance to the mountains of the Sierra Morena, between La Mancha and Andalucía.

[3]A historical figure of the thirteenth century.

done nothing to rouse him. When he woke he made another pass at the wineskin and found it somewhat flatter than it had been the night before, and his heart grieved, for it seemed to him they were not likely to remedy the lack very soon. Don Quixote did not wish to eat breakfast because, as has been stated, he meant to live on sweet memories. They continued on the road to Puerto Lápice, and at about three in the afternoon it came into view.

"Here," said Don Quixote when he saw it, "we can, brother Sancho Panza, plunge our hands all the way up to the elbows into this thing they call adventures. But be advised that even if you see me in the greatest danger in the world, you are not to put a hand to your sword to defend me, unless you see that those who offend me are baseborn rabble, in which case you certainly can help me; but if they are gentlemen, under no circumstances is it licit or permissible for you, under the laws of chivalry, to help me until you are dubbed a knight."

"There's no doubt, Señor," replied Sancho, "that your grace will be strictly obeyed in this; besides, as far as I'm concerned, I'm a peaceful man and an enemy of getting involved in quarrels or disputes. It's certainly true that when it comes to defending my person I won't pay much attention to those laws, since laws both human and divine permit each man to defend himself against anyone who tries to hurt him."

"I agree," Don Quixote responded, "but as for helping me against gentlemen, you have to hold your natural impulses in check."

"Then that's just what I'll do," replied Sancho, "and I'll keep that precept as faithfully as I keep the Sabbath on Sunday."

As they were speaking, there appeared on the road two Benedictine friars mounted on two dromedaries, for the two mules they rode on were surely no smaller than that. They wore their traveling masks and carried sunshades. Behind them came a carriage, accompanied by four or five men on horseback, and two muledrivers on foot. In the carriage, as was learned later, was a Basque lady going to Sevilla, where her husband was preparing to sail for the Indies to take up a very honorable post. The friars were not traveling with her, although their route was the same, but as soon as Don Quixote saw them, he said to his squire:

"Either I am deceived, or this will be the most famous adventure ever seen, because those black shapes you see there must be, and no doubt are, enchanters who have captured some princess in that carriage, and I needs must do everything in my power to right this wrong."

"This will be worse than the windmills," said Sancho. "Look, Señor, those are friars of St. Benedict, and the carriage must belong to some travelers. Look carefully, I tell you, look carefully at what you do, in case the devil is deceiving you."

"I have already told you, Sancho," replied Don Quixote, "that you know very little about the subject of adventures; what I say is true, and now you will see that it is so."

And having said this, he rode forward and stopped in the middle of the road that the friars were traveling, and when they were close enough so that he thought they could hear what he said, he called to them in a loud voice:

"You wicked and monstrous creatures, instantly unhand the noble princesses you hold captive in that carriage, or else prepare to receive a swift death as just punishment for your evil deeds."

The friars pulled on the reins, taken aback as much by Don Quixote's appearance as by his words, and they responded:

"Señor, we are neither wicked nor monstrous, but two religious of St. Benedict who are traveling on our way, and we do not know if there are captive princesses in that carriage or not."

"No soft words with me; I know who you are, perfidious rabble," said Don Quixote.

And without waiting for any further reply, he spurred Rocinante, lowered his lance, and attacked the first friar with so much ferocity and courage that if he had not allowed himself to fall off the mule, the friar would have been thrown to the ground and seriously injured or even killed. The second friar, who saw how his companion was treated, kicked his castle-size mule and began to gallop across the fields, faster than the wind.

Sancho Panza, who saw the man on the ground, quickly got off his donkey, hurried over to the friar, and began to pull off his habit. At this moment, two servants of the friars came over and asked why he was stripping him. Sancho replied that these clothes were legitimately his, the spoils of the battle his master, Don Quixote, had won. The servants had no sense of humor and did not understand anything about spoils or battles, and seeing that Don Quixote had moved away and was talking to the occupants of the carriage, they attacked Sancho and knocked him down, and leaving no hair in his beard unscathed, they kicked him breathless and senseless and left him lying on the ground. The friar, frightened and terrified and with no color in his face, did not wait another moment but got back on his mule, and when he was mounted, he rode off after his companion, who was waiting for him a good distance away, wondering what the outcome of the attack would be; they did not wish to wait to learn how matters would turn out but continued on their way, crossing themselves more than if they had the devil at their backs.

Don Quixote, as has been said, was talking to the lady in the carriage, saying:

"O beauteous lady, thou canst do with thy person as thou wishest, for the arrogance of thy captors here lieth on the ground, vanquished by this my mighty arm; and so that thou mayest not pine to know the name of thy emancipator, know that I am called Don Quixote of La Mancha, knight errant in search of adventures, and captive of the beauteous and peerless Doña Dulcinea of Toboso, and as recompense for the boon thou hast received from me, I desire only that thou turnest toward Toboso, and on my behalf appearest before this lady and sayest unto her what deeds I have done to gain thy liberty."

One of the squires accompanying the carriage was a Basque, who listened to everything that Don Quixote was saying; and seeing that he would not allow the carriage to move forward but said it would have to go to Toboso, the squire approached Don Quixote and, seizing his lance, in bad Castilian and even worse Basque, he said:

"Go on, mister, you go wrong; by God who make me, if don't let carriage go, as I be Basque I kill you."

Don Quixote understood him very well and replied with great serenity:

"If you were a gentleman, as you are not, I would already have punished your foolishness and audacity, unhappy creature."

To which the Basque replied:

"Not gentleman me? As Christian I make vow to God you lie. Throw away lance and pull out sword and soon see which one make horse drink. Basque by land, noble by sea, noble by devil, if say other thing you lie."

"Now you will see, said Agrajes,"[4] replied Don Quixote.

And after throwing his lance to the ground, he drew his sword, grasped his shield, and attacked the Basque, determined to take his life. The Basque, who saw him coming at him in this manner, wanted to get off the mule, which, being one of the inferior ones for hire, could not be trusted, but all he could do was draw his sword; it was his good fortune, however, to be next to the carriage, and he seized one of the pillows and used it as a shield, and the two of them went at each other as if they were mortal enemies. The rest of the people tried to make peace between them but could not, because the Basque said in his tangled words that if they did not allow him to finish his fight, he himself would kill his mistress and everyone else who got in his way. The lady in the carriage, stunned and fearful at what she saw, had the coachman drive some distance away, and from there she watched the fierce contest, in the course of which the Basque went over Don Quixote's shield and struck a great blow with his sword to his shoulder, and if it had not been protected by armor, he would have opened it to the waist. Don Quixote, who felt the pain of that enormous blow, gave a great shout, saying:

"O lady of my soul, Dulcinea, flower of beauty, come to the aid of this thy knight, who, for the sake of thy great virtue, finds himself in grave peril!"

Saying this, and grasping his sword, and protecting himself with his shield, and attacking the Basque were all one, for he was determined to venture everything on the fortune of a single blow.

The Basque, seeing him attack in this fashion, clearly understood the courage in this rash act and resolved to do the same as Don Quixote. And so he waited for him, shielded by his pillow, and unable to turn the mule one way or the other, for the mule, utterly exhausted and not made for such foolishness, could not take another step.

As has been said, Don Quixote was charging the wary Basque with his sword on high, determined to cut him in half, and the Basque, well-protected by his pillow, was waiting for him, his sword also raised, and all the onlookers were filled with fear and suspense regarding the outcome of the great blows they threatened to give to each other, and the lady in the carriage and all her maids were making a thousand vows and offerings to all the images and houses of devotion in Spain so that God would deliver the squire and themselves from the great danger in which they found themselves.

But the difficulty in all this is that at this very point and juncture, the author of the history leaves the battle pending, apologizing because he found nothing else written about the feats of Don Quixote other than what he has already re-counted. It is certainly true that the second author[5] of this work did not want to believe that so curious a history would be subjected to the laws of oblivion, or that the great minds of La Mancha possessed so little interest that they did not have in their archives or writing tables a few pages that dealt with this famous knight; and so, with this thought in mind, he did not despair of finding the conclusion to this gentle history, which, with heaven's help, he discovered in the manner that will be revealed in part two.[6]

MOLIÈRE

from *Tartuffe*

Tartuffe, one of Molière's most popular plays, satirizes both religious hypocrisy and fraudulence. It ridicules the obsessive fanaticism and blind gullibility of those who are duped by the deceitful and the selfish. The following is the opening scene of the play, in which Molière immediately sets the tone and course of hilarious action to come.

> MADAME PERNELLE, *Orgon's mother*
> ORGON, *Elmire's husband*
> ELMIRE, *Orgon's wife*
> DAMIS, *Orgon's son, Elmire's stepson*
> MARIANE, *Orgon's daughter; Elmire's stepdaughter, in love with Valère*
> VALÈRE, *in love with Mariane*
> CLÉANTE, *Orgon's brother-in-law*
> TARTUFFE, *a hypocrite*
> DORINE, *Mariane's lady's-maid*
> MONSIEUR LOYAL, *a bailiff*
> A POLICE OFFICER
> FLIPOTE, *Madame Pernelle's maid*

The Scene throughout: OORGON'S *house in Paris.*

ACT I

Scene I

MADAME PERNELLE *and* FLIPOTE, *her maid,* ELMIRE, MARIANE, DORINE, DAMIS, CLÉANTE

MADAME PERNELLE   Come, come, Flipote; it's time I left this place.
ELMIRE   I can't keep up, you walk at such a pace.
MADAME PERNELLE   Don't trouble, child; no need to show me out.
  It's not your manners I'm concerned about.
ELMIRE   We merely pay you the respect we owe.   5
  But Mother, why this hurry? Must you go?
MADAME PERNELLE   I must. This house appalls me.
  No one in it
  Will pay attention for a single minute.
  Children, I take my leave much vexed in spirit.

---

[4]Agrajes, a character in *Amadís of Gaul*, would say these words before doing battle; it became a proverbial expression used at the beginning of a fight.

[5]The "second author" is Cervantes (that is, the narrator), who claims, in the following chapter, to have arranged for the translation of another (fictional) author's book. This device was common in novels of chivalry.
[6]Cervantes originally divided the 1605 novel (commonly called the "first part" of *Don Quixote*) into four parts. The break in the narrative action between parts was typical of novels of chivalry.

I offer good advice, but you won't hear it. 10
You all break in and chatter on and on.
It's like a madhouse with the keeper gone.

DORINE   If . . .

MADAME PERNELLE   Girl, you talk too much, and I'm
    afraid.
    You're far too saucy for a lady's-maid. 15
    You push in everywhere and have your say.

DAMIS   But . . .

MADAME PERNELLE   You, boy, grow more foolish every
    day.
    To think my grandson should be such a dunce!
    I've said a hundred times, if I've said it once, 20
    That if you keep the course on which you've started,
    You'll leave your worthy father broken-hearted.

MARIANE   I think . . .

MADAME PERNELLE   And you, his sister, seem so pure,
    So shy, so innocent, and so demure. 25
    But you know what they say about still waters.
    I pity parents with secretive daughters.

ELMIRE   Now, Mother . . .

MADAME PERNELLE   And as for you, child, let me add
    That your behavior is extremely bad, 30
    And a poor example for these children, too.
    Their dear, dead mother did far better than you.
    You're much too free with money, and I'm distressed
    To see you so elaborately dressed.
    When it's one's husband that one aims to please, 35
    One has no need of costly fripperies.

CLÉANTE   Oh, Madam, really . . .

MADAME PERNELLE   You are her brother, Sir,
    And I respect and love you; yet if I were
    My son, this lady's good and pious spouse, 40
    I wouldn't make you welcome in my house.
    You're full of worldly counsels which, I fear,
    Aren't suitable for decent folk to hear.
    I've spoken bluntly, Sir; but it behooves us
    Not to mince words when righteous fervor moves us. 45

DAMIS   Your man Tartuffe is full of holy speeches . . .

MADAME PERNELLE   And practices precisely what he
    preaches.
    He's a fine man, and should be listened to.
    I will not hear him mocked by fools like you.

DAMIS   Good God! Do you expect me to submit 50
    To the tyranny of that carping hypocrite?
    Must we forgo all joys and satisfactions
    Because that bigot censures all our actions?

DORINE   To hear him talk—and he talks all the time—
    There's nothing one can do that's not a crime. 55
    He rails at everything, your dear Tartuffe.

MADAME PERNELLE   Whatever he reproves deserves re-
    proof.
    He's out to save your souls, and all of you
    Must love him, as my son would have you do.

DAMIS   Ah no, Grandmother, I could never take 60
    To such a rascal, even for my father's sake.
    That's how I feel, and I shall not dissemble.
    His every action makes me seethe and tremble
    With helpless anger, and I have no doubt
    That he and I will shortly have it out. 65

DORINE   Surely it is a shame and a disgrace
    To see this man usurp the master's place—
    To see this beggar who, when first he came,
    Had not a shoe or shoestring to his name
    So far forget himself that he behaves 70
    As if the house were his, and we his slaves.

MADAME PERNELLE   Well, mark my words, your souls
    would fare far better
    If you obeyed his precepts to the letter.

DORINE   You see him as a saint.
    I'm far less awed; 75
    In fact, I see right through him. He's a fraud.

MADAME PERNELLE   Nonsense!

DORINE   His man Laurent's the same, or worse;
    I'd not trust either with a penny purse. 80

MADAME PERNELLE   I can't say what his servant's
    morals may be;
    His own great goodness I can guarantee.
    You all regard him with distaste and fear
    Because he tells you what you're loath to hear,
    Condemns your sins, points out your
    moral flaws, 85
    And humbly strives to further Heaven's cause.

DORINE   If sin is all that bothers him, why is it
    He's so upset when folk drop in to visit?
    Is Heaven so outraged by a social call
    That he must prophesy against us all? 90
    I'll tell you what I think: if you ask me,
    He's jealous of my mistress' company.

MADAME PERNELLE   Rubbish! (*To* ELMIRE:) He's not
    alone, child, in complaining
    Of all of your promiscuous entertaining.
    Why, the whole neighborhood's upset, I know, 95
    By all these carriages that come and go,
    With crowds of guests parading in and out
    And noisy servants loitering about.
    In all of this, I'm sure there's nothing vicious;
    But why give people cause to be suspicious? 100

CLÉANTE   They need no cause; they'll talk in any case.
    Madam, this world would be a joyless place
    If, fearing what malicious tongues might say,
    We locked our doors and turned our friends away.
    And even if one did so dreary a thing, 105
    D'you think those tongues would cease their chattering?
    One can't fight slander; it's a losing battle;
    Let us instead ignore their tittle-tattle.
    Let's strive to live by conscience' clear decrees,
    And let the gossips gossip as they please. 110

DORINE   If there is talk against us, I know the source:
    It's Daphne and her little husband, of course.
    Those who have greatest cause for guilt and shame
    Are quickest to besmirch a neighbor's name.
    When there's a chance for libel, they never miss it;
    When something can be made to seem illicit 116
    They're off at once to spread the joyous news,
    Adding to fact what fantasies they choose.
    By talking up their neighbor's indiscretions
    They seek to camouflage their own transgressions,
    Hoping that others' innocent affairs 120
    Will lend a hue of innocence to theirs,

Or that their own black guilt will come to seem
Part of a general shady color-scheme.
MADAME PERNELLE   All that is quite irrelevant. I doubt *125*
That anyone's more virtuous and devout
Than dear Orante; and I'm informed that she
Condemns your mode of life most vehemently.
DORINE   Oh, yes, she's strict, devout, and has no taint
Of worldliness; in short, she seems a saint.   *130*
But it was time which taught her that disguise;
She's thus because she can't be otherwise.
So long as her attractions could enthrall,
She flounced and flirted and enjoyed it all,
But now that they're no longer what they were   *135*
She quits a world which fast is quitting her,
And wears a veil of virtue to conceal
Her bankrupt beauty and her lost appeal.
That's what becomes of old coquettes today:
Distressed when all their lovers fall away,   *140*
They see no recourse but to play the prude,
And so confer a style on solitude.
Thereafter, they're severe with everyone,
Condemning all our actions, pardoning none,
And claiming to be pure, austere, and zealous   *145*
When, if the truth were known, they're merely jealous,
And cannot bear to see another know
The pleasures time has forced them to forgo.
MADAME PERNELLE   *(initially to* ELMIRE)
That sort of talk is what you like to hear;
Therefore you'd have us all keep still, my dear,   *150*
While Madam rattles on the livelong day.
Nevertheless, I mean to have my say.
I tell you that you're blest to have Tartuffe
Dwelling, as my son's guest, beneath this roof;
That Heaven has sent him to forestall its wrath   *155*
By leading you, once more, to the true path;
That all he reprehends is reprehensible,
And that you'd better heed him, and be sensible.
These visits, balls, and parties in which you revel
Are nothing but inventions of the Devil.   *160*
One never hears a word that's edifying:
Nothing but chaff and foolishness and lying,
As well as vicious gossip in which one's neighbor
Is cut to bits with epee, foil, and saber.
People of sense are driven half-insane   *165*
At such affairs, where noise and folly reign
And reputations perish thick and fast.
As a wise preacher said on Sunday last,
Parties are Towers of Babylon, because
The guests all babble on with never a pause;   *170*
And then he told a story which, I think . . .
(To CLÉANTE)
I heard that laugh, Sir, and I saw that wink!
Go find your silly friends and laugh some more!
Enough; I'm going; don't show me to the door.
I leave this household much dismayed and vexed;   *175*
I cannot say when I shall see you next.
(Slapping FLIPOTE)
Wake up, don't stand there gaping into space!
I'll slap some sense into that stupid face.
Move, move, you slut.

JOHN DONNE

The Flea

One of John Donne's best known poems, "The Flea" is notable for its dramatic situation, its wit, and its humor. Unlike the typical Renaissance love poem, "The Flea" presents an unconventional seduction. Readers may infer that the woman at first resists the speaker's various strategies, as evidenced by what occurs in the "space" between the second and third stanzas. In its modernization of a conventional poetic fashion, "The Flea" exhibits Baroque characterizations of dramatic action and playful exaggeration.

Mark but this flea, and mark in this
How little that which thou deny'st me is;
It sucked me first, and now sucks thee,
And in this flea our two bloods mingled be;
Thou know'st that this cannot be said   *5*
A sin, nor shame, nor loss of maidenhead;
        Yet this enjoys before it woo,
        And pampered swells with one blood made of two,
        And this, alas, is more than we would do.

Oh stay, three lives in one flea spare,   *10*
Where we almost, yea, more than married are.
This flea is you and I, and this
Our marriage bed and marriage temple is;
Though parents grudge, and you, we are met
        And cloistered in these living walls of jet.   *15*
        Though use make you apt to kill me,
        Let not to that, self-murder added be,
        And sacrilege, three sins in killing three.

Cruel and sudden, hast thou since
Purpled by nail in blood of innocence?   *20*
Wherein could this flea guilty be,
Except in that drop which it sucked from thee?
Yet thou triumph'st and say'st that thou
Find'st not thyself, nor me the weaker now,
        Tis true. Then learn how false fears be: *25*
        Just so much honour, when thou yield'st to me,
        Will waste, as this flea's death took life from thee.

ANNE BRADSTREET

A Letter to Her Husband, Absent upon Public Employment

The following poem, although less complex than Donne's conceit-governed "A Valediction: Forbidding Mourning," is in directness and openness of feeling more moving. Like Donne's "Valediction," Bradstreet's poem reflects developments in modern science. Bradstreet was aware of the earth's rotation on its axis and the effect of this rotation on the seasons. The poet/speaker compares her husband to the sun, and his absence is like the sun's moving southward into "Capricorn"—that is, winter. She is herself like the frozen earth, and "in this dead time" even her children seem remote to her. She wishes her husband/sun might return home and once again cause to "burn" the "Cancer"—or Summer—of "her glowing breast."

My head, my heart, mine eyes, my life, nay, more,
My joy, my magazine of earthly store,

If two be one, as surely thou and I,
How stayest thou there, whilst I at Ipswich lie?
So many steps, head from the heart to sever,   *5*
If but a neck, soon should we be together.
I, like the Earth this season, mourn in black,
My Sun is gone so far in's zodiac,
Whom whilst I 'joyed, nor storms, nor frost I felt,
His warmth such frigid colds did cause to melt,   *10*
Return, return, sweet Sol, from Capricorn,
I this dead time, alas, what can I more
Than view those fruits which through thy heat I bore?
Which sweet contentment yield me for a space,
True living pictures of their father's face.   *15*
O strange effect! now thou art southward gone,
I weary grow the tedious day so long;
But when thou northward to me shalt return,
I wish my Sun may never set, but burn
Within the Cancer of my glowing breast,   *20*
The welcome house of him my dearest guest.
Where ever, ever stay, and go not thence,
Till nature's sad decree shall call thee hence;
Flesh of thy flesh, bone of thy bone,
I here, thou there, yet both but one.   *25*

THOMAS HOBBES

from *Leviathan*

Thomas Hobbes is best known for his Leviathan, *a book of political philosophy whose subtitle conveys its central concerns: "The Matter, Form, and Power of a Commonwealth, Ecclesiastical and Civil." A defense of secular monarchy, written during the Puritan Commonwealth rule of England, the work contains Hobbes's theory of the sovereign state. The remedy for the state of natural affairs in which individual human life is described as "solitary, poor, nasty, brutish and short" is for individuals to cede voluntarily their freedom to do whatever they want to a community, an assembly of others, which will collectively provide safety and security. Hobbes establishes a contract theory as a justification for political authority.*

OF THE NATURAL CONDITION OF MANKIND

Nature has made men so equal, in the faculties of body and mind, that though there be found one man sometimes manifestly stronger in body or of quicker mind than another, yet when all is reckoned together, the difference between man and man is not so considerable that one man can thereupon claim to himself any benefit to which another may not pretend as well as he . . .

From this equality of ability arises equality of hope in the attaining of our ends. And therefore if any two men desire the same thing, which nevertheless they cannot both enjoy, they become enemies; and in the way to their end (which is principally their own conservation, and sometimes their delectation only) endeavour to destroy or subdue one another. And from hence it comes to pass that where an invader has no more to fear than another man's single power, if one plant, sow, build, or possess a convenient seat, others may probably be expected to come prepared with forces united to dispossess, and deprive him, not only of the fruit of his labour, but also of his life, or liberty. And the invader again is in the like danger of another.

And from this diffidence[1] of one another, there is no more reasonable way for any man to secure himself than anticipation; that is, by force, or wiles, to master the persons of all men he can, until he sees no other power great enough to endanger him. And this is no more than his own conservation requires, and is generally allowed. Also, because there are some who take pleasure in contemplating their own power in the acts of conquest (which they pursue farther than their security requires), if others, that otherwise would be glad to be at ease within modest bounds, should not by invasion increase their power, they would not be able, long time, by standing only on their defence, to subsist. And by consequence, such augmentation of dominion over men, being necessary to a man's conservation, it ought to be allowed him.

Again, men have no pleasure (but on the contrary a great deal of grief) in keeping company, where there is no power able to over-awe them all. For every man looks that his companion should value him at the same rate he sets upon himself. And upon all signs of contempt, or undervaluing, naturally endeavours, as far as he dares (which amongst them that have no common power to keep them in quiet, is far enough to make them destroy each other), to extort a greater value from his contemners, by damage, and from others, by the example.

So that in the nature of man, we find three principal causes of quarrel: first, competition; secondly, diffidence; thirdly, glory.

The first, makes men invade for gain; the second, for safety; and the third, for reputation. The first use violence, to make themselves masters of other men's persons, wives, children, and cattle; the second, to defend them; the third, for trifles, as a word, a smile, a different opinion, and any other sign of undervalue, either direct in their persons, or by reflection in their kindred, their friends, their nation, their profession, or their name.

Hereby it is manifest, that during the time men live without a common power to keep them all in awe, they are in that condition which is called war; and such a war as is of every man against every man. For war consists not in battle only, or the act of fighting, but in a tract of time, wherein the will to contend by battle is sufficiently known; and therefore the notion of *time* is to be considered in the nature of war, as it is in the nature of weather. For as the nature of foul weather lies not in a shower or two of rain, but in an inclination thereto of many days together, so the nature of war consists not in actual fighting, but in the known disposition thereto, during all the time there is no assurance to the contrary. All other time is peace.

Whatsoever therefore is consequent to a time of war, where every man is enemy to every man, the same is consequent to the time wherein men live without other security than what their own strength and their own invention shall furnish them with. In such condition, there is no place for industry, because the fruit thereof is uncertain; and consequently

---

[1]diffidence: distrust.

no culture of the earth, no navigation, nor use of the commodities that may be imported by sea; no commodious building; no instruments of moving and removing such things as require much force; no knowledge of the face of the earth; no account of time; no arts; no letters; no society; and which is worst of all, continual fear, and danger of violent death; and the life of man, solitary, poor, nasty, brutish, and short.

It may seem strange to some man, that has not well weighed these things, that nature should thus dissociate, and render men apt to invade and destroy one another; and he may therefore, not trusting to this inference, made from the passions, desire perhaps to have the same confirmed by experience. Let him therefore consider with himself, when taking a journey, he arms himself, and seeks to go well accompanied; when going to sleep, he locks his doors; when even in his house he locks his chests; and this when he knows there be laws, and public officers, armed, to revenge all injuries shall be done him: what opinion he has of his fellow subjects, when he rides armed; of his fellow citizens, when he locks his doors; and of his children, and servants, when he locks his chests. Does he not there as much accuse mankind by his actions, as I do by my words? But neither of us accuse man's nature in it. The desires, and other passions of man, are in themselves no sin. No more are the actions that proceed from those passions, till they know a law that forbids them: which till laws be made they cannot know; nor can any law be made, till they have agreed upon the person that shall make it.

It may peradventure be thought there was never such a time, nor condition of war as this; and I believe it was never generally so, over all the world; but there are many places where they live so now. For the savage people in many places of America, except the government of small families (that concord whereof depends on natural lust) have no government at all; and live at this day in that brutish manner, as I said before. Howsoever, it may be perceived what manner of life there would be, where there were no common power to fear, by the manner of life which men that have formerly lived under a peaceful government tend to degenerate into, in a civil war . . .

To this war of every man against every man, this also is consequent: that nothing can be unjust. The notions of right and wrong, justice and injustice, have there no place. Where there is no common power, there is no law: where no law, no injustice. Force and fraud are, in war, the two cardinal virtues. Justice and injustice are none of the faculties either of the body or mind. If they were, they might be in a man that were alone in the world, as well as his senses and passions. They are qualities that relate to men in society, not in solitude. It is consequent also to the same condition that there be no propriety, no dominion, no *Mine* and *Thine* distinct; but only that to be every man's, that he can get; and for so long as he can keep it. And thus much for the ill condition which man by mere nature is actually placed in; though with a possibility to come out of it, consisting partly in the passions, partly in his reason.

The passions that incline men to peace, are fear of death; desire of such things as are necessary to commodious living; and a hope by their industry to obtain them. And reason suggests convenient articles of peace, upon which men may be drawn to agreement. These articles are they, which otherwise are called the laws of nature . . .

OF THE FIRST AND SECOND NATURAL LAWS, AND OF CONTRACTS

The *right of nature* . . . is the liberty each man has to use his own power, as he will himself, for the preservation of his own nature, that is to say, of his own life; and consequently, of doing anything, which in his own judgement and reasons, he shall conceive to be the aptest means thereunto.

By *liberty* is understood, according to the proper signification of the word, the absence of external impediments: which impediments, may oft take away part of a man's power to do what he would; but cannot hinder him from using the power left him, according as his judgement and reason shall dictate to him.

A *law of nature* . . . is a precept, or general rule, found out by reason, by which a man is forbidden to do that which is destructive of his life, or takes away the means of preserving the same; and to omit that by which he thinks it may be best preserved. For though they that speak of this subject tend to confound *right* and *law*, yet they ought to be distinguished; because right consists in liberty to do, or to forbear, whereas law determines, and binds to one of them. So that law and right differ as much as obligation and liberty, which in one and the same matter are inconsistent.

And because the condition of man . . . is a condition of war of every one against every one—in which case every one is governed by his own reason, and there is nothing he can make use of that may not be a help unto him in preserving his life against his enemies—it follows that in such a condition every man has a right to everything, even to one another's body. And therefore, as long as this natural right of every man to every thing endures, there can be no security to any man (how strong or wise soever he be) of living out the time which nature ordinarily allows men to live. And consequently it is a precept, or general rule of reason, *that every man, ought to endeavour peace, as far as he has hope of obtaining it; and when he cannot obtain it, that he may seek, and use, all helps and advantages of war.* The first branch of which rule contains the first and fundamental law of nature; which is, to *seek peace, and follow it.* The second, the sum of the right of nature; which is, *by all means we can, to defend ourselves.*

From this fundamental law of nature, by which men are commanded to endeavour peace, is derived this second law: *That a man be willing, when others are so too, as far-forth as for peace, and defence of himself he shall think it necessary, to lay down this right to all things; and be contented with so much liberty against other men as he would allow other men against himself.* For as long as every man holds this right of doing anything he likes, so long are all men in the condition of war. But if other men will not lay down their right, as well as he, then there is no reason for any one to divest himself of his: For that were to expose himself to prey (which no man in bound to) rather than to dispose himself to peace. This is that law of the Gospel; *Whatsoever you require that others should do to you, that do ye to them.* And that law of all men, *Quod tibi fieri non vis, alteri ne feceris* ['Do not do to another what you do not want to be done to you'].

Whenever a man transfers his right, or renounces it, it is either in consideration of some right reciprocally transferred to himself, or for some other good he hopes for thereby. For it is a voluntary act; and of the voluntary acts of every man, the object is some *good to himself*. And therefore there be some rights which no man can be understood by any words, or other signs, to have abandoned, or transferred. As, first, a man cannot lay down the right of resisting them that assault him by force, or take away his life; because he cannot be understood to aim thereby at any good to himself . . . The mutual transferring of right, is that which men call *contract*.

OF THE CAUSES, GENERATION AND DEFINITION OF A COMMON-WEALTH

The final cause, end, or design of men (who naturally love liberty, and dominion over others) in the introduction of that restraint upon themselves (in which we see them live in common-wealths) is the foresight of their own preservation, and of a more contented life thereby; that is to say, of getting themselves out from that miserable condition of war, which is necessarily consequent (as has been shown) to the natural passions of men, when there is no visible power to keep them in awe, and tie them by fear of punishment to the performance of their covenants, and observation of [the] laws of nature . . .

For the laws of nature (as justice, equity, modesty, mercy, and (in sum), *doing to others, as we would be done to*) of themselves, without the terror of some power to cause them to be observed, are contrary to our natural passions, that carry us to partiality, pride, revenge, and the like. And covenants, without the sword, are but words, and of no strength to secure a man at all. Therefore notwithstanding the laws of nature (which everyone has then kept, when he has the will to keep them, when he can do it safely) if there be no power erected, or not great enough for our security, every man will, and may lawfully, rely on his own strength and art, for caution against all other men . . .

The only way to erect such a common power, as may be able to defend them from the invasion of foreigners, and the injuries of one another, and thereby to secure them in such sort, as that by their own industry, and by the fruits of the earth, they may nourish themselves and live contentedly, is to confer all their power and strength upon one man, or upon one assembly of men, that may reduce all their wills, by plurality of voices, unto one will. Which is as much as to say, to appoint one man, or assembly of men, to bear their person; and every one to own, and acknowledge himself to be author of whatsoever he that so bears their person, shall act, or cause to be acted, in those things which concern the common peace and safety; and therein to submit their wills, every one to his will, and their judgements to his judgement. This is more than consent or concord; it is a real unity of them all, in one and the same person, made by covenant of every man with every man, in such manner, as if every man should say to every man: *I authorize and give up my right of governing myself to this man, or to this assembly of men, on this condition, that you give up your right to him, and authorize all his actions in like manner.* This done, the multitude, so united in one person, is called a common-wealth, in Latin *civitas*. This is the generation of that great Leviathan, or rather (to speak more reverently) of that *mortal God*, to which we owe, under the *immortal God*, our peace and defence. For by this authority, given him by every particular man in the commonwealth, he has the use of so much power and strength conferred on him, that by terror thereof, he is enabled to form the wills of them all, to peace at home, and mutual aid against their enemies abroad. And in him consists the essence of the common-wealth; which (to define it) is *one person, of whose acts a great multitude, by mutual covenants one with another, have made themselves every one the author, to the end he may use the strength and means of them all, as he shall think expedient, for their peace and common defence.* And he that carries this person is called *sovereign* and said to have *sovereign power*; and every one besides, his *subject*.

JOHN LOCKE
from *Second Treatise of Civil Government*

John Locke follows the framework Hobbes devised for dealing with questions of political power and authority. The state of nature that Locke describes before the establishment of a political community is less savage than that of Hobbes. But, like Hobbes, Locke proposes the need for government as a protection, although not just or even primarily for safety and security, as Hobbes postulated, but for the fruits of labor, including private property. Protection for these cannot be assured without the establishment of a civil society, which involves a trade-off of individual rights and privileges to the authority of a protective government.

THE STATE OF NATURE

To understand political power aright, and derive it from its original, we must consider what state all men are naturally in, and that is, a state of perfect freedom to order their actions, and dispose of their possessions and persons, as they think fit, within the bounds of the law of nature, without asking leave, or depending upon the will of any other man.

A state also of equality, wherein all the power and jurisdiction is reciprocal, no one having more than another; there being nothing more evident than that creatures of the same species and rank, promiscuously born to all the same advantages of nature, and the use of the same faculties, should also be equal one amongst another, without subordination or subjection, unless the lord and master of them all should, by any manifest declaration of his will, set one above another, and confer on him, by an evident and clear appointment, an undoubted right to dominion and sovereignty . . .

But though this be a state of liberty, yet it is not a state of licence: though man in that state have an uncontrollable liberty to dispose of his person or possessions, yet he has not liberty to destroy himself, or so much as any creature in his possession, but where some nobler use than its bare preservation calls for it. The state of nature has a law of nature to govern it, which obliges everyone; and reason, which is that law, teaches all mankind who will but consult it, that being all equal and independent, no one ought to harm another in his life, health, liberty, or possessions. For men being all the workmanship of one omnipotent, and infinitely wise maker— all the servants of one sovereign master, sent into the world by his order, and about his business—they are his property, whose workmanship they are, made to last during his, not one another's pleasure; and being furnished with like faculties, sharing all in one community of nature, there cannot be supposed any such subordination among us, that may authorize us to destroy one another, as if we were made for one another's uses, as the inferior ranks of creatures are for ours. Every one, as he is bound to preserve himself, and not to quit his station wilfully, so by the like reason, when his own preservation comes not in competition, ought as much as he can to preserve the rest of mankind, and not, unless it be to do justice on an offender, take away, or impair the life, or what tends to the preservation of the life, the liberty, health, limb or goods of another . . .

THE STATE OF WAR

And here we have the plain difference between the state of nature and the state of war, which however some men have confounded, are as far distant as a state of peace, good will, mutual assistance, and preservation, and a state of enmity, malice, violence, and mutual destruction are one from another. Men living together according to reason without a common superior on earth, with authority to judge between them, are properly in the state of nature. But force, or a declared design of force upon the person of another, where there is no common superior on earth to appeal to for relief, is the state of war; and it is the want of such an appeal [that] gives a man the right of war even against an aggressor, though he be in society and a fellow subject. Thus, a thief whom I cannot harm, but by appeal to the law, for having stolen all that I am worth, I may kill when he sets on me to rob me but of my horse or coat, because the law, which was made for my preservation, where it cannot interpose to secure my life from present force (which if lost is capable of no reparation) permits me my own defence and the right of war—a liberty to kill the aggressor, because the aggressor allows not time to appeal to our common judge, nor the decision of the law, for remedy in a case where the mischief may be irreparable. Want of a common judge with authority puts all men in a state of nature; force without right upon a man's person makes a state of war both where there is, and is not, a common judge . . .

PROPERTY

Though the earth and all inferior creatures be common to all men, yet every man has a *property* in his own *person*. This nobody has any right to but himself. The *labour* of his body and the *work* of his hands, we may say, are properly his. Whatsoever, then, he removes out of the state that nature has provided and left it in, he has mixed his labour with it, and joined to it something that is his own, and thereby makes it his property. It being by him removed from the common state nature placed it in, it has by this labour something annexed to it that excludes the common right of other men. For this labour being the unquestionable property of the labourer, no man but he can have a right to what that is once joined to, at least where there is enough, and as good, left in common for others . . .

It will perhaps be objected to this, that if gathering the acorns or other fruits of the earth, etc., makes a right to them, then anyone may engross as much as he will. To which I answer, Not so. The same law of nature that does by this means give us property, does also bound that property too. *God has given us all things richly* (1 Timothy 6:12) is the voice of reason confirmed by inspiration. But how far has he given it us, *to enjoy?* As much as any one can make use of to any advantage of life before it spoils, so much he may by his labour fix a property in. Whatever is beyond this is more than his share, and belongs to others. Nothing was made by God for man to spoil or destroy . . .

But since gold and silver, being little useful to the life of man, in proportion to food, raiment, and carriage, has its value only from the consent of men, whereof labour yet makes in great part the measure, it is plain that men have agreed to disproportionate and unequal possession of the earth, they having by a tacit and voluntary consent found out a way how a man may fairly possess more land than he himself can use the product of by receiving, in exchange for the overplus, gold and silver, which may be hoarded up without injury to anyone, these metals not spoiling or decaying in the hands of the possessor. This partage of things, in an inequality of private possessions, men have made practicable out of the bounds of society, and without compact, only by putting a value on gold and silver and tacitly agreeing in the use of money. For in governments the laws regulate the right of property, and the possession of land is determined by positive constitutions . . .

THE BEGINNING OF POLITICAL SOCIETIES

Men being, as has been said, by nature all free, equal and independent, no one can be put out of this estate and subjected to the political power of another without his own consent, which is done by agreeing with other men, to join and unite into a community for their comfortable, safe and peaceable living, one amongst another, in a secure enjoyment of their properties, and a greater security against any that are not of it. This any number of men may do, because it injures not the freedom of the rest; they are left, as they were, in the liberty of the state of nature. When any number of men have so consented to make one community or government, they are thereby presently incorporated, and make one body politic, wherein the majority have a right to act and conclude the rest.

For, when any number of men have, by the consent of every individual, made a community, they have thereby made that community one body, with a power to act as one body, which is only by the will and determination of the majority. For that which acts any community being only the consent of the individuals of it, and [since] it (being one body) must move one way, it is necessary the body should move that way whither the greater force carries it, which is the consent of the majority; or else it is impossible it should act or continue one body, one community, which the consent of every individual that united into it agreed that it should; and so everyone is bound by that consent to be concluded[1] by the majority. And therefore we see that in assemblies empowered to act by positive laws, where no number is set by that positive law which empowers them, the act of the majority passes for the act of the whole, and of course determines as having, by the law of nature and reason, the power of the whole . . .

---

[1]concluded: determined, decided.

And thus every man, by consenting with others to make one body politic under one government, puts himself under an obligation to everyone of that society to submit to the determination of the majority, and to be concluded by it; or else this original compact, whereby he with others incorporates into one society, would signify nothing, and be no compact, if he be left free and under no other ties than he was in before in the state of nature. For what appearance would there be of any compact? What new engagement if he were no farther tied by any decrees of the society than he himself thought fit and did actually consent to? This would be still as great a liberty as he himself had before his compact, or anyone else in the state of nature has, who may submit himself and consent to any acts of it if he thinks fit.

For if the consent of the majority shall not in reason be received as the act of the whole, and conclude every individual, nothing but the consent of every individual can make anything to be the act of the whole; which, considering the infirmities of health and avocations of business, which (in a number though much less than that of a commonwealth) will necessarily keep many away from the public assembly; and the variety of opinions and contrariety of interests which unavoidably happen in all collections of men, it is next [to] impossible ever to be had . . .

Whosoever therefore out of a state of nature unite into a community, must be understood to give up all the power necessary to the ends for which they unite into society to the majority of the community, unless they expressly agreed in any number greater than the majority. And this is done by barely agreeing to unite into one political society, which is all the compact that is, or needs be, between the individuals that enter into or make up a commonwealth. And thus, that which begins and actually constitutes any political society is nothing but the consent of any number of freemen capable of a majority, to unite and incorporate into such a society. And this is that, and that only, which did or could give beginning to any lawful government in the world . . .

Every man being, as has been showed, naturally free, and nothing being able to put him into subjection to any earthly power, but only his own consent, it is to be considered what shall be understood to be a sufficient declaration of a man's consent to make him subject to the laws of any government. There is a common distinction of an *express* and a *tacit* consent, which will concern our present case. Nobody doubts but an express consent of any man, entering into any society, makes him a perfect member of that society, a subject of that government. The difficulty is, what ought to be looked upon as a tacit consent, and how far it binds, i.e., how far anyone shall be looked on to have consented, and thereby submitted to any government, where he has made no expressions of it at all. And to this I say, that every man that has any possession or enjoyment of any part of the dominions of any government doth thereby give his tacit consent, and is as far forth obliged to obedience to the laws of that government, during such enjoyment, as any one under it, whether this his possession be of land to him and his heirs for ever, or a lodging only for a week; or whether it be barely travelling freely on the highway; and, in effect, it reaches as far as the very being of anyone within the territories of that government . . .

THE ENDS OF POLITICAL SOCIETY AND GOVERNMENT

If man in the state of nature be so free as has been said; if he be absolute lord of his own person and possessions; equal to the greatest and subject to nobody, why will he part with his freedom? Why will he give up this empire, and subject himself to the dominion and control of any other power? To which it is obvious to answer, that though in the state of nature he has such a right, yet the enjoyment of it is very uncertain and constantly exposed to the invasion of others; for all being kings as much as he, every man his equal, and the greater part no strict observers of equity and justice, the enjoyment of the property he has in this state is very unsafe, very unsecure. This makes him willing to quit this condition which, however free, is full of fears and continual dangers; and it is not without reason that he seeks out and is willing to join in society with others who are already united, or have a mind to unite, for the mutual preservation of their lives, liberties, and estates, which I call by the general name, property . . .

The great end of men's entering into society being the enjoyment of their properties in peace and safety, and the great instrument and means of that being the laws established in that society, the first and fundamental positive law of all commonwealths is the establishing of the legislative power; as the first and fundamental natural law, which is to govern even the legislative itself, is the preservation of the society, and (as far as will consist with the public good) of every person in it. This legislative is not only the supreme power of the commonwealth, but sacred and unalterable in the hands where the community have once placed it; nor can any edict of anybody else, in what form soever conceived, or by what power soever backed, have the force and obligation of a law which has not its sanction from that legislative which the public has chosen and appointed; for without this the law could not have that which is absolutely necessary to its being a law, the consent of the society, over whom nobody can have a power to make laws but by their own consent and by authority received from them; and therefore all the obedience, which by the most solemn ties anyone can be obliged to pay, ultimately terminates in this supreme power, and is directed by those laws which it enacts. Nor can any oaths to any foreign power whatsoever, or any domestic subordinate power, discharge any member of the society from his obedience to the legislative, acting pursuant to their trust, nor oblige him to any obedience contrary to the laws so enacted or farther than they do allow, it being ridiculous to imagine one can be tied ultimately to obey any power in the society which is not the supreme . . .

THE SUBORDINATION OF THE POWERS OF THE COMMONWEALTH

Though in a constituted commonwealth, standing upon its own basis and acting according to its own nature, that is, acting for the preservation of the community, there can be but one supreme power, which is the legislative, to which all the rest are and must be subordinate; yet the legislative being only a fiduciary power to act for certain ends, there remains still in the people a supreme power to remove or alter the legislative when they find the legislative act contrary to the trust reposed in them. For all power given with trust for the attaining an end being limited by that end, whenever that end is manifestly neglected or opposed, the trust must necessarily be forfeited, and the power devolve into the hands of those that gave it, who may place it anew where they shall think best for their safety and security.

And thus the community perpetually retains a supreme power of saving themselves from the attempts and designs of anybody, even of their legislators, whenever they shall be so foolish or so wicked as to lay and carry on designs against the liberties and properties of the subject. For no man or society of men having a power to deliver up their preservation, or consequently the means of it, to the absolute will and arbitrary dominion of another, whenever any one shall go about to bring them into such a slavish condition, they will always have a right to preserve what they have not a power to part with, and to rid themselves of those who invade this fundamental, sacred, and unalterable law of self-preservation, for which they entered into society. And thus the community may be said in this respect to be always the supreme power, but not as considered under any form of government, because this power of the people can never take place till the government be dissolved.

JOHN MILTON

from *Paradise Lost*

The power and beauty of Milton's language in Paradise Lost *is awe-inspiring. All the elements of dramatic tragedy, religious fervor, and poetic zeal are found in the following excerpts. The first, from Book IV, describes Satan's decision to take revenge against God by visiting God's creation, Earth. The second, from Book IX, describes Satan's tempting of Eve to violate God's commandment.*

from Book IV

O for that warning voice, which he who saw
Th' Apocalypse heard cry in Heaven aloud,
Then when the dragon, put to second rout,
Came furious down to be revenged on men,
Woe to the inhabitants on Earth! that now,   *5*
While time was, our first parents had been warned
The coming of their secret foe, and scaped,
Haply so scaped, his mortal snare! for now
Satan, now first inflamed with rage, came down,
The tempter, ere th' accuser, of mankind,   *10*
To wreak on innocent frail man his loss
Of that first battle, and his flight to hell.
Yet not rejoicing in his speed, though bold
Far off and fearless, nor with cause to boast,
Begins his dire attempt; which, nigh the birth   *15*
Now rolling, boils in his tumultuous breast,
And like a devilish engine back recoils
Upon himself. Horror and doubt distract
His troubled thoughts, and from the bottom stir
The Hell within him; for within him Hell   *20*
He brings, and round about him, nor from Hell
One step, no more than from himself, can fly
By change of place. Now conscience wakes despair
That slumbered; wakes the bitter memory   *25*

Of what he was, what is, and what must be
Worse; of worse deeds worse sufferings must ensue
Sometimes towards Eden, which now in his view
Lay pleasant, his grieved look he fixes sad;
Sometimes towards heaven and the full-blazing sun,
Which now sat high in his meridian tower: *30*
Then, much revolving, thus in sighs began:—
"O thou that, with surpassing glory crowned,
Look'st from thy sole dominion like the god
Of this new world—at whose sight all the stars
Hide their diminished heads—to thee I call,   *35*
But with no friendly voice, and add thy name,
O sun, to tell thee how I hate thy beams,
That bring to my remembrance from what state
I fell, how glorious once above thy sphere,
Till pride and worse ambition threw me down,   *40*
Warring in Heaven against Heaven's matchless king!
Ah, wherefore? He deserved no such return
From me, whom he created what I was
In that bright eminence, and with his good
Upbraided none; nor was his service hard.   *45*
What could be less than to afford him praise,
The easiest recompense, and pay him thanks,
How due! Yet all his good proved ill in me,
And wrought but malice. Lifted up so high,
I 'sdained° subjection, and thought one step higher   *50*
Would set me highest, and in a moment quit°
The debt immense of endless gratitude,
So burdensome, still paying, still to owe;
Forgetful what from him I still received;
And understood not that a grateful mind   *55*
By owing owes not, but still pays, at once
Indebted and discharged—what burden then?
Oh, had his powerful destiny ordained
Me some inferior angel, I had stood
Then happy; no unbounded hope had raised   *60*
Ambition. Yet why not? Some other power
As great might have aspired, and me, though mean,
Drawn to his part. But other powers as great
Fell not, but stand unshaken, from within
Or from without to all temptations armed!   *65*
Hadst thou the same free will and power to stand?
Thou hadst. Whom hast thou then, or what, to accuse,
But Heaven's free love dealt equally to all?
Be then his love accursed, since, love or hate,
To me alike it deals eternal woe.   *70*
Nay, cursed be thou; since against his thy will
Chose freely what it now so justly rues.
Me miserable! which way shall I fly
Infinite wrath and infinite despair?
Which way I fly is Hell; myself am Hell;   *75*
And, in the lowest deep, a lower deep
Still threatening to devour me opens wide,
To which the Hell I suffer seems a Heaven.
O, then, at last relent! Is there no place
Left for repentance, none for pardon left?   *80*

---

[50]*'sdained*: scorned.
[51]*quit*: acquit.

None left but by submission; and that word
Disdain forbids me, and my dread of shame
Among the spirits beneath, whom I seduced
With other promises and other vaunts
Than to submit, boasting I could subdue   85
Th' omnipotent. Ay me! they little know
How dearly I abide that boast so vain,
Under what torments inwardly I groan.
While they adore me on the throne of Hell,
With diadem and scepter high advanced,   90
The lower still I fall, only supreme
In misery: such joy ambition finds!
But say I could repent, and could obtain,
By act of grace my former state, how soon
Would height recall high thoughts, how soon unsay   95
What feigned submission swore! Ease would recant
Vows made in pain, as violent and void
For never can true reconcilement grow
Where wounds of deadly hate have pierced so deep;
Which would but lead me to a worse relapse   100
And heavier fall: so should I purchase dear
Short intermission, bought with double smart.
This knows my punisher; therefore as far
From granting he, as I from begging, peace.
All hope excluded thus, behold, instead   105
Of us, outcast, exiled, his new delight,
Mankind, created, and for him this world!
So farewell hope, and, with hope, farewell fear,
Farewell remorse! All good to me is lost;
Evil, be thou my good: by thee at least   110
Divided empire with Heaven's king I hold,
By thee, and more than half perhaps will reign;
As man ere long, and this new world, shall know."
    Thus while he spake, each passion dimmed his face,
Thrice changed with pale—ire, envy, and despair;   115
Which marred his borrowed visage, and betrayed
Him counterfeit, if any eye beheld:
For heavenly minds from such distempers foul
Are ever clear. Whereof he soon aware
Each perturbation smoothed with outward calm,   120
Artificer of fraud; and was the first
That practiced falsehood under saintly show,
Deep malice to conceal, couched with revenge:
Yet not enough had practiced to deceive
Uriel, once warned; whose eye pursued him down   125
The way he went, and on th' Assyrian mount
Saw him disfigured, more than could befall
Spirit of happy sort: his gestures fierce
He marked and mad demeanor, then alone,
As he supposed, all unobserved, unseen.   130
    So on he fares, and to the border comes.
Of Eden, where delicious Paradise,
Now nearer, crowns with her enclosure green,
As with a rural mound, the champaign° head
Of a steep wilderness, whose hairy sides   135
With thicket overgrown, grotesque° and wild,

Access denied; and overhead up grew
Insuperable height of loftiest shade,
Cedar, and pine, and fir, and branching palm,
A sylvan scene, and, as the ranks ascend   140
Shade above shade, a woody theater
Of stateliest view. Yet higher than their tops
The verdurous wall of Paradise up sprung;
Which to our general sire° gave prospect large
Into his nether empire neighboring round.   145
And higher than that wall a circling row
Of goodliest trees, laden with fairest fruit,
Blossoms and fruits at once of golden hue,
Appeared, with gay enameled colors mixed;
On which the sun more glad impressed his beams   150
Than in fair evening cloud, or humid bow°,
When God hath showered the earth: so lovely seemed
That landscape. And of pure now purer air
Meets his approach, and to the heart inspires
Vernal delight and joy, able to drive   155
All sadness but despair. Now gentle gales,
Fanning their odoriferous wings, dispense
Native perfumes, and whisper whence they stole
Those balmy spoils. As when to them who sail
Beyond the Cape of Hope, and now are past   160
Mozambic, off at sea northeast winds blow
Sabean odors from the spicy shore
Of Araby the Blest, with such delay
Well pleased they slack their course, and many a league
Cheered with the grateful smell old Ocean smiles; 165
So entertained those odorous sweets the fiend
Who came their bane, though with them better pleased
Than Asmodeus with the fishy fume
That drove him, though enamored, from the spouse
Of Tobit's son, and with a vengeance sent   170
From Media post to Egypt, there fast bound.
    Now to th' ascent of that steep savage hill
Satan had journeyed on, pensive and slow;
But further way found none; so thick entwined,
As one continued brake, the undergrowth   175
Of shrubs and tangling bushes had perplexed
All path of man or beast that passed that way.
One gate there only was, and that looked east
On th' other side. Which when th' arch-felon saw,
Due entrance he disdained, and, in contempt,   180
At one slight bound high overleaped all bound
Of hill or highest wall, and sheer within
Lights on his feet. As when a prowling wolf,
Whom hunger drives to seek new haunt for prey,
Watching where shepherds pen their flocks at eve, 185
In hurdled cotes amid the field secure,
Leaps o'er the fence with ease into the fold;
Or as a thief, bent to unhoard the cash
Of some rich burgher, whose substantial doors,
Cross-barred and bolted fast, fear no assault,   190
In at the window climbs, or o'er the tiles;
So clomb this first grand thief into God's fold:

---

¹³⁴*champaign:* open countryside.
¹³⁶*grotesque:* picturesque.

¹⁴⁴*our general sire:* Adam.
¹⁵¹*bow:* rainbow.

So since into his church lewd hirelings climb.
Thence up he flew, and on the Tree of Life,
The middle tree and highest there that grew,   195
Sat like a cormorant; yet not true life
Thereby regained, but sat devising death
To them who lived; nor on the virtue thought
Of that life-giving plant, but only used
For prospect, what, well used, had been the pledge   200
Of immortality. So little knows
Any, but God alone, to value right
The good before him, but perverts best things
To worst abuse, or to their meanest use.
    Beneath him, with new wonder, now he views,   205
To all delight of human sense exposed,
In narrow room Nature's whole wealth; yea, more,
A Heaven on Earth; for blissful Paradise
Of God the garden was, by him in the east
Of Eden planted. Eden stretched her line   210
From Auran eastward to the royal towers
Of great Seleucia, built by Grecian kings,
Or where the sons of Eden long before
Dwelt in Telassar. In this pleasant soil
His far more pleasant garden God ordained.   215
Out of the fertile ground he caused to grow
All trees of noblest kind for sight, smell, taste;
And all amid them stood the Tree of Life,
High eminent, blooming ambrosial fruit
Of vegetable gold; and next to life,   220
Our death, the Tree of Knowledge, grew fast by—
Knowledge of good, bought dear by knowing ill.

from **Book IX**

    "Serpent, we might have spared our coming hither,
Fruitless to me, though fruit be here to excess,
The credit of whose virtue rest with thee;
Wondrous indeed, if cause of such effects!
But of this tree we may not taste nor touch: 5
God so commanded, and left that command
Sole daughter of his voice; the rest, we live
Law to ourselves; our reason is our law."
    To whom the Tempter guilefully replied:
"Indeed? Hath God then said that of the fruit   10
Of all these garden trees ye shall not eat,
Yet lords declared of all in Earth or air?"
To whom thus Eve, yet sinless: "Of the fruit
Of each tree in the garden we may eat,
But of the fruit of this fair tree amidst   15
The garden, God hath said, 'Ye shall not eat
Thereof, nor shall ye touch it, lest ye die.' "
    She scarce had said, though brief, when now more
        bold,
The tempter, but with show of zeal and love
To man, and indignation at his wrong,   20
New part puts on, and as to passion moved,
Fluctuates disturbed, yet comely, and in act
Raised, as of some great matter to begin.
As when of old some orator renowned
In Athens or free Rome, where eloquence   25
Flourished, since mute, to some great cause addressed,

Stood in himself collected, while each part,
Motion, each act, won audience ere the tongue,
Sometimes in height began, as no delay
Of preface brooking, through his zeal of right.   30
So standing, moving, or to height upgrown
The tempter all impassioned thus began:
    "O sacred, wise, and wisdom-giving plant,
Mother of science!° now I feel thy power
Within me clear, not only to discern   35
Things in their causes, but to trace the ways
Of highest agents, deemed however wise.
Queen of this universe! do not believe
Those rigid threats of death. Ye shall not die;
How should ye? By the fruit? it gives you life   40
To° knowledge; by the Threatener? look on me,
Me who have touched and tasted, yet both live,
And life more perfect have attained than Fate
Meant me, by venturing higher than my lot.
Shall that be shut to man, which to the beast   45
Is open? Or will God incense his ire
For such a petty trespass, and not praise
Rather your dauntless virtue, whom the pain
Of death denounced, whatever thing death be,
Deterred not from achieving what might lead   50
To happier life, knowledge of good and evil?
Of good, how just! Of evil, if what is evil
Be real, why not known, since easier shunned?
God therefore cannot hurt ye, and be just;
Not just, not God; not feared then, nor obeyed: 55
Your fear itself of death removes the fear.
Why then was this forbid? Why but to awe,
Why but to keep ye low and ignorant,
His worshippers? He knows that in the day
Ye eat thereof, your eyes that seem so clear,   60
Yet are but dim, shall perfectly be then
Opened and cleared, and ye shall be as gods,
Knowing both good and evil, as they know.
That ye should be as gods, since I as man,
Internal man, is but proportion meet,   65
I, of brute, human; ye, of human, gods.
So ye shall die perhaps, by putting off
Human, to put on gods: death to be wished,
Though threatened, which no worse than this can bring.
And what are gods that man may not become   70
As they, participating godlike food?
The gods are first, and that advantage use
On our belief, that all from them proceeds.
I question it; for this fair Earth I see,
Warmed by the sun, producing every kind,   75
Them nothing: If they all things, who enclosed
Knowledge of good and evil in this tree,
That whoso eats thereof forthwith attains
Wisdom without their leave? And wherein lies
Th' offense, that man should thus attain to know?   80
What can your knowledge hurt him, or this tree
Impart against his will if all be his?

---

[34]*science:* knowledge.
[41]*To:* as well as.

Or is it envy, and can envy dwell
In heavenly breasts? These, these, and many more
Causes import your need of this fair fruit.   85
Goddess humane, reach then, and freely taste!"
      He ended, and his words, replete with guile,
Into her heart too easy entrance won:
Fixed on the fruit she gazed, which to behold
Might tempt alone, and in her ears the sound   90
Yet rung of his persuasive words, impregned°
With reason, to her seeming, and with truth;
Meanwhile the hour of noon drew on, and waked
An eager appetite, raised by the smell
So savory of that fruit, which with desire,   95
Inclinable now grown to touch or taste,
Solicited her longing eye; yet first
Pausing a while, thus to herself she mused:
      "Great are thy virtues, doubtless, best of fruits,
Though kept from man, and worthy to be admired,   100
Whose taste, too long forborn, at first essay
Gave elocution to the mute, and taught
The tongue not made for speech to speak thy praise:
Thy praise he also who forbids thy use,
Conceals not from us, naming thee the Tree   105
Of Knowledge, knowledge both of good and evil;
Forbids us then to taste; but his forbidding
Commends thee more, while it infers the good
By thee communicated, and our want:
For good unknown, sure is not had, or had   110
And yet unknown, is as not had at all.
In plain then, what forbids he but to know?
Forbids us good, forbids us to be wise!
Such prohibitions bind not. But if Death
Bind us with after-bands, what profits then   115
Our inward freedom? In the day we eat
Of this fair fruit, our doom is, we shall die.
How dies the serpent? He hath eaten and lives,
And knows, and speaks, and reasons, and discerns,
Irrational till then. For us alone   120
Was death invented? Or to us denied
This intellectual food, for beasts reserved?
For beasts it seems: yet that one beast which first
Hath tasted, envies not, but brings with joy
The good befallen him, author unsuspect,   125
Friendly to man, far from deceit or guile.
What fear I then, rather what know to fear
Under this ignorance of good and evil,
Of God or death, of law or penalty?
Here grows the cure of all, this fruit divine,   130
Fair to the eye, inviting to the taste,
Of virtue° to make wise: what hinders then
To reach, and feed at once both body and mind?"
      So saying, her rash hand in evil hour,
Forth reaching to the fruit, she plucked, she eat.   135
Earth felt the wound, and Nature from her seat
Sighing through all her works gave signs of woe,
That all was lost. Back to the thicket slunk

The guilty serpent, and well might, for Eve
Intent now wholly on her taste, naught else   140
Regarded; such delight till then, as seemed,
In fruit she never tasted, whether true
Or fancied so, through expectation high
Of knowledge; nor was godhead from her thought.
Greedily she engorged without restraint,   145
And knew not eating death: satiate at length,
And heightened as with wine, jocund and boon,
Thus to herself she pleasingly began:
      "O sovereign, virtuous, precious of all trees
In Paradise! of operation blest   150
To sapience, hitherto obscured, infamed°,
And thy fair fruit let hang, as to no end
Created; but henceforth my early care,
Not without song each morning, and due praise
Shall tend thee, and the fertile burden ease   155
Of thy full branches offered free to all;
Till dieted by thee I grow mature
In knowledge, as the gods who all things know;
Though others envy what they cannot give:
For had the gift been theirs, it had not here   160
Thus grown. Experience, next to thee I owe,
Best guide; not following thee I had remained
In ignorance; thou open'st Wisdom's way,
And giv'st access, though secret she retire.
And I perhaps am secret; Heaven is high,   165
High and remote to see from thence distinct
Each thing on Earth; and other care perhaps
May have diverted from continual watch
Our great Forbidder, safe with all his spies
About him. But to Adam in what sort   170
Shall I appear? Shall I to him make known
As yet my change, and give him to partake
Full happiness with me, or rather not,
But keep the odds of knowledge in my power
Without copartner? so to add what wants   175
In female sex, the more to draw his love,
And render me more equal, and perhaps,
A thing not undesirable, sometime
Superior: for, inferior, who is free?
This may be well: but what if God have seen   180
And death ensue? Then I shall be no more,
And Adam, wedded to another Eve,
Shall live with her enjoying, I extinct;
A death to think. Confirmed then I resolve,
Adam shall share with me in bliss or woe: 185
So dear I love him, that with him all deaths
I could endure, without him live no life."
      So saying, from the tree her step she turned,
But first low reverence done, as to the power
That dwelt within, whose presence had infused   190
Into the plant sciental° sap, derived
From nectar, drink of gods. Adam the while
Waiting desirous her return, had wove
Of choicest flowers a garland to adorn

°[91]*impregned:* impregnated.
°[132]*virtue:* power.

°[151]*infamed:* defamed.
°[191]*sciental:* knowledge-giving.

Her tresses, and her rural labors crown,   195
As reapers oft are wont their harvest queen.
Great joy he promised to his thoughts, and new
Solace in her return, so long delayed:
Yet oft his heart, divine of something ill,
Misgave him; he the faltering measure felt;   200
And forth to meet her went, the way she took
That morn when first they parted. By the Tree
Of Knowledge he must pass; there he her met,
Scarce from the tree returning; in her hand
A bough of fairest fruit that downy smiled,   205
New gathered, and ambrosial smell diffused.
To him she hastened, in her face excuse
Came prologue, and apology to prompt,
Which with bland words at will she thus addressed:
    "Hast thou not wondered, Adam, at my stay?   210
Thee I have missed, and thought it long, deprived
Thy presence, agony of love till now
Not felt, nor shall be twice; for never more
Mean I to try, what rash untried I sought,
The pain of absence from thy sight. But strange   215
Hath been the cause, and wonderful to hear:
This tree is not as we are told, a tree
Of danger tasted, nor to evil unknown
Opening the way, but of divine effect
To open eyes, and make them gods who taste;   220
And hath been tasted such. The serpent wise,
Or not restrained as we, or not obeying,
Hath eaten of the fruit, and is become,
Not dead, as we are threatened, but thenceforth
Endued with human voice and human sense,   225
Reasoning to admiration, and with me
Persuasively hath so prevailed, that I
Have also tasted, and have also found
Th' effects to correspond—opener mine eyes
Dim erst, dilated spirits, ampler heart,   230
And growing up to godhead; which for thee
Chiefly I sought, without thee can despise.
For bliss, as thou hast part, to me is bliss,
Tedious, unshared with thee, and odious soon.
Thou therefore also taste, that equal lot   235
May join us, equal joy, as equal love;
Lest, thou not tasting, different degree
Disjoin us, and I then too late renounce
Deity for thee, when Fate will not permit."
Thus Eve with countenance blithe her story told;   240
But in her cheek distemper flushing glowed.
On th' other side, Adam, soon as he heard
The fatal trespass done by Eve, amazed,
Astonied stood and blank, while horror chill
Ran through his veins, and all his joints relaxed;   245
From his slack hand the garland wreathed for Eve
Down dropped, and all the faded roses shed.
Speechless he stood and pale, till thus at length
First to himself he inward silence broke:

    "O fairest of creation, last and best   250
Of all God's works, creature in whom excelled
Whatever can to sight or thought be formed,
Holy, divine, good, amiable, or sweet!
How art thou lost, how on a sudden lost,
Defaced, deflowered, and now to death devote?°   255
Rather how hast thou yielded to transgress
The strict forbiddance, how to violate
The sacred fruit forbidden! Some cursèd fraud
Of enemy hath beguiled thee, yet unknown,
And me with thee hath ruined, for with thee   260
Certain my resolution is to die.
How can I live without thee, how forgo
Thy sweet converse and love so dearly joined,
To live again in these wild woods forlorn?
Should God create another Eve, and I   265
Another rib afford, yet loss of thee
Would never from my heart; no, no! I feel
The link of nature draw me: flesh of flesh,
Bone of my bone thou art, and from thy state
Mine never shall be parted, bliss or woe."   270
    So having said, as one from sad dismay
Recomforted, and after thoughts disturbed
Submitting to what seemed remediless,
Thus in calm mood his words to Eve he turned:
    "Bold deed thou hast presumed, adventurous Eve   275
And peril great provoked, who thus hast dared
Had it been only coveting to eye
That sacred° fruit, sacred to abstinence,
Much more to taste it, under ban to touch.
But past who can recall, or done undo?   280
Not God omnipotent, nor Fate! Yet so
Perhaps thou shalt not die, perhaps the fact
Is not so heinous now, foretasted fruit,
Profaned first by the serpent, by him first
Made common and unhallowed ere our taste,   285
Nor yet on him found deadly; he yet lives,
Lives, as thou saidst, and gains to live as man
Higher degree of life: inducement strong
To us, as likely, tasting, to attain
Proportional ascent, which cannot be   290
But to be gods, or angels, demigods.
Nor can I think that God, Creator wise,
Though threatening, will in earnest so destroy
Us his prime creatures, dignified so high,
Set over all his works, which in our fall,   295
For us created, needs with us must fail,
Dependent made; so God shall uncreate,
Be frustrate, do, undo, and labor lose;
Not well conceived of God, who, though his power
Creation could repeat, yet would be loath   300

---

²⁵⁵*devote:* doomed.
²⁷⁸*sacred:* dedicated.

Us to abolish, lest the adversary
Triumph and say: 'Fickle their state whom God
Most favors; who can please him long? Me first
He ruined, now mankind; whom will he next?'
Matter of scorn, not to be given the foe.   305
However, I with thee have fixed my lot,
Certain to undergo like doom: if death

Consort with thee, death is to me as life;
So forcible within my heart I feel
The bond of nature draw me to my own,   310
My own in thee, for what thou art is mine;
Our state cannot be severed; we are one,
One flesh; to lose thee were to lose myself."

CHAPTER 16

HISTORY

1710	Leibniz invents new notations of calculus
1715	Louis XV ascends to French throne
1733	James Key invents flying shuttle
1735	Linnaeus establishes biological classification system
1740–48	War of the Austrian Succession
1756–63	Seven Years' War
1759	Wedgwood opens English pottery factory
1769	Watt patents steam engine
1775–83	American Revolution
1776	American Declaration of Independence
1787	Edmund Cartwright invents power loom
1789–99	French Revolution
1789	Declaration of the Rights of Man and Citizen
	Gathering of Estates General and declaration of National Assembly; fall of Bastille
1792	French monarchy abolished
1793	Louis XVI and Marie Antoinette executed
1799	Napoleon overthrows Directory
1804	Napoleonic Code established

ART, ARCHITECTURE, AND MUSIC

1717	Watteau, *Pilgrimage to Cythera*
1725	Burlington/Kent, Chiswick House
1744	Hogarth, *Marriage à la Mode*
1763	Chardin, *The Brioche*
1769	Jefferson designs Monticello
1770	West, *Death of General Wolfe*
1772	Haydn, *Farewell Symphony*
1777–80	Reynolds, *Lady Elizabeth Delmé and Her Children*
1785	David, *Oath of the Horatii*
1785	Kaufmann, *Cornelia Pointing to Her Children as Her Treasures*
1786	Mozart, *The Marriage of Figaro*
1787	Vigée-Lebrun, *Portrait of Marie Antoinette with Her Children*
1787	Mozart, *Don Giovanni*
1788	Labille-Guiard, *Louise-Elisabeth of France*
1788–92	Houdon, *George Washington*
1796–98	Beethoven, early piano sonatas, op. 1–14
1807–8	Beethoven, Symphony No. 5 in C Minor

LITERATURE AND PHILOSOPHY

1712	Pope, *The Rape of the Lock*
1726	Swift, *Gulliver's Travels*
1751–72	Diderot, *Encyclopédie*
1755	Voltaire, *Candide*
1762	Rousseau, *Social Contract*
1776	Smith, *Wealth of Nations*

The Eighteenth Century

Marie-Louise-Elisabeth Vigée-Lebrun, *The Artist and Her Daughter*, ca. 1785, oil on canvas, 4′ 3″ × 3′ 1″ (139.7 × 94 cm). Photo: G. Blot/C. Jean. Musée du Louvre, Paris. Photo credit: Reunion des Musées Nationaux/Art Resource, NY/Musée d'Orsay.

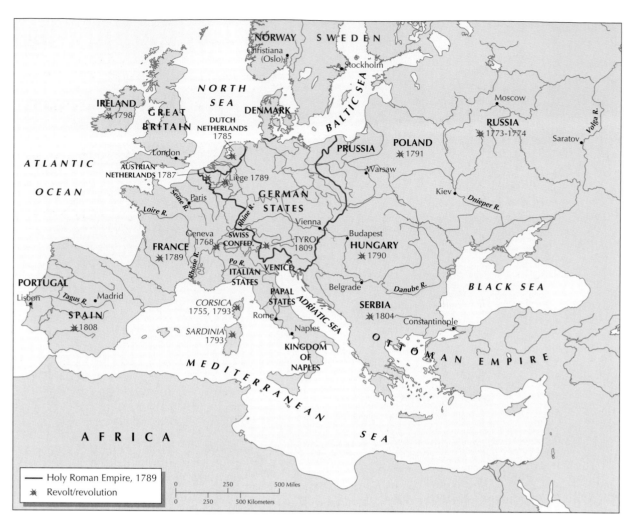

MAP 16.1   Revolts and revolutions in Europe, 1705–1809.

ENLIGHTENMENT

BETWEEN 1700 AND 1800, THE WORLD WAS transformed. At the beginning of the century, Louis XIV, the Sun King, had firm control of France. By the end of the century, the French monarchy had fallen, as Louis XVI (1754–93), the Sun King's great-grandson, and his Queen, MARIE ANTOINETTE [anntweh-NET] (1755–93), were executed by the National Assembly of the French Revolution.

The changes that occurred in the eighteenth century were swift and extreme, encompassing revolutions that were not only political, but intellectual, scientific, industrial, and social. Indeed, the eighteenth century has been called the "Age of Reason" because of the dominance of the intellectual revolution we have come to call the Enlightenment.

THE ENLIGHTENMENT

The term **Enlightenment** refers to the eighteenth-century European emphasis on the mind's power to reason, in contrast to the mind's yearning for religious faith, which a number of Enlightenment thinkers saw as superstition. The late seventeenth century through the eighteenth century saw two great movements: that of the "Age of Reason," which hallmarks the contemporary emphasis on rationality, and the Neoclassical, which testifies to the influence of classical antiquity.

The Enlightenment continued an emphasis on secular concerns that began during the Renaissance and continued with the rise of scientific and philosophical thought during the seventeenth century. Eighteenth-century political and philosophical ideals included freedom from tyranny and superstition, and a belief in the essential goodness of human nature and the equality of men (although not all men, and not women).

Enlightenment thinkers emphasized the common nature of human experience, ignoring differences in social, cultural, and religious values. Enlightenment composers sought universal musical forms. Enlightenment writers celebrated constancy and continuity, encouraging a respect for tradition and convention, especially in literature and the arts. Enlightenment artists and thinkers were not, however, simply supporters of the status quo. They used their analytical powers to attack the hypocrisies of the age. As much as they celebrated the powers of reason, they did not fail to notice when human behavior was guided by passion, selfishness, and irrationality. Voltaire, Swift, and Pope all composed scathing attacks on political and social misconduct.

The Philosophes. The Enlightenment was embodied in a group of intellectuals called by the French name **philosophes.** These thinkers believed that through reason, humankind could achieve a perfect society of perpetual peace, order, and harmony.

The philosophes championed the possibility of democratic rule; they feared tyranny most of all. The philosophes denounced intolerance in matters of religious belief which, since the Reformation, had continued to disrupt society, and they advocated public, as opposed to church-controlled, education.

Rational Humanism. **Rational humanism** is based on the belief that through rational, careful thought, progress—which is good and benefits everyone—is inevitable. Like the humanists of the Renaissance, the rational humanists believed progress is possible only through learning and through the individual's freedom to learn. Humans must, therefore, be free to think for themselves. This logic links the rational humanists with the two great political revolutions of the day, in America and in France, and with such political documents as the Declaration of Independence and the Declaration of the Rights of Man and Citizen as well as with the Constitution of the United States. The rational humanists believed that any political system that strives to suppress freedom of thought must be overthrown as an obstacle to progress.

REVOLUTIONS

THE AMERICAN REVOLUTION

Enlightenment ideals had a profound effect on eighteenth-century America. The first and most important was as a source of inspiration that spurred the colonists philosophically and politically to revolt against England. A later but no less significant Enlightenment influence was to keep religion separate from politics, leaving church and state to operate in distinct and separate realms.

But why did the American Revolution occur? What precipitated it? One major cause was the imposition of new taxes by the British in an attempt to exert more control over the colonies. Colonists were deeply angered over taxes on molasses, on publications and legal documents, and most famously, on tea. They also resented Britain's enforcement of laws requiring cargo to travel at sea in British vessels, and they objected to being required to house and accommodate British troops.

The colonists responded to Britain's authoritative stance by boycotting British products, attacking British officials, generating anti-British slogans like "no taxation without representation," and staging protests. The most famous of these was the "Boston Tea Party," in which colonists dumped a cargo of tea into Boston Harbor rather than pay the tax for it. Shortly afterward, colonists exchanged gunfire with British troops in Lexington, a suburb of Boston.

On July 4, 1776, the Continental Congress, which had been established two years earlier to coordinate resistance to British policies, adopted the Declaration of Independence. According to this important document inspired by Enlightenment ideas of liberty and sovereignty, "all men are created equal," and all are endowed by God with the "unalienable rights" of "Life, Liberty, and the Pursuit of Happiness." The Declaration also asserted that the colonists had the right to establish a government to secure these rights, and that the government derived its authority from the people.

The Declaration led to the colonists' armed resistance of Britain, and even though Britain was the preeminent economic and military power of the western world, the colonists prevailed, and the balance of world power was dramatically altered. The war lasted five years, with the surrender of British troops to General George Washington in 1781. Two years later, the Peace of Paris was signed, in which the British recognized American independence.

The Americans could not have won the war without the help of European nations, including France, Holland, and Spain, which all wanted to see Britain weakened. Another factor in the colonists' favor was that they were defending their own land and fighting for a set of principles, not the least of which was freedom.

Paine, Washington, Jefferson, and Franklin. Among the men who had a decisive impact leading up to the war with Britain, and who continued to exert a significant influence in America and beyond afterwards were Thomas Paine, George Washington, Thomas Jefferson, and Benjamin Franklin. Thomas Paine (1737–1809) was a journalist and pamphleteer whose writings roused readers' passions against the British and inspired them to believe that military resistance was both necessary and justified. The first of his famous pamphlets, *Common Sense*, begins with these rousing words: "These are the times that try men's souls; the summer soldier and sunshine patriot will, in this crisis, shrink from the service of their country, but he that stands by it now deserves the loving thanks of man and woman."

George Washington (1732–99) took charge of the army during the war. As a military leader, General Washington consistently outsmarted and outmaneuvered his British antagonists, culminating in their surrender to him. After the war, Washington served two terms, from 1789 to 1797, as the country's first President.

Thomas Jefferson (1743–1826) is credited as the primary author of the Declaration of Independence. Jefferson served as governor of Virginia, as U.S. minister to France, as Secretary of State under Washington, and as Vice President under John Adams, before becoming himself the third President of the United States. Jefferson was also a writer who argued that liberty was a God-given right. In addition, Jefferson founded the University of Virginia, which he planned, designed, and supervised.

The most versatile of the American Founding Fathers was Benjamin Franklin (1706–90), one of five men who helped draft the Declaration of Independence. Franklin was a statesman and diplomat, printer and writer, merchant and newspaper editor, and an inventor who experimented with electricity, and who invented both the lightning rod and bifocals. During a long and illustrious career, Franklin founded the first lending library in America, established the first fire company, and created a college that merged later with the University of Pennsylvania. Among his greatest accomplishments, however, was his service as Minister to friends prior to and during the Revolution. Franklin deserves much of the credit for securing a treaty with France, including financial support to secure American independence.

Enlightenment Thought and Women. During the eighteenth century, advocates for the rights of women were active in a number of countries, including Britain, Canada, France, and the United States. The British writer Mary Wollstonecraft was one of the best known, with her influential essay "A Vindication of the Rights of Women," published in 1792. Following John Locke's arguments for human freedom, Wollstonecraft argued that women would make better and more successful wives and mothers if they were educated, and that they would be fuller and abler participants in the political process.

In the United States, Elizabeth Cady Stanton would take up the cause for the full slate of women's rights, including the right to vote. The word *suffrage* means the right to vote, a right denied women in the United States and the United Kingdom until the suffragist movement in both countries reversed that denial. The movement for women's suffrage in the United States lasted more than seventy years, from the time of the first women's convention in Seneca Falls, NY, in 1848, until the passage of the nineteenth amendment to the U.S. Constitution in 1920. In the U.K., women were given restricted voting rights in 1918, and then full voting rights equal to those granted U.S. women, in 1928. (U.S. blacks had gained the right to vote with the ratification of the fifteenth amendment in 1870, although it took the Voting Rights Act of 1965 to make it a reality).

Propelling the movement for women's suffrage in the United States was the general movement for women's rights, including property rights and educational opportunities. These were announced at the Seneca Falls Convention in the Declaration of Sentiments. Fueling the movement for women's suffrage in the United Kingdom was the shortage of able-bodied men during World War I, requiring women to take on many traditional male roles and responsibilities, which led before long to a fuller understanding of the capabilities of women, and then to their being granted property, educational, and voting rights.

In other countries, too, women's rights were being contested. New Zealand gave women full voting rights in 1893, the first country to do so. In 1902 Australia gave women the right to vote in national elections. Other countries granting voting rights to women in the early 1900s included Canada, Finland, Germany, and Sweden.

THE FRENCH REVOLUTION

The executions of Louis XVI and Marie Antoinette in 1793 represented not only the death of the monarchy, but also an end to the privilege and extravagance that the monarchy had come to represent in the minds of the people. In death, all are equal. The century's growing belief in the equality of all, in the right of the individual to live free of tyranny, and in the right of humankind to self-governance, culminated in political **revolution,** the overthrow of the existing order for a new one. In fact, revolution itself seemed to many an "enlightened" course of action.

The American Revolution began to stir in 1774, when the colonists convened for the new Continental Congress. An American Declaration of Independence, authored by Thomas Jefferson (1743–1826), unified the colonies in their successful war against the British, and in the following years, a constitutional convention met in Philadelphia to draft a new charter for the American republic. At the convention, mechanisms were devised to assess and collect taxes, regulate commerce, and make enforceable laws, all within a government framework of "checks and balances." The legislative, judicial, and executive branches of government all had their own powers, but powers that were overseen by the other branches.

The French bourgeoisie watched with interest. They wanted a "National Assembly" like the Continental Congress; a document drafted along the same principles as the American Declaration; and a republican constitution that would give them life, liberty, and the right to own property. But the French situation was different from the American one. Where the American Revolution pitted against one another two groups with similar cultural values, one simply seeking economic autonomy from the other, the French Revolution was essentially an internal class struggle and, as such, expressed a clash in values.

Each of the French kings of the eighteenth century— Louis XIV (r. 1643–1715), Louis XV (r. 1715–74), and Louis XVI (r. 1774–93), guillotined on January 21, 1793— had successively led the country further into debt. In May 1789, Louis XVI, succumbing to mounting pressures to deal with the ever-increasing national debt, called for an assembly of the Estates General. This assembly of the clergy (the First Estate), the aristocrats (the Second Estate), and the bourgeois middle class (the Third Estate) resulted in the "The Declaration of the Rights of Man and Citizen," a document modeled on the American "Declaration of Independence."

THE NATIONAL ASSEMBLY

In the Estates General, each of the three estates had one vote. The Third Estate quickly realized it would be outvoted 2–1 on every question. Thus, on June 20, 1789, the deputies of the Third Estate along with their aristocratic sympathizers declared a "National Assembly" in a building called the Jeu de Paume, the king's tennis court. Together they swore they would not separate until France had a new constitution; Jacques-Louis David, a painter who recorded the revolution, captured the moment in *The Tennis Court Oath* (fig. 16.1).

Rumors that the king was planning to overthrow the National Assembly led to the formation of a volunteer bourgeois militia, which, on July 14, 1789, went to the Bastille prison in Paris in search of arms and gunpowder. The prison governor panicked and ordered his guard to fire on the militia, killing ninety-eight and wounding seventy-three. An angry mob quickly formed and stormed the Bastille, decapitating its governor and slaughtering six of the guards. The next day, Louis XVI asked if the incident had been a riot. "No, your majesty," was the reply, "it was a revolution."

The National Assembly continued to meet while rioting spread throughout the French countryside, and finally, on August 4, 1789, in a night session, the viscount of Nouilles and then the duke of Aiguillon renounced their feudal privileges and revenues. Other nobles did the same, and the clergy in attendance relinquished their tithes. By the end of the evening, all French people suddenly found themselves subject to the same laws and taxes. On August 27, 1789, the Assembly ratified its Declaration of the Rights of Man and Citizen, and a constitutional monarchy was established.

THE DEMISE OF THE MONARCHY

Despite the events of August 27, as early as October 5, 1789, Parisian women were back in the streets demonstrating for bread. It was on this day that Marie Antoinette is supposed to have declared, notoriously, "Let them eat cake!"—an exclamation some historians doubt was ever made. The women marched on the palace at Versailles and invaded the inner rooms, causing the queen to flee for her life, but Louis and Marie Antoinette were escorted back to Paris later that day.

The king ostensibly cooperated for a while with the National Assembly, but in June 1791 he attempted to flee with his family to Luxembourg. The royal retinue was captured and returned to Paris. Then, in April 1792, Austria and Prussia took the opportunity to declare war on the weakened nation, and the Prussian duke of Brunswick declared he would restore Louis XVI to full sovereignty, revealing an already widespread suspicion that the king was collaborating with the enemy. And so the bourgeois leaders, aided by the working class, invaded the Louvre on August 10, 1792, butchering the king's guard and the royal servants, and over the next forty days arrested and executed more than a thousand priests, aristocrats, and royalist sympathizers. On September 21, 1792, a newly assembled National Convention abolished the monarchy in France, and on January 21, 1793, Louis XVI was executed by guillotine

FIGURE 16.1   Jacques Louis David, *The Tennis Court Oath*, 1789–91, unfinished, pen and brown ink and brown wash on paper, 26 × 42″ (66 × 107 cm), Musée du Louvre, Paris. Reunion des Musées Nationaux, Art Resource/NY. Spectators peer down on the Third Estate, which takes its oath as the "winds of freedom" blow through the windows above.

in the Place de la Révolution, known today as the Place de la Concorde.

The situation continued to deteriorate. In the summer of 1793, a Committee of Public Safety was formed, headed by MAXIMILIEN DE ROBESPIERRE [ROBES-pea-air] (1758–94). For fifteen months, France endured the committee's Reign of Terror. The Terror had three goals: to win the war with Austria and Prussia; to establish a "Republic of Virtue"; and to suppress all its enemies. To achieve the latter, the Revolutionary Tribunal of Paris alone handed out 2,639 death sentences, including that of Marie Antoinette, who by this time was referred to simply as "the widow Capet." Throughout France, an estimated twenty thousand people were executed.

NAPOLEON BONAPARTE

In 1795, when the term of the National Convention expired, a political body known as the Directory succeeded to power. It managed to establish peace, but otherwise France was effectively rudderless. Finally, in November 1799, General NAPOLEON BONAPARTE [BONE-ah-part] (1769–1821) staged a coup d'état, abolishing the Di-

rectory and installing himself, on the Roman model, as First Consul (fig. 16.2).

Napoleon was a common man who rose to power through talent and civic sacrifice. Yet he was also a man of uncommon presence. He had no shortage of ego, either, for in 1802 he inquired of the people, "Is Napoleon Bonaparte to be made Consul for Life?" The people answered in the affirmative by 3.5 million votes to 8,000. After another election in 1804, he declared himself Emperor for Life, and was crowned Emperor Napoleon I in December 1804. France had, effectively, restored the monarchy.

Napoleon's power and appeal tell us much about the Enlightenment itself. He was the very model of enlightened leadership that the philosophes longed for, although his decision to crown himself emperor disillusioned many of his republican supporters. Under Napoleon's regime, the economy boomed again, and he vigorously supported industrial expansion. Cotton production, for instance, quadrupled between 1806 and 1810. In 1800, Napoleon created the Bank of France, which made government borrowing a far easier and more stable matter. But his greatest achievement was the **Napoleonic Code**, which provided a uniform system of law for the entire country. This code was brief and clear, with the aim that every cit-

Then & Now

THE RIGHTS OF WOMEN

When the French National Assembly ratified the Declaration of the Rights of Man and Citizen on August 27, 1789, its members did not include women among the "citizens." In 1791, Olympe de Gouges (1748–93) wrote a "Declaration of the Rights of Women" and demanded that the National Assembly act on it. This stated that "Woman is born free and remains equal to man in rights," arguing that "the only limit on the exercise of woman's natural rights is the perpetual tyranny wielded by men; these limits must be reformed by the law of nature and the law of reason." The declaration continued with the then radical claim that women were "equally entitled to all honors, places, and public employments according to their abilities, without any other distinction than that of their virtues and their talents."

The Englishwoman Mary Wollstonecraft (1759–97) wrote another important revolutionary manifesto supporting women's rights. *A Vindication of the Rights of Woman*, published in 1792, is a treatise embodying Enlightenment faith in reason and in the revolutionary concepts of change and progress. Wollstonecraft held that women, having an equal capacity for reason, should have an equal standing in society. She offered a scathing critique of the social forces that kept women in a position of inferiority. Wollstonecraft developed her revolutionary ideas in the company of a radical group of English artists and writers, including Tom Paine and William Godwin, who sympathized with the aims of the French Revolution.

To the contemporary American, these demands may seem reasonable enough, but it is worth remembering that women did not gain the right to vote in the United States until 1920. And women continue to fight for equality in the workplace, both in competing for jobs on an equal footing and receiving comparable pay for comparable work. Such demands were certainly not considered reasonable at the time of the French Revolution. De Gouges was charged with treason by the National Assembly and sentenced to the guillotine in 1793.

---

izen should be capable of understanding it. Together with the Declaration of Independence, the U.S. Constitution, and the Declaration of the Rights of Man, the Napoleonic Code is one of the great monuments of Enlightenment thought.

The causes of the revolution were complex, ranging from a resentment of royal absolutism, a desire for liberty in tune with enlightenment ideals, to gross economic class inequities, a scarcity of food, and the king's failure to deal with precipitating crises. The consequences of the French Revolution were momentous; the revolution was, in fact, a turning point in French history, with significant consequences for Europe. It marked a pronounced shift from monarchy and absolutism to republicanism and democracy. Furthermore, enlightenment ideals embodied in both the French and American revolutions, especially freedom, equality, and sovereignty, spurred revolutionary movements in the Caribbean and in Central and South America, especially in Bolivia, Haiti, and Mexico.

THE INDUSTRIAL REVOLUTION

The Birth of the Factory.   On May 1, 1759, in Staffordshire, England, a twenty-eight-year-old man named Josiah Wedgwood (1730–95) opened his own pottery manufacturing plant. Wedgwood initially specialized in unique pottery made by hand, but began to produce ceramic tableware on which designs were printed by mechanical means. In the same year, Wedgwood's friend Matthew Boulton (1728–1809) inherited his father's toy factory (small metal objects such as belt buckles, buttons, and clasps were known as "toys"). Soon he had built a factory in London, employing six hundred people in mechanized large-scale production. The steam engine, patented by James Watt in 1769, transformed the way in which these new factories could be powered. Mechanical looms were soon introduced into the cotton cloth industry, powered by Watt's steam engines. Where once workers had woven fabric at home as piecework, they now watched over giant looms that did the work for them, in a fraction of the time. Mass manufacturing, and with it what we have come to call the **Industrial Revolution,** had begun.

Adam Smith.   In 1776, the Scotsman Adam Smith (1727–90) provided the rationale for the entire enterprise. His *Inquiry into the Nature and Cause of the Wealth of Nations* barely mentioned manufacturing, concentrating instead on agriculture and trade, but the businesspeople who ran the new factories saw in his writings the justification for their practices. In a free-market system based on private property, Smith argued that prices and profits would automatically be regulated to the benefit, theoretically, of everyone, not just the factory owners. He contended that the economy would operate as if with an "invisible hand" beneficently guiding it. The new "working class" that arose out of the Industrial Revolution, however, would find that the free-market system benefited the factory owners a great deal more than themselves, and by the dawn of the nineteenth

FIGURE 16.2   Jacques Louis David, *Napoleon in His Study*, 1812, oil on canvas 7′4″ × 4′2½″, (2.05 × 1.28 m). Coll. Napoleon, Paris. Giraudon/Art Resource, NY. In this prime example of art as political propaganda, Napoleon is shown working all night for the people of France while surrounded by objects that refer to his accomplishments. Napoleon compared himself to the leaders of ancient Rome; his portrait deserves comparison to that of Emperor Augustus (fig. 4.8).

century, the factory owners had become the new "kings" of industrial culture—as spendthrift and tyrannical as the monarchs of the previous age.

THE SCIENTIFIC REVOLUTION

Isaac Newton.   The positivism of the age was driven by advances in scientific learning. The philosophes seized on the discovery by Isaac Newton (1642–1727) of the principle of gravitation, the first physical description of the forces holding the known universe together. The earth and its moon, Jupiter and its four moons, the sun and its planets all formed a harmonious system, with each celestial body

relying on the others to maintain its place and position. Transferring this vision to human society, the philosophes suggested that with a comparable system of mutual reliance humans could live in harmony. Throughout the eighteenth century, scientists explored the natural world to such a degree that new sciences had to be defined: geology (1795), mineralogy (1796), zoology (1818), and biology (1819).

Denis Diderot and Carolus Linnaeus.   The French essayist DENIS DIDEROT [DEED-eh-roe] (1713–84) conceived of an idea for an **Encyclopédie**, twentyeight volumes designed to encompass the whole of human knowledge, from science and technology to philosophical thought. The volumes contain thousands of illustrations showing the mechanical principles of production and commerce.

In the middle of the century, CAROLUS LINNAEUS [leh-NAY-us] (1707–78) established the biological classification system that is still used to identify species. Both Linnaeus's classification system and the *Encyclopédie* are undertakings that reveal the optimism of the age, the result of two hundred years of scientific advances that had convinced many people that humankind could in fact eventually know everything—and catalog it.

ROCOCO

The Rococo style of art was, in the eyes of many, entirely decadent and self-serving. It was commissioned by the same powerful aristocratic French families who were seen as suppressors of the people's freedom. Its abundant extravagance was interpreted as a reflection of its patrons' self-aggrandizement. The Rococo art of this aristocracy, the poetry, architecture, painting, and sculpture of the court of Louis XV (r. 1715–74), is precisely what the Enlightenment came to define itself against.

The name **Rococo** is thought to come from the French word *rocaille*, a type of decorative work or grotto work made from pebbles and shells. It is also very likely a pun on the Italian word for the Baroque, *barocco;* the style's connection to certain elements of the Baroque is strong. Associated especially with the reign of Louis XV of France, Rococo artists reshaped and refined the more elaborate aspects of the Baroque style.

Table 16–1   EIGTHEENTH-CENTURY TECHNOLOGICAL ADVANCES
The steam engine: United States, 1769
The flush toilet: England, 1775
The bicycle: France, 1779
The hot air balloon: France, 1783
The flintlock musket: United States, 1793

FRENCH MUSIC

Couperin and Rameau.   Next to the drama and grandeur of Baroque music, Rococo music is playful and light. The gallantry and polish of Rococo painting are echoed in Rococo music, especially music written for harpsichord by Francis Couperin (1668–1733) and Jean-Philippe Rameau (1683–1764).

During the mid-to-late eighteenth century, when the Rococo style was in full bloom, France successfully resisted the influence of foreign musical styles. King Louis XIV, in his effort to establish things French as the epitome of taste and culture, subjected the arts to a consistent national policy and set up an operatic monopoly that excluded foreign composers. A tight musicians' guild effectively limited outsiders from participating through strict apprenticeship and accreditation requirements. In addition, creative efforts in music, as in the other arts, were concentrated in areas approved and supported by the court. Thus music during the reign of Louis XIV was largely designed to accompany court functions, ceremonies, and entertainments. Couperin and Rameau supplied much of this music.

FRENCH PAINTING

Jean-Antoine Watteau.   JEAN-ANTOINE WATTEAU [WAH-toe] (1684–1721) was most noted for his ***fêtes galantes,*** depictions of elegant out-of-doors parties known for their amorous conversations, graceful fashion, and social gallantry.

Watteau's *Pilgrimage to Cythera* (fig. 16.3), of 1717, is a mythologized vision of just such an event. The party takes place on Cythera, the birthplace of Venus and the island of love. Lovers go there to honor Venus, portrayed by a statue on the far right. Cupids fly above the crowd, the sun is low, and the lovers are boarding the boat that will return them to the real world. The departure is sad; some people glance back, reluctant to leave the idyllic setting.

Watteau's painting gained entry into the Royal Academy of Painting and Sculpture even though it did not adhere to Academy rules of size or subject. It is relatively small, and the subject was neither history nor religion nor portraiture, the subjects the Academy favored. Watteau did not glorify the state or flatter the king. Nonetheless, the Academy recognized Watteau's achievement, and in a moment of triumph for the *rubéniste* sensibility, it created a new official category expressly for *fêtes galantes.*

By the time Louis XV assumed personal rule of the country in 1743, the court had enjoyed a free rein for many years. The king essentially adapted himself to its carefree ways, dismissing state officials at whim. In thirty years of personal rule, he had fourteen chief fiscal officers and eighteen different foreign secretaries, creating ceaseless instability in government. Part of the problem can be attributed to France's growing fiscal crisis and the high costs of government and court life. Nonetheless, life, for Louis XV, was something of an endless *fête galante.* He surrounded

FIGURE 16.3   Jean-Antoine Watteau, *Pilgrimage to Cythera*, 1717, oil on canvas, 4′3″ × 6′4½″ (1.30 × 1.90 m), Musée du Louvre, Paris. Reunion des Musées Nationaux/Art Resource, NY. The Rococo style is characterized by lightness both of content and of color; romantic pastimes are portrayed in an atmosphere of lighthearted aristocratic hedonism.

himself with mistresses, at least one of whom, Madame de Pompadour, wielded as much, or more, power than the king himself.

François Boucher. Madame de Pompadour's favorite painter was FRANÇOIS BOUCHER [boo-SHAY] (1703–70), who began his career, in 1725, by copying the Watteau paintings owned by Jean de Jullienne, the principal collector of the artist's work. Jullienne had conceived of the notion of having all of Watteau's works engraved so they could be enjoyed by a wider public. Boucher was the best of the printmakers hired by Jullienne to undertake the task. With his earnings, he set off for Rome in 1727 to study the masters. But he found Raphael "trite" and Michelangelo "hunchbacked," so he returned to Paris. By 1734, he was an established member of the Academy, specializing in *fêtes galantes* and other similar subjects. Soon he was appointed director of the Royal Academy and first painter to Louis XV, and patrons of society clamored after his work.

Boucher's painting of the *Bath of Diana* (fig. 16.4), of 1742, displays the delicate French grace and charming Rococo sentiment that made him so successful. Boucher painted many female nudes, then a popular subject; but on this occasion, to make it socially acceptable, he presented the figure as the mythological Diana. His goddess of the hunt, however, is hardly strong or powerful. She is aristo-

cratic, delicate, and soft, seemingly straight from the hairdresser. The curving shapes are characteristic of the Rococo style, as are the lush colors that he favors—tender pinks, blues, and soft whites. The artist's friends likened his colors to "rose petals floating in milk." The overall effect is one of quiet sensuality, conveying an air of relaxed indiscretion.

Jean-Honoré Fragonard. The other great painter of the Parisian Rococo was JEAN-HONORE FRAGONARD [frah-goh-NAR] (1732–1806), Boucher's student, whose work is even more overtly erotic than his teacher's. Sensuous nudes inhabit his paintings, and they are depicted in an equally sensual style, much like that of Rubens in its use of strong fluid color and areas of light and shade. Fragonard is noted for his rapid brushwork—sometimes he could paint an entire work inside an hour. His figures float softly, ever graceful, always courtly. Fragonard's most famous work, however, was a series of fourteen canvases commissioned around 1771 by Madame du Barry, Louis XV's last mistress. Designed to decorate her château, they depict a series of encounters between lovers in garden settings, like the gardens of the château itself. *The Meeting* (fig. 16.5) has elements characteristic of the whole series. Below a statue of Venus, a young woman waits to meet her lover, who is climbing over the garden wall. Depictions of flirtation and romance, enjoyed by elegantly attired aristocrats in imaginary garden settings, are typically Rococo.

FIGURE 16.4 François Boucher, *Bath of Diana*, 1742, oil on canvas, $22\frac{1}{2}''$ × $28\frac{3}{4}''$ (57.2 × 73 cm), Musée du Louvre, Paris. Reunion de Musées Nationaux. Gabriel Ojeda/Art Resource, NY. The portrayal of female nudity was made acceptable by the antique context in which it was presented. The female type admired was not athletic or rugged but pale and pampered.

FIGURE 16.5   Jean-Honoré Fragonard, *The Meeting*, 1771–73, oil on canvas, 10′ 5¼″ × 7′ ⅝″ (3.18 × 2.15 m), Frick Collection, New York. The pastel colors, delicate graceful gestures, and curving forms—including the twisting pose of the statue of Venus—are Rococo characteristics.

FIGURE 16.6   Marie-Louise-Elisabeth Vigée-Lebrun, *The Artist and Her Daughter*, ca. 1785, oil on canvas, 4′ 3″ × 3′ 1″ (139.7 × 94 cm). Musée du Louvre, Paris. Photo: G. Blot/ C. Jean./ Photo credit: Reunion des Musées Nationaux/Art Resource, NY/Musée d'Orsay. Vigée-Lebrun's style coincided perfectly with upper-class tastes, making her the highest paid portrait painter in France (by the age of twenty!) and court painter to Queen Marie Antoinette.

Fragonard endured constant interruption by Madame du Barry, and in the end the paintings were rejected, perhaps because the Rococo was becoming increasingly unpopular. Seen by many as the embodiment of the decadence of the aristocracy, the style was on the wane.

Marie-Louise-Elisabeth Vigée-Lebrun.   Paintings like *The Artist and Her Daughter* (fig. 16.6) by MARIE-LOUISE-ELISABETH VIGEE-LEBRUN [vee-JHAY le-BRUN] (1755–1842) signaled the arrival of a more restrained and naturalistic classical style. Her father died when she was young, and Vigée-Lebrun supported her mother and brother by her painting. She was a child prodigy; by the time she was twenty, her portraits were commanding the highest prices in France. Highly sought after, Vigée-Lebrun painted portraits of all the important members of the aristocracy, including Louis XVI's queen, Marie Antoinette. Vigée-Lebrun was able to con-

vey a sense of power combined with grace and intimacy. Her subjects often seem to be turning to glance at the viewer, as if the viewer just happened into their presence a moment ago. Closely linked to royalty, Vigée-Lebrun fled France during the revolution, spent many years traveling and painting in Europe, and published three volumes of memoirs, which give an insight into her art and era.

Adélaïde Labille-Guiard.   Like her contemporary Vigée-Lebrun. ADÉLAÏDE LABILLE-GUIARD [ahd-LAID la-BEE ghee-YAR] (1749–1803) was a French portraitist who received commissions from some of the same patrons. Both were admitted to the French Academy on the same day in 1783. Whether their rivalry was real or invented by the hostility of other artists is unknown. Several of Labille-Guiard's pupils went on to notable artistic careers. She was active in promoting the rights of women artists.

In her capacity as the Peintre des Mesdames (Painter of the Ladies) to Louis XVI, she was commissioned to portray *Louise-Elisabeth of France* (fig. 16.7) in 1788. This is a commemorative portrait, as Louise-Elisabeth had died almost thirty years earlier of smallpox when only thirty-two years old. In this poignant memorial, her expression is almost wistful as she looks out at the viewer, while her son reaches up to take her hand. Although shown on a balcony, the sweep of red drapery was customary in portraiture.

The New Hôtels.   In almost all things, the French court indulged its newfound sense of freedom. When Louis XIV died, and the Duc d'Orléans assumed the role of regent

FIGURE 16.7   Adélaïde Labille-Guiard *Posthumous portrait of Louise-Elisabeth of France, Duchess of Parma.* 1788, oil on canvas, 8′ 9″ × 5′ 3′ (2.72 × 1.6 m). Musée du Louvre. Paris. Chateaux de Versailles et de Trianon, Versailles, France. Reunion des Musees Nationaux/Art Resource, NY. This is a memorial portrait to a member of the family of Louis XVI, the former Duchess of Parma, who died of smallpox leaving the young son seen here, Don Ferdinand, the future Duke of Parma. Labille-Guiard evokes the viewer's sympathy by the child's gaze and gesture and especially by the use of shadows, as that across her face, for the sun is symbolically low and soon to set.

for the child-king, Louis XV, Versailles was immediately abandoned. The court was reestablished in Paris, although not so much at the Palace of the Louvre, as in **hôtels,** or townhouses, where clever hostesses oversaw weekly **salons,** fashionable social gatherings of notable people. These salons were the scene of conversations that turned, very often, into battles of wit and intelligence, or dwelt on matters of love and courtship. Musicians, frequently the finest of the day, entertained the guests.

The hostesses were free to pursue their own tastes in Paris, unhampered by any official court style such as they had experienced at Versailles, and they decorated their *hôtels* elaborately. One salon was created for the Princess de Soubise (fig. 16.8). Designed by France's royal architect, GABRIEL-GERMAIN BOFFRAND [boo-FRAHN] (1667–1754), it displays the typical Rococo pale pastel colors, small details, and concern for melding ceiling and walls into one curvilinear flow of delicate ornament and grace.

ENGLISH PAINTING

William Hogarth.   William Hogarth (1697–1764) painted series of pictures that were equivalent to scenes in a play or chapters in a novel. He used similar details to help viewers interpret the different scenes of his works, which were much like morality plays. He sought to teach by example, referring to his narratives as "modern moral subjects." A social critic, he satirized the decadent customs of his day by exposing the "character" of society. Thus, unlike his French counterparts, who painted the life of the aristocracy in an unabashedly erotic and glowing light, Hogarth's view of England's aristocracy is overtly critical and moralistic. The engravings he made of these paintings were sold to the public and became wildly popular. Hogarth's financial success was based on the fact that lurid stories sell well.

Hogarth's *Marriage à la Mode* is a series of paintings made in 1744. The first scene, called *The Marriage Contract* (fig. 16.9), introduces the cast of characters. On the right sits the father of the groom, a nobleman who points to his family tree. Through this arranged marriage, he is trading his social position for money that will ensure the mortgage on his estate is paid off. The bride's father, a wealthy tradesman, inspects the contract. On the left, the engaged couple have their backs to each other. The groom preens himself in the mirror. The bride talks to the lawyer, counselor Silvertongue.

In the five scenes that follow, the marriage, as expected, sours. Husband and wife are both unfaithful. When the husband finds his wife with Silvertongue, the lover stabs him. The wife is disgraced and takes poison. As she is dying, her father, mercenary to the end, removes her valuable rings. In *Marriage à la Mode* the guilty go unpunished.

Sir Joshua Reynolds.   One of the leading painters of London society was Sir Joshua Reynolds (1723–92). Thought-

FIGURE 16.8 Salon de la Princesse, Hôtel de Soubise, Paris, ca. 1737–38, decorated by Gabriel-Germain Boffrand. Turning away from the vast spaces of Baroque architecture, Rococo architects preferred small rooms, as demonstrated by those in this elegant townhouse. This room measures ca. 33 × 26′ (ca. 10.06 × 7.92 m), an ideal space in which to cultivate the art of conversation.

FIGURE 16.9   William Hogarth, *Marriage à la Mode: The Marriage Contract*, 1744, oil on canvas, 35 × 27″ (89 × 69 cm), National Gallery, London. Through a series of paintings, comparable to scenes in a play, Hogarth told moralizing tales focusing on the hypocritical or dishonest practices of his day. *Marriage à la Mode* shows the disastrous outcome of a marriage arranged for the benefit of the parents of the bride and groom.

ful, intelligent, and hard working, Reynolds was named the first president of the Royal Academy of London in 1768 and was knighted the following year. Favoring an academic art similar to that championed by Lebrun in France a century earlier, Reynolds developed a set of theories and rules in his fifteen *Discourses*, positioning history painting as the highest form of art.

The majority of Reynolds's works, however, are portraits, presumably because portrait painting was lucrative. His style is seen in his portrait *Lady Elizabeth Delmé and Her Children* (fig. 16.11), executed 1777–80 at the peak of his career. Reynolds often portrayed aristocratic ladies as elegant and gracious, refined and dignified. Lady Delmé sits on a rock and embraces her oldest children. All are

fashionably dressed. The colors and textures are lush in Reynolds's "Grand Manner"—indeed, the canvas itself is enormous and the figures almost life size.

Reynolds painted rapidly with full, free brushstrokes, without first making sketches. In his fourth *Discourse*, he says a portrait painter should give a general idea of his subject and "leave out all the minute breaks and peculiarities in the face . . . rather than observing the exact similitude of every feature." Thus Reynolds painted people the way he thought they should look, rather than how they actually did look.

Thomas Gainsborough. Reynolds's chief rival was Thomas Gainsborough (1727–88). Although Gainsborough began as a landscape painter, a subject he always

Connections

DIDEROT AS ART CRITIC

One of the very first art critics—certainly the first art critic of any substance—was Denis Diderot (1713–84), the philosophe. He enjoyed art, and his enjoyment is evident in every page of his essays, called the *Salons*. He reviewed all the exhibitions sponsored by the French Academy from 1759 on for a private newspaper, *La Correspondance littéraire*. Subscribers to this newspaper were the elite of Europe—princesses and princes—and it was intended to keep potential patrons abreast of the latest news from Paris.

Although he considered Boucher the most talented painter of his generation, Diderot generally disapproved of his subjects, and went so far as to condemn him and his contemporaries in the *Salon of 1767* for the essentially erotic content of most of what was on display. Four years earlier he had asked, "Haven't painters used their brushes in the service of vice and debauchery long enough, too long indeed?" He preferred what he called "moral" painting that sought "to move, to educate, to improve us, and to induce us to virtue." Diderot could also be cruel. Addressing a now-forgotten painter by the name of Challe, he asked,

"Tell me, Monsieur Challe, why are you a painter? There are so many other professions in which mediocrity is actually an advantage."

Anticipating the Impressionists a century later, he celebrated a **still life** painting entitled *The Brioche* (fig. 16.10) by JEAN-BAPTISTE-SIMEON CHARDIN [shar-DAN] (1699–1779), "Such magic leaves one amazed. There are thick layers of superimposed color, and their effect rises from below to the surface.... Come closer, and everything becomes flat, confused, and indistinct; stand back again, and everything springs back into life and shape."

Diderot's writing style is anything but as direct as his criticisms. Some of his *Salons* are so long that they cannot be read at a single sitting. They exercise every excuse for a digression. Still, their acuteness of vision and moral purpose continue to influence art criticism.

FIGURE 16.10   Jean-Baptiste-Siméon Chardin, *The Brioche*, 1763, oil on canvas, 18½" × 22" (47 × 55.9 cm), Musée du Louvre, Paris. Reunion des Musées Nationaux. Herve Lewandowski/Art Resource, NY. A master of still life, which in his day was considered the lowest form of painting, Chardin was nevertheless recognized by his contemporaries as applying paint and color as no one before him had ever done. But his technique was not, he thought, what mattered most. "Who told you that one paints with colors?" he once asked a fellow artist. "One uses colors, but one paints with feelings."

preferred, he painted portraits to make a living and became the most fashionable portraitist in British society. Gainsborough's *Mary, Countess Howe* (fig. 16.12), of 1765, like most eighteenth-century portraiture, flatters the subject. Set in a landscape worthy of Watteau, Gainsborough depicts the countess of Howe as if she were strolling in a *fete galante*. She is impeccably dressed, elegant, possessing social poise and a self-confident air of distinction. Painting with dash and freedom, using a fresh and fluid technique emphasizing lush textures in decorative colors, Gainsborough displays a technical virtuosity typical of the Rococo.

FIGURE 16.11   Sir Joshua Reynolds, *Lady Elizabeth Delmé and Her Children*, 1777–80, oil on canvas, 7′10″ × 4′12⅛″ (2.39 × 1.48 m), National Gallery of Art, Washington, D.C. Andrew W. Mellon Collection. Photograph © Board of Trustees, Reynolds, Gainsborough's rival, places his aristocratic subjects in a landscape setting indicative of the eighteenth-century appreciation of nature.

FIGURE 16.12   Thomas Gainsborough, *Mary, Countess Howe*, 1765, oil on canvas, 8′ × 5′ (2.59 × 1.52 m), London County Council, Kenwood House (Iveagh Bequest). English Heritage, London. Although he thought of himself first and foremost as a landscape painter, Gainsborough is best known for largescale portraits that present his subjects as aristocratic and refined.

LITERATURE OF RATIONALISM

During the eighteenth century, literary works throughout Europe reflected the rationalism of the Enlightenment. The emphasis on reason occurred across genres, from essays and fiction to poetry and drama. Benjamin Franklin and Thomas Paine wrote essays that relied on careful reasoning and incisive logic to support their claims about human political and social behavior as well as humanity's irrational beliefs, especially those concerning religious faith. Novelists and satirists, including Daniel Defoe and Jonathan Swift, often used irony to satirize humans' claim to reason. Swift suggested, in fact, that although human

beings are theoretically capable of being rational, few actually behave rationally. English poets in particular employed irony and sarcasm as weapons in their fiercely satirical verses on all manner of subjects, especially the behavior of courtiers.

Samuel Johnson's "Club."   The London of Hogarth's day was, above all, a city of contrasts. On the one hand, there was Fleet Street, largely rebuilt after the Great Fire of 1666 and dominated at one end by Wren's St. Paul's Cathedral. Fleet Street was the gathering place of the Club, a group of London intellectuals, writers, editors, and publishers. One of its founders was Samuel Johnson (1709–84), author of the 1755 *Dictionary of the English Lan-*

guage and editor of Shakespeare's complete plays. The Club was also home to members of refined society. Artists, too, among them Sir. Joshua Reynolds, sought each other's company at the Cock Tavern or at Ye Olde Cheshire Cheese. "When a man is tired of London, a man is tired of life," Johnson boasted of the city's intellectual and cultural stimulation.

On the other hand, there was Grub Street, a lane just outside the London Wall. As Johnson put it in his *Dictionary*, Grub Street was "inhabited by writers of small histories, dictionaries, and temporary poems"—the hacks of the burgeoning publishing trade. A world of difference lay between it and Fleet Street; Newgate Prison was between them, and Bethlehem Royal Hospital, known as Bedlam, the lunatic asylum, was nearby. This was the monstrous side of London, a side that members of Johnson's Club witnessed every day as they strolled from Fleet Street to the tavern where they met. On the way, they passed through Covent Garden, where the city's street-walkers plied their trade.

Alexander Pope.   Alexander Pope (1688–1744) set the standard for satiric poetry in eighteenth-century England. No work captures the spirit of Grub Street better than Pope's *Dunciad*, written in 1743. Pope equates the Grub Street writers with the lunacy of the city itself, and the poem ends with a "dunces" parade through the city.

In the face of the monstrosities of Grub Street, Pope writes, "Morality expires." Satire was Pope's chief tool, and the lowly hacks of Grub Street were by no means his only target. Like Hogarth, he attacked the morality of the aristocracy. Perhaps his most famous poem is *The Rape of the Lock*. This is a **mock epic**—that is, it treats a trivial incident in a heroic manner and style more suited to the traditional epic subjects of war and nation building. *The Rape of the Lock* is based on an actual incident in which a young man from a prominent family clipped a lock of hair from one Miss Arabella Fermor, an event that caused her family considerable consternation. Pope describes the gentlemen and ladies of polite society in the same terms as the heroes and heroines of Homer's epic *Iliad* and *Odyssey*, his translations of which first established his reputation. Pope's "war" is chiefly one of the words and deeds exchanged between the sexes, all described in heroic style. Applied to the frivolous world of snuffboxes, porcelain, and cosmetics, the effect is undeniably comical, as if Sir Joshua Reynolds's Grand Manner had been brought low.

Jonathan Swift.   A far crueler satirist was Jonathan Swift (1667–1745). Born in Ireland, Swift traveled to London, where he became a renowned poet and political writer, as well as an Anglican clergyman. After his appointment as dean of St. Patrick's Cathedral in Dublin in 1713, he spent the rest of his life in Ireland. Best known for his satirical prose work *Gulliver's Travels*, Swift for many years was considered a cynical misanthrope—a person who hates the human race. Much has been made of a comment from *Gulliver's Travels*, spoken by the King of Brobdingnag (the land of the giants). Addressing Lemuel Gulliver, Swift's

MAP 16.2   The Enlightenment in America and Europe.

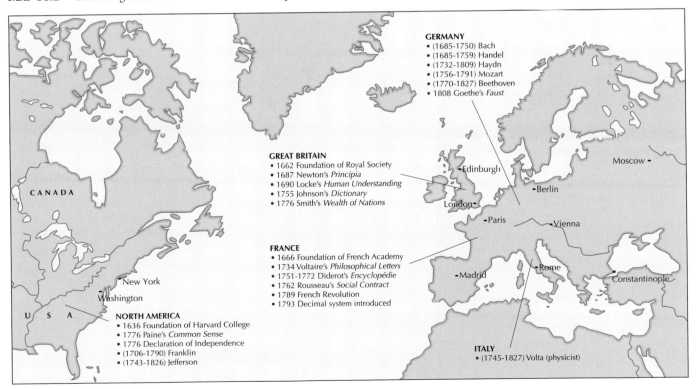

representative of humanity, the Brobdingnagian king describes human beings as "the most pernicious race of little odious vermin that Nature ever suffered to crawl upon the face of the earth."

This bitter satirical strain, however, is only one side of Swift's literary persona; his satirical imagination also had a lighter, more playful dimension. *Gulliver's Travels* is full of fantastic and marvelous events, delightful even to children. The book recounts the adventures of a ship's physician, Lemuel Gulliver, over four voyages. His first voyage takes him to Lilliput, where the people are only six inches tall; the second to Brobdingnag, the land of giants; the third to Laputa, a region where thought and intellect are privileged; and the fourth and final voyage to the land inhabited by the Yahoos and their masters the Houyhnhnms, horselike creatures whose lives are governed by reason, intelligence, and common sense. Nonetheless, throughout *Gulliver's Travels*, Swift uses his hero's adventures to satirize the political, social, and academic institutions of his own time and country, with their abundant display of human folly, stupidity, baseness, and greed. Thus he contrasts the sensible and wise Houyhnhnms with both the ignorant and filthy Yahoos and with the impractical and eccentric Laputians, who are so far from living effectively in the real world that they carry a large sack filled with a multitude of objects, which they need to communicate with one another.

VOLTAIRE'S PHILOSOPHY OF CYNICISM

One of the most important thinkers of the eighteenth century, François Marie Arouet, known by his pen name VOLTAIRE [Vole-TAIR] (1694–1778), shared Swift's general sense of human folly, as well as Hogarth and Pope's recognition of the moral bankruptcy of the aristocracy. Voltaire was deeply influenced by English political thought, especially by the freedom of ideas that, among other things, allowed writers such as Pope and Swift to publish without fear. Voltaire himself was jailed for a year, then exiled to England in 1726, for criticizing the morality of the French aristocracy. When he returned to France, in 1729, he promptly published his *Philosophical Letters Concerning the English*, in which, once more, he criticized French political and religious life. This time, his publisher was jailed, and Voltaire himself retreated to Lorraine, in eastern France, where he lived for the next fifteen years.

Voltaire's best known work, *Candide*, is a scathing indictment of those who agreed with the philosopher Leibniz that this is the best of all possible worlds, regardless of occasional misfortunes, and that everything that happens is part of the providential plan of a benevolent God. *Candide* was written just after the 1755 Lisbon earthquake, in which thousands were killed. Voltaire argued that those who explained the catastrophe away, minimizing its destructive consequences, were deceiving themselves. Voltaire reasoned that either God refused to prevent the existence of evil, in which case he was not benevolent, or he lacked the power to avert evil, in which case he was not omnipotent. Voltaire also rejected the Christian notion of a personal God. Voltaire was a Deist, one who subscribed to a belief system that envisioned a divine being as the maker of the universe, but a creator who lacked interest in the world once it had been created. According to Deism, the creator was like a clockmaker and the world like a complex machine, which was set in motion by the creator but into which he did not intervene. For Voltaire, religious traditions such as biblical Christianity that promise eternal joy, happiness, and salvation were responsible for creating unrealistic expectations and vain hopes. In fact, one of the strongest impetuses for rationalism was a disillusionment with religious belief—faith and revelation—because differences among religious factions had accounted for more than 150 years of bloody war throughout Europe.

NEOCLASSICISM

Many people in France were suspicious of the behavior and tastes of their own aristocracy. To painters, it seemed as if the sensuous color and brushwork of the *rubénistes* had led not merely to the excesses of the Rococo but had themselves become the visual sign of a general moral decline. Thus *poussinistes* once again began to take hold. Poussin's intellectual classicism offered not merely an alternative style to the Rococo but, in its rigor and orderliness, a corrective to the social ills of the state.

As early as 1746, in reviews of the exhibition of the French Academy, critics bemoaned the fact that the grandiose history paintings had disappeared, replaced by the Rococo fantasies Diderot abhorred. Prompted in large measure by the rediscovery of the ancient Roman cities of Herculaneum and Pompeii, in 1738 and 1748 respectively, which were partially excavated from the ashes and volcanic mud that had buried them when volcanic Mt. Vesuvius erupted in 79 C.E., many people began to reestablish classical values in art and state. People indentified with the public-minded values of the Greek and Roman heroes who placed moral virtue, patriotic self-sacrifice, and "right action" above all else, and they wanted to see these virtues displayed in painting. By 1775, the French Academy was routinely turning down Rococo submissions to its biennial Salon in favor of more classical subjects, just as Madame du Barry was rejecting Fragonard's panels for her new château. A *new* classicism—a **Neoclassicism**—replaced the Rococo almost overnight.

PAINTING

Jacques-Louis David.   The French artist JACQUES-LOUIS DAVID [dah-VEED] (1748–1825) was a follower of Nicolas Poussin. When he left to study in Rome in

1775, David asserted that antique art lacked fire and passion; but, in fact, he was to be thoroughly seduced by it. David offered his stark, simple painting as an antidote to Rococo frivolity.

His first major commission was for Louis XVI, the *Oath of the Horatii* (fig. 16.13). Three brothers from Rome, the Horatii, pledge an oath upon their weapons, which are being held by their father. They vow to fight to the death against the Curatii, three brothers from Alba, to resolve a conflict between the two cities. All figures are accurately drawn, carefully modeled in cold light, as solid as sculpture. In accordance with Neoclassical ideals, the scene is set against the severe architecture of the Roman revival. David, like Poussin, constructed his composition in a series of horizontal planes arranged parallel to the picture plane. Also like Poussin, David subordinated color to line, because he believed clarity of statement was most important and was best achieved by drawing. As a result, his paintings appear to be drawings that have been colored. David's subject is a display of Roman heroic stoicism and high principles. The Horatii place patriotic duty above concern for themselves and their family.

When the painting was exhibited at the Salon of 1785, it caused an immediate sensation, not so much because of its Neoclassical style, but because it promoted values that many people recognized were lacking in the king and his court. By the time of the French Revolution in 1789, the painting was read almost universally as an overtly anti-monarchist statement, although David probably did not originally intend it as such. Interpreted as a call for a new moral commitment on the part of the French state, David's art quickly became that most closely associated with the revolution. David himself was soon planning parades gala festivals, and public demonstrations, all designed to rally the people behind the revolution's cause. He persuaded the revolutionary government to abolish the French Academy, and in its stead to create a panel of experts charged with reforming the public taste.

Angelica Kauffmann. The work of ANGELICA KAUFFMANN [KOFF-mahn] (1741–1807) provides an even clearer example of painterly representation of virtuous behavior and high moral conduct. The Swiss-born Kauffmann was trained in Italy, where she modeled her

FIGURE 16.13 Jacques-Louis David, *Oath of the Horatii*, 1785, oil on canvas, 4′3″ × 6′5¼″ (1.30 × 1.96 cm), Musée du Louvre, Paris, RMN Reunion des Musées Nationaux/Art Resource, NY. Neoclassical artists favored subjects taken from ancient literature and history that illustrated high principles or ideals. Excavation of the ancient Roman cities of Herculaneum and Pompeii generated a renewed and widespread interest in the antique.

figures after the wall paintings at Pompeii and Hercula-neum. In 1766, she moved to England, and, with her friend Sir Joshua Reynolds, helped found the new British Royal Academy.

Kauffmann's *Cornelia Pointing to Her Children as Her Treasures* (fig. 16.14), of 1785, champions family values, simple dress, and austere interiors. Gone are Rococo de-pictions of women wearing the elegant and refined dress of the Rococo salon. Instead, when a visitor asks to see her family treasures, Cornelia points with pride to her two sons (the Gracchi), both of whom were to grow up to be-come leaders of the Roman Republic, repossessing public land from the decadent Roman aristocracy and redistrib-

uting it to the poor—precisely the spirit that drove the leaders of the French Revolution.

John Singleton Copley.   An American expatriate work-ing in London, JOHN SINGLETON COPLEY [COP-lee] (1738–1815) of Boston was New England's leading portraitist. Copley went to England in 1774, studied in London, gained admission to the Royal Academy, and re-mained there the rest of his life. Copley's *Watson and the Shark* (fig. 16.15), of 1778, depicts a contemporary event with a kind of immediacy and realism that anticipates the painting of the next century. The event depicted was real: A man named Brook Watson had indeed encountered a

FIGURE 16.14   Angelica Kauffmann, *Cornelia Pointing to Her Children as Her Treasures*, 1785, oil on canvas, 3′ 4″ × 4′ 2″ (1.02 × 1.27 m), Virginia Museum of Fine Arts, Richmond. The Adolph D. and Wilkins C. Williams Fund. Photo: Katherine Wetzel. In contrast to Rococo frivolity, Neoclassical art was intended to serve a public role in encouraging virtue. In this story from ancient republican Rome, when asked about her treasures, Cornelia points to her children, who went on to do good deeds on behalf of the poor.

FIGURE 16.15   John Singleton Copley, *Watson and the Shark*, 1778, oil on canvas, $6'\frac{1}{2}'' \times 7'6\frac{1}{4}''$ (1.84 × 2.29 m). Museum of Fine Arts, Boston. Gift of Mrs. George von Lengerke Meyer. Reproduced with permission. © Museum of Fine Arts, Boston. All Rights Reserved. Copley's painting has all the drama of a modern adventure film—a struggle for survival against nature depicted at the climactic moment and with the outcome left uncertain— combined with heroic nudity.

shark while swimming in the harbor of Havana, Cuba. The painting shows the shark lunging for Watson while two men reach out for him, straining, their faces showing their anguish, and another man grasps the shirt of one to prevent him from falling overboard. The drama is increased by the dramatic lighting and the dynamic diagonal movements. Copley paints a cliff-hanger—the viewer is left wondering whether Watson will survive. In fact, Watson had long escaped the shark when he commissioned the painting years later as a publicity ploy while running for political office.

SCULPTURE

Jean-Antoine Houdon.   One of France's greatest sculptors was JEAN-ANTOINE HOUDON [ooh-DON] (1741–1828), born at the Palace of Versailles where his father was a servant. Later his father became the caretaker for the school for advanced students in the French Academy of Painting and Sculpture, enabling Houdon to associate with artists from the time he was eight years old. It

is said that as a child he would sneak into class, steal some clay, and imitate what he saw. He learned well, for he won the Prix de Rome, which enabled him to study in Italy from 1764 to 1769.

Houdon was unrivaled in his day as a portrait sculptor. Even Americans ventured forth to commission him while they were in Paris: Benjamin Franklin (1778), John Paul Jones (1780), and Thomas Jefferson (1789). To create lifelike images, Houdon took precise measurements of his sitters and usually made a terra cotta model while working with the sitter. This model was given to his assistants, who blocked out the form in marble; then Houdon did the fine carving and polishing.

In order to portray George Washington (fig. 16.16), Houdon went to America and stayed for two weeks in October 1785 as a guest in Washington's home at Mount Vernon, Virginia. Houdon made a cast of Washington's face and a plaster bust, but returned to Paris to carve the life-size figure in stone, working on the project from 1788 to 1792.

During that time Houdon also made a statue of Washington in classical garb. Although the version finally selected shows Washington wearing contemporary attire, it, too, has

FIGURE 16.16   Jean-Antoine Houdon, *George Washington*, State Capitol, Richmond, Virginia, 1788–92, marble, height 6′ 2″ (1.88 m). Calm, composed, and commanding, this version of Washington in his general's attire was favored over another version in classical garb. Still, antique echoes are seen in the *contrapposto* pose and the thirteen *fasces* (rods) bound together, representing the states of the Union.

links to the classical past. Washington stands in the antique *contrapposto* pose. His left hand rests on thirteen bound rods, or ancient *fasces*, symbolizing both the original states of the Union and the power and authority of ancient Rome. Behind the *fasces* are sword and plow, representing war and peace.

ARCHITECTURE

Chiswick House.   Chiswick House (fig. 16.17) is an excellent example of Neoclassical architecture in England. It was begun in 1725, built by Lord Burlington (1694–1753)

FIGURE 16.17   Lord Burlington and William Kent, Chiswick House, west London, begun 1725. The architectural lineage of this house, with its central dome, triangular pediment, and columnar portico, can be traced back to the ancient Roman Pantheon (see Chapter 4).

and William Kent (1685–1748). Burlington was himself an amateur architect, but his team included trained architects.

Like its prototypes, including the Roman Pantheon (see fig. 4.13) and Palladio's Villa Rotundo in Vicenza, Italy (see fig. 13.46), Chiswick House is geometrically simple yet stately. The classical vocabulary and proportions are most important. Symmetry is maintained at all costs, even when it makes things inconvenient within the home. In the academic Neoclassical style, regularity, reason, and logic dominate imaginative variation. This is in marked contrast to the emotion and drama of the Baroque and Rococo styles. In Neoclassical buildings, the walls are flat and the decoration relatively austere compared to that of Rococo interiors, with their abundantly ornamented, animated, even undulating architectural elements.

La Madeleine.   In France, the Neoclassical style was promulgated in particular by Napoleon, who longed to rebuild Paris as the new Rome. The church of La Madeleine in Paris (fig. 16.18) had been started by Louis XVI, but Napoleon rededicated it in 1806 as a Temple of Glory to be designed by PIERRE-ALEXANDRE VIGNON [VEE-nyonh] (1762–1829).

Napoleon conceived of La Madeleine as a monument to his military victories and as a repository for his trophies. Reflecting the great interest in archaeology at this time, the exterior is an accurate reconstruction of an ancient Roman temple. It has a raised base, steps across the front only, a colonnade of the Corinthian order, entablature, pediments, and a peaked roof. Although highly dignified, there is something stark about La Madeleine's archaeological accuracy. Individual imagination seems absent. The interior belies the exterior, for its ceiling consists of three consec-

FIGURE 16.18   Pierre-Alexandre Vignon, La Madeleine, Paris, 1806–42, main facade, length 350′ (106.68 m), width 147′ (44.81 m), height of podium 23′ (7.01 m), height of columns 63′ (19.20 m). La Madeleine is based on the ancient rectangular temple type, such as the Greek Parthenon (see fig. 3.3).

utive domes; thus, unlike its ancient Greek and Roman prototypes, the exterior and interior are not coordinated. After Napoleon's death the building was once again used as a church.

Monticello.   The Neoclassical style of architecture was prominent in the United States, where the new American presidents, believing it to embody enlightened democratic leadership, championed its use in public architecture. One of the most notable Neoclassical designs in the United States is the private home of President Thomas Jefferson (1743–1826), known as Monticello [MON-tih-CHELL-o], in Charlottesville, Virginia (fig. 16.19). Jefferson drew up the designs for it himself in 1769. An adaptation of Burlington and Kent's Chiswick House, it was built between 1770 and 1806. Monticello is constructed of brick and wood and capped with a polygonal dome. The deep portico, or porch, here supported on Doric columns, was to become very popular in the southern United States, as seen in some of the great antebellum homes in Mississippi. In southern climates the portico provided protection from

the sun and added dignity and splendor to the building; the northern equivalent was much shallower. The plan of Monticello is almost perfectly symmetrical, with entrances on each of the four sides, and the rooms laid out on either side of a central hall and drawing room.

A leading architect of his time, Jefferson fostered classical ideas in America. He studied the ancient Roman temple known as the Maison Carrée in Nîmes, France, and used it as the model for the Virginia state capitol (1785–98). An example of austere Neoclassicism, it represents a deliberate rejection of the Baroque and the Rococo.

LITERATURE

The Rise of the Novel.   Although the novel can be said to have originated in the ancient world with stories told by Greek and Roman writers, it did not rise to significance as a literary genre until the eighteenth century in Europe. Preceding the rise of the novel as a major literary genre were occasional earlier prose fiction masterpieces, most

FIGURE 16.19   Thomas Jefferson, Monticello, Charlottesville, Virginia, main facade, 1770–1806.
Neoclassical architecture was favored in America for its formal symmetry and antique associations.
At Monticello a temple of stone and concrete, the ancient Roman Pantheon (see fig 4.13), via
Chiswick House (fig. 16.17), has been translated into a home of brick and wood.

notably Miguel Cervantes' *Don Quixote*, the picaresque tales of the famous knight of the woeful countenance and his comic sidekick the paunchy Sancho Panza.

But Cervantes' book and occasional other works of prose fiction did not manage to create an audience with an appetite for longer works of fiction. That did not happen until a leisured class of educated readers emerged in eighteenth century Europe, particularly in England and France. These readers had the time and the interest to read longer prose fictional works created by writers such as Henry Fielding and Samuel Richardson in England and Chaderlos la Clos in France. Fielding's *Tom Jones*, Richardson's *Pamela*, and La Clos' *The Dangerous Liaisons (Les Liaisons Dangereux)* were immensely popular works. They were published in stages, one part at a time, and offered to

readers in periodicals, or magazines that come out monthly or quarterly, thus keeping readers' interest keen as to what was to happen in forthcoming episodes.

All of these novelists and many that followed in both France and England wrote about a handful of basic subjects—mostly about love and marriage, money and class status. Novelists offered a panorama of society by depicting the various social classes interacting with each other. Novelists recreated in fictional form their social worlds, capturing the aura and ethos of city life and country life, of the rich and the poor, of social changes that occurred during their lifetimes, as for example the shift from an agricultural to an industrial economy. What these eighteenth century novelists began in earnest continued through the nineteenth century, in England with Jane Austen and

Critical Thinking

THE POPULARITY OF THE NOVEL

The novel became a popular literary genre in the eighteenth century with the serial publication of books such as *Tom Jones* in England and *Les Liaisons Dangereux* in France. These novels told the stories of fictional characters whose adventures their authors chronicled as if the characters were real and their stories biography rather than fiction. In the case of Defoe's *Robinson Crusoe* and *A Journal of the Plague Year*, as well as with the case of his novel, *Moll Flanders*, the characters and events seem as real as any actual person's life story or any actual historical chronicle of events.

To what extent do you think that the novel's popularity in the eighteenth century can be attributed to authors' attempts to make their books appear factual—either as biography or as history? What other factors contributed to the appeal of novels for readers then? To what extent do you think those appealing aspects of novels continue to make the novel popular in the twenty-first century? And, finally, as with the eighteenth century, so today, the majority of novel readers are women. Why do you think this genre has always been more popular with women than with men?

Charles Dickens among many other notable English novelists, and with Honoré de Balzac and Gustave Flaubert, among noteworthy French novelists of the next century.

One of the great paradoxes of the rise of the novel in Europe was the extent to which novelists made an effort, largely successful, to invest their characters with life-likeness, to the extent of giving them historical and biographical ballast. Daniel Defoe, the author of *Robinson Crusoe*, another famous eighteenth century novel, based his fiction on a factual account of a man, Alexander Selkirk, who experienced some of what Defoe describes as happening to Crusoe. In another novel, *A Journal of the Plague Year*, Defoe pretends to be chronicling actual history—what happened in London during the Great Plague in the 1660s, in which a large percentage of the city's population succumbed to the ravages of the disease. In one case Defoe writes fiction as a kind of biography and in another as a kind of history. And yet both works are fiction.

Jane Austen. One of the most important novelists of her day, Jane Austen (1775–1817) was the daughter of a clergyman and spent the first twenty-five years of her life at her parents' home in Hampshire, where she wrote her first novels, *Northanger Abbey*, *Sense and Sensibility*, and *Pride and Prejudice*. None of these works was actually published until the second decade of the nineteenth century, when Austen was almost forty. She came from a large and affectionate family, and her novels reflect a delight in family life; they are essentially social comedies. Above all else, they are about manners, good and bad. They advocate the behavioral norms by which society deemed decent must and should operate. They are also deeply romantic books that have marriage as their goal and end. Austen was not so naive as to believe good marriages could come from alliances built solely on social advantage; it is her scenes showing romantic love, not expedient matrimony, that draw the reader's sympathy.

Austen called herself a "miniaturist," by which she meant her ambition was to capture realistic and intimate portraits of her characters and the time in which they lived. Many readers have found that her presentation of human beings, with all their foibles, attempting to enjoy and prosper in life with one another, is utterly convincing.

CLASSICAL MUSIC

The Classical period of music is distinguished by the growth of a popular audience for serious music, highlighted by the rise of the public concert. A middle class began to demand from composers a more accessible and recognizable musical language than that provided by the complex patterns of, say, a Baroque fugue. The classical composers Haydn and Mozart developed this new musical language by reshaping old forms like the concerto and establishing new forms, such as the symphony.

The Symphony. The **symphony** is known as a large form: It consists of several distinct parts, called movements, that proceed in a predictable pattern. The challenge the composer faces is to create fresh and inventive compositions without diverging from the predictable format. A symphony typically consists of four movements:

First movement: The pace of the movement is fast, usually *allegro*, and its mood usually dramatic.
Second movement: This movement is slow (*adagio* or *andante*, for instance), and its mood reflective.
Third movement: The pace picks up moderately, and the period's most popular dance, the stately and elegant aristocratic minuet, often serves as the basis for the movement.
Fourth movement: Once again, the fourth movement is fast (*allegro*), spirited (*vivace*), or light and happy.

Over the course of the eighteenth century, audiences became educated in these conventions; in part the excitement of hearing a new composition centered on the anticipation the listeners felt as the composer moved inventively through this predictable pattern.

Each symphonic movement also possessed its own largely predictable internal form. The first and fourth movements usually employed a **sonata** (or sonata-allegro) form, the second was sometimes in this form but just as often a **theme and variations** or a **rondo,** and the third was generally a **minuet and trio.**

The word sonata derives from the Italian *sonare,* "to sound," as distinguished from cantata, which derives from the Italian *cantare,* meaning "to sing." Sonata form itself consists of three sections: exposition, development, and recapitulation, the last of which is sometimes followed by a coda, or tailpiece. The overall structure suggests a pattern of departure and return. The exposition introduces the movement's themes, the development section modifies and advances them, and the recapitulation returns home to the main theme.

Each of the other movements of the symphony employs this pattern of departure and return but in slightly different terms. In the theme and variations (a second movement form), the main theme is introduced and then recurs again and again in varied form. In a rondo, used in the second and fourth movements, a single theme repeats itself with new material added between each repetition. The minuet and trio (a third movement form) possesses an ABA structure. That is, a minuet ("A") is presented, followed by a contrasting trio section ("B"), before the return of the minuet ("A"). The trio section contrasts with the minuet in that it is written for fewer instruments, although not necessarily for three instruments, as the name suggests.

Franz Joseph Haydn.   Raised as a choirboy at St. Stephen's Cathedral in Vienna, FRANZ JOSEPH HAYDN [HIGH-din] (1732–1809) served as a court musician for Prince Esterházy for nearly thirty years, beginning in 1761. Haydn composed so many symphonies—more than a hundred—in so many variations that he is known as the "father" of the form. It is Haydn to whom we are indebted for the classical characteristics of musical clarity, balance, and restraint. As his nickname implies, Papa Haydn developed the basic classic form of the sonata, the symphony, and the string quartet. He set the guidelines for the classical style while adapting his music to his patrons' needs and desires. His career not only defines this transition from court to public music, but it also marks the moment when musicians and composers finally attained the social status that painters, sculptors, and architects had enjoyed since as early as the Renaissance.

Haydn's "Farewell" Symphony no. 45 of 1772 was conceived as an explicit protest at the living conditions at Eisenstadt palace, about thirty miles south of Vienna, where the court musicians lived in isolation. Esterházy did not allow his musicians to bring their families to the palace. Thus, living in crowded servant quarters, they were forced to be away from their loved ones for long periods at a time. Performing one evening at court, the musicians played the symphony's three uneventful movements, but in the middle of the fourth movement, the second horn player and the first oboist suddenly stopped playing, packed up their instruments, blew out the candles that illuminated their scores, and left the hall. Slowly, the rest of the orchestra followed suit until no one was left except two violinists, who finished the symphony. The prince immediately understood the implications of the performance and granted his musicians an extended leave to visit their families.

When Esterházy died in 1790, his son, who did not much care for music, disbanded the orchestra, and Haydn returned to Vienna. By now he was internationally renowned. A concert promoter from London, Johann Peter Salomon, offered him a commission, and in 1791, he left Vienna for England. There, he was received by the royal court, awarded an honorary doctorate at Oxford, and began to reap the financial benefits by conducting public subscription concerts of new work, particularly the famous "London" symphonies, which were acclaimed by the public as no other symphonic music had been before.

Wolfgang Amadeus Mozart.   Perhaps the greatest of the Classical composers was WOLFGANG AMADEUS MOZART [MOAT-zart] (1756–91), born and raised in Salzburg, Austria. His first music teacher was his father, Leopold, himself an accomplished musician and composer. Young Mozart's musical genius was immediately evident in his early piano and violin playing and in his composing, which he began at the age of five. Although he had enormous musical gifts, Mozart suffered from depression and illness and as an adult had a difficult time securing a regular income. He achieved stunning successes in Vienna, especially with his operas, but when he died at the age of thirty-five he was heavily in debt.

During his brief life, Mozart composed more than six hundred works. He wrote forty-one symphonies along with twenty-seven piano concertos and nine concertos for other instruments. He composed large numbers of chamber works and a significant volume of choral music, including his great *Requiem,* or mass for the dead, which remained unfinished at his death. Mozart also composed some of the most popular operas ever written, including *The Marriage of Figaro* (1786), *Don Giovanni* (1787), and *The Magic Flute* (1791). Reviving the drama of the Baroque, he created operas in both opera seria (usually with historical or mythological stories) or opera buffa (comic operas). His singspiels, which combined spoken dialogues and arias, duets and ensembles, were his main contribution to German opera.

Don Giovanni is based on the story of the legendary Spanish nobleman, Don Juan, who was notorious for his seduction of women. Mozart, well aware of the amorous goings-on in all the great courts of Europe, subtly mocks them in this work. His opera begins with Don Giovanni killing the outraged father of a young noblewoman he has just seduced. At the end of the opera, the dead man returns in the form of a statue that comes sufficiently alive to drag Don Giovanni down to hell. Between these two dramatic episodes, Mozart portrays Don Giovanni's seduction of three women, blending seriousness with humor.

An early scene from Act I reveals Don Giovanni at work in music that captures the Don's persuasive appeal for the peasant girl Zerlina (fig. 16.20), whom he has promised to marry if she comes to his palace. Mozart has the would-be lovers sing a duet entitled "*Là ci darem la mano*" ("There, you will give me your hand"). Don Giovanni begins with an attractive image of their intertwined future. Zerlina's ambivalent response indicates her desire for the Don and her fear that he may be tricking her. Following this initial exchange, Mozart speeds up their interaction to show Zerlina's increasing acquiescence and then blends their voices to suggest their final mutual accord. The scene is doubly pleasing. It portrays an actual seduction, one that any audience can enjoy, and it exposes Don Giovanni for the rake that he is, thus allowing the audience both to warm to and detest Mozart's antihero. The wide range of feelings typifies Mozart's music and in part accounts for his enduring popularity.

TOWARD ROMANTICISM

BEETHOVEN: FROM CLASSICAL TO ROMANTIC

LUDWIG VAN BEETHOVEN [BAY-tove-in] (1770–1827) was born during the age of the Enlightenment, came to maturity during a period of political and social revolu-

FIGURE 16.20   A scene from *Don Giovanni* by Wolfgang Amadeus Mozart. The opera premiered in 1787. Here, in Act I, Don Giovanni (played by Sherrill Milnes) seduces the innocent Zerlina (Teresa Stratas) in the duet "*Là ci darem la mano.*"

tion, and died as the **Romantic** era was in full flower. His work and his life reveal a tension between the Classical style of the past and the newly emerging Romantic tendencies in art. In his middle period, Beethoven enlarged the scope of the Classical style; in his later works, he transcended it, moving in new musical directions.

Beethoven was born and raised in Bonn, in the German Rhineland. At the age of twenty-one he went to Vienna, where he remained for the rest of his life. He became known for his prodigious ability on the piano, especially for his improvisational skill. By the time he was thirty, Beethoven was recognized as an innovative and creative composer. Unlike other musicians and composers of his time, he was determined to remain a free artist, and, with the help of a number of sympathetic patrons, he supported himself solely through composing and performing his music. Beethoven was aided by the growth of music publishing and an increase in concert life fueled by the rise of a middle-class public with an appetite for serious music.

Among the most significant experiences of Beethoven's life was the onset of deafness, which began to afflict him around 1800, just as his music was attracting serious acclaim. He nearly committed suicide. In 1802, he wrote his famous Heiligenstadt testament, an agonized letter to his brother describing his suicidal thoughts and his eventual victory over them: "I would have ended my life—it was only my art that held me back. Ah, it seemed to me impossible to leave the world until I had brought forth all that I felt was within me."

Living through this traumatic experience strengthened Beethoven, and the music he wrote afterward exhibited a new depth of feeling and imaginative power. By 1815, Beethoven was almost entirely deaf, but this did not stop him from composing and conducting his music. In the end, Beethoven's deafness was more of a social affliction than a musical one. He increasingly separated himself from society, for which his rebellious and fiery temperament ill suited him.

Beethoven produced an abundance of music, including thirty-two piano sonatas and nine symphonies, which set the standard against which the symphonic efforts of all subsequent composers have been measured.

The Three Periods of Beethoven's Music.   Beethoven's music can be divided into three periods, each reflecting differences in stylistic development. During the first period, which lasted until about 1802, Beethoven wrote works mainly in the Classical style, adhering to the formal elements established by Haydn and perfected by Mozart before him. In the middle period (1803–14), referred to as the "heroic" phase, his works become more dramatic; they are also noticeably longer than those of his Classical predecessors, as they begin to stretch the requirements of Classical form. The first movement of the Third Symphony is, for instance, as long as many full symphonies of Haydn and Mozart. And his compositions in

Cross Currents

TURKISH MILITARY MUSIC AND VIENNESE COMPOSERS

Western Europeans had long been fascinated with the so-called **exotic.** During the eighteenth century there was increased cultural interaction with Turkey, then part of the Ottoman empire. Although at the time it represented a threat to Austria, the Austrian Hapsburg empire enjoyed a taste for things Turkish and Ottoman. Viennese cuisine reflected the influence of Turkish spices. Viennese fashion exhibited Turkish influence in flowing garments and brightly decorative ribbons and braiding in women's attire. Viennese music incorporated elements of the music of Turkish military bands, composed of musicians mounted on horseback playing drums and shawms, long-tubed horns used in medieval Western as well as medieval Turkish music. In the seventeenth century, trumpets, cymbals, bells, and additional types of drums were added to Turkish military bands. Later, during the nineteenth century, some pianos were equipped with a special pedal for creating unusual percussive effects reminiscent of these instruments.

All three of the great Viennese composers of the time reveal the influence of the Turkish military band. Haydn wrote three military symphonies, whose titles reflect the martial nature of their music, including the "Drum Roll" and the "Military." Mozart included Turkish percussive musical elements in his opera *The Abduction from the Seraglio.* He also entitled the rondo movement from his piano sonata K. 331 "Rondo alla Turca," a spirited piece with a section reflective of Turkish military music. Beethoven was also inspired by Turkish music, as is evidenced by his *Turkish March* and in themes from the fourth movement of his Ninth Symphony. Moreover, inspired by the whirling dance of Islamic Turks, Beethoven wrote his *Chorus for Whirling Dervishes,* a work whose theme is repeated in increasing intensity and in quicker tempos, imitating the trance induced by the whirling dance of the Sufi dervishes (see Chapter 6).

---

this period modulate between the most gentle and appealing melodies and the most dynamic and forceful writing—not only between works, but within each work.

Beethoven's final period of composition spans the years 1815–27, during which he was almost completely deaf. In this period, Beethoven not only departed from the constraints of Classical compositional practice, but also entered new musical territory and reached new levels of spiritual profundity. Works from the late period include, among many others, his Ninth Symphony, considered by many the greatest symphony ever written; the last piano sonatas; and the deeply spiritual *Missa Solemnis.*

Symphony no. 5 in C Minor; op. 67. Beethoven's most famous work remains his middle period Symphony no. 5 in C Minor, op. 67, a work that defines the idea of the symphony in the popular imagination. He completed it in 1808. One of the most tightly unified compositions Beethoven ever wrote, its opening four-note motif is perhaps the best known of all symphonic themes. Out of that brief fragment of musical material, Beethoven constructs a dramatic and intense opening movement. He uses its rhythmic pattern of three short notes followed by a longer one in each remaining movement and further unifies the work by returning to the theme of the third movement during a dramatic passage in the fourth movement. Overall, the symphony moves from struggle and dramatic conflict to triumphant and majestic exultation.

The first movement, marked *Allegro con brio,* "fast with spirit," opens abruptly with the famous "Fate knocking on the door" theme—short-short-short-long:

Beethoven repeats this musical motif relentlessly throughout the exposition before a bridge passage leads to a second, contrasting, and more lyrical theme, which is accompanied in the cellos and basses by the first fournote theme. Additional musical ideas fill out the movement, including a development section that breaks the main theme

into smaller and smaller units and a recapitulation that features a surprising lyrical oboe solo.

The second movement, in theme and variations form, provides relief from the unabating tension created in the first. Two themes dominate the movement, the first sung by cellos and violas, the second by clarinets. Both receive extensive variation throughout the movement. The overall effect combines noble grandeur with sheer lyrical beauty.

The third movement, a scherzo, begins with a mysterious theme introduced quietly by cellos and basses, followed by a loud theme blared out by the horns on a single repeated note. Instead of a break between movements, Beethoven creates a sense of tension with a long sustained tone that forms a bridge to the fourth and final movement.

The fourth movement, a scherzo, in C major, is cast in sonata form, with an extensive coda, one of the most dra-

Cultural Impact

Politically and socially, the eighteenth century was a period of dramatic change. Government by aristocracy gave way to more democratic political structures. Although absolutist forms of government persisted in Europe, they were challenged by republican advocates of divided, complementary forms of political organization and by supporters of democratic rule. The seeds of democratic government were sown not only in America, but also in Europe, where democracy would eventually emerge as the prevalent form of government in the modern Western world.

The Enlightenment had a profound impact on the development of Western civilization. It was during this period that the ideals of "liberty, equality, and fraternity" animated the French Revolution. Similar ideals of "life, liberty, and the pursuit of happiness" provided the new American nation with its foundational principles.

The arts saw a return to the aesthetic ideals of classical antiquity, especially order, balance, symmetry, and proportion. Aspects of eighteenth-century architecture, for example, are modeled after that of ancient Greece and Rome. Enormously influential, the Neoclassical style is seen in government and public buildings constructed in the nineteenth and twentieth centuries in the United States and around the world.

Classical ideals of balance, symmetry, and proportion were also important in music and literature. So were qualities of wit and elegance: The spirit of the music and literature of the age is reflected in a propensity for irony, in sparkling dialogue between characters in novels, plays, and operas, and in a strong tendency toward satire. Concern for elegance in the formal structure of musical and literary works remains an important legacy of the Enlightenment.

---

matic Beethoven wrote. For this, he enlarged the orchestra: A high-pitched piccolo extends the orchestral range upward, a low-pitched contrabassoon extends it downward, and three extra trombones add power. Beethoven presents four themes first, then a stunning coda that appears to end a number of times before he finally brings the movement and the symphony to a triumphant conclusion.

It is perhaps because Beethoven became isolated from the natural world by his deafness that he was able to redefine the creative act of composition. It was no longer, as it had been for centuries, considered a function of objective laws and rules of harmony, but the expression of deeply personal and often introspective feelings. It is to this interior world that artists of the nineteenth century, the so-called Romantics, turned their attention.

KEY TERMS

Enlightenment	Rococo	Napoleonic Code	rondo
philosophes	*fêtes galantes*	Neoclassicism	minuet and trio
rational humanism	*hôtels*	novel	requiem
revolution	salons	symphony	Romantic
Industrial Revolution	still life	sonata	
Encyclopédie	mock epic	theme and variations	

www. WEBSITES FOR FURTHER STUDY

http://www.infidels.org/library/historical/john_remsburg/six_historic_americans/chapter_2.html
(This is a site entitled Six Historic Americans, which includes Thomas Jefferson, as written by John E. Remsburg.)

http://csep10.phys.utk.edu/astr161/lect/history/newtongrav.html
(A good physics site on Sir Issac Newton and studies on gravity.)

http://artchive.com/artchive/W/watteau.html
(This is the Artchive, a website with virtually every major artist in every style from every era in art history. It is an excellent resource.)

http://w3.rz-berlin.mpg.de/cmp/mozart.html
(A good site on Wolfgang Amadeus Mozart's biography.)

READINGS

ALEXANDER POPE

from *An Essay on Man*

An Essay on Man (1733) presents Pope's view of moral virtue as a basis for happiness. In this poem Pope celebrates virtue and reason as twin sources of stability and harmony, the kind of balance and orderliness that Pope himself struggled to achieve in his life as well as in his art. An example of Pope's fine ear for rhyme along with his sure sense of how sound echoes sense can be heard in the following passage from An Essay on Man, *a passage that also reflects the eighteenth-century tendency toward satire as it simultaneously suggests Pope's view of humankind's place in the order of creation.*

Awake, my ST. JOHN! leave all meaner things
To low ambition, and the pride of Kings.
Let us (since Life can little more supply
Than just to look about us and to die)
Expatiate free o'er all this scene of Man;   5
A mighty maze! but not without a plan;
A Wild, where weeds and flow'rs promiscuous shoot,
Or Garden, tempting with forbidden fruit.
Together let us beat this ample field,
Try what the open, what the covert yield;   10
The latent tracts, the giddy heights explore
Of all who blindly creep, or sightless soar;
Eye Nature's walks, shoot Folly as it flies,
And catch the Manners living as they rise;
Laugh where we must, be candid where we can;   15
But vindicate the ways of God to Man.
I. Say first, of God above, or Man below,
What can we reason, but from what we know?
Of Man what see we, but his station here,
From which to reason, or to which refer?   20
Thro' worlds unnumber'd tho' the God be known,
'Tis ours to trace him only in our own.
He, who thro' vast immensity can pierce,
See worlds on worlds compose one universe,
Observe how system into system runs,   25
What other planets circle other suns,
What vary'd being peoples ev'ry star,
May tell why Heav'n has made us as we are.
But of this frame the bearings, and the ties,
The strong connections, nice dependencies,   30
Gradations just, has thy pervading soul
Look'd thro'? or can a part contain the whole?
   Is the great chain, that draws all to agree,
And drawn supports, upheld by God, or thee?   34
II. Presumptuous Man! the reason wouldst thou find,
Why form'd so weak, so little, and so blind!
First, if thou canst, the harder reason guess,
Why form'd no weaker, blinder, and no less!
Ask of thy mother earth, why oaks are made
Taller or stronger than the weeds they shade?   40
Or ask of yonder argent fields above,
Why JOVE's Satellites are less than JOVE?

Of Systems possible, if 'tis confest
That Wisdom infinite must form the best,
Where all must full or not coherent be,   45
And all that rises, rise in due degree;
Then, in the scale of reas'ning life, 'tis plain
There must be, somewhere, such a rank as Man;
And all the question (wrangle e'er so long)
Is only this, if God has plac'd him wrong?   50
   Respecting Man, whatever wrong we call,
May, must be right, as relative to all.
In human works, tho' labour'd on with pain,
A thousand movements scarce one purpose gain;
In God's, one single can its end produce;   55
Yet serves to second too some other use.
So Man, who here seems principal alone,
Perhaps acts second to some sphere unknown,
Touches some wheel, or verges to some goal;
'Tis but a part we see, and not a whole.   60
   When the proud steed shall know why Man restrains
His fiery course, or drives him o'er the plains;
When the dull Ox, why now he breaks the clod,
Is now a victim, and now Ægypt's God:
Then shall Man's pride and dulness comprehend   65
His actions', passions', being's, use and end;
Why doing, suff'ring, check'd, impell'd; and why
This hour a slave, the next a deity.
   Then say not Man's imperfect, Heav'n in fault;
Say rather, Man's as perfect as he ought;   70
His knowledge measur'd to his state and place,
His time a moment, and a point his space.
If to be perfect in a certain sphere,
What matter, soon or late, or here or there?
The blest today is as completely so,   75
As who began a thousand years ago.
   III. Heav'n from all creatures hides the book of Fate,
All but the page prescrib'd, their present state;
From brutes what men, from men what spirits know:
Or who could suffer Being here below?   80
The lamb thy riot dooms to bleed to-day,
Had he thy Reason, would he skip and play?
Pleas'd to the last, he crops the flow'ry food,
and licks the hand just rais'd to shed his blood.
Oh blindness to the future! kindly giv'n,   85
That each may fill the circle mark'd by Heav'n;
Who sees with equal eye, as God of all,
A hero perish, or a sparrow fall,
Atoms or systems into ruin hurl'd,
And now a bubble burst, and now a world.   90
   Hope humbly then; with trembling pinions soar;
Wait the great teacher Death, and God adore!
What future bliss, he gives not thee to know,
But gives that Hope to be thy blessing now.
Hope springs eternal in the human breast: 95
Man never Is, but always To be blest:
The soul, uneasy and confin'd from home,
Rests and expatiates in a life to come.
   Lo! the poor Indian, whose untutor'd mind
Sees God in clouds, or hears him in the wind;   100
His soul proud Science never taught to stray
Far as the solar walk, or milky way;
Yet simple Nature to his hope has giv'n,

Behind the cloud-topt hill, an humbler heav'n;
Some safer world in depth of woods embrac'd, 105
Some happier island in the watry waste,
Where slaves once more their native land behold,
No fiends torment, no Christians thirst for gold!
To Be, contents his natural desire,
He asks no Angel's wing, no Seraph's fire; 110
But thinks, admitted to that equal sky,
His faithful dog shall bear him company.
    IV. Go, wiser thou! and in thy scale of sense
Weigh thy Opinion against Providence;
Call Imperfection what thou fancy'st such, 115
Say, here he gives too little, there too much;
Destroy all creatures for thy sport or gust,
Yet cry, If Man's unhappy, God's unjust;
If Man alone ingross not Heav'n's high care,
Alone made perfect here, immortal there: 120
Snatch from his hand the balance and the rod,
Re-judge his justice, be the GOD of GOD!
In Pride, in reas'ning Pride, our error lies;
All quit their sphere, and rush into the skies.
Pride still is aiming at the blest abodes, 125
Men would be Angels, Angels would be Gods.
Aspiring to be Gods, if Angels fell,
Aspiring to be Angels, Men rebel;
And who but wishes to invert the laws
Of ORDER, sins against th' Eternal Cause. 130
    V. Ask for what end the heav'nly bodies shine,
Earth for whose use? Pride answers, 'Tis for mine:
For me kind Nature wakes her genial pow'r,
Suckles each herb, and spreads out ev'ry flow'r;
Annual for me, the grape, the rose renew 135
The juice nectareous, and the balmy dew;
For me, the mine a thousand treasures brings;
For me, health gushes from a thousand springs;
Seas roll to waft me, suns to light me rise;
My foot-stool earth, my canopy the skies.' 140
    But errs not Nature from this gracious end,
From burning suns when livid deaths descend,
When earthquakes swallow, or when tempests sweep
Towns to one grave, whole nations to the deep?
'No ('tis reply'd) the first Almighty Cause 145
Acts not by partial, but by gen'ral laws;
Th' exceptions few; some change since all began,
And what created perfect?'—Why then Man?
If the great end be human Happiness,
Then Nature deviates; and can Man do less? 150
As much that end a constant course requires
Of show'rs and sun-shine, as of Man's desires;
As much eternal springs and cloudless skies,
As Men for ever temp'rate, calm, and wise.
If plagues or earthquakes break not Heav'n's design, 155
Why then a Borgia, or a Catiline?
Who knows but he, whose hand the light'ning forms,
Who heaves old Ocean, and who wings the storms,
Pours fierce Ambition in a Caesar's mind,
Or turns young Ammon loose to scourge mankind? 160
From pride, from pride, our very reas'ning springs;
Account for moral as for nat'ral things:
Why charge we Heav'n in those, in these acquit?
In both, to reason right is to submit.

Better for Us, perhaps, it might appear, 165
Were there all harmony, all virtue here;
That never air or ocean felt the wind;
That never passion discompos'd the mind:
But ALL subsists by elemental strife;
And Passions are the elements of Life. 170
The gen'ral ORDER, since the whole began,
Is kept in Nature, and is kept in Man.
    VI. What would this Man? Now upward will he soar,
And little less than Angel, would be more;
Now looking downwards, just as griev'd appears 175
To want the strengths of bulls, the fur of bears.
Made for his use all creatures if he call,
Say what their use, had he the pow'rs of all?
Nature to these, without profusion kind,
The proper organs, proper pow'rs assign'd; 180
Each seeming what compensated of course,
Here with degrees of swiftness, there of force;
All in exact proportion to the state;
Nothing to add, and nothing to abate.
Each beast, each insect, happy in its own; 185
Is Heav'n unkind to Man, and Man alone?
Shall he alone, whom rational we call,
Be pleas'd with nothing, if not bless'd with all?
    The bliss of Man (could Pride that blessing find)
Is not to act or think beyond mankind; 190
No pow'rs of body or of soul to share,
But what his nature and his state can bear.
Why has not Man a microscopic eye?
For this plain reason, Man is not a Fly.
Say what the use, were finer optics giv'n, 195
T' inspect a mite, not comprehend the heav'n?
Or touch, if trembling alive all o'er,
To smart and agonize at ev'ry pore?
Or quick effluvia darting thro' the brain,
Die of a rose in aromatic pain? 200
If nature thunder'd in his op'ning ears,
And stunn'd him with the music of the spheres,
How would he wish that Heav'n had left him still
The whisp'ring Zephyr, and the purling rill?
Who finds not Providence all good and wise, 205
Alike in what it gives, and what it denies?
    VII. Far as Creation's ample range extends,
The scale of sensual, mental pow'rs ascends:
Mark how it mounts, to Man's imperial race,
From the green myriads in the peopled grass: 210
What modes of sight betwixt each wide extreme,
The mole's dim curtain, and the lynx's beam:
Of smell, the headlong lioness between,
And hound sagacious on the tainted green:
Of hearing, from the life that fills the flood, 215
To that which warbles thro' the vernal wood:
The spider's touch, how exquisitely fine!
Feels at each thread, and lives along the line:
In the nice bee, what sense so subtly true
From pois'nous herbs extracts the healing dew: 220
How Instinct varies in the grov'ling swine,
Compar'd, half-reas'ning elephant, with thine:
'Twixt that, and Reason, what a nice barrier;
For ever sep'rate, yet for ever near!
Remembrance and Reflection how ally'd; 225

What thin partitions Sense from Thought divide:
And Middle natures, how they long to join,
Yet never pass th' insuperable line!
Without this just gradation, could they be
Subject these to those, or all to thee?   *230*
The pow'rs of all subdu'd by thee alone,
Is not thy Reason all these pow'rs in one?
   VIII. See, thro' this air, this ocean, and this earth,
All matter quick, and bursting into birth.
Above, how high progressive life may go!   *235*
Around, how wide! how deep extend below!
Vast chain of being, which from God began,
Natures æthereal, human, angel, man,
Beast, bird, fish, insect! what no eye can see,
No glass can reach! from Infinite to thee,   *240*
From thee to Nothing!—On superior pow'rs
Were we to press, inferior might on ours:
Or in the full creation leave a void,
Where, one step broken, the great scale's destroy'd:
From Nature's chain whatever link you strike,   *245*
Tenth or ten thousandth, breaks the chain alike.
   And if each system in gradation roll,
Alike essential to th' amazing whole;
The least confusion but in one, not all
That system only, but the whole must fall.   *250*
Let Earth unbalanc'd from her orbit fly,
Planets and Suns run lawless thro' the sky,
Let ruling Angels from their spheres be hurl'd,
Being on being wreck'd, and world on world,
Heav'n's whole foundations to their centre nod,   *255*
And Nature tremble to the throne of God:
All this dread ORDER break—for whom? for thee?
Vile worm!—oh Madness, Pride, Impiety!
   IX. What if the foot, ordain'd the dust to tread,
Or hand to toil, aspir'd to be the head?   *260*
What if the head, the eye, or ear repin'd
To serve mere engines to the ruling Mind?
Just as absurd for any part to claim
To be another, in this gen'ral frame:
Just as absurd, to mourn the tasks or pains   *265*
The great directing MIND OF ALL ordains.
   All are but parts of one stupendous whole,
Whose body, Nature is, and God the soul;
That, chang'd thro' all, and yet in all the same,
Great in the earth, as in th' æthereal frame,   *270*
Warms in the sun, refreshes in the breeze,
Glows in the stars, and blossoms in the trees,
Lives thro' all life, extends thro' all extent,
Spreads undivided, operates unspent,
Breathes in our soul, informs our mortal part,   *275*
As full, as perfect, in a hair as heart;
As full, as perfect, in vile Man that mourns,
As the rapt Seraph that adores and burns;
To him no high, no low, no great, no small;
He fills, he bounds, connects, and equals all.   *280*
   X. Cease then, nor ORDER Imperfection name:
Our proper bliss depends on what we blame.
Know thy own point: This kind, this due degree
Of blindness, weakness, Heav'n bestows on thee.
Submit—In this, or any other sphere,   *285*
Secure to be as blest as thou canst bear:

Safe in the hand of one disposing Pow'r,
Or in the natal, or the mortal hour.
All Nature is but Art, unknown to thee;
All Chance, Direction, which thou canst not see;   *290*
All Discord, Harmony, not understood;
All partial Evil, universal Good:
And, spite of Pride, in erring Reason's spite,
One truth is clear, 'Whatever IS, is RIGHT.'

JONATHAN SWIFT
A Modest Proposal[1]

Jonathan Swift's A Modest Proposal *began life as a pamphlet, whose title only hints at its satirical impulse:* A Modest Proposal for Preventing the Children of Poor People in Ireland from being a Burden to their Parents or Country, and for making them beneficial to the Publick. *Once readers learn the proposal—that the poor should bear and rear children to be killed and sold for food for the rich, and to have their body parts used for clothing, including the skin for fine gloves—they realize Swift is using the rhetorical strategies of irony and satire to condemn the economic practices and the social prejudices of his time.*

A Modest Proposal

for Preventing the Children of poor People in *Ireland,* from being a Burden to their Parents or Country; and for making them beneficial to the Publick.

Written in the year 1729

It is a melancholy object to those who walk through this great town,[2] or travel in the country, when they see the streets, the roads, and cabin-doors crowded with beggars of the female sex, followed by three, four, or six children, all in rags, and importuning every passenger for an alms. These mothers, instead of being able to work for their honest livelihood, are forced to employ all their time in strolling to beg sustenance for their helpless infants: who, as they grow up, either turn thieves for want of work, or leave their dear native country to fight for the Pretender in Spain, or sell themselves to the Barbadoes.[3]

   I think it is agreed by all parties, that this prodigious number of children in the arms, or on the backs, or at the heels of their mothers, and frequently of their fathers, is, in the present deplorable state of the kingdom, a very great additional grievance; and, therefore, whoever could find out a fair, cheap, and easy method of making these children sound and useful members of the commonwealth, would deserve so well of the public, as to have his statue set up for a preserver of the nation.

---

[1]The complete text edited by Herbert Davis.
[2]Dublin.
[3]At this time a British possession, with a prosperous sugar industry. Workers were needed in the sugar plantations. *The Pretender:* James Edward (1688–1766), son of the Catholic king James II of England, called the "Old Pretender" (in distinction to his son Charles, nine years old at the time of this work, called the "Young Pretender"). Many thought him a legitimate claimant to the throne.

But my intention is very far from being confined to provide only for the children of professed beggars; it is of a much greater extent, and shall take in the whole number of infants at a certain age, who are born of parents in effect as little able to support them as those who demand our charity in the streets.

As to my own part, having turned my thoughts for many years upon this important subject, and maturely weighed the several schemes of other projectors,[4] I have always found them grossly mistaken in their computation. It is true, a child, just dropped from its dam, may be supported by her milk for a solar year with little other nourishment; at most, not above the value of two shillings, which the mother may certainly get, or the value in scraps, by her lawful occupation of begging; and it is exactly at one year old that I propose to provide for them in such a manner, as, instead of being a charge upon their parents or the parish, or wanting food and raiment for the rest of their lives, they shall, on the contrary, contribute to the feeding, and partly to the clothing, of many thousands.

There is likewise another advantage in my scheme, that it will prevent those voluntary abortions, and that horrid practice of women murdering their bastard children, alas, too frequent among us, sacrificing the poor innocent babes, I doubt more to avoid the expense than the shame, which would move tears and pity in the most savage and inhuman breast.

The number of souls in this kingdom being usually reckoned one million and a half, of these I calculate there may be about two hundred thousand couple whose wives are breeders; from which number I subtract thirty thousand couples, who are able to maintain their own children (although I apprehend there cannot be so many, under the present distresses of the kingdom); but this being granted, there will remain a hundred and seventy thousand breeders. I again subtract fifty thousand for those women who miscarry, or whose children die by accident or disease within the year. There only remain a hundred and twenty thousand children of poor parents annually born. The question therefore is how this number shall be reared and provided for? which, as I have already said, under the present situation of affairs, is utterly impossible by all the methods hitherto proposed. For we can neither employ them in handicraft or agriculture; we neither build houses (I mean in the country) nor cultivate land: they can very seldom pick up a livelihood by stealing until they arrive at six years old, except where they are of towardly parts;[5] although I confess they learn the rudiments much earlier; during which time they can, however, be properly looked upon only as probationers; as I have been informed by a principal gentleman in the county of Cavan, who protested to me, that he never knew above one or two instances under the age of six, even in a part of the kingdom so renowned for the quickest proficiency in that art.

I am assured by our merchants that a boy or a girl before twelve years old is no saleable commodity; and even when they come to this age they will not yield above three pounds or three pounds and half-a-crown at most, on the exchange; which cannot turn to account either to the parents or kingdom, the charge of nutriment and rags having been at least four times that value.

I shall now, therefore, humbly propose my own thoughts, which I hope will not be liable to the least objection.

I have been assured by a very knowing American of my acquaintance in London, that a young healthy child, well nursed, is, at a year old, a most delicious, nourishing, and wholesome food, whether stewed, roasted, baked, or boiled; and I make no doubt that it will equally serve in a fricassee or a ragout.

I do therefore humbly offer it to public consideration, that of the hundred and twenty thousand children already computed, twenty thousand may be reserved for breed, whereof only one-fourth part to be males, which is more than we allow to sheep, black cattle, or swine; and my reason is, that these children are seldom the fruits of marriage, a circumstance not much regarded by our savages, therefore one male will be sufficient to serve four females. That the remaining hundred thousand may, at a year old, be offered in sale to the persons of quality and fortune through the kingdom; always advising the mother to let them suck plentifully in the last month, so as to render them plump and fat for a good table. A child will make two dishes at an entertainment for friends; and when the family dines alone, the fore or hind quarter will make a reasonable dish, and, seasoned with a little pepper or salt, will be very good boiled on the fourth day, especially in winter.

I have reckoned, upon a medium,[6] that a child just born will weigh twelve pounds, and in a solar year, if tolerably nursed, increaseth to twenty-eight pounds.

I grant this food will be somewhat dear,[7] and therefore very proper for landlords, who, as they have already devoured most of the parents, seem to have the best title to the children.

Infants' flesh will be in season throughout the year, but more plentifully in March, and a little before and after: for we are told by a grave author, an eminent French physician,[8] that fish being a prolific diet, there are more children born in Roman Catholic countries about nine months after Lent than at any other season; therefore, reckoning a year after Lent, the markets will be more glutted than usual, because the number of popish infants is at least three to one in this kingdom; and therefore it will have one other collateral advantage, by lessening the number of papists among us.

I have already computed the charge of nursing a beggar's child (in which list I reckon all cottagers, labourers, and four-fifths of the farmers) to be about two shillings per annum,[9] rags included; and I believe no gentleman would repine to give ten shillings for the carcass of a good fat child, which, as I have said, will make four dishes of excellent nutritive meat, when he has only some particular friend, or his own family, to dine with him. Thus the squire will learn to be a good landlord, and grow popular among his tenants; the mother will have eight shillings net profit, and be fit for work till she produces another child.

---

[4]Planners.
[5]Particularly talented, unusually gifted.
[6]Average.
[7]Expensive.
[8]François Rabelais (1494?–1553), French satirist and author of *Gargantua and Pautagruel* (1532–52).
[9]Per year (Latin).

Those who are more thrifty (as I must confess the times require) may flay the carcass; the skin of which, artificially dressed, will make admirable gloves for ladies, and summer-boots for fine gentlemen.

As to our city of Dublin, shambles[1] may be appointed for this purpose in the most convenient parts of it, and butchers we may be assured will not be wanting; although I rather recommend buying the children alive, and dressing them hot from the knife, as we do roasting pigs.

A very worthy person, a true lover of his country, and whose virtues I highly esteem, was lately pleased, in discoursing on this matter, to offer a refinement upon my scheme. He said, that many gentlemen of this kingdom, having of late destroyed their deer, he conceived that the want of venison might be well supplied by the bodies of young lads and maidens, not exceeding fourteen years of age, nor under twelve; so great a number of both sexes in every country being now ready to starve for want of work and service; and these to be disposed of by their parents, if alive, or otherwise by their nearest relations. But, with due deference to so excellent a friend, and so deserving a patriot, I cannot be altogether in his sentiments; for as to the males, my American acquaintance assured me from frequent experience, that their flesh was generally tough and lean, like that of our schoolboys, by continual exercise, and their taste disagreeable; and to fatten them would not answer the charge. Then as to the females, it would, I think, with humble submission, be a loss to the public, because they soon would become breeders themselves: and besides, it is not improbable that some scrupulous people might be apt to censure such a practice (although indeed very unjustly) as a little bordering upon cruelty; which, I confess hath always been with me the strongest objection against any project, how well soever intended.

But in order to justify my friend, he confessed that this expedient was put into his head by the famous Psalmanazar,[2] a native of the island Formosa, who came from thence to London above twenty years ago; and in conversation told my friend, that in his country, when any young person happened to be put to death, the executioner sold the carcass to persons of quality as a prime dainty; and that in his time the body of a plump girl of fifteen, who was crucified for an attempt to poison the emperor, was sold to his Imperial Majesty's prime minister of state, and other great mandarins of the court, in joints from the gibbet,[3] at four hundred crowns. Neither indeed can I deny, that if the same use were made of several plump young girls in this town, who, without one single groat to their fortunes, cannot stir abroad without a chair,[4] and appear at playhouse and assemblies in foreign fineries which they never will pay for, the kingdom would not be the worse.

Some persons of a desponding spirit are in great concern about the vast number of poor people who are aged, diseased, or maimed; and I have been desired to employ my thoughts what course may be taken to ease the nation of so grievous an encumbrance. But I am not in the least pain upon that matter, because it is very well known, that they are every day dying, and rotting, by cold and famine, and filth and vermin, as fast as can be reasonably expected. And as to the younger labourers, they are now in almost as hopeful a condition: they cannot get work, and consequently pine away for want of nourishment, to a degree, that if at any time they are accidentally hired to common labour, they have not strength to perform it; and thus the country and themselves are happily delivered from the evils to come.

I have too long digressed, and therefore shall return to my subject. I think the advantages by the proposal which I have made are obvious and many, as well as of the highest importance.

For first, as I have already observed, it would greatly lessen the number of papists, with whom we are yearly over-run, being the principal breeders of the nation as well as our most dangerous enemies; and who stay at home on purpose with a design to deliver the kingdom to the Pretender, hoping to take their advantage by the absence of so many good Protestants, who have chosen rather to leave their country than stay at home and pay tithes against their conscience to an idolatrous Episcopal curate.

Secondly, the poorer tenants will have something valuable of their own, which by law may be made liable to distress,[5] and help to pay their landlord's rent; their corn and cattle being already seized, and money a thing unknown.

Thirdly, whereas the maintenance of an hundred thousand children, from two years old and upwards, cannot be computed at less than ten shillings a piece per annum, the nation's stock will be thereby increased fifty thousand pounds per annum; besides the profit of a new dish introduced to the tables of all gentlemen of fortune in the kingdom who have any refinement in taste. And the money will circulate among ourselves, the goods being entirely of our own growth and manufacture.

Fourthly, the constant breeders, besides the gain of eight shillings sterling per annum by the sale of their children, will be rid of the charge of maintaining them after the first year.

Fifthly, this food would likewise bring great custom to taverns; where the vinters will certainly be so prudent as to procure the best receipts[6] for dressing it to perfection, and, consequently, have their houses frequented by all the fine gentlemen, who justly value themselves upon their knowledge in good eating: and a skilful cook, who understands how to oblige his guests, will contrive to make it as expensive as they please.

Sixthly, this would be a great inducement to marriage, which all wise nations have either encouraged by rewards, or enforced by laws and penalties. It would increase the care and tenderness of mothers towards their children, when they were sure of a settlement for life to the poor babes, provided in some sort by the public, to their annual profit instead of expense. We should soon see an honest emulation among the married women, which of them could bring the fattest child to the market. Men would become as fond of their wives during the time of their pregnancy, as they are now of their mares

---

[1]Slaughterhouses.
[2]George Psalmanazar (1679?–1763), a literary impostor born in southern France who claimed to be a native of Formosa and a recent Christian convert. He published a catechism in an invented language that he called Formosan, as well as a description of Formosa with an introductory autobiography.
[3]The post from which the bodies of criminals were hung in chains after execution. *Joints*: portions of a carcass carved up by a butcher.
[4]I.e., a sedan chair, an enclosed seat carried on poles by men.

---

[5]The legal seizing of goods to satisfy a debt, particularly for unpaid rent.
[6]Recipes.

in foal, their cows in calf, or sows when they are ready to farrow; nor offer to beat or kick them (as is too frequent a practice) for fear of a miscarriage.

Many other advantages might be enumerated. For instance, the addition of some thousand carcasses in our exportation of barrelled beef; the propagation of swine's flesh, and improvement in the art of making good bacon, so much wanted among us by the great destruction of pigs, too frequent at our tables, which are no way comparable in taste or magnificence to a wellgrown, fat yearling child, which, roasted whole, will make a considerable figure at a Lord Mayor's feast, or any other public entertainment. But this, and many others, I omit, being studious of brevity.

Supposing that one thousand families in this city would be constant customers for infants' flesh, besides others who might have it at merry meetings, particularly weddings and christenings. I compute that Dublin would take off annually about twenty thousand carcasses; and the rest of the kingdom (where probably they will be sold somewhat cheaper) the remaining eighty thousand.

I can think of no one objection that will possibly be raised against this proposal, unless it should be urged, that the number of people will be thereby much lessened in the kingdom. This I freely own, and it was indeed one principal design in offering it to the world. I desire the reader will observe that I calculate my remedy *for this one individual kingdom of Ireland, and for no other that ever was, is, or I think ever can be, upon earth.* Therefore let no man talk to me of other expedients: *of taxing our absentees at five shillings a pound: of using neither clothes nor household-furniture except what is of our own growth and manufacture: of utterly rejecting the materials and instruments that promote foreign luxury: of curing the expensiveness of pride, vanity, idleness, and gaming in our women; of introducing a vein of parsimony, prudence, and temperance: of learning to love our country, wherein we differ even from Laplanders, and the inhabitants of Topinamboo:*[7] of quitting our animosities and factions, nor act any longer like the Jews,[8] who were murdering one another at the very moment their city was taken: of being a little cautious not to sell our country and consciences for nothing: of teaching landlords to have at least one degree of mercy towards their tenants: lastly, of putting a spirit of honesty, industry, and skill into our shopkeepers; who, if a resolution could now be taken to buy only our native goods, would immediately unite to cheat and exact upon us in the price, the measure, and the goodness, nor could ever yet be brought to make one fair proposal of just dealing, though often and earnestly invited to it.[9]

Therefore I repeat, let no man talk to me of these and the like expedients, till he hath at least some glimpse of hope that there will ever be some hearty and sincere attempts to put them in practice.

But, as to myself, having been wearied out for many years with offering vain, idle, visionary thoughts, and at length utterly despairing of success, I fortunately fell upon this proposal; which, as it is wholly new, so it hath something solid and real, of no expense and little trouble, full in our own power, and whereby we can incur no danger in disobliging England. For this kind of commodity will not bear exportation, the flesh being of too tender a consistence to admit a long continuance in salt, although perhaps I could name a country[1] which would be glad to eat up our whole nation without it.

After all, I am not so violently bent upon my own opinion as to reject any offer proposed by wise men which shall be found equally innocent, cheap, easy, and effectual. But before something of that kind shall be advanced in contradiction to my scheme, and offering a better, I desire the author, or authors, will be pleased maturely to consider two points. First, as things now stand, how they will be able to find food and raiment for a hundred thousand useless mouths and backs? And, secondly, there being a round million of creatures in human figure throughout this kingdom, whose whole subsistence put into a common stock would leave them in debt two millions of pounds sterling, adding those who are beggars by profession, to the bulk of farmers, cottagers, and labourers, with the wives and children who are beggars in effect; I desire those politicians who dislike my overture, and may perhaps be so bold as to attempt an answer, that they will first ask the parents of these mortals, whether they would not at this day think it a great happiness to have been sold for food at a year old, in the manner I prescribe, and thereby have avoided such a perpetual scene of misfortunes as they have since gone through, by the oppression of landlords, the impossibility of paying rent without money or trade, the want of common sustenance, with neither house nor clothes to cover them from the inclemencies of weather, and the most inevitable prospect of entailing the like, or greater miseries, upon their breed for ever.

I profess, in the sincerity of my heart, that I have not the least personal interest in endeavouring to promote this necessary work, having no other motive than the public good of my country, by advancing our trade, providing for infants, relieving the poor, and giving some pleasure to the rich. I have no children by which I can propose to get a single penny; the youngest being nine years old, and my wife past childbearing.

VOLTAIRE

from *Candide*

In Candide *(1759), an innocent young man is introduced to pain, suffering, violence, and corruption, in a series of misfortunes that include witnessing decapitations, betrayals, murders, rapes, and natural disasters. He eventually realizes that his teacher's philosophy, that "all is for the best," is vain and nonsensical. Having tried scrupulously to live by this motto, he at last gives up hope of finding happiness, of discovering the ideal woman, and of understanding the world. Instead he returns to his country home to cultivate his garden, Voltaire's way of suggesting that the most human beings can do is live simply and reconcile themselves to fate.*

Translated from the German of Doctor Ralph with the additions that were found in the Doctor's pocket, when he died at Minden in the year of grace 1759.

---

[7]In Brazil.
[8]Referring to the factionalism under Herod Agrippa II at the time of the destruction of Jerusalem by the Roman emperor Titus.
[9]The italicized proposals are Swift's serious suggestions for remedying the situation of Ireland.

[1]England.

CHAPTER I

How Candide was reared in a beautiful castle, and how he came to be ejected

Living at the Baron Thunder-ten-tronckh's castle in Westphalia was a young man who was as mild and inoffensive as a lamb. His face was as simple as his soul was unsophisticated. For this reason, I think, he had been named Candide. The old retainers of the house surmised that he was the son, by the baron's sister, of an aristocratic neighbour, of exemplary character, whom this young lady always refused to marry, because, Time having wrought serious ravages on his genealogical tree, he could show only seventy-one quarterings to his escutcheon.

The baron was one of the most powerful lords in Westphalia, for his castle had both a door and windows. His great hall, too, was hung with tapestry. At a pinch, the mongrels in his backyard were a pack of hounds, and his stable-boy the whipper-in. The village curate was his Lord-High-Almoner. Everyone called him *Monseigneur*, and laughed when he told them stories.

The baroness, who weighed twenty-five stone, was much esteemed therefor, and the dignity with which she did the honours of her household made her seem still more respectable. Her daughter, Cunégonde, aged seventeen, was rosy-cheeked, plump, and attractive. The baron's son quite deserved to have the baron for father. Pangloss, the tutor, was the castle's oracle, to whose counsel little Candide listened with all the credulity of his age and temperament.

Pangloss taught metaphysico-theologo-cosmolonigology. He proved admirably that there is no effect without a cause, and that, in this best of all possible worlds, the baron's castle was the most beautiful of all castles, and the baroness the best of all possible baronesses.

"It is evident," said he, "that things cannot possibly be otherwise, for, as everything has been made with an object, that object must necessarily be the best of all possible objects. Take note that noses were made to carry spectacles; accordingly, we have spectacles. Legs were obviously designed to fill stockings; hence we have stockings. Stones were intended to be cut and used for building into castles; my lord baron has a very beautiful castle. The mightiest baron in the province must be the best lodged; and pigs being made to be eaten, we feed on pork all the year round. Consequently, those who aver that everything in this world is good, talk nonsense: what they should say is—'everything is the best possible.'"

Candide, who listened attentively, innocently believed all this; for he considered Mlle. Cunégonde extremely beautiful, although he had never had the courage to tell her so. He judged that, after the joy of being born Baron Thunder-ten-tronckh, the second degree of happiness was to be Mlle. Cunégonde; the third, to see her every day; and the fourth, to listen to Doctor Pangloss, the greatest Philosopher in the province, and, consequently, in the whole world.

One day, Cunégonde, while walking near the Castle in the little wood they called the park, saw between the bushes Doctor Pangloss giving a lesson in experimental physics to her mother's chambermaid, a gentle and very pretty little dark-haired girl. As Mlle. Cunégonde had a considerable liking for science, she quietly studied the repeated experiments of which she was witness. She saw clearly the Doctor's self-sufficient reasons, the effects and the causes, and went back home quite agitated and thoughtful, filled with the desire to be a learned woman, reflecting that she might well be the self-sufficient reason for young Candide, who in his turn might be also the self-sufficient reason for her.

On returning to the castle she met Candide, and blushed: Candide blushed also. She said good-morning to him in a strangled voice, and Candide spoke to her without knowing what he said. The following day, on leaving table after dinner, they happened to stop behind a screen. Cunégonde let her handkerchief fall, Candide picked it up. She guilelessly took his hand, the young man innocently kissed the young lady's fingers with a quite especial liveliness, tenderness, and grace. Their lips met, their eyes kindled, their knees trembled, their hands strayed. The Baron Thunder-ten-tronckh passed close by the screen and, seeing these causes and these effects, ejected Candide from the castle with tremendous kicks on the behind. Cunégonde fainted: when she came to, the baroness boxed her ears, and consternation reigned in the most beautiful and agreeable of all possible castles.

CHAPTER II

What happened to Candide among the Bulgars

Candide, expelled from his terrestrial paradise, wandered about aimlessly for a long time, weeping, raising his eyes to heaven, turning them often to the most beautiful of all possible castles, wherein dwelt the most beautiful of all possible daughters of barons. Without supping, he laid down to sleep in a field, between two furrows. Snow fell in big flakes.

Next morning, quite benumbed, famished and weary without a penny in his pocket, he dragged himself to a neighbouring village called *Valberg-hoff-trarbk-dikdorff*, and halted sadly before a cabaret. Two men, dressed in blue, noticed him. "Look mate!" said one of them. "There's a very well-built young man, and tall enough too." They went up to Candide, and very civilly asked him to dine with them.

"You do me great honour, gentlemen," said Candide, with charming modesty; "but I haven't the money to pay my share."

"That's all right!" replied one of the men in Blue. "Men of your stamp and attainments never need worry about money; why, you stand five foot five in your socks, don't you?"

"That's so," replied Candide with a bow.

"Well then, come and feed with us; we will not only pay for your meal, but will see also that you get some money: men should help one another."

"You're quite right," said Candide. "That's what Doctor Pangloss always told me, and it's quite clear that everything's for the best in this best of all possible worlds."

They begged him to accept a few crowns. He took them, and wished to make out an I.O.U., which they refused. They all sat down to the table.

"I suppose you love and honour . . . ?" said one of the men.

"Oh, yes!" replied Candide. "I love and honour Mlle. Cunégonde: I adore her."

"No, no!" said the other. "What we mean is—do you love and honour your King—the King of the Bulgars?"

"Love the King of the Bulgars? Good heavens, no! Why, I've never even seen him."

"What, never seen the King of the Bulgars! He's the best of all kings. You must drink his health."

"Willingly, gentlemen;" and he drank.

"That's all right, then," they said. "You're the defender, supporter, protector, of the Bulgars: you're their hero. Your fame's assured, and your fortune's made."

Without more ado, they put irons on his feet, and took him to the barracks. There, he was made to turn to the right and to the left, shoulder arms, present arms, port arms, fire, and march at the double. Then they gave him thirty strokes with the cat. The next day he did the exercises better, and received only twenty strokes: the day after that, only ten. His comrades thought him a marvel, but he was somewhat bewildered, as he could not quite make out how he was a hero.

One fine spring morning he took it into his head to go for a walk, in the belief that human beings, like other animals, were privileged to use their legs for pleasure. He had not covered a couple of leagues before four other six-foot heroes overtook him, bound him, and threw him into a dungeon. He was asked judicially whether he would prefer to be flogged thirty-six times successively by the entire regiment, or receive twelve leaden bullets in his brain all at once. He was very inclined to say that, as wishes are free, he preferred neither the one nor the other; but he had to make a choice, and was permitted (by virtue of that gift of God called Freewill) to choose to pass thirty-six times under the rod. He stood two floggings. The regiment membered two thousand men. That meant four thousand blows, which laid bare the muscles and sinews from the nape of his neck to the small of his back. As they were about to start on the third flogging, Candide, not being able to stand any more, begged that in pity they would be so kind as to kill him outright. This favour was granted. They bound his eyes, and forced him to his knees. At that moment, the King of the Bulgars passed by and was informed of the culprit's crime. Being a very intelligent king, however, he understood from everything that was told him about Candide that here was a young metaphysician completely ignorant of the ways of the world. He offered the prisoner a free pardon, therefore, and generously expressed his willingness to remit the remainder of the sentence. Such clemency will certainly be applauded by every newspaper for ever and ever.

A worthy doctor healed Candide in three weeks with the emollients prescribed by Dioscoridos. New skin had already started to grow, and Candide was able to walk, when the King of the Bulgars declared war on the King of the Abars.

CHAPTER III

How Candide escaped from the Bulgars, and what became of him

Never was anything so beautiful, so clever, so thrilling, and so well-arranged, as the two armies. The trumpets, fifes, hautboys, drums and cannons, made a harmony the like of which had never been heard in Hell. The cannons knocked down straightaway nearly six thousand men on each side. Then the muskets removed from this best of all possible worlds some nine or ten thousand blackguards who infected its surface. The bayonet also was sufficient reason for the death of a few

thousands. The total was in easy reach of thirty thousand souls. Candide, trembling like a philosopher, hid himself as best he could during this heroic slaughter.

At last, while the two kings were singing Te Deums in their respective camps, Candide made up his mind to go to reason effects and causes elsewhere. He clambered over the pile of dead and dying, and reached, first of all, the ashes of an Abar village, which the Bulgars had burned according to the laws of public justice. Here, old men, riddled with holes, watched their butchered wives dying with babes at their bleeding breasts. There, disembowelled girls, having satisfied the natural needs of a few heroes, were breathing their last. Others, half burned, begged for death. Brains were spattered on the ground beside bits of arms and legs.

Candide fled as quickly as possible to the next village, which, belonging to the Bulgars, had been treated by the Abars in precisely the same way. Stepping continually on quivering limbs, and walking always over ruins, he at last got out of the theatre of war, with a little food in his knapsack and an unfading picture of Mlle. Cunégonde in his memory. When he reached Holland, his food supply gave out; but having heard that everyone in that country was rich, and Christian, he did not doubt that he would be treated as well there as he had been in the baron's castle, before being ejected on account of Mlle. Cunégonde's beautiful eyes.

He begged charity from several sedate people, who all replied that, if he continued begging as a profession, they would have him put in the lockup in order that he might learn how to make a living out in the world.

After this, he approached a man who, for an hour on end, had been discoursing to a large gathering on the subject of charity. This orator looked him up and down. "What do you intend doing in this country?" he asked. "Have you good cause for being here?"

"There's no effect without a cause," replied Candide, modestly. "Everything's necessarily linked up and arranged for the best possible possible object. It was absolutely necessary a few days ago that I should be kicked from Mlle. Cunégonde's side and flogged by the entire regiment, and it is absolutely necessary now that I should beg bread until I get it. Nothing of all this could have happened differently."

"My friend," said the orator. "Do you believe that the Pope is Antichrist?"

"I've never heard anyone say he was," answered Candide. "But whether he is or whether he isn't, I want some bread to eat."

"You don't deserve to eat," returned the other. "Away with you, you rascal! Away, you vagabond! And don't come near me again, or it'll be the worse for you!"

At this point, the orator's wife put her head out of the window, and, on learning that here was a man who doubted that the Pope was Antichrist, emptied over his head a full . . . Oh, heavens! to what excesses does religious ardour bring women.

A man who had never been baptised, a good Anabaptist named Jacques, seeing the cruel and ignominious treatment thus meted out to one of his brethren, a featherless biped with an immortal soul, took him home, washed him, gave him bread and beer, presented him with two florins, and even wished to teach him the manufacture of Persian fabrics, which are made in Holland.

"Oh!" cried Candide, falling at his feet. "Doctor Pangloss well said that everything was for the best in this best of all possible worlds. I am infinitely more touched by your great generosity than by the harshness shown me by that black-coated man and his wife."

While out walking next day, he came across a beggar all covered with sores, with eyes glazed, the end of his nose eaten away, mouth twisted, teeth black; who spoke in a hoarse voice, and spat out a tooth every time his racking cough tormented him.

CHAPTER IV

How Candide met Doctor Pangloss, his former master of philosophy, and what came of their meeting

Candide, more moved by pity than by horror, gave this terrible beggar the two florins he had received from that honest Anabaptist, Jacques. The spectre fixed him with a glance, shed some tears, and tried to embrace him. Candide drew back in alarm.

"Alas!" said the one poor wretch to the other. "Don't you recognise me? I'm your old friend, Pangloss."

"What! You, my old master! You, in this horrible state! What on earth's happened to you? Why aren't you still in the most beautiful of all possible castles? What's become of that priceless pearl, that masterpiece of nature, Mlle. Cunégonde?"

"I'm absolutely worn out," said Pangloss.

Candide at once led him to the Anabaptist's outhouse, and made him eat a little bread. When Pangloss had revived somewhat, he resumed his catechism.

"Well, what about Cunégonde?"

"She's dead," replied Pangloss.

Candide fainted. His friend brought him round with a little sour vinegar that happened to be in the shed. Candide slowly opened his eyes.

"Cunégonde dead!" he wailed. "Oh, best of all worlds, where are you? But what did she die of? Surely not from seeing me toed out of her father's beautiful castle?"

"No," said Pangloss, calmly. "Some Bulgar soldiers raped her as much as anyone could be raped, and then ripped her stomach open. The baron tried to defend her, and had his head split for his pains. The baroness was torn to pieces. As for the castle, not a stone remains, not a barn, not a sheep, not a duckling, not a tree even. But we were well revenged, for the Abars did just as much damage in the next estate, which belonged to a Bulgar lord."

On hearing all this, Candide fainted again.

Having regained consciousness once more, he lamented to his heart's content, and then inquired: what causes, what effects, and what self-sufficient reasons, had brought Pangloss to his present piteous pass.

"It was Cupid!" said Pangloss, sadly. "Love! the consoler of the human race, the saviour of the universe, the stimulant to action of every sentient creature—sweet, tender, precious, beautiful Love!"

"Yes," said Candide regretfully. "Yes, I've met this Love, this ruler of our hearts, this essence of our being . . . but it was never worth more to me than one kiss on the mouth, and twenty kicks on the backside. Tell me, how did this beautiful cause come to produce in you such an abominable effect?"

"It was like this," replied Pangloss. "Do you remember, my dear Candide, that the baroness had a pretty little chamber-maid, called Paquette? Well, it was in her arms that I tasted those heavenly ecstasies which have produced the hellish torments with which you see me ravaged. She had the pest, and has already died from it, maybe. Paquette received this present from a very learned Franciscan friar, who acquired it with an unbroken pedigree, for he had it from an old countess, who got it from a cavalry captain, who owed it to a marquise, who received it from a page, who derived it from a Jesuit, who, while a novice, had it in direct descent from one of the companions of Christopher Columbus. As for me, I shan't give it to anybody, because I'm dying."

"Oh, Pangloss!" cried Candide. "What a strange ancestry! The devil must have founded that family."

"Strange? Not at all!" replied the great man. "That ancestry was an indispensable ingredient of this best of all possible worlds, an essential constituent, because, if Columbus had missed catching in America this malady which taints the source of procreation, which often even stops procreation altogether, and is obviously opposed to nature's great purpose, we should have neither chocolate nor cochineal. Notice also that, up to date, this disease is peculiar to us in our continent. The Turks, Indians, Persians, Chinese, Siamese and Japanese, are still ignorant of its existence even; but there is a self-sufficient reason for supposing that, in a few centuries, they in their turn will make its acquaintance. Meanwhile, among us, the malady has made marvellous progress, especially in those large armies of fine, heroic mercenaries, which decide the destinies of nations. You can be certain that when thirty thousand men are thrown at war against another thirty thousand, about twenty thousand on each side die from the pox."

"That's excellent," said Candide. "But now you've got to be cured."

"And how can I be cured?" asked Pangloss. "I haven't a sou, my friend, and no doctor on this earth will bleed me or treat me free of charge."

These last words decided Candide. He went and threw himself at the feet of that charitable Anabaptist, Jacques, and painted so touching a picture of the condition to which his friend was reduced, that the good man hastened to assist Doctor Pangloss, and had him cured at his own expense. As a result of the cure, Pangloss lost only an eye and an ear.

As the Doctor read well, and knew arithmetic perfectly, Jacques made him his book-keeper, and having, after a couple of months, to go to Lisbon on business, he took the two philosophers with him on his ship. Pangloss explained to him how this was the best of all possible worlds. Jacques did not agree.

"I think men must have corrupted nature somewhat," said he. "They were not born wolves, yet they have become wolves. God never gave them either cannons or bayonets, yet they've made cannons and bayonets in order to destroy themselves. I might quote the parallel of Bankruptcy and the Justice which seizes the goods of the bankrupt in order to disappoint the creditors."

"All that's absolutely necessary," replied the one-eyed doctor. "Individual misfortunes make for the general good, so that the more trouble a man has, the better it is for everyone else."

"While he was discoursing, the sky became clouded, the wind blew from the four corners of the globe, and the ship was struck by a terrific storm, in full sight of the port of Lisbon.

THOMAS JEFFERSON

DECLARATION OF INDEPENDENCE

Thomas Jefferson (1743–1826) was the third president of the United States. Jefferson was a remarkable figure—an Enlightenment intellectual, a prolific writer, an architect, a scientist, an agriculturalist, an educational theorist, a diplomat, a politician, and a leader. One of America's "founding fathers," Jefferson is credited with having drafted the "Declaration of Independence," which states in language both eloquent and powerful the guiding principles upon which the American nation was founded. In its bold assertion of freedom from tyranny, it details the reasons American political leaders established their own government separate from that of its colonial master; England. The Declaration was adopted by Congress on July 4, 1776.

THE DECLARATION OF INDEPENDENCE AS ADOPTED BY CONGRESS

In Congress July 4, 1776

The Unanimous Declaration of the Thirteen United States of America

When in the Course of human events, it becomes necessary for one people to dissolve the political bands which have connected them with another, and to assume among the powers of the earth, the separate and equal station to which the Laws of Nature and of Nature's God entitle them, a decent respect to the opinions of mankind requires that they should declare the causes which impel them to the separation. We hold these truths to be self-evident, that all men are created equal, that they are endowed by their Creator with certain unalienable Rights, that among these are Life, Liberty and the pursuit of Happiness. That to secure these rights, Governments are instituted among Men, deriving their just powers from the consent of the governed, That whenever any Form of Government becomes destructive of these ends, it is the Right of the People to alter or to abolish it, and to institute new Government, laying its foundation on such principles and organizing its powers in such form, as to them shall seem most likely to effect their Safety and Happiness. Prudence, indeed, will dictate that Governments long established should not be changed for light and transient causes; and accordingly all experience hath shewn, that mankind are more disposed to suffer, while evils are sufferable, than to right themselves by abolishing the forms to which they are accustomed. But when a long train of abuses and usurpations, pursuing invariably the same Object evinces a design to reduce them under absolute Despotism, it is their right, it is their duty, to throw off such Government, and to provide new Guards for their future security. Such has been the patient sufferance of these Colonies; and such is now the necessity which constrains them to alter their former Systems of Government. The history of the present King of Great Britain is a history of repeated injuries and usurpations, all having in direct object the establishment of an absolute Tyranny over these States. To prove this, let Facts be submitted to a candid world. He has refused his Assent to Laws, the most wholesome and necessary for the public good. He has forbidden his Governors to pass Laws of immediate and pressing importance, unless suspended in their operation till his Assent should be obtained; and when so suspended, he has utterly neglected to attend to them. He has refused to pass other Laws for the accommodation of large districts of people, unless those people would relinquish the right of Representation in the Legislature, a right inestimable to them and formidable to tyrants only. He has called together legislative bodies at places unusual, uncomfortable, and distant from the depository of their public Records, for the sole purpose of fatiguing them into compliance with his measures. He has dissolved Representative Houses repeatedly, for opposing with manly firmness his invasions on the rights of the people. He has refused for a long time, after such dissolutions, to cause others to be elected; whereby the Legislative powers, incapable of Annihilation, have returned to the People at large for their exercise; the State remaining in the mean time exposed to all the dangers of invasion from without, and convulsions within. He has endeavoured to prevent the population of these States; for that purpose obstructing the Laws for Naturalization of Foreigners; refusing to pass others to encourage their migrations hither, and raising the conditions of new Appropriations of Lands. He has obstructed the Administration of Justice, by refusing his Assent to Laws for establishing Judiciary powers. He has made Judges dependent on his Will alone, for the tenure of their offices, and the amount and payment of their salaries. He has erected a multitude of New Offices, and sent hither swarms of Officers to harrass our people, and eat out their substance. He has kept among us, in times of peace, standing Armies without the Consent of our legislatures. He has affected to render the Military independent of and superior to the Civil power. He has combined with others to subject us to a jurisdiction foreign to our constitution, and unacknowledged by our laws; giving his Assent to their Acts of pretended Legislation: For Quartering large bodies of armed troops among us: For protecting them, by a mock Trial, from punishment for any Murders which they should commit on the Inhabitants of these States: For cutting off our Trade with all parts of the world: For imposing Taxes on us without our Consent: For depriving us in many cases of the benefits of Trial by Jury: For transporting us beyond Seas to be tried for pretended offences: For abolishing the free System of English Laws in a neighbouring Province, establishing therein an Arbitrary government, and enlarging its Boundaries so as to render it at once an example and fit instrument for introducing the same absolute rule into these Colonies: For taking away our Charters, abolishing our most valuable Laws, and altering fundamentally the Forms of our Governments: For suspending our own Legislatures, and declaring themselves invested with power to legislate for us in all cases whatsoever. He has abdicated Government here, by declaring us out of his Protection and waging War against us. He has plundered our seas, ravaged our Coasts, burnt our towns, and destroyed the Lives of our people. He is at this time transporting large Armies of foreign Mercenaries to compleat the works of death, desolation and tyranny, already begun with circumstances of Cruelty & perfidy scarcely paralleled in the most barbarous ages, and totally unworthy the Head of a civilized nation. He has constrained our fellow Citizens taken

Captive on the high Seas to bear Arms against their Country, to become the executioners of their friends and Brethren, or to fall themselves by their Hands. He has excited domestic insurrections amongst us, and has endeavoured to bring on the inhabitants of our frontiers, the merciless Indian Savages, whose known rule of warfare, is an undistinguished destruction of all ages, sexes and conditions. In every stage of these Oppressions We have Petitioned for Redress in the most humble terms: Our repeated Petitions have been answered only by repeated injury. A Prince, whose character is thus marked by every act which may define a Tyrant, is unfit to be the ruler of a free people. Nor have We been wanting in attentions to our Brittish brethren. We have warned them from time to time of attempts by their legislature to extend an unwarrantable jurisdiction over us. We have reminded them of the circumstances of our emigration and settlement here. We have appealed to their native justice and magnanimity, and we have conjured them by the ties of our common kindred to disavow these usurpations, which, would inevitably interrupt our connections and correspondence. They too have been deaf to the voice of justice and of consanguinity. We must, therefore, acquiesce in the necessity, which denounces our Separation, and hold them, as we hold the rest of mankind, Enemies in War, in Peace Friends.

We, therefore, the Representatives of the united States of America, in General Congress, Assembled, appealing to the Supreme Judge of the world for the rectitude of our intentions, do, in the Name, and by Authority of the good People of these Colonies, solemnly publish and declare, That these United Colonies are, and of Right ought to be Free and Independent States; that they are Absolved from all Allegiance to the British Crown, and that all political connection between them and the State of Great Britain, is and ought to be totally dissolved; and that as Free and Independent States, they have full Power to levy War, conclude Peace, contract Alliances, establish Commerce, and to do all other Acts and Things which Independent States may of right do. And for the support of this Declaration, with a firm reliance on the protection of divine Providence, we mutually pledge to each other our Lives, our Fortunes and our sacred Honor.

DECLARATION OF THE RIGHTS OF MAN AND CITIZEN

In August 1789, the National Constituent Assembly of France decided to declare a new set of political principles. The French Declaration of the Rights of Man and Citizen was clearly a product of the Age of Reason, with noticeable influences from Jefferson's American Declaration of Independence, Locke's theory of inalienable human rights ("life, liberty, and property"), and the constitutional principles recently established in England. Like the American declaration, France's document proclaimed civic equality, rights to own property, rights to security, and the protection from oppression. And like the American declaration, all of these innate rights applied only to men, not to women. It was for this reason that women like Olympe de Gouges and Mary Wollstonecraft found it necessary to speak out for female rights.

The representatives of the French people, organized in National Assembly, considering that ignorance, forgetfulness, or contempt of the rights of man are the sole causes of public misfortunes and of the corruption of governments, have resolved to set forth in a solemn declaration the natural, inalienable, and sacred rights of man, in order that such declaration, continually before all members of the social body, may be a perpetual reminder of their rights and duties; in order that the acts of the legislative power and those of the executive power may constantly be compared with the aim of every political institution and may accordingly be more respected; in order that the demands of the citizens, founded henceforth upon simple and incontestable principles, may always be directed towards the maintenance of the Constitution and the welfare of all.

Accordingly the National Assembly recognizes and proclaims, in the presence and under the auspices of the Supreme Being, the following rights of man and citizen.

1. Men are born and remain free and equal in rights; social distinctions may be based only upon general usefulness.

2. The aim of every political association is the preservation of the natural and inalienable rights of man; these rights are liberty, property, security, and resistance to oppression.

3. The source of all sovereignty resides essentially in the nation; no group, no individual may exercise authority not emanating expressly therefrom.

4. Liberty consists of the power to do whatever is not injurious to others; thus the enjoyment of the natural rights of every man has for its limits only those that assure other members of society the enjoyment of those same rights; such limits may be determined only by law.

5. The law has the right to forbid only actions which are injurious to society. Whatever is not forbidden by law may not be prevented, and no one may be constrained to do what it does not prescribe.

6. Law is the expression of the general will; all citizens have the right to concur personally, or through their representatives, in its formation; it must be the same for all, whether it protects or punishes. All citizens, being equal before it, are equally admissible to all public offices, positions, and employments, according to their capacity, and without other distinction than that of virtues and talents.

7. No man may be accused, arrested, or detained except in the cases determined by law, and according to the forms prescribed thereby. Whoever solicit, expedite, or execute arbitrary orders, or have them executed, must be punished; but every citizen summoned or apprehended in pursuance of the law must obey immediately; he renders himself culpable by resistance.

8. The law is to establish only penalties that are absolutely and obviously necessary; and no one may be punished except by virtue of a law established and promulgated prior to the offence and legally applied.

9. Since every man is presumed innocent until declared guilty, if arrest be deemed indispensable, all unnecessary severity for securing the person of the accused must be severely repressed by law.

10. No one is to be disquieted because of his opinions, even religious, provided their manifestation does not disturb the public order established by law.

11. Free communication of ideas and opinions is one of the most precious of the rights of man. Consequently, every

citizen may speak, write, and print freely, subject to responsibility for the abuse of such liberty in the cases determined by law.

12. The guarantee of the rights of man and citizen necessitates a public force; such a force, therefore, is instituted for the advantage of all and not for the particular benefit of those to whom it is entrusted.

13. For the maintenance of the public force and for the expenses of administration a common tax is indispensable; it must be assessed equally on all citizens in proportion to their means.

14. Citizens have the right to ascertain, by themselves or through their representatives, the necessity of the public tax, to consent to it freely, to supervise its use, and to determine its quota, assessment, payment, and duration.

15. Society has the right to require of every public agent an accounting of his administration.

16. Every society in which the guarantee of rights is not assured or the separation of powers not determined has no constitution at all.

17. Since property is a sacred and inviolable right, no one may be deprived thereof unless a legally established public necessity obviously requires it, and upon condition of a just and previous indemnity.

JANE AUSTEN

from *Pride and Prejudice*

Jane Austen's Pride and Prejudice *(1813) beautifully exemplifies her ironic tone and her incisive intelligence. The novel's opening sentence cuts immediately to the issues at the heart of Austen's world: money, status, marriage, and family relations. Although the author anchors these concerns in the particularities of early nineteenth-century pre-industrial England, her book is still relevant today for its insight into human nature.*

In the following passage readers are introduced to the Bennet family—father, mother, and daughters—and within the space of a few pages, Austen has characterized each distinctively. She also conveys crisply her attitude toward them, making comedy out of their anxieties, their habits, and their dispositions. In fact, the novel can be described as a comedy of manners.

CHAPTER 1

It is a truth universally acknowledged, that a single man in possession of a good fortune, must be in want of a wife.

However little known the feelings or views of such a man may be on his first entering a neighbourhood, this truth is so well fixed in the minds of the surrounding families, that he is considered as the rightful property of some one or other of their daughters.

"My dear Mr Bennet," said his lady to him one day, "have you heard that Netherfield Park is let at last?"

Mr Bennet replied that he had not.

"But it is," returned she; "for Mrs Long has just been here, and she told me all about it."

Mr Bennet made no answer.

"Do not you want to know who has taken it?" cried his wife impatiently.

"*You* want to tell me, and I have no objection to hearing it."

This was invitation enough.

"Why, my dear, you must know, Mrs Long says that Netherfield is taken by a young man of large fortune from the north of England; that he came down on Monday in a chaise and four to see the place, and was so much delighted with it that he agreed with Mr Morris immediately; that he is to take possession before Michaelmas, and some of his servants are to be in the house by the end of next week."

"What is his name?"

"Bingley."

"Is he married or single?"

"Oh! single, my dear, to be sure! A single man of large fortune; four or five thousand a year. What a fine thing for our girls!"

"How so? how can it affect them?"

"My dear Mr Bennet," replied his wife, "how can you be so tiresome! You must know that I am thinking of his marrying one of them."

"Is that his design in settling here?"

"Design! nonsense, how can you talk so! But it is very likely that he *may* fall in love with one of them, and therefore you must visit him as soon as he comes."

"I see no occasion for that. You and the girls may go, or you may send them by themselves, which perhaps will be still better, for as you are as handsome as any of them, Mr Bingley might like you the best of the party."

"My dear, you flatter me. I certainly *have* had my share of beauty, but I do not pretend to be any thing extraordinary now. When a woman has five grown up daughters, she ought to give over thinking of her own beauty."

"In such cases, a woman has not often much beauty to think of."

"But, my dear, you must indeed go and see Mr Bingley when he comes into the neighbourhood."

"It is more than I engage for, I assure you."

"But consider your daughters. Only think what an establishment it would be for one of them. Sir William and Lady Lucas are determined to go, merely on that account, for in general you know they visit no new comers. Indeed you must go, for it will be impossible for *us* to visit him, if you do not."

"You are over scrupulous surely. I dare say Mr Bingley will be very glad to see you; and I will send a few lines by you to assure him of my hearty consent to his marrying which ever he chuses of the girls; though I must throw in a good word for my little Lizzy."

"I desire you will do no such thing. Lizzy is not a bit better than the others; and I am sure she is not half so handsome as Jane, nor half so good humored as Lydia. But you are always giving *her* the preference."

"They have none of them much to recommend them," replied he; "they are all silly and ignorant like other girls; but Lizzy has something more of quickness than her sisters."

"Mr Bennet, how can you abuse your own children in such a way? You take delight in vexing me. You have no compassion on my poor nerves."

"You mistake me, my dear. I have a high respect for your nerves. They are my old friends. I have heard you mention them with consideration these twenty years at least."

"Ah! you do not know what I suffer."

"But I hope you will get over it, and live to see many young men of four thousand a year come into the neighbourhood."

"It will be no use to us, if twenty such should come since you will not visit them."

"Depend upon it, my dear, that when there are twenty, I will visit them all."

Mr Bennet was so odd a mixture of quick parts, sarcastic humour, reserve, and caprice, that the experience of three and twenty years had been sufficient to make his wife understand his character. *Her* mind was less difficult to develop. She was a woman of mean understanding, little information, and uncertain temper. When she was discontented she fancied herself nervous. The business of her life was to get her daughters married; its solace was visiting and news.

Chapter 2

Mr Bennet was among the earliest of those who waited on Mr Bingley. He had always intended to visit him, though to the last always assuring his wife that he should not go; and till the evening after the visit was paid, she had no knowledge of it. It was then disclosed in the following manner. Observing his second daughter employed in trimming a hat, he suddenly addressed her with,

"I hope Mr Bingley will like it Lizzy."

"We are not in a way to know *what* Mr Bingley likes," said her mother resentfully, "since we are not to visit."

"But you forget, mama," said Elizabeth, "that we shall meet him at the assemblies, and that Mrs Long has promised to introduce him."

"I do not believe Mrs Long will do any such thing. She has two nieces of her own. She is a selfish, hypocritical woman, and I have no opinion of her."

"No more have I," said Mr Bennet; "and I am glad to find that you do not depend on her serving you."

Mrs Bennet deigned not to make any reply; but unable to contain herself, began scolding one of her daughters.

"Don't keep coughing so, Kitty, for heaven's sake! Have a little compassion on my nerves. You tear them to pieces."

"Kitty has no discretion in her coughs," said her father; "she times them ill."

"I do not cough for my own amusement," replied Kitty fretfully.

"When is your next ball to be, Lizzy?"

"To-morrow fortnight."

"Aye, so it is," cried her mother, "and Mrs Long does not come back till the day before; so, it will be impossible for her to introduce him, for she will not know him herself."

"Then, my dear, you may have the advantage of your friend, and introduce Mr Bingley to *her.*"

"Impossible, Mr Bennet, impossible, when I am not acquainted with him myself; how can you be so teazing?"

"I honour your circumspection. A fortnight's acquaintance is certainly very little. One cannot know what a man really is by the end of a fortnight. But if *we* do not venture, somebody else will; and after all, Mrs Long and her nieces must stand their chance; and therefore, as she will think it an act of kindness, if you decline the office, I will take it on myself."

The girls stared at their father. Mrs Bennet said only, "Nonsense, nonsense!"

"What can be the meaning of that emphatic exclamation?" cried he. "Do you consider the forms of introduction, and the stress that is laid on them, as nonsense? I cannot quite agree with you *there*. What say you, Mary? for you are a young

lady of deep reflection I know, and read great books, and make extracts."

Mary wished to say something very sensible, but knew not how.

"While Mary is adjusting her ideas," he continued, "Let us return to Mr Bingley."

"I am sick of Mr Bingley," cited his wife.

"I am sorry to hear that; but why did not you tell me so before? If I had known as much this morning, I certainly would not have called on him. It is very unlucky; but as I have actually paid the visit, we cannot escape the acquaintance now."

The astonishment of the ladies was just what he wished; that of Mrs Bennet perhaps surpassing the rest; though when the first tumult of joy was over, she began to declare that it was what she had expected all the while.

"How good it was in you, my dear Mr Bennet! But I knew I should persuade you at last. I was sure you loved your girls too well to neglect such an acquaintance. Well, how pleased I am! and it is such a good joke, too, that you should have gone this morning, and never said a word about it till now."

"Now, Kitty, you may cough as much as you choose," said Mr Bennet; and, as he spoke, he left the room, fatigued with the raptures of his wife.

"What an excellent father you have, girls," said she, when the door was shut. "I do not know how you will ever make him amends for his kindness; or me either, for that matter. At our time of life, it is not so pleasant I can tell you, to be making new acquaintance every day; but for your sakes, we would do any thing. Lydia, my love, though you *are* the youngest, I dare say Mr Bingley will dance with you at the next ball."

"Oh!" said Lydia stoutly, "I am not afraid; for though I *am* the youngest, I'm the tallest."

The rest of the evening was spent in conjecturing how soon he would return Mr Bennet's visit, and determining when they should ask him to dinner.

MARY WOLLSTONECRAFT

from *A Vindication of the Rights of Woman*

Wollstonecraft's Vindication *is a polemic, an argumentative discourse, whose central purpose is to persuade readers of the unjust treatment of women in late-eighteenth-century British society. Wollstonecraft's strategy is to compare the plight of women to that of the working poor and to show that women's grievances and oppression were equal to if not greater than those of the working class. Her essay, an early and influential analysis of social roles, became an important model for later feminist discourse.*

Women in Society

. . . The preposterous distinctions of rank, which render civilization a curse, by dividing the world between voluptuous tyrants and cunning envious dependents, corrupt, almost equally, every class of people, because respectability is not attached to the discharge of the relative duties of life, but to the station, and when the duties are not fulfilled the affections cannot gain sufficient strength to fortify the virtue of which they are the natural reward. Still there are some loopholes out of which a man may creep, and dare to think and act for himself; but for a woman it is an herculean task, because she has difficulties peculiar to her sex to overcome, which require almost superhuman powers.

A truly benevolent legislator always endeavours to make it the interest of each individual to be virtuous; and thus private virtue becoming the cement of public happiness, an orderly whole is consolidated by the tendency of all the parts towards a common centre. But the private or public virtue of woman is very problematical, for Rousseau, and a numerous list of male writers, insist that she should all her life be subjected to a severe restraint, that of propriety. Why subject her to propriety—blind propriety—if she be capable of acting from a nobler spring, if she be an heir of immortality? Is sugar always to be produced by vital blood? Is one half of the human species, like the poor African slaves, to be subjected to prejudices that brutalize them, when principles would be a surer guard, only to sweeten the cup of man? Is not this indirectly to deny woman reason? for a gift is a mockery, if it be unfit for use.

Women are, in common with men, rendered weak and luxurious by the relaxing pleasures which wealth procures; but added to this they are made slaves to their persons, and must render them alluring that man may lend them his reason to guide their tottering steps aright. Or should they be ambitious, they must govern their tyrants by sinister tricks, for without rights there cannot be any incumbent duties. The laws respecting woman . . . make an absurd unit of a man and his wife; and then, by the easy transition of only considering him as responsible, she is reduced to a mere cipher.

The being who discharges the duties of its station is independent; and, speaking of women at large, their first duty is to themselves as rational creatures, and the next, in point of importance, as citizens, is that, which includes so many, of a mother. The rank in life which dispenses with their fulfilling this duty, necessarily degrades them by making them mere dolls. Or should they turn to something more important than merely fitting drapery upon a smooth block, their minds are only occupied by some soft platonic attachment; or the actual management of an intrigue may keep their thoughts in motion; for when they neglect domestic duties, they have it not in their power to take the field and march and counter-march like soldiers, or wrangle in the senate to keep their faculties from rusting.

I know that, as a proof of the inferiority of the sex, Rousseau has exultingly exclaimed, How can they leave the nursery for the camp! And the camp has by some moralists been proved the school of the most heroic virtues, though I think it would puzzle a keen casuist to prove the reasonableness of the greater number of wars that have dubbed heroes. I do not mean to consider this question critically; because, having frequently viewed these freaks of ambition as the first natural mode of civilization, when the ground must be torn up, and the woods cleared by fire and sword, I do not choose to call them pests; but surely the present system of war has little connection with virtue of any denomination, being rather the school of *finesse* and effeminacy than of fortitude.

Yet, if defensive war, the only justifiable war, in the present advanced state of society, where virtue can show its face and ripen amidst the rigours which purify the air on the mountain's top, were alone to be adopted as just and glorious, the true heroism of antiquity might again animate female bosoms. But fair and softly, gentle reader, male or female, do not alarm thyself, for though I have compared the character of a modern soldier with that of a civilized woman, I am not going to advise them to turn their distaff into a musket, though I sincerely wish to see the bayonet converted into a pruning-hook. I only re-created an imagination, fatigued by contemplating the vices and follies which all proceed from a feculent stream of wealth that has muddied the pure rills of natural affection, by supposing that society will some time or other be so constituted, that man must necessarily fulfil the duties of a citizen, or be despised, and that while he was employed in any of the departments of civil life, his wife, also an active citizen, should be equally intent to manage her family, educate her children, and assist her neighbours.

But to render her really virtuous and useful, she must not, if she discharge her civil duties, want individually the protection of civil laws; she must not be dependent on her husband's bounty for her subsistence during his life, or support after his death; for how can a being be generous who has nothing of its own? or virtuous who is not free? The wife, in the present state of things, who is faithful to her husband, and neither suckles nor educates her children, scarcely deserves the name of a wife, and has no right to that of a citizen. But take away natural rights, and duties become null.

Women then must be considered as only the wanton solace of men, when they become so weak in mind and body that they cannot exert themselves unless to pursue some frothy pleasure, or to invent some frivolous fashion. What can be a more melancholy sight to a thinking mind, than to look into the numerous carriage that drive helter-skelter about this metropolis in a morning full of pale-faced creatures who are flying from themselves! I have often wished, with Dr Johnson, to place some of them in a little shop with half a dozen children looking up to their languid countenances for support. I am much mistaken, if some latent vigour would not soon give health and spirit to their eyes, and some lines drawn by the exercise of reason on the blank cheeks, which before were only undulated by dimples, might restore lost dignity to the character, or rather enable it to attain the true dignity of its nature. Virtue is not to be acquired even by speculation, much less by the negative supineness that wealth naturally generates.

Besides, when poverty is more disgraceful than even vice, is not morality cut to the quick? Still to avoid misconstruction, though I consider that women in the common walks of life are called to fulfil the duties of wives and mothers, by religion and reason, I cannot help lamenting that women of a superior cast have not a road open by which they can pursue more extensive plans of usefulness and independence. I may excite laughter, by dropping a hint, which I mean to pursue, some future time, for I really think that women ought to have representatives, instead of being arbitrarily governed without having any direct share allowed them in the deliberations of government.

But, as the whole system of representation is now, in this country, only a convenient handle for despotism, they need not complain, for they are as well represented as a numerous class of hard-working mechanics, who pay for the support of royalty when they can scarcely stop their children's mouths with bread. How are they represented whose very sweat supports the splendid stud of an heir-apparent, or varnishes the chariot of some female favourite who looks down on shame? Taxes on the very necessaries of life, enable an endless tribe of idle princes and princesses to pass with stupid pomp before a gaping crowd, who almost worship the very parade which costs them so dear. This is mere gothic grandeur, something like the barbarous useless parade of having sentinels on horseback at Whitehall, which I could never view without a mixture of contempt and indignation.

How strangely must the mind be sophisticated when this sort of state impresses it! But, till these monuments of folly are levelled by virtue, similar follies will leaven the whole mass. For the same character, in some degree, will prevail in the aggregate of society; and the refinements of luxury, or the vicious repinings of envious poverty, will equally banish virtue from society, considered as the characteristic of that society, or only allow it to appear as one of the stripes of the harlequin coat, worn by the civilized man.

In the superior ranks of life, every duty is done by deputies, as if duties could ever be waived, and the vain pleasures which consequent idleness forces the rich to pursue, appear so enticing to the next rank, that the numerous scramblers for wealth sacrifice everything to tread on their heels. The most sacred trusts are then considered as sinecures, because they were procured by interest, and only sought to enable a man to keep *good company*. Women, in particular, all want to be ladies. Which is simply to have nothing to do, but listlessly to go they scarcely care where, for they cannot tell what.

But what have women to do in society? I may be asked, but to loiter with easy grace; surely you would not condemn them all to suckle fools and chronicle small beer! No. Women might certainly study the art of healing and be physicians as well as nurses. And midwifery, decency seems to allot to them though I am afraid the word midwife, in our dictionaries, will soon give place to *accoucheur*, and one proof of the former delicacy of the sex be effaced from the language.

They might also study politics, and settle their benevolence on the broadest basis; for the reading of history will scarcely be more useful than the perusal of romances, if read as mere biography; if the character of the times, the political improvements, arts, etc., be not observed. In short, if it be not considered as the history of man; and not of particular men, who filled a niche in the temple of fame, and dropped into the black rolling stream of time, that silently sweeps all before it into the shapeless void called—eternity.—For shape, can it be called, 'that shape hath none'?

Business of various kinds, they might likewise pursue, if they were educated in a more orderly manner, which might save many from common and legal prostitution. Women would not then marry for a support, as men accept of places under Government, and neglect the implied duties; nor would an attempt to earn their own subsistence, a most laudable one! sink them almost to the level of those poor abandoned creatures who live by prostitution. For are not milliners and mantuamakers reckoned the next class? The few employments open to women, so far from being liberal, are menial; and when a superior education enables them to take charge of the education of children as governesses, they are not treated like the tutors of sons, though even clerical tutors are not always treated in a manner calculated to render them respectable in the eyes of their pupils, to say nothing of the private comfort of the individual. But as women educated like gentlewomen, are never designed for the humiliating situation which necessity sometimes forces them to fill; these situations are considered in the light of a degradation; and they know little of

the human heart, who need to be told, that nothing so painfully sharpens sensibility as such a fall in life.

Some of these women might be restrained from marrying by a proper spirit of delicacy, and others may not have had it in their power to escape in this pitiful way from servitude; is not that Government then very defective, and very unmindful of the happiness of one-half of its members, that does not provide for honest, independent women, by encouraging them to fill respectable stations? But in order to render their private virtue a public benefit, they must have a civil existence in the State, married or single; else we shall continually see some worthy woman, whose sensibility has been rendered painfully acute by undeserved contempt, droop like 'the lily broken down by a plowshare'.

It is a melancholy truth; yet such is the blessed effect of civilization! the most respectable women are the most oppressed; and, unless they have understandings far superior to the common run of understandings, taking in both sexes, they must, from being treated like contemptible beings, become contemptible. How many women thus waste life away the prey of discontent, who might have practised as physicians, regulated a farm, managed a shop, and stood erect, supported by their own industry, instead of hanging their heads surcharged with the dew of sensibility, that consumes the beauty to which it at first gave lustre; nay, I doubt whether pity and love are so near akin as poets feign, for I have seldom seen much compassion excited by the helplessness of females, unless they were fair; then, perhaps, pity was the soft handmaid of love, or the harbinger of lust.

How much more respectable is the woman who earns her own bread by fulfilling any duty, than the most accomplished beauty!—beauty did I say!—so sensible am I of the beauty of moral loveliness, or the harmonious propriety that attunes the passions of a well-regulated mind, that I blush at making the comparison; yet I sigh to think how few women aim at attaining this respectability by withdrawing from the giddy whirl of pleasure, or the indolent calm that stupefies the good sort of women it sucks in.

Proud of their weakness, however, they must always be protected, guarded from care, and all the rough toils that dignify the mind. If this be the fiat of fate, if they will make themselves insignificant and contemptible, sweetly to waste 'life away', let them not expect to be valued when their beauty fades, for it is the fate of the fairest flowers to be admired and pulled to pieces by the careless hand that plucked them. In how many ways do I wish, from the purest benevolence, to impress this truth on my sex; yet I fear that they will not listen to a truth that dear bought experience has brought home to many an agitated bosom, nor willingly resign the privileges of rank and sex for the privileges of humanity, to which those have no claim who do not discharge its duties.

Those writers are particularly useful, in my opinion, who make man feel for man, independent of the station he fills, or the drapery of factitious sentiments. I then would fain convince reasonable men of the importance of some of my remarks; and prevail on them to weigh dispassionately the whole tenor of my observations. I appeal to their understandings; and, as a fellow-creature, claim, in the name of my sex, some interest in their hearts. I entreat them to assist to emancipate their companion, to make her a *helpmeet* for them.

Would men but generously snap our chains, and be content with rational fellowship instead of slavish obedience, they would find us more observant daughters, more affectionate sisters, more faithful wives, more reasonable mothers—in a word, better citizens. We should then love them with true affection, because we should learn to respect ourselves; and the peace of mind of a worthy man would not be interrupted by the idle vanity of his wife, nor the babes sent to nestle in a strange bosom, having never found a home in their mother's.

THOMAS PAINE

Thomas Paine (1737–1809), revolutionary writer, is best known for his pamphlet Common Sense, *published in Philadelphia in 1776, which argued for the colonies' independence from Britain. His* The Rights of Man, *published in England fifteen years later, was written in support of the French Revolution. Paine's ideas about religion were published in* The Age of Reason, *the first chapter of which appears here.*

from Age of Reason, Part First, Section 1

It has been my intention, for several years past, to publish my thoughts upon religion. I am well aware of the difficulties that attend the subject, and from that consideration, had reserved it to a more advanced period of life. I intended it to be the last offering I should make to my fellow-citizens of all nations, and that at a time when the purity of the motive that induced me to it, could not admit of a question, even by those who might disapprove the work.

The circumstance that has now taken place in France of the total abolition of the whole national order of priesthood, and of everything appertaining to compulsive systems of religion, and compulsive articles of faith, has not only precipitated my intention, but rendered a work of this kind exceedingly necessary, lest in the general wreck of superstition, of false systems of government, and false theology, we lose sight of morality, of humanity, and of the theology that is true.

As several of my colleagues and others of my fellow-citizens of France have given me the example of making their voluntary and individual profession of faith, I also will make mine; and I do this with all that sincerity and frankness with which the mind of man communicates with itself.

I believe in one God, and no more; and I hope for happiness beyond this life.

I believe in the equality of man; and I believe that religious duties consist in doing justice, loving mercy, and endeavoring to make our fellow-creatures happy.

But, lest it should be supposed that I believe in many other things in addition to these, I shall, in the progress of this work, declare the things I do not believe, and my reasons for not believing them.

I do not believe in the creed professed by the Jewish church, by the Roman church, by the Greek church, by the Turkish church, by the Protestant church, nor by any church that I know of. My own mind is my own church.

All national institutions of churches, whether Jewish, Christian or Turkish, appear to me no other than human inventions, set up to terrify and enslave mankind, and monopolize power and profit.

I do not mean by this declaration to condemn those who believe otherwise; they have the same right to their belief as I have to mine. But it is necessary to the happiness of man, that he be mentally faithful to himself. Infidelity does not consist in believing, or in disbelieving; it consists in professing to believe what he does not believe.

It is impossible to calculate the moral mischief, if I may so express it, that mental lying has produced in society. When a man has so far corrupted and prostituted the chastity of his mind, as to subscribe his professional belief to things he does not believe, he has prepared himself for the commission of every other crime. He takes up the trade of a priest for the sake of gain, and in order to qualify himself for that trade, he begins with a perjury. Can we conceive any thing more destructive to morality than this?

Soon after I had published the pamphlet Common Sense, in America, I saw the exceeding probability that a revolution in the system of government would be followed by a revolution in the system of religion. The adulterous connection of church and state, wherever it had taken place, whether Jewish, Christian, or Turkish, had so effectually prohibited by pains and penalties, every discussion upon established creeds, and upon first principles of religion, that until the system of government should be changed, those subjects could not be brought fairly and openly before the world; but that whenever this should be done, a revolution in the system of religion would follow. Human inventions and priestcraft would be detected; and man would return to the pure, unmixed and unadulterated belief of one God, and no more.

Every national church or religion has established itself by pretending some special mission from God, communicated to certain individuals. The Jews have their Moses; the Christians their Jesus Christ, their apostles and saints; and the Turks their Mahomet, as if the way to God was not open to every man alike.

Each of those churches show certain books, which they call revelation, or the word of God. The Jews say, that their word of God was given by God to Moses, face to face; the Christians say, that their word of God came by divine inspiration: and the Turks say, that their word of God (the Koran) was brought by an angel from Heaven. Each of those churches accuse the other of unbelief; and for my own part, I disbelieve them all.

As it is necessary to affix right ideas to words, I will, before I proceed further into the subject, offer some other observations on the word revelation. Revelation, when applied to religion, means something communicated immediately from God to man.

No one will deny or dispute the power of the Almighty to make such a communication, if he pleases. But admitting, for the sake of a case, that something has been revealed to a certain person, and not revealed to any other person, it is revelation to that person only. When he tells it to a second person, a second to a third, a third to a fourth, and so on, it ceases to be a revelation to all those persons. It is revelation to the first person only, and hearsay to every other, and consequently they are not obliged to believe it.

It is a contradiction in terms and ideas, to call anything a revelation that comes to us at second-hand, either verbally or in writing. Revelation is necessarily limited to the first communication—after this, it is only an account of something which that person says was a revelation made to him; and though he may find himself obliged to believe it, it cannot be incumbent on me to believe it in the same manner; for it was not a revelation made to me, and I have only his word for it that it was made to him.

When Moses told the children of Israel that he received the two tables of the commandments from the hands of God, they were not obliged to believe him, because they had no other authority for it than his telling them so; and I have no other authority for it than some historian telling me so. The commandments carry no internal evidence of divinity with them; they contain some good moral precepts, such as any man qualified to be a lawgiver, or a legislator, could produce himself, without having recourse to supernatural intervention. NOTE

BENJAMIN FRANKLIN

Benjamin Franklin (1706–90) American statesman, diplomat, scientist, publisher, and writer was one of America's founding fathers, and a signer of the Declaration of Independence. Throughout his life, Franklin sought to improve himself, as he was a conscious perfectionist. The following passage from his autobiography reveals his determination to achieve moral perfection and a method he used to make his attempt.

from Autobiography

It was about this time that I conceiv'd the bold and arduous Project of arriving at moral Perfection. I wish'd to live without committing any Fault at any time; I would conquer all that either Natural Inclination, Custom, or Company might lead me into. As I knew, or thought I knew, what was right and wrong, I did not see why I might not *always* do the one and avoid the other. But I soon found I had undertaken a Task of more Difficulty than I had imagined: While my Care was employ'd in guarding against one Fault, I was often surpriz'd by another. Habit took the Advantage of Inattention. Inclination was sometimes too strong for Reason. I concluded at length, that the mere speculative Conviction that it was our Interest to be compleatly virtuous, was not sufficient to prevent our Slipping, and that the contrary Habits must be broken and good Ones acquired and established, before we can have any Dependance on a steady uniform Rectitude of Conduct. For this purpose I therefore contriv'd the following Method.

In the various Enumerations of the moral Virtues I had met with in my Reading, I found the Catalogue more or less numerous, as different Writers included more or fewer Ideas under the same Name. Temperance, for Example, was by some confin'd to Eating and Drinking, while by others it was extended to mean the moderating every other Pleasure, Appetite, Inclination or Passion, bodily or mental, even to our Avarice and Ambition. I propos'd to myself, for the sake of Clearness, to use rather more Names with fewer Ideas annex'd to each, than a few Names with more Ideas; and I included after Thirteen Names of Virtues all that at that time occurr'd to me as necessary or desirable, and annex'd to each a short Precept, which fully express'd the Extent I gave to its Meaning.

These Names of Virtues with their Precepts were

1. *Temperance.* Eat not to Dulness. Drink not to Elevation.
2. *Silence.* Speak not but what may benefit others or your self. Avoid trifling conversation.
3. *Order.* Let all your Things have their Places. Let each Part of your Business have its Time.
4. *Resolution.* Resolve to perform what you ought. Perform without fail what you resolve.
5. *Frugality.* Make no Expence but to do good to others or yourself: i.e. Waste nothing.
6. *Industry.* Lose no Time. Be always employ'd in something useful. Cut off all unnecessary Actions.
7. *Sincerity.* Use no hurtful Deceit. Think innocently and justly; and, if you speak; speak accordingly.
8. *Justice.* Wrong none, by doing Injuries or omitting the Benefits that are your Duty.
9. *Moderation.* Avoid Extreams. Forbear resenting Injuries so much as you think they deserve.
10. *Cleanliness.* Tolerate no Uncleanness in Body, Cloaths or Habitation.
11. *Tranquility.* Be not disturbed at Trifles, or at Accidents common or unavoidable.
12. *Chastity.* Rarely use Venery but for Health or Offspring; Never to Dulness, Weakness, or the Injury of your own or another's Peace or Reputation.
13. *Humility.* Imitate Jesus and Socrates.

My intention being to acquire the *Habitude* of all these Virtues, I judg'd it would be well not to distract my Attention by attempting the whole at once, but to fix it on one of them at a time, and when I should be Master of that, then to proceed to another, and so on till I should have gone thro' the thirteen. And as the previous Acquisition of some might facilitate the Acquisition of certain others, I arrang'd them with that View as they stand above. *Temperance* first, as it tends to procure that Coolness and Clearness of Head, which is so necessary where constant Vigilance was to be kept up, and Guard maintained, against the unremitting Attraction of ancient Habits, and the Force of perpetual Temptations. This being acquir'd and establish'd, *Silence* would be more easy, and my Desire being to gain Knowledge at the same time that I improv'd in Virtue, and considering that in Conversation it was obtain'd rather by the Use of the Ears than of the Tongue, and therefore wishing to break a Habit I was getting into of Prattling, Punning and Joking, which only made me acceptable to trifling Company, I gave *Silence* the second Place. This, and the next, *Order*, I expected would allow me more Time for attending to my Project and my Studies; RESO-LUTION once become habitual, would keep me firm in my Endeavors to obtain all the subsequent Virtues; *Frugality* and *Industry*, by freeing me from my remaining Debt, and producing Affluence and Independance would make more easy the Practice of *Sincerity* and *Justice*, etc. etc. Conceiving then that agreable to the Advice of Pythagoras in his Golden Verses, daily examination would be necessary, I contriv'd the following Method for conducting that Examination.

I made a little Book in which I allotted a Page for each of the Virtues. I rul'd each Page with red Ink so as to have seven Columns, one for each Day of the Week, marking each Column with a Letter for the Day. I cross'd these Columns with thirteen red Lines, marking the Beginning of each Line with the first Letter of one of the Virtues, on which Line and in its

TEMPERANCE							
Eat not to Dulness.							
Drink not to Elevation.							
	S	M	T	W	T	F	S
T							
S	••	•		•		•	
O	•	•	•		•	•	•
R			•			•	
F		•			•		
I			•				
S							
J							
M							
Cl.							
T							
Ch.							
H							

proper Column I might mark by a little black Spot every Fault I found upon Examination, to have been committed respecting that Virtue upon that Day.

I determined to give a Week's strict Attention to each of the Virtues successively. Thus in the first Week my great Guard was to avoid every the least Offence against Temperance, leaving the other Virtues to their ordinary Chance, only marking every Evening the faults of the Day. Thus if in the first Week I could keep my first Line marked T clear of Spots, I suppos'd the Habit of that Virtue so much strengthen'd and its opposite weaken'd, that I might venture extending my Attention to include the next, and for the following Week keep both Lines clear of Spots. Proceeding thus to the last, I could go thro' a Course compleat in Thirteen Weeks, and four Courses in a Year. And like him who having a Garden to weed, does not attempt to eradicate all the bad Herbs at once, which would exceed his Reach and his Strength, but works on one of the Beds at a time, and having accomplish'd the first proceeds to a second; so I should have, (I hoped) the encouraging Pleasure of seeing on my Pages the Progress I made in Virtue, by clearing successively my Lines of their Spots, till in the End by a Number of Courses,

I should be happy in viewing a clean Book after a thirteen Weeks daily Examination. . . .

CHAPTER 17

HISTORY

1789–99	French Revolution
1804	Napoleon declared emperor
1848	Revolutions spread through Europe
1854	Pasteur develops pasteurization
1860s	American Civil War
1868	German empire proclaimed

ART, ARCHITECTURE, AND MUSIC

1814	Ingres, *La Grande Odalisque*
1814–15	Goya, *The Third of May*
1819	Gericault, *Raft of the Medusa*
1821	Constable, *The Haywain*
1824	Delacroix, *Scenes from the Massacres at Chios*
1830	Berlioz, *Symphonie Fantastique*
1830	New York Philharmonic founded
1833–36	Rude, *La Marseillaise*
1836	Barry and Pugin, Houses of Parliament
1840	Turner, *The Slave Ship*
1842	Chopin, Polonaise in A — flat, Op. 53
1849	Mozart's *Requiem* played at Chopin's funeral
1849	Bonheur, *Plowing in the Nievernais*
1851	Paxton, Crystal Palace
1863	Manet, *Luncheon on the Grass*
1868	Brahms' "Lullaby"
ca. 1872	Lewis, *The Old Indian Arrow Maker*
1875	Whitney, Charles Sumner
1887	Verdi, *Otello*
1887	Brownscombe, *Love's Young Dream*

LITERATURE AND PHILOSOPHY

1798	Wordsworth and Coleridge, *Lyrical Ballads*
1808	Goethe, *Faust*
1819–24	Lord Byron, *Don Juan*
1836	Emerson, *Nature*
1838	Dickens, *Oliver Twist*
1851	Melville, *Moby Dick*
1854	Thoreau, *Walden*
1855	Whitman, *Leaves of Grass*
1856	Flaubert, *Madame Bovary*
1859	Darwin, *On the Origin of the Species*
1860s	Dickinson, *Poems*
1872	Rousseau, *Confessions*
1877	Tolstoy, *Anna Karenina*
1881	Dostoyevsky, *The Brothers Karamazov*

Romanticism and Realism

Théodore Géricault, *Raft of the Medusa*, 1818–19, oil on canvas, 16′ 1″ × 23′ 6″ (4.9 × 7.16 m).
Musée du Louvre, Paris. Reunion des Musées Nationaux. Anauder/Art Resource, NY.

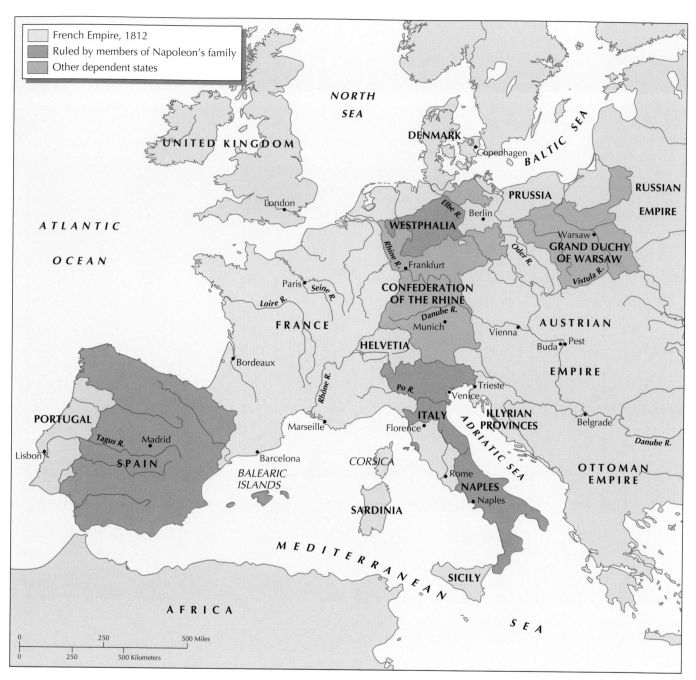

Legend:
- French Empire, 1812
- Ruled by members of Napoleon's family
- Other dependent states

MAP 17.1 Napoleon's Empire 1812

CHAPTER OVERVIEW

ROMANTICISM
The imagination runs wild

REALISM
The European sociopolitical scene turns the arts to everyday life

ROMANTICISM

BY 1800, NEOCLASSICISM WAS THE dominant style in European art and architecture, which suited Napoleon well. As early as 1805, Napoleon had begun to speak of his "Grand Empire," conceiving of it as a modern version of the Holy Roman Empire. In 1808, as part of his strategy to subdue the entire European continent, his troops crossed the Pyrenees into Spain, ostensibly on their way to Portugal, which was closely allied with the British. But once in Spain, Napoleon took advantage of the abdication of the unpopular Charles IV, refused to recognize his successor, Ferdinand VII, and took control of the country. At first, there was little resistance, but Napoleon discovered that just because the Spanish did not care for their king did not mean they were prepared to be ruled by a French emperor. Skirmishes broke out across the country. These "little wars," or *guerrillas* (the origin of our word for guerrilla warfare), forced Napoleon to withdraw large numbers of troops from Germany to fight in Spain, and soon full-scale war broke out.

In the meantime, an emerging new movement, **Romanticism,** provided a countertendency to the Neoclassical style. Romanticism is an attitude more than a style, but it depends on a growing trust in subjective experience, particularly in the emotions and feelings of individuals. The Romantics had a love for anything that elicits such feelings: the fantastic world of dreams, the exotic world of the Orient, the beauty of nature revealed in a sudden vista of hills exposed around a turn in an English garden, the forces of nature in a magnificent or unpredictable moment, such as a sunset after a storm.

Inexactitude and indeterminacy characterize this view of the world, and it can be discovered everywhere in this period. The Romantic painter Eugène Delacroix loved the **études** by a contemporary composer, Frédéric Chopin, for "their floating, indefinite contour . . . destroying the rigid frameworks of form . . . like sheets of mist." Mist was actually a favorite subject of many Romantic painters (fig. 17.1).

The Romantic attitude depends particularly on the concept of **originality.** Just as no aspect of an English garden should be like any other, no painter or author should imitate any other. The new Romantic genius stands alone, different from the rest, and unsurpassed—a true original.

In addition, the Romantic attitude is a mixture of belief in the natural goodness of man as expressed by Rousseau and in the autonomy of rational beings. Emanating from these central Romantic conceptions was empathy for the disadvantaged and the downtrodden apparent in the writings of William Blake and the paintings of Géricault, Turner, and Goya. The ethical law of Immanuel Kant (1724–1804) never to treat another human being as a object bolsters these conceptions, as does Kant's advice to behave as if the maxim that guides your action were to become a universal law.

FIGURE 17.1 Caspar David Friedrich, *The Wanderer Above a Sea of Fog*, ca. 1817–18, oil on canvas, $2'5\frac{1}{2}'' \times 3'1\frac{1}{4}''$ (74.8 × 94.8 cm). Hamburger Kunsthalle, Hamburg, Germany. Bildarchiv Preussischer Kulturbesitz/Art Resource, NY. Friedrich was the greatest of the German Romantic painters, noted for his depictions of Gothic cathedrals in ruin, bleak metaphors for the crisis in religious faith experienced by many people of the era.

The Romantic glorification of the self found expression in many ways. Artists, composers, and writers were seen as divinely inspired visionaries with Promethean powers of inspiration and illumination. Many compared the creative power of the artist to the power of the biblical creator. They saw God's power as residing within their own creative genius.

Romantic artists were fascinated by the strange and the marvelous, by dreams and the occult. They celebrated the commonplace, seeing the extraordinary in the ordinary, infinity in a grain of sand and eternity in an hour, to paraphrase William Blake. In addition, Romantic artists expressed an abiding interest in folk traditions. And they were preoccupied as well with the uncanny and the irrational, a fascination that would lead, by the end of the century, in the person of Sigmund Freud, to the rise of psychiatry as a respected branch of medicine. Accommodating all these varied tendencies, Romantic art is multiplicitous, as various as the temperaments that created it.

PAINTING

Francisco Goya.   The Spaniard FRANCISCO GOYA [GOY-uh] (1746–1828) began his career as a favorite portraitist of Madrid society and in 1789 was made a court painter to Charles IV of Spain. Goya was a social and political revolutionary, whose sympathies were with the Enlightenment and the failed French Revolution; he worked for the king not out of loyalty but in order to make a good living. In 1794, a serious illness left him totally deaf, and within the isolation produced by his deafness he became ever more introspective. Slowly, gaiety and exuberance were replaced by bitterness.

At first, Goya was in favor of Napoleon's invasion of Spain, hoping Spain would be modernized as a consequence. But on May 2, 1808, the civilians of Madrid rose up in a guerrilla action against the French, and on the following day one of Napoleon's generals executed his Spanish hostages in retaliation. That execution is the subject of one of Goya's most powerful works, *The Third of May,*

1808 (fig. 17.2). Painted several years after the event, the painting marks Goya's change of heart. The French presence had brought Spain only savage atrocity, death, famine, and violence.

The soldiers on the right, faceless, inhuman, and machine-like, turn their backs to the viewer in anonymity and raise their weapons to destroy. The lighting of this night scene is theatrical; the square light in front of the soldiers illuminates their next victim. Christlike, with arms extended, his portrayal here evokes the image of the Savior, but he is simply one man among many. Several lie dead in their own pools of blood to his right, and those about to die await their turn. *The Third of May, 1808* is a painting that gives visual form to a sense of hopelessness. Although it possesses all the emotional intensity of religious art, here people die for liberty rather than for God; and they are killed by political tyranny, not Satan.

The terror depicted in *The Third of May, 1808* is no match for the series of eighty-two prints known as *Los Desastres de la Guerra* (*The Disasters of War*), produced be-

FIGURE 17.2   Francisco Goya, *The Third of May, 1808*, 1814–15, oil on canvas, 8′ 9″ × 13′ 4″ (2.67 × 4.06 m), Museo del Prado, Madrid. One of the most powerful antiwar statements ever made, Goya's painting documents the execution of Madrid citizens for resisting the French occupation of their city. The killers are faceless, dehumanized, mechanized; the victim, Christlike in pose, dies for liberty rather than religion.

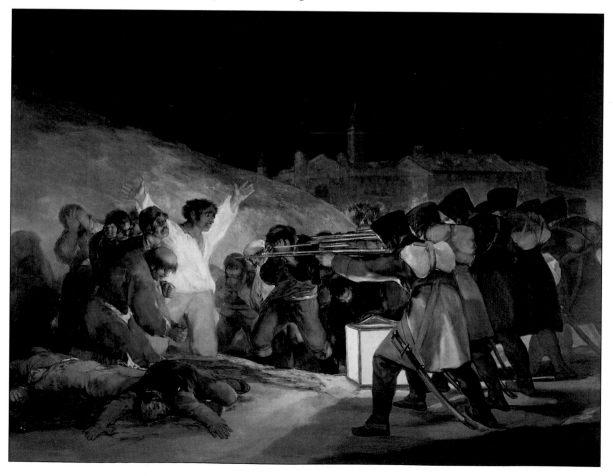

FIGURE 17.3   Francisco Goya, *Great Courage! Against Corpses!*, from *The Disasters of War*, 1810–23, $5\frac{1}{2}'' \times 7\frac{1}{4}''$ (13.6 × 18.6 cm), © Copyright The British Museum, London. As in his paintings, Goya works in areas of light and dark in this etching, the stark contrast emphasizing the brutality of the subject. Few artists have approached Goya's fury.

tween 1810 and 1823. *The Disasters of War* was inflammatory, since it showed both the French and the Spanish as unheroic. Goya found nothing noble or heroic in war. Instead, war was the very image of human brutality, even bestiality, as his prints demonstrate. Number thirty-nine in the series, called *Great Courage! Against Corpses!* (fig. 17.3), shows war for what it is—a powerful demonstration of humanity's inhumanity.

Théodore Géricault.   Goya's equal among the French painters of the Romantic movement is THÉODORE GÉRICAULT [jay-ree-COH] (1791–1824). Like Goya, Géricault painted subjects that affected him emotionally. His most famous painting, the *Raft of the Medusa* (fig. 17.4), painted 1818–19, was inspired by an infamous incident in 1816. The government ship *Medusa* set sail overloaded with settlers and soldiers bound for Senegal. When it sank on a reef off the coast of North Africa, the ship's captain and officers saved themselves in the six available lifeboats and left the 150 passengers and crew members to fend for themselves on a makeshift raft. These people

FIGURE 17.4   Théodore Géricault, *Raft of the Medusa*, 1818–19, oil on canvas, 16′ 1″ × 23′ 6″ (4.9 × 7.16 m). Musée du Louvre, Paris. Réunion des Musées Nationaux. Anauder/Art Resource, NY. In this moving depiction of a tragedy in which many lives were lost after days at sea, the impact is enhanced by the raft jutting obliquely into the viewer's space, by the proximity of extremely realistic dead bodies, and by the dramatic contrasts of light and shadow.

spent twelve days at sea before being rescued; only fifteen survived, the others having died from exposure and starvation. Some went insane and there were even reports of cannibalism. The actions of the captain and officers were judged criminally negligent and intentionally cruel, and the entire incident reflected poorly on the French monarchy, newly restored to the throne after Napoleon's defeat. The captain had been commissioned on the basis not of his ability but of his noble birth. His decision to save himself was considered an act inspired by his belief in aristocratic privilege.

Géricault completed the enormous painting (16′ 1″ × 23′ 6″) in nine months. In an attempt to portray accurately the raft and the people on it, Géricault interviewed survivors, studied corpses in the morgue, and even had the ship's carpenter build a model raft, which he then floated. His search for the uncompromising truth led him to produce a vividly realistic painting of powerfully heroic drama. Géricault elected to portray the moment of greatest emotional intensity—when the survivors first sight the ship that will eventually rescue them, just visible on the horizon. It is a scene of extraordinary tension, a thrilling combination of hope and horror. Those who have died or given up are shown at the bottom of the composition, close to the viewer, large, and extremely realistic. The strongest struggle hysterically upward, led by a black man in a diagonal surge of bodies that rises toward the upper right.

THE JULY MONARCHY

For Romantic painters such as Géricault and his friend EUGENE DELACROIX [duh-lah-KWA] (1798–1863), who served as the model for the central corpse lying face down below the mast in the *Raft of the "Medusa,"* art could serve as an effective social and political tool.

In France particularly, the plight of the working people was at issue throughout the reign of Louis-Philippe, who became king shortly after July 28, 1830, when violent fighting broke out in the streets of Paris, supported by almost every segment of society, and the rule of Charles X quickly came to an end. Within days, Louis-Philippe, who was the former king's cousin, was named the head of what would come to be called the July Monarchy. Eugène Delacroix quickly went to work on a large painting to celebrate this new revolution, so reminiscent of the glorious days of 1789.

Delacroix named his painting *The Twenty-Eighth of July: Liberty Leading the People* (fig. 17.5). It was finished in time for the Salon of 1831, but instead of the accolades he thought he would receive, Delacroix was roundly attacked for the painting. It was purchased by the new government of Louis-Philippe and quickly removed to storage. The scene is set in barricades of the kind traditionally built by Parisians by piling cobblestones up in the street, thus creating lines of defense against the advance of government troops. Behind it, to the right, are the towers of Notre-Dame Cathedral, seen through the smoke of battle across the Seine River. The composition rises in a pyramid of human forms, the dead sprawled along the base of the painting, and Liberty herself, waving the French tricolor, crowns the composition. Beside Liberty is a youth of the streets. To Liberty's right, a working-class rebel in white and a bourgeois gentleman, distinguished by his tie, coat, and top hat, advance with her. Delacroix depicts the cross-section of society that actually took part in the uprising.

Jean-Auguste-Dominque Ingres.   A pupil of David, JEAN-AUGUSTE-DOMINIQUE INGRES [AN-gruh] (1780–1867) is perhaps the last Neoclassical painter, for he opposed all Romantics of his day, particularly Delacroix. Stubborn and plodding, he was described as a "pedantic tyrant." Through his position as head of the French Academy, he restricted official art for generations.

In Ingres's approach, precision of line is all important. His *La Grande Odalisque* (fig. 17.6), the word **odalisque** meaning "harem woman" in Turkish, painted in 1814, is the kind of exotic subject also favored by the Romantics. The odalisque is not an individual, and her anatomy is neither academic nor accurate. The elongated, large-hipped proportions recall the Mannerist style (see Chapter 13) rather than the classical ideal. Ingres perhaps had more in common with the Romantics than he would have liked to admit, since it is hard to remove *all* sensuality from such a subject. He was shocked when the Neoclassical painters found his work unclassical.

Still, compared to a Delacroix *Odalisque* (fig. 17.7) of 1845–50, Ingres's painting seems positively tame. Delacroix's nude is unabashedly sensual. His painting style is loose, physical, not at all intellectual. Where Ingres explores the external human form, Delacroix explores the internal emotions the body can generate.

John Constable.   In England, painters were attracted to the physical aspects of nature. John Constable (1776–1837) immersed himself in the scenery of his native land and painted places he knew and loved such as Suffolk and Essex. The valley of the River Stour, which divides Suffolk from Essex, was his special haunt.

In the 1820s, Constable began painting a series of "six-footers," which were large ambitious landscapes celebrating rural life. *The Haywain* (fig. 17.8), of 1821, depicts a wagon mired beside Willy Lott's cottage in the millstream at Flatford that ran beside the Stour proper, adjacent to Constable's own property. Willy Lott lived in this cottage for eighty years and spent only four nights away from it during his entire life. He embodied, for Constable, the enduring attachment to place so fundamental to rural life. Constable was interested in the transience of nature, the momentary effects of atmosphere and light, of storm and sunlight, and the contrast of dense foliage and open field.

J. M. W. Turner.   Constable's love of nature was shared by his fellow Englishman Joseph Mallord William Turner

FIGURE 17.5   Eugène Delacroix, *The Twenty-Eighth of July: Liberty Leading the People*, 1830, oil on canvas, 8′6⅜″ × 10′8″ (2.59 × 3.25 m), Musée du Louvre, Paris. Reunion des Musées Nationaux. Herve Lewandowski/Art Resource, NY. In this romanticized representation of the Revolution of 1830, Liberty is personified by a seminaked woman leading her followers through Paris. The revolution resulted in the abdication of Charles X and the formation of a new government under Louis-Philippe.

FIGURE 17.6   Jean-Auguste-Dominique Ingres, *La Grande Odalisque*, 1814, oil on canvas, 2′11¼″ × 5′3¾″ (89.7 × 162 cm), Musée du Louvre, Paris. Reunion des Musées Nationaux. Art Resource, NY. The treatment of the anatomy of this odalisque (harem woman), an exotic and erotic subject, is less academic than Ingres might have liked to believe. In fact, she has much in common with the smooth elongated bodies created by Mannerist artists, such as Parmigianino's *Madonna with the Long Neck* (fig. 13.37).

FIGURE 17.7   Eugène Delacroix, *Odalisque*, 1845–50, oil on canvas, $14\frac{7}{8}'' \times 18\frac{1}{4}''$ (37.6 × 46.4 cm). Fitzwilliam Museum, Cambridge, England. It is hard to say which is more sensual in Delacroix's painting, the subject or the brushwork. There is an obvious contrast with Ingres's treatment of an odalisque subject thirty-odd years earlier (see fig. 17.6). Whereas in Ingres's version the emphasis is very much on line, Delacroix is a *rubéniste* and delights in an ecstatic use of color.

(1775–1851). The son of a barber, Turner had no formal education but was interested in art from childhood. His talent was quickly recognized for he was already a full member of the Royal Academy in 1802, when he was only twenty-seven. Opposing the Academy's classicism, he was to become England's leading Romantic painter.

Although Turner worked from nature, he took even greater liberties with the facts than Constable did. Consequently, it is not always possible to recognize his sites or fully to comprehend his subject. For example, Turner's painting *The Slave Ship* (fig. 17.9), of 1840, originally titled *Slavers Throwing Overboard the Dead and Dying—Typhoon Coming On*, illustrates a specific contemporary event with all the outrage of Géricault and Delacroix. A ship's captain had thrown overboard slaves who were sick or dying from an epidemic that had broken out on board. The captain was insured against loss of slaves at sea, but not against their loss owing to disease.

Turner's figures are lost in the wash of colors of sea and sky, and the political subject threatens to become, in Turner's hands, an excuse for a study of atmosphere. The forms dissolve into a haze of mist. The swirl of storm and colored light is the result of layers of oil glazes. So radical

FIGURE 17.8   John Constable, *The Haywain*, 1821, oil on canvas, $4'3\frac{1}{4}'' \times 6'1''$ (1.30 × 1.90 m), National Gallery, London. The English penchant for landscape painting indicates a growing interest in nature and weather conditions that prefigures late-nineteenth-century Impressionism. Although Constable sketched from nature, he did the final painting in his studio.

FIGURE 17.9 Joseph Mallord William Turner, *The Slave Ship*, 1840, oil on canvas, $2'11\frac{3}{4}'' \times 4'$ (90.5 × 122 cm), Museum of Fine Arts, Boston. Henry Lillie Pierce Fund. Reproduced with permission, © 2005, All Rights Reserved. Constable called Turner's paintings "tinted steam." The original title, *Slavers Throwing Overboard the Dead and Dying—Typhoon Coming On*, in spite of its unusual length, hardly clarifies the subject, which is, above all, Turner's Romantic response to nature.

was Turner's style that he was dubbed "the over-Turner." His distortion of the subject and interest in nature and light would pave the way to Impressionism.

Thomas Cole. American landscape painting often focuses on solitude. When figures are included in a scene, as, for instance, in *American Lake Scene* of 1844 (fig. 17.10) by Thomas Cole (1801–48), they are barely visible, dwarfed by the landscape that surrounds them. Here a lone Native American warrior sits between two trees on a small island where he has brought his canoe to rest. We share his view, enthralled by the combination of open space and light that fills the scene. In an analogous moment, Cole described his feelings as he looked out across two lakes in Franconia Notch in the New Hampshire mountains, saying: "I was overwhelmed with an emotion of the sublime such as I have rarely felt. It was not that the jagged precipices were lofty, that the encircling woods were of the dimmest shade, or that the waters were profoundly deep; but that over all, rocks, wood, and water, brooded the spirit of repose, and

FIGURE 17.10 Thomas Cole, *American Lake Scene*, 1844, oil on canvas, $18\frac{1}{4}'' \times 24\frac{1}{2}''$ (46.4 × 62.2 cm). Detroit Institute of Arts, Detroit. Gift of Douglas F. Roby. Although his landscape paintings were a popular success, they seemed less important to Cole than his historical and allegorical works, which were not as enthusiastically received.

Then & Now

AMERICA'S NATIONAL PARKS

In the early eighteenth century, the new American nation prided itself on its political system, but it lagged far behind Europe in cultural achievement. Rather than in authors and artists, the country took pride in the one thing it had in abundance—land. After Thomas Jefferson purchased the Louisiana territory from Napoleon in 1803, the American landscape became, in effect, the nation's cultural inheritance. And as the country was subsequently explored, the treasures it held, in beauty as well as gold, excited the American populace.

It was the artists and photographers who accompanied the expeditions to the West who publicized the beauty of the landscape. The painter ALBERT BIERSTADT [BEER-shtaht] (1830–1902) accompanied Colonel Frederick Lander to the Rockies in 1859. The photographer C. E. Watkins (1829–1916) traveled to Yosemite in 1861. The painter Thomas Moran (1837–1926) went with Colonel Ferdinand V. Hayden of the National Geographic Survey through the Rockies to Yellowstone in 1871.

Bierstadt's paintings and Watkins's photographs were the primary reason that Lincoln signed into law a bill establishing Yosemite as a national preserve in 1864. In 1872, Congress purchased Moran's *Grand Canyon of the Yellowstone* (fig. 17.11) for $10,000 and later hung the massive painting in the lobby of the Senate. On March 1, 1872, President Ulysses S. Grant signed the Yellowstone Park Act into law, establishing the national park system.

Today the national park system is increasingly threatened. Automobiles have been banned from Yosemite, parts of Mesa Verde, and other parks as well. In the early 1980s, developers proposed building a geothermal power plant fifteen miles west of Upper Geyser Basin and "Old Faithful" Geyser in Yellowstone. The project was halted only because no one could demonstrate the exact boundaries of the Yellowstone geothermal reservoirs. In 1980, the National Park Service explained the situation this way: "Yellowstone, Great Smoky Mountains, Everglades, and Glacier—most of these great parks were at one time pristine areas surrounded and protected by vast wilderness regions. Today, with their surrounding buffer zones gradually disappearing, many of these parks are experiencing significant and widespread adverse effects associated with external encroachment."

The nation is losing one of its myths—the myth that people can live harmoniously with nature, which was illustrated in the landscapes of American Romantic painters.

FIGURE 17.11   Thomas Moran, *Grand Canyon of the Yellowstone*, 1872, oil on canvas, 7′ × 12′ (2.13 × 3.66 m), Smithsonian Institution, Washington, D.C., Art Resource, NY. Lent by the Department of the Interior Museum. Smithsonian American Art Museum, On a visit to England in 1862, Moran studied and copied the paintings of J. M. W. Turner, whose use of light and color he particularly admired.

the silent energy of nature stirred the soul to its inmost depths." The same spirit of repose infuses this depiction of rock, wood, and water.

SCULPTURE

Perhaps surprisingly, during the Romantic era, sculpture fell out of favor. In fact, in 1846, the poet Charles Baudelaire argued that the idea of Romantic sculpture was impossible. Sculpture, he suggested, can neither arouse subjective feelings in the viewer nor express the personal sensibility of the artist because, as a three-dimensional object, it asserts its objective reality too thoroughly. Baudelaire summed up Romantic sculpture in the title of his essay, "Why Sculpture Is Boring."

Baudelaire did argue, however, that sculpture could escape this fate in the service of architecture; attached to a larger whole, it could evoke profound feelings. One example is *The Departure of the Volunteers of 1792*, popularly known as *La Marseillaise* (fig. 17.12), by François Rude (1784–1855), a huge stone sculpture made for the Arc de Triomphe in Paris. Although sculpted between 1833 and 1836, the subject refers to an event that occurred in 1792—the defense of the French Republic by volunteers rallying

FIGURE 17.12 François Rude, *La Marseillaise (The Departure of the Volunteers of 1792)*, Arc de Triomphe, Place de l'Etoile, Paris, 1833–36, limestone, ca. 42′ × 26′ (12.80 × 7.90 m). The use of a triumphal arch to commemorate a military victory, as well as the use of a winged female figure to represent victory, derives from Greek and Roman antiquity.

to repel invaders from abroad. For Rude, the subject was deeply emotional because his own father had been among the volunteers.

The figures are costumed in both ancient and medieval armor, and the nude youth in front is Neoclassical in pose and physique. A winged female figure representing Victory (as in antiquity) leads the soldiers forward, and the group below appears to surge upward with a diagonal force that points in the direction of the tip of her sword. Thus, in a rectangular format necessitated by the architecture of the arch itself, Rude created a dynamic triangular thrust to the left that creates an emotional thrust as well, one that many French people associate with their national anthem to this day.

ARCHITECTURE

Like painting and sculpture, architecture of the Romantic era also borrowed freely from the past, creating revivals of earlier architectural styles. The Gothic and the Baroque,

in particular, were revived, and often several styles were combined.

Houses of Parliament. The Gothic Revival is seen in the Houses of Parliament in London (fig. 17.13), begun 1836, by Sir Charles Barry (1795–1860) and Augustus W. N. Pugin (1812–52). The Gothic revival was strongest in England, where it was mistakenly believed to have originated. In fact, as discussed in Chapter 12, the Gothic style originated in France and was associated primarily with ecclesiastical architecture. Somewhat incongruously, this style was applied to the buildings of the British government. Gothic features on the Houses of Parliament are the irregular silhouette, broken surface, incessant accenting of the vertical, and multiplicity of small delicate surface forms. The whole was designed to evoke the spiritual and ethical values of the Middle Ages.

Opéra. In contrast, it was the Baroque that provided the inspiration for Charles Garnier (1825–98) when he designed the Opéra in Paris (fig. 17.14) between 1861 and 1874. Made to accommodate large audiences, the Opéra was built on a grand scale. The quantity of sculptured ornament is neo-Baroque, and the overall effect is of extreme sumptuousness. The three-story facade consists of a series of arches, surmounted by a story with two sizes of orders, topped by an ornamental attic. The forward-jutting corner pavilions are typically French.

By the second half of the nineteenth century, new technological achievements, particularly the development of cast iron as a construction material, offered architects and sculptors new possibilities. In fact, two of the most innovative works of the day, Crystal Palace in London and the Statue of Liberty in New York harbor, were considered by some to be more feats of engineering than works of art.

Crystal Palace. Built for the Great Exhibition of 1851, Crystal Palace (fig. 17.15) was designed by Joseph Paxton (1803–65), who was once gardener to the duke of Devonshire and was trained neither as an architect nor as an engineer. When Prince Albert called for a competition to design the exhibition site, the judges, among them Charles Barry, who had designed the Gothic Revival Houses of Parliament, deemed none of the large number of entries suitable. The judges themselves prepared a design, but it, too, was rejected. Finally Paxton offered his proposal. Instead of a giant brick edifice, as everyone else had proposed, Paxton extended the concept of the glassframe greenhouse. Employing a cast-iron prefabricated modular framework—the first such building of its kind—Paxton used glass for his walls. Over 900,000 square feet of glass— nearly a third of Britain's total annual production—were fitted into a building 1,851 feet long and 408 feet wide. The result was not only in harmony with the building's site in Hyde Park, but offered the simplest solution to the problem of lighting the interior of a vast exhibition space. Soon Paxton's model was adapted to other similar spaces, particularly to railway stations.

FIGURE 17.13   Sir Charles Barry and Augustus Welby Northmore Pugin, Houses of Parliament, London, 1836–60, length 940′ (286.5 m). The delicacy of Gothic religious architecture is applied to government office buildings. Among the plethora of pointed pinnacles, turrets, and towers is the clock known as Big Ben.

FIGURE 17.14   Charles Garnier, Opéra, facade, Paris, 1861–74, width ca. 200′ (62.96 m), height 95′ (28.96 m). The Opera, with its Neo-Baroque combination of arcades, colonnades, and luxuriously opulent ornament, is well suited to performance of opera, a Baroque form of music.

FIGURE 17.15   Joseph Paxton, Crystal Palace, London, 1851, cast iron and glass, length 1851′ (564.18 m), width 408′ (124.36 m), height 108′ (32.92 m). Designed by a gardener, Crystal Palace was, in its time, the largest enclosed space ever created. Built as an exhibition hall to display industrial and technological accomplishments, it was in itself an impressive demonstration of new technology.

PHILOSOPHY

Jean-Jacques Rousseau and the Concept of Self.   The autobiographical *Confessions* of the French philosophical writer JEAN-JACQUES ROUSSEAU [roo-SEW] (1712–78) was the first and most influential exploration of the self in the West outside the tradition of religious autobiography. As a Romantic rather than an Enlightenment figure, Rousseau stood in stark contrast to many of his contemporaries, particularly Swift and Voltaire. Rousseau believed in the basic goodness of humanity, in naturally positive instincts rather than naturally negative ones. Society, he felt, corrupted a person's basic instincts, making people competitive, greedy, and uncaring. Like the Romantic poets and painters who were to follow, he celebrated the claims of the imagination above all else.

Rousseau was most interested in the subjectivity of the self. His early works concern social themes. In his *Discourse on Inequality* (1754), he provides a critique of the philosophy of Thomas Hobbes, who argued that human beings are spurred by self-interest and that to exist in a state of nature is to exist in a state of war (see Chapter 15). Rousseau argued that although humans are motivated by self-interest, they also possess a natural instinct of compassion.

Rousseau's *Confessions* serves as a powerful example of reflective self-analysis, a model for future philosophical self-explorations. This celebration of the self became so prevalent during the Romantic era that even in the face of crisis, as with the dashed hopes of many in Britain and France at the outcome of the French Revolution, there was a belief that those aspirations could be profitably redefined. If the revolution did not create a better society, then the revolutionary ideal should be transferred from the social realm to the personal one to create a better mind. If a transformation of political reality was more complicated than had been imagined, then a transformation of human consciousness could at least be effected.

Hegel and Historical Change.   Another key thinker of the Romantic era, German philosopher George Friedrich Wilhelm Hegel (1770–1831) saw reality and history as a dynamic process rather than a series of static ideals. For Hegel, historical change reflects a dialectical process in which opposing ideas collide to produce a new result, or synthesis, that combines elements of the original two contradictory forces. Every thesis has its antithesis, with the conflict between them resulting in a synthesis, which becomes the basis for a further synthesis, resulting in freedom and rationality. Originally designed to explain the conflicting ideas and ideals of great men, Hegel's dialectic was later adapted to explain opposing economic forces and class conflicts between owner/managers and labor. Karl Marx and Friedrich Engels, in *The Communist Manifesto* (1844), argued for the influence of economic factors on all aspects of human experience, including social, political, and intellectual matters.

Ralph Waldo Emerson and Transcendentalism.   The sentiments about nature expressed by the Romantic painters were quickly adopted in the United States, where in the nineteenth century more people lived in close communion with nature than in Europe. The union of humanity with nature was a special theme of Ralph Waldo Emerson (1803–82), author of the widely influential essay "Nature," first published in 1836. Emerson was one of a number of American thinkers who called themselves Transcendentalists. The Transcendentalists built a philosophical perspective from the poetry of William Wordsworth, on the one hand, and the philosophy of the German Immanuel Kant (1724–1804), on the other. Kant had argued there are two basic elements, "those that we receive through impressions, and those that our faculty of knowledge supplies from itself." The first he called **phenomena,** the second **noumena.** We can never truly know the essence of the things that the mind creates for itself. "In the world of sense, however far we may carry our investigation, we can never have anything before us but mere phenomena . . . The transcendental object remains unknown to us." The "transcendental object" is known only through intuition. Emerson was able to intuit the transcendental in nature. As he puts it in the most famous passage in "Nature": "Standing on the bare ground,—my head bathed by the blithe air, and uplifted into infinite space,—all mean egotism vanishes. I become a transparent eyeball; I am nothing; I see all; the currents of the Universal Being circulate through me; I am part or particle of God. . . . In the wilderness, I find something more dear and connate than in streets or villages. In the tranquil landscape, and especially in the distant line of the horizon, one beholds somewhat as beautiful as one's own nature."

Henry David Thoreau.   The American wilderness was raw and vast, and even along the eastern seaboard, where civilization had taken firm hold, it was still easy to leave the city behind, as Henry David Thoreau (1817–62) did at Walden Pond. "I went to the woods," Thoreau wrote in *Walden* (1854), "because I wished to live deliberately, to front only the essential facts of life, and see if I could not learn what it had to teach, and not, when I came to die, discover that I had not lived." Living close to nature was, for Thoreau, the very source of humankind's strength. In an essay entitled "Walking" he echoed the sentiments Emerson had expressed in "Nature":

> What I have been preparing to say is, that in Wildness is the preservation of the world. Every tree sends its fibres forth in search of the Wild. . . . From the forest and wilderness come the tonics and barks which brace mankind. Our ancestors were savages. The story of Romulus and Remus being suckled by a wolf is not a meaningless fable. The founders of every State which has risen to eminence have drawn their nourishment and vigor from a similar wild source. It was because the children of the Empire were not suckled by the wolf that they were conquered and displaced by the children of the Northern

forests who were. I believe in the forest, and in the meadow, and in the night in which the corn grows.

THE ANTISLAVERY MOVEMENT

The growth of humanitarian feeling during the eighteenth century Age of Enlightenment and the spreading of democratic ideals through revolutions in France and the Americas led to increased criticism of the slave trade. In the United States, the prohibition of the foreign slave trade was not realized until 1805. In Britain, slavery was abolished with the Abolition Act of 1833, which was followed by its gradual abolition in all lands under British control.

In the northern United States a group opposed to slavery emerged, with members calling themselves "abolitionists." Believing that slavery was evil, the abolitionists fought for its eradication on idealistic moral grounds, arguing against its spread to the western U.S. territories and in favor of its elimination in all states where it existed. Among the most famous of the abolitionists were William Lloyd Garrison, who published an abolitionist newspaper, *The Liberator*, for thirty-five years, and Frederick Douglass, a former slave, whose *Narrative of the Life* revealed the shocking brutality and degradation slavery encouraged. Douglass's autobiographical work was complemented by Harriet Beecher Stowe's immensely successful novel *Uncle Tom's Cabin* (1852), the best-selling novel of the nineteenth century. Upon meeting the author, President Abraham Lincoln is said to have remarked: "So this is the little lady who wrote the big book that started this great war."

In other countries the emancipation of slaves was also at issue. As South American countries acquired their independence, they abolished slavery. Some countries, such as Chile (1823), Mexico (1829), and Bolivia (1831) made the prohibition against slavery absolute. In other countries, however, including Argentina (1810), Colombia (1814), and Venezuela (1821), the abolition of slavery was more gradual. In Brazil, the issue was explosive, and although slavery was abolished in 1888, fierce opposition fueled revolution there in 1889.

THE CIVIL WAR

Civil War erupted in the United States over slavery and a suite of other factors, social, political, and economic. With the election of Abraham Lincoln as president in 1860, a number of tensions came to a head. Prominent among them was the issue of slavery, with Lincoln a firm believer that slavery was immoral and in need of abolishment. Equally important political issues, such as states rights versus the authority of the federal government, and the competing claims of the agrarian south versus the industrial northern states, drove a wedge between the two parts of the country.

A firm believer in the sacredness of the Union, Lincoln refused to allow the southern states to secede, which they considered their right. Believing that they could sustain a separate southern union of states on the backs of their slaves, eleven southern states withdrew from the Union in 1860 and 1861. The war followed swiftly and became the bloodiest ever fought on American soil, lasting four agonized years, until 1865.

Midway through the war, President Lincoln announced his *Emancipation Proclamation*, which promised freedom to slaves and the abolition of the institution of slavery in all the United States. When the northern states finally prevailed, slavery was ended as an institution in the country, and the central government was strengthened. The issues that divided the country, however, would do so in attenuated form for more than another century, as the problem of freed slaves during the Reconstruction era and the rights of blacks would become and long remain major social and political issues.

THE CRIMEAN WAR

During the nineteenth century, European imperialist tendencies increased. The first major Ottoman war, the Crimean War occurred from 1854 to 1856, with Russia, which had been annexing Muslim lands in Central Asia. Eager to absorb Muslim provinces in Eastern Europe, Russia attacked the Ottomans ostensibly over the right to defend Christian sites in the Holy Land. Alarmed at further Russian expansionist tendencies, Britain and France sided with the Ottomans and declared war on Russia. Although the Turks and their allies were victorious, both sides suffered heavy casualties.

The Crimean War initiated a decline in Ottoman power and influence. It was the first Ottoman war in which the Ottomans did not control the outcome. After the Crimean War, the European powers no longer considered the Ottomans a serious global political and military force. For Russia, the effects of the war were equally disastrous. In addition to losing more than 100,000 men and suffering humiliating military defeat on its own soil, Russia could no longer sustain its expansionist ambitions. The war clearly showed that Russia's agrarian economy based on the labor of serfs was no match for the European industrial powers.

LITERATURE

The theme of much nineteenth-century literature is our ignorance of things. In Herman Melville's (1819–91) novel *Moby Dick* (1851), Captain Ahab is bent on capturing the great white whale, which comes to stand, in his imagination, for something close to a final truth or a first cause. But the whale eludes him, and even when Ahab does indeed "capture" it, the whale drags him to his death. He seeks a knowledge he cannot possess.

Robert Louis Stevenson (1850–94), another important author of the era, wrote a short novel, *Dr. Jekyll and Mr. Hyde* (1886), which embodies the conflict between the classical mind, with its urge for order, and the new Romantic mind, and in which the rational, scientific Dr. Jekyll has to battle with his alter ego, the violent, irrational Mr. Hyde. In other popular literature, the mystery tale rises into fashion in France in the 1830s and is seen in America a decade later, but culminates, at the end of the century, in the English writer Sir Arthur Conan Doyle's great detective, Sherlock Holmes. In the typical mystery, everyone is, metaphorically, thrown into a fog by murder. No one knows "who done it," a situation that has excited the passions of readers ever since. As a sort of Enlightenment hero, the detective penetrates the fog, clarifies the situation, resolves the conflict, and explains it logically. If our Romantic spirit is excited by inexactitude and indeterminacy, we nonetheless long to be rescued from them.

William Blake.   A product of the industrial slums, the poet and artist William Blake (1757–1827) was born in poverty and, unable to attend school, taught himself to read and studied engravings of paintings by such Renaissance masters as Raphael, Dürer, and Michelangelo. At the age of twenty-two, Blake entered the Royal Academy as an engraving student, but unsettling clashes over artistic differences returned him to a life of nonconformist study.

Blake insisted that his "great task" as a poet was "To open the Eternal Worlds, to open the immortal Eyes of Man inwards into the Worlds of Thought." His was a poetry of revelation, not technique. As a boy Blake saw "a tree filled with angels, bright angelic wings bespangling every bough with stars." This ability to see beyond the physical, what he called his "double vision," fueled Blake's imaginative and poetic flights (fig. 17.16).

Blake saw himself as a prophet, and he drew heavily on both the Hebrew and the Christian sacred texts. At the core of Blake's work are two contrary archetypal states of the human soul: innocence and experience. Humanity's oscillation between these states forms the focus of much of his poetry.

For Blake, innocence and experience are psychological states that carry political implications. "The Chimney Sweeper" in *Songs of Innocence* is a young boy who rationalizes his misery and naively declares, "Those that do their duty need not fear harm." Historically, nothing could have been further from the truth. Young sweeps who endured this forced labor rarely lived to reach adulthood. The irony of his final pronouncement escapes the innocent boy, unaware of the horrors of the Industrial Revolution. Readers would have understood the implications nonetheless.

William Wordsworth and Samuel Taylor Coleridge.
The year 1798 saw the publication of the *Lyrical Ballads*, co-authored by William Wordsworth (1770–1850) and Samuel Taylor Coleridge (1772–1834). Turning their backs on the sophisticated syntax and vocabulary of Neoclassical writing, they insisted that the language of poetry should be natural; as natural, in fact, as its subject, nature—both

FIGURE 17.16   William Blake, frontispiece to *Europe: A Prophecy*, 1794, $12\frac{1}{4}'' \times 9\frac{1}{2}''$ (31.1 × 24.1 cm), © The British Museum, London. British Museum Great Court Ltd. Blake's idea of God, Urizen, is depicted here on the second day of Creation. He holds a pair of compasses as he measures out and delineates the firmament.

human nature and the natural world. Coleridge was particularly interested in folk idioms and songs. Wordsworth's ear was tuned to the everyday language of common folk, "a language really used by men," as he put it. He wrote about everyday subjects, a poetry of the individual, of the inner life and "the essential passions of the heart."

Exactly how the human imagination delineates a sense of place in nature, and by extension in daily reality, also underlies Wordsworth's lyric "I Wandered Lonely as a Cloud." According to his sister Dorothy's journal of April 15, 1802, they had gone for a walk "in the woods beyond Gowbarrow Park." Together they stumbled upon a stretch of daffodils that "grew among the mossy stones . . . some rested their heads upon these stones as on a pillow for weariness; and the rest tossed and reeled and danced, and seemed as if they verily laughed with the wind, that flew upon them over the Lake; they looked so gay, ever glancing, ever changing." The daffodils of Wordsworth's poem are the personified flowers of Dorothy's journal entry, but in the end brother and sister witness different events. Whereas Dorothy draws simple pleasure from her walk among the flowers, the poet's attention becomes fixed on how the imagination interacts with nature. For although Wordsworth takes pleasure in his walk, the "wealth" the poem refers to comes into focus only with the "inward eye" of the imagination. The poem reflects many of Wordsworth's Romantic preoccupations, particularly the power of nature and of remembered experience to restore the human spirit.

John Keats. Probably no poet of the period was more aware of his inability to know the world fully, yet at the same time more compelled to explore it, than John Keats (1795–1821). Like Wordsworth, Keats believed in the vitality of sensation but did not limit himself to sight and sound. Keats often uses imagery designating one sense in place of imagery suggesting another. For example, he writes of "fragrant and enwreathed light," "pale and silver silence," "scarlet pain," and "the touch of scent." Keats's images register on palate and fingertip as well as within the ear and eye, making the world, the poet, and the poem one complete sensation. This blurring of borders reflects the empathic power Keats termed "negative capability," the poet's ability to empathize with other characters, or entities, living or imagined, animate or inanimate.

Perhaps the most affecting of Keats's efforts at negative capability is "This Living Hand," written shortly before he died of tuberculosis at the age of twenty-five:

> This living hand, now warm and capable
> Of earnest grasping, would, if it were cold
> And in the icy silence of the tomb,
> So haunt thy days and chill thy dreaming nights
> That thou wouldst wish thine own heart dry of blood
> So in my veins red life might stream again,
> And thou be conscience-calmed—see here it is—hold it
> towards you.

Lord Byron. Another great English Romantic poet, George Gordon, Lord Byron (1788–1824), embodies the Romantic self. A free spirit, he was notorious for his unconventional behavior. One of his first books of poems, *Hours of Idleness* (1807), was subjected to severe criticism in the *Edinburgh Review*, to which Byron retorted, in 1809, with a biting satire in the style of Swift and Pope, entitled *English Bards and Scotch Reviewers.* It won him instant fame. That same year, he left England to travel extensively in Spain, Portugal, Italy, and the Balkans (fig. 17.17). Good-looking and flamboyant, Byron socialized with a variety of upper-class and aristocratic women. His most famous poem, *Don Juan* (1819–24), portrayed the seducer already well known to most audiences. Most of his followers assumed the poem to be semiautobiographical, since it was begun soon after he formed a relationship with Contessa Teresa Guicioli in Italy, who remained his mistress for the rest of his life. As one female friend said of him, not without some real admiration, "He is mad, bad, and dangerous

FIGURE 17.17 Thomas Philips, *Lord Byron in Albanian Costume*, 1814, oil on canvas, $29\frac{1}{2}''\times 24\frac{1}{2}''$ (75 × 62 cm), National Portrait Gallery, London. Byron looks particularly dashing in this costume, which signifies the love of the exotic and interest in the cultures of the Balkans reflected in his writing.

to know." Byron died in the Balkans fighting for the Greeks in the war against Turkey in 1824, the same year that Delacroix painted his *Massacres at Chios.*

Emily Brontë. *Wuthering Heights* (1847), the masterpiece of EMILY BRONTË [BRON-tay] (1818–48), is organized with the same structural care in the classical manner of Jane Austen, but it is a fully Romantic work that breaks new ground in the violence of its scenes and the extravagance of its style.

Gone is the decorum that marked Austen's world (the "artificial rudeness" of the English garden) and in its place is a world of storm and turmoil. The novel's central characters display passionate and socially disruptive tendencies entirely at odds with the rational and serene world of the Enlightenment, and it is as if the landscape around them responds. Reason and social decorum are replaced by intense feeling and individual expression. The demands and needs of the self are paramount. Nature is untamed, unruly, and grand, exhibiting patterns of storm followed by calm, similar to the contrasting emotions displayed by Brontë's characters, and analogous to the alternation of quiet lyricism and passionate drama heard in Romantic music such as Schubert's. Moreover, in the work of both artists, drama explodes in the midst of serenity and calm, suggesting thereby the potential for abrupt change in both inner and outer weather.

Johann Wolfgang von Goethe.
Perhaps the most influential writer of the Romantic era was JOHANN WOLF-GANG VON GOETHE [GUR-tuh] (1749–1832), who lived half his life during the Enlightenment and half during the Romantic era. He witnessed the shift in consciousness from the Enlightenment emphasis on reason, objectivity, and scientific fact to the Romantic concern for emotion, subjectivity, and imaginative truth.

Born and raised in Frankfurt, Goethe studied law at the University of Strasbourg, where he met the German critic and thinker J. G. Herder. With Herder and Friedrich Schiller, Goethe contributed to the beginnings of German Romanticism in the 1770s, leading what was called the **Sturm und Drang** (storm and stress) movement. Goethe's contribution to this movement was his novel *The Sorrows of Young Werther* (1774). Enormously influential throughout Europe, the work expressed discontent with Enlightenment ideals of objectivity, rationality, and restraint. In it, an educated young man, Werther, gives up a government position to search for greater meaning in his life. He becomes alienated and unhappy until he meets and falls in love with a young woman, who is unfortunately engaged to a businessman, whom she marries. Werther becomes obsessed with her and finally commits suicide.

The work for which Goethe is best known, *Faust* (1808), is based on the life of the medieval German scholar Johann Faust, who is reputed to have sold his soul to the devil in exchange for knowledge. *Faust* has been described as a defining work of European Romanticism, one that epitomizes the temper and spirit of the Romantic era and serves to represent the anxiety-ridden Romantic imagination in all its teeming aspiration.

Throughout his life and literary career, Goethe was torn between the intellectual ideals of the Enlightenment and the emotional passions of the Romantic period. In *Faust*, readers confront alternative perspectives on life, represented by the characters Faust and the devil, Mephistopheles. Faust is a man of the mind, a knowledgeable scholar, who abandons himself to the exploration of physical experience, represented by Mephistopheles, who offers Faust the chance to live a more active life of sensation. Faust remains a divided figure, one who cannot integrate harmoniously the two different aspects of his consciousness—his scientific rationalism and his poetic intuition.

Walt Whitman.
Of the American poets writing during the nineteenth century, two stand out above all others: Walt Whitman (1819–92) and Emily Dickinson. Unlike Dickinson, whose idiosyncratic and elliptical style has found few imitators, Whitman greatly influenced later American poets. William Carlos Williams emulated Whitman's attention to the commonplace and his experiments with the poetic line. Wallace Stevens displayed the meditative, philosophical cast of mind found in poems such as Whitman's "Crossing Brooklyn Ferry." Later, Allen Ginsberg exhibited something of Whitman's early extravagance and outrageousness.

Instead of using the poetic structures of his day, Whitman developed more open, fluid forms. And rather than using old-fashioned poetic diction, he wrote in familiar and informal language, following Wordsworth's "language really used by men." Whitman also mixed exalted language with common speech, resulting in, as he remarked, a "new style . . . necessitated by new theories, new themes," far removed from European models. Whitman's stylistic innovations in *Leaves of Grass*, which he wrote and revised over nearly fifty years and once described as "a language experiment," were intended to "give something to our literature which will be our own . . . strengthening and intensifying the national." In this he was like many nineteenth-century artists who expressed their nationalistic tendencies in music, painting, and literature.

Emily Dickinson.
In his exalted ambition, Whitman differed markedly from Emily Dickinson (1830–86), whose poetic inclination gravitated inward. Although Whitman and Dickinson each brought something strikingly original to American poetry, their poems could not be more different. A glance at a page of their poetry reveals a significant visual difference. Whitman's poems are expansive, with long lines and ample stanzas. Dickinson's poems, by contrast, are very tight, with four-line stanzas that distill feeling and thought.

The openness of Whitman's form is paralleled by the openness of his stance, his outgoing public manner. Dickinson's poetry, in contrast, is much more private. Her meditative poems are rooted partly in the metaphysical poetry of seventeenth-century writers such as John Donne and partly in the tradition of Protestant hymnology. Dickinson made frequent and ingenious use of Protestant hymn meters and followed their usual stanzaic pattern. Her adaptation of hymn meter accords with her adaptation of the traditional religious doctrines of orthodox Christianity. For although many of her poems reflect her Calvinist heritage—particularly in the ways their religious disposition intersects with intensely felt psychological experience—Dickinson was not an orthodox Christian. "Some keep the Sabbath going to Church," she wrote. "I keep it, staying at Home." Her love of nature separates her from her Puritan precursors, allying her instead with such Transcendentalist contemporaries as Emerson, Thoreau, and Whitman, although her vision of life was starker than theirs.

Dickinson spent nearly all of her life in one town, Amherst, Massachusetts, living as a near recluse and dying in the house where she was born. Dickinson's poems probe deeply into a few experiences—love, death, doubt, and faith. In examining her experience, Dickinson makes a scrupulous effort to tell the truth, but she tells it "slant," as one of her poems puts it: "Tell all the Truth but tell it slant." Part of her artistry includes the way she invites readers to share her search for truth. Her poems' qualified assertions, along with their riddles and questioning stance, cumulatively suggest that life is mysterious and complex, as it was for so many Romantic artists.

MUSIC

Because it seems capable of unleashing emotions beyond mere words or images, music is perhaps the most "romantic" of Romantic art forms. Romantic music was not a break with the classical ideas of Haydn and Mozart but an expansion of techniques to express emotion in symphonies and other absolute musical forms. Both in length and substance, Romantic music served as an aural palette of new colors and expression. Romantic composers wrote music that expressed individuality and innovation, exalted nature, and broke new ground formally, harmonically, and stylistically. They also developed a musical language that reflected changing political and social attitudes. Their concern was with freedom and self-expression, with the grandeur of nature, with folk traditions, and with the vicissitudes of romantic love. And above all, their music expressed intense feeling.

Some features of Romantic music resulted from technological advances, such as the invention of valves for brass instruments and key systems for woodwinds, which increased their orchestral prominence, and the development of thicker strings for the piano, which deepened and enhanced the instrument's tonal properties. Other features of the Romantic style reflected social changes, such as the movement of musical performance from church and palace to the public concert hall, which occasioned opportunities for musical compositions of larger scope performed by bigger orchestras and choruses. This type of change enriched the orchestral sound, along with new timbres.

Although some Romantic works tended to be, on the whole, larger and longer than their counterparts from earlier centuries, there developed alongside the monumental impulse one toward the miniature. Chopin and Schubert, for example, wrote numerous short piano pieces of only a few minutes' duration. Schubert and Schumann, among others, developed the **Lied** (or art song), also a small form, designed for performance by a singer and accompanist in a room in someone's house. The monumentality of Romantic music is evident in the size of the orchestra needed to perform symphonic and choral works and the sheer magnitude of some of the works themselves. Some symphonies of Gustave Mahler (1860–1911), for example, last two hours, and require more than a hundred orchestral players as well as a hundred choral singers. And four operas of Richard Wagner (1813–83) create a linked cycle, the *Ring of the Niebelung*, which takes thirteen hours to perform.

Program Music.   Program music is a characteristic form of Romantic composition. As opposed to **absolute music,** which does not refer to anything outside of musical sound, form, and tone color, **program music** describes, in musical tones, a scene, story, event, or other nonmusical situation. Exploiting the mind's capacity to suggest and evoke, program music attempts to imitate something beyond the music itself by emphasizing an instrument's special properties or tone.

Earlier composers had used the flute to imitate birdsong, as did the Baroque composer Antonio Vivaldi in *The Four Seasons*. Renaissance composers such as Thomas Weelkes had imitated human sighing with a downward melodic motion. But composers of the Romantic era developed the idea of musical description into something far more ambitious, creating a musical program that governed an entire symphonic movement or work. In his Symphony no. 6, nicknamed "the Pastoral Symphony," for example, Beethoven provides all five movements with descriptive titles, including "Awakening of joyful feelings upon arriving in the country" and "The thunderstorm."

Hector Berlioz.   One of the most innovative of Romantic composers was HECTOR BERLIOZ [BEAR-lee-ohz] (1803–69). After pursuing a medical degree, he turned instead to music, analyzing scores, attending operas, giving lessons, singing in a theater chorus, and composing. Not long out of the Paris Conservatory of Music, Berlioz wrote his *Symphonie Fantastique*, a work that shocked Parisian audiences with its innovative orchestration, its musical recreation of a bizarre witches' sabbath, and its autobiographical theme about Berlioz's own "endless and unquenchable passion" for the English actress, Harriet Smithson, whom he pursued and married against the wishes of both their families.

The *Symphonie Fantastique* contains five movements: (1) Reveries, Passions; (2) A Ball; (3) Scene in the Country; (4) March to the Scaffold; and (5) Dream of a Witches' Sabbath. Each movement uses distinctive musical material. The first movement, for example, combines a mood of reverie with an agitated and impassioned section that employs dramatic crescendos and obsessive repetitions of a musical theme Berlioz used throughout this movement and the entire symphony. This "fixed idea," or **idée fixe,** as he called it, exemplifies musically the image of "the beloved one herself [who] becomes for him a melody, a recurrent theme that haunts him everywhere." Berlioz transforms the beloved's theme of the *idée fixe* in each movement according to the needs of the program. The *idée fixe* unifies the symphony and carries it forward to a tragic conclusion. Throughout, Berlioz continually expands the orchestral palette, introducing a wide range of instruments including bells, cymbals, sponge-tipped drumsticks, a snare drum, and four harps.

Franz Schubert and Johannes Brahms.   Inspired by the outburst of lyric poetry of the age, many composers turned to writing songs. FRANZ SCHUBERT [SHU-bert] (1797–1828) lived in Vienna and was a contemporary of Beethoven's. Over the course of his career, he wrote more than six hundred songs, many of which were settings of Goethe's verse. He also wrote three **song cycles,** or groups of linked songs, including *Die Schöne Müllerin* (*The Pretty Miller-Maid*) of 1824, which tells the story of a love affair that starts joyously only to end in tragedy.

Song was also one of the favorite forms of Johannes Brahms (1833–97), who composed later in the century. As a boy he played piano in the bars and coffeehouses of his native Hamburg, and during the Hungarian uprising of 1848, when the city was inundated with refugees, he became particularly intrigued by gypsy songs and melodies. His most famous song, known today as "Brahms's Lullaby," was written in 1868 for the baby son of a woman who sang in the Hamburg choir. Only just over two minutes long, the song is one of the most peaceful and serene ever written.

In addition to his songs, Brahms wrote three significant concertos, two for piano and one for violin and orchestra. He composed four important symphonies, along with a multitude of chamber works and pieces for solo piano. His orchestral music especially reflects the formalist Romantic style, hewing more closely to classical musical structures inherited from Beethoven.

Clara Schumann and Fanny Mendelssohn.

Two composers of the nineteenth century, whose works have been overshadowed in one case by a husband and in another by a brother, are Clara Wieck Schumann, wife of Robert Schumann, and Fanny Mendelssohn Hensel, sister of Felix Mendelssohn. Fanny Mendelssohn (1805–47) was a German pianist and a composer of Lieder and chamber music. Her works were long neglected, but in recent years have begun to be published and performed. Her songs are particularly accomplished, with the well-crafted piano accompaniments playing an important role as settings for the poetic texts set to music. Their lyricism appears as well in her "songs without words," short piano pieces in the style of the Lied, a genre in which her brother Felix was also accomplished and which he is often credited with having invented (though Fanny may have an equal claim to that honor).

Clara Schumann (1819–96), like her husband Robert and also like Fanny Mendelssohn, was a pianist and composer. Clara Schumann's first public appearance as a pianist was at age nine, followed by a complete recital at age eleven, and a concert tour a year later. Over the objections of her father, Clara Wieck married Robert Schumann when she was twenty-one, and became a close musical collaborator, studying symphonic and chamber music scores with him, and composing some pieces together, including a series of songs with their Lied settings intertwined. Johannes Brahms was a friend of both Robert and Clara Schumann, and was acknowledged to have been in love with her. After Robert Schumann's death, Clara continued to champion his music, as well as that of Brahms, and is believed to have been a direct influence on the music of both composers.

Chopin and the Piano.

If Berlioz represents one pole of the Romantic composer's spectrum, FREDERIC CHOPIN [SHOW-Pan] (1810–49) represents the other. Where Berlioz wrote mostly in large forms, Chopin wrote in small ones. Where Berlioz composed for orchestra, Chopin wrote almost exclusively for the piano. During the eighteenth and the early nineteenth centuries, the **piano** (then called the pianoforte) was a smaller instrument than the concert version of today. Throughout the Romantic period, it was used as a solo instrument for short lyric pieces, as an accompaniment to songs, and for orchestral use. Unlike the harpsichord, which plucks its strings, the piano strikes them with small felt-tipped hammers, giving the musician the ability to modulate between soft and loud simply by exerting more or less pressure on the keys—hence the name, *piano* (soft) *forte* (loud), later shortened simply to *piano*.

Chopin composed two piano concertos, two large-scale piano sonatas, and a series of semilong works for solo piano, as well as two sets of études (or studies), a group of **preludes** in different keys, a set of **nocturnes** (or night pieces) mostly melancholy in tone, along with **waltzes,** polonaises, and mazurkas, which capture the spirit and flavor of the Parisian salon and of the Polish peasant world. The **polonaises** and the **mazurkas** reflect Chopin's nationalistic spirit during a time when Poland was partly under Russian domination. The majestic Polonaise in A Flat, op. 53, one of Chopin's best known pieces, expresses both joy and pride in a spirit of noble grandeur. The spirit of the polonaise ennobles it, its melody makes it memorable, and its technical demands make it a bravura piece for the piano virtuoso.

Among his most lyrical and sensuous pieces, Chopin's nocturnes conjure up images of moonlight and reverie. Nocturne no. 2 in E Flat, for example, is slow and suffused with a sense of melancholy that is sustained and embellished throughout. A brief expression of excitement is followed by a quiet ending in keeping with the work's pervasive mood of bittersweet and pensive sadness. Chopin's ability to bring out the piano's rich palette of sound and to exploit its resonant musical possibilities revolutionized the way later composers wrote for the instrument.

Giuseppe Verdi and Grand Opera.

Opera first appeared as a distinct form early in the seventeenth century in Italy. Its popularity was increased by Claudio Monteverdi, who further contributed to its development. During the eighteenth century, it became popular in England and Austria, with Mozart composing his consummate operatic masterpieces, including *Don Giovanni* and *The Marriage of Figaro*. It was during the nineteenth century, however, that opera became

Connections

GOETHE AND SCHUBERT: POETRY AND SONG

During the nineteenth century there occurred an explosion of lyric poetry fueled by the Romantic movement. In England, France, and Germany especially, poetry poured from the pens of writers such as William Wordsworth, Samuel Taylor Coleridge, John Keats, Lord Byron, Alfred de Musset, Victor Hugo, and Heinrich Heine, among many others. Of the German poets, the poetry of Johann Wolfgang von Goethe was especially inspiring to the young Viennese composer Franz Schubert.

Schubert set many poems to music, perfecting a form of musical art called the *Lied* (plural *Lieder*). The Lied was a type of art song set to an accompaniment, usually for piano, that suited the tone, mood, and details of a poem. Schubert composed more than six hundred Lieder, more than fifty of them to poems by Goethe. Among the most accomplished of Schubert's settings of Goethe texts is a song he wrote as a teenager: *Erlkönig (The Erlking)*.

Based on a Danish legend, Goethe's narrative poem has the Romantic qualities of strangeness and awe. The poem tells the story of a boy who is pursued, charmed, then violently abducted by the king of the elves, as the child rides on horseback through the forest with his father.

FATHER   My son, why hide your face so anxiously?
SON   Father, don't you see the Erlking?
The Erlking with his crown and his train?
FATHER   My son, it is a streak of mist.
ERLKING   Dear child, come, go with me!
I'll play the prettiest games with you.
Many colored flowers grow along the shore,
My mother has many golden garments.
SON   My father, my father, and don't you hear
The Erlking whispering promises to me?
FATHER   Be quiet, stay quiet, my child;
The wind is rustling in the dead leaves.
. . .
ERLKING   I love you, your beautiful figure delights me!
And if you're not willing, then I shall use force!
SON   My father, my father, now he is taking hold of me!
The Erlking has hurt me!
NARRATOR   The father shudders, he rides swiftly on;
He holds in his arms the groaning child,

He reaches the courtyard weary and anxious:
In his arms the child—was dead.

In setting Goethe's poem, Schubert was faced with the challenge of delineating in music the lines and voices of four characters—father, son, narrator, and Erlking. His response to the challenge exhibits his early musical genius. Schubert differentiates the poem's characters by giving them very different melodies and by putting their music in different vocal registers. The child's vocal line is high pitched and fearful. The father's is in a lower register and conveys confidence. The Erlking's melody is lilting and seductive. Schubert also characterizes the horse by using galloping triplets in the piano accompaniment. Throughout the alternation of the characters' lines, Schubert builds tension by raising the child's vocal line in pitch and increasing its intensity. By altering the character of the Erlking's music toward the end, he suggests the Erlking's shift from charm and seduction to threatening menace.

Throughout his setting of Goethe's poem, Schubert finds musical analogues for the poet's language, imagery, and story. One of his more dramatic strategies is to slow down the music at the end, and he actually stops singer and accompanist in a dramatic pause in the middle of the final line: "In his arms the child—was dead."

---

internationally popular, with Romantic composers of many countries participating in the grand flowering of the genre.

The rise of the middle class after 1820 helped usher in a new kind of opera, grand opera, which appealed to the masses because of its spectacle as much as its music. Alongside the drama and passion of grand opera there remained comic opera, which continued to flourish as it had in the previous century.

Italy's greatest and most important Romantic composer of any kind was GIUSEPPE VERDI [VAIR-dee] (1813–1901), whose music epitomizes dramatic energy, power, and passion. Born in northern Italy near Parma, Verdi had little formal musical training. Verdi's career began with a series of early operas in the 1850s—*Rigoletto*, *Il Trovatore*, and *La Traviata;* continued with a series of popular operas in the 1860s—*Un Ballo in Maschere, La*

Forza del Destino, and *Don Carlos;* and concluded triumphantly with a series of grand operas in the 1870s and 1880s—*Aida, Otello* (based on Shakespeare's *Othello*), and *Falstaff* (based on Shakespeare's *Merry Wives of Windsor*).

Rigoletto, composed in 1851, is one of Verdi's most dramatic works. Based on a play by the French Romantic writer Victor Hugo, *Rigoletto* depicts intense passion and violence in a tale of seduction, revenge, and murder. Rigoletto is a court jester, a hunchback who serves the duke of Mantua. When the Duke seduces his daughter Gilda, Rigoletto plans to kill him in revenge and lures the Duke to a quiet inn with Maddalena, the sister of his hired assassin, Sparafucile. He hopes that Gilda will renounce her love for the Duke when she sees him attempt to seduce Maddalena. His hopes, however, are dashed when Gilda sacrifices her own life to save the Duke.

The melodies Verdi provides for his characters perfectly express their feelings. The Duke sings one of the most famous of all operatic arias, "*La donna è mobile*" ("Woman is fickle"), which perfectly captures his frivolous and pleasure-loving nature. Following this song, Verdi provides a quartet for the Duke, Maddalena, Gilda, and Rigoletto, giving voice to their individual concerns. In response to the Duke's elegantly seductive melodic line, Maddalena voices a series of sharp broken laughs. Gilda's melody is fraught with pain and sorrow; Rigoletto's reveals his heated anger as he curses the Duke. Verdi deftly balances the individual singers so their ensemble singing is blended into a unified and dramatic expression of feeling.

Richard Wagner. As Beethoven had dominated the musical world of the first half of the nineteenth century, RICHARD WAGNER [VAHG-ner] (1813–83) dominated the musical world of the second half. It was, in fact, through intense study of Beethoven's works that Wagner became a composer. Late in life, Wagner explained that he had wanted to do for opera what Beethoven had done for symphonic music—to make it express a wide range of experience and to have it achieve overwhelming emotional effects. Wagner called the new kind of opera he would create "music drama." Unlike Beethoven, whose works express a profound hope in human possibility, Wagner displays a more pessimistic attitude toward life, emphasizing the blind forces of irrationality and passion that drive human behavior. Wagner's works include the comic *Die Meistersinger von Nürenberg*, the mystical *Lohengrin*, and the sensuous *Tristan and Isolde*, which influenced subsequent European musical style perhaps more than any work of the late nineteenth century. His operas portray characters whose lives are made unhappy by circumstances they cannot control, as in *Tristan and Isolde*, in which the two lovers are kept apart only to be finally united in death.

Wagnerian music drama brings together song and instrumental music, dance and drama and poetry in a single unbroken stream of art. Wagner's ambitious goals were to restore the importance of music in opera, to establish a better balance between orchestra and singers, and to raise the quality of the librettos, or texts of operas. This last Wagner accomplished by finding his subjects in medieval legend and Nordic mythology and by writing his own librettos, or little books, for his operatic music.

Designed to do more than simply provide beautiful accompaniments for arias, Wagner's operatic orchestral writing was meant to arouse intense emotion, to comment on stage action, to be associated with incidents in the plot, and to reflect characters' behavior. Wagner accomplished these goals in part by using what were called **leitmotifs**. These were usually brief fragments of melody or rhythm that, when played, would remind the listeners of particular characters and actions, somewhat in the way a movie or television theme triggers associations in the mind of the audience.

Wagner's tetralogy *The Ring of the Niebelung*, which is generally considered his greatest work, includes four operas—*The Rhinegold*, *The Valkyries*, *Siegfried*, and *The Twilight of the Gods*. Based on Norse myth, the opera is a profusion of grandeur, in the story it tells, in its singing and orchestration, and in its staging, sets, and costumes (fig. 17.18).

MUSIC IN RUSSIA

Before Peter the Great's Europeanization drive in the eighteenth century, Russian music consisted primarily of religious and folk music. After the czar's return from the West, however, European music, particularly that composed during the eighteenth and nineteenth centuries, greatly influenced what was being produced in Russia. Among the composers who were able to synthesize the two musical styles were Modest Mussorgsky, whose operas commemorate great Russian leaders, and Peter Ilyich Tchaikovsky, whose ballets, operas, symphonies, and chamber works made him an internationally acclaimed figure.

Modest Mussorgsky. Supporting himself by working as a government clerk, MODEST MUSSORGSKY (moo-ZORG-skee) (1839–81) composed relatively few works; although each reflected important qualities of the Russian national character. Mussorgsky led the school of Russian nationalist music in the 1860s that incorporated elements of Russian folk music into its compositions and used ancient Russian church modes in addition to the Western major and minor scales.

Most prominent among Mussorgsky's works is *Boris Godunov*, an opera that reveals the human soul in all its profundity. *Boris Godunov* is based on a poem by the Russian Alexander Pushkin (1799–1837). It is in four acts and opens with a prologue that contains two important choral scenes, set in front of the Kremlin churches, which convey the national and religious spirit of old Russia. Mussorgsky includes the sound of the church bells, almost as important an emblem of Russian religious fervor as religious icons.

Peter Tchaikovsky. If Mussorgsky is to be considered one of the most nationalistic of Russian composers, PETER ILYICH TCHAIKOVSKY [cheye-KOV-skee] (1840–93) can be said to be one of the most European. At the age of thirty, Tchaikovsky was introduced to a wealthy patron, Nadezhda von Meck. His patron agreed to attend to his material needs on condition that they never meet but only correspond. The more than three thousand letters they exchanged have given us an intimate picture of Tchaikovsky, the artist and the man. Although he was often reproached for his excessive sentimentality, his six symphonies are some of the most beautiful examples of Western influence on a Russian composer. Tchaikovsky was one of the first Russian composers to visit America, and his music remains popular in the United States as well as in his homeland today. A favorite among Americans, his *1812 Overture* was commissioned to celebrate the seventieth anniversary of Russia's victory over Napoleon. With booming cannons, familiar tunes, ringing bells, and fireworks,

FIGURE 17.18   Brunhilde enveloped in fire, in the 1989 staging of Wagner's tetralogy *The Ring of the Niebelung* at the Royal Opera House, Covent Garden, London.

Table 17-1   ROMANTIC COMPOSERS AND REPRESENTATIVE WORKS
Ludwig von Beethoven (1770–1827): Symphony no. 5
Franz Schubert (1797–1828): *The Erlking* (Lied or art song)
Hector Berlioz (1803–69): *Symphonie Fantastique*
Frederic Chopin (1810–49): Revolutionary Etude (piano piece)
Richard Wagner (1813–83): *Tristan and Isolde* (music drama)
Giuseppe Verdi (1813–1901): *La Bohème* (opera)
Johannes Brahms (1833–97): Piano Concerto # 2
Peter Ilyich Tchaikovsky (1840–93): *The Nutcracker* (ballet)

this piece is frequently performed at Fourth of July celebrations.

Tchaikovsky is best known for his ballet music, such as *Swan Lake, Sleeping Beauty,* and *The Nutcracker.* His work exhibits a gift for melodic invention and demonstrates his skill as an orchestrator, highlighting the tonal color and varied expressive qualities of the full range of orchestral instruments. In its sense of drama and intense emotion, Tchaikovsky's music shares important affinities with other nineteenth-century Romantic composers from France, Italy, Germany, and Austria.

REALISM

Realism is the term used to describe a development in the arts in which many artists tried to convey in a non-idealized way the realities of modern life. The artist's role was no longer simply to reveal the beautiful and the sublime, but to open the public's eyes to the world around them, not just its grandeur but its brute reality as well. In Realist art and literature, the aim is to tell the truth, not

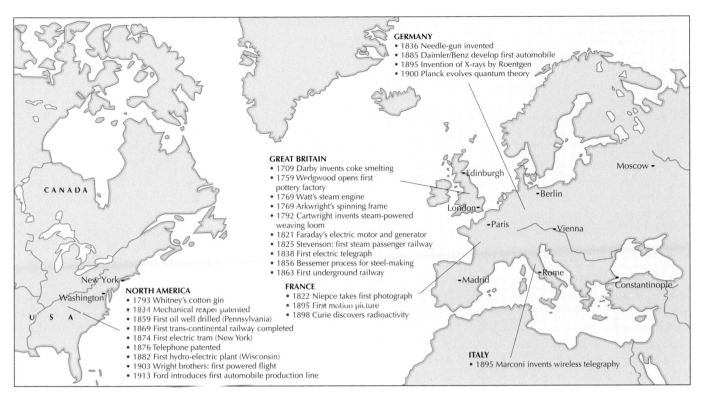

GERMANY
• 1836 Needle-gun invented
• 1885 Daimler/Benz develop first automobile
• 1895 Invention of X-rays by Roentgen
• 1900 Planck evolves quantum theory

GREAT BRITAIN
• 1709 Darby invents coke smelting
• 1759 Wedgwood opens first
  pottery factory
• 1769 Watt's steam engine
• 1769 Arkwright's spinning frame
• 1792 Cartwright invents steam-powered
  weaving loom
• 1821 Faraday's electric motor and generator
• 1825 Stevenson: first steam passenger railway
• 1838 First electric telegraph
• 1856 Bessemer process for steel-making
• 1863 First underground railway

NORTH AMERICA
• 1793 Whitney's cotton gin
• 1834 Mechanical reaper patented
• 1859 First oil well drilled (Pennsylvania)
• 1869 First trans-continental railway completed
• 1874 First electric tram (New York)
• 1876 Telephone patented
• 1882 First hydro-electric plant (Wisconsin)
• 1903 Wright brothers: first powered flight
• 1913 Ford introduces first automobile production line

FRANCE
• 1822 Niepce takes first photograph
• 1895 First motion picture
• 1898 Curie discovers radioactivity

ITALY
• 1895 Marconi invents wireless telegraphy

MAP 17.2   The Industrial Revolution in Europe and America.

to be true to some higher, perfect ideal. Ordinary events and objects were, to the Realist, as interesting as heroes or the grand events of history. Increasingly, after the revolution of 1789, it was no longer the aristocracy who made history, but the ordinary working class people. And so it was to the lives of the working class that Realist art turns for its inspiration.

In Lyons in 1831, silk workers had gone on strike for better wages. The situation fomented for three years until, in 1834, strikers fought police and national troops in a six-day battle that resulted in hundreds of deaths. A few days later, Louis-Philippe suspended publication of a radical newspaper and arrested the leaders of the working-class Society of the Rights of Man. In protest, workers again took to the streets, battling with government troops. In one working-class neighborhood, troops invaded an apartment building from which, they claimed, shots had been fired.

Honoré Daumier.   The cartoonist HONORÉ DAU-MIER [DOME-yay] (1801–79) depicted the aftermath in a lithograph exhibited in a storefront window a few days later, *Rue Transonain, April 15, 1834* (fig. 17.19). A father, in a nightshirt, lies dead by his bed. Beneath him, face down, lies his child. His wife is sprawled in the shadows, and another, older man, perhaps the child's grandfather, lies to the right. Such a slaughter of the innocent outraged not only the Parisian working class but the intelligentsia as well.

KARL MARX AND FRIEDRICH ENGELS

It was precisely such conditions, common across Europe, that influenced the thinking of Karl Marx (1818–83) and his colleague Friedrich Engels (1820–95). Workers, they realized, had no effective political voice other than revolution and, alienated from their labor by an increasingly mechanized industrial system from which they also received no real economic benefit, they were bound to rebel.

FIGURE 17.19   Honoré Daumier, *Rue Transonain, April 15, 1834*, 1834, lithograph, $11\frac{1}{2}'' \times 17\frac{5}{8}''$ (29.2 × 44.8 cm), The Art Institute of Chicago. Charles Derring Fund, 1953. 530. Photograph © 2005, All Rights Reserved. Daumier wrote that "One must be part of one's times." This stark and moving image records the repression of the people by the troops of Louis-Philippe.

"The bourgeoisie . . . has converted the physician, the lawyer, the priest, the poet, the people of science into its paid wage-laborers," they wrote in *The Communist Manifesto* (1848). "Constant revolutionizing of production, uninterrupted disturbance of all social conditions, everlasting uncertainty and agitation distinguish the bourgeois epoch. . . . All that is solid melts into air, all that is holy is profaned, and one is at last compelled to face, with sober senses, the real conditions of life."

Even as Marx was writing these words, Europe was undergoing an unprecedented economic decline. Revolution quickly followed, first in France in February 1848, then in Germany, Austria, Hungary, Poland, and Italy. In France, the government formed National Workshops, known as **ateliers,** in order to put the people back to work. But enrollment quickly swelled to a size that the government could not handle—120,000 by June—and, fearing they had inadvertently created an army of the dissatisfied and unemployed, the government disbanded the workshops. The reaction was swift and, on June 23, the working class rebelled. Three days later, after some of the bloodiest street fighting in European history, the rebels found themselves surrounded in their neighborhoods, with an estimated ten thousand dead. More died in the struggles that followed, and eleven thousand others were imprisoned and deported to the French colonies, particularly to North Africa. It was, Marx wrote, "the first great battle . . . between the two classes that split modern society." For

a few brief weeks, Delacroix's *Liberty Leading the People* was removed from storage and put on public view, and on December 10, 1848, Louis Napoleon Bonaparte, nephew of the first emperor, was elected president of France in a landslide election.

FRENCH PAINTING

Rosa Bonheur. One of the first truly successful painters of working class subjects was ROSA BONHEUR [BON-ur] (1822–99). She disliked life in Paris, where she had grown up, preferring the rural life. A student of zoology, Bonheur made detailed studies out of doors and even painted there, directly from nature, which was not yet common practice. When studying the anatomy of animals at the Paris slaughterhouses or when observing horses at the Paris horse fairs, Bonheur dressed in men's suits because, she explained, women's clothing interfered with her work. By dressing as a man she was able to move in a world from which she would have otherwise been excluded. She described herself as of a "brusque and almost savage nature," as well as "perfectly feminine" and proud of being a woman.

After winning a first-class medal at the 1848 French Salon, Bonheur was commissioned in 1849 by the French government to paint *Plowing in the Nievernais: The Dressing of the Vines* (fig. 17.20), which established her as a leading painter in France. The painting portrays peasant life in harmony with nature, especially with the animal kingdom.

FIGURE 17.20   Rosa Bonheur, *Plowing in the Nivernais: The Dressing of the Vines*, 1849, oil on canvas, 5′ 9″ × 8′ 8″ (1.75 × 2.64 m), F. R. 64. Musée d'Orsay, Paris. Erich Lessing/Art Resource, NY. Bonheur studied directly from her subject to create this factual record of nature's grandeur. Previously, such subject matter was not considered worthy of an artist's attention and certainly would not have been depicted on such a large scale.

Depicted with almost photographic realism is a scene of the good agrarian life in which the soil is fertile, the oxen are strong, and the weather is favorable. It seems to illustrate lines written by Bonheur's contemporary George Sand (another woman who dressed in men's clothing) in her 1846 novel *The Devil's Pond*, which describes "a truly beautiful sight, a noble subject for a painter. At the far end of the flat ploughland, a handsome young man was driving a magnificent team [of] oxen."

Gustave Courbet.   While Sand and Bonheur admired the French peasantry, GUSTAVE COURBET [koor-BAY] (1819–77) refused to idealize working life. A Realist, Courbet preferred simply to tell things as they were. A group of large paintings he exhibited in the Paris Salon of 1850–51 outraged conservative critics, and Courbet found himself defending not only his works but the "honest truth" of the people who were their subjects. He had, in fact, returned to his native village, Ornans, in 1849, after the revolution and painted the realities of life experienced by the peasant farmers.

A Burial at Ornans (fig. 17.21) angered the public in part because it seemed, at the very least, pretentious. At 10′ 3″ × 20′ 10″, it is of a size generally reserved for only the most serious allegories and histories. A distant relative of Courbet's, one C. E. Teste, is being buried, and the mayor of Ornans, the justice of the peace, Courbet's father, and his three sisters are among the mourners who line up across the painting, echoing the horizon line's con-

tour. Even the grave seems an extension of the Loue valley that cuts through the plateau behind them. Nevertheless, the painting is emotionally unfocused. No one's eyes are fixed on the same place, not even on the grave or the coffin. The dog stares away uninterestedly. The religious import of the scene is undermined by the way the cross seems to sit askew on the far horizon. The emotional impact of death is entirely deromanticized as well. We are witness here to a simple matter of fact.

The work's lack of idealism is especially evident if we compare it to Bonheur's *Plowing in the Nivernais*. Where the figures in Courbet's painting seem static, forming an almost flat wall of humanity in front of the viewer, Bonheur's similarly horizontal format is dynamic. On the left, the hills lead downward and away from the viewer; on the right, the oxen move upward and toward the viewer.

Edouard Manet.   The most characteristic Realist painter was EDOUARD MANET [man-AY] (1832–83). Born into a well-to-do family, Manet was a sensitive and cultured man who studied literature and music (he married his piano teacher). After Manet twice failed the entrance exam to the Naval Training School, his family permitted him to study art. Manet had an academic training, which included copying paintings at the Louvre. He particularly admired the artists Hals, Velázquez, and Goya, all of whom worked in a painterly style, letting the brushstrokes show.

His *Luncheon on the Grass* (fig. 17.22), often referred to by its French title *Le Déjeuner sur l'herbe*, was painted in 1863.

FIGURE 17.21   Gustave Courbet, *A Burial at Ornans*, 1849, oil on canvas, ca. 10′ 3″ × 20′ 10″ (3.10 × 6.40 m). Musée du Louvre, Paris. Reunion de Musées Nationaux. Art Resource, NY. The extremely hostile reaction of the public to this painting was due to the fact that the subject was not elevated, glorified, or romanticized—Courbet referred to this as the burial of Romanticism. He said, "Show me an angel and I'll paint one."

FIGURE 17.22   Edouard Manet, *Luncheon on the Grass (Le Déjeuner sur l'herbe)*, 1863, oil on canvas, 7′ × 8′ 10″ (2.10 × 2.60 m), Musée d'Orsay, Paris. An outraged public deemed this painting indecent for depicting a naked woman out of doors with two clothed men. Actually painted in Manet's studio from models, it was based on a print by Marcantonio Raimondi after a painting by Raphael, ca. 1520, of the *Judgment of Paris*.

That year, the official Salon jury rejected over four thousand paintings, producing such an uproar from disappointed painters and their supporters that Napoleon III set up a separate salon to exhibit the rejected paintings, the Salon des Refusés (Salon of the Rejected). Thus, there were two salons, and the monopoly of academicism had been broken. But even at the Salon des Refusés, *Luncheon on the Grass* was regarded as shocking and scandalous by many. In fact, Manet had not painted an actual event, as the public thought; instead, his sources were highly respectable. The poses of the three central figures were derived from an engraving made about 1520 by the Italian artist Marcantonio Raimondi after a painting of the *Judgment of Paris* by Raphael.

It was his painting style, above all, that offended many. He painted directly on the canvas with thinned oil paint, which permitted him to wipe off any mistakes, the traces of which may sometimes still be seen. When the compo-

sition was determined, he executed the final painting directly with large brushstrokes. Instead of the smooth surfaces admired by the public, Manet's brushstrokes were strong, quick, and remain fully visible.

Manet's way of painting was fresh and direct. Rather than using carefully wrought highlights and shadows to make forms appear three dimensional, Manet intentionally flattened forms and used rapid, loose brushwork. This was criticized as carelessness or incompetence by many critics.

AMERICAN PAINTING

Winslow Homer.   During the time that France and the rest of Europe were enduring class struggle and adjusting to the new industrial world, Americans had one thing on their minds—the Civil War, which gave impetus to American Realism. Recording events in the Civil War for

Critical Thinking

REALISM AND FEMINISM

In the last quarter century, feminist scholars of literature, music, and art began an intensive study of works created by women. Bringing sociological, economic, and historical approaches to the study of works by women, feminist scholars raised questions about the ways in which women have been portrayed in art created by men. One example of this concern is the extent to which paintings that include both men and women may show the men clothed and the women nude, as Edouard Manet's *Le Dejeuner sur l'herbe* (fig. 17.22). In this painting, two fully clothed men sit in a park-like setting with a nude woman. Why, we might ask, are the men clothed, yet the woman unclothed? Why is the nude woman looking directly out at the viewer? Why is there a second woman, clothed, in the background? What is suggested about the relations of the men and women in the painting? What roles are assumed by each?

To what extent do feminist considerations enhance your understanding and appreciation of a painting like *Le Dejeuner sur l'herbe?* To what extent does the painting reflect a particularly male or masculine sensibility? To what extent does the representation of women (and men) in the painting reflect the time and place in which it was created?

Harper's Weekly was a young illustrator named Winslow Homer (1836–1910). He specialized in camp life and avoided the brutal scenes of battle captured by the new medium of photography. Homer's painting career began soon after the war with *Prisoners from the Front* (fig. 17.23), of 1866. This work depicts the surrender of three Confederate soldiers to a Union officer, a recognizable portrait of General Francis Channing Barlow, a distant cousin of Homer's. The painting was considered remarkable, even at the time, for the unrepentant, even arrogant attitude of the central figure, who, hand on hip, stares defiantly at General Barlow. Here, some felt, was an image of a nation at odds with itself.

After the painting's exhibition at the National Academy of Design in 1866, it was displayed in Paris at the World Exposition of 1867. Homer accompanied it and, once there, became acquainted with the work of Gustave Courbet and Edouard Manet. Manet's willingness to paint everyday life in a direct and informal way especially appealed to Homer. His later paintings continued to evoke the aesthetics of photography, but they also showed brilliant color and brushwork, borrowed from Manet, which insisted on their status as paintings by emphasizing the quality of pigment on canvas.

Thomas Eakins.
Another American Realist was THOMAS EAKINS [AY-kins] (1844–1916). Eakins, from Philadelphia, referred to himself as a scientific realist. He was interested in human anatomy, in the construction of the human body, its muscles and bones, saying that he learned more from watching his fellow students wrestling in the studio than he did from drawing a posed model. He even took medical courses in anatomy at Jefferson Medical College in Philadelphia for two years. He saw no reason for artists to study the antique, as was customary in his time, favoring instead the study of nature, saying that nature is "just as varied and just as beautiful in our day as she was in the time of Phidias," noting that "the Greeks did not study the antique."

In *The Swimming Hole* (fig. 17.24), painted 1883–85, Eakins creates a composition around a series of studies of nude boys seen from different angles and in different poses, some still and other more active—especially the boy caught in mid-air as he dives off the rocks. Eakins was fascinated by the human body and dedicated to depicting it accurately in motion. He used photographs in his figure studies. Eakins taught at the Pennsylvania Academy of Fine Arts in Philadelphia from 1870 to 1886, until forced to resign because of a scandal he created by introducing a nude male model to a women's drawing class. Eakins had a serious personality and his approach was intellectual and methodical. But his realism was too harsh for most people and he sold few paintings during his lifetime.

Jennie Augusta Brownscombe.
Another American. Jennie Augusta Brownscombe (1850–1936), after the death of her father when she was eighteen, earned a living by selling her paintings to be reproduced on Christmas cards and calendars. Consequently, her art became widely known. She moved to Manhattan, studied art, and was one of the founders of the Art Students League, where she later taught.

The setting in her *Love's Young Dream* (fig. 17.25), painted in 1887, must have been familiar to her, for she was born in rural Pennsylvania in a log cabin. She often depicts country life, family, and tradition in sentimental ways. Her narrative paintings are realistic, the details enhancing the appeal of a charming story—as the cat playing with the ball of yarn that has fallen from the lap of the older woman, presumably the mother in this family—which also recalls the artist's own, as Brownscombe was an only child.

FIGURE 17.23   Winslow Homer, *Prisoners from the Front*, 1866, oil on canvas, 24″ × 38″
(60.9 × 96.5 cm), signed and dated (lower right): HOMER 1866. Metropolitan Museum of
Art, New York, gift of Mrs. Frank B. Porter, 1922. (22.207). Photograph © 1985 The Metropolitan Museum of Art, NY. For such factual narrative depictions of aspects of life in America,
Homer was known during his lifetime as "the greatest American artist."

FIGURE 17.24   Thomas Eakins, *The Swimming Hole*, ca.
1883–85, oil on canvas, 27″ × 36″ (68.5 × 91.4 cm), Purchased
by the Friends of Art, Fort Worth Art Association, 1925; acquired by Amon Carter Museum, 1990 from the Modern Art
Museum of Fort Worth through grants and donations. As part
of his quest for realistic factuality, in the foreground, Eakins
painted himself as part of the group.

FIGURE 17.25   Jennie Augusta Brownscombe, *Love's Young
Dream*, 1887, oil on canvas, 21¼″ × 32½″ (54 × 81.6 cm), National Museum of Women in the Arts, Washington, D.C. Gift
of Wallace and Wilhelmina Holladay. Brownscombe suggests
complex stories and relationships through simple compositions
painted in a realistic detailed style.

THE RISE OF PHOTOGRAPHY

Photography was invented simultaneously in England and France: in 1839 by William Henry Fox Talbot (1800–77) and LOUIS-JACQUES-MANDE DAGUERRE [duh-GARE] (1787–1851). Before photography, an image could *look* spontaneous and immediate; now it could *be* spontaneous and immediate. Moreover, because the photographic image was the product of a machine, it had the aura, at least, of being purely objective, lacking the subjective intervention of the artist. Talbot's images made on sensitized paper between 1833 and 1839 were precursors of modern photographic prints.

Daguerreotypes. Through competition from photography, painted portraits underwent a rapid decline and photographs largely replaced them for a while. The **daguerreotype,** named for Daguerre's process, was the earliest photograph, produced on silver or silver-covered copper plate. In Paris in 1849 alone, over a hundred thousand photographic daguerreotypes, mostly portraits, were sold to people of every rank and class. In England, photography studios sprang up everywhere to satisfy the craze for photographic portraits (fig. 17.26). The photograph

had the advantage of capturing reality accurately and immediately, and as its technology rapidly developed, making it easier and easier to use, it captured the Realist imagination.

Mathew B. Brady. The American Civil War was the first war to be documented in the new medium of photography. It was not action, however, that the photographers captured—the time required to expose film was still too long to permit that. Instead, it was the aftermath of war they recorded, and it was a gruesome sight. Mathew B. Brady (ca. 1823–96) was the best known of the war photographers, and his *On the Antietam Battlefield* (fig. 17.27) of 1862 is representative of his work. In the battle at Antietam, Maryland, on September 17, nearly five thousand men died and eighteen thousand were wounded. Brady makes dramatic use of the single vantage point that the camera eye so rigorously asserts: Bodies lie beneath the fenceline, stretching as if to infinity. This was the reality of war as it had never before been seen.

Eadweard Muybridge. As camera technology quickly improved, it revealed more and more about the nature of reality. When, in 1872, the former governor of California, Leland Stanford, bet a friend $25,000 that a running horse had all four feet off the ground when either trotting or galloping, he hired EADWEARD MUYBRIDGE [MWE-bridge] (1830–1904) to photograph one of his horses in motion. Along a racetrack at Stanford's ranch in Palo Alto, California, Muybridge lined up a series of cameras with trip wires that would snap the shutter as the horse ran by. For the first time, the muscular and physical

FIGURE 17.26 Richard Beard, *Maria Edgeworth*, 1841, daguerreotype, $2\frac{1}{8}'' \times 1\frac{3}{4}''$ (5.4 × 4.4 cm), National Portrait Gallery, London. Beard's was the first British portrait studio, and the author Edgeworth one of his earliest customers. "It is a wonderful mysterious operation," she wrote. Daguerre's process was used until the end of the nineteenth century.

FIGURE 17.27 Mathew B. Brady, *On the Antietam Battlefield*, 1862, photograph, Library of Congress. In addition to his documentary photographs of the battle's results, Brady photographed President Lincoln so often that he became known as "the President's Cameraman."

FIGURE 17.28   Eadweard Muybridge, *Annie G. Cantering, Saddled*, 1887, collotype print, sheet: 19″ × 24″; image: 7½″ × 16¼″ (19 × 41.3 cm), Philadelphia Museum of Art, City of Philadelphia Trade and Convention Center, Dept. of Commerce (Commercial Museum). Muybridge's sequence studies would lead to the invention of the motion picture by the century's end.

movements of an animal in motion were recorded. Muybridge's studies of animal (fig. 17.28) and human locomotion at the University of Pennsylvania in 1883 would have a major impact on later painters.

Alfred Stieglitz.   Photographer Alfred Stieglitz (1864–1946) had been interested in European modernist work since the turn of the century. Stieglitz was the first American to buy a Picasso. His own photographic talents captured the early modern era, its hustle, streets, and skylines. One classic photograph, *Winter, Fifth Avenue* (fig. 17.29), records Manhattan's main thoroughfare. Even progress and the growth of industry cannot protect those unlucky enough to be caught in this fierce snowstorm.

Gertrude Stanton Käsebier.   The American Gertrude Stanton Käsebier (1852–1934) is considered among the finest photographers. She opened a portrait studio on Fifth Avenue, the most fashionable street in Manhattan. The studio was an immediate success with clients, and her own work exhibited there received favorable reviews.

Using photography as an aesthetic rather than a documentary medium, her subjects were frequently landscapes and figure compositions. This approach, known as **pictorialism,** is seen in *The Manger* (fig. 17.30), a print made around 1899. The lines are softened, the image intentionally slightly out of focus, the details obscured. This differs from the more frequent use of photography to capture a detailed record of a temporary scene. In fact, it has been questioned if there was even a baby in this posed photo. The reference to the birth of Jesus in a stable (the setting was a stable in Newport, RI) is evident.

FIGURE 17.29   Alfred Stieglitz, *Winter, Fifth Avenue*, 1893, photogravure, 8⅝″ × 6 1/16″ (21.9 × 15.4 cm), Museum of Modern Art, New York/Licensed by SCALA, Art Resource, NY. Stieglitz was not only the leading photographer of his day but, through his Gallery 291 in New York, the person most responsible for introducing European *avant-garde* art to the United States.

FIGURE 17.30 Gertrude Stanton Käsebier (1852–1934), American, *The Manger (Ideal Motherhood)*, ca. 1899, platinum print, $7\frac{5}{8}'' \times 5\frac{1}{2}''$ (19.4 × 14 cm), National Museum of Women in the Arts, Washington. D.C. Gift of the Holladay Foundation. One of the most popular photographs taken by Käsebier, this is an example of pictorialism in which photography is used, like other artistic media, to create an aesthetically satisfying image, rather than a documentary record.

FIGURE 17.31 Frédéric-Auguste Bartholdi, *Statue of Liberty (Liberty Enlightening the World)*, Liberty Island, New York Harbor, 1875–84, copper sheeting over iron armature, height of figure 151' 6" (46.18 m). A gift of the French people, the *Statue of Liberty* has become the symbol of the United States. The monument portrays a crowned woman in classical garb, holding the torch high, while breaking underfoot the shackles of tyranny.

Working with the photographer Alfred Stieglitz (fig. 17.29). Käsebier founded the Photo-Secession in 1902, which encouraged the pictorial, rather than the documentary, use of photography.

SCULPTURE

The Statue of Liberty. In 1875, a year before the centennial celebration of the American Revolution, organizers in France conceived the idea of commemorating the event with a colossal statue. A Franco-American Union was founded to raise funds, and the architect Frédéric-Auguste Bartholdi (1834–1904) was hired to design the work. *Liberty Enlightening the World*, commonly known as the *Statue of Liberty* (fig. 17.31), was the result. Bartholdi first made a nine-foot model of the sculpture, and then GUSTAVE EIFFEL [EE-FELL] (1832–1923)—the French engineer who created the Eiffel Tower—designed a huge iron framework to support the giant sheets of copper, molded in

the shape of Bartholdi's model. All the components were transported across the ocean, and in 1884, construction began on Liberty Island in New York Harbor. The sculpture, dedicated in 1886, is itself over 151 feet high and rests on a 150-feet-high concrete pedestal faced with granite. Sculpture and pedestal in turn sit on an eleven-point star, the walls of which are part of old Fort Wood. The Statue of Liberty remains a symbol of welcome and freedom to generations of people immigrating to the United States.

Edmonia Lewis. Among the more interesting sculptors of the era was Edmonia Lewis (1845–after 1911), an American, born outside Albany, to an American Indian mother and an African-American father. After both parents died while she was still a child, she was raised by aunts on her mother's side. Her brother financed her education, and, in 1859, she entered Oberlin College in Ohio. There, however, she was accused of poisoning two classmates, beaten, tried, and acquitted. She moved to Boston and then on to Rome in 1865, were she was highly successful as a sculptor.

FIGURE 17.32 Edmonia Lewis, *The Old Arrow Maker and His Daughter*, ca. 1872, carved marble, $21\frac{1}{2}'' \times 12\frac{5}{8}'' \times 13\frac{3}{8}''$ ($54.75 \times 34.5 \times 34$ cm) Smithsonian Institution, American Art Museum, Washington D.C.; Art Resource, NY. Lewis's mixed racial heritage is referenced in several of her sculptures. This work relates to her mother, a Chippewa Indian, while Lewis's *Forever Free*, the title referring to the end of slavery, relates to her father, an African-American.

FIGURE 17.33 Anne Whitney, *Charles Sumner*, Harvard Square, Cambridge, MA, modeled 1875, cast 1902, bronze, ca. 7′ 1″ × 3′ 2″ × 4′ 8″ ($2.16 \times .97 \times 1.4$ m) (without base). This realistic portrayal of the abolitionist senator is in the Neoclassical style, which returned to the ideals of harmony and balance of the ancient Greeks and Romans, here used to create a sense of stately, noble grandeur.

Lewis carved a variety of subjects, including portraits and religious themes, but perhaps most notable are those that relate to her biracial family background, such as *The Old Arrow Maker and his Daughter* (Fig. 17.32), ca. 1872. Lewis created, a series of contrasts with exquisite carving, between flesh and muscle structure of old and young, male and female. The natural poses of the figures, their attention seemingly caught by the viewer's presence, convey a sense of latent energy.

Anne Whitney. From a very different background was another American who moved to Rome to sculpt. ANNE WHITNEY (1821–1915), from Massachusetts, turned from writing poetry to creating sculpture when she was in her thirties. Independently wealthy and politically liberal, she was a member of a group of expatriate American women sculptors working in Rome. She returned to the United States in 1871, and made the model for the figure of the abolitionist senator *Charles Sumner* (fig. 17.33) in 1875, although it was not cast in bronze until 1902. She

won the competition held by the Boston Art Committee for this commission, but it was rescinded when the Committee learned that Whitney was a woman. She completed the piece independently, many years later; it was her final work. In the Neoclassical style, the monument is grand in scale, and Sumner impressively powerful in Whitney's straightforward depiction.

LITERATURE

Honoré de Balzac. Like the painters of modern life, Realist writers aimed, above all, to represent contemporary life and manners with precision. In the case of HONORÉ DE BALZAC [BALL-zak] (1779–1850), the project was extensive: Balzac sought to represent contemporary life with encyclopedic completeness. In the nearly one hundred novels and stories that make up his series *La Comédie humaine*, Balzac touched on virtually every aspect of French society, from the urban working class and the country peasant, to the middle-class merchant, the new industrialists, and the bankrupt aristocracy. By 1816, while working as a law clerk in Paris, he would spend his evenings wandering through the streets, gathering details for his novels. "In listening to these people," he later recalled, "I felt I could champion their lives. I felt their rags upon my back. I walked with my feet in their tattered shoes; their desires, their wants—everything passed into my soul." His characters—there are over two thousand—often appear in more than one novel, establishing a sense of the interconnectedness of French life. Chief among them is Eugéne Rastignac, the son of a poor provincial family who comes to Paris, mixes with nobility, builds a career as a politician, and generally leads a life of gambling and debauchery. At the climax of *Le Père Goriot*, Rastignac climbs to the top of the hill at Père Lachaise cemetery and, in one of the most famous moments in French literature, faces the city that threatens to consume him: "There lay the glittering world that he had hoped to conquer. He stared at the humming hive as if sucking out its honey in advance and pronounced these impressive words, 'It's you or me now!'" Rastignac's moment on the top of the hill is entirely Romantic. Pitting himself against the world, he is caught in the web of his own Romanticism: from a Realist's point of view, a self-indulgent fate.

Gustave Flaubert.

The Realist novel that represents the most thorough attack on the Romantic sensibility is *Madame Bovary*, published in 1857 after five years in the writing, by GUSTAVE FLAUBERT [floh-BEAR] (1821–80). Flaubert's heroine—if, indeed, *heroine* is a word that can be used to describe her, she is such a banal figure—is Emma Bovary, the wife of a country doctor who seeks to reinvent her life in the manner of the romantic novels she reads so voraciously.

Emma desperately takes lovers to overcome the incessant boredom of everyday life, spends money as if she were nobility, falls into the deepest debt, and finally, in the most romantic gesture of all, commits suicide by swallowing arsenic.

The novel took five years to write because Flaubert sought, in every sentence, to find what he called "*le mot juste*," exactly the right word needed to describe each situation. In this, Flaubert felt, he was proceeding like the modern scientist, investigating the lives of his characters in precisely the same way that the scientist pursues research through careful and systematic observation.

Emile Zola.

Flaubert's scientific approach to writing became the standard for all subsequent French Realist writing, particularly the work of the so-called French naturalists, who emphasized the influence of heredity and environment in determining the fate of the literary characters they created. A prominent naturalist, EMILE ZOLA [ZOH-la] (1840–1902) saw society as a kind of grand laboratory and the people in it as data for his study of the ways in which humans were determined. In books such as *Germinal*, which chronicled the life of French miners, and *Nana*, which detailed the life of a prostitute, Zola used naturalistic techniques to reflect his fatalistic vision of the world.

Realist Writing.

Important English Realist novelists of the time include Charles Dickens (1812–70), Anthony Trollope (1815–82), and George Eliot (1819–80), the pen name of Mary Ann Evans. Eliot's *Middlemarch* (1872) is a portrayal of nineteenth-century life in an English country village. Trollope, an inspector of rural mail deliveries, created an imaginary English country called Barsetshire, the cathedral town of which he named Barchester, and he set a long series of novels in and around this fictional locale. The Barchester novels capture the spirit of nineteenth-century rural life in a series of similarly interconnected tales. Where Trollope and Eliot chronicled country life, Dickens wrote mostly about the increasingly dark urban environment epitomized by London, attacking conditions in the English workhouses in *Oliver Twist*, published serially in 1837–38, and the evils brought on by industrialization in *Hard Times* (1854). Like their continental counterparts, the English novelists wrote about the world in which they lived and that they knew most thoroughly.

In America, nineteenth-century fiction writers tended toward Romantic themes and styles until very late in the century. While Realism was spreading through Europe, American writers, such as Edgar Allan Poe (1809–49), Nathaniel Hawthorne (1804–64), and Herman Melville (1819–91), wrote fiction characterized, in Hawthorne's terms, as "romances" rather than as "novels." In the fiction of these romance writers, characters and settings were not depicted with the social realism of their European counterparts. In Hawthorne, dialogue borders on the archaic and in Melville on the theatrical. Description in the works of both is highly symbolic and often poetic, rather than serving as a vehicle for a sharp-edged realism.

RUSSIAN LITERATURE

One of the glories of Russian art is the development of the Russian novel in the middle to late nineteenth century. Of the many novels written during this half-century period, those of Fyodor Dostoyevsky and Leo Tolstoy tower above the rest. Among the most accomplished of Realist writers, they wrote novels on a grand scale, covering all aspects of Russian culture and society.

Fyodor Dostoyevsky.

FYODOR DOSTOYEVSKY [doss-toh-YEF-skee] (1821–81) was the son of a Moscow doctor and landowner who was murdered by his serfs when Fyodor was eighteen. After studying military engineering, Dostoyevsky spent a year in the army before taking up a literary career, the most dramatic event of which was his arrest and imprisonment for conspiring to set up a secret printing press and discussing political and social ideas

Then & Now

EMERSON, THOREAU, AND THE AMERICAN ENVIRONMENT

During the nineteenth century, the American landscape was considered a source of consolation as well as of sustenance. Nature was celebrated in poems and letters, essays, lectures, and books, most notably by the New England Transcendentalist writers Ralph Waldo Emerson and Henry David Thoreau. For Emerson, nature was a moral teacher, a guide that contained lessons in how to live life properly. Nature was intimately connected with the life of humanity, and thus was not something to be conquered or contested but a dimension of reality to bond with. For Emerson, nature was less to be used as a resource than to be treasured as a gift from God.

Emerson's embrace of the spirit of nature reflects the reverence felt toward the natural world by those who have long made their living from its bountiful resources. And his perspective is shared by a number of contemporary groups concerned with finding the physical, spiritual, and intellectual common ground necessary for sustaining the earth's life.

Emerson's spiritual counterpart in appreciating nature, Henry David Thoreau, was less mystical in his attachment to the natural world but no less devoted to it. Thoreau loved to ramble in the woods, to scrutinize their every nook and cranny to see what he could find there. At the same time, Thoreau found in nature time to deliberate about those few essentials things in life that really matter. "Let us spend one day as deliberately as Nature," he admonishes his readers in *Walden*. For Thoreau, perhaps even more than for Emerson, nature provided an escape from the corruptions of civilization, a place to retreat for spiritual recreation.

In the thought and work of Emerson and Thoreau lie the seeds of the modern environmental movement. Today's Sierra Club and other ecologically minded groups are working to preserve the American land, to conserve the country's resources. They continue the tradition of valuing the natural world not for the profits that can be made from it or even for the solace it can provide, but simply for itself, for its beauty. Environmentalists lament the heedless destruction of natural resources, recognizing they are limited. Environmentalists also view nature as a treasure to be preserved, enjoyed by all and owned by none, most truly possessed by those who have learned to understand the glory and the grandeur Emerson and Thoreau discovered in nature.

---

banned by the czarist regime. After eight months, Dostoyevsky was sentenced to death, only to receive a last-minute reprieve; his sentence was commuted to four years of hard labor and an additional four years of military service. His prison reading was restricted to the New Testament, which he read avidly, and which informs the novels he wrote upon his release, especially *Crime and Punishment* (1866) and *The Brothers Karamazov* (1881).

Dostoyevsky's realism (which he described as a "higher realism") is underpinned by the psychological rather than the social. His interest lies not so much in presenting a panorama of Russian urban life, but in probing the tensions and anxieties that animate and motivate behavior.

His narrative impulse is richly dramatic, realizing itself forcefully in scenes of conflict. The interview scenes with the ax-murderer Raskolnikov and the detective Porfiry Petrovich in *Crime and Punishment* exemplify the drama inherent in his dialogue. Raskolnikov's behavior throughout the novel reflects Dostoyevsky's acute understanding of human psychology, and reveals the author's belief that any transgression of the moral law—in Raskolnikov's case, murder—no matter how reasonable it may appear, results in the guilt of a tormented conscience. The punishment is internal, undeniable, and tortuous.

Leo Tolstoy.
LEO TOLSTOY [TOHL-stoy] (1828–1910) was born into an aristocratic world, one replete with the trappings of high society, including servants, fine cuisine, extravagant clothing, and the manifold opportunities that come with great wealth. As a young man, Tolstoy studied oriental languages at the University of Kazan, but left without taking a degree, returning to run the family estate in Yosnaya Polyana, south of Moscow.

War and Peace was published in 1869. Set in the Napoleonic age, the novel explores the nature of history and the role that great men play in influencing the development of historical events. The book combines speculation on philosophical questions, such as necessity and free will, causation, and human destiny, with social concerns, such as agrarian reform. It also dramatizes ideas about the nature of the Russian state, as well as being a chronicle of the lives of several Russian families, with an emphasis on the philosophy of marriage. The novel contrasts the glories of nature and the simple life with the superficiality and artifice of civilization, celebrating the natural, privileging intuition over analysis, and emphasizing hope in the basic goodness of life rather than more studied forms of civilized learning and behavior.

During the writing of his second masterpiece, *Anna Karenina* (1873–77), Tolstoy experienced a moral and religious crisis that set him on a course that would change his life. *Anna Karenina* possesses all the realism of Tolstoy's earlier novel, but during its writing, the author began to have doubts about the book's secular emphasis, and so in-

Critical Thinking

MEMOIR, FACT, AND TRUTH

Autobiography and memoir have long been important as an overlapping literary genre. Among the earliest autobiographies, St. Augustine's *Confessions* set the standard for self-analysis and self-reflection. Autobiography continued to be of interest to readers, particularly autobiographies of great men, such as those of the religious writer John Bunyan, the historian Edward Gibbon, the scientist Charles Darwin, and the social philosopher, such as Jean-Jacques Rousseau. Autobiography and memoir continue to draw readers into the twenty-first century. Some recent critics believe that these nonfiction prose genres have now outstripped the novel in popularity and importance as a literary genre—though other critics contest that claim.

But there is no question as to the popular appeal of memoir, so much so that the television host Oprah Winfrey chose a memoir, James Frey's *A Million Little Pieces* for her enormously popular and influential Oprah's Book Club. When reports surfaced that the author had fabricated significant portions of his memoir, wildly exaggerating some of his experiences and brazenly inventing others, Oprah withdrew her endorsement of the book. A national debate ensued about the extent to which an autobiographer or memoirist was obliged to tell the truth by sticking to facts and events, and leave invention and fiction to novelists—or to reclassify the work as a novel.

What is your view? To what extent do you think writers of autobiography and memoir should include in their books only actual facts and real events? Or should they, perhaps, identify them as fiction, instead? Is it possible for there to exist autobiographical works, such as memoirs, that contain some invented parts or that exaggerate some details to get at what their authors have called a "larger truth"?

troduced a tone of moral criticism into the work, not only of Anna's adultery, but also of other characters' violations of society's moral norms. Even so, Tolstoy keeps the didactic impulse from overwhelming his literary artistry. Although he disapproves of Anna's adulterous behavior, he portrays her as a powerfully attractive woman, the site of struggle between his artistic sympathy and his moral judgment.

Anton Chekhov.   The finest examples of Russian drama are the plays of its foremost dramatist, ANTON CHEKHOV [CHECK-off] (1860–1904). A short-story writer as well as a playwright, Chekhov began publishing fiction and sketches in newspapers and journals while studying medicine, in order to help support his large family. His fiction was well received, far better, initially, than the plays he would begin writing in the 1880s. Although Chekhov is celebrated as a major influence for later writers such as James Joyce and Ernest Hemingway, his plays are heralded in their own right as Modernist masterpieces and as precursors of important trends in modern theater.

Chekhov's plays, such as *The Three Sisters* and *The Cherry Orchard*, lack the intense melodramatic character of those by other realist dramatists, such as Henrik Ibsen. They don't tell stories, nor do they build toward tragic climaxes. Instead, Chekhov creates characters that are very lifelike in their inability to find happiness, their uncertainty about the future, and their indecisiveness in achieving their desires.

Because Chekhov was writing at a time when the old social order in Russia was dying, his plays have often been seen as dramatizations of the disappearance of the land-owning gentry as a source of authority and cultural value. Yet the playwright's interest lies in human nature, in individuals caught in a world undergoing great transformation. The characters in plays like *The Three Sisters* and *The Cherry Orchard* are neither heroes nor villains. They do not operate as mouthpieces for the dramatist's views. Indeed, their very inability to articulate their feelings, or even to act on them, adds poignancy to their suffering. Chekhov's insight into the truths of human experience is unmatched in modern drama.

THE NEW SCIENCES: PASTEUR AND DARWIN

The interest in the precise, objective description of things evidenced in Realist painting and literature was shared as well by the philosophers and scientists of the age. In France, the scientist LOUIS PASTEUR [pass-TER] (1822–95) began to look at organisms smaller than the eye can see—micro-organisms that he claimed were responsible for the spread of disease. Sterile practices could radically reduce the chance of infection in medical procedures, and by heating food, spoilage could be eliminated, a process that led to the **pasteurization** of milk.

But by far the most influential scientist of the age was Charles Darwin (1809–82). Darwin's *On the Origin of Species*, drafted in 1844 but not published until 1859, laid out his theory of **evolution** by **natural selection.** A landmark work, it had an immediate and profound impact on late-nineteenth-century thought.

Darwin noted that, in the struggle for existence, since nature cannot provide sufficiently for all the animals that

Cultural Impact

The Romantic era saw radical changes in the political makeup of Europe and America. Greece achieved independence; Germany and Italy became unified nations. America, which had gained its independence in the last quarter of the eighteenth century, became a political world power and established itself as a distinctive artistic presence, especially in painting, fiction, and poetry. France, which shared with America the revolutionary ideals of freedom and equality, established the Napoleonic Code, which continues to govern the legal system of the French-speaking world today.

Deep social changes took root during the Romantic age and throughout the nineteenth century. The primary cause of social change was the Industrial Revolution, which altered the way in which many people made their living; with the rise of industry, the demise of agrarian life began. Instead of living on farms and in small country villages, people began migrating to large urban centers, where they found work in manufacturing.

Romanticism profoundly influenced not only nineteenth-century political, social, and artistic concerns, but also twentieth-century attitudes toward these aspects of life. During the Romantic era, writers and artists continued to reflect the respect for human freedom that Enlightenment thinkers had celebrated, retaining the Enlightenment's belief in human possibility. With rare exception, Romantic artists and writers avoided the satiric thrust of Enlightenment art and literature; nor did they emphasize the importance of reason celebrated by the Enlightenment predecessors. Instead, Romantic-era artists and writers emphasized the primacy of feeling, making the heart as important as the head, emotion as significant a human experience as thought.

In music, the artistic forms and structures popular during the eighteenth century significantly changed. Beethoven's symphonies broke the mold of the classical symphonic form established by Haydn and perfected by Mozart, clearing the ground for more radical changes not only in musical forms, but also in harmony, rhythm, and musical texture. Wagnerian music drama took opera in new directions and was paralleled by the explosion of Romantic Italian opera, which extended the scope and range of opera far beyond what Handel and Mozart had envisioned.

The literature of the Romantic era also reflected a significant break with the past. Wordsworth and Coleridge changed the direction of English poetry by describing familiar scenes from everyday life in common, everyday language. The Romantic literary and artistic revolution had as significant an impact on literature and art as the political and industrial revolutions had on society. The legacy of all four types of revolutions continues to affect the way life is lived and art is produced and enjoyed throughout the world today.

come into being, only the fittest will survive, suggesting that more than simple luck accounted for the survival of individual members of a species. Darwin proposed that, in any given environment, those individuals best able to adapt to that environment, have the greatest chance of surviving. He suggested it was the strongest members of the species that survive long enough to breed and pass on to future generations genes enabling them to survive as well. He also suggested that as an environment changes, those individual members of a species that adapt to the changes will survive to pass on their genetic inheritance.

Darwin's emphasis on the mechanism of natural selection undermined conventional theological and philosophical assumptions about the special place of human beings in the divine order of creation. Instead of a world providentially designed by God with humankind as its guardian and guide, Darwin postulated a world that followed the blind laws of chance and saw human beings simply as a species of animal that has successfully adapted to its world, ensuring its capacity for survival. Moreover, there was no indication that humans were the highest point of creation, nor was their survival assured in future centuries.

Darwin did not deny that humankind represented the high point of creation so far, only that its origins were other than had been believed for centuries. His *The Descent of Man* (1871) suggested that humans were derived from lower life-forms that evolved. The distinguishing feature of humans, their spiritual nature and their consciousness, was diminished to emphasize their biological origins and their relationship to their simian ancestors. At stake in this revolutionary shift was humanity's ultimate place in the cosmos. At stake, too, were theological beliefs that had withstood the scientific revolution of the seventeenth century, but which seemed incompatible with Darwinian scientific explanation and the profusion of evidence he brought to support it.

KEY TERMS

Romanticism
études
originality
odalisque
phenomena/noumena
Sturm und Drang
Lied

absolute music
program music
idée fixe
song cycles
piano
prelude

nocturnes
waltz
polonaise
mazurka
leitmotif
Realism

atelier
daguerreotype
pictorialism
pasteurization
evolution
natural selection

www. WEBSITES FOR FURTHER STUDY

http://artchive.com/artchive/I/ingres.html
(This is the Artchive, a website with virtually every major artist in every style from every era in art history. It is an excellent resource.)

http://www.beautiful-london.co.uk/big-ben.htm
(An excellent site on the Houses of Parliament and many other London landmarks.)

http://www.wabash.edu/Rousseau/home.htm
(The Rousseau Association, where one can find a biography, his written works, and many associated links.)

http://www.r-cube.co.uk/fox-talbot/history.html
(William Henry Fox Talbot, philosopher, classicist, Egyptologist, mathematician, philologist, transcriber and translator of Syrian and Chaldean cuneiform text, physicist, and photographer.)

http://www.wagnersocietyny.org/
(The Wagner Society of New York, with many links and information about one of the greatest opera composers of all time.)

READINGS

JEAN-JACQUES ROUSSEAU

from *Confessions*

In his Confessions, *Rousseau explained himself to himself. His very conception of the largeness and importance of the "Self" has been his greatest influence. One of the great ironies of the* Confessions *is that, for all his effort to present himself honestly and faithfully, Rousseau included some self-excusing rationalizations of his conduct. He was criticized for making himself out to be more generous and more deeply feeling than he actually was. Rousseau countered that he had only his feelings and his sense of himself to guide him and that no objective measure could justly portray any individual.*

I am commencing an undertaking, hitherto without precedent, and which will never find an imitator. I desire to set before my fellows the likeness of a man in all the truth of nature, and that man myself.

Myself alone! I know the feelings of my heart, and I know men. I am not made like any of those I have seen; I venture to believe that I am not made like any of those who are in existence. If I am not better, at least I am different. Whether Nature has acted rightly or wrongly in destroying the mould in which she cast me, can only be decided after I have been read.

Let the trumpet of the Day of Judgment sound when it will, I will present myself before the Sovereign Judge with this book in my hand. I will say boldly: "This is what I have done, what I have thought, what I was. I have told the good and the bad with equal frankness. I have neither omitted anything bad, nor interpolated anything good. If I have occasionally made use of some immaterial embellishments, this has only been in order to fill a gap caused by lack of memory. I may have assumed the truth of that which I knew might have been true, never of that which I knew to be false. I have shown myself as I was: mean and contemptible, good, high-minded and sublime, according as I was one or the other. I have unveiled my inmost self even as Thou hast seen it, O Eternal Being. Gather round me the countless host of my fellow-men; let them hear my confessions, lament for my unworthiness, and blush for my imperfections. Then let each of them in turn reveal, with the same frankness, the secrets of his heart at the foot of the Throne, and say, if he dare, '*I was better than that man!*'"

I was born at Geneva, in the year 1712, and was the son of Isaac Rousseau and Susanne Bernard, citizens. The distribution of a very moderate inheritance amongst fifteen children had reduced my father's portion almost to nothing; and his only means of livelihood was his trade of watch-maker, in which he was really very clever. My mother, a daughter of the Protestant minister Bernard, was better off. She was clever and beautiful, and my father had found difficulty in obtaining her hand. Their affection for each other had commenced almost as soon as they were born. When only eight years old, they walked every evening upon the Treille; at ten, they were inseparable. Sympathy and union of soul strengthened in them the feeling produced by intimacy. Both, naturally full of tender sensibility, only waited for the moment when they should find the same disposition in another—or, rather, this moment waited for them, and each abandoned his heart to the first which opened to receive it. Destiny, which appeared to oppose their passion, only encouraged it. The young lover, unable to obtain possession of his mistress, was consumed by grief. She advised him to travel, and endeavour to forget her. He travelled, but without result, and returned more in love than ever. He found her whom he loved still faithful and true. After this trial of affection, nothing was left for them but to love each other all their lives. This they swore to do, and Heaven blessed their oath.

Gabriel Bernard, my mother's brother, fell in love with one of my father's sisters, who only consented to accept the hand of the brother, on condition that her own brother married the sister. Love arranged everything, and the two marriages took place on the same day. Thus my uncle became the husband of my aunt, and their children were doubly my first cousins. At the end of a year, a child was born to both, after which they were again obliged to separate.

My uncle Bernard was an engineer. He took service in the Empire and in Hungary, under Prince Eugène. He distinguished himself at the siege and battle of Belgrade. My father, after the birth of my only brother, set out for Constantinople, whither he was summoned to undertake the post of watchmaker to the Sultan. During his absence, my mother's beauty, intellect and talents gained for her the devotion of numerous admirers. M. de la Closure, the French Resident, was one of the most eager to offer his. His passion must have been great, for, thirty years later, I saw him greatly affected when speaking to me of her. To enable her to resist such advances, my mother had more than her virtue: she loved her husband tenderly. She pressed him to return; he left all, and returned. I was the unhappy fruit of this return. Ten months later I was born, a weak and ailing child; I cost my mother her life, and my birth was the first of my misfortunes.

I have never heard how my father bore this loss, but I know that he was inconsolable. He believed that he saw his wife again in me, without being able to forget that it was I who had robbed him of her; he never embraced me without my perceiving, by his sighs and the convulsive manner in which he clasped me to his breast, that a bitter regret was mingled with his caresses, which were on that account only the more tender. When he said to me, "Jean Jacques, let us talk of your mother," I used to answer, "Well, then, my father, we will weep!"—and this word alone was sufficient to move him to tears. "Ah!" said he, with a sigh, "give her back to me, console me for her loss, fill the void which she has left in my soul. Should I love you as I do, if you were only my son?" Forty years after he had lost her, he died in the arms of a second wife, but the name of the first was on his lips and her image at the bottom of his heart.

Such were the authors of my existence. Of all the gifts which Heaven had bestowed upon them, a sensitive heart is the only one they bequeathed to me; it had been the source of their happiness, but for me it proved the source of all the misfortunes of my life.

from On Social Contract or Principles of Political Right

—foederis aequas
Dicamus leges.
Aeneid XI[1]

On Social Contract, published in 1762, sets out Rousseau's social and political philosophy in systematic fashion. The following passage excerpts its early chapters, conveying Rousseau's belief that a state becomes legitimate through its members' freedom to enact their own laws. The tradeoff for them is that they yield the state their unqualified obedience.

Foreword

This little treatise is extracted from a more extensive work, undertaken in the past without having considered my strength, and long since abandoned. Of the various fragments that might have been taken from what was completed, this is the most important and seemed to me the least unworthy of being offered to the public. The rest no longer exists.

Book I

I wish to discover if, in the civil order, there can be any legitimate and fixed rule of administration, taking men as they are and laws as they can be.[2] I shall, in this inquiry, always strive to reconcile what right permits with what interest prescribes, so that justice and utility may not be divided.

I broach the subject without giving proof of its importance. I shall be asked if I am a prince or a lawmaker, since I am writing on politics. I answer that I am neither, and that this is precisely why I am writing on politics. If I were a prince or a lawmaker, I would not waste my time talking about what ought to be done; I would either do it or remain silent.

I was born the citizen of a free state and a member of the sovereign, and, however feeble an influence my voice may have in public affairs, my right to vote on them suffices to make it my duty to inform myself on such matters. I am always happy, whenever I reflect upon the nature of government, to find in my inquiries new reasons for loving that of my own country!

Chapter 1 The Subject of This First Book

Man is born free, and everywhere he is in chains.[3] Anyone who thinks himself the master of others is no less a slave than they. How has this change come about? I do not know. What can make it legitimate? I believe I can resolve this question.

If I were to consider only force and its effects, I would say that as long as a people is compelled to obey and does so, it does well; as soon as it can shake off the yoke and does so, it does even better, for, either this people, in recovering its liberty by the same right as the one by which it was stolen, is entitled to regain it, or no one was entitled to take it away. But the social order is a sacred right which serves as the basis of all the others. Yet, this right is not derived from nature; it is, therefore, founded upon agreements. It is a question of knowing what these agreements are. Before coming to that, however, I must prove what I have just asserted.

Chapter 2 On the First Societies

The oldest of all societies and the only natural one is that of the family. Even so, the children remain bound to their father only as long as they need him to survive. As soon as this need ceases to exist, the natural bond is dissolved. The children, free from having to obey their father, and the father, free from having to care for his children, return all alike to a state of independence. If they continue to remain united, they do so not naturally but voluntarily, and the family itself is maintained only by agreement.

This common liberty is a consequence of man's nature. His first law is to see to his own preservation; his first concerns are those he owes to himself, and, as soon as he reaches the age of reason, being then the sole judge of the proper means of preserving himself, he thereby becomes his own master.

The family, therefore, is, if you will, the first model for political societies; the leader is like the father and the people like his children; and all, having been born free and equal, alienate their liberty only for their own advantage. The main difference is that, in the family, the father's love for his children repays him for the care he provides them, whereas in the state, the pleasure of commanding replaces a love that the leader does not feel for his peoples.

Grotius denies that all human power is established for the benefit of those who are governed; he cites slavery as an example.[4] His most usual manner of arguing is always to establish rights on the basis of fact.[5] It is possible to argue in a more consistent manner, but not in one more favorable to tyrants.

It is therefore uncertain, according to Grotius, whether the human race belongs to a hundred men or so, or whether these hundred men or so belong to the human race, and, all through his book, he appears to lean towards the first view; this is also Hobbes's opinion. Thus, we find the human race divided into herds of cattle, each with a leader who keeps watch over it in order to devour it.

Just as the herdsman is superior by nature to his herd, so the shepherds of men, who are their leaders, are superior by na-

---

[1] Rousseau cites Virgil's *Aeneid*, XI. 436, where, after the funeral rites and mourning for his son Pallas, King Latinus, finding himself without allies, proposes to end the violence by drawing up an equitable treaty ("Let us make equitable treaty terms"), so that both Latins and Trojans may live in peace as citizens in Italy.

[2] Rousseau is not concerned with the administrative function of government, as the phrase "rule of administration" might suggest. His subject is basic constitutional arrangements.

[3] This sentence distills two of Rousseau's claims in the *Discourse on Inequality* that social life robs us of our natural freedom, and that this loss is irreversible. Rousseau will argue in the eighth chapter of this book that in a just society a new sort of freedom is attained. In the present chapter and the three that follow, he rejects four traditional tests for a state's legitimacy. Neither familial descent, nor physical prowess, nor military success, nor ownership of slaves gives a ruler the right to be obeyed.

[4] Hugo Grotius (1583–1645) was a Dutch jurist and statesman. Rousseau refers here and elsewhere to his *De jure belli ac pacis* (On the Law of War and Peace), first published in 1625.

[5] "Scholarly research in public law is often only the history of former abuses; and anyone who takes the trouble to study it too deeply is misguidedly obstinate." (*Treatise on the Interests of France in Relation to Her Neighbors* by the Marquis d'Argenson, printed at Rey publishers in Amsterdam). This is precisely what Grotius did* [Rousseau's note, with 1782 correction].
* All of Rousseau's notes to *On Social Contract* have been included. His additions to the 1782 edition are also indicated by date.

ture to their peoples. In Philo's account, the emperor Caligula reasoned in this manner and concluded appropriately enough for this analogy that either kings were gods or that peoples were beasts.[6]

Caligula's reasoning comes down to that of Hobbes and Grotius.[7] Before any of them, Aristotle also had said that men are not naturally equal but that some are born to be slaves and others to be masters.[8]

Aristotle was right, but he mistook the effect for the cause. Every man born into slavery is born to be a slave; nothing is more certain. Slaves lose everything in their chains, even the desire to escape from them; they love their servitude as Ulysses's companions loved their brutishness.[9] If there are, therefore, slaves by nature, it is because there have been slaves against nature. Force created the first slaves; their cowardice has perpetuated their condition.

I have said nothing of King Adam or Emperor Noah, father of three great monarchs who divided the world among themselves, as did the children of Saturn, with whom they have been compared. I hope that my moderation will be appreciated, for, being the direct descendant of one of these princes, and perhaps of the eldest branch, how do I know whether I might not find myself the legitimate king of the human race through a verification of titles? Be that as it may, it cannot be denied that Adam was sovereign of the world, just as Robinson was of his island, as long as he was its only inhabitant, and what was most agreeable about this empire was that the monarch, secure on his throne, had nothing to fear from rebellions, wars, or conspirators.[1]

Chapter 3 On the Right of the Strongest

The strongest man is never strong enough to remain forever the master, unless he transforms his might into right and obedience into duty. Hence, the right of the strongest, a right that is ostensibly understood ironically and actually established as a principle. But will anyone ever explain this word to us? Force is a physical power; I do not see what kind of morality can result from its effects. Yielding to force is an act of necessity, not of will; it is, at most, an act of prudence. In what sense could this be a duty?

Let us suppose for a moment that this alleged right exists. I say that nothing but inexplicable nonsense results from it, for as soon as might makes right, the effect changes along with the cause; any new force that overcomes the first also inherits its rights. As soon as it becomes possible to disobey with impunity, it is possible to disobey legitimately; and since the strongest is always in the right, it is only a question of be-

having so that one may be the strongest. But what kind of right is one which perishes when the force behind it ceases to exist? If force makes it necessary to obey, it is no longer necessary to obey out of a sense of duty; if a person is no longer forced to obey, he is no longer obligated to do so. We can see, therefore, that this word right adds nothing to force; in this context, it means nothing at all.

Obey the powers that be. If that means to yield to force, the precept is good but superfluous; I answer that it will never be violated. All power comes from God,[2] I admit, but every illness comes from him as well. Is this to say that calling a doctor is forbidden? If a thief surprises me in a corner of the woods, I am forced to give him my purse, but am I, in conscience, obligated to give it to him when I could hide it? For, after all, the pistol in his hand is also a kind of power.

Let us agree, therefore, that might does not make right, and that we are obligated to obey only legitimate powers. Thus, my original question always recurs.[3]

Chapter 4 On Slavery[4]

Since no individual has natural authority over his fellow man, and since force creates no rights, agreements remain the basis of all legitimate authority among men.

If a private individual, says Grotius, can alienate his liberty and make himself the slave of a master, why could not an entire people alienate its liberty and make itself the subject of a king? There are a good many equivocal words in this statement which need explanation, but let us confine ourselves to the word *alienate*. To alienate means to give or to sell. Now, a man who makes himself another's slave does not give himself; at the very least, he sells himself for his subsistence, but for what purpose does a people sell itself? Far from furnishing his subjects with their subsistence, a king only derives his own from them, and, according to Rabelais, a king does not live on little. Do subjects, then, give up their persons on condition that their property will also be taken? I do not see what they have left to keep.

It will be said that the despot guarantees his subjects civil tranquillity.[5] That may be, but what do they gain by that, if the wars which his ambition brings upon them, his insatiable greed, and the vexations of his administration devastate them more than their own dissensions? What do they gain, if that very tranquillity is one of their miseries? Living in dungeons is also tranquil: is that enough to make them appealing? The Greeks confined in the Cyclop's cave lived tranquilly there while awaiting their turn to be devoured.[6]

---

[6]Philo Judaeus (25 B.C.—A.D. 54) was a Jewish philosopher from Alexandria, who offered his readers an outsider's view of Rome.

[7]Rousseau is a bit short with Hobbes, who thought men equal in the important sense that they are equally able to harm one another.

[8]See Aristotle's (384–322 B.C.) discussion of slavery in *Politics* 1. 4–8, where he claims some men are slaves by nature.

[9]See a short treatise by Plutarch entitled: *That Beasts Employ Reason* [Rousseau's note].

[1]Rousseau is pointedly satirizing the doctrine of the divine right of kings espoused by royalists like Sir Robert Filmer, author of *Patriarcha, or the Natural Power of Kings* (London 1680), in which he defends absolute monarchy by tracing royal authority back to the domestic absolutism of Noah and Adam.

[2]See Romans 13:1 and Paul's discussion of the secular government of Rome.

[3]This question concerns the characteristics of a legitimate state, one that deserves to be obeyed.

[4]The purpose of this chapter is less to attack slavery than to dispose of the argument, advanced above all by Grotius, that people who voluntarily agree to obey a state ought to obey it, even if it deprives them of their freedom.

[5]Rousseau disputes Hobbes's claims that an unlimited government is the best means of achieving domestic peace, and that such peace is the principle aim of the social contract.

[6]Locke also develops this theme in *Two Treatises of Government*. II. xix. 228: both arguments are inspired by the Polyphemus episode in Book IX of Homer's *Odyssey*.

To say that a man gives himself for nothing is to say something absurd and inconceivable, such an act is illegitimate and invalid, if only because anyone who does such a thing is not in his right mind. To say the same thing of an entire people is to suppose a nation of madmen: madness does not make right.

Even if each individual could alienate himself, he cannot alienate his children, for they are born men and free; their liberty belongs to them, and no one has the right to dispose of it but they themselves. Before they reach the age of reason, the father can, in their name, stipulate conditions for their preservation and well-being, but he cannot give them to someone else irrevocably and unconditionally, since such a gift is contrary to nature's ends and exceeds the rights of fatherhood. In order, then, for an arbitrary government to be legitimate, the people in each generation would have to be free to accept or reject it, but, then, this government would no longer be arbitrary.

To renounce one's liberty is to renounce one's humanity, the rights of humanity and even its duties. No compensation is possible for someone who renounces everything. Such a renunciation is incompatible with man's nature, and to strip him of all freedom of will is to strip his actions of all morality.[7] In short, an agreement that stipulates absolute authority on one hand and unlimited obedience on the other is vain and contradictory. Is it not clear that one is not committed in any way to a person from whom one has the right to demand everything, and does not this single condition, this lack of equality or mutual obligation, suggest the meaninglessness of such an act? For, since all that he has belongs to me, what rights would my slave have against me, and, since his rights are mine, what sense is there in this idea that I have a right against myself?

Grotius and the others find in war another origin for this supposed right of slavery. Since the victor, according to them, has the right to kill the vanquished, the latter can buy back his life at the cost of his liberty, an agreement all the more legitimate because it is advantageous to both parties.

But it is clear that this supposed right to kill the vanquished in no way results from the state of war. If only because, living in their original state of independence, they lack the constant intercourse necessary to constitute either a state of peace or a state of war, men are not naturally enemies. It is the relation of things and not of men that constitutes war; and since the state of war cannot arise from simple personal relations, but only from proprietary relations, private war, that is, the war of man against man, cannot exist either in the state of nature, where there is no established property, or in the social state, where everything is under the authority of the laws.

Individual combats, duels, and encounters are acts that do not constitute a state of war, and, with regard to those private wars authorized by the Establishments of Louis IX, king of France, and suspended by the Peace of God, they are abuses of feudal government, an absurd system if ever there was one,

contrary to the principles of natural right and to every good political organization.

War is not, therefore, a relation of man to man but a relation of state to state, in which individuals are enemies only by accident, not as men or even as citizens,[8] but as soldiers, not as members of the homeland, but as its defenders. In short, the enemies of each state can only be other states and not men, inasmuch as true relations cannot be established between things of different natures.

This principle is even in conformity with the general maxims established in every age and with the invariable practice of all civilized peoples. Declarations of war are warnings not so much to the powers that be as to their subjects. Whether a king, a private individual, or a people, the foreigner who robs, kills, or detains the subjects without declaring war on the prince is not an enemy but a brigand. Even in open war, a just prince rightly takes possession of all that belongs to the public in the enemy country, but he respects the person and property of private individuals; he respects the rights upon which his own are founded. Since the purpose of war is the destruction of the enemy state, one has the right to kill its defenders as long as they bear arms, but as soon as they lay them down and surrender, ceasing to be enemies or instruments of the enemy, they become once again simply men, and no one has any further right over their lives. Sometimes it is possible to kill the state without killing a single one of its members, but war confers no right except that which is necessary to its purpose. These principles are not those of Grotius; they are not founded upon the authority of poets, but they are derived from the nature of things and are founded upon reason.

With regard to the right of conquest, it has no foundation other than the law of the strongest. If war does not give the victor the right to slaughter the vanquished, this right, which he does not actually possess, cannot be the basis of a right to enslave them. We have the right to kill the enemy only when we cannot enslave him; the right to enslave him does not, therefore, come from the right to kill him; it is, then, an unjust exchange to make him purchase his life, over which no one has any right, at the price of his liberty. In establishing the right of life and death upon the right of slavery, and the right of slavery upon the right of life and death, are we not clearly arguing in a vicious circle?

Even assuming this terrible right to kill everyone, I say that a slave created by war or a conquered people is under no obligation of any sort toward a master, except to obey him as

---

[7]Rousseau here grounds his argument against unlimited government on his commitment to the value of moral responsibility. Unlimited government is illegitimate because, by depriving us of freedom, it deprives us of the responsibility for our acts, and, hence, of our very humanity. This same commitment to moral responsibility will be central to his defense of direct democracy.

[8]The Romans, who have understood and respected the right of war better than any nation in the world, carried their scruples so far in this regard that no citizen was permitted to serve as a volunteer without having expressly enlisted against the enemy, and specifically against such and such an enemy. When a legion in which Cato the Younger [Cato the Elder's son], took up his first arms under Popillius was formed anew, Cato the Elder wrote to Popillius that, if he was willing for his son to continue to serve under him, he would have to make him swear a new military oath, because, once the first was annulled, he could no longer bear arms against the enemy. And the same Cato wrote to his son to take care not to present himself for combat until he had taken this new oath. I know that some will oppose my argument with the example of the siege of Clusium and other particular cases, but I am citing laws, customs. The Romans are the ones who have less often transgressed their laws than other nations; and they are the only ones who have had such fine ones [Rousseau's note, 1782].

long as force makes it necessary. In taking the equivalent of a man's life, the victor has not really spared him anything: instead of killing him for no good purpose, he has killed him profitably. So far is he, therefore, from having acquired any authority over this slave other than that created by force, that the state of war subsists between them as before; their relationship is indeed the result of it, and the custom of the right of war presupposes no peace treaty. They have made an agreement, it is true, but far from putting an end to the state of war, this agreement presupposes its continuation.

Thus, however we view the matter, the right of slavery is invalid, not only because it is illegitimate but also because it is absurd and meaningless. These words, *slavery* and *right*, are contradictory; they are mutually exclusive. Whether spoken by one man to another or by one man to an entire people, the following statement will always be equally nonsensical: *I am making an agreement with you wholly at your expense and wholly for my benefit, which I shall observe as long as I please and which you will observe as long as I please.*

Chapter 5 That We Must Always Go Back to a First Agreement[9]

Even if I were to grant all that I have so far refuted, the supporters of despotism would not find their cause any further advanced. There will always be a great difference between subduing a multitude and governing a society. Where isolated individuals are successively enslaved by a single man, whatever their number may be, I see there only a master and his slaves, not a people and its leader; it is an aggregation, if you will, but not an association; in it, there is neither public good nor body politic. Even if such a man had enslaved half the world, he is still only a private individual; his interest, separate from that of the others, is still only a private interest. If this same man happens to die, his empire is left broken up and disunited after him, just as an oak disintegrates and falls into a heap of ashes after it has been consumed by fire.

A people, says Grotius, can give itself to a king. According to Grotius, a people is therefore a people before giving itself to a king. That gift is in itself a civil act; it presupposes a public decision. Therefore, before examining the act by which a people elects a king, it would be good to examine the act by which a people becomes a people, for, since this act is necessarily prior to the other, it is the true foundation of society.[1]

Indeed, if there were no prior agreement, why, unless the election were unanimous, would the minority have an obligation to submit to the choice of the majority, and why do a hundred men who want a master have the right to vote on behalf of ten who do not? The law of majority rule is itself established by agreement and presupposes unanimity on at least one occasion.

Chapter 6 On the Social Pact

I assume men to have reached the point at which the obstacles to their preservation in the state of nature have a resistance greater than the forces each individual can use to maintain himself in that state.[2] At this point, that primitive state could no longer subsist, and the human species would perish if it did not change its way of living.

Now, since men cannot engender new forces but merely unite and direct the existing ones, they have no other means of preserving themselves than to form by aggregation a sum of forces that can overcome this resistance, bring them into play by means of a single motive power, and make them act in concert.

This sum of forces can arise only from the cooperation of several men, but since each man's strength and liberty are the primary instruments of self-preservation, how will he commit them without harming himself and without neglecting the care he owes himself? This difficulty, in relation to my subject, can be set forth in these terms:

"To find a form of association that defends and protects the person and possessions of each associate with all the common strength, and by means of which each person, joining forces with all, nevertheless obeys only himself and remains as free as before." Such is the fundamental problem to which the social contract furnishes the solution.

The clauses of this contract are so determined by the nature of the act that the slightest modification would render them null and void, so that, although they have never perhaps been formally enunciated, they are everywhere the same, everywhere tacitly admitted and recognized, until the social pact is violated, and each person regains his original rights and recovers his natural liberty, losing the civil liberty for which he renounced it.[3]

Rightly understood, these clauses can all be reduced to one alone, namely, the total alienation of each associate with all his rights to the whole community.[4] For, in the first place, since each person gives himself entirely, the condition is equal for all, and since the condition is equal for all, no one has an interest in making it burdensome for the others.

Furthermore, since the alienation is made without reservation, the union is as perfect as it can be, and no associate has anything more to claim. For, if some rights were left to private individuals, and there were no common superior who could decide between them and the public, each person, being in some respects his own judge, would soon claim to be so in

---

[9]The previous three chapters have refuted some standard views of what makes a state legitimate. In this chapter. Rousseau introduces his contractualist claim that in a legitimate state, obedience is based on free and rational agreement.

[1]In this paragraph, Rousseau announces a theme that grows in importance as he proceeds. It is the relations among the members of society, rather than their relations to officials, that are crucial for the legitimacy of a state.

[2]The dire conflict to which Rousseau alludes here is described in the *Discourse on Inequality* as arising from the competition engendered by social life. Rousseau's concern in that work is to show how existing states control this struggle by depriving subjects of their freedom. In this case, however, his aim is prescriptive to show how a state should be organized to make its subjects free as well as safe.

[3]Note that for Rousseau what makes a state legitimate is not that its subjects expressly agree to the terms of this contract, but that it abides by these terms, whether they expressly agree to them or not.

[4]Taken alone, this sentence makes Rousseau sound like a partisan of intolerable tyranny, but the elaboration of this sentence in this and the next two paragraphs shows that he envisages nothing sinister when he calls for total alienation to the community. The community to which we should submit turns out to be a democratic community of equals in whose operation each has an equal and effective share. Cf. below. Book II. chapter 4.

every instance; the state of nature would subsist, and the association would necessarily become tyrannical or ineffectual.

Finally, each person, in giving himself to all, gives himself to no one, and as there are no associates over whom he does not acquire the same right as he concedes to them over himself, he gains the equivalent of all that he loses and more force to preserve what he has.

If, then, we eliminate whatever is not essential to the social pact, we shall find that it can be reduced to the following terms: *Each of us puts his person and all his power in common under the supreme control of the general will, and, as a body, we receive each member as an indivisible part of the whole.*[5]

In place of the private person of each contracting party, this act of association at once produces a collective and artificial body, composed of as many members as the assembly has votes, which receives from this same act its unity, its collective self, its life, and its will. This public person, which is thus formed by the union of all the other persons, formerly took the name of *city*[6] and now takes that of *republic* or *body politic*, and its members call it a *state* when it is passive, a *sovereign* when it is active, and a *power* when comparing it to others of its kind. As for the associates, they collectively take the name of the *people*, and, individually, they are called *citizens*, when they participate in the sovereign authority, and *subjects* when they are subject to the laws of the state. But these terms are often confused and mistaken for one another; it is enough to know how to distinguish them when they are used with absolute precision.

WILLIAM WORDSWORTH
I Wandered Lonely as a Cloud

Because of his inclination toward inwardly directed explorations, Wordsworth has often been considered one of the first great poets of the inner life. His poetry is rooted in psychological insight leading to self-realization and celebrating the growth of the mind.

I wandered lonely as a cloud
That floats on high o'er vales and hills,
When all at once I saw a crowd,

---

[5] Ought we obey the general will, as Rousseau recommends? No answer is possible until we learn more about the nature of the general will and about how to know what it prescribes. Much of Book II of *On Social Contract*, as well as chapters one to three of Book IV, give the information needed for an intelligent response.

[6] The true meaning of this word has been almost entirely effaced among the moderns; most take a town for a city, and a townsman for a citizen. They do not know that houses make the town but that citizens make the city. This same error formerly cost the Carthaginians dearly. I have not read that the title of *cives* has ever been given to the subject of any prince, not even formerly to the Macedonians, nor, in our times, to the English, although they are nearer liberty than all the rest. Only the French construe this term *citizen* quite loosely, because they have no real idea of its meaning, as we can see in their dictionaries; otherwise, they would, by usurping this word, fall into the crime of high treason; among them, this name expresses a virtue and not a right. When Bodin endeavored to speak of our citizens and townsmen, he committed a gross blunder, by mistaking the former for the latter. Mr. D'Alembert was not mistaken, and, in his article *Geneva*, properly distinguished the four orders of men (even five, counting simple strangers) in our town, of which two alone compose the Republic. No other French author, as far as I know, has understood the real meaning of the word *citizen* [Rousseau's note].

A host, of golden daffodils;
Beside the lake, beneath the trees,   5
Fluttering and dancing in the breeze.

Continuous as the stars that shine
And twinkle on the milky way,
They stretched in never-ending line
Along the margin of a bay: 10
Ten thousand saw I at a glance,
Tossing their heads in sprightly dance.

The waves beside them danced; but they
Outdid the sparkling waves in glee:
A poet could not but be gay,   15
In such a jocund company:
I gazed—and gazed—but little thought
What wealth the show to me had brought:

For oft, when on my couch I lie
In vacant or in pensive mood,   20
They flash upon that inward eye
Which is the bliss of solitude;
And then my heart with pleasure fills,
And dances with the daffodils.

WILLIAM BLAKE
The Chimney Sweeper

In his two poems about chimney sweeps, William Blake presents contrasting visions based on the themes of innocence and experience that govern his early collection of poems, Songs of Innocence and Experience: Showing the Two Contrary States of the Human Soul *(1794). Even as Blake focuses in turn on innocence and on experience, he complicates each poem with suggested elements of the opposite state.*

The Chimney Sweeper (Innocence)

When my mother died I was very young,
And my father sold me while yet my tongue,
Could scarcely cry "'weep! 'weep! 'weep! 'weep!"
So your chimneys I sweep & in soot I sleep.

There's little Tom Dacre, who cried when his head   5
That curl'd like a lamb's back, was shav'd, so I said.
"Hush Tom never mind it, for when your head's bare,
You know that the soot cannot spoil your white hair."

And so he was quiet, & that very night,
As Tom was a-sleeping he had such a sight,   10
That thousands of sweepers Dick, Joe, Ned & Jack,
Were all of them lock'd up in coffins of black;

And by came an Angel who had a bright key,
And he open'd the coffins & set them all free;
Then down a green plain leaping laughing they run,   15
And wash in a river and shine in the Sun.

Then naked & white, all their bags left behind,
They rise upon clouds, and sport in the wind.

And the Angel told Tom if he'd be a good boy,
He'd have God for his father & never want joy. *20*

The Chimney Sweeper (Experience)

A little black thing among the snow:
Crying "'weep, 'weep," in notes of woe!
"Where are thy father & mother? say?"
"They are both gone up to the church to pray.

"Because I was happy upon the heath, *5*
And smil'd among the winter's snow:
They clothed me in the clothes of death,
And taught me to sing the notes of woe.

"And because I am happy, & dance & sing,
They think they have done me no injury: *10*
And are gone to praise God & his Priest & King
Who make up a heaven of our misery."

JOHN KEATS

Ode to a Nightingale

During the last year of his life, Keats composed six great odes. In the "Ode to a Nightingale," Keats's speaker loses himself completely in the nightingale's song, only to be called back at the end to a state of solitary sadness.

1

My heart aches, and a drowsy numbness pains
        My sense, as though of hemlocks[1] I had drunk,
Or emptied some dull opiate to the drains[2]
        One minute past, and Lethe-wards[3] had sunk:
'Tis not through envy of thy happy lot, *5*
        But being too happy in thine happiness—
                That thou, light-wingéd Dryad[4] of the trees,

In some melodious plot
        Of beechen green, and shadows numberless,
                Singest of summer in full-throated ease. *10*

2

O, for a draught of vintage! that hath been
        Cooled a long age in the deep-delvéd earth,
Tasting of Flora and the country green,
        Dance, and Provençal song, and sunburnt mirth!
O for a beaker full of the warm South, *15*
        Full of the true, the blushful Hippocrene,[5]
With beaded bubbles winking at the brim,

And purple-stainéd mouth;
        That I might drink, and leave the world unseen,
                And with thee fade away into the forest dim: *20*

3

Fade far away, dissolve, and quite forget
        What thou among the leaves hast never known,
The weariness, the fever, and the fret
        Here, where men sit and hear each other groan;
Where palsy shakes a few, sad, last gray hairs, *25*
        Where youth grows pale, and spectre-thin, and dies,
                Where but to think is to be full of sorrow

And leaden-eyed despairs,
        Where Beauty cannot keep her lustrous eyes,
                Or new Love pine at them beyond
        tomorrow. *30*

4

Away! away! for I will fly to thee,
        Not charioted by Bacchus and his pards,[6]
But on the viewless[7] wings of Poesy,
        Though the dull brain perplexes and retards:
Already with thee! tender is the night, *35*
        And haply[8] the Queen-Moon is on her throne,
Clustered around by all her starry Fays;[9]

But here there is no light,
        Save what from heaven is with the breezes blown
                Through verdurous glooms and winding
        mossy ways. *40*

5

I cannot see what flowers are at my feet,
        Nor what soft incense hangs upon the boughs,
But, in embalméd darkness, guess each sweet
        Wherewith the seasonable month endows
The grass, the thicket, and the fruit tree wild; *45*
        White hawthorn, and the pastoral eglantine;
                Fast fading violets covered up in leaves;

And mid-May's eldest child,
        The coming musk-rose, full of dewy wine,
                The murmurous haunt of flies on summer
        eves. *50*

6

Darkling I listen; and for many a time
        I have been half in love with easeful Death,
Called him soft names in many a muséd rhyme,
        To take into the air my quiet breath;
Now more than ever seems it rich to die, *55*
        To cease upon the midnight with no pain,
                While thou art pouring forth thy soul abroad

---

[1] *hemlock:* a poisonous drug.
[2] *drains:* dregs.
[3] *Lethe-wards:* toward Lethe, the river of forgetfulness.
[4] *Dryad:* tree nymph.
[5] *true . . . Hippocrene:* wine.

[6] *Bacchus . . . pards:* the god of wine and revelry and the leopards who drew his chariot.
[7] *viewless:* invisible.
[8] *haply:* perhaps.
[9] *Fays:* fairies.

In such an ecstasy!
  Still wouldst thou sing, and I have ears in vain—
   To thy high requiem become a sod.   *60*

7

Thou wast not born for death, immortal Bird!
  No hungry generations tread thee down;
The voice I hear this passing night was heard
  In ancient days by emperor and clown:
Perhaps the selfsame song that found a path *65*
  Through the sad heart of Ruth, when, sick for home,
   She stood in tears amid the alien corn;

The same that ofttimes hath
  Charmed magic casements, opening on the foam
   Of perilous seas, in faery lands forlorn. *70*

8

Forlorn! the very word is like a bell
  To toll me back from thee to my sole self!
Adieu! the fancy cannot cheat so well
  As she is famed to do, deceiving elf.
Adieu! adieu! thy plaintive anthem fades *75*
  Past the near meadows, over the still stream,
  Up the hill side; and now 'tis buried deep

In the next valley-glades:
  Was it a vision, or a waking dream?
   Fled is that music:—Do I wake or sleep? *80*

WALT WHITMAN

from *Song of Myself*

The longest and most important poem in Leaves of Grass, Song of Myself *offers a Romantic perspective that can be compared with Emerson's and Thoreau's perspectives on nature and the self. Its fifty-two sections span a wide range of topics, including nature, the individual self, the social self, democratic brotherhood, and the organic relationship between life and death, humanity, and the natural world.*

1

I celebrate myself,
And what I assume you shall assume,
For every atom belonging to me as good belongs to you.
I loafe and invite my soul,
I lean and loafe at my ease observing a spear of
  summer grass. *5*

2

Houses and rooms are full of perfumes . . . the shelves
  are crowded with perfumes,
I breathe the fragrance myself, and know it and like it,
The distillation would intoxicate me also, but I shall
  not let it.

The atmosphere is not a perfume . . . it has no taste of
  the distillation . . . it is odorless,

It is for my mouth forever . . . I am in love with it, *10*
I will go to the bank by the wood and become
  undisguised and naked,
I am mad for it to be in contact with me.

The smoke of my own breath,
Echoes, ripples, and buzzed whispers . . . loveroot,
  silkthread, crotch and vine,
My respiration and inspiration . . . the beating of my heart
  . . . the passing of blood and air through
  my lungs, *15*
The sniff of green leaves and dry leaves, and of the shore
  and darkcolored sea-rocks, and of hay in the barn,
The sound of the belched words of my voice . . . words
  loosed to the eddies of the wind,
A few light kisses . . . a few embraces . . . a reaching
  around of arms,
The play of shine and shade on the trees as the supple
  boughs wag,
The delight alone or in the rush of the streets, or along
  the fields and hillsides, *20*
The feeling of health . . . the full-moon trill . . . the song
  of me rising from bed and meeting the sun.
Have you reckoned a thousand acres much? Have you
  reckoned the earth much?
Have you practiced so long to learn to read?
Have you felt so proud to get at the meaning of poems?

Stop this day and night with me and you shall possess
  the origin of all poems, *25*
You shall possess the good of the earth and sun . . . there
  are millions of suns left,
You shall no longer take things at second or third hand
  . . . nor look through the eyes of the dead . . . nor
  feed on the spectres in books,
You shall not look through my eyes either, nor take
  things from me,
You shall listen to all sides and filter them from yourself.

3

I have heard what the talkers were talking . . . the talk of
  the beginning and the end, *30*

But I do not talk of the beginning or the end.
There was never any more inception than there is now,
Nor any more youth or age than there is now;
And will never be any more perfection than there is now,
Nor any more heaven or hell than there is now. *35*

Urge and urge and urge,
Always the procreant urge of the world.

Out of the dimness opposite equals advance . . . Always
  substance and increase,
Always a knit of identity . . . always distinction . . .
  always a breed of life.

To elaborate is no avail . . . Learned and unlearned feel
  that it is so. *40*

Sure as the most certain sure . . . plumb in the uprights,
    well entretied, braced in the beams,
Stout as a horse, affectionate, haughty, electrical,
I and this mystery here we stand.

Clear and sweet is my soul . . . and the unseen is proved
    by the seen,   *44*
Till that becomes unseen and receives proof in its turn.
Showing the best and dividing it from the worst, age
    vexes age,
Knowing the perfect fitness and equanimity of things,
    while they discuss I am silent, and go bathe and
    admire myself.

Welcome is every organ and attribute of me, and of any
    man hearty and clean,
Not an inch nor a particle of an inch is vile, and none
    shall be less familiar than the rest.

I am satisfied . . . I see, dance, laugh, sing;   *50*
As God comes a loving bedfellow and sleeps at my side
    all night and close on the peep of the day,
And leaves for me baskets covered with white towels
    bulging the house with their plenty,
Shall I postpone my acceptation and realization and
    scream at my eyes,
That they turn from gazing after and down the road,
And forthwith cipher and show me to a cent,
Exactly the contents of one, and exactly the contents of
    two, and which is ahead?   *55*

21

I am the poet of the body,
And I am the poet of the soul.
The pleasures of heaven are with me, and the pains of
    hell are with me,
The first I graft and increase upon myself . . . the latter I
    translate into a new tongue.

I am the poet of the woman the same as the man,   *60*
And I say it as great to be a woman as to be a man,
And I say there is nothing greater than the mother of men.

I chant a new chant of dilation or pride,
We have had ducking and deprecating about enough,
I show that size is only development.   *65*

Have you outstript the rest? Are you the President?
It is a trifle . . . they will more than arrive there every
    one, and still pass on.

I am he that walks with the tender and growing night;
I call to the earth and sea half-held by the night.

Press close barebosomed night! Press close magnetic
    nourishing night!   *70*
Night of south winds! Night of the large few stars!
Still nodding night! Mad naked summer night!
Smile O voluptuous coolbreathed earth!

Earth of the slumbering and liquid trees!
Earth of departed sunset! Earth of the mountains
    misty-top!   *75*
Earth of the vitreous pour of the full moon just tinged
    with blue!
Earth of shine and dark mottling the tide of the river!
Earth of the limpid gray of clouds brighter and clearer
    for my sake!
Far-swooping elbowed earth! Rich apple-blossomed earth!
Smile, for your lover comes!   *80*

Prodigal! you have given me love! . . . therefore I to
    you give love!
O unspeakable passionate love!

Thruster holding me tight and that I hold tight!
We hurt each other as the bridegroom and the bride
    hurt each other.
                            . . .

48

I have said that the soul is not more than the body,   *85*
And I have said that the body is not more than the soul
And nothing, not God, is greater to one than one's-self is,
And whoever walks a furlong without sympathy walks to
    his own funeral, dressed in his shroud,
And I or you pocketless of a dime may purchase the pick
    of the earth,
And to glance with an eye or show a bean in its pod
    confounds the learning of all times,   *90*
And there is no trade or employment but the young man
    following it may become a hero,
And there is no object so soft but it makes a hub for the
    wheeled universe,
And any man or woman shall stand cool and supercilious
    before a million universes.

And I call to mankind, Be not curious about God,
For I who am curious about each am not curious
    about God,   *95*
No array of terms can say how much I am at peace about
    God and about death.

I hear and behold God in every object, yet I understand
    God not in the least,
Nor do I understand who there can be more wonderful
    than myself.

Why should I wish to see God better than this day?   *100*
I see something of God each hour of the twenty-four,
    and each moment then,
In the faces of men and women I see God, and in my
    own face in the glass;
I find letters from God dropped in the street, and every
    one is signed by God's name,
And I leave them where they are, for I know that others
    will punctually come forever and ever.
                            . . .

51

The past and present wilt . . . I have filled them and
    emptied them,   *105*
And proceed to fill my next fold of the future.
Listener up there! Here you . . . what have you to
    confide to me?
Look in my face while I snuff the sidle of evening,
Talk honestly, for no one else hears you, and I stay only
    a minute longer.
Do I contradict myself?   *110*
Very well then . . . I contradict myself;
I am large . . . I contain multitudes.

I concentrate toward them that are nigh . . . I wait on
    the door-slab.

Who has done his day's work and will soonest be
    through with his supper?
Who wishes to talk with me?   *115*

Will you speak before I am gone? Will you prove al-
    ready too late?

52

The spotted hawk swoops by and accuses me . . . he
    complains of my gab and my loitering.

I too am not a bit tamed . . . I too am untranslatable,
I sound my barbaric yawp over the roofs of the world.

The last scud of day holds back for me,   *120*
It flings my likeness after the rest and true as any on the
    shadowed wilds,
It coaxes me to the vapor and the dusk.

I depart as air . . . I shake my white locks at the runaway
    sun,
I effuse my flesh in eddies and drift it in lacy jags.

I bequeath myself to the dirt to grow from the grass I
    love,   *125*
If you want me again look for me under your bootsoles.

You will hardly know who I am or what I mean,
But I shall be good health to you nevertheless,
And filter and fibre your blood.

Failing to fetch me at first keep encouraged,   *130*
Missing me one place search another,
I stop some where waiting for you.

EMILY DICKINSON

Five Poems

Emily Dickinson remained preoccupied throughout her work with these major themes: love, death, faith, doubt, nature, and hope. Her poems reveal a consummate linguistic intelligence, and interpreting them requires painstaking attention to every word and phrase and every mark of punctuation. Each detail contributes to her range of implication and meaning. The images of Dickinson's poems carry their meaning in concrete form—the slanting light and shadows of 258; the drum beat and broken plank of 280; the chorister and dome of 324; the tomb and moss of 449; and the sound and light of 465.

258

There's a certain Slant of light,
Winter Afternoons—
That oppresses, like the Heft
Of Cathedral Tunes—

Heavenly Hurt, it gives us—   *5*
We can find no scar,
But internal difference,
Where the Meanings, are—
None may teach it—Any—
'Tis the Seal Despair—   *10*
An imperial affliction
Sent us of the Air—

When it comes, the Landscape listens—
Shadows—hold their breath—
When it goes, 'tis like the Distance   *15*
On the look of Death—

280

I felt a Funeral, in my Brain,
And Mourners to and fro
Kept treading—treading—till it seemed
That Sense was breaking through—

And when they all were seated,   *5*
A Service, like a Drum—
Kept beating—beating—till I thought
My Mind was going numb—

And then I heard them lift a Box
And creak across my Soul   *10*
With those same Boots of Lead, again,
Then Space—began to toll,

As all the Heavens were a Bell,
And Being, but an Ear,
And I, and Silence, some strange Race   *15*
Wrecked, solitary, here—

And then a Plank in Reason, broke,
And I dropped down, and down—
And hit a World, at every plunge,
And Finished knowing—then—   *20*

324

Some keep the Sabbath going to Church—
I keep it, staying at Home—
With a Bobolink for a Chorister—
And an Orchard, for a Dome—

Some keep the Sabbath in Surplice—   *5*
I just wear my Wings—
And instead of tolling the Bell, for Church,
Our little Sexton—sings.

God preaches, a noted Clergyman—
And the sermon is never long,   *10*
So instead of getting to Heaven, at last—
I'm going, all along.

449

I died for Beauty—but was scarce
Adjusted in the Tomb
When One who died for Truth, was lain
In an adjoining Room—
He questioned softly "Why I failed"?   *5*
"For Beauty", I replied—
"And I—for Truth—Themself are One—
We Brethren, are", He said—

And so, as Kinsmen, met a Night—
We talked between the Rooms—   *10*
Until the Moss had reached our lips—
And covered up—our names—

465

I heard a Fly buzz—when I died—
The Stillness in the Room
Was like the Stillness in the Air—
Between the Heaves of Storm—

The Eyes around—had wrung them dry—   *5*
And Breaths were gathering firm
For that last Onset—when the King
Be witnessed—in the Room—

I willed my Keepsakes—Signed away
What portion of me be   *10*
Assignable—and then it was
There interposed a Fly—

With Blue—uncertain stumbling Buzz—
Between the light—and me—
And then the Windows failed—and then   *15*
I could not see to see—

CHARLES DARWIN

from *The Descent of Man*

Darwin's The Descent of Man *challenged a belief upheld by the Christian religion for centuries, namely that Adam and Eve were the first parents and that these parents were created fully formed by God to please him. Darwin's principles implied human beings were descended from baser living organisms. He had previously outlined his ideas of evolution of plants and animals in* On the Origin of Species *(1859), but he had not discussed human beings as one of the species.*

His theory of human evolution became inextricably tied to the origin of humanity. It was the subject of courtroom debate in the Scopes trial of 1927, in which a biology teacher, John T. Scopes, was tried for teaching Darwinism in a Dayton, Tennessee, public school. Scopes was convicted but later released on a technicality. In the 1950s, Jerome Lawrence and Robert E. Lee wrote a dynamic play about the trial, Inherit the Wind.

The main conclusion arrived at in this work, namely, that man is descended from some lowly organised form, will, I regret to think, be highly distasteful to many. But there can hardly be a doubt that we are descended from barbarians. The astonishment which I felt on first seeing a party of Fuegians on a wild and broken shore will never be forgotten by me, for the reflection at once rushed into my mind—such were our ancestors. These men were absolutely naked and bedaubed with paint, their long hair was tangled, their mouths, frothed with excitement, and their expression was wild, startled, and distrustful. They possessed hardly any arts, and like wild animals lived on what they could catch; they had no government, and were merciless to every one not of their own small tribe. He who has seen a savage in his native land will not feel much shame, if forced to acknowledge that the blood of some more humble creature flows in his veins. For my own part I would as soon be descended from that heroic little monkey, who braved his dreaded enemy in order to save the life of his keeper, or from that old baboon, who descending from the mountains, carried away in triumph his young comrade from a crowd of astonished dogs—as from a savage who delights to torture his enemies, offers up bloody sacrifices, practises infanticide without remorse, treats his wives like slaves, knows no decency, and is haunted by the grossest superstitions.

Man may be excused for feeling some pride at having risen, though not through his own exertions, to the very summit of the organic scale; and the fact of his having thus risen, instead of having been aboriginally placed there, may give him hope for a still higher destiny in the distant future. But we are not here concerned with hopes or fears, only with the truth as far as our reason permits us to discover it; and I have given the evidence to the best of my ability. We must, however, acknowledge, as it seems to me, that man with all his noble qualities, with sympathy which feels for the most debased, with benevolence which extends not only to other men but to the humblest living creature, with his god-like intellect which has penetrated into the movements and constitution of the solar system—with all these exalted powers—Man still bears in his bodily frame the indelible stamp of his lowly origin.

KARL MARX AND FRIEDRICH ENGELS

from *The Communist Manifesto*

According to Karl Marx, the structure and values of a society are determined by the way it organizes the production of goods and services. Marx thought that an inescapable conflict existed between the classes in the capitalist system, in which those who owned and controlled the means of production (the bourgeoisie) would inevitably be in opposition to the people who worked for them (the proletariat or working class). He believed the Industrial Revolution would mean more machines, which would mean, in turn, more workers. Thus a greater and stronger proletariat would eventually overthrow the capitalists and redistribute the wealth in a just and classless society in which capital would be shared by everyone.

The Communist Manifesto (1848) was written by Marx in collaboration with Friedrich Engels, a German socialist who had once owned a factory in Manchester, England, and who exposed Marx to the economic conditions of the working class. It appealed to many in Russia who were disillusioned with the czarist regime, and the Russian peasants, and workers were quick to embrace its ideals. The authors' urging seemed like a call to action: "Let the ruling classes tremble at a Communistic revolution. The proletarians have nothing to lose but their chains." Indeed, when they wrote, "Working Men of all Countries, Unite!," the workers did.

Bourgeois and Proletarians

THE HISTORY OF HITHERTO EXISTING SOCIETY IS THE HISTORY OF CLASS STRUGGLES

Freeman and slave, patrician and plebeian, lord and serf, guildmaster and journeyman, in a word, oppressor and oppressed, stood in constant opposition to one another, carried on an uninterrupted, now hidden, now open fight, a fight that each time ended, either in a revolutionary reconstitution of society at large, or in the common ruin of the contending classes.

In the earlier epochs of history, we find almost everywhere a complicated arrangement of society into various orders, a manifold gradation of social rank. In ancient Rome we have patricians, knights, plebeians, slaves; in the Middle Ages, feudal lords, vassals, guild-masters, journeymen, apprentices, serfs; in almost all of these classes, again, subordinate gradations.

The modern bourgeois society that has sprouted from the ruins of feudal society has not done away with class antagonisms. It has but established new classes, new conditions of oppression, new forms of struggle in place of the old ones.

Our epoch, the epoch of the bourgeoisie, possesses, however, this distinctive feature: it has simplified the class antagonisms. Society as a whole is more and more splitting up into two great hostile camps, into two great classes directly facing each other: Bourgeoisie and Proletariat.

From the serfs of the Middle Ages sprang the chartered burghers of the earliest towns. From these burgesses the first elements of the bourgeoisie were developed.

The discovery of America, the rounding of the Cape, opened up fresh ground for the rising bourgeoisie. The East-Indian and Chinese markets, the colonisation of America, trade with these colonies, the increase in the means of exchange and in commodities generally, gave to commerce, to navigation, to industry, an impulse never before known, and thereby, to the revolutionary element in the tottering feudal society, a rapid development.

The feudal system of industry, under which industrial production was monopolised by closed guilds, now no longer sufficed for the growing wants of the new markets. The manufacturing system took its place. The guildmasters were pushed on one side by the manufacturing middle class; division of labour between the different corporate guilds vanished in the face of division of labour in each single workshop.

Meantime the markets kept ever growing, the demand ever rising. Even manufacture no longer sufficed. There-upon, steam and machinery revolutionised industrial production. The place of manufacture was taken by the giant, Modern Industry, the place of the industrial middle class, by industrial millionaires, the leaders of whole industrial armies, the modern bourgeois.

Modern industry has established the world-market, for which the discovery of America paved the way. This market has given an immense development to commerce, to naviga-tion, to communication by land. This development has, in its turn, reacted on the extension of industry; and in proportion as industry, commerce, navigation, railways extended, in the same proportion the bourgeoisie developed, increased its capital, and pushed into the background every class handed down from the Middle Ages.

We see, therefore, how the modern bourgeoisie is itself the product of a long course of development, of a series of revolutions in the modes of production and of exchange.

Each step in the development of the bourgeoisie was accompanied by a corresponding political advance of that class. An oppressed class under the sway of the feudal nobility, an armed and self-governing association in the mediaeval commune; here independent urban republic (as in Italy and Germany), there taxable "third estate" of the monarchy (as in France), afterwards, in the period of manufacture proper, serving either the semi-feudal or the absolute monarchy as a counterpoise against the nobility, and, in fact, corner-stone of the great monarchies in general, the bourgeoisie has at last, since the establishment of Modern Industry and of the world-market, conquered for itself, in the modern representative State, exclusive political sway. The executive of the modern State is but a committee for managing the common affairs of the whole bourgeoisie.

The bourgeoisie, historically, has played a most revolutionary part.

The bourgeoisie, whenever it has got the upper hand has put an end to all feudal, patriarchal, idyllic relations. It has pitilessly torn asunder the motley feudal ties that bound man to his "natural superiors," and has left remaining no other nexus between man and man than naked self-interest, than callous "cash payment." It has drowned the most heavenly ecstasies of religious fervour, of chivalrous enthusiasm, of philistine sentimentalism, in the icy water of egotistical calculation. It has resolved personal worth into exchange value and in place of the numberless indefeasible chartered freedoms, has set up that single, unconscionable freedom—Free Trade. In one word, for exploitation, veiled by religious and political illusions, it has substituted naked, shameless, direct, brutal exploitation.

The bourgeoisie has stripped of its halo every occupation hitherto honoured and looked up to with reverent awe. It has converted the physician, the lawyer, the priest, the poet, the man of science, into its paid wage-labourers.

The bourgeoisie has torn away from the family its sentimental veil, and has reduced the family relation to a mere money relation.

FYODOR DOSTOYEVSKY

from *The Brothers Karamazov*

The following passage is the opening chapter of The Brothers Karamazov *(1881). Here, Dostoyevsky creates drama and interest while introducing the characters and supplying the preliminary information necessary for understanding them. Even though the chapter compresses a considerable amount of information and condenses a long stretch of narrative time in a few pages, a wide range of action and feeling is apparent. The ironic tone of the first book, "A Nice Little Family," provides an example of the way the author blends humor, pathos, and tragedy in the novel. Dostoyevsky also implicates his readers in the action, inviting them in the final lines of the chapter to consider the extent to which the world of his characters is theirs as well.*

Alexey Fyodorovitch Karamazov was the third son of Fyodor Pavlovitch Karamazov, a landowner well known in our district in his own day, and still remembered among us owing to his gloomy and tragic death, which happened thirteen years ago, and which I shall describe in its proper place. For the present I will only say that this "landowner"—for so we used to call him, although he hardly spent a day of his life on his own estate—was a strange type, yet one pretty frequently to be met with, a type abject and vicious and at the same time senseless. But he was one of those senseless persons who are very well capable of looking after their worldly affairs, and, apparently, after nothing else. Fyodor Pavlovitch, for instance, began with next to nothing; his estate was of the smallest; he ran to dine at other men's tables, and fastened on them as a toady, yet at his death it appeared that he had a hundred thousand roubles in hard cash. At the same time, he was all his life one of the most senseless, fantastical fellows in the whole district. I repeat, it was not stupidity—the majority of these fantastical fellows are shrewd and intelligent enough—but just senselessness, and a peculiar national form of it.

He was married twice, and had three sons, the eldest, Dmitri, by his first wife, and two, Ivan and Alexey, by his second. Fyodor Pavlovitch's first wife, Adelaïda Ivanovna, belonged to a fairly rich and distinguished noble family, also landowners in our district, the Miüsovs. How it came to pass that an heiress, who was also a beauty, and moreover one of those vigorous, intelligent girls, so common in this generation, but sometimes also to be found in the last, could have married such a worthless, puny weakling, as we all called him, I won't attempt to explain. I knew a young lady of the last "romantic" generation who after some years of an enigmatic passion for a gentleman, whom she might quite easily have married at any moment, invented insuperable obstacles to their union, and ended by throwing herself one stormy night into a rather deep and rapid river from a high bank, almost a precipice, and so perished, entirely to satisfy her own caprice, and to be like Shakespeare's Ophelia. Indeed, if this precipice, a chosen and favourite spot of hers, had been less picturesque, if there had been a prosaic flat bank in its place, most likely the suicide would never have taken place. This is a fact, and probably there have been not a few similar instances in the last two or three generations. Adelaïda Ivanovna Miüsov's action was similarly, no doubt, an echo of other people's ideas, and was due to the irritation caused by lack of mental freedom. She wanted, perhaps, to show her feminine independence, to override class distinctions and the despotism of her family. And a pliable imagination persuaded her, we must suppose, for a brief moment, that Fyodor Pavlovitch, in spite of his parasitic position, was one of the bold and ironical spirits of that progressive epoch, though he was, in fact, an ill-natured buffoon and nothing more. What gave the marriage piquancy was that it was preceded by an elopement, and this greatly captivated Adelaïda Ivanovna's fancy. Fyodor Pavlovitch's position at the time made him specially eager for any such enterprise, for he was passionately anxious to make a career in one way or another. To attach himself to a good family and obtain a dowry was an alluring prospect. As for mutual love it did not exist apparently, either in the bride or in him, in spite of Adelaïda Ivanovna's beauty. This was, perhaps, a unique case of the kind in the life of Fyodor Pavlovitch, who was always of a voluptuous temper, and ready to run after any petticoat on the slightest encouragement. She seems to have been the only woman who made no particular appeal to his senses.

Immediately after the elopement Adelaïda Ivanovna discerned in a flash that she had no feeling for her husband but contempt. The marriage accordingly showed itself in its true colours with extraordinary rapidity. Although the family accepted the event pretty quickly and apportioned the run-away bride her dowry, the husband and wife began to lead a most disorderly life, and there were everlasting scenes between them. It was said that the young wife showed incomparably more generosity and dignity than Fyodor Pavlovitch who, as is now known, got hold of all her money up to twenty-five thousand roubles as soon as she received it, so that those thousands were lost to her for ever. The little village and the rather fine town house which formed part of her dowry he did his utmost for a long time to transfer to his name, by means of some deed of conveyance. He would probably have succeeded, merely from her moral fatigue and desire to get rid of him, and from the contempt and loathing he aroused by his persistent and shameless importunity. But, fortunately, Adelaïda Ivanovna's family intervened and circumvented his greediness. It is known for a fact that frequent fights took place between the husband and wife, but rumour had it that Fyodor Pavlovitch did not beat his wife but was beaten by her, for she was a hot-tempered, bold, dark-browed, impatient woman, possessed of remarkable physical strength. Finally, she left the house and ran away from Fyodor Pavlovitch with a destitute divinity student, leaving Mitya, a child of three years old, in her husband's hands. Immediately Fyodor Pavlovitch introduced a regular harem into the house, and abandoned himself to orgies of drunkenness. In the intervals he used to drive all over the province, complaining tearfully to each and all of Adelaïda Ivanovna's having left him, going into details too disgraceful for a husband to mention in regard to his own married life. What seemed to gratify him and flatter his self-love most was to play the ridiculous part of the injured husband, and to parade his woes with embellishments.

"One would think that you'd got a promotion, Fyodor Pavlovitch, you seem so pleased in spite of your sorrow," scoffers said to him. Many even added that he was glad of a new comic part in which to play the buffoon, and that it was simply to make it funnier that he pretended to be unaware of his ludicrous position. But, who knows, it may have been simplicity. At last he succeeded in getting on the track of his run-away wife. The poor woman turned out to be in Petersburg, where she had gone with her divinity student, and where she had thrown herself into a life of complete emancipation. Fyodor Pavlovitch at once began bustling about, making preparations to go to Petersburg, with what object he could not himself have said. He would perhaps have really gone; but having determined to do so he felt at once entitled to fortify himself for the journey by another bout of reckless drinking. And just at that time his wife's family received the news of her death in Petersburg. She had died quite suddenly in a garret, according to one story, of typhus, or as another version had it, of starvation. Fyodor Pavlovitch was drunk when he heard of his wife's death, and the story is that he ran out into the street and began shouting with joy, raising his hands to Heaven: "Lord, now lettest Thou Thy servant depart in peace," but others say he wept without restraint like a little child, so much so that people were sorry for him, in spite of the repulsion he inspired. It is quite possible that both versions were true, that he rejoiced at his release, and at the same time wept for her who released him. As a general rule, people, even the wicked, are much more naive and simple-hearted than we suppose. And we ourselves are, too.

LEO TOLSTOY

from *Anna Karenina*

Tolstoy's Anna Karenina *(1877), a novel he later repudiated for its immorality, is one of the world's greatest works of fiction. Its opening sentence identifies the theme and sets the tone for the entire monumental work. The novel explores family dynamics across a range of social standings, from the world of Russian peasantry to the splendor of the aristocracy. Tolstoy's novel pits the simple virtues of country life, linked with the cycle of nature, against the perversions and immorality of urban aristocrats. The opening chapter in a few swiftly executed paragraphs introduces readers to the complex and intricate world of family life.*

Part One

I

All happy families are alike; each unhappy family is unhappy in its own way.

All was confusion in the Oblonskys' house. The wife had found out that the husband was having an affair with their former French governess, and had announced to the husband that she could not live in the same house with him. This situation had continued for three days now, and was painfully felt by the couple themselves, as well as by all the members of the family and household. They felt that there was no sense in their living together and that people who meet accidentally at any inn have more connection with each other than they, the members of the family and household of the Oblonskys. The wife would not leave her rooms, the husband was away for the third day. The children were running all over the house as if lost; the English governess quarrelled with the housekeeper and wrote a note to a friend, asking her to find her a new place; the cook had already left the premises the day before, at dinner-time; the kitchen-maid and coachman had given notice.

On the third day after the quarrel, Prince Stepan Arkadyich Oblonsky—Stiva, as he was called in society—woke up at his usual hour, that is, at eight o'clock in the morning, not in his wife's bedroom but in his study, on a morocco sofa. He rolled his full, well-tended body over on the springs of the sofa, as if wishing to fall asleep again for a long time, tightly hugged the pillow from the other side and pressed his cheek to it; but suddenly he gave a start, sat up on the sofa and opened his eyes.

'Yes, yes, how did it go?' he thought, recalling his dream. 'How did it go? Yes! Alabin was giving a dinner in Darmstadt—no, not in Darmstadt but something American. Yes, but this Darmstadt was in America. Yes, Alabin was giving a dinner on glass tables, yes—and the tables were singing *Il mio tesoro*, only it wasn't *Il mio tesoro* but something better, and there were some little carafes, which were also women,' he recalled.

Stepan Arkadyich's eyes glittered merrily, and he fell to thinking with a smile. 'Yes, it was nice, very nice. There were many other excellent things there, but one can't say it in words, or even put it into waking thoughts.' And, noticing a strip of light that had broken through the side of one of the heavy blinds, he cheerfully dropped his feet from the sofa, felt for the slippers trimmed with gold morocco that his wife had embroidered for him (a present for last year's birthday), and, following a nine-year-old habit, without getting up, reached his hand out to the place where his dressing gown hung in the bedroom. And here he suddenly remembered how and why he was sleeping not in his wife's bedroom but in his study: the smile vanished from his face, and he knitted his brows.

'Oh, oh, oh! Ohh!. . .' he moaned, remembering all that had taken place. And in his imagination he again pictured all the details of his quarrel with his wife, all the hopelessness of his position and, most painful of all, his own guilt.

'No, she won't forgive me and can't forgive me! And the most terrible thing is that I'm the guilty one in it all—guilty, and yet not guilty. That's the whole drama,' he thought. 'Oh, oh, oh!' he murmured with despair, recalling what were for him the most painful impressions of this quarrel.

Worst of all had been that first moment when, coming back from the theatre, cheerful and content, holding a huge pear for his wife, he had not found her in the drawing room; to his surprise, he had not found her in the study either, and had finally seen her in the bedroom with the unfortunate, all-revealing note in her hand.

She—this eternally preoccupied and bustling and, as he thought, none-too-bright Dolly—was sitting motionless, the note in her hand, looking at him with an expression of horror, despair and wrath.

'What is this? this?' she asked, pointing to the note.

And, in recalling it, as often happens, Stepan Arkadyich was tormented not so much by the event itself as by the way he had responded to these words from his wife.

What had happened to him at that moment was what happens to people when they are unexpectedly caught in something very shameful. He had not managed to prepare his face for the position he found himself in with regard to his wife now that his guilt had been revealed. Instead of being offended, of denying, justifying, asking forgiveness, even remaining indifferent—any of which would have been better than what he did!—his face quite involuntarily ('reflexes of the brain', thought Stepan Arkadyich, who liked physiology) smiled all at once its habitual, kind and therefore stupid smile.

That stupid smile he could not forgive himself. Seeing that smile, Dolly had winced as if from physical pain, burst with her typical vehemence into a torrent of cruel words, and rushed from the room. Since then she had refused to see her husband.

'That stupid smile is to blame for it all,' thought Stepan Arkadyich.

'But what to do, then? What to do?' he kept saying despairingly to himself, and could find no answer.

CHAPTER 18

Impressionism
and Post-Impressionism

Claude Monet, *Impression, Sunrise*, 1872, oil on canvas, $17\frac{3}{4}'' \times 21\frac{3}{4}''$ (48 × 63 cm),
Musée Marmottan, Paris.

MAP 18.1 Europe in 1871.

CHAPTER OVERVIEW

IMPRESSIONISM
Art and science converge

POST-IMPRESSIONISM
Technology and nature influence the arts

IMPRESSIONISM

Before 1848, Paris was characterized by narrow streets and dark alleys, a maze that had been fortified with rebel barricades nine times since 1830.

GEORGES EUGENE HAUSSMANN [OUSE-mun] (1809–91) was commissioned to rebuild the city. He had three principal aims, the first being "to disencumber the large buildings, palaces, and barracks in such a way as to make them more pleasing to the eye, afford easier access on days of celebration, and a simplified defense on days of riot." Second, he recognized that slum conditions had a detrimental effect on public health, a situation he sought to rectify by the "systematic destruction of infected alleyways and centers of epidemics." Finally, he stated his plans "to assure public peace by the creation of large boulevards which will permit the circulation not only of air and light but also of troops." By the time Haussmann had completed his work in 1870, hundreds of miles of streets had been widened, new water and sewage systems were in place, the boulevards of modern Paris had been built, the banks of the Seine cleared of hovels, new bridges built, and tens of thousands of working-class poor evicted to the suburbs.

Due to Baron Haussmann, Paris was suddenly nearly as much a park as it was a city. It was, moreover, purged of its politically dangerous working class. In 1850, there were forty-seven acres of parkland in the city; by 1870, there were over 4,500, an increase of almost 100-fold. Haussmann doubled the number of trees lining the streets to over 100,000. The Bois de Boulogne, a neglected royal hunting ground to the west of the city, was redesigned between 1852 and 1858 as a giant English garden, with twisting, meandering paths, and a racecourse, Longchamp, which was built to please the politically powerful Jockey Club.

PAINTING

In 1874, a group of artists organized a show of their work. They included Mary Cassatt, Edgar Degas, Claude Monet, Berthe Morisot, Camille Pissarro, Pierre Renoir, and Alfred Sisley. Although he did not exhibit with them, Edouard Manet, who was particularly good friends with Monet, worked closely with the Impressionists. Manet most clearly bridges the gap between the Realists and the Impressionists. His Realist painting of 1863, *Luncheon on the Grass* (see fig. 17.22) was a precursor of the new Impressionist movement.

Claude Monet. The term **"Impressionism"** was derived from a painting by CLAUDE MONET [moh-NAY] (1840–1926) shown at the first exhibition of Impressionist art. Painted in 1872, it was called *Impression, Sunrise* (fig. 18.1). The painting encapsulates many of the features characteristic of Impressionist art. The *way* the Impressionist painters worked was as important to them as the subjects they painted. The traditional method of oil painting was to begin with a dark background color and work up to the lighter colors. The Impressionists reversed this, beginning with a white canvas and building up to dark colors. To convey a sense of natural light, they painted in the open air, rather than in the studio. They also tried to depict

FIGURE 18.1 Claude Monet, *Impression, Sunrise*, 1872, oil on canvas, $17\frac{3}{4}'' \times 21\frac{3}{4}''$ (48 × 63 cm), Musée Marmottan, Paris. The term "Impressionism," originally meant as an insult, derives from the title of this painting. Critics objected to the style, saying artists created *merely* an impression of a scene, without detail or compositional structure.

a momentary impression of nature's transitory light, atmosphere, and weather conditions; in Monet's painting the sun rises on a misty day over the harbor at Le Havre on the northern French coast. Behind this painting, and Impressionism as a whole, there also lies a major technological advance—the availability of oil paint in small, portable tins and tubes, which allowed painters to transport their paints out of doors.

Monet's brushwork is deliberately sketchy, consisting of broad dashes and dabs of paint. He suggests waves in the water with strokes of black. He shows the reflection of the sunrise in a series of orange and white strokes mixed together while still wet, right on the canvas. Although Monet's brushwork is loose, his composition is tightly controlled. Everything is carefully placed within a grid, defined horizontally by the horizon and vertically by the masts and the pattern of light and shadow that forms vertical bands across the composition.

Monet embarked on a number of projects designed to investigate the way in which changes in light and weather alter what we see by repeatedly painting the same subject at different times of the day and in different seasons: Rouen Cathedral, poplars, water lillies, and haystacks. Among the most famous of these projects, begun in 1888, is the series of paintings of haystacks. In *Haystacks at Giverny* (fig. 18.2), the color actually creates a feeling of heat. Monet realized that natural light changes color constantly and that many different colors make up what is perceived to be a single one. The myriad dabs of "broken" color are intended to blend in the viewer's eyes, creating sparkle and vibration. When a group of fifteen of these paintings was exhibited in Paris in 1891, they caused an immediate sensation. As the critic Gustave Geffroy wrote in the introduction to the show's catalog, "[Monet] knows that the artist can spend his life in the same place and look around himself without exhausting the constantly renewed spectacle. . . . These stacks, in this deserted field, are transient objects whose surfaces, like mirrors, catch the mood of the environment, the states of the atmosphere with the errant breeze, the sudden glow."

Pierre-Auguste Renoir. PIERRE-AUGUSTE RENOIR [ren-WAH] (1841–1919) was a good friend of Monet when both were poor and struggling, and the two often painted together in Paris and at Argenteuil where Renoir was a frequent visitor. His joyous personality and his zest for living, which reflect the age itself, inform his paintings.

Impressionists changed the focus of artistic subject matter. In turning away from traditional religious, mythological, historical, and literary subjects, they were similar to the Realists in temperament, but instead of looking objectively at the ordinary life of the working class, they looked to the good life and the entertainments of the middle class in a new "beautiful age"—the **belle époque.** It was an age of pleasure-seeking in which life focused on Paris's *grands boulevards*, weekend outings in its suburbs and gardens, a day at the races, boating on the Seine, the theatre, or dancing.

Dance at the Moulin de la Galette (fig. 18.3), of 1876, is a good example. The painting, of a restaurant and open-air dance hall in Montmartre, a northern section of Paris, captures the sense of gaiety that marks the belle époque.

FIGURE 18.2   Claude Monet, *Haystacks at Giverny (end of summer, morning)*, 1891, oil on canvas, $23\frac{3}{4}$" × $39\frac{1}{2}$" (60.5 × 100 cm), Musée d'Orsay, Paris. Reunion des Musées Nationaux. B. Hatala/Art Resource, NY. Rather than painting in the studio as did earlier artists, Monet painted out of doors. Instead of mixing colors on a palette beforehand, he applied paint in dabs of pure color, referred to as "broken color."

FIGURE 18.3   Pierre-Auguste Renoir, *Dance at the Moulin de la Galette*, 1876, oil on canvas, $4'3\frac{1}{2}'' \times 5'9''$ (1.30 × 1.80 m), Musée d'Orsay, Paris. Reunion des Musées Nationaux. Herve Lewandowski/Art Resource, NY. © 2005 Artists Rights Society (ARS), NY. Instead of choosing traditional subjects, the Impressionists depicted pleasant places where people congregated. In Renoir's paintings the people are always attractive and the weather is usually good—here the sun falls in patches through the leaves.

Renoir painted outdoors, working rapidly with his colors to capture the atmosphere of the moment. Light comes through the trees, falling in patches, dappling the surface—note the pattern of round splotches of light on the back of the man in the foreground. Renoir's figures appear relaxed, rather than stiffly posed. Interestingly, the couple dancing on the left gaze at the viewer. They seem aware they are being watched, a photographic effect that lends the painting an aura of spontaneity. They are, in fact, friends of the artist: Margot, one of his models, and Solares, a Cuban painter. As in all of his paintings, the men are handsome, the women are pretty, the activity in which they engage is pleasant, and the sun is shining. According to Renoir, "A picture ought to be a lovable thing, joyous and pretty, yes, pretty. There are enough boring things in this world without our making more."

Berthe Morisot.   The only woman to exhibit at the first Impressionist exhibition was BERTHE MORISOT [more-ee-SOH] (1841–95). Married to Manet's younger brother Eugène, her work was almost immediately given the negative label "feminine" by the critics, perhaps because her subject matter was, almost exclusively, women and children. Whatever she depicted, it is clear she was the most daring of all the Impressionist painters. *Summer's Day* (fig. 18.4), exhibited at the fifth show in 1880, is remarkable for the looseness of its brushwork, which is hardly contained within the contours of the forms it depicts. It zigs and zags across the surface in a seemingly arbitrary manner. Yet in the small rapid movements of her strokes, we can almost feel the breeze on the water, see the lapping and splashing of the water on the oars, and hear the wisps of conversation between the two women as they enjoy their outing.

FIGURE 18.4 Berthe Morisot, *Summer's Day*, 1879, oil on canvas, 18″ × 29¾″ (45.7 × 75.2 cm), National Gallery, London. Note in particular Morisot's handling of the three ducks swimming on the right. They are so loosely painted that they have become almost unrecognizable.

Edgar Degas. A very different type of French Impressionism was created by EDGAR DEGAS [DAY-GAH] (1834–1917). An aristocrat from a banking family, Degas was independently wealthy and therefore able to paint to suit himself. Many other painters disliked him, and with reason, for he was snobbish and unfriendly, with a nasty wit. Politically and socially conservative, Degas did not think art should be available to the lower class.

Degas's strict academic training resulted in a style based on draftsmanship. In 1865, he met Ingres, then eighty-five years old. Ingres told him to "do lines and more lines, from nature or from memory, and you will become a good artist." Because of this approach, Degas has been called a "linear Impressionist," which may seem at first to be a contradiction. Degas, however, hated the word "Impressionist" because of the negative connotations of "accidental" or "incomplete." He worked methodically, sometimes determining the proportions of the work by ruling off squares and often making many sketches before painting. He once remarked, "No art was ever less spontaneous than mine. What I do is the result of reflection and study of the great masters; of inspiration, spontaneity, temperament, I know nothing."

What makes Degas an Impressionist, nonetheless, is the *sense* of spontaneity visible in his work, not only in the looseness of his brushwork, but also in the choice and treatment of his subject matter. However calculatingly hard he worked, he aimed to *appear* unstudied. His effect is one of instantaneous and immediate vision. Degas seems to have been influenced by photography, and by the snapshot in particular. His paintings often appear severely cropped, cutting figures in half, as if they are just entering or leaving the viewfinder of a camera.

In Degas's depictions of ballet dancers, for which he is perhaps best known, he takes us behind the scenes. In *The Dancing Class* (fig. 18.5), of about 1874, he seems to have tried deliberately to capture the dancers at their least grace-

FIGURE 18.5 Edgar Degas, *The Dancing Class*, ca. 1874, oil on canvas, 33½″ × 29½″ (85 × 75 cm), Musée d'Orsay, Paris. Degas was called a "linear Impressionist"—seemingly an oxymoron. Interested in figures in motion, he made many pictures of ballerinas. He seems to have preferred them at their least graceful, as when leaning tired against the barre, stooping over their aching feet, or adjusting their costumes.

ful—straining, stretching, scratching, and yawning. Known for his unusual compositions, Degas constructs a boxlike space in which the walls are not parallel to the picture plane but instead on oblique angles. The point of view from which the scene is recorded is striking—from above and to the side. It anticipates, in effect, the freedom of perspective that photographers would discover with the handheld camera, an invention that the Kodak Corporation had introduced by the end of the century.

Mary Cassatt. In addition to French Impressionist painters, there were a number of American Impressionists. One of the foremost was MARY CASSATT [kah-SAHT] (1844–1925), who left her wealthy Pittsburgh family and moved to Europe where she became absorbed in the art world. Her parents opposed her study of art so strongly that her father is reported to have said, "I would almost rather see you dead." She soon gained recognition, however—she was called a madwoman because of her style. Cassatt was a close friend of Degas, who claimed he never would have believed a woman could draw so well. As early as 1879, Cassatt was exhibiting with the Impressionists.

Cassatt's *The Boating Party* (fig. 18.6), painted 1893–94, was criticized when first shown, for the foreground figure has rudely turned his back on for the viewer. Rather than

FIGURE 18.6   Mary Cassatt, *The Boating Party*, 1893–94, oil on canvas, $35\frac{1}{2}''\times 46\frac{1}{8}''$ (90 × 117 cm), National Gallery of Art, Washington, DC, Chester Dale Collection. Photograph © Board of Trustees, 1963. 10. 94 (1758)/PA. An American working in France, Cassatt paints a typical Impressionist subject—pleasant and out of doors. The composition directs the viewer's eyes to the squirming child.

being the center of attention, however, he acts as a compositional device directing the viewer's gaze into the composition. His arm and oar point inward, and he looks toward the mother and child, just as the viewer does. The contours of the boat and sail also lead to the mother and child. A sense of realism is achieved in the squirming movement of the child.

The influence of Japanese prints is apparent in the asymmetrical composition, the emphasis on sharp silhouettes and linear rhythms, the broad flat areas of color, the snapshot quality of the scene, the high positioning of the horizon, and, moreover, the unusual perspective—we look down into the boat, which is abruptly cut off. The brilliant light effects so typical of Impressionism are not achieved through the use of broken color. Instead, Cassatt juxtaposes large areas of bright color. The light appears intense, but is not realistic: the interior of the boat should, in fact, be dark. Facts are manipulated for art, and in this respect Cassatt's painting, and that of other Impressionists, can be seen as anticipating the art of the next century.

James Abbott McNeill Whistler.   The work of another expatriate American, James Abbott McNeill Whistler (1834–1903), also foreshadows twentieth-century art. After a disappointing stint at West Point, and being fired from a government job in Washington, D.C., Whistler went to Paris in 1855, where he lived as a bohemian art student. Then in 1859, he moved to London, and was to remain there for the rest of his life. He visited Paris several times and learned about Impressionism, but he never used Impressionistic broken color or light effects.

FIGURE 18.7   James Abbott McNeill Whistler, *Arrangement in Black and Gray: The Artist's Mother*, 1871, oil on canvas, $4'9''\times 5'4\frac{1}{4}''$ (1.50 × 1.60 m), Musée d'Orsay, Paris. Reunion des Musées Nationaux. Jean Shormars/Art Resource, NY. Whistler's mother, as subject, is treated much the same as the other elements in this intellectual arrangement in restricted colors.

In 1863, his mother came to keep house for him (she supported him financially), and in 1871 he immortalized her in a work entitled *Arrangement in Black and Gray: The Artist's Mother* (fig. 18.7), known popularly as *Whistler's Mother*. Whistler referred to his paintings by musical terms such as nocturnes, symphonies, and harmonies. This painting is first and foremost an "arrangement," and only secondarily a portrait. Abstract and formal, the pictorial space is flattened, depth receives little emphasis, and light, shadow, and modeling are minimal. Whistler maintained that art should not be concerned with morality, education, or storytelling, but should appeal to the aesthetic sense. He believed in art for art's sake.

LITERATURE

The Symbolists.   Like the Impressionists, the **Symbolist** poets also attempted to convey reality by impression and sensation. They felt liberated by their medium, words, and from the necessity of rendering the "facts" of vision. Words, they believed, could do more than simply portray these "facts" of external experience; indeed, they could capture a sense of the shifting and fluid nature of our entire mental experience. Language could encompass not only our perceptions of the outside world, but our internal lives as well. The Symbolists sought to evoke states of mind and feeling beyond the surface of everyday reality. And because they did not believe they could successfully

Connections

DEBUSSY AND MALLARMÉ: IMPRESSIONIST AND SYMBOLIST

Claude Debussy's chamber orchestral composition *Prelude to the Afternoon of a Faun* was inspired by Stéphane Mallarmé's poem "The Afternoon of a Faun." Both composer and poet convey the faun's experience through suggestive uses of sound and language. Mallarmé's poem describes the reveries of a creature from classical mythology, with the body of a man and the horns, ears, legs, and tail of a goat. The poem's dreamlike tone raises the question as to whether the faun has actually been chasing nymphs or whether he has only been dreaming about doing so. Equally ambiguous is the poem's sense of time and place. Debussy's composition does not attempt to portray the content of the poem so much as to evoke its atmosphere of languor and fantasy.

Debussy wrote the music to suggest "the successive scenes through which pass the desires and dreams of the faun in the heat of [an] afternoon." He accomplishes this with a musical language that includes the sounds of woodwind and harp while excluding those of trumpets and trombones. Rather than the clearly articulated, symmetrical themes of the Classical and Romantic styles that were developed and recapitulated, Debussy creates a more dreamlike and evocative music. His themes appear and disappear, often in misty fragments and brief orchestral swells. The music ebbs and flows continuously in a series of subtly shifting rhythms, the flute suggesting the musical pipes associated with the mythological faun. The overall musical effect is one of reverie, which suits the mood of Mallarmé's poem.

---

render the external world objectively, they were free to present it from their own unique and idiosyncratic perspectives. Reality was at best, they argued, an irretrievably personal affair.

Poetry, they felt, had long been mired in the ordinary, caught up in conventions of meaning and usage that blinded the reader to language's potential to reveal the extraordinary and the unknown. For the Symbolists, an image or symbol did not so much stand for something as suggest a cluster of ideas and feelings. They preferred the vagueness of symbolic suggestion to a more precise rendering of experience. As Stéphane Mallarmé wrote, "To name an object is to do away with three-quarters of the enjoyment of the poem, which is derived from the satisfaction of guessing little by little; to suggest it, to evoke it, this is what charms the imagination."

Among the poets associated with the Symbolist movement, CHARLES BAUDELAIRE [bow-duh-LAIR] (1821–67) is an important precursor, but STÉPHANE MALLARMÉ [mal-are-MAY] (1842–98) was the group's leading theoretician and its most influential practitioner. Both Baudelaire and Mallarmé attempted to create poems using images that fuse the senses and attain the expressiveness of music. In Baudelaire's "Hair," for example, the speaker pays homage to a lover's hair by describing it as "A port resounding where, in draughts untold, / My soul may drink in colour, scent, and sound." A similar combination of the senses occurs in Mallarmé's "Windows," in lines such as "His eye on the horizon gorged with light, / Sees golden ships, fine as swans, / On a scented river of purple." In addition to this attempt to convey the rich sensuousness of imagined experience, Symbolist poets tried to make their verse musical, so the sounds of the words themselves would be suggestive in a musical sense rather than purely representational, a characteristic difficult to demonstrate in translation.

Naturalism. The impulse toward Romanticism in the nineteenth century was countered by the writing of a number of American women. Writers such as Sarah Orne Jewett (1849–1909), Charlotte Perkins Gilman (1851–1904), and KATE CHOPIN [SHOW-panh] (1851–1904) all deal with the concerns of middle-class women in naturalistic detail, with a psychological realism often reminiscent of Freud. Jewett's stories center on the everyday lives of New England characters; Gilman focuses on the ways in which nineteenth-century attitudes toward women kept them physically and psychologically imprisoned; and Chopin's fiction depicts strong women who insist upon their independence and their right to determine their own destinies.

Kate Chopin was especially adept at depicting the lives of the Creole, Cajun, African American, and Native American communities of Louisiana, and her popularity soared as readers consumed her stories filled with local customs and dialects. Chopin's best known work is the short novel *The Awakening*, published in 1899. It is intensely psychological in its portrayal of its heroine Edna Pontellier's passionate emotional life, her boredom with her constricting marriage, and her flirtatious adventures with another man. But the novel was considered virtually obscene in its day, banned from most libraries, and Chopin's reputation suffered until the 1950s, when the work was rediscovered.

Drama, too, began to develop along naturalistic lines, especially in Europe. Among the great nineteenth-century realist dramatists was the Norwegian playwright Henrik Ibsen (1828–1906), whose plays touched on such themes as the roles and rights of women (*A Doll House*), the scourge of venereal disease (*Ghosts*), and the death of a child (*Little Eyolf*). Ibsen's dramatic intensity and electrifying revelations were matched by the Swedish playwright August Strindberg (1849–1912), whose plays *The Father*, *Creditors*, and *Comrades* were all written in a strongly realistic style. The plays of Russian writer ANTON CHEKHOV [CHECK-off] (1860–1904), such as *The Three Sisters* and *The Cherry Orchard*, lack the intense melodramatic character of those by Ibsen and Strindberg. They don't have a clear cause and effect plot structure, and they do not build toward tragic climaxes. Instead, Chekhov's characters are lifelike in their inability to find happiness, their uncertainty about the future, and their indecisiveness in achieving their desires.

The plays of Ibsen, Strindberg, Chekhov, and the numerous other naturalist dramatists of the time were staged to emphasize the authenticity of the characters, settings, and situations. Chekhov's plays were produced at the Moscow Art Theater, which was run by Konstantin Stanislavsky, whose theory of acting asked actors to "live" their roles based on their own psychological reactions to the characters. Chekhov's plays, with their complex portraits of character relationships, were particularly suited to the Stanislavsky system. Together, Chekhov and Stanislavsky profoundly influenced subsequent modern realistic theater in the West.

MUSIC

Debussy's Musical Impressionism. The composer CLAUDE DEBUSSY [day-byou-SEE] (1862–1918) revolutionized his artistic medium. Just as Claude Monet altered the way external reality was rendered in pigment, so Debussy altered the way music suggested extramusical sensations and impressions. Working with a palette of sound instead of color, he mixed musical tones, combining them in ways never heard before, thus influencing the music that would be written after him.

Debussy insisted that "French music is clearness, elegance, simple and natural declamation. French music aims first of all to give pleasure." This he did in a wide range of compositions—some for orchestra, such as *Fêtes* (*Festivals*) and *La Mer* (*The Sea*), and others for piano, including the popular *Clair de Lune* (*Moonlight*), inspired by the Symbolist poet Paul Verlaine. Rather than duplicating the poem's images or details, Debussy created a parallel or analogous musical image of moonlight through beautiful sounds and suggestive harmonies, without a long lyrical melodic line.

Debussy rejected the dramatic dynamics of theme employed by Classical and Romantic composers in favor of greater tonal variety. He accomplished this effect partly by encouraging the use of the piano's damper pedal, which allows the strings for different notes to resonate simultaneously, creating a hazy but rich blend of sounds. He complemented this with a fluctuating sense of rhythm. In masking the basic musical pulse, Debussy created music that avoided the familiar melodic, harmonic, and rhythmic patterns of the past. At the Paris International Exposition in 1889, Debussy heard Javanese and Southeast Asian music that he could not duplicate on Western instruments. In response, he explored a scale of six whole tones, entirely of whole-step intervals. The effect of using such a scale was to make all the scale tones equal in weight, without the strong pull of any one home key. The unfocused quality of music that resulted from a whole-tone scale is comparable to the effects Impressionist painters used in creating a shimmering atmosphere across a canvas, and to the lack of representation achieved by Symbolist poets in their deliberate avoidance of strict linguistic referentiality.

POST-IMPRESSIONISM

As the nineteenth century came to a close, the Western world was overtaken by a sense that an era was ending. It was a time of extraordinary material innovation: In the 1880s and 1890s, the telegraph, telephone, bicycle, automobile, typewriter, phonograph, elevator, and electric lamp all came into being. At the 1889 World Fair in Paris, which marked the one hundredth anniversary of the revolution, the engineer Gustave Eiffel (1832–1923) constructed the tallest structure in the world, a tower that stood 984 feet high (fig. 18.8). At first, many Parisians hated it. The author Guy de Maupaussant, for instance, preferred to lunch at the restaurant in the Eiffel Tower because, he said, "It's the only place in Paris where I don't have to see it." Despite the negative reception, its skeletal iron frame prepared the way for the most prevalent of twentieth-century buildings—the skyscraper—which would define the terms of the new urban workplace as surely as the telephone and the typewriter.

The end of the century was also a time of profound and disturbing social unrest and, to many, one of moral decay. Starting in the 1880s, severe economic depression in England marked the beginning of the end of the country's supremacy as a world power. The Dockers' Strike of 1889 led to the unionization of unskilled workers, and by 1900, the Labour Party had been founded. In France, meanwhile, the working classes, it seemed, turned more and more to alcohol for pleasure. Beginning in 1891 and continuing for twenty more years, three thousand new bistros opened in Paris every year, and by 1910, there was one for every eighty-two Parisians. By 1906, most French workmen drank over three liters of wine a day. Drug use was on the rise, with opium, and its derivative morphine, finding special favor. With addiction and poverty came crime, so much so that electric light was championed more for its ability to deter criminal behavior than for anything else.

FIGURE 18.8   Gustave Eiffel, Eiffel Tower, Paris, 1889. This demonstration of engineering technology, which was extremely controversial when erected and has remained unique, is now considered the symbol of France. An elevator takes tourists up to enjoy a spectacular view of Paris.

The period also witnessed a challenge on the part of European intellectuals to the accepted code of moral behavior of the day. Some writers styled themselves "decadents." Oscar Wilde (1854–1900) flaunted his homosexuality. This identifiable "type" suddenly became visible to such a point that in Vienna, in 1905, Sigmund Freud would include homosexuality in his *Three Essays on the Theory of Sexuality*. George Sand and Rosa Bonheur had worn men's clothing in midcentury, but now, in the 1890s, many women, particularly intellectuals, wore trousers, and they were consequently decried for betraying their sex. Moreover, they asked with increasing intensity for the right to vote. In the late nineteenth century, many conventional standards of behavior were being questioned and reevaluated.

AMERICAN EXPANSION

Throughout the nineteenth century, the United States engaged in territorial expansion. Territories had been added through purchase, most famously with Thomas Jefferson's negotiated purchase of the Louisiana Territory from the French in 1803, and later the purchase of Alaska from Russia in 1867. In addition to these land purchases, under the banner of "manifest destiny," Native American Indians were routinely displaced from their lands and relegated to reservations. Many lost their lives in the Indian Wars.

Other kinds of expansion proved equally troublesome. When the United States accepted Texas, which had seceded from Mexico in 1836, into the union, Mexico protested and the resulting tensions led to the Mexican American War of 1845–48. The main result of this war was Mexico's sale of its territories in California and New Mexico and its recognition of the U.S. annexation of Texas.

One place where the United States did not succeed in expanding was north into Canada. During the War of 1812 between the United States and Britain, Canadians consistently repelled U.S. incursions, serving to unite the previously splintered French and British Canadians, and propelling Canada toward political sovereignty.

The United States also had mixed experiences in expanding its territory into other areas. The Hawaiian islands were annexed in 1898, after the last Hawaiian monarch was ousted in 1893. The United States took possession of Cuba and Puerto Rico after a brief military encounter with Spain in the Spanish American War of 1898–99. Each of these has had a different fate, with Hawaii becoming the fiftieth U.S. state in 1959, Puerto Rico rejecting U.S. statehood and remaining a U.S.-associated commonwealth, and Cuba becoming independent.

Spain also lost its colonial possessions in the Pacific to the United States, with the Guam and the Philippine islands coming under U.S. control in 1898. As a result of the Spanish American War, Spain lost control of the last remnants of its overseas colonial empire, with a new imperialist force, the United States, recognized as a major world power.

THE BOER WAR

Seeking gold in South African mines, thousands of prospectors from Britain and other countries came to South Africa. British imperialism also found expression in the Boer Wars, especially the Second Boer War, also known as the South African War (1899–1902). The war was fought between the British Empire and the two independent Boer Republics in South Africa. Victorious, Britain absorbed into the British Empire the Orange Free

State and the Transvaal Republic, as the Union of South Africa.

Although the war was fought among whites, many black Africans who served on both sides were killed. British concentration camps held as many as 100,000 black Africans, 10,000 of whom died. Other groups who suffered from severe treatment were Chinese laborers, or "coolies," who, employed by the British colonial governor after the war, were poorly paid, segregated from the local population, and left to live in appalling conditions.

NEW SCIENCE AND NEW TECHNOLOGIES

Even as prosperity seemed to promise a limitless future, the technology it spawned contributed to the breakdown of established patterns of social organization. New means of communication, such as the telephone, and new forms of transportation, such as the automobile, complicated life rather than simplifying it. The rules of the road remained largely uncodified, and the continuing process of industrialization spurred the growth of urban centers at the expense of agrarian life. Modern intellectual developments greatly accelerated the transformation of traditional ways of thinking. In particular, discoveries in quantum physics and depth psychology transformed twentieth-century thought. The most important of these developments were Freud's invention of psychoanalysis and Einstein's promulgation of his theory of relativity.

The Theory of Relativity.
In 1905, Albert Einstein (1879–1955) proposed that space and time are not absolute as they appear to be, but are instead relative to each other in a "space-time continuum." Not until 1919 could the mathematical equations central to Einstein's special theory of relativity be confirmed through scientific experiment. Subsequent experiments further established the legitimacy of his ideas. All modern developments in space technology were influenced by his discoveries, those developments proving the accuracy of his theory right into the 1980s. Einstein's notion of relativity was widely circulated even though it undermined traditional ways of thinking about the universe, similar to the way in which Copernicus's theory had overturned the Ptolemaic concept of the universe.

The Atom.
Equally important in its implications was the work of J. J. Thomson (1856–1940) in Cambridge, England, who between 1897 and 1899 managed to detect the existence of separate components, which he called electrons, in the structure of the **atom,** which had previously been thought indivisible. By 1911, his colleague Ernest Rutherford (1871–1937) had introduced his revolutionary new model of the atom. It consisted of a small positively charged nucleus, which contained most of the atom's mass, around which its electrons orbited. To many, the world no longer seemed a solid whole.

PHILOSOPHY AT THE TURN OF THE CENTURY

Friedrich Nietzsche.
The philosopher FRIEDRICH NIETZSCHE [NEE-chuh] (1844–1900) emphasized the rebellious nature of the **superman,** a superhuman being who refused to be confined within the traditional structures of nationalist ideology, Christian belief, scientific knowledge, and bourgeois values. Proclaiming "God is dead," Nietzsche asserted the complete freedom of the individual, who could now begin to channel **Dionysian** (instinctual) and **Apollonian** (intellectual) tendencies in ways that were unrestricted by social conventions. Early modernist art, in part, owes its rebellious antiauthoritarianism to Nietzsche's example. So too, in part, do developments in literary theory and in philosophy, especially existentialism.

Sigmund Freud.
The psychology of SIGMUND FREUD [FROYD] (1856–1939) further influenced modernist trends in culture and the arts. Freud's analysis of unconscious motives and his description of instinctual drives reflected an antirationalist perspective that undermined faith in the apparent order and control in human individual and social life. His emphasis on the irrational provided a quasi-scientific explanation of impulses and behaviors that had formerly been displayed in works of literature, which could now be analyzed with the language and concepts of **psychoanalysis** he developed. Freud's splitting of the human psyche into the **ego,** the **id,** and the **superego** provided a psychoanalytical analogue for the growing concern with social fragmentation and cultural disharmony, the distressing feeling that all was not well, even if the period was known as the belle époque.

POST-IMPRESSIONIST PAINTING

By the early 1890s, the Impressionist style of painting was widely accepted. However, since the time of Courbet, painters had defined themselves against the mainstream of approved art. The next wave of artists to challenge the public's expectations were called the Post-Impressionists.

The term **Post-Impressionism** is, in fact, an extremely broad one, for the Post-Impressionists did not band together but worked in isolation. Rather than a rejection of Impressionism, Post-Impressionism, which began in France in the 1880s, was an attempt to improve on it and to extend it. The Post-Impressionists considered Impressionism too objective, too impersonal, and lacking control. They did not think that recording a fleeting moment or portraying atmospheric conditions was sufficient. Placing greater emphasis on composition and form, the Post-Impressionists worked to control reality, to organize, arrange, and formalize. The Post-Impressionist painters wanted more personal interpretation and expression, as well as greater psychological depth.

Paul Cézanne. PAUL CÉZANNE [say-ZAHN] (1839–1906) was in Paris at the beginning of the Impressionist phenomenon. Introverted to the point of being reclusive, he led an almost completely isolated existence in the south of France from 1877 to 1895. People there considered him a madman and jeered at him. He became ever more irritable as a consequence and turned increasingly inward.

Reacting against the loose and unstructured quality of Impressionist art, Cézanne's greatest interest was in order, stability, and permanence. He said he wanted "to make of Impressionism something solid and durable, like the art of the museums." All of Cézanne's paintings are carefully constructed. His usual technique was to sketch with thin blue paint and then apply the colors directly. He washed his brush between strokes so that each color would be distinct, sometimes taking as long as twenty minutes between brushstrokes. In fact, he referred to his brushstrokes as "little planes." An apple, for example, is viewed as a spherical form consisting of a series of small planes—each plane is a specific color according to the apple's form. This revolutionary style of painting would lead to the innovative ideas of the early twentieth century. Indeed, some historians feel Cézanne was the first artist to profoundly redirect painting since Giotto (see Chapter 12) in the early fourteenth century.

Cézanne's favorite subjects were still life and landscape, and indeed, landscape may be regarded as enlarged still life. Inanimate objects permitted Cézanne's intensive and lengthy study. In his painting of *Mount Sainte-Victoire from the Large Pine Tree* (fig. 18.9), of 1885–87, one of several paintings he

FIGURE 18.10   Paul Cézanne, *Still Life with Peppermint Bottle*, ca. 1894, oil on canvas, 26″ × 32⅜″ (66 × 82.3 cm), National Gallery of Art, Washington, DC, Chester Dale Collection, Photograph © Board of Trustees. Post-Impressionists perpetuated the bright colors of Impressionism, but for different purposes. Using broken color in a more scientific and studied way, Cézanne referred to each brushstroke as a "little plane," which he used to establish the contours of an object in space.

made of this mountain, Cézanne used his "little planes" to analyze and carefully construct the view. Tree trunks mark the foreground plane, yet the curves of their branches echo the silhouette of the most distant hills, linking foreground and background, compressing pictorial space.

In his *Still Life with Peppermint Bottle* (fig. 18.10), of ca. 1894, Cézanne makes apparent that the subject was not as important to him as *how* he painted it, and he often combined unrelated objects in his still lifes. No attempt at photographic reproduction was made, for he consciously distorted edges and shapes, emphasizing the contours and the space between objects. Disregarding the conventions of perspective, he created a tension between the three-dimensional subject and the two-dimensional surface.

Always striving, yet chronically dissatisfied with his work, Cézanne felt he did not reach his goal. "I am the primitive of the way I have discovered," he claimed. Yet much of early twentieth-century painting is indebted to Cézanne, who has been called the "Father of Abstract Art." His phrase, "You must see in nature the cylinder, the sphere, and the cone," became the basis of the Cubist painting of Pablo Picasso and Georges Braque.

Georges Seurat.   Another important French Post-Impressionist artist, GEORGES SEURAT [sir-AH] (1859–91), had an approach to painting that was still more intellectual and scientific, for he believed that art could be created by a system of rules. Like Cézanne, he made many sketches and studies before painting and worked very slowly.

Sunday Afternoon on La Grande Jatte (fig. 18.11), painted between 1884 and 1886, is a monumental work. The sub-

FIGURE 18.9   Paul Cézanne, *Mount Sainte-Victoire from the Large Pine Tree*, 1887, oil on canvas, 23½″ × 28½″ (60 × 73 cm), The Phillips Collection, Washington, DC, acquired 1925. Cézanne's innovative approach to depicting objects in space, without using traditional methods of perspective, would prove to be influential for twentieth-century painting.

Then & Now

POINTILLISM AND TELEVISION

Seurat's Pointillist technique involved putting small dabs of different colored paint next to one another and allowing the eye to blend them into a single tone. Television works in much the same way. A standard set contains one picture tube and three electron guns. Each gun makes a complete picture on the screen in one of the primary light colors—red, blue, and green (not yellow as in surface primary colors). The screen itself is made of small dots, each dot capable of being hit by only one of the guns. When the three primary colors are projected simultaneously through the dots on the screen, they blend, projecting a full range of colors to the viewer's eye. If you look at the screen of a color television with a magnifying glass before turning it on, you can see the pattern of dots. Then look at the screen after turning it on, and you can see how the manufacturer has arranged the different primary colors (every manufacturer employs a different pattern) in an array intended to create vivid color images.

FIGURE 18.11   Georges Seurat, *A Sunday Afternoon on La Grande Jatte*, 1884–86, oil on canvas, 6'9¾" × 10'1¼" (2 × 3m), The Art Institute of Chicago. Helen Birch Bartlett Memorial Collection. Photograph © 2005, All Rights Reserved. Seurat systematically applied bright color in tiny dots intended to blend in the viewer's eyes when the painting is seen from a distance. The technique is scientific, and the composition is carefully unified by the repetition of curving shapes.

Cross Currents

JAPANESE PRINTS AND WESTERN PAINTERS

The influence of the Japanese prints on Western painters of the nineteenth century, especially on the Impressionists, is the direct result of the opening of Japan to trade with the West after Commodore Matthew Perry sailed into Tokyo Bay in 1853, demanding that Japanese ports be opened to foreigners. Perry's arrival ended over two hundred years of Japanese isolationism, which had started as a result of the negative reception of Christian ideas introduced into the country by foreign missionaries.

After trade began, Japanese prints flooded Europe to such an extent that they became commonplace. Western artists were attracted especially to the flatness of Japanese forms, the compressed pictorial space, and the oblique perspective that characterizes Japanese prints. The cropped but close-up renderings of occurrences in everyday life that so enthralled the Japanese artists influenced, in particular, the work of Edgar Degas and Mary Cassatt.

Claude Monet discovered the first of the many Japanese prints that would decorate his house at Giverny wrapped around a cheese purchased at the market. What especially attracted him to Japanese landscapes were the ways in which they organized the natural elements, such as rocks and trees. Perhaps the clearest example of Monet's enthusiasm for Japanese art and culture is the garden he created at Giverny and the paintings it inspired. The Far Eastern influence is evident in the small pond he created, which was spanned by a little arched bridge, with blue wisteria flowers arranged so as to hang down on either side. There were irises, bamboo, and willows, all common plants in Japanese paintings.

Perhaps the artist most thoroughly influenced by the Japanese print was Vincent van Gogh. He owned hundreds of prints, and one of the reasons he went to Arles in 1888 was that he believed he would find a landscape there similar to that of Japan. His letters to his brother Theo repeatedly refer to his idealized image of Japanese life, in which painters and printmakers lived in close contact with ordinary people and in harmony with the rhythms and cycles of nature. While still in Paris, in 1887, van Gogh copied a print by Ando Hiroshige, *Plum Estate*, of 1857. Van Gogh's painting, entitled *Japonaiserie: The Tree* (fig. 18.12), is an almost exact copy. What particularly impressed van Gogh was the relation between the tree in the foreground,

and the space behind it, the gulf between the nearby detail and the landscape beyond. This is an effect that would dominate his paintings in the future.

FIGURE 18.12   Vincent van Gogh, *Japonaiserie: The Tree*, 1887, oil on canvas, $21\frac{5}{8}'' \times 18\frac{1}{8}''$ (55 × 46 cm), National Museum Vincent van Gogh, Amsterdam. Van Gogh was influenced in this painting and in others by the unusual vantage point, flat pattern, and dark outlines characteristic of Japanese prints.

ject is the type favored by the Impressionists—a sunny afternoon in a public park with a gathering of French society. Yet, in an effort to give structure to the disintegrating forms of Impressionism, Seurat solidified and simplified them and defined their boundaries. Edges reappear and silhouettes are sharp. All is tidy, balanced, and arranged with precision.

Seurat's working method was first to create silhouettes of simple lines and precise contours. He then organized the composition's surface and depth. Spaces between figures and shadows were considered part of the composition, and shapes were repeated for unity. Finally, he painted in his *petits points*, a technique called "Pointillism," although Seurat called it "divisionism." **Pointillism** is the almost mathematical application of paint to the canvas in small dots or points of uniform size, each dot precisely placed. This technique is underpinned by color theory—

Seurat believed the human eye could optically mix the different colors he applied as dots. Thus, where a blue dot was placed next to a red dot, theoretically the eye would see purple. It is difficult to imagine the patience required to paint in this technique, which Seurat even used to sign his name and to paint the frames. Each shape, its color, size, and location, is calculated—very different from Impressionism's informal, seemingly accidental quality.

Vincent van Gogh.   In contrast to Seurat, VINCENT VAN GOGH [van GOH] (1853–90) is famed for his rapidly executed paintings, which use expressive and emotional color. Dutch by birth, van Gogh lived and worked in France for most of his life. His brother Theo, director of a small art gallery, supported him. Van Gogh met the Impressionists and used their bright colors and vivid contrasts, not to capture light effects but to convey emotion.

Critical Thinking

ARTISTS' LIVES

One question that has interested readers of literature and viewers of art for centuries is the relationship between a writer's or artist's work and his or her life. Some scholars believe that a thorough knowledge of an artist's or writer's life is essential to understanding a particular book or painting. Others contend, on the contrary, that such biographical knowledge is not vital for such understanding, and that it may actually distract readers and viewers from the literary and artistic achievement of the work alone. Still others argue that a work can be appreciated and understood without knowing the details of an author's or artist's actual life, but that such biographical knowledge enriches that appreciation and understanding without either distracting us from or displacing the work aesthetically.

We might consider, for example, the weight we might give the knowledge that William Wordsworth wrote his poem "I Wandered Lonely as a Cloud" after having read in his sister Dorothy's journal, an account of a walk he had taken with her some years earlier. Or, to take another example, we might consider the relevance of Vincent van Gogh's suicide for an analysis of his paintings, particularly those he painted near the end of his life. How important is what van Gogh wrote in a letter to his brother Theo in connection with his painting *The Starry Night?* "I go out at night to paint the stars, and I dream always of a picture like of the house with a group of figures. . . . I have a terrible lucidity at moments when nature is so beautiful; I am not conscious of myself any more, and the pictures come to me as in a dream."

Van Gogh's *Starry Night* (fig. 18.13), of 1889, was painted on a hillside overlooking St.-Rémy, a small town just south of Arles. *Starry Night* is anything but calm. In this unusually turbulent landscape, his highly expressive brushwork implies the precarious balance of his emotions. Pigment appears slapped on, sometimes applied with a brush, sometimes a palette knife, sometimes squeezed directly from the tube—as if van Gogh were desperate to get his ideas on canvas as quickly as possible. This appears spontaneous, almost as if he started painting and could not stop himself. The result is an emotional landscape, frenzied, passionate, flamelike, undulating, the sky swirling and writhing. Yet, in fact, the composition was planned in advance and is organized and balanced by traditional methods. The composition flows from left to right, the trees and church steeple slowing the movement down, with the hills rising on the right-hand side of the picture for balance. Vincent wrote to Theo explaining his working method, saying he would think everything out "down to the last detail" and then quickly paint a number of canvases.

Van Gogh suffered from extreme emotional swings. During one of his periods of depression, he shot himself in a field in Auvers. He died two days later, on July 21, 1890, in Theo's arms. He was thirty-seven years old. He never knew fame, but today he is one of the most celebrated of all painters.

Paul Gauguin. Fellow Post-Impressionist PAUL GAUGUIN [go-GAN] (1848–1903) was born to a Peruvian mother and a French father. A successful banker and stockbroker in Paris, Gauguin had a personal crisis at the age of thirty-five. He decided to become a full-time artist, leave his wife and five children, and embark on an exotic life, which he recorded in his autobiography, *Noa Noa (Fragrance)*. Gauguin shared with the Symbolist poets a desire to escape the everyday world and retreat into what Mallarmé called metaphorically "the afternoon of a faun." To that end, he auctioned off about thirty of his paintings and sailed to Tahiti in 1891. There he lived in a wooden hut, painted all day, naked, and referred to himself as Monsieur Sauvage (Mr. Savage). He learned the native language and myths, took a Tahitian wife, and had a son.

Gauguin wrote about his painting *Manao Tupapau (Spirit of the Dead Watching)* (fig. 18.14), of 1892, in *Noa*

FIGURE 18.13 Vincent van Gogh, *Starry Night*, 1889, oil on canvas, $28\frac{3}{4}'' \times 36\frac{1}{2}''$ (73 × 92 cm), The Museum of Modern Art, NY, acquired through the Lillie P. Bliss Bequest, Licensed by SCALA Art Resource, NY. Although seemingly conceived and executed without restraint, as if painted in a fevered rush, this painting was actually preceded by a complete preliminary drawing.

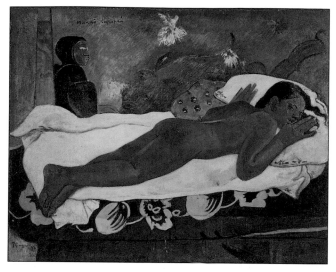

FIGURE 18.14 Paul Gauguin, *Manao Tupapau (Spirit of the Dead Watching)*, 1892, oil on burlap mounted on canvas, $28\frac{1}{2}'' \times 36\frac{3}{8}''$ (72.4 × 92.5 cm), Albright-Knox Art Gallery, Buffalo. A. Conger Goodyear Collection, 1965, The phosphorescent spots were believed by the Maoris to signify the spirits of the dead. In spite of his claims, Gauguin remained a sophisticated artist, drawing more on the art of the museums than from his surroundings.

Noa. One night, he returned to his hut, only to find it in complete darkness. Lighting a match, he found Tehura lying as shown, terror-stricken by the dark. The woman in the background is the "Spirit of the Dead." The white areas in the background are phosphorescent fungi which, according to Maori legend, symbolize the spirits of ancestors. Gauguin wrote that he tried to convey fear through "somber, sad, frightening" colors. The painting is treated as a pattern of rhythmically arranged colored shapes. Rather than emphasizing the three-dimensional-

ity of solid forms, the picture plane is emphasized by the areas of flat color and by the stress on outline.

Gauguin called this style of painting *Synthetism*, characterized by heightened color, flattened forms, and heavy outlines. The style is also called **Symbolism**, the intent being to give concrete form to abstract ideas—Gauguin is considered the leader of the French Symbolist movement. Gauguin's willingness to distort shapes and colors for symbolic purposes was important for the future of painting. By turning away from realistic academic painting, Gauguin led others to use arbitrary shape and color, and to free art from the restraints of nature.

NEW DIRECTIONS IN SCULPTURE AND ARCHITECTURE

Auguste Rodin. For the better part of the nineteenth century, many sculptural concepts had amounted to little more than variations on classicism, but toward the end of the century a major sculptor appeared. The Frenchman AUGUSTE RODIN [roh-DAN] (1840–1917) became the most influential sculptor in Europe. He studied the human form from nude models in his studio, but rather than having them remain immobile as was the tradition, Rodin's models walked around so he could study the human body in motion.

Rodin's bronze sculpture *The Thinker* (fig. 18.15), made between 1879 and 1889, was intended to form part of a larger work for the entrance to the Museum of Decorative Arts in Paris, *The Gates of Hell*, based on Dante's *Inferno* (see Chapter 12), with *The Thinker* looking down on hell, brooding over the gates. Rodin's superb understanding of "body language" can be seen in the details, for example, in the tension in the toes of the figure that seem to grip the base.

Also created for this entrance was an over-lifesize marble sculpture called *The Kiss* (fig. 18.16), made between

Table 18–1	IMPORTANT PAINTINGS OF IMPRESSIONISM AND POST-IMPRESSIONISM	
	Artist	**Painting and Date**
Impressionism	Whistler	*Arrangement in Black and Gray,* 1871
	Degas	*The Dancing Class,* ca. 1874
	Renoir	*Dance at the Moulin de la Galette,* 1876
	Morisot	*Summer's Day,* 1879
	Monet	*Haystacks at Giverny,* 1891
	Cassatt	*The Boating Party,* 1893–94
Post-Impressionism	Seurat	*Sunday Afternoon on La Grande Jatte,* 1884–86
	van Gogh	*Starry Night,* 1889
	Gauguin	*Spirit of the Dead Watching,* 1892
	Cézanne	*Still Life with Peppermint Bottle,* ca. 1894

FIGURE 18.15 Auguste Rodin, *The Thinker*, 1879–89, bronze, height 27½″ (69.8 cm), Metropolitan Museum of Art, NY. Gift of Thomas F. Ryan Like the Impressionist painters' concern with light flickering over forms, Rodin's broken surface creates a similarly dappled and unfinished effect.

FIGURE 18.16 Auguste Rodin, *The Kiss*, 1886–98, marble, over-lifesize, height 6′ 2″ (1.90 m), Musée Rodin, Paris. The seemingly warm soft flesh is emphasized in contrast to the hard cold stone from which it was carved.

1886 and 1898. In this work Rodin displays a sensuous love of the body as well as virtuosity in carving two intertwined figures. The completed sculpture has portions of stone that have been intentionally left rough, thereby emphasizing a contrast of textures between the illusion of soft skin and the hard marble from which it came. Some of Michelangelo's work also has this contrast, but this is because he lacked time to finish his work. Rodin, in contrast, did this as a conscious aesthetic.

Camille Claudel. Rodin's art was closely linked with that of the French sculptor CAMILLE CLAUDEL [ka-ME claw-DEL] (1864–1943). She was a prodigy; when only thirteen years old she was presented to the Director of the École Nationale des Beaux-Arts. Claudel and Rodin both focused on the human body as a vehicle for emotional expression. Their styles were so similar that there were instances in which he signed her work—and she was furious.

Twenty-four years younger than Rodin, Claudel was first his student, then his collaborator, and soon his lover.

Claudel created a sculpture of a couple dancing, but, because the nudity of the figures shocked the public, she added the costumes, creating the version of *The Waltz* seen in fig. 18.17 in 1892. The work was very well received when it was exhibited in 1893 and various versions were created in later years.

After Claudel's definitive split with Rodin in 1898, she freed herself from his influence and was at her most creative. Although she thrived artistically, she suffered emotionally, and concerns about her mental health began with initial signs of paranoia. In her "madness," as it was called, she destroyed what she had created. At her family's request, she was institutionalized for the last thirty years of her life.

American Architecture. Toward the end of the nineteenth century, a new style developed in architecture. It

FIGURE 18.17 Camille Claudel, French, *The Waltz*, 1892, bronze, height $9\frac{7}{8}''$ (25 cm), Bayerische Staatsgemaldesammlungen, Neue Pinakothek, Munich. Claudel, long in the shadow of Rodin—her teacher, collaborator, and lover—was certainly his artistic equal. Her work is unmatched for the exquisite refinement of the forms and the graceful fluidity of the movements.

FIGURE 18.18 Louis Sullivan, Wainwright Building, St. Louis, Missouri, 1890–91. Moving in the direction of the skyscraper, the Wainwright Building has an underlying steel skeleton and brick skin. The architect Louis Sullivan's now famous phrase, "form follows function" sums up his beliefs.

was the public and commercial buildings—the stores, offices, and apartments—that defined the new architectural style. The use of iron, steel, concrete, and large sheets of glass radically changed architectural language. As steel construction and concrete forms were developed, thick masonry walls were no longer required to support the whole structure of a building. Expression was given freely to the new underlying skeletal frames. The idea of the building as a solid closed space was replaced by that of the building as an open airy environment. As height could be more easily increased, tall buildings began to define the city skyline.

The American architect Louis Sullivan (1856–1924) designed such a structure with the Wainwright Building in St. Louis, Missouri (fig. 18.18). Built between 1890 and 1891, it uses a supporting steel structure and has a brick exterior. Sullivan's design stresses the continuous verticals that reflect the internal steel supports, thus emphasizing the building's height. Sullivan doubled the number of piers

necessary, creating a dense effect. The corners are stressed and thereby visually strengthened. Horizontals at the top and bottom provide a visual frame—in a sense, a start and a conclusion to the compostion.

Sullivan saw a building as being like the human body: The steel is the bone; the brick is the flesh and skin. It was Sullivan who coined the phrase "form follows function." Yet this does not mean the decorative elements of the design are integral to the architectural design. For Sullivan, "the function of all functions is the Infinite Creative Spirit," and this spirit could be revealed in the rhythm of growth and decay we find in nature. Thus the elaborate organic forms that cover his building were intended to evoke the infinite. For Sullivan, the primary function of a building was to elevate the spirit of those who worked in it. His ideas led to a new school of Functionalist architecture.

Art Nouveau. Sullivan's belief in nature was mirrored in **Art Nouveau** (literally, New Art), a short-lived style that

FIGURE 18.19 Victor Horta, staircase, Dr. Tassel's house, Brussels, 1893. Art Nouveau favored forms derived from nature such as foliage and curling tendrils. To achieve a certain harmony, Horta designed everything in the house, from the furniture and rugs down to the small details such as the hinges.

FIGURE 18.20 Antoní Gaudí, Casa Milá Apartment Building, Barcelona, 1905–07. Although made of traditional cut stone, the forms appear eroded by nature, weathered into curves, and the metal balcony railings look like seaweed.

Cultural Impact

During the second half of the nineteenth century, Romanticism gave way to Realism and then to Impressionism and Post-Impressionism. These artistic changes occurred in a climate of political and social unrest. In America, the Civil War raged from 1861 to 1865, with a death toll of more than 658,000. The war was a watershed in American history, and its legacy continues in issues of race and regionalism in contemporary America. In Europe, German unification resulted in increased military and economic power, a precursor to the German might of the Hitler era and to the consolidation of German political and economic enterprises following the collapse of communism and the fall of the Berlin Wall in 1989.

Of intellectual currents important during the later nineteenth century, none has been more significant than Darwin's theory of evolution through the process of natural selection. Darwin's ideas profoundly affected how human beings thought about themselves, unsettling their religious beliefs and challenging their understanding of science and history. Karl Marx's adaptation of Hegel's theory of historical change through conflict and resolution provided the foundation for the Russian Revolution of 1917. Finally, the emergence of liberalism as an applied political philosophy encouraged the spread of middle-class values, including thrift, ambition, and work, as well as an emphasis on the value of the individual.

The rise of the middle class created an audience for fiction and propelled it to primacy among the literary genres. In the later nineteenth century, drama too became increasingly popular as Ibsen and Strindberg, among others, wrote plays that reflected the issues of the time, including individual rights, inherited diseases, and the struggle for power between men and women. Realism continues to be enormously influential. In some senses, Realism has never gone out of style, although other styles have emerged to compete with it.

The Impressionist painters Claude Monet and Auguste Renoir enabled people to look at the everyday world in new ways, and their experiments with light, color, and atmosphere redirected the history of painting. In music, too, Impressionism was a significat stylistic development: The French composers Claude Debussy and Maurice Ravel achieved the sonorous equivalent of the color and light of Impressionist painting. Debussy created new harmonies and introduced new melodic possibilities, partly influenced by the music of other cultures, especially those of Asia. Ravel exploited instrumental sonorities of individual instruments and combined them in ways that expanded the orchestral sound palette.

The literary analogue of Impressionism was Symbolism, which sought to achieve with words effects similar to those of Impressionist painting and music. French Symbolist poetry attempted to create musicality with verbal sounds, inspiring Impressionist composers such as Debussy, in turn, to create musical equivalents of Symbolist poems. The work of Impressionist and Symbolist artists continue to influence contemporary painters, composers, and poets.

---

began in Europe and was popular from the 1890s to the early 1900s. It is characterized by decoration, especially curvilinear patterns, based on the forms of nature. The influence of Art Nouveau extended beyond architecture to include home furnishings, clothing, and typography.

The home of Dr. Tassel in Brussels, designed by the architect VICTOR HORTA [OAR-ta] (1861–1947) and built 1893, is an ideal example of the Art Nouveau style. Horta liked to be able to design "each piece of furniture, each hinge and door-latch, the rugs and the wall decoration." Consequently, in the Tassel house every part is in harmony, characterized by curve and counter-curve, by its small scale, grace, and charm. The staircase (fig. 18.19) is illuminated by a skylight and made with large amounts of glass and metal, used both for ornamentation and for structure. It is especially characteristic of the Art Nouveau style with its swirling and sensuous forms.

In Spain, another exponent of Art Nouveau was ANTONÍ GAUDÍ [GOW-dee] (1852–1926), the architect of the Casa Milá in Barcelona (fig. 18.20), built 1905–07. This apartment building bears no relation to anything that had gone before. Gaudí's Art Nouveau style has few flat areas or straight lines, favoring instead constantly curving lines and asymmetry over symmetry. Although made of cut stone, the Casa Milá looks like it was molded from soft clay. Gaudí created an organic style influenced by the forms of the natural world. The building appears eroded, as if nature has worn away all the sharp angles. The facade seems to ripple around the corner of the building, and the roof seems to undulate. The chimneys look like abstract sculptures. Gaudí did much of his designing on the actual building site, which was unusual then (as it is now), and produced a highly personal and eccentric style.

KEY TERMS

Impressionism	superman	ego	Pointillism
belle époque	Dionysian	id	Symbolism
Symbolists	Apollonian	superego	Art Nouveau
atom	psychoanalysis	Post-Impressionism	

WWW. WEBSITES FOR FURTHER STUDY

http://www.artchive.com/artchive/M/manet.html
(This is the Artchive, a website with virtually every major artist in every style from every era in art history. It is an excellent resource.)

http://www.accd.edu/sac/english/bailey/jewett.html
(This is the Sarah Orne Jewett website, one of the more important woman authors of the late nineteenth century.)

http://www.npr.org/programs/specials/milestones/991110.motm.riteofspring.html
(A National Public Radio site featuring Stravinsky's Rite of Spring, including an audio excerpt of the work.)

http://www.hf.uio.no/ibsensenteret/index_eng.html
(A comprehensive site on Henrik Ibsen, dramatist and author, with many links.)

http://www.westegg.com/einstein/
(An excellent, comprehensive site on all the work of Albert Einstein.)

READINGS

CHARLES BAUDELAIRE

Correspondences

The following poem by this prominent French Symbolist illustrates some of the ways in which the Symbolists attempted to associate the language of poetry with other sensory experience, such as shapes, sounds, and colors. In "Correspondences" Baudelaire sets up a series of connections between sounds and tastes, colors and scents, religion and nature, the spiritual and the sensuous. Baudelaire's work reflects the Symbolist concern for suggesting meaning through image, metaphor, and symbolic association rather than by means of direct statement.

Nature is a temple from whose living columns
Commingling voices emerge at times;
Here man wanders through forests of symbols
Which seem to observe him with familiar eyes.

Like long-drawn echoes afar converging   5
In harmonies darksome and profound,
Vast as the night and vast as light,
Colors, scents and sounds correspond.

There are fragrances fresh as the flesh of children,
Sweet as the oboe, green as the prairie,   10
—And others overpowering, rich and corrupt,

Possessing the pervasiveness of everlasting things,
Like benjamin, frankincense, amber, myrrh,
Which the raptures of the senses and the spirit sing.

STÉPHANE MALLARMÉ

from The Afternoon of a Faun

Stéphane Mallarmé's poem "The Afternoon of a Faun" (1876) directly inspired Claude Debussy's orchestral composition. It describes the reveries of a faun from classical mythology with an almost Romantic languor. However, Mallarmé's use of language and metaphor is Symbolist.

Eclogue

The Faun

These nymphs, I would make them endure.

Their delicate flesh-tint so clear,

it hovers yet upon the air
heavy with foliage of sleep.

Was it a dream I loved? My doubt,   5
hoarded of old night, culminates
in many a subtle branch, that stayed
the very forest's self and proves

alas! that I alone proposed
the ideal failing of the rose   10
as triumph of my own. Think now . . .
and if the women whom you gloze
picture a wish of your fabled senses!
Faun, the illusion takes escape
from blue cold eyes, like a spring in tears,   15
of the purer one: and would you say
of her, the other, made of sighs,
that she contrasts, like the day breeze
warmly astir now in your fleece!
No! through the moveless, half-alive   20
languor that suffocates in heat
freshness of morning, if it strive,
no water sounds save what is poured
upon the grove sparged with accords
by this my flute; and the sole wind   25
prompt from twin pipes to be exhaled
before dispersal of the sound
in arid shower without rain
is—on the unwrinkled, unstirred
horizon—calm and clear to the eye,   30
the artificial breath of in-
spiration, which regains the sky.

Sicilian shores of a calm marsh,
despoilèd by my vanity
that vies with suns, tacit beneath   35
the flower-sparkle, now RELATE
how here I cut the hollow reeds
that talent tames; when, on pale gold
of distant greens that dedicate
their vine to fountains, undulates   40
an animal whiteness in repose:
and how at sound of slow prelude
with which the pipes first come to life
this flight of swans, no! naiads flees
or plunges . . .   45

Limp in the tawny hour
all is afire but shows no trace
by what art those too many brides
longed-for by him who seeks the *A*
all at once decamped; then shall I wake   50
to the primal fire, alone and straight,
beneath an ancient surge of light,
even as one of you, lilies!
by strength of my simplicity.

Other than the soft nothingness   55
their lips made rumor of, the kiss,
which gives assurance in low tones
of the two perfidious ones,
my breast, immaculate of proof,
attests an enigmatic bite,   60
imputed to some august tooth;
leave it! such mystery made choice
of confidant: the vast twinned reed—
beneath blue sky we give it voice:
diverting to itself the cheek's   65
turmoil, it dreams, in a long solo,
that we amused the beauty here-

about by false bewilderments
between it and our naïve song;
dreams too that from the usual dream 70
of back or flawless flank traced by
my shuttered glances, it makes fade,
tempered to love's own pitch, a vain,
monotonous, sonorous line.

KATE CHOPIN

The Storm

Kate Chopin is best known for her short fiction and her novel of 1899, The Awakening, *which generated a storm of criticism for its frank portrayal of female sexuality and its depiction of an extramarital love affair. The following story displays her ability to convey in brief compass the power of sexual attraction and the apparently beneficial effects the indulged passion has for all concerned, including the cuckolded husband.*

1

The leaves were so still that even Bibi thought it was going to rain. Bobinôt, who was accustomed to converse on terms of perfect equality with his little son, called the child's attention to certain sombre clouds that were rolling with sinister intention from the west, accompanied by a sullen, threatening roar. They were at Friedheimer's store and decided to remain there till the storm had passed. They sat within the door on two empty kegs. Bibi was four years old and looked very wise.

"Mama'll be 'fraid, yes," he suggested with blinking eyes.

"She'll shut the house. Maybe she got Sylvie helpin' her this evenin'," Bobinôt responded reassuringly.

"No; she ent got Sylvie. Sylvie was helpin' her yistiday," piped Bibi.

Bobinôt arose and going across to the counter purchased a can of shrimps, of which Calixta was very fond. Then he returned to his perch on the keg and sat stolidly holding the can of shrimps while the storm burst. It shook the wooden store and seemed to be ripping great furrows in the distant field. Bibi laid his little hand on his father's knee and was not afraid.

2

Calixta, at home, felt no uneasiness for their safety. She sat at a side window sewing furiously on a sewing machine. She was greatly occupied and did not notice the approaching storm. But she felt very warm and often stopped to mop her face on which the perspiration gathered in beads. She unfastened her white sacque at the throat. It began to grow dark, and suddenly realizing the situation she got up hurriedly and went about closing windows and doors.

Out on the small front gallery she had hung Bobinôt's Sunday clothes to air and she hastened out to gather them before the rain fell. As she stepped outside, Alcée Laballière rode in at the gate. She had not seen him very often since her marriage, and never alone. She stood there with Bobinôt's coat in her hands, and the big rain drops began to fall. Alcée rode his horse under the shelter of a side projection where the chickens had huddled and there were plows and a harrow piled up in the corner.

"May I come and wait on your gallery till the storm is over, Calixta?" he asked.

"Come 'long in, M'sieur Alcée."

His voice and her own startled her as if from a trance, and she seized Bobinôt's vest. Alcée, mounting to the porch, grabbed the trousers and snatched Bibi's braided jacket that was about to be carried away by a sudden gust of wind. He expressed an intention to remain outside, but it was soon apparent that he might as well have been out in the open: the water beat in upon the boards in driving sheets, and he went inside, closing the door after him. It was even necessary to put something beneath the door to keep the water out.

"My! what a rain! It's good two years since it rain' like that," exclaimed Calixta as she rolled up a piece of bagging and Alcée helped her to thrust it beneath the crack.

She was a little fuller of figure than five years before when she married; but she had lost nothing of her vivacity. Her blue eyes still retained their melting quality; and her yellow hair, dishevelled by the wind and rain, kinked more stubbornly than ever about her ears and temples.

The rain beat upon the low, shingled roof with a force and clatter that threatened to break an entrance and deluge them there. They were in the dining room—the sitting room—the general utility room. Adjoining was her bed room, with Bibi's couch along side her own. The door stood open, and the room with its white, monumental bed, its closed shutters, looked dim and mysterious.

Alcée flung himself into a rocker and Calixta nervously began to gather up from the floor the lengths of a cotton sheet which she had been sewing.

"If this keeps up, *Dieu sait* if the levees goin' to stan' it!" she exclaimed.

"What have you got to do with the levees?"

"I got enough to do! An' there's Bobinôt with Bibi out in that storm—if he only didn' left Friedheimer's!"

"Let us hope, Calixta, that Bobinôt's got sense enough to come in out of a cyclone."

She went and stood at the window with a greatly disturbed look on her face. She wiped the frame that was clouded with moisture. It was stiflingly hot. Alcée got up and joined her at the window, looking over her shoulder. The rain was coming down in sheets obscuring the view of far-off cabins and enveloping the distant wood in a grey mist. The playing of the lightning was incessant. A bolt struck a tall chinaberry tree at the edge of the field. It filled all visible space with a blinding glare and the crash seemed to invade the very boards they stood upon.

Calixta put her hands to her eyes, and with a cry, staggered backward. Alcée's arm encircled her, and for an instant he drew her close and spasmodically to him.

"*Bonté!*" she cried, releasing herself from his encircling arm and retreating from the window. "the house'll go next! If I only knew w'ere Bibi was!" She would not compose herself; she would not be seated. Alcée clasped her shoulders and looked into her face. The contact of her warm, palpitating body when he had unthinkingly drawn her into his arms, had aroused all the old-time infatuation and desire for her flesh.

"Calixta," he said, "don't be frightened. Nothing can happen. The house is too low to be struck, with so many tall trees standing about. There! aren't you going to be quiet? say, aren't you?" He pushed her hair back from her face that was warm and steaming. Her lips were as red and moist as pomegranate seed. Her white neck and a glimpse of her full, firm bosom disturbed him powerfully. As she glanced up at him the fear in her liquid blue eyes had given place to a drowsy gleam that unconsciously betrayed a sensuous desire. He looked down into her eyes and there was nothing for him to do but to gather her lips in a kiss. It reminded him of Assumption.

"Do you remember—in Assumption, Calixta?" he asked in a low voice broken by passion. Oh! she remembered; for in Assumption he had kissed her and kissed and kissed her; until his senses would well nigh fail, and to save her he would resort to a desperate flight. If she was not an immaculate dove in those days, she was still inviolate; a passionate creature whose very defenselessness had made her defense, against which his honor forbade him to prevail. Now—well, now—her lips seemed in a manner free to be tasted, as well as her round, white throat and her whiter breasts.

They did nor heed the crashing torrents, and the roar of the elements made her laugh as she lay in his arms. She was a revelation in that dim, mysterious chamber, as white as the couch she lay upon. Her firm, elastic flesh that was knowing for the first time its birthright, was like a creamy lily that the sun invites to contribute its breath and perfume to the undying life of the world.

The generous abundance of her passion, without guile or trickery, was like a white flame which penetrated and found response in depths of his own sensuous nature that had never yet been reached.

When he touched her breasts they gave themselves up in quivering ecstasy, inviting his lips. Her mouth was a fountain of delight. And when he possessed her, they seemed to swoon together at the very borderland of life's mystery.

He stayed cushioned upon her, breathless, dazed, enervated, with his heart beating like a hammer upon her. With one hand she clasped his head, her lips lightly touching his forehead. The other hand stroked with a soothing rhythm his muscular shoulders.

The growl of the thunder was distant and passing away. The rain beat softly upon the shingles, inviting them to drowsiness and sleep. But they dared not yield.

The rain was over; and the sun was turning the glistening green world into a palace of gems. Calixta, on the gallery, watched Alcée ride away. He turned and smiled at her with a beaming face; and she lifted her pretty chin in the air and laughed aloud.

3

Bobinôt and Bibi, trudging home, stopped without at the cistern to make themselves presentable.

"My! Bibi, w'at will yo' mama say! You ought to be ashame'. You oughtn' put on those good pants. Look at 'em! An' that mud on yo' collar! How you got that mud on yo' collar, Bibi? I never saw such a boy!" Bibi was the picture of pathetic resignation. Bobinôt was the embodiment of serious solicitude as he strove to remove from his own person and his son's the signs of their tramp over heavy roads and through wet fields. He scraped the mud off Bibi's bare legs and feet with a stick and carefully removed all traces from his heavy brogans. Then, prepared for the worst—the meeting with an over-scrupulous housewife, they entered cautiously at the back door.

Calixta was preparing supper. She had set the table and was dripping coffee at the hearth. She sprang up as they came in.

"Oh, Bobinôt! You back! My! but I was uneasy. W'ere you been during the rain? An' Bibi? he ain't wet? he ain't hurt?" She had clasped Bibi and was kissing him effusively. Bobinôt's explanations and apologies which he had been composing all along the way, died on his lips as Calixta felt him to see if he were dry, and seemed to express nothing but satisfaction at their safe return.

"I brought you some shrimps, Calixta," offered Bobinôt, hauling the can from his ample side pocket and laying it on the table.

"Shrimps! Oh, Bobinôt! you too good fo' anything!" and she gave him a smacking kiss on the cheek that resounded. "*J'vous reponds*, we'll have a feas' to-night! umph-umph!"

Bobinôt and Bibi began to relax and enjoy themselves, and when the three seated themselves at table they laughed much and so loud that anyone might have heard them as far away as Laballière's.

4

Alcée Laballière wrote to his wife, Clarisse, that night. It was a loving letter, full of tender solicitude. He told her not to hurry back, but if she and the babies liked it at Biloxi, to stay a month longer. He was getting on nicely; and though he missed them, he was willing to bear the separation a while longer—realizing that their health and pleasure were the first things to be considered.

5

As for Clarisse, she was charmed upon receiving her husband's letter. She and the babies were doing well. The society was agreeable; many of her old friends and acquaintances were at the bay. And the first free breath since her marriage seemed to restore the pleasant liberty of her maiden days. Devoted as she was to her husband, their intimate conjugal life was something which she was more than willing to forego for a while.

So the storm passed and everyone was happy.

HENRIK IBSEN

from *A Doll House*

Henrik Ibsen, the Norwegian playwright, is one of the giants of modern drama. He wrote many plays during his long career, of which A Doll House *(1879) has been one of his most enduring theatrical successes. The play explores the marriage of Nora and Torvald Helmer, a middle-class Norwegian couple living in the middle of the nineteenth century. Nora, confined by what society has determined a woman should be—dutiful wife and devoted mother—experiences a personal crisis, undergoes a spiritual transformation, and leaves her husband and family in search of a new identity and life. The following passage, from Act III, follows Nora's departure to the final slamming of the door.*

NORA   It is true. I have loved you beyond all else in the world.
HELMER   Pshaw—no silly evasions.
NORA   (a step nearer him). Torvald—!

HELMER   Wretched woman! what have you done?

NORA   Let me go—you shall not save me. You shall not take my guilt upon yourself.

HELMER   I don't want any melodramatic airs. (Locks the door). Here you shall stay and give an account of yourself. Do you understand what you have done? Answer. Do you understand it?

NORA   (looks at him fixedly, and says with a stiffening expression). Yes; now I begin fully to understand it.

HELMER   (walking up and down). Oh, what an awful awakening! During all these eight years—she who was my pride and my joy—a hypocrite, a liar—worse, worse— a criminal. Oh! The hideousness of it! Ugh! Ugh! (Nora is silent, and continues to look fixedly at him.) I ought to have foreseen something of the kind. All your father's dishonesty—be silent! I say all your father's dishonesty you have inherited—no religion, no morality, no sense of duty. How I am punished for shielding him! I did it for your sake and you reward me like this.

NORA   Yes—like this!

HELMER   You have destroyed my whole happiness. You have ruined my future. Oh! It's frightful to think of! I am in the power of a scoundrel; he can do whatever he pleases with me, demand whatever he chooses, and I must submit. And all this disaster is brought upon me by an unprincipled woman.

NORA   When I'm gone, you will be free.

HELMER   Oh, no fine phrases. Your father, too, was always ready with them. What good would it do to me if you were "gone" as to say? No good in the world! He can publish the story all the same; I might even be suspected of collusion. People will think I was at the bottom of it all and egged you on. And for all this I have you to thank—you whom I have done nothing but pet and spoil during our whole married life. Do you understand now what you have done to me?

NORA   (with cold calmness). Yes.

HELMER   It's incredible. I can't grasp it. But we must come to an understanding. Take that shawl off. Take it off I say. I must try to pacify him in one way or the other—the secret must be kept, cost what it may. As for ourselves, we must live as we have already done; but of course only in the eyes of the world. Of course you will continue to live here. But the children cannot be left in your care. I dare not trust them to you—Oh, to have to say this to one I have loved so tenderly—whom I still—but that must be a thing of the past. Henceforward there can be no question of happiness, but merely of saving the ruins, the shreds, the show of it! (A ring; Helmer starts.) What's that? So late! Can it be the worst? Can he—? Hide yourself, Nora; say you are ill. (Nora stands motionless. Helmer goes to the door and opens it.)

ELLEN   (half dressed, in the hall). Here is a letter for you. ma'am.

HELMER   Give it to me. (Seizes letter and shuts the door.) Yes, from him. You shall not have it. I shall read it.

NORA   Read it!

HELMER   (by the lamp). I have hardly courage to. We may be lost, both you and I. Ah! I must know. (Tears the letter hastily open; reads a few lines, looks at an en-

closure; a cry of joy.) Nora. (Nora looks interrogatively at him.) Nora! Oh! I must read it again. Yes, yes, it is so. I am saved! Nora, I am saved!

NORA   And I?

HELMER   You too, of course; we are both saved, both of us. Look here, he sends you back your promissory note. He writes that he regrets and apologizes—that a happy turn in his life—Oh, what matter what he writes. We are saved, Nora! No one can harm you. Oh! Nora, Nora—no, first to get rid of this hateful thing. I'll just see—(Glances at the I.O.U.) No, I won't look at it; the whole thing shall be nothing but a dream to me. (Tears the I.O.U and both letters in pieces, throws them into the fire and watches them burn.) There, it's gone. He wrote that ever since Christmas Eve—Oh, Nora, they must have been three awful days for you!

NORA   I have fought a hard fight for the last three days.

HELMER   And in your agony you saw no other outlet but— no; we won't think of that horror. We will only rejoice and repeat—it's over, all over. Don't you hear, Nora? You don't seem to be able to grasp it. Yes, it's over. What is this set look on your face? Oh, my poor Nora, I understand; you can't believe that I have forgiven you. But I have, Nora; I swear it. I have forgiven everything. I know what you did was all for love of me.

NORA   That's true.

HELMER   You loved me as a wife should love her husband. It was only the means you misjudged. But do you think I love you the less for your helplessness? No, no, only lean on me. I will counsel and guide you. I should be no true man if this very womanly helplessness did not make you doubly dear in my eyes. You mustn't think of the hard things I said in my first moment of terror, when the world seemed to be tumbling about my ears. I have forgiven you, Nora—I swear I have forgiven you.

NORA   I thank you for your forgiveness. (Goes out, right.)

HELMER   No, stay. (Looks in.) What are you going to do?

NORA   (inside). To take off my doll's dress.

HELMER   (in doorway). Yes, do, dear. Try to calm down, and recover your balance, my sacred little songbird. You may rest secure, I have broad wings to shield you. (Walking up and down near the door.) Oh, how lovely—how cosy our home is, Nora. Here you are safe; here I can shelter you like a hunted dove, whom I have saved from the claws of the hawk. I shall soon bring your poor beating heart to rest, believe me, Nora, I will. To-morrow all this will seem quite different—everything will be as before; I shall not need to tell you again that I forgive you; you will feel for yourself that it is true. How could I find it in my heart to drive you away, or even so much as to reproach you? Oh, you don't know a true man's heart, Nora. There is something indescribably sweet and soothing to a man in having forgiven his wife—honestly forgiven her from the bottom of his heart. She becomes his property in a double sense. She is as though born again; she has become, so to speak, at once his wife and his child. That is what you shall henceforth be to me, my bewildered, helpless darling.

Don't worry about anything, Nora; only open your heart to me, and I will be both will and conscience to you. (Nora enters, crossing to table in everyday dress.) Why, what's this? Not gone to bed? You have changed your dress.

NORA Yes, Torvald; now I have changed my dress.

HELMER But why now so late?

NORA I shall not sleep to-night.

HELMER But, Nora dear—

NORA (looking at her watch). It's not so late yet. Sit down, Torvald, you and I have much to say to each other. (She sits on one side of the table.)

HELMER Nora, what does this mean; your cold, set face—

NORA Sit down. It will take some time; I have much to talk over with you. (Helmer sits at the other side of the table.)

HELMER You alarm me; I don't understand you.

NORA No, that's just it. You don't understand me; and I have never understood you—till to night. No, don't interrupt. Only listen to what I say. We must come to a final settlement, Torvald!

HELMER How do you mean?

NORA (after a short silence). Does not one thing strike you as we sit here?

HELMER What should strike me?

NORA We have been married eight years. Does it not strike you that this is the first time we two, you and I, man and wife, have talked together seriously?

HELMER Seriously! Well, what do you call seriously?

NORA During eight whole years and more—ever since the day we first met—we have never exchanged one serious word about serious things.

HELMER Was I always to trouble you with the cares you could not help me to bear?

NORA I am not talking of cares. I say that we have never yet set ourselves seriously to get to the bottom of anything.

HELMER Why, my dear Nora, what have you to do with serious things?

NORA There we have it! You have never understood me. I have had great injustice done me, Torvald, first by my father and then by you.

HELMER What! by your father and me?—by us who have loved you more than all the world?

NORA (shaking her head). You have never loved me. You only thought it amusing to be in love with me.

HELMER Why, Nora, what a thing to say!

NORA Yes, it is so, Torvald. While I was at home with father he used to tell me all his opinions and I held the same opinions. If I had others I concealed them, because he would not have liked it. He used to call me his doll child, and play with me as I played with my dolls. Then I came to live in your house—

HELMER What an expression to use about our marriage!

NORA (undisturbed). I mean I passed from father's hands into yours. You settled everything according to your taste; and I got the same tastes as you; or I pretended to—I don't know which—both ways perhaps. When I look back on it now, I seem to have been living here like a beggar, from hand to mouth. I lived by performing tricks for you, Torvald. But you would have it so. You and father have done me a great wrong. It's your fault that my life has been wasted.

HELMER Why, Nora, how unreasonable and ungrateful you are. Haven't you been happy here?

NORA No, never; I thought I was, but I never was.

HELMER Not—not happy?

NORA No, only merry. And you have always been so kind to me. But our house has been nothing but play-room. Here I have been your doll-wife, just as at home I used to be papa's doll-child. And the children in their turn have been my dolls. I thought it fun when you played with me, just as the children did when I played with them. That has been our marriage, Torvald.

HELMER There is some truth in what you say, exaggerated and overstrained though it be. But henceforth it shall be different. Playtime is over; now comes the time for education.

NORA Whose education? Mine, or the children's.

HELMER Both my dear Nora.

NORA Oh, Torvald, you can't teach me to be a fit wife for you.

HELMER And you say that?

NORA And I—am I fit to educate the children?

HELMER Nora!

NORA Did you not say yourself a few minutes ago you dared not trust them to me.

HELMER In the excitement of the moment! Why should you dwell upon that?

NORA No—you are perfectly right. That problem is beyond me. There's another to be solved first—I must try to educate myself. You are not the one to help me in that. I must set about it alone. And that is why I am leaving you!

HELMER (jumping up). What—do you mean to say—

NORA I must stand quite alone to know myself and my surroundings; so I cannot stay with you.

HELMER Nora! Nora!

NORA I am going at once. Christine will take me in for to-night—

HELMER You are mad. I shall not allow it. I forbid it.

NORA It's no use your forbidding me anything now. I shall take with me what belongs to me. From you I will accept nothing, either now or afterward.

HELMER What madness!

NORA To-morrow I shall go home.

HELMER Home!

NORA I mean to what was my home. It will be easier for me to find some opening there.

HELMER Oh, in your blind experience—

NORA I must try to gain experience, Torvald.

HELMER To forsake your home, your husband, and your children! You don't consider what the world will say.

NORA I can pay no heed to that! I only know that I must do it.

HELMER It's exasperating! Can you forsake your holiest duties in this way?

NORA What do you call my holiest duties?

HELMER Do you ask me that? Your duties to your husband and your children.

NORA I have other duties equally sacred.

HELMER Impossible! What duties do you mean?

NORA My duties towards myself.

HELMER Before all else you are a wife and a mother.

NORA   That I no longer believe. I think that before all else I am a human being, just as much as you are—or, at least, I will try to become one. I know that most people agree with you, Torvald, and that they say so in books. But henceforth I can't be satisfied with what most people say, and what is in books. I must think things out for myself and try to get clear about them.

HELMER   Are you not clear about your place in your own home? Have you not an infallible guide in questions like these? Have you not religion?

NORA   Oh, Torvald, I don't know properly what religion is.

HELMER   What do you mean?

NORA   I know nothing but what our clergyman told me when I was confirmed. He explained that religion was this and that. When I get away from here and stand alone I will look into the matter too. I will see whether what he taught me is true, or, at any rate, whether it is true for me.

HELMER   Oh, this is unheard of! But if religion cannot keep you right, let me appeal to your conscience—I suppose you have some moral feeling? Or, answer me, perhaps you have none?

NORA   Well, Torvald, it's not easy to say. I really don't know—I am all at sea about these things. I only know that I think quite differently from you about them. I hear, too, that the laws are different from what I thought; but I can't believe that they are right. It appears that a woman has no right to spare her dying father, or to save her husband's life. I don't believe that.

HELMER   You talk like a child. You don't understand the society in which you live.

NORA   No, I don't. But I shall try to. I must make up my mind which is right—society or I.

HELMER   Nora, you are ill, you are feverish. I almost think you are out of your senses.

NORA   I never felt so much clearness and certainty as to-night.

HELMER   You are clear and certain enough to forsake husband and children?

NORA   Yes I am.

HELMER   Then there is only one explanation possible.

NORA   What is that?

HELMER   You no longer love me.

NORA   No, that is just it.

HELMER   Nora! Can you say so?

NORA   Oh, I'm so sorry, Torvald; for you've always been so kind to me. But I can't help it. I do not love you any longer.

HELMER   (keeping his composure with difficulty). Are you clear and certain on this point too?

NORA   Yes, quite. That is why I won't stay here any longer.

HELMER   And can you also make clear to me, how I have forfeited your love?

NORA   Yes, I can. It was this evening, when the miracle did not happen. For then I saw you were not the man I had taken you for.

HELMER   Explain yourself more clearly; I don't understand.

NORA   I have waited so patiently all these eight years; for, of course, I saw clearly enough that miracles do not happen every day. When this crushing blow threatened me, I said to myself, confidently, "Now comes the miracle!" When Krogstad's letter lay in the box, it never occurred to me that you would think of submitting to that man's conditions. I was convinced that you would say to him, "Make it known to all the world," and that then—

HELMER   Well? When I had given my own wife's name up to disgrace and shame—?

NORA   Then I firmly believed that you would come forward, take everything upon yourself, and say, "I am the guilty one."

HELMER   Nora!

NORA   You mean I would never have accepted such a sacrifice? No, certainly not. But what would my assertions have been worth in opposition to yours? That was the miracle that I hoped for and dreaded. And it was to hinder that that I wanted to die.

HELMER   I would gladly work for you day and night, Nora—bear sorrow and want for your sake—but no man sacrifices his honour, even for one he loves.

NORA   Millions of women have done so.

HELMER   Oh, you think and talk like a silly child.

NORA   Very likely. But you neither think nor talk like the man I can share my life with. When your terror was over—not for me, but for yourself—when there was nothing more to fear,—then it was to you as though nothing had happened. I was your lark again, your doll—whom you would take twice as much care of in the future, because she was so weak and fragile. (Stands up.) Torvald, in that moment it burst upon me, that I had been living here these eight years with a strange man, and had borne him three children—Oh! I can't bear to think of it—I could tear myself to pieces!

HELMER   (sadly). I see it, I see it; an abyss has opened between us—But, Nora, can it never be filled up?

NORA   As I now am, I am no wife for you.

HELMER   I have strength to become another man.

NORA   Perhaps—when your doll is taken away from you.

HELMER   To part—to part from you! No, Nora, no; I can't grasp the thought.

NORA   (going into room, right). The more reason for the thing to happen. (She comes back with out-door things and a small travelling bag, which she puts on a chair.)

HELMER   Nora, not now! Wait till to-morrow.

NORA   (putting on cloak). I can't spend the night in a strange man's house.

HELMER   But can't we live here as brother and sister?

NORA   (fastening her hat). You know very well that would not last long. Good-bye, Torvald. No, I won't go to the children. I know they are in better hands than mine. As I now am, I can be nothing to them.

HELMER   But some time, Nora—some time—

NORA   How can I tell? I have no idea what will become of me.

HELMER   But you are my wife, now and always?

NORA   Listen, Torvald—when a wife leaves her husband's house, as I am doing, I have heard that in the eyes of the law he is free from all the duties towards her. At any rate I release you from all duties. You must not feel yourself bound any more than I shall. There must be perfect freedom on both sides. There, there is your ring back. Give me mine.

HELMER   That too?

NORA   That too.

HELMER   Here it is.

NORA   Very well. Now it is all over. Here are the keys. The servants know about everything in the house, better than I do. To-morrow, when I have started, Christina will come to pack up my things. I will have them sent after me.

HELMER   All over! All over! Nora, will you never think of me again?

NORA   Oh, I shall often think of you, and the children— and this house.

HELMER   May I write to you, Nora?

NORA   No, never. You must not.

HELMER   But I must send you—

NORA   Nothing, nothing.

HELMER   I must help you if you need it.

NORA   No, I say. I take nothing from strangers.

HELMER   Nora, can I never be more than a stranger to you?

NORA   (taking her travelling bag). Oh, Torvald, then the miracle of miracles would have to happen.

HELMER   What is the miracle of miracles?

NORA   Both of us would have to change so that—Oh, Torvald, I no longer believe in miracles.

HELMER   But I will believe. We must so change that—?

NORA   That communion between us shall be a marriage. Good-bye. (She goes out.)

HELMER   (sinks in a chair by the door with his face in his hands). Nora! Nora! (He looks around and stands up.) Empty. She's gone! (A hope inspires him.) Ah! The miracle of miracles—?! (From below is heard the reverberation of a heavy door closing.)

FRIEDRICH NIETZSCHE

from *The Birth of Tragedy*

Known for his ruthless ability to dissect the moral assumptions of his time, Friedrich Wilhelm Nietzsche turned his attention, in The Birth of Tragedy *(1909), to Western cultural beliefs about classical antiquity. Specifically, he challenged the received view that Greek art embodied an ideal world based on principles of noble simplicity and tranquil grandeur. Instead, Nietzsche saw much more turbulent and psychologically powerful forces at work, forces he labeled the "Apollonian" and the "Dionysian." This selected passage illustrates what Nietzsche meant by these terms.*

We shall have gained much for the science of aesthetics, once we perceive not merely by logical inference, but with the immediate certainty of vision, that the continuous development of art is bound up with the *Apollonian* and *Dionysian* duality— just as procreation depends on the duality of the sexes, involving perpetual strife with only periodically intervening reconciliations. The terms Dionysian and Apollonian we borrow from the Greeks, who disclose to the discerning mind the profound mysteries of their view of art, not, to be sure, in concepts, but in the intensely clear figures of their gods. Through Apollo and Dionysus, the two art deities of the Greeks, we come to recognize that in the Greek world there existed a tremendous opposition, in origin and aims, between the Apollonian art of sculpture, and the nonimagistic, Dionysian art of music. These two different tendencies run parallel to each other, for the most part openly at variance; and they continually incite each other to new and more powerful births, which perpetuate an antagonism, only superficially reconciled by the common term "art"; till eventually, by a metaphysical miracle of the Hellenic "will," they appear coupled with each other, and through this coupling ultimately generate an equally Dionysian and Apollinian form of art— Attic tragedy.

In order to grasp these two tendencies, let us first conceive of them as the separate art worlds of *dreams* and *intoxication*. These physiological phenomena present a contrast analogous to that existing between the Apollonian and the Dionysian. It was in dreams, says Lucretius, that the glorious divine figures first appeared to the souls of men.

The beautiful illusion of the dream worlds, in the creation of which every man is truly an artist, is the prerequisite of all plastic art, and, as we shall see, of an important part of poetry also. In our dreams we delight in the immediate understanding of figures; all forms speak to us; there is nothing unimportant or superfluous. But even when this dream reality is most intense, we still have, glimmering through it, the sensation that it is *mere appearance:* at least this is my experience, and for its frequency—indeed, normality—I could adduce many proofs, including the sayings of the poets.

This joyous necessity of the dream experience has been embodied by the Greeks in their Apollo: Apollo, the god of all plastic energies, is at the same time the soothsaying god. He, who (as the etymology of the name indicates) is the "shining one," the deity of light, is also ruler over the beautiful illusion of the inner world of fantasy. The higher truth, the perfection of these states in contrast to the incompletely intelligible everyday world, this deep consciousness of nature, healing and helping in sleep and dreams, is at the same time the symbolical analogue of the soothsaying faculty and of the arts generally, which make life possible and worth living.

Schopenhauer has depicted for us the tremendous *terror* which seizes man when he is suddenly dumbfounded by the cognitive form of phenomena because the principle of sufficient reason, in some one of its manifestations, seems to suffer an exception. If we add to this terror the blissful ecstasy that wells from the innermost depths of man, indeed of nature, at this collapse of the *principium individuationis*, we steal a glimpse into the nature of the *Dionysian*, which is brought home to us most intimately by the analogy of intoxication.

Either under the influence of the narcotic draught, of which the songs of all primitive men and peoples speak, or with the potent coming of spring that penetrates all nature with joy, these Dionysian emotions awake, and as they grow in intensity everything subjective vanishes into complete self-forgetfulness. In the German Middle Ages, too, singing and dancing crowds, ever increasing in number, whirled themselves from place to place under this same Dionysian impulse. In these dancers of St. John and St. Vitus, we rediscover the Bacchic choruses of the Greeks, with their prehistory in Asia Minor, as far back as Babylon and the orgiastic Sacaea. There are some who, from obtuseness or lack of experience, turn away from such phenomena as from "folkdiseases," with contempt or pity born of the consciousness of their own "healthy-mindedness." But of course such poor wretches have no idea how corpselike and ghostly their socalled "healthy-mindedness" looks when the glowing life of the Dionysian revelers roars past them.

Under the charm of the Dionysian not only is the union between man and man reaffirmed, but nature which has become alienated, hostile, or subjugated, celebrates once more her reconciliation with her lost son, man. Freely, earth proffers her gifts, and peacefully the beasts of prey of the rocks and desert approach. The chariot of Dionysus is covered with flowers and garlands; panthers and tigers walk under its yoke. Transform Beethoven's "Hymn to Joy" into a painting; let your imagination conceive the multitudes bowing to the dust; awestruck—then you will approach the Dionysian. Now the slave is a free man; now all the rigid, hostile barriers that necessity, caprice, or "impudent convention" have fixed between man and man are broken. Now, with the gospel of universal harmony, each one feels himself not only united, reconciled, and fused with his neighbor, but as one with him, as if the veil of *maya* had been torn aside and were now merely fluttering in tatters before the mysterious primordial unity.

In song and in dance man expresses himself as a member of a higher community; he has forgotten how to walk and speak and is on the way toward flying into the air, dancing. His very gestures express enchantment. Just as the animals now talk, and the earth yields milk and honey, supernatural sounds emanate from him, too: he feels himself a god, he himself now walks about enchanted, in ecstasy, like the gods he saw walking in his dreams. He is no longer an artist, he has become a work of art: in these paroxysms of intoxication the artistic power of all nature reveals itself to the highest gratification of the primordial unity. The noblest clay, the most costly marble, man, is here kneaded and cut, and to the sound of the chisel strokes of the Dionysian world-artist rings out the cry of the Eleusinian mysteries: "Do you prostrate yourselves, millions? Do you sense your Maker, world?"

FRIEDRICH NIETZSCHE

from Beyond Good and Evil

In Beyond Good and Evil, *Nietzsche offers a provocative critique of moral systems based on religious principles. Nietzsche sees the impetus to love others and sacrifice for them as a form of weakness; he urges a morality that calls for privileging the strong, who discard conventional morality in an assertion of individual will.*

Every choice human being strives instinctively for a citadel and a secrecy where he is saved from the crowd, the many, the great majority—where he may forget 'men who are the rule,' being their exceptions—excepting only the one case in which he is pushed straight to such men by a still stronger instinct, as a seeker after knowledge in the great and exceptional sense. Anyone who, in intercourse with men, does not occasionally glisten in all the colours of distress, green and grey with disgust, satiety, sympathy, gloominess and loneliness, is certainly not a man of elevated tastes; supposing, however, that he does not take all this burden and disgust upon himself voluntarily, that he persistently avoids it, and remains, as I said, quietly and proudly hidden in his citadel, one thing is certain: he was not made, he was not predestined, for knowledge. If he were,

he would one day have to say to himself: 'The devil take my good taste! but the rule is more interesting than the exception—than myself, the exception!' And he would go *down* and above all, he would go 'inside.' The long and serious study of the *average* man, and consequently much disguise, self-overcoming, familiarity, and bad contact (all contact is bad except with one's equals)—this constitutes a necessary part of the life history of every philosopher, perhaps the most disagreeable, odious and disappointing part . . .

Independence is for the very few; it is a privilege of the strong. And whoever attempts it even with the best right but without inner constraint proves that he is probably not only strong, but also daring to the point of recklessness. He enters into a labyrinth, he multiplies a thousandfold the dangers which life brings with it in any case, not the least of which is that no one can see how and where he loses his way, becomes lonely, and is torn piecemeal by some minotaur of conscience. Supposing one like that comes to grief, this happens so far from the comprehension of men that they neither feel it nor sympathize. And he cannot go back any longer. Nor can he go back to the pity of men . . .

During the longest part of human history—so-called prehistorical times—the value or disvalue of an action was derived from its consequences. The action itself was considered as little as its origin. It was rather the way a distinction or disgrace still reaches back today from a child to its parents, in China: it was the retroactive force of success or failure that led men to think well or ill of an action. Let us call this period the *pre-moral* period of mankind: the imperative 'Know thyself!' was as yet unknown.

In the last ten thousand years, however, one has reached the point, step by step, in a few large regions on the earth, where it is no longer the consequences but the origin of an action that one allows to decide its value. On the whole this is a great event which involves a considerable refinement of vision and standards; it is the unconscious after-effect of the rule of aristocratic values and the faith in 'descent'—the sign of a period that one may call *moral* in the narrower sense. It involves the first attempt at self-knowledge. Instead of the consequences, the origin: indeed a reversal of perspective! Surely, a reversal achieved only after long struggles and vacillations. To be sure, a calamitous new superstition, an odd narrowness of interpretation, thus become dominant: the origin of an action was interpreted in the most definite sense as origin in an *intention;* one came to agree that the value of an action lay in the value of the intention. The intention as the whole origin and prehistory of an action—almost to the present day this prejudice dominated moral praise, blame, judgement, and philosophy on earth.

But today—shouldn't we have reached the necessity of once more resolving on a reversal and fundamental shift in values, owing to another self-examination of man, another growth in profundity? Don't we stand at the threshold of a period which should be designated negatively, to begin with, as *extra-moral?* After all, today at least we immoralists have the suspicion that the decisive value of an action lies precisely in what is *unintentional* in it, while everything about it that is intentional, everything about it that can be seen, known, 'conscious', still belongs to its surface and skin—which, like every skin, betrays something but *conceals* even more. In short, we believe that the intention is merely a sign and symptom that still requires interpretation—moreover, a sign that means too much and therefore, taken by itself alone, almost nothing. We believe that morality in the traditional sense, the morality of intentions, was a prejudice, precipitate and perhaps provisional—something on the order of astrology and alchemy—but in any case something that must be overcome. The overcoming of morality, in a certain sense even the self-overcoming of morality—let this be the name for that long secret work which has been saved up for the finest and most honest, also the most malicious, consciences of today, as living touchstones of the soul.

There is no other way: the feelings of devotion, selfsacrifice for one's neighbour, the whole morality of selfdenial must be questioned mercilessly and taken to court - no less than the aesthetics of 'contemplation devoid of all interest' which is used today as a seductive guise for the emasculation of art, to give it a good conscience. There is too much charm and sugar in these feelings of 'for others', '*not* for myself', for us not to need to become doubly suspicions at this point and to ask: 'are these not perhaps—*seductions?*' That they *please*—those who have them and those who enjoy their fruits, and also the mere spectator—this does not yet constitute an argument in their *favour* but rather invites caution. So let us be cautions . . .

No one is very likely to consider a doctrine true merely because it makes people happy or virtuous—except perhaps the lovely 'idealists' who become effusive about the good, the true and the beautiful and allow all kinds of motley, clumsy, and benevolent disiderata to swim around in utter confusion in their pond. Happiness and virtue are no arguments. But people like to forget—even sober spirits—that making unhappy and evil are no counter-arguments. Something might be true while being harmful and dangerous in the highest degree. Indeed, it might be a basic characteristic of existence that those who would know it completely would perish, in which case the strength of a spirit should be measured according to how much of the 'truth' one could still barely endure—or to put it more clearly, to what degree one would *require* it to be thinned down, shrouded, sweetened, blunted, falsified.

But there is no doubt at all that the evil and unhappy are more favoured when it comes to the discovery of certain *parts* of truth, and that the probability of their success here is greater—not to speak of the evil who are happy, a species the moralists bury in silence. Perhaps hardness and cunning furnish more favourite conditions for the origin of the strong, independent spirit and philosopher than that gentle, fine, conciliatory good-naturedness and art of taking things lightly which people prize, and prize rightly, in a scholar. Assuming first of all that the concept 'philosopher' is not restricted to the philosopher who writes books—or makes books of *his* philosophy . . .

The moral sentiment in Europe today is as refined, old, diverse, irritable and subtle, as the 'science of morals' that accompanies it is still young, raw, clumsy and butterfingered—an attractive contrast that occasionally becomes visible and incarnate in the person of a moralist. Even the term 'science of morals' is much too arrogant considering what it designates, and offends *good* taste—which always prefers more modest terms.

One should own up in all strictness to what is still necessary here for a long time to come, to what alone is justified so far: to collect material, to conceptualize and arrange a vast realm of subtle feelings of value and differences of value which are alive, grow, beget and perish—and perhaps attempts to present vividly some of the more frequent and recurring forms of such living crystallizations—all to prepare a *typology* of morals.

To be sure, so far one has not been so modest. With a stiff seriousness that inspires laughter, all our philosophers demanded something far more exalted, presumptuous, and solemn from themselves as soon as they approached the study of morality: they wanted to supply a *rational foundation* for morality—and every philosopher so far has believed that he has provided such a foundation. Morality itself, however, was accepted as 'given'. How remote from their clumsy pride was that task which they considered insignificant and left in dust and must—the task of description although the subtlest fingers and senses can scarcely be enough for it.

Just because our moral philosophers knew the facts of morality only very approximately in arbitrary extracts or in accidental epitomes for example as the morality of their environment, their class, their church, the spirit of their time, their climate and part of the world—just because they were poorly informed and not even very curious about different peoples, times and past ages—they never laid eyes on the real problems of morality; for these emerge only when we compare *many* moralities. In all 'science of morals' so far one thing was *lacking*, strange as it may sound: the problem of morality itself; what was lacking was any suspicion that there was something problematic here. What the philosophers called 'a rational foundation for morality' and tried to supply was, seen in the right light, merely a scholarly variation of the common *faith* in the prevalent morality; a new means of *expression* for this faith; and thus just another fact within a particular morality; indeed, in the last, analysis a kind of denial that this morality might ever be considered problematic—certainly the very opposite of an examination, analysis, questioning, and vivisection of this very faith . . .

As long as the utility reigning in moral value judgements is solely the utility of the herd, as long as one considers only the preservation of the community, and immorality is sought exactly and exclusively in what seems dangerous to the survival of the community—there can be no morality of 'neighbour-love'. Supposing that even then there was a constant little exercise of consideration, pity, fairness, mildness, reciprocity of assistance; supposing that even in that state of society all those drives are active that later receive the honorary designation of 'virtues' and eventually almost coincide with the concept of 'morality'—in that period they do not yet at all belong in the realm of moral valuations; they are still *extra-moral*. An act of pity, for example, was not considered either good or bad, moral or immoral, in the best period of the Romans; and even when it was praised, such praise was perfectly compatible with a kind of disgruntled disdain as soon as it was juxtaposed with an action that served the welfare of the whole, of the *res publica* [commonwealth].

In the last analysis, 'love of the neighbour' is always something secondary, partly conventional and arbitrary-illusory in relation to *fear of the neighbour*. After the structure of society is fixed on the whole and seems secure against external dangers, it is this fear of the neighbour that again creates new perspectives of moral valuation. Certain strong and dangerous drives, like an enterprising spirit, foolhardiness, vengefulness, craftiness, rapacity, and the lust to rule, which had so far not merely been honoured in so far as they were socially useful under different names, to be sure, from those chosen here—but had to be trained and cultivated to make them great (because one constantly needed them in view of the dangers to the whole community, against the enemies of the community), are now experienced as doubly dangerous, since the channels to divert them are lacking, and, step upon step, they are branded as immoral and abandoned to slander.

Now the opposite drives and inclinations receive moral honours; step upon step, the herd instinct draws its conclusions. How much or how little is dangerous to the community, dangerous to equality, in an opinion, in a state or affect, in a will, in a talent—that now constitutes the moral perspective here, too, fear is again the mother of morals.

The highest and strongest drives, when they break out passionately and drive the individual far above the average and the flats of the herd conscience, wreck the self-confidence of the community, its faith in itself, and it is as if its spine snapped. Hence just these drives are branded and slandered most. High and independent spirituality, the will to stand alone, even a powerful reason are experienced as dangers. Everything that elevates an individual above the herd, and intimidates the neighbour is henceforth called *evil;* and the fair, modest, submissive, conforming mentality, the *mediocrity* of desires attains moral designations and honours. Eventually, under very peaceful conditions, the opportunity and necessity for educating one's feelings to severity and hardness is lacking more and more; and even severity, even injustice, begins to disturb the conscience; any high and hard nobility and self-reliance is almost felt to be an insult and arouses mistrust; the 'lamb' even more than the 'sheep', gains in respect.

There is a point in the history of a society when it becomes so pathologically soft and tender that among other things it sides even with those who harm it, criminals, and does this quite seriously and honestly. Punishing somehow seems unfair to it, and it is certain that imagining 'punishment' and 'being supposed to punish' hurts it, arouses fear in it. 'Is it not enough to render him *undangerous?* Why still punish? Punishing itself is terrible.' With this question, herd morality, the morality of timidity, draws its ultimate consequence. Supposing that one could altogether abolish danger, the reason for fear, this morality would thereby be abolished too: it would no longer be needed, it would no longer *consider itself* necessary.

Whoever examines the conscience of the European today will have to pull the same imperative out of a thousand moral folds and hideouts—the imperative of herd timidity: 'we want that some day there should be *nothing any more to be afraid of!*' Some day—throughout Europe, the will and way to this day is now called 'progress' . . .

We have a different faith; to us the democratic movement is not only a form of the decay of political organization but a form of the decay, namely the diminution, of man, making him mediocre and lowering his value. Where, then, must *we* reach with our hopes?

Toward *new philosophers;* there is no choice; toward spirits strong and original enough *to* provide the stimuli for opposite valuations and to revalue and invert 'eternal values'; toward forerunners, toward men of the future who in the present tie the knot and constraint that forces the will of millennia upon *new* tracks. To teach man the future of man as

his *will*, as dependent on a human will, and to prepare great ventures and over-all attempts of discipline and cultivation by way of putting an end to that gruesome dominion of nonsense and accident that has so far been called 'history'—the nonsense of the 'greatest number' is merely its ultimate form: at some time new types of philosophers and commanders will be necessary for that, and whatever has existed on earth of concealed, terrible and benevolent spirits, will look pale and dwarfed by comparison. It is the image of such leaders that we envisage: may I say this out loud, you free spirits? The conditions that one would have partly to create and partly to exploit for their genesis; the probable ways and tests that would enable a soul to grow to such a height and force that it would feel the *compulsion* for such tasks; a revaluation of values under whose new pressure and hammer a conscience would be steeled, a heart turned to bronze, in order to endure the weight of such responsibility; on the other hand, the necessity of such leaders, the frightening danger that they might fail to appear or that they might turn out badly or degenerate— these are *our* real worries and gloom—do you know that, you free spirits?—these are the heavy distant thoughts and storms that pass over the sky of *our* life.

SIGMUND FREUD

Sigmund Freud (1856–1939) was an Austrian neurologist who founded psychoanalysis. Much of modern psychological and psychoanalytical terminology derives from Freud's work, including the terms ego, id, and superego, and notions such as repression and sublimation. Author of many works and cases studies, Freud turns his analytical method on civilization in the following excerpt from his Civilization and Its Discontents.

from *Civilization and Its Discontents*

Chapter III

Our enquiry concerning happiness has not so far taught us much that is not already common knowledge. And even if we proceed from it to the problem of why it is so hard for men to be happy, there seems no greater prospect of learning anything new. We have given the answer already by pointing to the three sources from which our suffering comes: the superior power of nature, the feebleness of our own bodies and the inadequacy of the regulations which adjust the mutual relationships of human beings in the family, the state and society. In regard to the first two sources, our judgement cannot hesitate long. It forces us to acknowledge those sources of suffering and to submit to the inevitable. We shall never completely master nature; and our bodily organism, itself a part of that nature, will always remain a transient structure with a limited capacity for adaptation and achievement. This recognition does not have a paralysing effect. On the contrary, it points the direction for our activity. If we cannot remove all suffering, we can remove some, and we can mitigate some: the experience of many thousands of years has convinced us of that. As regards the third source, the social source of suffering, our attitude is a different one. We do not admit it at all; we cannot see why the regulations made by ourselves should not, on the contrary, be a protection and a benefit for every one of us. And yet, when we consider how unsuccessful we have been in precisely this field of prevention of suffering, a suspicion dawns on us that here, too, a piece of unconquerable nature may lie behind—this time a piece of our own psychical constitution.

When we start considering this possibility, we come upon a contention which is so astonishing that we must dwell upon it. This contention holds that what we call our civilization is largely responsible for our misery, and that we should be much happier if we gave it up and returned to primitive conditions. I call this contention astonishing because, in whatever way we may define the concept of civilization, it is a certain fact that all the things with which we seek to protect ourselves against the threats that emanate from the sources of suffering are part of that very civilization.

How has it happened that so many people have come to take up this strange attitude of hostility to civilization?[1] I believe that the basis of it was a deep and long-standing dissatisfaction with the then existing state of civilization and that on that basis a condemnation of it was built up, occasioned by certain specific historical events. I think I know what the last and the last but one of those occasions were. I am not learned enough to trace the chain of them far back enough in the history of the human species; but a factor of this kind hostile to civilization must already have been at work in the victory of Christendom over the heathen religions. For it was very closely related to the low estimation put upon earthly life by the Christian doctrine. The last but one of these occasions was when the progress of voyages of discovery led to contact with primitive peoples and races. In consequence of insufficient observation and a mistaken view of their manners and customs, they appeared to Europeans to be leading a simple, happy life with few wants, a life such as was unattainable by their visitors with their superior civilization. Later experience has corrected some of those judgements. In many cases the observers had wrongly attributed to the absence of complicated cultural demands what was in fact due to the bounty of nature and the ease with which the major human needs were satisfied. The last occasion is especially familiar to us. It arose when people came to know about the mechanism of the neuroses, which threaten to undermine the modicum of happiness enjoyed by civilized men. It was discovered that a person becomes neurotic because he cannot tolerate the amount of frustration which society imposes on him in the service of its cultural ideals, and it was inferred from this that the abolition or reduction of those demands would result in a return to possibilities of happiness.

There is also an added factor of disappointment. During the last few generations mankind has made an extraordinary advance in the natural sciences and in their technical application and has established his control over nature in a way never before imagined. The single steps of this advance are common knowledge and it is unnecessary to enumerate them. Men are proud of those achievements, and have a right to be. But they seem to have observed that this newly-won power over space and time, this subjugation of the forces of nature, which is the fulfillment of a longing that goes back thousands of years, has not increased the amount of pleasurable satisfaction which they may expect from life and has not made them feel happier. From the recognition of this fact we ought

to be content to conclude that power over nature is not the *only* precondition of human happiness, just as it is not the *only* goal of cultural endeavour; we ought not to infer from it that technical progress is without value for the economics of our happiness. One would like to ask: is there, then, no positive gain in pleasure, no unequivocal increase in my feeling of happiness, if I can, as often as I please, hear the voice of a child of mine who is living hundreds of miles away or if I can learn in the shortest possible time after a friend has reached his destination that he has come through the long and difficult voyage unharmed? Does it mean nothing that medicine has succeeded in enormously reducing infant mortality and the danger of infection for women in childbirth, and, indeed, in considerably lengthening the average life of a civilized man? And there is a long list that might be added to benefits of this kind which we owe to the much-despised era of scientific and technical advances. But here the voice of pessimistic criticism makes itself heard and warns us that most of these satisfactions follow the model of the 'cheap enjoyment' extolled in the anecdote—the enjoyment obtained by putting a bare leg from under the bedclothes on a cold winter night and drawing it in again. If there had been no railway to conquer distances, my child would never have left his native town and I should need no telephone to hear his voice; if travelling across the ocean by ship had not been introduced, my friend would not have embarked on his sea-voyage and I should not need a cable to relieve my anxiety about him. What is the use of reducing infantile mortality when it is precisely that reduction which imposes the greatest restraint on us in the begetting of children, so that, taken all round, we nevertheless rear no more children than in the days before the reign of hygiene, while at the same time we have created difficult conditions for our sexual life in marriage, and have probably worked against the beneficial effects of natural selection? And, finally, what good to us is a long life if it is difficult and barren of joys, and if it is so full of misery that we can only welcome death as a deliverer?

It seems certain that we do not feel comfortable in our present-day civilization, but it is very difficult to form an opinion whether and in what degree men of an earlier age felt happier and what part their cultural conditions played in the matter. We shall always tend to consider people's distress objectively—that is, to place ourselves, with our own wants and sensibilities, in *their* conditions, and then to examine what occasions we should find in them for experiencing happiness or unhappiness. This method of looking at things, which seems objective because it ignores the variations in subjective sensibility, is, of course, the most subjective possible, since it puts one's own mental states in the place of any others, unknown though they may be. Happiness, however, is something essentially subjective. No matter how much we may shrink with horror from certain situations—of a galley-slave in antiquity, of a peasant during the Thirty Years' War, of a victim of the Holy Inquisition, of a Jew awaiting a pogrom—it is nevertheless impossible for us to feel our way into such people—to divine the changes which original obtuseness of mind, a gradual stupefying process, the cessation of expectations, and cruder or more refined methods of narcotization have produced upon their receptivity to sensations of pleasure and unpleasure. Moreover, in the case of the most extreme possibility of suffering, special mental protective devices are brought into operation. It seems to me unprofitable to pursue this aspect of the problem any further.

---

[1][Freud had discussed this question at considerable length two years earlier, in the opening chapters of *The Future of an Illusion* (1927*c*).]

It is time for us to turn our attention to the nature of this civilization on whose value as a means to happiness doubts have been thrown. We shall not look for a formula in which to express that nature in a few words, until we have learned something by examining it. We shall therefore content ourselves with saying once more that the word 'civilization'[2] describes the whole sum of the achievements and the regulations which distinguish our lives from those of our animal ancestors and which serve two purposes—namely to protect men against nature and to adjust their mutual relations.[3] In order to learn more, we will bring together the various features of civilization individually, as they are exhibited in human communities. In doing so, we shall have no hesitation in letting ourselves be guided by linguistic usage or, as it is also called, linguistic feeling, in the conviction that we shall thus be doing justice to inner discernments which still defy expression in abstract terms.

The first stage is easy. We recognize as cultural all activities and resources which are useful to men for making the earth serviceable to them, for protecting them against the violence of the forces of nature, and so on. As regards this side of civilization, there can be scarcely any doubt. If we go back far enough, we find that the first acts of civilization were the use of tools, the gaining of control over fire and the construction of dwellings. Among these, the control over fire stands out as a quite extraordinary and unexampled achievement,[4] while the others opened up paths which man has followed ever since, and the stimulus to which is easily guessed. With every tool man is perfecting his own organs, whether motor or sensory, or is removing the limits to their functioning. Motor power places gigantic forces at his disposal, which, like his muscles, he can employ in any direction; thanks to ships and aircraft neither water nor air can hinder his movements; by means of spectacles he corrects defects in the lens of his own eye; by means of the telescope he sees into the far distance; and by means of the microscope he overcomes the limits of visibility set by the structure of his retina. In the photographic camera he has created an instrument which retains the fleeting visual impressions, just as a gramophone disc retains the equally fleeting auditory ones; both are at bottom materializations of the power he possesses of recollection, his memory. With the help of the telephone he can hear at distances which would be respected as unattainable even in a fairy tale. Writing was in its origin the voice of an absent person; and the dwellinghouse was a substitute for the mother's womb, the first lodging, for which in all likelihood man still longs, and in which he was safe and felt at ease.

These things that, by his science and technology, man has brought about on this earth, on which he first appeared as a feeble animal organism and on which each individual of his species must once more make its entry ('oh inch of nature!'[5]) as a helpless suckling—these things do not only sound like a fairy tale, they are an actual fulfilment of every—or of almost every—fairy-tale wish. All these assets he may lay claim to as his cultural acquisition. Long ago he formed an ideal conception of omnipotence and omniscience which he embodied in his gods. To these gods he attributed everything that seemed unattainable to his wishes, or that was forbidden to him. One may say, therefore, that these gods were cultural ideals. To-day he has come very close to the attainment of this ideal, he has almost become a god himself. Only, it is true, in the fashion in which ideals are usually attained according to the general judgement of humanity. Not completely; in some respects not at all, in others only half way. Man has, as it were, become a kind of prosthetic[6] God. When he puts on all his auxiliary organs he is truly magnificent; but those organs have not grown on to him and they still give him much trouble at times. Nevertheless, he is entitled to console himself with the thought that this development will not come to an end precisely with the year 1930 A.D. Future ages will bring with them new and probably unimaginably great advances in this field of civilization and will increase man's likeness to God still more. But in the interests of our investigations, we will not forget that present-day man does not feel happy in his Godlike character.

We recognize, then, that countries have attained a high level of civilization if we find that in them everything which can assist in the exploitation of the earth by man and in his protection against the forces of nature—everything, in short, which is of use to him—is attended to and effectively carried out. In such countries rivers which threaten to flood the land are regulated in their flow, and their water is directed through canals to places where there is a shortage of it. The soil is

---

[2] '*Kultur.*' For the translation of this word see the Editor's Note to *The Future of an Illusion.*

[3] See *The Future of an Illusion.*

[4] Psycho-analytic material, incomplete as it is and not susceptible to clear interpretation, nevertheless admits of a conjecture—a fantastic-sounding one—about the origin of this human feat. It is as though primal man had the habit, when he came in contact with fire, of satisfying an infantile desire connected with it, by putting it out with a stream of his urine. The legends that we possess leave no doubt about the originally phallic view taken of tongues of flame as they shoot upwards. Putting out fire by micturating—a theme to which modern giants, Gulliver in Lilliput and Rabelais' Gargantua, still hark back—was therefore a kind of sexual act with a male, an enjoyment of sexual potency in a homosexual competition. The first person to renounce this desire and spare the fire was able to carry it off with him and subdue it to his own use. By damping down the fire of his own sexual excitation, he had tamed the natural force of fire. This great cultural conquest was thus the reward for his renunciation of instinct. Further, it is as though woman had been appointed guardian of the fire which was held captive on the domestic hearth, because her anatomy made it impossible for her to yield to the temptation of this desire. It is remarkable, too, how regularly analytic experience testifies to the connection between ambition, fire and urethral erotism.—[Freud had pointed to the connection between urination and fire as early as in the 'Dora' case history (1905*e* [1901]). The connection with ambition came rather later. A full list of references will be found in the Editor's Note to the later paper on the subject, 'The Acquisition and Control of Fire' (1932*a*).]

[5] [In English in the original. This very Shakespearean phrase is not in fact to be found in the canon of Shakespeare. The words 'Poore inch of Nature' occur, however, in a novel by George Wilkins, *The Painfull Adventures of Pericles Prince of Tyre*, where they are addressed by Pericles to his infant daughter. This work was first printed in 1608, just after the publication of Shakespeare's play, in which Wilkins has been thought to have had a hand. Freud's unexpected acquaintance with the phrase is explained by its appearance in a discussion of the origins of *Pericles* in Georg Brandes's well-known book on Shakespeare, a copy of the German translation of which had a place in Freud's library (Brandes, 1896). He is known to have greatly admired the Danish critic (cf. Jones, 1957, 120), and the same book is quoted in his paper on the three caskets (1913*f*).]

[6] [A prosthesis is the medical term for an artificial adjunct to the body, to make up for some missing or inadequate part: e.g. false teeth or a false leg.]

carefully cultivated and planted with the vegetation which it is suited to support; and the mineral wealth below ground is assiduously brought to the surface and fashioned into the required implements and utensils. The means of communication are ample, rapid and reliable. Wild and dangerous animals have been exterminated, and the breeding of domesticated animals flourishes. But we demand other things from civilization besides these, and it is a noticeable fact that we hope to find them realized in these same countries. As though we were seeking to repudiate the first demand we made, we welcome it as a sign of civilization as well if we see people directing their care too to what has no practical value whatever, to what is useless—if, for instance, the green spaces necessary in a town as playgrounds and as reservoirs of fresh air are also laid out with flower-beds, or if the windows of the houses are decorated with pots of flowers. We soon observe that this useless thing which we expect civilization to value is beauty. We require civilized man to reverence beauty wherever he sees it in nature and to create it in the objects of his handiwork so far as he is able. But this is far from exhausting our demands on civilization. We expect besides to see the signs of cleanliness and order. We do not think highly of the cultural level of an English country town in Shakespeare's time when we read that there was a big dung-heap in front of his father's house in Stratford; we are indignant and call it 'barbarous' (which is the opposite of civilized) when we find the paths in the Wiener Wald[7] littered with paper. Dirtiness of any kind seems to us incompatible with civilization. We extend our demand for cleanliness to the human body too. We are astonished to learn of the objectionable smell which emanated from the *Roi Soleil*;[8] and we shake our heads on the Isola Bella[9] when we are shown the tiny wash-basin in which Napoleon made his morning toilet. Indeed, we are not surprised by the idea of setting up the use of soap as an actual yardstick of civilization. The same is true of order. It, like cleanliness, applies solely to the works of man. But whereas cleanliness is not to be expected in nature, order, on the contrary, has been imitated from her. Man's observation of the great astronomical regularities not only furnished him with a model for introducing order into his life, but gave him the first points of departure for doing so. Order is a kind of compulsion to repeat which, when a regulation has been laid down once and for all, decides when, where and how a thing shall be done, so that in every similar circumstance one is spared hesitation and indecision. The benefits of order are incontestable. It enables men to use space and time to the best advantage, while conserving their psychical forces. We should have a right to expect that order would have taken its place in human activities from the start and without difficulty; and we may well wonder that this has not happened—that, on the contrary, human beings exhibit an inborn tendency to carelessness, irregularity and unreliability in their work, and that a laborious training is needed before they learn to follow the example of their celestial models.

Beauty, cleanliness and order obviously occupy a special position among the requirements of civilization. No one will maintain that they are as important for life as control over the forces of nature or as some other factors with which we shall become acquainted. And yet no one would care to put them in the background as trivialities. That civilization is not exclusively taken up with what is useful is already shown by the example of beauty, which we decline to omit from among the interests of civilization. The usefulness of order is quite evident. With regard to cleanliness, we must bear in mind that it is demanded of us by hygiene as well, and we may suspect that even before the days of scientific prophylaxis the connection between the two was not altogether strange to man. Yet utility does not entirely explain these efforts; something else must be at work besides.

No feature, however, seems better to characterize civilization than its esteem and encouragement of man's higher mental activities—his intellectual, scientific and artistic achievements—and the leading role that it assigns to ideas in human life. Foremost among those ideas are the religious systems, on whose complicated structure I have endeavoured to throw light elsewhere.[10] Next come the speculations of philosophy; and finally what might be called man's 'ideals'—his ideas of a possible perfection of individuals, or of peoples or of the whole of humanity, and the demands he sets up on the basis of such ideas. The fact that these creations of his are not independent of one another, but are on the contrary closely interwoven, increases the difficulty not only of describing them but of tracing their psychological derivation. If we assume quite generally that the motive force of all human activities is a striving towards the two confluent goals of utility and a yield of pleasure, we must suppose that this is also true of the manifestations of civilization which we have been discussing here, although this is easily visible only in scientific and aesthetic activities. But it cannot be doubted that the other activities, too, correspond to strong needs in men—perhaps to needs which are only developed in a minority. Nor must we allow ourselves to be misled by judgements of value concerning any particular religion, or philosophic system, or ideal. Whether we think to find in them the highest achievements of the human spirit, or whether we deplore them as aberrations, we cannot but recognize that where they are present, and, in especial, where they are dominant, a high level of civilization is implied.

The last, but certainly not the least important, of the characteristic features of civilization remains to be assessed: the manner in which the relationships of men to one another, their social relationships, are regulated—relationships which affect a person as a neighbour, as a source of help, as another person's sexual object, as a member of a family and of a State. Here it is especially difficult to keep clear of particular ideal demands and to see what is civilized in general. Perhaps we may begin by explaining that the element of civilization enters on the scene with the first attempt to regulate these social relationships. If the attempt were not made, the relationships would be subject to the arbitrary will of the individual: that is to say, the physically stronger man would decide them in the sense of his own interests and instinctual impulses. Nothing would be changed in this if this stronger man should in his turn meet

---

[7][The wooded hills on the outskirts of Vienna.]
[8][Louis XIV of France.]
[9][The well-known island in Lake Maggiore, visited by Napoleon a few days before the battle of Marengo.]

[10][Cf. *The Future of an Illusion* (1927c).]

someone even stronger than he. Human life in common is only made possible when a majority comes together which is stronger than any separate individual and which remains united against all separate individuals. The power of this community is then set up as 'right' in opposition to the power of the individual, which is condemned as 'brute force'. This replacement of the power of the individual by the power of a community constitutes the decisive step of civilization. The essence of it lies in the fact that the members of the community restrict themselves in their possibilities of satisfaction, whereas the individual knew no such restrictions. The first requisite of civilization, therefore, is that of justice—that is, the assurance that a law once made will not be broken in favour of an individual. This implies nothing as to the ethical value of such a law. The further course of cultural development seems to tend towards making the law no longer an expression of the will of a small community—a caste or a stratum of the population or a racial group—which, in its turn, behaves like a violent individual towards other, and perhaps more numerous, collections of people. The final outcome should be a rule of law to which all—except those who are not capable of entering a community—have contributed by a sacrifice of their instincts, and which leaves no one—again with the same exception—at the mercy of brute force.

The liberty of the individual is no gift of civilization. It was greatest before there was any civilization, though then, it is true, it had for the most part no value, since the individual was scarcely in a position to defend it. The development of civilization imposes restrictions on it, and justice demands that no one shall escape those restrictions. What makes itself felt in a human community as a desire for freedom may be their revolt against some existing injustice, and so may prove favourable to a further development of civilization; it may remain compatible with civilization. But it may also spring from the remains of their original personality, which is still untamed by civilization and may thus become the basis in them of hostility to civilization. The urge for freedom, therefore, is directed against particular forms and demands of civilization or against civilization altogether. It does not seem as though any influence could induce a man to change his nature into a termite's. No doubt he will always defend his claim to individual liberty against the will of the group. A good part of the struggles of mankind centre round the single task of finding an expedient accommodation—one, that is, that will bring happiness—between this claim of the individual and the cultural claims of the group; and one of the problems that touches the fate of humanity is whether such an accommodation can be reached by means of some particular form of civilization or whether this conflict is irreconcilable.

By allowing common feeling to be our guide in deciding what features of human life are to be regarded as civilized, we have obtained a clear impression of the general picture of civilization; but it is true that so far we have discovered nothing that is not universally known. At the same time we have been careful not to fall in with the prejudice that civilization is synonymous with perfecting, that it is the road to perfection preordained for men. But now a point of view presents itself which may lead in a different direction. The development of civilization appears to us as a peculiar process which mankind undergoes, and in which several things strike us as familiar. We may characterize this process with reference to the changes which it brings about in the familiar instinctual dispositions of human beings, to satisfy which is, after all, the economic task of our lives. A few of these instincts are used up in such a manner that something appears in their place which, in an individual, we describe as a character-trait. The most remarkable example of such a process is found in the anal erotism of young human beings. Their original interest in the excretory function, its organs and products, is changed in the course of their growth into a group of traits which are familiar to us as parsimony, a sense of order and cleanliness—qualities which, though valuable and welcome in themselves, may be intensified till they become markedly dominant and produce what is called the anal character. How this happens we do not know, but there is no doubt about the correctness of the finding.[11] Now we have seen that order and cleanliness are important requirements of civilization, although their vital necessity is not very apparent, any more than their suitability as sources of enjoyment. At this point we cannot fail to be struck by the similarity between the process of civilization and the libidinal development of the individual. Other instincts [besides anal erotism] are induced to displace the conditions for their satisfaction, to lead them into other paths. In most cases this process coincides with that of the *sublimation* (of instinctual aims) with which we are familiar, but in some it can be differentiated from it. Sublimation of instinct is an especially conspicuous feature of cultural development; it is what makes it possible for higher psychical activities, scientific, artistic or ideological, to play such an important part in civilized life. If one were to yield to a first impression, one would say that sublimation is a vicissitude which has been forced upon the instincts entirely by civilization. But it would be wiser to reflect upon this a little longer. In the third place,[12] finally, and this seems the most important of all, it is impossible to overlook the extent to which civilization is built up upon a renunciation of instinct, how much it presupposes precisely the non-satisfaction (by suppression, repression or some other means?) of powerful instincts. This 'cultural frustration' dominates the large field of social relationships between human beings. As we already know, it is the cause of the hostility against which all civilizations have to struggle. It will also make severe demands on our scientific work, and we shall have much to explain here. It is not easy to understand how it can become possible to deprive an instinct of satisfaction. Nor is doing so without danger. If the loss is not compensated for economically, one can be certain that serious disorders will ensue.

But if we want to know what value can be attributed to our view that the development of civilization is a special process, comparable to the normal maturation of the individual, we must clearly attack another problem. We must ask ourselves to what influences the development of civilization owes its origin, how it arose, and by what its course has been determined.[13]

---

[11]Cf. my 'Character and Anal Erotism' (1908*b*), and numerous further contributions, by Ernest Jones [1918] and others.

[12][Freud had already mentioned two other factors playing a part in the 'process' of civilization: character-formation and sublimation.]

[13][Freud returns to the subject of civilization as a 'process' below, on p. 82 and again on p. 97ff. He mentions it once more in his open letter to Einstein, *Why War?* (1933*b*).]

CHAPTER 19

HISTORY

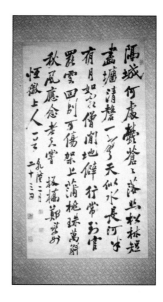

ARTS AND ARCHITECTURE

LITERATURE AND PHILOSOPHY

Chinese Civilization
after the Thirteenth Century

The Forbidden City, Beijing, seen from north.

MAP 19.1 China under the Qing Dynasty, ca. 1840.

CHAPTER OVERVIEW

LATER CHINESE CULTURE
An isolated China reluctantly absorbs Western ideas

LATER CHINESE CULTURE

The last of the great medieval dynasties of China was the Yuan, a Mongol dynasty. In 1271, the Mongolian leader KUBLAI KHAN [koob-lie KON] (1214–94), a grandson of Genghis Khan, adopted the Chinese dynastic name Yuan. By 1279, Kublai Khan had conquered the Southern Song and ruled from Beijing [bay-JHING] as emperor of China. He turned Beijing into a walled city and extended the Grand Canal to provision it. The Mongol ruling class

kept the principal offices of governmental administration to themselves, but appointed Chinese to the lowest posts. Although the Mongols wanted to maintain their ethnic separateness during their rule, they nonetheless needed Chinese officials to maintain order, collect taxes, and settle disputes.

The period of Yuan rule was the shortest of China's major dynasties, but it was culturally significant. A subtle and quiet resistance to the uneasy foreign occupation pervaded almost every aspect of Chinese life, including its painting. *Bamboo* (fig. 19.1) by WU ZHEN [WOO JUN]

FIGURE 19.1 Wu Zhen, *Bamboo*, Yuan dynasty, 1350, album leaf, ink on paper, 16 × 21″ (40.5 × 53.3 cm), National Palace Museum, Taipei, Taiwan. Despite Mongol rule, Wu Zhen worked in an intensely intellectual Chinese environment, dominated on the one hand by gatherings organized for the appreciation and criticism of poetry, calligraphy, painting, and wine, and, on the other, by deep interest in Buddhist and Taoist thought.

(1280–1354), one of the "Four Masters" of the Yuan dynasty, is ostensibly a simple representation of the plant, but its social significance was widely recognized. Bamboo, one of the strongest of materials and a symbol of survival, is like the Chinese under foreign rule: They might bend, but they would never break. Similarly, orchids, which nurture themselves without soil surrounding their roots, are a common symbol of Chinese culture in this period. Like the nation, the orchid could survive, even though the native Chinese soil had been stolen by the Mongol invaders. In 1368, Zhu Yuanzhang drove the last Yuan emperor north into the deserts and declared himself the first emperor of the new Ming dynasty. China was once again ruled by the Chinese.

MING AND QING DYNASTIES

The Ming (1368–1644) and Qing [CHING] (1644–1911), China's last dynasties, maintained the centralized bureaucratic political organization developed by the earlier Tang and Song dynasties. Although the Qing was ruled by Manchus, rather than ethnic Chinese, the Ming and Qing were remarkably alike in their reliance on Confucian ideals and in their high level of cultural achievement. The patriarchal nature of Confucian society (see Chapter 8) was evident at every level: The family, headed by the father, was the model unit. Politically, the emperor, as the Son of Heaven, was the father of the country. The magistrates, who carried out the rule of the emperor, also served as authority figures. The entire Ming–Qing system, one of unity and integration, benefited from the ability and commitment of its governing officials, who became known as *mandarins*, or counselors. These officials, trained in poetry and calligraphy as well as Confucianism, also helped create and support many arts.

Later Ming emperors reinforced the Great Wall, originally built by the first Qin Emperor in the third century B.C.E. The Ming emperors made the wall a century-long project, using thousands of workers to extend and repair the 1,500-mile-long wall that reached heights of thirty to fifty feet, and which included watchtowers, signal towers, and accommodations for troops.

The Ming dynasty ended in 1644 with the invasion of the Manchu from the north, who created the Qing ("pure") dynasty, which ruled until 1911. Two of the Manchu emperors, Kanxi (1661–1772) and Qianlong (1736–95) solidified Manchu control of China. Both of these emperors were sophisticated and learned men, accomplished in the arts, while also being brilliant diplomats and military tacticians. These and other Qing emperors continued the governmental structure developed by their Ming predecessors, with a highly centralized state under the administrative control of Confucian mandarin scholars. These scholar-bureaucrats, who earned their rank through a complex series of competitive civil services examinations, controlled the political and social life of the country. By focusing exclusively on Confucian classics and neo-Confucianist commentaries on them, the examination system ensured the continued importance of Confucianism to the cultural history of China.

Among the many and varied developments that occurred during Qing rule was the arrival of Jesuit Catholic missionaries. Most notable of the Jesuits who came to China was Matteo Ricci (1552–1610), a frequent presence at the Ming courts, a consequence of his mastery of the Chinese language and the Confucian classics. Among the many ways that Ricci and his Jesuit colleagues and successors charmed their Chinese hosts was with their mathematical, scientific, and technical knowledge. Through these and other forms of Western knowledge brought by the Jesuits to China, the Jesuits gained access. Although this did not yield many converts, it did serve to build a metaphorical bridge of knowledge and understanding between China and Europe, the first since the time of Marco Polo.

Although China was generally self-sufficient during these centuries, it gradually became apparent that technical and scientific advances in the West had left China behind. By the end of the nineteenth century, China was politically weak, and European countries had established trading relations that were decidedly unfavorable to China. Something had to be done, and in the early twentieth century, China abandoned the tradition of imperial rule that had provided social stability for many centuries. First, Confucian ideals of governance began to be discarded.

Then, with the overthrow of the Qing dynasty in 1911, came a period of political instability that lasted until the establishment of the communist state in 1949.

Communism remains the dominant political system in contemporary China. Despite the tumultuous Cultural Revolution in the late 1960s—a period of upheaval in all aspects of Chinese culture and society—and despite the Tiananmen Square protests in 1989, which sought greater democratic liberties for the Chinese people, the Communist Party has maintained its political control. Nevertheless, a more liberal attitude toward capitalistic economic growth has led in the last decades to many changes in China, including modernization and emergence into the network of world trade.

Until a hundred years ago, however, the system that kept China organized was based on the national examination system. The examination system allowed the brightest and most capable men to join and advance in government, and these scholar-officials were most influential in the arts.

Ming Furniture The Ming dynasty is renowned for many things, not the least of which is the gracefully beautiful furniture that was created during its reign. Often completely unornamented, Ming dynasty furniture exhibits a perfection of line and an elegance of form unique in its austere beauty. The precious woods used to construct Ming furniture were typically left unlacquered, unlike furniture from other periods, including that of the later Qing dynasty.

Ming furniture is constructed with complex joinery without the use of nails or glue. The pieces are held together with elaborate mitre, mortise, and tenon joints, which enable them to be disassembled readily, which was of great importance for their original Chinese mandarin owners who were obligated to move on a regular basis.

The woods used in Ming dynasty furniture are especially beautiful and have long been highly valued. Most Ming furniture was made from dense tropical hardwoods, called "Ying mu," which were notable for their striking color and grain. One of the most popular woods and highly sought after today is Huali, which includes Huanghuali and Xinhuali. Though other woods were used, such as the dark and striking zitan, as well as jichi and Elmwood, Huanghuali is the wood most frequently seen in museum-quality Ming dynasty furniture. Different woods and design variations gave each piece a unique character.

Ming furniture mingled form with function. Furniture was designed to reflect and dramatize the purposes for which it was designed. Ming beds, for example, were considered miniature houses with their covered tops and semi-enclosed sides, and were envisioned as places where sons were conceived. Ming tables were designed for the use of scholars to write and paint as well as to dine. And Ming chairs were designed less for comfort than for elegance of design and strength of structure. Chairs were placed and positioned according to the rank of the sitters. Where you sat indicated who you were in terms of social rank.

As striking as Ming dynasty furniture is to behold, it needs to be considered in light of the houses—the architecture—in which it was placed. The interior of a room was often undivided, and when partitioned, was done so in ways that made it easy to revise the interior spatial configuration.

LITERATI PAINTING

Many of the most important paintings created in China after the thirteenth century were by the scholar-official amateurs called **literati**, such as Wu Zhen (see fig. 19.1). During the Yuan, Ming, and Qing periods, these poet-artists utilized brushwork to express their understanding of humankind and nature, usually communicating their poetic vision in landscapes.

Shen Zhou. The literati movement in the Ming dynasty was exemplified by SHEN ZHOU [SHUN JOH] (1427–1509), who was less a professional artist than a gentleman scholar. Unlike a typical member of his social class, he never held an official government position. Described as a "poet of the brush," Shen Zhou was the founder of the Wu school, a group of amateur scholar-painters for whom painting was an intimate expression of personal feeling. (The name "Wu" derives from Wuhsien, the Yangtze river delta where Shen Zhou and other painters lived and worked.)

FIGURE 19.2 Zitan wood, Southern Official's Hat Armchair, late Ming dynasty, before 1644. Height 36.75″ (93.5 cm), seat dimensions: height 18.5″ (47 cm), width 22.5″ (57 cm), depth 18.5″ (47 cm). Courtesy of Ming Furniture, Ltd., Inc. This is a graceful and elegant example of a Ming dynasty chair.

FIGURE 19.3 *The Studio of Gratifying Discourse,* Qing dynasty, 1797, wood, ceramic tile, stone, lacquer. Minneapolis Institute of Arts, gift of Ruth and Bruce Dayton. Scholar's study with desk and footrest in center and window grate looking out to garden.

Among Shen Zhou's most striking compositions is *Poet on a Mountaintop* (fig. 19.4), one of five album paintings mounted as a hand scroll. Using black ink with a few touches of color, the artist balances white spaces (unpainted paper) with bold strokes and spots of black, to define the forms of rocks, trees, and other vegetation. He sets off the poet and the mountain in the center against lighter surroundings—washes of soft ink and white space. The poet, tiny and simply sketched, stands poised at the edge of a cliff on an inclined plane, propped up by his walking staff. Tucked away on the right is a mountain pavilion, a part of the natural scene, which is used as a place for people to put themselves in tune with the natural surroundings. Unlike many of his predecessors, Shen Zhou does not attempt to portray nature in an especially beautiful fashion, nor render the natural scene in carefully drawn, realistic detail. Instead, his painting conveys a sense of nature's serene grandeur.

Shitao. The paintings of SHITAO (Shee-DOW) (1641–1707) are more overtly expressive than those of Shen Zhou, reflecting an adventurous life in which he trav-eled extensively through China, became a Ch'an (Zen) monk, and finally returned to secular life. He became known for his eccentricities, such as naming one of his paintings, *"Ten Thousand Ugly Ink Dots."* He excelled in **wet-brush technique** in which the ink and colors merge and fuzz out on the paper or silk as in his work *Searching for the Past* (fig. 19.5). His dramatic compositions often seem to put the viewer directly into the scene.

Like many literati, Shitao wrote about painting, emphasizing that one could not rely on following the past styles of painting, but must find one's own way based on timeless truths. His ideas rely on Taoist and Zen ideals (see Chapter 8) but apply them in a new way to art. He wrote, "In ancient times there were no methods, since the state of natural simplicity had not been shattered. But when this state was dispersed, methods arose. What was their basis? The true single stroke of the brush! This is the origin of all methods for depicting anything in existence and it is the root of all images. Revealed through the spirit, it is innate in all people but they do not realize this. I have established for myself this method of no-method, from which all methods emerge." More specifically, he

FIGURE 19.4 Shen Zhou, *Poet on a Mountaintop*, Ming dynasty, ca. 1500, album painting mounted as a hand scroll, ink and color on paper, $15\frac{1}{4} \times 23\frac{3}{4}''$ (38.1 × 60.2 cm), Nelson-Atkins Museum of Art, Kansas City, MO. Like much Chinese nature painting, this work portrays human beings as a small element within a large natural scene.

wrote, "When the wrist does not move freely, the painting will not be alive, but if each single stroke is created without hesitation, all methods are mastered."

Zhu Da. Another eccentric artist of the seventeenth century was ZHU DA (Joo-DAH) (also called Bada Shanren,

FIGURE 19.5 Daoji, 1641–1707, *Reminiscences of the Qin-Huai River*. Qing dynasty, 1704. From album of eight leaves. Ink and light color on paper, $10\frac{1}{3} \times 8''$ (25.5 × 20.2 cm). © The Cleveland Museum of Art, John L. Severence Fund, 1966. 31.8. The scholar-sage is walking along the river, and according to his poem, he is searching for the remains of past dynasties while composing poems.

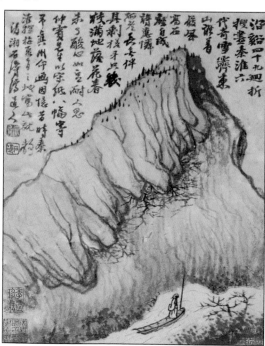

1626–1705). Related to the Ming imperial family, he was raised in wealth and privilege. At the age of eighteen, however, he saw the downfall of the Ming dynasty to the Manchus and he became, or pretended to be, dumb for some years. He served as a Buddhist monk but began to act as though he were insane; scholars still debate whether he was truly mad or was pretending in order to live his life without constraints. In his final years he turned more and more to painting, sometimes depicting landscapes but more often birds, animals, and plants in a distinctive ink style all his own. His painting *Fish and Rocks* (fig. 19.6) illustrates his unique style.

CALLIGRAPHY

The Chinese have long believed that the flexible brush is the perfect means to express one's inner spirit. Thus calligraphy with ink on paper or silk, whether by scholars, poets, monks, or government leaders, is often considered the highest form of art. Great masterworks from earlier periods such as the Tang dynasty were used as models for the proper style and proportion of the more than fifty thousand Chinese characters. There were also a number of different scripts to choose from. Ancient seal script, used even today for carving seals (or "chops"), conveys an archaic flavor, as does clerical script, developed in the Han Dynasty by clerks to record government documents. Calligraphy, however, could also be written in regular (printed), running (more rapid), or cursive (with strokes joined together) script, not unlike our own choices in English—for example, most of us do not write the small letter *a* in this printed form, but in more rapid pencil or pen movement. Similarly, Chinese calligraphers usually preferred less formal and more dramatic styles of brushwork to regular script. Some masters, however, combined scripts, such as the painter-poet-calligrapher ZHENG XIE [CHENG SHEE-EH] (1693–1765), who enjoyed mixing clerical, regular, running, and cursive scripts. Zheng's eight-line verse (fig. 19.7) reflects the nostalgia for country life felt by the official who must live and work in the city.

A COUNTRY TEMPLE

Outside the city, where is the foliage most lush?
By the decorated walls where the setting sunlight filters
  through the pine forest.
A single note comes from the pure sounding-stone, the
  sky seems like water;
On the evening river, the reflection of the moon is like
  frost.
The monks are calm at this remote place, and I often visit,
Floating like a cloud from my government office; I am
  pained when I must depart.
On the trellis are grapes like ten thousand pearls:
The autumn wind must have remembered that this old
  man loves to eat them.

FIGURE 19.6   Pa-ta-shan-jen (Chu Ta), 1626–1705, *Fish and Rocks*, hanging scroll, ink on paper, 53 × 23 7/8″ (134.6 × 60.6 cm), Metropolitan Museum of Art, NY, Bequest of John M. Crawford, Jr., 1988 (1988. 363.137) Photograph © 1995 The Metropolitan Museum of Art, NY. The fish swim around animistic rocks that seem to float in space, resembling the heads of rabbits. The artist hides his skill with seemingly child-like strokes of the brush, but the result is hauntingly powerful as well as whimsical.

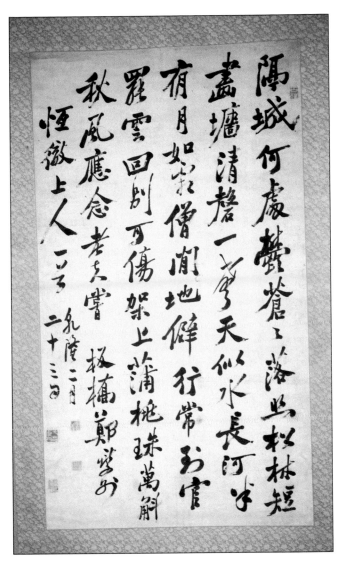

FIGURE 19.7   Zheng Xie, *A Country Temple*, Qing Dynasty, ca. 1740, hanging scroll, ink on paper, 62 × 34 3/4″ (162.3 × 88.2 cm), Hsiao Hua Collection. Chinese is written in columns from top to bottom and then right to left, so this poem begins in the upper right and ends with the seals on the lower left.

Chinese Scholars' Rocks   In early times, prized rocks were placed in the garden, but by the Song dynasty, favored rocks were also taken into a scholar's study. These most beautiful of rocks served as objects of contemplation. Like landscape paintings, the scholars' rocks reflected the universe in microcosm, providing the scholar with a stimulus to meditation on nature while remaining in the confines of his study. The rocks' abstract qualities appealed to Chinese scholar aesthetes, much in the way that abstract sculpture might appeal to a Western aesthete today. (See fig. 19.8).

The rocks range in size from miniatures of a few inches high to larger than human size, with the commonest being small enough to place on a desk or table. Typically made of limestone, they are often found in caves that have been eroded by underground streams. Scholars' rocks differ from garden rocks in exhibiting a higher degree of complex interior surfaces. They are also placed on carved wooden stands that elevate them and complement their unique forms. The literati class that collected beautiful and interesting rock specimens for their studies believed that Nature engaged in creating art by producing such strange and evocative forms.

ARCHITECTURE: CITY PLANNING

Architecture in traditional China signified the connection between the rule of the emperor and the order of the universe. Cities were constructed on a grid system, surrounded by walls, which represented stability. The ruler's palace was generally situated at the north end, looking south, so the emperor's back was turned against the north from which evil (including the Mongol invaders) was always believed to come, and so his gaze overlooked and protected the people, who lived in the city's southern half. The emperor looked down on the city just as the Pole Star,

from its permanent position in the north, looks down on the cosmos. So long as the emperor fulfilled his function as the Son of Heaven, peace and harmony, it was believed, would be enjoyed by all.

Under the rule of the Yongle Emperor (reigned 1402–24), present-day Beijing was reconstructed as the imperial capital (fig. 19.9). Following traditional architectural plans, the principal buildings and gates of the government district, called the Imperial City, faced south, and almost all structures were arranged in a gridded square (fig. 19.10). The palace enclosure where the emperor and his court lived, called the Forbidden City, was approached through a series of gates: The Gate of Heavenly Peace (called Tiananmen) is first, then the Noon Gate, which opens into a giant courtyard. Next, the Meridian Gate leads into the city's walled enclosure and opens out onto the first spacious courtyard, which has a waterway with five arched marble bridges. These bridges represent the five Confucian relationships as well as the five virtues (see Chapter 8). Past the bridges, high on a marble platform, stands the Gate of Supreme Harmony. Beyond the gate is the largest courtyard with three ceremonial halls. The most important is the Hall of Supreme Harmony, used for the emperor's audiences and special ceremonies.

With its series of interlocking gates and courtyards, its walled-in sections within larger walled-in areas, Beijing gives the visitor a different experience from Western cityscapes, which have open vistas with numerous opportunities to see up and down thoroughfares. An analogy can be made by comparing a Western landscape painting, which is seen in totality from a fixed perspective, to a Chinese landscape hand scroll, which must be viewed section by section as it is unrolled. In Chinese architecture and in such scrolls, the viewer experiences a series of discrete visual incidents, which only cumulatively provide an impression of totality.

FIGURE 19.8 *Chinese Scholar's Rock.* Legend has it that during the Ming dynasty the only Lingbis found were green rather than black.

FIGURE 19.9 The Forbidden City, Beijing seen from the north.

Then & Now

HONG KONG

The history of Hong Kong, the island city just off the coast of the Chinese mainland, has long been important to China's relations with the West. In the nineteenth century, the West began to pursue colonial ambitions in Asia, and the emperors of the declining Qing dynasty were forced to make trade and territorial concessions to encroaching Western powers. Defeated by Great Britain in the Opium War (1840–42), China ceded Hong Kong to Britain by the Treaty of Nanking (Nanjing) in 1842. In a renegotiated settlement in 1898, Hong Kong, along with two other local Chinese territories, was "leased" to Britain until 1997, when control of the city reverted to China.

With one of the greatest deep-water harbors in the world, Hong Kong has always been a trading center, in part because the land is unsuitable for agriculture and lacks minerals and other natural resources. Since the 1960s, Hong Kong has developed one of the most successful economies in Asia, outperforming those of some Western countries, including Great Britain. As Hong Kong's economic value has increased, the city became a symbolic bone of contention between China and Britain. Although the countries share an interest in Hong Kong's stability and prosperity, they had contrasting visions of Hong Kong's purpose and management. For Britain, Hong Kong represented the crowning achievement of its global economic expansion. For China, Hong Kong stands as an economic catalyst for the rest of the country.

In 1984, an agreement between China and Britain called for the termination of British rule in Hong Kong while maintaining its capitalist economy and democratic governmental structure until 2047. Since 1997, with Hong Kong officially incorporated into the People's Republic of China, it ostensibly retains a social structure and democratic government elected by the people of Hong Kong. However, Beijing's control over the transitional governing council, and its increasing disregard for Hong Kong's democratic political culture, raise questions about the city's future as an engine of free economic enterprise. It remains to be seen whether, with its new political status, Hong Kong will sustain its economic vitality and global influence.

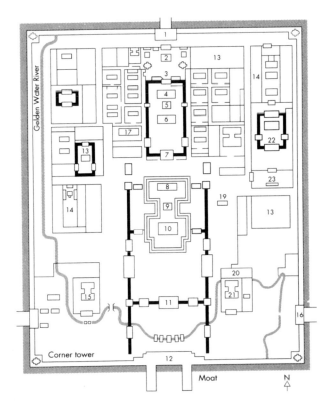

FIGURE 19.10 Plan of the Imperial Palace, Beijing. Outside the palace enclosure is Tiananmen Square. 1 Gate of Divine Pride; 2 Pavilion of Earthly Peace; 3 Imperial Garden; 4 Palace of Earthly Tranquillity; 5 Hall of Union; 6 Palace of Heavenly Purity; 7 Gate of Heavenly Purity; 8 Hall of the Preservation of Harmony; 9 Hall of Perfect Harmony; 10 Hall of Supreme Harmony; 11 Gate of Supreme Harmony, 12 Meridian Gate; 13 Kitchens; 14 Gardens; 15 Former Imperial Printing House; 16 Flower Gate; 17 Palace of the Culture of the Mind; 18 Hall of the Worship of the Ancestors; 19 Pavilion of Arrows; 20 Imperial Library; 21 Palace of Culture; 22 Palace of Peace and Longevity; 23 Nine Dragon Screen.

Critical Thinking

FENG SHUI

When the British handed Hong Kong over to the Chinese in 1997, the new Chinese governor of the province, Tung Chee-hwa, had to select a site for his offices. In order to do so, he brought with him a Feng Shui (Fung-SHWAY) master, who advised him regarding the appropriateness of various prospective office locations. Feng Shui, which combines the Chinese words for "wind" and "water," is the Chinese art of harmonizing people and their environment. With its origins in Daoism and a three-thousand-year-old heritage, Feng Shui addresses the design and layout of cities and villages as well as houses and public buildings to achieve harmony with the environment.

Feng Shui is grounded in the idea that influences in the natural environment affect people's fortunes. In deciding where to build a temple or a home, or where to situate a grave, the topography of terrain, its hills and fields and bodies of water, and their relationships to each other are analyzed. Such considerations and calculations can be quite complex; hence the need for an expert geomancer with the requisite esoteric knowledge.

Feng Shui, though not so popular among young Chinese in the People's Republic, is still used in rural China, Hong Kong, Taiwan, Singapore, and Malaysia, and it has practitioners in Japan and Korea as well. One example of a building purportedly built with Feng Shui in mind is the Citigroup building in Hong Kong, which was designed with a curved façade to shield it from and deflect negative elements emanating from a neighboring Bank of China building. Another is the Cheonk Kung Tower, which is a "green" building inside and built with its major entrance facing east because the Feng Shui master, who advised the Li Ka Shing family who own it, believed it would have a favorable effect on their wealth and fortune.

What do you think of the idea of Feng Shui and the beliefs associated with it? To what extent do you agree that it is important to consider the placement of a home, tomb, or building with respect to its natural environment? And how does this concept of Feng Shui compare with the principles guiding the work of an architect such as Frank Lloyd Wright, especially in the location of homes that he designed?

In recent years, the practice of Feng Shui has become quite popular in the West. Decisions in the West, however, about where to build offices and houses, may need to take into account historical factors or practical environmental considerations. How important do you think these other factors are, and why?

LITERATURE

Traditional Poetry. Much of the poetry written during the Ming dynasty was used in other art forms such as drama, fiction, music, and painting. The calligraphy at the upper left of Shen Zhou's *Poet on a Mountaintop* (fig. 19.4) is, in fact, a poem. Shen Zhou was not only an accomplished painter but a fine poet and, like many of his fellow artists of the Yuan and Ming dynasties, he was skilled at many of the literati arts, which include music, seal carving, and prose essays. Shen Zhou's poem reads:

> White clouds like a belt encircle the mountain's waist
> A stone ledge flying in space and the far thin road.
> I lean alone on my bramble staff and gazing contented into
> space
> Wish the sounding torrent would answer your flute.

Not only does the poem express an affinity for nature, it contrasts the speaker's isolation with the need for companionship, the sound of the flute announcing the arrival of a companion along the "far thin road" shrouded in mist. The comparison of the fog to a belt, furthermore, transforms the landscape into human terms. Removing the belt of clouds would cause the landscape's robe to fall open and reveal its natural beauty to the poet's eye, offering the promise of human intimacy—which the image on its own does not even begin to suggest.

Yuan Hong-dao. Shen Zhou's poem continues a long tradition of Chinese poetry and fits comfortably within it. But by the late Ming dynasty, poetry began to change. The finest poet of the era was Yuan Hong-dao (1568–1610), who wrote, "The good painter learns from things, not from other painters. The good philosopher learns from his mind, not from some doctrine. The good poet learns from the panoply of images, not from writers of the past." Yuan served, as did so many literati, as an official, but he semihumorously complained that "Superiors visit you like gathering clouds, travelers stop by like drops of rain, papers pile up like mountains, and oceans of taxes in cash or grain must be collected; if you work and write morning and night, you still can't keep up with all of it! Misery, misery!" Nevertheless Yuan was able to write a number of poems as well as prose on subjects as unusual as spider fights, before his death at the age of forty-two. His brother Yuan Zhong-dao was also an excellent poet, and he too sometimes chose unusual subjects for his verse: One poem, for example, is about keeping a pet rooster.

The Chinese poetry tradition continued into the Qing dyasty, including among the Manchus who now ruled the country. Almost all of the emperors themselves were poets, and some wrote vast quantities. For example, over 42,000 poems have been attributed to the emperor Qianlong (1736–96). However, prose fiction, focusing on the lives of merchants, servants, and petty officials, was the most innovative literary development of the Qing dynasty.

Cao Xueqin's Dream of the Red Chamber. The most important work of Chinese literature written in the eighteenth century, considered by some the greatest Chinese novel, is *The Dream of the Red Chamber* by CAO XUE-QIN [TSAO SOOEH-CHIN] (1715–63). The novel is enormous, with 120 chapters. The "red chamber" is where the female characters live; the "dream" refers to the foretelling of the fates of these characters.

The Dream of the Red Chamber has been read as a story about the decline of a family, an allegory of Buddhist attitudes toward the world, and an autobiographical fiction adhering closely to the life of its author. It has also been considered a love story, a search for identity, and a quest for understanding the purpose of human existence. The book can be seen as a reflection of the many elements of mid-Qing elite life, including politics and religion, economics and aesthetics, love and family. Blending realism with dream and fantasy, *The Dream of the Red Chamber* has been hailed as one of the most revealing works ever written about Chinese civilization.

Modern Chinese Poetry. Although fiction and drama have long been a part of Chinese literary tradition, pride of place has always been accorded to poetry. Even when poets swerved away from refined classical Chinese and began to write in the modern vernacular, poetry continued to command more respect than other literary genres. While frequently working within ancient Chinese traditions, modern Chinese poets have also experimented with free verse and other styles and forms that emerged in Europe during the nineteenth and twentieth centuries. Without directly imitating the literature of the Western world, modern Chinese writers absorbed Western influences to express contemporary Chinese cultural experiences, including the political circumstances of the age. Chairman MAO ZEDONG [ZAY-DUNG] (1893–1976), the father of Chinese communism, wrote a number of poems celebrating the revolutionary ideal. Also political, but in direct opposition to the established order of contemporary China, the poems of BEI DAO [BAY DOW] (b. 1949) repudiate the oppressiveness of a society that, if it does not execute its dissenters, jails them. The Tiananmen Square massacre of 1989 gives urgent meaning to the sentiments expressed in the poems by Bei and other contemporary

Chinese poets, who sometimes feel lost between old traditions and new realities.

I'M FOREVER A STRANGER

I'm forever a stranger
to this world.
I don't understand its language.
It doesn't understand my silence.
As if we'd met in a mirror,
a shadow of contempt
is all we exchange.
I'm forever a stranger
to myself.
Afraid of the dark,
I block with my body
the only light.
My only lover is my shadow,
my only enemy my heart.

MUSIC

Chinese Theater Music. From the fourteenth through the seventeenth centuries, Chinese music was largely associated with drama, especially with a form of musical drama known as ***Hsi-wen,*** which included musical arias or lyrical songs, spoken dialogue, dance, and mime—all with instrumental accompaniment. Two different styles developed. There was a northern style, ***'ei-chu,*** in which a pearshaped lute (*pipa*) was the primary instrument for accompaniment, and singing was performed by one individual. In the southern style, ***ti,*** the transverse flute (*dizi*) was the primary instrument for accompaniment and nearly all the characters sang.

During the 1500s, these two styles of musical drama merged in the Kun opera, which incorporated elaborate poetic texts and intricate plots with numerous scenes. Although Kun opera became a more or less elitist form of musical drama owing to its intricacy and complexity, it did have an influence on more popular forms of musical drama that emerged in later centuries, including the Beijing opera, a nineteenth-century development.

Beijing Opera. Beijing opera has become one of the most popular musical forms of the twentieth century. Incorporating traditional styles of acting absorbed from the history of Chinese drama, Beijing opera possesses a distinctive liveliness, with colorful, fast-paced scenes based on ancient Chinese myths, legends, and fables.

The dramatic action of Beijing opera is highly stylized. There are, for example, twenty-six distinct ways to laugh and thirty-nine specific ways to manipulate the twenty different types of beards. The performers' roles are divided into four major categories: male (**sheng**), female (**dan**), painted male face (**jing**), and clown (**chou**). The male and female roles, all performed by men, are subdivided into roles for old men

Connections

KANGXI AND QIANLONG: CHINESE RULERS, WRITERS, AND SCHOLARS

Two of the most important Chinese emperors, KANGXI [KANNG-shi] (1661–1722) and QIANLONG [SHIEN- lahng] (1736–95), reigned during the Qing dynasty (1644–1911). Both were members of the Manchu, a people from Manchuria, who had been given important court responsibilities under the Ming emperors (1368–1644), especially toward the end of Ming rule, when Manchu rulers supplanted them. Manchu rulers preserved their own cultural identity by outlawing intermarriage with Chinese and by forbidding the Chinese to travel to Manchuria or to learn the Manchus' language.

The emperor Kangxi was a strong ruler, who helped the Manchus consolidate their power early in the Qing dynasty. He expanded the Qing empire, absorbing the island of Taiwan, conquering nomadic peoples of Mongolia and central China, and establishing a protectorate in Tibet. A voracious reader, Kangxi was also a poet, and an advocate of the Confucian classics, whose teachings he incorporated into his political policies. His agricultural program of flood control, for example, was based on Confucian precepts. In addition, he was an avid supporter of Confucian schools.

Kangxi's grandson, Qianlong, continued his grandfather's expansion of the empire into Turkestan and made Vietnam, Burma, and Nepal vassal states. Like Kangzi, Qianlong was well versed in scholarship. In addition to being a more prolific poet than his grandfather (he is reputed to have composed 100,000 poems), Qianlong was a connoisseur of painting and calligraphy. Under his reign, China prospered, remaining a well-organized, efficient, and extremely wealthy country.

and roles without beards for young men, including the flirtatious female and the lady of propriety (fig. 19.11).

The music for Beijing opera is performed by an orchestra arranged in two parts: a percussion section composed of gongs and drums, and a melodic section of strings and wind instruments. The percussion instruments play introductory music prior to the characters' entrances; they also play between the singing and acting. The melodic instruments accompany the singing. Although the melodies for the Beijing opera arias derive from traditional music, there is often originality in their embellishment.

With the founding of the Communist People's Republic of China in 1949, Chinese music was directed toward social revolutionary purposes. Mao Zedong conscripted all the arts, remarking that they "operate as powerful weapons in unifying and educating the people and for attacking and destroying the enemy." Mao introduced two influential artistic directives: (1) a return to folk tradition and (2) an emphasis on political ideals and content in music. From 1966 to 1969, at the height of the Cultural Revolution, the only opera performances permitted in

FIGURE 19.11   An actor from the Beijing opera performing as the heroine Mu Guiying, a popular character who comes from the Yang family of the eleventh century. She is the most important of the women generals of the family—women who fought their enemies from the north.

Table 19–1   CHINESE ARTS

Landscape painting: Shen Zhou

Calligraphy: Zheng Xie

City planning: The Forbidden City

Theater music: Beijing Opera

Fiction: *The Dream of the Red Chamber*

Poetry: Bei Dao

Cross Currents

THE PIPA AND THE GUITAR

The pipa is a four-stringed lute of middle-eastern origin with a pear-shaped body of different sizes and which included differing numbers of frets, as few as 10 and as many as 30. The pipa's frets are made of wood, ivory, or jade and its strings are made of silk. The pipa's history is a long one, being mentioned in texts dating from the Han dynasty (206 B.C.E.–220 C.E.). Since the Tang dynasty, the pipa has been among the most popular of Chinese musical instruments, maintaining its appeal as both a chamber instrument and as a solo instrument.

The popularity of the pipa can be compared to that of the Spanish or classical guitar. Both instruments are plucked with the fingernails, with the pipa producing a sound resembling that of a harpsichord. They have three open-string tunings in common: A, D, and E. And performers on the two instruments share some plucking techniques, including rapidly wheeling the fingers of the right hand over a string to create a sustained tremolo effect.

Contemporary professional players of the pipa perform both traditional music and modern compositions written for the instrument. They also play music of other cultures, including western music, both popular and classical. The contemporary performers Wu Man and Liu Fang play pieces that embrace a variety of world music, including the Indian music of Ravi Shankar, as well as music from Korea, Japan, Ethiopia, Europe, and the United States. Both of these artists also play traditional Chinese music, such as "Dance of the Yi People," a popular favorite often required by conservatory juries of prospective students.

Another Chinese professional musician, Xuefei Yang, a classical guitarist, plays traditional Western classical guitar repertoire and also makes her own arrangements for guitar of traditional Chinese music as well as contemporary music of Chinese composers. A recent album, Si Ji, which translates as "Four Seasons," is an example of this kind of musical cross current. Sharon Isbin, still another contemporary classical guitarist, has played in concert and has recorded a guitar concerto by the contemporary Chinese composer Tan Dun. In her live and recorded performances of this music, she has, in certain moments, attempted to imitate the sound of the pipa with her guitar, yet another example of how these two stringed instruments, one of ancient Chinese lineage, and the other developing its repertory in nineteenth-century Spain, continue to influence each other.

FIGURE 19.12 Wu Man playing the Chinese pipa during a performance of "Night Banquet," directed by Cher Shi-Zheng, Lincoln Center Festival, LaGuardia Concert Hall, NY. Photograph © 2002 Linda Vartoogian/FrontRowPhotos. All Rights Reserved. Since her move to the United States, in 1990, Ms. Wu has greatly expanded her repertory and knowledge of world music.

Cultural Impact

China's impact on the rest of the world continues to be felt in many ways. Politically, China has developed its own version of Marxist-Leninist communism. Economically, it has become a major player on the international scene, having joined the World Trade Organization and established trade relationships with a number of important African, Asian, and European countries.

Chinese cultural influence has extended into Asian countries, including Korea and Vietnam. Korean ceramics owe a debt to China's long tradition of ceramic ware, having been influenced especially by the ceramic artisans of the Tang, Song, and Ming dynasties. The impact of China on Vietnam has been both cultural and political. Well into the eighteenth century, the most important Vietnamese poetry, including the country's epic, *The Tale of Kieu,* existed primarily in Chinese. Politically, modern Vietnam inherited Chinese communism. In addition, both Vietnam and Korea exhibit the influence of Confucianism and Taoism, although Buddhism is a stronger religious presence in Vietman.

The impact of the Chinese aesthetic ideal has been felt in the West as well, particularly in interior design and decor, with modern and contemporary architects and interior designers following Chinese aesthetic principles of simplicity, balance, elegance, and harmony. Chinese furniture of the Ming dynasty continues to be popular in Western countries, as do various period styles of ceramic ware. In the earlier twentieth century, Chinese poetry, with its emphasis on images rather than discursiveness, influenced American poets such as Ezra Pound, T. S. Eliot, and William Carlos Williams.

China were eight revolutionary works deemed pure of the taint of so-called bourgeois ideas and influences.

Music played an important role throughout the Cultural Revolution in extolling the glories of China and providing ceremonial background to public events. One early revolutionary song has been adapted for several purposes. "East Is Red" was written by a peasant in 1946 and performed by three thousand workers, students, and soldiers in 1964 to celebrate the fifteenth anniversary of the Proletarian Republic of China. This same song played as background music in radio broadcasts of the time and as a wake-up call—from loudspeakers in the streets—every morning. China's best known composer, XIAN XING-HAI (SHEE-EN SHINH-he) (1905–40), wrote *Yellow River Cantata,* which continued the persistent theme of revolutionary music by combining folk songs that extolled the beauty of China and memorialized the hardships of the people.

In the late twentieth and early twenty-first centuries, the necessity for such strict adherence to political ideology for musical composition and performance has diminished. Although revolutionary themes dominate many modern Chinese musical works, Western influences, instruments, and performance practices are now apparent.

KEY TERMS

literati	*'ei-chu*	sheng	chou
wet-brush technique	*ti*	dan	pipa
Hsi-wen	*Ching-hsi*	jing	feng shui

www. WEBSITES FOR FURTHER STUDY

http://www-chaos.umd.edu/history/imperial3.html
(An article that summarizes the Mongol and Ming dynasties ruling in China.)

http://www.chinats.com/beijing/index.html
(The Forbidden City, Beijing, China.)

http://www.sinologic.com/literature.html
(A page devoted to the poetry of Bei Dao and a brief biography.)

READINGS

YUAN HONG-DAO

The 'Slowly, Slowly' Poem, playfully inscribed on a wall

It was a custom of Chinese poets occasionally to inscribe their poems on walls where passersby might enjoy them. Here the poet begins with a bittersweet commentary on nature and his own life, and he ends with a philosophical sense of the alternations of the world.

The bright moon slowly, slowly rises,
The green mountains slowly, slowly descend.
The flowering branches slowly, slowly redden,
The spring colors slowly, slowly fade.
My salary slowly, slowly increases,
My teeth slowly, slowly fall out.
My lover's waist slowly, slowly expands,
My complexion slowly, slowly ages.

We are low in society in the days of our greatest health,
Our pleasure comes when we are no longer young.
The Goddess of Good Luck and the Dark Lady of Bad
    Luck
Are with us every step we take.
Even heaven and earth are imperfect
And human society is full of ups and downs.

Where do we look for real happiness?
—Bow humbly, and ask the Master of Taoist Arts.

YUAN ZHONG-DAO

Keeping a Pet Rooster

The less famous brother of Yuan Hong-dao, Zhong-dao was also a fine poet, as this unusual verse attests.

I have a friend in the capital
Who has made me a gift of a pet rooster.
He has sharp spurs, a high comb,

And colorful markings—a fine appearance!
He beats his wings and crows out loud,
Flies over the walls and into my room.
He sheds feathers on the bookcase
And leaves scratches all over my zither.
Suddenly I hear the sound of a knife being sharpened;
Tears come into my eyes, and I sigh,
"I can do without the taste of fowl,
But it's a matter of life and death for him!"
I throw down my book, run to the kitchen,
And hold back my servant, with scolding and curses.
The rooster is still terrified:
He cowers in a dark corner of the room.
Chirping, chirping—the bird in the cage
Wants to fly away, and has wings.
Glistening, glistening—the fish in the net
Plunges back in the water as soon as there's a chance.
I want to let the rooster go
But he'll never escape the butcher's knife.
The best thing to do is to keep him
And let him stay always on his favorite perch.
Don't say it's another mouth to feed—
A few kernels of grain in a bowl—
        How much is that to spare?

CAO XUEQIN

from *The Dream of the Red Chamber*

The first great example of realistic fiction produced in China, The Dream of the Red Chamber is the ancestor of the family saga and depicts with psychological realism and sociological accuracy a wide range of characters in a richly textured social world. The following passage opens the work.

Chapter One

In which Chen Shih-yin meets the Stone of Spiritual Understanding and Chia Yu-tsun encounters a maid of unusual discernment

WHEN the Goddess Nügua undertook to repair the Dome of Heaven, she fashioned at the Great Mythical Mountain under the Nonesuch Bluff 36,501 pieces of stone, each 120 feet high and 240 feet around. Of these she used only 36,500 and left the remaining piece in the shadow of the

Green Meadows Peak. However, the divine hands of Nügua had touched off a spark of life in the Stone and endowed it with supernatural powers. It was able to come and go as it pleased and change its size and form at will. But it was not happy because it alone had been rejected by the Goddess, and it was given to sighing over its ill fortune.

As it was thus bemoaning its fate one day, it saw coming toward it a Buddhist monk and a Taoist priest, both of uncommon appearance. They were talking and laughing and, when they reached the shadow of the Peak, they sat down by the side of the Stone and continued their conversation. At first they talked about cloud-wrapped mountains and mistcovered seas and the mysteries of immortal life, but presently they changed the topic of their conversation and spoke of the wealth and luxury and the good things of life in the Red Dust. This stirred the earthly strain in the Stone and aroused in it a desire to experience for itself the pleasures of mortal life. Therefore, it addressed the monk and the priest thus:

"Venerable sirs, forgive me for intruding. I could not help overhearing your conversation and I should like very much to have a taste of the pleasures of the Red Dust of which you spoke. Though I am crude in substance, I am not without some degree of understanding or a sense of gratitude. If you, venerable sirs, would be kind enough to take me for a turn in the Red Dust and let me enjoy for a few years its pleasures and luxuries, I shall be grateful to you for eons to come."

"It is true that the Red Dust has its joys," the two immortals answered with an indulgent smile, "but they are evanescent and illusory. Moreover, there every happiness is spoiled by a certain lack, and all good things are poisoned by the envy and covetousness of other men, so that in the end you will find the pleasure outweighed by sorrow and sadness. We do not advise such a venture."

But the fire of earthly desires, once kindled, could not easily be extinguished. The Stone ignored the warning of the immortals and continued to importune them, until the Buddhist monk said to his companion with a sigh, "We have here another instance of Quiescence giving way to Activity and Non-Existence yielding to Existence." Then turning to the Stone, he said, "We shall take you for a turn in the Red Dust if you insist, but don't blame us if you do not find it to your liking."

"Of course not, of course not," the Stone assured them eagerly.

Then the monk said, "Though you are endowed with some degree of understanding, your substance needs improvement. If we take you into the world the way you are, you will be kicked about and cursed like any ordinary stumbling block. How would you like to be transformed into a substance of quality for your sojourn in the Red Dust and then be restored to your original self afterward?"

The Stone agreed, and thereupon the monk exercised the Infinite power of the Law and transformed the Stone into a piece of pure translucent jade, oval in shape and about the size of a pendant. The monk held it on his palm and smiled as he said, "You will be treasured now as a precious object, but you still lack real distinguishing marks. A few characters must be engraved upon you so that everyone who sees you will recognise you as something unique. Only then shall we take you down to some prosperous land, where you will enjoy the advantages of a noble and cultured family and all the pleasures that wealth and position can bring."

The Stone was overjoyed on hearing this and asked what characters were to be engraved upon it and where it was to be taken, but the monk only smiled and said, "Don't ask what and where now; you will know when the time comes." So saying, he tucked the Stone in his sleeve and disappeared with the priest to we know not where.

Nor do we know how many generations or epochs it was afterward that the Taoist of the Great Void passed by the Great Mythical Mountain, the Nonesuch Bluff, and the Green Meadows Peak and came upon the Stone, now restored to its original form and substance. Engraved on it was a long, long story. The Taoist read it from beginning to end and found that it was the self-same Stone that was first carried into the Red Dust and then guided to the Other Shore by the Buddhist of Infinite Space and the Taoist of Boundless Time. The story was that of the Stone itself. The land of its descent, the place of its incarnation, the rise and fall of fortunes, the joys and sorrows of reunion and separation—all these were recorded in detail, together with the trivial affairs of the family, the delicate sentiments of the maidens' chambers, and a number of poems and conundrums which one usually finds in such stories.

LU XUN

Lu Xun (1881–1906) is considered the finest Chinese writer of his generation. Lu Xun, pen name of Zhou Shuren, was born to a family of scholar-administrators in southeast China and received a traditional Confucian classical education, later after spending some years in Japan, returning to China to work in the Ministry of Education. He is best known as a novelist, essayist, and short story writer. In his brief sketch, "A Small Incident" Lu Xun describes a scene whose reverberations echo with personal questions of ethics and humanity.

A Small Incident

Six years have slipped by since I came from the country to the capital. During that time the number of so-called affairs of state I have witnessed or heard about is far from small, but none of them made much impression. If asked to define their influence on me, I can only say they made my bad temper worse. Frankly speaking, they taught me to take a poorer view of people every day.

One small incident, however, which struck me as significant and jolted me out of my irritability, remains fixed even now in my memory.

It was the winter of 1917, a strong north wind was blustering, but the exigencies of earning my living forced me to be up and out early. I met scarcely a soul on the road, but eventually managed to hire a rickshaw to take me to S— Gate. Presently the wind dropped a little, having blown away the drifts of dust on the road to leave a clean broad highway, and the rickshaw man quickened his pace. We were just approaching S— Gate when we knocked into someone who slowly toppled over.

It was a grey-haired woman in ragged clothes. She had stepped out abruptly from the roadside in front of us, and although the rickshaw man had swerved, her tattered padded waistcoat, unbuttoned and billowing in the wind, had caught on the shaft. Luckily the rickshaw man had slowed down, otherwise she would certainly have had a bad fall and it might have been a serious accident.

She huddled there on the ground, and the rickshaw man stopped. As I did not believe the old woman was hurt and as no one else had seen us, I thought this halt of his uncalled for, liable to land him in trouble and hold me up.

"It's all right," I said. "Go on."

He paid no attention—he may not have heard—but set down the shafts, took the old woman's arm and gently helped her up.

"Are you all right?" he asked.

"I hurt myself falling."

I thought: I saw how slowly you fell, how could you be hurt? Putting on an act like this is simply disgusting. The rickshaw man asked for trouble, and now he's got it. He'll have to find his own way out.

But the rickshaw man did not hesitate for a minute after hearing the old woman's answer. Still holding her arm, he helped her slowly forward. Rather puzzled by this I looked ahead and saw a police-station. Because of the high wind, there was no one outside. It was there that the rickshaw man was taking the old woman.

Suddenly I had the strange sensation that his dusty retreating figure had in that instant grown larger. Indeed, the further he walked the larger he loomed, until I had to look up to him. At the same time he seemed gradually to be exerting a pressure on me which threatened to overpower the small self hidden under my fur-lined gown.

Almost paralysed at that juncture I sat there motionless, my mind a blank, until a policeman came out. Then I got down from the rickshaw.

The policeman came up to me and said. "Get another rickshaw. He can't take you any further."

On the spur of the moment I pulled a handful of coppers from my coat pocket and handed them to the policeman. "Please give him this," I said.

The wind had dropped completely, but the road was still quiet. As I walked along thinking, I hardly dared to think about myself. Quite apart from what had happened earlier, what had I meant by that handful of coppers? Was it a reward? Who was I to judge the rickshaw man? I could give myself no answer.

Even now, this incident keeps coming back to me. It keeps distressing me and makes me try to think about myself. The politics and the fighting of those years have slipped my mind as completely as the classics I read as a child. Yet this small incident keeps coming back to me, often more vivid than in actual life, teaching me shame, spurring me on to reform, and imbuing me with fresh courage and fresh hope.

BEI DAO

Bei Dao (b. 1949) is one of China's most gifted and controversial poets to emerge during the last half of the twentieth century. His poetry reflects and criticizes China's Cultural Revolution of the 1960s and 1970s. "Declaration" is one of his best known and highly regarded poems.

Declaration[1]

For *Yu Luoke*

Perhaps the final hour is come
I have left no testament
Only a pen, for my mother
I am no hero
In an age without heroes   5
I just want to be a man

[1]Translated by Bonnie S. McDougall.

The still horizon
Divides the ranks of the living and the dead
I can only choose the sky
I will not kneel on the ground   10
Allowing the executioners to look tall
The better to obstruct the wind of freedom

From the star-like bullet holes shall flow
A blood-red dawn.

CHAPTER 20

Japanese Culture
after the Fifteenth Century

Katsushika Hokusai, *The Great Wave of Kanagawa*, from the series *Thirty-Six Views of Mount Fuji*, Tokugawa period, ca. 1831, color woodblock print, $9\frac{7}{8} \times 14\frac{5}{8}''$ (25.5 × 37.1 cm). Private Collection, Art Resource, NY.

Japan in 1853, when Commodore Perry reopened trade with the West.

CHAPTER OVERVIEW

LATER JAPANESE CULTURE

Japan carefully gleans from the West what will make it an international power, while maintaining its own cultural identity

LATER JAPANESE CULTURE

Toward the end of over a century of feudal warfare, known as the Warring States period (1477–1600), TOKUGAWA IEYASU [TOH-KOO-GAH-WA HYEH-YAH-SOO] (1542–1616) became the **shogun,** or military ruler, of a newly unified Japan. The Tokugawa family ruled the country from 1600 until 1868, retaining emperors as cultural and symbolic figures in Kyoto while making Edo (present-day Tokyo) the effective capital of the country. Under Confucian influence, society was ordered into classes of **samurai** (who during an age of peace became government officials), farmers, artisans, and merchants, who theoretically had the lowest status but who rose in power and importance in this period. The Tokugawa **shogunate** both unified the country and isolated it from the outside world. Only the Dutch, relegated to a small island off Nagasaki, were permitted to trade with Japanese merchants. It was through Dutch traders that Japan was apprised of developments in the West, but the government did its best to preserve Japan's distinctive national culture and identity almost immune to outside influence.

After the American military expedition led by Commodore Perry forced the Tokugawa regime to open its trade doors in the 1850s, Japan began to look to the West, instead of to China, in its effort to transform itself into a modern nation-state. In 1868, Japan returned to rule by an emperor and a parliament, inaugurating a period known as the Meiji era (1868–1912), during which it enjoyed rapid economic development and a growth in national power. Japan adopted a constitution modeled on that of Germany; it eliminated the power of the shogunate, the samurai, and their local vassals; and it began programs of industrialization and universal education.

Japan also began to exert its influence throughout the western Pacific. Through its victory in the war with China of 1894–95, it acquired the island of Taiwan (then called Formosa) and gained influence over Korea. After its triumph in the Russo-Japanese War (1904–5) and its alliance with the victorious nations in World War I, Japan colonized Korea and parts of the Chinese mainland. When Japan had to face the consequences of its defeat after World War II, it turned to economic rather than military means to achieve international power and influence.

THE SHINTO REVIVAL

With the rise of the Tokugawa dynasty, Shinto was resurrected as a state religion. **Shinto,** which literally means "the way of the gods," is a belief system indigenous to Japan; it involves rituals and veneration of local deities, known as *kami*. In its most general sense, Shinto is a "religion" of Japanese patriotism. Less a system of doctrines than a reverential attitude toward things Japanese, Shinto emphasizes the beauty of the Japanese landscape, especially its mountain regions, and views the Japanese land and people as superior to all others.

Accompanying the revival of Shinto was the rise of the feudal knight, or samurai, who was idealized as a native hero. Much like the medieval knight of Christendom, the samurai was held to a strict code of conduct that emphasized loyalty, self-sacrifice, and honor. The rejuvenation of Shinto and of the samurai reflected an intense Japanese ethnocentrism and contributed to the isolationism of the Tokugawa dynasty.

LANDSCAPE PAINTING

The respect for the land that distinguishes the Shinto religion, combined with literati and Zen Chinese **ink-style painting** traditions, were developed in the landscape painting of the Muromachi period (1392–1568), which shows reverence for the grace and grandeur of nature and the humble place of human beings within it. Japanese painting suggests less a naturalistically rendered scene than an extension of unseen vistas beyond the explicitly depicted view. This pictorial tradition characterizes the Zen ideal of "capturing the principle of things as they move on."

Sesshu. Of Japanese Muromachi artists, the priest/painter SESSHU [SES-SHU] (1420–1506), more than anyone else, took Chinese ink-style painting and made it Japanese. In 1467–69, he traveled to China, where examples of landscape painting greatly influenced his work. However, Sesshu was to put a distinctive, Zenlike mark upon the tradition, writing on his return that he had learned more from viewing China's mountains than from its painters, and the Japanese monk-artists of the past were his true teachers.

His *Winter Landscape* (fig. 20.1) suggests the cold, brittle mood that the season inspires. Sesshu's bold brushstrokes and diagonal lines suggest the power of nature, as patches of blank paper signify snow and depict winter's starkness. In striking contrasts of black and white, the painting's bold angular outlines convey a chilly strength; the tiny figure travels through this dynamic scene as a pilgrim through the world.

Sesshu's landscape scrolls possess some of the boldness of his Chinese contemporary, Shen Zhou. Sesshu's work, however, emphasizes strong lines. His extended vistas are consistently subordinated to visual drama and experience, reflecting the Zen qualities of immediate apprehension and intuitive understanding.

In Sesshu's era, the shogunate favored Zen painting, just as they favored Zen monks as advisers and teachers. After 1600, however, the government turned to neo-Confucianists to be their advisers and teachers, and Zen became less dominant as a cultural force, although it was still significant. Instead of painter-monks, the leading Zen masters now created paintings and calligraphy for their followers, rather than to decorate palaces, mansions, and castles.

FIGURE 20.1 Sesshu, *Winter Landscape*, Japan, Ashikaga period, ca. 1470s, hanging scroll, ink and slight color on paper, $18\frac{1}{4} \times 11\frac{1}{2}''$ (46.3 × 29.3 cm), Tokyo National Museum, Tokyo. The harshness of the pictorial style, seen in this unsentimental representation of a wintry world, is characteristic of Sesshu.

Hakuin Ekaku and Zen. Hakuin Ekaku (1685–1769) is considered the most important Zen master of the past five hundred years. Hakuin reached a wide audience, from farmers to samurai, with his paintings and writings.

Hakuin was only seven or eight years old when his mother, a devout Buddhist, took him to a fire-and-brimstone sermon by a famous traveling preacher. Deeply affected by the sermon. Hakuin determined that in order to save his soul he would become a monk. He began his formal Buddhist training at the age of fourteen, learning classical Chinese texts and Zen practice. He continued his training for many years, practicing *zazen* (seated Zen meditation) and meditating on the *koan* (Zen riddle) in which the Zen master Joshu is asked, "Does a dog have the Buddha-nature?" Although all living beings possess this Buddha-nature, Joshu replies, "*Mu*" (literally, "no" or "nothing").

FIGURE 20.2 Hakuin Ekaku (1685–1768), *Meditating Daruma*, 49 × 21'' (126 × 55 cm), ink on paper, Chikusei Collection. The inscription comes from words attributed to Bodhidharma (Daruma), the first Zen Patriarch: "Pointing directly to the human heart/See your own nature and become Buddha."

This koan is traditionally the first that Zen monks begin meditating on trying to break though to their own Buddha-nature. Such koans, seemingly nonsensical questions and statements, are used by Zen masters to help their students achieve enlightenment by breaking through the barriers of rational dualistic thought. Students do not solve koans logically, but rather dissolve them by transcending their illogicality without providing a logical explanation. In understanding a koan, students bypass logic to arrive at an intuitive understanding.

Hakuin began having enlightenment experiences at the age of twenty-four and eventually established himself as a Zen master and teacher. He strove to convert complex Zen ideas into everyday form by writing folk songs and poems that could be easily understood, such as his *Song of Meditation*. Just as significantly, he painted images that conveyed Zen teachings clearly, simply, directly, and often humorously. Hakuin produced thousands of paintings and calligraphies and gave them to his monk and lay followers to help guide them on their own Zen journeys. In his painting of *Daruma Meditating* (fig. 20.2), Hakuin reveals the intense concentration of the first Zen patriarch with bold brushstrokes and a tight composition.

Hakuin also created his own Zen koan, "What is the sound of one hand clapping?" which has gained notoriety in contemporary Western society. Although Hakuin stressed the importance of traditional *zazen* and *koan* study, he also strongly believed Zen should not be an isolated, solitary experience, but should take place within every aspect of one's existence. He taught that meditation within the activities of daily life was just as important as seated silent meditation, and his influence continues to the present day.

WOODBLOCK PRINTS

During the seventeenth and eighteenth centuries, a style of art called **ukiyo-e** became especially associated with woodblock prints. *Ukiyo* means "floating world" in the Buddhist sense of "transient" or "evanescent," and *ukiyo-e* means "pictures of the floating world." The Impressionist painters of nineteenth-century Europe admired *ukiyo-e* prints enormously because, like them, Japanese artists were concerned with the world of everyday life, particularly of cultural enjoyments, such as dance, theater, music, games, and travel.

Prior to the seventeenth century, woodblock prints were used almost exclusively to make inexpensive Buddhist images for the public. With the increased interest in everyday life of the Tokugawa period, the subject matter of prints expanded, and the spread of literacy meant a wider public for woodblock-printed books, often with illustrations. Gradually, single-sheet prints of the "floating world" became popular, and new techniques for color reproduction were developed.

For the expanding public in big cities such as Edo (Tokyo) with an appetite for entertainment, color woodblock prints represented the world of human pleasures. Many eighteenth-century prints celebrated the beautiful courtesans of the Yoshiwara, the pleasure district of Tokyo; a significant percentage of prints were erotic. In the nineteenth century, artists also turned their attention to the Japanese landscape, providing fresh interpretations of nature.

Woodblock prints were closely linked with the world of the Kabuki theater, which had a large and enthusiastic audience. Prints of Kabuki actors were popular, as were posters and programs featuring the actors in Kabuki roles. In fact, print publishers frequently asked artists to create up-to-date images of the actors to sell during the run of a play. These prints usually showed the most dramatic moments, such as when an actor paused in a crucial action to cross his eyes and hold a dramatic pose.

Utamaro Kitagawa. Of the artists producing woodblock prints for popular consumption, UTAMARO KITAGAWA [OO-TAH-MAH-ROH] (1753–1806) is among the best known. Utamaro's elegant, willowy, and languorous women are typically rendered in full-length portraits characterized by delicacy and refinement, but he also helped to develop the close-up print showing little more than the face of some beautiful courtesan, often with a mica background to enhance the decorative quality of the portraits. One of the full-color woodblock prints, *Painting the Lips* (fig. 20.3), shows a woman who has just blackened her teeth now applying color to her lips before a mirror. She has not shaved her eyebrows, however, which women did when they married, so she can be identified as a courtesan. The slightly turned position of her head and torso adds visual drama without disrupting the elegance of her posture.

Hokusai Katsushika. HOKUSAI KATSUSHIKA [HOK-KOO-SAI] (1760–1849), created a multitude of designs and prints, which were produced in large editions. Hokusai created some of his finest works after age seventy, including his popular series *Thirty-Six Views of Mount Fuji*. His *The Great Wave off Kanagawa* (fig. 20.4) is remarkable for its depiction of the power of nature, with Mount Fuji, a symbol of Japan's enduring beauty and stability, small in the distance. Although almost centered in the print, Fuji is dwarfed by a giant wave, which threatens to crash on the boat beneath it. In this image, which is now known worldwide, Hokusai contrasts the transience of everyday existence, the fragility of life, to the more enduring majesty of Fuji.

Ando Hiroshige. HIROSHIGE [HE-ROH SHEE-GUH] (1797–1858), like Hokusai preferred landscapes to portraits. Also like Hokusai, Hiroshige produced many prints as parts of various series of woodblock prints of landscapes. Among his most famous and important works are the series of prints *One Hundred Views of Edo*. Number 58 of that series shows a characteristic scene of high summer when the humid heat dissolves into streaking slanting rain. Hiroshige captures the suddenness of the downpour, showing elegant ladies and bare-legged men caught unawares on a bridge, while other figures are depicted crouching under umbrellas, huddling under straw capes, or rushing for the nearest protection.

FIGURE 20.3 Utamaro Kitagawa, *Kuchi-bini* (Painting the Lips), Tokugawa period, color woodcut with printed glue, ca.1794–95. $14\frac{1}{3} \times 9\frac{3}{4}''$ (36.5 × 24.8 cm). New York Public Library Photographic Services, Art Resource, NY. The strong composition contrasts with the delicate face of this woman as she applies her makeup.

FIGURE 20.4 Katsushika Hokusai, *The Great Wave of Kanagawa*, Japan, from the series *Thirty-Six Views of Mount Fuji*, Tokugawa period, ca. 1831, color woodblock print, $9\frac{7}{8} \times 14\frac{5}{8}''$ (25.5 × 37.2 cm), Private Collection, Art Resource, NY. Among the best known of all Japanese woodblock prints, this image, an icon representing Japan, contrasts the powerful energy of the ocean's waves with the stable serenity of the distant snow-capped mountain in the background.

FIGURE 20.5 Ando Hiroshige, Sudden Shower Over Atake, Number 58 of One Hundred Views of Edo, 1857. Woodblock print, color, $10\frac{1}{2} \times 15''$ (26.7 × 38 cm). British Museum, London. As with many of Hiroshige's masterpieces, this mint represents not just the view, but also mood and atmosphere.

ARCHITECTURE

Architectural styles in early modern Japan differ from those of previous eras and from one another. During the Muromachi period, the Ashikaga shoguns attempted to fuse styles inherited from their predecessors. During the next era, the Momoyama era, secular architecture became increasingly grandiose and elaborate. This architectural exuberance was tempered during the Tokugawa, with a more restrained aesthetic.

The Temple of the Golden Pavilion (Kinkakuji). One of the most interesting and elegant buildings constructed during the Muromachi period was the Kyoto landmark, Kinkakuji, known as the Temple of the Golden Pavilion (fig. 20.6). Erected in 1397 under the shogun Yoshimitsu (1358–1408), the Golden Pavilion, so named because parts of the exterior are covered with gold leaf, was originally a private chapel designed for Yoshimitsu's villa in Kyoto. After his death, it was converted into a Buddhist temple

FIGURE 20.6 Temple of the Golden Pavilion (Kinkakuji), Kyoto, Muromachi period, 1397. The building was constructed for the shogun as a retreat and converted to a temple after his retirement.

and monastery, with a Zen meditation hall and rooms for contemplating the landscape and the moon. Its three stories culminate in a curving Chinese-pyramidal and Japanese-shingled roof. The pavilion is set on a platform that juts into a pond surrounded by trees, which are carefully planted to create a look of natural variety and profusion. The structure seems simultaneously set off from and into the landscape in a harmonious blending of nature and civilization. The overall effect is one of spontaneous simplicity.

Himeji Castle. In contrast to the elegant simplicity of Muromachi religious and domestic architecture, military architecture developed in the Momoyama period. In earlier military fortresses, the living quarters of the ***daimyo,*** or lord, were separated from the defensive fortifications. During the Momoyama, home and fortifications were combined into a single massive edifice designed to discourage attack. The interior, however, was richly decorated to impress visitors with its owner's wealth.

Himeji (fig. 20.7), begun by the shogun Hideyoshi in 1581 and enlarged and completed in 1609, is an

FIGURE 20.7 Himeji Castle, Hyogo (near Osaka), Momoyama period (1581–1609). Popularly known as White Heron Castle, Himeji was built as a fortress by powerful Japanese warlords.

Cross Currents

Of contemporary Japanese composers, among the best known in the West is TAKEMITSU TORU [TAH-KEY-MEET-SOO] (1930–1996). Takemitsu wrote for film and television as well as for the concert hall. His concert works include symphonic orchestral pieces, compositions for chamber orchestras, and works for voices. Takemitsu scored his orchestral works for both Western and traditional Japanese instruments such as the **biwa** (lute) and the **shakuhachi** (bamboo flute originally played by Zen monks).

Takemitsu became known in the West through Igor Stravinsky (see Chapter 18), who championed his work, and Aaron Copland (see Chapter 21), who considered him "one of the outstanding composers of our time." Serving as a bridge between East and West, Takemitsu brought works by Japanese composers to the attention of Western performers and introduced Western musical innovations to Japan. He was also instrumental in organizing cultural exchanges between Japan and the United States. Takemitsu enriched his harmonic palette through the influence of French Impressionist composers such as Debussy. He also found inspiration for his music in nature, at one time describing himself as "a gardener of music," a title that reflects his interest in the combination of natural beauty and cultured formality typical of Japanese landscape gardens. Titles of his works often reflect connotations of nature, as in "Riverrun," "Eclipse," and "Toward the Sea."

outstanding example of castle architecture. The exterior of the castle's main building is constructed of massive masonry, made necessary by the introduction of Western firearms and cannons. The castle rises from a moat, with towers soaring fifty to sixty feet above the water. Atop this impregnable masonry foundation sits a four-story wooden structure reminiscent of temple architecture.

THE JAPANESE GARDEN

The Japanese garden is essentially landscape architecture. Aesthetically, it is tied to Japanese painting. Many Muromachi gardens were designed by prominent artists, including Sesshu, who shaped the raw materials of nature to appear like a carefully inked scroll. Some gardens were designed for contemplation, others for meandering. In either case, with their neatly raked patterns of sand and carefully positioned shrubs and stones, Japanese gardens are conducive to meditation.

Larger-scale gardens might also be carved out of nature in the manner of the large glen surrounding the Golden Pavilion of Kinkakuji. Other types include moss gardens, which present nature in microcosm. A Zen-style "dry" garden might be designed with sand, which was used to suggest water, punctuated by "islands" of rocks.

One of the most famous of the Zen-inspired gardens is the Daisen-in monastery garden (fig. 20.8) in Kyoto, designed by the painter Soami (d. 1525). This 1,100-square-foot garden lies alongside the priest's house. Its vertical rocks represent cliffs; horizontal stones represent embankments and bridges. The trees in the background symbolize distant mountains.

Larger, more elaborate Japanese gardens include bridges and pagodas as well as plants. These designs are meant to evoke the essence of the Japanese landscape as well as to follow representations of nature in Japanese art. As a result, gardens reflect Japanese cultural aesthetics, including asymmetrical balance, subtle proportion, overall unity, and visual harmony.

LITERATURE

Prior to 1600, literature in Japan had been aristocratic or religious in focus, written by court figures or monks for an educated audience. After 1600, however, literature developed more popular subject matter and was produced by writers from a wider social spectrum.

Saikaku Ihara. While Murasaki's twelfth-century *The Tale of Genji* (see Chapter 9) is generally considered the first great Japanese novel, the novels of SAIKAKU IHARA [SIGH-KAY-KOO] (1642–1693), especially his *The Life of an Amorous Man, The Life of an Amorous Woman,* and *Five Women Who Loved Love,* achieved great popularity in their day. Earlier adventure novels had explored sexuality, but Saikaku's inventive technical experiments with style and point of view were largely responsible for the legitimization of the subject matter.

Five Women Who Loved Love remains Saikaku's most highly regarded book. By exploring the desires of his five female protagonists, Saikaku suggests their kinship with the court ladies of earlier Japanese literature. His merchant wives experience the same passions as courtesans, but they are more willing to sacrifice everything, even their lives, for love. Although modeled on actual people, Saikaku's five heroines are not as highly individualized as characters from nineteenth-century European novels such as Flaubert's Emma Bovary or Tolstoy's Anna Karenina.

THE SAMURAI CODE

The code of the samurai consisted of five aspects: loyalty, hierarchy, bravery, self-control, and shame. Samurai were loyal to their aristocratic lords, who rewarded them with land in return for military service. The samurai themselves were warrior aristocrats with a keen sense of rank and hierarchy. And although the age of the samurai ended in the late twelfth century during the Kamakura shogunate, the samurai ideal has had a strong influence on Japanese culture, both in peacetime and during wartime. Many samurai values, in fact, remain embedded in the fabric of contemporary Japanese society.

The importance of loyalty, for example, can be seen in the way Japanese workers and businesspeople bind themselves to a single company for their working lives. Japanese baseball players, too, play for a single team in Japan rather than looking for better and better deals with different teams, as players do in the United States. To some extent, this kind of total loyalty is beginning to break down, as global markets undermine Japanese businesses and some Japanese ball players come to America to play in the major leagues. Nonetheless the cultural ideal of loyalty to a single entity remains pervasive in Japan.

Hierarchy, too, remains pervasive in Japanese culture. It can be found in relationships in every sector and level of society, from business and government to university life, from religion to the military, and among spouses and relatives of those holding positions of rank and authority. The flip side of the emphasis on rank carries with it a set of responsibilities such that honor is always at stake. In situations where an individual has failed or disappointed his superiors, there is a sense of shame and dishonor. In medieval times, the failed samurai warrior would commit ritual suicide with his own sword. During the financial setbacks of the 1990s, a number of Japanese businessmen committed suicide for failing their companies, families, and coworkers.

The Japanese warrior code, *bushido*, was apparent during World War II as Japanese kamikaze pilots defended the honor of country and emperor by flying their airplanes on suicide missions into enemy ships. And although contemporary Japanese are questioning their allegiance to the ancient samurai code of *bushido*, its cultural values continue to exert a strong pull, even in the midst of cultural change.

FIGURE 20.8 Attributed to Kagaku Soku, Garden of the Daisen-in monastery, Daitokuji temple, Kyoto, Japan, sixteenth century. Although used primarily for meditation, this garden served also as a place of assembly for Zen priests and samurai to compose *renga*, linked verses of poetry composed communally.

Saikaku's characters, however, are engaging figures, whose actions anticipate the behavior of more modern Japanese fictional heroines.

Haiku. Haiku are three-line poems consisting of a total of 17 syllables in a pattern of 5, 7, and 5 syllables per line. In the past four hundred years, haiku has been the most popular form of poetry in Japan, and in the past century it has also been extremely influential in the West. The essence of a good haiku is a momentary, implicitly spiritual, insight presented without explicit comment. According to conventions established in the seventeenth century, the haiku must have imagery from nature, and usually includes reference to a season while avoiding rhyme. The haiku poet attempts to create an emotional response in the reader by penetrating to the heart of the poem's subject, thus evoking a sudden moment of awareness.

Basho Matsuo. Haiku reached its greatest artistic heights with the poems of BASHO MATSUO [BAH-SHOH] (1644–94). Basho began his life as a member of the samurai class, but he gave up this life to become a wandering poet. Strongly influenced by the Tang masters Du Fu and Li Bai (see Chapter 3), Basho took from his Chinese predecessors their austerity and loneliness while absorbing their sense of humor. His poems, like theirs, convey an enjoyment of life and express regret at life's impermanence, in Basho's case with a minimum of words and images.

In his desire to distance himself from the clever haiku popular in his day, Basho developed a distinctive style that reflected the realities of everyday living while suggesting spiritual depths and intellectual insights. Humor is readily apparent in this haiku, written on a journey Basho made in 1689. On the road he saw a monkey caught in a sudden rain shower, and moved by its evident distress, he composed the following:

hatsushigure	First rain of winter—
saru mo komino wo	the monkey too seems to want
hoshige nari	a little straw raincoat.

Even in this humorous vision, we can detect Basho's profound sense of what the Latin poet Virgil called "the tears of things." When Basho was ill and approaching death, he composed the following haiku, which evokes his sense of solitude.

tabi ni yande	Sick on a journey,
yume wa kareno wo	my dreams wander over
kakemeguru	withered fields.

This haiku, the last Basho ever wrote, was titled "Composed in Illness" by the poet. Providing a title was highly unusual; Basho knew the severity of his illness. He used the image of the journey both literally, for he became ill

while traveling, and metaphorically, for the journey of life. The final word *kakemeguru*, translated here as "withered fields," brings home with precision and elegance the inevitable fact of his dying.

Yosa Buson and Kobayashi Issa. Haiku master Yosa Buson (1716–1784) was equally well known as a literati painter. Many of his haiku have a strong visual element. Buson taught that the poet should use ordinary language to express what is beyond the ordinary.

Shojo to shite	Bleak and lonely
Ishi ni hi no ireru	the sun penetrates the rocks
kareno kana	in the withered field

Poet Kobayashi Issa (1763–1827) lived a tragic life; his wife and several children died before he did. Issa, who invested his poetry with great compassion for all living creatures, may be the best loved of all Japanese poets.

Yare utsu na	"Don't hit me!"
hae ga te wo suru	the fly wrings his hands
ashi wo suru	and wrings his feet

In more modern times, the poet and critic Masaoka Shiki (1867–1902) admired Buson for his ability to express emotion through imagery; his own haiku often convey a tinge of melancholy. One of Shiki's finest haiku has been misattributed to Buson:

Yuku ware ni	For me leaving
todomaru nare ni	and you staying—
aki futatsu	two autumns

Haiku in modern Japan has gone in two directions. A great number of poets strive to follow the traditional rules of seventeen syllables and a seasonal reference; others advocate an approach that breaks the formal rules in order to follow the spirit of haiku: a subtle expression of meaning through natural images through which the reader becomes an equal partner with the poet.

The monk Taneda Santoka (1882–1940) was a leading exponent of free haiku. He wrote of himself, "A foolish traveler, I have only a life of wandering, like grasses floating from one bank to the other, the shadows of my heart changing as life provides for me." One of his rule-breaking poems has a combination of eight and seven syllables in its two lines:

Yama no shizukasa e	To the mountain silence—
shikuzanaru ae	silent rain

Haiku has become the most international of all forms of poetry. Most writers in other countries do not follow the 5-7-5 rule, since languages such as English compress more meaning in fewer syllables, but the ideal of brief poems expressing meaning indirectly through images from nature, including human nature, continues to inspire people all over the world.

Modern Fiction. Modern Japanese literature is traditionally dated from the beginning of the reign of the Meiji

Connections

BUNRAKU: JAPANESE PUPPET THEATER

Although puppets were used in Japanese ceremonies and festivals at least as early as the eleventh century, it was during the Tokugawa period that the puppet theater, or **Bunraku,** developed and flourished. The texts of Bunraku plays were more distinguished than those of Kabuki, with the best of them composed by CHIKAMATSU MONZAEMON [CHICK-A-MAHT-SU] (1653–1724), who is considered by many the greatest Japanese dramatist. Written in poetic language, Chikamatsu's Bunraku plays had a narrator and were accompanied by a *samisen* (three-string banjo) player, both of whom typically sit on a dais set off to the side of the stage. Unlike Kabuki actors, who are the main attraction for a Kabuki audience, the puppeteers, the *samisen* accompanist, and the narrator are all self-effacing. Their job is not to impress the audience and win applause, but rather to bring the play to the audience in such a way that they are all but forgotten while the audience concentrates on the action of the puppets and the language of the play.

In its reliance on the rhythmic pacing of the stringed *samisen* and the narrator's chanting, Bunraku can be compared with the earliest Greek dramas, in which a single actor-speaker recounts tales from the ancient myths and legends. In Bunraku the narrator is the voice of all the puppets, whose movements are controlled by puppet masters dressed in black. Like their ancient Greek counterparts, the early Bunraku plays celebrate ancient tales of Japanese culture, such as stories from *The Tale of Genji* (see Chapter 9). Chikamatsu, however, shifted the grounds of Bunraku from an emphasis on heroic stories of the past to situations involving ordinary people in his own time. Foreigners who view Bunraku are usually amazed how much depth of feeling can be evoked in a form of theater that in the West is usually performed as entertainment for children.

emperor in 1868. During the Meiji era (1868–1912) a number of Westernizing reforms were introduced into Japanese economic, social, educational, and cultural life. Literacy was increasing dramatically, and writers began to use colloquial Japanese rather than the language of classical Japan. These changes, which parallel those in China at the turn of the twentieth century, inaugurated a period of modern fiction that is recognized for its elegance, subtlety, and grace. Japanese authors, such as Nobel Prize winner Oe Kenzaburo, have frequently written what are called "confessional novels" centering on the experience of the protagonist told from his or her own point of view. In most cases, however, modern Japanese novels reflect a larger-scale struggle between traditional Japanese values and new influences from the Western world.

The fiction of modern Japan therefore reflects a strong concern with identity, both cultural and individual. Prizing communal values, Japanese have wondered at the Western emphasis on the autonomy of the individual self. TANIZAKI JUN'ICHIRO [TAH-NEE-ZAH-KEE] (1886–1965) explored these themes. Depicting Japan's changing cultural terrain, his works examine the consequences individuals face when set free from cultural constraints to pursue personal ambitions and desires. Many of Tanizaki's characters live as modern Japanese, and the results of their self-assertion and self-aggrandizement produce guilt and alienation: guilt for abandoning long-valued cultural norms, and alienation as a result of being cut off from the solidarity of the group.

THEATER

There are two primary types of Japanese music for theater: Noh and Kabuki. Each is a distinctive form, with different musical conventions. Noh drama was developed in the fifteenth century, during the age of warrior control; Kabuki theater emerged in the seventeenth century under the influence of merchant culture.

Noh. Literally meaning "an accomplishment," **Noh** consists of dances, dialogue and songs by the main actors, and music from a *ji,* or chorus. The instruments used to accompany the singing are collectively referred to as the *hayashi.* The *hayashi* ensemble consists of a *nokan,* or flute; an *o-tsuzumi,* a type of hourglass drum held on the hip; a *ko-tsuzumi,* a shoulder drum; and a *taiko,* or stick drum on a stand. During the entire time actors perform a Noh drama, the musicians of the *hayashi* remain on stage, their musical actions choreographed as part of the drama alongside the words and gestures of the actors.

Noh is distinguished from other forms of drama by its solemnity. Even the happier moments are performed with a seriousness and gravity that make them sound ritualistic. Originally, Noh plays were performed by Shinto priests to placate the gods. Later, from the fourteenth through the seventeenth centuries, the plays were performed by professional actors wearing masks, one of the genre's distinguishing features. The limited plot action, the highly poetic texts, and the understated stylized gestures differentiate Noh plays from the realistic plays of Western theater.

Cross Currents

EAST MEETS WEST: THE FILMS OF AKIRA KUROSAWA

One of the greatest Japanese film directors, producers, and screenwriters, Akira Kurosawa (1910–98), is also one of the most popular in the West. His *Rashomon* (1950) was remade by Hollywood as *The Outrage* (1964) and his *Seven Samurai* (1954) as the *Magnificent Seven* (1960). Both Hollywood versions of Kurosawa's films were Westerns, a cinematic form that Kurosawa himself knew well and to which he was deeply indebted. *Seven Samurai*, notable for its dramatic and violent action, closeups, moving cameras, and contrasting scenes of lyricism, presents a Japanese variation on the opposition between Western ranchers and farmers familiar from American Westerns. The film depicts the breakdown of social barriers, as aristocratic samurai fight victoriously alongside peasants against an alien enemy.

Rashomon, based on a story by Ryunosuke Akutagawa, is a very different kind of film. Set in the Heian period (794–1184), the film depicts an encounter between a husband, wife, and bandit, during which the wife is raped and the husband killed. The film's narrative action is described four times from four points of view, that of each of its three protagonists and a fourth narrated by a woodcutter who witnessed the event. Kurosawa's film calls truth and objectivity into question, as each of the four tells a different version of the story. Replete with ambiguity, uncertainty, and contradiction, the four versions undercut the attempt to fix the truth with any certainty.

A number of Kurosawa's films were inspired by, or adapted from, Western literary works. His *Throne of Blood* was inspired by Shakespeare's *Macbeth; Ran* by *King Lear*; and *The Bad Sleep Well* by *Hamlet*. Tolstoy's *The Death of Ivan Ilych* inspired Kurosawa's *Ikiru*, and another of his films adapted Dostoyevsky's *The Idiot*. In addition, Kurosawa was influenced by the American film maker John Ford, who made many Westerns, and Kurosawa was himself a significant influence on a number of American filmmakers, including George Lucas, maker of the *Star Wars* films.

Kabuki. During the first years of the Tokugawa period, a type of theater that includes more lively song and dance was performed in Kyoto. The first **Kabuki** were short dramatic dances, performed by women, accompanied by song and percussion, that celebrated the exploits of heroes, especially the samurai. However, scandals concerning relations between noblemen and the actresses led to this form of theater, like Noh, being performed only by men. During the eighteenth century, with the works of Chikamatsu, Kabuki developed a repertoire of plays based on the daily lives of peasants and merchants. Unlike Noh drama, which looked back to the glories of the Middle Ages, Kabuki focused on the present. In contrast to the solemnity and decorum of Noh drama, Kabuki performances were melodramatic and suggestive of the actors' seductive charms. Developed in response to the needs of an urban audience, Kabuki includes popular drama along with various types of dance and music, some of which are performed onstage and some offstage.

Cinema/Anime. Japan has long had a vibrant film industry and a proud cinematic tradition. In the early twentieth century, most Japanese films were simply cinematic renditions of staged plays and other theatrical performances. During the 1920s, however, Japanese films began to deal with both period and modern themes and to exist independently of theater productions. Samurai films became a staple, and they remain an important film genre to this day.

The golden era of Japanese filmmaking began in 1950 with the production of *Rashomon* by the acclaimed director Akira Kurosawa, which won a number of international prizes. Kurosawa also based a number of films on the plays of Shakespeare, most notably, perhaps, *Throne of Blood*, a modernized samurai adaptation of *Macbeth*. Other Japanese directors of the 1950s include Mizoguchi Kenji, whose *Tales of Ugetsu* and *The Life of Oharu* joined Kurosawa's *Seven Samurai* as popular films in both Japan and abroad.

A contemporary cinematic development in Japan is **anime,** a word derived from French and English and denoting highly sophisticated animated films. In Japan animated films occupy a place of pride in the film genre hierarchy, and they are taken as seriously as any other kind of film. Anime films in Japan are not just cartoons for children, but rather extend to many genres, including science fiction, action and adventure films, as well as romantic films and historical dramas. Targeting all age groups,

---

Table 20–1   JAPANESE ARTS

Landscape painting: Sesshu

Woodblock prints: Hokusai

Architecture: Golden Pavilion

Landscape gardens: Garden of the Daisen-in Monastery

Haiku poetry: Basho

Theater: Noh and Kabuki

Critical Thinking

THE ECONOMIC FUTURE OF JAPAN

After the Second World War, Japan embarked on a program of education and business innovation that led the country to develop one of the world's most successful economies. Japanese auto manufacturers modeled their products on luxury cars made in Germany, and before long were taking a large percentage of the high-end auto market from the Germans, after having successfully taken much of the lower and mid-dle range auto market from American auto manufacturers.

Japan had a similar success with consumer electronics goods, especially with televisions, radios, and the "Sony Walkman," at least until the Apple Computer Corporation displaced the Walkman with its ubiquitous and wildly successful Ipod. Japan is facing fierce competition in consumer electronics both from American companies like Apple and from South Korean companies like Samsung, which has surpassed Japan as the leading electronics company. And it is also facing competition in the auto market both from a resurgence of makers of luxury cars, including Mercedes, Audi, and BMW, as well as from South Korean manufacturers of mid and lower priced cars, such as Hyundai.

What does Japan need to regain its position as a market leader in these industries? To what extent is it possible for Japan to become a world leader again? To what extent does the rise of China as an economic power complicate Japan's economic future? How much time, effort, initiative, and investment will be needed for Japan to achieve economic success?

---

anime films explore philosophical questions and social issues, develop complex plots, and provide stunningly realistic animated visuals.

The World of the Geisha. Historically, **geisha,** or women who served as "professional entertainers," or "artist entertainers," were skilled at art, music, dance, storytelling, and even a simple kind of juggling. They are typically hired to attend parties, sometimes at tea houses, sometimes at traditional Japanese restaurants. Arrangements are made through a geisha union office. Geisha originated as skilled professional entertainers, with most of them being male. Over time, the number of male geisha dwindled, and by the early nineteenth century, female geisha vastly outnumbered them.

Popular Western misconceptions of geisha confuse them with prostitutes. However, this has not, historically, been the case, but rather the exception. This confusion has been exacerbated by Japanese prostitutes, who have traded on the image of the geisha by presenting themselves to tourists as "geisha." Additional confusion has resulted from the portrayal of geishas in popular novels and films like the recent *Memoirs of a Geisha.*

Like other kinds of work involving the development of skills, such as the skilled trades in western countries, the path for the **maika,** or geisha in training, to full geisha status was long and arduous. It required dedication and commitment over a span of many years. Traditionally, geisha began their training while very young, with some girls sold to geisha houses as children. Today, however, many women begin their careers as geisha in adulthood, while others begin their training after high school. Geisha, today, still study traditional Japanese musical instruments, such as the shamisen and the shakuhachi, and they still learn classical Japanese dance, the tea ceremony, flower arranging (ike-bana), along with literature, especially poetry, which has long been popular in Japan.

CONTEMPORARY MUSIC

Oe Hikari. The story of the contemporary composer OE HIKARI [OH-AY HEE-KAH-REE] (b. 1963), son of the Nobel Laureate for Literature in 1994, Oe Kenzaburo, is one of the more unusual accounts of the making of an artist. Oe Hikari was born with a life-threatening growth on his brain. Against the advice of doctors, his parents decided to have the growth removed, even though part of Hikari's brain had to be sacrificed. The surgery saved his life but left him severely brain damaged, so that it was difficult for him to communicate using language. He did not make a sound until the age of six, when he responded to bird calls in the wild by imitating them perfectly, an early indication that he possessed an unusual aural ability. His parents soon realized he had memorized more than seventy distinctive bird calls from a recording given to him at the age of four.

Although Oe's verbal language remains limited, his imagination has allowed him to compose music, beginning after piano lessons at the age of eleven. His work shows an instinctive appreciation of melody and an inclination toward the harmonic traditions of Western music from the seventeenth through the nineteenth centuries. Oe's music is deeply indebted to the musical styles of Bach, Mozart, and Chopin. Most of his compositions are brief and lyrical, conveying sorrow and joy, serenity and exuberance.

Koto Music. Like much else in Japanese culture, a predecessor of the koto came to Japan from China during the late seventh and early eighth centuries. Chinese and

Korean musicians came with this zither-like instrument to play it in the Japanese court orchestra. About two hundred years later, the koto was being used as a solo instrument of the aristocracy. The earliest extant koto music dates from the sixteenth century and was used in Buddhist temple ceremonies. Performance of koto music at that time was restricted to priests, scholars, and aristocrats.

The best known and most important traditional koto music dates from the Edo period (1615-1868) when Japan's capital moved to Edo, currently Tokyo. Although Japanese society was isolated during most of this period, Japanese merchants served as catalysts for artistic developments in music, kabuki, and woodblock prints. Music for the koto during the early Edo was intended for entertainment rather than to accompany religious ceremonies. It was composed not by priests or scholars but by professional musicians, most of whom were blind, and who belonged to a special guild. As with other crafts, the koto repertoire was passed down through apprenticeship and was played from memory. The most famous of the koto masters was a blind musician named Yatsuhashi Kengyo, considered the father of modern koto music; like other koto masters, he was also a teacher of young women from wealthy Japanese families.

The koto is used for solos, for duets, often with the shakuhachi, a five-holed end-blown bamboo flute, and for vocal accompaniments. It is also sometimes coupled with the shamisen, a plucked lute-like instrument with three strings. Most koto music is based on pentatonic (five-tone) scales that correspond to CDEGA or CDE♭GA♭ on the piano. In fact, the koto is to Japanese music what the piano is to western music—an extremely important instrument.

FIGURE 20.9   Yuki Yamada, playing the Japanese koto with the Kifu Mitsuhashi Ensemble at the Japan Society, NY. Photograph © 2003 Jack Vartoogian/FrontRowPhotos. All Rights Reserved.

Cultural Impact

Japan's impact on the rest of the world continues to be felt in various ways. Since the 1950s, Japan has been an important world economic power and a significant trading partner of the United States and Europe as well as of Asian countries. Its dominance of electronics, particularly CD players, radios, speakers, and stereo equipment, is paralleled by the popularity of its automobiles across a range of price categories, from the Lexus and Infiniti at higher prices to its Hondas and Toyotas at midrange.

In the previous century, European painters, in particular Claude Monet and Vincent van Gogh, were inspired by Japanese woodblock prints, especially those of Hokusai, to produce paintings that imitated particular Hokusai prints or incorporated details from them. Monet produced a number of paintings on Japanese themes, emphasizing the elegance and graceful lines of Japanese art. Van Gogh collected Hokusai's woodblock prints, many of which can be seen today, hanging alongside van Gogh's own paintings in the van Gogh museum in Amsterdam. Other Western painters, including the American James McNeill Whistler, introduced Japanese elements into their works.

Japanese music influenced Western composers of both the nineteenth and twentieth centuries. The Impressionist composers Claude Debussy and Maurice Ravel experimented with Japanese melodic and harmonic elements. Contemporary composers such as Steve Reich incorporate Japanese musical motifs into their compositions. Japanese music for flute, especially, remains popular, as CDs by flutists Jean Pierre Rampal and James Galway attest.

In filmmaking, director Akiru Kurosawa's samurai films have influenced American Westerns, especially the films of John Ford and Sam Peckinpah, and can be seen in the recent *The Last Samurai*, although Kurosawa's influence extends beyond this genre. His *Rashomon*, which presents a single story told from the perspectives of a narrator and each of its three characters, remains influential as an example of multiple perspectivism and the relativity of truth.

Finally, the influence of Zen continues to reverberate in both Europe and America. Zen meditation practices have been adapted by contemporary spiritual and psychological movements such as EST. Zen aesthetics, especially floral arranging and the tea ceremony, continue to have their adherents in the West, as does Zen-inspired calligraphy, painting, and poetry, particularly haiku.

KEY TERMS

shogun	*koan*	*samisen*	*taiko*
samurai	*ukiyo-e*	Noh	Kabuki
shogunate	*daimyo*	*ji*	anime
Shinto	*hiwa*	*hayashi*	maika
kami	*shakuhachi*	*nokan*	geisha
ink-style painting	haiku	*o-tsuzumi*	
zazen	Bunraku	*ko-tsuzumi*	

WWW. WEBSITES FOR FURTHER STUDY

http://www.japan-zone.com/omnibus/shinto.shtml
(A history of Shinto: from its early history through the revival and to modern Shinto.)

http://web-japan.org/atlas/architecture/arc16.html
(Himeji Castle, Hyogo [near Osaka], Japan, Momoyama period, 1581–1609.)

http://web.kyoto-inot.or.jp/org/orion/eng/hstj/histj.html
(History of architecture in Kyoto, including the Daisen-in Gardens.)

R E A D I N G S

HAKUIN EKAKU

Song of Meditation

Hakuin's Song of Meditation *is an example of how he took Zen to everyday people through any means possible, including paintings, calligraphy, and poetry.*

All living beings are originally Buddhas, just like
    water and ice:
Without water there is no ice, and outside living beings
    there is no Buddha.
Not knowing how near it is, people seek it outside them-
    selves; what a pity!
Like someone in the middle of water crying out in thirst,
Or the child of a rich man wandering around like a beggar,
We are bound to the six worlds because we are lost in
    the darkness of ignorance;
Following dark path after dark path, when shall we es-
    cape birth and death?

The Zen meditation of Mahayana Buddhism is beyond
    all words of praise;
The virtues of charity, morality, invoking the Buddha,
    repentance, training,
And all other worthy actions have their source in medi-
    tation.
Even those who sit in zazen only once will destroy evil
    karma,
How then can there be false paths? The Pure Land is
    now very close.
Listen with reverence to this teaching, praise embrace it,
    and you will find merit;
Better yet, look within and find the self-nature beyond
    the self
And you will transcend words and explanations.

When you open the gate of cause-and-effect,
You will discover a path beyond duality or multiplicity;
When you abide in the form which is no-form,
Whether going or returning, you will always be at home;
When you take thought as non-thought,
You will sing and dance to the music of Buddhist truth.
Boundless as the sky, radiant as the moon, is the four-
    fold wisdom,
At this moment, what do you lack? Nirvana is right in
    front of you,
This very place is the Lotus Land, this body is the body
    of Buddha.

SAIKAKU IHARA

from *Five Women Who Loved Love*

The following passage is excerpted from "Gengobei, The Mountain of Love," the final novella in Saikaku's Five Women Who Loved Love. *The story focuses on a young woman, Oman, who loves a Buddhist monk named Gengobei. The following sections reveal Saikaku's penetrating analysis of human behavior and his fascination with the variety and complexity of human love. Like the other heroines of Saikaku's book, Oman is a determined woman, one who not only knows what she wants but knows how to get it as well.*

People themselves are the most despicable and heartless of all creatures. If we stop to think and look about us in the world, we find that everyone—ourselves as well as others— talks of giving up his life on the spot when some great misfortune occurs, when a young man dies in the prime of his youthful beauty, or when a wife to whom one has pledged undying love passes away early in life. But even in the midst of tears unseemly desires are ever with us. Our hearts slip off to seek treasure of all kinds or give way to sudden impulses.

Thus it is with the woman whose husband has hardly breathed his last before she is thinking of another man to marry—watching, listening, scheming for one. She may have the dead man's younger brother take his place when he is gone. She may look for a pleasing match among close relatives or, in the dizzy chase, discard completely those with whom she has long been most intimate. She will say one short prayer to Amida—so much for her obligations. She will bring flowers and incense, just so that others may see her do it.

But one can hardly notice when she paints a little powder on her face, impatient to be done with mourning before thirty-five days have passed. Her hair soon regains its luster, glistening with oil, and is all the more attractive because the wanton locks fall free of any hairdress. Then too, her underclothes run riot with color beneath a simple, unadorned garment—so unobtrusive, yet so seductive.

And there is the woman who, feeling the emptiness of life because of some sad episode, shaves her head in order to spend the rest of her days in a secluded temple, where she will have only the morning dew to offer in memory of her husband, asleep beneath the grass. Among the things she must leave behind is a gown with fawn-spot designs and beautiful embroidery. "I shall not need this anymore. It should be made into a canopy or an altarcloth or a temple pennant." But in her heart the lady is thinking: "Too bad these sleeves are just a little too small. I might still wear them."

Nothing is more dreadful than woman. No one can keep her from doing what her heart is set upon, and he who tries will be frightened off by a great demonstration of tears. So it is that widows vanish from the earth like ghosts, for none will long be true to a dead man's ghost. And so it is with certain men, except that a man who has killed off three or five wives will not be censured for taking another.

But it was not so with Gengobei. Having seen two lovers die, he was led by true devotion to sequester himself in a grass hut on the mountainside, there to seek earnestly the way to salvation in the afterlife, and to seek naught else, for he had admirably determined to quit the way of the flesh.

At that time in Hama-no-Machi, on the Bay of Satsuma, lived a man from the Ryukyus who had a daughter named Oman. She was fifteen, graced with such beauty that even the moon envied her, and of a gentle, loving disposition. Every man who looked upon her, so ripe for love, wanted her for himself. But in spring of the past year Oman had fallen in love with that flower of manhood, Gengobei. She pined away for him and wrote him many letters, which a messenger delivered in secret. Still there was no answer from Gengobei, who had never in his life given a thought to girls.

It was heartbreaking for Oman. Night and day, day after day, she thought only of him and would consider offers of marriage from no other quarter. She went so far as to feign sudden illness, which puzzled everyone, and she said many wild things to offend people, so that they thought her quite mad. Oman still did not know that Gengobei had become a priest, until one day she heard someone mention the fact. It was a cruel blow, but she tried to console herself, saying that a day would come for her to fulfil her desires, a vain hope indeed, which soon turned to bitter resentment.

"Those black robes of his—how I hate them! I must go to see him just once and let him know how I feel."

With this in mind, Oman bade farewell to her friends as if to leave the world for a nunnery. In secret she clipped her own hair to make it look like a boy's. She had already taken care to get suitable clothing and was able to transform herself completely into a mannish young lover. Then, quietly, stealthily, she set out, bound for the Mountain of Love.

As Oman stepped along she brushed the frost of the bamboo grass, for it was October, the Godless Month, yet here was a girl true to her love. A long way she went, far from the village into a grove of cedars which someone had described to her. At the end of it could be seen the wild crags of a cliff and off to the west a deep cavern, in the depths of which one's mind would get lost thinking about it. Across a stream lay some rotten logs—two, three, four of them, which were barely enough to support her. A treacherous bridge, Oman thought, as she looked down at the rapids below and saw crashing waves which would dash her to pieces. Beyond, on a little piece of flat land, was a lean-to sloping down from the cliff, its eaves all covered with vines from which water dripped, as if it were a "private rain."

On the south side of the hut a window was open. Oman peeped in to find that it was the poorest sort of abode. There was one rickety stove, in which lay a piece of green wood, only half burnt up. There were two big teacups, but no other utensils, not even a dipper or ladle.

"How dismal!" she sighed as she looked around from outside. "Surely the Buddha must be pleased with one who lives in such miserable quarters."

She was disappointed to find the priest gone. "I wonder where to?" she asked, but there was no one there to tell her, nothing at all but the lonely pines, and nothing for her to do but wait, pining among the pines.

Then she tried the door. Luckily it was open. Inside she found a book on his reading table. *The Waiting Bed* it was called, a book which described the origins of manly love.

"Well," she observed, "I see he still has not given up this kind of love."

She thought she would read while waiting for him to return, but soon it grew dark and she could hardly see the words. There was no lamp for her to use and she felt more and more lonely, waiting by herself in the darkness. True love is such that one will endure almost anything for it.

It must have been about midnight when the bonze Gengobei came home, finding his way by the faint light of a torch. He had almost reached the hut, where Oman waited eagerly for him, when it seemed to her as if two handsome young men came toward him out of the withered underbrush. Each was as beautiful as the other. Either one could have been justly called a "flower of spring" or a "maple leaf in fall." And they seemed to be rivals in love, for one looked resentful and the other deeply hurt. They both made ardent advances toward Gengobei, but he was just one and they were two, and he was helpless to choose between them.

Seeing the agitated, tortured expression on Gengobei's face, Oman could not help feeling a tender sympathy for him. Nevertheless, it was a discouraging sight for her.

"So he has love enough for many men," she said bitterly. "Still, I am committed to this affair and cannot leave it as it stands. I shall simply have to open my heart to him."

Oman went toward him, looking so determined that the two young men took fright and vanished into the night. She, in turn, was startled at their disappearance, and Gengobei at seeing her.

"What sort of young man are you?" he asked.

"As you can see I am one who has taken up the way of manly love. I have heard so much about you, Sir Priest, that I came all the way to meet you at the risk of my life. But these many loves of yours—I knew nothing of them. I have loved you in vain. It was all a mistake."

In the midst of her wailing Gengobei clapped his hands in delight. "How could I fail to appreciate such love as that!" he exclaimed as his fickle heart went out to her. "Those two lovers you saw are dead—just illusions."

Oman wept and he with her. "Love me in their stead," she begged. "Do not turn me away."

"Love is hard to pass up," he replied coyly, "even for a priest."

Perhaps Buddha would forgive him. After all, Gengobei did not know his lover was a girl.

"When I first entered the religious life," Gengobei was saying, "I promised Buddha that I would give up completely the love of women. But I knew it would be very hard to give up the love of young men, and I asked him to be lenient with me in this. Now there is no one who can censure me for it, because I made it all plain to the Buddha from the beginning. Since you loved me enough to come all the way in search of me, you must never forsake me later on."

Gengobei said these things half in jest, but it was doubly a joke for Oman. She pinched her thigh and held her breast to keep from laughing.

RYUNOSUKE AKUTAGAWA

Ryunosuke Akutagawa (1892–1927) is a prolific Japanese short-story writer and essayist. Among his most famous and influential works is the story "Rashomon" (The Rasho Gate), which he published in a university magazine in 1915. Set in the Heian period (794–1184), the strange story uses multiple perspectives to convey the illusory nature of truth. This story, combined with another, "In a Grove," were made into an important film by the Japanese film director Akira Kurosawa.

Rashōmon[1]

It was a chilly evening. A servant of a samurai stood under the Rashōmon, waiting for a break in the rain.

---

[1]Translated by T. Kojima.

No one else was under the wide gate. On the thick column, its crimson lacquer rubbed off here and there, perched a cricket. Since the Rashōmon stands on Sujaku Avenue, a few other people at least, in sedge hat or nobleman's headgear, might have been expected to be waiting there for a break in the rain storm. But no one was near except this man.

For the past few years the city of Kyōto had been visited by a series of calamities, earthquakes, whirlwinds, and fires, and Kyōto had been greatly devastated. Old chronicles say that broken pieces of Buddhist images and other Buddhist objects, with their lacquer, gold, or silver leaf worn off, were heaped up on roadsides to be sold as firewood. Such being the state of affairs in Kyōto, the repair of the Rashōmon was out of the question. Taking advantage of the devastation, foxes and other wild animals made their dens in the ruins of the gate, and thieves and robbers found a home there too. Eventually it became customary to bring unclaimed corpses to this gate and abandon them. After dark it was so ghostly that no one dared approach.

Flocks of crows flew in from somewhere. During the daytime these cawing birds circled round the ridgepole of the gate. When the sky overhead turned red in the after-light of the departed sun, they looked like so many grains of sesame flung across the gate. But on that day not a crow was to be seen, perhaps because of the lateness of the hour. Here and there the stone steps, beginning to crumble, and with rank grass growing in their crevices, were dotted with the white droppings of crows. The servant, in a worn blue kimono, sat on the seventh and highest step, vacantly watching the rain. His attention was drawn to a large pimple irritating his right cheek.

As has been said, the servant was waiting for a break in the rain. But he had no particular idea of what to do after the rain stopped. Ordinarily, of course, he would have returned to his master's house, but he had been discharged just before. The prosperity of the city of Kyōto had been rapidly declining, and he had been dismissed by his master, whom he had served many years, because of the effects of this decline. Thus, confined by the rain, he was at a loss to know where to go. And the weather had not a little to do with his depressed mood. The rain seemed unlikely to stop. He was lost in thoughts of how to make his living tomorrow, helpless incoherent thoughts protesting an inexorable fate. Aimlessly he had been listening to the pattering of the rain on the Sujaku Avenue.

The rain, enveloping the Rashōmon, gathered strength and came down with a pelting sound that could be heard far away. Looking up, he saw a fat black cloud impale itself on the tips of the tiles jutting out from the roof of the gate.

He had little choice of means, whether fair or foul, because of his helpless circumstances. If he chose honest means, he would undoubtedly starve to death beside the wall or in the Sujaku gutter. He would be brought to this gate and thrown away like a stray dog. If he decided to steal . . . His mind, after making the same detour time and again, came finally to the conclusion that he would be a thief.

But doubts returned many times. Though determined that he had no choice, he was still unable to muster enough courage to justify the conclusion that he must become a thief.

After a loud fit of sneezing he got up slowly. The evening chill of Kyōto made him long for the warmth of a brazier. The wind in the evening dusk howled through the columns of the gate. The cricket which had been perched on the crimson-lacquered column was already gone.

Ducking his neck, he looked around the gate, and drew up the shoulders of the blue kimono which he wore over his thin underwear. He decided to spend the night there, if he could find a secluded corner sheltered from wind and rain. He found a broad lacquered stairway leading to the tower over the gate. No one would be there, except the dead, if there were any. So, taking care that the sword at his side did not slip out of the scabbard, he set foot on the lowest step of the stairs.

A few seconds later, halfway up the stairs, he saw a movement above. Holding his breath and huddling cat-like in the middle of the broad stairs leading to the tower, he watched and waited. A light coming from the upper part of the tower shone faintly upon his right cheek. It was the cheek with the red, festering pimple visible under his stubbly whiskers. He had expected only dead people inside the tower, but he had only gone up a few steps before he noticed a fire above, about which someone was moving. He saw a dull, yellow, flickering light which made the cobwebs hanging from the ceiling glow in a ghostly way. What sort of person would be making a light in the Rashōmon . . . and in a storm? The unknown, the evil terrified him.

As quietly as a lizard, the servant crept up to the top of the steep stairs. Crouching on all fours, and stretching his neck as far as possible, he timidly peeped into the tower.

As rumor had said, he found several corpses strewn carelessly about the floor. Since the glow of the light was feeble, he could not count the number. He could only see that some were naked and others clothed. Some of them were women, and all were lolling on the floor with their mouths open or their arms outstretched showing no more signs of life than so many clay dolls. One would doubt that they had ever been alive, so eternally silent they were. Their shoulders, breasts, and torsos stood out in the dim light; other parts vanished in shadow. The offensive smell of these decomposed corpses brought his hand to his nose.

The next moment his hand dropped and he stared. He caught sight of a ghoulish form bent over a corpse. It seemed to be an old woman, gaunt, gray-haired, and nunnish in appearance. With a pine torch in her right hand, she was peeping into the face of a corpse which had long black hair.

Seized more with horror than curiosity, he even forgot to breathe for a time. He felt the hair of his head and body stand on end. As he watched, terrified, she wedged the torch between two floor boards and, laying hands on the head of the corpse, began to pull out the long hairs one by one, as a monkey kills the lice of her young. The hair came out smoothly with the movement of her hands.

As the hair came out, fear faded from his heart, and his hatred toward the old woman mounted. It grew beyond hatred, becoming a consuming antipathy against all evil. At this instant if anyone had brought up the question of whether he would starve to death or become a thief—the question which had occurred to him a little while ago—he would not have hesitated to choose death. His hatred toward evil flared up like the piece of pine wood which the old woman had stuck in the floor.

He did not know why she pulled out the hair of the dead. Accordingly, he did not know whether her case was to be put down as good or bad. But in his eyes, pulling out the hair of the dead in the Rashōmon on this stormy night was an unpardonable crime. Of course it never entered his mind that a little while ago he had thought of becoming a thief.

Then, summoning strength into his legs, he rose from the stairs and strode, hand on sword, right in front of the old creature. The hag turned, terror in her eyes, and sprang up from the floor, trembling. For a small moment she paused, poised there, then lunged for the stairs with a shriek.

"Wretch! Where are you going?" he shouted, barring the way of the trembling hag who tried to scurry past him. Still she attempted to claw her way by. He pushed her back to prevent her . . . they struggled, fell among the corpses, and grappled there. The issue was never in doubt. In a moment he had her by the arm, twisted it, and forced her down to the floor. Her arms were all skin and bones, and there was no more flesh on them than on the shanks of a chicken. No sooner was she on the floor than he drew his sword and thrust the silver-white blade before her very nose. She was silent. She trembled as if in a fit, and her eyes were open so wide that they were almost out of their sockets, and her breath come in hoarse gasps. The life of this wretch was his now. This thought cooled his boiling anger and brought a calm pride and satisfaction. He looked down at her, and said in a somewhat calmer voice:

"Look here, I'm not an officer of the High Police Commissioner. I'm a stranger who happened to pass by this gate. I won't bind you or do anything against you, but you must tell me what you're doing up here."

Then the old woman opened her eyes still wider, and gazed at his face intently with the sharp red eyes of a bird of prey. She moved her lips, which were wrinkled into her nose, as though she were chewing something. Her pointed Adam's apple moved in her thin throat. Then a panting sound like the cawing of a crow came from her throat:

"I pull the hair . . . I pull out the hair . . . to make a wig."

Her answer banished all unknown from their encounter and brought disappointment. Suddenly she was only a trembling old woman there at his feet. A ghoul no longer: only a hag who makes wigs from the hair of the dead—to sell, for scraps of food. A cold contempt seized him. Fear left his heart, and his former hatred entered. These feelings must have been sensed by the other. The old creature, still clutching the hair she had pulled off the corpse, mumbled out these words in her harsh broken voice:

"Indeed, making wigs out of the hair of the dead may seem a great evil to you, but these that are here deserve no better. This woman, whose beautiful black hair I was pulling, used to sell cut and dried snake flesh at the guard barracks, saying that it was dried fish. If she hadn't died of the plague, she'd be selling it now. The guards liked to buy from her, and used to say her fish was tasty. What she did couldn't be wrong, because if she hadn't, she would have starved to death. There was no other choice. If she knew I had to do this in order to live, she probably wouldn't care."

He sheathed his sword, and, with his left hand on its hilt, he listened to her meditatively. His right hand touched the big pimple on his cheek. As he listened, a certain courage was born in his heart—the courage which he had not had when he sat under the gate a little while ago. A strange power was driving him in the opposite direction of the courage which he had had when he seized the old woman. No longer did he wonder whether he should starve to death or become a thief. Starvation was so far from his mind that it was the last thing that would have entered it.

"Are you sure?" he asked in a mocking tone, when she finished talking. He took his right hand from his pimple, and, bending forward, seized her by the neck and said sharply:

"Then it's right if I rob you. I'd starve if I didn't."

He tore her clothes from her body and kicked her roughly down on the corpses as she struggled and tried to clutch his leg. Five steps, and he was at the top of the stairs. The yellow clothes he had wrested off were under his arm, and in a twinkling he had rushed down the steep stairs into the abyss of night. The thunder of his descending steps pounded in the hollow tower, and then it was quiet.

Shortly after that the hag raised up her body from the corpses. Grumbling and groaning, she crawled to the top stair by the still flickering torchlight, and through the gray hair which hung over her face, she peered down to the last stair in the torch light.

Beyond this was only darkness . . . unknowing and unknown.

YOSANO AKIKO

Yosano Akiko is one of Japan's most engaging contemporary poets. Her use of traditional poetic forms with highly charged subject matter has gained her poetry both attention and notoriety.

1134

Ah, my black hair,
the thousand strands of my hair,
my tangled hair:
my thoughts entangled as well
   in the tangle of my thoughts.

1136

"The springtime is so short,
and who ever heard of a life
   that lasts forever?"
So I said, and filled his hands
   with the power of my breasts.

1137

Of the way—say nothing.
Of the future—think nothing.
Of fame—ask nothing.
Now I see just you and me—
one loving, the other loving back.

CHAPTER 21

HISTORY

1900	Labour Party founded in England
1905	Einstein formulates theory of relativity
1908	Ford introduces Model T
1913	Assembly line introduced at Ford plant
1914	World War I begins
1917	Russian Revolution
1920	Nineteenth Amendment grants women the right to vote
1920s	Harlem Renaissance flourishes
1920s	"Roaring Twenties" and prohibition
1927	Lindbergh's solo flight across Atlantic Ocean
1929	Stock Market crashes; Depression begins
1933	FDR introduces New Deal
	Nazis gain control of Germany
1935	WPA begun: FSA begins photography program
1936–39	Spanish Civil War
1939	World War II begins
1941	United States enters World War II

ARTS AND ARCHITECTURE

1905	Matisse, *Woman with a Hat*
1907	Picasso, *Les Demoiselles d'Avignon*
1913	Stravinsky, *The Rite of Spring*
1915	Severini, *Suburban Train Arriving at Paris*
1917	Duchamp, *Fountain*
1920	Mondrian, *Composition in Red, Yellow, and Blue*
1924	Gershwin, *Rhapsody in Blue*
1926	O'Keeffe, *Yellow Calla*
1928	Armstrong, *West End Blues*
1928	Brancusi, *Bird in Space*
1931	Dali, *The Persistence of Memory*
1931	Schoenberg, *Variations for Orchestra*
1933	Rivera, *Detroit Industry*
1936	Oppenheim, *Breakfast in Fur*
1937	Picasso, *Guernica*
1938	Moore, *Recumbent Figure*
1939–41	Lawrence, *The Migration of the Negro*
1940	Ellington, *Concerto for Cootie*
1942	Hopper, *Nighthawks*
1944	Copland, *Appalachian Spring*

LITERATURE AND PHILOSOPHY

1905	Freud, *Three Essays on the Theory of Sexuality*
1922	Eliot, *The Waste Land*
1922	Joyce, *Ulysses*
1926	Hemingway, *The Sun Also Rises*
1927	Woolf, *To the Lighthouse*
1929	Cocteau, *Les Enfants Terribles*
1929	Faulkner, *The Sound and the Fury*
1939	Steinbeck, *The Grapes of Wrath*

Early Twentieth Century

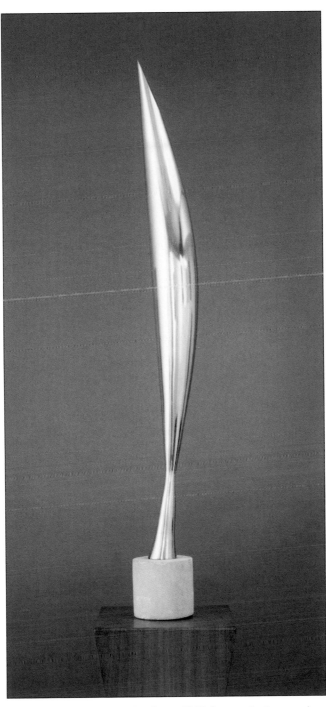

Constantin Brancusi, *Bird in Space*, 1920, bronze (unique cast), 54 × 8½ × 6½″ (137.2 × 21.6 × 16.5 cm). Museum of Modern Art/Licensed by SCALA-Art Resource, NY. Given Annonymously. Photograph © 2000 The Museum of Modern Art, NY. © 2000 Artists Rights Society (ARS), New York ADAGP, Paris.

MAP 21.1 Europe after World War I, ca. 1920.

CHAPTER OVERVIEW

NEW DIRECTIONS IN THE ARTS
Picasso and Cubism impact the arts

THE GREAT WAR AND AFTER
Changes in a civilization altered by war

REPRESSION AND DEPRESSION
The thirties: global instability infuses the arts

NEW DIRECTIONS IN THE ARTS

PICASSO AND CUBISM IMPACT THE ARTS

By the early twentieth century, the Impressionist and Post-Impressionists were no longer regarded as radical or shocking; they were now accepted by the official French Salon that had previously scorned them. In 1901, a huge retrospective exhibition of van Gogh's work was held in Paris. The 1907 Salon featured Cézanne's paintings. The Impressionists and Post-Impressionists were now the leaders of art that went against tradition and expectation, preferring to seek what was unique and innovative, even startling or shocking, the **avant garde.** In the never-ending quest for the new, movement after movement, "ism" after "ism," came and went. Thus, Romanticism, Realism, Impressionism, and Post-Impressionism were followed in the early twentieth century by **Fauvism, Cubism, Futurism,** and **German Expressionism.** In general, the later nineteenth-century trend toward abstraction of the visual world, the willingness to distort its form and color, was still more extreme in early twentieth-century art.

The interest in **abstraction** takes three forms: (1) an *expressive* art that is emotional, gestural, and free in its use of color; (2) a *formalist* art that is concerned with structure and order; and (3) an art of *fantasy* that is concerned with the individual imagination and the realm of dreams. In all three, the world of surface appearances is gradually left behind. Abstract art is based less and less on the artist's *perception* and increasingly on the artist's *conception* of things.

FAUVISM

The 1905 Salon d'Automne (Autumn Salon) in Paris was liberal in its acceptance policy and included a room of paintings by Henri Matisse, Maurice de Vlaminck, André Derain, Georges Rouault, and others who were exhibiting together for the first time. The art critic Louis Vauxcelles reviewed the show and was quick to label these artists *Les Fauves* (The Wild Beasts) because of their paintings' violent and arbitrary colors. The artists who launched **Fauvism,** like van Gogh and Gauguin, believed color could be an expressive force in its own right and it could correspond, not to reality, but to what van Gogh had called "the artist's temperament." Furthermore, they rejected the small "dots and dashes" of color that characterized Impressionist painting and, particularly, the Post-Impressionist paintings of Seurat. Their work was intended to shock the viewer, visually and psychologically, with its intensely surprising color. It was, above all, new.

Henri Matisse. The leader of the Fauves was HENRI MATISSE [mah-TEES] (1869–1954). At the age of twenty-two, Matisse had abandoned a career in law for one in art. At the 1905 Autumn Salon, he exhibited *Woman with a Hat* (fig. 21.1), a portrait of Madame Matisse. It ap-

FIGURE 21.1 Henri Matisse, *Woman with a Hat*, 1905, oil on canvas, $32\frac{1}{4} \times 23''$ (82 × 60.5 cm), Collection of Mrs. Walter A. Haas, San Francisco. Visual Arts Library/Artephot/Faillet, © Succession Ho Matisse/DACS 1998. © 2005 Artists Rights Society (ARS), NY. The American author Getrude Stein and her brother Leo purchased this painting at the Autumn Salon in 1905, inaugurating one of the greatest collections of modern art in Paris in the twentieth century. Americans, in particular, flocked to Stein's evening gatherings in her apartment on the Rue des Fleurs to see the work of Matisse and Picasso and to meet the artists themselves, who were in regular attendance.

peared to many viewers to be little more than a smearing of brilliant, arbitrary, and unnatural colors across the subject's face and background. In its subject matter, this could be an Impressionist painting depicting Madame Matisse dressed for an outing in gloves and an enormous hat, yet it bears almost no resemblance to any earlier work. Rather than employing dabs of color, Matisse broke the color into broad zones. Not only are the colors seemingly arbitrary, the artist makes no attempt to harmonize them. Red, green, and purple are used at maximum intensity.

Matisse soon realized that *Woman with a Hat* lacked something that profoundly interested him—drawing. Beyond depicting raw contrasts of pure color in flat planes, he wanted to emphasize line. Through the expressive use of color and line, Matisse gave even the most ordinary subject expressive force. *Harmony in Red (Red Room)* (fig. 21.2),

FIGURE 21.2 Henri Matisse, *Harmony in Red (Red Room)*, 1908–1909, oil on canvas, 5′11¼″ × 8′7⅞″ (1.81 × 2.46 m), State Hermitage Museum, St. Petersburg, Russia. © 2005 Artists Rights Society, NY. Traditional methods of creating an illusion of three dimensions on a two-dimensional surface are not used in many twentieth-century paintings. Here, indications that the table top is horizontal and the wall vertical are avoided, creating a flat and decorative effect.

painted 1908–09, is an everyday scene distinguished by pattern and harmony between the colors, shapes, and lines. This painting oscillates between two-dimensional pattern and three-dimensional representation. The tablecloth and the wall share the same pattern and colors; the only indication Matisse provides that the table is a horizontal surface is the placement of fruit on it. Are we looking out of a window on the left or at a flat painting hanging on the wall? Every object plays a role in forming an overall surface pattern. This differs from the efforts made by earlier artists to construct an illusion of space behind the picture plane. Matisse, like many later painters, intentionally compressed the space and emphasized the picture plane, making clear this is a painting, not an illusion of the visible world.

CUBISM

The Fauvist emphasis on the reality of the picture plane is also apparent in the work of the Cubist painters. Derived from Cézanne's famous dictum, "You must see in nature the cylinder, the sphere, and the cone," **Cubism** differs, first, in its depiction of objects in their most reduced geometric form, particularly, as its name implies, in cubes. It differs, secondly, in the way in which objects are represented simultaneously from several different points of view. Rather than presenting the object from a single vantage point, the Cubists wanted to present all aspects of the object simultaneously. Reality, they argued, is not just what we see, but what we know about what we see, in the same way that when we see a person's back, we can infer that person's face.

Cubism was the invention of two relatively unknown painters at the time, Pablo Picasso and Georges Braque, both of whom arrived separately at the same conclusions about the nature of our experience of the world. They soon discovered one another's shared convictions and proceeded to work together for seven years until the outbreak of World War I.

Pablo Picasso. Often considered the single most important painter of the twentieth century, PABLO PICASSO [pi-KAH-soh] (1881–1973) never ceased searching for the new. He went through many styles in his long life and worked in a wide variety of media including painting, graphics, sculpture, and ceramics. He might draw and paint with extraordinary realism one day and with a high degree of abstraction the next—although he never abandoned a subject entirely.

Picasso's famous *Les Demoiselles d'Avignon* (*The Ladies of Avignon*) (fig. 21.3), of 1907, was a turning point in the history of painting. Although the word *demoiselles* means "gentlewomen," here it refers to prostitutes, and Avignon refers to Avignon Street in Barcelona rather than the city of the popes in southern France. The anatomy of the figures shows distorted proportions, their bodies turned into rhythmic shapes and broken angular pieces. Space is treated in the same way. Solid and void are depicted in terms of structural units, similar to Cézanne's "little planes." The style is also deliberately "primitive." African sculpture, particularly masks, inundated Paris in the first decade of the century, and Picasso took full advantage of their expressive force.

Georges Braque. One of the first people to see *Les Demoiselles*, and to approve of it, was GEORGES BRAQUE [BRAHK] (1882–1963). Braque had worked with Matisse as a member of the Fauves, and it was probably Matisse, who was himself horrified by *Les Demoiselles*, who introduced him to Picasso. But Braque saw in it a flattening and simplification of form that he believed Cézanne had championed.

Braque's *The Portuguese* (fig. 21.4), of 1911, depicts a guitarist playing at a café, but there is no fully realized figure. We can see the guitar's soundhole and strings in the lower-middle part of the painting. There are fragments of lettering—OCO and BAL—and something is offered at a price of 10.40 francs. A rope is wrapped around a post, and perhaps that is the guitarist's broad smile in the upper-middle part of the piece. All is a fleeting glance as if seen through a window in which the reflections of activity and movement outside distort everything seen inside.

Both Braque and Picasso began to introduce recognizable pieces of material reality into their compositions, asking the questions: What is real and what is art? If something is real, can it be art? And vice versa, if something is art, is it real? By pasting real materials on the canvas they engaged in a technique called **collage** (from the French word *coller*, "to glue" or "to paste"). Picasso's *Still Life with Chair Caning* (fig. 21.5), of 1912, contains rope and a piece of oilcloth with imitation chair caning printed on it, a cigarette, and a fragment of a newspaper (*Le Journal*). All we see are the first three letters, a fragment of the whole, but this fragment tells us much about Braque and Picasso's intentions. The letters "jou" also form the beginning of the verb *jouer*, the French for "to play." Collage became the new playground of the artist.

Sonia Terk Delaunay. Sonia Terk Delaunay (1885–1979) was born Sarah Stern in the Ukraine, but grew up in St. Petersburg under the care of a relative, the art collector Heinrich Terk. In 1909, she married an art dealer, Wilhelm Uhde, who exhibited her work in his Paris gallery. In 1910, she married again, now to the artist Robert Delaunay, with whom she formed a long creative partnership.

The couple developed a style of abstract painting called **Simultanéisme** based on color theory, using vivid colors and geometric shapes, intended to be experienced simultaneously. Sonia Delaunay's *Tango au Bal Bullier* (fig. 21.6), 1913, conveys the rapid graceful movement of dancers, including a sense of their animation and energy. She applied this style to clothing created from various materials, thereby combining art and attire, blurring the traditional distinction between Fine Art and Applied Art. She designed costumes for Diaghilev's Russian Ballet and for Tristna Tzara's play *Le Coeur à Gaz*. With the fashion designer Jacques Heim, she opened the Boutique Simultané in Paris in 1925, featuring garments and accessories in this style.

FUTURISM

The **Futurism** movement, based in Italy before World War I, used Cubist forms in a dynamic way. It was the first art movement to have been founded almost exclusively in the popular press, conceived by its creator, the poet FILIPPO MARINETTI [mah-ri-NET-ee] (1876–1944), in his "Manifesto of Futurism," published on February 20, 1909, in the French newspaper *Le Figaro*.

The "Manifesto" outlines an eleven-point pledge, including the Futurists' intention to "sing the love of danger," to "affirm that the world's magnificence has been enriched by a new beauty, the beauty of speed," to "glorify war—the world's only hygiene," to "destroy the museums, libraries, and academies of every kind," and, finally, to "sing of great crowds excited by work, by pleasure, and by riot."

Gino Severini. In February 1910, seven painters, including GINO SEVERINI [sev-err-EE-nee] (1883–1966), signed a "Manifesto of Futurist Painters" that pledged, among other things, "to rebel against the tyranny of terms like 'harmony' and 'good taste,' " "to demolish the works of Rembrandt, of Goya, and of Rodin," and, most importantly, "to express our whirling life of steel, of pride, of

FIGURE 21.3 Pablo Picasso, *Les Demoiselles d'Avignon*, 1907, oil on canvas, 8′ × 7′ 8″ (2.40 × 2.30 m), Museum of Modern Art, New York. With motifs that echo African art, the angular lines and overlapping planes of this painting initiated a new way of analyzing three-dimensional forms in space. The work's primitive energy sent shock waves through the art world when it was first shown in Paris, allying it with Stravinsky's *Rite of Spring*, which had a similar effect on the world of music six years later.

fever, and of speed." The Furturists wanted, they claimed, to render "universal dynamism" in painting.

The Futurists' interest in expressing speed was aided by the forms of Cubism. Severini's *Suburban Train Arriving at Paris* (fig. 21.7), of 1915, depicts speed as a sequence of positions of multifaceted forms. Similar to a series of movie stills, or to a multiple exposure photograph, the artist expresses the direction of the force by the abstract fragmentation of the speeding forms. The Futurists valued simultaneous perspective, as did the Cubists, but the Futurists recorded the various aspects of a moving object, whereas the analytical Cubists recorded those of a static one.

FIGURE 21.4 Georges Braque, *The Portuguese*, 1911, oil on canvas, $45\frac{1}{8}''$ × $32\frac{1}{8}''$ (114.5 × 81.5 cm), Kunstmuseum, Basel, Switzerland. © 2005 Artists Rights Society (ARS), NY. © ADAGP, Paris and DACS, London 1998. In cubism the forms are broken and faceted as if portions of cubes, and the forms are portrayed from multiple viewpoints. The range of color is restricted so it will not distract from this new way of analyzing form in space.

FIGURE 21.5 Pablo Picasso, *Still Life with Chair Caning*, 1912, oil, oilcloth, and pasted paper simulating chair caning on canvas, rope frame, $10\frac{1}{2}$ × $13\frac{3}{4}''$ (26.7 × 35 cm), Musée Picasso, Paris. Reunion des Musées Nationaux. Art Resource, NY. © 2005 Estate of Pablo Picasso/Artists Rights Society (ARS), NY. This collage (from the French for "to paste" or "to gluc") is created from scraps of ordinary materials that became art when arranged into a composition.

GERMAN EXPRESSIONISM

The last of the great prewar avant-garde movements was **German Expressionism** which consisted of two separate branches, *Die Brücke* (The Bridge), established in Dresden in 1905, and *Der Blaue Reiter* (The Blue Rider) formed in Munich in 1911. Both were directly indebted to the example of the Fauves in Paris, especially in terms of the liberation of color and the celebration of sexuality.

Emil Nolde. One of the most daring members of *Die Brücke* was EMIL NOLDE [NOHL-(duh)] (1867–1956). What distinguishes his *Dancing Around the Golden Calf* (fig. 21.8) from the work of Matisse and the Fauves is the painting's lack of contour and outline. Instead, emphasis is on the use of color, which fully exploits the dissonances between its bright reds, orange-yellows, and red-violets. The energy of this style—almost slapdash in comparison to

Matisse—helps create a sense of violence, fury, and wanton sexuality that is alien to Matisse's vision. This rough-hewn, purposefully inelegant approach is typical of *Die Brücke* work, and it owes much to the example of Picasso's *Les Demoiselles* and its so-called primitivism.

Vassily Kandinsky. The leader of *Der Blaue Reiter* was VASSILY KANDINSKY [kan-DIN-skee] (1866–1944), who was born in Moscow. A practicing lawyer with a professorship in Moscow, Kandinsky saw one of Monet's *Haystacks* paintings in 1895 and was so moved by the experience that he traveled to Munich to study art. He became friendly with the Fauves and the Cubists, bringing their work to Germany in 1911 for a major exhibition.

The name *Der Blaue Reiter* refers to St. George slaying the dragon, the image that appeared on the city emblem of Moscow. Tradition held that Moscow would be the capital of the world during the millennium, the thousand-year reign of Jesus on earth after the Apocalypse. *Improvisation No. 30 (Warlike Theme)* (fig. 21.9) includes, at the bottom of the composition, two firing cannons, which announce the second coming of Jesus. Crowds of people march toward the millennium across the canvas. Above them are the churches of the Kremlin and, circling around the horizon, the streets of Moscow itself. Kandinsky did not so much want to convey the meaning of his work through its imagery as through its color. Color, he believed, caused "vibrations (in German, *Klangen*) in the soul," and his painting was designed, he wrote in 1912 in his *Concerning the Spiritual in Art*, to "urge" the viewer to a spiritual awakening in preparation for the second coming.

FIGURE 21.6   Sonia Delaunany-Terk, *Tango au Bal Bullier*, 1913, oil on canvas 3′ 2″ ×
12′ 8″ (97 × 390 cm), Musée National d'Art Moderne, Centre National d'Art et de Culture,
Georges Pompidou. Philippe Megeat/Reunion des Musées Nationaux/Art Resource, NY. The
title of this painting is the name of a dance hall in Paris where the artist danced the tango wearing
her *simultanéiste* costumes, which her husband Robert Delaunay described as "living paintings."

MUSIC

Igor Stravinsky.   IGOR STRAVINSKY [strah-VIN-
skee] (1882–1971) is considered the most influential composer of the modern era. His works revolutionized
twentieth-century musical styles and affected artists such
as Picasso, writers such as T. S. Eliot, and ballet choreographers such as George Balanchine. Stravinsky was born in
Russia, near St. Petersburg. Although groomed for a law
career, Stravinsky studied music and achieved early success composing for the Ballets Russes, a Russian ballet
troupe performing in Paris under the artistic direction of
Serge Diaghilev. His early scores, *The Firebird* (1910) and
Petrushka (1911), were both ballets based on Russian
themes and musically influenced by Debussy.

The Rite of Spring.   The most spectacular of Stravinsky's early ballet scores was *Le Sacre du Printemps (The Rite*

of Spring) of 1913. *The Rite of Spring* broke new ground.
The music was filled with harmonic shifts, rhythmic surprises, and melodic irregularities. The public was shocked
by the near violence of the sound and by its disruption of
their emotional expectations.

The origin of *The Rite of Spring* came to Stravinsky in
a vision: "a solemn pagan rite: wise elders, seated in a circle, watch a young girl dance herself to death. They are
sacrificing her to propitiate the god of spring." Stravinsky linked this vision to his childhood memories of the
"violent Russian spring that seemed to begin in an hour
and was like the whole earth cracking." The work depicts the fertility rites of a primitive tribe in pagan Russia. The first part, "The Fertility of the Earth," opens
with a suggestion of the rebirth of spring. A bassoon solo
begins the introductory section and is soon followed by
other woodwinds, and then the brasses that play the
melody, all without a home key, that is, without a har-

FIGURE 21.7   Gino Severini, *Suburban Train Arriving at
Paris*, 1915, oil on canvas, 35 × 45½″ (88.6 × 115.6 cm), Tate
Gallery, London. © 2005 Artists Rights Society (ARS), NY.
The Italian Futurists sought to destroy museums and anything
old, praised what they called the "beauty of speed," glorified
war and machinery, and favored the "masculine" over the
"feminine."

FIGURE 21.8   Emil Nolde, *Dancing Around the Golden Calf*,
1910, oil on canvas, 34¾″ × 39½″ (88 × 100 cm), Staatsgalerie
Moderner Kunst, Munich. Much of the shock of this painting
derives from its depiction of a biblical subject in such openly
sexual terms.

FIGURE 21.9   Vassily Kandinsky, *Improvisation No. 30 (Warlike Theme)*, 1913, oil on canvas, $43\frac{1}{4}''\times43\frac{1}{4}''$ (110 × 110 cm), Art Institute of Chicago. Photograph © 2005, All Rights Reserved. © 2005 Artists Rights Society (ARS), NY. Although Kandinsky did produce completely nonrepresentational paintings, beginning in 1910, that were intended to stir the viewer's emotions, this painting includes recognizable subjects having political and religious implications.

monic center. The music builds to a climax and then abruptly stops, leaving the solo bassoon to echo the introductory notes.

Without pause, a brief four-note theme repeated softly by the violins opens the second part, "The Sacrifice." Immediately comes the "Dance of the Youths and Maidens," in which Stravinsky builds intensity through the heavy use

of percussion, sharply irregular rhythmic accents, and the shrill syncopation of the horns. All this is emphasized further by both polytonal harmonies and strong dissonance. Stravinsky's "Introduction" to *The Rite of Spring* reflects the modern composer's new directions in melody and harmony; "The Dance of the Youths and Maidens" displays a corresponding rhythmic freedom.

THE GREAT WAR AND AFTER

"ON OR ABOUT DECEMBER 1910 HUMAN character changed," wrote English novelist Virginia Woolf. "All human relations shifted, those between masters and servants, husbands and wives, parents and children. And when human relations shift there is at the same time a change in religion, conduct, politics and literature." These changes were dramatized by the Great War (as World War I was then called), which began in August 1914. As another English novelist, D. H. Lawrence, wrote, "in 1915 the old world ended." The war gave frightening meaning to the radical changes of the early twentieth century. It was a time of "disorder and early sorrow," as German writer Thomas Mann wrote in one of his stories; where "things fall apart; the centre cannot hold," as the Irish poet William Butler Yeats noted. Change, disorder, sorrow, and disintegration: These forebodings ushered in an age of anxiety.

WORLD WAR I

On June 28, 1914, a Serbian nationalist named Gavrilo Princip assassinated the Habsburg archduke, Francis Ferdinand, heir to the throne of Austria and Hungary, and his wife, Sophie Chotek, on the street in Sarajevo, Bosnia. Within weeks, Europe was at war, the Central Powers (Austria, Hungary, Germany, Turkey, and later, Bulgaria) against the Allies (Serbia, Russia, France, and Britain, and later, the United States).

It is hard to overstate the impact of the Great War on the public in the West. It took the lives of over eight million soldiers in action, and many millions more through malnutrition and disease. Along the Western Front, which extended from the English Channel to the Swiss border with Alsace, near Basel, hundreds of thousands of soldiers faced each other in parallel trenches across a stationary line. British historian Charles Carrington (1897–1981) remembers life in the trenches on the Somme, as a young man barely twenty years of age:

> The killed and wounded were all lost by harassing fire, mostly on their way up or down the line. Once in position . . . you could not show a finger by daylight, and by night every path by which you might be supposed to move was raked by machine-guns which had been trained on it by day. . . . If you could reach your funk-hole and crouch in it, there was a fair chance of your coming out of it alive next day to run the gauntlet . . . again. In your funk-hole, with no room to move, no hot food, and no chance of getting any, there was nothing worse to suffer than a steady drizzle of wintry rain and temperature just above the freezing point. A little colder and the mud would have been more manageable. Life was entirely numbed; you could do nothing. There could be no fighting since the combatants could not get at one another, no improvement of the trenches since any new work would instantly be demolished by a storm of shell-fire.

Another chronicler of the war, the German Erich Maria Remarque, described in his novel *All Quiet on the Western Front* (1929) the sense of doom that dominated the German lines: "Monotonously the lorries sway, monotonously come the calls, monotonously falls the rain. It falls on our heads and on the heads of the dead up the line, on the body of the little recruit with the wound that is so much too big for his hip; it falls on Kemerich's grave; it falls in our hearts." After the Great War, it seemed as if the whole world mourned, a mood evoked in this lithograph by the German artist KATHE KOLLWITZ [KOL-vits] (1867–1945) (fig. 21.10).

THE RUSSIAN REVOLUTION AND AFTER

The influence of the West on Russia, so evident in St. Petersburg, was counterbalanced by later political developments that undermined the autocratic monarchy of the Tsars. The Russian Revolution officially began when the last Russian Tsar, Nicholas II, abdicated in 1917. However, it had in fact started earlier, on Bloody Sunday, January 9, 1905, when government troops fired on a peaceful demonstration by workers outside the Winter Palace in St. Petersburg. The workers quickly organized themselves into "soviets," or councils of workers elected in the factories, while the police responded swiftly by arresting dissenters. Most leaders were either sent to Siberia or chose self-imposed exile, as did Lenin, removing himself with many others to Switzerland.

Yet it was World War I that precipitated the real crisis. The Russian army was crushed in the fight with Germany, resulting in over five million casualties between 1914 and

FIGURE 21.10   Kathe Kollwitz, *The Mothers*, 1919, lithograph, $17\frac{3}{4} \times 23''$ (45 × 58.4 cm), Philadelphia Museum of Art. © DACS 1998. © 2005 Artists Rights Society (ARS), NY. Kollwitz captures the tragedy of World War I in this image of lower-class German mothers left to fend for themselves and their children after the war. The black-and-white medium emphasizes the harshness of their reality.

1917. Germany penetrated deep into western Russia. The flow of refugees into Moscow could almost not be supported.

In February 1917, popular demonstrations forced Nicholas from power. (He and his family were later executed on the night of July 16, 1918.) A democracy was promised, the nature of which was to be determined by a constituent assembly, elected by the people at the earliest opportunity. From February to October 1917, Russia was ruled by a provisional government, but in October, to cries of "all power to the soviets," the Bolshevik party seized power, led by Vladimir Ilyich Lenin (1870–1924). The Bolsheviks were Marxists—that is, those who believed in the writings of Karl Marx and called for a new society ruled by the proletariat, the working class. In Marx and Engels's words, from *The Communist Manifesto:* "In place of the old bourgeois society, with its classes and class antagonisms, we shall have an association, in which the free development of each is the condition for the free development of all."

Within a few months, Russia was embroiled in a bitter civil war, which would last for three years. The war pitted the Red Army of the working proletariat against the White Army of the anti-Bolshevik bourgeoisie. The Reds won, but since Britain and France had openly supported the Whites, and Japan and the United States had sent troops to Siberia, the new Bolshevik government was almost totally isolated from the West. It nationalized almost all industry, organizing the workers, and created what it called a "dictatorship of the proletariat." Yet a deep economic crisis soon followed, and Lenin, recognizing that he had moved too quickly, inaugurated a New Economic Policy (NEP) in 1921, legalizing private trade, abandoning the nationalization of industry, and allowing the private sector of the economy to reestablish itself. It was a full retreat from Communist principles, but one necessitated, Lenin believed, by reality.

Meanwhile, the new Soviet bureaucracy began to establish itself. Rising to the position of General Secretary of the Bolshevik party was Joseph Stalin (1879–1953). When Lenin died in 1924, Stalin overcame his rival Leon Trotsky (1879–1940) and took over, making it clear that the primary goal of the Soviet Union was industrialization. His Five-Year Plan, implemented in 1929, modernized the country and built the basic structure of Soviet society, which remained intact until December 1991.

The Russian Revolution created a new order that affected not only Russians, but other peoples around the globe. Its complex web of causes included popular grievances, radical ideas espoused by intellectuals, idealism coupled with a lust for power, and a breakdown of public order. Its consequences included helping to prevent the restoration of peace after World War I—which contributed to the rise of Nazi Germany and the outbreak of World War II—and increasing world tension throughout the twentieth century, resulting in a "cold war."

DADA

The war had an immense impact on art. Profoundly affected by the destruction, a group of artists, writers, and musicians founded a new art movement—**Dada,** from a nonsense word indicating a child's first utterance of 'Da, da' or 'yes, yes' to life. Beginning in Zurich and New York during the war, it flourished in Paris and Germany after it.

As early as 1916, artists and intellectuals who had escaped the war gathered regularly at the Café Voltaire in Zurich. Swiss sculptor Hans Arp (1886–1966) defined Dada in the following way: "Repelled by the slaughterhouses of the world war, we turned to art. We searched for an elementary art that would, we thought, save mankind from the furious madness of these times." This it attempted to do in an irreverent manner. Arp himself made relief sculptures by dropping liquid into a series of small puddles, outlining each, and then cutting out wooden replicas and finally putting them together. His *Portrait of Tristan Tzara* (fig. 21.11) portrays his friend, a Dada poet. TRISTAN TZARA [ZAHR-ah] (1896–1963) wrote poems using these same "laws of chance." Tzara would cut up a newspaper article word by word, then draw the words out

FIGURE 21.11   Hans Arp, *Portrait of Tristan Tzara*, 1916, relief of painted wood, $20\frac{1}{8} \times 19\frac{3}{4} \times 4''$ (51 × 50 × 10 cm). Jean-Marc Yersin/Musée d'Art et d'Histoire, Geneva, Inv. No 1982/13 ©2005 Artists Rights Society (ARS), NY. Like Dada poetry created by random combinations of words, this so-called portrait is created by combining random shapes and colors.

of a hat, and write a poem. Tzara also performed a kind of poetry at the Café Voltaire—*bruitisme*, he called it, after the French word for "noise"—consisting of vowels, consonants, and guttural sounds, strung together in a nonsense parody of German *Lieder* (songs). The Dadaists thought that if tradition was responsible for the madness of the Great War, then tradition deserved no respect. The childlike, absurd behavior of the Dadaists was a conscious attempt to start again from square one.

Marcel Duchamp. One of the most important Dadaists, MARCEL DUCHAMP [doo-SHAHM] (1883–1968), worked as a painter before the war. When Duchamp arrived in New York in 1915, he said that Dada meant "hobby horse" in French (yet another meaning), and claimed he had picked the word at random from a French dictionary (yet another conflicting story of its origins). Duchamp saw Dada as a kind of **anti-art** one that embodied imagination, chance, and irrationality, and opposed all recognized values in art and literature.

In 1917, Duchamp submitted a "sculpture" to the Independents exhibition in New York. Entitled *Fountain* (fig. 21.12), it was a porcelain urinal signed with a pseudonym, "R. Mutt." It caused an uproar. Duchamp let it be known that he was "Mutt" himself, suggesting that what mattered most about a "work of art" was not aesthetic concerns, but who made it. Furthermore, the significance of the urinal changed in different contexts. It was one thing in a plumbing shop or bathroom, quite another on a plinth in an art exhibition, demonstrating that where things were seen changed how they were understood. Duchamp had taken something mundane and, by reframing it, had revealed its aesthetic dimension.

Duchamp engaged in many other demonstrations and attacks on traditional aesthetics. He retouched a poster of Leonardo da Vinci's *Mona Lisa*, (see fig. 13.21) adding a mustache and goatee, and a series of letters which, when pronounced phonetically result in an off-color pun. Duchamp used puns in many of his works because he thought that wordplay undermined the stability of meaning, and in so doing encouraged new ways of seeing.

FIGURE 21.12 Marcel Duchamp, *The Fountain*, 1917, height $24\frac{5}{8}$″ (62.2 cm), porcelain urinal Photograph by Alfred Stieglitz in *The Blind Man, no. 2*, May 1917; original lost. © Philadelphia Museum of Art: The Louise and Walter Arensberg Collection. Duchamp argued that he "created a new thought for that object" by forcing the viewer to see it in a new context. He labeled such works "ready-mades."

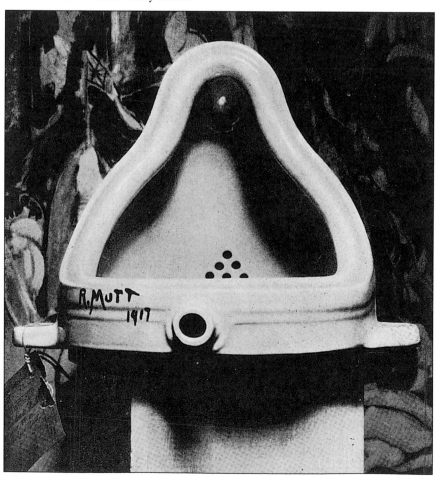

SURREALISM

The spirit of the *avant-garde* continued to thrive after the war. Paris was its center, "the laboratory of ideas in the arts," as the American poet Ezra Pound put it. Tristan Tzara organized a massive Dada festival in Paris in 1920. In May 1917, Diaghilev's Ballets Russes performed *Parade*, a dance with music by French composer Eric Satie and complete with the sounds of dynamos, sirens, express trains, airplanes, and typewriters. The stage set was designed by Picasso (fig. 21.13). The whole creation seemed to the poet Guillaume Apollinaire like the space of a *surréalisme*, or "super-realism."

In 1924, the poet André Breton appropriated the word *sur-réalisme* to name his own new movement in the arts. Delighting in the irrational, and its lack of "aesthetic or moral concern," **Surrealism** was indebted to Dada. Where it differed was in its fascination with the realm of dreams, supported by a willful misunderstanding of Freud. Where Freud considered neurosis as an illness demanding psychoanalysis and cure, Breton found it liberating. The neurotic person, for Breton, was free to behave in any manner, and the dreams opened up whole new vistas of subject matter, many of them previously taboo.

There were two approaches to this new subject matter: one abstract, the other representational. The abstract vein was based on Breton's notion of psychic **automatism**—that is, drawing liberated from the necessity of plan. Surrealists, according to this idea, should accept any apparent accident as psychologically predetermined and therefore revelatory. The second approach was focused on representing the world of dreams accurately, deliberately, and particularly without self-censorship.

Joan Miró. One of the practitioners of automatism is JOAN MIRO [mee-ROH] (1893–1983). Although Miró never called himself a Surrealist, he acknowledged the Surrealist influence on his art. Soon after arriving in Paris from his native Spain in 1922, he was, he said, "carried

FIGURE 21.13 Pablo Picasso, curtain for the ballet *Parade*, 1917, tempera, $35'3\frac{1}{3}'' \times 57'6''$ (10.60 × 17.24 m), Musées Nationaux, Paris. © Succession Picasso/DACS 1998. Art Resource, NY. © 2005 Estate of Pablo Picasso/Artist Rights Society (ARS) NY. The ballet was based on a poem by Jean Cocteau, another member of the avant-garde circle. It is a "realistic ballet," meaning its concerns arise within an everyday street setting, complete with street musicians and performers, car horns and sirens, businesspeople, tabloids, and skyscrapers.

FIGURE 21.14   Joan Miró, *Painting*, 1933, oil on canvas, $4'3\frac{1}{4}'' \times 5'3\frac{1}{2}''$ (1.30 × 1.61 m), Wadsworth Atheneum, Hartford, Connecticut. © 2005 Artists Rights Society (ARS) NY. ADAGP, Paris/DACS, London 1998. One of the reasons this painting, when it is seen in real life, seems so alive, as if inhabited by abstract creatures, is that it is very large, so the forms depicted in it are on a human scale.

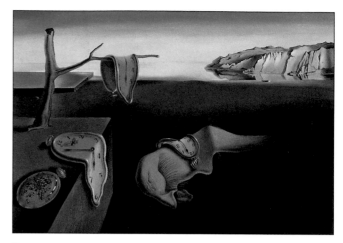

FIGURE 21.15   Salvador Dali, *The Persistence of Memory*, 1931, oil on canvas, $9\frac{1}{2} \times 13''$ (24.1 × 33 cm). Museum of Modern Art, NY. Licensed by Scala/Art Resource, NY. (162. 1934). Given anonymously. © 2002 Kingdom of Spain. © 2005 Salvador Dail, Gala/Salvador Dali Foundation/Artists Rights Society (ARS), NY. Combining psychology and art, Surrealist artists sought to express the unconscious. Intentionally enigmatic and mysterious, Dali's painting depicts the impossible and irrational with absolute conviction.

away" by their example, and by 1925 "was drawing almost entirely from hallucinations. At the time I was living on a few dried figs a day."

His *Painting* (fig. 21.14) of 1933 is a rendering of machine forms he saw in a catalog, transformed into abstract shapes, more organic than mechanical. The two bands of color in the background create a landscape, which the forms inhabit, existing at the very edge of rational thought.

Salvador Dali.   The most famous Surrealist is SALVADOR DALI [DAH-lee] (1904–89), also from Spain, who arrived in Paris in 1929 and consciously invented himself as a Surrealist cult figure. He manipulated his foot-long mustache into various shapes. He claimed he could remember life in his mother's womb. He had himself buried and resurrected. Dali's life of irrational behavior garnered fame and fortune—highly rational results.

Dali's painting *The Persistence of Memory* (fig. 21.15), of 1931, depicts four watches that are limp, corroded by rust, and attacked by ants. What can this puzzling vision mean? Is time itself wilting, even as it causes decay and destruction? Has time become flexible, or is it distorted? Can the artist "bend time"? Is creativity a means to immortality? Can art defeat time? Such are the questions the painting seems to pose.

The slug-like object on the ground, appears to be a distorted self-portrait. "I want to paint like a madman," Dali said. As he pointed out, if Surrealism were to investigate the unconscious, then it had to explore whatever the unconscious had to offer. In this painting and others, Dali depicted illogically juxtaposed objects, impossibly distorted forms, and undefined spatial settings. Yet when rendered

with his meticulous technique, the inconceivable becomes real.

Méret Oppenheim.   Surrealist artists did not limit themselves to painting. One of the best-known Surrealist works is the *Object (Le Déjeuner en Fourrure) (Luncheon in Fur)* (fig. 21.16), 1936, created by MÉRET OPPENHEIM [OP-pen-hime] (1913–1985). Born in Berlin, she moved to

FIGURE 21.16   Méret Oppenheim, *Object (Le Déjeuner en Fourrure) (Luncheon in Fur)*, 1936, fur-covered cup, saucer, and spoon, diameter of saucer $9\frac{3}{8}''$ (23.7 cm), overall height $2\frac{7}{8}''$ (7.3 cm), Museum of Modern Art, NY/Licenced by Scala Art Resource, NY. © 2007 Artists Rights Society. In this paradigm of the peculiar, this icon of incongruous materials, Oppenheim combined tableware and fur, making this one of the most memorable examples of Surrealist sculpture.

her mother's native Switzerland, and continued on to Rome when eighteen or nineteen years old, to study art. As Surrealist painters combined ordinary objects in extraordinary ways, Oppenheim combined the refined teacup, saucer, and spoon with the wildness of animal fur. This evokes the intentionally disturbing thought of drinking from a fur-lined cup: imagine the sensation of sipping tea through the fur of a Chinese gazelle. Or might the fur keep the tea warm? The title of the work, *Le Déjeuner en fourrure*, was given by Andre Breton, one of the leaders of the Surrealists, as a reference to *Le Déjeuner sur l'herbe* painted by Manet in 1863 (fig. 17.22), which certainly disturbed the public when first exhibited. Oppenheim also created Surrealist drawings, paintings, sculptures, appliances, furniture, and clothing as well as poems and descriptions of dreams.

DE STIJL

If Dada represents a nihilistic reaction to World War I, **De Stijl** ("The Style" in Dutch), sometimes called **Neo-Plasticism,** represents an affirmative, hopeful response. Founded in 1917 in Holland, the movement sought to integrate painting, sculpture, architecture, and industrial design, and championed a "pure" abstraction. In the movement's first manifesto, the De Stijl artists wrote, "The war is destroying the old world with its contents. . . . The new art has brought forward what the new consciousness of the time contains: balance between the universal and the individual."

Piet Mondrian. The leading painter of the De Stijl school was PIET MONDRIAN [MON-dree-on] (1872–1944). Dutch by birth, he moved to Paris in 1912 and turned his attention to Cubism, which he quickly took to its logical conclusion. His work referred less and less to nature, until it finally became completely nonobjective abstraction.

By 1920, Mondrian had defined a mature style, as seen in *Composition in Red, Yellow, and Blue* (fig. 21.17). Believing the flat plane was integral to painting and that it must be respected rather than falsified by perspective, and seeking perfection within strictly imposed limitations, Mondrian created a surface grid of horizontal and vertical lines; the rectangle and square are its basic shapes. The colors are restricted to the primary colors—red, yellow, and blue—plus black, white, and, in a few places, gray. Using these simple elements, Mondrian established a sense of balance. As he would assert, while writing about a drawing of this time, "If one does not represent things, a place remains for the Divine."

ABSTRACTION IN SCULPTURE

A number of sculptors sought to explore the possibilities of abstraction in three dimensions. They created shapes that were organic and fluid, suggesting natural forms. Thus

FIGURE 21.17 Piet Mondrian, *Composition in Red, Yellow, and Blue*, 1920, oil on canvas, $20\frac{1}{2} \times 23\frac{5}{8}''$ (52 × 60 cm), Stedelijk Museum, Amsterdam. Giraudon/Art Resource, NY/© 2004 Mondrian/Holtzman Trust. Mondrian actually called his style Neo-Plasticism, but the name *De Stijl*, the title of the Dutch magazine that published not only his own but also the writings of other figures from the movement, is now generally used.

their work appears mysterious and elemental, universal in its simplicity.

Constantin Brancusi. A Romanian who moved to Paris in 1904, CONSTANTIN BRANCUSI [Bran-KOO-zee] (1876–1957) "rediscovered" primitive sculpture while working with the Expressionist painters. Brancusi favored simple geometric forms—rectangles, ovals, and verticals. His *Bird in Space* (fig. 21.18), in polished bronze, for example, is an elongated vertical shape. Its purity of form does not depict a bird, but rather evokes the flight of the bird. The work is completely abstract; its expressive quality is completed by our knowing the title. "Don't look for obscure formulas or mystery," Brancusi said of his work. "It is pure joy that I am giving you."

Barbara Hepworth. The British sculptor Barbara Hepworth (1903–1975) perfected abstraction. Her *Three Forms* (fig. 21.19) was carved in 1935 of white serravezza marble. Hepworth's sculptures have a biological quality, as if nature created this organic abstraction of three egglike ovoids, molding and shaping not only the masses but also the spaces between them. Hepworth said she was "absorbed . . . in tensions between forms." Although these forms are simplified to the point of severity, they are gently rounded, the surfaces perfectly finished.

Henry Moore. The human figure was the point of departure for British sculptor Henry Moore (1898–1986). Yet Moore's figures are so simplified and abstract that they are barely identifiable, often appearing to be forms of nature, capable of growth but beaten by the elements. He

FIGURE 21.18   Constantin Brancusi, *Bird in Space*, 1920, bronze (unique cast), 54 × 8½ × 6½″ (137.2 × 21.6 × 16.5 cm). Museum of Modern Art, NY/Licensed by Scala/Art Resource, NY. Given anonymously. Photograph © 2000 The Museum of Modern Art, NY. One of Brancusi's *Bird in Space* sculptures was the center of a battle between Brancusi and the U.S. Customs Office in 1927. Customs officials called it "bric-à-brac" and said it should therefore be taxed, whereas Brancusi said it was a work of art and was thus duty free. Brancusi won—a victory for modern art, now officially recognized as abstract art.

FIGURE 21.19   Barbara Hepworth, *Three Forms*, 1935, marble, Tate Gallery, London. Art Resource, NY. Hepworth created this soon after the birth of her triplets in 1934. Her work achieves a timelessness—primitive in its elemental simplicity, classical in its subtle refinement while simultaneously modern in its organic quality and tense spatial relationships.

admired prehistoric Stonehenge and similar forms eroded by nature and time. His *Recumbent Figure* (fig. 21.20), of 1938, looks weathered and suggests the power of natural forces at work. Moore's sculptures are often more effective when seen in a park than in a museum.

Moore's smooth flowing forms include large openings and hollows. He shapes the solids but gives equal importance to the voids. The masses can be viewed as "positive volumes" and the depressions and holes may be seen as "negative spaces."

ARCHITECTURE

Unlike the other modern arts, in architecture a single **international style** developed over the first half of the twentieth century that almost all architects acknowledged, if not wholly accepted. The Museum of Modern Art in New York held an exhibition of modern architecture in 1932 that identified a new "International Style . . . based primarily on the nature of modern materials and structure . . . slender steel posts and beams, and concrete reinforced by steel." Many leading architects fled the worsening situation in Europe in the 1930s and came to the United States. The booming economic climate after the war called for many new buildings.

Walter Gropius.   A leading architect in Germany before World War II, Walter Gropius (1883–1969) directed the **Bauhaus** art school in Dessau, Germany, and designed its chief buildings (fig. 21.21), built 1925–26. When Adolf Hitler closed the Bauhaus, Gropius moved to America and became the chair of the Architecture Department at Harvard University.

The main principle of the Bauhaus was to interrelate art, science, and technology so there was no dividing line between the fine arts, architecture, and industrially pro-

FIGURE 21.20   Henry Moore, *Recumbent Figure*, 1938, green hornton stone, length 55″ (141 cm), Henry Moore Foundation/Tate Picture Gallery, London. Moore's monumental figure, although in a classical reclining pose, appears to have been weathered into this organic shape.

FIGURE 21.21   Walter Gropius, Bauhaus, Dessau, Germany, 1925–26. Museum of Modern Art/Licensed by SCALA/Art Resource, NY. The Bauhaus (House of Building), closed by the Nazis in 1933, was a school that sought to adapt to the modern world by combining the methods and disciplines of fine art, craft, graphic design, architecture, and industry. Built of reinforced concrete, steel, and glass, the Bauhaus building itself looked like a painting by Mondrian made three dimensional.

FIGURE 21.22   Le Corbusier (Charles Edouard Jeanneret), Savoye House, Poissy-sur-Seine, France, 1929–30. Le Corbusier called the functional homes he designed *machines à habiter*—"machines for living." Made of reinforced concrete and glass in simple geometric shapes, this home is an example of the International Style of the 1920s.

duced functional objects. The artist, the architect, the craftsperson, and the engineer were brought together.

The Bauhaus building is essentially a cage of glass. Its steel frame makes possible walls entirely of glass because the walls do not support the structure. The cornice at the top is not functionally necessary to protect a building of glass, steel, and concrete from the elements, but it is aesthetically necessary as a visual conclusion to the architectural composition, to frame the building.

Le Corbusier.   Another influential architect of the international style was Charles Edouard Jeanneret, known as LE CORBUSIER [cor-BOO-see-ay] (1886–1965). The Savoye House in Poissy-sur-Seine in France (fig. 21.22), built 1929–30, is a private home that caused a revolution in domestic architecture. Corbusier called such houses he designed *machines à habiter* ("machines for living"), reflecting Corbusier's admiration for the neatness and precision of machines.

The Savoye House is elevated on stilts of **reinforced concrete.** Smooth walls in pure geometric shapes enclose space in an abstract composition of simple planes and clean lines, like a large sculpture that can be inhabited. Because the house is elevated, outsiders cannot see in, although the inhabitants can see out. The materials used are ornamental, without extraneous decoration.

Frank Lloyd Wright.   The American Frank Lloyd Wright (1867–1959) believed that a building must be related to its site and blend with the terrain. Contrary to critics who call modern architecture "impersonal," Wright used the term "organic" to describe his buildings. Wright's best known home is Fallingwater, in Bear Run, Pennsylvania (fig. 21.23), built in 1936 for the Kaufmann family. The house projects out over a waterfall and blends into the rising cliffs of the landscape. Inside, Fallingwater is open and

is oriented to the outdoors with windows that extend floor to ceiling. Walls are made of screens. The furniture, as in other Wright homes, is largely built-in.

AMERICAN MODERNISM

In 1913, just before World War I, a number of American artists worked together to plan an International Exhibition of Modern Art at the 69th Street Regiment Armory, in New York City. Thousands of people jammed into what was soon known as "the Armory Show" to see the Post-Impressionist, Fauve, and Cubist works. Most visitors gawked at the show and ridiculed it, but some American artists were inspired, especially those who frequented the New York City gallery known simply as 291, run by Alfred Stieglitz.

Georgia O'Keeffe.   Among the painters most influenced by Stieglitz's style was Georgia O'Keeffe (1887–1986). Born in Wisconsin, O'Keeffe was a student at the Art Institute of Chicago and the Art Students League in New York. When, in 1915, she sent Stieglitz a bundle of drawings and watercolors, he immediately exhibited them. They later married.

Favoring flowers and animal bones as her subjects, O'Keeffe is best known for the type of painting represented by *Yellow Calla* (fig. 21.25), of 1929, a large-scale abstraction of a natural form. *Yellow Calla* is a flower seen close up and painted large scale, emphasizing its abstract form and pattern. Simple yet carefully designed, O'Keeffe's painting makes use of shading to create filmy, translucent, fluttering forms that are rich and sensuous. Intrigued by light and color, she said, "Color is one of the great things in the world that makes life worth living to me." Although many saw

Cross Currents

RUSSIA AND THE WEST: THE BALLETS RUSSES

Ballet as a dance form did not originate in Russia, but it certainly flourished there. The most influential nineteenth-century choreographer in Russia was the French-born MARIUS PETIPA [PET-ee-pah] (1819–1910), who worked for the czar in St. Petersburg. Petipa collaborated with Tchaikovsky on both *Sleeping Beauty* and *The Nutcracker* to create two of the most popular ballets ever. After Petipa, Michel Fokine rose to prominence and became the principal choreographer of the Ballets Russes, a Russian dance company set up in Paris under the direction of the impresario SERGEI DIAGHILEV [dee-AHG-uh-LEF] (1872–1929), who was responsible for popularizing ballet throughout Europe.

Diaghilev set himself the goal of bringing Russian culture to the attention of the West, moving to Paris to do so. In 1906, he held a large-scale exhibition of Russian art, and in 1907, he began a series of concerts of Russian music. It was his presentation of Mussorgsky's *Boris Godunov* in 1908 that dazzled Western audiences with its originality and splendor. In 1909, he ventured a second season, which featured some ballets that included scenes from Borodin's opera *Prince Igor*, arranged for dancers rather than singers. The Russian ballerina Tamara Karsavina and her male counterpart, Vaslav Nijinsky, so stunned and enthralled Parisian audiences that they streamed onto the stage during the intermission of the first performance.

With dancers like Nijinsky and choreographers that included George Balanchine, and with set designs commissioned by painters such as Pablo Picasso and Henri Matisse, the Ballets Russes brought together a wealth of talent from a wide range of cultures and art forms. Composers who produced music for the Russian ballet included Claude Debussy, Maurice Ravel, and the Russian Serge Prokofiev.

The international acclaim of Russian ballet was furthered when George Balanchine defected from Russia in 1924 and eventually came to the United States in 1933 to choreograph. He founded and directed his own company, The New York City Ballet, and his own school. Here, Balanchine created a style of ballet that suited the American ethos—fast, sleek, conceptual, and thoroughly modern. During the communist era, many dancers, including Rudolf Nureyev and Mikhail Barishnikov, defected from the Soviet Union to enjoy the artistic freedom of the West, much to the delight of Western audiences.

FIGURE 21.23   Frank Lloyd Wright, Fallingwater, Bear Run, Pennsylvania, 1936. Seeking to unite structure and site, Wright used cantilevered construction to build this home over a waterfall. As in contemporary painting and structure, solid and void are given equal consideration in this composition.

sexual symbols in her work, O'Keeffe repeatedly made clear that this was not true. She was, she explained a painter of nature and of nature's forms and colors.

The same year she painted *Yellow Calla*, O'Keeffe began spending her summers near Taos, New Mexico. After Stieglitz's death in 1946, she moved there permanently. The forms of the desert Southwest became her primary subject matter and its colors her palette.

Charles Demuth.   Among the other American artists championed by Stieglitz was Charles Demuth (1883–1935). Unlike O'Keeffe, whose primary interest was in natural forms and colors, Demuth was concerned with the architectural forms of the American scene. He reduced them to flat compositions in a manner reminiscent of the Cubist landscape paintings of Picasso and Braque. In *Aucassin and Nicolette* (fig. 21.26), of 1921, for instance, the geometric shapes of the industrial landscape near Demuth's home in Lancaster, Pennsylvania, are rendered in flat, hard-edged forms, the lines of which extend into the sky like facets on a polished gem.

MODERNIST LITERATURE

American expatriates flocked to Paris and Europe to escape Prohibition and other social restrictions at home. There, they discovered liberation from what they considered the stultifying Puritanism of America.

Connections

GRAHAM AND NOGUCHI: THE SCULPTURE OF DANCE

For the pioneer of modern dance Martha Graham (1894–1991), modern sculpture proved to be a useful way of thinking about the movement of the body in space. Dance was, for Graham, a trajectory into space, a composition of mass moving through void. She also perceived that set design could move from its position as backdrop to occupy the territory of the dance itself. Dancers could move in it, around it, over it, under it, through it, and beside it. They could lean on it, jump over it, hide behind it.

Her dances showed humans interacting with art.

In 1935, for the dance *Frontier* (fig. 21.24), Graham initiated what was to be a long-lasting relationship with Isamu Noguchi. (See Chapter 23, fig. 23.12) Noguchi devised a simple fence, set at center stage, with two ropes attached to it, extending from each end of the fence forward and upward to the portals of the theater. This giant V shape created the illusion of space when viewed from a traditional, single-point perspective, receding in a steep plane toward a vanishing point below and behind the fence rail. "It's not the rope that is the sculpture,"

Noguchi later explained, "but the space that it creates that is the sculpture. It is an illusion of space. . . . It is in that spatial concept that Martha moves and creates her dances. In that sense, Martha is a sculptor herself." Graham herself forms the apex of the V as the dance opens, and as she moves forward and backward in front of the fence, it is as if she is in a vast landscape, the prairies and basins of the American frontier.

"Isamu Noguchi's vision of space," Graham later said, "and the integral meaning of his sculpture set me on a direction which sustained me throughout my career."

FIGURE 21.24 Martha Graham in *Frontier*, set by Isamu Noguchi, 1935. © ADAGP Paris and DACS, London 1998. Noguchi designed over thirty-five sets for Graham, this being his first. To create sculptural forms with her body, Graham had her costume designed with a full circle skirt to swoop and arc through the air, creating linear curves as she moved.

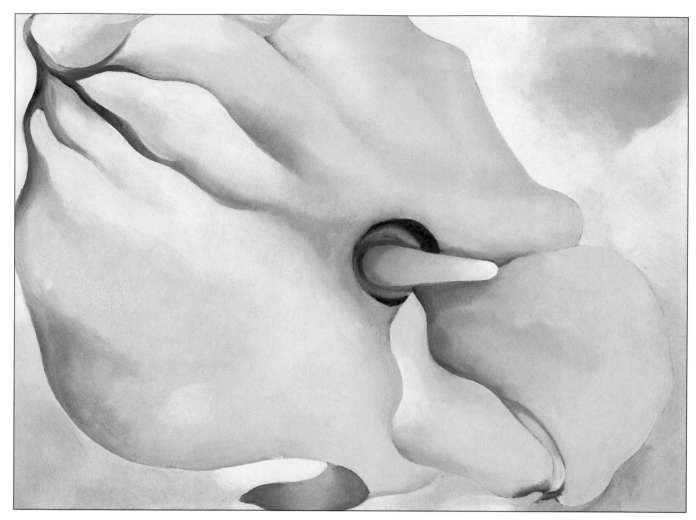

FIGURE 21.25 Georgia O'Keeffe, *Yellow Calla*, 1926, oil on fiberboard, 9 × 12¾″ (22.9 × 32.4 cm), Smithsonian American Art Museum, Washington, D.C. © 2005 Artists Rights Society (ARS), NY. Concerned with expressive organic abstractions of nature throughout her long career, O'Keeffe made it clear she was an artist—not a "woman artist."

During and after the war the most adventurous new writing in English was published in Paris: James Joyce's *Ulysses*, in 1922, banned for obscenity in America and Britain until 1933; T. S. Eliot's *The Waste Land*, in 1922; William Carlos Williams's prose and poetry *Spring and All*, in 1923; F. Scott Fitzgerald's *The Great Gatsby*, in 1925; Ezra Pound's first sixteen *Cantos*, in 1926; and Ernest Hemingway's *The Sun Also Rises*, also in 1926. It was Hemingway who defined the mood of what he called the "lost generation."

Ezra Pound and T. S. Eliot. Ezra Pound (1885–1972) and T. S. Eliot (1888–1965), two influential American Modernist poets, wrote complex, multifaceted poems that were technically innovative and densely allusive. Pound and Eliot relied heavily on rapidly shifting images, typically presented without explanation. Readers are left to make connections among the poems' images and allusions and to arrive at understanding for themselves.

Pound and Eliot are sometimes considered difficult for all but the most learned and experienced readers. Both poets believed poetry *should* be difficult, in part to reflect the difficulty of experience, especially that of World War I, which Eliot once described as an "immense panorama of futility and anarchy." Eliot's most influential poem, *The Waste Land*, burst onto the literary scene in 1922. Eliot was aided in his work by his friend Ezra Pound, who cut more than a hundred lines from an early draft and suggested alterations to help unify the poem. In appreciation Eliot dedicated the poem to Pound and honored him further as *il miglior fabbro* ("the better maker").

"I had not thought death," Eliot writes in the poem, "had undone so many," speaking of the benumbed people inhabiting the "unreal city" of postwar London. To Eliot, London seemed as if it had been stricken by the gas warfare on the Western Front. His poem is but a holding action, to stop the bleeding, so to speak—"frag-

FIGURE 21.26 Charles Demuth, *Aucassin and Nicolette*, 1921, oil on canvas, $23\frac{9}{16} \times 19\frac{1}{9}''$ (59.8 × 49.5 cm), Ferdinand Howland Collection, Columbus Gallery of Fine Arts, Columbus, Ohio. The painting's ironic title, referring to the famous lovers of medieval romance, is attributed to another member of the Stieglitz circle during World War I, Marcel Duchamp. In fact, Demuth records the industrialization of rural Pennsylvania.

ments I have shored against my ruin," as he describes it at poem's end.

Pound's early poetry is a concerted attack on World War I. The five-part "Hugh Selwyn Mauberley," published in 1920, ends with this indictment of the cause the soldiers had been fighting for:

> There died a myriad,
> And of the best, among them,
> For an old bitch gone in the teeth,
> For a botched civilization . . .

So disillusioned was Pound with the political and economic policies of England, France, and the other Allies that, when Mussolini took power in Italy in the early 1930s, he became one of his champions. Fascism, and the anti-Semitism that went with it, appealed to Pound, and he supported Mussolini throughout World War II. After the war he was imprisoned, tried for treason, and certified insane. For thirteen years, he was kept at St. Elizabeth's mental hospital in Washington, D.C. Finally, at the request of

writers including Hemingway, Williams, and Eliot, he was released, and returned to Italy, where he died in 1972.

James Joyce. James Joyce (1882–1941) accomplished for modern fiction what T. S. Eliot did for modern poetry: He changed its direction by introducing startling innovations. Like Eliot, who employed abundant and wide-ranging literary and historical allusions in *The Waste Land*, Joyce, in his monumental *Ulysses*, published in the same year, complicated the texture and structure of his narrative with intricate mythic and literary references.

Joyce used a **stream of consciousness** narrative technique to take readers into the minds of his characters. His innovations include shifting abruptly from one character's mind to another; moving from description of an action to a character's response to it; mixing different styles and voices in a single paragraph or sentence; combining events from the past and the present in one passage. These and similar devices convey a sense of a mind alive, a consciousness that is absorbing and connecting the experiences it perceives—what one critic has described as "the shifting, kaleidoscopic nature of human awareness." In his *Portrait of the Artist as a Young Man*, for example, Joyce uses stream of consciousness to recreate the early memories of his protagonist partly by imitating the toddler's baby talk and partly by emphasizing the sights, smells, and tastes of a young child's consciousness. Despite the modernist style, Joyce still casts his novel in the tradition of the *bildungsroman*, or the novel of education, the preferred genre of eighteenth- and nineteenth-century novelists.

Ulysses grows out of the tradition of the nineteenth-century realist novel. Combining a microscopic factual accuracy in depicting Dublin with a rich language, it is an intricate recreation of the events of one day (June 16, 1904) in the life of Leopold Bloom. Organized into eighteen increasingly complex chapters, it echoes major events in Homer's *Odyssey*.

Virginia Woolf. As James Joyce was experimenting with techniques in fiction, Virginia Woolf (1882–1941), one of the founders of the Bloomsbury group in London, was developing ways of rendering a literary character's inner thoughts. Both writers explored techniques for conveying stream of consciousness, the representation of the flow of mental impressions and perceptions through an individual's consciousness, conveying a sense of his or her subjective psychic reality. Woolf, in particular, was interested in revealing a character's inner being through what that character thinks and feels, rather than what that character says or does.

Mrs. Dalloway (1925) and *To the Lighthouse* (1927) are two of Woolf's novels that illustrate her use of the stream of consciousness technique. Like Joyce, Woolf in *Mrs. Dalloway* focuses on a single day in the life of a person, in this case a middle-aged Englishwoman, Clarissa Dalloway. Readers overhear Mrs. Dalloway's thoughts and feelings as she reflects on her life, especially her marriage. External events are indicated only through the characters' subjective impressions of them. The novel's point of view shifts among a series of characters, including Septimus Warren Smith, a shell-shocked war veteran, who functions to a certain extent as her alter ego.

In *To the Lighthouse*, Woolf commemorates her mother Julia Stephen, who had died in 1895. The novel explores aspects of gender and sexual difference by contrasting Mrs. Ramsay, the book's central character, with her husband, a philosopher. Another central character, Lily Briscoe, is an artist who paints a portrait of Mrs. Ramsay. As critic Lyall Gordon notes, "The artist behind her easel, the biographer behind her novel reproduce the action of the lighthouse: together they light up a woman's uncharted nature." *To the Lighthouse* is a masterpiece of literary modernism, full of the subjective experiences of a central character who is at odds with the world, and replete with poetic symbols that reveal the character's true nature.

Ernest Hemingway.   One of the most imitated American writers, Ernest Hemingway (1899–1961) wrote novels and short stories in a manner that came to characterize one pole of the modern fictional idiom. His language is laconic and spare. His plots are simple. The complexity of his fiction lies in its suggestiveness, in the implications of what is said and of what is left unspoken. Hemingway believed fiction should reveal less rather than more, like an iceberg with only its tip exposed above water.

Thus Hemingway's style, tone, and manner provide the index to his literary achievement. His first significant book, *In Our Time* (1925), is a series of sketches depicting the realities of war and the violence, skill, and grace of bullfighting. The book's eighteen vignettes range in length from a paragraph to a page. The following is a typical example.

INTERCHAPTER VII

While the bombardment was knocking the trench to pieces at Fossalta, he lay very flat and sweated and prayed oh jesus christ get me out of here. Dear jesus please get me out. Christ please please please christ. If you'll only keep me from getting killed I'll do anything you say. I believe in you and I'll tell every one in the world that you are the only one that matters. Please please dear jesus. The shelling moved further up the line. We went to work on the trench and in the morning the sun came up and the day was hot and muggy and cheerful and quiet. The next night back at Mestre he did not tell the girl he went upstairs with at the Villa Rossa about Jesus. And he never told anybody.

Concise and direct, this sketch is remarkable for its modernist assumptions. An unglamorous pair of incidents demythologizes war, love, and religion. Instead of courage, there is fear; instead of love, a casual encounter with a prostitute. And instead of religious faith, the narrator bargains with a God he forgets once he is out of danger. In a few swift strokes, Hemingway delineates the modern attitude, so different from the past.

Franz Kafka.   The fiction of Franz Kafka (1883–1924) does not form part of a school; nor does it represent a particular type of technical innovation. Kafka's fiction is so distinctive—a blend of the real and the fanciful, the ordinary and the fantastic—that a word has been coined to characterize it: *Kafkaesque*. This term also refers to nightmarish events that wheel out of control and to individuals who, driven by guilt and anxiety, experience a sense of alienation and helplessness in the face of forces they can neither explain nor control. Kafka's is a frightening universe, one in which characters suffer without cause, looking for answers they never find.

Despite the small output, Kafka's writings loom large in modern literature. His three novels, *The Trial* (1925), *The Castle* (1926), and *Amerika* (1927), were all published posthumously—against his wishes, for he had left instructions that his manuscripts be destroyed. The best known of these, *The Trial*, is the only one that contains an ending. Its beginning, one of the most frightening in modern literature, presents Joseph K., a man accused of a crime whose nature is never revealed to him. As he awaits his trial and execution one year later, Joseph K. tries to understand what has happened to him, eventually coming to believe in his guilt. He gradually realizes his guilt or innocence is immaterial, since he feels he deserves his punishment. Kafka renders a world riddled with anxiety and incomprehension, irrational, absurd, confused, lonely, and lost.

RUSSIAN FILM

SERGEI EISENSTEIN [EYE-zen-stine] (1898–1948) was a film theorist as well as a film director. His wideranging knowledge of history, philosophy, science, and the arts is reflected in his films. For Eisenstein, film was the most complete of the arts. It included all the various artistic expressions of conflict—the kinetic conflict of dance, the visual conflict of painting, the verbal conflict of literature and theater, and the conflicts of character essential to fiction and drama.

Eisenstein built his films shot by shot and frame by frame, calculating the dramatic tension until it finally exploded on film. Eisenstein achieved striking effects with lighting, time lapses, designs, and backgrounds in various camera shots, using narratives that were loosely structured and episodic in construction.

In his silent film *Battleship Potemkin*, first shown in 1926, Eisenstein dramatizes the mutiny on board the czarist ship *Potemkin* in 1905, and the ensuing street demonstrations in the port of Odessa. Eisenstein was commissioned to make the film as part of the twentieth anniversary celebrations of the 1905 Revolution. Eisenstein structures his film like a symphony. The first section presents the bloody mutiny and the conditions that precipitated it. The second provides a respite as the ship drops anchor in the harbor after the revolt. Following this lull, a third section

Then & Now

ROBIN HOOD AT THE MOVIES

The adventures of Robin Hood are often retold in movies, and Robin Hood is one of the most popular screen characters of all time. When the 1938 version, *The Adventures of Robin Hood*, appeared, audiences raved about the charismatic Errol Flynn as Robin Hood and Olivia de Haviland as the demure Maid Marian (fig. 21.27).

An earlier version had been made in 1922 with Douglas Fairbanks and Mary Pickford, two of the four co-founders of United Artists. It ran 170 minutes, long for a silent film. It cost over $1.5 million—unheard of in 1922; even Warner Brothers lavished only $2 million on the Flynn remake in 1938.

The Warner Brothers version, in 1938, added sound and color, and Robin Hood came to life. Filmed in Technicolor, it contained deep blacks, dark purples, and luscious greens, and utilized stunning contrasts of light and dark that dazzled audiences. The addition of sound made it possible to speed up the pace, since a silent film required many stills of narrative and dialogue.

Perhaps the greatest contrast between the two early versions lies in the change in the country's ethos and in the studio system's effort to promote Errol Flynn as the embodiment of the hero. In the depressed 1930s, Americans needed a man who "steals from the rich to give to the poor." Flynn's flashing smile and good looks reinforced the appeal. When the film was released, newspapers and magazines covered it, radio shows dramatized parts of the story, and a paperback edition was published with Errol Flynn as Robin Hood on the cover.

Over the years, new versions have been produced. Disney created an animated feature in 1973 in which Robin Hood is a fox. Mel Brooks spoofed the legend in *Robin Hood: Men in Tights* (1993). Brooks's film parodied a previous film, *Robin Hood: Prince of Thieves* (1991), directed by Kevin Costner, in which Robin and his band of Merry Men are portrayed as politically correct rebels.

FIGURE 21.27   Errol Flynn and Olivia de Haviland in Warner Brothers' 1938 movie *The Adventures of Robin Hood.*

---

focuses on the people of Odessa. Here Eisenstein creates his most brilliant editing effects, alternating between the panic-stricken and defenseless masses who support the mutinous sailors and the Cossack soldiers, armed with bayonets, who march relentlessly through the crowd, massacring those who fall in their path. The final section shows the ship returning to sea, with cheers coming from other ships in the fleet. It marks a call to action.

Eisenstein's Odessa sequence (fig. 21.28) includes a formal technique called **montage,** a set of impressions edited to achieve dramatic effect or, here, to increase tension to the point of "emotional saturation." Eisenstein believed viewer tension would find release in an emotional bonding with the victims depicted on screen. Yet, for all its innovations, the film is intentional propaganda and was made to legitimize and celebrate the revolution.

MODERN MUSIC

Music too embodied the discord and disharmony of this anxious age. Before the war, Stravinsky's *The Rite of Spring* had shaken the foundations of tonality, and hence traditional harmony. Stravinsky's use of multiple tonal centers created dissonance and harmonic disorientation. Fleeing to Switzerland during the war, and returning to Paris in 1920, Stravinsky began work on a new ballet for Diaghilev, entitled *Pulcinella*. Taking a number of sonatas by Classical composers, Stravinsky reworked their harmonies to make them dissonant, changed their phrase lengths to make them irregular, and altered their rhythms to make them lively and syncopated. "*Pulcinella*," he would later admit, "was my discovery of the past." But his was a past thoroughly modernized.

Arnold Schoenberg.   The Viennese composer ARNOLD SCHOENBERG [SHONE-berg] (1874–1951) undermined the stability of Western classical music even further by writing music that lacked a *tonal center*, or home key. **Atonality,** he called it. Much of this work was done before the war and badly received. He was convinced tonality was a "straitjacket," but also realized that atonality was structureless. Consequently, he developed a twelve-tone musical scale, as used in the *Variation for Orchestra* (1931). The twelve-tone scale was based on the traditional octave, counting all the half steps. Twelve-tone composition would "level" each tone, giving none more weight

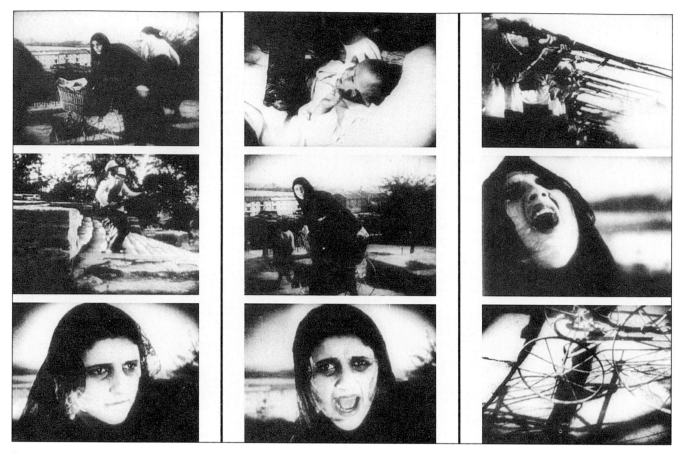

FIGURE 21.28 These consecutive film stills from Sergei Eisenstein's *Battleship Potemkin* (1924) reveal the director's dramatic use of close-up and the contrast between human and inanimate images.

than any other, by predetermining the order in which the tones would be played. This order would be used for the entire composition, sequence after sequence.

The music is difficult to listen to for audiences accustomed to traditional harmony, but, given the proper theme, it can be moving. Jewish by birth, Schoenberg based many of his works on Jewish liturgy, including his opera *Moses und Aaron* (1923), which is based on a single twelve-tone series.

REPRESSION AND DEPRESSION: THE THIRTIES

World War I was meant to be "the war to end all wars." Instead it left a sense of disillusionment and fear that led many to crave security. Some found security in authoritarian leadership and in inflated national pride, which blamed adverse conditions on others. Although the end of the war brought a semblance of peace, it did not bring harmony. As the Russian communist experiment took hold, it threatened other nations. Workers throughout Europe looked to the Russian communists for a new vision and

identity. When worldwide economic depression struck in 1929, simplistic explanations, such as blaming bankers for all economic woes, appealed to many.

FASCISM IN EUROPE

Benito Mussolini. In many respects, BENITO MUSSOLINI [moo-soh-LEE-nee] (1883–1945) is responsible for the invention of fascism, which was first established in Italy. Expelled from the Italian Socialist Party for advocating Italian entry into World War I, Mussolini formed groups of so-called *fasci* (from the Latin word for the bundle of rods that symbolize the Roman Republic). These groups consisted of young men like himself who called for Italy's entry into the war in 1915.

Mussolini's power base expanded rapidly after the war. He organized Italians who were dissatisfied with the government and who opposed the socialist cause as Bolshevik. Mussolini's fascist bands, with the support of the Italian police, openly attacked labor union offices, opposition newspapers, and antifascist politicians. Nearly two thousand people were killed between October 1920 and October 1922. Meanwhile, Mussolini gained power, and on

October 29, 1922, he was named premier. By the late 1920s, the government was totally controlled by the Fascist Party, and Mussolini had become more dictator than premier, both head of the party and chief of state. He outlawed emigration, advocated the largest possible families by reducing taxes with each successive child, and taxed bachelors in an attempt to encourage them to marry. His dream was to create, in a single generation, a huge Italian army and a country thoroughly loyal to the goals of the fascist state. Education, from textbooks to professors, became a propaganda arm of the government itself. The police sought out dissenters and eliminated them.

Adolf Hitler. Meanwhile, the fascist approach to government spread to Germany, where Adolf Hitler (1889–1945) took advantage of public despair over the state of Germany's economy after World War I. In 1923,

the value of the German currency decreased from a few thousand marks to the dollar to literally trillions of marks to the dollar by the end of the year. Lifetime savings were suddenly worthless. Workers found themselves earning starvation wages as even the price of bread rocketed. In Munich, Adolf Hitler created the National Socialist Party of the German Workers—the **Nazi** (abbreviation for "National") Party.

In 1921, Hitler named himself *führer* (or leader) of the Nazi Party. He became chancellor of the Nazi Party in January 1933, backed by the party's new *Schutzstaffel*, or *SS* (literally, "Defense Force"), an elite honor guard, and by the *Sturmabteilung*, or *SA* (literally, "Storm Troops"), a huge private army. A month later, a fire broke out in the Reichstag, the central buildings of German government, and Hitler quickly blamed it on the communists. By noon the next day, four thousand members of the Communist

MAP 21.2   Left- and right-wing Europe, 1918–39.

Party had been arrested, and their citizenship rights had been suspended.

In August 1934, Hitler became president and chancellor of Germany. Every political party that opposed him was banned. Like Mussolini in Italy, Hitler was convinced the Bolsheviks were responsible for the catastrophic state of the German economy. The Jews became Hitler's primary target. The "Nuremberg Laws" of September 1935 defined a Jew as anyone with one Jewish grandparent. It denounced marriage between Jews and non-Jews as "racial pollution" and prohibited it. Jews were forbidden to teach in educational institutions and were banned from writing, publishing, acting, painting, and performing music. Nor were they allowed to work in hospitals or banks, bookstores or law offices. In November 1938, after a seventeen-year-old Jewish boy shot and killed the secretary of the German Embassy in Paris, mobs looted and burned Jewish shops and synagogues all over Germany. They swept through the streets, entering Jewish homes, beating the occupants, and stealing their possessions. After this night, known as *Kristallnacht* (literally, "Night of Glass"), the extent of German anti-Semitism was apparent to the world.

From the beginning, Hitler's Nazi Party was militaristic in its discipline, organization, and goals. Nazis were proponents of the policy of **Lebensraum** ("living space"), which they claimed justified the geographic expansion of the state into other countries' territories to make room for what they believed was the "superior" German race of people. By the mid-1930s, Hitler was preparing for war.

Francisco Franco. Spain had been in disarray since the king's overthrow in 1931. Spain's Popular Front, consisting of a coalition of Republicans, Socialists, labor unions, Communists, and anarchists, won an electoral victory in February 1936. Shortly thereafter, however, Spain's right formed the Falange ("Phalanx"), a coalition of monarchists, clerics (whose church schools had been closed), and the military, who desired to overthrow the new Republican government. At the Falange's head was General Francisco Franco (1892–1975), who on July 17, 1936, with his right-wing army, led a coordinated revolt in Spanish Morocco and in a number of towns in mainland Spain—Córdoba, Seville, and Burgos, among them.

The Spanish Civil War had begun. Within a few weeks, about a third of the country was under Franco's control, but Barcelona, Madrid, and Valencia remained Republican strongholds, as did the Basque provinces in the north. The Soviet Union supported the Republican cause, furnishing them with military advisers and organizing international brigades of volunteers (among them Ernest Hemingway).

Mussolini and Hitler supported Franco. Hitler even provided Franco with an air force. On April 26, 1937, Wolfram von Richthofen, the cousin of the German ace Manfred von Richthofen, the Red Baron of World War I, planned an attack on the town of Guernica in northern Spain, where Basque Republican forces were retreating.

Beginning at half past four in the afternoon and lasting for three and a half hours, a strike force of thirty-three planes, each loaded with three thousand pounds of bombs, pummeled the city. By the time the fires subsided three days later, the town center had been razed to the ground—fifteen square blocks—and a thousand innocent citizens had been killed. As news of the event spread, Pablo Picasso, living in Paris, began work on a giant canvas commemorating the massacre, a disaster that foreshadowed the bombing of cities in World War II.

Guernica (fig. 21.29) is the culmination of Picasso's Surrealist style. Painted only in black, white, and grays, it contains a Pietà theme, and many elements of Surrealist dream symbolism. The horse, speared and dying in anguish, represents the fate of creativity. The entire scene is surveyed by a bull, which represents Spain and the bullfight—the struggle of life and death. The bull also represents the Minotaur, the bull-man of Greek mythology, which stands for the animalistic forces of the human psyche. The electric light bulb, at the top center of the painting, and the oil lamp, held by the woman reaching out of the window, have been much debated, and represent, on a fundamental level, old and new ways of seeing.

Franco captured the Republican strongholds of Madrid and Barcelona in 1939 and ruled Spain as a fascist dictator until his death in 1975. The attack on Guernica and other fascist victories in Spain outraged the Allies, but they proved to Hitler just how effective his military forces and tactics were. While the Spanish Civil War was winding down, Hitler sent troops into Czechoslovakia, in March 1939. Meeting with little or no resistance, shortly thereafter Hitler set his designs on Poland—and the world.

FRANKLIN DELANO ROOSEVELT AND THE NEW DEAL

Throughout the 1920s, the United States had enjoyed unprecedented prosperity, fueled by speculation on the stock market and the extraordinary expansion of the industrial infrastructure. For the first time in history, a country could define itself not as an agricultural society, nor as an industrial one, but as a consumer society. Houses, automobiles, and everyday goods were purchased on credit, in an almost unregulated economic climate. Unfortunately, this prosperity was built on a house of cards, and on October 29, 1929, it all came tumbling down in a stock market crash. Many of the wealthiest people in America were devastated, as $30 billion of assets disappeared within two weeks. Faced with massive withdrawals they could not sustain, banks closed. Families lost their life savings. By the early 1930s, over sixteen million American men were unemployed, nearly a third of the workforce. To make matters worse, whole areas of the Midwest suffered severe drought. The effect, exacerbated by overplowing, was the creation of a giant **Dust Bowl**. Whole populations left the

FIGURE 21.29 Pablo Picasso, *Guernica*, 1937, oil on canvas, 11′5 $\frac{1}{2}$″ × 25′5 $\frac{1}{4}$″ (3.49 × 7.75 m). Centro de Arte Reina Sofia, Madrid/Licensed by SCALA/Art Resource, NY. © 2005 Estate of Pablo Picasso/Artists Rights Society, NY. After Franco's victory in 1939, *Guernica* was exhibited at the Museum of Modern Art in New York where Picasso placed it on "extended loan." He did, however, affirm that the painting belonged "to the Spanish Republic," but he forbade its return to Spain until such time that democracy and "individual liberties" were restored there. With the death of Franco in 1975, the subsequent crowning of Juan Carlos as constitutional monarch in 1977, and the adoption of a democratic constitution in 1978, the painting was finally returned to Spain in 1981.

hardest hit areas of Arkansas and Oklahoma for California, an exodus depicted by John Steinbeck in his novel *The Grapes of Wrath*.

Fearing that economic catastrophe would lead to the rise of fascism as seen in Europe, or worse, communism, the U.S. government decided to intervene. President Franklin Delano Roosevelt (1882–1945), or "FDR" as he was called, declared a bank holiday in 1933; gradually those institutions that were financially sound reopened. Roosevelt recognized that at the root of the **Depression** was a deep imbalance between the haves and the have-nots. He wanted to give the have-nots what he called a "New Deal." In 1935, a Social Security Act inaugurated unemployment insurance and old-age pensions. Tax codes were revised to increase the tax burden on wealthier Americans in an effort to close the gap. Agricultural subsidies were given to farmers to maintain agricultural production and to steady the economy. For the arts, the Works Progress Administration (WPA) was established to subsidize authors, artists, and musicians.

PHOTOGRAPHY AND THE FSA

To create a sense of national consensus for Roosevelt's social reforms, photographers were subsidized by the Farm Security Administration (FSA) to portray the plight of American farmers and sharecroppers devastated by Depression and drought.

Dorothea Lange. One of the photographers to be part of the plan was Dorothea Lange (1895–1965). Lange's documentary style, although seemingly objective, was driven by a social reformist impulse. Lange's most famous photograph, *Migrant Mother, Nipomo, California* (fig. 21.30), depicts a young widow with three of her ten forlorn children, migrants on the way to California, the sort that Steinbeck described. She stares into space, pensive and anxious, her glance avoiding the camera. She looks much older than her thirty-two years. Her children turn inward, seeking shelter beside their mother, who has none for herself. The picture's grainy gray tones complete the mood of resignation.

Walker Evans. Another FSA photographer, Walker Evans (1903–1975), is best known for his photographs for *Let Us Now Praise Famous Men* by James Agee published in 1941, which details Evans and Agee's life with a family of sharecroppers in Hale County, Alabama, in 1936. Agee's "famous" men are the forgotten people of poverty. He describes, for instance, the sharecroppers' house as nightfall creeps over it: "The house and all that was in it had now descended deep beneath the gradual spiral it had sunk through; it lay formal under the order of entire silence."

FIGURE 21.30 Dorothea Lange, *Migrant Mother; Nipomo, California*, 1936, gelatin silver print, Library of Congress, Washington, D.C. Lange chose to include only three of the mother's ten children in this photograph because she did not want to add to widespread resentment in wealthier parts of American society about overpopulation among the poor.

FIGURE 21.31 Walker Evans, *Washroom and Dining Area of Floyd Burroughs's Home, Hale County, Alabama*, 1936, photograph, Library of Congress, Washington, D.C. The power of this photograph rests not only in its formal coherence, but in it stunning focus, its ability to capture the texture of wood, cloth, glass, and vinyl in a manner that makes everything almost real enough to touch.

Evans's *Washroom and Dining Area of Floyd Burroughs's Home, Hale County, Alabama* (fig. 21.31) is dominated by a grid of verticals and horizontals, punctuated by a single oval washbowl on the right and an oil lamp on the left. The work echoes Mondrian's "pure" abstractions. As it embodies the stark poverty of a sharecropper's life, Evans's photograph reveals a dignity in the clean lines of this sparse world, a dignity that also marks Agee's accompanying prose.

Margaret Bourke-White.   Like Evans, Margaret Bourke-White (1904–1971) collaborated with a writer, her husband Erskine Caldwell, to depict the social realities of the Depression. Their best known project is *You Have Seen Their Face* (1937). But it was Bourke-White's photo-journalism that earned her worldwide recognition. One of the first photographers hired by *Life* magazine after its founding in 1936, Bourke-White came to define the profession.

Her photographs of the Depression depict the harsh conditions of the time. *At the Time of the Louisville Flood* (fig. 21.32) records the aftermath of the great flood of the Ohio River in January 1937. Inundating Louisville, Kentucky, it left over nine hundred people dead or injured. On

assignment for *Life*, Bourke-White arrived on the last flight before the airfield was closed, and she hitchhiked on rescue rowboats shooting photo after photo of the scene. *At the Time of the Louisville Flood* juxtaposes a soup line of African Americans displaced by disaster against the government billboard behind them, thus seeming to indict the American dream as mere government propaganda.

Bourke-White worked throughout the world, covering World War II and the Korean War as a correspondent. She was the first woman photographer attached to the U.S. armed forces, and the only U.S. photographer to cover the siege of Moscow in 1941.

Louise Dahl-Wolfe.   The American LOUISE DAHL-WOLFE (1895–1989), although known for her fashion photography, preferred portraiture. Her photograph of

FIGURE 21.32 Margaret Bourke-White, *At the Time of the Louisville Flood*, 1937, photograph. *Life* magazine offered many photographers the opportunity to work professionally. Reacting to the arrival of *Life* magazine on the publishing scene, Bourke-White said, "I could almost feel the horizon widening and the great rush of wind sweeping in. . . . This was the kind of magazine that could be anything we chose to make it."

Colette (fig. 21.33) is among those of famous writers Dahl-Wolfe took while on staff for many years (1936–58) at the magazine *Harper's Bazaar*. This casual and intimate portrait shows Colette, the French novelist, interrupted while writing in bed, in her apartment in Paris. Known for her technical perfection, Dahl-Wolfe developed her photographs

FIGURE 21.33 Louise Dahl-Wolfe, American, *Colette*, 1951, gelatin silver print, $10\frac{7}{8} \times 13\frac{1}{8}''$ (27.6 × 33.3 cm), National Museum of Women in the Arts, Washington, D.C. Gift of Helen Cumming Ziegler. © 1989 Center for Creative Photography, Arizona Board of Regents. As Colette glances up, pen in hand, Dahl-Wolfe's photo skillfully and subtly suggests that the viewer is standing very close to the famous French author—and has disturbed her as she writes.

herself and was among the first to work with color photography. She enjoyed her many successes during a long and productive life.

Lola Alvarez Bravo. Born Dolores (Lola) Martinez Vianda in Jalisco. Mexico, an orphan at the age of eight, Lola Alvarez Bravo (1907–93) married the Mexican photographer Manuel Alvarez Bravo, from whom she was later divorced. Her photographs record daily life in Mexico, in the city as well as in the country, for example, her print *From Generation to Generation* (fig. 21.34), taken around 1950, and of the famous people as well as of the ordinary. Highly successful as a photographer, Bravo also had an art gallery in Mexico City where, in 1953, she gave Frida Kahlo a one-woman exhibition—the only one held in Mexico during Kahlo's lifetime. Bravo taught photography at the Academia de San Carlos in Mexico City.

FIGURE 21.34 Lola Alvarez Bravo, *From Generation to Generation*, gelatin silver print, ca. 1950, $9 \times 6\frac{1}{8}''$ (22.9 × 15.6 cm). National Museum of Women in the Arts, Washington, D.C. In this charming photo, a wide-eyed child stares inquisitively at the viewer. Bravo created a contrast between young and old, small and large, front and back. Aesthetically striking, this could be analyzed as a carefully composed arrangement in blacks, grays, and whites.

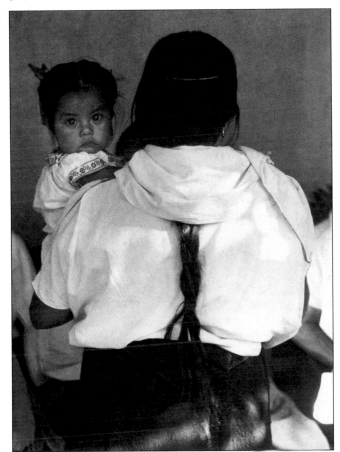

Critical Thinking

PHOTOGRAPHY AND TRUTH

A picture, it has been said, is worth a thousand words. And it has often been remarked how photographs capture the truth of a scene, rendering it as the scene exists in real life. However, we might want to ask a few questions about these commonly accepted notions.

To what extent do photographs, snapshots of a moment of time, tell the truth?

To what extent are photographs limited by the moment of their shooting? By the angle or perspective from which they are taken?

To what extent can photographs be "arranged" to suggest something that supposedly happened spontaneously, but was actually "staged" by the photographer? How would you go about deciding what was "staged" and what was unvarnished reality? And can a "staged" or "arranged" photograph convey the truth of a situation, such as a love relationship or a social situation, such as racial harmony or racial tension, for example? How would you determine if a photograph was telling the "truth," or if it was revealing only a partial, and therefore slanted, truth? How do you distinguish between photographs that portray truth and those that convey propaganda?

REGIONALISM IN AMERICAN PAINTING

The success achieved by photographers working for the FSA was underpinned by the realist impulse in American culture. Many American artists, especially in the Midwest, rejected abstraction and turned instead to a more naturalistic representation of the American experience through regional scenes.

Edward Hopper. Although he had traveled to Europe several times between 1906 and 1910, for his 1933 exhibition at the Museum of Modern Art, Edward Hopper (1882–1967) wrote, "A nation's art is greatest when it most reflects the character of its people. . . . We are not French and never can be and any attempt to be so is to deny our inheritance and to try to impose upon ourselves a character that can be nothing but a veneer upon surface."

Hopper's paintings record the American scene. Its cafés, restaurants, stores, and barber-shops are his subject matter. Hopper paints places inhabited by the middle class, representing ordinary things that had previously been deemed unworthy of an artist's attention. He is adept at conveying disquieting isolation and regret. *Nighthawks* (fig. 21.35), of 1942, portrays the bleak loneliness and the alienation of city life after hours. Stark and still, few human figures appear in Hopper's paintings; often, there is no one at all.

Thomas Hart Benton. The regionalist impulse was supported by the Works Progress Administration (WPA), which initiated a mural project to decorate public buildings across the country. The murals were to represent American themes and experiences. Over two thousand murals were painted between 1935 and 1939, and among the best were those by Thomas Hart Benton (1889–1975). Benton was radically anti-European. "The fact that our art was arguable in the language of the street," he wrote, "was proof to us that we had succeeded in separating it from the hothouse atmosphere of an imported, and for our country, functionless aesthetic."

One of his most ambitious undertakings was a set of murals for the Missouri State Capitol, recording the social history of Missouri (fig. 21.36). Almost every aspect of Missouri life is depicted. In a domestic scene, an old woman rolls out dough while an old man reads and a young boy drinks a glass of milk. To the left are various farming scenes; a cow is milked; pigs are fed; a farmer sits atop his tractor. To the right a lawyer argues a case before the jury in a courtroom.

Jacob Lawrence. Another, earlier migration, reminiscent of the migration of Oklahoma farmworkers, was that of African Americans after World War I. They moved steadily from the South to the North seeking employment in rapidly expanding industries. Between 1916 and 1923, the African American population in major northern cities doubled. African-American artist Jacob Lawrence (1917–2000), supported by the WPA, captured this movement in a series of tempera paintings, *The Migration of the Negro*, made between 1939 and 1941.

Those who migrated first found jobs in the north because of labor shortages resulting from World War I, but as others followed, life in the north soon revealed itself to be little different from life in the south. The *Migration* series depicts the entire saga. The migrants arriving in Chicago, St. Louis, Pittsburgh, and New York encounter injustice, racism, and inadequate housing. Race riots result. In one panel, *They Also Found Discrimination* (fig. 21.37), Lawrence depicts the racial divide the African Americans encountered in the north. A subtle, yet startling effect is the facelessness of the African Americans. They are anonymous, undifferentiated, "invisible," to use the word of African American writer Ralph Ellison, who explored this experience in his classic novel, *Invisible Man*.

FIGURE 21.35   Edward Hopper, *Nighthawks*, 1942, oil on canvas, 2′6″ × 4′8$\frac{11}{16}$″ (76.2 × 143.9 cm), Friends of American Art Collection, 1942. 1 © 1997 Art Institute of Chicago. Photograph © 2005, The Art Institute of Chicago. All Rights Reserved. Using carefully constructed compositions to depict ordinary subjects, especially the loneliness of urban life, the artist documented the American scene.

SOUTHERN REGIONALIST WRITING

Regionalism is also identifiable in American fiction between the two world wars. Especially in the South, a distinct brand of writing developed. The South's "tall-tale" tradition was enhanced by colorful dialect and usage and, in no small part, by the memory of the Civil War, which fostered a sense of hurt pride and regional identity. The writing of southern regionalists is marked by violent and grotesque characters who are often treated with colloquial humor. It is also distinguished, in particular, by a sense of place.

William Faulkner.   Unlike Hemingway, who chose fictional settings in various parts of the world, William Faulkner (1897–1962) chose to remain a chronicler of the American South. Set in fictional Yoknapatawpha County—very much like his native Lafayette County, Mississippi—Faulkner's work describes the decline of local families. His work, which ranges widely in style, tone, and technique, earned him a Nobel Prize in 1950.

Faulkner novels experiment with narrative. In *The Sound and the Fury*, for instance, he tells the story of the increasing misfortunes of the Compson family from four

Table 21–1   IMPORTANT STYLES OF PAINTING DURING THE AGE OF ANXIETY

Style	Artist	Painting and Date
Dada	Arp	*Portrait of Tristan Tzara*, 1916
De Stijl	Mondrian	*Composition in Red, Yellow, and Blue*, 1920
Surrealism	Miró	*Painting*, 1933
	Dali	*The Persistence of Memory*, 1931
American modernism	O'Keeffe	*Yellow Calla*, 1926
	Demuth	*Aucassin and Nicolette*, 1921
American regionalism	Hopper	*Nighthawks*, 1942
	Benton	*Missouri Mural*, 1936
	Lawrence	*They Also Found Discrimination*, 1940–41

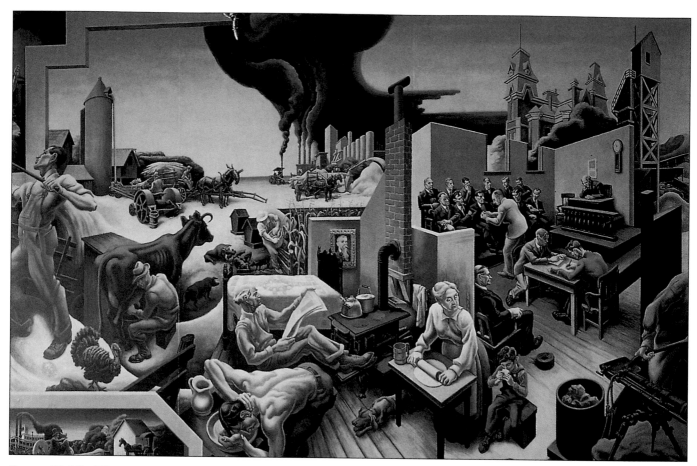

FIGURE 21.36 Thomas Hart Benton, *Missouri Mural* (section), 1936, Missouri State Capitol, Jefferson City, Missouri, oil on canvas, © T.H. Benton and R.P. Benton Testamentary Trusts/ Licensed by VAGA, New York, NY. The WPA's mural project was directly inspired by the example of the Mexican muralists, one of whom, Diego Rivera, is discussed in the Cross Currents box in this chapter, and whose efforts were supported by the Mexican government.

different points of view. Each narrative perspective provides a context for the others, so the whole story becomes known through compilation. He also uses a stream of consciousness technique.

Faulkner understood that in exploring the world close to him he was also exploring ideas that resonated beyond the locales he was describing. As he himself put it, "I discovered that my own little postage stamp of native soil was worth writing about and that I would never live long enough to exhaust it." For all its experimental form and rhetorical brilliance, Faulkner's work derives its power from his depiction of characters, whose struggle to endure remains familiar and remarkable. In his Nobel Prize acceptance speech, Faulkner noted that "man will not merely endure: he will prevail . . . because he has a soul, a spirit capable of compassion and sacrifice and endurance."

Flannery O'Connor. The stories of Flannery O'Connor (1925–64) explore humor, irony, and paradox, especially the paradox of evil and redemption. O'Connor's social

satires challenge American attitudes about violence, race, and class.

Although O'Connor set her fiction in the South, she explored Christian beliefs that transcend the confines of one region. "The woods are full of regional writers," she once said, "and it is the great horror of every serious Southern writer that he will become one of them." Several of O'Connor's stories begin with a comic protagonist who indulges in fantasies of moral or social superiority or who has a false sense of the certainty of things. The protagonist then has a traumatic encounter with other characters or with ironic situations that suggest a disturbing and incomprehensible universe. Although her stories blend comedy and tragedy, several end quite gruesomely.

THE AMERICAN SOUND

Just as American painters and writers evoked the distinct character of America's regions, a number of composers and musicians sought to convey their own sense of a dis-

FIGURE 21.37 Jacob Lawrence, *They Also Found Discrimination*, from the series *The Migration of the Negro*, panel 49. 1940–41, tempera on wood, $21\frac{1}{4} \times 18''$ (54 × 45.7 cm), Philips Collection, Washington, DC. Courtesy of the Jacob and Gwendolyn Lawrence Foundation. When the series was exhibited in 1941, Lawrence achieved instant fame, and the series was purchased jointly by the Philips Collection and the Museum of Modern Art, in New York, who divided the panels between them. It was reassembled as a complete series in the mid-1990s when it toured the country—once again to national acclaim.

tinctively American "sound." For over two centuries, people had brought their own musical customs and instruments from many different countries, and, as they settled into communities, different folk sounds developed across the land. Spirited banjo and fiddle music grew popular in the Appalachian mountains; cowboy songs thrived on the American prairie; gospel music arose in African American communities in the South; and jazz, which developed in New Orleans, spread to big cities around the country, including New York, Chicago, and Los Angeles.

Charles Ives. Charles Ives (1874–1954) was an American original, an insurance executive who was at the same time an innovative composer. While steeped in the classi-

cal music tradition, Ives wrote distinctively American music, which, like the poetry of Walt Whitman, expresses the multiplicity of American life. Ives's music echoes American folk songs, marches, fiddle tunes, spirtuals, and patriotic songs while also evoking snatches of Beethoven and Brahms. Like Whitman, Ives could "hear America singing," and he captured a multitude of American voices in his collection *114 Songs*, which includes sentimental ballads, war songs, street songs, religious songs, folk tunes, cowboy songs, humorous songs, and dramatic poems.

Ives was influenced by the writings of the American Transcendentalists, especially Ralph Waldo Emerson and Henry David Thoreau. Transcendentalism's optimism, its belief in the innate goodness of human beings, its emphasis on individualism and self-reliance, and its appreciation of nature all captured Ives's imagination. These ideals find expression in Ives's songs and symphonies, and especially in his *Concord Sonata* for piano, with its movements devoted to Emerson and Thoreau, in his *Unanswered Question*, subtitled philosophically "A Cosmic Landscape," and in his *Universe Symphony*, which Ives once described as "a presentation and contemplation in tones . . . of the mysterious creation of the earth and firmament, the evolution of all life in nature, in humanity to the Divine."

Aaron Copland. Born in Brooklyn, New York, AARON COPLAND [COPE-land] (1900–90) is an esteemed American composer. After his early training, Copland went to Paris for four years, where he experienced firsthand the artistic energy of Picasso, Stravinsky, Hemingway, Pound, and many other modernist writers, artists, and composers. Returning to America in the mid-1920s, Copland was determined to compose music with a distinctively American style that would appeal to a wide audience. He achieved this with a series of ballet scores that relied on American folk elements. Copland worked with two leading choreographers who were themselves striving for uniquely American dance aesthetics. Agnes de Mille choreographed the ballet *Rodeo* to Copland's music in 1942; in 1944, Martha Graham choreographed *Appalachian Spring*. De Mille went on to arrange the stage dance for several leading Broadway musicals, including *Oklahoma!* (1943) and had her own touring company for years.

Although Copland's score for the ballet *Rodeo* has been a favorite among American audiences, his *Appalachian Spring* is performed more frequently as a concert piece. The work's subject is, as he said, "a pioneer celebration in spring around a newly built farmhouse in the Pennsylvania hills" in the early nineteenth century. A bride and groom, their neighbor, and a preacher and his congregation constitute the piece's characters. Copland's music imitates American fiddle tunes and hymns, including *Simple Gifts*, the traditional Shaker hymn.

George Gershwin. Inspired by African-American blues and jazz, George Gershwin (1898–1937) fused classical

Connections

ART AS POLITICS

An art as abstract as that of Malevich and El Lissitzky might seem ineffectual as a political tool, but it was conceived in quite the opposite terms, as a means of bringing art to the masses. In the late nineteenth century, a number of St. Petersburg artists, calling themselves the Wanderers, sought to champion the newly emancipated peasant class by bringing art to the people through traveling exhibitions. This initiative took new form soon after the disturbances of 1905, when the Bolsheviks began to use wall posters extensively: They were inexpensive, and appealed to the mostly illiterate masses. By 1917, the poster was a major Russian art form. El Lissitzky's *Beat the Whites with the Red Wedge* (fig. 21.38), of 1919, is a perfect example. Using basic geometric shapes, the Red Army is represented by the triangle that pierces the circular form, which in turn represents the White Army. The sense of aggression, originating both figuratively and literally from "the left," is unmistakable.

Such propaganda art was soon disseminated throughout Russia, primarily by means of Agit-trains. These consisted of seven or eight railway cars sent "to establish ties between the localities and the center, to agitate, to carry out propaganda, to bring information, and to supply literature." Each was also equipped with a film projector. The peasants were

fascinated by film, and Lenin quickly realized the power of the medium as propaganda. Sitting on the train, the people watched newsreels of Lenin—entertained, but also indoctrinated in the Bolshevik cause.

At first, the Agit-trains were decorated with abstract Russian art, but the peasants objected. So they were repainted with pictures of soldiers, workers, and peasants, a development that foreshadowed the fate of Russian modernist art as a whole. Abstraction did not speak to the masses after all. At the end of the first Five-Year Plan in 1932, Stalin outlawed independent artistic organizations, and in 1934 he proclaimed "Socialist Realism" as the official Soviet style. Abstraction was permanently banned in the Soviet Union.

FIGURE 21.38   El Lissitzky, *Beat the Whites with the Red Wedge*, 1919–20, lithograph, $20\frac{7}{8} \times 27\frac{1}{2}''$ (53 × 70 cm), Stedelijk Van Abbemuseum, Eindhoven, The Netherlands. Russian poster design would soon begin to incorporate photographic images in photomontages.

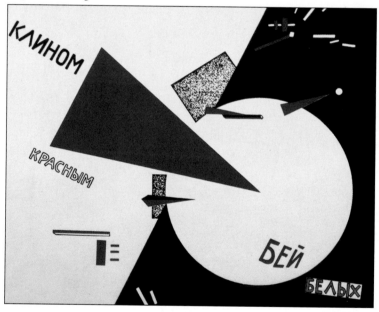

and jazz elements, mingling a wide range of sounds. Gershwin's work stands for the sound of the modern age, as signified by the four taxi horns in *An American in Paris* (1928), his tribute to the expatriate scene.

An accomplished jazz pianist himself, Gershwin's *Rhapsody in Blue* (1924) and his *Piano Concerto in F* (1925) were both composed with a view to taking advantage of his own skill at the keyboard, and both include long piano solos accompanied by full orchestra. Gershwin is best known for *Porgy and Bess* (1935), one of the earliest and most important American operas (fig. 21.40). It addresses the lives of poor black people in Charleston, South Carolina, and contains some of the most widely heard songs of the 1930s, including the hit "Summertime." Gershwin

traveled to South Carolina to familiarize himself with the local dialect and the region's performance rituals, witnessed in church services and public gatherings.

THE JAZZ AGE

The origins of American **jazz** go back to the rhythms and songs of Africa. In vocal music, the call and response pattern of ritual tribal practice, in which the leader sings a phrase to which the community replies, can be heard in gospel, jazz, and even rock and roll. The jazz **riff,** a short phrase improvised over and over, often unifies the music, as can the so-called samples that are the basis of today's rap and hip-hop. Syncopated and offbeat rhythms, to-

Cross Currents

DIEGO RIVERA AND THE DETROIT MURALS

In the early 1920s, the Mexican government initiated a mural movement designed to give the Mexican people a sense of identity and national pride. A leading painter of this movement, Diego Rivera (1886–1957), had lived in Paris, studying the work of Picasso and Braque, and had developed a fluid Cubist style. But when confronted with the task of creating a national revolutionary art, he traveled to Italy to study the Italian fresco and immersed himself in Mexico's pre-Columbian heritage.

In 1931, Rivera was commissioned by Edsel B. Ford and the Detroit Institute of Arts to create a series of frescoes depicting Detroit for the museum's Garden Court. Being fascinated by both the promise of modern industry and the plight of industrial workers, Rivera decided to represent Detroit's industry—its famous automobile factories, pharmaceutical and chemical companies, its aviation facilities and power plants.

Working from drawings and photographs, Rivera made panels for all four walls of the court, with large panels for the north and south walls. At the top of the north panel (fig. 21.39) are depictions of two of what he regarded as the four races of humanity—the Native American and the African American. Opposite them, on the south panel, are images of the Caucasian and Asian races. The main part of the north panel depicts the assembly line of automobile manufacturing, showing people molding engine blocks, boring cylinders, and making the final touches. At the bottom left, a line of workers punch into a time clock. At the bottom right, they eat lunch. Between the two, Rivera captures the extraordinary exertion and strength required of these workers, all day, every day.

FIGURE 21.39 Diego Rivera, *Detroit Industry* (north wall), 1932–33, fresco, main panel 17′8½″ × 45′ (5.40 × 13.20 m). Detroit Institute of Arts. Gift of Edsel B. Ford. © 2003 Banco de Mexico, Diego Rivera & Frida Kahlo Museums Trust. D.F. Reproduction authorized by the Instituto National de Bellas Artesy Literatura. At once a celebration of industry and an exposé of the workers' plight, Rivera's mural is a relatively optimistic plea for social and economic reform through, and by means of, industrial progress.

gether with improvisation of a basic melody or phrase, are the characteristic features of jazz.

Scott Joplin. Scott Joplin (1868–1917) made famous **ragtime,** a type of jazz piano composition in which the left hand plays a steady beat while the right improvises on a melody in a syncopated rhythm. **Syncopation** means accenting a beat where it is not expected, in particular off beat or in between beats. Joplin, the son of a slave, began his career as the pianist at the Maple Leaf Saloon in Sedalia, Missouri. His score of the "Maple Leaf Rag," published in 1899, quickly sold hundreds of thousands of copies and ranks as one of the first pop hits.

Louis Armstrong. One of the best-loved jazz musicians of all time is Louis Armstrong (1900–71). Also known as "Satchmo," Armstrong was a vocalist and a trumpeter. Born and raised in New Orleans, a mecca for jazz in America, Armstrong first played in a New Orleans jazz combo. A few years later, Armstrong left to play cornet in Chicago with King Oliver's Creole Jazz Band. In no time, he was recording with his own bands and secured his place as the premier jazz trumpeter.

A stunning improviser, Armstrong could take a simple melody and transform it into a singing, swinging piece by changing its rhythm and altering its pitches. He could also play the trumpet in higher registers than anyone else, and he made his music distinctive with an array of vibratos and note-altering variations.

His gravelly voice, neither elegant nor beautiful, conveyed spirit and fire. Among his vocal techniques was **scat**

FIGURE 21.40   A scene from a production of George Gershwin's *Porgy and Bess* at Glyndebourne, England.

singing, in which Armstrong vocalized nonsense syllables on a melody. Ella Fitzgerald, after him, was to take scat to new heights.

Duke Ellington.   The great jazz pianist and arranger Edward Kennedy ("Duke") Ellington (1899–1974) was a composer and conductor of a jazz ensemble, or swing band (fig. 21.41). Unlike the New Orleans–style combo featuring improvisations by each of the five to eight members of the group, **swing** music was played by big bands of approximately fifteen musicians arranged in three groups: saxophones/clarinets, brasses (trumpets/trombones), and rhythm (piano, percussion, guitar, and bass). Although swing often included improvised solos, its music was most often arranged due to the larger size of the group. The members of the swing band did more ensemble playing, with each section taking its turn: saxes, brasses, and rhythm, playing in unison. The saxophone became a popular solo instrument during the swing era (1925–45), with percussion instruments and the piano also becoming prominent instruments of jazz expression.

Ellington composed mini-concertos within pieces. One example, his *Concerto for Cootie* (1940), showcases Ellington's trumpeter Cootie Williams, whose command of tonal color differed markedly from Louis Armstrong.

FIGURE 21.41   The Duke Ellington Orchestra in 1949. Ellington was a dynamic and creative performer. He and his band were immensely popular at the famous Cotton Club in Harlem.

Cultural Impact

The early Modernist spirit took root in the first years of the twentieth century when late-nineteenth-century artistic styles seemed tame in comparison with styles such as Fauvism and Cubism. Early Modernism was a time of cultural energy and artistic revolution. Braque and Picasso pushed painting toward abstraction. Severini's seemingly animate painting typified the energy of the period, as did the hard-driving propulsive music of Igor Stravinsky. Modernism celebrated the speed and energy of modern life. Literary artists, such as Joyce and Wolfe, Eliot and Pound, in their fiction and poetry, respectively, captured something of the complexity of modern life.

With the advent of Einsteinian physics and Freudian psychology, conceptions of the external world of nature and the internal world of human nature were fundamentally altered. Fixed points of reference gave way to a relativity of perspective, both physically and psychologically. Conventional explanations made way for psychological forces derived from early childhood experience and manifested in dreams. Old certainties were undermined and new forms of explanation and representation were emerging.

The greatest legacy of Modernism, perhaps, was this uprooting and upheaval of the past. Painting was no longer required to be representational. Poetry no longer required rhyme and symmetrical stanzas. Music moved past harmony and tonality into dissonance and atonality. Because of Modernism, contemporary artists, whatever their medium of expression, have a multitude of options in pursuing their art.

KEY TERMS

avant garde	Dada	reinforced concrete	Depression
Fauvism	anti-art	stream of consciousness	jazz
Cubism	Surrealism	montage	riff
collage	automatism	atonality	ragtime
Futurism	De Stijl (Neo-Plasticism)	Nazi	syncopation
Simultanéisme	International style	*Lebensraum*	scat
German Expressionism	Bauhaus	Dust Bowl	swing

WWW. WEBSITES FOR FURTHER STUDY

http://artchive.com/artchive/P/picasso.html
(This is the Artchive, a website with virtually every major artist in every style from every era in art history. It is an excellent resource.)

http://collections.sfmoma.org/obj2583$12965
(Perhaps no work is more singularly identified with the transformation of art in the twentieth century than Fountain [1917] by Marcel Duchamp [1887–1968].)

http://www.mcs.csuhayward.edu/~malek/Surrealism/index.html
(An unusual but interestingly good site on Surrealism.)

http://www.masters-of-photography.com/S/stieglitz/stieglitz_equivalent_1926.html
(A good site on Stieglitz and photography in general.)

http://www.allaboutjazz.com/timeline.htm
(This site features a brief history of jazz with associated links, written by Doug Ronallo and Michael Ricci.)

READINGS

FRANZ KAFKA

Franz Kafka (1883–1924), an Austrian writer born in Prague who wrote in German, worked for an insurance company in Prague. His visionary, metaphorical, and psychologically complex fiction expressed the anxiety and alienation of modern life, so much so that the word "Kafkaesque" has been coined to convey its surreal and absurdist qualities. "Before the Law" is one of his many parables; this one has affinities with his novel The Trial *in quality of strangeness, confused guilt, and nightmare.*

Before the Law[1]

Before the Law stands a doorkeeper. To this doorkeeper there comes a man from the country and prays for admittance to the Law. But the doorkeeper says that he cannot grant admittance at the moment. The man thinks it over and then asks if he will be allowed in later. "It is possible," says the doorkeeper, "but not at the moment." Since the gate stands open, as usual, and the doorkeeper steps to one side, the man stoops to peer through the gateway into the interior. Observing that, the doorkeeper laughs and says: "If you are so drawn to it, just try to go in despite my veto. But take note: I am powerful. And I am only the least of the doorkeepers. From hall to hall there is one doorkeeper after another, each more powerful than the last. The third doorkeeper is already so terrible that even I cannot bear to look at him." These are difficulties the man from the country has not expected; the Law, he thinks, should surely be accessible at all times and to everyone, but as he now takes a closer look at the doorkeeper in his fur coat, with his big sharp nose and long, thin, black Tartar beard, he decides that it is better to wait until he gets permission to enter. The doorkeeper gives him a stool and lets him sit down at one side of the door. There he sits for days and years. He makes many attempts to be admitted, and wearies the doorkeeper by his importunity. The doorkeeper frequently has little interviews with him, asking him questions about his home and many other things, but the questions are put indifferently, as great lords put them, and always finish with the statement that he cannot be let in yet. The man, who has furnished himself with many things for his journey, sacrifices all he has, however valuable, to bribe the doorkeeper. The doorkeeper accepts everything, but always with the remark: "I am only taking it to keep you from thinking you have omitted anything." During these many years the man fixes his attention almost continuously on the doorkeeper. He forgets the other doorkeepers, and this first one seems to him the sole obstacle preventing access to the Law. He curses his bad luck, in his early years boldly and loudly, later, as he grows old, he only grumbles to himself. He becomes childish, and since in his yearlong contemplation of the doorkeeper he has come to know even the fleas in his fur collar, he begs the fleas as well to help him and to change the doorkeeper's mind. At length

[1]Translated by Edwin and Willa Muir.

his eyesight begins to fail, and he does not know whether the world is really darker or whether his eyes are only deceiving him. Yet in his darkness he is now aware of a radiance that streams inextinguishably from the gateway of the Law. Now he has not very long to live. Before he dies, all his experiences in these long years gather themselves in his head to one point, a question he has not yet asked the doorkeeper. He waves him nearer, since he can no longer raise his stiffening body. The doorkeeper has to bend low towards him, for the difference in height between them has altered much to the man's disadvantage. "What do you want to know now?" asks the doorkeeper; "you are insatiable." "Everyone strives to reach the Law," says the man, "so how does it happen that for all these many years no one but myself has ever begged for admittance?" The doorkeeper recognizes that the man has reached his end, and to let his failing senses catch the words roars in his ear: "No one else could ever be admitted here, since this gate was made only for you. I am now going to shut it."

ANNA AKHMATOVA

Anna Akhmatova (1889–1966) suffered greatly under Stalinist repression during the 1930s. For almost two decades Akhmatova was prohibited from publishing her work. During the Stalinist purges both her husband and her son were arrested on political charges, an experience that provided the stimulus for her poem Requiem, *which is excerpted here.*

1

At dawn they came and took you away.
You were my dead: I walked behind.
In the dark room children cried,
the holy candle gasped for air.
Your lips were chill from the ikon's kiss,   *5*
sweat bloomed on your brow—those deathly flowers!
Like the wives of Peter's troopers in Red Square
I'll stand and howl under the Kremlin towers.

                    —1935

2

Quietly flows the quiet Don;
into my house slips the yellow moon.   *10*
It leaps the sill, with its cap askew,
and balks at a shadow, that yellow moon.

This woman is sick to her marrow-bone,
this woman is utterly alone,

with husband dead, with son away   *15*
in jail. Pray for me. Pray.

3

Not, not mine: it's somebody else's wound.
I could never have borne it. So take the thing
that happened, hide it, stick it in the ground.
Whisk the lamps away . . .   *20*
           Night.

4

They should have shown you—mocker,
delight of your friends, hearts' thief,
naughtiest girl of Pushkin's town—
this picture of your fated years,   25
as under the glowering wall you stand,
shabby, three hundredth in the line,
clutching a parcel in your hand,
and the New Year's ice scorched by your tears.
See there the prison poplar bending!   30
No sound. No sound. Yet how many
innocent lives are ending. . . .

5

For seventeenth months I have cried aloud,
calling you back to your lair.
I hurled myself at the hangman's foot.   35
You are my son, changed into nightmare.
Confusion occupies the world,
and I am powerless to tell
somebody brute from something human,
or on what day the word spells, "Kill!"   40
Nothing is left but dusty flowers,
the tinkling thurible, and tracks
that lead to nowhere. Night of stone,
whose bright enormous star
stares me straight in the eyes,   45
promising death, ah soon!

6

The weeks fly out of mind,
I doubt that it occurred:
how into your prison, child,
the white nights, blazing, stared;   50
and still, as I draw breath,
they fix their buzzard eyes
on what the high cross shows,
this body of your death.

OSIP MANDELSTAM

Osip Mandelstam (1891–1938), along with Anna Akhmotova, is one of Russia's greatest modern poets. A literary theorist and prose writer as well as a poet, Mandelstam wrote many poems celebrating classical and medieval culture, including poems about Homer, Dante, and Villon, as well as poems about the great cathedral Notre Dame *in Paris and the great cathedral converted to mosque and museum,* Hagia Sophia *in Istanbul. His poem "The Stalin Epigram," one of his overt political poems, precipitated his arrest in 1934.*

The Stalin Epigram[1]

Our lives no longer feel ground under them.
At ten paces you can't hear our words.

But whenever there's a snatch of talk
it turns to the Kremlin mountaineer,

---

[1] Translated by Clarence Brown and W. S. Merwin.

the ten thick worms his fingers,   5
his words like measures of weight,

the huge laughing cockroaches on his top lip,
the glitter of his boot-rims.

Ringed with a scum of chicken-necked bosses
he toys with the tributes of half-men.   10

One whistles, another meouws, a third snivels.
He pokes out his finger and he alone goes boom.

He forges decrees in a line like horseshoes,
One for the groin, one the forehead, temple, eye.

He rolls the executions on his tongue like berries.   15
He wishes he could hug them like big friends from home.

T. S. ELIOT

The Love Song of J. Alfred Prufrock

Eliot's most popular poem, The Love Song of J. Alfred Prufrock, *portrays an inhibited, insecure man unable to engage truly in life. In a series of self-deprecatory asides, he reveals his fear of human contact, identifying himself as a diminished, ineffectual person who cannot declare his feelings for a woman. Eliot's Prufrock is the prototype of a human caught in the seeming futility of the modern age of anxiety.*

> *S'io credesse che mia risposta fosse*
> *A persona che mai tornasse al mondo,*
> *Questa fiamma staria senza più scosse.*
> *Ma perciocche giammai di questo fondo*
> *Non tornò vivo alcun, s'i'odo il vero,*
> *Senza tema d'infamia ti rispondo.°*

Let us go then, you and I,
When the evening is spread out against the sky
Like a patient etherized upon a table;
Let us go, through certain half-deserted streets,
The muttering retreats   5
Of restless nights in one-night cheap hotels
And sawdust restaurants with oyster-shells:
Streets that follow like a tedious argument
Of insidious intent
To lead you to an overwhelming question. . .   10
Oh, do not ask, "What is it?"
Let us go and make our visit.

In the room the women come and go
Talking of Michelangelo.

Epigraph from Dante's Inferno, canto XXVII, 61–66. The words are spoken by Guido da Montefeltro when asked to identify himself. "If I thought my answer were given to anyone who could ever return to the world, this flame would shake no more; but since none ever did return above from this depth, if what I hear is true, without fear of infamy I answer thee."

The yellow fog that rubs its back upon the window-
    panes,   *15*
The yellow smoke that rubs its muzzle on the window-
    panes,

Licked its tongue into the corners of the evening,
Lingered upon the pools that stand in drains,
Let fall upon its back the soot that falls from chimneys,
Slipped by the terrace, made a sudden leap,   *20*
And seeing that it was a soft October night,
Curled once about the house, and fell asleep.

And indeed there will be time
For the yellow smoke that slides along the street
Rubbing its back upon the window-panes;   *25*
There will be time, there will be time
To prepare a face to meet the faces that you meet;
There will be time to murder and create,
And time for all the works and days of hands
That lift and drop a question on your plate;   *30*
Time for you and time for me,
And time yet for a hundred indecisions,
And for a hundred visions and revisions,
Before the taking of a toast and tea.

In the room the women come and go   *35*
Talking of Michelangelo.

And indeed there will be time
To wonder, "Do I dare?" and, "Do I dare?"
Time to turn back and descend the stair,
With a bald spot in the middle of my hair—   *40*
(They will say: "How his hair is growing thin!")
My morning coat, my collar mounting firmly to the chin,
My necktie rich and modest, but asserted by a simple pin—
(They will say: "But how his arms and legs are thin!")
Do I dare   *45*
Disturb the universe?
In a minute there is time
For decisions and revisions which a minute will reverse.

For I have known them all already, known them all—
Have known the evenings, mornings, afternoons,   *50*
I have measured out my life with coffee spoons;
I know the voices dying with a dying fall°
Beneath the music from a farther room.
      So how should I presume?

And I have known the eyes already, known them all—
The eyes that fix you in a formulated phrase,   *56*
And when I am formulated, sprawling on a pin,
When I am pinned and wriggling on the wall,
Then how should I begin
To spit out all the butt-ends of my days and ways?   *60*
      And how should I presume?
And I have known the arms already, known them all—

Arms that are braceleted and white and bare
(But in the lamplight, downed with light brown hair!)
Is it perfume from a dress   *65*
That makes me so digress?
Arms that lie along a table, or wrap about a shawl.
      And should I then presume?
      And how should I begin?
    . . . .

Shall I say, I have gone at dusk through narrow streets *70*
And watched the smoke that rises from the pipes
Of lonely men in shirt-sleeves, leaning out of
    windows?. . .

I should have been a pair of ragged claws
Scuttling across the floors of silent seas.
    . . . .

And the afternoon, the evening, sleeps so peacefully! *75*
Smoothed by long fingers,
Asleep. . . tired. . . or it malingers,
Stretched on the floor, here beside you and me.
Should I, after tea and cakes and ices,
Have the strength to force the moment to its crisis? *80*
But though I have wept and fasted, wept and prayed,
Though I have seen my head (grown slightly bald)
    brought in upon a platter,°
I am no prophet—and here's no greater matter;
I have seen the moment of my greatness flicker,
And I have seen the eternal Footman hold my coat, and
    snicker,   *85*
And in short, I was afraid.

And would it have been worth it, after all,
After the cups, the marmalade, the tea,
Among the porcelain, among some talk of you and me,
Would it have been worth while,   *90*
To have bitten off the matter with a smile,
To have squeezed the universe into a ball
To roll it towards some overwhelming question,
To say: "I am Lazarus,° come from the dead,
Come back to tell you all, I shall tell you all"—   *95*
If one, settling a pillow by her head,
    Should say: "That is not what I meant at all.
    That is not it, at all."

And would it have been worth it, after all,
Would it have been worth while,   *100*
After the sunsets and the dooryards and the sprinkled
    streets,
After the novels, after the teacups, after the skirts that
    trail along the floor—
And this, and so much more?—
It is impossible to say just what I mean!
But as if a magic lantern threw the nerves in patterns on
    a screen: *105*

---

⁵²*I know . . . dying fall:* this echoes the first lines of Shakespeare's *Twelfth Night* I, i, 1–4. "If music be the food of love, play on;/Give me excess of it, that, surfeiting/The appetite may sicken, and so die./That strain again! it had a dying fall."

⁸²*my head . . . upon a platter:* John the Baptist was beheaded at the order of King Herod to please his wife, Herodias, and daughter, Salome. His head was offered to his daughter on a platter. See Matthew 14: 1–11.
⁹⁴*Lazarus:* Lazarus was raised from the dead by Jesus. See John 11: 1–44.

Would it have been worth while
If one, settling a pillow or throwing off a shawl,
And turning toward the window, should say:
        "That is not it at all,
        That is not what I meant, at all."   *110*

        . . . .

No! I am not Prince Hamlet, nor was meant to be;
Am an attendant lord, one that will do
To swell a progress,° start a scene or two,
Advise the prince; no doubt, an easy tool,
Deferential, glad to be of use,   *115*
Politic, cautious, and meticulous;
Full of high sentence, but a bit obtuse;
At times, indeed, almost ridiculous—
Almost, at times, the Fool.

I grow old. . .I grow old. . .   *120*
I shall wear the bottoms of my trousers rolled.

Shall I part my hair behind? Do I dare to eat a peach?
I shall wear white flannel trousers, and walk upon the
        beach.
I have heard the mermaids singing, each to each.

I do not think that they will sing to me.   *125*

I have seen them riding seaward on the waves
Combing the white hair of the waves blown back
When the wind blows the water white and black.

We have lingered in the chambers of the sea
By sea-girls wreathed with seaweed red and brown   *130*
Till human voices wake us, and we drown.

LANGSTON HUGHES

I, Too, Sing America

*Langston Hughes (1902–67) was the voice of two generations of
African Americans during the early to mid twentieth century. He
was a leading figure in New York's "Harlem Renaissance," a wave
of astonishing African American creativity in literature and the
arts. Strongly influenced by music, especially the blues, Hughes captured its rhythms and sadness in many of his poems.*

I, too, sing America
I am the darker brother.
They send me to eat in the kitchen
When company comes,
But I laugh,   *5*
And eat well,
And grow strong.

Tomorrow,
I'll be at the table
When company comes.   *10*
Nobody'll dare
Say to me,

"Eat in the kitchen,"
Then.

Besides,   *15*
They'll see how beautiful I am
And be ashamed—

I, too, am America.

VIRGINIA WOOLF

from *To the Lighthouse*

*With its wide-ranging stream of consciousness techniques and its
evocative poetic symbols,* To the Lighthouse *(1927) is generally
considered one of the seminal masterpieces of literary modernism.
The following passage from the first section of Woolf's novel describes a single day at the Ramsay family's country home near the
sea. Woolf's central character, Mrs. Ramsay, is a woman with an
open and generous spirit, who is crushed by the clipped severity of her
repressed husband, a distinguished philosopher.*

"Yes, of course, if it's fine tomorrow," said Mrs. Ramsay. "But
you'll have to be up with the lark," she added.

To her son these words conveyed an extraordinary joy, as
if it were settled, the expedition were bound to take place,
and the wonder to which he had looked forward, for years
and years it seemed, was, after a night's darkness and a day's
sail, within touch. Since he belonged, even at the age of six,
to that great clan which cannot keep this feeling separate from
that, but must let future prospects, with their joys and sorrows, cloud what is actually at hand, since to such people even
in earliest childhood any turn in the wheel of sensation has the
power to crystallise and transfix the moment upon which its
gloom or radiance rests, James Ramsay, sitting on the floor
cutting out pictures from the illustrated catalogue of the Army
and Navy Stores, endowed the picture of a refrigerator, as his
mother spoke, with heavenly bliss. It was fringed with joy.
The wheelbarrow, the lawnmower, the sound of poplar trees,
leaves whitening before rain, rooks cawing, brooms knocking,
dresses rustling—all these were so coloured and distinguished
in his mind that he had already his private code, his secret
language, though he appeared the image of stark and uncompromising severity, with his high forehead and his fierce
blue eyes, impeccably candid and pure, frowning slightly at
the sight of human frailty, so that his mother, watching him
guide his scissors neatly round the refrigerator, imagined him
all red and ermine on the Bench or directing a stern and momentous enterprise in some crisis of public affairs.

"But," said his father, stopping in front of the drawingroom
window, "it won't be fine."

Had there been an axe handy, or a poker, any weapon that
would have gashed a hole in his father's breast and killed him,
there and then, James would have seized it. Such were the extremes of emotion that Mr. Ramsay excited in his children's
breasts by his mere presence; standing, as now, lean as a knife,
narrow as the blade of one, grinning sarcastically, not only
with the pleasure of disillusioning his son and casting ridicule
upon his wife, who was ten thousand times better in every
way than he was (James thought), but also with some secret
conceit at his own accuracy of judgement. What he said was

°¹¹³ *progress*: a procession or journey made by members of the royal court.

true. It was always true. He was incapable of untruth; never tampered with a fact; never altered a disagreeable word to suit the pleasure or convenience of any mortal beings least of all of his own children, who, sprung from his loins, should be aware from childhood that life is difficult; facts uncompromising; and the passage to that fabled land where our brightest hopes are extinguished, our frail barks founder in darkness (here Mr. Ramsay would straighten his back and narrow his little blue eyes upon the horizon), one that needs, above all, courage, truth, and the power to endure.

"But it may be fine—I expect it will be fine," said Mrs. Ramsay, making some little twist of the reddish brown stocking she was knitting, impatiently. If she finished it tonight, if they did go to the Lighthouse after all, it was to be given to the Lighthouse keeper for his little boy, who was threatened with a tuberculous hip; together with a pile of old magazines, and some tobacco, indeed, whatever she could find lying about, not really wanted, but only littering the room, to give those poor fellows, who must be bored to death sitting all day with nothing to do but polish the lamp and trim the wick and rake about on their scrap of garden, something to amuse them. For how would you like to be shut up for a whole month at a time, and possibly more in stormy weather, upon a rock the size of a tennis lawn? she would ask; and to have no letters or newspapers, and to see nobody; if you were married, not to see your wife, not to know how your children were,—if they were ill, if they had fallen down and broken their legs or arms; to see the same dreary waves breaking week after week, and then a dreadful storm coming, and the windows covered with spray, and birds dashed against the lamp, and the whole place rocking, and not be able to put your nose out of doors for fear of being swept into the sea? How would you like that? she asked, addressing herself particularly to her daughters. So she added, rather differently, one must take them whatever comforts one can.

"It's due west," said the atheist Tansley, holding his bony fingers spread so that the wind blew through them, for he was sharing Mr. Ramsay's evening walk up and down, up and down the terrace. That is to say, the wind blew from the worst possible direction for landing at the Lighthouse. Yes, he did say disagreeable things, Mrs. Ramsay admitted; it was odious of him to rub this in, and make James still more disappointed; but at the same time, she would not let them laugh at him. "The atheist," they called him; "the little atheist." Rose mocked him; Prue mocked him; Andrew, Jasper, Roger mocked him; even old Badger without a tooth in his head had bit him, for being (as Nancy put it) the hundred and tenth young man to chase them all the way up to the Hebrides when it was ever so much nicer to be alone.

"Nonsense," said Mrs. Ramsay, with great severity. Apart from the habit of exaggeration which they had from her, and from the implication (which was true) that she asked too many people to stay, and had to lodge some in the town, she could not bear incivility to her guests, to young men in particular, who were poor as church mice, "exceptionally able," her husband said, his great admirers, and come there for a holiday. Indeed, she had the whole of the other sex under her protection; for reasons she could not explain, for their chivalry and valour, for the fact that they negotiated treaties, ruled India, controlled finance; finally for an attitude towards herself which no woman could fail to feel or to find agreeable, something

trustful, childlike, reverential; which an old woman could take from a young man without loss of dignity, and woe betide the girl—pray Heaven it was none of her daughters!—who did not feel the worth of it, and all that it Implied, to the marrow of her bones!

She turned with severity upon Nancy. He had not chased them, she said. He had been asked.

They must find a way out of it all. There might be some simpler way, some less laborious way, she sighed. When she looked in the glass and saw her hair grey, her cheek sunk, at fifty she thought, possibly she might have managed things better—her husband; money; his books. But for her own part she would never for a single second regret her decision, evade difficulties, or slur over duties. She was now formidable to behold, and it was only in silence, looking up from their plates, after she had spoken so severely about Charles Tansley, that her daughters, Prue, Nancy, Rose—could sport with infidel ideas which they had brewed for themselves of a life different from hers; in Paris, perhaps; a wilder life; not always taking care of some man or other; for there was in all their minds a mute questioning of deference and chivalry, of the Bank of England and the Indian Empire, of ringed fingers and lace, though to them all there was something in this of the essence of beauty, which called out the manliness in their girlish hearts, and made them, as they sat at table beneath their mother's eyes, honour her strange severity, her extreme courtesy, like a Queen's raising from the mud to wash a beggar's dirty foot, when she thus admonished them so very severely about that wretched atheist who had chased them—or, speaking accurately, been invited to stay with them—in the Isles of Skye.

ERNEST HEMINGWAY
Hills Like White Elephants

The following short story from 1927 illustrates Hemingway's style: detailed yet laconic, and close to the bone. It opens with the symbolic image of mountains rising from the plain, but the reader must glean Hemingway's meaning. Hemingway lets his images speak for themselves. His dialogue is remarkable for what his characters do not say. The details of the conversation, as well as those of the landscape, reinforce the contrast between sterility and fertility, life and death.

The hills across the valley of the Ebro were long and white. On this side there was no shade and no trees and the station was between two lines of rails in the sun. Close against the side of the station there was the warm shadow of the building and a curtain, made of strings of bamboo beads, hung across the open door into the bar, to keep out flies. The American and the girl with him sat at a table in the shade, outside the building. It was very hot and the express from Barcelona would come in forty minutes. It stopped at this junction for two minutes and went on to Madrid.

"What should we drink?" the girl asked. She had taken off her hat and put it on the table.

"It's pretty hot," the man said.

"Let's drink beer."

"Dos cervezas," the man said into the curtain.

"Big ones?" a woman asked from the doorway.

"Yes. Two big ones."

The woman brought two glasses of beer and two felt pads. She put the felt pads and the beer glasses on the table and looked at the man and the girl. The girl was looking off at the line of hills. They were white in the sun and the country was brown and dry.

"They look like white elephants," she said.

"I've never seen one," the man drank his beer.

"No, you wouldn't have."

"I might have," the man said. "Just because you say I wouldn't have doesn't prove anything."

The girl looked at the bead curtain. "They've painted something on it," she said. "what does it say?"

"Anis del Toro. It's a drink."

"Could we try it?"

The man called "Listen" through the curtain. The woman came out from the bar.

"Four reales."

"We want two Anis del Toro."

"With water?"

"Do you want it with water?"

"I don't know," the girl said. "Is it good with water?"

"It's all right."

"You want them with water?" asked the woman.

"Yes, with water."

"It tastes like licorice," the girl said and put the glass down.

"That's the way with everything."

"Yes," said the girl. "Everything tastes of licorice. Espe cially all the things you've waited so long for, like absinthe."

"Oh, cut it out."

"You started it," the girl said. "I was being amused. I was having a fine time."

"Well, let's try and have a fine time."

"All right. I was trying. I said the mountains looked like white elephants. Wasn't that bright?"

"That was bright."

"I wanted to try this new drink. That's all we do, isn't it— look at things and try new drinks?"

"I guess so."

The girl looked across at the hills.

"They're lovely hills," she said. "They don't really look like white elephants. I just meant the coloring of their skin through the trees."

"Should we have another drink?"

"All right."

The warm wind blew the bead curtain against the table.

"The beer's nice and cool," the man said.

"It's lovely," the girl said.

"It's really an awfully simple operation, Jig," the man said. "It's not really an operation at all."

The girl looked at the ground the table legs rested on.

"I know you wouldn't mind it, Jig. It's really not anything. It's just to let the air in."

The girl did not say anything.

"I'll go with you and I'll stay with you all the time. They just let the air in and then it's all perfectly natural."

"Then what will we do afterward?"

"We'll be fine afterward. Just like we were before."

"What makes you think so?"

"That's the only thing that bothers us. It's the only thing that's made us unhappy."

The girl looked at the bead curtain, put her hand out and took hold of two of the strings of beads.

"And you think then we'll be all right and be happy."

"I know we will. You don't have to be afraid. I've known lots of people that have done it."

"So have I," said the girl. "And afterward they were all so happy."

"Well," the man said, "if you don't want to you don't have to. I wouldn't have you do it if you didn't want to. But I know it's perfectly simple."

"And you really want to?"

"I think it's the best thing to do. But I don't want you to do it if you don't really want to."

"And if I do it you'll be happy and things will be like they were and you'll love me?"

"I love you now. You know I love you."

"I know. But if I do it, then it will be nice again if I say things are like white elephants, and you'll like it?"

"I'll love it. I love it now but I just can't think about it. You know how I get when I worry."

"If I do it you won't ever worry?"

"I won't worry about that because it's perfectly simple."

"Then I'll do it. Because I don't care about me."

"What do you mean?"

"I don't care about me."

"Well, I care about you."

"Oh, yes. But I don't care about me. And I'll do it and then everything will be fine."

"I don't want you to do it if you feel that way."

The girl stood up and walked to the end of the station. Across on the other side, were fields of grain and trees along the banks of the Ebro. Far away, beyond the river, were moun tains. The shadow of a cloud moved across the field of grain and she saw the river through the trees.

"And we could have all this," she said. "And we could have everything and every day we make it more impossible."

"What did you say?"

"I said we could have everything."

"We can have everything."

"No, we can't."

"We can have the whole world."

"No, we can't."

"We can go everywhere."

"No, we can't. It isn't ours any more."

"It's ours."

"No, it isn't. And once they take it away, you never get it back."

"But they haven't taken it away."

"We'll wait and see."

"Come on back in the shade," he said. "You mustn't feel that way."

"I don't feel any way," the girl said. "I just know things."

"I don't want you to do anything that you don't want to do—"

"Nor that isn't good for me," she said. "I know. Could we have another beer?"

"All right. But you've got to realize—"

"I realize," the girl said. "Can't we maybe stop talking?"

They sat down at the table and the girl looked across at the hills on the dry side of the valley and the man looked at her and at the table.

"You've got to realize," he said, "that I don't want you to do it if you don't want to. I'm perfectly willing to go through with it if it means anything to you."

"Doesn't it mean anything to you? We could get along."

"Of course it does. But I don't want anybody but you. I don't want any one else. And I know it's perfectly simple."

"Yes, to you it's perfectly simple."

"It's all right for you to say that, but I do know it."

"Would you do something for me now?"

"I'd do anything for you."

"Would you please please please please please please please stop talking?"

He did not say anything but looked at the bags against the wall of the station. There were labels on them from all the hotels where they had spent nights.

"But I don't want you to," he said, "I don't care anything about it."

"I'll scream," the girl said.

The woman came out through the curtains with two glasses of beer and put them down on the damp felt pads. "The train comes in five minutes," she said.

"What did she say?" asked the girl.

"That the train is coming in five minutes."

The girl smiled brightly at the woman, to thank her.

"I'd better take the bags over to the other side of the station," the man said. She smiled at him.

"All right. Then come back and we'll finish the beer."

He picked up the two heavy bags and carried them around the station to the other tracks. He looked up the tracks but could not see the train. Coming back, he walked through the barroom, where people waiting for the train were drinking. He drank an Anis at the bar and looked at the people. They were all waiting reasonably for the train. He went out through the bead curtain. She was sitting at the table and smiled at him.

"Do you feel better?" he asked.

"I feel fine," she said. "There's nothing wrong with me. I feel fine."

JAMES JOYCE

Araby

James Joyce's "Araby" is one of his most eloquent stories. Like other stories in Dubliners, *"Araby" focuses on adolescence, particularly on the transition from the innocence of youth to the more complex realities of young adult experience. The story is constructed so as to conclude with an epiphany, or moment of blinding awareness, in which Joyce conveys the power of the protagonist's shocking realization of what he has seen and experienced.*

North Richmond Street, being blind, was a quiet street except at the hour when the Christian Brothers' School set the boys free. An uninhabited house of two storeys stood at the blind end, detached from its neighbours in a square ground. The other houses of the street, conscious of decent lives within them, gazed at one another with brown imperturbable faces.

The former tenant of our house, a priest, had died in the back drawing-room. Air, musty from having been long enclosed, hung in all the rooms, and the waste room behind the kitchen was littered with old useless papers. Among these I found a few paper-covered books, the pages of which were curled and damp: *The Abbot*, by Walter Scott, *The Devout Communicant* and *The Memoirs of Vidocq*. I liked the last best because its leaves were yellow. The wild garden behind the house contained a central apple-tree and a few straggling bushes under one of which I found the late tenant's rusty bicycle-pump. He had been a very charitable priest; in his will he had left all his money to institutions and the furniture of his house to his sister.

When the short days of winter came dusk fell before we had well eaten our dinners. When we met in the street the houses had grown sombre. The space of sky above us was the colour of ever-changing violet and towards it the lamps of the street lifted their feeble lanterns. The cold air stung us and we played till our bodies glowed. Our shouts echoed in the silent street. The career of our play brought us through the dark muddy lanes behind the houses where we ran the gantlet of the rough tribes from the cottages, to the back doors of the dark dripping gardens where odours arose from the ashpits, to the dark odorous stables where a coachman smoothed and combed the horse or shook music from the buckled harness. When we returned to the street light from the kitchen windows had filled the areas. If my uncle was seen turning the corner we hid in the shadow until we had seen him safely housed. Or if Mangan's sister came out on the doorstep to call her brother in to his tea we watched her from our shadow peer up and down the street. We waited to see whether she would remain or go in and, if she remained, we left our shadow and walked up to Mangan's steps resignedly. She was waiting for us, her figure defined by the light from the half-opened door. Her brother always teased her before he obeyed and I stood by the railings looking at her. Her dress swung as she moved her body and the soft rope of her hair tossed from side to side.

Every morning I lay on the floor in the front parlour watching her door. The blind was pulled down to within an inch of the sash so that I could not be seen. When she came out on the doorstep my heart leaped. I ran to the hall, seized my books and followed her. I kept her brown figure always in my eye and, when we came near the point at which our ways diverged, I quickened my pace and passed her. This happened morning after morning. I had never spoken to her, except for a few casual words, and yet her name was like a summons to all my foolish blood.

Her image accompanied me even in places the most hostile to romance. On Saturday evenings when my aunt went marketing I had to go to carry some of the parcels. We walked through the flaring streets, jostled by drunken men and bargaining women, amid the curses of labourers, the shrill litanies of shop-boys who stood on guard by the barrels of pigs' cheeks, the nasal chanting of street-singers, who sang a *come-all-you* about O'Donovan Rossa, or a ballad about the troubles in our native land. These noises converged in a single sensation of life for me: I imagined that I bore my chalice safely through a throng of foes. Her name sprang to my lips at moments in strange prayers and praises which I myself did not understand. My eyes were often full of tears (I could not tell why) and at times a flood from my heart seemed to pour itself out into my bosom. I thought little of the future. I did not know whether I would ever speak to her or not or, if I spoke to her, how I could tell her of my confused adoration. But my body was like a harp and her words and gestures were like fingers running upon the wires.

One evening I went into the back drawing-room in which the priest had died. It was a dark rainy evening and there was no sound in the house. Through one of the broken panes I heard the rain impinge upon the earth, the fine incessant needles of water playing in the sodden beds. Some distant lamp or lighted window gleamed below me. I was thankful that I could see so little. All my senses seemed to desire to veil themselves and, feeling that I was about to slip from them, I pressed the palms of my hands together until they trembled, murmuring: *O love! O love!* many times.

At last she spoke to me. When she addressed the first words to me I was so confused that I did not know what to answer. She asked me was I going to *Araby*. I forget whether I answered yes or no. It would be a splendid bazaar, she said; she would love to go.

—And why can't you? I asked.

While she spoke she turned a silver bracelet round and round her wrist. She could not go, she said, because there would be a retreat that week in her convent. Her brother and two other boys were fighting for their caps and I was alone at the railings. She held one of the spikes, bowing her head towards me. The light from the lamp opposite our door caught the white curve of her neck, lit up her hair that rested there and, falling, lit up the hand upon the railing. It fell over one side of her dress and caught the white border of a petticoat, just visible as she stood at ease.

—It's well for you, she said.

—If I go, I said, I will bring you something.

What innumerable follies laid waste my waking and sleeping thoughts after that evening! I wished to annihilate the tedious intervening days. I chafed against the work of school. At night in my bedroom and by day in the classroom her image came between me and the page I strove to read. The syllables of the word *Araby* were called to me through the silence in which my soul luxuriated and cast an Eastern enchantment over me. I asked for leave to go to the bazaar Saturday night. My aunt was surprised and hoped it was not some Freemason affair. I answered few questions in class. I watched my master's face pass from amiability to sternness; he hoped I was not beginning to idle. I could not call my wandering thoughts together. I had hardly any patience with the serious work of life which, now that it stood between me and my desire, seemed to me child's play, ugly monotonous child's play.

On Saturday morning I reminded my uncle that I wished to go to the bazaar in the evening. He was fussing at the hall-stand, looking for the hat-brush, and answered me curtly:

—Yes, boy, I know.

As he was in the hall I could not go into the front parlour and lie at the window. I left the house in bad humour and walked slowly towards the school. The air was pitilessly raw and already my heart misgave me.

When I came home to dinner my uncle had not yet been home. Still it was early. I sat staring at the clock for some time and, when its ticking began to irritate me, I left the room. I mounted the staircase and gained the upper part of the house.

The high cold empty gloomy rooms liberated me and I went from room to room singing. From the front window I saw my companions playing below in the street. Their cries reached me weakened and indistinct and, leaning my forehead against the cool glass, I looked over at the dark house where she lived. I may have stood there for an hour, seeing nothing but the brown-clad figure cast by my imagination, touched discreetly by the lamplight at the curved neck, at the hand upon the railings and at the border below the dress.

When I came downstairs again I found Mrs Mercer sitting at the fire. She was an old garrulous woman, a pawn-broker's widow, who collected used stamps for some pious purpose. I had to endure the gossip of the tea-table. The meal was prolonged beyond an hour and still my uncle did not come. Mrs Mercer stood up to go: she was sorry she couldn't wait any longer, but it was after eight o'clock and she did not like to be out late, as the night air was bad for her. When she had gone I began to walk up and down the room, clenching my fists. My aunt said:

—I'm afraid you may put off your bazaar for this night of Our Lord.

At nine o'clock I heard my uncle's latchkey in the halldoor. I heard him talking to himself and heard the hallstand rocking when it had received the weight of his overcoat. I could interpret these signs. When he was midway through his dinner I asked him to give me the money to go to the bazaar. He had forgotten.

—The people are in bed and after their first sleep now, he said.

I did not smile. My aunt said to him energetically:

—Can't you give him the money and let him go? You've kept him late enough as it is.

My uncle said he was very sorry he had forgotten. He said he believed in the old saying: *All work and no play makes Jack a dull boy.* He asked me where I was going and, when I had told him a second time he asked me did I know *The Arab's Farewell to his Steed*. When I left the kitchen he was about to recite the opening lines of the piece to my aunt.

I held a florin tightly in my hand as I strode down Buckingham Street towards the station. The sight of the streets thronged with buyers and glaring with gas recalled to me the purpose of my journey. I took my seat in a third-class carriage of a deserted train. After an intolerable delay the train moved out of the station slowly. It crept onward among ruinous houses and over the twinkling river. At Westland Row Station a crowd of people pressed to the carriage doors; but the porters moved them back, saying that it was a special train for the bazaar. I remained alone in the bare carriage. In a few minutes the train drew up beside an improvised wooden platform. I passed out on to the road and saw by the lighted dial of a clock that it was ten minutes to ten. In front of me was a large building which displayed the magical name.

I could not find any sixpenny entrance and, fearing that the bazaar would be closed, I passed in quickly through a turnstile, handing a shilling to a weary-looking man. I found myself in a big hall girdled at half its height by a gallery. Nearly all the stalls were closed and the greater part of the hall was in darkness. I recognised a silence like that which pervades a church after a service. I walked into the centre of the bazaar timidly. A few people were gathered about the stalls which were still open. Before a curtain, over which the words *Café Chantant* were written in coloured lamps, two men were counting money on a salver. I listened to the fall of the coins.

Remembering with difficulty why I had come I went over to one of the stalls and examined porcelain vases and flowered tea-sets. At the door of the stall a young lady was talking and laughing with two young gentlemen. I remarked their English accents and listened vaguely to their conversation.

—O, I never said such a thing!

—O, but you did!

—O, but I didn't!

—Didn't she say that?

—Yes, I heard her.

—O, there's a . . . fib!

Observing me the young lady came over and asked me did I wish to buy anything. The tone of her voice was not encouraging; she seemed to have spoken to me out of a sense of duty. I looked humbly at the great jars that stood like eastern guards at either side of the dark entrance to the stall and murmured:

—No, thank you.

The young lady changed the position of one of the vases and went back to the two young men. They began to talk of the same subject. Once or twice the young lady glanced at me over her shoulder.

I lingered before her stall, though I knew my stay was useless, to make my interest in her wares seem the more real. Then I turned away slowly and walked down the middle of the bazaar. I allowed the two pennies to fall against the sixpence in my pocket. I heard a voice call from one end of the gallery that the light was out. The upper part of the hall was now completely dark.

Gazing up into the darkness I saw myself as a creature driven and derided by vanity; and my eyes burned with anguish and anger.

WILLIAM BUTLER YEATS

William Butler Yeats (1865–1939) is Ireland's greatest poet and one of the most important of Modernist poets. In his "The Second Coming," Yeats describes the state of the modern world as one in which "things fall apart; the centre cannot hold." During the early decades of the twentieth century, the traditional religious, moral, and philosophical certainties began to lose their influence. Yeats images the loss of control with the falcon's flying beyond the call of the falconer and the onset of a period of destruction with the ominous acknowledgment of the arrival of a "great beast."

In "Sailing to Byzantium," Yeats explores a contrast between the transient world of physical materiality and change and that of the eternal changelessness and timelessness of art. Images of flesh and mortality are balanced and blended with those of things unaffected by time and change. In this respect, Yeats's poem can be compared with Keats's "Ode on a Grecian Urn" (Chapter 17).

The Second Coming

Turning and turning in the widening gyre
The falcon cannot hear the falconer;
Things fall apart; the center cannot hold;
Mere anarchy is loosed upon the world,
The blood-dimmed tide is loosed, and everywhere
The ceremony of innocence is drowned;
The best lack all conviction, while the worst
Are full of passionate intensity.
Surely some revelation is at hand;

Surely the Second Coming is at hand;　　　　10
The Second Coming! Hardly are those words out
When a vast image out of *Spiritus Mundi*
Troubles my sight: somewhere in sands of the desert
A shape with lion body and the head of a man,
A gaze blank and pitiless as the sun,
Is moving its slow thighs, while all about it
Reel shadows of the indignant desert birds.
The darkness drops again; but now I know
That twenty centuries of stony sleep
Were vexed to nightmare by a rocking cradle,　　20
And what rough beast, its hour come round at last,
Slouches towards Bethlehem to be born?

Sailing to Byzantium

1

That is no country for old men. The young
In one another's arms, birds in the trees
—Those dying generations—at their song,
The salmon-falls, the mackerel-crowded seas,
Fish, flesh, or fowl, commend all summer long　　5
Whatever is begotten, born, and dies.
Caught in that sensual music all neglect
Monuments of unaging intellect.

2

An aged man is but a paltry thing,
A tattered coat upon a stick, unless　　　　　10
Soul clap its hands and sing, and louder sing
For every tatter in its mortal dress,
Nor is there singing school but studying
Monuments of its own magnificence;
And therefore I have sailed the seas and come　　15
To the holy city of Byzantium.

3

O sages standing in God's holy fire
As in the gold mosaic of a wall,
Come from the holy fire, perne° in a gyre°,
And be the singing-masters of my soul.　　　　20
Consume my heart away; sick with desire
And fastened to a dying animal
It knows not what it is; and gather me
Into the artifice of eternity.

4

Once out of nature I shall never take　　　　25
My bodily form from any natural thing,
But such a form as Grecian goldsmiths make
Of hammered gold and gold enameling

---

¹⁹ *perne:* descend; *gyre:* spiral.

To keep a drowsy Emperor awake;
Or set upon a golden bough to sing 30
To lords and ladies of Byzantium
Of what is past, or passing, or to come.

RAINER MARIA RILKE

Selected Poems

Rainer Maria Rilke (1875–1926) is one of Germany's most important modern poets. His "Archaic Torso of Apollo," a Petrarchan sonnet, is based on a fifth-century B.C.E. Greek sculpture displayed in the Louvre Museum in Paris. Rilke invites readers to experience the sensuality of the marble torso as well as the brilliant radiance of its imagined face. In "Buddha in Glory," Rilke transforms the seated image of a Buddha with its outwardly calm physical appearance into a deeply imagined passionate spirituality that is the poet's true subject. Both "Archaic Torso of Apollo" and "Buddha in Glory" blend Rilke's acute visual description with a penetrating vision of other levels of existence.

Archaic Torso of Apollo

We never knew his head and all the light
that ripened in his fabled eyes. But
his torso still glows like a candelabra,
in which his gazing, turned down low,

holds fast and shines. Otherwise the surge
of the breast could not blind you, nor a smile
run through the slight twist of the loins
toward that center where procreation thrived.

Otherwise this stone would stand deformed and curt
under the shoulders' invisible plunge
and not glisten just like wild beasts' fur;

and not burst forth from all its contours
like a star: for there is no place
that does not see you. You must change your life.

Buddha in Glory

Center of all centers, core of cores,
almond, that closes tightly in and sweetens,—
this entire world out to all the stars
is your fruit-flesh: we greet you.

Look, you feel how nothing any longer
clings to you; your husk is in infinity,
and there the strong juice stands and crowds.
And from outside a radiance assists it,

for high above, your suns in full splendor
have wheeled blazingly around.
Yet already there's begun inside you
what lasts beyond the suns.

CHAPTER 22

Modern Africa and Latin America

David Alfaro Siqueiros, *Cuauhtémoc Against the Myth*, Teepan Union Housing Project,
Tlatelco, Mexico, 1944, mural, pyroxylin on celtex and plywood, 1,000 sq. ft. (92.9 sq. m).
Photo by Dr. Desmond Rochfort. © Estate of David Alfaro Siqueiros/SOMAAP/Licensed by
VAGA, NY. Reproduction authorized by the Institute Nacional de Bellas Artes y Literatura.

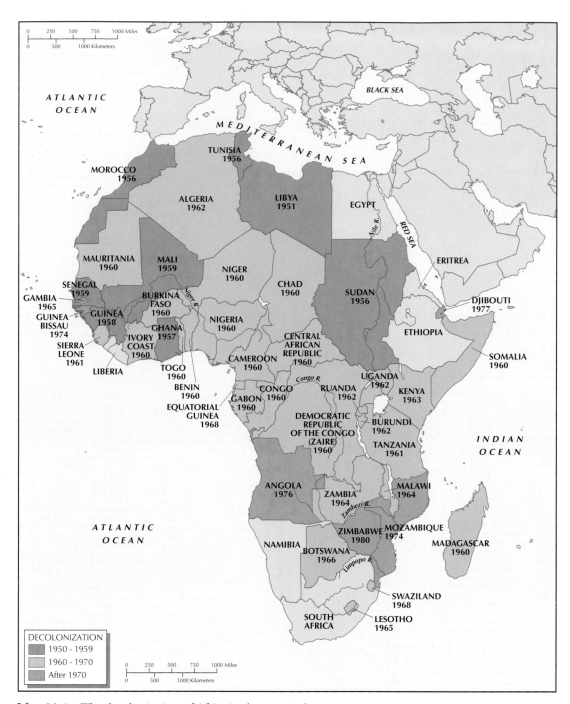

MAP 22.1 The decolonization of Africa in the twentieth century

CHAPTER OVERVIEW

MODERN AFRICA

The "Dark Continent" moves into the light of modern culture despite European attempts at colonialism

MODERN LATIN AMERICA

Central American culture is enriched through a multiracial society composed of indigenous and colonial peoples

MODERN AFRICA

IN 1800, THE TRANSATLANTIC SLAVE TRADE was reaching its peak, with nearly 100,000 enslaved Africans transported to the Americas each year. Most were destined for Brazil and the Carribean, although some 5 percent were taken to North America. Profits from this trade were high for slave traders; the cost was high for Africa. Where once the inhabitants of Western and Central Africa had provided largely for their own needs in terms of industry, the economy of the regions had increasingly turned toward slave trading. Now, rather than making iron, textiles, and household implements, many African states chose to capture slaves and sell them in exchange for materials and finished goods from European traders. Firearms, in particular, were an important part of this system of exchange. Ironically, even those African states that determined the trade in human beings to be immoral, such as Benin in south-central Nigeria, were eventually forced to take part, since one of the few ways to acquire enough firearms and powder to protect their people from enslavement was to sell slaves. Many historians believe the increased sense of insecurity created by the slave trade undermined existing systems of political legitimacy because new rulers were increasingly selected only for their ability to organize military force. Such a political system tended to concentrate power in the hands of the few, rather than the many.

Changing economics and the rise of an abolitionist movement in Europe and the Americas, however, began to turn the tide against the slave trade in the early 1800s. In 1807, Great Britain and the United States unilaterally outlawed the transatlantic slave trade, treating any slave ship found on the high seas as a pirate vessel (neither country outlawed slavery within its borders for some decades, however). By the 1820s, a large percentage of the British navy was involved in interdicting the slave trade. After 1850, the Atlantic slave trade had been reduced to a trickle, with only a few Portuguese, Brazilian, and Cuban slave traders risking the antislaving squadrons. Notably, any enslaved Africans rescued on the high seas were dropped at the small British protectorate of Sierra Leone in West Africa, creating a remarkable pan-African society known as "Krio" [KREE-oh] **(creole).** The era of the slave trade gave way to a period known as "Legitimate Trade." Running roughly from 1850 to 1880, the regions of West and Central Africa saw substantial economic growth as European demand shifted from human labor to commodities such as palm oil (used to lubricate machinery), latex (natural rubber), and gum arabic (a dye fixer).

THE SCRAMBLE FOR AFRICA AND COLONIAL RULE

By the latter 1800s, the relationship between Africa and Europe was changing once again. For centuries, European traders had been largely relegated to the coastlines of Africa's tropical regions because of a disease environment particularly hostile to peoples with no resistance to either malaria or yellow fever. Similarly, a relative technological parity between Africans and Europeans meant European military forces were unlikely to defeat African armies. The few examples of European attempts to penetrate beyond the coasts of Africa before the 1870s generally met with failure. For example, in 1824, a British army was defeated when it attempted to attack the Asante kingdom in the Gold Coast (now modern Ghana). However, three important technological innovations changed this balance of power. The first was the discovery of quinine, a drug that allowed Europeans to both prevent and cure malaria. Interestingly, quinine was originally used by Andean societies in South America, and it was not so much discovered as it was refined by Europeans after they witnessed its use. Nonetheless, now Europeans could hope to live in malarial regions without it being the equivalent of a death sentence. Second was the development of breech-loading cartridgefiring rifles. These weapons were far more reliable than flintlocks, especially in wet environments, and they also allowed individual soldiers to fire more rapidly and with greater range and accuracy than before. European soldiers, even in small numbers, were now far more deadly than their counterparts anywhere else in the world. Finally, the development of steam power and metalhulled boats allowed the rapid transport of European troops anywhere in the world, including up previously unnavigable rivers.

Thus, by the 1880s, there was, for the first time, a possibility that tropical Africa could be conquered by Europeans. Growing competition among European states, particularly Great Britain, France and Germany, for African trade and territories was leading to tension and even the threat of war. To prevent such a conflict, Bismark, the German chancellor, called the "Conference of Berlin." Held from 1884 to 1885, this meeting resulted in a division of the continent among Great Britain, France, Germany, Belgium, Italy, Portugal, and Spain. Areas were assigned to different European states based on a variety of criteria, ranging from previous explorations of the regions by European agents to treaties allegedly signed by African leaders who surrendered their sovereignty over to European "protectors." By and large, most African rulers had no idea they had been labeled as subjects of the various European powers. Ironically, the European powers involved declared they were partitioning the continent for the Africans' own good, specifically stating they were doing so to help bring an end to slavery and to bring the benefits of civilization to Africa.

Of course, declaring the partition of Africa on paper was different from actually colonizing the continent, and the final declaration of the Conference of Berlin demanded that the various European states establish "effective occupation" of the regions assigned to them if the other states were to respect the assigned boundaries. The outcome was, in effect, a declaration of war on Africans by Europeans. From the mid-1880s to the early 1900s, European armies (sometimes largely consisting of African troops under European command) sought to establish European control over the areas allotted by the Conference of Berlin. These campaigns were often bloody and hard fought. Even with their newfound technology, European armies were not guaranteed an easy victory. For example, a West African leader named Samori Ture led his people against the French from 1882 to 1898, winning numerous battles before eventually being overcome by his enemies. In 1896, the Ethiopians successfully defeated the Italians at the Battle of Adowa, guaranteeing their independence from colonial occupation. They were the only African country to do so. However, even stateless societies, such as the Igbo of Nigeria or the Herero of Namibia, often proved particularly difficult for European forces to defeat, in part because the absence of a single leader or even a capital made it hard to overthrow these societies' flexible systems of political authority. As a result the British spent more than a decade before defeating the Igbo.

The horrors of colonialism did not come to a close with the successful military occupation of the continent. Under even the most benevolent colonial regimes, African subjects were faced with a denial of the most basic rights enjoyed by the citizens of the states that had colonized them. Colonial governments used forced labor, a sort of temporary slavery, to build roads, railways, and harbors that helped facilitate the export of African commodities and the import of finished goods from Europe. Similarly, African farmers were often required to grow fixed quantities of crops (such as cotton, cocoa, peanuts, or palm oil) in demand in Europe and sell them to the new colonial government at non-negotiable prices. All colonial powers sought to make colonialism profitable by supporting industries in Europe with cheap materials from Africa and control over African markets.

Perhaps the greatest abuse of colonial political and economic power came in the Congo Free State, a Central African region roughly the size of Western Europe that the Conference of Berlin made the personal property of King Leopold of Belgium. The potential wealth of the Congo Free State was largely in the form of latex (natural rubber). Following the imposition of colonial rule, the traders and agents of the Congo Free State ordered adult males in the colony to produce a weekly quota of latex. If a town or village failed to meet its collective quota, women and children might be taken hostage and homes might be burned down. If production still failed to meet demand, the hostages could be shot—with their hands cut off and returned to company officials along with the spent bullet casing—just to prove no ammunition had been wasted. As demand for latex in Europe and the United States skyrocketed in the 1890s and early 1900s (thanks to the growing demand for bicycle tires), the Congo Free State's administrators simply increased the quotas demanded of the region's inhabitants. So great was the demand that hundreds of thousands died each year from overwork, starvation, or in rebellion against the colony's brutal policies. Not until missionaries helped expose the brutality of the system did other colonial powers raise protests. Dubbed the "red rubber scandal," this situation resulted in the dissolution of the Congo Free State and the creation of a Belgian government-run colony in the region. King Leopold and his agents had already left their mark, however. At least a million people had died (some estimate the total as high as ten million) as a result of policies that had greatly enriched the Belgian king and his government.

VARIETIES OF COLONIAL RULE

The various colonial powers shared similar economic goals, but they often had very different ideas about the sort of political and administrative systems to use to attain these financial ends. In general, these policies can be distinguished as direct rule, as practiced by the French, Germans, Belgians, and Portuguese, and indirect rule, as practiced by the British. Under direct rule, the colonial power established a top-to-bottom bureaucracy staffed with nationals of the ruling country and organized along European lines. Thus, for a French West African colony such as Senegal, a post office would be run by a French postal officer, a police detachment by a French lieutenant, and a court presided over by a French judge. Each of these officials probably oversaw numerous African clerks and functionaries, but the immediate source of authority was still a French official. Similarly, all laws, rules and practices were as French as possible. More so, the language of government was French as well. Thus, in order to have any interaction with the new colonial state, Africans under French colonial authority had to learn to speak French.

The principle behind this system was known as *assimilation*, the idea that the more French (or Belgian or Portuguese) the Africans learned to act, the more civilized they were considered. Such standards included not just language, but what and how people ate, how they dressed, the music they listened to, and so on. The colonial powers practicing direct rule argued that once Africans assimilated, they would be granted full rights of citizenship, and the colonies would eventually become, for example, part of an expanded "Greater France." In reality, very few Africans were ever deemed adequately assimilated to receive full rights. By 1922, only about a hundred Africans had been granted French citizenship, for example. Nonetheless, with all government jobs and even schools biased toward the exclusion of those who did not accept and embrace the culture of the ruling country, there was considerable pressure to adopt some degree of European culture. Not surprisingly, in former French, Belgian, and Portuguese colonies (the Germans lost their colonies after World War I), a wide variety of European cultural practices are to be found. Anywhere in former French Africa, for example, it is easy to buy French bread and even croissants for breakfast. Similarly, French is the near universal language in former French colonies. In Belgian colonies, in particular, the Catholic Church was used as a major tool to help people assimilate, and it continues to be very influential in those regions today.

Quite different from direct rule was the British policy of indirect rule, based on the assumption it was better to rule through existing African systems of political authority than to replace them with European-style bureaucracies. Thus, wherever possible, the British incorporated local rulers into the British colonial governments. For example, after defeating the Sokoto Caliphate (a precolonial state located largely in the region of contemporary northern Nigeria) and killing the sultan of Sokoto in 1903, the British then built the administration of the region around the structures of the Caliphate, keeping the local **emirs** (kings) as the heads of local government and tasking them with such duties as maintaining police forces and courts and collecting taxes. Thus, rather than overthrowing local political systems, the British often reinforced them. Notably, however, in regions previously inhabited by stateless societies, the British created "chiefs" where none had existed before, simply as a means to facilitate colonial administration. In general, British rule rested more lightly on the shoulders of colonized Africans, in part because it was more familiar and not so culturally disruptive. Rather than demanding that Africans learn to speak English, for example, British colonial officers were required to learn local languages themselves.

COLONIALISM AND CULTURE

Religion.   Many of the outcomes of colonialism, however, were different from what the colonial powers expected. Although the British, French, and Belgians ultimately held political and economic power, they were often at a loss to control the cultural path of their colonies. For example, although European missionaries sought to bring established European churches to the continent, Africans soon created their own independent forms of Christianity. Indeed, the most successful forms of Christianity in Africa came to be known as "independent churches," which had no institutional ties to European denominations of Christianity. Today, for example, the Aladura churches are prevalent in coastal West Africa and the Zion churches are found throughout southern Africa. Both denominations emphasize ecstatic possession by the Holy Spirit, the power of God to heal the sick, and the ability of belief to protect church members from witchcraft. Colonialism certainly introduced Christianity to many Africans, but it could not define the final form Christianity would take.

Another outcome of colonialism, interestingly, was the rapid expansion of Islam in Africa. Islam had long been established in North Africa, the West African savannahs, and the East African coast, but its expansion elsewhere in the continent had been slow. Colonialism, however, changed this situation. In only a few decades, colonial rule facilitated the spread of Islam deep into the East African interior and also into the forest and coastal regions of West Africa. This growth occurred for two main reasons. First, colonial economic systems, no matter how abusive, served to help connect regions of Africa previously separated by distance and natural barriers. As such, rail lines extending from the coastal ports to the interior were not only conduits for goods, but also culture. Muslim traders not only exported products from the West African savannahs, but they also brought Islam to the people of the coastline. Conversely, Swahili Muslims used similar railway links in East Africa to carry Islam into the interior. Similarly, since assimilationist colonial powers saw Islam as a potential barrier to making Africans "more European," they often sought to repress or restrict the religion, which often had the effect of making conversion to Islam a means of resisting colonial cultural imperialism.

Nationalism.   One of the most important cultural developments that came out of Africa's colonization was African identity and nationalism. Faced with the common experience of colonization, and also taking advantage of the expanded opportunities for travel and communication afforded by colonial infrastructures, an increasingly large number of Africans, particularly those who were able to acquire European-style educations, began to think of themselves as a single people.

For example, the Senegalese scholar (and later president) Leopold Senghor was one of the few Africans granted full French citizenship. Nonetheless, he became a leading founder of the movement called **negritude,** which, beginning in the 1930s, stressed the cultural unity and achievements of all people of African descent. Elsewhere, many Western-educated Africans began to use the very rhetoric of colonialism as a tool to destroy it. It did not take long for Africans who read about democracy, human rights, or free-market capitalism to understand that they were receiving little of these so-called benefits of modernization under colonial rule. Thus African nationalists such as Kwame Nkruma (who would become president of Ghana) and Jomo Kenyatta (first president of Kenya) were able to use the very underpinnings of Western philosophy to demand an end to colonialism. It was an argument that European democracies could not deny.

Beginning in the 1940s and becoming increasingly vocal in the 1950s, these nationalists built upon Europe's weakened position following World War II to demand greater self-determination and even an end to colonialism. In this they shared in the mid-twentieth-century phenomenon of liberation movements that included the end of colonialism in Asia and the Middle East and the civil rights and women's rights movements in the United States.

By 1960, it was clear the winds of change were blowing in Africa, and most colonial powers took steps to end their formal administrations in Africa. Portugal, itself ruled by a fascist dictatorship, refused to relinquish its African colonies despite years of war. Only with the overthrow of the Salazar government in 1974 did Portugal withdraw from Africa. The white minority government of Southern Rhodesia was replaced with a new nonracial government following years of bloody conflict in 1980. In South Africa, decades of internal and international protest against the system of racial oppression and segregation known as **apartheid** came to a head when Nelson Mandela was released from prison in 1990 after twenty-seven years of incarceration. Mandela was soon elected president of a new South Africa.

INDEPENDENT AFRICA

Euphoria greeted African independence in the 1960s. Decades of colonial occupation and exploitation were finally at an end, and the expectations for economic growth and improved quality of life were great. For most Africans, however, these hopes have not yet come to pass. The reasons for this failure lie both outside of Africa and within. Externally, the Cold War made it difficult for new countries to find their footing, particularly in Africa. During this period the United States and the Soviet Union both interfered in African political affairs, often arming and shoring up brutal dictators and fostering civil wars to pursue their own international political and economic agendas. Internally, many of Africa's new rulers focused on enriching themselves rather than helping the people they were elected to serve. One-party states and military regimes increasingly became the norm in Africa over the course of the latter twentieth century. Many, such as Idi Amin in Uganda and Robert Mugabe in Zimbabwe, oversaw brutal abuses of human rights. Some countries, such as Somalia and the Democratic Republic of the Congo, effectively collapsed from the combined pressures of international meddling and internal corruption, leaving large areas under the control of local warlords. In recent years, the pandemic of HIV has added greatly to Africa's suffering, especially in the southern regions of the continent, where infection rates sometimes exceed 25 percent of the population.

There have been notable success stories, however. Despite an economic collapse in the 1970s, Ghana's economy has rebounded in recent years. The country also returned to democracy in 1992, after over a decade of military rule. Current annual "happiness surveys" now list Ghanaians as among the most cheerful people on the face of the earth. Similarly, in countries such as Uganda, aggressive public-education campaigns have helped reverse the spread of HIV. Elsewhere the end of apartheid in South Africa and a resurgence of democratically elected governments around the continent have been seen as signs that Africa's postindependence fortunes may be changing.

Africa's economic and political upheaval, however, has not meant Africa has failed to make a substantial cultural contribution to the modern world. Indeed, the artistic expression of African artists, authors, and musicians continues to change and develop in response to new influences and contemporary needs.

SCULPTURE

As we saw in Chapter 10, Africans have long produced significant works of sculpture in wood, metal, and clay. Modern African sculpture reflects both the preservation of local sculptural traditions and the introduction of styles and techniques from outside the continent. For example, the **gelede** masking tradition (fig. 22.1) shows the continuity of older artistic forms even in the present. Indeed, the *gelede* performances of the Yoruba are still popular, and the masks continue to be made. Other forms of physical art are quite innovative. African art enjoys huge markets in the West, and African artists have responded by creating *tourist art*, which combines African styles with the expectations of international customers. Still, some art historians argue that even as the form of the artwork changes, the purpose of the art remains consistent. Susan Vogel, a prominent African art historian, explains,

> Content . . . is of prime importance for African artists, critics and audiences, who tend to share an expectation that works of art will have a readable message or story. African art of all kinds is likely to be explainable in terms of a narrative or a religious, social or political text known to both

FIGURE 22.1 Mask, Yoruba, Republic of Benin, polychrome, wood, height $14\frac{1}{2}''$ (37 cm), Musée du Quai Branley. Paris, reserved rights. The reference to the moon in the crescent-shaped horns of this mask echoes a *gelede* song that begins, "All-powerful mother, mother of the night bird."

artists and audiences. . . . All forms of contemporary African art are seen as functional, or as serving some common good. . . . Most kinds of African art . . . seem to have a kind of seriousness, a higher mission than pleasure or decoration alone. The general consensus is that it must honor, instruct, uplift, clarify, or even scold, expose and ridicule, to push people to be what they must be. Even at its most lighthearted, it is never trivial.

The coffins of KANE KWEI [KWHY] (b. 1924) of Ghana are a good example. Kwei never received any formal training as a carpenter. In the mid-1970s, a dying uncle, who had worked as a fisherman, asked him to produce a coffin in the shape of a boat. Kwei's work delighted the entire community, and he was soon creating many types of coffins—fish and whales (for fishermen), hens with chicks (for women with large families), Mercedes-Benz coffins (for the wealthy), and cash crops (for farmers), among them the cocoa bean (fig. 22.2). These coffins disappeared underground soon after they were made. Coffins in Ghana are seen as serving the community and also have a spiritual purpose: They celebrate the successful life of the person and form part of the traditional Ghanaian funeral celebrations that often last for days. In 1974, an American art dealer exhibited Kwei's coffins in San Francisco, and now Kwei's large workshop turns out coffins for both funerals and the art market.

MUSIC

Africa is home to a great variety of musical traditions, encompassing a diversity of rhythmic and melodic styles. As discussed in Chapter 10, some West and Central African musical styles were carried by enslaved Africans to the Americas, where they interacted with European and Native American musical traditions to form such musical styles as rumba, blues, and jazz. Of particular influence was the West African minor pentatonic scale. This scale differs from the eight-note European chromatic scale (do-re-mi) in that it has five key notes, the third and fifth of which are flat, known to blues and jazz players as the "blue notes." Critical to the development of not only blues and jazz, this five-note scale often plays a significant role in gospel, country, folk, and rock and roll. Further, rather than stressing only the pure notes, African music often explores the tonal spaces in between. Thus many African instruments or musical styles encourage the musician to bend notes. For example, the **talking drum,** an instrument that also blurs the line between melody and rhythm, constantly slides between notes, as do the slide guitars so popular in blues, country, and rock music. Similarly, many African musical forms include a **call-and-response format** in which lines are called out by a leader and sung back by the band, chorus, or audience. As previously noted, African musical styles also emphasize participation by a community rather than performance to an audience, and call and response is a critical way that nonmusicians are made a part of the music.

African music is also rhythmically complex. Rather than just making sure the instruments play in unison, as is the function of the beat in classical Western music, African beats serve to both propel the music and serve as instruments in their own right. Critical to this is the interplay between multiple rhythms, a form known as **polyrhythms.** Here, multiple rhythms, such as a 4/4 and a 3/4 beat, are intertwined—intersecting at certain times and diverging at others in a complex musical interplay. But this complexity

FIGURE 22.2 Kane Kwei (Teshi tribe, Ghana, Africa), *Coffin, Orange, in the Shape of a Cocoa Pod*, ca. 1970, polychrome, wood, 34″ × 105½″ × 29″ (86.4 × 268 × 61 cm). Fine Arts Museums of San Francisco, gift of Vivian Burns, Inc. 74.8. When reproduced in a photograph, as it is here, Kwei's coffin seems smaller than it actually is. It is, literally, a coffin, over 8½ feet long.

Connections

THE MASK AS DANCE

For the Baule [BOW-LAY] carvers of the Ivory Coast, the helmet mask illustrated here (fig. 22.3) is a pleasing and beautiful object but has another significance as well. It is the Dye sacred mask. As the carver explained to Susan Vogel, "The god is a dance of rejoicing for me. So when I see the mask, my heart is filled with joy. I like it because of the horns and the eyes. The horns curve nicely, and I like the placement of the eyes and ears. In addition, it executes very interesting and graceful dance steps. . . . This is a sacred mask danced in our village."

The Baule carver pays attention to the physical features of the mask, and he also sees the mask *as* dance. In its features, he sees its performance. A mask is thus more than an ornament disguising or hiding the face. These Africans have no separate word for mask; rather the word *mask* includes the whole person performing the dance. In this sense, masks can be said to dance, and the mask or the dancer is a vehicle through which the spirit of the place passes.

FIGURE 22.3   Helmet mask. Baule style, Ivory Coast, nineteenth—twentieth century, polychrome, wood, length 38″ (95.8 cm), Metropolitan Museum of Art, NY. Michael C. Rockefeller Memorial Collection, gift of Adrian Pascal LaGamma, 1993. This African mask "makes us happy when we see it," explains a Baule carver.

is not random, and the musicians use the synergy and tension inherent in the cross rhythms to guide the songs. Like the minor pentatonic scale, the powerful nature of African rhythms has had a powerful influence on contemporary music. Although few modern musicians invest the time necessary to master the complexity of polyrhythms, the prevalence of a strong **backbeat** and the omnipresence of the drum set in popular music are testimonies to the influence of African music on the global stage.

Inside Africa, musical forms have continued to develop as African musicians have embraced instruments and styles from elsewhere in the world. Electric guitars, drum machines, and electronic keyboards are now ubiquitous in African popular music. Contemporary musicians like SONNY OKOSUN [OAK-ka-sun] (b. 1947) blend African and Western sounds. Okosun's work is based on a brand of Ghanaian music known as *highlife*, itself a blend of local rhythms and melodies with Western musical forms. Indeed, African-influenced musical forms such as jazz and country music have been of great influence in Africa. **Soukous** styles in Central Africa themselves reflect the popularity of Afro-Cuban music reintroduced to Africa in the 1950s and 1960s. African bands also often perform versions of Johnny Cash songs. In the 1970s, funk music from the United States greatly influenced the development of **Afrobeat** music in Nigeria and Ghana. In recent years, hip-hop has become a significant musical influence in Africa. For example, young Ghanaian musicians have combined hip-hop with local highlife styles to create a new musical form called **hip life.**

Like most African artwork, African music often makes overt political commentary. Chimurenga songs, for example, were a key form of protest against white minority rule in Southern Rhodesia. Anti-apartheid music was produced throughout the continent. Sonny Okosun produced *Fire in Soweto* in 1978, despite the fact that he is from Ghana. The song and album became a popular statement against apartheid throughout Africa. Perhaps no musician better represents the political side of African music, however, than Nigeria's FELA KUTI [KOO-ti]. Born into a wealthy Western-educated family, Kuti studied jazz and classical music in London. Returning to Nigeria in the late 1960s, he not only helped create the musical style of Afrobeat, but also repeatedly attacked the Nigerian government for corruption. Albums such as *Coffin for Head of State*, *VIP (Vagabonds in Power)*, and *Africa Stealing* landed him in jail repeatedly, and made him a popular hero in Nigeria.

The Lion King: The Saga of a Song.   One of the most popular songs of the twentieth century, "The Lion Sleeps Tonight," originated in Africa. A centerpiece of the 1994 Disney movie *The Lion King*, as well as the Broadway show later developed from the hit film, the original song upon which it was based was written decades earlier by a Zulu

Then & Now/Timbuktu

Timbuktu (also Timbuctu or Timbuctoo) is a city in the West African country of Mali, about eighty miles from the Niger River. Its location made it a logical meeting point for local African populations and nomadic Arab peoples to the north. Timbuktu was for many years a trading post linking Africa with Jewish and Islamic traders throughout North Africa, and through them, with European traders. Its most enduring contribution to world civilization is scholarship, with important books and manuscripts written, copied, and preserved in its well-endowed library. It is also known for the Great Mosque of Timbuktu, which is actually located in the nearby village of Djenne. In modern times, especially in the West, Timbuktu has become a metaphor for the exotic and far away, as in the expression "from here to Timbuktu."

FIGURE 22.4 Great Mosque of Timbuktu, also known as the Great Mosque of Djénné.

musician, Solomon Linda. Linda's original song, "Mbube," which is Zulu for lion, and which was recorded in 1939, includes simple lyrics, background chanting, and harmonies that made it an immediate popular success initially in Africa and then around the world.

When the American folk singer Pete Seeger recorded it, "Mbube" became "wimoweh," a mispronunciation that became standard in subsequent renderings of the song by American and European artists. An American songwriter adapted the song, adding lyrics that began his version with the words, "In the jungle, the mighty jungle, the lion sleeps tonight." This version was recorded by the Tokens and became a worldwide phenomenon. Since then, more than 150 artists have recorded it, and it lives on in its stage and screen versions.

One unfortunate fact of the song's saga is that its originator, Solomon Linda, earned less than one dollar when he sold the rights to "Mbube" in 1952. Millions of dollars have been made by singers, songwriters, record producers and studios since. Recently, though, Mr. Linda's family was awarded royalties reverting to 1987 and onward.

LITERATURE

In the modern era, many African authors have continued a tradition of protest begun by early African nationalists. Jomo Kenyatta's famous ethnography/autobiography *Facing Mount Kenya* is a prime example of how early au-

thors used literature to challenge colonialism. In more recent years, African authors have turned their pens on their own rulers when they deemed them corrupt. An example of this theme is Ayi Kwei Armah's *The Beautiful Ones Are Not Yet Born*, which indicts the corruption of early independence in Ghana in the 1960s.

Chinua Achebe. Nigerian CHINUA ACHEBE (ah-CHAY-bay) (b. 1930) has set his most famous works in the fictional town of Umofia. They deal with the coming of colonial rule or trace the lives of a series of characters from Umofia as they cope with the changing economic, political, and cultural situation in their country. These novels include *Things Fall Apart*, *Arrow of God*, *A Man of the People*, *No Longer at Ease*, and *Anthills of the Savannah* and roughly chronicle the fate of Nigeria from the advent of colonialism in the latter 1800s to independence and the struggle for stability in the 1990s. By tracing the development of Nigeria over such a long span of time, Achebe is able to critically examine the complex interactions of African and European cultures. A profound realist, Achebe is perfectly willing to attack what he sees as the shortcomings of Igbo or Nigerian culture, just as he assaults the inequities of colonialism and international economics.

Wole Soyinka. WOLE SOYINKA [shoy-INK-ah] (b. 1934) from Nigeria became the first African writer to win the Nobel Prize for Literature in 1986. Although best

Then & Now

TWINS

The Yoruba have one of the highest rates of twin births in the world. Yet, for the Yoruba, twins remain "gifts of the gods" who possess, or rather are possessed by, the deities of creativity. They are empowered by their inborn ability to perceive a dimension beyond the everyday, communicating with a universe beyond our own.

The Yoruba believe a mother is blessed with twins as a reward for her patience and virtue, and hence, after their birth, she is treated as if she were a member of the highest royalty. Indeed, any woman who gives birth to twins three times is considered the most powerful person of all, higher than kings. This is a particularly remarkable honor given that the Yoruba have a patriarchal culture, in which the oldest male member leads his entire clan.

For some time, it has been Yoruba tradition to have images carved of the twins, or *ere ibeji*, which are kept in case one of the twins should die, which sometimes happens, since twins are often smaller and more fragile than single babies. Until the twentieth century, these figures were carved out of wood, but they have been increasingly replaced by mass-produced Western dolls (fig. 22.5). The mother cares for the "twin" doll of the dead child as if it were still alive, placing it in a shrine in her bedroom. Its spirit, the Yoruba believe, will bring good fortune to the family.

FIGURE 22.5 Dolls used as *ere ibeji*, mid-twentieth century, unknown factory (Nigeria), molded plastic and metal, height $9\frac{4}{5}''$ (25 cm), Dennis J. Nervig, Fowler Museum of Cultural History, UCLA. *Ere ibeji* dolls, images of twins; represent hope for the future to the Yoruba.

---

known as a playwright, Soyinka is also a poet, essayist, political activist, social critic, and literary scholar. His poetry and plays are deeply political: as he noted in a *New York Times* interview, "I cannot conceive of my existence without political involvement."

During the Nigerian Civil War, Soyinka was imprisoned and kept in solitary confinement for his antigovernment activism. There he composed *Poems from Prison* (1969) and *The Man Died: Prison Notes of Wole Soyinka* (1988), both written in secret on toilet paper and later smuggled out. During the 1960s he worked tirelessly to develop a Nigerian national drama. Two of his best-known plays depict political intrigue in an imaginary kingdom, *Death and the King's Horseman* (1976) and *A Play for Giants* (1984), a satire on African dictators.

John Maxwell Coetzee. The South African author J. M. Coetzee (b. 1940) first came to international prominence with his novel *Waiting for the Barbarians* in 1980 and for *Life and Times of Michael K.* in 1983. A South African of Afrikaaner (Dutch) and English descent, Coetzee nonetheless uses his novels as a platform for a thinly veiled criticism of apartheid, the white South African government's policy of racial segregation and oppression, although he generally sets his novels in fictional surroundings that could be anywhere in the world. Coetzee's books are bleak and unremittingly realistic, sometimes brutally so. They chronicle the inhuman cruelties that powerful human beliefs inflict on the weak, the marginalized, and the disenfranchised. And yet for all their unflinching honesty, Coetzee's novels offer testimony to human beings' power to survive, to endure in the face of even the most oppressive hardships. He twice won the prestigious British Booker Prize (the first author to do so), and in 2003 was awarded the Nobel Prize for Literature.

MODERN LATIN AMERICA

Like Africa, Latin America had long been under the rule of colonial Europeans—chiefly the Spanish and Portuguese. Then, in the early nineteenth century, grassroots movements fueled wars of independence throughout the region and inspired the Latin American social elite to break the economic trade monopolies of the colonial rulers while preserving the existing social structure.

Latin America is marked by the collision and intermingling of two separate cultural and economic traditions. The colonists and their heirs are largely well-to-do Roman Catholics, whereas the diverse indigenous peoples maintain their own traditional cultural practices and make up an underprivileged, subsistence-based social class. A variety of types of societies developed among different Latin American countries. In Argentina and Uruguay, the few natives were essentially wiped out by European diseases in the early years of colonization. A **Eurocentric** culture developed when over one million Europeans, mostly Spanish and Italian, emigrated to these countries between 1905 and 1910. In Central America and Peru, in contrast, strong native communities, of Mayan and Incan ancestry, survive to this day, with their own thriving indigenous cultures.

PAINTING

Colonial Art.   The joining of Native American and European traditions is evident in much of the art and architecture produced during the colonial period. In Mexico, for instance, Baroque architecture flourished, but with a native exuberance and love for naturalistic detail that far exceeds most Baroque architecture in Europe (see Chapter 15). In painting, native artists combined their own traditions with those of the Catholic Church.

A depiction of a Corpus Christi procession in Santa Ana, Peru (fig. 22.6) shows European and Native American traditions converging. The work was painted in about 1660 by the followers of QUISPE TITO [TEE-toh] (1611–81), a painter of Inca origin, who worked in Cuzco, Peru. At the head of the procession, on the left, is an Indian leader in royal Inca dress, wearing a headdress decorated with a combination of Spanish and pre-Conquest symbols, including a bird, which, for the Incas, had magical significance (a live bird, with brilliant plumage, also sits on the wall above his head). Following the Inca leader are the priest and acolytes, then the Corpus Christi glory cart with a statue of the parish saint holding onto a palm tree with a cupidlike angel on his shoulder. To the right are the native parishioners. Behind the scene, the European elite watch from their balconies, from which hang brightly colored sheets from Spain.

The Mexican Mural Movement.   Despite the merging of traditions evident in colonial art, the church and the

FIGURE **22.6**   Followers of Quispe Tito, *Corpus Christi Procession with the Parishioners of Santa Ana* (detail), ca. 1660, fresco, Damian Bayon/Museo de Arte Hatun Rumiyoc, Cuzco, Peru/ Embassy of Peru. Another section of this fresco depicts a giant altar erected especially for the occasion, decorated with silver-framed paintings and sculptures of angels who wear feathered helmets derived from Inca tradition.

European cultural elite wanted to suppress native customs. In Mexico particularly, where strong native populations had begun to rebel against the European elite by the early twentieth century, these customs were a source of identity and pride. Beginning in 1910 with a violent revolt against the regime of Porfirio Díaz, Mexico was rocked by social and political unrest. Civil war lasted until the inauguration of the revolutionary leader, Alvaro Obregón, as president in 1920. Obregón believed the aesthetic faculty, and the appreciation of painting in particular, could lead the way to revolutionary change. He also believed in restoring Mexico's indigenous cultural identity. He thus began a vast mural project designed to cover the walls of public spaces across the country with images celebrating Mexico's past and future. By the mid-1920s, the mural movement was in the hands of three painters, *Los Tres Grandes*, as they were called, "The Three Giants"—DIEGO RIVERA [rih-VAY-rah] (1886–1957), JOSE CLEMENTE OROZCO [oh-ROZ-coe] (1883–1949), and DAVID ALFARO SIQUEIROS [see-KAYR-ohs] (1896–1974).

All three artists began their careers painting **al fresco,** but the sun, rain, and humidity of the Mexican climate damaged their efforts. In 1937, Siqueiros organized a workshop in New York City, close to the chemical industry, to develop and experiment with new synthetic paints. One of the first media used in the workshop was **pyroxylin,** commonly known as Duco, a lacquer developed as an automobile paint. It is used in the large-scale mural by Siqueiros, *Cuauhtémoc Against the Myth* (fig. 22.7), which was painted in 1944 on panel so it could withstand earthquakes and is housed today in the Union Housing Project at Tlatelco, Mexico. It depicts the story of the Aztec hero who shattered the myth that the Spanish army could not be conquered. This message had great significance for the people: The indigenous people could regain power. Siqueiros also meant it as a commentary on the susceptibility to defeat of the Nazis in Europe.

Frida Kahlo. Rivera was married to another prominent Mexican painter, FRIDA KAHLO [KAH-loh] (1910–54), whose work was initially overshadowed by that of her husband, but whose reputation has increased to such a degree that she is now considered the greater artist and is surely the more famous. Kahlo is best known for her highly distinctive self-portraits in a wide range of circumstances and settings. "I paint self-portraits because I am so often alone," she once said, "because I am the person I know best." Her self-portraits, it has been argued, created a series of alternative selves that helped exorcise life's pains. She suffered almost her entire life: first from polio, which she contracted at age six and left her with a withered right leg; then from a bus and trolley collision at age eighteen, in which her pelvis and spinal column were broken, her foot was crushed, and her abdomen and uterus were pierced by a steel handrail, resulting in a life-long series of operations; and finally from her volatile relationship with

Rivera, whose many adulterous affairs, including one with her own sister, hurt her deeply.

The Two Fridas (fig. 22.8), 1939, alludes to Kahlo's mixed ancestry, physical suffering, and troubled marriages to Rivera. On the left is the European Frida, a reference to her German-Jewish father; on the right is the Mexican Frida, a reference to her Mexican mother. The two Fridas are linked by their clasped hands and the shared artery between their hearts. The Mexican Frida holds a tiny image of Rivera, while the European Frida tries to stop herself from bleeding, without success.

Wilfredo Lam. The work of Cuban painter Wilfredo Lam (1902–82), of Chinese and mulatto ancestry, demonstrates the close connection between European and Latin American cultures. Lam left for Europe in 1923 at the age of twenty-one and did not return to the Caribbean for eighteen years, until 1941, when he was sent by the Nazis to a prison camp in Martinique. Within forty days, he was released and sent back to Havana, where he discovered that the idyllic Cuba of his childhood had been destroyed by the collapse of sugar prices.

Lam's masterpiece, *The Jungle* (fig. 22.9), painted in 1943, is a record of his reaction. It is almost exactly the same size as *Les Demoiselles d'Avignon* (see fig. 18.26) by Picasso, who had befriended Lam in Paris in 1939. The faces of Lam's totemic figures are based, like Picasso's, on African masks. But crucially different from Picasso's painting is the density of Lam's image. Every space is occupied, not only by shoots of sugarcane and jungle foliage, but by the figures themselves, whose arms and hands seem to reach to the ground. This natural world is inhabited by a mysterious, mythical virgin-beast, both productive and destructive, whose origins are to be found in Lam's fascination with the world of **santería** or voodoo.

Fernando Botero. Columbian artist FERNANDO BOTERO [bo-TAIR-oh] (b. 1932) is known for his "swollen" or "inflated" figures that fill the canvas like balloons and satirize the Latin American ruling elite. "When I inflate things," he has explained, "I enter a subconscious world rich in folk images." *Mona Lisa at the Age of Twelve* (fig. 22.10), painted in 1959, condenses three images: Leonardo da Vinci's original painting (see fig. 13.21), the Infanta Margarita in Diego Velázquez's *Maids of Honor* (see fig. 15.25), and *Alice in Wonderland*. Mona Lisa's oft-noted "inscrutable" smile here becomes grotesquely piglike, Botero revealing in it the gluttony of the Latin American aristocracy and their ability to "consume" the land and its people.

MUSIC

Latin America has a rich musical heritage, both popular and traditional. The most prevalent forms of popular music are those associated with dance. The tango came

FIGURE 22.7   David Alfaro Siqueiros, *Cuauhtémoc Against the Myth*, Teepan Union Housing Project, Tlatelco, Mexico, 1944, mural, pyroxylin on celtex and plywood, 1,000 sq. ft. (92.9 sq. m). Photo by Dr. Desmond Rochfort. © Estate of David Alfaro Siqueiros/SOMAAP/ Licensed by VAGA, NY. Reproduction authorized by the Insituto Nacional de Bellas Artes y Literatura. Siqueiros's experimentation with synthetic paints would lead to the invention of acrylics, much in use today.

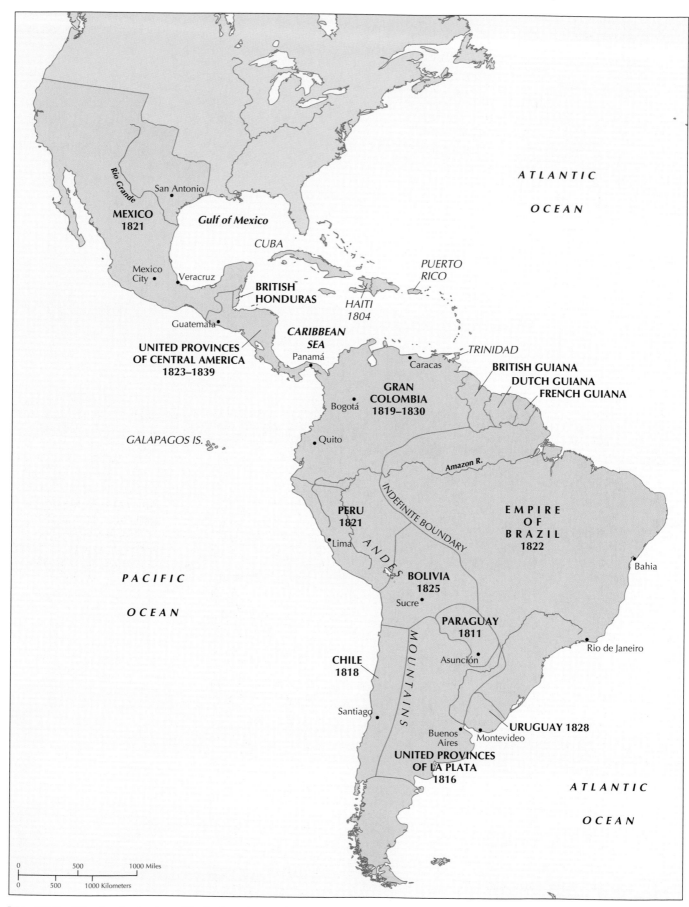

MAP 22.2 The decolonization of Latin America 1800–36.

FIGURE 22.8 Frida Kahlo, *The Two Fridas*, 1939, oil on canvas, 5′9″ square (1.73 m square), Museo Nacional de Arte Moderno, Mexico City, © 2001 Banco de Mexico, Diego Rivera & Frida Kahlo Museums Trust. Av. Cinco de Mayo No. 2, Col. Centro, Del. Cuanhtemoc 06059, Mexico, D.F. Reproduction authorized by the Instituto Nacional de Bellas Artes y Literatura. Bob Schalkwijk/Art Resource, NY. The marriage between the artists Rivera and Kahlo was described by her parents as "like the marriage between an elephant and a dove." Kahlo described marriage to Rivera as her "second accident"—a nearly fatal traffic collision at the age of eighteen was her first.

FIGURE 22.9 Wilfredo Lam, *The Jungle*, 1943, gouache on paper, mounted on canvas, 7′10″ × 7′6½″ (2.39 × 2.30 m), Museum of Modern Art, NY, Inter-American Fund, Licensed by SCALA-Art Resource, NY. © 2005 Artists Rights Society, NY. The son of a Chinese immigrant and an Afro-Cuban mother, Lam studied African art in Paris and adopted Picasso's style in an attempt to explore his own origins.

Cross Currents

BACH IN BRAZIL

One interesting musical cross current between Latin America and Europe is Villa-Lobos's *Bachianas Brasileiras*, a piece inspired by the German Baroque composer Johann Sebastian Bach and written as a tribute to his memory and legacy. In this work, Villa-Lobos couples Brazilian rhythms with Bachian counterpoint to create a fusion of Latin and Germanic musical styles that spans cultures, oceans, and centuries.

Bach was the archetypal composer for Villa-Lobos, since Bach also drew inspiration from simple folk melodies, which he then developed into complex polyphonic compositions. *Bachianas Brasileiras* consists of nine parts, each scored for different instrumental combinations. No. 1, for example, is scored for eight cellos, No. 3 for piano and orchestra, No. 6 for flute and bassoon.

One of the most notable parts of *Bachianas Brasileiras* is No. 5, which includes a beautiful aria based on a Brazilian folk song. Villa-Lobos sets this piece for soprano and eight cellos, with a solo cello line. Its elegant beauty in the alternative arrangements is but one example of the way cultures interact to produce new and exciting artistic forms and styles.

---

from Argentina, the **samba** from Brazil, and the pasillo from Colombia. Latin-inspired dances include the Caribbean **calypso**, the Cuban rumba, the Brazilian lambada, and even the macarena.

One of the most popular instruments used in Latin American music is the guitar, which has a long history in Spain and Spanish American cultures. The guitar has been used both in folk and classical music, by many composers, including the Brazilian HEITOR VILLALOBOS [VEE-yah LOW-bows] (1887–1959).

Latin America's best known classical composer, Villa-Lobos was born in Rio de Janeiro. After studying music with his father, he earned a living by playing the cello in cafés. He researched and collected authentic folk and Indian songs, both of which he later used as melodies in his classical compositions. Villa-Lobos believed that folk music reveals the special vitality and spirit of a people, their unique essence, and he conveys this in his large works for chorus and orchestra.

FIGURE 22.10 Fernando Botero, *Mona Lisa at the Age of Twelve*, 1959, oil and tempera on canvas, 6′ 11″ × 6′ 5″ (2.11 × 1.96 m), Museum of Modern Art, NY, Inter-American Fund. Licensed by Scala/Art Resource, NY. In the 1970s, Botero moved to Paris, where he began to make large bronze sculptures of his swollen figures.

LITERATURE

The literature of Latin America is written primarily in two languages, Spanish and Portuguese. Yet the plurality of voices and visions that emerge in modern and contemporary Latin American fiction is staggering. A concern many writers share is an exploration of the imagination. Three writers in particular can be singled out for special attention: the Argentinean novelist, essayist, and short-story writer Jorge Luis Borges; the contemporary Colombian novelist and short-story writer Gabriel García Márquez; and the Chilean novelist Isabel Allende.

Jorge Luis Borges. JORGE LUIS BORGES [BOR-haze] (1899–1986) is best known for what he calls his *ficciones*—short, enigmatic fictional works that invite philosophical reflection, especially speculation about the mysterious universe that human beings inhabit. Borges's fiction is situated at the interface between the genres of essay and autobiography; he mixes facts and names from his family chronicles with reflections on philosophical matters. His stories frequently involve a central character confronted

Critical Thinking

MAGIC REALISM

Magic Realism is a term that was coined to attempt to describe the literary movement that began in South America and had its greatest and most sustained success there. It refers to a style of writing (and also films and paintings) that mixes sharply etched realistic descriptive details with fantastic and dreamlike elements, that include motifs from myths and fairy tales. Related to surrealism, a movement in art primarily and secondarily in literature that combines elements of dreams and myth with everyday experience, magic realism hews more closely to everyday experiential reality, without pretending to supersede, surpass, or transcend it. Magic realism includes the following aspects:

- elements of the fantastic or marvelous
- a lack of discursive explanation
- an acceptance of the irrational and nonlogical
- an abundance of sensory images and details
- temporal distortions and causal inversions
- elements of folklore and legend
- multiple perspectives and points of view
- ambiguity and uncertainty

Why do you think writers and other artists in the twentieth century developed such an approach to their art? How might elements of magic realism, such as those identified in the list above, contribute to meaningful literary and artistic productions and performances? What is your own personal response to works that employ elements of magic realism?

with a puzzle or problem, which has to be unraveled much in the manner of detective stories.

One of Borges's most powerful metaphors is that of the labyrinth, a maze into which the central character (and the reader) is placed, and from which extrication comes as the character gains realization about the imaginative world. Borges often merges the "real" with the imaginary, what is historical with what is invented, so his readers become disoriented and are forced to reconsider the relationship between fiction and reality.

Gabriel García Márquez. If Borges is the master of the short story, GABRIEL GARCÍA MÁRQUEZ [gar-SEE-ah MAR-kez] (b. 1928) is the master of the novel. His *One Hundred Years of Solitude* (1967) blends the "real" with the imaginary in unpredictable yet convincing ways, in a style that has come to be known as **magic realism.** Magic realism weaves realistic events together with incredible and fantastic ones, in an attempt to convey the truths of life. In magic realism, key events do not necessarily have a logical explanation; mystery is an integral part of experience. Remarking that "There's not a single line in all my work that does not have a basis in reality," García Márquez, like other magic realists, sees his work as conveying simultaneously the truths of the imagination and those of "reality."

Isabel Allende. In the same year that García Márquez won the Nobel Prize for Literature, ISABEL ALLENDE [ay-END-eh] (b. 1942) published her noteworthy novel *The House of Spirits* (1982). Like García Márquez's *One Hun-*

Table 22-1 MODERN AFRICAN AND LATIN AMERICAN WRITERS

African Writers

Chinua Achebe (b. 1930), Nigeria, *Things Fall Apart; Arrow of God* (novels)

Wole Soyinka (b. 1938), Nigeria, *Poems from Prison; Death and the King's Horseman* (play)

J. M. Coetzee (b. 1940), South Africa, *Waiting for the Barbarians; Disgrace* (novels)

Latin American Writers

Jorge Luis Borges (1899–1966), Argentina, *Ficciones* (stories)

Gabriel García Márquez (b. 1928), Colombia, *One Hundred Years of Solitude* (novel)

Isabel Allende (b. 1942), Chile, *The House of Spirits* (novel)

Cultural Impact

Twentieth-century Africa has been a continent in flux. Its political makeup has shifted from a continent of European colonial empires to one of modern nation-states. It has been a battleground for competing ideologies, both native and foreign, including Marxist-inspired revolutions, Christian proselytizing, and Islamic cultural incursions.

Parts of contemporary Africa continue to suffer from a high incidence of contagious diseases, including malaria and AIDS. Some African countries are becoming increasingly modernized, and some increasingly democratic. Recent developments in South Africa testify to the vitality and influence of the continent's impact politically, socially, and economically. Artistically, African music continues to influence Western composers and performers, and African music and dance groups perform to acclaim around the world, especially in the United States.

Modern Latin America has undergone significant social and political change. Revolutions in a number of countries, including Argentina, Brazil, and Mexico, occurred early in the century. Among later centers of unrest, the Mexican revolution of 1910 was the most successful in reorganizing social structures and fostering economic and political renewal.

The legacy of Latin American arts continues to influence painters, writers, and musicians around the globe. The social scope and political focus of the Mexican mural tradition has had a major impact on twentieth-century artists in the Americas and in Europe. The psychological complexity of Mexican portrait painting, especially in the paintings of Frida Kahlo, has had a lasting influence on the art world. In addition, the magic realism of South American novelists, especially in the work of Gabriel García Márquez, has been imitated and adapted by writers worldwide. Finally, the music of Latin America continues to be among the most internationally influential of any in the world.

---

dred Years of Solitude, Allende's novel creates a fictional world that reconstructs the history of a country—in her case, modern Chile, her homeland, from which she was exiled when her uncle, President Salvador Allende of Chile, was assassinated in 1975. Like García Márquez, Allende uses techniques of magic realism to weave realistic events with incredible and fantastic ones to convey the truths of life.

Allende explains that she uses these techniques because, as she says, "in Latin America, we value dreams, passions, obsessions, emotions." It is also partly attributable to, as she says, "our sense of family, our sense of religion, of superstition, too." But mostly it is because "Fantastic things happen every day in Latin America—it's not that we make them up."

KEY TERMS

creole	talking drum	Afrobeat	*santería*
emirs	call-and-response format	hip life	samba
negritude	polyrhythms	Eurocentric	calypso
apartheid	backbeat	al fresco	magic realism
gelede	Soukous	pyroxylin	

www. WEBSITES FOR FURTHER STUDY

http://cti.itc.virginia.edu/%7Ebcr/Bayly/Bayly.html
(African art from the Bayly Museum.)

http://globetrotter.berkeley.edu/Elberg/Soyinka/soyinka-con0.html
(Harry Kreisler interviews Nobel Laureate Wole Soyinka about writing, theater arts, and political activism.)

http://www.rdpl.red-deer.ab.ca/villa/heller.html
(An excellent website featuring the life and works of composer Heitor Villa-Lobos.)

http://www.themodernword.com/gubo/
(An extensive site on one of the world's greatest writers, Gabriel García Márquez.)

READINGS

CHINUA ACHEBE

from *Things Fall Apart*

The following passage constitutes the opening of Achebe's best known novel, Things Fall Apart, *which dramatizes the encounter of traditional Ibo life with colonialism and Christianity at the beginning of the twentieth century. Achebe's portrait of pre-Christian tribal life became depicts a society in transition and emphasizes the importance of communication to avert misunderstanding.*

Okonkwo was well known throughout the nine villages and even beyond. His fame rested on solid personal achievements. As a young man of eighteen he had brought honor to his village by throwing Amalinze the Cat. Amalinze was the great wrestler who for seven years was unbeaten, from Umuofia to Mbaino. He was called the Cat because his back would never touch the earth. It was this man that Okonkwo threw in a fight which the old men agreed was one of the fiercest since the founder of their town engaged a spirit of the wild for seven days and seven nights.

The drums beat and the flutes sang and the spectators held their breath. Amalinze was a wily craftsman, but Okonkwo was as slippery as a fish in water. Every nerve and every muscle stood out on their arms, on their backs and their thighs, and one almost heard them stretching to breaking point. In the end Okonkwo threw the Cat.

That was many years ago, twenty years or more, and during this time Okonkwo's fame had grown like a bush-fire in the harmattan. He was tall and huge, and his bushy eye-brows and wide nose gave him a very severe look. He breathed heavily, and it was said that, when he slept, his wives and children in their houses could hear him breathe. When he walked, his heels hardly touched the ground and he seemed to walk on springs, as if he was going to pounce on somebody. And he did pounce on people quite often. He had a slight stammer and whenever he was angry and could not get his words out quickly enough, he would use his fists. He had no patience with unsuccessful men. He had had no patience with his father.

Unoka, for that was his father's name, had died ten years ago. In his day he was lazy and improvident and was quite incapable of thinking about tomorrow. If any money came his way, and it seldom did, he immediately bought gourds of palm-wine, called round his neighbors and made merry. He always said that whenever he saw a dead man's mouth he saw the folly of not eating what one had in one's lifetime. Unoka was, of course, a debtor, and he owed every neighbor' some money, from a few cowries to quite substantial amounts.

He was tall but very thin and had a slight stoop. He wore a haggard and mournful look except when he was drinking or playing on his flute. He was very good on his flute, and his happiest moments were the two or three moons after the harvest when the village musicians brought down their instruments, hung above the fireplace. Unoka would play with them, his face beaming with blessedness and peace. Sometimes another village would ask Unoka's band and their dancing *egwugwu* to come and stay with them and teach them their tunes. They would go to such hosts for as long as three or four markets, making music and feasting. Unoka loved the good fare and the good fellowship, and he loved this season of the year, when the rains had stopped and the sun rose every morning with dazzling beauty. And it was not too hot either, because the cold and dry harmattan was wind blowing down from the north. Some years the harmattan was very severe and a dense haze hung on the atmosphere. Old men and children would then sit round log fires, warming their bodies. Unoka loved it all, and he loved the first kites that returned with the dry season, and the children who sang songs of welcome to them. He would remember his own childhood, how he had often wandered around looking for a kite sailing leisurely against the blue sky. As soon as he found one he would sing with his whole being, welcoming it back from its long, long journey, and asking it if it had brought home any lengths of cloth.

That was years ago, when he was young. Unoka, the grown-up, was a failure. He was poor and his wife and children had barely enough to eat. People laughed at him because he was a loafer, and they swore never to lend him any more money because he never paid back. But Unoka was such a man that he always succeeded in borrowing more, and piling up his debts.

One day a neighbor called Okoye came in to see him. He was reclining on a mud bed in his hut playing on the flute. He immediately rose and shook hands with Okoye, who then unrolled the goatskin which he carried under his arm and sat down. Unoka went into an inner room and soon returned with a small wooden disc containing a kola nut, some alligator pepper and a lump of white chalk.

"I have kola," he announced when he sat down, and passed the disc over to his guest.

"Thank you. He who brings kola brings life. But I think you ought to break it," replied Okoye, passing back the disc.

"No, it is for you, I think," and they argued like this for a few moments before Unoka accepted the honor of breaking the kola. Okoye, meanwhile, took the lump of chalk, drew some lines on the floor, and then painted his big toe.

As he broke the kola, Unoka prayed to their ancestors for life and health, and for protection against their enemies. When they had eaten they talked about many things: about the heavy rains which were drowning the yams, about the next ancestral feast and about the impending war with the village of Mbaino. Unoka was never happy when it came to wars. He was in fact a coward and could not bear the sight of blood. And so he changed the subject and talked about music, and his face beamed. He could hear in his mind's ear the bloodstirring and intricate rhythms of the *ekwe* and the *udu* and the *ogene*, and he could hear his own flute weaving in and out of them, decorating them with a colorful and plaintive tune. The total effect was gay and brisk, but if one picked out the flute as it went up and down and then broke up into short snatches one saw that there was sorrow and grief there.

Okoye was also a musician. He played on the *ogene*. But he was not a failure like Unoka. He had a large barn full of yams and he had three wives. And now he was going to take the Idemili title, the third highest in the land. It was a very expensive ceremony and he was gathering all his resources together. That was in fact the reason why he had come to see Unoka. He cleared his throat and began:

"Thank you for the kola. You may have heard of the title I intend to take shortly."

Having spoken plainly so far, Okoye said the next half a dozen sentences in proverbs. Among the Ibo the art of conversation is regarded very highly, and proverbs are the palm-oil with which words are eaten. Okoye was a great talker and he spoke for a long time, skirting round the subject and then hitting it finally. In short, he was asking Unoka to return the two hundred cowries he had borrowed from him more than two years before. As soon as Unoka understood what his friend was driving at, he burst out laughing. He laughed loud and long and his voice rang out clear as the *ogene*, and tears stood in his eyes. His visitor was amazed, and sat speechless. At the end, Unoka was able to give an answer between fresh outbursts of mirth.

"Look at that wall," he said, pointing at the far wall of his hut, which was rubbed with red earth so that it shone. "Look at those lines of chalk;" and Okoye saw groups of short perpendicular lines drawn in chalk. There were five groups, and the smallest group had ten lines. Unoka had a sense of the dramatic and so he allowed a pause, in which he took a pinch of snuff and sneezed noisily, and then he continued: "Each group there represents a debt to someone, and each stroke is one hundred cowries. You see, I owe that man a thousand cowries. But he has not come to wake me up in the morning for it. I shall pay you, but not today. Our elders say that the sun will shine on those who stand before it shines on those who kneel under them. I shall pay my big debts first." And he took another pinch of snuff, as if that was paying the big debts first. Okoye rolled his goatskin and departed.

When Unoka died he had taken no title at all and he was heavily in debt. Any wonder then that his son Okonkwo was ashamed of him? Fortunately, among these people a man was judged according to his worth, and not according to the worth of his father. Okonkwo was clearly cut out for great things. He was still young but he had won fame as the greatest wrestler in the nine villages. He was a wealthy farmer and had two barns full of yams, and had just married his third wife. To crown it all he had taken two titles and had shown incredible prowess in two inter-tribal wars. And so although Okonkwo was still young, he was already one of the greatest men of his time. Age was respected among his people, but achievement was revered. As the elders said, if a child washed his hands he could eat with kings. Okonkwo had clearly washed his hands and so he ate with kings and elders. And that was how he came to look after the doomed lad who was sacrificed to the village of Umuofia by their neighbors to avoid war and bloodshed. The ill-fated lad was called Ikemefuna.

JORGE LUIS BORGES
The Garden of Forking Paths

One of Borges's best known and most intriguing stories, this work contains a labyrinth, which serves as a metaphor for the difficulty of knowing anything with certainty. Here, using this image, the author is able to blend history and fiction, the real and the imaginary. He once described his preoccupation with the labyrinth during an interview. "I discovered the labyrinth in a book published in France by Garnier that my father had in his library. The book had a very odd engraving that took a whole page and showed a building that resembled an amphitheater. I remember that it had cracks and seemed tall, taller than the cypresses and the men that stood around it. My eyesight was not perfect—I was very myopic—but I

thought that if I used a magnifying glass, I would be able to see a minotaur within the building. That labyrinth was, besides, a symbol of bewilderment, a symbol of being lost in life. I believe that all of us, at one time or another, have felt that we are lost, and I saw in the labyrinth the symbol of that condition. Since then, I have held that vision of the labyrinth."

On page 22 of Liddell Hart's *History of World War I* you will read that an attack against the Serre-Montauban line by thirteen British divisions (supported by 1,400 artillery pieces), planned for the 24th of July, 1916, had to be postponed until the morning of the 29th. The torrential rains, Captain Liddell Hart comments, caused this delay, an insignificant one, to be sure.

The following statement, dictated, reread and signed by Dr. Yu Tsun, former professor of English at the *Hochschule* at Tsingtao, throws an unsuspected light over the whole affair. The first two pages of the document are missing.

". . . and I hung up the receiver. Immediately afterwards, I recognized the voice that had answered in German. It was that of Captain Richard Madden. Madden's presence in Viktor Runeberg's apartment meant the end of our anxieties and—but this seemed, *or should have seemed*, very secondary to me—also the end of our lives. It meant that Runeberg had been arrested or murdered.[1] Before the sun set on that day, I would encounter the same fate. Madden was implacable. Or rather, he was obliged to be so. An Irishman at the service of England, a man accused of laxity and perhaps of treason, how could he fail to seize and be thankful for such a miraculous opportunity: the discovery, capture, maybe even the death of two agents of the German Reich? I went up to my room; absurdly I locked the door and threw myself on my back on the narrow iron cot. Through the window I saw the familiar roofs and the cloud-shaded six o'clock sun. It seemed incredible to me that that day without premonitions or symbols should be the one of my inexorable death. In spite of my dead father, in spite of having been a child in a symmetrical garden of Hai Feng, was I—now—going to die? Then I reflected that everything happens to a man precisely, precisely *now*. Centuries of centuries and only in the present do things happen; countless men in the air, on the face of the earth and the sea, and all that really is happening is happening to me . . . The almost intolerable recollection of Madden's horselike face banished these wanderings. In the midst of my hatred and terror (it means nothing to me now to speak of terror, now that I have mocked Richard Madden, now that my throat yearns for the noose) it occurred to me that the tumultuous and doubtless happy warrior did not suspect that I possessed the Secret. The name of the exact location of the new British artillery park on the River Ancre. A bird streaked across the grey sky and blindly I translated it into an airplane and that airplane into many (against the French sky) annihilating the artillery station with vertical bombs. If only my mouth, before a bullet shattered it, could cry out that secret name so it could be heard in Germany . . . My human voice was very weak. How might I make it carry to the ear of the Chief? To the ear of that sick and hateful man who knew nothing of

[1]An hypothesis both hateful and odd. The Prussian spy Hans Rabener, alias Victor Runeberg, attacked with drawn automatic the bearer of the warrant for his arrest, Captain Richard Madden. The latter, in self-defense, inflicted the wound which brought about Runeberg's death.

Runeberg and me save that we were in Staffordshire and who was waiting in vain for our report in his arid office in Berlin, endlessly examining newspapers . . . I said out loud: *I must flee.* I sat up noiselessly, in a useless perfection of silence, as if Madden were already lying in wait for me. Something—perhaps the mere vain ostentation of proving my resources were nil—made me look through my pockets. I found what I knew I would find. The American watch, the nickel chain and the square coin, the key ring with the incriminating useless keys to Runeberg's apartment, the notebook, a letter which I resolved to destroy immediately (and which I did not destroy), a crown, two shillings and a few pence, the red and blue pencil, the handkerchief, the revolver with one bullet. Absurdly, I took it in my hand and weighed it in order to inspire courage within myself. Vaguely I thought that a pistol report can be heard at a great distance. In ten minutes my plan was perfected. The telephone book listed the name of the only person capable of transmitting the message; he lived in a suburb of Fenton, less than a half hour's train ride away.

I am a cowardly man. I say it now, now that I have carried to its end a plan whose perilous nature no one can deny. I know its execution was terrible. I didn't do it for Germany, no. I care nothing for a barbarous country which imposed upon me the abjection of being a spy. Besides, I know of a man from England—a modest man—who for me is no less great than Goethe. I talked with him for scarcely an hour, but during that hour he was Goethe . . . I did it because I sensed that the Chief somehow feared people of my race—for the innumerable ancestors who merge within me. I wanted to prove to him that a yellow man could save his armies. Besides, I had to flee from Captain Madden. His hands and his voice could call at my door at any moment. I dressed silently, bade farewell to myself in the mirror, went downstairs, scrutinized the peaceful street and went out. The station was not far from my home, but I judged it wise to take a cab. I argued that in this way I ran less risk of being recognized; the fact is that in the deserted street I felt myself visible and vulnerable, infinitely so. I remember that I told the cab driver to stop a short distance before the main entrance. I got out with voluntary, almost painful slowness; I was going to the village of Ashgrove but I bought a ticket for a more distant station. The train left within a very few minutes, at eight-fifty. I hurried; the next one would leave at nine-thirty. There was hardly a soul on the platform. I went through the coaches; I remember a few farmers, a woman dressed in mourning, a young boy who was reading with fervor the *Annals* of Tacitus, a wounded and happy soldier. The coaches jerked forward at last. A man whom I recognized ran in vain to the end of the platform. It was Captain Richard Madden. Shattered, trembling, I shrank into the rear corner of the seat, away from the dreaded window.

From this broken state I passed into an almost abject felicity. I told myself that the duel had already begun and that I had won the first encounter by frustrating, even if for forty minutes, even if by a stroke of fate, the attack of my adversary. I argued that this slightest of victories foreshadowed a total victory. I argued (no less fallaciously) that my cowardly felicity proved that I was a man capable of carrying out the adventure successfully. From this weakness I took strength that did not abandon me. I foresee that man will resign himself each day to more atrocious undertakings; soon there will be no one but warriors and brigands; I give them this counsel: *The author of an atrocious undertaking ought to imagine that he has already accomplished it, ought to impose upon himself a future as irrevocable as the past.* Thus I proceeded as my eyes of a man already dead registered the elapsing of that day, which was perhaps the last, and the diffusion of the night. The train ran gently along, amid ash trees. It stopped almost in the middle of the fields. No one announced the name of the station. "Ashgrove?" I asked a few lads on the platform. "Ashgrove," they replied. I got off.

A lamp enlightened the platform but the faces of the boys were in shadow. One questioned me, "Are you going to Dr. Stephen Albert's house?" Without waiting for my answer, another said, "The house is a long way from here, but you won't get lost if you take this road to the left and at every crossroads turn again to your left." I tossed them a coin (my last), descended a few stone steps and started down the solitary road. It went downhill, slowly. It was of elemental earth; overhead the branches were tangled; the low, full moon seemed to accompany me.

For an instant, I thought that Richard Madden in some way had penetrated my desperate plan. Very quickly, I understood that that was impossible. The instructions to turn always to the left reminded me that such was the common procedure for discovering the central point of certain labyrinths. I have some understanding of labyrinths: not for nothing am I the great grandson of that Ts'ui Pên who was governor of Yunnan and who renounced worldly power in order to write a novel that might be even more populous than the *Hung Lu Meng* and to construct a labyrinth in which all men would become lost. Thirteen years he dedicated to these heterogeneous tasks, but the hand of a stranger murdered him—and his novel was incoherent and no one found the labyrinth. Beneath English trees I meditated on that lost maze; I imagined it inviolate and perfect at the secret crest of a mountain; I imagined it erased by rice fields or beneath the water; I imagined it infinite, no longer composed of octagonal kiosks and returning paths, but of rivers and provinces and kingdoms . . . I thought of a labyrinth of labyrinths, of one sinuous spreading labyrinth that would encompass the past and the future and in some way involve the stars. Absorbed in these illusory images, I forgot my destiny of one pursued. I felt myself to be, for an unknown period of time, an abstract perceiver of the world. The vague, living countryside, the moon, the remains of the day worked on me, as well as the slope of the road which eliminated any possibility of weariness. The afternoon was intimate, infinite. The road descended and forked among the now confused meadows. A high-pitched, almost syllabic music approached and receded in the shifting of the wind, dimmed by leaves and distance. I thought that a man can be an enemy of other men, of the moments of other men, but not of a country: not of fireflies, woods, gardens, streams of water, sunsets. Thus I arrived before a tall, rusty gate. Between the iron bars I made out a poplar grove and a pavilion. I understood suddenly two things, the first trivial, the second almost unbelievable: the music came from the pavilion, and the music was Chinese. For precisely that reason I had openly accepted it without paying it any heed. I do not remember whether there was a bell or whether I knocked with my hand. The sparkling of the music continued.

From the rear of the house within a lantern approached: a lantern that the trees sometimes striped and sometimes eclipsed, a paper lantern that had the form of a drum and the color of the moon. A tall man bore it. I didn't see his face for the light blinded me. He opened the door and said slowly, in my own language: "I see that the pious Hsi P'êng persists in correcting my solitude. You no doubt wish to see the garden?"

I recognized the name of one of our consuls and I replied, disconcerted, "The garden?"

"The garden of forking paths."

Something stirred in my memory and I uttered with incomprehensible certainty, "The garden of my ancestor Ts'ui Pên."

"Your ancestor? Your illustrious ancestor? Come in."

The damp path zigzagged like those of my childhood. We came to a library of Eastern and Western books. I recognized bound in yellow silk several volumes of the Lost Encyclopedia, edited by the Third Emperor of the Luminous Dynasty but never printed. The record on the phonograph revolved next to a bronze phoenix. I also recall a *famille rose* vase and another, many centuries older, of that shade of blue which our craftsmen copied from the potters of Persia . . .

Stephen Albert observed me with a smile. He was, as I have said, very tall, sharp-featured, with gray eyes and a gray beard. He told me that he had been a missionary in Tientsin "before aspiring to become a Sinologist."

We sat down—I on a long, low divan, he with his back to the window and a tall circular clock. I calculated that my pursuer, Richard Madden, could not arrive for at least an hour. My irrevocable determination could wait.

"An astounding fate, that of Ts'ui Pên," Stephen Albert said. "Governor of his native province, learned in astronomy, in astrology and in the tireless interpretation of the canonical books, chess player, famous poet and calligrapher—he abandoned all this in order to compose a book and a maze. He renounced the pleasures of both tyranny and justice, of his populous couch, of his banquets and even of erudition—all to close himself up for thirteen years in the Pavilion of the Limpid Solitude. When he died, his heirs found nothing save chaotic manuscripts. His family, as you may be aware, wished to condemn them to the fire; but his executor—a Taoist or Buddhist monk—insisted on their publication."

"We descendants of Ts'ui Pên," I replied, "continue to curse that monk. Their publication was senseless. The book is an indeterminate heap of contradictory drafts. I examined it once: in the third chapter the hero dies, in the fourth he is alive. As for the other undertaking of Ts'ui Pên, his labyrinth . . ."

"Here is Ts'ui Pên's labyrinth," he said, indicating a tall lacquered desk.

"An ivory labyrinth!" I exclaimed. "A minimum labyrinth."

"A labyrinth of symbols," he corrected. "An invisible labyrinth of time. To me, a barbarous Englishman, has been entrusted the revelation of this diaphanous mystery. After more than a hundred years, the details are irretrievable; but it is not hard to conjecture what happened. Ts'ui Pên must have said once: *I am withdrawing to write a book.* And another time: *I am withdrawing to construct a labyrinth.* Every one imagined two works; to no one did it occur that the book and the maze were one and the same thing. The Pavilion of the Limpid Solitude stood in the center of a garden that was perhaps intricate; that circumstance could have suggested to the heirs a physical labyrinth. Ts'ui Pên died; no one in the vast territories that were his came upon the labyrinth; the confusion of the novel suggested to me that *it* was the maze. Two circumstances gave me the correct solution of the problem. One: the curious legend that Ts'ui Pên had planned to create a labyrinth which would be stictly infinite. The other: a fragment of a letter I discovered."

Albert rose. He turned his back on me for a moment he opened a drawer of the black and gold desk. He faced me and in his hands he held a sheet of paper that had once been crimson, but was now pink and tenuous and cross-sectioned. The fame of Ts'ui Pên as a calligrapher had been justly won. I read, uncomprehendingly and with fervor, these words written with a minute brush by a man of my blood: *I leave to the various futures (not to all) my garden of forking paths.* Wordlessly, I returned the sheet. Albert continued:

"Before unearthing this letter, I had questioned myself about the ways in which a book can be infinite. I could think of nothing other than a cyclic volume, a circular one. A book whose last page was identical with the first, a book which had the possibility of continuing indefinitely. I remembered too that night which is at the middle of the Thousand and One Nights when Scheherazade (through a magical oversight of the copyist) begins to relate word for word the story of the Thousand and One Nights, establishing the risk of coming once again to the night when she must repeat it, and thus on to infinity. I imagined as well a Platonic, hereditary work, transmitted from father to son, in which each new individual adds a chapter or corrects with pious care the pages of his elders. These conjectures diverted me; but none seemed to correspond, not even remotely, to the contradictory chapters of Ts'ui Pên. In the midst of this perplexity, I received from Oxford the manuscript you have examined. I lingered, naturally, on the sentence: *I leave to the various futures (not to all) my garden of forking paths.* Almost instantly, I understood: 'the garden of forking paths' was the chaotic novel; the phrase 'the various futures (not to all)' suggested to me, the forking in time, not in space. A broad rereading of the work confirmed the theory. In all fictional works, each time a man is confronted with several alternatives, he chooses one and eliminates the others: in the fiction of Ts'ui Pên he chooses—simultaneously all of them. *He creates,* in this way, diverse a futures, diverse times which themselves also proliferate and fork. Here, then, is the explanation of the novel's contradictions. Fang, let us say, has a secret; a stranger calls at his door; Fang resolves to kill him. Naturally, there are several possible outcomes: Fang can kill the intruder, the intruder can kill Fang, they both can escape, they both can die, and so forth. In the work of Ts'ui Pên, all possible outcomes occur; each one is the point of departure for other forkings. Sometimes, the paths of this labyrinth converge: for example, you arrive at this house, but in one of the possible pasts you are my enemy, in another, my friend. If you will resign yourself to my incurable pronunciation, we shall read a few pages."

His face, within the vivid circle of the lamplight, was unquestionably that of an old man, but with something unalterable about it, even immortal. He read with slow precision two versions of the same epic chapter. In the first, an army marches to a battle across a lonely mountain; the horror of the rocks and shadows makes the men undervalue their lives and they gain an easy victory. In the second the same army traverses a palace where a great festival is taking place; the resplendent battle seems to them a continuation of the celebration and they win the victory. I listened with proper veneration to these ancient narratives, perhaps less admirable in themselves than the fact that they had been created by my blood and were being restored to me by a man of a remote empire, in the course of a desperate adventure, on a Western isle. I remember the last words, repeated in each version like a secret commandment: *Thus fought the heroes, tranquil their admirable hearts, violent their swords, resigned to kill and to die.*

From that moment on, I felt about me and within my dark body an invisible, intangible swarming. Not the swarming of the divergent, parallel and finally coalescent armies, but a more inaccessible, more intimate agitation that they in some manner prefigured. Stephen Albert continued:

"I don't believe that your illustrious ancestor played idly with these variations. I don't consider it credible that he would sacrifice thirteen years to the infinite execution of a rhetorical experiment. In your country, the novel is a subsidiary form of literature; in Ts'ui Pên's time it was a despicable form. Ts'ui Pên was a brilliant novelist, but he was also a man of letters who doubtless did not consider himself a mere novelist. The testimony of his contemporaries proclaims—and his life fully confirms—his metaphysical and mystical interests. Philosophic controversy usurps a good part of the novel. I know that of all problems, none disturbed him so greatly nor worked upon him so much as the abysmal problem of time. Now then, the latter is the only problem that does not figure in the pages of the *Garden*. He does not even use the word that signifies time. How do you explain this voluntary omission?"

I proposed several solutions—all unsatisfactory. We discussed them. Finally, Stephen Albert said to me:

"In a riddle whose answer is chess, what is the only prohibited word?"

I thought a moment and replied, "The word *chess.*"

"Precisely," said Albert. "*The Garden of Forking Paths* is an enormous riddle, or parable, whose theme is time; this recondite cause prohibits its mention. To omit a word always, to resort to inept metaphors and obvious periphrases, is perhaps the most emphatic way of stressing it. That is the tortuous method preferred, in each of the meanderings of his indefatigable novel, by the oblique Ts'ui Pên. I have compared hundreds of manuscripts, I have corrected the errors that the negligence of the copyists has introduced. I have guessed the plan of this chaos, I have re-established—I believe I have re-established—the primordial organisation, I have translated the entire work: it is clear to me that not once does he employ the word 'time.' The explanation is obvious: *The Garden of Forking Paths* is an incomplete, but not false, image of the universe as Ts'ui Pên conceived it. In contrast to Newton and Schopenhauer, your ancestor did not believe in a uniform, absolute time. He believed in an infinite series of times, in a growing, dizzying net of divergent, convergent and parallel times. This network of times which approached one another, forked, broke off, or were unaware of one another for centuries, embraces *all* possibilities of time. We do not exist in the majority of these times; in some you exist, and not I; in others I, and not you; in others, both of us. In the present one, which a favorable fate has granted me, you have arrived at my house; in another, while crossing the garden, you found me dead; in still another, I utter these same words, but I am a mistake, a ghost."

"In every one," I pronounced, not without a tremble to my voice, "I am grateful to you and revere you for your recreation of the garden of Ts'ui Pên."

"Not in all," he murmured with a smile. "Time forks perpetually toward innumerable futures. In one of them I am your enemy."

Once again I felt the swarming sensation of which I have spoken. It seemed to me that the humid garden that surrounded the house was infinitely saturated with invisible persons. Those persons were Albert and I, secret, busy and multiform in other dimensions of time. I raised my eyes and the tenuous nightmare dissolved. In the yellow and black garden there was only one man; but this man was as strong as a statue . . . this man was approaching along the path and he was Captain Richard Madden.

"The future already exists," I replied, "but I am your friend. Could I see the letter again?"

Albert rose. Standing tall, he opened the drawer of the tall desk; for the moment his back was to me. I had readied the revolver. I fired with extreme caution. Albert fell uncomplainingly, immediately. I swear his death was instantaneous—a lightning stroke.

The rest is unreal, insignificant. Madden broke in, arrested me. I have been condemned to the gallows. I have won out abominably; I have communicated to Berlin the secret name of the city they must attack. They bombed it yesterday; I read it in the same papers that offered to England the mystery of the learned Sinologist Stephen Albert who was murdered by a stranger, one Yu Tsun. The Chief had deciphered this mystery. He knew my problem was to indicate (through the uproar of the war) the city called Albert, and that I had found no other means to do so than to kill a man of that name. He does not know (no one can know) my innumerable contrition and weariness.

PABLO NERUDA

Pablo Neruda (1904–73) was a Chilean poet and diplomat. Among his diplomatic positions was consul in Buenos Aires, Argentina, and ambassador to Mexico. Neruda published numerous books of poetry spanning nearly fifty years. He won the Nobel Prize for literature in 1971. Among his many poems were a series of odes, loosely organized poems that celebrate and comment on a wide range of everyday objects. His "Ode to the Americas" conveys his attitude toward both nature and politics in the lands of South America.

Ode to the Americas

Oh, pure Americas,
ocean-guarded lands
kept
purple and intact,
centuries of silent apiaries,
pyramids and earthen vessels,
rivers of bloodstained butterflies,
yellow volcanos
and silent peoples,
shapers of pitchers,
workers of stone.

Today, Paraguay, water-formed
turquoise, buried rose,
you have become a prison.
Peru, heart of the world,

eagles'
aerie,
are you alive?
Venezuela, Colombia,
no one hears
your happy voices.
What has become of
your silvery morning chorus?
Only the birds
of ancient plumage,
only the waterfalls,
display their diadems.
Prison bars have
multiplied.
In the humid kingdom of
fire and emerald,
between
paternal rivers,
each day
a new despot arises and with his saber
lops off mortgages and auctions your treasure.
Brother begins
to hunt brother.
Stray shots sound in the ports.
Experts arrive
from Pennsylvania,
the new
conquistadors,
meanwhile,
our blood
feeds
the putrid
plantations and the buried mines,
the dollars flow,
and
our silly young girls
slip a disk learning the dance
of the orangutan.
Oh, pure Americas,
sacred lands,
what sadness!
A Machado dies and a Batista is born.
A Trujillo remains in power.
So much room
for sylvan freedom,
Americas,
so much
purity, ocean
waters,
solitary pampas, dizzying
geography, why do
insignificant blood merchants
breed and multiply?
What is happening?
How can the
silence continue
interrupted
by bloodthirsty parrots
perched in the branches
of Pan-American greed?
Americas, assailed
by broadest expanse of foam,

by felicitous seas
redolent
of the pepper of the archipelagos,
dark
Americas,
in our orbit
the star of the people
is rising,
heroes are being born,
new paths being garlanded
with victory,
the ancient nations
live again,
autumn passes
in the most radiant light,
new flags
flutter on the wind.
May your voice and your deeds,
America,
rise free from your
green girdle,
may there be an end
to love imprisoned,
may your native dignity
be restored,
may your grain rise toward the sky
awaiting with other nations
the inevitable dawn.

JULIO CORTÁZAR

Julio Cortázar (1914–84) was an Argentine novelist, short-story writer, and translator who was born in Brussels and raised in Buenos Aires. Cortázar left Argentina in 1951 in opposition to the Perón government and lived in self-imposed exile in France for the rest of his life. Considered a germinator of the Latin American novel, Cortázar, along with Gabriel Garciá Márques, was one of the major writers of "El Boom," the explosion of Latin American fiction on the world literary scene in the 1950s and 1960s. Characteristic of Cortázar's fiction, "Continuity of Parks" mixes the commonplace and the bizarre in a surreal combination that surprises and discomfits.

Continuity of Parks[1]

He had begun to read the novel a few days before. He had put it down because of some urgent business conferences, opened it again on his way back to the estate by train; he permitted himself a slowly growing interest in the plot, in the characterizations. That afternoon, after writing a letter giving his power of attorney and discussing a matter of joint ownership with the manager of his estate, he returned to the book in the tranquility of his study which looked out upon the park with its oaks. Sprawled in his favorite armchair, its back toward the door—even the possibility of an intrusion would have irritated him, had he thought of it—he let his left hand caress repeatedly the green velvet upholstery and set to reading the final chapters. He remembered effortlessly the names and his mental image of the characters; the novel spread its glamour over him almost at once. He tasted the almost perverse pleasure of disengaging himself line by line from the things around

---

[1]Translated by Paul Blackburn.

him, and at the same time feeling his head rest comfortably on the green velvet of the chair with its high back, sensing that the cigarettes rested within reach of his hand, that beyond the great windows the air of afternoon danced under the oak trees in the park. Word by word, licked up by the sordid dilemma of the hero and heroine, letting himself be absorbed to the point where the images settled down and took on color and movement, he was witness to the final encounter in the mountain cabin. The woman arrived first, apprehensive; now the lover came in, his face cut by the backlash of a branch. Admirably, she stanched the blood with her kisses, but he rebuffed her caresses, he had not come to perform again the ceremonies of a secret passion, protected by a world of dry leaves and furtive paths through the forest. The dagger warmed itself against his chest, and underneath liberty pounded, hidden close. A lustful, panting dialogue raced down the pages like a rivulet of snakes, and one felt it had been decided from eternity. Even to those caresses which writhed about the lover's body, as though wishing to keep him there, to dissuade him from it; they sketched abominably the frame of that other body it was necessary to destroy. Nothing had been forgotten: alibis, unforeseen hazards, possible mistakes. From this hour on, each instant had its use minutely assigned. The cold-blooded, twice-gone-over re-examination of the details was barely broken off so that a hand could caress a check. It was beginning to get dark.

Not looking at one another now, rigidly fixed upon the task which awaited them, they separated at the cabin door. She was to follow the trail that led north. On the path leading in the opposite direction, he turned for a moment to watch her running, her hair loosened and flying. He ran in turn, crouching among the trees and hedges until, in the yellowish fog of dusk, he could distinguish the avenue of trees which led up to the house. The dogs were not supposed to bark, they did not bark. The estate manager would not be there at this hour, and he was not there. He went up the three porch steps and entered. The woman's words reached him over the thudding of blood in his ears: first a blue chamber, then a hall, then a carpeted stairway. At the top, two doors. No one in the first room, no one in the second. The door of the salon, and then, the knife in hand, the light from the great windows, the high back of an armchair covered in green velvet, the head of the man in the chair reading a novel.

GABRIEL GARCÍA MÁRQUEZ

from *One Hundred Years of Solitude*

Gabriel García Márquez is the godfather of magic realism, a literary style and movement that began and flowered in Latin America, and for which García Marquéz is considered the premier practitioner. The following passage constitutes the opening chapter of his masterpiece, One Hundred Years of Solitude, *the book that made his name and for which he continues to be best known. Even from a single chapter you can gain a sense of the marvelous imagination that characterizes Márquez's storytelling.*

Many years later, as he faced the firing squad, Colonel Aureliano Buendía was to remember that distant afternoon when his father took him to discover ice. At that time Macondo was a village of twenty adobe houses, built on the bank of a river of clear water that ran along a bed of polished stones, which were white and enormous, like prehistoric eggs. The world was so recent that many things lacked names, and in order to indicate them it was necessary to point. Every year during the month of March a family of ragged gypsies would set up their tents near the village, and with a great uproar of pipes and kettledrums they would display new inventions. First they brought the magnet. A heavy gypsy with an untamed beard and sparrow hands, who introduced himself as Melquíades, put on a bold public demonstration of what he himself called the eighth wonder of the learned alchemists of Macedonia. He went from house to house dragging two metal ingots and everybody was amazed to see pots, pans, tongs, and braziers tumble down from their places and beams creak from the desperation of nails and screws trying to emerge, and even objects that had been lost for a long time appeared from where they had been searched for most and went dragging along in turbulent confusion behind Melquíades' magical irons. "Things have a life of their own," the gypsy proclaimed with a harsh accent. "It's simply a matter of waking up their souls." José Arcadio Buendía, whose unbridled imagination always went beyond the genius of nature and even beyond miracles and magic, thought that it would be possible to make use of that useless invention to extract gold from the bowels of the earth. Melquíades, who was an honest man, warned him: "It won't work for that." But José Arcadio Buendía at that time did not believe in the honesty of gypsies, so he traded his mule and a pair of goats for the two magnetized ingots. Úrsula Iguarán, his wife, who relied on those animals to increase their poor domestic holdings, was unable to dissuade him. "Very soon we'll have gold enough and more to pave the floors of the house," her husband replied. For several months he worked hard to demonstrate the truth of his idea. He explored every inch of the region, even the riverbed, dragging the two iron ingots along and reciting Melquíades' incantation aloud. The only thing he succeeded in doing was to unearth a suit of fifteenth-century armor which had all of its pieces soldered together with rust and inside of which there was the hollow resonance of an enormous stone-filled gourd. When José Arcadio Buendía and the four men of his expedition managed to take the armor apart, they found inside a calcified skeleton with a copper locket containing a woman's hair around its neck.

In March the gypsies returned. This time they brought a telescope and, a magnifying glass the size of a drum, which they exhibited as the latest discovery of the Jews of Amsterdam. They placed a gypsy woman at one end of the village and set up the telescope at the entrance to the tent. For the price of five reales, people could look into the telescope and see the gypsy woman an arm's length away. "Science has eliminated distance," Melquíades proclaimed. "In a short time, man will be able to see what is happening in any place in the world without leaving his own house." A burning noonday sun brought out a startling demonstration with the gigantic magnifying glass: they put a pile of dry hay in the middle of the street and set it on fire by concentrating the sun's rays. José Arcadio Buendía, who had still not been consoled for the failure of his magnets, conceived the idea of using that invention as a weapon of war. Again Melquíades tried to dissuade him, but he finally accepted the two magnetized ingots and three colonial coins in exchange for the magnifying glass. Úrsula wept in consternation. That money was from a chest of gold coins that her father had put together over an entire life of privation and that she had buried underneath her bed in hopes of a proper occasion to make use of it. José Arcadio Buendía made no attempt to console her, completely absorbed in his tactical experiments with the abnegation of a scientist and even at the risk of his own life. In an attempt to show the effects of the glass on enemy troops, he exposed himself to the concentration of the sun's rays and suffered burns which turned into sores that took a long time to heal. Over the protests of his wife, who was alarmed at such a dangerous invention, at one point he was ready to set the house on fire. He would spend hours on end in his room, calculating the strategic possibilities of his novel weapon until he succeeded in putting together a manual of startling instructional clarity and an irresistible power of conviction. He sent it to the government, accompanied by numerous descriptions of his experiments and several pages of explanatory sketches, by a messenger who crossed the mountains, got lost in measureless swamps, forded stormy rivers, and was on the point of perishing under the lash of despair, plague, and wild beasts until he found a route that joined the one used by the mules that carried the mail. In spite of the fact that a trip to the capital was little less than impossible at that time, José Arcadio Buendía promised to undertake it as soon as the government ordered him to so that he could put on soiree practical demonstrations of his invention for the military authorities and could train them himself in the complicated art of solar war. For several years he waited for an answer. Finally, tired of waiting, he bemoaned to Melquíades the failure of his project and the gypsy then gave him a convincing proof of his honesty: he gave him back the doubloons in exchange for the magnifying glass, and he left him in addition some Portuguese maps and several instruments of navigation. In his own hand-writing he set down a concise synthesis of the studies by Monk Hermann, which he left José Arcadio so that he would be able to make use of the astrolabe, the compass, and the sextant. José Arcadio Buendía spent the long months of the rainy season shut up in a small room that he had built in the rear of the house so that no one would disturb his experiments. Having completely abandoned his domestic obligations, he spent entire nights in the courtyard watching the course of the stars and he almost contracted sunstroke from trying to establish an exact method to ascertain noon. When he became an expert in the use and manipulation of his instruments, he conceived a notion of space that allowed him to navigate across unknown seas, to visit uninhabited territories, and to establish relations with splendid beings without having to leave his study. That was the period in which he acquired the habit of talking to himself, of walking through the house without paying attention to anyone, as Úrsula and the children broke their backs in the garden, growing banana and caladium, cassava and yams, ahuyama roots and eggplants. Suddenly, without warning, his feverish activity was interrupted and was replaced by a kind of fascination. He spent several days as if he were bewitched, softly repeating to himself a string of fearful conjectures without giving credit to his own understanding. Finally, one Tuesday in December, at lunchtime, all at once he released the whole weight of his torment. The children would remember for the rest of their lives the august solemnity with which their father, devastated by his prolonged vigil and by the wrath of his imagination, revealed his discovery to them:

"The earth is round; like an orange."

Úrsula lost her patience. "If you have to go crazy, please go crazy all by yourself!" she shouted. "But don't try to put your gypsy ideas into the heads of the children." José Arcadio Buendía, impassive, did not let himself be frightened by the desperation of his wife, who, in a seizure of rage, smashed the astrolabe against the floor. He built another one, he gathered the men of the village in his little room, and he demonstrated to them, with theories that none of them could understand, the possibility of returning to where one had set out by consistently sailing east. The whole village was convinced that José Arcadio Buendía had lost his reason, when Melquíades returned to set things straight. He gave public praise to the intelligence of a man who from pure astronomical speculation had evolved a theory that had already been proved in practice, although unknown in Macondo until then, and as a proof of his admiration he made him a gift that was to have a profound influence on the future of the village: the laboratory of an alchemist.

By then Melquíades had aged with surprising rapidity. On his first trips he seemed to be the same age as José Arcadio Buendía. But while the latter had preserved his extraordinary strength, which permitted him to pull down a horse by grabbing its ears, the gypsy seemed to have been worn down by some tenacious illness. It was, in reality, the result of multiple and rare diseases contracted on his innumerable trips around the world. According to what he himself said as he spoke to José Arcadio Buendía while helping him set up the laboratory, death followed him everywhere, sniffing at the cuffs of his pants, but never deciding to give him the final clutch of its claws. He was a fugitive from all the plagues and catastrophes that had ever lashed mankind. He had survived pellagra in Persia, scurvy in the Malayan archipelago, leprosy in Alexandria, beriberi in Japan, bubonic plague in Madagascar, an earthquake in Sicily, and a disastrous shipwreck in the Strait of Magellan. That prodigious creature, said to possess the keys of Nostradamus, was a gloomy man, enveloped in a sad aura, with an Asiatic look that seemed to know what there was on the other side of things. He wore a large black hat that looked like a raven with widespread wings, and a velvet vest across which the patina of the centuries had skated. But in spite of his immense wisdom and his mysterious breadth, he had a human burden, an earthly condition that kept him involved in the small problems of daily life. He would complain of the ailments of old age, he suffered from the most insignificant economic difficulties, and he had stopped laughing a long time back because scurvy had made his teeth drop out. On that suffocating noontime when the gypsy revealed his secrets, José Arcadio Buendía had the certainty that it was the beginning of a great friendship. The children were startled by his fantastic stories. Aureliano, who could not have been more than five at the time, would remember him for the rest of his life as he saw him that afternoon, sitting against the metallic and quivering light from the window, lighting up with his deep organ voice the darkest reaches of the imagination, while down over his temples there flowed the grease that was being melted by the heat. José Arcadio, his older brother, would pass on that wonderful image as a hereditary memory to all of his descendants. Úrsula, on the other hand, held a bad memory of that visit, for she had entered the room just as Melquíades had carelessly broken a flask of bichloride of mercury.

"It's the smell of the devil," she said.

"Not at all," Melquíades corrected her. "It has been proven that the devil has sulphuric properties and this is just a little corrosive sublimate."

Always didactic, he went into a learned exposition of the diabolical properties of cinnabar, but Úrsula paid no attention to him, although she took the children off to pray. That biting odor would stay forever in her mind linked to the memory of Melquíades.

The rudimentary laboratory—in addition to a profusion of pots, funnels, retorts, filters, and sieves—was made up of a primitive water pipe, a glass beaker with a long, thin neck, a reproduction of the philosopher's egg, and a still the gypsies themselves had built in accordance with modern descriptions of the three-armed alembic of Mary the Jew. Along with those items, Melquíades left samples of the seven metals that corresponded to the seven planets, the formulas of Moses and Zosimus for doubling the quantity of gold, and a set of notes and sketches concerning the processes of the Great Teaching that would permit those who could interpret them to undertake the manufacture of the philosopher's stone. Seduced by the simplicity of the formulas to double the quantity of gold, José Arcadio Buendía paid court to Úrsula for several weeks so that she would let him dig up her colonial coins and increase them by as many times as it was possible to subdivide mercury. Úrsula gave in, as always, to her husband's unyielding obstinacy. Then José Arcadio Buendía threw three doubloons into a pan and fused them with copper filings, orpiment, brimstone, and lead. He put it all to boil in a pot of castor oil until he got a thick and pestilential syrup which was more like common caramel than valuable gold. In risky and desperate processes of distillation, melted with the seven planetary metals, mixed with hermetic mercury and vitriol of Cyprus, and put back to cook in hog fat for lack of any radish oil, Úrsula's precious inheritance was reduced to a large piece of burnt hog cracklings that was firmly stuck to the bottom of the pot.

When the gypsies came back, Úrsula had turned the whole population of the village against them. But curiosity was greater than fear, for that time the gypsies went about the town making a deafening noise with all manner of musical instruments while a hawker announced the exhibition of the most fabulous discovery of the Naciancenes. So that everyone went to the tent and by paying one cent they saw a youthful Melquíades, recovered, unwrinkled, with a new and flashing set of teeth. Those who remembered his gums that had been destroyed by scurvy, his flaccid cheeks, and his withered lips trembled with fear at the final proof of the gypsy's supernatural power. The fear turned into panic when Melquíades took out his teeth, intact, encased in their gums, and showed them to the audience for an instant—a fleeting instant in which he went back to being the same decrepit man of years past—and put them back again and smiled once more with the full control of his restored youth. Even José Arcadio Buendía himself considered that Melquíades' knowledge had reached unbearable extremes, but he felt a healthy excitement when the gypsy explained to him alone the workings of his false teeth. It seemed so simple and so prodigious at the same time that overnight he lost all interest in his experiments in alchemy. He underwent a new crisis of bad humor. He did not go back to eating regularly, and he would spend the day walking through the house. "Incredible things are happening in the world," he said to Úrsula. "Right there across the river there are all kinds of magical instruments while we keep on living like donkeys." Those who had known

him since the foundation of Macondo were startled at how much he had changed under Melquíades' influence.

At first José Arcadio Buendía had been a kind of youthful patriarch who would give instructions for planting and advice for the raising of children and animals, and who collaborated with everyone, even in the physical work, for the welfare of the community. Since his house from the very first had been the best in the village, the others had been built in its image and likeness. It had a small, well-lighted living room, a dining room in the shape of a terrace with gaily colored flowers, two bedrooms, a courtyard with a gigantic chestnut tree, a well-kept garden, and a corral where goats, pigs, and hens lived in peaceful communion. The only animals that were prohibited, not just in his house but in the entire settlement, were fighting cocks.

Úrsula's capacity for work was the same as that of her husband. Active, small, severe, that woman of unbreakable nerves who at no moment in her life had been heard to sing seemed to be everywhere, from dawn until quite late at night, always pursued by the soft whispering of her stiff, starched petticoats. Thanks to her the floors of tamped earth, the unwhitewashed mud walls, the rustic, wooden furniture they had built themselves were always clean, and the old chests where they kept their clothes exhaled the warm smell of basil.

José Arcadio Buendía, who was the most enterprising man ever to be seen in the village, had set up the placement of the houses in such a way that from all of them one could reach the river and draw water with the same effort, and he had lined up the streets with such good sense that no house got more sun than another during the hot time of day. Within a few years Macondo was a village that was more orderly and hardworking than any known until then by its three hundred inhabitants. It was a truly happy village where no one was over thirty years of age and where no one had died.

Since the time of its founding, José Arcadio Buendía had built traps and cages. In a short time he filled not only his own house but all of those in the village with troupials, canaries, bee eaters, and redbreasts. The concert of so many different birds became so disturbing that Úrsula would plug her ears with beeswax so as not to lose her sense of reality. The first time that Melquíades' tribe arrived, selling glass balls for headaches, everyone was surprised that they had been able to find that village lost in the drowsiness of the swamp, and the gypsies confessed that they had found their way by the song of the birds.

That spirit of social initiative disappeared in a short time, pulled away by the fever of the magnets, the astronomical calculations, the dreams of transmutation, and the urge to discover the wonders of the world. From a clean and active man, José Arcadio Buendía changed into a man lazy in appearance, careless in his dress, with a wild beard that Úrsula managed to trim with great effort and a kitchen knife. There were many who considered him the victim of some strange spell. But even those most convinced of his madness left work and family to follow him when he brought out his tools to clear the land and asked the assembled group to open a way that would put Macondo in contact with the great inventions.

José Arcadio Buendía was completely ignorant of the geography of the region. He knew that to the east there lay an impenetrable mountain chain and that on the other side of the mountains there was the ancient city of Riohacha, where in times past—according to what he had been told by the first

Aureliano Buendía, his grandfather—Sir Francis Drake had gone crocodile hunting with cannons and that he repaired them and stuffed them with straw to bring to Queen Elizabeth. In his youth, José Arcadio Buendía and his men, with wives and children, animals and all kinds of domestic implements, had crossed the mountains in search of an outlet to the sea, and after twenty-six months they gave up the expedition and founded Macondo, so they would not have to go back. It was, therefore, a route that did not interest him, for it could lead only to the past. To the south lay the swamps, covered with an eternal vegetable scum, and the whole vast universe of the great swamp, which, according to what the gypsies said, had no limits. The great swamp in the west mingled with a boundless extension of water where there were softskinned cetaceans that had the head and torso of a woman, causing the ruination of sailors with the charm of their extraordinary breasts. The gypsies sailed along that route for six months before they reached the strip of land over which the mules that carried the mail passed. According to José Arcadio Buendía's calculations, the only possibility of contact with civilization lay along the northern route. So he handed out clearing tools and hunting weapons to the same men who had been with him during the founding of Macondo. He threw his directional instruments and his maps into a knapsack, and he undertook the reckless adventure.

During the first days they did not come across any appreciable obstacle. They went down along the stony bank of the river to the place where years before they had found the soldier's armor, and from there they went into the woods along a path between wild orange trees. At the end of the first week they killed and roasted a deer, but they agreed to eat only half of it and salt the rest for the days that lay ahead. With that precaution they tried to postpone the necessity of having to eat macaws, whose blue flesh had a harsh and musky taste. Then, for more than ten days, they did not see the sun again. The ground became soft and damp, like volcanic ash, and the vegetation was thicker and thicker, and the cries of the birds and the uproar of the monkeys became more and more remote, and the world became eternally sad. The men on the expedition felt overwhelmed by their most ancient memories in that paradise of dampness and silence, going back to before original sin, as their boots sank into pools of steaming oil and their machetes destroyed bloody lilies and golden salamanders. For a week, almost without speaking, they went ahead like sleepwalkers through a universe of grief, lighted only by the tenuous reflection of luminous insects, and their lungs were overwhelmed by a suffocating smell of blood. They could not return because the strip that they were opening as they went along would soon close up with a new vegetation that almost seemed to grow before their eyes. "It's all right," José Arcadio Buendía would say. "The main thing is not to lose our bearings." Always following his compass, he kept on guiding his men toward the invisible north so that they would be able to get out of that enchanted region. It was a thick night, starless, but the darkness was becoming impregnated with a fresh and clear air. Exhausted by the long crossing, they hung up their hammocks and slept deeply for the first time in two weeks. When they woke up, with the sun already high in the sky, they were speechless with fascination. Before them, surrounded by ferns and palm trees, white and powdery in the silent morning light, was an enormous Spanish galleon. Tilted slightly to the starboard, it had hanging from

its intact masts the dirty rags of its sails in the midst of its rigging, which was adorned with orchids. The hull, covered with an armor of petrified barnacles and soft moss, was firmly fastened into a surface of stones. The whole structure seemed to occupy its own space, one of solitude and oblivion, protected from the vices of time and the habits of the birds Inside, where the expeditionaries explored with careful intent, there was nothing but a thick forest of flowers.

The discovery of the galleon, an indication of the proximity of the sea, broke José Arcadio Buendía's drive. He considered it a trick of his whimsical fate to have searched for the sea without finding it, at the cost of countless sacrifices and suffering, and to have found it all of a sudden without looking for it, as if it lay across his path like an insurmountable object. Many years later Colonel Aureliano Buendía crossed the region again, when it was already a regular mail route, and the only part of the ship he found was its burned-out frame in the midst of a field of poppies. Only then, convinced that the story had not been some product of his father's imagination, did he wonder how the galleon had been able to get inland to that spot. But José Arcadio Buendía did not concern himself with that when he found the sea after another four days' journey from the galleon. His dreams ended as he faced that ashen, foamy, dirty sea, which had not merited the risks and sacrifices of the adventure.

"God damn it!" he shouted. "Macondo is surrounded by water on all sides."

The idea of a peninsular Macondo prevailed for a long time, inspired by the arbitrary map that José Arcadio Buendía sketched on his return from the expedition. He drew it in rage, evilly, exaggerating the difficulties of communication, as if to punish himself for the absolute lack of sense with which he had chosen the place. "We'll never get anywhere," he lamented to Úrsula. "We're going to rot our lives away here without receiving the benefits of science." That certainty, mulled over for several months in the small room he used as his laboratory, brought him to the conception of the plan to move Macondo to a better place. But that time Úrsula had anticipated his feverish designs. With the secret and implacable labor of a small ant she predisposed the women of the village against the flightiness of their husbands, who were already preparing for the move. José Arcadio Buendía did not know at what moment or because of what adverse forces his plan had become enveloped in a web of pretexts, disappointments, and evasions until it turned into nothing but an illusion. Úrsula watched him with innocent attention and even felt some pity for him on the morning when she found him in the back room muttering about his plans for moving as he placed his laboratory pieces in their original boxes. She let him finish. She let him nail up the boxes and put his initials on them with an inked brush, without reproaching him, but knowing now that he knew (because she had heard him say so in his soft monologues) that the men of the village would not back him up in his undertaking. Only when he began to take down the door of the room did Úrsula dare ask him what he was doing, and he answered with a certain bitterness. "Since no one wants to leave, we'll leave all by ourselves." Úrsula did not become upset.

"We will not leave," she said. "We will stay here, because we have had a son here."

"We have still not had a death," he said. "A person does not belong to a place until there is someone dead under the ground."

Úrsula replied with a soft firmness:

"If I have to die for the rest of you to stay here, I will die."

José Arcadio Buendía had not thought that his wife's will was so firm. He tried to seduce her with the charm of his fantasy with the promise of a prodigious world where all one, had to do was sprinkle some magic liquid on the ground and the plants would bear fruit whenever a man wished, and where all manner of instruments against pain were sold at bargain prices. But Úrsula was insensible to his clairvoyance.

"Instead of going around thinking about your crazy inventions, you should be worrying about your sons," she replied. "Look at the state they're in, running wild just like donkeys."

José Arcadio Buendía took his wife's words literally. He looked out the window and saw the barefoot children in the sunny garden and he had the impression that only at that instant had they begun to exist, conceived by Úrsula's spell. Something occurred inside of him then, something mysterious and definitive that uprooted him from his own time and carried him adrift through an unexplored region of his memory. While Úrsula continued sweeping the house, which was safe now from being abandoned for the rest of her life, he stood there with an absorbed look, contemplating the children until his eyes became moist and he dried them with the back of his hand, exhaling a deep sigh of resignation.

"All right," he said. "Tell them to come help me take the things out of the boxes."

José Arcadio, the older of the children, was fourteen. He had a square head, thick hair, and his father's character. Although he had the same impulse for growth and physical strength, it was early evident that he lacked imagination. He had been conceived and born during the difficult crossing of the mountains, before the founding of Macondo, and his parents gave thanks to heaven when they saw he had no animal features. Aureliano, the first human being to be born in Macondo, would be six years old in March. He was silent and withdrawn. He had wept in his mother's womb and had been born with his eyes open. As they were cutting the umbilical cord, he moved his head from side to side, taking in the things in the room and examining the faces of the people with a fearless curiosity. Then, indifferent to those who came close to look at him, he kept his attention concentrated on the palm roof, which looked as if it were about to collapse under the tremendous pressure of the rain. Úrsula did not remember the intensity of that look again until one day when little Aureliano, at the age of three, went into the kitchen at the moment she was taking a pot of boiling soup from the stove and putting it on the table. The child, perplexed, said from the doorway, "It's going to spill." The pot was firmly placed in the center of the table, but just as soon as the child made his announcement, it began an unmistakable movement toward the edge, as if impelled by some inner dynamism, and it fell and broke on the floor. Úrsula, alarmed, told her husband about the episode, but he interpreted it as a natural phenomenon. That was the way he always was, alien to the existence of his sons, partly because he considered childhood as a period of mental insufficiency, and partly because he was always too absorbed in his fantastic speculations.

But since the afternoon when he called the children in to help him unpack the things in the laboratory, he gave them his best hours. In the small separate room, where the walls were gradually being covered by strange maps and fabulous drawings, he taught them to read and write and do sums, and he spoke to them about the wonders of the world, not only where his learning had extended, but forcing the limits of his imagination to extremes. It was in that way that the boys ended up learning that in the southern extremes of Africa there were men so intelligent and peaceful that their only pastime was to sit and think, and that it was possible to cross the Aegean Sea on foot by jumping from island to island all the way to the port of Salonika. Those hallucinating sessions remained printed on the memories of the boys in such a way that many years later, a second before the regular army officer gave the firing squad the command to fire, Colonel Aureliano Buendía saw once more that warm March afternoon on which his father had interrupted the lesson in physics and stood fascinated, with his hand in the air and his eyes motionless, listening to the distant pipes, drums, and jingles of the gypsies, who were coming to the village once more, announcing the latest and most startling discovery of the sages of Memphis.

They were new gypsies, young men and women who knew only their own language, handsome specimens with oily skins and intelligent hands, whose dances and music sowed a panic of uproarious joy through the streets, with parrots painted all colors reciting Italian arias, and a hen who laid a hundred golden eggs to the sound of a tambourine, and a trained monkey who read minds, and the multiple-use machine that could be used at the same time to sew on buttons and reduce fevers, and the apparatus to make a person forget his bad memories, and a poultice to lose time, and a thousand more inventions so ingenious and unusual that José Arcadio Buendía must have wanted to invent a memory machine so that he could remember them all. In an instant they transformed the village. The inhabitants of Macondo found themselves lost in their own streets, confused by the crowded fair.

Holding a child by each hand so as not to lose them in the tumult, bumping into acrobats with gold-capped teeth and jugglers with six arms, suffocated by the mingled breath of manure and sandals that the crowd exhaled, José Arcadio Buendía went about everywhere like a madman, looking for Melquíades so that he could reveal to him the infinite secrets of that fabulous nightmare. He asked several gypsies, who did not understand his language. Finally he reached the place where Melquíades used to set up his tent and he found a taciturn Armenian who in Spanish was hawking a syrup to make oneself invisible. He had drunk down a glass of the amber substance in one gulp as José Arcadio Buendía elbowed his way through the absorbed group that was witnessing the spectacle, and was able to ask his question. The gypsy wrapped him in the frightful climate of his look before he turned into a puddle of pestilential and smoking pitch over which the echo of his reply still floated: "Melquíades is dead." Upset by the news, José Arcadio Buendía stood motionless, trying to rise above his affliction, until the group dispersed, called away by other artifices, and the puddle of the taciturn Armenian evaporated, completely. Other gypsies confirmed later on that Melquíades had in fact succumbed to the fever on the beach at Singapore and that his body had been thrown into the deepest part of the Java Sea. The children had no interest in the news. They insisted that their father take them to see the overwhelming novelty of the sages of Memphis that was being advertised at the entrance of a tent that, according to what was said, had belonged to King Solomon. They insisted so much that José Arcadio Buendía paid the thirty reales and led them into the center of the tent, where there was a giant with a hairy torso and a shaved head, with a copper ring in his nose and a heavy iron chain on his ankle, watching over a pirate chest. When it was opened by the giant, the chest gave off a glacial exhalation. Inside there was only an enormous, transparent block with infinite internal needles in which the light of the sunset was broken up into colored stars. Disconcerted, knowing that the children were waiting for an immediate explanation, José Arcadio Buendía ventured a murmur:

"It's the largest diamond in the world."

"No," the gypsy countered. "It's ice."

José Arcadio Buendía, without understanding, stretched out his hand toward the cake, but the giant moved it away. "Five reales more to touch it," he said. José Arcadio Buendía paid them and put his hand on the ice and held it there for several minutes as his heart filled with fear and jubilation at the contact with mystery. Without knowing what to say, he paid ten reales more so that his sons could have that prodigious experience. Little José Arcadio refused to touch it. Aureliano, on the other hand, took a step forward and put his hand on it, withdrawing it immediately. "It's boiling," he exclaimed, startled. But his father paid no attention to him. Intoxicated by the evidence of the miracle, he forgot at that moment about the frustration of his delirious undertakings and Melquíades' body, abandoned to the appetite of the squids. He paid another five reales and with his hand on the cake, as if giving testimony on the holy scriptures, he exclaimed:

"This is the great invention of our time."

J. M. COETZEE

from *Disgrace*

J. M. Coetzee's novels have won worldwide acclaim for the brilliance of their language, the honesty of their descriptions, and the sheer power of their narratives. The following passage is the beginning of Coetzee's prizewinning novel, Disgrace. *This brief opening chapter sets the stage for what will become a harrowing tale of racial, sexual, and generational tension and suffering. The clarity and focus of this opening chapter are but one measure of Coetzee's seriousness of purpose.*

For a man of his age, fifty-two, divorced, he has, to his mind, solved the problem of sex rather well. On Thursday afternoons he drives to Green Point. Punctually at two p.m. he presses the buzzer at the entrance to Windsor Mansions, speaks his name, and enters. Waiting for him at the door of No. 113 is Soraya. He goes straight through to the bedroom, which is pleasant-smelling and softly lit, and undresses. Soraya emerges from the bathroom, drops her robe, slides into bed beside him. 'Have you missed me?' she asks. 'I miss you all the time,' he replies. He strokes her honey-brown body, unmarked by the sun; he stretches her out, kisses her breasts; they make love.

Soraya is tall and slim, with long black hair and dark, liquid eyes. Technically he is old enough to be her father; but then, technically, one can be a father at twelve. He has been on her books for over a year; he finds her entirely satisfactory. In the desert of the week Thursday has become an oasis of *luxe et volupté*.

In bed Soraya is not effusive. Her temperament is in fact rather quiet, quiet and docile. In her general opinions she is surprisingly moralistic. She is offended by tourists who bare their breasts ('udders', she calls them) on public beaches; she thinks vagabonds should be rounded up and put to work sweeping the streets. How she reconciles her opinions with her line of business he does not ask.

Because he takes pleasure in her, because his pleasure is unfailing, an affection has grown up in him for her. To some degree, he believes, this affection is reciprocated. Affection may not be love, but it is at least its cousin. Given their unpromising beginnings, they have been lucky, the two of them: he to have found her, she to have found him.

His sentiments are, he is aware, complacent, even uxorious. Nevertheless he does not cease to hold to them.

For a ninety-minute session he pays her R400, of which half goes to Discreet Escorts. It seems a pity that Discreet Escorts should get so much. But they own No. 113 and other flats in Windsor Mansions; in a sense they own Soraya too, this part of her, this function.

He has toyed with the idea of asking her to see him in her own time. He would like to spend an evening with her, perhaps even a whole night. But not the morning after. He knows too much about himself to subject her to a morning after, when he will be cold, surly, impatient to be alone.

That is his temperament. His temperament is not going to change, he is too old for that. His temperament is fixed, set. The skull, followed by the temperament: the two hardest parts of the body.

Follow your temperament. It is not a philosophy, he would not dignify it with that name. It is a rule, like the Rule of St Benedict.

He is in good health, his mind is clear. By profession he is, or has been, a scholar, and scholarship still engages, intermittently, the core of him. He lives within his income, within his temperament, within his emotional means. Is he happy? By most measurements, yes, he believes he is. However, he has not forgotten the last chorus of *Oedipus*: Call no man happy until he is dead.

In the field of sex his temperament, though intense, has never been passionate. Were he to choose a totem, it would be the snake. Intercourse between Soraya and himself must be, he imagines, rather like the copulation of snakes: lengthy, absorbed, but rather: abstract, rather dry, even at its hottest.

Is Soraya's totem the snake too? No doubt with other men she becomes another woman: *la donna è mobile*. Yet at the level of temperament her affinity with him can surely not be feigned.

Though by occupation she is a loose woman he trusts her, within limits. During their sessions he speaks to her, with a certain freedom, even on occasion unburdens himself. She knows the facts of his life. She has heard the stories of his two marriages, knows about his daughter and his daughter's ups and downs. She knows many of his opinions.

Of her life outside Windsor Mansions Soraya reveals nothing. Soraya is not her real name, that he is sure of. There are signs she has borne a child, or children. It may be that she is not a professional at all. She may work for the agency only one or two afternoons a week, and for the rest live a respectable life in the suburbs, in Rylands or Athlone. That would be unusual for a Muslim, but all things are possible these days.

About his own job he says little, not wanting to bore her. He earns his living at the Cape Technical University, formerly Cape Town University College. Once a professor of modern languages, he has been, since Classics and Modern Languages were closed down as part of the great rationalization, adjunct professor of communications. Like all rationalized personnel, he is allowed to offer one special-field course a year, irrespective of enrolment, because that is good for morale. This year he is offering a course in the Romantic poets. For the rest he teaches Communications 101, 'Communication Skills', and Communications 201, 'Advanced Communication Skills'.

Although he devotes hours of each day to his new discipline, he finds its first premise, as enunciated in the Communications 101 handbook, preposterous: 'Human society has created language in, order that we may communicate our thoughts, feelings and intentions to each other.' His own opinion, which he does not air, is that the origins of speech lie in song, and the origins of song in the need to fill out with sound the overlarge and rather empty human soul.

In the course of a career stretching back a quarter of a century he has published three books, none of which has caused a stir or even a ripple: the first on opera (*Boito and the Faust Legend: The Genesis of Mefistofele*), the second on vision as eros (*The Vision of Richard of St Victor*), the third on Wordsworth and history (*Wordsworth and the Burden of the Past*).

In the past few years he has been playing with the idea of a work on Byron. At first he had thought it would be another book, another critical opus. But all his sallies at writing it have bogged down in tedium. The truth is, he is tired of criticism, tired of prose measured by the yard. What he wants to write is music: *Byron in Italy*, a meditation on love between the sexes in the form of a chamber opera.

Through his mind, while he faces his Communications classes, flit phrases, tunes, fragments of song from the unwritten work. He has never been much of a teacher; in this transformed and, to his mind, emasculated institution of learning he is more out of place than ever. But then, so are other of his colleagues from the old days, burdened with upbringings inappropriate to the tasks they are set to perform; clerks in a post-religious age.

Because he has no respect for the material he teaches, he makes no impression on his students. They look through him when he speaks, forget his name. Their indifference galls him more than he will admit. Nevertheless he fulfils to the letter his obligations toward them, their parents, and the state. Month after month he sets, collects, reads, and annotates their assignments, correcting lapses in punctuation, spelling and usage, interrogating weak arguments, appending to each paper a brief, considered critique.

He continues to teach because it provides him with a livelihood; also because it teaches him humility, brings it home to him who he is in the world. The irony does not escape him: that the one who comes to teach learns the keenest of lessons, while those who come to learn learn nothing. It is a feature of his profession on which he does not remark to Soraya. He doubts there is an irony to match it in hers.

In the kitchen of the flat in Green Point there are a kettle, plastic cups, a jar of instant coffee, a bowl with sachets of sugar. The refrigerator holds a supply of bottled water. In the bathroom there is soap and a pile of towels, in the cupboard clean bedlinen. Soraya keeps her makeup in an overnight bag. A place of assignation, nothing more, functional, clean, well regulated.

The first time Soraya received him she wore vermilion lipstick and heavy eyeshadow. Not liking the stickiness of the makeup, he asked her to wipe it off. She obeyed, and has never worn it since. A ready learner, compliant, pliant.

He likes giving her presents. At New Year he gave her an enamelled bracelet, at Eid a little malachite heron that caught his eye in a curio shop. He enjoys her pleasure, which is quite unaffected.

It surprises him that ninety minutes a week of a woman's company are enough to make him happy, who used to think he needed a wife, a home, a marriage. His needs turn out to be quite light, after all, light and fleeting, like those of a butterfly. No emotion, or none but the deepest, the most unguessed-at: a ground bass of contentedness, like the hum of traffic that lulls the city-dweller to sleep, or like the silence of the night to countryfolk.

He thinks of Emma Bovary, coming home sated, glazen-eyed, from an afternoon of reckless fucking. *So this is bliss!*, says Emma, marvelling at herself in the mirror. *So this is the bliss the poets speak of!* Well, if poor ghostly Emma were ever to find her way to Cape Town, he would bring her along one Thursday afternoon to show her what bliss can be: a moderate bliss, a moderated bliss.

Then one Saturday morning everything changes. He is in the city on business; he is walking down St George's Street when his eyes fall on a slim figure ahead of him in the crowd. It is Soraya, unmistakably, flanked by two children, two boys. They are carrying parcels; they have been shopping.

He hesitates, then follows at a distance. They disappear into Captain Dorego's Fish Inn. The boys have Soraya's lustrous hair and dark eyes. They can only be her sons.

He walks on, rums back, passes Captain Dorego's a second time. The three are seated at a table in the window. For an instant, through the glass, Soraya's eyes meet his.

He has always been a man of the city, at home amid a flux of bodies where eros stalks and glances flash like arrows. But this glance between himself and Soraya he regrets at once.

At their rendezvous the next Thursday neither mentions the incident. Nonetheless, the memory hangs uneasily over them. He has no wish to upset what must be, for Soraya, a precarious double life. He is all for double lives, triple lives, lives lived in compartments. Indeed, he feels, if anything, greater tenderness for her. *Your secret is safe with me*, he would like to say.

But neither he nor she can put aside what has happened. The two little boys become presences between them, playing quiet as shadows in a corner of the room where their mother and the strange man couple. In Soraya's arms he becomes, fleetingly, their father: foster-father, step-father, shadow-father. Leaving her bed afterwards, he feels their eyes flicker over him covertly, curiously.

His thoughts turn, despite himself, to the other father, the real one. Does he have any inkling of what his wife is up to, or has he elected the bliss of ignorance?

He himself has no son. His childhood was spent in a family of women. As mother, aunts, sisters fell away, they were replaced in due course by mistresses, wives, a daughter. The company of women made of him a lover of women and, to an extent, a womanizer. With his height, his good bones, his olive skin, his flowing hair, he could always count on a degree of magnetism. If he looked at a woman in a certain way, with a certain intent, she would return his look, he could rely on that. That was how he lived; for years, for decades, that was the backbone of his life.

Then one day it all ended. Without warning his powers fled. Glances that would once have responded to his slid over, past, through him. Overnight he became a ghost. If he wanted a woman he had to learn to pursue her; often, in one way or another, to buy her.

He existed in an anxious flurry of promiscuity. He had affairs with the wives of colleagues; he picked up tourists in bars on the waterfront or at the Club Italia; he slept with whores.

His introduction to Soraya took place in a dim little sitting-room of the front office of Discreet Escorts, with Venetian blinds over the windows, pot plants in the corners, stale smoke hanging in the air. She was on their books under 'Exotic'. The photograph showed her with a red passion-flower in her hair and the faintest of lines at the corners of her eyes. The entry said 'Afternoons only'. That was what decided him: the promise of shuttered rooms, cool sheets, stolen hours.

From the beginning it was satisfactory, just what he wanted. A bull's eye. In a year he has not needed to go back to the agency.

Then the accident in St George's Street, and the strangeness that has followed. Though Soraya still keeps her appointments, he feels a growing coolness as she transforms herself into just another woman and him into just another client.

He has a shrewd idea of how prostitutes speak among themselves about the men who frequent them, the older men in particular. They tell stories, they laugh, but they shudder too, as one shudders at a cockroach in a washbasin in the middle of the night. Soon, daintily, maliciously, he will be shuddered over. It is a fate he cannot escape.

On the fourth Thursday after the incident, as he is leaving the apartment, Soraya makes the announcement he has been steeling himself against. 'My mother is ill. I'm going to take a break to look after her. I won't be here next week.'

'Will I see you the week after?'

'I'm not sure. It depends on how she gets on. You had better phone first.'

'I don't have a number.'

'Phone the agency. They'll know.'

He waits a few days, then telephones the agency. Soraya? Soraya has left us, says the man. No, we cannot put you in touch with her, that would be against house rules. Would you like an introduction to another of our hostesses? Lots of exotics to choose from—Malaysian, Thai, Chinese, you name it.

He spends an evening with another Soraya—Soraya has become, it seems, a popular *nom de commerce*—in a hotel room in Long Street. This one is no more than eighteen, unpractised, to his mind coarse. 'So what do you do?' she says as she slips off her clothes. 'Export-import,' he says. 'You don't say,' she says.

There is a new secretary in his department. He takes her to lunch at a restaurant a discreet distance from the campus and listens while, over shrimp salad, she complains about her sons' school. Drug-pedlars hang around the playing-fields, she says, and the police do nothing. For the past three years she and her husband have had their name on a list at the New Zealand consulate, to emigrate. 'You people had it easier. I mean, whatever the rights and wrongs of the situation, at least you knew where you were.'

'You people?' he says. 'What people?'

'I mean your generation. Now people just pick and choose which laws they want to obey. It's anarchy. How can you bring up children when there's anarchy all around?'

Her name is Dawn. The second time he takes her out they stop at his house and have sex. It is a failure. Bucking and clawing, she works herself into a froth of excitement that in the end only repels him. He lends her a comb, drives her back to the campus.

After that he avoids her, taking care to skirt the office where she works. In return she gives him a hurt look, then snubs him.

He ought to give up, retire from the game. At what age, he wonders, did Origen castrate himself? Not the most graceful of solutions, but then ageing is not a graceful business. A clearing of the decks, at least, so that one can turn one's mind to the proper business of the old: preparing to die.

Might one approach a doctor and ask for it? A simple enough operation, surely: they do it to animals every day, and animals survive well enough, if one ignores a certain residue of sadness. Severing, tying off: with local anaesthetic and a steady hand and a modicum of phlegm one might even do it oneself, out of a textbook. A man on a chair snipping away at himself: an ugly sight, but no more ugly, from a certain point of view, than the same man exercising himself on the body of a woman.

There is still Soraya. He ought to close that chapter. Instead, he pays a detective agency to track her down. Within days he has her real name, her address, her telephone number. He telephones at nine in the morning, when the husband and children will be out. 'Soraya?' he says: 'This is David. How are you? When can I see you again?'

A long silence before she speaks. 'I don't know who you are,' she says. 'You are harassing me in my own house. I demand you will never phone me here again, never.'

Demand. She means *command.* Her shrillness surprises him: there has been no intimation of it before. But then, what should a predator expect when he intrudes into the vixen's nest, into the home of her cubs?

He puts down the telephone. A shadow of envy passes over him for the husband he has never seen.

CHAPTER 23

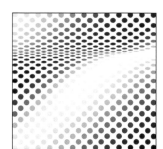

Mid-Twentieth Century
and Later

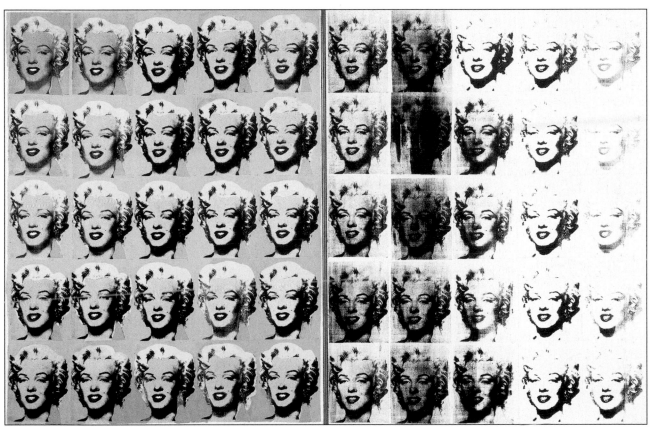

Andy Warhol, *Marilyn Diptych*, 1962, oil on canvas, in two panels, 6′ 10″ × 9′ 6″ (2.08 × 2.90 m), Tate Gallery, London, Art Resource, NY. © 2003 Andy Warhol Foundation for the Visual Arts (ARS), NY, (TM) 2002 Marilyn Monroe LLC under license authorized by CMG World-wide, Inc., Indianopolis, IN.

MAP 23.1 Post-war Europe, 1949.

CHAPTER OVERVIEW

MID-TWENTIETH CENTURY AND LATER
The existential and the abstract change the face of the humanities

POP CULTURE
Modern society and art exchange ideas and influences

MID-TWENTIETH CENTURY AND LATER

More than seventeen million soldiers died fighting World War II, and eighteen million civilians died because of it. The economies of Europe and Asia were decimated. The Allied victory was undermined by a mistrust of the Soviets, wartime allies whose ideology demonized capitalism. Only one thing was certain: humankind was now capable of total self-destruction.

On May 10, 1940, nine months after Hitler's invasion of Poland had forced France and Britain to declare war on Germany, German troops moved north into the Low Countries. From Belgium, German troops poured into France, driving not directly to Paris but to the English Channel, thus separating France from its British allies. More than 300,000 French and British troops trapped on the beaches at Dunkirk retreated to England, and then Hitler marched on Paris. On June 13, the French declared Paris an open city and evacuated without a fight. On June 22, Marshal Henri Pétain signed an armistice with the Germans, handing over two-thirds of the country to German control, leaving himself in charge of the Mediterranean areas. His headquarters were in the small resort community of Vichy, and his government, despised as collaborators after the war, was known as Vichy France.

Hitler believed that, without France's support, Britain would give in as well, but Britain did nothing of the kind. Britain's new prime minister, Winston Churchill (1874–1965), addressed the House of Commons with these words:

> I have nothing to offer but blood, toil, tears, and sweat. We have before us an ordeal of the most grievous kind. We have before us many, many long months of struggle and of suffering. You ask, what is our policy? I will say: It is to wage war, by sea, land, and air, with all our might and with all the strength that God can give us; to make war against a monstrous tyranny, never surpassed in the dark, lamentable catalogue of human crime. That is our policy.
>
> You ask, what is our aim? I can answer in one word: It is victory, victory at all costs, victory in spite of all terror, victory, however long and hard the road may be; for without victory there is no survival.

In August and September 1940, Hitler tested the British resolve with full-scale bomber attacks on the country. But, in what Churchill would label Great Britain's "finest hour," Germany failed to win air superiority over Britain, and British resolve strengthened.

Meanwhile, in the Pacific, Japanese leaders, who had struck a deal with Vichy France, invaded French Indochina (Vietnam) and pressed into China. The Japanese Emperor Hirohito (1901–89) agreed to enter the war in alliance with Hitler if the United States joined the Allied forces and entered the war in Europe. Forcing the issue, Japanese forces attacked the American naval base at Pearl Harbor, Hawaii, on December 7, 1941. An outraged United States immediately declared war on Japan, and Germany honored its alliance with Japan and declared war on the United States. By the end of 1941, the world was at war.

Slowly, the Allies gained the upper hand both in Europe and the Pacific. There were many turning points. In North Africa, Allied troops defeated the German general Erwin Rommel, the "Desert Fox." In Russia, the Soviets turned back the Germans at Stalingrad (Volgograd). In Italy, the Allied invasion of Sicily soon took Italy out of the war. Then came D-Day on June 6, 1944, and the Allies regained the beaches of northern France (fig. 23.1). A decisive factor in

FIGURE 23.1 Allied troops landing in Normandy. This photograph, taken two days after D-Day, on June 6, 1944, shows reinforcements arriving on French soil. The dimension of the Allied effort is evident.

Critical Thinking

The weekend as we know it in the West today did not always exist. Although scattered religious holidays were celebrated from the Middle Ages, and though there was, traditionally, no working on the Sabbath, the two-day weekend did not materialize until the late nineteenth century, when workers in some places took Saturday afternoons off. It did not become standardized and extended to two full days until the mid-twentieth century.

Why do you think the weekend eventually became commonplace in Western societies? Why do you think it took so long to become what it is today? And to what extent do you think new technologies like email and the cell phone have begun to erode it? And, finally, do you think the weekend is a good idea, one that should be preserved? Why or why not?

---

defeating Germany was Allied air superiority, which demolished Germany's industrial base and oil production capabilities, halting its resupply of troops in the field.

As Allied troops overran Berlin, Hitler shot himself in defeat, having started a war that had resulted in millions of military and civilian deaths, including between six and seven million Jews in death camps such as Auschwitz, in Poland, where as many as twelve thousand Jews were executed in a single day. On May 8, 1945, Churchill and the American President, Harry S Truman (1884–1972), declared victory in Europe. The United States dropped its newly developed atom bomb on the Japanese cities of Hiroshima, on August 6, 1945, and, three days later, on Nagasaki. On September 2, 1945, Japan surrendered as well.

COLD WAR AND ECONOMIC RECOVERY

Many historians view World War II as a rekindling of unresolved hostilities from World War I. In this light, the 1920s and 1930s can be viewed as an extended truce. So devastating was the war that Europe lost its central place in world politics and culture, and Japan was left so battered that its emperor, Hirohito, referred to the situation as "the unendurable that must be endured."

The rebuilding of Europe and Japan required a huge investment. The American secretary of state, George C. Marshall (1880–1959), conceived the idea of providing economic aid to the European countries on the condition they work together for their mutual benefit. It was called the Marshall Plan, and it fostered unprecedented prosperity and affluence in Europe. In Japan, General Douglas MacArthur (1880–1964) oversaw a new democratic constitution forbidding the manufacture of arms for "land, sea, or air force . . . [and] other war potential." Japan thus became the only world power without a significant defense budget, which freed its economy.

Europe became the focal point of a struggle for world power called the Cold War, fought without open warfare between the United States and the Soviet Union. The United States had as its ally much of Western Europe while the Soviet Union dominated Eastern Europe. By 1950, the former imperial powers of Europe lost control of most of their empires overseas, and many of these countries—in Southeast Asia, Africa, and Latin America—became points of conflict in the U.S./Soviet power struggle.

Even as Western Europe lost political clout, it developed a strong economic union, the European Community, or the Common Market as it was known (it has now been renamed once more as the European Union), which brought wealth to the continent. As opposed to Eastern Europe, where shortages of food and goods remained a constant of the Soviet regime, both Western Europe and the United States enjoyed fifty years of economic expansion. Japan, too, unburdened by military expenditures in accordance with its new constitution, turned its attention to its economy, and by 1970, it led the world in the production of consumer goods. By 1996, its gross national product (GNP) was nearly four times that of France and three times that of Germany.

The period after World War II can thus be viewed as a movement from destruction and devastation to affluence and prosperity. Anything seemed possible. Visionaries speculated that one day every family might own a television. Music might be played in stereophonic sound. People might fly to the moon. Computers might interpret data, drive cars, or clean houses. More importantly, racism might end, women might achieve equality, world peace might be possible. Such were the dreams. The reality was more complicated.

THE VIETNAM WARS

Vietnam has a long history of domination by foreign powers. Throughout its history, Vietnam engaged in continued resistance, against China in the eighteenth and nineteenth centuries, and in the mid-twentieth century, against France. After the defeat of the French at Dien Bien Phu in 1945, the United States provided support to the non-Communist government of South Vietnam, which was at war with the Communist North. The United States became increasingly implicated in the war, first through supplying money and war materials, later sending American

MAP 23.2

military advisors, and finally sending American soldiers to fight alongside the South Vietnamese army.

Gradually, however, due to strong political dissatisfaction with America's presence in Vietnam, U.S. forces were withdrawn and peace agreements signed in 1973. Two years, later, however, the North Vietnamese army marched on Saigon and captured the capital. One year later the country was united as the Republic of Vietnam, and Saigon was renamed Ho Chi Minh City.

THE PHILOSOPHY OF EXISTENTIALISM

The horrible reality of the German concentration camps, of "man's inhumanity to man," and, in France particularly, of the fact that thousands had collaborated with the Nazis

in the Vichy government or, at the least, turned their eyes from Nazi atrocities, fueled a discourse about the individual's responsibility to make choices—**existentialism.** Its seeds lay in the ideas of the Danish philosopher **SØREN KIERKEGAARD** [KEAR-kah-gard] (1813–55), who insisted on the irreducibly subjective and personal dimension of human life. Kierkegaard used the term the "existing individual" to characterize the subjective perspective, and from this the term "existential" later developed. Kierkegaard emphasized the essentially ethical nature of human life, with each individual responsible for making choices and commitments. Kierkegaard insisted that these choices require respect for other people, virtuous behavior on their behalf, and a faith in spiritual things that transcends the limitations and vicissitudes of material life.

Jean-Paul Sartre. Like Kierkegaard, the French philosopher JEAN-PAUL SARTRE [SAHR-truh] (1905–80) emphasized the ethical aspect of existential thought. Unlike Kierkegaard, however, Sartre, who was an atheist, disavowed the spiritual or religious dimension. The central tenets of Sartre's philosophy begin with his idea that "existence precedes essence," which suggests that human beings are defined by their choices and actions. Nothing is fixed or preestablished in human nature. What is important is what human beings become, what they make of themselves through their choices, decisions, and commitments, which are always in question and never finally settled.

This fundamental idea is related to another: Human beings exist relative to one another; they exist in interpersonal and social situations that affect them, situations that also involve repeated decisive choices. The choices human beings make are necessary and inescapable. Those choices, moreover, not only make individuals who they are, since a person is what he or she does, but they also make people responsible for each other as well as for themselves. When people evade responsibility for themselves or for others, they exist in a state that Sartre describes as "bad faith," which results from denying their freedom to do, think, act, or be otherwise than they are.

Sartre developed his philosophy in context of World War II, including the Nazi occupation of France. During that time he came to recognize the ways one's physical freedom could be curtailed and one's life endagered. Nonetheless, he remained uncompromising in his insistence that, regardless of one's situation, one always had the conscious power to negate it and to transcend it in thought. What people make of such situations, much as what they make of themselves through the many roles they perform in life, determines who they become. It is not the situations themselves or the roles people find themselves in that fix their identities but the choices they make in response to those roles and situations.

Simone de Beauvoir. SIMONE DE BEAUVOIR [boh-VWAHR] (1908–1966) shared with Sartre ideas about the necessity for responsibility in choosing what one makes of one's life. De Beauvoir stressed more than Sartre the ambiguity that is frequently a factor in the ethical decisions people need to make.

De Beauvoir's most important contribution involves her study of women. In her groundbreaking book *The Second Sex*, she reviewed history and myth, bringing them to bear on the situation of women at midcentury. She also analyzed the biological bases of female experience, concluding that although biological differences between men and women are incontrovertible, it is social differentiation that determines their very different life experiences. De Beauvoir was especially eloquent on women's need to distinguish themselves from men, to break the pattern of being seen only in relation to them. She was ahead of her time in advancing the belief that, in a man's world, women need to band together to assert pressure for change.

ABSTRACTION IN AMERICAN ART

Existentialism became the dominant postwar philosophy, and the arts began to emphasize individual expression. In the United States, in particular, a brand of highly personal and subjective painting developed that became known as **abstract expressionism**. Although varied in style, the work of the Abstract Expressionists, was unified in its emphasis on expressive gesture and its rejection of art as representation.

During the 1930s, many artists were not working on the kind of mural painting supported by the WPA, and the government recognized this. As part of the New Deal, an easel painting project was initiated that paid artists $95 a month. Although hardly a fortune, this was living wage, and some of the artists under this plan became the focal point of the American avant-garde of the 1940s, among them Jackson Pollock, Willem de Kooning, and Mark Rothko.

Jackson Pollock. Jackson Pollock (1912–56) was born in Wyoming, moved to New York in the 1930s, and studied with Thomas Hart Benton, whose interest in large-scale work influenced him. By the mid-1940s, Pollock had begun developing a body of work sometimes referred to as "drip" paintings for which he was dubbed "Jack the Dripper." When he created them, he was in psychoanalysis and was interested in the role of the unconscious in art. Pollock was intrigued by the notion of psychic automatism, imported by the Surrealists who had escaped war in Europe, seeking asylum in the United States. In addition, he had been especially affected by Picasso's *Guernica* (see Chapter 21) when it was first displayed in New York in 1939.

His working method, the results of which are seen in *Autumn Rhythm: Number 30* (fig. 23.2), of 1950, was to unroll a huge canvas on the floor and throw, drip, and splatter paint onto it as he moved around it. Although Pollock said he knew what he was trying to achieve before starting on a canvas, his compositions appear accidental. There is no clear top or bottom: Pollock determined this only when he signed it. The entirety is a web of countless swirling marks, seemingly pushing and pulling one another.

Pollock's style became known as **action painting** because it conveys the artist's physical activity. Pollock swung his arms and moved his entire body when making his drip paintings. For him, the act of getting paint onto the canvas was the important part; the "work" is not so much a finished product as the process of making it.

Lee Krasner. Lee Krasner (1908–84) was born in Brooklyn, NY, into an Orthodox Jewish family. After studying art in various New York schools, she joined the American Abstract Artists Group in 1939. She worked with Jackson

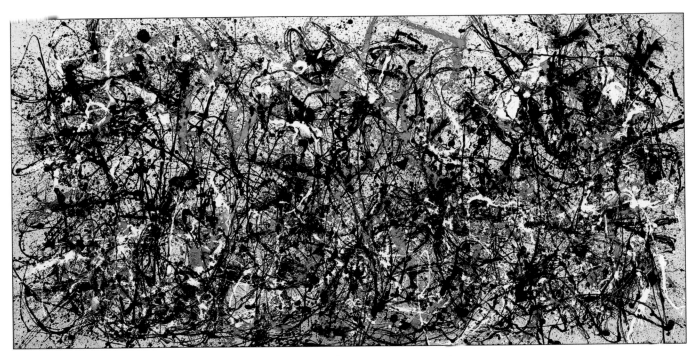

FIGURE 23.2 Jackson Pollock, *Autumn Rhythm: Number 30*, 1950, oil on canvas, 8'9" × 17'3" (2.66 × 5.25 m), Metropolitan Museum of Art, NY. George A. Hearn Fund, 1957. © 2005, ARS, NY. Because there is no recognizable subject, such work is referred to as "abstract expressionism." Pollock's personal technique is known as "action painting" because of the highly active physical process—he splattered, flung, and dripped paint onto canvas unrolled on the floor, the result being largely accidental.

Pollock in 1941 when both participated in an exhibition held in New York the following year. At this time, she was the better known of the two artists and provided him with access to the Manhattan art world. Krasner married Pollock in 1945; by the following year they were influencing each other's art.

Both worked in styles that gave visual expression to the physical energy of painting. Her *Flowering Limb* (fig. 23.3), painted in 1963, several years after Pollock's death, shows her work, by comparison, to be more controlled than his. Although her paint is applied with a brush rather than dripped onto the canvas, Krasner, too, eliminated the handcrafted quality of careful brushwork, which may be seen as an aspect of the artist's detachment from an actual subject.

Willem de Kooning.   Similarly, the paintings of Willem de Kooning (1904–97) reveal an interest not so much in representing a preconceived idea but rather in experiencing the act of painting. When de Kooning emigrated to the United States from his native Holland in 1926, he was a figure painter, albeit one deeply influenced by the Cubists. Soon, he was influenced by the Surrealists and began painting with broad, slashing strokes. In *Excavation* (fig. 23.4), of 1950, interlocking, neutral-colored shapes, simultaneously organic and geometric, arise from a multicolored ground. Identifiable items can be detected, at various points: sets of teeth, eyes, and even, in the very middle, a red, white, and blue area that suggests an American flag. De Kooning's aim was to create an afocal surface, that is, one on which the eye can never quite come to rest. For de Kooning, this disorientation, comparable to the disorientation felt by immigrants and refugees, represents the modern condition.

Mark Rothko.   The **color field** abstraction of Mark Rothko (1903–70), is characterized by an absence of a recognizable figurative subject, an absence of an illusion of space, and large areas of flat color. A Russian who moved to America, Rothko was an introspective artist whose anguish about himself and his work led to his eventual suicide in his studio in 1970. *Red, Brown, and Black* (fig. 23.5), of 1958, is characteristic of the canvases covered with rectangles of subtle, rich colors for which Rothko is best known. Working with layers of thin paint, Rothko made the edges of his rectangles fuzzy and soft, rendering the rectangles cloudlike, seemingly able to float one on top of another. These subtle color harmonies hover in an ambiguous space, sometimes advancing and sometimes receding. Rothko wished to evoke the emotions "tragic and timeless." He thought of his canvases as backdrops before which viewers experience their feelings, ranging from calm to happy to sad.

FIGURE 23.3   Lee Krasner, *Flowering Limb*, 1963, oil on canvas $57\frac{3}{4}''\times 45\frac{3}{4}''$ (146.7 $\times$ 116.2 cm). Photograph courtesy of Robert Miller Gallery, NY. Estate of Lee Krasner © 2008 Artists Rights Society (ARS), NY. The degree of abstraction is such that the viewer is unlikely to suspect that this painting portrays a tree branch in bloom prior to reading the title. The dense pattern, almost a form of abstract calligraphy, seems to spread beyond the edges of the canvas, suggesting an ongoing expansive space.

Helen Frankenthaler.   Rothko's color field painting, with its chromatic subtleties, is given freer form by the American artist Helen Frankenthaler (b. 1928), a second-generation Abstract Expressionist. Her *Mauve District* (fig. 23.6), of 1966, is an example of this nonobjective style of painting. Like Pollock, Frankenthaler worked on raw, or unprimed canvas, that is, canvas without glue and gesso (white paint) primer. Like Pollock, she worked on huge canvases laid out flat rather than placed on an easel. Unlike Pollock, however, Frankenthaler poured paint onto the canvas, soaking and staining the canvas. At first she used oil paint, thinned with turpentine until it was very

fluid. Later she used acrylic paints, which are thinned with water and handled much like watercolor. Frankenthaler's experiments resulted in soft, silky biomorphic shapes in color harmonies producing floating lyrical effects with a look of ease and spontaneity. Some areas of the canvas are left unpainted, defining the painted areas abutting them.

Lois Mailou Jones.   Of special interest is the black American textile designer, painter, teacher, and ambassador, Lois Mailou Jones (1905–98). She was born in Boston and graduated with honors from the School of the Museum of Fine Arts. In Washington, D.C., she taught at Howard Uni-

FIGURE 23.4   Willem de Kooning, *Excavation*, 1950, oil on canvas, $6'8\frac{1}{2}'' \times 8'4\frac{1}{8}''$ (2.04 × 2.54 m). Art Institute of Chicago, Gift of Mr. and Mrs. Noah Goldowsky and Edgar Kaufmann, Jr., Mr. & Mrs. Frank G. Logan Purchase Prize, 1952. 1. Photograph © 1997 All Rights Reserved. © 2005 Artists Rights Society (ARS), NY. Fragments of human anatomy seem to reveal themselves behind, through, and across the webbed surfaces of many de Kooning paintings.

versity for many years—from 1930 to 1977. In the 1930s, she began to utilize motifs from African tribal art in her painting, and was influenced also by the strong colors patterns of Haitian art—her husband was Haitian. In 1970 she became the United States Information Agency's cultural ambassador to Africa. This experience is reflected in her works such as *Ode to Kinshasa* (fig. 23.7) of 1972. Simple forms, bright colors, and the various textures of the materials pasted onto the canvas are combined with both simplicity and sophistication.

ARCHITECTURE

Ludwig Mies van der Rohe.   Among Walter Gropius's colleagues at the Bauhaus in Dessau was LUDWIG MIES VAN DER ROHE [mees van-duh-ROW] (1887–1969). When Hitler closed the school, Mies moved to Chicago where he concentrated his efforts on designing a new campus for the Illinois Institute of Technology. Later Mies created what we now think of as the modern skyscraper.

Typical of his work are the Lake Shore Drive Apartment Houses (fig. 23.8), built 1950–52. Mies's motto, "Less

is more," is embodied in these buildings. The steel frame skeleton provides the surface pattern; ornament is avoided. The extreme simplicty approaches austerity. Solid and void are aesthetic equals.

Le Corbusier   The work of Le Corbusier was introduced in chapter 21, with the Savoye House (fig. 21.22). He designed the church of Notre-Dame-du-Haut at Ronchamp, France (fig. 23.9), 1950–55. The name of the church refers to its location on a mountaintop. Built of masonry and sprayed concrete, the rough surfaces appear to be sheets of a soft material that has been cut with enormous scissors and bent into these concave and convex shapes. Unlike traditional religious architecture, symmetry has been abandoned. Le Corbusier does use light and stained glass, as in a Gothic cathedral (see Chapter 12), but the effect is new. Windows of different sizes and shapes are set into the thickness of the wall, and form an abstract arrangement.

Frank Lloyd Wright.   Perhaps the most influential architect of the age was the American Frank Lloyd Wright whose Fallingwater was discussed in Chapter 21 (fig. 21.23).

FIGURE 23.5 Mark Rothko, *Red, Brown, and Black*, 1958, oil on canvas, 8′1″ × 9′9″ (2.72 × 2.97 m), Museum of Modern Art, NY. Mrs. Simon Guggenheim Fund, Licensed by Scala/Art Resource, NY. © ARS, NY. Working in a style known as color field painting, Rothko produced a series of paintings consisting of soft-edged rectangles of various colors that are theoretical and philosophical representations of contrasting states of emotion and discipline.

FIGURE 23.6 Helen Frankenthaler, *Mauve District*, 1966, polymer on unprimed canvas, 8′7″ × 7′11″ (2.62 × 2.41 m), Museum of Modern Art, NY. Mrs. Donald Straus Fund, Licensed by Scala/Art Resource, NY. Frankenthaler was deeply impressed by the work of Jackson Pollock. However, where Pollock's oil paint was thick, Frankenthaler achieved soft stained effects, similar to watercolor, by painting with thinned paint on absorbent raw canvas.

Wright's works included not only private homes, but also public spaces, such as office buildings, churches, hotels, and museums. His Guggenheim Museum in New York City (fig. 23.10), designed 1942–43 and built 1957–60, is visually arresting. Constructed of reinforced concrete, the shape derives from the ramp inside. Visitors ride an elevator to the top and then view the art while circling down the long spiral walkway.

MODERN DRAMA

Modern drama begins in the nineteenth century with the plays of the Norwegian dramatist Henrik Ibsen (see Chapter 17), whose realism shocked his contemporaries and propelled the theater in new directions. Ibsen's emphasis on the psychology of his characters was developed by later playwrights to depict the new existential thought.

An existentialist sense of the absurd dominated postwar theater. A full-blown Theater of the Absurd substituted storyless action for well-contrived plots and disconnected dialogue for witty responses and grand speeches. Absurdist dramatists rejected the idea that characters can be understood or that plot should be structured, just as they rejected the order and coherence of character and action in everyday life.

Cross Currents

ABSTRACT EXPRESSIONISM IN JAPAN

In the summer of 1955, a group of young Japanese artists who called themselves the Gutai Art Association organized a thirteen-day, twenty-four-hour-a-day, outdoor exhibition in a pine grove park along the beach in Ashiya, a small town outside Osaka. Their name, Gutai, literally means "concreteness," but more importantly it derives from two separate characters, *gu*, meaning "tool" or "means," and *tai*, meaning "body" or "substance." Taking Jackson Pollock's physical approach to painting as a starting point, they approached their work with their entire bodies, literally throwing themselves into it.

They called the exhibition in Ashiya the *Experimental Outdoor Exhibition of Modern Art to Challenge the Mid-Summer Sun*. A year later, in Tokyo, Gutai held another exhibition. They applied paint to canvas with watering cans and remote control toys. Shimamato Shozo, wearing goggles and dressed for combat, threw jars of paint against rocks positioned across a canvas in a manner reminiscent of a Japanese Zen garden. The finished works were encrusted with paint and glass. Shiraga Kazuo painted on large canvases stretched across the floor, in the manner of Pollock, but used his feet as his brush as he slid through the oil paint. In a piece called *Challenging Mud*, he submerged himself half naked in a pile of dense mud. Rolling in it, squeezing it, wrestling with it, he created a sculptural version of his physical presence. Murakami Saburo built large paper screens six feet high by twelve feet wide, and then flung himself through them.

As violent as these activities were, they were also rooted in Zen. Concrete enactments of the individual's being unite the physical and spiritual in a single image.

FIGURE 23.7 Lois Mailou Jones, *Ode to Kinshasa*, 1972, mixed media on canvas, 48 × 36″ (27.9 × 20.3 cm), National Museum of Women in the Arts, Washington, DC. Gift of the artist. The title of this painting refers to the African republic of Congo (formerly Zaire), which Jones, a black American, had visited in 1970 as the United States cultural ambassador.

FIGURE 23.8 Ludwig Mies van der Rohe, Lake Shore Drive Apartment Houses, Chicago, 1950–52. Modern office and apartment buildings favor simplified and standardized rectangular buildings of steel and glass, the vertical emphasized and the structural frame made obvious.

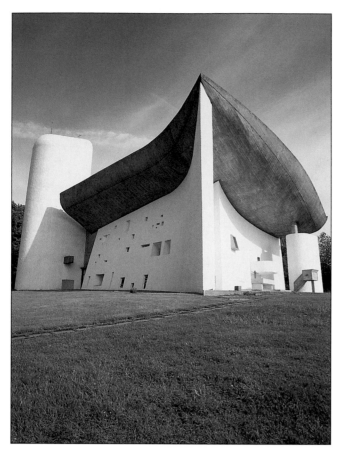

FIGURE 23.9 Le Corbusier (Charles Edouard Jenneret), Notre-Dame-du-Haut, Ronchamp, France, 1950–55. Le Corbusier turned away from the International Style and designed this extraordinary pilgrimage church. Thick masonry walls are covered with sprayed concrete to form curved sculptural surfaces that appear natural and organic rather than rigid and stiff.

The Irish-born playwright Samuel Beckett (1906–89) is best known for *Waiting for Godot* and *Endgame*. Beckett mixes humor with pathos. Relying on the farcical gestures of vaudeville performers and circus clowns, Beckett's characters display a dark intelligence and bleakly pessimistic view of their tragicomic situation. Lacking in purpose and meaning, they wait for the inevitable.

Waiting for Godot (1952) portrays two tramps, Vladimir and Estragon, who wait for someone who never comes. As they wait, the tramps quarrel, contemplate suicide, separation, and departure. They wait until they become dependent on waiting itself. Two additional characters, a master and servant named Pozzo and Lucky, share the stage for a time with the tramps. The rich Pozzo mistreats Lucky cruelly, until Pozzo becomes blind, at which point he needs the now mute Lucky to lead him. Each pair has nothing more in life than one another. Beckett's theatrical genius is in depicting the human will to survive, despite the direst of circumstances, in all its starkness and humor.

SCULPTURE

Alexander Calder. A new kind of sculpture was created by the American Alexander Calder (1898–1976), whose father was also a sculptor. The younger Calder first gained recognition as a toy maker in Paris in the 1930s with a miniature circus that fascinated the Surrealists, particularly Miró. By this time, Calder was already making **mobiles,** sculptural forms suspended from the ceiling that are driven by the air itself (fig. 23.11). Although many people today know what a mobile is, it was Calder who invented the form and Marcel Duchamp who gave it its name. Because a mobile moves in the faintest breeze, its form is always changing, the simple shapes constantly forming new relationships. A mobile uses color, shape, composition, motion, time, and space. The artist must be concerned with each.

Isamu Noguchi. A student of Brancusi's in Paris in the 1920s, Japanese-American sculptor ISAMU NOGUCHI [No-GOO-chee] (1904–88) was particularly influenced by Brancusi's sense of sculpture as possessing an inherent expressive power. Noguchi drew on his own Japanese heritage in an attempt to discover in stone what the Japanese call *wabi*—the "ultimate naturalness" of an object.

Kouros (fig. 23.12) is one of Noguchi's works from the period of World War II, during which time he voluntarily entered a Japanese internment facility at Poston, Arizona, in order to help those being held there. "Kouros" is the ancient Greek term for "boy" or "young man" and refers to life-size sculptures of the nude male that began to appear in Greece in the seventh century B.C.E. (see Chapter 2). Despite the title, the form of Noguchi's work is more obviously related to that of the Surrealists, particularly Arp and Miró. The piece unites two opposing techniques for, on the one hand, it is carved while, on the other, it is constructed. When viewed from two different angles—that is, from the front and from the side—it appears to be two entirely different works of art. In other words, it induces, or indeed demands, the viewer's movement.

POP CULTURE

In the 1950s and 1960s, the material dreams of the post-war era seemed to be coming true. Society was rapidly becoming a consumer culture. In 1947, 75,000 homes in the United States were equipped with television sets. By 1967, over 55 million sets were in operation and over 95 per cent of American families owned at least one. That same year, Swanson introduced the first frozen TV Dinner—turkey, mashed potatoes, and peas. In 1955, McDonald's was founded, inaugurating the fast-food industry. The growth of the automobile industry, which made fast food possible, was staggering. By 1949, Detroit was producing 5 million automobiles a year, a year later 8 million, and the number continued to grow. In response to this, shopping patterns

Then & Now

COFFEE: THE BEAN THAT WAKES UP THE WORLD

Coffee is one drink that people enjoy the world over. Coffee was first used by nomads in Ethiopia, where, according to legend, it was discovered by a goatherd who noticed that goats exhibited unusual energy after eating the red berries. The goatherd, named Kaldi, tried the berries himself and experienced an energy surge. A monk from a nearby monastery boiled the berries to make a drink, the ancestor of coffee as we know it today. Sometime between 1000 and 1300, coffee was made into a beverage. And although some authorities date coffee's earliest cultivation to late-sixth-century Yemen, coffee isn't mentioned in literature until the end of the first millenium.

The medicinal properties of coffee were first described by the Arabic philosopher/physician Avicenna. By the late fifteenth century, coffee had spread to the Muslim cities of Mecca and Medina, and by the seventeenth century it had been introduced to the Netherlands and to North America. During the eighteenth century, coffee became daily fare of people throughout the world, soon leading to a plethora of coffeehouses and coffee bars throughout Europe and ultimately, to the phenomenon of Starbucks and other specialty coffee merchants today.

Some highlights from the annals of coffee: Sultan Selim I introduces coffee to Constantinople in 1517; the first coffeehouses open in Venice (1645), Oxford (1650), and New York (1696); the English bring coffee cultivation to Jamaica in 1730; the New York Coffee Exchange opens in 1882; decaffeinated coffee is invented in Germany in 1910; instant coffee is invented in the United States in 1938.

FIGURE 23.10 Frank Lloyd Wright, Guggenheim Museum, New York, designed 1942–43, built 1957–60. Wright believed people are greatly influenced by their architectural surroundings. Essentially an enormous concrete spiral, a sort of sculpture one can enter, the Guggenheim Museum is itself a work of art.

FIGURE 23.11   Alexander Calder, *Red Gongs*, completed 1950, hanging mobile, painted aluminum, brass, steel rod and wire, overall size 4′11″ × 12′1⅓″ (1.50 × 3.70 m), Metropolitan Museum of Art, NY. Calder invented this type of hanging sculpture, called a "mobile" because its component parts, highly responsive to the environment, are moved by the faintest breeze. He also made "stabiles" out of similar thin flat shapes that did not move.

changed. In 1950, just north of Seattle, Washington, the Northgate Shopping Center opened, accessible only by car and consisting of forty shops clustered around a Bon Marché department store. Six years later, the first covered shopping mall, Southdale Center, opened in Minneapolis. In 1953, the Kinsey Report on sexual behavior in the United States was published, and by 1966, the sexual revolution had taken firm hold as an **oral contraceptive,** popularly called "the Pill," became widely available.

As consumerism increasingly preoccupied American life, artists and intellectuals turned their attention to the cycle of production, consumption, and waste that defined experience. Like the Dadaists of a previous generation, they realized that art might be almost anything.

A theoretician of this point of view was the composer John Cage (1912–95), who first taught at Black Mountain College in North Carolina in the early 1950s, and at the New School in New York City in the late 1950s. For instance, his piece 4′3″ is four minutes and thirty-three seconds of actual silence, during which the audience becomes aware of sound in the room—"traffic sounds," in the words of one audience member at a performance at the Carnegie Recital Hall in New York, "chairs creaking, people cough-

ing, rustling of clothes, then giggles . . . a police car with its siren running . . . the elevator in the building . . . the air conditioning going through the ducts." These sounds comprise the "music" of the piece. First performed at Woodstock, New York, on August 29, 1952, the work possesses three influential features: minimal elements—silence; commonplace chance events, which links the piece to Surrealism; uniqueness in time—two performances are never alike.

ARTISTS OF THE EVERYDAY

Robert Rauschenberg.   One Black Mountain student, Robert Rauschenberg (b. 1925), influenced by Cage's composition of the everyday, began making **assemblages,** a variation on the idea of the collage (see Chapter 21), taking things one would normally discard and combining them to create "art." Creation, he said, is "the process of assemblage." *Odalisk* (fig. 23.13), made between 1955 and 1958, is compiled of a stuffed rooster, a pillow, magazine illustrations (including nude photographs), and paint, all on wood. The title is a pun, combining "odalisque" (harem girl) and "obelisk," a four-sided stone pillar capped by a small pyramid.

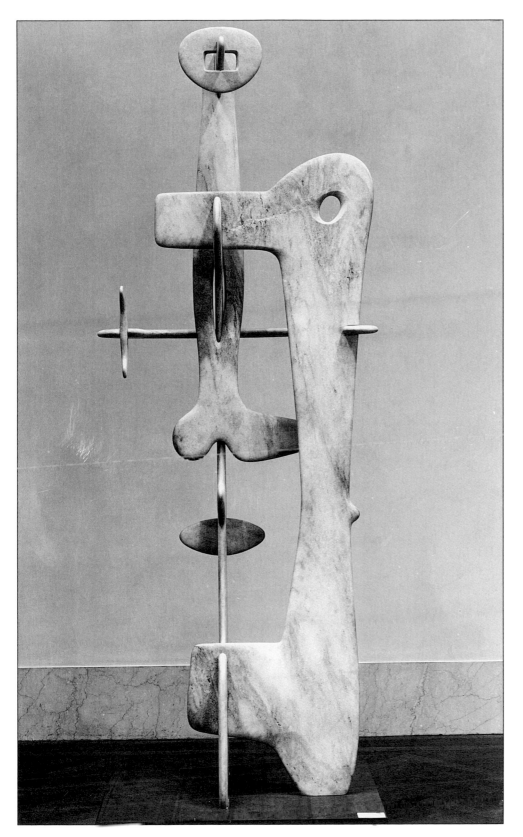

FIGURE 23.12 Isamu Noguchi, *Kouros*, 1944–45, pink Georgia marble, height 9′9″ (2.97 m), Metropolitan Museum of Art, NY, Fletcher Fund, 1953 (53.87a-i). Noguchi turned to these flat slabs of marble because, used in the commercial building industry for facades, countertops, and the like, they were inexpensive and widely available.

Like Cage, Rauschenberg brings together daily life and art. It is a messy art, an art of disorder, of chance, indeterminate, unpredictable, and multilayered. The images are not arranged neatly but are made to overlay, one intruding upon another. Rauschenberg called this work "combine painting."

Louise Nevelson. A different type of assemblage was created by Louise Nevelson (1899–1988), who was born in Kiev, Russia, and moved to Maine as a child. Nevelson studied many arts—music, dance, theater, painting, and printmaking. In her fifties, she began assembling small wooden objects, scraps and remnants that she found in furniture shops. She nailed and glued these fragments together, creating compositions within wooden boxes, which were then stacked together to create walls of a kind of large-scale relief. The entire assemblage was painted one color—black most often, or white, or gold.

Nevelson's *Sky Cathedral* (fig. 23.14), made in 1958, is painted black. According to the artist, black is the most aristocratic color and "encompasses all colors." This single color unifies what would otherwise appear fragmentary into an environment that looks like a city of many compartments, all compressed into a single plane.

Andy Warhol. The most "everyday" objects of the 1950s and 1960s were images of popular culture itself—advertising images, celebrated entertainers, product labels, and highway billboards. All of these, were "packaged," as one young artist, Andy Warhol (1928–87), recognized. Starting in commercial art in the late 1950s, he turned his studio into what he called The Factory, where he began churning out large editions of prints, as well as unique paintings. His work mimics the world of mass production—Campbell's soup cans, Coca-Cola bottles, dollar bills, and images of Elvis Presley and Marilyn Monroe (fig. 23.15). The style was quickly labeled **Pop Art**—popular art.

Warhol's images raise everyday objects and icons to artistic status; behind this lies an ironic resignation to widespread banality. The duplicate impressions of Marilyn Monroe in Warhol's diptych suggest that she became the image Hollywood created, and that her suicide was a desperate escape. Warhol brooded frequently about the violence of American society, creating images of electric chairs, automobile accidents, the Kennedy assassination, and, late in his career, endangered species.

Roy Lichtenstein. The same underlying despair combines with cartoonlike presentation in the work of Roy Lichtenstein (b. 1923). Lichtenstein painted large-scale imitations of two kinds of comic strips—war comics, depicting men in battle, and romance comics, akin to television soap operas, portraying the lives of young women. *Drowning Girl* (fig. 23.16) depicts with deadpan humor an absurd relationship dilemma.

A basis of Lichtenstein's style is the printer's dot—the so-called ben-day dot—used to print color in the comic strips. The style may be seen as a parody of Seurat's pointil-

FIGURE 23.13 Robert Rauschenberg, *Odalisque*, 1955–58, assemblage, including stuffed rooster, pillow, and paint, on wood, 6′9″ × 25″ × 25″ (205.7 × 63.5 × 63.5 cm), Museum Ludwig, Cologne. Rheinisches Bildarchiv, Cologne. © Robert Rauschenberg/Licensed by VAGA, NY. This construction, or assemblage, is not carved or modeled but compiled, the materials left as found rather than transformed. Rauschenberg works with materials not traditionally used in creating fine art, materials that one would normally discard.

MID-TWENTIETH CENTURY AND LATER **435**

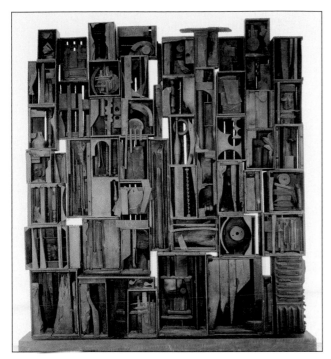

FIGURE 23.14 Louise Nevelson, *Sky Cathedral*, 1958, assemblage, wood, painted black, 11'3½" × 10'¼" × 1'6" (3.44 × 3.05 × 0.46 m) Museum of Modern Art, NY © 2005 Artists Rights Society (ARS), NY. Art Resource, NY. From a series of small compositional units made of pieces of wooden furniture and furnishings, Nevelson compiled wallsize assemblages, which she unified by painting a single solid color.

list technique (see Chapter 18). Lichtenstein asks us both to laugh and to take it seriously.

Claes Oldenburg. In December 1961, at 107 East Second Street in New York City, Claes Oldenburg (b. 1929), a Yale graduate and son of a Norwegian diplomat, opened an exhibition of painted plaster replicas of commodities—meat, vegetables, candy, cakes, pies, ice cream sundaes—in a shop front that he named "The Store." One replica was *Two Cheeseburgers, with Everything (Dual Hamburgers)* (fig. 23.17). At Oldenburg's store a plate of meat cost $399.98 and a sandwich $149.98. "I do things that are contradictory," Oldenburg explained. "I try to make the art look like it's part of the world around it. At the same time I take great pains to show that it doesn't function as part of the world around it." The following summer, Oldenburg recast some objects in giant scale and redid others as soft sculptures, sewn and stuffed with foam rubber. What should be soft—a hamburger, for instance—was hard plaster. What should be hard—a typewriter—was suddenly soft and sagging. Oldenburg's work jokes about audience expectations. In Oldenburg's world, consumable goods cannot be consumed, and giant versions of clothespins, spoons, electric plugs, scissors, trowels, and faucets transform the everyday into the monumental.

Marisol Escobar. The Pop Art sculptor MARISOL [ESCOBAR] (1930–) is an American who was born in Paris, although her parents were Venezuelan. She moved to Los Angeles, back to Paris, and then to Manhattan. Here, her work humorously satirizing social and political aspects of life, was well received. A well-known example is *Women*

FIGURE 23.15 Andy Warhol, *Marilyn Diptych*, 1962, acrylic on canvas, in two panels, 6'10" × 9'6" (2.08 × 2.90 m), Tate Gallery, London, Art Resource, NY. © 2003 Andy Warhol Foundation for the Visual Arts/ARS, New York. (TM) 2002 Marilyn Monroe LLC under License authorized by CMG Worldwide, Inc., Indianapolis, IN. The way in which Marilyn Monroe's face is both obliterated and fades away in the right-hand panel epitomized, for Warhol, her own tragic end.

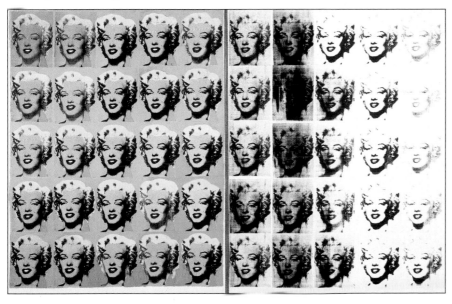

FIGURE 23.16 Roy Lichtenstein, *Drowning Girl*, 1963, oil and synthetic polymer paint on canvas, 5'7⅝" × 5'6¾" (1.72 × 1.70 m), Museum of Modern Art, NY/Licensed by SCALA-Art Resource, NY. Philip Johnson Fund and Gift of Mr. and Mrs. Bagley Wright. Photograph © 2005 Museum of Modern Art, NY. Lichtenstein recognized that, even though his audience would laugh at a cartoon image such as this, they would identify with the image as well.

and Dog (fig. 23.18) of 1964. Here are three women, a child, and a dog, perhaps out for a stroll. Two of the women have multiple faces, suggesting that they are glancing in all directions.

Although essentially wooden sculpture, the wood is only minimally carved; the block shapes are retained. The effect depends less on carving than on painting with strong colors, the composition unified by the repetition of the pattern on a skirt and a blouse, the size changed and the color scheme inverted.

Happenings. Allan Kaprow (b. 1927) believed Cage's work suggested a new "total art." Kaprow's vision sprang from an "event" that Cage staged at Black Mountain College in 1952, entitled *Theater Piece #1*, that combined music, film, art, poetry, and dance. Kaprow envisaged "an assemblage of events . . . [which] unlike a stage play, may occur at a supermarket, driving along a highway, under a pile of rags, and in a friend's kitchen, either at once or sequentially." He called such a work a **Happening.** "It is art," he said, "but seems closer to life."

MINIMAL AND CONCEPTUAL ART

Cage's **minimalism** also attracted sculptors, who saw principles relevant to their work in it. First, they saw that a formal but minimal sculptural statement would be interpreted varyingly according to its situation; and, second,

FIGURE 23.17 Claes Oldenburg, *Two Cheeseburgers, with Everything (Dual Hamburgers)*, 1961, burlap soaked in plaster, painted with enamel, 7 × 14¾" (17.8 × 37.5 cm), Museum of Modern Art, NY, Philip Johnson Fund, Licensed by Scala/Art Resource, NY. Pop Art seems simultaneously to laud and laugh at popular culture. Should art reflect the most characteristic aspects of a culture, or strive to raise the level of culture?

that the repetition of a sculptural statement, as in mass manufacture, changes the meaning of the form.

Donald Judd. Beginning in 1965, minimalist sculptor Donald Judd (b. 1928) created a series of uniform, modular sheet-metal boxes that he called "Specific Objects." Judd cantilevered these boxes from the wall arranged in equally spaced vertical columns or horizontal lines. Without reference to figure or landscape, the boxes insist on themselves, so to speak. By the late 1960s, Judd presented boxes as freestanding floor pieces (fig. 23.19), made of copper, brass, and stainless steel, often polished so as to reflect the surrounding space, each other, and the viewer. He also began to paint these pieces, especially their interiors, with enamel or lacquer, and sometimes sealed them on top and bottom with sheets of colored plexiglas. These simple, pure geometric shapes with sleek surfaces achieve a certain elegance.

Sol LeWitt. Also working in modular units, Sol LeWitt (b. 1928) created cubic frameworks of white, baked enamel

Table 23–1	IMPORTANT STYLES OF PAINTING DURING THE AGE OF AFFLUENCE	
Style	**Artist**	**Painting and Date**
Abstract Expressionism	Pollock	*Autumn Rhythm*, 1950
	de Kooning	*Excavation*, 1950
	Rothko	*Red, Brown, and Black*, 1958
	Frankenthaler	*Mauve District*, 1966
Pop Art	Warhol	*Marilyn Diptych*, 1962
	Lichtenstein	*Drowning Girl*, 1963
Op Art	Riley	*Hesitate*, 1964

FIGURE 23.19 Donald Judd, *Untitled*, 1969, anodized aluminum and blue plexiglas, each of four units, $47\frac{1}{2} \times 59\frac{7}{8} \times 11\frac{7}{8}''$ (121 × 152 × 30 cm), Missouri Art Museum. © Jack Mitchell/St. Louis. Judd's work may be thought of in terms of existentialism, as a kind of "pure being," but without existentialism's sense of moral imperative.

FIGURE 23.18 Marisol [Escobar], *Women and Dog*, 1964, plaster, synthetic polymer, wood, taxidermed dog head and miscellaneous items, overall: 72 × 85 × 48″ (182.9 × 215.9 × 121.9 cm). Whitney Museum of American Art, NY. Purchase, with funds from the Friends of the Whitney Museum of American Art 64.17 a–g. © Marisol Escobar/Licensed by VAGA, NY. Pop Art artists treat ordinary, everyday aspects of life in ways that may surprise, entertain, or even amuse the viewer—perhaps causing us to reconsider some things we tend to overlook or take for granted.

beams arranged and repeated according to various mathematical formulas. *Open Modular Cube* (fig. 23.21), for instance, appears quite straightforward. But over the course of a day, its shadows change and its appearance also changes as the viewer moves around it; thus the appearance of LeWitt's apparently stable structure is constantly changing.

For LeWitt, a work of art is "pure information," and could exist simply *as* information rather than as an object. That is, it could exist solely as a *concept*. LeWitt soon started making verbal instructions for artworks rather than making art itself. For a wall drawing, he might say, "Draw lines from the middle of the edge to a point in the center, in each of four colors, one color for each side," and so on. Then the drawing would be executed by whomever at whatever site, each work different.

Bridget Riley. Although associated with **Op Art** (a shortening of *Optical Art*), or retinal painting, a nonrepresen-

tational style of painting concerned with optics, the British painter Bridget Riley (b. 1931) explained that she never studied optics, relying instead on "empirical analyses and syntheses." Op Art is not emotional but intellectual, characterized by meticulous patterns, precisely painted, frequently in brilliant contrasting colors or in black and white.

Hesitate (fig. 23.22) is one of a group of black, gray, and white paintings Riley created in 1964. Other titles in this series include *Disturbance* and *Pause*, suggesting deeper implications. That the wavelike patterns appear to undulate and pulsate, creating illusions of three dimensions on the flat surface without using traditional methods of perspective, Riley notes "is purely fortuitous." Instead, she is concerned with polarities such as "static and active, or fast and slow," explaining that "repetition, contrast, calculated reversal and counterpoint also parallel the basis of our emotional structure."

Christo and Jeanne-Claude. Large scale wrapping or draping places temporarily in fabric is the hallmark of the site-specific artists Christo (b. 1935) and Jeanne-Claude (b. 1935), a husband and wife team.

Central Park Gates (fig. 23.23). installed in the park of this name in Manhattan for several weeks, consisted of a series of large hanging banners of bright orange fabric, carefully spaced and placed along the paths of the park, delineating the curves and contours of the landscape. The many visitors walked beneath the open tunnels thus created. Jean-Claude and Christo said that this was to be a gift to the city of Manhattan, and indeed it was—people of all ages and ethnicities (as well as their pets) were brought together in the park to share the common experience this environment created.

Connections

RAUSCHENBERG, CAGE, AND CUNNINGHAM

At Black Mountain College, artist Robert Rauschenberg, composer John Cage, and choreographer Merce Cunningham began a series of collaborations that lasted over three decades. At their collaboration's heart was a belief in, as one critic described Rauschenberg's combine paintings, "an aesthetics of heterogeneity." Together they trusted that, in the chance encounter of diverse materials, moments of revelation will be generated.

Both Cage and Rauschenberg were willing to admit almost anything into their work. So was Cunningham:

> In classical ballet, the space was observed in terms of the proscenium stage, it was frontal. What if, as in my pieces, you decide to make any point on the stage equally interesting? I used to be told that you see the center of the space as the most important: that was the center of interest. But in many modern paintings this was not the case and the sense of space was different. . . . When I happened to read that sentence of Albert Einstein's: 'There are no fixed points in space,' I thought, indeed, if there are no fixed points, then every point is equally interesting and equally changing.'

An example of such a dance is the 1958 *Summerspace* (fig. 23.20), with sets by Rauschenberg. "When I spoke to Bob

FIGURE 23.20   Merce Cunningham, *Summerspace*, 1958. Dancers: Robert Kovich and Chris Komar. Cunningham tries to devise dances in which so much is happening at once that the effect is not unlike trying to watch all three rings of a circus simultaneously.

Rauschenberg—for the decor—I said, 'One thing I can tell you about this dance is that it has no center . . .' So he made a pointillist backdrop and costumes." In another piece, *Variations V,* the dancer triggers sensors, which in turn trigger an "orchestra" of tape recorders, record players, and radio receivers containing sounds "composed" by Cage. A member of Cunningham's dance company, Gordon Mumma, describes the result as "a superbly poly: -chromatic, -genic, -phonic, -morphic, -pagic, -technic, -valent, multi-ringed circus."

The works of Christo and Jean-Claude are funded through the sales of their prints and preparatory drawings. To create a work such as this requires the cooperation of lawyers, government organizations, environmentalists, and many more—including the team of actual workers who were largely volunteers. Christo and Jean-Claude consider these procedural obstacles to be part of their controversial installations.

ARCHITECTURE

Richard Rogers and Renzo Piano.   Intentionally extraordinary, the Pompidou Center in Paris, built 1971–77 by Richard Rogers and Renzo Piano (fig. 23.24), is a famous—or infamous—example of modern architecture. In essence, a building turned inside out, its mechanical parts—usually hidden from view—have been oversized, put on the outside of the building, and painted bright colors according to their function: red for vertical transportation; green for water; yellow for electricity; white for ventilation, and blue for air conditioning. The escalator looks like a huge caterpillar inching its way along the facade. The Pompidou Center emphasizes the ordinary, the everyday, the commonplace—much like Pop Art.

Likewise, in his book *Learning from Las Vegas*, the architect Robert Venturi suggests the collision of styles, signs, and symbols that marks the American commercial strip can be seen as composing a new sort of unity. On the strip, anything goes, unlike traditional architectural practice, in which the architect harmonizes the building with its environment.

FIGURE 23.23   Christo and Jean-Claude, *Central Park Gates*, temporary installation, Central Park, New York City, NY, 2005. The artists "environmental art," which has included wrapping large buildings such as the Reicshstag in Berlin and the Pont Neuf in Paris, is intentionally both grand in scale and transitory, and often involves vast lengths of brightly colored fabric. The creation of a work such as the *Central Park Gates* requires the organization and cooperation of many people, the result being an event available to large numbers of visitors.

FIGURE 23.21   Sol LeWitt, *Open Modular Cube*, 1966. Painted aluminum, 5′ × 5′ × 5′ (1.52 × 1.52 × 1.52 m). Art Gallery of Ontario, Toronto. © 2005 ARS, NY. The simplest geometric shape, the square, is repeated countless times, creating a complex composition comparable to a monochromatic Mondrian (see fig. 21.27) in three dimensions.

FIGURE 23.22   Bridget Riley, *Hesitate*, 1964, emulsion on board, $43\frac{3}{8} \times 45\frac{1}{2}''$ (1.07 × 1.12 m), © Tate Gallery, London/Art Resource, NY. Tricking the eye, Op Art plays with the optical mechanics of human visual perception, the patterns appearing to vibrate and vacillate forward and backward. Riley said this effect was ancillary to her intentions, for she wanted the entire painting to be seen as a "field" rather than in individual parts, and compared it to painting a landscape.

Frank Gehry.   No architect's work epitomizes pop culture's collision of styles more than that of Frank Gehry (b. 1929). His own home, in Santa Monica, California, which he purchased and began to remodel in 1976, is a conscious version of Venturi's principles (fig. 23.25). Bored with the typical 1940s two-story frame house he had purchased, but unable to afford anything more, Gehry decided to surround the original with a new one, making the division between old and new visually clear. His building materials—plywood, concrete blocks, corrugated metal, and chainlink fence—are the everyday materials of popular culture. Needing a new kitchen, he built it at ground level, outside the original house's dining room on an asphalt pad (fig. 23.26). The new design included a long corrugated metal side that faced the street and offended his neighbors, but Gehry did not want his house to fit in. It announced that Gehry was different, and that difference was, perhaps, a good thing.

LITERATURE: THE BEATS

Not everyone felt the consumer culture developing in the United States during the 1950s was such a good thing. The so-called **Beat** generation of writers saw material prosperity as leading to conformity, complacency, and oppression. Theirs was the first in a series of critiques of America after World War II, critiques that would surface again in the civil rights and anti–Vietnam War movements in the 1960s and the feminist movement in the 1970s.

Jack Kerouac.   For Jack Kerouac (1922–69), the Beats were a resurgence of the lost American type, the "wild

FIGURE 23.24 Richard Rogers and Renzo Piano, Center National d'Art et Culture Georges Pompidou, Paris, 1971–77. Musée National d'Art Moderne. Reunion des Musées Nationaux/Art Resource, NY. The novelty of this museum of modern art is that the mundane mechanical parts are made the focal point, emphasized by their size, colors, and, above all, their location on the exterior rather than hidden within the walls in the usual manner. This glorification of the ordinary is the architectural equivalent of Pop Art.

self-believing" who had founded the country. In *On the Road*, written in 1951 and published in 1957, Kerouac reinvents the American archetype of the frontiersman and cowboy, as his narrator, Sal Paradise, a "wild yea-saying overburst of American joy," seeks to escape the confines of American civilization in Denver's skid row and Cheyenne, Wyoming's Wild West Week.

Kerouac wrote in "spontaneous prose," as he called it, with roots in the automatic writing of Surrealism and the expressive gesture of the Abstract Expressionist painters. The poet Allen Ginsberg described Kerouac's prose as "completely personal, [that] comes from the writer's own person—his person defined as his body, his breathing rhythm, his actual talk."

Allen Ginsberg. This style is, essentially, the style of Allen Ginsberg (1926–97) himself. His long poem *Howl* (1956)—of which the first section and part of the third were drafted in one day in August 1955, in San Francisco, the rest following shortly after—is indeed a rush of language, as its title suggests. It is an outcry against a system that turns individuals into abstractions, an outcry against a world in which parents turn their children over to the ancient god Moloch (a figure standing for American cul-

FIGURE 23.25 Frank Gehry, Gehry house, Santa Monica, 1977–78. Gehry's house represents the consciously assembled style of past and present elements that has come to distinguish what is known as postmodern architecture.

Then & Now

THE MOVIES PAST AND PRESENT

In the early twentieth century, the first films made were silent. The characters' speech was not heard; instead, music accompanied the action. Among the most important of early filmmakers was David Ward Griffith (1875–1948). Like the Russian director Sergei Eisenstein, Griffith believed that editing held the key to cinematography. In 1915, Griffith produced his first full-length film, *The Birth of a Nation*, which offered a romanticized view of the antebellum South and the struggle of white Southerners to survive the devastating effects of the Civil War. Griffith employed a full range of cinematic techniques to create suspense and human interest, including close-ups, cross-cuts, tracking, and panoramic shots, along with scenes of fast-paced suspenseful action, including just-in-time rescues.

Another master filmmaker and actor of the silent era was Charlie Chaplin (1889–1977). Chaplin became famous for the Tramp figure, who with his bowler hat, baggy pants, floppy shoes, and cane, was the supreme social outsider. In *The Tramp*, Chaplin's character saves a beautiful woman and her father from danger. But instead of being rewarded by them, he is ousted when her handsome boyfriend returns. The film ends with Chaplin's signature conclusion: The Tramp, clearly disappointed, returning to the road, walking slowly, his back to the camera, then jumping up and clicking his heels together before walking briskly away.

The silent film Chaplin wished to be remembered for was *The Gold Rush* (1925). In its most famous scene, Chaplin's Tramp character is starving and cooks his shoe, roasting and carving it as if it were a delectable piece of meat, and sucking the nails in its sole as if they were small chicken bones. He even twirls the shoelaces like spaghetti. *The Gold Rush* presents a social view that both celebrates and criticizes money and material success, suggesting that the Tramp continues to desire the very material possessions that have corrupted others.

Like the great films of the silent era, the movies of today continue to use sophisticated cinematic techniques to tell stories, portray human relationships, and offer perspectives on social issues. Like the silent films of Griffith and Chaplin, today's movies are designed to entertain audiences and to make money. Like the older films, those of today provide opportunities for audiences to escape into imagined worlds, such as the fantasy world of the *Lord of the Rings* movies. And like older films, today's connect with viewers' everyday experience to stimulate laughter, arouse emotion, awaken moral sensibility, and prompt reflection.

Other connections between the films of the past and those of the present involve their emphasis on star actors and celebrity directors, whose association with a film guarantee high production costs, large marketing campaigns, extensive distribution, and a variety of merchandising tie-ins.

FIGURE 23.26   Axonometric drawing of the Gehry house.

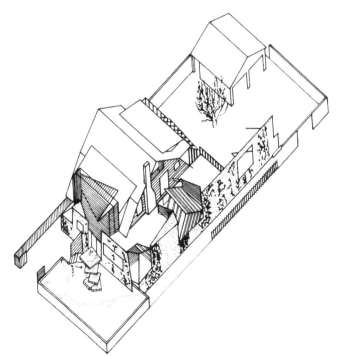

ture as a whole), who consumes them. Dedicated to Carl Solomon, a patient in a mental hospital in New York—and in Ginsberg's mind, a sort of political prisoner—the poem is a celebration of madness. Madness, for Ginsberg, is a sign of salvation, a sign of rebellion against the all-consuming American Moloch. By rejecting reason, and accepting the innate rhythms of the body itself, *Howl* seeks to transcend the constrictions of civilization.

THE POPULARIZATION OF CLASSICAL MUSIC

The Boston Pops.   In the 1950s and 1960s, in a culture defined by the consumer, music too responded to the demands of a popular audience. The Boston Pops Orchestra, led by Arthur Fiedler (1894–1979), became a national institution, famous for its concerts of folk tunes, marches such as John Philip Sousa's "Stars and Stripes Forever," and classical hits such as George Gershwin's *Rhapsody in Blue*. Bridging the gap between popular song and classical repertoire, the pops served as "the door through which young people enter into the magic domain of musical comprehension," as one critic put it.

Critical Thinking

THE POPULARITY OF THE BEATLES

During the 1960s, a rock group from Britain took that country and then the United States by storm. The Beatles began their musical journey in Liverpool, a working class city, playing locally there before receiving acclaim in London and throughout England. The Beatles included four musicians, the drummer Ringo Starr, the accomplished guitarist George Harrison, and the lead singers and guitarists Paul McCartney and John Lennon, who also wrote most of the group's songs. Each of the four had a distinct personality and an individual musical identity, yet they blended into a cohesive and wonderfully identifiable group identity unlike any before in the realm of pop/rock music.

But what was it that made the Beatles the phenomenon they became? What elements combined to make them the premier pop combo of their generation not only in England and the United States, but beyond? To what extent was it the personas they created and purveyed? To what extent was it their musicianship, their originality, and their unique sound? To what extent was their popularity attributable to the musical innovations they introduced, such as the "concept album," in which all the songs on a disk were related to an overarching topical theme? To what extent was their success a function of the times in which they rose to fame—an era when teenage girls went wild over young rock stars? And why is it that the Beatles continue to remain popular today—in Britain, the United States, and Europe?

Musical Theater   Like opera in the nineteenth century, musical theater became a popular form in the mid twentieth century. Despite the new tonalities, experimentation with rhythms and forms, and a dissonant harmony expressing the "age of anxiety" in classical composition, the music-listening public gravitated to this lighter type of musical entertainment. Unlike opera, not all words are sung in musical theater; music is interspersed between spoken dialogue. The mood of musicals is usually uplifting and the songs singable and memorable.

During the early part of the century, Victor Herbert and George M. Cohan wrote musicals about the war to entertain a popular audience. By the end of World War II, Richard Rodgers and Oscar Hammerstein had captivated audiences with *Carousel* and *Oklahoma*. By the early 1950s, Broadway had become the center of popular theatrical music in America. With the production of *West Side Story* by Leonard Bernstein in the late 1950s (see description next) the musical had matured to more complex harmonies and rhythms with libretti that were more psychological and darker than before.

Leonard Bernstein.   Successful at both popularizing classical music and classicizing popular music, Leonard Bernstein (1918–90) was a composer, conductor, pianist, and mentor. His lecture demonstrations with the New York Philharmonic Orchestra introduced a generation of children to the world of classical music and were later published as the *Young People's Guide to the Orchestra*.

Bernstein's genius for composing popular and classical music sets him apart. He is best known for his works for the musical theater: *Candide* (1956) and, especially, *West Side Story* (1957), a version of *Romeo and Juliet*, in a contemporary setting with intercultural tensions. Bernstein transforms Shakespeare's warring Capulet and Montague families into two rival gangs from New York City's Spanish Harlem, the Jets and the Hispanic Sharks. Like Tchaikovsky, whose *Romeo and Juliet Fantasy Overture* was also inspired by Shakespeare's play, Bernstein writes music that is both lyrical and dramatic. Songs like "Maria," a lyrical love song, intermingle with Latin-inspired pieces such as "America" and "Tonight," set in quasi-operatic style for four voices.

Andrew Lloyd Weber.   One of the most successful of contemporary composers for the musical theater has been Andrew Lloyd Weber (b. 1948), who is responsible for many hit shows produced in England and the United States. Among them are *Joseph and His Amazing Technicolor Dreamcoat* (1968), based on the story of Joseph and his brothers in the biblical book of Genesis; *Jesus Christ Superstar* (1970), a rock opera based on the last seven days of Jesus's life; *Evita* (1976), based on the life of Eva Peron, wife of an Argentinian dictator; *Cats* (1981), based on poetry by T. S. Eliot; and *Phantom of the Opera* (1986), based on a 1911 French novel by Gaston Leroux. Half of his sixteen musicals have been made into films, including *Cats, Evita,* and *Phantom of the Opera.* Translated into nearly a dozen languages, *Cats* has played in more than twenty countries and over 250 cities, and *Phantom* has been seen by more than eighty million people in over two dozen countries, recently surpassing *Cats* in number of performances.

Songs from his musicals have become famous worldwide, especially "Memory," from *Cats*, "The Music of the Night," from *Phantom of the Opera*, and "Don't Cry for Me, Argentina," from *Evita*. He also has the distinction of having been knighted by the Queen of England, and of having composed a *Requiem* mass, a classical work, one of whose songs, "Pie Jesu," became a popular success.

LATE MODERN MUSIC

Music in the late twentieth century was influenced by the thinking of John Cage and others, who believed experimentation was the key to finding a "new voice." While elite groups tended to follow and promoted this avant-garde music, the general pubblic rejected much of this experimentation.

Returning to tonal composition, composers such as Philip Glass and Steven Reich simplified their sound by minimalizing melody, rhythm, and form. Played in simple sequences with much repetition most minimalistic music is written for the synthesizer, a machine that can replicate the tones of almost all instruments. Blending sounds of Western and Eastern music traditions, Glass's music draws the listener into a soothing state and opens the mind at a meditative level. Phillip Glass has also produced operas such as *Einstein on the Beach* and *Akhenaten*, and popular music for theater, dance, and movies.

ROCK AND ROLL

Sometimes rock and roll music seems to be the very center of American culture. With roots in African-American rhythm and blues, rock music began as a separate form in the 1950s and has evolved into a wide variety of subtypes. The early rock of Elvis Presley and Chuck Berry appealed to the yearnings of the American teen. With the 1960s British bands such as the Beatles, rock music began to have international stature. Folk rock, and later psychedelic rock, experimented with timbres and lyrics to make antiestablishment political statements following the mood of the country. Jazz and Latin American music influenced dance music of the 1970s as well as reggae, punk rock, and rhythm and blues. The "selling of America" via advances in audiovisual technology led to a worldwide explosion on the pop rock scene in the 1980s with the advent of CDs and MTV.

Alternative rock bands rebelled against society with music that explored social and sexual taboos, and subcultures of heavy metal, rap, and world music gained popularity in the 1990s rock scene.

Cultural Impact

The social developments and cultural impulses that emerged at the beginning of the century continued. Automobiles, developed at the start of the century, fundamentally changed transportation, and the assembly line on which they were built revolutionized the organization of work, warfare, and consumption. Cinema, a development of photography emerged early in the century, and continued to be refined by improvements in technology. Early silent films gave way to talkies; black-and-white films were superseded by those in color; and today computer animated backgrounds and characters replace real places and actors; often, animated and real materials are combined side by side.

In music and art no single dominant style or trend has dominated. Later modernism has expanded the approaches of early modernism. Contemporary artists, in all media, benefit from the broadening of perspective and the artistic possibilities opened up by the modernists.

One legacy of the collaborations between composers and dancers working together in ballet and film was the Broadway musical, a distinctively American form of entertainment. Musicals, along with films, provide a staple of contemporary entertainment, with such long-running shows as *Cats*, *Les Miserables*, *The Phantom of the Opera*, *Oklahoma*, *Beauty and the Beast*, and *The Lion King* on stages in the United States and around the world.

KEY TERMS

existentialism
abstract expressionism
action painting

color field
oral contraceptive
mobiles

assemblage
Pop Art
Happening

minimalism
Op Art
Beat

WWW.WEBSITES FOR FURTHER STUDY

http://www.tameri.com/csw/exist/
(An excellent site on existentialism with all the major philosophers and many links.)

http://www.bauhaus.de/english/bauhaus1919/architektur/
(In 1919, the Bauhaus manifesto proclaims that the ultimate aim of all creative activity is a building.)

http://www.witcombe.sbc.edu/ARTH ILinks.html
(Art history resources on the Web by Chris Witcombe.)

READINGS

JEAN-PAUL SARTRE

from *Existentialism and Humanism*

In the following essay, Sartre raises questions about what it means to be human. His advocacy of existentialism as the quintessential way to express one's humanity highlights the necessity for human beings to be responsible for their choices and their actions. This essay is largely a response to a series of criticisms leveled against Sartre's version of existentialism, and accordingly Sartre defines what he means by key terms, including "existentialism" itself, and distinguishes himself from others who use the existential label differently. He also explains what he means by the subjectivity of human experience, which is a central tenet of Sartre's philosophy.

It is to various reproaches that I shall endeavor to reply today; that is why I have entitled this brief exposition, *Existentialism and Humanism*. Many may be surprised at the mention of humanism in this connection, but we shall try to see in what sense we understand it. In any case, we can begin by saying that existentialism, in our sense of the word, is a doctrine that does render human life possible; a doctrine, also, which affirms that every truth and every action imply both an environment and a human subjectivity. The essential charge laid against us is, of course, that of overemphasis upon the evil side of human life. I have lately been told of a lady who, whenever she lets slip a vulgar expression in a moment of nervousness, excuses herself by exclaiming, "I believe I am becoming an existentialist." So it appears that ugliness is being identified with existentialism. Those who appeal to the wisdom of the people—which is a sad wisdom—find ours sadder still. Indeed their excessive protests make me suspect that what is annoying them is not so much our pessimism, but, much more likely, our optimism. For at bottom, what is alarming in the doctrine that I am about to try to explain to you is—is it not? that it confronts man with a possibility of choice. To verify this, let us review the whole question upon the strictly philosophic level. What, then, is this that we call existentialism?

Most of those who are making use of this word would be highly confused if required to explain its meaning. For since it has become fashionable, people cheerfully declare that this musician or that painter is "existentialist." A columnist in Clartes signs himself "The Existentialist," and, indeed, the word is now so loosely applied to so many things that it no longer means anything at all. It would appear that, for the lack of any novel doctrine such as that of surrealism, all those who are eager to join in the latest scandal or movement now seize upon this philosophy in which, however, they can find nothing to their purpose. For in truth this is of all teachings the least scandalous and the most austere; it is intended strictly for experts and philosophers. All the same, it can easily be defined.

The question is only complicated because there are two kinds of existentialists. There are, on the one hand, the Christian existentialists and on the other hand the existential atheists, among whom I place myself. What they have in common is simply the fact that they believe that existence comes before essence—or, if you will, that we must begin from the subjective.

What do we mean by saying that existence precedes essence? We mean that man first of all exists, encounters himself, surges up in the world—and defines himself afterwards. If man is as the existentialist sees him, as not definable, it is because to begin with he is nothing. He will not be anything until later, and then he will be what he makes of himself. Thus, there is no human nature, because there is no God to have a conception of it. Man simply is. Not that he is simply what he conceives himself to be, but he is what he wills, and as he conceives himself after already existing—as he wills to be after that leap towards existence. Man is nothing else but that which he makes of himself. That is the first principle of existentialism. And this is what people call its "subjectivity," using the word as a reproach against us. But what do we mean to say by this, but that man is of a greater dignity than a stone or a table? For we mean to say that man primarily exists—that man is, before all else, something which propels itself towards a future and is aware that it is doing so. Man is, indeed, a project which possesses a subjective life, instead of being a kind of moss, or a fungus, or a cauliflower. Before that projection of the self nothing exists; not even in the heaven of intelligence; man will only attain existence when he is what he proposes to be. Thus, the first effort of existentialism is that it puts every man in possession of himself as he is, and places the entire responsibility for his existence squarely upon his own shoulders. And when we say that man is responsible for himself, we do not mean that he is responsible only for his own individuality, but that he is responsible for all men.

The word "subjective" is to be understood in two senses, and our adversaries play upon only one of them. Subjectivism means, on the one hand, the freedom of the individual subject and, on the other, that man cannot pass beyond human subjectivity. It is the latter which is the deeper meaning of existentialism. When we say that man chooses himself, we do mean that everyone of us must choose himself; but by that we also mean that in choosing for himself he chooses for all men. For in effect, of all the actions a man may take in order to create himself as he wills to be, there is not one which is not creative, at the same time, of an image of man such as he believes he ought to be. To choose between this or that is at the same time to affirm the value of that which is chosen, for we are unable ever to choose the worse. What we choose is always the better; and nothing can be better for us unless it is better for all. If moreover, existence precedes essence and we will to exist at the same time as we fashion our image, that image is valid for all and for the entire epoch in which we find ourselves. Our responsibility is thus much greater than we had supposed, for it concerns mankind as a whole. I am thus responsible for myself and for all men, and I am creating a certain image of man as I would have him be. "In fashioning myself I fashion man."

This may enable us to understand what is meant by such terms—perhaps a little grandiloquent—as anguish, abandonment, and despair. As you will soon see, it is very simple. First, what do we mean by anguish? The existentialist frankly states that man is in anguish. His meaning is as follows—When a man commits himself to anything, fully realizing that he is not only choosing what he will be, but is thereby at the same time a legislator deciding for the whole of mankind—in such a moment a man cannot escape from the sense of complete and profound responsibility. There are many, indeed, who show no such anxiety. But we affirm that they are merely disguising their anguish or are in flight from it. Certainly, many people think that in what they are doing they commit no one but themselves to anything; and if you ask them, "What would happen if everyone did so?" they shrug their shoulders and reply, "Everyone does not do so." But in truth, one ought always to ask oneself what would happen if everyone did as one is doing; nor can one escape from that disturbing thought except by a kind of self-deception. The man who lies in self-excuse, by saying "Everyone will not do it" must be ill at ease in his conscience for the act of lying implies the universal value which it denies. By its very disguise his anguish reveals itself. This is the anguish that Kierkegaard called "the anguish of Abraham." You know the story: An angel commanded Abraham to sacrifice his son: and obedience was obligatory, if it really was an angel who had appeared and said "Thou, Abraham, shalt sacrifice thy son." But anyone in such a case would wonder, first, whether it was indeed an angel and secondly, whether I am really Abraham. Where are the proofs?

I shall never find any proof whatever; there will be no sign to convince me of it. If a voice speaks to me, it is still I myself who must decide whether the voice is or is not that of an angel. If I regard a certain course of action as good, it is only I who choose to say that it is good and not bad. There is nothing to show that I am Abraham; nevertheless, I also am obliged at every instant to perform actions which are examples. Everything happens to every man as though the whole human race had its eyes fixed upon what he is doing and regulated its conduct accordingly. So every man ought to say. "Am I really a man who has the right to act in such a manner that humanity regulates itself by what I do?" If a man does not say that, he is dissembling his anguish. Clearly, the anguish with which we are concerned here is not one that could lead to quietism or inaction. It is anguish pure and simple, of the kind well known to all those who have borne responsibilities. Far from being a screen which could separate us from action, it is condition of action itself.

And when we speak of "abandonment"—a favourite word of Heidegger—we only mean to say that God does not exist, and that it is necessary to draw the consequences of his absence right to the end. The existentialist is strongly opposed to a certain type of secular moralism which seeks to suppress God at the least possible expense. Toward 1880, when the French professors endeavored to formulate a secular morality, they said something like this—God is a useless and costly hypothesis, so we will do without it. However, if we are to have morality, a society, and a law-abiding world, it is essential that certain values should be taken seriously; they must have an *a priori* existence ascribed to them. It must be considered obligatory *a priori* to be honest, not to lie, not to beat one's wife, to bring up children, and so forth; so we are going to do a little work on this subject, which will enable us to show that these values exist all the same, inscribed in an intelligible heaven although, of course, there is no God. In other words—and this is, I believe, the purport of all we in France call radicalism—nothing will be changed if God does not exist; we shall rediscover the same norms of honesty, progress, and humanity, and we shall have disposed of God as an out-of-date hypothesis which will die away quietly of itself.

The existentialist, on the contrary, finds it extremely embarrassing that God does not exist, for there disappears with Him all possibility of finding values in an intelligible heaven. There can no longer be any good *a priori* since there is no infinite and perfect consciousness to think it. It is nowhere written that "the good" exists, that one must be honest or must not lie, since we are now upon the plane where there are only men. Dostoevski once wrote, "If God did not exist, everything would be permitted"; and that, for existentialism, is the starting point. Everything is indeed permitted if God does not exist, and man is in consequence forlorn, for he cannot find anything to depend upon either within or outside himself. He discovers forthwith that he is without excuse. For if indeed existence precedes essence, one will never be able to explain one's action by reference to a given and specific human nature; in other words, there is no determinism—man is free, man is freedom.

You are free, therefore choose—that is to say, invent. No rule of general morality can show you what you ought to do; no signs are vouchsafed in this world. That is what "abandonment" implies, that we ourselves decide our being. And with this abandonment goes anguish.

As for "despair" the meaning of this expression is extremely simple. It merely means that we limit ourselves to a reliance upon that which is within our wills, or within the sum of the probabilities which render our action feasible. Whenever one wills anything, there are always these elements of probability. If I am counting upon a visit from a friend, who may be coming by train or by tram, I presuppose that the train will arrive at the appointed time, or that the tram will not be derailed. I remain in the realm of possibilities; but one does not rely upon any possibilities beyond those that are strictly concerned in one's action, beyond the point at which the possibilities under consideration cease to affect my action. I ought to disinterest myself. For there is no God and no prevenient design which can adapt the world and all its possibilities to my will. When Descartes said, "Conquer yourself rather than the world," what he meant was, at bottom, the same—that we should act without hope.

In the light of all this, what people reproach us with is not, after all, our pessimism but the sternness of our optimism. If people condemn our works of fiction, in which we describe characters that are base, weak, cowardly, and sometimes even frankly evil, it is not only because those characters are base, weak, cowardly or evil. For suppose that, like Zola, we showed that the behaviour of these characters was caused by their heredity, or by the action of their environment upon them, or by determining factors, psychic or organic. People would be reassured, they would say, "You see, that is what we are like, no one can do anything about it." But the existentialist, when he portrays a coward, shows him as responsible for his cowardice. The existentialist says that the coward makes himself cowardly, the hero makes himself heroic; and that there is always a possibility for the coward to give up cowardice and for the hero to stop being a hero. What counts is the total commitment, and it is not by a particular case or particular action that you are committed altogether.

We have now, I think, dealt with a certain number of the reproaches against existentialism. You have seen that it cannot be regarded as a philosophy of quietism since it defines man by his action; nor as a pessimistic description of man, for no doctrine is more optimistic, the destiny of man is placed within himself. Nor is it an attempt to discourage man from action since it tells him that there is no hope except in his action, and that the one thing which permits him to have life is the deed. Upon this level therefore, what we are considering is an ethic of action and self-commitment.

Man makes himself; he is not found ready-made; he makes himself by the choice of his morality, and he cannot but choose a morality, such is the pressure of circumstances upon him. We define man only in relation to his commitments; it is therefore absurd to reproach us for irresponsibility in our choice. And moreover, to say that we invent values means neither more nor less than this; that there is no sense in life *a priori*. Life is nothing until it is lived; but it is yours to make sense of, and the value of it is nothing else but the sense that you choose. Therefore, you can see that there is a possibility of creating a human community. I have been reproached for suggesting that existentialism is a form of humanism.

Man is all the time outside of himself; it is in projecting and losing himself beyond himself that he makes man to exist; and, on the other hand, it is by pursuing transcendent aims that he himself is able to exist. Since man is thus self-surpassing, and can grasp objects only in relation to his self-surpassing, he is himself the heart and centre of his transcendence. There is no other universe except the human universe, the universe of subjectivity. This relation of transcendence as constitutive of man (not in the sense that God is transcendent, but in the sense of self-surpassing) with subjectivity (in such a sense that man is not shut up in himself but forever present in a human universe)—it is this that we call existential humanism. This is humanism, because we remind man that there is no legislator but himself; that he himself, thus abandoned, must decide for himself; also because we show that it is not by turning back upon himself, but always by seeking, beyond himself, an aim which is one of liberation or of some particular realization, that man can realize himself as truly human.

ALLEN GINSBERG

Howl

A descendant of Walt Whitman's Leaves of Grass, *Allen Ginsberg's* Howl *revitalized the oral tradition in American poetry by incorporating the rhythms of everyday American speech into the poem's long lines. In fact, Ginsberg's readings, complete with harmonium and finger cymbal accompaniments, Buddhist mantras, and audience response, soon transformed the poetry reading from formal recital to communal performance.*

I

I saw the best minds of my generation destroyed by
    madness, starving hysterical naked,
dragging themselves through the negro streets at dawn
    looking for an angry fix,
angelheaded hipsters burning for the ancient heavenly
    connection to the starry dynamo in the
    machinery of night,
who poverty and tatters and hollow-eyed and high sat
    up smoking in the supernatural darkness of cold-
    water flats floating across the tops of cities
    contemplating jazz,

who bared their brains to Heaven under the El° and
    saw Mohammedan angels staggering on tenement
    roofs illuminated,   5
who passed through universities with radiant cool eyes
    hallucinating Arkansas and Blake-light tragedy
    among the scholars of war.
who were expelled from the academies for crazy &
    publishing obscene odes on the windows of the skull,
who cowered in unshaven rooms in underwear, burning
    their money, in wastebaskets and listening to the
    Terror through the wall,
who got busted in their pubic beards returning through
    Laredo with a belt of marijuana for New York,
who ate fire in paint hotels or drank turpentine in
    Paradise Alley,° death, or purgatoried their torsos
    night after night   10
with dreams, with drugs, with waking nightmares,
    alcohol and cock and endless balls,
incomparable blind streets of shuddering cloud and
    lightning in the mind leaping toward poles of
    Canada & Paterson, illuminating all the motionless
    world of Time between,
Peyote solidities of halls, backyard green tree cemetery
    dawns, wine drunkenness over the rooftops,
    storefront boroughs of teahead joyride neon blinking
    traffic light, sun and moon and tree vibrations in the
    roaring winter dusks of Brooklyn, ashcan rantings
    and kind king light of mind,
who chained themselves to subways for the endless ride
    from Battery to holy Bronx on benzedrine until the
    noise of wheels and children brought them down
    shuddering mouth-wracked and battered bleak of
    brain all drained of brilliance in the drear light of
    Zoo,
who sank all night in submarine light of Bickford's°
    floated out and sat through the stale beer afternoon
    in desolate Fugazzi's,° listening to the crack of doom
    on the hydrogen jukebox,   15
who talked continuously seventy hours from park to pad
    to bar to Bellevue to museum to the Brooklyn
    Bridge,
a lost battalion of platonic conversationalists jumping
    down the stoops off fire escapes off windowsills off
    Empire State out of the moon,
yacketayakking screaming vomiting whispering facts
    and memories and anecdotes and eyeball kicks and
    shocks of hospitals and jails and wars,
whole intellects disgorged in total recall for seven days
    and nights with brilliant eyes, meat for the
    Synagogue cast on the pavement,
who vanished into nowhere Zen° New Jersey leaving a
    trail of ambiguous picture postcards of Atlantic City
    Hall,   20

---

[5] *El:* Elevated railway
[10] *Paradise Alley:* This was in New York's Lower East Side and the setting for one of Beat writer Jack Kerouac's novels.
[15] *Bickford's:* A café where Ginsberg once worked. *Fugazzi's:* A bar in Greenwich Village.
[20] *Zen:* Zen Buddhism, an Eastern philosophy of great importance to the Beats in the 1950s.

suffering Eastern sweats and Tangerian bonegrindings
    and migraines of China under junkwithdrawal
    in Newark's bleak furnished room,
who wandered around and around at midnight in the
    railroad yard wondering where to go, and went,
    leaving no broken hearts,
who lit cigarettes in boxcars boxcars boxcars racketing
    through snow toward lonesome farms in
    grandfather night,
who studied Plotinus Poe St. John of the Cross
    telepathy and bop kabbalah° because the cosmos
    instinctively vibrated at their feet in Kansas,
    who loned it through the streets of Idaho seeking
    visionary indian angels who were visionary indian
    angels,   *25*
who thought they were only mad when Baltimore
    gleamed in supernatural ecstasy,
who jumped in limousines with the Chinaman of
    Oklahoma on the impulse of winter midnight
    streetlight smalltown rain,
who lounged hungry and lonesome through Houston
    seeking jazz or sex or soup, and followed the brilliant
    Spaniard to converse about America and Eternity, a
    hopeless task, and so took ship to Africa,
who disappeared into the volcanoes of Mexico leaving
    behind nothing but the shadow of dungarees and the
    lava and ash of poetry scattered in fireplace Chicago,
who reappeared on the West Coast investigating the
    FBI in beards and shorts with big pacifist eyes sexy
    in their dark skin passing out incomprehensible
    leaflets,   *30*
who burned cigarette holes in their arms protesting the
    narcotic tobacco haze of Capitalism,
who distributed Supercommunist pamphlets in Union
    Square weeping and undressing while the sirens of
    Los Alamos wailed them down, and wailed down
    Wall, and the Staten Island ferry also wailed,
who broke down crying in white gymnasiums naked
    and trembling before the machinery of other
    skeletons,
who bit detectives in the neck and shrieked with delight
    in policecars for committing no crime but their own
    wild cooking pederasty and intoxication,
who howled on their knees in the subway and were
    dragged off the roof waving genitals and
    manuscripts,   *35*
who let themselves be fucked in the ass by saintly
    motorcyclists, and screamed with joy,
who blew and were blown by those human seraphim,
    the sailors, caresses of Atlantic and Caribbean love,
who balled in the morning in the evenings in
    rosegardens and the grass of public parks and
    cemeteries scattering their semen freely to
    whomever come who may,
who hiccuped endlessly trying to giggle but wound up
    with a sob behind a partition in a Turkish Bath
    when
    the blond & naked angel came to pierce them with
    a sword,

who lost their loveboys to the three old shrews of fate
    the one eyed shrew of the heterosexual dollar the
    one eyed shrew that winks out of the womb and the
    one eyed shrew that does nothing but sit on her ass
    and snip the intellectual golden threads of the
    craftsman's loom,   *40*
who copulated ecstatic and insatiate with a bottle of
    beer a sweetheart a package of cigarettes a candle
    and fell off the bed, and continued along the floor
    and down the hall and ended fainting on the wall
    with a vision of ultimate cunt and come eluding the
    last gyzym of consciousness,
who sweetened the snatches of a million girls trembling
    in the sunset and were red eyed in the morning but
    prepared to sweeten the snatch of the sunrise,
    flashing buttocks under barns and naked in the lake,
who went out whoring through Colorado in myriad
    stolen nightcars, N.C.,° secret hero of these poems,
    cocksman and Adonis of Denver—joy to the
        memory
    of his innumerable lays of girls in empty lots & diner
    backyards, moviehouses' rickety rows, on
    mountaintops in caves or with gaunt waitresses in
    familiar roadside lonely petticoat upliftings &
    especially secret gas-station solipsisms of johns, &
    hometown alleys too,
who faded out in vast sordid movies, were shifted in
    dreams, woke on a sudden Manhattan, and picked
    themselves up out of basements hungover with
    heartless Tokay and horrors of Third Avenue iron
    dreams & stumbled to unemployment offices,
who walked all night with their shoes full of blood on
    the snowbank docks waiting for a door in the East
    River to open to a room full of steamheat and
        opium,   *45*
who created great suicidal dramas on the apartment
    cliff-banks of the Hudson under the wartime blue
    floodlight of the moon & their heads shall be
    crowned with laurel in oblivion,
who ate the lamb stew of the imagination or digested
    the crab at the muddy bottom of the rivers of
    Bowery,°
who wept at the romance of the streets with their
    pushcarts full of onions and bad music,
who sat in boxes breathing in the darkness under the
    bridge, and rose up to build harpsichords in their
    lofts,
who coughed on the sixth floor of Harlem crowned
    with flame under the tubercular sky surrounded by
    orange crates of theology,   *50*
who scribbled all night rocking and rolling over lofty
    incantations which in the yellow morning were
    stanzas of gibberish,
who cooked rotten animals lung heart feet tail borsht &
    tortillas dreaming of the pure vegetable kingdom,
who plunged themselves under meat trucks looking for
    an egg,

---

[24]*Plotinus . . . kabbalah:* The names of people and texts that are traditionally associated with mystical religious experience.

[43]*N.C.:* Neal Cassady (1926–68), a Beat writer who traveled with Jack
Kerouac and was memorialized as the character Dean Morioarty in Kerouac's novel *On the Road* (1957).
[47]*Bowery:* A district known in New York for its alcoholics and down-and-outs.

who threw their watches off the roof to cast their ballot
for Eternity outside of Time, & alarm clocks fell on
their heads every day for the next decade,

who cut their wrists three times successively
unsuccessfully, gave up and were forced to open
antique stores where they thought they were
growing old and cried,   55

who were burned alive in their innocent flannel suits on
Madison Avenue amid blasts of leaden verse & the
tanked-up clatter of the iron regiments of fashion &
the nitroglycerine shrieks of the fairies of advertising
& the mustard gas of sinister intelligent editors, or
were run down by the drunken taxicabs of Absolute
Reality,

who jumped off the Brooklyn Bridge this actually
happened and walked away unknown and forgotten
into the ghostly daze of Chinatown soup alleyways &
firetrucks, not even one free beer,

who sang out of their windows in despair, fell out of the
subway window, jumped in the filthy Passaic, leaped
on negroes, cried all over the street, danced on
broken wineglasses barefoot smashed phonograph
records of nostalgic European 1930s German jazz
finished the whiskey and threw up groaning into the
bloody toilet, moans in their ears and the blast of
colossal steamwhistles,

who barreled down the highways of the past journeying
to each other's hotrod—Golgotha jail—solitude
watch or Birmingham jazz incarnation,

who drove crosscountry seventytwo hours to find out if
I had a vision or you had a vision or he had a vision
to find out Eternity,   60

who journeyed to Denver, who died in Denver, who
came back to Denver & waited in vain, who watched
over Denver & brooded & loned in Denver and
finally went away to find out the Time & now
Denver is lonesome for her heroes,

who fell on their knees in hopeless cathedrals praying
for each other's salvation and light and breasts, until
the soul illuminated its hair for a second,

who crashed through their minds in jail waiting for
impossible criminals with golden heads and the
charm of reality in their hearts who sang sweet blues
to Alcatraz,

who retired to Mexico to cultivate a habit, or Rocky
Mount to tender Buddha or Tangiers to boys or
Southern Pacific to the black locomotive or Harvard
to Narcissus to Woodlawn to the daisychain or
grave,

who demanded sanity trials accusing the radio of
hypnotism & were left with their insanity & their
hands & a hung jury,   65

who threw potato salad at CCNY lecturers on Dadaism
and subsequently presented themselves on the
granite steps of the madhouse with shaven heads and
harlequin speech of suicide, demanding
instantaneous lobotomy,

and who were given instead the concrete void of insulin
Metrazol electricity hydrotherapy psychotherapy
occupational therapy pingpong & amnesia,

who in humorless protest overturned only one symbolic
pingpong table, resting briefly in catatonia,

returning years later truly bald except for a wig of
blood, and tears and fingers, to the visible madman
doom of the wards of the madtowns of the East,

Pilgrim° State's Rockland's and Greystone's foetid halls,   70
bickering with the echoes of the soul, rocking and
rolling in the midnight solitude—bench dolmen—
realms of love, dream of life a nightmare, bodies
turned to stone as heavy as the moon,

with mother finally ******° and the last fantastic book
flung out of the tenement window, and the last door
closed at 4 A.M. and the last telephone slammed at
the wall in reply and the last furnished room emptied
down to the last piece of mental furniture, a yellow
paper rose twisted on a wire hanger in the closet,
and even that imaginary nothing but a hopeful little
bit of hallucination—

ah, Carl, while you are not safe I am not safe, and now
you're really in the total animal soup of time—

and who therefore ran through the icy streets obsessed
with a sudden flash of the alchemy of the use of the
ellipse the catalog the meter & the vibrating plane,

who dreamt and made incarnate gaps in Time & Space
through images juxtaposed, and trapped the
archangel of the soul between 2 visual images and
joined the elemental verbs and set the noun and dash
of consciousness together jumping with sensation of
Pater Omnipotens Aeterna Deus°

to recreate the syntax and measure of poor human prose
and stand before you speechless and intelligent and
shaking with shame, rejected yet confessing out the
soul to conform to the rhythm of thought in his
naked and endless head,   75

the madman bum and angel beat in Time, unknown,
yet putting down here what might be left to say in
time come after death,

and rose reincarnate in the ghostly clothes of jazz in the
goldhorn shadow of the band and blew the suffering
of America's naked mind for love into an eli eli
lamma lamma sabacthani° saxophone cry that
shivered the cities down to the last radio

with the absolute heart of the poem of life butchered
out of their own bodies good to eat a thousand years.

EUGENE IONESCO

The Gap

Eugene Ionesco (1912–94), a Rumanian-born French dramatist, is best known for Rhinoceros, a play in the tradition of the Theater of the Absurd. In the following one-act play, The Gap, a professor; learns of a gap in his education. Even though he has earned numerous advanced diplomas, he is required to take an examination to complete his undergraduate degree. Ionesco uses irony and exaggeration to satirize the illogical rigidities of an absurd bureaucracy.

---

[70]*Pilgrim: . . . Greystone's:* The names of mental hospitals.
[71]****** : Ginsberg's mother Naomi was hospitalized for paranoia and died in 1956.
[74]*Pater Omnipoteus Aeterna Deus:* "Father omnipotent, eternal God."
[77]*eli eli lamma . . . sabacthani:* "My God, my God, why have you forsaken me?"—the words spoken by Christ on the cross.

THE FRIEND: I don't know what to say.

THE WIFE: I know.

THE FRIEND: I heard the news last night. I did not want to call you. At the same time I couldn't wait any longer. Please forgive me for coming so early with such terrible news.

THE WIFE: He didn't make it! How terrible! We were still hoping. . . .

THE FRIEND: It's hard. I know. He still had a chance. Not much of one. We had to expect it.

THE WIFE: I didn't expect it. He was always so successful. He could always manage somehow, at the last moment.

THE FRIEND: In that state of exhaustion. You shouldn't have let him!

THE WIFE: What can we do, what can we do! . . . How awful!

THE FRIEND: Come on, dear friend, be brave. That's life.

THE WIFE: I feel faint: I'm going to faint. (She falls in one of the armchairs.)

THE FRIEND   (holding her, gently slapping her cheeks and hands): I shouldn't have blurted it out like that. I'm sorry.

THE WIFE: No, you were right to do so. I had to find out somehow or other.

THE FRIEND: I should have prepared you, carefully.

THE WIFE: I've got to be strong. I can't help thinking of him, the wretched man. I hope they won't put it in the papers. Can we count on the journalists' discretion?

THE FRIEND: Close your door. Don't answer the telephone. It will still get around. You could go to the country. In a couple of months, when you are better, you'll come back, you'll go on with your life. People forget such things.

THE WIFE: People won't forget so fast. That's all they were waiting for. Some friends will feel sorry, but the others, the others. . . .

[*The academician comes in, fully dressed: uniform, chest covered with decorations, his sword on his side.*]

THE ACADEMICIAN: Up so early, my dear? (to the friend) You've come early too. What's happening? Do you have the final results?

THE WIFE: What a disgrace!

THE FRIEND: You mustn't crush him like this, dear friend. (to the academician) You have failed.

THE ACADEMICIAN: Are you quite sure?

THE FRIEND: You should never have tried to pass the baccalaureate examination.

THE ACADEMICIAN: They failed me. The rats! How dare they do this to me!

THE FRIEND: The marks were posted late in the evening.

THE ACADEMICIAN: Perhaps it was difficult to make them out in the dark. How could you read them?

THE FRIEND: They had set up spotlights.

THE ACADEMICIAN: They're doing everything to ruin me.

THE FRIEND: I passed by in the morning: the marks were still up.

THE ACADEMICIAN: You could have bribed the concierge into pulling them down.

THE FRIEND: That's exactly what I did. Unfortunately the police were there. Your name heads the list of those who failed. Everyone's standing in line to get a look. There's an awful crush.

THE ACADEMICIAN: Who's there? The parents of the candidates?

THE FRIEND: Not only they.

THE WIFE: All your rivals, all your colleagues must be there. All those you attacked in the press for ignorance: your undergraduates, your graduate students, all those you failed when you were chairman of the board of examiners.

THE ACADEMICIAN: I am discredited! But I won't let them. There must be some mistake.

THE FRIEND: I saw the examiners. I spoke with them. They gave me your marks. Zero in mathematics.

THE ACADEMICIAN: I had no scientific training.

THE FRIEND: Zero in Greek, zero in Latin.

THE WIFE   (to her husband): You, a humanist, the spokesman for humanism, the author of that famous treatise "The Defense of Poesy and Humanism."

THE ACADEMICIAN: I beg your pardon, but my book concerns itself with twentieth-century humanism: (to the friend) What about composition? What grade did I get in composition?

THE FRIEND: Nine hundred. You have nine hundred points.

THE ACADEMICIAN: That's perfect. My average must be all the way up.

THE FRIEND: Unfortunately not. They're marking on the basis of two thousand. The passing grade is one thousand.

THE ACADEMICIAN: They must have changed the regulations.

THE WIFE: They didn't change them just for you. You have a frightful persecution complex.

THE ACADEMICIAN: I tell you they changed them.

THE FRIEND: They went back to the old ones, back to the time of Napoleon.

THE ACADEMICIAN: Utterly outmoded. Besides, when did they make those changes? It isn't legal. I'm chairman of the Baccalaureate Commission of the Ministry of Public Education. They didn't consult me, and they cannot make any changes without my approval. I'm going to expose them. I'm going to bring government charges against them.

THE WIFE: Darling, you don't know what you're doing. You're in your dotage. Don't you recall handing in your resignation just before taking the examination so that no one could doubt the complete objectivity of the board of examiners?

THE ACADEMICIAN: I'll take it back.

THE WIFE: You should never have taken that test. I warned you. After all, it's not as if you needed it. But you have to collect all the honors, don't you? You're never satisfied. What did you need this diploma for? Now all is lost. You have your Doctorate, your Master's, your high school diploma, your elementary school certificate, and even the first part of the baccalaureate.

THE ACADEMICIAN: There was a gap.

THE WIFE: No one suspected it.

THE ACADEMICIAN: But *I* knew it. Others might have found out. I went to the office of the Registrar and asked for a transcript of my record. They said to me: "Certainly Professor, Mr. President, Your Excellency. . . ." Then they looked up my file, and the Chief Registrar came back looking embarrassed, most embarrassed indeed. He said: "There's something peculiar, very peculiar.

You have your Master's, certainly, but it's no longer valid." I asked him why, of course. He answered: "There's a gap behind your Master's. I don't know how it happened. You must have registered and been accepted at the University without having passed the second part of the baccalaureate examination."

THE FRIEND: And then?

THE WIFE: Your Master's degree is no longer valid?

THE ACADEMICIAN: No, not quite. It's suspended. "The duplicate you are asking for will be delivered to you upon completion of the baccalaureate. Of course you will pass the examination with no trouble." That's what I was told, so you see now that I had to take it.

THE FRIEND: Your husband, dear friend, wanted to fill the gap. He's a conscientious person.

THE WIFE: It's clear you don't know him as I do. That's not it at all. He wants fame, honors. He never had enough. What does one diploma more or less matter? No one notices them anyway, but he sneaks in at night, on tiptoe, into the living room, just to look at them, and count them.

THE ACADEMICIAN: What else can I do when I have insomnia?

THE FRIEND: The questions asked at the baccalaureate are usually known in advance. You were admirably situated to get this particular information. You could also have sent in a replacement to take the test for you. One of your students, perhaps. Or if you wanted to take the test without people realizing that you already knew the questions, you could have sent your maid to the black market, where one can buy them.

THE ACADEMICIAN: I don't understand how I could have failed in my composition. I filled three sheets of paper. I treated the subject fully, taking into account the historical background. I interpreted the situation accurately . . . at least plausibly. I didn't deserve a bad grade.

THE FRIEND: Do you recall the subject?

THE ACADEMICIAN: Hum . . . let's see . . .

THE FRIEND: He doesn't even remember what he discussed.

THE ACADEMICIAN: I do . . . wait . . . hum.

THE FRIEND: The subject to be treated was the following: "Discuss the influence of Renaissance painters on novelists of the Third Republic." I have here a photostatic copy of your examination paper. Here is what you wrote.

THE ACADEMICIAN: (grabbing the photostat and reading): "The trial of Benjamin: After Benjamin was tried and acquitted, the assessors holding a different opinion from that of the President murdered him, and condemned Benjamin to the suspension of his civic rights, imposing on him a fine of nine hundred francs. . . ."

THE FRIEND: That's where the nine hundred points come from.

THE ACADEMICIAN: "Benjamin appealed his case . . . Benjamin appealed his case." I can't make out the rest. I've always had bad handwriting. I ought to have taken a typewriter along with me.

THE WIFE: Horrible handwriting, scribbling and crossing out; ink spots didn't help you much.

THE ACADEMICIAN   (goes on with his reading after having retrieved the text his wife had pulled out of his hand): "Benjamin appealed his case. Flanked by policemen dressed in zouave uniforms . . . in zouave uniforms. . . ." It's getting dark. I can't see the rest. . . . I don't have my glasses.

THE WIFE: What you've written has nothing to do with the subject.

THE FRIEND: Your wife's quite right, friend. It has nothing to do with the subject.

THE ACADEMICIAN: Yes, it has. Indirectly.

THE FRIEND: Not even indirectly.

THE ACADEMICIAN: Perhaps I chose the second question.

THE FRIEND: There was only one.

THE ACADEMICIAN: Even if there was only that one, I treated another quite adequately. I went to the end of the story. I stressed the important points, explaining the motivations of the characters, highlighting their behavior. I explained the mystery, making it plain and clear. There was even a conclusion at the end. I can't make out the rest. (to the friend) Can you read it?

THE FRIEND: It's illegible. I don't have my glasses either.

THE WIFE   (taking the text): It's illegibile and I have excellent eyes. You pretended to write. Mere scribbling.

THE ACADEMICIAN: That's not true. I've even provided a conclusion. It's clearly marked here in heavy print: "Conclusion or sanction . . . Conclusion or sanction . . ." They can't get away with it. I'll have this examination rendered null, and void.

THE WIFE: Since you treated the wrong subject, and treated it badly, setting down only titles, and writing nothing in between, the mark you received is justified. You'd lose your case.

THE FRIEND: You'd most certainly lose. Drop it. Take a vacation.

THE ACADEMICIAN: You're always on the side of the Others.

THE WIFE: After all, these professors know what they're doing They haven't been granted their rank for nothing. They passed examinations, received serious training. They know the rules of composition.

THE ACADEMICIAN: Who was on the board of examiners?

THE FRIEND: For Mathematics, a movie star. For Greek, one of the Beatles. For Latin, the champion of the automobile race, and many others.

THE ACADEMICIAN: But these people aren't any more qualified than I am. And for composition?

THE FRIEND: A woman, a secretary in the editorial division of the review *Yesterday, the Day Before Yesterday, and Today.*

THE ACADEMICIAN: Now I know. This wretch gave me a poor grade out of spite because I never joined her political party. It's an act of vengeance. But I have ways and means of rendering the examination null and void. I'm going to call the President.

THE WIFE: Don't. You'll make yourself look even more ridiculous. (to the friend) Please try to restrain him. He listens to you more than to me. (the friend shrugs his shoulders, unable to cope with the situation. the wife turns to her husband, who has just lifted the receiver off the hook.) Don't call!

THE ACADEMICIAN   (on the telephone): Hello, John? It is I . . . What? . . . What did you say? . . . But, listen, my dear friend . . . but, listen to me . . . Hello! Hello! (Puts down the receiver.)

THE FRIEND: What did he say?

THE ACADEMICIAN: He said . . . He said. . . . "I don't want
to talk to you. My mummy won't let me make friends
with boys at the bottom of the class." Then he hung
up on me.

THE WIFE: You should have expected it. All is lost. How
could you do this to me? How could you do this to me?

THE ACADEMICIAN: Think of it! I lectured at the Sorbonne,
at Oxford, at American universities. Ten thousand theses have been written on my work; hundreds of critics
have analyzed it. I hold an *honoris causa* doctorate from
Amsterdam as well as a secret university Chair with the
Duchy of Luxembourg. I received the Nobel Prize
three times. The King of Sweden himself was amazed
by my erudition. A doctorate *honoris causa, honoris causa*
and I failed the baccalaureate examination!

THE WIFE: Everyone will laugh at us!

[*the academician takes off his sword and breaks it on his knee.*]

THE FRIEND   (picking up the two pieces): I wish to preserve these in memory of our ancient glory.

[*the academician meanwhile in a fit of rage is tearing down his
decorations, throwing them on the floor, and stepping on them.*]

THE WIFE   (trying to salvage the remains): Don't do this!
Don't! That's all we've got left.

WISLAWA SYMBORSKA

Selected Poems

*Wislawa Symborska was born in Poland in 1923, where she con-
tinues to live. Having worked as a poetry editor, columnist, and
translator, she is best known as a poet. She won the Nobel Prize for
Literature in 1996. Her poems are notable for their wit, playfulness, and intelligence.*

The End and the Beginning

After every war
someone has to tidy up.
Things won't pick
themselves up, after all.

Someone has to shove
the rubble to the roadsides
so the carts loaded with corpses
can get by.

Someone has to trudge
through sludge and ashes,
through the sofa springs,
the shards of glass,
the bloody rags.

Someone has to lug the post
to prop the wall,
someone has to glaze the window,
set the door in its frame.

No sound bites, no photo opportunities,
and it takes years.
All the cameras have gone
to other wars.

The bridges need to be rebuilt,
the railroad stations, too.

Shirtsleeves will be rolled
to shreds.

Someone, broom in hand,
still remembers how it was.
Someone else listens, nodding
his unshattered head.

But others are bound to be bustling nearby
who'll find all that
a little boring.

From time to time someone still must
dig up a rusted argument
from underneath a bush
and haul it off to the dump.

Those who knew
what this was all about
must make way for those
who know little.
And less than that.
And at last nothing less than nothing.

Someone has to *lie* there
in the grass that covers up
the causes and effects
with a cornstalk in his teeth,
gawking at clouds.

Nothing Twice

Nothing can ever happen twice.
In consequence, the sorry fact is
that we arrive here improvised
and leave without the chance to practice.

Even if there is no one dumber,
if you're the planet's biggest dunce,
you can't repeat the class in summer:
this course is only offered once.

No day copies yesterday,
no two nights will teach what bliss is
in precisely the same way,
with exactly the same kisses.

One day, perhaps, some idle tongue
mentions your name by accident:
I feel as if a rose were flung
into the room, all hue and scent.

The next day, though you're here with me,
I can't help looking at the clock:
A rose? A rose? What could that be?
Is it a flower or a rock?

Why do we treat the fleeting day
with so much needless fear and sorrow?
It's in its nature not to stay:
Today is always gone tomorrow.

With smiles and kisses, we prefer
to seek accord beneath our star,
although we're different (we concur)
just as two drops of water are.

CHAPTER 24

HISTORY

1954	*Brown v. Board of Education*
1965	Major buildup of U.S. troops in Vietnam
1966	National Organization for Women founded
	The Pill (oral contraceptive) becomes available in the United States
1989	Berlin Wall dismantled
1991	Communism in the USSR collapses

ARTS AND ARCHITECTURE

1974–79	Chicago, *The Dinner Party*
1982	Lin, Vietnam Veterans' Memorial
1982	Basquiat, *Charles the First*
1991	Smith, *Paper Dolls for a Post-Columbian World*
1995	Fifield, *Ghost Dancers Ascending*
1999	Mori, *Dream Temple*

LITERATURE AND PHILOSOPHY

Late 60s	Barthes, structuralism
	Derrida, deconstruction
1963	Friedan, *The Feminine Mystique*
1969	Momaday, *The Way to Rainy Mountain*
	Morrison, *The Bluest Eye*
1976	Kingston, *The Woman Warrior*
1994	Cisneros, *House on Mango Street*

Diversity
in Contemporary Life

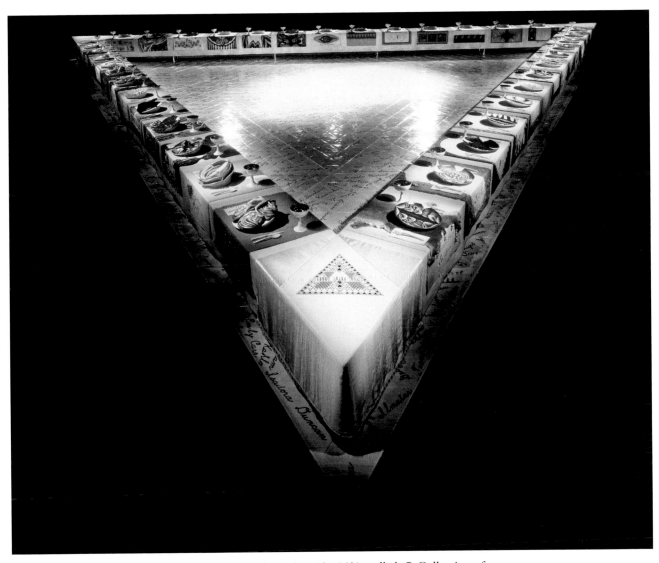

Judy Chicago, *The Dinner Party*, 1979, mixed media, 48′ × 42′ × 38′ installed. © Collection of the Booklyn Museum of Art, Gift of Elizabeth A. Sackler Foundation. Photograph © Donald Woodman/Through the Flower.

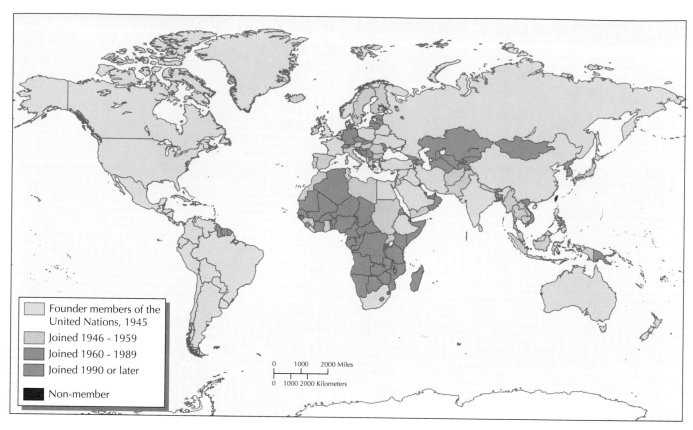

MAP 24.1 World membership of the United Nations.

DIVERSITY IN THE UNITED STATES

Women artists rise to prominence
The Internet connects the world

THE GLOBAL VILLAGE

Technology reaches out to all the ends of the earth, bringing humanity together

DIVERSITY IN THE UNITED STATES

THROUGHOUT THE 1960S AND INTO THE 1970s, American society underwent a profound shift in attitude. As a result of the civil rights movement, the Vietnam War, and the women's movement, Americans examined and questioned long-held customs and values. The quest for rights for African Americans and for women, especially, caused an increased awareness of the meaning and power of diversity.

POSTMODERNISM

Although the term **postmodernism** is intended to represent a break from, or rejection of, the preceding modernists (the *avant-garde*), the term's meaning is imprecise

and a subject of argument. Postmodernism focuses on the period between approximately 1960 (essentially post Pop Art) and the 1990s, and on the changes that occurred in politics, philosophy, art, and architecture.

Postmodernism is skeptical, even critical. In its quest for the nontraditional, it is anti-convention, anti-authority, and anti-establishment. Yet it is far from an organized, consistent, or even definable style; instead, postmodernism refers to many different ways of questioning tradition. Postmodern artists turned away from pure abstraction toward a more conceptual art that often dealt with socially conscious issues. Aspects of "postmodernism" are found in "modernism"—as in Dada and Surrealism—and in other earlier styles.

Semiotics, the study of signs and symbols, which began in the earlier twentieth century, was used as a postmodernist philosophy to propound a relativist philosophy derived from the structuralist's theorie of language. Postmodernists point out that our view of reality is molded by the ways in which information about reality comes to us—for example, via commercial media. This is the key break from the modernist tradition of belief in absolutes. Postmodernists skeptically question the mode of transmission and the place of reception before they accept the message. According to postmodernists, a work of art is actually the work of many people: Nothing an artist creates can be truly original, because it is based on those countless representations the artist has seen. Postmodernism encourages us to look at ways in which the meaning of symbols or signs, which consist of concepts (the "signified") and their sound images (the "signifiers"), changes depending on context, to determine ("deconstruct") the manner in which meaning is constructed. **Deconstructionism** rejects universals. Readers are free to interpret an author's words in their own way. Deconstructionists prefer written words to spoken words, intentionally seeking the obscure and complex rather than the obvious and logical.

PAINTING AND SCULPTURE

Diverse visions have had a considerable impact in art. The single most important development in the art world in recent decades has been the rise to prominence of visions previously excluded from the mainstream. This has been, in part, a function of the art world's quest for innovative approaches to experience, but it is also true that the art world has become increasingly willing to acknowledge the "outsider's" point of view.

The photographer Cindy Sherman (b. 1954) creates a fictional persona in order to investigate different aspects of the self. Beginning in the late 1970s, Sherman photographed herself in a variety of self-portraits called *Untitled Film Stills* (fig. 24.1). In each, Sherman wears a different costume, makes herself up to look a different part, stages herself, and announces, in effect, that the "self" is a fictionalized construction. We are whoever we choose to look like. And what we choose to look like, is one or another of a series of media images. Her work undermines the very idea of an "authentic" personality behind our repertoire of selves.

Similarly critical of modernism's quest for individual innovation, Sherrie Levine "appropriated" (i.e., copied) a photo taken by Walker Evans and claimed it as her own work of art by giving it the title *After Walker Evans*, thereby both questioning and mocking art's traditional adulation of originality as, instead, an assertion of the ego.

Other artists emphasized the reuse of images. Julian Schnabel's large-scale work of the early 1980s incorporated incongruent images taken from other forms of representation—from film, photography, even religious imagery. By putting the old into a new context created for these eclectic images, the unexpected and unfamiliar jux-

FIGURE 24.1   Cindy Sherman, *Untitled Film Still #35*, 1979, black-and-white photograph. In this version of herself, Sherman takes on the appearance of Sophia Loren playing the part of a bedraggled Italian housewife. In other words, Sherman depicts a media image, not a real person.

taposition of images (recalling Dada in this regard) leaves their meaning unclear. David Salle created similar amalgamations of disparate imagery and media, intentionally seeking to challenge established assumptions about art.

The long-standing dominance of white upper-class males in the fine arts was questioned by Andreas Huyssen. Instead, he suggested that art should be more inclusive and comprehensive, based on identities, of which he defined four: national, sexual, environmental, and ethnic (non-Western). Art that focuses on these identities has traditionally been considered lesser, lower, popular art—not fine art. These identities are relevant to postmodernism, which frequently deals with political, social, and gender issues and activism—such as feminism.

Judy Chicago.   The feminist artist Judy Chicago (b. 1939, Judy Gerowitz), working with many other women, created *The Dinner Party*, 1974–79 (fig. 24.2), a history of

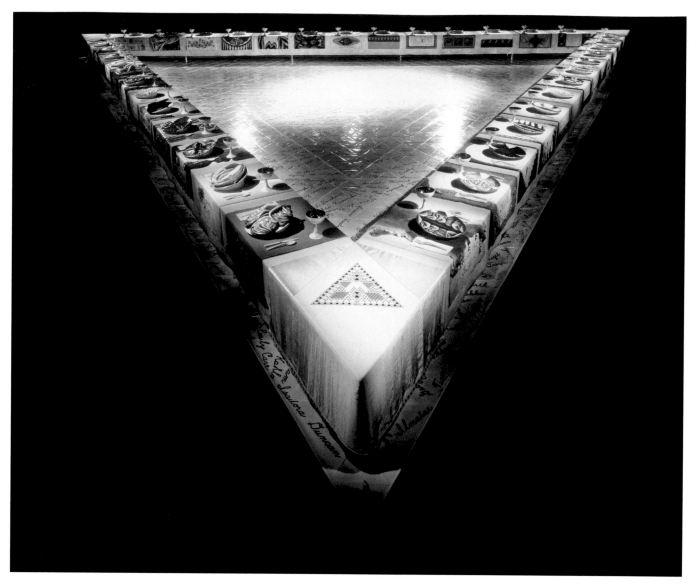

FIGURE 24.2 Judy Chicago, *The Dinner Party,* 1979, mixed media, 48′ × 48′ × 48′, (14.63 × 14.63 × 14.63 m), installed. Brooklyn Museum of Art, NY. Gift of the Elizabeth A. Sackler Foundation. Photograph © Donald Woodman/Through the Flower. This visually striking large-scale postmodern work is a monument to the myriad accomplishments of women through the ages.

women's accomplishments. Each place setting at a triangular table represents a specific woman, from prehistoric and ancient Minoan goddesses to the modern novelist Virginia Woolf and the painter Georgia O'Keeffe. The thirty-nine place settings are arranged with thirteen on each side, recalling depictions of Jesus's Last Supper. The names of 999 additional women are written on the table's runner.

The Dinner Party took what had routinely been dismissed as woman's domain and transformed it into a monumental sculpture that brought public attention to women's art. Carrie Richey wrote in *Artforum* magazine in 1981 that *The Dinner Party* "is a glossary of the so-called 'lesser arts'—tatting, lace[making], weaving, making ceramic household vessels, embroidering. . . . All these crafts

have been brought together. . . . *The Dinner Party* . . . proposes that the sum of the lesser arts is great art."

Guerrilla Girls. The impact of women on the art world has increased significantly in recent years. In 1970–71, only 13.5 percent of the artists exhibiting in New York were women. In the 1970s, only 10 percent of the shows devoted to living artists were one-person exhibitions by women. In 1982, the Coalition of Women's Art Organizations reported that only 2 percent of museum exhibitions by living artists were devoted to women. This imbalance was the focus of a socially active group of women known as the Guerrilla Girls, their identity hidden by their gorilla masks. Beginning in 1985, they plastered

FIGURE 24.3   Guerrilla Girls, *Do Women Have to be Naked to Get into the Met. Museum?*, 1989, poster, 11 × 28″ (27.9 × 71.1 cm), private collection. The Guerrilla Girls' posters document an art scene that was, as late as the mid-1980s, still dominated by men, where women were either excluded or underacknowledged.

New York City with posters (fig. 24.3), publicly questioning the inequity with which women are represented, exhibited, and funded in the arts.

Eleanor Antin.   Women artists have increasingly turned to new media, especially performance art. One innovator in performance art is Eleanor Antin (b. 1935), who has developed a series of characters, including Eleanora Antinova, a fictional black ballerina in Diaghilev's Ballets Russes. By playing Antinova, Antin freed herself to investigate hidden aspects of her own situation. A drawing from her memoir, *Being Antinova* (fig. 24.4), shows how removed Antinova is from the traditional Western ballet world. Not only is Antinova black, but her own sense of physical freedom contradicts the regimen and routine of ballet. Imagine, she points out, a black ballerina in *Swan Lake*. The world of ballet is, in her words, a "white machine."

Susan Rothenberg.   Among the many women painters who have achieved a place in American painting since the early 1980s is Susan Rothenberg (b. 1945), who works in New Mexico. Rothenberg achieved success early with her first exhibition in New York in 1976. It is for her images of horses, such as *Axes* (fig. 24.5), painted in 1976, that she is best known. In this painting a lone animal is moving,

FIGURE 24.4   Eleanor Antin, drawing from *Being Antinova*, 1983. Courtesy Ronald Feldman Fine Arts. NY. The physical freedom expressed by Antinova in this drawing differentiates her from other dancers in the troupe.

FIGURE 24.5   Susan Rothenberg, *Axes*, 1976, synthetic polymer paint and gesso on canvas, $5'4\frac{5}{8}'' \times 8'8\frac{7}{8}''$ (1.64 × 2.66 m), Museum of Modern Art, NY. Art Resource, NY/Licensed by SCALA-Art Resource, NY. © 2005 Artists Rights Society, NY. In this Neo-Expressionist work, form is suggested rather than specified, hinted at rather than defined. The perfect balance within the rectangle of the canvas is based upon the horse's implied movement to the left.

stark and ghostly, a hallucination, an apparition, a dream. Both primal and sophisticated, Rothenberg's work is characterized by rough strokes from which forms emerge, as if through a heavy fog. In *Axes*, the axis of the center of the canvas and the axis of the horse's body are not aligned, an imbalance animates the canvas.

Betye Saar.   Artist Betye Saar (b. 1926) created the Pop Art-like construction entitled *The Liberation of Aunt Jemima* (fig. 24.6) in 1972. Saar's image "converts a popular" conception of the African-American "mammy"—the smiling Aunt Jemima of pancake and syrup fame. As Aunt Jemima takes up arms, raising the fist of black power over the scene, the white baby is not merely unhappy, but terrified. "Mammy's" politics are revealed; this advertising image, once servant and slave, takes matters into her own hands. The painting announces the necessity—the actuality—of change for the African American.

Jean-Michel Basquiat.   As a teenager in New York, Jean-Michel Basquiat (1960–88) achieved notoriety as "Samo," a graffiti artist writing on walls in Soho and Tribeca. By early 1981, gallery owners in New York, Zurich, and Milan had convinced him to apply his graffiti to canvas, and he soon became an art world media darling. The value of his paintings rose with meteoric speed. By the time he was twenty-three years old, his work had already sold at auction for $19,000. Basquiat, the son of a middle-class Haitian-born accountant and his Puerto Rican wife, possessed an authenticity—raw, direct, unmediated by tradition.

In *Charles the First* (fig. 24.7), Basquiat's homage to jazz saxophonist Charlie Parker, the immediacy of Basquiat's style is in his "mistakes." As one of Basquiat's heroes, Parker is a king—hence the painting's title, the crown, and

FIGURE 24.6 Betye Saar, *The Liberation of Aunt Jemima*, 1972, mixed media, $11\frac{3}{4} \times 8 \times 2\frac{3}{4}''$ (29.8 × 20.3 × 6.9 cm), University Art Museum, University of California, Berkeley. Saar's image not only attacks racism but sexism as well, and the expectations of the dominant culture.

FIGURE 24.7 Jean-Michel Basquiat, *Charles the First*, 1982, acrylic and oilstick on canvas, triptych, $6'6'' \times 5'2\frac{1}{4}''$ (1.98 × 1.58 m), Robert Miller Gallery, New York. © 2005 Artists Rights Society (ARS), NY. © The Estate of Jean-Michel Basquiat. The "X" crossing out elements in Basquiat's work is never entirely negative. In a book on symbols, Basquiat discovered a section on "Hobo Signs," marks left, like graffiti, by hobos to inform their brethren about the locality. In this graphic language, an "X" means "O.K. All right."

the word "Thor" (the god of Norwegian myth). At the bottom is Basquiat's admonition to kings; the word "young" is crossed out. Parker's fall from grace is everywhere in the painting: in the drips that fall from the blue field in the middle of the painting and in the way that, above the word "Cherokee" (the name of one of Parker's most important compositions), one of the feathers (Parker was known as "Bird") falls into a dollar sign.

Much of Basquiat's art protests against the exploitation of black heroes—Sugar Ray Robinson, Hank Aaron, Cassius Clay, Dizzy Gillespie, and Louis Armstrong. Basquiat identified with them, as if he knew his own meteoric rise would end in tragedy. He died, age twenty-seven, of a drug overdose.

Judith F. Baca. The mural painting of Chicana artist Judith F. Baca (b. 1948) asserts its independence from traditional approaches to painting, even as it recovers and revitalizes the Mexican mural tradition of "Los Tres Grandes"—Rivera, Orozco, and Siquieros (see Chapter 22).

In 1974, Baca inaugurated the Citywide Mural Project in Los Angeles, which completed 250 murals, 150 of which

she directed herself. Since then she has continued to sponsor and direct murals through SPARC, the Social and Public Art Resource Center, which she founded. The *Great Wall of Los Angeles*, begun in 1976, is her most ambitious project. Nearly a mile long, it is located in the Tujunga Wash of the Los Angeles river, which was entirely lined in concrete as Los Angeles grew. This concrete conduit is, says Baca, "a giant scar across the land which served to further divide an already divided city. . . . Just as young Chicanos tattoo battle scars on their bodies, *Great Wall of Los Angeles* is a tattoo on a scar where the river once ran." The wall narrates a history of Los Angeles not told in textbooks. It recounts the history of indigenous peoples, immigrant minorities—Portuguese, Chinese, Japanese, Korean, and Basque, as well as Chicano—and of women from prehistory to the present. The detail reproduced here (fig. 24.8) depicts how four freeways intersected the East Los Angeles Chicano communities, dividing them, weakening them, and turning them against each other. To the right a Mexican woman protests the building of Dodger

FIGURE 24.8   Judith F. Baca, *Great Wall of Los Angeles* (detail: Division of the Barrios and Chavez Ravine), Tujunga Wash, Los Angeles, California, 1976–continuing, mural, height 13′ (3.96 m) (whole mural over a mile long). Photo © SPARC, Venice, CA. The collaborative process of making murals is, in Baca's words, "the transforming of pain . . . rage . . . and shame."

Stadium, which displaced a Mexican community in Chavez Ravine.

Baca worked on the *Great Wall* project as director and facilitator, but nearly four hundred inner-city youths, many from the juvenile justice system, did the actual painting and design. Rival gang members, of different races and from different neighborhoods, representing a divided city, found themselves working on the project together. For Baca, the collaborative mural process heals wounds, brings people together, and helps recreate communities for, as she said, "Collaboration is a requirement."

Lisa Fifield.   Lisa Fifield (b. 1957), of Iroquois-Oneida descent, portrays the traditions and beliefs of Native American peoples. Fifield painted a series of canvases based on the slaughter at Wounded Knee, by the U. S. Army, of Native American men, women, and children. One such painting *Ghost Dancers Ascending* (fig. 24.9), depicts the spirits of the dead rising above the earth. The Plains Indians developed the Ghost Dance in the 1890s after they had lost their ancestral lands and been relegated to reservations. They danced for the return of warriors, for the return of the bison, and for the reestablishment of their former way of life. In the painting, the attire worn by the figures is based on that worn by those killed at Wounded Knee, clothing they mistakenly believed could not be pierced by bullets. With reverential spirit, Fifield depicts their spirits transcending the material fact of death in vibrant primary colors.

Maya Lin and the Vietnam Veterans' Memorial.   The Vietnam Veterans' Memorial in Washington, D.C. (fig. 24.10) was constructed and dedicated in 1982. Funded by contributions from corporations, foundations, unions,

FIGURE 24.9   Lisa Fifield, *Ghost Dancers Ascending*, 1995, watercolor on paper, 30 × 22″ (76.2 × 55.9 cm), private collection. Fifield depicts the spirits rising above the earth at Wounded Knee, their powerful colors and effortless floating making them seem to transcend their tragic deaths.

FIGURE 24.10   Maya Lin, Vietnam Veterans' Memorial, Washington, D.C., 1982, black granite, length 250′ (820.21 m). Known simply as "the Wall," this memorial tribute to those killed in the Vietnam War has become a national symbol of recognition and reconciliation.

veterans, civic organizations, and nearly three million individuals, the memorial achieved the wishes of the foundation that established it, which was to begin a process of national reconciliation.

The memorial was designed by Maya Ying Lin (b. 1960), at the time a twenty-one-year-old graduate architectural student at Yale University. Lin, an American woman of Chinese descent, won a national competition that included more than 1,400 design submissions. Inscribed on the surface of the memorial's polished black granite walls are the more than 58,000 names of servicemen and -women killed during the Vietnam War or missing in action. The wall is shaped like a giant V, whose vertex is set at an angle of approximately 125 degrees. The names of the casualties are listed beginning at one end of the wall in the chronological order of their deaths, encompassing the span of U.S. involvement in the war. The wall provides each name an honored place in the nation's memory. As Maya Lin said about the design, "The names would become the memorial."

Despite some dissenting voices at first, the Vietnam Veterans' War Memorial has won national approval and respect. Thousands visit the memorial every year. When looking at the names on the memorial's granite slabs, which are polished to a mirrorlike sheen, viewers can see themselves reflected in the wall's surface. Visitors are

Table 24–1   CONTEMPORARY AMERICAN WOMAN ARTISTS
Betye Saar (b. 1926), *The Liberation of Aunt Jemima*
Eleanor Antin (b. 1935), *Being Antinova*
Judy Chicago (b. 1939), *The Dinner Party*
Susan Rothenberg (b. 1945), *Axes*
Judith F. Baca (b. 1948), *Great Wall of Los Angeles*
Cindy Sherman (b. 1954), *Untitled Film Still #35*
Lisa Fifield (b. 1957), *Ghost Dancers Ascending*
Maya Lin (b. 1960), *Vietnam Veterans' Memorial*

moved by the wall's profound homage and sense that here healing can begin.

Mariko Mori. The Japanese multi-media installation artist Mariko Mori (1967–) was born in Tokyo and lives both there and in Manhattan. Similarly, her art consists of contrasts: Aspects of the traditional religions of Buddhism and Shintoism are combined with the most modern technology. She produces photographs, videos, and entire productions, in which she often features herself dressed in extreme costumes. Entire production crews may be employed to stage these performances.

Her *Dream Temple* (fig. 24.11), 1999, creates an environment unlike anything previously created by artists and is distant from Nature's forms and materials. The visitor can literally enter into Mori's vision. The meaning of such a work derives from a fusion of religion, philosophy, and modern popular technology.

STRUCTURALISM AND DECONSTRUCTION

Beginning in the late 1960s, a number of French intellectuals made the case for the plurality of experience and developed strategies for challenging accepted traditions. One of these thinkers was Roland Barthes [BAR(t)] (1915–80), whose early work was on "structural" linguistics, and whose approach to culture was thus called **structuralism.** At the heart of structural linguistics is an approach to "meaning" based on the notion of the plurality of the "sign." The "sign" is the ratio between the so-called signifier and the signified. For instance, the word "tree" is a signifier and a tree itself is the signified object. In French, the word for tree is *arbre;* in Swahili, it is *mti.* The signifier (the word) changes from language to language. In addition, the signified encompasses all possible trees. The signified is so plural and various that, on contemplation, it seems astonishing that language enables us

FIGURE 24.11   Mariko Mori, *Dream Temple*, 1999, audio, metal, glass, glass fiber threads, Vision Dome. 3-D semi-circular display, height 16′5″ (5 m), diameter 32′ 10″ (10 m). The shape of this futuristic structure derives from an eighth-century temple, although here there is no god. Mori's work has been described as "Cyborg Surrealism."

to communicate meaningfully at all. What determines the particulars of the tree we are talking about when we say or write the word "tree" is the context of the tree. The pine tree in the backyard is different from the oak tree in the square. Context determines meaning. It follows then that when we consider any object, the object's meaning is determined not by its existence alone but by the situation in which we observe it. And this situation is always subject to change. Thus "meaning" is never absolute. It is as diverse as the situations in which it comes to exist.

What is known as "poststructuralist" thought is an application of this way of thinking, based on the assumption that speech—the meaning of which is never fully "determined"—can as easily mask reality as reveal it. The chief practitioner of poststructuralist thought is the French philosopher JACQUES DERRIDA [dare-ree-DAH] (b. 1930). Derrida's method, known as **deconstruction,** consists of taking apart received traditions on the assumption that all thoughts include leaps in logic and inconsistencies, the revelation of which tells us more about the thought than the thought itself does. That is, in philosophy what is not said is at least as important as what is said. For Derrida, even the self is a fiction or construction, built out of unexamined assumptions, and it, too, must be deconstructed for true understanding. In sum, in the poststructuralist mind, there are no facts, only interpretations. Such a philosophical stance, which amounts to a profound skepticism, has led to a critical revision of much of Western thought.

THE DIVERSITY OF AMERICAN VOICES

Adrienne Rich.   Poet Adrienne Rich (b. 1929) is a passionate spokeswoman for feminist consciousness. Her prose and poetry, rooted in radical feminist ideology, dramatizes the freedom of self-discovery. At her best, Rich is less a polemicist and publicist than an artist who challenges preconceptions about women and their relationships to men and to one another.

In "When We Dead Awaken: Writing as Re-Vision," Rich describes how she needed to change the images that represented her ideals of both woman and poet, since her images of both had been dominated by men. She explores the concept of re-vision, which she calls "the act of looking back, of seeing with fresh eyes," as essential for writers, and as essential for women living in a male-dominated society. Re-vision is "an act of survival."

Maxine Hong Kingston.   One characteristic of contemporary writing is the combination of elements from different genres. The autobiographical novel *The Woman Warrior* (1976), by Chinese American writer Maxine Hong Kingston (b. 1940), has been described by the author as "the book of her mother," since it is filled with stories her mother told her about her Chinese ancestors, especially the women whom Kingston describes as the ghosts of her

girlhood. A second book, *China Men* (1980), is her father's book; it tells the stories of her male ancestors, including her father and grandfathers, although she learned these male stories from women, mostly from her mother. Mixing fact and fiction, autobiography and legend, Kingston's books combine family history with fictional invention. Kingston's identity as a Chinese American woman and her attempts to create images of her experience reveal her relationship to her ancestral past.

The stories Kingston recounts and invents in *The Woman Warrior* and in *China Men* derive from the Chinese "talk story," a Cantonese oral tradition kept alive mainly by woman. The books' talk-story narrators tell their stories in multiple versions, varying the amount of detail each reveals. These stories contain silences that invite the reader to engage in the imaginative world of the writer, who occasionally hints at her fictionalizing with cues such as "I wonder," "perhaps," and "may have."

By writing her mother's stories and adding variants of her own, Kingston marks the talk-story tradition with her own distinctive imprint. In the process, these stories entertain readers outside the Chinese cultural tradition. Kingston's work appeals because she gives voice to things women had spoken only in private or not at all. She also transmits her Cantonese heritage. Kingston animates a world and constructs a self that are at once strange and familiar, both "other" and inherently recognizable.

Toni Morrison.   The 1996 Nobel Prize winner Toni Morrison (b. 1931) writes novels that focus on the complex balance between personal identity and social identity in African-American communities. Mixing feminist concerns with racial and cultural issues, Morrison's fiction explores the cultural inheritance of African Americans facing hardship and conflict through memory, relationships, and actions.

In her first novel, *The Bluest Eye* (1969), Morrison explores what it is like to be of mixed—white and black—descent and thus light-skinned, capturing not only the hurt of prejudices based on color but also the tragedy of unrecognized beauty. In *Sula* (1973), she portrays the family consequences of a woman achieving her own independence and freedom, and in *Song of Solomon* (1977), she portrays a black man's attempt to come to terms with his roots. The power of eroticism is the subject of *Tar Baby* (1981), and *Beloved* (1987) explores the degrading effects of slavery. Although every book is embedded in pain, Morrison's work is about survival, and her urgency to write is her quest to survive. "I think about what black writers do," she has said, "as having a quality of hunger and disturbance that never ends."

Judith Ortiz Cofer.   From Puerto Rico, JUDITH ORTIZ COFER [CO-fur] (b. 1952) has published poetry and prose, in volumes such as *Silent Dancing* and *The Latin Deli.* These display Cofer's knack for conveying the experience of the lives of immigrants. Her stories, both auto-

Cross Currents

THE SCULPTURE OF WEN-YING TSAI

Cybernetic sculpture fuses art and technology. Through electronic feedback control systems that include high-frequency lights, microphones, and harmonic vibration, Wen-Ying Tsai's *Cybernetic Sculpture, 1979* comes to life when music is played or hands are clapped in its presence (fig. 24.12). The photograph here makes the figure appear two dimensional, but it is a three-dimensional sculpture.

Cybernetic Sculpture is constructed of a series of fiberglass rods about 10 feet in height. Each rod is set on a base under which is a small motor. With the motors beneath each base switched on, the rods vibrate slowly but remain perfectly vertical. When stimulated by sound and light, they vibrate synchronously in gently swaying arcs. As long as the stimuli continue, the rods undulate in dancelike movement.

Tsai's cybernetic sculptures are self-organizing systems that maintain equilibrium whether in motion or at rest. His works blend not only art and technology, but also Eastern and Western traditions. In fulfilling what Hsieh Ho, a fifth-century Chinese master, identifies as the primary requirement of all art—"rhythmic vitality, a kind of spiritual rhythm expressed in the movement of life"—Tsai's cybernetic sculpture takes its place in a long-established Chinese aesthetic.

Tsai's cybernetic sculpture also reflects Chinese aesthetic ideals in its harmonious blending of the human, the mechanical, and the natural. Each element contributes harmoniously to the unity of the whole. The spirit of his sculpture is Taoist, as are its effects—a refined equilibrium that merges wisdom with wit, seriousness with humor, mysticism with modernity.

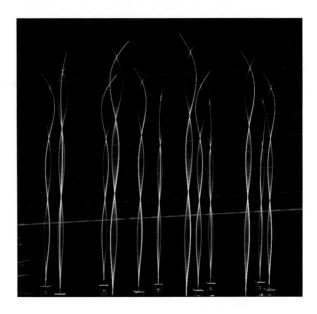

FIGURE 24.12 Wen-Ying Tsai, *Cybernetic Sculpture*, 1979, fiberglass mounted on steel plates covering an electronic feedback system, 10 × 10′ (3.05 × 3.05 m) National Palace Museum, Taipei. The work responds to changes in light and sound by vibrating with graceful, dancelike undulations.

---

biographical and fictional, show characters' conflicts with their new lives in mainland America and their memories of Puerto Rico. Elegant, lyrical, and convincing, Cofer's stories, poems, and autobiographical essays analyze and celebrate the double perspective of seeing life through the lenses of two cultures and languages.

Oscar Hijuelos. Hispanic Caribbean writer OSCAR HIJUELOS [hi-YAIL-oss] (b. 1951) captures the pre-Castro immigrant experience in the United States, particularly in New York. His novel *The Mambo Kings Play Songs of Love* won the Pulitzer Prize in 1990, the first book by a writer of Hispanic origin to win the prestigious award. In chronicling the lives of Cuban immigrants, their quest for the American dream, and their ultimate disillusionment, Hijuelos evokes the atmosphere of the 1950s. Throughout his work Hijuelos explores the influence of Hispanic culture on American popular culture. His fascination with the diverse cultural threads woven into the fabric of contemporary American life brims over in his pages. An important influence on younger Hispanic Caribbean and Latino writers, Hijuelos captures and celebrates the spirit of place, in which his values are rooted. Hijuelos emphasizes the necessity for preserving cultural heritage, yet he also revels in the way life reflects a mosaic of cultural inflections.

N. Scott Momaday. The works of N. SCOTT MOMADAY [MOHM-ah-day] (b. 1934) were among the first by a Native American to garner a wide audience. Born in Oklahoma of Kiowa ancestry, Momaday has written poetry, fiction, and autobiography. His 1969 novel, *House Made of Dawn*, won a Pulitzer Prize. In it a young Native American man returns from military service in Vietnam to find himself without a place in either Indian society or mainstream America. Momaday's two autobiographical works, *The Way to Rainy Mountain* (1969) and *The Names* (1976), mingle Kiowa legends with American history and his family's personal experience.

Connections

VACLAV HAVEL, PLAYWRIGHT AND POLITICIAN

During the 1960s and 1970s, Vaclav Havel, the first president of the post-Soviet Czech Republic, was best known as a playwright. Born in Prague, Czechoslovakia, in 1936, into a family of engineers, Havel became interested in philosophy and literature as a teenager and during the 1960s studied at the Academy of the Performing Arts. His best known plays include *The Garden Party* (1963), *The Memorandum* (1965), and *The Increased Difficulty of Concentration* (1968), which focus on political themes, especially on oppressive and threatening political environments. Havel has also written books about his political imprisonment, including *Living in Truth* (1989), *Disturbing the Peace* (1990), and *Letters to Olga* (1990).

Havel became known as a political dissident during the 1960s when he publicly criticized his country's Writer's Union for acting "as a broker between politics and literature," rather than "defending the right of literature to be literature." At that time he published an article arguing for the end of single-party rule in Czechoslovakia. The communist government responded by banning his writings.

During the 1970s, Havel helped establish an underground press to publish government-censored works. He continued to write pieces critical of the totalitarian regime, including "The Power of the Powerless," an essay on totalitarianism and dissent. Havel was arrested and imprisoned in the early 1970s and again in the early 1980s.

With the collapse of the communist system in Eastern Europe in 1991, and with the division of Czechoslovakia into separate Czech and Slovak republics in 1993, democratic government was introduced. Imprisoned again in 1989 for dissident activities, Havel was released, and by the end of the year was elected president of Czechoslovakia. In 1993, he became the first president of the new Czech Republic. Havel's political reputation grew to include that of a courageous leader, one with a vision of tolerant coexistence of people of different cultures and identities. Havel's social vision and political leadership were of a piece with the moral themes of his plays. His literary works effected social and political change, not the least of which was Havel's election to the presidency of his country.

Leslie Marmon Silko. Leslie Marmon Silko (b. 1948) has written poetry and prose that reflects her mixed ancestry: She is descended from the Laguna tribe but has white and Mexican ancestry as well. Her novel *Ceremony* (1978) and her collection of prose and poetry *Storyteller* (1981) both emphasize the cultural values and spirit of her Pueblo ancestors. *Ceremony* makes a connection between the shared cultural heritage of the tribal community and the experience of a Native American Indian veteran of the Vietnam War, who returns to the reservation to reclaim a sense of identity. *Storyteller*, a collection of folktales, family anecdotes, photographs, stories, and poems, reflects the intersection of the spiritual and material worlds, as well as connections between history and personal experience. The relationship between nature and culture permeates this work, emphasizing the way Native American peoples have lived in harmony with the natural world, the land being part of their identity, not merely a place to live.

THE GLOBAL VILLAGE

The opening of the Berlin Wall in November 1989 and, in turn, the collapse of the communist regime in the Soviet Union two years later symbolized the awakening of tolerance among diverse cultures in the contemporary world. For the first time since World War II, the citizens of East and West Germany were able to come together freely and openly. As Vaclav Havel (b. 1936), the president of the Czech Republic, put it in 1993: "All of us—whether from the west, the east, the south, or the north of Europe—can agree that the common basis of any effort to integrate Europe is the wealth of values and ideas we share. . . . All of us respect the principle of unity in diversity and share a determination to foster creative cooperation between the different nations and ethnic, religious, and cultural groups—and the different spheres of civilization— that exist in Europe." Havel's message can easily be extended to the globe as a whole. We have come to recognize and accept a worldwide imperative: We live in a pluralistic community of nearly five billion people. To survive and thrive, we need to communicate and share with one another as if we lived in a single village.

GLOBALIZATION

A major trend among the world's economies came to a head in the 1990s—the emergence of globalization, or the massive movement of information, technology, and goods across national borders. Globalization is one of a number of factors influencing changes in the general world order that present challenges to the relationships between and among nations and cultures worldwide. Fueling the fires

Then & Now

NAVIGATING THE WEB

Perhaps no single technological development has succeeded in shrinking the globe more than the **Internet** and its network, the World Wide Web. Not only is text available on the Web, but so are images, videos, sound, and film. Over five hundred museum and gallery sites are accessible on the Web, including such sites as the A.I.R. Gallery in New York (women artists), the Andy Warhol Museum in Pittsburgh, and the Louvre in Paris, where one can view such works as Leonardo's *Mona Lisa* (see Chapter 13) and Géricault's *Raft of the "Medusa"* (see Chapter 17). By browsing the sites of museums and galleries around the globe, it is possible to view old and new work by artists from over fifty countries. You can browse the collection of the Ho-Am Art Museum in Seoul, Korea, viewing masterpieces from its painting, ceramics, and bronze collections, or you can tour galleries in Taipei, Taiwan.

You can watch a video clip of a war dance by the Anlo-Ewe people of Ghana, West Africa, or listen to music samples from the newest CD releases in South America. Alternatively, you could browse the current issue of *Critical Inquiry*, a scholarly journal in the United States, or check out *LIVEculture*, the online publication of the Institute for Learning Technologies at Columbia University, which focuses on contemporary art, literature, media, communications, and cultural studies. The possibilities are endless, and the availability of information about almost anything is unprecedented. The World Wide Web promises to change the way in which we think about ourselves and learn about the world around us.

---

of economic globalization are a series of technological developments, especially in communications, that have erased geographic distance and accelerated time. In addition, a number of economic agreements were made in the mid- to late twentieth century, including the General Agreement on Free Trade and Tariffs (GATT), signed by 23 countries in 1947, and which now includes 123 signatories. In 1995 GATT gave way to the World Trade organization (WTO), with the most important recent country addition being China.

The most important practical economic development has been the emergence of global corporations, which have spread their operations around the world, as they seek business efficiencies, especially the lowest possible operating costs. The integration of world economies and the globalization of companies have been complemented by the rapid rise of Asian economies, including those of Hong Kong, Singapore, South Korea, and Taiwan, as well as those of China and India, two sleeping giants whose economies have only recently begun to awaken.

Other global economic intiatives include the North American Free Trade Agreement (NAFTA) signed by Canada, Mexico, and the United States; the Organization of Petroleum Exporting Countries (OPEC) in the Middle East; the Association of Southeast Asian Nations (ASEAN), and the European Union (EU).

In addition to economic globalization, the late twentieth and early twenty-first centuries have seen increasing cross-cultural exchanges in ideas, arts, and cultural practices. The English language has become the world's main language of communication, especially when people of different language groups work together. The world's cultures are being brought closer together with developments in technology, including the Internet, email, and the cell phone. However, as countries and regions struggle to preserve their own cultures, languages, and identities, inevitable tensions have resulted. The threat of cultural homogenization with franchises like McDonald's and Starbucks marketing their products seemingly everywhere is compounded by other kinds of global threats, from diseases like bird flu to terrorist attacks. With more people traveling around the world for business and pleasure, the possibility of the rapid spread of disease has increased dramatically—one negative to the many positive benefits of global travel, such as the increased awareness and appreciation of other cultures.

MAGICIANS OF THE EARTH

In 1989, an exhibition in Paris announced itself as "the first worldwide exhibition of contemporary art." Called *Magiciens de la terre*, or *Magicians of the Earth*, the show consisted of works by one hundred artists, fifty from the traditional "centers" of Western culture (Europe and America) and fifty from Asia, South America, Australia, Africa, and, incidentally, Native American art from North America. It was, in the words of Thomas McEvilley, an American art critic, "a major event in the social history of art," if not in its aesthetic history.

Although it was difficult for most viewers to detect coherent themes or influences among artists and cultures, the exhibition underscored the diversity and plurality of world art. As the exhibition's chief curator, Jean-Hubert Martin, put it, "Rather than showing that abstraction is a universal language, or that the return to figuration is now happening everywhere in the world, I want to show the *real differences* and the specificity of different cultures."

Critical Thinking

THE PROS AND CONS OF GLOBALIZATION

One of the challenges of the late twentieth and the early twenty-first century has been globalization—what one analyst has termed the "flattening of the world." By this he means a number of things: (1) the way communications technology allows for instantaneous transfer and sharing of information and data around the world; (2) the economic interdependence of countries upon one another; (3) the ways that work that used to be done in one and only one place can now be "outsourced" to faraway places due to advances in technology, as for example a hospital outsourcing to India its radiological analysis of X-rays or the outsourcing of call centers to Ireland or Bangalore to answer customer questions from the United States.

Globalization is here to stay. There is no question about that. The question is how to deal with the effects of a globalized world—whether those effects involve economics and world trade, political and social influences, or something as dangerous as world terrorism. What is your view of how globalization has altered the way we live now? What can or should be done to ensure that the positive benefits of globalization outweigh its negative possibilities?

THE EXAMPLE OF AUSTRALIAN ABORIGINAL PAINTING

Ceremonial body, rock, and ground paintings have been made for millennia by the Aboriginal peoples of Central Australia's Western Desert region. The sand painting in the installation view of the *Magicians of the Earth* (fig. 24.13) is one such work, executed on the spot by the Yuendumu community. Today, Aboriginal artists are known for their acrylic paintings, which were not produced in the region until 1971. In that year, an art teacher named Geoff Bardon arrived in Papunya, a settlement organized by the government to provide health care, education, and housing for the Aborigines on the edge of the Western Desert. Several older Aboriginal men became interested in Bardon's classes, and he encouraged them to paint in acrylic, using traditional motifs. Between July 1971 and August 1972, they produced 620 paintings.

Each painted design has traditional ceremonial power connected with the identity of who made it. The organizing logic of most Aboriginal art is the "Dreaming," a system of belief unique to the Australian Aborigines. The Dreaming is not literal dreaming, not what goes on in our sleep. For the Aborigine, the Dreaming is the presence, or mark, of an ancestral being in the world. Images of these beings—representations of the myths about them, maps of their travels, depictions of the places and landscapes they inhabited—make up the great bulk of Aboriginal art. In fact, the Australian landscape is thought of as a series of marks made by the Dreaming. Thus geography itself *is* meaning and history. The paintings speak the concise vocabulary conceived to map this geography.

Each painting depicts a Dreaming for which the artist is *kirda*. Artists are *kirda* if they have inherited the "rights" to the Dreaming from their father. Each Dreaming is also inherited through the mother's line, and a person who is related to a Dreaming in this way is said to be *kurdungurlu*. *Kurdungurlu* must ensure that the *kirda* fulfill their proper obligations to the Dreaming. As a result, several people usually work on any given painting. The person that Westerners designate as the "artist"—a distinction not employed in Aboriginal culture before the advent of acrylic painting—is generally the person who has chosen the specific Dreaming to be depicted.

Erna Motna's *Bushfire and Corroboree Dreaming* (fig. 24.14) depicts the preparations for a *corroboree*, or celebration ceremony. The circular features at the top and bottom of the painting represent small bushfires that have been started by women. As small animals run from the fire

FIGURE 24.13   Installation view of *Magiciens de la terre (Magicians of the Earth)*, La Villette, Paris, 1989. This exhibition attempted to put works from the developing countries beside works from the West in a nonjudgmental way. Here a sand painting by the Australian aboriginal Yuendumu community lies on the floor beneath English artist Richard Long's *Red Earth Circle*.

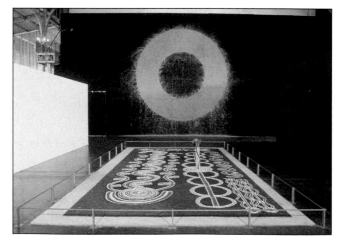

FIGURE 24.14   Erna Motna, *Bushfire and Corroboree Dreaming*, 1988, acrylic on canvas, 48 × 32″ (121.9 × 81.3 cm), Australia Gallery, New York. Surrounding each of the three fires—the white circles in the painting—are a number of weapons used to kill larger animals: boomerangs, spears, *nulla nullas* (clubs), and *woomeras* (spear throwers).

Cultural Impact

Just a few years into the twenty-first century, America continues to experience an influx of immigrants from around the world. European immigration has risen from the previous decades, partly due to the collapse of Soviet communism. Asian immigration, from India, China, Korea, and Vietnam, continues unabated, with students from Asian countries making up the majority of those studying at U.S. universities from abroad. Even larger numbers of immigrants, however, have come to the United States from the Caribbean and from Central and South America, so much so that Spanish is rapidly becoming an unofficial second language in the country.

These diverse groups of people bring a rich array of languages and cultures, which have a significant impact on the cultural life of contemporary America. African-American poets, playwrights, and novelists have altered the literary landscape. African-American musicians maintain an extensive presence and exert a powerful influence on the music of the day, from hip-hop to rock, from jazz to gospel and blues. Latin American and Caribbean musicians, performers, and composers have also made a lasting impact on American cultural life. And Latin American and Caribbean writers have left a similarly extensive legacy for the future, with works in both Spanish and in English.

The legacy of Native Americans has also recently begun to be appreciated, spurred by the renewed study of Native American history and culture in the past few decades. The popularity of Native American crafts, art, and artifacts, such as Navajo blankets and southwest Indian basketry, pottery, and jewelry, have influenced contemporary style. Native American artists and writers have had a decisive impact on contemporary attitudes toward the environment; the Native American approach to living in harmony with nature may, in fact, be the greatest of its cultural legacies.

The full force of contemporary cultural ideas can only be assessed in the future. Certain features of the contemporary landscape, however, reflect cultural values that are becoming increasingly evident. Among these are a broadening of cultural perspective and a deepening of cultural awareness to include a wider range of voices and visions than had been previously accommodated socially and artistically. Women continue to achieve greater recognition for their accomplishments. Minorities of all cultural, racial, ethnic, and linguistic backgrounds continue to have an impact on contemporary cultural and artistic values.

(symbolized by the small red dots at the edge of each circle), they are caught by the women and hit with digging sticks, also visible around each fire, and then carried with fruit and vegetables to the central fire, the site of the *corroboree* itself. Unlike most forms of Aboriginal art, acrylic paintings are permanent and not destroyed after serving the ceremony for which they were produced.

A difference between Western art and the art of non-Western cultures, as Aboriginal painting suggests, is that the latter seems more participatory and ceremony based. Even when we can identify the "artist"—Erna Motna, for instance—it is his or her relationship to the whole community that is emphasized as well as the work's ceremonial place in community life. In the West, in contrast, the work of art tends to be a commodity, the artist a solitary individual, and the audience nonparticipatory spectators.

Still, aspects of each approach inform most art made today in the global village. On the wall behind the Yuendumu sand painting at the *Magicians of the Earth* exhibition is a large circle created by English artist Richard Long. Made of mud that Long had collected on a visit to the Yuendumu community, its juxtaposition with the sand painting bestowed on it a power it might have otherwise lacked. As Jean-Hubert Martin explained, "Successful and dominant countries impose their laws and styles on other countries, but they also borrow from them and so become permeated by other ways of life. The notion of cultural identity . . . is the product of a static concept of human activity, whereas culture is always the result of an ever-moving dynamic of exchanges."

KEY TERMS

postmodernism   structuralism   Internet
semiotics   deconstructionism   globalization

www. WEBSITES FOR FURTHER STUDY

http://www.judychicago.com/
(A website on Judy Chicago, a major contemporary force in women associated with art.)

http://www.johnseed.com/basquiat.html
(An informative site on Jean-Michel Basquiat, graffiti artist-cum-master, whose meteoric fame
for portraying black heroes was tragically cut short by an early death.)

http://www.greatbuildings.com/buildings/Vietnam_Veterans_Memorial.html
(GreatBuildings.com site on Maya Lin's Vietnam memorial.)

http://www.uncp.edu/home/canada/work/canam/kingston.htm
(A basic site on Maxine Hong Kingston, one of the most important woman writers of our time.)

http://www.aboriginal-art.com/desert_pages/yuendumu_thumb.html#yuendumu2
(A site on Central Australia's Western Desert Aboriginal region, featuring the art of the
Yuendumu and Lajamanu communities.)

READINGS

ADRIENNE RICH
"XIII (Dedications)"

In this section from An Atlas of the Difficult World, *Adrienne Rich addresses her readers directly, reassuring them of the value and importance of what they are doing as they go about their lives. The speaker/poet embraces a variety of imagined readers, none of them great, or wise, or rich, but still hungry for truth and understanding of a world that weighs heavily on each of us.*

I know you are reading this poem
late, before leaving your office
of the one intense yellow lamp-spot and the
    darkening window
in the lassitude of a building faded to quiet
long after rush-hour. I know you are reading this poem 5
standing up in a bookstore far from the ocean
on a grey day of early spring, faint flakes driven
across the plains' enormous spaces around you.
I know you are reading this poem
in a room where too much has happened for you to bear 10
where the bedclothes lie in stagnant coils on the bed
and the open valise speaks of flight
but you cannot leave yet. I know you are reading this
    poem
as the underground train loses momentum and before
    running up the stairs
toward a new kind of love   15
your life has never allowed.
I know you are reading this poem by the light
of the television screen where soundless images jerk and
    slide
while you wait for the newscast from the *intifada*.
I know you are reading this poem in a waiting-room   20
of eyes met and unmeeting, of identity with strangers.
I know you are reading this poem by fluorescent light
in the boredom and fatigue of the young who are
    counted out,
count themselves out, at too early an age. I know
you are reading this poem through your failing
    sight, the thick   25
lens enlarging these letters beyond all meaning yet
    you read on
because even the alphabet is precious.
I know you are reading this poem as you pace beside the
    stove
warming milk, a crying child on your shoulder, a book in
    your hand
    because life is short and you too are thirsty.   30
I know you are reading this poem which is not in your
    language
guessing at some words while others keep you reading
and I want to know which words they are.
I know you are reading this poem listening for
    something, torn between bitterness and hope

turning back once again to the task you cannot
    refuse.   35
I know you are reading this poem because there is
    nothing else left to read
there where you have landed, stripped as you are.

MAXINE HONG KINGSTON

from *The Woman Warrior*

In the following section from Kingston's The Woman Warrior, *readers overhear a story reputedly told by Kingston's mother to the young writer, a story she was not to repeat, and haunts her all her life. This section of the book describes the tension between the Chinese culture of Kingston's ancestors and her own American cultural world. Kingston emphasizes the cultural distance between China and America, past and present, and the divided worlds of men and women.*

NO NAME WOMAN

"You must not tell anyone," my mother said, "what I am about to tell you. In China your father had a sister who killed herself. She jumped into the family well. We say that your father has all brothers because it is as if she had never been born.

"In 1924 just a few days after our village celebrated seventeen hurryup weddings—to make sure that every young man who went 'out on the road' would responsibly come home—your father and his brothers and your grandfather and his brothers and your aunt's new husband sailed for America, the Gold Mountain. It was your grandfather's last trip. Those lucky enough to get contracts waved goodbye from the decks. They fed and guarded the stowaways and helped them off in Cuba, New York, Bali, Hawaii. "We'll meet in California next year," they said. All of them sent money home.

I remember looking at your aunt one day when she and I were dressing; I had not noticed before that she had such a protruding melon of a stomach. But I did not think, "She's pregnant," until she began to look like other pregnant women, her shirt pulling and the white tops of her black pants showing. She could not have been pregnant, you see, because her husband had been gone for years. No one said anything. We did not discuss it. In early summer she was ready to have the child, long after the time when it could have been possible.

"The village had also been counting. On the night the baby was to be born the villagers raided our house. Some were crying. Like a great saw, teeth strung with lights, files of people walked zigzag across our land, tearing the rice. Their lanterns doubled in the disturbed black water, which drained away through the broken bunds. As the villagers closed in, we could see that some of them, probably men and women we knew well, wore white masks. The people with long hair hung it over their faces. Women with short hair made it stand up on end. Some had tied white bands around their foreheads, arms, and legs.

"At first they threw mud and rocks at the house. Then they threw eggs and began slaughtering our stock. We could hear the animals scream their deaths—the roosters, the pigs, a last great roar from the ox. Familiar wild heads flared in our night windows; the villagers encircled us. Some of the faces stopped to peer at us, their eyes rushing like searchlights. The hands flattened against the panes, framed heads, and left red prints.

"The villagers broke in the front and the back doors at the same time, even though we had not locked the doors against them. Their knives dripped with the blood of our animals. They smeared blood on the doors and walls. One woman swung a chicken, whose throat she had slit, splattering blood in red arcs about her. We stood together in the middle of our house, in the family hall with the pictures and tables of the ancestors around us and looked straight ahead.

"At that time the house had only two wings. When the men came back we would build two more to enclose our courtyard and a third one to begin a second courtyard. The villagers pushed through both wings, even your grandparents' rooms, to find your aunt's, which was also mine until the men returned. From this room a new wing for one of the younger families would grow. They ripped up her clothes and shoes and broke her combs, grinding them underfoot. They tore her work from the loom. They scattered the cooking fire and rolled the new weaving in it. We could hear them in the kitchen breaking our bowls and banging the pots. They overturned the great waist-high earthenware jugs; duck eggs, pickled fruits, vegetables burst out and mixed in acrid torrents. The old woman from the next field swept a broom through the air and loosed the spirits-of-the-broom over our heads. "Pig." "Ghost." "Pig," they sobbed and scolded while they ruined our house.

"When they left, they took sugar and oranges to bless themselves. They cut pieces from the dead animals. Some of them took bowls that were not broken and clothes that were not torn. Afterward we swept up the rice and sewed it back up into sacks. But the smells from the spilled preserves lasted. Your aunt gave birth in the pigsty that night. The next morning when I went up for the water, I found her and the baby plugging up the family well.

"Don't let your father know that I told you. He denies her. Now that you have started to menstruate, what happened to her could happen to you. Don't humiliate us. You wouldn't like to be forgotten as if you had never been born. The villagers are watchful."

Whenever she had to warn us about life, my mother told stories that ran like this one, a story to grow up on. She tested our strength to establish realities. Those in the emigrant generations who could not reassert brute survival died young and far from home. Those of us in the first American generations have had to figure out how the invisible world the emigrants built around our childhoods fit in solid America.

The emigrants confused the gods by diverting their curses, misleading them with crooked streets and false names. They must try to confuse their offspring as well, who, I suppose, threaten them in similar ways—always trying to get things straight, always trying to name the unspeakable. The Chinese I know hide their names; sojourners take new names when their lives change and guard their real names with silence.

Chinese-Americans, when you try to understand what things in you are Chinese, how do you separate what is peculiar to childhood, to poverty, insanities, one family, your mother who marked your growing with stories, from what is Chinese? What is Chinese tradition and what is the movies?

If I want to learn what clothes my aunt wore, whether flashy or ordinary, I would have to begin, "Remember Father's drowned-in-the-well sister?" I cannot ask that. My mother has told me once and for all the useful parts. She will add nothing unless powered by Necessity, a riverbank that guides her life. She plants vegetable gardens rather than lawns; she carries the odd-shaped tomatoes home from the fields and eats food left for the gods.

Whenever we did frivolous things, we used up energy; we flew high kites. We children came up off the ground over the melting cones our parents brought home from work and the American movie on New Years' Day—Oh, You Beautiful Doll with Betty Grable one year, and She Wore a Yellow Ribbon with John Wayne another year. After the one carnival ride each, we paid in guilt; our tired father counted his change on the dark walk home.

Adultery is extravagance. Could people who hatch their own chicks and eat the embryos and the heads for delicacies and boil the feet in vinegar for party food, leaving only the gravel, eating even the gizzard lining—could such people engender a prodigal aunt? To be a woman, to have a daughter in starvation time was a waste enough. My aunt could not have been the lone romantic who gave up everything for sex. Women in the old China did not choose. Some man had commanded her to lie with him and be his secret evil. I wonder whether he masked himself when he joined the raid on her family.

Perhaps she encountered him in the fields or on the mountain where the daughters-in-law collected fuel. Or perhaps he first noticed her in the marketplace. He was not a stranger because the village housed no strangers. She had to have dealings with him other than sex. Perhaps he worked an adjoining field, or he sold her the cloth for the dress she sewed and wore. His demand must have surprised, then terrified her. She obeyed him; she always did as she was told.

When the family found a young man in the next village to be her husband, she stood tractably beside the best rooster, his proxy, and promised before they met that she would be his forever. She was lucky that he was her age and she would be the first wife, an advantage secure now. The night she first saw him, he had sex with her. Then he left for America. She had almost forgotten what he looked like. When she tried to envision him, she only saw the black and white face in the group photograph the men had had taken before leaving.

The other man was not, after all, much different from her husband. They both gave orders: she followed. "If you tell your family, I'll beat you. I'll kill you. Be here again next week." No one talked sex, ever. And she might have separated the rapes from the rest of living if only she did not have to buy her oil from him or gather wood in the same forest. I want her fear to have lasted just as long as rape lasted so that the fear could have been contained. No drawn-out fear. But women at sex hazarded birth and hence lifetimes. The fear did not stop but permeated everywhere. She told the man, "I think I'm pregnant." He organized the raid against her.

On nights when my mother and father talked about their life back home, sometimes they mentioned an "outcast table" whose business they still seemed to be settling, their voices tight. In a commensal tradition, where food is precious, the powerful older people made wrongdoers eat alone. Instead of letting them start separate new lives like the Japanese, who could become samurais and geishas, the Chinese family, faces averted but eyes glowering sideways, hung on to the offenders and fed them leftovers. My aunt must have lived in the same house as my parents and eaten at an outcast table. My mother spoke about the raid as if she had seen it, when she and my aunt, a daughter-in-law to a different household, should not have been living together at all. Daughters-in-law lived with their husbands' parents, not their own; a synonym for marriage in Chinese is "taking a daughter-in-law." Her husband's parents could have sold her, mortgaged her, stoned her. But they had sent her back to her own mother and father, a mysterious act hinting at disgraces not told me. Perhaps they had thrown her out to deflect the avengers.

She was the only daughter; her four brothers went with her father, husband, and uncles "out on the road" and for some years became western men. When the goods were divided among the family, three of the brothers took land, and the youngest, my father, chose an education. After my grandparents gave their daughter away to her husband's family, they had dispensed all the adventure and all the property. They expected her alone to keep the traditional ways, which her brothers, now among the barbarians, could fumble without detection. The heavy, deep-rooted women were to maintain the past against the flood, safe for returning. But the rare urge west had fixed upon our family, and so my aunt crossed boundaries not delineated in space.

The work of preservation demands that the feelings playing about in one's guts not be turned into action. Just watch their passing like cherry blossoms. But perhaps my aunt, my forerunner, caught in a slow life, let dreams grow and fade and after some months or years went toward what persisted. Fear at the enormities of the forbidden kept her desires delicate, wire and bone. She looked at a man because she liked the way the hair was tucked behind his ears, or she liked the question-mark line of a long torso curving at the shoulder and straight at the hip. For warm eyes or a soft voice or a slow walk—that's all—a few hairs, a line, a brightness, a sound, a pace, she gave up family. She offered us up for a charm that vanished with tiredness, a pigtail that didn't toss when the wind died. Why, the wrong lighting could erase the dearest thing about him.

It could very well have been, however, that my aunt did not take subtle enjoyment of her friend, but, a wild woman, kept rollicking company. Imagining her free with sex doesn't fit, though. I don't know any women like that, or men either. Unless I see her life branching into mine, she gives me no ancestral help.

To sustain her being in love, she often worked at herself in the mirror, guessing at the colors and shapes that would interest him, changing them frequently in order to hit on the right combination. She wanted to look back.

On a farm near the sea, a woman who tended her appearance reaped a reputation for eccentricity. All the married women blunt-cut their hair in flaps about their ears or pulled it back in tight buns. No nonsense. Neither style blew easily into heart-catching tangles. And at their weddings they displayed themselves in their long hair for the last time. "It brushed the backs of my knees," my mother tells me. "It was braided, and even so, it brushed the backs of my knees."

At the mirror my aunt combed individuality into her bob. A bun could have been contrived to escape into black stream-ers blowing in the wind or in quiet wisps about her face, but only the older women in our picture album wear buns. She brushed her hair back from her forehead, tucking the flaps behind her ears. She looped a piece of thread, knotted into a circle between her index fingers and thumbs, and ran the double strand across her forehead. When she closed her fingers as if she were making a pair of shadow geese bite, the string twisted together catching the little hairs. Then she pulled the thread away from her skin, ripping the hairs out neatly, her eyes watering from the needles of pain. Opening her fingers, she cleaned the thread, then rolled it along her hairline and the tops of the eyebrows. My mother did the same to me and my sisters and herself. I used to believe that the expression "caught by the short hairs" meant a captive held with a depilatory string. It especially hurt at the temples, but my mother said we were lucky we didn't have to have our feet bound when we were seven. Sisters used to sit on their beds and cry together, she said, as their mothers or their slave removed the bandages for a few minutes each night and let the blood gush back into their veins. I hope that the man my aunt loved appreciated a smooth brow, that he wasn't just a tits-and-ass man.

Once my aunt found a freckle on her chin, at a spot that the almanac said predestined her for unhappiness. She dug it out with a hot needle and washed the wound with peroxide.

More attention to her looks than these pullings of hairs and pickings at spots would have caused gossip among the villagers. They owned work clothes and good clothes, and they wore good clothes for feasting the new seasons. But since a woman combing her hair hexes beginnings, my aunt rarely found an occasion to look her best. Women looked like great sea snails—the corded wood, babies, and laundry they carried were the whorls on their backs. The Chinese did not admire a bent back; goddesses and warriors stood straight. Still there must have been a marvelous freeing of beauty when a worker laid down her burden and stretched and arched.

Such commonplace loveliness, however, was not enough for my aunt. She dreamed of a lover for the fifteen days of New Year's, the time for families to exchange visits, money, and food. She plied her secret comb. And sure enough she cursed the year, the family, the village, and herself.

Even as her hair lured her imminent lover, many other men looked at her. Uncles, cousins, nephews, brothers would have looked, too, had they been home between journeys. Perhaps they had already been restraining their curiosity, and they left, fearful that their glances, like a field of nesting birds, might be startled and caught. Poverty hurt, and that was their first reason for leaving. But another, final reason for leaving the crowded house was the never-said.

She may have been unusually beloved, the precious only daughter, spoiled and mirror-gazing because of the affection the family lavished on her. When her husband left, they welcomed the chance to take her back from the in-laws; she could live like the little daughter for just a while longer. There are stories that my grandfather was different from other people, "crazy ever since the little Jap bayoneted him in the head." He used to put his naked penis on the dinner table, laughing. And one day he brought home a baby girl, wrapped up inside his brown western-style greatcoat. He had traded one of his sons, probably my father, the youngest, for her. My grandmother made him trade back. When he finally got a daughter of his own, he doted on her. They must have all loved her, except perhaps my father, the only brother who never went back to China, having once been traded for a girl.

Brothers and sisters, newly men and women, had to efface their sexual color and present plain miens. Disturbing hair and eyes, a smile like no other, threatened the ideal of five generations living under one roof. To focus blurs, people shouted face to face and yelled from room to room. The immigrants I know have loud voices, unmodulated to American tones even after years away from the village where they called their friendships out across the fields. I have not been able to stop my mother's screams in public libraries or over telephones. Walking erect (knees straight, toes pointed forward, not pigeon-toed, which is Chinese-feminine) and speaking in an inaudible voice, I have tried to turn myself American-feminine. Chinese communication was loud, public. Only sick people had to whisper. But at the dinner table, where the family members came nearest one another, no one could talk, not the outcasts nor any eaters. Every word that falls from the mouth is a coin lost. Silently they gave and accepted food with both hands. A preoccupied child who took his bowl with one hand got a sideways glare. A complete moment of total attention is due everyone alike. Children and lovers have no singularity here, but my aunt used a secret voice, a separate attentiveness.

She kept the man's name to herself throughout her labor and dying; she did not accuse him that he be punished with her. To save her inseminator's name she gave silent birth.

He may have been somebody in her own household, but intercourse with a man outside the family would have been no less abhorrent. All the village were kinsmen, and the titles shouted in loud country voices never let kinship be forgotten. Any man within visiting distance would have been neutralized as a lover—"brother," "younger brother," "older brother"—115 relationship titles. Parents researched birth charts probably not so much to assure good fortune as to circumvent incest in a population that has but one hundred surnames. Everybody has eight million relatives. How useless then sexual mannerisms, how dangerous.

As if it came from an atavism deeper than fear, I used to add "brother" silently to boys' names. It hexed the boys, who would or would not ask me to dance, and made them less scary and as familiar and deserving of benevolence as girls.

But, of course, I hexed myself also—no dates. I should have stood up, both arms waving, and shouted out across libraries, "Hey, you! Love me back." I had no idea, though, how to make attraction selective, how to control its direction and magnitude. If I made myself American-pretty so that the five or six Chinese boys in the class fell in love with me, everyone else—the Caucasian, Negro, and Japanese boys—would too. Sisterliness, dignified and honorable, made much more sense.

Attraction eludes control so stubbornly that whole societies designed to organize relationships among people cannot keep order, not even when they bind people to one another from childhood and raise them together. Among the very poor and the wealthy, brothers married their adopted sisters, like doves. Our family allowed some romance, paying adult brides' prices and providing dowries so that their sons and daughters could marry strangers. Marriage promises to turn strangers into friendly relatives—a nation of siblings.

In the village structure, spirits shimmered among the live creatures, balanced and held in equilibrium by time and land. But one human being flaring up into violence could open up a black hole, a maelstrom that pulled in the sky. The frightened villagers, who depended on one another to maintain the real, went to my aunt to show her a personal, physical representation of the break she made in the "roundness." Misallying couples snapped off the future, which was to be embodied in true offspring. The villagers punished her for acting as if she could have a private life, secret and apart from them.

If my aunt had betrayed the family at a time of large grain yields and peace, when many boys were born, and wings were being built on many houses, perhaps she might have escaped such severe punishment. But the men—hungry, greedy, tired of planting in dry soil, cuckolded—had been forced to leave the village in order to send food-money home. There were ghost plagues, bandit plagues, wars with the Japanese, floods. My Chinese brother and sister had died of an unknown sickness. Adultery, perhaps only a mistake during good times, became a crime when the village needed food.

The round moon cakes and round doorways, the round tables of graduated size that fit one roundness inside another, round windows and rice bowls—these talismans had lost their power to warn this family of the law: A family must be whole, faithfully keeping the descent line by having sons to feed the old and the dead who in turn look after the family. The villagers came to show my aunt and lover-in-hiding a broken house. The villagers were speeding up the circling of events because she was too shortsighted to see that her infidelity had already harmed the village, that waves of consequences would return unpredictably, sometimes in disguise, as now, to hurt her. This roundness had to be made coinsized so that she would see its circumference: Punish her at the birth of her baby. Awaken her to the inexorable. People who refused fatalism because they could invent small resources insisted on culpability. Deny accidents and wrest fault from the stars.

After the villagers left, their lanterns now scattering in various directions toward home, the family broke their silence and cursed her. "Aiaa, we're going to die. Death is coming. Death is coming. Look what you've done. You've killed us. Ghost! Dead Ghost! Ghost! You've never been born." She ran out into the fields, far enough from the house so that she could no longer hear their voices, and pressed herself against the earth, her own land no more. When she felt the birth coming, she thought that she had been hurt. Her body seized together. "They've hurt me too much," she thought. "This is gall, and it will kill me." With forehead and knees against the earth, her body convulsed and then relaxed. She turned on her back, lay on the ground. The black well of sky and stars went out and out forever; her body and her complexity seemed to disappear. She was one of the stars, a bright dot in blackness, without home, without a companion, in eternal cold and silence. An agoraphobia rose in her, speeding higher and higher, bigger and bigger; she would not be able to contain it; there would be no end to fear.

Flayed, unprotected against space, she felt pain return, focusing her body. This pain chilled her—a cold, steady kind of surface pain. Inside, spasmodically, the other pain, the pain of the child, heated her. For hours she lay on the ground, alternately body and space. Sometimes a vision of normal comfort obliterated reality: She saw the family in the evening gambling at the dinner table, the young people massaging their elders' backs. She saw them congratulating one another, high joy on the mornings the rice shoots came up. When these pictures burst, the stars drew yet further apart. Black space opened.

She got to her feet to fight better and remembered that old-fashioned women gave birth in their pigsties to fool the jealous, pain-dealing gods, who do not snatch piglets. Before the next spasms could stop her, she ran to the pigsty, each step a rushing out into emptiness. She climbed over the fence and knelt in the dirt. It was good to have a fence enclosing her, a tribal person alone.

Laboring, this woman who had carried her child as a foreign growth that sickened her every day, expelled it at last. She reached down to touch the hot, wet, moving mass, surely smaller than anything human, and could feel that it was human after all—fingers, toes, nails, nose. She pulled it up on to her belly, and it lay curled there, butt in the air, feet precisely tucked one under the other. She opened her loose shirt and buttoned the child inside. After resting, it squirmed and thrashed and she pushed it up to her breast. It turned its head this way and that until it found her nipple. There, it made little snuffling noises. She clenched her teeth at its preciousness, lovely as a young calf, a piglet, a little dog.

She may have gone to the pigsty as a last act of responsibility: She would protect this child as she had protected its father. It would look after her soul, leaving supplies on her grave. But how would this tiny child without family find her grave when there would be no marker for her anywhere, neither in the earth nor the family hall? No one would give her a family hall name. She had taken the child with her into the wastes. At its birth the two of them had felt the same raw pain of separation, a wound that only the family pressing tight could close. A child with no descent line would not soften her life but only trail after her, ghostlike, begging her to give it purpose. At dawn the villagers on their way to the fields would stand around the fence and look.

Full of milk, the little ghost slept. When it awoke, she hardened her breasts against the milk that crying loosens. Toward morning she picked up the baby and walked to the well.

Carrying the baby to the well shows loving. Otherwise abandon it. Turn its face into the mud. Mothers who love their children take them along. It was probably a girl; there is some hope of forgiveness for boys.

"Don't tell anyone you had an aunt. Your father does not want to hear her name. She has never been born." I have believed that sex was unspeakable and words so strong and fathers so frail that "aunt" would do my father mysterious harm. I have thought that my family, having settled among immigrants who had also been their neighbors in the ancestral land, needed to clean their name, and a wrong word would incite the kinspeople even here. But there is more to this silence: They want me to participate in her punishment. And I have.

In the twenty years since I heard this story I have not asked for details nor said my aunt's name; I do not know it. People who comfort the dead can also chase after them to hurt them further—a reverse ancestor worship. The real punishment was not the raid swiftly inflicted by the villagers, but the family's deliberately forgetting her. Her betrayal so maddened them, they saw to it that she would suffer forever, even after death. Always hungry, always needing, she would have to beg food from other ghosts, snatch and steal it from those whose living descendants give them gifts. She would have to fight the ghosts massed at crossroads for the buns a few thoughtful citizens leave to decoy her away from village and home so that the ancestral spirits could feast unharassed. At peace, they could act like gods, not ghosts, their descent lines providing them with paper suits and dresses, spirit money, paper houses, paper automobiles, chicken, meat, and rice into eternity—essences delivered up in smoke and flames, steam and incense rising from each rice bowl. In an attempt to make the Chinese care for people outside the family, Chairman Mao encourages us now to give our paper replicas to the spirits of outstanding soldiers and workers, no matter whose ancestors they may be. My aunt remains forever hungry. Goods are not distributed evenly among the dead.

My aunt haunts me—her ghost drawn to me because now, after fifty years of neglect, I alone devote pages of paper to her, though not origamied into houses and clothes. I do not think she always means me well. I am telling on her, and she was a spite suicide, drowning herself in the drinking water. The Chinese are always very frightened of the drowned one, whose weeping ghost, wet hair hanging and skin bloated, waits silently by the water to pull down a substitute.

N. SCOTT MOMADAY

from *The Way to Rainy Mountain*

In the following passage from his autobiographical The Way to Rainy Mountain, *N. Scott Momaday describes his Kiowa grandmother. Momaday provides a sense of what has been lost from his grandmother's Kiowa heritage. One of the most striking elements of the piece is Momaday's description of his grandmother chanting her prayers, an image that reveals powerfully the cultural difference between the values of Momaday's grandmother's culture and those of the modern white world that supplanted it. Through an emphasis on the land and history of his Kiowa ancestors, Momaday conveys a sense of the value of his heritage.*

A single knoll rises out of the plain in Oklahoma, north and west of the Wichita range. For my people, the Kiowas, it is an old landmark, and they gave it the name Rainy Mountain. The hardest weather in the world is there. Winter brings blizzards, hot tornadic winds arise in the spring, and in summer the prairie is an anvil's edge. The grass turns brittle and brown, and it cracks beneath your feet. There are green belts along the rivers and creeks, linear groves of hickory and pecan, willow and witch hazel. At a distance in July or August the steaming foliage seems almost to writhe in fire. Great green and yellow grasshoppers are everywhere in the tall grass, popping up like corn to sting the flesh, and tortoises crawl about on the red earth, going nowhere in the plenty of time. Loneliness is an aspect of the land. All things in the plain are isolate; there is no confusion of objects in the eye, but *one* hill or *one* tree or *one* man. To look upon that landscape in the early morning, with the sun at your back, is to lose the sense of proportion. Your imagination comes to life, and this, you think, is where Creation was begun.

I returned to Rainy Mountain in July. My grandmother had died in the spring, and I wanted to be at her grave. She had lived to be very old and at last infirm. Her only living daughter was with her when she died, and I was told that in death her face was that of a child.

I like to think of her as a child. When she was born, the Kiowas were living the last great moment of their history. For more than a hundred years they had controlled the open range from the Smoky Hill River to the Red, from the headwaters of the Canadian to the fork of the Arkansas and Cimarron. In alliance with the Comanches, they had ruled the whole of the Southern Plains. War was their sacred business, and they were the finest horsemen the world has ever known. But warfare for the Kiowas was preeminently a matter of disposition rather than of survival, and they never understood the grim, unrelenting advance of the U.S. Cavalry. When at last, divided and ill provisioned, they were driven onto the Staked Plains in the cold of autumn, they fell into panic. In Palo Duro Canyon they abandoned their crucial stores to pillage and had nothing then but their lives. In order to save themselves, they surrendered to the soldiers at Fort Sill and were imprisoned in the old stone corral that now stands as a military museum. My grandmother was spared the humiliation of those high gray walls by eight or ten years, but she must have known from birth the affliction of defeat, the dark brooding of old warriors.

Her name was Aho, and she belonged to the last culture to evolve in North America. Her forebears came down from the high country in western Montana nearly three centuries ago. They were a mountain people, a mysterious tribe of hunters whose language has never been classified in any major group. In the late seventeenth century they began a long migration to the south and east. It was a journey toward the dawn, and it led to a golden age. Along the way the Kiowas were befriended by the Crows, who gave them the culture and religion of the Plains. They acquired horses, and their ancient nomadic spirit was suddenly free of the ground. They acquired Tai-me, the sacred sun-dance doll, from that moment the object and symbol of their worship, and so shared in the divinity of the sun. Not least, they acquired the sense of destiny, therefore courage and pride. When they entered upon the Southern Plains they had been transformed. No longer were they slaves to the simple necessity of survival; they were a lordly and dangerous society of fighters and thieves, hunters and priests of the sun. According to their origin myth, they entered the world through a hollow log. From one point of view, their migration was the fruit of an old prophecy, for indeed they emerged from a sunless world.

Though my grandmother lived out her long life in the shadow of Rainy Mountain, the immense landscape of the continental interior lay like memory in her blood. She could tell of the Crows, whom she had never seen, and of the Black Hills, where she had never been. I wanted to see in reality what she had seen more perfectly in the mind's eye, and drove fifteen hundred miles to begin my pilgrimage.

A dark mist lay over the Black Hills, and the land was like iron. At the top of a ridge I caught sight of Devil's Tower upthrust against the gray sky as if in the birth of time the core of the earth had broken through its crust and the motion of the world was begun. There are things in nature that engender an awful quiet in the heart of man; Devil's Tower is one of them. Two centuries ago, because of their need to explain it, the Kiowas made a legend at the base of the rock. My grandmother said:

"Eight children were there at play, seven sisters and their brother. Suddenly the boy was struck dumb; he trembled and began to run upon his hands and feet. His fingers became claws, and his body was covered with fur. There was a bear where the boy had been. The sisters were terrified; they ran, and the bear after them. They came to the stump of a great tree, and the tree spoke to them. It bade them climb upon it, and as they did so, it began to rise into the air. The bear came to kill them, but they were just beyond its reach. It reared against the tree and scored the bark all around with its claws. The seven sisters were borne into the sky, and they became the stars of the Big Dipper." From that moment, and so long as the legend lives, the Kiowas have kinsmen in the night sky. Whatever they were in the mountains, they could be no more. However tenuous their well-being, however much they had suffered and would suffer again, they had found a way out of the wilderness.

My grandmother had a reverence for the sun, a holy regard that now is all but gone out of mankind. There was a wariness in her, and an ancient awe. She was a Christian in her later years, but she had come a long way about, and she never forgot her birthright. As a child she had been to the sun dances, she had taken part in that annual rite, and by it she had learned the restoration of her people in the presence of Tai-me. She was about seven when the last Kiowa sun dance was held in 1887 on the Washita River above Rainy Mountain Creek. The buffalo were gone. In order to consummate the ancient sacrifice—to impale the head of a buffalo bull upon the Tai-me tree—a delegation of old men journeyed into Texas, there to beg and barter for an animal from the Goodnight herd. She was ten when the Kiowas came together for the last time as a living sun-dance culture. They could find no buffalo; they had to hang an old hide from the sacred tree. Before the dance could begin, a company of soldiers rode out from Fort Sill under orders to disperse the tribe. Forbidden without cause the essential act of their faith, having seen the wild herds slaughtered and left to rot upon the ground, the Kiowas backed away forever from the tree. That was July 20, 1890, at the great bend of the Washita. My grandmother was there. Without bitterness, and for as long as she lived, she bore a vision of deicide.

Now that I can have her only in memory, I see my grandmother in the several postures that were peculiar to her: standing at the wood stove on a winter morning and turning meat in a great iron skillet; sitting at the south window, bent above her beadwork, and afterwards when her vision failed, looking down for a long time into the fold of her hands; going out upon a cane, very slowly as she did when the weight of age came upon her; praying. I remember her most often at prayer. She made long, rambling prayers out of suffering and hope, having seen many things. I was never sure that I had the right to hear, so exclusive were they of all mere custom and company. The last time I saw her she prayed standing by the side of her bed at night, naked to the waist, the light of a kerosene lamp moving upon her dark skin. Her long black hair, always drawn and braided in the day, lay upon her shoulders and against her breasts like a shawl. I do not speak Kiowa, and I never understood her prayers, but there was something inherently sad in the sound, some merest hesitation upon the syllables of sorrow. She began in a high and descending pitch, exhausting her breath to silence; then again and again—and always the same intensity of effort, of something that is, and is not, like urgency in the human voice. Transported so in the dancing light among the shadows of her room, she seemed beyond the reach of time. But that was illusion; I think I knew then that I should not see her again.

Houses are like sentinels in the plain, old keepers of the weather watch. There, in a very little while, wood takes on the appearance of great age. All colors wear soon away in the wind and rain, and then the wood is burned gray and the grain appears and the nails turn red with rust. The window panes are black and opaque; you imagine there is nothing within, and indeed there are many ghosts, bones given up to the land. They stand here and there against the sky, and you approach them for a longer time than you expect. They belong in the distance; it is their domain.

Once there was a lot of sound in my grandmother's house, a lot of coming and going, feasting and talk. The summers there were full of excitement and reunion. The Kiowas are a summer people; they abide the cold and keep to themselves, but when the season turns and the land becomes warm and vital they cannot hold still: an old love of going returns upon them. The aged visitors who came to my grandmother's house when I was a child were made of lean and leather, and they bore themselves upright. They wore great black hats and bright ample shirts that shook in the wind. They rubbed fat upon their hair and wound their braids with strips of colored cloth. Some of them painted their faces and carried the scars of old and cherished enmities. They were an old council of warlords, come to remind and be reminded of who they were. Their wives and daughters served them well. The women might indulge themselves; gossip was at once the mark and compensation of their servitude. They made loud and elaborate talk among themselves, full of jest and gesture, fright and false alarm. They went abroad in fringed and flowered shawls, bright beadwork and German silver. They were at home in the kitchen, and they prepared meals that were banquets.

There were frequent prayer meetings, and nocturnal feasts. When I was a child I played with my cousins outside, where the lamplight fell upon the ground and the singing of the old people rose up around us and carried away into the darkness. There were a lot of good things to eat, a lot of laughter and surprise. And afterwards, when the quiet returned, I lay down with my grandmother and could hear the frogs away by the river and feel the motion of the air.

Now there is a funereal silence in the rooms, the endless wake of some final word. The walls have closed in upon my grandmother's house. When I returned to it in mourning, I saw for the first time in my life how small it was. It was late at night, and there was a white moon, nearly full. I sat for a long time on the stone steps by the kitchen door. From there I could see out across the land; I could see the long row of trees by the creek, the low light upon the rolling plains, and the stars of the Big Dipper. Once I looked at the moon and caught sight of a strange thing. A cricket had perched upon the handrail, only a few inches away. My line of vision was such that the creature filled the moon like a fossil. It had gone there, I thought, to live and die, for there, of all places, was its small definition made whole and eternal. A warm wind rose up and purled like the longing within me.

The next morning, I awoke at dawn and went out on the dirt road to Rainy Mountain. It was already hot, and the grasshoppers began to fill the air. Still, it was early in the morning, and birds sang out of the shadows. The long yellow grass on the mountain shone in the bright light, and a scissortail hied above the land. There, where it ought to be, at the end of a long and legendary way, was my grandmother's grave. She had at last succeeded to that holy ground. Here and there on the dark stones were ancestral names. Looking back once, I saw the mountain and came away.

LESLIE SILKO

Yellow Woman

Leslie Silko (b. 1948), a major figure in the Native American Indian Renaissance, was brought up on a Pueblo Reservation in New Mexico. Her essays, poems, and stories center on the traditions of her people, celebrating Native American culture. Her short story, "Yellow Woman," mixes legendary materials with realistic details to create a mysterious and mythic fable.

I

My thigh clung to his with dampness, and I watched the sun rising up through the tamaracks and willows. The small brown water birds came to the river and hopped across the mud, leaving brown scratches in the alkali-white crust. They bathed in the river silently. I could hear the water, almost at our feet where the narrow fast channel bubbled and washed green ragged moss and fern leaves. I looked at him beside me, rolled in the red blanket on the white river sand. I cleaned the sand out of the cracks between my toes, squinting because the sun was above the willow trees. I looked at him for the last time, sleeping on the white river sand.

I felt hungry and followed the river south the way we had come the afternoon before, following our footprints that were already blurred by lizard tracks and bug trails. The horses were still lying down, and the black one whinnied when he saw me but he did not get up—maybe it was because the corral was made out of thick cedar branches and the horses had not yet felt the sun like I had. I tried to look beyond the pale red mesas to the pueblo. I knew it was there, even if I could not see it, on the sandrock hill above the river, the same river that moved past me now and had reflected the moon last night.

The horse felt warm underneath me. He shook his head and pawed the sand. The bay whinnied and leaned against the gate trying to follow, and I remembered him asleep in the red blanket beside the river. I slid off the horse and tied him close to the other horse. I walked north with the river again, and the white sand broke loose in footprints over footprints.

"Wake up."

He moved in the blanket and turned his face to me with his eyes still closed. I knelt down to touch him.

"I'm leaving."

He smiled now, eyes still closed. "You are coming with me, remember?" He sat up now with his bare dark chest and belly in the sun.

"Where?"

"To my place."

"And will I come back?"

He pulled his pants on. I walked away from him, feeling him behind me and smelling the willows.

"Yellow Woman," he said.

I turned to face him. "Who are you?" I asked.

He laughed and knelt on the low, sandy bank, washing his face in the river. "Last night you guessed my name, and you knew why I had come."

I stared past him at the shallow moving water and tried to remember the night, but I could only see the moon in the water and remember his warmth around me.

"But I only said that you were him and that I was Yellow Woman—I'm not really her—I have my own name and I come from the pueblo on the other side of the mesa. Your name is Silva and you are a stranger I met by the river yesterday afternoon."

He laughed softly. "What happened yesterday has nothing to do with what you will do today, Yellow Woman."

"I know—that's what I'm saying—the old stories about the ka'tsina spirit and Yellow Woman can't mean us."

My old grandpa liked to tell those stories best. There is one about Badger and Coyote who went hunting and were gone all day, and when the sun was going down they found a house. There was a girl living there alone, and she had light hair and eyes and she told them that they could sleep with her. Coyote wanted to be with her all night so he sent Badger into a prairie-dog hole, telling him he thought he saw something in it. As soon as Badger crawled in, Coyote blocked up the entrance with rocks and hurried back to Yellow Woman.

"Come here," he said gently.

He touched my neck and I moved close to him to feel his breathing and to hear his heart. I was wondering if Yellow Woman had known who she was—if she knew that she would become part of the stories. Maybe she'd had another name that her husband and relatives called her so that only the ka'tsina from the north and the storytellers would know her as Yellow Woman. But I didn't go on; I felt him all around me, pushing me down into the white river sand.

Yellow Woman went away with the spirit from the north and lived with him and his relatives. She was gone for a long time, but then one day she came back and she brought twin boys.

"Do you know the story?"

"What story?" He smiled and pulled me close to him as he said this. I was afraid lying there on the red blanket. All I could know was the way he felt, warm, damp, his body beside me. This is the way it happens in the stories, I was thinking, with no thought beyond the moment she meets the ka'tsina spirit and they go.

"I don't have to go. What they tell in stories was real only then, back in time immemorial. Eke they say."

He stood up and pointed at my clothes tangled in the blanket. "Let's go," he said.

I walked beside him, breathing hard because he walked fast, his hand around my wrist. I had stopped trying to pull away from him, because his hand felt cool and the sun was high, drying the river bed into alkali. I will see someone, eventually I will see someone, and then I will be certain that he is only a man—some man from nearby—and I will be sure that

I am not Yellow Woman. Because she is from out of time past and I live now and I've been to school and there are highways and pickup trucks that Yellow Woman never saw.

It was an easy ride north on horseback. I watched the change from the cottonwood trees along the river to the junipers that brushed past us in the foothills, and finally there were only piñons, and when I looked up at the rim of the mountain plateau I could see pine trees growing on the edge. Once I stopped to look down, but the pale sandstone had disappeared and the river was gone and the dark lava hills were all around. He touched my hand, not speaking, but always singing softly a mountain song and looking into my eyes.

I felt hungry and wondered what they were doing at home now—my mother, my grandmother, my husband, and the baby. Cooking breakfast, saying, "Where did she go?—maybe kidnapped," and Al going to the tribal police with the details: "She went walking along the river."

The house was made with black lava rock and red mud. It was high above the spreading miles of arroyos and long mesas. I smelled a mountain smell of pitch and buck brush. I stood there beside the black horse, looking down on the small, dim country we had passed, and I shivered.

"Yellow Woman, come inside where it's warm."

2

He lit a fire in the stove. It was an old stove with a round belly and an enamel coffeepot on top. There was only the stove, some faded Navajo blankets, and a bedroll and cardboard box. The floor was made of smooth adobe plaster, and there was one small window facing east. He pointed at the box.

"There's some potatoes and the frying pan." He sat on the floor with his arms around his knees pulling them close to his chest and he watched me fry the potatoes. I didn't mind him watching me because he was always watching me—he had been watching me since I came upon him sitting on the river bank trimming leaves from a willow twig with his knife. We ate from the pan and he wiped the grease from his fingers on his Levis.

"Have you brought women here before?" He smiled and kept chewing, so I said, "Do you always use the same tricks?"

"What tricks?" He looked at me like he didn't understand.

"The story about being a ka'tsina from the mountains. The story about Yellow Woman."

Silva was silent; his face was calm.

"I don't believe it. Those stories couldn't happen now," I said.

He shook his head and said softly, "But someday they will talk about us, and they will say, 'Those two lived long ago when things like that happened.' "

He stood up and went out. I ate the rest of the potatoes and thought about things—about the noise the stove was making and the sound of the mountain wind outside. I remembered yesterday and the day before, and then I went outside.

I walked past the corral to the edge where the narrow trail cut through the black rim rock. I was standing in the sky with nothing around me but the wind that came down from the blue mountain peak behind me. I could see faint mountain images in the distance, miles across the vast spread of mesas and valleys and plains. I wondered who was over there to feel the mountain wind on those sheer blue edges—who walks on the pine needles in those blue mountains.

"Can you see the pueblo?" Silva was standing behind me. I shook my head. "We're too far away."

"From here I can see the world." He stepped out on the edge. "The Navajo reservation begins over there." He pointed to the east. "The Pueblo boundaries are over here." He looked below us to the south, where the narrow trail seemed to come from. "The Texans have their ranches over there, starting with that valley, the Concho Valley. The Mexicans run some cattle over there too."

"Do you ever work for them?"

"I steal from them," Silva answered. The sun was dropping behind us and shadows were filling the land below. I turned away from the edge that dropped forever into the valleys below.

"I'm cold," I said; "I'm going inside." I started wondering about this man who could speak the Pueblo language so well but who lived on a mountain and rustled cattle. I decided that this man Silva must be Navajo, because Pueblo men didn't do things like that.

"You must be a Navajo."

Silva shook his head gently. "Little Yellow Woman," he said, "you never give up, do you? I have told you who I am. The Navajo people know me, too." He knelt down and unrolled the bedroll and spread the extra blankets out on a piece of canvas. The sun was down, and the only light in the house came from outside—the dim orange light from sundown.

I stood there and waited for him to crawl under the blankets.

"What are you waiting for?" he said, and I lay down beside him. He undressed me slowly like the night before beside the river—kissing my face gently and running his hands up and down my belly and legs. He took off my pants and then he laughed.

"Why are you laughing?"

"You are breathing so hard."

I pulled away from him and turned my back to him.

He pulled me around and pinned me down with his arms and chest. "You don't understand, do you, little Yellow Woman? You will do what I want."

And again he was all around me with his skin slippery against mine, and I was afraid because I understood that his strength could hurt me. I lay underneath him and I knew that he could destroy me. But later, while he slept beside me, I touched his face and I had a feeling—the kind of feeling for him that overcame me that morning along the river. I kissed him on the forehead and he reached out for me.

When I woke up in the morning he was gone. It gave me a strange feeling because for a long time I sat there on the blankets and looked around the little house for some object of his—some proof that he had been there or maybe that he was coming back. Only the blankets and the cardboard box remained. The .30–30 that had been leaning in the corner was gone, and so was the knife I had used the night before. He was gone, and I had my chance to go now. But first I had to eat, because I knew it would be a long walk home.

I found some dried apricots in the cardboard box, and I sat down on a rock at the edge of the plateau rim. There was no wind and the sun warmed me. I was surrounded by silence.

I drowsed with apricots in my mouth, and I didn't believe that there were highways or railroads or cattle to steal.

When I woke up, I stared down at my feet in the black mountain dirt. Little black ants were swarming over the pine needles around my foot. They must have smelled the apricots. I thought about my family far below me. They would be wondering about me, because this had never happened to me before. The tribal police would file a report. But if old Grandpa weren't dead he would tell them what happened—he, would laugh and say, "Stolen by a ka'tsina, a mountain spirit. She'll come home—they usually do." There are enough of them to handle things. My mother and grandmother will raise the baby like they raised me. Al will find someone else, and they will go on like before, except that there will be a story about the day I disappeared while I was walking along the river. Silva had come for me, he said he had. I did not decide to go. I just went. Moonflowers blossom in the sand hills before dawn, just as I followed him. That's what I was thinking as I wandered along the trail through the pine trees.

It was noon when I got back. When I saw the stone house I remembered that I had meant to go home. But that didn't seem important any more, maybe because there were little blue flowers growing in the meadow behind the stone house and the gray squirrels were playing in the pines next to the house. The horses were standing in the corral, and there was a beef carcass hanging on the shady side of a big pine in front of the house. Flies buzzed around the clotted blood that hung from the carcass. Silva was washing his hands in a bucket full of water. He must have heard me coming because he spoke to me without turning to face me.

"I've been waiting for you."

"I went walking in the big pine trees."

I looked into the bucket fall of bloody water with brown-and-white animal hairs floating in it. Silva stood there letting his hands drip, examining me intently.

"Are you coming with me?"

"Where?" I asked him.

"To sell the meat in Marquez."

"If you're sure it's O.K."

"I wouldn't ask you if it wasn't," he answered.

He sloshed the water around in the bucket before he dumped it out and set the bucket upside down near the door. I followed him to the corral and watched him saddle the horses. Even beside the horses he looked tall, and I asked him again if he wasn't Navajo. He didn't say anything; he just shook his head and kept cinching up the saddle.

"But Navajos are tall."

"Get on the horse," he said, "and let's go."

The last thing he did before we started down the steep trail was to grab the .30–30 from the corner. He slid the rifle into the scabbard that hung from his saddle.

"Do they ever try to catch you?" I asked.

"They don't know who I am."

"Then why did you bring the rifle?"

"Because we are going to Marquez where the Mexicans live."

3

The trail leveled out on a narrow ridge that was steep on both sides like an animal spine. On one side I could see where the trail went around the rocky gray hills and disappeared into the southeast where the pale sandrock mesas stood in the distance near my home. On the other side was a trail that went west, and as I looked far into the distance I thought I saw the little town. But Silva said no, that I was looking in the wrong place, that I just thought I saw houses. After that I quit looking off into the distance; it was hot and the wildflowers were closing up their deep-yellow, petals. Only the waxy cactus flowers bloomed in the bright sun, and I saw every color that a cactus blossom can be; the white ones and the red ones were still buds, but the purple and the yellow were blossoms, open full and the most beautiful of all.

Silva saw him before I did. The white man was riding a big gray horse, coming up the trail toward us. He was traveling fast and the gray horse's feet sent rocks rolling off the trail into the dry tumbleweeds. Silva motioned for me to stop and we watched the white man. He didn't see us right away, but finally his horse whinnied at our horses and he stopped. He looked at us briefly before he loped the gray horse across the three hundred yards that separated us. He stopped his horse in front of Silva, and his young fat face was shadowed by the brim of his hat. He didn't look mad, but his small, pale eyes moved from the blood-soaked gunny sacks hanging from my saddle to Silva's face and then back to my face.

"Where did you get the fresh meat?" the white man asked.

"I've been hunting," Silva said, and when he shifted his weight in the saddle the leather creaked.

"The hell you have, Indian. You've been rustling cattle. We've been looking for the thief for a long time."

The rancher was fat, and sweat began to soak through his white cowboy shirt and the wet cloth stuck to the thick rolls of belly fat. He almost seemed to be panting from the exertion of talking, and he smelled rancid, maybe because Silva scared him.

Silva turned to me and smiled. "Go back up the mountain, Yellow Woman."

The white man got angry when he heard Silva speak in a language he couldn't understand. "Don't try anything, Indian. Just keep riding to Marquez. We'll call the state police from there."

The rancher must have been unarmed because he was very frightened and if he had a gun he would have pulled it out then. I turned my horse around and the rancher yelled, "Stop!" I looked at Silva for an instant and there was something ancient and dark—something I could feel in my stomach—in his eyes, and when I glanced at his hand I saw his finger on the trigger of the .30–30 that was still in the saddle scabbard. I slapped my horse across the flank and the sacks of raw meat swung against my knees as the horse leaped up the trail. It was hard to keep my balance, and once I thought I felt the saddle slipping backward; it was because of this that I could not look back.

I didn't stop until I reached the ridge where the trail forked. The horse was breathing deep gasps and there was a dark film of sweat on its neck. I looked down in the direction I had come from, but I couldn't see the place. I waited. The wind came up and pushed warm air past me. I looked up at the sky, pale blue and full of thin clouds and fading vapor trails left by jets.

I think four shots were fired—I remember hearing four hollow explosions that reminded me of deer hunting. There could have been more shots after that, but I couldn't have heard them because my horse was running again and the loose rocks were making too much noise as they scattered around his feet.

Horses have a hard time running downhill, but I went that way instead of uphill to the mountain because I thought it was safer. I felt better with the horse running southeast past the round gray hills that were covered with cedar trees and black lava rock. When I got to the plain in the distance I could see the dark green patches of tamaracks that grew along the river; and beyond the river I could see the beginning of the pale sandrock mesas. I stopped the horse and looked back to see if anyone was coming; then I got off the, horse and turned the horse around, wondering if it would go back to its corral under the pines on the mountain. It looked back at me for a moment and then plucked a mouthful of green tumbleweeds before it trotted back up the trail with its ears pointed forward, carrying its head daintily to one side to avoid stepping on the dragging reins. When the horse disappeared over the last hill, the gunny sacks full of meat were still swinging and bouncing.

4

I walked toward the river on a wood-hauler's road that I knew would eventually lead to the paved road. I was thinking about waiting beside the road for someone to drive by but by the time I got to the pavement I had decided it wasn't very far to walk if I followed the river back the way Silva and I had come.

The river water tasted good, and I sat in the shade under a cluster of silvery willows. I thought about Silva, and I felt sad at leaving him; still, there was something strange about him, and I tried to figure it out all the way back home.

I came back to the place on the river bank where he had been sitting the first time I saw him. The green willow leaves that he had trimmed from the branch were still lying there, wilted in the sand. I saw the leaves and I wanted to go back to him—to kiss him and to touch him—but the mountains were too far away now. And I told myself, because I believe it, he will come back sometime and be waiting again by the river.

I followed the path up from the river into the village. The sun was getting low, and I could smell supper cooking when I got to the screen door of my house. I could hear their voices inside—my mother was telling my grandmother how to fix the Jell-O and my husband, Al, was playing with the baby. I decided to tell them that some Navajo had kidnapped me, but I was sorry that old Grandpa wasn't alive to hear my story because it was the Yellow Woman stories he liked to tell best.

SANDRA CISNEROS

Sandra Cisneros (b. 1954), the daughter of a Mexican father and Mexican-American mother, writes poetry and fiction that focus on the lives of the poor. Her short story, "Barbie-Q," which plays on the southwestern food, barbeque, and which centers on the long popular American icon, the Barbie doll, comically raises a number of serious questions about class and money and values.

Barbie-Q

Yours is the one with mean eyes and a ponytail. Striped swimsuit, stilettos, sunglasses, and gold hoop earrings. Mine is the one with bubble hair. Red swimsuit, stilettos, pearl earrings, and a wire stand. But that's all we can afford, besides one extra outfit apiece. Yours, "Red Flair," sophisticated A-line coat-dress with a Jackie Kennedy pillbox hat, white gloves, handbag, and heels included. Mine, "Solo in the Spotlight," evening elegance in black glitter strapless gown with a puffy skirt at the bottom like a mermaid tail, formal-length gloves, pink chiffon scarf, and mike included. From so much dressing and undressing, the black glitter wears off where her titties stick out. This and a dress invented from an old sock when we cut holes here and here and here, the cuff rolled over for the glamorous, fancy-free, off-the-shoulder look.

Every time the same story. Your Barbie is roommates with my Barbie, and my Barbie's boyfriend comes over and your Barbie steals him, okay? Kiss kiss kiss. Then the two Barbies fight. You dumbbell! He's mine. Oh no he's not, you stinky! Only Ken's invisible, right? Because we don't have money for a stupid-looking boy doll when we'd both rather ask for a new Barbie outfit next Christmas. We have to make do with your mean-eyed Barbie and my bubblehead Barbie and our one outfit apiece not including the sock dress.

Until next Sunday when we are walking through the flea market on Maxwell Street and *there!* Lying on the street next to some tool bits, and platform shoes with the heels all squashed, and a fluorescent green wicker wastebasket, and aluminum foil, and hubcaps, and a pink shag rug, and windshield wiper blades, and dusty mason jars, and a coffee can full of rusty nails. *There!* Where? Two Mattel boxes. One with the "Career Gal" ensemble, snappy black-and-white business suit, three-quarter-length sleeve jacket with kick-pleat skirt, red sleeveless shell, gloves, pumps, and matching hat included. The other, "Sweet Dreams," dreamy pink-and-white plaid nightgown and matching robe, lace-trimmed slippers, hairbrush and hand mirror included. How much? Please, please, please, please, please, please, please, until they say okay.

On the outside you and me skipping and humming but inside we are doing loopity-loops and pirouetting. Until at the next vendor's stand, next to boxed pies, and bright orange toilet brushes, and rubber gloves, and wrench sets, and bouquets of feather flowers, and glass towel racks, and steel wool, and Alvin and the Chipmunks records, *there!* And *there!* And *there!* And *there!* and *there!* and *there!* and *there!* Bendable Legs Barbie with her new page-boy hairdo. Midge, Barbie's best friend. Ken, Barbie's boyfriend. Skipper, Barbie's little sister. Tutti and Todd, Barbie and Skipper's tiny twin sister and brother. Skipper's friends, Scooter and Ricky. Alan, Ken's buddy. And Francie, Barbie's MOD'ern cousin.

Everybody today selling toys, all of them damaged with water and smelling of smoke. Because a big toy warehouse on Halsted Street burned down yesterday—see there?—the smoke still rising and drifting across the Dan Ryan expressway. And now there is a big fire sale at Maxwell Street, today only.

So what if we didn't get our new Bendable Legs Barbie and Midge and Ken and Skipper and Tutti and Todd and Scooter and Ricky and Alan and Francie in nice clean boxes and had to buy them on Maxwell Street, all water-soaked and sooty. So what if our Barbies smell like smoke when you hold them up to your nose even after you wash and wash and wash them. And if the prettiest doll, Barbie's MOD'ern cousin Francie with real eyelashes, eyelash brush included, has a left foot that's melted a little—so? If you dress her in her new "Prom Pinks" outfit, satin splendor with matching coat, gold belt, clutch, and hair bow included, so long as you don't lift her dress, right?—who's to know?

MICHAEL HOGAN

Michael Hogan is the author of fourteen books of fiction, poetry, and non fiction, including the seminal work on the Irish Soldiers in the Mexican War of 1846–1848. His poetry and prose have been published in a number of prominent literary magazines, including The Paris Review, The Harvard Review, The Iowa Review, *and the* American Poetry Review. *The poems that follow touch on large themes by means of ordinary details. They also suggest a strong link between the natural and the human, the local and the universal.*

On Translating a Mexican Poet

No es el mismo decir ventana que "window."
—CAMILO JOSÉ CELA

Outside the hummingbird blinks
among blossoming jasmine
to leap a stucco wall
sparkling (from broken glass)
in the always vertical sun
below Cancer. *Cerrada.*

North, ice is a silver ornament
intricate as quartz.
In fair weather Windex gleam and slant rays
for panicked wrens
to break their necks on. Closed.

Ventana abierta.
The postman's two-note whistle
the cowbells for *basura*
dry briskness of the morning brooms
church bells, taco smells.

Open windows.
What do you expect? Neighbors
at it again, incessant car alarms
horns along the avenue
someone's Sunday bacon frying.

Ventana, windspace, *ventus*, opening
for the wind to flow.
Window, *windeye, vind-auga*
lens to watch it by.
Ventana: I am here.
Window: I am watching.

What do we translate here?
What do we mean?
Here is a poem of a third thing.
Language trapped in between.

The Patio at Dusk

In the late afternoon
when the stucco walls still hold
their heat like two lovers
clinging after the act of their joining,

the day pauses.
It waits with whatever hope remains
for the unfolding of the tenacious ivy
for the drooping eye of the jasmine finally to close
for the tender sheathing
of the gentle sex of the hibiscus.

It watches the sun
sagely unbusying himself
as the deepening shade of the palm
opens like a hand over the wall
as the hummingbirds scatter like neon fragments
back to their breathless nests.

For the second time I take
a battered blue teapot
and carry it brimming from the sink.
I go out and water the fig tree
watch its roots draw the liquid
like a desiccated sponge
like a green magnet
like a man
finding a lost spring in a desert
when he had almost surrendered desire.

How easy to love this place
this time without time

in the peace of its darkening
where already the cool breeze of the Sierras
has set the branches trembling
and death itself, simply
another side of a leaf.

Spring

Ice has been cracking all day
and small boys on the shore
pretending it is the booming of artillery
lie prone clutching imaginary carbines.

Inside the compound returning birds
peck at bread scraps from the mess hall.

Old cons shiver in cloth jackets
as they cross the naked quadrangle.
They know the inside perimeter is exactly
two thousand eighty-four steps
and they can walk it five more times
before a steam whistle blows for count.

Above them a tower guard dips his rifle
then raises it again dreamily.
He imagines a speckled trout
coming up shining and raging with life.

Glossary

Note: Words in **boldface** indicate terms defined elsewhere in the glossary.

a cappella (ah kuh-PELL-uh) Italian for "chapel style." In music, a composition for voices only, not accompanied by any other instruments.

absolute music Instrumental composition that does not attempt to tell a story or describe a scene, but deals only with musical sound, form, and tone color. Compare **program music.**

Abstract Expressionism Mid-twentieth-century painting style that rejected realistic representation and emphasized the artist's spontaneous and emotional interaction with the work.

abstraction Art that does not portray the actual appearance of a subject but reflects an artist's nonrepresentational conception of it.

acrylic Paint made of pigment in a solution of a synthetic resin.

action painting Mid-twentieth-century painting style popularized by Pollock in which the artist throws, drops, or splatters paint on a canvas to convey a sense of physical activity.

adagio (uh-DAH-joe; uh-DAH-jee-oh) Musical direction for an "easy" or slow **tempo.**

aesthetic Related to the appreciation of beauty in the arts.

Afrobeat Complex pattern of musical rhythms characteristic of some forms of African music, particularly from Nigeria and Ghana, and of their influence on other musical styles.

agit-trains Trains that disseminated propaganda art in postrevolutionary Russia.

aisle A long side passageway of a church. Aisles run parallel to the central **nave.**

alla prima (AH-la PREE-ma) To paint without making any preliminary drawing.

allegro Musical direction for a fast **tempo.**

altarpiece Painted or carved panel or panels behind or above the **altar** of a church.

altar Raised platform or table at which religious ceremonies take place. It is where the Eucharist is celebrated in Christian churches.

alto In music, the range of the lowest female voice.

anime Sophisticated Japanese animated films.

apartheid Policy of racial segregation practiced in the Republic of South Africa, involving political, legal, and economic discrimination against non-whites.

Apollonian Style of culture and art characterized by clarity, harmony, and restraint, and in the philosophy of Friedrich Nietzsche, as embodying the power of critical reason. See also **Dionysian.**

arch In architecture, the curved or pointed structure spanning the top of an open space, such as a doorway.

aria (AHR-ee-ah) Section of an **opera, oratorio,** or **cantata** for a solo singer, usually with orchestral accompaniment.

Art Nouveau (art new-VOE) French for "new art." A late nineteenth- and early twentieth-century movement noted for its ornamental decoration based on the forms of nature, especially the frequent use of curvilinear and floral patterns.

art song Song in which words and music are artistically combined so the composition reflects the tone, mood, and meaning of the lyrics.

atelier (AT-ul-yay) French for an artist's workshop.

atonality Lack of a home key or **tonal center** in a musical composition.

automatism Surrealist artistic technique of the early twentieth century in which the artist gives up intellectual control over his or her work, allowing the subconscious to take over.

avant-garde (ah-vahnt GUARD) Literally, "advance guard" in French. Military term used to describe artists on the cutting edge, especially those vanguard artists of the early twentieth century in France who focused on **abstraction.**

backbeat Steady, rhythmic background musical beat.

baldacchino (ball-dah-KEY-noh) Italian for, in architecture, a canopy placed over a sacred space, such as an altar.

ballad In poetry, a narrative poem, often of folk origin, written in four-line stanzas. In music, a song that tells a story, often about love and loss.

balustrade In architecture, a carved railing supported by small posts, or balusters, as along a staircase or roof line.

Bantu Member of any of a large number of linguistically related peoples of central and southern Africa. The word means "people" in the Bantu language.

baptistery Small building or room where baptisms are performed.

Baroque (bah-ROKE) Seventeenth-century artistic period characterized by opulence, emotionalism, theatricality, and large scale. In music, a composition style of the seventeenth and eighteenth centuries characterized by ornamentation and rigid structure.

bass In music, the range of the lowest male voice.

Bauhaus Early twentieth-century German art school led by Gropius that attempted to blend all forms of art, science, and technology.

beat Unit of rhythm in a musical composition, or the accent in that rhythm.

Beats Short for Beatniks; members of the Beat generation espoused unconventional attitudes, ideas, and behavior during the 1950s.

Beijing opera Chinese musical drama developed in the nineteenth century that featured fast-paced, stylized scenes based on ancient Chinese myths.

belle époque (bell-lay-PUCK) French for "beautiful age," used to refer to the era of elegance in Paris during the late nineteenth and early twentieth centuries.

blank verse Unrhymed verse in iambic pentameter, frequently used in Elizabethan drama.

brass instrument Musical instrument, such as a trumpet or tuba, played by blowing through a detachable brass mouthpiece.

Bunraku (boon-RAH-koo) Traditional Japanese puppet theater featuring large puppets and puppeteers on stage, and a samisen accompanist and narrator who sit just off the side of the stage.

buttress In architecture, a projecting support or reinforcement of stone.

call and response Style of chanting and/or singing that involves one or more leaders and a group of chanter/singers who respond with their own verses. Popular in African music.

Calvinism Theological belief system, based on John Calvin's (1509–1564) writings, that held that some individuals—the Elect—are predestined to be saved; noted for its strict moral code.

calypso Type of music that originated in the West Indies, characterized by improvised lyrics often on humorous topics.

camera obscura (ub-SKOOR-a) Crude cameralike device for verifying perspective, first used in the Renaissance. It consisted of a box with a tiny hole in one side through which a beam of light passes, projecting the scene, now inverted, on the opposite wall of the box.

campanile Italian for "bell tower."

cantata From the Italian verb "to sing." Small-scale musical work for a solo singer or small group of singers and accompanying instruments. Compare **sonata**

cantilever In architecture, a self-supporting extension from a wall.

canzone; canzoni (can-TSOE-neh; can-TSOE-nee) A song, especially one performed by troubadours in the eleventh through thirteenth centuries and using a love poem as text.

capital In architecture, the decorative top part of a column that supports the **entablature.**

cast iron Cast alloy of iron with silicon and carbon.

chanson (shawn-SEWN or SHANN-sen) French for "song." A general term for a song with French lyrics, especially one performed by troubadours in the eleventh through sixteenth centuries.

chanson de geste (shawn-SAWN duh JZEST) French for "song of deeds." A

medieval **epic** poem that celebrates the actions of historical figures or heroes.

château French for "castle."

chiaroscuro (key-are-oh-SKOO-roe) From the Italian *chiaro*, "clear" or "light," and *oscuro*, "obscure" or "dark." In painting, a method of modeling that uses subtle shifts of light to dark to give the impression of depth.

chorale Simple Protestant hymn sung in unison by a church congregation.

chorus In ancient Greek drama, the group of actors who spoke or chanted in unison, often while moving in a stylized dance; the chorus provided a commentary on the action. Later, the term was generalized to mean a company of singers.

Christian humanism Sixteenth-century belief system that combined the ideals of classical **humanism** with biblical morality.

Classical Artistic style of ancient Greece or Rome that emphasized balance, restraint, and quest for perfection. In music, the eighteenth-century style characterized by accessibility, balance, and clarity.

classicism Any later artistic style reminiscent of the ancient Greek or Roman **Classical** style and its values of balance, restraint, and quest for perfection.

coda Repeated section of music at the end of a movement in **sonata form.**

collage From the French word for "gluing" or "pasting." A visual art form in which bits of familiar objects, such as rope or a piece of newspaper, are glued on a surface.

colonnade In architecture, a row of columns placed side by side, usually to support a roof or series of **arches.**

color field Twentieth-century abstract painting style, popularized by Rothko, that featured large rectangles of flat color intended to evoke an emotional response.

comedy Amusing play or novel with a happy ending, usually including a marriage.

comic opera Light **opera,** especially of the **Classical** era, that featured simple music, an amusing plot, and spoken dialogue.

complementary colors Combination of one primary color and one secondary color formed by the two other primary colors. Red and green, blue and orange, and yellow and purple are complementary colors. See also **primary colors; secondary colors.**

Conceptual art Twentieth-century artistic style whose works were conceived in the mind of the artist, often submitted in a written proposal, and did not originate in the commercial art scene.

concerto (kun-CHAIR-toe) Musical composition for solo instrument and orchestra, usually in three contrasting movements in the pattern fast–slow–fast.

continuous narration In art, simultaneous depiction of events that occurred sequentially.

contrapposto (CONE-truh-POSE-toe) In sculpture and painting, an asymmetrical positioning of the human body in which the weight rests on one leg, elevating the hip and opposite shoulder.

Corinthian Ancient Greek order of architecture characterized by a **capital** ornamented with acanthus leaves.

cornice In architecture, a horizontal molding that forms the uppermost, projecting part of an **entablature.**

Counter-Reformation Sixteenth-century Roman Catholic response of reform to the Protestant **Reformation.**

counterpoint In music, weaving two or more independent melodies into one harmonic texture.

Creole Pan-African societal group in Sierra Leone, in West Africa.

Cubism Early twentieth-century painting and sculpture style characterized by geometric depiction of objects, and faceted multiple views of one object; leading Cubists were Picasso and Braque.

cupola (KYOO-puh-luh) In architecture, a small dome.

Dada Artistic and literary movement during and just after World War I that rejected tradition and championed the irrational and absurd.

daguerreotype (duh-GARE-oh-type) Early photograph form, produced on silver or silver-coated copper plates. Named for Daguerre, the French painter who invented the method.

daimyo Lord, in Japan, of a fortress or castle.

decadents Label that *fin-de-siècle* writers used for themselves to describe their moral decadence, mannered style, and fascination with morbid or perverse subject matter.

deconstruction Twentieth-century philosophical approach, especially in linguistics, of breaking apart the whole, assuming that in all systems there are gaps or inconsistencies and those gaps reveal the most about the whole system.

Deism (DEE-izm) Belief system based on the premise of a God who created the universe and then left it to run by itself.

Depression Often referred to as the Great Depression, a period of drastic international economic decline in the 1930s.

Der Blaue Reiter German for "The Blue Rider." A branch of early twentieth-century German **Expressionist** art characterized by abstract forms and pure colors.

deus ex machina In Greek and Roman drama, a god lowered by stage machinery to resolve a play's plot or extricate a protagonist from a difficult situation. In later literature, the ending of a work that includes an unexpected or improbable device or event to conclude it.

Die Brücke German for "The Bridge." A branch of early-twentieth-century German **Expressionist** art characterized by abstract forms and pure colors.

Dionysian Of an ecstatic, orgiastic, or irrational nature—after the Greek god of wine and revelry, Dionysius—in contrast to a critical and rational emphasis. See **Apollonian.**

diptych Painting or relief consisting of two panels that are hinged together and may be closed like a book.

dissonance In music, a chord or interval that sounds unfinished and seems to need resolution in a harmonious chord.

dome A hemispherical **vault.**

Doric Ancient Greek order of architecture characterized by a **capital** consisting of a square block supported by a cushion shape.

drum In architecture, a circular wall, usually topped by a **dome,** or one of the several cylindrical stones used to construct a column.

Duco Brand name for pyroxylin, a lacquer first developed for automobiles and commonly used as a painting medium in Mexican murals.

egg tempera Paint consisting of ground pigment and egg yolk.

ego Latin word for "I," designating the self as distinct from the world and others. In **psychoanalysis,** the conscious aspect of the self that relates to external reality.

emir Prince, chieftain, king, or other governing leader.

engraving Type of print made by cutting an image onto metal and inking the recesses of the image.

Enlightenment Eighteenth-century European intellectual movement that emphasized the mind's power to reason, challenged the traditional, and favored social reform.

entablature In architecture, the horizontal structure above the columns and **capitals** and below the roof.

epic Extended narrative poem written in a dignified style about a heroic character or characters.

ere ibeji Yoruban carvings of twins, who are believed to be gifts of the gods.

essay French for "attempt." A short literary composition, usually expressing the author's personal views.

etching Type of print made by incising an image on a waxed metal plate, corroding the exposed metal in an acid bath, removing the wax, then inking the recessed design.

étude (AY-tood) Solo musical study focusing on a particular technique.

existentialism Twentieth-century philosophy that emphasizes the uniqueness and isolation of individual experience in an indifferent world and stresses freedom of choice and responsibility for one's actions.

Expressionism Modern artistic and literary movement characterized by emotional expression, often with agitated strokes, intense colors, and themes of sexuality. See also *Die Brücke; Der Blaue Reiter.*

facade Front face of a building.

feng shui The Chinese art of harmonizing people with their environment.

fête galante In Rococo painting, a depiction of an elegant outdoor party, featuring amorous conversations, graceful fashion, and social gallantry.

ficciones Term coined by Borges for his short puzzling fictional works that invite philosophical reflection.

fin de siècle (fan duh SYEH-cle) French for "end of the century." Describes the last years of the nineteenth century, generally noted for inventiveness, social unrest, and artistic activity.

finial Decorative part at the top of a spire, gable, lamp, or piece of furniture.

flâneur (flah-NERR) Type of a person in *belle époque* Paris noted for his or her lifestyle of leisure, fine manners, elegant attire, idle strolling, and light conversation.

foreshortening In painting and relief sculpture, to reduce a form that is not parallel to the picture plane, thereby creating an illusion of three dimensionality.

free verse Poetry that uses the natural rhythm of words and phrases instead of a consistent pattern of meter and rhyme.

fresco Painting technique in which ground pigment mixed with water is applied to wet lime plaster.

fugue (FYOOG) Musical composition of three or four highly independent parts in which one voice states a theme that is then imitated in succession by each of the other voices in **counterpoint.**

Functionalism Architectural theory that a building's design should be adapted to its function.

Futurism Early twentieth-century artistic movement that rejected conventional art and sought to show the fast-paced, dynamic nature of modern life and the machine age, often by portraying various views of a moving object.

geisha Professional Japanese female entertainers.

gelede Traditional Yoruban masked ritual, performed to appease "the mothers," women thought to possess special powers.

genre (JON-ruh) Category of art, music, or literature, such as portrait, bust, symphony, and novel.

genre painting Scene in which the subject is taken from everyday life.

glaze Thin, transparent layer of oil paint, usually applied on top of another layer or over a painted surface to achieve a glowing or glossy look. In ceramics, a glasslike surface coating.

grand opera Nineteenth-century form of **opera** that appealed to the audience because of its spectacle.

Greek cross In architecture, a floor plan with four arms of equal length. Compare to **Latin cross.**

guild Association of people in the same craft or trade, formed during the Middle Ages or Renaissance to give economic and political power to its members and to control the trade's standards.

haiku (HIGH-koo) Japanese poetry form in three lines, with seventeen syllables in the pattern five, seven, and five syllables per line; usually features imagery from nature, includes a reference to a season, and avoids rhyme.

Happening An art form of the 1960s that incorporated theater, performance, visual arts, and audience involvement.

Harlem Renaissance Mid-twentieth-century literary and artistic movement centered in the African-American community of New York City's Harlem neighborhood.

harmony In music, playing or singing two or more tones at the same time, especially when the resulting sound is pleasing to the ear; generally, the arrangement of chords.

hayashi Instruments as a group used to accompany Japanese Noh drama.

highlife Style of contemporary African music featuring a fusion of indigenous dance rhythms and melodies with Western marches, sea chanties, and church hymns.

homophony; homophonic In music, the playing or singing of a single melodic line with harmonic accompaniment.

hôtel French for "townhouse."

humanism Belief system, especially during the Renaissance, that stressed the worth, dignity, and accomplishments of the individual. Stemmed from renewed interest in **Classical** values of ancient Greece and Rome.

icon Religious image, such as a figure from the Bible, used as a sacred reminder of important elements of Christianity.

iconoclasm; iconoclastic controversy (eye-KON-o-KLAZ-em) Opposition to the use of religious images; the systematic destruction of religious **icons.**

iconography In visual arts, the symbols used to communicate meaning.

iconophile A lover of artistic images, at odds with iconoclasts in the **iconoclastic controversy** of the Byzantine era.

iconostasis Panel of **icons** that typically separates the priests from the rest of the congregation in the Eastern Orthodox Church.

id Latin for "thing"; in Freudian theory the unconscious part of the psyche and the source of instinctual impulses, including sexual desires.

idée fixe (ee-day FEEKS) French for "fixed idea." In music, a recurring musical theme or idea used throughout a movement or entire composition, as in Berlioz's *Symphonie Fantastique.*

illusionism Appearance of reality in art; specifically, the technique used to make a created work look like a continuation of the surrounding architecture.

impasto (im-POSS-toe) Paint applied thickly so an actual texture is created on the painted surface.

Impressionism Late nineteenth-century artistic style that sought to portray a fleeting view of the world, usually by applying paint in short strokes of pure color. In music, a style that suggested moods and places through lush and shifting harmonies and vague rhythms.

Industrial Revolution Rapid emergence of modern industrial production during the late eighteenth and early nineteenth centuries.

International style Twentieth-century architectural style focusing primarily on modern materials, especially steel and concrete, and boxlike shapes.

Ionic Ancient Greek order of architecture characterized by a capital in the shape of a curling volute scroll.

jazz Category of music, first developed by African Americans in the early twentieth century, that usually features **syncopated** rhythms and improvisation of the melody or a phrase.

Jesuits Members of the Society of Jesus, an order of Roman Catholic priests established by St. Ignatius of Loyola in 1540.

Ji Chorus for Japanese Noh drama.

Kabuki (kuh-BOO-key) Japanese musical theater developed in the seventeenth century, noted for its melodramatic dancing, lively drama, and instrumental accompaniment. Traditionally performed by an all-male cast.

kami Local deities in the Japanese Shinto system of belief.

koan Riddle in the form of a paradox used in Zen as an aid to meditation and intuitive understanding.

koto A Japanese stringed instrument something like a zither.

lantern In architecture, an open or windowed structure placed on top of a roof to allow light to enter below.

Latin cross In architecture, a floor plan with three short arms and one long one. Compare to **Greek cross.**

Lebensraum Additional territory deemed necessary to a nation, especially Nazi Germany, for its continued existence or economic well-being.

leitmotif (LIGHT-moe-teef) German for "leading motive." In Wagnerian opera, brief fragments of melody or rhythm that trigger the audience to think of particular characters, actions, or objects.

Les Fauves; **Fauvism** (FOVE; FOVE-izm) French for "wild beasts." Early twentieth-century artistic movement characterized by violent, arbitrary colors as seen in the paintings of Matisse.

libretto Words for an opera or other textual vocal work.

Lied; Lieder (LEED; LEED-er) Romantic German **art song** designed for a vocalist and accompanist performing in a room of a home.

literati Literary intelligentsia or leading literary figures of a country.

lithograph Type of print made when an image, drawn with a greasy substance on a stone block, is first wetted, then inked. Because the greasy areas repel water, only the image accepts the ink.

liturgy Religious rite used in public organized worship.

loggia (LOH-juh) In architecture, a covered open air gallery.

Lutheranism Theological belief system and denomination founded by Martin Luther (1483–1546) that holds that salvation is delivered by faith, not by personal achievement.

lyric poetry Poems that have a songlike quality; usually emotional in nature.

madrigal **Polyphonic** music composed for a small group of singers, usually based on short **secular lyric** poems and sung with no accompaniment.

magic realism Latin American literary style that weaves together realistic events with incredible and fantastic ones to convey the often mysterious truths of life.

Mannerism Artistic style of the sixteenth century that rejected Renaissance aesthetic principles; noted for its obscure subject matter, unbalanced compositions, distorted bodies and poses, strange facial expressions, confusing spatial constructions, and harsh colors.

mass Central religious ritual, principally in the Roman Catholic Church; a musical setting of this ritual.

mazurka Lively Polish dance in triple meter.

Minimal art (or Minimalism) Twentieth-century artistic style featuring a small number of shapes arranged in a simple, often repeated, pattern.

minuet Slow, elegant dance in triple meter.

minuet and trio form Organizing structure for a musical work in the pattern minuet-trio-minuet. Usually the form of the third movement of a **symphony.** See also **minuet; trio.**

mobile Sculptural form suspended from the ceiling, mechanized or moved by air currents; invented by Calder in the 1930s.

mock epic Extended narrative poem that treats a trivial incident in a heroic manner. See also **epic.**

model In painting, to create the illusion of depth by using light and shadow. In sculpture, to shape a pliable substance into a three-dimensional object.

Modernism; the modern Artistic and literary movement of the late nineteenth and twentieth centuries that sought to find new methods of artistic expression for the modern, dynamic world, and rejected the traditions of the past.

monastery Residence for monks.

monophony Musical texture with a single melody and no accompaniment. Compare **polyphony.**

montage In film, a set of abruptly edited images used for dramatic effect.

mosaic Image created by inlaying small pieces of colored glass, stone, or tile in mortar; mosaics are usually placed on floors, walls, or ceilings.

motet In Renaissance music, a multi-voiced composition, usually based on a sacred Latin text and sung *a cappella.*

muezzin (myoo-EZ-in) Crier who calls the Muslim faithful to prayer five times a day.

mural A large wall painting.

music drama Musical term first used by Wagner to describe his operas that combined song, instrumental music, dance, drama, and poetry with no interruptions and without breaking the opera up into conventional arias or recitatives.

naturalism Late nineteenth-century literary movement that strove to depict characters in naturalistic, objective detail, focusing on the authenticity of characters, setting, and situations; emphasized biological and cultural determinants for the behavior and fate of literary characters.

natural selection The idea that nature chooses or selects organisms with natural characteristics best able to survive. Natural selection is the mechanism at the basis of Charles Darwin's theory of evolution.

Nazi Member of Hitler's German National Socialist Party.

Neoclassicism Late-eighteenth-century artistic style that revived an interest in the ancient **Classical** ideals. Developed as a reaction to the more ornate Rococo style,

Neoplatonism Revival of the philosophy of Plato, developed by Plotinus in the third century C.E. and prevalent during the Renaissance; based on the belief that the psyche is trapped within the body and philosophical thought is the only way to ascend from the material world to union with the single, higher source of existence.

niche In architecture, a recess in a wall, often used to hold a statue or vase.

nocturne Musical composition for the night, usually melancholy in tone and for solo piano.

Noh (NO) Japanese musical theater developed in the fifteenth century, noted for its solemnity, highly poetic texts, stylized gestures, and masked actors.

nokan Japanese flute used in Noh theater.

novel Literary form based on social and psychological descriptions of the world and individual people, including a plot unfolded by the actions and thoughts of fictional characters. Although the novel became a dominant kind of literature in eighteenth-century England, its antecedents include *Don Quixote,* in seventeenth-century Spain, and *The Tale of Genji,* at the beginning of the second millennium, in Japan.

obelisk In architecture, a four-sided shaft topped by a pyramid.

octave Eight-line section of a poem, particularly the first section in a **Petrarchan sonnet;** in music, an eight-note interval.

odalisque Harem woman.

ode Lyric poem, usually addressed to a person or object and written in a dignified style.

opera Italian for "a work." Musical form, first introduced in the **Baroque** era, that combines drama, a text set to vocal music, and orchestral accompaniment.

oracle A religious professional and prophet who interpreted the will of the gods.

Oratorians Group of lay Catholics, founded in 1575 by St. Philip Ncri, who met for spiritual conversation, study, and prayer.

oratories Places for prayer, such as private chapels, and associated with the Oratorians, a religious movement of priests and lay persons, founded by St. Philip Neri during the Counter-Reformation in the sixteenth century.

oratorio Sacred opera performed without costume or acting, featuring solo singers, a chorus, and an orchestra.

oratory Prayer hall.

orthogonal In visual arts, a receding line perpendicular to the picture plane. In linear perspective, orthogonals converge and disappear at a **vanishing point.**

o-tsuzumi Type of hourglass drum held on the hip and used in Japanese Noh theater.

palette Artist's choice of colors for a particular work of art, or the surface on which such colors are placed and mixed.

patron Person who sponsors art or artists financially.

pediment In **Classical** architecture, a triangular space at the end of a building, formed by the **cornice** and the ends of the sloping roof.

percussion instrument Musical instrument, such as a timpani or bass drum, played by hitting or shaking.

peristyle In architecture, a continuous row of columns, forming an enclosure around a building or courtyard.

perspective A method of creating the illusion of three-dimensional space on a two-dimensional surface. Achieved by methods such as *atmospheric perspective,* using slight variations in color and sharpness of the subject, or *linear perspective,* creating a horizon line and **orthogonals,** which meet at **vanishing points.**

Petrarchan sonnet Italian sonnet poem of an octave of eight lines, which introduces a situation or problem scene, and sestet of six lines, which expands on the scene or resolves the problem. The octave rhymes *abba abba* (or *abab abab*), and the sestet rhymes *cde cde* (or *cde ced; cde dce;* or *cd cd cd*). Devised by the poet Petrarch in the fourteenth century. See also **Shakespearean sonnet.**

phenomena (fuh-NOM-uh-nuh) In Kantian philosophy, elements as they are perceived by worldly senses, not as they really are.

philosophes (fill-uh-SOFF) Group of intellectuals of the **Enlightenment** who believed that, through reason, humans could achieve a perfect society.

pianoforte (pee-ANN-oh-FOR-tay) Literally, "soft loud" in Italian. Name originally used for the piano because of its ability to differentiate between soft and loud tones, which the harpsichord could not do.

picaresque In literature, a narrative form that originated in Spain and details the adventurous life of a *pícaro*, a rogue hero.

pier In architecture, a vertical support structure similar to a column, but usually square or rectangular in shape, rather than cylindrical.

pietà (pee-ay-TAH) Italian for "pity." In visual arts, a work that shows Mary mourning over her dead son Jesus in her lap.

pilaster In architecture, a flat decorative pillar attached to a wall, projecting just slightly, that may reinforce the wall.

pipa A Chinese lute.

plainchant; plainsong In music, the **monophonic,** unmetered vocal music of the early Christian church, as in **Gregorian chant.**

Pointillism Post-Impressionist technique developed by Seurat that uses an almost exact application of paint in small dots or points, intended to blend in the viewer's eyes.

polonaise Stately, proud Polish dance in triple meter.

polyphony Simultaneous playing or singing of several independent musical lines. Compare **monophony.**

polyptych (POL-ip-tick) Painting or relief with four or more panels, often hinged so panels can be folded. See also **triptych.**

polyrhythms Multiple rhythms played or sung simultaneously within the same musical composition.

Pop Art Mid twentieth-century artistic style in which subjects were taken from everyday items from the mass media or were mass produced, such as comic strips, soup cans, or images of famous figures.

portal In architecture, an entrance or doorway.

portico In architecture, a porch or walkway covered by a roof supported by columns. It often marks an entrance to the main building.

prelude (PRELL-yood) Short instrumental composition that usually precedes a larger musical work.

primary colors The colors red, yellow, and blue. See also **secondary colors.**

program music Instrumental composition that musically describes a scene, story, or other nonmusical situation. Popularized in the Romantic era. Compare **absolute music.**

proscenium arch In theater, the framing device that separates the stage from the audience.

psychoanalysis Method of therapy originated by Sigmund Freud in which free association, dream interpretation, and analysis of resistance and transference are used to explore repressed or unconscious impulses, anxieties, and internal conflicts.

ragtime Jazz piano composition in which the left hand plays a steady beat while the right hand improvises on a melody using a **syncopated** rhythm.

rational humanism Philosophical belief system of the **Enlightenment** based on the idea that progress is possible only through learning and through the individual's freedom to learn.

Realism Nineteenth-century artistic and literary movement that attempted to convey to the public the realities of modern life, not just to depict the beautiful.

recitative (ress-uh-tuh-TEEV) In **opera,** a form of musically heightened speech halfway between spoken dialogue and melodic singing.

requiem Mass for a deceased person and the music for such a mass.

rib In architecture, a curved, projecting **arch** used for support or decoration in a **vault.**

riff In **jazz,** a short phrase repeated frequently during improvisation.

ritornello (rit-or-NELL-low) Musical passage that will recur several times throughout a **concerto** movement.

rondo form Organizing structure for a musical work in which the main theme repeats itself frequently, with new, contrasting material added between each repetition. Often the form of the second or last movements of a **concerto.**

salon; Salon Large reception room in a townhouse, or the social gathering held in such rooms; an annual exhibition of works of art, especially by the French Academy in the eighteenth and nineteenth centuries.

Salon des Refusés French for "Salon of the Rejected." Artistic **salon** established by Napoleon III in 1863 to exhibit paintings rejected by the official French Academy Salon.

samba Brazilian dance.

samurai Ruler-warriors of Japan, especially during the feudal era.

satire Literary or dramatic work that exposes vice or follies with ridicule or sarcasm, often in a humorous way.

scat Method of vocal singing in nonsense syllables.

score Written or published version of a musical composition showing parts for all instruments and voices.

scroll In Chinese and Japanese art, a painting or text drawn on paper or silk. The scroll is conventionally kept rolled and tied except on special occasions. Some are vertical *hanging scrolls;* others are horizontal *hand scrolls.* Japanese narrative scrolls are called *emaki-mano.*

secondary colors The colors orange, green, and purple, formed when two primary colors (red, yellow, or blue) are mixed. See also **primary colors.**

secular Not sacred or religious.

sestet Six-line section of a poem, particularly the last section in a **Petrarchan sonnet.**

sestina Verse form developed by Renaissance troubadours that employs six-line stanzas and a three-line concluding envoy, with the six end words of the first stanza repeated throughout the other five stanzas and envoy.

sfumato (sfoo-MA-toe) The Italian word for "smoky." In painting, the intentional blurring of the outline of a figure in a hazy, almost smoky atmosphere.

Shakespearean sonnet; English sonnet Poem of three four-line stanzas and a final two-line couplet, usually rhyming *abab cdcd efef gg.* See also **Petrarchan sonnet.**

Shinto Principal and former state religion of Japan characterized by rituals and venerations for local deities and strong patriotism.

shogun Hereditary military dictator of Japan; originally, commander-in-chief of the **samurai.**

Socialist Realism Artistic style declared by Stalin in 1934 as the official Soviet style; it rejected **abstraction** and focused on images of soldiers, workers, and peasants.

soliloquy (suh-LILL-uh-kwee) In drama, a character's private reflections spoken aloud toward the audience, but not to the other characters.

sonata From the Italian verb "to sound." Musical composition for one or two instruments, usually in three or four movements. Compare **cantata.**

sonata form Organizing structure for a musical work with three main sections: exposition, development, and recapitulation, sometimes followed by a **coda.** Usually the form of the first and fourth movements of a **symphony.**

song cycle Popularized during the nineteenth century by German *Lied* composers, a group of songs based on a single theme or story.

sonnet Renaissance lyric poetic form invented by Petrarch in Italy and imitated by English Renaissance poets, including Shakespeare. A sonnet includes fourteen lines in iambic pentameter with one of two predominant structural and rhyming patterns: (1) the **Italian** or **Petrarchan sonnet** comprising an eight-line octave and six-line sestet, with a rhyme pattern of abba abba cde cde, or cd cd cd (or a variation on these); (2) the **English** or **Shakespearean sonnet** comprising three quatrains and a concluding couplet—typically rhyming abab cdcd efef gg.

soprano In music, the range of the highest voice of females or young boys.

still life Painting or sculpture representing inanimate subjects such as flowers, fruit, or objects.

stream of consciousness Modern literary technique that records the free flow of a character's mental impressions.

Sumo A style of Japanese wrestling in which the object is to push an opponent out of the ring or throw him down within it.

superman In the philosophy of Friedrich Nietzsche, the superior being, the over or super person who is exempt from legal and moral constraints that bind ordinary people.

swing Jazz style of big bands of the 1930s and 1940s, usually fast and arranged instead of improvised.

Symbolists Poets of the late nineteenth century who used symbolic words and figures to express ideas, impressions, and emotions and rejected the realistic depiction of the external world.

symphony Large orchestral work, usually in four distinct movements.

syncopation Musical rhythm in which **beats** that are normally unaccented are stressed.

synoptic gospels The **gospels** of Matthew, Mark, and Luke, which are similar. The gospel of John is unique.

taiko Stick drum on a stand; used in Japanese Noh theater.

talking drum Type of African drum whose sound blurs the line between melody and rhythm.

tango Popular Argentinian dance and the music affiliated with it.

tenebrism Painting technique that dramatically contrasts light and dark and makes little use of middle tones.

tenor In music, the range of the highest male voice, which usually carries the melody; also, the bottom, slower line of an **organum duplum.**

theme and variations form Organizing structure for a musical work in which a theme is presented and repeated several more times, each time in a slightly varied way. Often the form of the first and fourth movements of a **symphony.**

theocracy Political entity ruled by a religious figure or group claiming to have divine authority.

tonal center Home key of a musical composition.

tragedy Serious literary or theatrical work about a central character's problems, with an unhappy ending.

Transcendentalism Romantic philosophical theory that an ideal reality transcends the material world, known only through intuition, especially in nature. See also **phenomena.**

triptych Painting or relief consisting of three panels, with the side panels hinged so they can be folded over the center panel.

trompe-l'oeil (trump-LOY) French for "trick the eye." An artistic effect that creates an optical illusion of reality.

twelve-tone composition Musical composition style developed by Schoenberg that uses a twelve-note scale, which is the traditional octave plus all internal half steps; each tone is used equally and in a highly organized manner.

ukiyo-e Japanese for "pictures of the floating world." Style of Japanese woodblock prints of the seventeenth and eighteenth centuries noted for their everyday subject matter.

unities In Greek drama, and in attenuated form in later Renaissance theater, the rules that a play's action should take place within a single day, at a single location, and focus on a single central plot.

vanishing point In linear perspective, a point on the horizon line at which the **orthogonals** appear to converge. See drawing in Starter Kit on p. xxii.

vault Arched masonry roof or ceiling. A **barrel** (or tunnel) **vault,** is an uninterrupted semicircular vault made of a series of **arches.** A **cross** or **groin vault** is created by the intersection of two barrel vaults set at right angles. A *ribbed vault* is a form of groin vault in which the groins formed by the intersection of curved sides are reinforced by raised **ribs.** See drawing in Starter Kit on p. xxvi.

verisimilitude (ver-uh-si-MILL-uh-tude) Appearance of being true to reality.

vernacular Common language spoken in a particular country or region.

waltz Ballroom dance in triple meter.

whole tone; whole step In music, the **interval** between any two consecutive white keys on the piano, when a black key intervenes. A whole step is made up of two half steps.

woodcut Print made by carving a design into a wooden block, inking the raised surfaces, placing a piece of paper on the inked surface, and applying pressure to transfer the ink to the paper.

woodwind instrument Musical instrument, such as a flute or clarinet, played by blowing through a reed or mouthpiece attached to the main body of the instrument.

word painting In Renaissance music, a composition style that emphasizes the meaning of words through the accompanying music. For example, the word "weep" might be expressed by a descending melodic line.

zazen Meditation as practiced in Zen Buddhism.

Picture Credits and Further Information

Introduction
0.1 Nasjonalmuseet for Kunst/Nasjonalgalleriet, Oslo. © 2003 The Munch Museum/The Munch-Ellingsen Group/Artists Rights Society (ARS), NY/ADAGP, Paris. J. Lathion/© Nasjonalgalleriet; 0.3 Robert Harding World Imagery

Chapter Thirteen
13.1 SCALA/Art Resource, NY; 13.2 Galleria degli Uffizi, Florence. SCALA/Art Resource, NY; 13.3 Bodleian Library, University of Oxford; 13.4 SCALA/Art Resource, NY; 13.6 Ralph Lieberman/Canali PhotoBank; 13.7 ALINARI/Art Resource, NY; 13.8 SCALA/Art Resource, NY; 13.9 SCALA/Art Resource, NY; 13.10 Museo Nazionale del Bargello, Florence. SCALA/Art Resource, NY; 13.11 Museo dell'Opera del Duomo, Florence. SCALA/Art Resource, NY; 13.12 SCALA/Art Resource, NY; 13.13 SCALA/Art Resource, NY; 13.14 Galleria degli Uffizi, Florence. SCALA/Art Resource, NY; 13.15 Galleria degli Uffizi, Florence. SCALA/Art Resource, NY; 13.16 SCALA/Art Resource, NY; 13.17 Galleria degli Uffizi, Florence. SCALA/Art Resource, NY; 13.18 Galleria degli Uffizi, Florence. SCALA/Art Resource, NY; 13.19 SCALA/Art Resource, NY; 13.20 SuperStock, Inc.; 13.21 © Musée du Louvre/Reunion des Musées Nationaux/Art Resource, NY; 13.22; ALINARI/Art Resource, NY; 13.23 Giancarlo Costa/Brera Gallery, Milan. Ministero per i Beni e le Attivita Culturali; 13.24 Kunsthistorisches Museum, Vienna. Erich Lessing/Art Resource, NY, 13.25 Vatican Museums, Rome, Italy; 13.26 Araldo de Luca/Fabbrica di San Pietro. Vatican Museums, Rome, Italy; 13.27 SCALA/Art Resource, NY; 13.28 Bridgeman Art Library International; 13.29 Vatican Museums, Rome, Italy; 13.30 ALINARI/Art Resource, NY; 13.31 Janetta Rebold Benton, Prof. of Fine Arts, Pace University; 13.33 ALINARI/Art Resource, NY; 13.34 Cameraphoto Arte di Codato G.P. & C.snc; 13.35 Erich Lessing/Museo del Prado, Madrid, Spain/Art Resource, NY; 13.36 J. G. Berizzi. Musée du Louvre, Paris/Reunion des Musées Nationaux, France/Art Resource, NY; 13.37 Uffizi Gallery, Florence, ALINARI/Art Resource, NY; 13.38 © The National Gallery Company, Ltd., London; 13.39 San Giorgio Maggiore, Venice. SCALA/Art Resource, NY; 13.40 Archivo Fotographico Oronoz, Madrid; 13.41 Larry Sander, Milwaukee Art Museum. Gift of the Family of Mrs. Fred Vogel, Jr.; 13.42 National Museum of Women in the Arts, Washington, DC. Gift of Wallace and Wilhelmina Holladay; 13.43 Kunsthistorisches Museum, Vienna, Austria; 13.44 SCALA/Art Resource, NY; 13.45 SCALA/Art Resource, NY; 13.46 Janetta Rebold Benton, Prof. of Fine Arts, Pace University

Chapter Fourteen
14.1 The Cloisters Collection, Metropolitan Museum of Art, NY; 14.2 © St. Baafskathedraal, Gent/© Paul M. R. Maeyert Photographie; 14.3 © St. Baafskathedraal, Gent/© Paul M. R. Maeyert Photographie; 14.4 Erich Lessing/Art Resource, NY; 14.5 Museo del Prado, Madrid/The Bridgeman Art Library International; 14.6 Derechos reservados © Museo Nacional Del Prado, Madrid; 14.7 Uffizi Gallery, Florence. Cranach. SCALA/Art Resource, NY; 14.8 Galleria Nazionale d'Arte Antica, Rome. SCALA/Art Resource, NY; 14.9 Alte Pinakothek, Munich, Germany/A. K. G., Berlin/SuperStock, Inc.; 14.10 Gift of Junius S. Morgan, Metropolitan Museum of Art, NY; 14.11 Philadelphia Museum of Art; 14.12 Musée du Louvre, Paris. Reunion des Musées Nationaux/Art Resource, NY; 14.13 © The National Gallery Company Ltd.; 14.14 Rogers Fund, Metropolitan Museum of Art, NY; 14.15 Erich Lessing/Kunsthistorisches Museum, Vienna/Art Resource, NY; 14.16 Nils-Johan Norenlind/AGE Fotostock America, Inc.; 14.17 © Eric Crichton/CORBIS, NY. All Rights Reserved; 14.18 The Royal Collection © 2004 Her Majesty Queen Elizabeth II, Royal Collection Enterprises Ltd.; 14.19 Reproduced by permission of The Huntington Library Art Collections and Botanical Gardens, San Marino, California; 14.20 Giraudon/The Bridgeman Art Library International; 14.21 C. Walter Hodges, "Shakespeare and the Players," London 1948

Chapter Fifteen
15.1 Janetta Rebold Benton, Prof. of Fine Arts, Pace University; 15.3 © Gianni Dagli Orti/CORBIS/Bettmann; 15.4 Araldo de Luca/Embassy of Italy; 15.5 Araldo de Luca/Embassy of Italy; 15.6 SCALA/Art Resource, NY; 15.7 Musei Vaticani, Pinacoteca, Rome, SCALA/Art Resource, NY; 15.8 Galleria degli Uffizi, Florence, SCALA/Art Resource, NY; 15.9 National Museum of Women in the Arts, Washington, DC, Gift of Wallace and Wilhelmina Holladay. Conservation funds generously provided by the Southern California State Committee of the National Museum of the Arts; 15.10 SCALA/Art Resource, NY; 15.11 SCALA/Art Resource, NY; 15.12 Rijksmuseum, Amsterdam; 15.13 Nationalmuseum, Stockholm, 15.14 Rijksmuseum, Amsterdam; 15.15 Metropolitan Museum of Art, NY, bequest of Mrs. H. O. Havermeyer, The H. O. Havermeyer Collection; 15.16 Royal Picture Gallery Mauritshuis, The Hague; 15.17 Widener Collection, © Board of Trustees, National Gallery of Art, Washington, DC; 15.18 Gift of Henry G. Marquand, Metropolitan Museum of Art, NY; 15.19 National Museum of Women in the Arts, Washington, DC. Gift of Wallace and Wilhelmina Holladay; 15.20 Jean Lewandowski, Musée du Louvre, Paris/Reunion des Musées Nationaux/Art Resource, NY; 15.21 Derechos reservados © Museo Nacional Del Prado, Madrid; 15.22 Musée du Louvre, Paris/Reunion des Musées Nationaux/Art Resource, NY; 15.23 Erich Lessing/Art Resource, NY, Museo del Prado, Madrid; 15.24 Erich Lessing/Bodleian Library, University of Oxford; 15.25 Derechos reservados © Museo Nacional Del Prado, Madrid; 15.26 Metropolitan Museum of Art, NY; 15.27 The Norton Simon Foundation; 15.28 James Austin/Art Resource/Musée du Louvre; 15.29 Massimo Listri/CORBIS, NY; 15.30 A. F. Kersting; 15.31 Robert Harding/Metropolitan Museum of Art, NY; 15.32 The Crosby Brown Collection of Musical Instruments/Embassy of Mexico; 15.33 The Bancroft Library; 15.34 The Bancroft Library; 15.35 Museum of Science, Florence, SCALA/Art Resource, NY

Chapter Sixteen
16.1 Musée du Louvre, Paris, Reunion des Musées Nationaux/Art Resource, NY; 16.2 Giraudon/Art Resource, NY; 16.3 Musée du Louvre, Paris, Reunion des Musées Nationaux, Gerard Blott/Art Resource, NY; 16.4 Musée du Louvre, Paris, Reunion des Musées Nationaux, Gabriel Ojeda/Art Resource, NY; 16.5 Frick Art Reference Library/The Frick Collection, NY; 16.6 G. Blot/C. Jean, Musée du Louvre, Paris, Reunion des Musées Nationaux/Art Resource, NY/Musée d'Orsay; 16.7 Reunion des Musées Nationaux, RMN/Art Resource, NY; 16.8 Ets J. E. Bulloz; 16.9 © The National Gallery, London; 16.10 Musée du Louvre, Paris/Reunion des Musées Nationaux, Herve Lewandowski/Art Resource, NY; 16.11 Andrew W. Mellon Collection. Photograph © Board of Trustees, National Gallery of Art, Washington, DC; 16.12 London County Council, Kenwood House (Iveagh Bequest). English Heritage/National Monuments Record, London; 16.13 © Musée du Louvre/RMN Reunion des Musées Nationaux/Art Resource, NY; 16.14 Virginia Museum of Fine Arts, Richmond. The Adolph D. and Wilkins C. Williams Fund. Photo: Katherine Wetzel; 16.15 Gift of Mrs. George von Lengerke Meyer. Reproduced with permission. © Museum of Fine Arts, Boston. All Rights Reserved; 16.16 The Library of Virginia; 16.17 Janetta Robold Benton, Prof. of Fine Arts, Pace University; 16.18 Paul M. R. Maeyaert, Photographie; 16.19 © David R. Frazier Photolibrary, Inc./Alamy Images; 16.20 Photostage, Ltd.

Chapter Seventeen
17.1 Hamburger Kunsthalle, Hamburg, Germany, Bildarchiv Preussischer Kulturbesitz/Art Resource, NY; 17.2 Derechos reservados © Museo Nacional Del Prado, Madrid; 17.3 © Copyright The British Museum, London; 17.4 Herve Lewandowski, Musée du Louvre, Paris/Reunion des Musées Nationaux; 17.5 Musée du Louvre, Paris/Reunion des Musées Nationaux, Herve Lewandowski/Art Resource, NY; 17.6 Musée du Louvre, Paris/Reunion Musées Nationaux, Art Resource, NY; 17.7 Fitzwilliam Museum; 17.8 © The National Gallery, London; 17.9 Henry Lillie Pierce Fund. Reproduced with permission. © 2005 Museum of Fine Arts, Boston. All Rights Reserved; 17.10 Gift of Douglas F. Roby. Detroit Institute of Arts; 17.11 Lent by the Department of the Interior Museum. Smithsonian American Art Museum, Smithsonian Institution, Washington, DC/Art Resource, NY; 17.12 Ets J. E. Bulloz; 17.13 Ed Pritchard, Getty Images, Inc.–Stone Allstock; 17.14 Robert Harding Associates; 17.15 By permission of The British Library; 17.16 The British Museum Great Court Ltd. Copyright © The British Museum; 17.17 By courtesy of the National Portrait Gallery, London; 17.18 Photostage, Ltd.; 17.19 Charles Deering Fund, Photograph © 2005, The Art Institute of Chicago, All Rights Reserved; 17.20 Musée d'Orsay, Paris, France. Erich Lessing/Art Resource, NY; 17.21 Herve Lewandowski. © Musée d'Orsay, Paris, France/Reunion des Musées Nationaux, Art Resource, NY; 17.22 Musée d'Orsay, Paris/Giraudon, Paris/SuperStock, Inc.; 17.23 Gift of Mrs. Frank B. Porter. Photograph © 1985 The Metropolitan Museum of Art, NY; 17.24 Purchased by the Friends of Art, Fort Worth Art Association, acquired by Amon Carter Museum, from the Modern Art Museum of Fort Worth through grants and donations; 17.25 National Museum of Women in the Arts, Washington, DC, Gift of Wallace and Wilhelmina Holladay; 17.26 By courtesy of the National Portrait Gallery, London; 17.27 Courtesy of the Library of Congress; 17.28 Philadelphia Museum of Art/City of Philadelphia, Trade & Convention Center, Dept. of Commerce (Commercial Museum); 17.29 Museum of Modern Art, NY/Licensed by SCALA, Art Resource, NY; 17.30 National Museum of Women in the Arts, Washington, DC, Gift of the Holladay Foundation; 17.31 Peter Bennet/Ambient Images; 17.32 Smithsonian American Art Museum, Washington, DC/Art Resource, NY; 17.33 Ulrike Welsch Photography

Chapter Eighteen
18.1 Erich Lessing/(ARS) Artists Rights Society, NY/© Estate of Claude Monet; 18.2 Musée d'Orsay, Paris/Reunion des Musées Nationaux, B. Hatala/Art Resource, NY; 18.3 Musée du Louvre/Art Resource, NY © 2004 (ARS) Artists Rights Society, NY; 18.4 © The National Gallery, London; 18.5 © The National Gallery, London; 18.6 Chester Dale Collection. Photograph © Board of Trustees, National Gallery of Art, Washington, DC; 18.7 Musée d'Orsay, Paris/Reunion des Musées Nationaux, Jean Schormans/Art Resource, NY; 18.8 Janetta Rebold Benton, Prof. of Fine Arts, Pace University, 18.9 Acquired 1925, The Phillips Collection, Washington, DC; 18.10 Chester Dale Collection. Photograph © Board of Trustees, National Gallery of Art, Washington, DC; 18.11 Helen Birch Bartlett Memorial Collection. Photograph © 2005, The Art Institute of Chicago, All Rights Reserved; 18.12 Bequest of Stephen Carlton Clark, B. A., 1903. Yale University Art Gallery, New Haven, CT; 18.13 Acquired through the Lillie P. Bliss Bequest, The Museum of Modern Art/Licensed by SCALA/Art Resource, NY; 18.14 A. Conger Goodyear Collection, Albright–Knox Art Gallery, Buffalo; 18.15 Gift of Thomas F. Ryan, Metropolitan Museum of Art, NY; 18.16 Rodin Museum, Paris, France; 18.17 Bayerisch Staatsgemaldesammlungen/Alte Pinakothek, Munich; 18.18 Emil Boehl/Missouri Historical Society, St. Louis; 18.19 Copyright © 2005 Artists Rights Society (ARS), NY/SOFAM, Brussels. Photo by Ch. Bastin & J. Evrard; 18.20 Gala/SuperStock, Inc.; 18.20 Gala/SuperStock, Inc.

Chapter Nineteen
19.1 National Palace Museum, Taipei, Taiwan; 19.2 Ming Furniture Ltd., Inc.; 19.3 The Minneapolis Institute of Arts, Gift of Ruth and Bruce Dayton; 19.4 The Nelson-Atkins Museum of Art, Kansas City, MO; 19.5 © The Cleveland Museum of Art, John L. Severence Fund; 19.6 Bequest of John M. Crawford, Jr./Photograph © 1995 The Metropolitan Museum of Art, NY; 19.7 Stephen Addiss/Hsaio Hua Collection; 19.8 ChinaStock Photo Library; 19.9 © Liu Liqun, CORBIS/Bettmann; 19.11 Photostage, Ltd.; 9.12 Jack Vartoogian/Photograph © 2002 Linda Vartoogian/FrontRowPhotos. All Rights Reserved

Chapter Twenty
20.1 Tokyo National Museum, DNP Archives.com Co., Ltd.; 20.2 Stephen Addiss/Chikusei Collection; 20.3 New York Public Library Photographic Services/Art Resource, NY; 20.4 Private Collection/Art Resource, NY; 20.5 Art Resource, NY; 20.6 Spectrum Pictures; 20.7 Spectrum Pictures; 20.8 Catherine Karnow/CORBIS/Bettmann; 20.9 Photograph © 2003 Jack Vartoogian/FrontRowPhotos, All Rights Reserved

Chapter Twenty-One
21.1 Collection of Mrs. Walter A. Haas, San Francisco, Visual Arts Library/Artephot/Faillet, © Succession H. Matisse/DACS 1998, © 2005 Artists Rights Society (ARS), NY; 21.2 The State Hermitage Museum, St. Petersburg, Russia, © 2005 Artists Rights Society (ARS), NY; 21.3 Acquired through the Lillie P. Bliss

Literature Credits

Chapter Thirteen
Pico della Mirandola, *Oration on the Dignity of Man*, Regnery Publishing; Petrarch, *Sonnet*, from *The Italian Renaissance Reader*, edited by Julia Conaway Bondanella & Mark Musa, translated by Julia Conaway Bondanella & Mark Musa, Copyright © 1987 by Julia Conaway Bondanella & Mark Musa. Used by permission of Dutton Signet, a division of Penguin Group (USA) Inc.; Francois Villon *Ballade of Forgiveness* from *The Mindreader*, English translation Copyright © by Richard Wilber, reprinted by permission of Harcourt; *I Live on This Depraved and Lonely Cliff* by Vittoria da Colonna, from *A Book of Women Poets from Antiquity to Now* by Aliki Barnstone and Willis Barnstone, Copyright © 1980 by Schocken Books, a division of Random House, Inc.; From *The Book of the Courtier* by Baldesar Castiglione, translated by George Bull, Penguin, 1967, Copyright © George Bull, 1967; From *The Prince* by Niccolo Machiavelli, translated by George Bull (Penguin Classics 1961, Third revised edition 1983) Copyright © George Bull, 1961, 1975, 1981, 1983; From *The Autobiography of Benvenuto Cellini* by Benvenuto Cellini, translated by George Bull (Penguin, 1956), translation © George Bull, 1956

Chapter Fourteen
The Praise of Folly and Other Writings by Desiderus Erasmus, translated by Robert M. Adams. Copyright © 1989 by W. W. Norton & Company, Inc. Used by permission

of W. W. Norton & Company, Inc.; *Ninety-Five Theses* from *Luther's Works*, Volume 31, ed. Harold Grimm © 1957 Fortress Press, used by permission of Augsburg Fortress; Louise Labe, Sonnet 18, *Kiss me again, rekiss me, kiss me more*, from *A Book of Woman Poets from Antiquity to Now*, eds. Aliki and Willis Barnstone, Copyright © 1980 by Schocken Books, a division of Random House, Inc. Used by permission of Random House, Inc.; Michel de Montaigne, *Of Cannibals*, from *The Complete Essays of Montaigne*, translated by Donald M. Frame. Copyright © 1958 by the Board of Trustees of the Leland Stanford, Jr. University, with permission of Stanford University Press

Chapter Fifteen
The Fifth Exercise by Ignatius of Loyola, from *St. Ignatius' Spiritual Exercises*, translated by Anthony Mottola, Copyright © 1964 by Doubleday, a division of Random House, Inc. Used by permission of Doubleday, a division of Random House; From *Don Quixote* by Miguel de Cervantes: A new translation by Edith Grossman, Introduction by Harold Bloom. Translation Copyright © 2003 by Edith Grossman, Introduction © 2003 by Harold Bloom. Reprinted by permission of HarperCollins Publishers, Inc.; *Tartuffe* by Moliere, English translation Copyright © 1963, 1962, 1961 and renewed 1991, 1990 and 1989 by Richard Wilbur, reprinted by permission of Harcourt, Inc. CAUTION: Professionals and amateurs

are hereby warned that this translation, being fully protected under the Copyright laws of the United States of America, the British Empire, including the Dominion of Canada, and all other countries which are signatories to the Universal Copyright Convention and the International Copyright Union, are subject to royalty. All rights, including professional, amateur, motion pictures, recitation, lecturing, public reading, radio broadcasting, and television, are strictly reserved. Particular emphasis is laid on the question of readings, permission for which must be secured from the author's agent in writing. Inquiries on professional rights (except for amateur rights) should be addressed to Mr. Peter Franklin, William Morris Agency, 1325 Avenue of the Americas, New York, NY 10019. Inquiries on translation rights should be addressed to Harcourt, Inc., Permissions Department, Orlando, FL 32887. The stock and amateur acting rights of TARTUFFE are controlled exclusively by the Dramatists Play Service, Inc., 440 Park Avenue South, New York, NY. No amateur performances of the play may be given without obtaining in advance the written permission of the Dramatist Play Service, Inc., and paying the requisite fee

Chapter Seventeen
On Social Contract: Book I from *Confessions* by Jean-Jacques Rousseau, translated by Julia Conaway Bondanella, Norton Critical Edition, Cambridge University Press.

Index